PETERSON'S COLLEGES IN THE MIDWEST

2005

THOMSON

PETERSON'S

Australia • Canada • Mexico • Singapore • Spain • United Kingdom • United States

About Thomson Peterson's

Thomson Peterson's (www.petersons.com) is a leading provider of education information and advice, with books and online resources focusing on education search, test preparation, and financial aid. Its Web site offers searchable databases and interactive tools for contacting educational institutions, online practice tests and instruction, and planning tools for securing financial aid. Thomson Peterson's serves 110 million education consumers annually.

For more information, contact Thomson Peterson's, 2000 Lenox Drive, Lawrenceville, NJ 08648; 800-338-3282; or find us on the World Wide Web at www.petersons.com/about.

Editor: Fern A. Oram; Production Editor: Linda Seghers; Copy Editors: Bret Bollmann, Jim Colbert, Michele N. Firestone, Michael Haines, Sally Ross, Jill C. Schwartz, Pam Sullivan, Valerie Bolus Vaughan; Research Project Manager: Daniel Margolin; Research Associates: Mary Meyer-Penniston, Jared A. Stein, Amy L. Weber; Programmer: Phyllis Johnson; Manufacturing Manager: Judy Coleman; Composition Manager: Linda M. Williams; Client Relations Representatives: Mimi Kaufman, Lois Regina Milton, Mary Ann Murphy, Jim Swinarski, Eric Wallace.

ISSN 1525-3813
ISBN 0-7689-1385-3

Printed in the United States of America

10 9 8 7 6 5 4 3 2 1   06 05 04

Twentieth Edition

CONTENTS

A Note from the Peterson's Editors

Welcome to the world of college decision making. This guide can be an invaluable tool as you think about college and where to apply. You are probably considering at least one college that is relatively near your home. It may surprise you to learn that the majority of all students go to college within a 300-mile radius of where they live. Because of that factor, we publish this series of college guides that focuses on the colleges in each of six regions of the country so that students can easily compare the colleges in their own area. (Two-year public and proprietary colleges are not included because their admission patterns are significantly different from other colleges.)

For advice and guidance in the college search and selection process, just turn the page. "Surviving Standardized Tests" describes the most frequently used test and lists test dates for 2004–05. Of course, part of the college selections process involves visiting the schools themselves and "The Whys and Whats of College Visits" is just the planner you need to make those trips well worth your while. Next, "Applying 101" provides advice on how best to approach the application phase of the process. If you've got questions about transferring, "Successful Transfer" has got the answers you need. "Who's Paying for This? Financial Aid Basics" and the "Financial Aid Programs for Schools in the Midwest" articles provide you with the essential information on how to meet your educational expenses. "Searching for Four-Year Colleges Online" gives you all the tips you'll need to integrate the Web into your college search. Lastly, you'll want to read through the "How to Use This Guide" and learn how to use all the information presented in this volume.

Following these articles are the **Profiles of Colleges** sections. The college profiles are easy to read and should give you a good sense of whether a college meets your basic needs and should be considered further. This consistently formatted collection of data can provide a reference balance to the individual mailings you are likely to receive from colleges. The profiles appear in geographical order by state.

In a number of the profiles (those marked with a U.S. map icon), you will find helpful information about social life, academic life, campus visits, and interviews. These **Special Messages to Students** are written in each case by a college admissions office staff member. You will find valuable insights into what each writer considers special about his or her institution (both socially and academically), what is expected of you during your interview at that college, and how important the interview is there. You will also be alerted to outstanding attractions on campus or nearby so you can plan a productive visit. In many cases travel information (nearest commercial airport and nearest interstate highway) is included that will be of help on your campus visit.

And if you still thirst for even more information, look for the two-page narrative descriptions appearing in the **In-Depth Descriptions of Colleges** sections of the book. These descriptions are written by admissions deans and provide great detail about each college. They are edited to provide a consistent format across entries for your ease of comparison.

The **Indexes** at the back of the book ("Majors and Degrees," "Athletic Programs and Scholarships," and "ROTC Programs") enable you to pinpoint colleges listed in the profiles according to their specific offerings. Additionally, there is an "Alphabetical Listing of Colleges and Universities" to enable you to quickly find a school that you may have already determined meets your criteria.

We hope you will find this information helpful. Try to remember that admission directors are as interested in you and the possibility of your attending their college as you are in the possibility of applying. They spend most of their time reaching out to students, explaining their colleges' programs and policies, and easing the application process whenever they can. If you think of them as people who like students and if you can picture them taking the time to carefully provide the information in this book for you, it might help to lessen any anxiety you are feeling right now about applying.

Our advice is to relax, enjoy high school, and do as well as you can in your courses. Give yourself enough time during the early stages of your search to think about what kind of person you are and what you want to become so you can choose colleges for the right reasons. Read all college materials with an open mind, and visit as many campuses as you can. Plan ahead so you do not rush through your applications. If you can keep yourself in balance during this process, it need not become the panic period you may have seen some friends go through. We urge you to contact admission staff members at any college in which you are interested. They are all willing to help you. In fact, the admission people whose names you will find in this book hope to hear from you. We at Peterson's wish you success and happiness wherever you enroll.

The College Admissions Process

Surviving Standardized Tests

WHAT ARE STANDARDIZED TESTS?

Colleges and universities in the United States use tests to help evaluate applicants' readiness for admission or to place them in appropriate courses. The tests that are most frequently used by colleges are the ACT Assessment of American College Testing, Inc., and the College Board's SAT. In addition, the Educational Testing Service (ETS) offers the TOEFL test, which evaluates the English-language proficiency of nonnative speakers. The tests are offered at designated testing centers located at high schools and colleges throughout the United States and U.S. territories and at testing centers in various countries throughout the world. The ACT Assessment test and the SAT tests are each taken by more than a million students each year. The TOEFL test is taken by more than 700,000 students each year.

Upon request, special accommodations for students with documented visual, hearing, physical, or learning disabilities are available. Examples of special accommodations include tests in Braille or large print and such aids as a reader, recorder, magnifying glass, or sign language interpreter. Additional testing time may be allowed in some instances. Contact the appropriate testing program or your guidance counselor for details on how to request special accommodations.

College Board SAT Program

Currently, the SAT Program consists of the SAT I Reasoning Test and the SAT II Subject Tests. The SAT I is a 3-hour test made up of seven sections, primarily multiple-choice, that measures verbal and mathematical abilities. The three verbal sections test vocabulary, verbal reasoning, and critical reading skills. Emphasis is placed on reading passages, which are 400–850 words in length. Some reading passages are paired; the second opposes, supports, or in some way complements the point of view expressed in the first. The three mathematics sections test a student's ability to solve problems involving arithmetic, algebra, and geometry. They include questions that require students to produce their own responses, in addition to questions that students can choose from four or five answer choices. Calculators may be used on the SAT I mathematics sections. Beginning in the spring of 2005, the SAT will be a 3-hour and 35-minute test that focuses on college success skills of writing, critical reading, and mathematics. The new writing component will measure grammar and usage and include a short, student-written essay.

The SAT II Subject Tests are 1-hour tests, primarily multiple-choice, in specific subjects that measure students' knowledge of these subjects and their ability to apply that knowledge. Some colleges may require or recommend these tests for placement, or even admission. The Subject Tests measure a student's academic achievement in high school and may indicate readiness for certain college programs. Tests offered include Writing, Literature, U.S. History, World History, Mathematics Level IC, Mathematics Level IIC, Biology E/M (Ecological/Molecular), Chemistry, Physics, French, German, Modern Hebrew, Italian, Latin, and Spanish, as well as Foreign Language Tests with Listening in Chinese, French, German, Japanese, Korean, Spanish, and English Language Proficiency (ELPT). The Mathematics Level IC and IIC tests require the use of a scientific calculator.

SAT scores are automatically sent to each student who has taken the test. On average, they are mailed about three weeks after the test. Students may request that the scores be reported to their high schools or to the colleges to which they are applying.

DON'T FORGET TO . . .

- Take the SAT or ACT Assessment before application deadlines.
- Note that test registration deadlines precede test dates by about six weeks.
- Register to take the TOEFL test if English is not your native language and you are planning on studying at a North American college.
- Practice your test-taking skills with **Peterson's Ultimate SAT Tool Kit, Peterson's Ultimate ACT Tool Kit,** and **Peterson's TOEFL Success** (all available with software).
- Contact the College Board or American College Testing, Inc., in advance if you need special accommodations when taking tests.

ACT Assessment Program

The ACT Assessment Program is a comprehensive data collection, processing, and reporting service designed to assist in educational and career planning. The ACT Assessment instrument consists of four academic tests, taken under timed conditions, and a Student Profile Section and Interest Inventory, completed when students register for the ACT Assessment.

The academic tests cover four areas—English, mathematics, reading, and science reasoning. The ACT Assessment consists of 215 multiple-choice questions and takes approximately 3 hours and 30 minutes to complete with breaks (testing time is actually 2 hours and 55 minutes). They are designed to assess the student's educational development and readiness to handle college-level work. The minimum standard score is 1, the maximum is 36, and the national average is 21. Students should note that beginning in February 2005, an optional writing test will be offered.

The Student Profile Section requests information about each student's admission and enrollment plans, academic and out-of-class high school achievements and aspirations, and high school course work. The student is also asked to supply biographical data and self-reported high school grades in the four subject-matter areas covered by the academic tests.

The ACT Assessment has a number of career planning services, including the ACT Assessment Interest Inventory, which is designed to measure six major dimensions of student interests–business contact, business operations, technical, science, arts, and social service. Results are used to compare the student's interests with those of college-bound students who later majored in each of a wide variety of areas. Inventory results are also used to help students compare their work-activity preferences with work activities that characterize twenty-three "job families."

Because the information resulting from the ACT Assessment Program is used in a variety of educational settings, American College Testing, Inc., prepares three reports for each student: the Student Report, the High School Report, and the College Report. The Student Report normally is sent to the student's high school, except after the June test date, when it is sent directly to the student's home address. The College Report is sent to the colleges the student designates.

Early in the school year, American College Testing, Inc., sends registration packets to high schools across the country that contain all the information a student needs to

2004–05 ACT ASSESSMENT AND SAT TEST DATES

ACT Assessment
September 25, 2004*
October 23, 2004
December 11, 2004
February 12, 2005**
April 9, 2005
June 11, 2005

SAT
October 9, 2004 (SAT I and SAT II)
November 6, 2004 (SAT I, SAT II, and Language Tests with Listening, including ELPT*)
December 4, 2004 (SAT I and SAT II)
January 22, 2005 (SAT I, SAT II, and ELPT)
March 12, 2005 (SAT I only)** NEW SAT
May 7, 2005 (SAT I and SAT II) NEW SAT
June 4, 2005 (SAT I and SAT II) NEW SAT

All test dates fall on a Saturday. Tests are also given on the Sundays following the Saturday test dates for students who cannot take the test on Saturday because of religious reasons. The basic ACT Assessment registration fee for 2003–04 was $26 ($29 in Florida and $42 outside of the U.S.).

*The September test is available only in Arizona, California, Florida, Georgia, Illinois, Indiana, Maryland, Nevada, North Carolina, Pennsylvania, South Carolina, Texas, and Washington.

**The February test date is not available in New York.

For the 2003–04 academic year, the basic fee for the SAT I Reasoning Test was $28.50, which included the $16 basic registration and reporting fee. The basic fee for the SAT II Subject Tests was $16 for the Writing Test, $13 for the Language Tests with Listening, and $8 each for all other Subject Tests. Students can take up to three SAT II Subject Tests on a single date, and a $16 basic registration and reporting fee should be added for each test date. Tests are also given on the Sundays following the Saturday test dates for students who cannot take the test on Saturday because of religious reasons. Fee waivers are available to juniors and seniors who cannot afford test fees.

*Language Tests with Listening (including the English Language Proficiency Test, or ELPT) are only offered on November 6; the ELPT is offered on November 6 and January 22 at some test centers. See the Registration Bulletin for details.

**The March 12 test date is only available in the U.S. and its territories.

register for the ACT Assessment. High school guidance offices also receive a supply of *Preparing for the ACT Assessment*, a booklet that contains a complete practice test, an answer key, and general information about preparing for the test.

Test of English as a Foreign Language (TOEFL)

The TOEFL test is used by various organizations, such as colleges and universities, to determine English proficiency. The test is mainly offered in a computer-based format (TOEFL CBT), although the paper-based test is still offered in some areas. Eventually, the TOEFL will be completely computer-based.

The TOEFL tests students in the areas of listening, structure, reading comprehension, and writing. Score requirements are set by individual institutions. For more information on TOEFL, and to obtain a copy of the Information Bulletin, contact the Educational Testing Service.

Peterson's *TOEFL CBT Success* can help you prepare for the exam. The CD version of the book includes a TOEFL practice test and adaptive English skill building exercise. An online CBT test can also be taken for a small fee at petersons.com.

Contact your secondary school counselor for full information about the SAT and ACT Assessment programs and the TOEFL test.

The Whys and Whats of College Visits

Dawn B. Sova, Ph.D.

The campus visit should not be a passive activity for you and your parents, and you will have to take the initiative and use all of your senses to gather information beyond that provided in the official tour. You will see many important indicators during your visit that will tell you more about the true character of a college and its students than the tour guide will reveal. Know what to look for and how to assess the importance of such indicators.

WHAT SHOULD YOU ASK AND WHAT SHOULD YOU LOOK FOR?

Your first stop on a campus visit is the visitor center or admissions office, where you will probably have to wait to meet with a counselor. Colleges usually plan to greet visitors later than the appointed time in order to give them the opportunity to review some of the campus information that is liberally scattered throughout the visitor waiting room. Take advantage of the time to become even more familiar with the college by arriving 15 to 30 minutes before your appointment to observe the behavior of staff members and to browse through the yearbooks and student newspapers that will be available.

If you prepare in advance, you will have already reviewed the college catalog and map of the campus. These materials familiarize you with the academic offerings and the physical layout of the campus, but the true character of the college and its students emerges in other ways.

Begin your investigation with the visitor center staff members. As a student's first official contact with the college, they should make every effort to welcome prospective students and to project a friendly image.

- How do they treat you and other prospective students who are waiting? Are they friendly and willing to speak with you, or do they try their hardest to avoid eye contact and conversation?
- Are they friendly with each other and with students who enter the office, or are they curt and unwilling to help?
- Does the waiting room have a friendly feeling or is it cold and sterile?

If the visitor center staff members seem indifferent to *prospective* students, there is little reason to believe that they will

be warm and welcoming to current students. View such behavior as a warning to watch very carefully the interaction of others with you during the tour. An indifferent or unfriendly reception in the admissions office may be simply the first of many signs that attending this college will not be a pleasant experience.

Look through several yearbooks and see the types of activities that are actually photographed, as opposed to the activities that colleges promise in their promotional literature. Some questions are impossible to answer if the college is very large, but for small and moderately sized colleges the yearbook is a good indicator of campus activity.

- Has the number of clubs and organizations increased or decreased in the past five years?
- Do the same students appear repeatedly in activities?
- Do sororities and fraternities dominate campus activities?
- Are participants limited to one sex or one ethnic group or are the participants diverse?
- Are all activities limited to the campus, or are students involved in activities in the community?

Use what you observe in the yearbooks as a means of forming a more complete understanding of the college, but don't base your entire impression on just one facet. If time permits, look through several copies of the school newspaper, which should reflect the major concerns and interests of the students. The paper is also a good way to learn about the campus social life.

- Does the paper contain a mix of national and local news?
- What products or services are advertised?
- How assertive are the editorials?
- With what topics are the columnists concerned?
- Are movies and concerts that meet your tastes advertised or reviewed?
- What types of ads appear in the classified section?

The newspaper should be a public forum for students, and, as such, should reflect the character of the campus and of the student body. A paper that deals only with seemingly safe and well-edited topics on the editorial page and in regular feature columns might indicate administrative censorship. A lack of ads for restaurants might indicate either a lack of good places to eat or that area restaurants do not welcome student business. A limited mention of movies, concerts, or other entertainment might reveal a severely limited campus social life. Even if ads and reviews are included, you can also learn a lot about how such activities reflect your tastes.

You will have only a limited amount of time to ask questions during your initial meeting with the admissions counselor, for very few schools include a formal interview in the initial campus visit or tour. Instead, this brief meeting is often just a nicety that allows the admissions office to begin a file for the student and to record some initial impressions. Save your questions for the tour guide and for campus members that you meet along the way.

HOW CAN YOU ASSESS THE TRUE CHARACTER OF A COLLEGE AND ITS STUDENTS?

Colleges do not train their tour guides to deceive prospective students, but they do caution guides to avoid unflattering topics and campus sites. Does this mean that you are condemned to see only a sugarcoated version of life on a particular college campus? Not at all, especially not if you are observant.

Most organized campus visits include such campus facilities as dormitories, dining halls, libraries, student activity and recreation centers, and the health and student services centers. Some may only be pointed out, while you will walk through others. Either way, you will find that many signs of the true character of the college emerge if you keep your eyes open.

Bulletin boards in dormitories and student centers contain a wealth of information about campus activities, student concerns, and campus groups. Read the posters, notices, and messages to learn what *really* interests students. Unlike ads in the school newspaper, posters put up by students advertise both on- and off-campus events, so they will give you an idea of what is also available in the surrounding community.

Review the notices, which may cover either campuswide events or events that concern only small groups of students. The catalog may not mention a performance group, but an individual dormitory with its own small theater may offer regular productions. Poetry readings, jam sessions, writers' groups, and other activities may be announced and shows diversity of student interests.

Even the brief bulletin board messages offering objects for sale and noting objects that people want to purchase reveal a lot about a campus. Are most of the items computer related? Or do the messages specify compact discs, audio equipment, or musical instruments? Are offers to barter goods or services posted? Don't ignore the "ride wanted" messages. Students who want to share rides home during a break may specify widely diverse geographical locations. If so, then you know that the student body is not limited to only the immediate area or one locale. Other messages can also enhance your knowledge of the true character of the campus and its students.

As you walk through various buildings, examine their condition carefully.

- Is the paint peeling, and do the exteriors look worn?
- Are the exteriors and interiors of the building clean?
- Is the equipment in the classrooms up-to-date or outdated?

Pay particular attention to the dormitories, especially to factors that might affect your safety. Observe the appearance of the structure, and ask about the security measures in and around the dormitories.

- Are the dormitories noisy or quiet?
- Do they seem crowded?
- How good is the lighting around each dormitory?
- Are the dormitories spread throughout the campus or are they clustered in one main area?
- Who has access to the dormitories in addition to students?
- How secure are the means by which students enter and leave the dormitory?

While you are on the subject of dormitory safety, you should also ask about campus safety. Don't expect that the guide will rattle off a list of crimes that have been committed in the past year. To obtain that information, access the recent year of issues of *The Chronicle of Higher Education* and locate its yearly report on campus crime. Also ask the guide about safety measures that the campus police take and those that students have initiated.

- Can students request escorts to their residences late at night?
- Do campus shuttle buses run at frequent intervals all night?
- Are "blue-light" telephones liberally placed throughout the campus for students to use to call for help?
- Do the campus police patrol the campus regularly?

If the guide does not answer your questions satisfactorily, wait until after the tour to contact the campus police or traffic office for answers.

Campus tours usually just point out the health services center without taking the time to walk through. Even if you don't see the inside of the building, you should take a close look at the location of the health services center and ask the guide questions about services.

- How far is the health center from the dormitories?
- Is a doctor always on call?
- Does the campus transport sick students from their dormitories or must they walk?
- What are the operating hours of the health center?
- Does the health center refer students to a nearby hospital?

If the guide can't answer your questions, visit the health center later and ask someone there.

Most campus tours take pride in showing students their activities centers, which may contain snack bars, game rooms, workout facilities, and other means of entertainment. Should you scrutinize this building as carefully as the rest? Of course. Outdated and poorly maintained activity equipment contributes to your total impression of the college. You should also ask about the hours, availability, and cost (no, the activities are usually *not* free) of using the bowling alleys, pool tables, air hockey tables, and other items.

As you walk through campus with the tour, also look carefully at the appearance of the students who pass. The way in which both men and women groom themselves, the way they dress, and even their physical bearing communicate a lot more than any guidebook can. If everyone seems to conform to the same look, you might feel that you would be uncomfortable at the college, however nonconformist that look might be. On the other hand, you might not feel comfortable on a campus that stresses diversity of dress and behavior, and your observations now can save you discomfort later.

- Does every student seem to wear a sorority or fraternity t-shirt or jacket?
- Is everyone of your sex sporting the latest fad haircut?
- Do all of the men or the women seem to be wearing expensive name-brand clothes?
- Do most of the students seem to be working hard to look outrageous in regard to clothing, hair color, and body art?
- Would you feel uncomfortable in a room full of these students?

Is appearance important to you? If it is, then you should consider very seriously if you answer *yes* to any of the above questions. You don't have to be the same as everyone else on campus, but standing out too rigorously may make you unhappy.

As you observe the physical appearance of the students, also listen to their conversations as you pass them? What are they talking about? How are they speaking? Are their voices and accents all the same, or do you hear diversity in their speech? Are you offended by their language? Think how you will feel if surrounded by the same speech habits and patterns for four years.

WHERE SHOULD YOU VISIT ON YOUR OWN?

Your campus visit is not over when the tour ends because you will probably have many questions yet to be answered and many places to still be seen. Where you go depends upon the extent to which the organized tour covers the campus. Your tour should take you to view residential halls, health and student services centers, the gymnasium or field house, dining halls, the library, and recreational centers. If any of the facilities on this list have been omitted, visit them on your own and ask questions of the students and staff members you meet. In addition, you should step off campus and gain an impression of the surrounding community. You will probably become bored with life on campus and spend at least some time off campus. Make certain that you know what the surrounding area is like.

The campus tour leaves little time to ask impromptu questions of current students, but you can do so after the tour. Eat lunch in one of the dining halls. Most will allow visitors to pay cash to experience a typical student meal. Food may not be important to you now while you are living at home and can simply take anything you want from the refrigerator at any time, but it will be when you are away at college with only a meal ticket to feed you.

- How clean is the dining hall? Consider serving tables, floors, and seating.
- What is the quality of the food?
- How big are the portions?
- How much variety do students have at each meal?
- How healthy are the food choices?

While you are eating, try to strike up a conversation with students and tell them that you are considering attending their college. Their reactions and advice can be eye-opening. Ask them questions about the academic atmosphere and the professors.

- Are the classes large or small?
- Do the majority of the professors only lecture or are tutorials and seminars common?
- Is the emphasis of the faculty career-oriented or abstract?
- Are the teaching methods innovative and stimulating or boring and dull?
- Is the academic atmosphere pressured, lax, or somewhere in between?
- Which are the strong majors? The weak majors?
- Is the emphasis on grades or social life or a mix of both at the college?
- How hard do students have to work to receive high grades?

Current students can also give you the inside line on the true nature of the college social life. You may gain some idea through looking in the yearbook, in the newspaper, and on the bulletin boards, but students will reveal the true highs and lows of campus life. Ask them about drug use, partying, dating rituals, drinking, and anything else that may affect your life as a student.

- Which are the most popular club activities?
- What do students do on weekends? Do most go home?
- How frequently do concerts occur on campus? Which groups have recently performed?
- How can you become involved in specific activities (name them)?
- How strictly are campus rules enforced and how severe are penalties?
- What counseling services are available?
- Are academic tutoring services available?
- Do they feel that the faculty really cares about students, especially freshmen?

You will receive the most valuable information from current students, but you will only be able to speak with them after the tour is over. And you might have to risk rejection as you try to initiate conversations with students who might not want to reveal how they feel about the campus. Still, the value of this information is worth the chance.

If you have the time, you should also visit the library to see just how accessible research materials are and to observe the physical layout. The catalog usually specifies the days and hours of operation, as well as the number of volumes contained in the library and the number of periodicals to which it subscribes. A library also requires accessibility, good lighting, an adequate number of study carrels, and lounge areas for students. Many colleges have created 24-hour study lounges for students who find the residence halls too noisy for studying, although most colleges claim that they designate areas of the residences as "quiet study" areas. You may not be interested in any of this information, but when you are a student you will have to make frequent use of the campus library so you should know what is available. You should at least ask how extensive their holdings are in your proposed major area. If they have virtually

nothing, you will have to spend a lot of time ordering items via interlibrary loan or making copies, which can become expensive. The ready answer of students that they will obtain their information from the Internet is unpleasantly countered by professors who demand journal articles with documentation.

Make a point of at least driving through the community surrounding the college, because you will be spending time there shopping, dining, working in a part-time job, or attending events. Even the largest and best-stocked campus will not meet all of your social and personal needs. If you can spare the time, stop in several stores to see if they welcome college students.

- Is the surrounding community suburban, urban, or rural?
- Does the community offer stores of interest, such as bookstores, craft shops, and boutiques?
- Do the businesses employ college students?
- Does the community have a movie or stage theater?
- Are there several types of interesting restaurants?
- Do there seem to be any clubs that court a college clientele?
- Is the center of activity easy to walk to, or do you need a car or other transportation?

You might feel that a day is not enough to answer all of your questions, but even answering some questions will provide you with a stronger basis for choosing a college. Many students visit a college campus several times before making their decision, as you also should. Keep in mind that for the rest of your life you will be associated with the college that you attend. You will spend four years of your life at this college. The effort of spending several days to obtain the information to make your decision is worthwhile.

_____

Dawn B. Sova, Ph.D., is a former newspaper reporter and columnist, as well as the author of more than eight books and numerous magazine articles. She teaches creative and research writing, as well as scientific and technical writing, newswriting, and journalism.

Applying 101

The words "applying yourself" have several important meanings in the college application process. One meaning refers to the fact that you need to keep focused during this important time in your life, keep your priorities straight, and know the dates that your applications are due so you can apply on time. The phrase might also refer to the person who is really responsible for your application--you.

You are the only person who should compile your college application. You need to take ownership of this process. The intervention of others should be for advisement only. The guidance counselor is not responsible for completing your applications, and your parents shouldn't be typing them. College applications must be completed in addition to your normal workload at school, college visits, and SAT, ACT Assessment, or possibly, TOEFL testing.

THE APPLICATION

The application is your way of introducing yourself to a college admissions office. As with any introduction, you should try to make a good first impression. The first thing you should do in presenting your application is to find out what the college or university needs from you. Read the application carefully to find out the application fee and deadline, required standardized tests, number of essays, interview requirements, and anything else you can do or submit to help improve your chances for acceptance.

Completing college applications yourself helps you learn more about the schools to which you are applying. The information a college asks for in its application can tell you much about the school. State university applications often tell you how they are going to view their applicants. Usually, they select students based on GPAs and test scores. Colleges that request an interview, ask you to respond to a few open-ended questions, or require an essay are interested in a more personal approach to the application process and may be looking for different types of students than those sought by a state school.

In addition to submitting the actual application, there are several other items that are commonly required. You will be responsible for ensuring that your standardized test scores and your high school transcript arrive at the colleges to which you apply. Most colleges will ask that you submit teacher recommendations as well. Select teachers who know you and your abilities well and allow them plenty of time to

complete the recommendations. When all portions of the application have been completed and sent in, whether electronically or by mail, make sure you follow up with the college to ensure their receipt.

THE APPLICATION ESSAY

Some colleges may request one essay or a combination of essays and short-answer topics to learn more about who you are and how well you can communicate your thoughts. Common essay topics cover such simple themes as writing about yourself and your experiences or why you want to attend that particular school. Other colleges will ask that you show your imaginative or creative side by writing about a favorite author, for instance, or commenting on a hypothetical situation. In such cases, they will be looking at your thought processes and your level of creativity.

Whereas the other portions of your application—your transcript, test scores, and involvement in extracurricular activities—are a reflection of what you've accomplished up to this point, your application essay is an opportunity to present yourself in the here and now. The essay shows your originality and verbal skills and is very important. Test scores and grades may represent your academic results, but your essay shows how you approach a topic or problem and express your opinion.

Admissions officers, particularly those at small or mid-size colleges, use the essay to determine how you, as a student, will fit into life at that college. The essay, therefore, is a critical component of the application process. Here are some tips for writing a winning essay:

- Colleges are looking for an honest representation of who you are and what you think. Make sure that the tone of the essay reflects enthusiasm, maturity, creativity, the ability to communicate, talent, and your leadership skills.
- Be sure you set aside enough time to write the essay, revise it, and revise it *again*. Running the "spell check" feature on your computer will only detect a fraction of the errors you probably made on your first pass at writing it. Take a break and then come back to it and reread it. You will probably notice other style, content, and grammar problems—and ways that you can improve the essay overall.
- Always answer the question that is being asked, making sure that you are specific, clear, and true to your personality.
- Enlist the help of reviewers who know you well— friends, parents, teachers—since they are likely to be the most honest and will keep you on track in the presentation of your true self.

THE PERSONAL INTERVIEW

Although it is relatively rare that a personal interview is required, many colleges recommend that you take this opportunity for a face-to-face discussion with a member of the admissions staff. Read through the application materials to determine whether or not a college places great emphasis on the interview. If they strongly recommend that you have one, it may work against you to forego it.

In contrast to a group interview and some alumni interviews, which are intended to provide information about a college, the personal interview is viewed both as an information session and as further evaluation of your skills and strengths. You will meet with a member of the admissions staff who will be assessing your personal qualities, high school preparation, and your capacity to contribute to undergraduate life at the institution. On average, these meetings last about 45 minutes—a relatively short amount

of time in which to gather information and leave the desired impression—so here are some suggestions on how to make the most of it.

Scheduling Your Visit. Generally, students choose to visit campuses in the summer or fall of their senior year. Both times have their advantages. A summer visit, when the campus is not in session, generally allows for a less hectic visit and interview. Visiting in the fall, on the other hand, provides the opportunity to see what campus life is like in full swing. If you choose the fall, consider arranging an overnight trip so that you can stay in one of the college dormitories. At the very least, you should make your way around campus to take part in classes, athletic events, and social activities. Always make an appointment and avoid scheduling more than two college interviews on any given day. Multiple interviews in a single day hinder your chances of making a good impression, and your impressions of the colleges will blur into each other as you hurriedly make your way from place to place.

Preparation. Know the basics about the college before going for your interview. Read the college viewbook or catalog in addition to this guide. You will be better prepared to ask questions that are not answered in the literature and that will give you a better understanding of what the college has to offer. You should also spend some time thinking about your strengths and weaknesses and, in particular, what you are looking for in a college education. You will find that as you get a few interviews under your belt, they will get easier. You might consider starting with a college that is not a top contender on your list, where the stakes are not as high.

Asking Questions. Inevitably, your interviewer will ask you, "Do you have any questions?" Not having one may suggest that you're unprepared or, even worse, not interested. When you do ask questions, make sure that they are ones that matter to you and that have a bearing on your decision about whether or not to attend. The questions that you ask will give the interviewer some insight into your personality and priorities. Avoid asking questions that can be answered in the college literature—again, a sign of unpreparedness. Although the interviewer will undoubtedly pose questions to you, the interview should not be viewed merely as a question-and-answer session. If a conversation evolves out of a particular question, so much the better. Your interviewer can learn a great deal about you from how you sustain a conversation. Similarly, you will be able to learn a great deal about the college in a conversational format.

Separate the Interview from the Interviewer. Many students base their feelings about a college solely on their impressions of the interviewer. Try not to characterize a college based only on your personal reaction, however, since your impressions can be skewed by whether you and your interviewer hit it off. Pay lots of attention to everything else that you see, hear, and learn about a college. Once on campus, you may never see your interviewer again.

In the end, remember to relax and be yourself. Don't drink jitters-producing caffeinated beverages prior to the interview, and suppress nervous fidgets like leg-wagging, finger-drumming, or bracelet-jangling. Your interviewer will expect you to be somewhat nervous, which will relieve some of the pressure. Consider this an opportunity to put forth your best effort and to enhance everything that the college knows about you up to this point.

THE FINAL DECISION

Once you have received your acceptance letters, it is time to go back and look at the whole picture. Provided you received more than one acceptance, you are now in a position to compare your options. The best way to do this is to compare your original list of important college-ranking criteria with what you've discovered about each college along the way. In addition, you and your family will need to factor in the financial aid component. You will need to look beyond these cost issues and the quantifiable pros and cons of each college, however, and know that you have a good feeling about your final choice. Before sending off your acceptance letter, you need to feel confident that the college will feel like home for the next four years. Once the choice is made, the only hard part will be waiting for an entire summer before heading off to college!

Successful Transfer

Adrienne Aaron Rulnick

Transfer students need and deserve detailed and accurate information but often lack direction as to where it can be obtained. Few general college guides offer information about transfer deadlines and required minimum grade point averages for transfer admission. College catalogs are not always clear about the specific requirements and procedures for transfer students who may be confused about whether they need to present high school records, SAT I or ACT Assessment scores, or a guidance counselor's recommendation, particularly if they have been out of high school for several years. Transfer advisers are not available to those enrolled at a baccalaureate institution; at community and junior colleges, the transfer advising function may be performed by a designated transfer counselor or by a variety of college advisers who are less clearly identified.

The challenge for transfer students is to determine what they need to know in order to make good, informed decisions and identify the individuals and resources that can provide that information. An organized research process is very much at the heart of a successful transfer.

HOW TO BEGIN

Perhaps the most important first step in this process is one of self-analysis. Adopting a consumer approach is appropriate—higher education is a formidable purchase, no matter how it is financed. The reputation of the college from which you obtain your degree may open doors to future jobs and careers; friendships and contacts you make at college can provide a significant network for lifelong social and professional relationships. The environment of a transfer school may be the perfect opportunity for you to test out urban living or the joys of country life, explore a different area of the country, experience college residential living for the first time, or move out of the family nest into your first apartment. Like any major purchase in your life, there are costs and benefits to be weighed. Trade-offs include cost, distance, rigor of academic work, extra time in school required by a cooperative education program, and specific requirements, such as foreign language competence at a liberal arts institution or courses in religion at an institution with a denominational affiliation.

USE EXPERIENCE AS A GUIDE

The wise consumer reflects on his or her own experience with a product (i.e., your initial college or colleges) and then seeks out people who have firsthand experience with the new product being considered. Talk to friends and family members who have attended the colleges you are considering; ask college faculty members you know to tell you about the colleges they attended and how they view these schools. Talk to people engaged in the careers you are considering: what are their impressions of the best programs and schools in their field? Make sure you sample a variety of opinions, but beware of dated experiences. An engineering department considered top-notch when Uncle Joe attended college twenty years ago might be very different today!

THE NITTY-GRITTY

Once your list is reduced to a manageable number of schools, usually fewer than ten, it is important to identify academic requirements, requisite grade point averages for admission, and deadline dates. Most schools admit for both the fall and spring semesters; those on a trimester system may have winter and summer admissions as well. Some schools have rolling admission policies and will process applications as they are received; others, particularly the more selective colleges, have firm deadlines because their admission process involves a committee review, and decisions are made on a competitive basis. It is helpful to know how many transfer students are typically accepted for the semester you wish to begin, whether the minimum grade point average is indicative of the actual average of accepted students (this can vary widely), and whether the major you are seeking has special prerequisites and admission procedures. For example, fine arts programs admission procedures usually require portfolios or auditions. For engineering, computer science, and some business majors, there are specific requirements in mathematics that must be met before a student is considered for admission. Many specialized health-care programs, including nursing, may only admit once a year. Some schools have different standards for sophomore and junior transfers or for in-state and out-of-state students.

Other criteria that you should identify include whether college housing and financial aid are available for transfer students. Some colleges have special transfer scholarships that require separate applications and references, while others simply award aid based on applications that indicate a high grade point average or membership in a nationally recognized junior and community college honor society, such as Phi Theta Kappa. There are also scholarships for transfer students who demonstrate accomplishment in specified academic and performance areas; the latter may be based on talent competitions or accomplishment evidenced in a portfolio or audition.

NONTRADITIONAL STUDENTS

For the nontraditional student, usually defined as anyone beyond the traditional college age of 18 to 23, there may be additional aspects to investigate. Some colleges award credit based on demonstrated life experience; many colleges grant credit for qualifying scores on the CLEP exams or for participation in the DANTES program. Experience in industry may yield college credit as well. If you are ready and able to pursue further college work but are not in a position to attend regular classes at a senior college, there are a variety of distance learning options at fully accredited colleges. Other colleges provide specialized support services for nontraditional students and may allow students the opportunity to attend part-time if they have family and work responsibilities. In some cases, usually at large universities, there may be married student housing or family housing available. More and more schools have established daycare facilities, although the waiting lists are often very long.

APPLYING

Once you have identified the schools that meet the needs you have established as priorities, it is time to begin the application process. Make sure you observe all the indicated deadlines: it never hurts to have everything in early, as there are consequences, such as closed-out majors and the loss of housing and financial aid, if you submit your application late. Make appointments with faculty members and others who are providing references; make sure they understand what is required of them and when and where their references must be sent. It is your responsibility to follow through to make sure all of your credentials are received, including transcripts from all colleges previously attended, even if you only took one summer course or attended for less than a semester. If you have not yet had the opportunity to visit the schools to which you are applying, now is the time to do so. Arrange interviews wherever possible, and make sure to include a tour of the campus and visits to the department and career offices to gain a picture of the facilities and future opportunities. If you have questions about financial aid, schedule an appointment in the financial aid office, and make sure you are aware of all the deadlines and requirements and any scholarship opportunities for which you are eligible.

MAKING YOUR CHOICE

Congratulations! You have been accepted at the colleges of your choice. Now what? Carefully review the acceptance of your previous college credit and how it has been applied. You are entitled to know how many transfer credits you have received and your expected date of graduation. Compare financial aid packages and housing options. The best choice should emerge from this review process. Then, send a note to the schools you will not be attending. Acknowledge your acceptance, but indicate that you have chosen to attend elsewhere. Carefully read everything you have received from the college of your choice. Return required deposits within the deadline, reserve time to attend transfer orientation, arrange to have your final transcript sent from the college you currently attend, and review the financial picture. This is the time to finalize college loan applications and make sure you are in a position to meet all the costs entailed at this college. Don't forget to include the costs of travel and housing.

You've done it! While many transfer students reflect on how much work was involved in the transfer admission process, those who took the time to follow all of the steps outlined above report a sense of satisfaction with their choices and increased confidence in themselves. We wish you an equally rewarding experience.

_____

Adrienne Aaron Rulnick is a Transfer Counselor at Berkshire Community College.

Who's Paying for This? Financial Aid Basics

A college education can be expensive—costing more than $100,000 for four years at some of the higher priced private colleges and universities. Even at the lower cost state colleges and universities, the cost of a four-year education can approach $50,000. Determining how you and your family will come up with the necessary funds to pay for your education requires planning, perseverance, and learning as much as you can about the options that are available to you.

Paying for college should not be looked on as a four-year financial commitment. For most families, paying the total cost of a student's college education out of current savings is usually not realistic. For families that have planned ahead and have financial savings established for higher education, the burden is a lot easier. But for most, meeting the cost of college requires the pooling of current income and assets and investing in longer-term loan options. These family resources, together with possible financial assistance from the state, federal, and institutional resources enable millions of students each year to attend the institution of their choice.

HOW NEED-BASED FINANCIAL AID IS AWARDED

When you apply for aid, your family's financial situation is analyzed using a government-approved formula called the Federal Methodology. This formula looks at five items:

1. Demographic information of the family.
2. Income of the parents.
3. Assets of the parents.
4. Income of the student.
5. Assets of the student.

This analysis determines the amount you and your family are expected to contribute toward your college expenses, called your Expected Family Contribution or EFC. If the EFC is equal to or more than the cost at a particular college, then you do not demonstrate financial need. However, even if you don't have financial need, you may still qualify for aid, as there are grants, scholarships, and loan programs that are not need-based.

If the cost of your education is greater than your EFC, then you do demonstrate financial need and qualify for assistance. The amount of your financial need that can be met varies from school to school. Some are able to meet your full need, while others can only cover a certain percentage of need. Here's the formula:

Cost of Attendance
– Expected Family Contribution
= Financial Need

The EFC remains constant, but your need will vary according to the costs of attendance at a particular college. In general, the higher the tuition and fees at a particular college, the higher the cost of attendance will be. Expenses for books and supplies, room and board, and other miscellaneous costs are included in the overall cost of attendance. It is important to remember that you do not have to be "needy" to qualify for financial aid. Many middle and upper-middle income families qualify for need-based financial aid.

SOURCES OF FINANCIAL AID

The largest single source of aid is the federal government, which awards almost $84 billion to more than 8.9 million students each year.

The next largest source of financial aid is found in the college and university community. Institutions award an estimated $20 billion to students each year. Most of this aid is awarded to students who have a demonstrated need based on the Federal Methodology. Some institutions use a different formula, the Institutional Methodology, to award their own funds in conjunction with other forms of aid. Institutional aid may be either need-based or non-need based. Aid that is not based on need is usually awarded for a student's academic performance (merit awards), specific talents or abilities, or to attract the type of students a college seeks to enroll.

Another source of financial aid is from state government, awarding more than $5.6 billion per year. All states offer grant and/or scholarship aid, most of which is need-based. However, more and more states are offering substantial merit-based aid programs. Most state programs award aid only to students attending college in their home state.

Other sources of financial aid include:

- Private agencies
- Foundations
- Corporations
- Clubs
- Fraternal and service organizations
- Civic associations
- Unions
- Religious groups that award grants, scholarships, and low-interest loans
- Employers that provide tuition reimbursement benefits for employees and their children

More information about these different sources of aid is available from high school guidance offices, public libraries, college financial aid offices, directly from the sponsoring organizations and on the Web at www.finaid.org.

APPLYING FOR FINANCIAL AID

Every student must complete the Free Application for Federal Student Aid (FAFSA) to be considered for financial aid. The FAFSA is available from your high school guidance office, many public libraries, colleges in your area, or directly from the U.S. Department of Education.

Students also can apply for federal student aid over the Internet using the interactive FAFSA on the Web. FAFSA on the Web can be accessed at http:www.fafsa.ed.gov. Both the student and at least one parent must apply for a federal pin number at http://www.pin.ed.gov. The pin number serves as your electronic signature when applying for aid on the Web.

To award their own funds, some colleges require an additional application, the Financial Aid PROFILE® form. The PROFILE asks supplemental questions that some colleges and awarding agencies feel provide a more accurate assessment of the family's ability to pay for college. It is up to the college to decide whether it will use only the FAFSA or both the FAFSA and the PROFILE. PROFILE applications are available from the high school guidance office and on the Web. Both the paper application and the Web site list those colleges and programs that require the PROFILE application.

If Every College You're Applying to for Fall 2005 Requires Just the FAFSA

. . . then it's pretty simple: Complete the FAFSA after January 1, 2005, being certain to send it in before any college-imposed deadlines. (You are not permitted to send in the 2005-06 FAFSA before January 1, 2005.) Most college FAFSA application deadlines are in February or early March. It is easier if you have all your financial records for the previous year available, but if that is not possible, you are strongly encouraged to use estimated figures.

After you send in your FAFSA, either with the paper application or electronically, you'll receive a Student Aid Report (SAR) that includes all of the information you reported and shows your EFC. If you provided an e-mail address, the SAR is sent to you electronically; otherwise, you will receive a paper copy in the mail. Be sure to review the SAR, checking to see if the information you reported is accurate. If you used estimated numbers to complete the FAFSA, you may have to resubmit the SAR with any corrections to the data. The college(s) you have designated on the FAFSA will receive the information you reported and will use that data to make their decision. In many instances, the colleges you've applied to will ask you to send copies of your and your parents' federal income tax returns for 2004, plus any other documents needed to verify the information you reported.

If a College Requires the PROFILE

Step 1: Register for the Financial Aid PROFILE in the fall of your senior year in high school.

Registering for the Financial Aid PROFILE begins the financial aid process. You can register by calling the College Scholarship Service at 1-800-778-6888 and providing basic demographic information, a list of colleges to which you are applying, and your credit card number to pay for the service. You can also apply for the PROFILE online at http://profileonline.collegeboard.com/index.jsp. Registration packets with a list of the colleges that require the PROFILE are available in most high school guidance offices. There is a fee for using the Financial Aid PROFILE application ($23 for the first college and $18 for each additional college). You must pay for the service by credit card when you register. If you do not have a credit card, you will be billed.

Step 2: Fill out your customized Financial Aid PROFILE.

A few weeks after you register, you'll receive in the mail a customized financial aid application that you can use to apply for institutional aid at the colleges you've designated, as well as from some private scholarship programs, like the National Merit Scholarship. (Note: If you've waited until winter and a college's financial aid application deadline is approaching, you can get overnight delivery by paying an extra fee.) The PROFILE contains all the questions necessary to calculate your "institutional" EFC, plus any additional questions that the colleges and organizations you've designated require you to answer. Your individualized packet will also contain a customized cover letter instructing you what to do and informing you about deadlines and requirements for the colleges and programs you designated when you registered for the PROFILE, codes that indicate which colleges wanted which additional questions, and supplemental forms (if any of the colleges to which you are applying require them—e.g. the Business/Farm Supplement for students whose parents own a business or farm or the Divorced/Separated Parents' Statement).

Make sure you submit your PROFILE by the earliest deadline listed. Two to four weeks after you do so, you will receive an acknowledgment and a report estimating your "institutional" EFC based on the data elements you provided on your PROFILE. Remember, this is a different formula from the federal system that uses the FAFSA.

FINANCIAL AID PROGRAMS

There are three types of financial aid:

1. Gift-aid—Scholarships and grants are funds that do not have to be repaid.
2. Loans—Loans must be repaid, usually after graduation; the amount you have to pay back is the total you've borrowed plus any accrued interest. This is considered a source of self-help aid.
3. Student employment—Student employment is a job arranged for you by the financial aid office. This is another source of self-help aid.

The federal government has two major grant programs—the Federal Pell Grant and the Federal Supplemental Educational Opportunity Grant. These grants are targeted to low-to-moderate income families with significant financial need. The federal government also sponsors a student employment program called Federal Work-Study, which offers jobs both on and off campus; and several loan programs, including those for students and for parents of undergraduate students.

There are two types of student loan programs, subsidized and unsubsidized. The Subsidized Stafford Loan and the Federal Perkins Loan are need-based, government-subsidized loans. Students who borrow through these programs do not have to pay interest on the loan until after they graduate or leave school. The Unsubsidized Stafford Loan and the Parent Loan Programs are not based on need, and borrowers are responsible for the interest while the student is in school. There are different methods on how these loans are administered. Once you choose your college, the financial aid office will guide you through this process.

After you've submitted your financial aid application and you've been accepted for admission, each college will send you a letter describing your financial aid award. Most award letters show estimated college costs, how much you and your family are expected to contribute, and the amount

and types of aid you have been awarded. Most students are awarded aid from a combination of sources and programs. Hence, your award is often called a financial aid "package."

IF YOU DON'T QUALIFY FOR NEED-BASED AID

If you are not eligible for need-based aid, you can still find ways to lessen the burden on your parents.

Here are some suggestions:

- Search for merit scholarships. You can start at the initial stages of your application process. College merit awards are becoming increasingly important as more and more colleges award these grants to students they especially want to attract. As a result, applying to a college at which your qualifications put you at the top of the entering class may give you a larger merit award. Another source of aid to look for is private scholarships that are given for special skills and talents. Additional information can be found at petersons.com and at www.finaid.org.
- Seek employment during the summer and the academic year. The student employment office at your college can help you locate a school-year job. Many colleges and local businesses have vacancies remaining after they have hired students who are receiving Federal Work-Study financial aid.
- Borrow through the Unsubsidized Stafford Loan programs. These are open to all students. The terms and conditions are similar to the subsidized loans. The biggest difference is that the borrower is responsible for the interest while still in college, although most lenders permit students to delay paying the interest right away and add the accrued interest to the total amount owed. You must file the FAFSA to be considered.
- After you've secured what you can through scholarships, working, and borrowing, your parents will be expected to meet their share of the college bill (the Expected Family Contribution). Many colleges offer monthly payment plans that spread the cost over the academic year. If the monthly payments are too high, parents can borrow through the Federal Parent Loan for Undergraduate Students (PLUS program), through one of the many private education loan programs available, or through home equity loans and lines of credit. Families seeking assistance in financing college expenses should inquire at the financial aid office about what programs are available at the college. Some families seek the advice of professional financial advisers and tax consultants.

HOW IS YOUR FAMILY CONTRIBUTION CALCULATED?

The chart on the next page makes the following assumptions:

- two parent family where age of older parent is 45
- lower income families will file the 1040A or 1040EZ tax form
- student income is less than $2300

- there are no student assets
- there is only one family member in college

All figures are estimates and may vary when the complete FAFSA or PROFILE application is submitted.

Approximate Expected Family Contribution

ASSETS / FAMILY SIZE	$20,000	30,000	40,000	50,000	60,000	70,000	80,000	90,000	100,000
$ 20,000									
3	$ 0	870	2,450	4,350	7,000	9,800	12,600	15,500	18,000
4	0	80	1,670	3,350	5,600	8,300	11,000	14,000	17,100
5	0	0	930	2,500	4,500	7,000	9,700	12,600	15,600
6	0	0	100	1,700	3,350	5,500	8,100	11,000	14,000
$ 30,000									
3	$ 0	870	2,450	4,350	7,000	9,800	12,600	15,500	18,000
4	0	80	1,670	3,350	5,600	8,300	11,000	14,000	17,100
5	0	0	930	2,500	4,500	7,000	9,700	12,600	15,600
6	0	0	100	1,700	3,350	5,500	8,100	11,000	14,000
$ 40,000									
3	$ 0	870	2,450	4,350	7,000	9,800	12,600	15,500	18,000
4	0	80	1,670	3,350	5,600	8,300	11,000	14,000	17,100
5	0	0	930	2,500	4,500	7,000	9,700	12,600	15,600
6	0	0	100	1,700	3,350	5,500	8,100	11,000	14,000
$ 50,000									
3	$ 0	870	2,450	4,350	7,500	10,300	13,000	16,000	19,000
4	0	80	1,670	3,350	6,000	8,800	11,500	14,400	17,500
5	0	0	930	2,500	4,700	7,400	10,100	13,000	16,100
6	0	0	100	1,700	3,600	5,900	8,500	11,400	14,500
$ 60,000									
3	$ 0	870	2,450	5,100	8,050	10,800	13,600	16,500	19,600
4	0	80	1,670	3,950	6,550	9,300	12,200	15,000	18,100
5	0	0	930	3,000	5,300	7,900	10,800	13,600	16,700
6	0	0	100	2,150	4,000	6,300	9,100	12,000	15,000
$ 80,000									
3	$ 0	870	2,450	6,000	9,200	12,000	14,800	17,600	20,700
4	0	80	1,670	4,700	7,600	10,500	13,200	16,100	19,200
5	0	0	930	3,700	6,100	9,000	11,800	14,700	17,800
6	0	0	100	2,700	4,700	7,400	10,200	13,100	16,200
$ 100,000									
3	$ 0	870	2,450	7,000	10,300	13,000	15,900	18,800	21,850
4	0	80	1,670	5,600	8,700	11,500	14,300	17,200	20,300
5	0	0	930	4,400	7,100	10,200	12,900	15,800	18,900
6	0	0	100	3,300	5,500	8,500	11,300	14,200	17,300
$ 120,000									
3	$ 0	870	2,450	8,100	11,400	14,200	17,000	19,900	23,000
4	0	80	1,670	6,600	9,800	12,600	15,500	18,400	21,500
5	0	0	930	5,300	8,200	11,300	14,100	17,000	20,000
6	0	0	100	4,000	6,500	9,700	12,500	15,300	18,400
$ 140,000									
3	$ 0	870	2,450	9,300	12,600	15,400	18,200	21,000	24,100
4	0	80	1,670	7,600	11,000	13,900	16,700	19,500	22,600
5	0	0	930	6,100	9,500	12,500	15,200	18,100	21,200
6	0	0	100	4,700	7,600	10,800	13,600	16,500	19,600

INCOME BEFORE TAXES heading spans income columns. *FAMILY SIZE* labels each asset block's rows (3, 4, 5, 6).

Financial Aid Programs for Schools in the Midwest

Each state government has established one or more state-administered financial aid programs for qualified students. The state programs may be restricted to legal residents of the state, or they also may be available to out-of-state students who are attending public or private colleges or universities within the state. In addition, other qualifications may apply.

The programs are described below in alphabetical order, along with information about how to determine eligibility and how to apply. The information refers to awards for 2003–04, unless otherwise stated. Students should write to the address given for each program to request that award details for 2004–05 be sent to them as soon as they are available.

ILLINOIS

Golden Apple Scholars of Illinois. 100 scholars are selected annually. Scholars receive $7,000 a year for 4 years. Applicants must be between 17 and 21 and maintain a GPA of 2.5. Eligible applicants must be residents of Illinois studying in Illinois. The deadline is December 1. Recipients must agree to teach in high-need Illinois schools. *Academic Fields/Career Goals:* Education. *Award:* Forgivable loan for use in freshman, sophomore, junior, or senior year; renewable. *Award amount:* $7000. *Number of awards:* up to 100. *Eligibility Requirements:* Applicant must be age 17-21; enrolled or expecting to enroll full-time at a four-year institution or university; resident of Illinois and studying in Illinois. Applicant must have 2.5 GPA or higher. Available to U.S. and non-U.S. citizens. *Application Requirements:* Application, autobiography, essay, interview, photo, references, test scores, transcript. *Deadline:* December 1. **Contact:** Pat Kilduff, Director of Recruitment and Placement, Golden Apple Foundation, 8 South Michigan Avenue, Suite 700, Chicago, IL 60603-3318. *E-mail:* kilduff@goldenapple. org. *Phone:* 312-407-0006 Ext. 105. *Fax:* 312-407-0344. *Web site:* www.goldenapple.org.

Grant Program for Dependents of Police, Fire, or Correctional Officers. Award for dependents of police, fire, and corrections officers killed or disabled in line of duty. Provides for tuition and fees at approved Illinois institutions. Must be resident of Illinois. Continuous deadline. Provide proof of status. *Award:* Grant for use in freshman, sophomore, junior, senior, graduate, or postgraduate years; renewable. *Award amount:* $3000–$4000. *Number of awards:* 50–55. *Eligibility Requirements:* Applicant must be enrolled or expecting to enroll at a two-year, four-year, or technical institution or university; resident of Illinois and studying

in Illinois. Applicant or parent of applicant must have employment or volunteer experience in police/firefighting. Available to U.S. and non-U.S. citizens. *Application Requirements:* Application, proof of status. *Deadline:* continuous. **Contact:** David Barinholtz, Client Information, Illinois Student Assistance Commission (ISAC), 1755 Lake Cook Road, Deerfield, IL 60015-5209. *E-mail:* cssupport@isac.org. *Phone:* 847-948-8500 Ext. 2385. *Web site:* www. collegezone.com.

Higher Education License Plate Program—HELP. Need-based grants for students at institutions participating in program whose funds are raised by sale of special license plates commemorating the institutions. Deadline: June 30. Must be Illinois resident. *Award:* Grant for use in freshman, sophomore, junior, or senior year; not renewable. *Award amount:* up to $2000. *Number of awards:* 175–200. *Eligibility Requirements:* Applicant must be enrolled or expecting to enroll full or part-time at a two-year or four-year institution or university; resident of Illinois and studying in Illinois. Available to U.S. and non-U.S. citizens. *Application Requirements:* Financial need analysis. *Deadline:* June 30. **Contact:** David Barinholtz, Client Information, Illinois Student Assistance Commission (ISAC), 1755 Lake Cook Road, Deerfield, IL 60015-5209. *E-mail:* cssupport@isac.org. *Phone:* 847-948-8500 Ext. 2385. *Web site:* www. collegezone.com.

Illinois College Savings Bond Bonus Incentive Grant Program. Program offers holders of Illinois College Savings Bonds a $20 grant for each year of bond maturity payable upon bond redemption if at least 70% of proceeds are used to attend college in Illinois. May not be used by students attending religious or divinity schools. *Award:* Grant for use in freshman, sophomore, junior, senior, graduate, or postgraduate years; not renewable. *Award amount:* $40–$220. *Number of awards:* 1200–1400. *Eligibility Requirements:* Applicant must be enrolled or expecting to enroll full or part-time at a two-year, four-year, or technical institution or university and studying in Illinois. Available to U.S. and non-U.S. citizens. *Application Requirements:* Application. *Deadline:* continuous. **Contact:** David Barinholtz, Client Information, Illinois Student Assistance Commission (ISAC), 1755 Lake Cook Road, Deerfield, IL 60015-5209. *E-mail:* cssupport@isac.org. *Phone:* 847-948-8500 Ext. 2385. *Web site:* www.collegezone.com.

Illinois Future Teachers Corps Program. Scholarships available for students planning to become teachers in Illinois. Students must be Illinois residents enrolled or accepted as a junior or above in a Teacher Education Program at an Illinois college or university. By receiving award, students agree to teach for 5 years at either a public, private, or parochial Illinois preschool, or at a public elementary or secondary school. For an application and further information, visit http://www.collegezone.com. *Academic Fields/Career Goals:* Education. *Award:* Forgivable loan for use in junior, senior, or graduate year; renewable. *Award amount:* up to $15,000. *Number of awards:* 1150. *Eligibility Requirements:* Applicant must be enrolled or expecting to enroll full or part-time at an institution or university; resident of Illinois and studying in Illinois. Available to U.S. citizens. *Application Requirements:* Application. *Deadline:* March 1. **Contact:** applications available at website, Illinois Student Assistance Commission (ISAC). *Web site:* www.collegezone.com.

Illinois Incentive for Access Program. Award for eligible first-time freshmen enrolling in approved Illinois institutions. One-time grant of up to $500 may be used for any educational expense. Using the FAFSA, applicants are encouraged to apply as quickly as possible after January 1st preceding the academic year. *Award:* Grant for use in freshman year; not renewable. *Award amount:* $300–$500. *Number of awards:* 19,000–22,000. *Eligibility Requirements:* Applicant must be enrolled or expecting to enroll full or part-time at a two-year, four-year, or technical institution or university; resident of Illinois and studying in Illinois. Available to U.S. and non-U.S. citizens. *Application Requirements:* Financial need analysis. *Deadline:* continuous. **Contact:** David Barinholtz, Client Information, Illinois Student Assistance Commission (ISAC), 1755 Lake Cook Road, Deerfield, IL 60015-5209. *E-mail:* cssupport@isac.org. *Phone:* 847-948-8500 Ext. 2385. *Web site:* www. collegezone.com.

Illinois Monetary Award Program. Award for eligible students attending Illinois public universities, private colleges and universities, community colleges, and some proprietary institutions. Applicable only to tuition and fees. Based on financial need. Applicants are encouraged to apply as soon after January 1st as possible. *Award:* Grant for use in freshman, sophomore, junior, or senior year; not renewable. *Award amount:* up to $4968. *Number of awards:* 135,000–145,000. *Eligibility Requirements:* Applicant must be enrolled or expecting to enroll full or part-time at a two-year, four-year, or technical institution or university; resident of Illinois and studying in Illinois. Available to U.S. and non-U.S. citizens. *Application Requirements:* Financial need analysis. *Deadline:* continuous. **Contact:** David Barinholtz, Client Information, Illinois Student Assistance Commission (ISAC), 1755 Lake Cook Road, Deerfield, IL 60015-5209. *E-mail:* cssupport@isac.org. *Phone:* 847-948-8500 Ext. 2385. *Web site:* www.collegezone.com.

Illinois National Guard Grant Program. Award for qualified National Guard personnel which pays tuition and fees at Illinois public universities and community colleges. Must provide documentation of service. Applications are due October 1 of the academic year for full year, March 1 for second/third term, or June 15 for the summer term. *Award:* Grant for use in freshman, sophomore, junior, senior, graduate, or postgraduate years; renewable. *Award amount:* $1300–$1700. *Number of awards:* 2000–3000. *Eligibility Requirements:* Applicant must be enrolled or expecting to enroll full or part-time at a two-year or four-year institution or university; resident of Illinois and studying in Illinois. Available to U.S. and non-U.S. citizens. Applicant must have served in the Air Force National Guard or Army National Guard. *Application Requirements:* Application, documentation of service. *Deadline:* varies. **Contact:** David Barinholtz, Client Information, Illinois Student Assistance Commission (ISAC), 1755 Lake Cook Road, Deerfield, IL 60015-5209. *E-mail:* cssupport@isac.org. *Phone:* 847-948-8500 Ext. 2385. *Web site:* www.collegezone.com.

Illinois Student-to-Student Program of Matching Grants. Award provides matching funds for need-based grants at participating Illinois public universities and community colleges. Deadlines are set by each institution. *Award:* Grant for use in freshman, sophomore, junior, or senior year; not renewable. *Award amount:* $300–$500. *Number of awards:* 2000–4000. *Eligibility Requirements:* Applicant must be enrolled or expecting to enroll full or part-time at a two-year or four-year institution or university; resident of Illinois and studying in Illinois. Available to U.S. and non-U.S. citizens. *Application Requirements:* Application, financial need analysis. *Deadline:* varies. **Contact:** David Barinholtz, Client Information, Illinois Student Assistance Commission (ISAC), 1755 Lake Cook Road, Deerfield, IL 60015-5209. *E-mail:* cssupport@ isac.org. *Phone:* 847-948-8500 Ext. 2385. *Web site:* www.collegezone. com.

Illinois Veteran Grant Program—IVG. Award for qualified veterans for tuition and fees at Illinois public universities and community colleges. Must provide documentation of service (DD214). Deadline is continuous. *Award:* Grant for use in freshman, sophomore, junior, senior, or graduate year; renewable. *Award amount:* $1400–$1600. *Number of awards:* 11,000–13,000. *Eligibility Requirements:* Applicant must be enrolled or expecting to enroll full or part-time at a two-year or four-year institution or university; resident of Illinois and studying in Illinois. Available to U.S. and non-U.S. citizens. Applicant must have general military experience.*Application Requirements:* Application, documentation of service. *Deadline:* continuous. **Contact:** David Barinholtz, Client Information, Illinois Student Assistance Commission (ISAC), 1755 Lake Cook Road, Deerfield, IL 60015-5209. *E-mail:* cssupport@ isac.org. *Phone:* 847-948-8500 Ext. 2385. *Web site:* www.collegezone. com.

Merit Recognition Scholarship (MRS) Program. Award for Illinois high school seniors graduating in the top 5% of their class and attending Illinois postsecondary institution. Students scoring in the top 5% in one of the college entrance tests among Illinois residents are also eligible. Contact for application procedures.*Award:* Scholarship for use in freshman year; not renewable. *Award amount:* up to $1000. *Number of awards:* 5000–6000. *Eligibility Requirements:* Applicant must be high school student; planning to enroll or expecting to enroll full or part-time at a two-year or four-year institution or university; resident of Illinois and studying in Illinois. Applicant must have 3.5 GPA or higher. Available to U.S. and non-U.S. citizens. *Application Requirements:* Application. *Deadline:* continuous. **Contact:** David Barinholtz, Client Information, Illinois Student Assistance Commission (ISAC), 1755 Lake Cook Road, Deerfield, IL 60015-5209. *E-mail:* cssupport@isac.org. *Phone:* 847-948-8500 Ext. 2385. *Web site:* www.collegezone.com.

MIA/POW Scholarships. One-time award for spouse, child, or step-child of veterans who are missing in action or were a prisoner of war. Must be enrolled at a state-supported school in Illinois. Candidate must be U.S. citizen. Must apply and be accepted before beginning of school. Also for children and spouses of veterans who are determined to be 100% disabled as established by the Veterans Administration.*Award:* Scholarship for use in freshman, sophomore, junior, senior, or graduate year; renewable. *Award amount:* varies. *Number of awards:* varies. *Eligibility Requirements:* Applicant must be enrolled or expecting to enroll full or part-time at a two-year or four-year institution or university; resident of Illinois and studying in Illinois. Available to U.S. citizens. Applicant or parent must meet one or more of the following requirements: general military experience; retired from active duty; disabled or killed as a result of military service; prisoner of war; or missing in action.*Application Requirements:* Application. *Deadline:* continuous. **Contact:** Ms. Tracy Mahan, Grants Section, Illinois Department of Veterans' Affairs, 833 South Spring Street, Springfield, IL 62794-9432. *Phone:* 217-782-3564. *Fax:* 217-782-4161. *Web site:* www.state.il.us/agency/dva.

Minority Teachers of Illinois Scholarship Program. Award for minority students planning to teach at an approved Illinois preschool, elementary, or secondary school. Deadline: March 1. Must be Illinois resident. *Academic Fields/Career Goals:* Education; Special Education. *Award:* Forgivable loan for use in freshman, sophomore, junior, senior, graduate, or postgraduate years; renewable. *Award amount:* up to $5000. *Number of awards:* 450–550. *Eligibility Requirements:* Applicant must be American Indian/Alaska Native, Asian/Pacific Islander, Black (non-Hispanic), or Hispanic; enrolled or expecting to enroll full or part-time at a two-year or four-year institution or university; resident of Illinois and studying in Illinois. Applicant must have 2.5 GPA or higher. Available to U.S. and non-U.S. citizens. *Application Requirements:* Application. *Deadline:* March 1. **Contact:** David Barinholtz, Client Information, Illinois Student Assistance Commission (ISAC), 1755 Lake Cook Road, Deerfield, IL 60015-5209. *E-mail:* cssupport@isac.org. *Phone:* 847-948-8500 Ext. 2385. *Web site:* www.collegezone.com.

Veterans' Children Educational Opportunities. Award is provided to each child age 18 or younger of a veteran who died or became totally disabled as a result of service during World War I, World War II, Korean, or Vietnam War. Must be an Illinois resident and studying in Illinois. Death must be service-connected. Disability must be rated 100% for two or more years. *Award:* Grant for use in freshman year; not renewable. *Award amount:* up to $250. *Number of awards:* varies. *Eligibility Requirements:* Applicant must be age 10-18; enrolled or expecting to enroll at an institution or university; resident of Illinois and studying in Illinois. Available to U.S. citizens. Applicant or parent must meet one or more of the following requirements: general military experience; retired from active duty; disabled or killed as a result of military service; prisoner of war; or missing in action. *Application Requirements:* Application. *Deadline:* June 30. **Contact:** Ms. Tracy Mahan, Grants Section, Illinois Department of Veterans' Affairs, 833 South Spring Street, Springfield, IL 62794-9432. *Phone:* 217-782-3564. *Fax:* 217-782-4161. *Web site:* www.state.il.us/agency/dva.

INDIANA

Charles A. Holt Indiana Wildlife Federation Endowment Scholarship. A $1000 scholarship will be awarded to an Indiana resident accepted for the study or already enrolled for the study of resource conservation or environmental education at the undergraduate level. For more details see Web site: http://www.indianawildlife.org. *Academic Fields/Career Goals:* Natural Resources. *Award:* Scholarship for use in sophomore, junior, or senior year; not renewable. *Award amount:* $1000. *Number of awards:* 1. *Eligibility Requirements:* Applicant must be enrolled or expecting to enroll full-time at a four-year institution or university; resident of Indiana and studying in Indiana. Available to U.S. citizens. *Application Requirements:* Application. *Deadline:* April 30. **Contact:** application available at Web site, Indiana Wildlife Federation Endowment. *Web site:* indianawildlife.org.

Child of Disabled Veteran Grant or Purple Heart Recipient Grant. Free tuition at Indiana state-supported colleges or universities for children of disabled veterans or Purple Heart recipients. Must submit Form DD214 or service record.*Award:* Grant for use in freshman, sophomore, junior, senior, graduate, or postgraduate years; renewable. *Award amount:* varies. *Number of awards:* varies.

Eligibility Requirements: Applicant must be enrolled or expecting to enroll full or part-time at a two-year or four-year institution or university; resident of Indiana and studying in Indiana. Available to U.S. citizens. Applicant or parent must meet one or more of the following requirements: general military experience; retired from active duty; disabled or killed as a result of military service; prisoner of war; or missing in action. *Application Requirements:* Application. *Deadline:* continuous. **Contact:** Jon Brinkley, State Service Officer, Indiana Department of Veterans' Affairs, 302 West Washington Street, Room E-120, Indianapolis, IN 46204-2738. *E-mail:* jbrinkley@dva.state.in.us. *Phone:* 317-232-3910. *Fax:* 317-232-7721. *Web site:* www.ai.org/veteran/index.html.

Culture Connection Foundation Scholarship. Scholarships available for students in single parent families. May be used for undergraduate or graduate study. Those interested in foreign languages, culture, and ethnic studies are encouraged to apply. Application deadline is August 1. *Academic Fields/Career Goals:* African Studies; Anthropology; Area/Ethnic Studies; Art History; Asian Studies; Education; European Studies; Foreign Language; International Studies; Law/Legal Services. *Award:* Scholarship for use in freshman, sophomore, junior, senior, or graduate year; renewable. *Award amount:* $4700. *Number of awards:* 1000. *Eligibility Requirements:* Applicant must be enrolled or expecting to enroll full or part-time at a two-year, four-year, or technical institution or university and single. Applicant must have 2.5 GPA or higher. Available to U.S. and non-U.S. citizens. *Application Requirements:* Application, essay, financial need analysis, interview, references, self-addressed stamped envelope, test scores, transcript, birth certificate, divorce decree. *Deadline:* August 1. **Contact:** Anna Leis, National Program Director, Culture Connection, 8888 Keystone Crossing, Suite 1300, Indianapolis, IN 46240. *E-mail:* annaleis@thecultureconnection.com. *Phone:* 317-547-7055. *Fax:* 317-547-7083. *Web site:* www.thecultureconnection.com.

Department of Veterans Affairs Free Tuition for Children of POW/MIA's in Vietnam. Renewable award for residents of Indiana who are the children of veterans declared missing in action or prisoner-of-war after January 1, 1960. Provides tuition at Indiana state-supported institutions for undergraduate study. *Award:* Grant for use in freshman, sophomore, junior, senior, graduate, or postgraduate years; renewable. *Award amount:* varies. *Number of awards:* varies. *Eligibility Requirements:* Applicant must be enrolled or expecting to enroll at a two-year or four-year institution or university; resident of Indiana and studying in Indiana. Available to U.S. citizens. Applicant or parent must meet one or more of the following requirements: general military experience; retired from active duty; disabled or killed as a result of military service; prisoner of war; or missing in action.*Application Requirements:* Application. *Deadline:* continuous. **Contact:** Jon Brinkley, State Service Officer, Indiana Department of Veterans' Affairs, 302 West Washington Street, Room E-120, Indianapolis, IN 46204-2738. *E-mail:* jbrinkley@dva.state.in.us. *Phone:* 317-232-3910. *Fax:* 317-232-7721. *Web site:* www.ai.org/veteran/index.html.

Hoosier Scholar Award. The Hoosier Scholar Award is a $500 nonrenewable award. Based on the size of the senior class, one to three scholars are selected by the guidance counselor(s) of each accredited high school in Indiana. The award is based on academic merit and may be used for any educational expense at an eligible Indiana institution of higher education. *Award:* Scholarship for use in freshman year; not renewable. *Award amount:* $500. *Number of awards:* 790–840. *Eligibility Requirements:* Applicant must be high school student; planning to enroll or expecting to enroll full-time at a two-year or four-year institution or university; resident of Indiana and studying in Indiana. Applicant must have 3.5 GPA or higher. Available to U.S. citizens. *Application Requirements:* References. *Deadline:* March 10. **Contact:** Ms. Ada Sparkman, Program Coordinator, State Student Assistance Commission of Indiana (SSACI), 150 West Market Street, Suite 500, Indianapolis, IN 46204-2805. *Phone:* 317-232-2350. *Fax:* 317-232-3260. *Web site:* www.ssaci.in.gov.

Indiana Freedom of Choice Grant. The Freedom of Choice Grant is a need-based, tuition-restricted program for students attending Indiana private institutions seeking a first undergraduate degree. It is awarded in addition to the Higher Education Award. Students (and parents of dependent students) who are U.S. citizens and Indiana residents must file the FAFSA yearly by the March 10 deadline.*Award:* Grant for use in freshman, sophomore, junior, or senior year; not renewable. *Award amount:* $200–$5915. *Number of awards:* 10,000–11,830. *Eligibility Requirements:* Applicant must be enrolled or expecting to enroll full-time at a four-year institution or university; resident of Indiana and studying in Indiana. Available to U.S. citizens. *Application Requirements:* Application, financial need analysis, FAFSA. *Deadline:* March 10. **Contact:** Grants Counselor, State Student Assistance Commission of Indiana (SSACI), 150 West Market Street, Suite 500, Indianapolis, IN 46204-2805. *E-mail:* grants@ssaci.state.in.us. *Phone:* 317-232-2350. *Fax:* 317-232-3260. *Web site:* www.ssaci.in.gov.

Indiana Higher Education Award. The Higher Education Award is a need-based, tuition-restricted program for students attending Indiana public, private, or proprietary institutions seeking a first undergraduate degree. Students (and parents of dependent students) who are U.S. citizens and Indiana residents must file the FAFSA yearly by the March 10 deadline. *Award:* Grant for use in freshman, sophomore, junior, or senior year; not renewable. *Award amount:* $200–$4700. *Number of awards:* 38,000–43,660. *Eligibility Requirements:* Applicant must be enrolled or expecting to enroll full-time at a two-year, four-year, or technical institution or university; resident of Indiana and studying in Indiana. Available to U.S. citizens. *Application Requirements:* Application, financial need analysis, FAFSA. *Deadline:* March 10. **Contact:** Grants Counselor, State Student Assistance Commission of Indiana (SSACI), 150 West Market Street, Suite 500, Indianapolis, IN 46204-2805. *E-mail:* grants@ssaci.state.in.us. *Phone:* 317-232-2350. *Fax:* 317-232-3260. *Web site:* www.ssaci.in.gov.

Indiana Minority Teacher and Special Education Services Scholarship Program. For Black or Hispanic students seeking teaching certification or for students seeking special education teaching certification or occupational or physical therapy certification. Must be a U.S. citizen and Indiana resident enrolled full-time in an eligible Indiana institution. Must teach in an Indiana-accredited elementary or secondary school after graduation. Contact institution for application and deadline. Minimum 2.0 GPA required. *Academic Fields/Career Goals:* Education; Special Education; Therapy/Rehabilitation. *Award:* Scholarship for use in freshman, sophomore, junior, or senior year; not renewable. *Award amount:* $1000–$4000. *Number of awards:* 280–370. *Eligibility Requirements:* Applicant must be Black (non-Hispanic) or Hispanic; enrolled or expecting to enroll full-time at a four-year institution or university; resident of Indiana and studying in Indiana. Available to U.S. citizens. *Application Requirements:* Application, financial need analysis. *Deadline:* continuous. **Contact:** Ms. Yvonne Heflin, Director, Special Programs, State Student Assistance Commission of Indiana (SSACI), 150 West Market Street, Suite 500, Indianapolis,

IN 46204-2805. *E-mail:* grants@ssaci.state.in.us. *Phone:* 317-232-2350. *Fax:* 317-232-3260. *Web site:* www.ssaci.in.gov.

Indiana National Guard Supplemental Grant. The award is a supplement to the Indiana Higher Education Grant program. Applicants must be members of the Indiana National Guard. All Guard paperwork must be completed prior to the start of each semester. The FAFSA must be received by March 10. Award covers certain tuition and fees at select public colleges. *Award:* Grant for use in freshman, sophomore, junior, or senior year; not renewable. *Award amount:* $200–$6516. *Number of awards:* 503–925. *Eligibility Requirements:* Applicant must be enrolled or expecting to enroll full or part-time at a two-year or four-year institution or university; resident of Indiana and studying in Indiana. Available to U.S. citizens. Applicant must have served in the Air Force National Guard or Army National Guard. *Application Requirements:* Application. *Deadline:* March 10. **Contact:** Grants Counselor, State Student Assistance Commission of Indiana (SSACI), 150 West Market Street, Suite 500, Indianapolis, IN 46204-2805. *E-mail:* grants@ssaci.state.in.us. *Phone:* 317-232-2350. *Fax:* 317-232-2360. *Web site:* www.ssaci.in.gov.

Indiana Nursing Scholarship Fund. Need-based tuition funding for nursing students enrolled full- or part-time at an eligible Indiana institution. Must be a U.S. citizen and an Indiana resident and have a minimum 2.0 GPA or meet the minimum requirements for the nursing program. Upon graduation, recipients must practice as a nurse in an Indiana health care setting for two years. *Academic Fields/Career Goals:* Nursing. *Award:* Scholarship for use in freshman, sophomore, junior, or senior year; not renewable. *Award amount:* $200–$5000. *Number of awards:* 490–690. *Eligibility Requirements:* Applicant must be enrolled or expecting to enroll full or part-time at a two-year or four-year institution or university; resident of Indiana and studying in Indiana. Available to U.S. citizens. *Application Requirements:* Application, financial need analysis. *Deadline:* continuous. **Contact:** Ms. Yvonne Heflin, Director, Special Programs, State Student Assistance Commission of Indiana (SSACI), 150 West Market Street, Suite 500, Indianapolis, IN 46204-2805. *Phone:* 317-232-2350. *Fax:* 317-232-3260. *Web site:* www.ssaci.in.gov.

Part-time Grant Program. Program is designed to encourage part-time undergraduates to start and complete their associate or baccalaureate degrees or certificates by subsidizing part-time tuition costs. It is a term-based award that is based on need. State residency requirements must be met and a FAFSA must be filed. Eligibility is determined at the institutional level subject to approval by SSACI. *Award:* Grant for use in freshman, sophomore, junior, or senior year; not renewable. *Award amount:* $50–$4000. *Number of awards:* 4680–6700. *Eligibility Requirements:* Applicant must be enrolled or expecting to enroll part-time at a two-year, four-year, or technical institution or university; resident of Indiana and studying in Indiana. Available to U.S. citizens. *Application Requirements:* Application, financial need analysis. *Deadline:* continuous. **Contact:** Grants Counselor, State Student Assistance Commission of Indiana (SSACI), 150 West Market Street, Suite 500, Indianapolis, IN 46204-2805. *E-mail:* grants@ssaci.state.in.us. *Phone:* 317-232-2350. *Fax:* 317-232-3260. *Web site:* www.ssaci.in.gov.

Twenty-first Century Scholars Award. Income-eligible 7th graders who enroll in the program, fulfill a pledge of good citizenship, and complete the Affirmation Form are guaranteed tuition for four years at any participating public institution. If the student attends a private institution, the state will award an amount comparable to that of a public institution. If the student attends a participating proprietary school, the state will award a tuition scholarship equal to that of Ivy Tech State College. FAFSA and affirmation form must be filed yearly by March 10. Applicant must be resident of Indiana. *Award:* Scholarship for use in freshman, sophomore, junior, or senior year; not renewable. *Award amount:* $1000–$6516. *Number of awards:* 2800–8100. *Eligibility Requirements:* Applicant must be enrolled or expecting to enroll full-time at a two-year, four-year, or technical institution or university; resident of Indiana and studying in Indiana. Applicant must have 2.5 GPA or higher. Available to U.S. citizens. *Application Requirements:* Application, financial need analysis, affirmation form. *Deadline:* March 10. **Contact:** Twenty-first Century Scholars Program Counselors, State Student Assistance Commission of Indiana (SSACI), 150 West Market Street, Suite 500, Indianapolis, IN 46204-2805. *Phone:* 317-233-2100. *Fax:* 317-232-3260. *Web site:* www.ssaci.in.gov.

IOWA

Governor Terry E. Branstad Iowa State Fair Scholarship. Up to four scholarships ranging from $500 to $1000 will be awarded to students graduating from an Iowa high school. Must actively participate at the Iowa State Fair. For more details see Web site: http://www.iowacollegeaid.org. *Award:* Scholarship for use in freshman year; not renewable. *Award amount:* $500–$1000. *Number of awards:* up to 4. *Eligibility Requirements:* Applicant must be high school student; planning to enroll or expecting to enroll at an institution or university; resident of Iowa and studying in Iowa. Available to U.S. citizens. *Application Requirements:* Application, essay, financial need analysis, references, transcript. *Deadline:* May 1. **Contact:** Brenda Easter, Director, Special Programs, Iowa College Student Aid Commission, 200 10th Street, 4th Floor, Des Moines, IA 50309-3609. *Phone:* 515-242-3380. *Fax:* 515-242-3388. *Web site:* www.iowacollegeaid.org.

Iowa Foster Child Grants. Grants renewable up to four years will be awarded to students graduating from an Iowa high school who are in Iowa foster care under the care and custody of the Iowa Department of Human Service. Must have a minimum GPA of 2.25 and have applied to an accredited Iowa college or university. For more details see Web site: http://www.iowacollegeaid.org. *Award:* Grant for use in freshman year; renewable. *Award amount:* $2000–$4200. *Number of awards:* varies. *Eligibility Requirements:* Applicant must be high school student; planning to enroll or expecting to enroll at a two-year or four-year institution or university; resident of Iowa and studying in Iowa. Available to U.S. citizens. *Application Requirements:* Application. *Deadline:* April 15. **Contact:** Brenda Easter, Director, Special Programs, Iowa College Student Aid Commission, 200 10th Street, 4th Floor, Des Moines, IA 50309-3609. *Phone:* 515-242-3380. *Fax:* 515-242-3388. *Web site:* www.iowacollegeaid.org.

Iowa Grants. Statewide need-based program to assist high-need Iowa residents. Recipients must demonstrate a high level of financial need to receive awards ranging from $100 to $1,000. Awards are prorated for students enrolled for less than full-time. Awards must be used at Iowa postsecondary institutions. *Award:* Grant for use in freshman, sophomore, junior, or senior year; not renewable. *Award amount:* $100–$1000. *Number of awards:* varies. *Eligibility Requirements:* Applicant must be enrolled or expecting to enroll full- or part-time at a two-year, four-year, or technical institution or university; resident of Iowa and studying in Iowa. Available to U.S. citizens. *Application Requirements:* Application, financial need analysis. *Deadline:* continuous. **Contact:** Julie Leeper, Director,

State Student Aid Programs, Iowa College Student Aid Commission, 200 10th Street, 4th Floor, Des Moines, IA 50309-3609. *E-mail:* icsac@max.state.ia.us. *Phone:* 515-242-3370. *Fax:* 515-242-3388. *Web site:* www.iowacollegeaid.org.

Iowa National Guard Education Assistance Program. Program provides postsecondary tuition assistance to members of Iowa National Guard Units. Must study at a postsecondary institution in Iowa. Contact for additional information.*Award:* Grant for use in freshman, sophomore, junior, or senior year; not renewable. *Award amount:* up to $1200. *Number of awards:* varies. *Eligibility Requirements:* Applicant must be enrolled or expecting to enroll full or part-time at a two-year, four-year, or technical institution or university; resident of Iowa and studying in Iowa. Available to U.S. citizens. Applicant must have served in the Air Force National Guard or Army National Guard. *Application Requirements:* Application. *Deadline:* continuous. **Contact:** Julie Leeper, Director, State Student Aid Programs, Iowa College Student Aid Commission, 200 10th Street, 4th Floor, Des Moines, IA 50309-3609. *E-mail:* icsac@max.state.ia.us. *Phone:* 515-242-3370. *Fax:* 515-242-3388. *Web site:* www.iowacollegeaid.org.

Iowa Teacher Forgivable Loan Program. Forgivable loan assists students who will teach in Iowa secondary schools. Must be an Iowa resident attending an Iowa postsecondary institution. Contact for additional information. *Academic Fields/Career Goals:* Education. *Award:* Forgivable loan for use in freshman, sophomore, junior, or senior year; not renewable. *Award amount:* $2686. *Number of awards:* varies. *Eligibility Requirements:* Applicant must be enrolled or expecting to enroll full or part-time at a four-year institution or university; resident of Iowa and studying in Iowa. Applicant or parent of applicant must have employment or volunteer experience in teaching. Available to U.S. citizens. *Application Requirements:* Application, financial need analysis. *Deadline:* continuous. **Contact:** Brenda Easter, Special Programs Administrator, Iowa College Student Aid Commission, 200 10th Street, 4th Floor, Des Moines, IA 50309-3609. *E-mail:* icsac@max.state.ia.us. *Phone:* 515-242-3380. *Fax:* 515-242-3388. *Web site:* www.iowacollegeaid.org.

Iowa Tuition Grant Program. Program assists students who attend independent postsecondary institutions in Iowa. Iowa residents currently enrolled, or planning to enroll, for at least three semester hours at one of the eligible Iowa postsecondary institutions may apply. Awards currently range from $100 to $4000. Grants may not exceed the difference between independent college and university tuition and fees and the average tuition and fees at the three public Regent universities. *Award:* Grant for use in freshman, sophomore, junior, or senior year; not renewable. *Award amount:* $100–$4000. *Number of awards:* varies. *Eligibility Requirements:* Applicant must be enrolled or expecting to enroll full or part-time at a two-year or four-year institution; resident of Iowa and studying in Iowa. Available to U.S. citizens. *Application Requirements:* Application, financial need analysis. *Deadline:* July 1. **Contact:** Julie Leeper, Director, State Student Aid Programs, Iowa College Student Aid Commission, 200 10th Street, 4th Floor, Des Moines, IA 50309-3609. *E-mail:* icsac@max.state.ia.us. *Phone:* 515-242-3370. *Fax:* 515-242-3388. *Web site:* www.iowacollegeaid. org.

Iowa Vocational Rehabilitation. Provides vocational rehabilitation services to individuals with disabilities who need these services in order to maintain, retain, or obtain employment compatible with their disabilities. Must be Iowa resident.*Award:* Grant for use in freshman, sophomore, junior, senior, graduate, or postgraduate years; renewable. *Award amount:* $500–$4000. *Number of awards:*

up to 5000. *Eligibility Requirements:* Applicant must be enrolled or expecting to enroll full or part-time at a two-year, four-year, or technical institution or university and resident of Iowa. Applicant must be hearing impaired, learning disabled, physically disabled, or visually impaired. Available to U.S. and non-U.S. citizens. *Application Requirements:* Application, interview. *Deadline:* continuous. **Contact:** Ralph Childers, Policy and Workforce Initiatives Coordinator, Iowa Division of Vocational Rehabilitation Services, Division of Vocational Rehabilitation Services, 510 East 12th Street, Des Moines, IA 50319. *E-mail:* rchilders@dvrs.state.ia.us. *Phone:* 515-281-4151. *Fax:* 515-281-4703. *Web site:* www.dvrs.state.ia.us.

Iowa Vocational-Technical Tuition Grant Program. Program provides need-based financial assistance to Iowa residents enrolled in career education (vocational-technical), and career option programs at Iowa area community colleges. Grants range from $150 to $650, depending on the length of program, financial need, and available funds. *Award:* Grant for use in freshman or sophomore year; not renewable. *Award amount:* $150–$650. *Number of awards:* varies. *Eligibility Requirements:* Applicant must be enrolled or expecting to enroll full or part-time at a technical institution; resident of Iowa and studying in Iowa. Available to U.S. citizens.*Application Requirements:* Application, financial need analysis. *Deadline:* July 1. **Contact:** Julie Leeper, Director, State Student Aid Programs, Iowa College Student Aid Commission, 200 10th Street, 4th Floor, Des Moines, IA 50309-3609. *E-mail:* icsac@max.state.ia.us. *Phone:* 515-242-3370. *Fax:* 515-242-3388. *Web site:* www.iowacollegeaid. org.

State of Iowa Scholarship Program. Program provides recognition and financial honorarium to Iowa's academically talented high school seniors. Honorary scholarships are presented to all qualified candidates. Approximately 1700 top-ranking candidates are designated State of Iowa Scholars every March, from an applicant pool of nearly 5000 high school seniors. Must be used at an Iowa postsecondary institution. Minimum 3.5 GPA required. *Award:* Scholarship for use in freshman year; not renewable. *Award amount:* up to $400. *Number of awards:* up to 1700. *Eligibility Requirements:* Applicant must be high school student; planning to enroll or expecting to enroll full-time at a two-year, four-year, or technical institution or university; resident of Iowa and studying in Iowa. Applicant must have 3.5 GPA or higher. Available to U.S. citizens. *Application Requirements:* Application, test scores. *Deadline:* November 1. **Contact:** Julie Leeper, Director, State Student Aid Programs, Iowa College Student Aid Commission, 200 10th Street, 4th Floor, Des Moines, IA 50309-3609. *E-mail:* icsac@max.state. ia.us. *Phone:* 515-242-3370. *Fax:* 515-242-3388. *Web site:* www. iowacollegeaid.org.

KANSAS

Kansas Educational Benefits for Children of MIA, POW, and Deceased Veterans of the Vietnam War. Full-tuition scholarship awarded to students who are children of veterans. Must show proof of parent's status as missing in action, prisoner of war, or killed in action in the Vietnam War. Kansas residence required of veteran at time of entry to service. Must attend a state-supported postsecondary school. *Award:* Scholarship for use in freshman, sophomore, junior, or senior year; not renewable. *Eligibility Requirements:* Applicant must be enrolled or expecting to enroll at a two-year, four-year, or technical institution or university and studying in Kansas. Available to U.S. citizens. Applicant or parent must meet one or more of the following requirements: general military experience; retired from active duty; disabled or killed as

a result of military service; prisoner of war; or missing in action. *Application Requirements:* Application, report of casualty, birth certificate, school acceptance letter. *Deadline:* continuous. **Contact:** Tony Floyd, Program Director, Kansas Commission on Veterans Affairs, 700 Southwest Jackson, Jayhawk Tower, #701, Topeka, KS 66603. *E-mail:* kcva004@ink.org. *Phone:* 785-291-3422. *Fax:* 785-296-1462. *Web site:* www.kcva.org.

Kansas National Guard Educational Assistance Award Program. Service scholarship for enlisted soldiers in the Kansas National Guard. Pays up to 100% of tuition and fees based on funding. Must attend a state-supported institution. Recipients will be required to serve in the KNG for three months for every semester of benefits after the last payment of state tuition assistance. Must not have over 15 years of service at time of application. Deadlines are January 15 and August 20. Contact KNG Education Services Specialist for further information. Must be Kansas resident.*Award:* Scholarship for use in freshman, sophomore, junior, or senior year; not renewable. *Award amount:* $250–$3500. *Number of awards:* up to 400. *Eligibility Requirements:* Applicant must be enrolled or expecting to enroll full or part-time at a two-year, four-year, or technical institution or university; resident of Kansas and studying in Kansas. Available to U.S. citizens. Applicant must have served in the Air Force National Guard or Army National Guard. *Application Requirements:* Application. *Deadline:* varies. **Contact:** Steve Finch, Education Services Specialist, Kansas National Guard Educational Assistance Program, Attn: AGKS-DOP-ESO, The Adjutant General of Kansas, 2800 South West Topeka Boulevard, Topeka, KS 66611-1287. *E-mail:* steve.finch@ ks.ngb.army.mil. *Phone:* 785-274-1060. *Fax:* 785-274-1609.

MICHIGAN

Michigan Adult Part-time Grant. Grant for part-time, needy, independent undergraduates at an approved, degree-granting Michigan college or university. Eligibility is limited to two years. Must be Michigan resident. Deadlines determined by college. *Award:* Grant for use in freshman, sophomore, junior, or senior year; not renewable. *Award amount:* up to $600. *Number of awards:* varies. *Eligibility Requirements:* Applicant must be enrolled or expecting to enroll part-time at a two-year or four-year institution or university; resident of Michigan and studying in Michigan. Available to U.S. citizens. *Application Requirements:* Application, financial need analysis. **Contact:** Program Director, Michigan Bureau of Student Financial Assistance, PO Box 30466, Lansing, MI 48909-7966. *Web site:* www.michigan.gov/mistudentaid.

Michigan Competitive Scholarship. Awards limited to tuition. Must maintain a C average and meet the college's academic progress requirements. Must file Free Application for Federal Student Aid. Deadline: March 1. Must be Michigan resident. Renewable award of $1300 for undergraduate study at a Michigan institution.*Award:* Scholarship for use in freshman, sophomore, junior, or senior year; renewable. *Award amount:* $100–$1300. *Number of awards:* varies. *Eligibility Requirements:* Applicant must be enrolled or expecting to enroll at a two-year or four-year institution or university; resident of Michigan and studying in Michigan. Available to U.S. citizens. *Application Requirements:* Application, financial need analysis, test scores, FAFSA. *Deadline:* March 1. **Contact:** Scholarship and Grant Director, Michigan Bureau of Student Financial Assistance, PO Box 30466, Lansing, MI 48909. *Web site:* www. michigan.gov/mistudentaid.

Michigan Educational Opportunity Grant. Need-based program for Michigan residents who are at least half-time undergraduates attending public Michigan colleges. Must maintain good academic standing. Deadline determined by college. Award of up to $1000. *Award:* Grant for use in freshman, sophomore, junior, or senior year; not renewable. *Award amount:* up to $1000. *Number of awards:* varies. *Eligibility Requirements:* Applicant must be enrolled or expecting to enroll full or part-time at a two-year or four-year institution or university; resident of Michigan and studying in Michigan. Available to U.S. citizens. *Application Requirements:* Application, financial need analysis. *Deadline:* varies. **Contact:** Program Director, Michigan Bureau of Student Financial Assistance, PO Box 30466, Lansing, MI 48909-7966. *Web site:* www.michigan.gov/mistudentaid.

Michigan Indian Tuition Waiver. Renewable´ award provides free tuition for Native-American of one-quarter or more blood degree who attend a Michigan public college or university. Must be a Michigan resident for at least one year. For more details and deadlines contact college financial aid office. *Award:* Scholarship for use in freshman, sophomore, junior, senior, graduate, or postgraduate years; renewable. *Award amount:* varies. *Number of awards:* varies. *Eligibility Requirements:* Applicant must be American Indian/Alaska Native; enrolled or expecting to enroll full or part-time at a two-year or four-year institution or university; resident of Michigan and studying in Michigan. Available to U.S. and Canadian citizens. *Application Requirements:* Application, driver's license. *Deadline:* continuous. **Contact:** Christin McKerchie, Executive Assistant to Programs, Inter-Tribal Council of Michigan, Inc., 405 East Easterday Avenue, Sault Ste. Marie, MI 49783. *E-mail:* christin@itcmi.org. *Phone:* 906-632-6896. *Fax:* 906-632-1810. *Web site:* www.itcmi.org.

Michigan Merit Award. Scholarship for students scoring well on state's standardized assessment tests. Students will have four years from high school graduation to use the award. *Award:* Scholarship for use in freshman year; not renewable. *Award amount:* $1000–$2500. *Number of awards:* varies. *Eligibility Requirements:* Applicant must be high school student; planning to enroll or expecting to enroll full or part-time at a two-year, four-year, or technical institution or university and resident of Michigan. Available to U.S. citizens. *Application Requirements:* Test scores. **Contact:** Program Director, Michigan Bureau of Student Financial Assistance, PO Box 30466, Lansing, MI 48909-7966. *Web site:* www.michigan.gov/mistudentaid.

Michigan Nursing Scholarship. For students enrolled in an LPN, associate degree in nursing, or bachelor of science in nursing programs. Colleges determine application procedure and select recipients. Recipients must fulfill in-state work commitment or repay scholarship. *Academic Fields/Career Goals:* Nursing. *Award:* Scholarship for use in freshman, sophomore, junior, or senior year; renewable. *Award amount:* up to $4000. *Number of awards:* varies. *Eligibility Requirements:* Applicant must be enrolled or expecting to enroll full or part-time at a two-year or four-year institution or university; resident of Michigan and studying in Michigan. Available to U.S. citizens. **Contact:** Program Director, Michigan Bureau of Student Financial Assistance, PO Box 30466, Lansing, MI 48909-7966. *Web site:* www.michigan.gov/mistudentaid.

Michigan Tuition Grants. Need-based program. Students must attend a Michigan private, nonprofit, degree-granting college. Must file the Free Application for Federal Student Aid and meet the college's academic progress requirements. Deadline: March 1. Must be Michigan resident. Renewable award of $2000. *Award:* Grant for use in freshman, sophomore, junior, or senior year; renewable. *Award amount:* $100–$2750. *Number of awards:* varies.

Eligibility Requirements: Applicant must be enrolled or expecting to enroll at a two-year or four-year institution or university; resident of Michigan and studying in Michigan. Available to U.S. citizens. *Application Requirements:* Application, financial need analysis, FAFSA. *Deadline:* March 1. **Contact:** Scholarship and Grant Director, Michigan Bureau of Student Financial Assistance, PO Box 30466, Lansing, MI 48909-7966. *Web site:* www.michigan.gov/mistudentaid.

Michigan Veterans Trust Fund Tuition Grant Program. Tuition grant of $2,800 for children of Michigan veterans who died on active duty or subsequently declared 100% disabled as the result of service-connected illness or injury. Must be 17 to 25 years old, be a Michigan resident, and attend a private or public institution in Michigan. *Award:* Grant for use in freshman, sophomore, junior, or senior year; renewable. *Award amount:* up to $2800. *Number of awards:* varies. *Eligibility Requirements:* Applicant must be age 17-25; enrolled or expecting to enroll full-time at a two-year, four-year, or technical institution or university; resident of Michigan and studying in Michigan. Applicant or parent must meet one or more of the following requirements: general military experience; retired from active duty; disabled or killed as a result of military service; prisoner of war; or missing in action. *Application Requirements:* Application. *Deadline:* continuous. **Contact:** Phyllis Ochis, Department of Military and Veterans Affairs, Michigan Veterans Trust Fund, 2500 South Washington Avenue, Lansing, MI 48913. *Phone:* 517-483-5469. *Web site:* www.michigan.gov/dmva.

Tuition Incentive Program (TIP)-Michigan. Award for Michigan residents who receive or have received Medicaid for required period of time through the Family Independence Agency. Scholarship provides two years tuition towards an associate's degree at a Michigan college or university. Apply before graduating from high school or earning General Education Development diploma. *Award:* Scholarship for use in freshman or sophomore year; renewable. *Number of awards:* varies. *Eligibility Requirements:* Applicant must be high school student; planning to enroll or expecting to enroll full or part-time at a two-year or four-year institution or university; resident of Michigan and studying in Michigan. Available to U.S. citizens. *Application Requirements:* Application, financial need analysis. *Deadline:* continuous. **Contact:** Program Director, Michigan Bureau of Student Financial Assistance, PO Box 30466, Lansing, MI 48909. *Web site:* www.michigan.gov/mistudentaid.

MINNESOTA

Donaldson Company, Inc. Scholarship Program. Scholarships for children of U.S. employees of Donaldson Company, Inc. Any form of accredited postsecondary education is eligible. Application deadline is March 12. *Award:* Scholarship for use in freshman, sophomore, junior, or senior year; renewable. *Award amount:* $1000–$3000. *Eligibility Requirements:* Applicant must be enrolled or expecting to enroll full-time at a two-year, four-year, or technical institution or university. Applicant or parent of applicant must be affiliated with Donaldson Company. Available to U.S. citizens. *Application Requirements:* Application, essay, financial need analysis, references, transcript. *Deadline:* March 12. **Contact:** Norm Linnell, Vice President, General Counsel, and Secretary, Donaldson Company, PO Box 1299, Minneapolis, MN 55440. *E-mail:* nlinnell@mail.donaldson.com. *Phone:* 952-887-3631. *Fax:* 952-887-3005. *Web site:* www.donaldson.com.

Leadership, Excellence and Dedicated Service Scholarship. Awarded to high school seniors who enlist in the Minnesota National Guard. The award recognizes demonstrated leadership, community services and potential for success in the Minnesota

---

National Guard. For more information, applicant may contact any Minnesota army national guard recruiter at 1-800-go-guard or visit the Web site http://www.dma.state.mn.us. *Award:* Scholarship for use in freshman year; not renewable. *Award amount:* $1000. *Number of awards:* 30. *Eligibility Requirements:* Applicant must be high school student and planning to enroll or expecting to enroll full or part-time at a two-year, four-year, or technical institution or university. Available to U.S. and non-U.S. citizens. Applicant must have served in the Air Force National Guard or Army National Guard. *Application Requirements:* Essay, resume, references, transcript. *Deadline:* March 15. **Contact:** Barbara O'Reilly, Education Services Officer, Minnesota Department of Military Affairs, Veterans Services Building, 20 West 12th Street, St. Paul, MN 55155-2098. *E-mail:* barbara.oreilly@mn.ngb.army.mil. *Phone:* 651-282-4508. *Web site:* www.dma.state.mn.us.

Minnesota Educational Assistance for War Orphans. War orphans may qualify for $750 per year. Must have lost parent through service-related death. Children of deceased veterans may qualify for free tuition at State university, college, or vocational or technical schools, but not at University of Minnesota. Must have been resident of Minnesota for at least two years. *Award:* Grant for use in freshman, sophomore, junior, or senior year; renewable. *Award amount:* $750. *Number of awards:* varies. *Eligibility Requirements:* Applicant must be enrolled or expecting to enroll full or part-time at a two-year, four-year, or technical institution or university; resident of Minnesota and studying in Minnesota. Available to U.S. citizens. Applicant or parent must meet one or more of the following requirements: general military experience; retired from active duty; disabled or killed as a result of military service; prisoner of war; or missing in action. *Application Requirements:* Application, financial need analysis. *Deadline:* continuous. **Contact:** Terrence Logan, Management Analyst IV, Minnesota Department of Veterans' Affairs, 20 West 12th Street, Second Floor, St. Paul, MN 55155-2079. *Phone:* 651-296-2562. *Fax:* 651-296-3954. *Web site:* www.state.mn.us/ebranch/mdva.

Minnesota Indian Scholarship Program. One time award for Minnesota Native-American. Applicant must be one quarter Native-American and a resident of Minnesota. Must re-apply for scholarship annually. *Award:* Scholarship for use in freshman, sophomore, junior, or senior year; not renewable. *Award amount:* up to $3300. *Number of awards:* varies. *Eligibility Requirements:* Applicant must be American Indian/Alaska Native; enrolled or expecting to enroll full or part-time at a two-year, four-year, or technical institution or university; resident of Minnesota and studying in Minnesota. Available to U.S. citizens. *Application Requirements:* Application, financial need analysis. *Deadline:* July 1. **Contact:** Lea Perkins, Director, Minnesota Indian Scholarship Office, Minnesota Department of Education, 1500 Highway 36W, Roseville, MN 55113-4266. *E-mail:* cfl.indianeducation@state.mn.us. *Phone:* 800-657-3927. *Web site:* www.mheso.state.mn.us.

Minnesota Nurses Loan Forgiveness Program. This program offers loan repayment to registered nurse and licensed practical nurse students who agree to practice in a Minnesota nursing home or an Intermediate Care Facility for persons with mental retardation for a minimum 3-year service obligation after completion of training. Candidates must apply while still in school. *Academic Fields/Career Goals:* Health and Medical Sciences; Nursing. *Award:* Grant for use in freshman, sophomore, junior, or senior year; not renewable. *Award amount:* $3000–$4000. *Number of awards:* 25–35. *Eligibility Requirements:* Applicant must be enrolled or expecting to enroll full or part-time at a two-year, four-year, or technical institu-

tion or university. Available to U.S. citizens. *Application Requirements:* Application, essay, resume. *Deadline:* continuous. **Contact:** Karen Welter, Minnesota Department of Health, 121 East Seventh Place, Suite 460, PO Box 64975, St. Paul, MN 55164-0975. *E-mail:* karen.welter@health.state.mn.us. *Phone:* 651-282-6302. *Web site:* www.health.state.mn.us.

Minnesota Reciprocal Agreement. Renewable tuition waiver for Minnesota residents. Waives all or part of non-resident tuition surcharge at public institutions in Iowa, Kansas, Michigan, Missouri, Nebraska, North Dakota, South Dakota, and Wisconsin. Deadline is last day of academic term. *Award:* Scholarship for use in freshman, sophomore, junior, senior, graduate, or postgraduate years; renewable. *Award amount:* varies. *Number of awards:* varies. *Eligibility Requirements:* Applicant must be enrolled or expecting to enroll full or part-time at a two-year, four-year, or technical institution or university; resident of Minnesota and studying in Iowa, Kansas, Michigan, Missouri, Nebraska, North Dakota, South Dakota, or Wisconsin. Available to U.S. citizens. *Application Requirements:* Application. *Deadline:* varies. **Contact:** Minnesota Higher Education Services Office, 1450 Energy Park Drive, Suite 350, St. Paul, MN 55108-5227. *Phone:* 651-642-0567 Ext. 1. *Web site:* www.mheso.state.mn.us.

Minnesota Safety Officers' Survivor Program. Grant for eligible survivors of Minnesota public safety officer killed in the line of duty. Safety officers who have been permanently or totally disabled in the line of duty are also eligible. Must be used at a Minnesota institution participating in State Grant Program. Write for details. Must submit proof of death or disability and Public Safety Officers Benefit Fund Certificate. Must apply each year. Can be renewed for four years. *Award:* Grant for use in freshman, sophomore, junior, or senior year; not renewable. *Award amount:* up to $8096. *Eligibility Requirements:* Applicant must be enrolled or expecting to enroll full or part-time at a two-year, four-year, or technical institution or university and studying in Minnesota. Applicant or parent of applicant must have employment or volunteer experience in police/firefighting. Available to U.S. citizens. *Application Requirements:* Application, proof of death/disability. *Deadline:* continuous. **Contact:** Minnesota Higher Education Services Office, 1450 Energy Park Drive, Suite 350, St. Paul, MN 55108-5227. *Phone:* 651-642-0567 Ext. 1. *Web site:* www.mheso.state.mn.us.

Minnesota State Grant Program. Need-based grant program available for Minnesota residents attending Minnesota colleges. Student covers 46% of cost with remainder covered by Pell Grant, parent contribution and state grant. Students apply with FAFSA and college administers the program on campus. *Award:* Grant for use in freshman, sophomore, junior, or senior year; not renewable. *Award amount:* $100–$7662. *Number of awards:* 71,000–75,000. *Eligibility Requirements:* Applicant must be age 17; enrolled or expecting to enroll full or part-time at a two-year, four-year, or technical institution or university; resident of Minnesota and studying in Minnesota. Available to U.S. citizens. *Application Requirements:* Application, financial need analysis. *Deadline:* varies. **Contact:** Minnesota Higher Education Services Office, 1450 Energy Park Drive, Suite 350, St. Paul, MN 55108. *Phone:* 651-642-0567 Ext. 1. *Web site:* www.mheso.state.mn.us.

Minnesota State Veterans' Dependents Assistance Program. Tuition assistance to dependents of persons considered to be prisoner-of-war or missing in action after August 1, 1958. Must be Minnesota resident attending Minnesota two- or four-year school. *Award:* Scholarship for use in freshman, sophomore, junior, or senior year; renewable. *Award amount:* varies. *Number of awards:*

varies. *Eligibility Requirements:* Applicant must be enrolled or expecting to enroll at a two-year or four-year institution; resident of Minnesota and studying in Minnesota. Available to U.S. citizens. Applicant or parent must meet one or more of the following requirements: general military experience; retired from active duty; disabled or killed as a result of military service; prisoner of war; or missing in action.*Application Requirements:* Application. *Deadline:* continuous. **Contact:** Minnesota Higher Education Services Office, 1450 Energy Park Drive, Suite 350, St. Paul, MN 55108-5227. *Web site:* www.mheso.state.mn.us.

Minnesota VA Educational Assistance for Veterans. One-time $750 stipend given to veterans who have used up all other federal funds, yet have time remaining on their delimiting period. Applicant must be a Minnesota resident and must be attending a Minnesota college or university, but not the University of Minnesota.*Award:* Grant for use in freshman, sophomore, junior, or senior year; not renewable. *Award amount:* $750. *Number of awards:* varies. *Eligibility Requirements:* Applicant must be enrolled or expecting to enroll full or part-time at a two-year, four-year, or technical institution or university; resident of Minnesota and studying in Minnesota. Available to U.S. citizens. Applicant must have general military experience. *Application Requirements:* Application, financial need analysis. *Deadline:* continuous. **Contact:** Terrence Logan, Management Analyst IV, Minnesota Department of Veterans' Affairs, 20 West 12th Street, Second Floor, St. Paul, MN 55155-2079. *Phone:* 651-296-2562. *Fax:* 651-296-3954. *Web site:* www.state.mn.us/ebranch/mdva.

Postsecondary Child Care Grant Program-Minnesota. One-time grant available for students not receiving MFIP. Based on financial need. Cannot exceed actual child care costs or maximum award chart (based on income). Must be Minnesota resident. For use at Minnesota two- or four-year school, including public technical colleges. *Award:* Grant for use in freshman, sophomore, junior, or senior year; not renewable. *Award amount:* $100–$2200. *Number of awards:* varies. *Eligibility Requirements:* Applicant must be enrolled or expecting to enroll full or part-time at a two-year, four-year, or technical institution or university; resident of Minnesota and studying in Minnesota. Available to U.S. citizens. *Application Requirements:* Application, financial need analysis. *Deadline:* continuous. **Contact:** Minnesota Higher Education Services Office, 1450 Energy Park Drive, Suite 350, St. Paul, MN 55108-5227. *Phone:* 651-642-0567 Ext. 1. *Web site:* www.mheso.state.mn.us.

MISSOURI

Charles Gallagher Student Assistance Program. Available to Missouri residents attending Missouri colleges or universities full-time. Must be undergraduates with financial need. May reapply for up to a maximum of ten semesters. Free Application for Federal Student Aid (FAFSA) or a renewal must be received by the federal processor by April 1 to be considered. *Award:* Grant for use in freshman, sophomore, junior, or senior year; not renewable. *Award amount:* $100–$1500. *Number of awards:* varies. *Eligibility Requirements:* Applicant must be enrolled or expecting to enroll full-time at a two-year, four-year, or technical institution or university; resident of Missouri and studying in Missouri. Available to U.S. citizens. *Application Requirements:* Financial need analysis. *Deadline:* April 1. **Contact:** MDHE Information Center, Missouri Department of Higher Education, 3515 Amazonas Drive, Jefferson City, MO 65109. *E-mail:* icweb@dhe.mo.gov. *Phone:* 800-473-6757 Ext. 1. *Fax:* 573-751-6635. *Web site:* www.dhe.mo.gov.

Marguerite Ross Barnett Memorial Scholarship. Applicant must be employed (at least 20 hours per week) and attending school part-time. Must be Missouri resident and enrolled at a participating Missouri postsecondary school. Awards not available during summer term. Minimum age is 18. *Award:* Scholarship for use in freshman, sophomore, junior, or senior year; not renewable. *Award amount:* $900–$1700. *Number of awards:* varies. *Eligibility Requirements:* Applicant must be age 18; enrolled or expecting to enroll part-time at a two-year or four-year institution or university; resident of Missouri and studying in Missouri. Available to U.S. citizens. *Application Requirements:* Application, financial need analysis. *Deadline:* April 1. **Contact:** MDHE Information Center, Missouri Department of Higher Education, 3515 Amazonas Drive, Jefferson City, MO 65109. *E-mail:* icweb@dhe.mo.gov. *Phone:* 800-473-6757 Ext. 1. *Fax:* 573-751-6635. *Web site:* www.dhe.mo.gov.

Missouri College Guarantee Program. Available to Missouri residents attending Missouri colleges full-time. Minimum 2.5 GPA required. Must have participated in high school extracurricular activities. *Award:* Scholarship for use in freshman, sophomore, junior, or senior year; not renewable. *Award amount:* $100–$4900. *Number of awards:* varies. *Eligibility Requirements:* Applicant must be enrolled or expecting to enroll full-time at a two-year or four-year institution or university; resident of Missouri and studying in Missouri. Applicant must have 2.5 GPA or higher. Available to U.S. citizens. *Application Requirements:* Financial need analysis, test scores. *Deadline:* April 1. **Contact:** MDHE Information Center, Missouri Department of Higher Education, 3515 Amazonas Drive, Jefferson City, MO 65109. *E-mail:* icweb@dhe.mo.gov. *Phone:* 800-473-6757 Ext. 1. *Fax:* 573-751-6635. *Web site:* www.dhe.mo.gov.

Missouri Higher Education Academic Scholarship (Bright Flight). Awards of $2000 for Missouri high school seniors. Must be in top 3% of Missouri SAT or ACT scorers. Must attend Missouri institution as full-time undergraduate. May reapply for up to ten semesters. Must be Missouri resident and U.S. citizen. *Award:* Scholarship for use in freshman, sophomore, junior, or senior year; not renewable. *Award amount:* $2000. *Number of awards:* varies. *Eligibility Requirements:* Applicant must be high school student; planning to enroll or expecting to enroll full-time at a two-year, four-year, or technical institution or university; resident of Missouri and studying in Missouri. Available to U.S. citizens. *Application Requirements:* Test scores. *Deadline:* July 31. **Contact:** MDHE Information Center, Missouri Department of Higher Education, 3515 Amazonas Drive, Jefferson City, MO 65109. *E-mail:* icweb@dhe.mo.gov. *Phone:* 800-473-6757 Ext. 1. *Fax:* 573-751-6635. *Web site:* www.dhe.mo.gov.

Missouri Minority Teaching Scholarship. Award may be used any year up to four years at an approved, participating Missouri institution. Scholarship is for minority Missouri residents in teaching programs. Recipients must commit to teach for five years in a Missouri public elementary or secondary school. Graduate students must teach math or science. Otherwise, award must be repaid. *Academic Fields/Career Goals:* Education. *Award:* Scholarship for use in freshman, sophomore, junior, senior, or graduate year; renewable. *Award amount:* $3000. *Number of awards:* 100. *Eligibility Requirements:* Applicant must be American Indian/Alaska Native, Asian/Pacific Islander, Black (non-Hispanic), or Hispanic; enrolled or expecting to enroll full-time at a two-year or four-year institution or university; resident of Missouri and studying in Missouri. Applicant must have 3.0 GPA or higher. Available to U.S. citizens. *Application Requirements:* Application, essay, financial need analysis, resume, references, test scores, transcript. *Deadline:* February 15.

Contact: Laura Harrison, Administrative Assistant II, Missouri Department of Elementary and Secondary Education, PO Box 480, Jefferson City, MO 65102-0480. *E-mail:* laura.harrison@dese.mo.gov. *Phone:* 573-751-1668. *Fax:* 573-526-3580. *Web site:* www.dese.state.mo.us.

Missouri Teacher Education Scholarship (General). Nonrenewable award for Missouri high school seniors or Missouri resident college students. Must attend approved teacher training program at a participating Missouri institution. Must rank in top 15 % of high school class on ACT/SAT. Merit-based award. Recipients must commit to teach in Missouri for five years at a public elementary or secondary school or award must be repaid. *Academic Fields/Career Goals:* Education. *Award:* Scholarship for use in freshman, sophomore, junior, or senior year; not renewable. *Award amount:* $2000. *Number of awards:* 200–240. *Eligibility Requirements:* Applicant must be enrolled or expecting to enroll full-time at a two-year or four-year institution or university; resident of Missouri and studying in Missouri. Applicant must have 3.5 GPA or higher. Available to U.S. citizens. *Application Requirements:* Application, essay, resume, references, test scores, transcript. *Deadline:* February 15. **Contact:** Laura Harrison, Administrative Assistant II, Missouri Department of Elementary and Secondary Education, PO Box 480, Jefferson City, MO 65102-0480. *E-mail:* laura.harrison@dese.mo.gov. *Phone:* 573-751-1668. *Fax:* 573-526-3580. *Web site:* www.dese.state.mo.us.

National Farmworker Jobs Program. The grant is from the Department of Labor. Renewable grant to low income seasonal farm workers and their dependents for tuition assistance. Must be a resident of Missouri. Must be paid wages for doing farm work. High school seniors may apply. Must attend a Missouri school. Minimum 2.5 GPA required. *Award:* Grant for use in freshman, sophomore, junior, or senior year; renewable. *Award amount:* up to $3000. *Number of awards:* varies. *Eligibility Requirements:* Applicant must be age 16; enrolled or expecting to enroll at a two-year, four-year, or technical institution or university; resident of Missouri and studying in Missouri. Applicant or parent of applicant must have employment or volunteer experience in agriculture, farming, or migrant worker. Applicant must have 2.5 GPA or higher. *Application Requirements:* Application. *Deadline:* continuous. **Contact:** Lynn Hatfield, Program Director, Rural Missouri, Inc., 1014 Northeast Drive, Jefferson City, MO 65109. *E-mail:* lynn@rmiinc.org. *Phone:* 800-234-4971. *Fax:* 573-635-5636. *Web site:* www.rmiinc.org.

Primary Care Resource Initiative for Missouri Loan Program. Forgivable loans for Missouri residents attending Missouri institutions pursuing a degree as a primary care physician or dentist, studying for a bachelors degree as a dental hygienist, or a master of science degree in nursing leading to certification as an Advanced Practice Nurse. To be forgiven participant must work in a Missouri health professional shortage area. *Academic Fields/Career Goals:* Dental Health/Services; Health and Medical Sciences; Nursing. *Award:* Forgivable loan for use in freshman, sophomore, junior, senior, graduate, or postgraduate years; not renewable. *Award amount:* $3000–$25,000. *Number of awards:* varies. *Eligibility Requirements:* Applicant must be enrolled or expecting to enroll full or part-time at a four-year institution or university; resident of Missouri and studying in Missouri. Available to U.S. citizens. *Application Requirements:* Application, driver's license. *Deadline:* July 1. **Contact:** Kristie Frank, Health Program Representative, Missouri Department of Health and Senior Services, PO Box 570,

Jefferson City, MO 65102-0570. *E-mail:* frank@dhss.mo.gov. *Phone:* 800-891-7415. *Fax:* 573-522-8146. *Web site:* www.dhss.state.mo.us.

NEBRASKA

Nebraska National Guard Tuition Credit. Renewable award for members of the Nebraska National Guard. Pays 75% of enlisted soldier's tuition until he or she has received a baccalaureate degree. *Award:* Scholarship for use in freshman, sophomore, junior, or senior year; renewable. *Number of awards:* up to 1200. *Eligibility Requirements:* Applicant must be enrolled or expecting to enroll full or part-time at a two-year, four-year, or technical institution or university; resident of Nebraska and studying in Nebraska. Applicant must have served in the Air Force National Guard or Army National Guard. *Application Requirements:* Application. *Deadline:* continuous. **Contact:** Cindy York, Administrative Assistant, Nebraska National Guard, 1300 Military Road, Lincoln, NE 68508-1090. *Phone:* 402-309-7143. *Fax:* 402-309-7128. *Web site:* www.neguard.com.

Nebraska State Grant. Available to undergraduates attending a participating postsecondary institution in Nebraska. Available to Pell Grant recipients only. Nebraska residency required. Awards determined by each participating institution. Contact financial aid office at institution for application and additional information.*Award:* Grant for use in freshman, sophomore, junior, or senior year; not renewable. *Award amount:* $100–$1032. *Number of awards:* varies. *Eligibility Requirements:* Applicant must be enrolled or expecting to enroll full or part-time at a two-year, four-year, or technical institution or university; resident of Nebraska and studying in Nebraska. Available to U.S. citizens. *Application Requirements:* Application, financial need analysis. *Deadline:* continuous. **Contact:** Financial Aid Office at college or university, State of Nebraska Coordinating Commission for Postsecondary Education. *Web site:* www.ccpe.state.ne.us.

NORTH DAKOTA

North Dakota Department of Transportation Engineering Grant. Educational grants for civil or construction engineering, or civil engineering technology, are awarded to students who have completed one year of course study at an institution of higher learning in North Dakota. Recipients must agree to work for the Department for a period of time at least equal to the grant period or repay the grant at 6% interest. Minimum 2.0 GPA required. *Academic Fields/Career Goals:* Civil Engineering; Engineering/Technology. *Award:* Grant for use in sophomore, junior, or senior year; renewable. *Award amount:* $1000–$6000. *Number of awards:* varies. *Eligibility Requirements:* Applicant must be enrolled or expecting to enroll full-time at a four-year, or technical institution and studying in North Dakota. Available to U.S. citizens. *Application Requirements:* Application, financial need analysis, interview, transcript. *Deadline:* continuous. **Contact:** Lorrie Pavlicek, Human Resources Manager, North Dakota Department of Transportation, 503 38th Street South, Fargo, ND 58103. *E-mail:* lpavlice@state.nd.us. *Phone:* 701-239-8934. *Fax:* 701-239-8939. *Web site:* www.state.nd.us/dot/.

North Dakota Indian Scholarship Program. Assists Native-American North Dakota residents in obtaining a college education. Priority given to full-time undergraduate students and those having a 3.5 GPA or higher. Certification of tribal enrollment required. For use at North Dakota institution. *Award:* Scholarship for use in freshman, sophomore, junior, senior, or graduate year;

renewable. *Award amount:* $600–$900. *Number of awards:* up to 150. *Eligibility Requirements:* Applicant must be American Indian/ Alaska Native; enrolled or expecting to enroll at a two-year or four-year institution or university; resident of North Dakota and studying in North Dakota. Applicant must have 3.5 GPA or higher. *Application Requirements:* Application, financial need analysis, transcript, proof of tribal enrollment. *Deadline:* July 15. **Contact:** Rhonda Schauer, Coordinator of American Indian Higher Education, State of North Dakota, 600 East Boulevard, Department 215, Bismarck, ND 58505-0230. *Phone:* 701-328-9661. *Web site:* www.ndus.nodak.edu.

North Dakota Scholars Program. Provides scholarships equal to cost of tuition at the public colleges in North Dakota for North Dakota residents. Must score at or above the 95th percentile on ACT and rank in top twenty percent of high school graduation class. Must take ACT in fall. For high school seniors with a minimum 3.5 GPA. Application deadline is the October or June ACT test date. *Award:* Scholarship for use in freshman, sophomore, junior, or senior year; renewable. *Award amount:* varies. *Number of awards:* 20. *Eligibility Requirements:* Applicant must be high school student; planning to enroll or expecting to enroll full-time at a two-year or four-year institution or university; resident of North Dakota and studying in North Dakota. Applicant must have 3.5 GPA or higher. Available to U.S. citizens. *Application Requirements:* Test scores. *Deadline:* varies. **Contact:** Peggy Wipf, Director of Financial Aid, State of North Dakota, 600 East Boulevard, Department 215, Bismarck, ND 58505-0230. *Phone:* 701-328-4114. *Web site:* www.ndus.nodak.edu.

North Dakota Student Financial Assistance Grants. Aids North Dakota residents attending an approved college or university in North Dakota. Must be enrolled in a program of at least nine months in length. *Award:* Grant for use in freshman, sophomore, junior, or senior year; not renewable. *Award amount:* up to $600. *Number of awards:* 2500–2600. *Eligibility Requirements:* Applicant must be enrolled or expecting to enroll full-time at a two-year or four-year institution or university; resident of North Dakota and studying in North Dakota. Available to U.S. citizens. *Application Requirements:* Financial need analysis, FAFSA. *Deadline:* March 15. **Contact:** Peggy Wipf, Director of Financial Aid, State of North Dakota, 600 East Boulevard, Department 215, Bismarck, ND 58505-0230. *Phone:* 701-328-4114. *Web site:* www.ndus.nodak.edu.

OHIO

Accountancy Board of Ohio Educational Assistance Program. Program intended for minority students or students with financial need. Applicant must be enrolled as accounting major at an accredited Ohio college or university in a five-year degree program. Applicant must be an Ohio resident. Please refer to Web site for further details: http://acc.ohio.gov/educasst.html. *Academic Fields/ Career Goals:* Accounting. *Award:* Scholarship for use in sophomore, junior, or senior year; not renewable. *Award amount:* $7700. *Number of awards:* varies. *Eligibility Requirements:* Applicant must be enrolled or expecting to enroll at a four-year institution or university; resident of Ohio and studying in Ohio. Available to U.S. citizens. *Application Requirements:* Application, financial need analysis, transcript, FAFSA. *Deadline:* varies. **Contact:** Kay Sedgmer, Scholarship Secretary, Accountancy Board of Ohio, Accountancy Board of Ohio, 77 South High Street, 18th Floor, Columbus, OH 43266-0301. *E-mail:* kay.sedgmer@acc.state.oh.us. *Phone:* 614-466-4135. *Fax:* 614-466-2628. *Web site:* acc.ohio.gov/.

Ohio Academic Scholarship Program. Award for academically outstanding Ohio residents planning to attend an approved Ohio college. Must be a high school senior intending to enroll full-time. Award is renewable for up to four years. Must rank in upper quarter of class or have a minimum GPA of 3.5. *Award:* Scholarship for use in freshman, sophomore, junior, or senior year; renewable. *Award amount:* $2205. *Number of awards:* 1000. *Eligibility Requirements:* Applicant must be high school student; planning to enroll or expecting to enroll full-time at a two-year or four-year institution; resident of Ohio and studying in Ohio. Applicant must have 3.5 GPA or higher. Available to U.S. citizens. *Application Requirements:* Application, test scores, transcript. *Deadline:* February 23. **Contact:** Sarina Wilks, Program Administrator, Ohio Board of Regents, PO Box 182452, Columbus, OH 43218-2452. *E-mail:* swilks@regents.state.oh.us. *Phone:* 614-752-9528. *Fax:* 614-752-5903. *Web site:* www.regents.state.oh.us.

Ohio Instructional Grant. Award for low- and middle-income Ohio residents attending an approved college or school in Ohio or Pennsylvania. Must be enrolled full-time and have financial need. Average award is $630. May be used for any course of study except theology. *Award:* Grant for use in freshman, sophomore, junior, or senior year; renewable. *Award amount:* $78–$5466. *Number of awards:* varies. *Eligibility Requirements:* Applicant must be enrolled or expecting to enroll full-time at a two-year or four-year institution or university; resident of Ohio and studying in Ohio or Pennsylvania. Available to U.S. citizens. *Application Requirements:* Application, financial need analysis. *Deadline:* October 1. **Contact:** Charles Shahid, Assistant Director, Ohio Board of Regents, PO Box 182452, Columbus, OH 43218-2452. *E-mail:* cshahid@regents.state.oh.us. *Phone:* 614-644-5959. *Fax:* 614-752-5903. *Web site:* www.regents.state.oh.us.

Ohio Missing in Action and Prisoners of War Orphans Scholarship. Renewable award aids children of Vietnam conflict servicemen who have been classified as missing in action or prisoner of war. Must be an Ohio resident, be 16-21, and be enrolled full-time at an Ohio college. Full tuition awards. *Award:* Scholarship for use in freshman, sophomore, junior, or senior year; renewable. *Award amount:* varies. *Number of awards:* 1–5. *Eligibility Requirements:* Applicant must be age 16-21; enrolled or expecting to enroll full-time at a two-year or four-year institution; resident of Ohio and studying in Ohio. Available to U.S. citizens. Applicant or parent must meet one or more of the following requirements: general military experience; retired from active duty; disabled or killed as a result of military service; prisoner of war; or missing in action. *Application Requirements:* Application. *Deadline:* July 1. **Contact:** Sarina Wilks, Program Administrator, Ohio Board of Regents, PO Box 182452, Columbus, OH 43218-2452. *E-mail:* swilks@regents.state.oh.us. *Phone:* 614-752-9528. *Fax:* 614-752-5903. *Web site:* www.regents.state.oh.us.

Ohio National Guard Scholarship Program. Scholarships are for undergraduate studies at an approved Ohio postsecondary institution. Applicants must enlist for six years of Selective Service Reserve Duty in the Ohio National Guard. Scholarship pays 100% instructional and general fees for public institutions and an average of cost of public schools is available for private schools. Must be 18 years of age or older. Award is renewable. Deadlines: July 1, November 1, February 1, April 1. *Award:* Scholarship for use in freshman, sophomore, junior, or senior year; renewable. *Award amount:* up to $3000. *Number of awards:* 3500–8000. *Eligibility Requirements:* Applicant must be age 18; enrolled or expecting to enroll full or part-time at a two-year, four-year, or technical institution or university and studying in Ohio. Available to U.S. citizens. Applicant must have served in the Air Force National Guard or Army National Guard. *Application Requirements:* Application. *Deadline:* varies. **Contact:** Mrs. Toni Davis, Grants Administrator, Ohio National Guard, 2825 West Dublin Granville Road, Columbus, OH 43235-2789. *E-mail:* toni.davis@tagoh.org. *Phone:* 614-336-7032. *Fax:* 614-336-7318.

Ohio Safety Officers College Memorial Fund. Renewable award covering up to full tuition is available to children and surviving spouses of peace officers and fire fighters killed in the line of duty in any state. Children must be under 26 years of age. Must be an Ohio resident and enroll full-time or part-time at an Ohio college or university. *Award:* Scholarship for use in freshman, sophomore, junior, or senior year; renewable. *Award amount:* varies. *Number of awards:* 50–65. *Eligibility Requirements:* Applicant must be age 25 or under; enrolled or expecting to enroll full or part-time at a two-year or four-year institution or university; resident of Ohio and studying in Ohio. Applicant or parent of applicant must have employment or volunteer experience in police/firefighting. Available to U.S. citizens. *Application Requirements: Deadline:* continuous. **Contact:** Barbara Metheney, Program Administrator, Ohio Board of Regents, PO Box 182452, Columbus, OH 43218-2452. *E-mail:* bmethene@regents.state.oh.us. *Phone:* 614-752-9535. *Fax:* 614-752-5903. *Web site:* www.regents.state.oh.us.

Ohio Student Choice Grant Program. Renewable award available to Ohio residents attending private colleges within the state. Must be enrolled full-time in a bachelor's degree program. Do not apply to state. Check with financial aid office of college. *Award:* Grant for use in freshman, sophomore, junior, or senior year; renewable. *Award amount:* up to $1002. *Number of awards:* varies. *Eligibility Requirements:* Applicant must be enrolled or expecting to enroll full-time at a four-year institution; resident of Ohio and studying in Ohio. Available to U.S. citizens. *Application Requirements: Deadline:* continuous. **Contact:** Barbara Metheney, Program Administrator, Ohio Board of Regents, PO Box 182452, Columbus, OH 43218-2452. *E-mail:* bmethene@regents.state.oh.us. *Phone:* 614-752-9535. *Fax:* 614-752-5903. *Web site:* www.regents.state.oh. us.

Ohio War Orphans Scholarship. Aids Ohio residents attending an eligible college in Ohio. Must be between the ages of 16-21, the child of a disabled or deceased veteran, and enrolled full-time. Renewable up to five years. Amount of award varies. Must include Form DD214. *Award:* Scholarship for use in freshman, sophomore, junior, or senior year; renewable. *Award amount:* varies. *Number of awards:* 300–450. *Eligibility Requirements:* Applicant must be age 16-21; enrolled or expecting to enroll full-time at a two-year or four-year institution; resident of Ohio and studying in Ohio. Available to U.S. citizens. Applicant or parent must meet one or more of the following requirements: general military experience; retired from active duty; disabled or killed as a result of military service; prisoner of war; or missing in action. *Application Requirements:* Application. *Deadline:* July 1. **Contact:** Sarina Wilks, Program Administrator, Ohio Board of Regents, PO Box 182452, Columbus, OH 43218-2452. *E-mail:* swilks@regents.state.oh.us. *Phone:* 614-752-9528. *Fax:* 614-752-5903. *Web site:* www.regents.state.oh.us.

Part-time Student Instructional Grant. Renewable grants for part-time undergraduates who are Ohio residents. Award amounts vary. Must attend an Ohio institution. *Award:* Grant for use in freshman, sophomore, or junior year; renewable. *Award amount:* varies. *Number of awards:* varies. *Eligibility Requirements:* Applicant must be enrolled or expecting to enroll part-time at a two-year or

four-year institution or university; resident of Ohio and studying in Ohio. Available to U.S. citizens. *Application Requirements:* Application, financial need analysis. *Deadline:* continuous. **Contact:** Barbara Metheney, Program Administrator, Ohio Board of Regents, PO Box 182452, Columbus, OH 43218-2452. *E-mail:* bmethene@regents.state.oh.us. *Phone:* 614-752-9535. *Fax:* 614-752-5903. *Web site:* www.regents.state.oh.us.

Robert C. Byrd Honors Scholarship. Renewable award for graduating high school seniors who demonstrate outstanding academic achievement. Each Ohio high school receives applications by January of each year. School can submit one application for every 200 students in the senior class. Application deadline is the second Friday in March. *Award:* Scholarship for use in freshman, sophomore, junior, or senior year; renewable. *Award amount:* up to $1500. *Number of awards:* varies. *Eligibility Requirements:* Applicant must be high school student; planning to enroll or expecting to enroll at a two-year or four-year institution or university and resident of Ohio. Applicant must have 3.5 GPA or higher. Available to U.S. citizens. *Application Requirements:* Application, test scores. *Deadline:* varies. **Contact:** Byrd Program Office, Ohio Department of Education, 25 South Front Street, Second Floor, Columbus, OH 43215. *Phone:* 614-466-4590. *Web site:* www. ode.state.oh.us.

OKLAHOMA

Academic Scholars Program. Encourages students of high academic ability to attend institutions in Oklahoma. Renewable up to four years. ACT or SAT scores must fall between 99.5 and 100th percentiles, or applicant must be designated as a National Merit scholar or finalist. *Award:* Scholarship for use in freshman, sophomore, junior, or senior year; renewable. *Award amount:* $3500–$5500. *Number of awards:* varies. *Eligibility Requirements:* Applicant must be high school student; planning to enroll or expecting to enroll full-time at a two-year or four-year institution or university and studying in Oklahoma. Available to U.S. and non-U.S. citizens. *Application Requirements:* Application, test scores, transcript. *Deadline:* continuous. **Contact:** Oklahoma State Regents for Higher Education, PO Box 108850, Oklahoma City, OK 73101-8850. *E-mail:* studentinfo@osrhe.edu. *Phone:* 800-858-1840. *Fax:* 405-225-9230. *Web site:* www.okhighered.org.

Future Teacher Scholarship-Oklahoma. Open to outstanding Oklahoma high school graduates who agree to teach in shortage areas. Must rank in top 15% of graduating class or score above 85th percentile on ACT or similar test, or be accepted in an educational program. Students nominated by institution. Reapply to renew. Must attend college/university in Oklahoma. Contact institution's financial aid office for application deadline. *Academic Fields/Career Goals:* Education. *Award:* Scholarship for use in freshman, sophomore, junior, senior, or graduate year; not renewable. *Award amount:* up to $1500. *Number of awards:* varies. *Eligibility Requirements:* Applicant must be enrolled or expecting to enroll full or part-time at a two-year or four-year institution or university; resident of Oklahoma and studying in Oklahoma. Available to U.S. and non-U.S. citizens. *Application Requirements:* Application, essay, test scores, transcript. *Deadline:* continuous. **Contact:** Oklahoma State Regents for Higher Education, PO Box 108850, Oklahoma City, OK 73101-8850. *Phone:* 800-858-1840. *Fax:* 405-225-9230. *Web site:* www.okhighered.org.

Oklahoma Tuition Aid Grant. Award for Oklahoma residents enrolled at an Oklahoma institution at least part time each semester in a degree program. May be enrolled in two- or four-year or approved vocational-technical institution. Award of up to $1000 per year. Application is made through FAFSA. *Award:* Grant for use in freshman, sophomore, junior, senior, or graduate year; renewable. *Award amount:* $200–$1000. *Number of awards:* 23,000. *Eligibility Requirements:* Applicant must be enrolled or expecting to enroll full or part-time at a two-year, four-year, or technical institution or university; resident of Oklahoma and studying in Oklahoma. Available to U.S. citizens. *Application Requirements:* Application, financial need analysis, FAFSA. *Deadline:* April 30. **Contact:** Oklahoma State Regents for Higher Education, PO Box 3020, Oklahoma City, OK 73101-3020. *E-mail:* otaginfo@otag.org. *Phone:* 405-225-9456. *Fax:* 405-225-9392. *Web site:* www.okhighered.org.

Regional University Baccalaureate Scholarship. Renewable award for Oklahoma residents attending one of 11 participating Oklahoma public universities. Must have an ACT composite score of at least 30 or be a National Merit semifinalist or commended student. In addition to the award amount, each recipient will receive a resident tuition waiver from the institution. Must maintain a 3.25 GPA. Deadlines vary depending upon the institution attended. *Award:* Scholarship for use in freshman, sophomore, junior, or senior year; renewable. *Award amount:* $3000. *Number of awards:* varies. *Eligibility Requirements:* Applicant must be enrolled or expecting to enroll full-time at an institution or university; resident of Oklahoma and studying in Oklahoma. Available to U.S. and non-U.S. citizens. *Application Requirements:* Application. *Deadline:* varies. **Contact:** Oklahoma State Regents for Higher Education, PO Box 108850, Oklahoma City, OK 73101-8850. *E-mail:* studentinfo@osrhe.edu. *Phone:* 800-858-1840. *Fax:* 405-225-9230. *Web site:* www.okhighered.org.

SOUTH DAKOTA

Education Benefits for Dependents of POWs and MIAs. Children and spouses of prisoners of war, or of persons listed as missing in action, are entitled to attend a state-supported school without the payment of tuition or mandatory fees provided they are not eligible for equal or greater federal benefits. Must use SDDVA form E-12 available at financial aid offices. Must be a South Dakota resident intending to study in South Dakota. *Award:* Scholarship for use in freshman, sophomore, junior, or senior year; not renewable. *Award amount:* varies. *Number of awards:* varies. *Eligibility Requirements:* Applicant must be enrolled or expecting to enroll at an institution or university; resident of South Dakota and studying in South Dakota. Available to U.S. citizens. Applicant or parent must meet one or more of the following requirements: general military experience; retired from active duty; disabled or killed as a result of military service; prisoner of war; or missing in action.*Application Requirements:* Application. *Deadline:* varies. **Contact:** Dr. Lesta V. Turchen, Senior Administrator, South Dakota Board of Regents, 306 East Capitol Avenue, Suite 200, Pierre, SD 57501-3159. *Phone:* 605-773-3455. *Fax:* 605-773-2422. *Web site:* www.ris.sdbor.edu.

Haines Memorial Scholarship. One-time scholarship for South Dakota public university students who are sophomores, juniors, or seniors having at least a 2.5 GPA and majoring in a teacher education program. Include resume with application. Must be South Dakota resident. *Academic Fields/Career Goals:* Education. *Award:* Scholarship for use in sophomore, junior, or senior year; not renewable. *Award amount:* $2150. *Number of awards:* 1. *Eligibility Requirements:* Applicant must be enrolled or expecting to enroll at an institution or university; resident of South Dakota and studying in South Dakota. Applicant must have 2.5 GPA or

higher.*Application Requirements:* Application, autobiography, essay, resume. *Deadline:* February 25. **Contact:** South Dakota Board of Regents, 306 East Capitol Avenue, Suite 200, Pierre, SD 57501-3159. *Web site:* www.ris.sdbor.edu.

South Dakota Aid to Dependents of Deceased Veterans. Program provides free tuition for children of deceased veterans who are under the age of 25, are residents of South Dakota, and whose mother or father was killed in action or died of other causes while on active duty. ("Veteran" for this purpose is as defined by South Dakota Codified Laws.) Parent must have been a bona fide resident of SD for at least six months immediately preceding entry into active service. Eligibility is for state-supported schools only. Must use SDDVA form E-12 available at financial aid offices. *Award:* Scholarship for use in freshman, sophomore, junior, or senior year; not renewable. *Award amount:* varies. *Number of awards:* varies. *Eligibility Requirements:* Applicant must be age 24 or under; enrolled or expecting to enroll at a two-year or four-year institution; resident of South Dakota and studying in South Dakota. Available to U.S. citizens. Applicant or parent must meet one or more of the following requirements: general military experience; retired from active duty; disabled or killed as a result of military service; prisoner of war; or missing in action.*Application Requirements:* Application. *Deadline:* varies. **Contact:** Dr. Lesta V. Turchen, Senior Administrator, South Dakota Board of Regents, 306 East Capitol Avenue, Suite 200, Pierre, SD 57501-3159. *Phone:* 605-773-3455. *Fax:* 605-773-2422. *Web site:* www.ris.sdbor.edu.

South Dakota Board of Regents Senior Citizens Tuition Assistance. Award for tuition assistance for any postsecondary academic year of study to senior citizens age 65 and older. Write for further details. Must be a South Dakota resident and attend a school in South Dakota. *Award:* Scholarship for use in freshman, sophomore, junior, or senior year; not renewable. *Award amount:* varies. *Number of awards:* varies. *Eligibility Requirements:* Applicant must be age 65; enrolled or expecting to enroll at an institution or university; resident of South Dakota and studying in South Dakota. *Application Requirements:* Application. *Deadline:* continuous. **Contact:** South Dakota Board of Regents, 306 East Capitol Avenue, Suite 200, Pierre, SD 57501-3159. *Web site:* www.ris.sdbor.edu.

South Dakota Board of Regents State Employee Tuition Assistance. Award for South Dakota state employees for any postsecondary academic year of study in South Dakota institution. Must be U.S. citizen. Write for requirements and other details. *Award:* Scholarship for use in freshman, sophomore, junior, or senior year; not renewable. *Award amount:* varies. *Number of awards:* varies. *Eligibility Requirements:* Applicant must be enrolled or expecting to enroll at an institution or university; resident of South Dakota and studying in South Dakota. Applicant or parent of applicant must have employment or volunteer experience in designated career field. Available to U.S. citizens. *Application Requirements:* *Deadline:* continuous. **Contact:** South Dakota Board of Regents, 306 East Capitol Avenue, Suite 200, Pierre, SD 57501-3159. *Web site:* www.ris.sdbor.edu.

South Dakota Education Benefits for National Guard Members. Guard members who meet the requirements for admission are eligible for a 50% reduction in undergraduate tuition charges at any state-supported school for up to a maximum of four academic years. Provision also covers one program of study, approved by the State Board of Education, at any state vocational school. Must be state resident and member of the SD Army or Air Guard throughout period for which benefits are sought. Must contact financial aid office for full details and forms at time of registration. *Award:* Scholarship for use in freshman, sophomore, junior, or senior year; not renewable. *Award amount:* varies. *Number of awards:* varies. *Eligibility Requirements:* Applicant must be enrolled or expecting to enroll at a two-year, four-year, or technical institution or university; resident of South Dakota and studying in South Dakota. Available to U.S. citizens. Applicant must have served in the Air Force National Guard or Army National Guard. *Application Requirements:* Application. *Deadline:* varies. **Contact:** Dr. Lesta V. Turchen, Senior Administrator, South Dakota Board of Regents, 306 East Capitol Avenue, Suite 200, Pierre, SD 57501-3159. *Phone:* 605-773-3455. *Fax:* 605-773-2422. *Web site:* www.ris.sdbor.edu.

South Dakota Education Benefits for Veterans. Certain veterans are eligible for free undergraduate tuition assistance at state-supported schools provided they are not eligible for educational payments under the GI Bill or any other federal educational program. Contact financial aid office for full details and forms. May receive one month of free tuition for each month of qualifying service (minimum one year, maximum four years). Must be resident of South Dakota. *Award:* Scholarship for use in freshman, sophomore, junior, or senior year; not renewable. *Award amount:* varies. *Number of awards:* varies. *Eligibility Requirements:* Applicant must be enrolled or expecting to enroll at an institution or university; resident of South Dakota and studying in South Dakota. Available to U.S. citizens. Applicant must have general military experience. *Application Requirements:* Application, DD Form 214. *Deadline:* varies. **Contact:** Dr. Lesta V. Turchen, Senior Administrator, South Dakota Board of Regents, 306 East Capitol Avenue, Suite 200, Pierre, SD 57501-3159. *Phone:* 605-773-3455. *Fax:* 605-773-2422. *Web site:* www.ris.sdbor.edu.

WISCONSIN

Handicapped Student Grant-Wisconsin. One-time award available to residents of Wisconsin who have severe or profound hearing or visual impairment. Must be enrolled at least half-time at a nonprofit institution. If the handicap prevents the student from attending a Wisconsin school, the award may be used out-of-state in a specialized college. Please refer to Web site for further details: http://www.heab.state.wi.us*Award:* Grant for use in freshman, sophomore, junior, or senior year; not renewable. *Award amount:* $250–$1800. *Number of awards:* varies. *Eligibility Requirements:* Applicant must be enrolled or expecting to enroll full or part-time at a two-year, four-year, or technical institution or university and resident of Wisconsin. Applicant must be hearing impaired or visually impaired. Available to U.S. citizens.*Application Requirements:* Application, financial need analysis. *Deadline:* continuous. **Contact:** Sandra Thomas, Program Coordinator, Wisconsin Higher Educational Aids Board, PO Box 7885, Madison, WI 53707-7885. *E-mail:* sandy.thomas@heab.state.wi.us. *Phone:* 608-266-0888. *Fax:* 608-267-2808. *Web site:* www.heab.state.wi.us.

Minnesota-Wisconsin Reciprocity Program. Wisconsin residents may attend a Minnesota public institution and pay the reciprocity tuition charged by Minnesota institution. All programs are eligible except doctoral programs in medicine, dentistry, and veterinary medicine. Please refer to Web site for further details: http://www.heab.state.wi.us*Award:* Scholarship for use in freshman, sophomore, junior, or senior year; renewable. *Award amount:* varies. *Number of awards:* varies. *Eligibility Requirements:* Applicant must be enrolled or expecting to enroll full or part-time at a two-year, four-year, or technical institution or university; resident of Wisconsin and studying in Minnesota. Available to U.S. citizens.

Application Requirements: Application. *Deadline:* continuous. **Contact:** Cindy Lehrman, Wisconsin Higher Educational Aids Board, PO Box 7885, Madison, WI 53707-7885. *E-mail:* cindy.lehrman@heab.state.wi.us. *Phone:* 608-267-2209. *Fax:* 608-267-2808. *Web site:* www.heab.state.wi.us.

Minority Retention Grant-Wisconsin. Provides financial assistance to African-American, Native-American, Hispanic, and former citizens of Laos, Vietnam, and Cambodia, for study in Wisconsin. Must be Wisconsin resident, enrolled at least half-time in a two-year or four-year nonprofit college, and must show financial need. Please refer to Web site for further details: http://www.heab.state.wi.us*Award:* Grant for use in sophomore, junior, senior, or graduate year; not renewable. *Award amount:* $250–$2500. *Number of awards:* varies. *Eligibility Requirements:* Applicant must be American Indian/Alaska Native, Asian/Pacific Islander, Black (non-Hispanic), or Hispanic; enrolled or expecting to enroll full or part-time at a two-year, four-year, or technical institution; resident of Wisconsin and studying in Wisconsin. Available to U.S. and non-U.S. citizens. *Application Requirements:* Application, financial need analysis. *Deadline:* continuous. **Contact:** Mary Lou Kuzdas, Program Coordinator, Wisconsin Higher Educational Aids Board, PO Box 7885, Madison, WI 53707-7885. *E-mail:* mary.kuzdas@heab.state.wi.us. *Phone:* 608-267-2212. *Fax:* 608-267-2808. *Web site:* www.heab.state.wi.us.

Nursing Student Loan Program. Provides forgivable loans to students enrolled in a nursing program. Must be a Wisconsin resident studying in Wisconsin. Application deadline is last day on which student is enrolled. Please refer to Web site for further details: http://www.heab.state.wi.us *Academic Fields/Career Goals:* Nursing. *Award:* Forgivable loan for use in freshman, sophomore, junior, or senior year; renewable. *Award amount:* $250–$3000. *Number of awards:* 150–1800. *Eligibility Requirements:* Applicant must be enrolled or expecting to enroll full or part-time at a two-year, four-year, or technical institution or university; resident of Wisconsin and studying in Wisconsin. Available to U.S. citizens. *Application Requirements:* Application, financial need analysis. **Contact:** Cindy Lehrman, Program Coordinator, Wisconsin Higher Educational Aids Board, PO Box 7885, Madison, WI 53707-7885. *E-mail:* cindy.lehrman@heab.state.wi.us. *Phone:* 608-267-2209. *Fax:* 608-267-2808. *Web site:* www.heab.state.wi.us.

Talent Incentive Program Grant. Assists residents of Wisconsin who are attending a nonprofit institution in Wisconsin and have substantial financial need. Must meet income criteria, be considered economically and educationally disadvantaged and be enrolled at least half-time. Please refer to Web site for further details: http://www.heab.state.wi.us*Award:* Grant for use in freshman, sophomore, junior, or senior year; renewable. *Award amount:* $250–$1800. *Number of awards:* varies. *Eligibility Requirements:* Applicant must be enrolled or expecting to enroll full or part-time at a two-year, four-year, or technical institution or university; resident of Wisconsin and studying in Wisconsin. Available to U.S. citizens.*Application Requirements:* Financial need analysis, nomination. *Deadline:* continuous. **Contact:** John Whitt, Program Coordinator, Wisconsin Higher Educational Aids Board, PO Box 7885, Madison, WI 53707-7885. *E-mail:* john.whitt@heab.state.wi.us. *Phone:* 608-266-1665. *Fax:* 608-267-2808. *Web site:* www.heab.state.wi.us.

Teacher of the Visually Impaired Loan Program. Provides forgivable loans to students who enroll in programs that lead to be certified as a teacher of the visually impaired or an orientation and mobility instructor. Must be a Wisconsin resident. For study in

Wisconsin, Illinois, Iowa, Michigan, and Minnesota. Please refer to Web site for further details: http://www.heab.state.wi.us *Academic Fields/Career Goals:* Special Education. *Award:* Forgivable loan for use in freshman, sophomore, junior, senior, graduate, or postgraduate years; not renewable. *Award amount:* $250–$10,000. *Number of awards:* varies. *Eligibility Requirements:* Applicant must be enrolled or expecting to enroll full or part-time at a two-year, four-year, or technical institution or university; resident of Wisconsin and studying in Illinois, Iowa, Michigan, Minnesota, or Wisconsin. Available to U.S. citizens. *Application Requirements:* Application, financial need analysis. *Deadline:* continuous. **Contact:** John Whitt, Program Coordinator, Wisconsin Higher Educational Aids Board, PO Box 7885, Madison, WI 53707-7885. *E-mail:* john.whitt@heab.state.wi.us. *Phone:* 608-266-0888. *Fax:* 608-267-2808. *Web site:* www.heab.state.wi.us.

Tuition and Fee Reimbursement Grants. Up to 100% tuition and fee reimbursement for Wisconsin veterans who were discharged from active duty within the last 10 years. Undergraduate courses must be completed at accredited Wisconsin schools. Those attending Minnesota public colleges, universities, and technical schools that have a tuition reciprocity agreement with Wisconsin also may qualify. Must meet military service requirements. Application must be received no later than 60 days after the completion of the course. *Award:* Grant for use in freshman, sophomore, junior, or senior year; renewable. *Award amount:* varies. *Number of awards:* varies. *Eligibility Requirements:* Applicant must be enrolled or expecting to enroll full-time at a two-year, four-year, or technical institution or university; resident of Wisconsin and studying in Minnesota or Wisconsin. Available to U.S. citizens. Applicant must have general military experience. *Application Requirements:* Application. *Deadline:* varies. **Contact:** Mike Keatley, Grants Coordinator, Wisconsin Department of Veterans Affairs, PO Box 7843, Madison, WI 53707-7843. *Phone:* 608-266-1311. *Web site:* dva.state.wi.us.

Wisconsin Academic Excellence Scholarship. Renewable award for high school seniors with the highest GPA in graduating class. Must be a Wisconsin resident. Award covers tuition for up to four years. Must maintain 3.0 GPA for renewal. Scholarships of up to $2250 each. Must attend a nonprofit Wisconsin institution full-time. Please refer to Web site for further details: http://www.heab.state.wi.us *Award:* Scholarship for use in freshman, sophomore, junior, or senior year; renewable. *Award amount:* up to $2250. *Number of awards:* 3445. *Eligibility Requirements:* Applicant must be enrolled or expecting to enroll full-time at a two-year, four-year, or technical institution or university; resident of Wisconsin and studying in Wisconsin. Applicant must have 3.5 GPA or higher. Available to U.S. citizens. *Application Requirements:* Transcript. *Deadline:* continuous. **Contact:** Alice Winters, Program Coordinator, Wisconsin Higher Educational Aids Board, PO Box 7885, Madison, WI 53707-7885. *E-mail:* alice.winters@heab.state.wi.us. *Phone:* 608-267-2213. *Fax:* 608-267-2808. *Web site:* www.heab.state.wi.us.

Wisconsin Department of Veterans Affairs Retraining Grants. Renewable award for veterans, unmarried spouses of deceased veterans, or dependents of deceased veterans. Must be resident of Wisconsin and attend an institution in Wisconsin. Veteran must be recently unemployed and show financial need. Must enroll in a vocational or technical program that can reasonably be expected to lead to employment. Course work at four-year colleges or universities does not qualify as retraining. *Award:* Grant for use in freshman or sophomore year; renewable. *Award amount:* up to $3000. *Number of awards:* varies. *Eligibility Requirements:* Applicant

must be enrolled or expecting to enroll full or part-time at a technical institution; resident of Wisconsin and studying in Wisconsin. Applicant or parent must meet one or more of the following requirements: general military experience; retired from active duty; disabled or killed as a result of military service; prisoner of war; or missing in action. *Application Requirements:* Application, financial need analysis. *Deadline:* varies. **Contact:** Mike Keatley, Grants Coordinator, Wisconsin Department of Veterans Affairs, PO Box 7843, Madison, WI 53707-7843. *Phone:* 608-266-1311. *Web site:* dva.state.wi.us.

Wisconsin Higher Education Grants (WHEG). Grants for residents of Wisconsin attending a campus of the University of Wisconsin or Wisconsin Technical College. Must be enrolled at least half-time and show financial need. Please refer to Web site for further details: http://www.heab.state.wi.us *Award:* Grant for use in freshman, sophomore, junior, or senior year; not renewable. *Award amount:* $250–$2500. *Number of awards:* varies. *Eligibility Requirements:* Applicant must be enrolled or expecting to enroll full or part-time at a two-year, four-year, or technical institution or university; resident of Wisconsin and studying in Wisconsin. Available to U.S. citizens. *Application Requirements:* Application, financial need analysis. *Deadline:* continuous. **Contact:** Sandra Thomas, Program Coordinator, Wisconsin Higher Educational Aids Board, PO Box 7885, Madison, WI 53707-7885. *E-mail:* sandy.thomas@heab.state.wi.us. *Phone:* 608-266-0888. *Fax:* 608-267-2808. *Web site:* www.heab.state.wi.us.

Wisconsin National Guard Tuition Grant. Renewable award for active members of the Wisconsin National Guard in good standing, who successfully complete a course of study at a qualifying school. Award covers full tuition, excluding fees, not to exceed undergraduate tuition charged by University of Wisconsin-Madison. Must have a minimum 2.0 GPA. *Award:* Grant for use in freshman, sophomore, junior, or senior year; renewable. *Award amount:* up to $1927. *Number of awards:* up to 4000. *Eligibility Requirements:* Applicant must be enrolled or expecting to enroll full or part-time at a two-year, four-year, or technical institution or university and resident of Wisconsin. Available to U.S. citizens. Applicant must have served in the Air Force National Guard or Army National Guard. *Application Requirements:* Application. *Deadline:* continuous. **Contact:** Karen Behling, Tuition Grant Administrator, Department of Military Affairs, PO Box 14587, Madison, WI 53708-0587. *E-mail:* karen.behling@dma.state.wi.us. *Phone:* 608-242-3159. *Fax:* 608-242-3154. *Web site:* wisconsinguard.com.

Wisconsin Native American Student Grant. Grants for Wisconsin residents who are at least one-quarter American-Indian. Must be attending a college or university within the state. Please refer to Web site for further details: http://www.heab.state.wi.us *Award:* Grant for use in freshman, sophomore, junior, senior, graduate, or postgraduate years; not renewable. *Award amount:* $250–$1100. *Number of awards:* varies. *Eligibility Requirements:* Applicant must be American Indian/Alaska Native; enrolled or expecting to enroll full or part-time at a two-year, four-year, or technical institution or university; resident of Wisconsin and studying in Wisconsin. Available to U.S. citizens. *Application Requirements:* Application, financial need analysis. *Deadline:* continuous. **Contact:** Sandra Thomas, Program Coordinator, Wisconsin Higher Educational Aids Board, PO Box 7885, Madison, WI 53707-7885. *E-mail:* sandy.thomas@heab.state.wi.us. *Phone:* 608-266-0888. *Fax:* 608-267-2808. *Web site:* www.heab.state.wi.us.

Wisconsin Tuition Grant Program. Available to Wisconsin residents who are enrolled at least half-time in degree or certificate programs at independent, nonprofit colleges or universities in Wisconsin. Must show financial need. Please refer to Web site for further details: http://www.heab.state.wi.us*Award:* Grant for use in freshman, sophomore, junior, or senior year; not renewable. *Award amount:* varies. *Number of awards:* varies. *Eligibility Requirements:* Applicant must be enrolled or expecting to enroll full or part-time at a four-year institution or university; resident of Wisconsin and studying in Wisconsin. Available to U.S. and non-U.S. citizens.*Application Requirements:* Application, financial need analysis. *Deadline:* continuous. **Contact:** Mary Lou Kuzdas, Program Coordinator, Wisconsin Higher Educational Aids Board, PO Box 7885, Madison, WI 53707-7885. *E-mail:* mary.kuzdas@heab.state.wi.us. *Phone:* 608-267-2212. *Fax:* 608-267-2808. *Web site:* www.heab.state.wi.us.

Wisconsin Veterans Part-time Study Reimbursement Grant. Open only to Wisconsin veterans. Renewable for continuing study. Contact office for more details. Application deadline is no later than sixty days after the course completion. Veterans may be reimbursed up to 100% of tuition and fees. *Award:* Grant for use in freshman, sophomore, junior, or senior year; renewable. *Award amount:* $300–$2000. *Number of awards:* varies. *Eligibility Requirements:* Applicant must be enrolled or expecting to enroll part-time at an institution or university; resident of Wisconsin and studying in Wisconsin. Available to U.S. citizens. Applicant or parent must meet one or more of the following requirements: general military experience; retired from active duty; disabled or killed as a result of military service; prisoner of war; or missing in action. *Application Requirements:* Application. *Deadline:* varies. **Contact:** Mike Keatley, Grants Coordinator, Wisconsin Department of Veterans Affairs, PO Box 7843, Madison, WI 53707-7843. *Phone:* 608-266-1311. *Web site:* dva.state.wi.us.

Searching for Four-Year Colleges Online

The Internet can be a great tool for gathering information about four-year colleges and universities. There are many worthwhile sites that are ready to help guide you through the various aspects of the selection process, including Peterson's Undergraduate Channel at www.petersons.com/ugchannel.

HOW PETERSON'S UNDERGRADUATE CHANNEL CAN HELP

Choosing a college involves a serious commitment of time and resources. Therefore, it is important to have the most up-to-date information about prospective schools at your fingertips. That is why Peterson's Undergraduate Channel is a great place to start your college search and selection process.

Find a College

Peterson's Undergraduate Channel is a comprehensive information resource that will help you make sense of the college admissions process. Peterson's Undergraduate Channel offers visitors enhanced search criteria and an easily navigable interface. The Channel is organized into various sections that make finding a program easy and fun. You can search for colleges based on name or location for starters, or do a detailed search on the following criteria:

- *Location*
- *Major*
- *Tuition*
- *Size*
- *Student/faculty ratio*
- *Average GPA*
- *Type of college*
- *Sports*
- *Religion*

Once you have found the school of your choice, simply click on it to get information about the institution, including majors, off-campus programs, costs, faculty, admission requirements, location, academic programs, academic facilities, athletics, student life, financial aid, student government, and application information and contacts.

E-mail the School

If, after looking at the information provided on Peterson's Undergraduate Channel, you still have questions, you can send an e-mail directly to the admissions department of the school. Just click on the "E-mail the School" button and send your message. In most instances, if you keep your questions short and to the point, you will receive an answer in no time at all.

School Web Site

For institutions that have provided information about their Web sites, simply click on the "School Web Site" button and you will be taken directly to that institution's Web page. Once you arrive at the school's Web site, look around and get a feel for the place. Often, schools offer virtual tours of the campus, complete with photos and commentary. If you have specific questions about the school, a visit to a school's Web site will often yield an answer.

Detailed Description

If the schools you are interested in have provided Peterson's with an **In-Depth Description,** you can do a keyword search on that description. Here, schools are given the opportunity to communicate unique features of their programs to prospective students.

Microsite

Several educational institutions provide students access to microsites, where more information about the types of resources and services offered can be found. In addition, students can take campus tours, apply for admissions, and explore academic majors.

Apply

The Apply link gives you the ability to directly apply to the school online.

Add to My List

The My List feature is designed to help you with your college planning. Here you can save the list of schools you're interested in, which you can then revisit at any time, access all the features of the site, and be reminded of important dates. You'll also be notified when new features are added to the site.

Get Recruited

Here's your chance to stop looking for colleges and let them find you with CollegesWantYou[SM] (www. collegeswantyou.com), the new approach to the search and selection process. Unlike other college search and selection tools, CollegesWantYou[SM] allows you to enter information on your preferences, test scores, and extracurricular activities into the online form, and before you know it, colleges that meet your specifications will be in touch with you. Registration is free, and all you need to do is complete a short profile indicating your preferences and then sit back and wait as colleges contact you directly!

Write Admissions Essays

This year, 500,000 college applicants will write 500,000 different admissions essays. Half will be rejected by their first-choice school, while only an 11 eleven percent will gain admission to the nation's most selective colleges. With acceptance rates at all-time lows, setting yourself apart requires more than just blockbuster SAT scores and impeccable transcripts--it requires the perfect application essay. Named "the world's premier application essay editing service" by the New York Times Learning Network and "one of the best essay services on the Internet" by the *Washington Post*, EssayEdge (www.essayedge.com) has helped more applicants write successful personal statements than any other company in the world. Learn more about EssayEdge and how it can give you an edge over hundreds of applicants with comparable academic credentials.

Practice for Your Test

At Peterson's, we understand that the college admissions process can be very stressful. With the stakes so high and the competition getting tighter every year, it's easy to feel like the process is out of your control. Fortunately, preparing for college admissions tests like the SAT, ACT, and PSAT helps you exert some control over the options you will have available to you. You can visit Peterson's Test Prep Channel (www.petersonstestprep.com) to learn more about how Peterson's can help you maximize your scores—and your options.

USE THE TOOLS TO YOUR ADVANTAGE

Choosing a college is an involved and complicated process. The tools available to you on www.petersons.com/ugchannel can help you to be more productive in this process. So, what are you waiting for? Fire up your computer; your future alma mater may be just a click away!

How to Use This Guide

This article provides an outline of the profile format, describing the items covered. All college information presented was supplied to Peterson's by the colleges themselves. Any information that does not apply to a particular college or for which no information was supplied is omitted from that college's profile. Colleges that were unable to supply usable data in time for publication are listed by name and, if available, address.

PROFILES OF COLLEGES IN THE MIDWEST

This section prints pertinent factual and statistical data for each college in a standard format for easy comparison.

General Information

The first paragraph gives a brief introduction to the college, covering following elements.

Type of student body: The categories are *men's* (100 percent of the student body), *primarily men's*, *women's* (100 percent of the student body), *primarily women's*, and *coed*. A college may be designated as coordinate with another institution, indicating that there are separate colleges or campuses for men and women, but facilities, courses, and institutional governance are shared.

Institutional control: A *public* college receives its funding wholly or primarily from the federal, state, and/or local government. The term *private* indicates an independent, nonprofit institution, that is, one whose funding comes primarily from private sources and tuition. This category includes independent, religious colleges, which may also specify a particular religious denomination or church affiliation. Profit-making institutions are designated as *proprietary*.

Institutional type: A *two-year college* awards associate degrees and offers the first two years of a bachelor's degree program. A *primarily two-year college* awards bachelor's degrees, the vast majority of students are enrolled in two-year programs. A *four-year college* awards bachelor's degrees may also award associate degrees, but it does not offer graduate (postbachelor's) degree programs. A *five-year college* is a five-year bachelor's program in a professional field such as architecture or pharmacy but does not award graduate degrees. An *upper-level institution* awards bachelor's degrees, but entering students must have at least two years of previous college-level credit; it may also offer graduate programs. A *comprehensive institution* awards bachelor's degrees and may also award associate degrees; graduate degree programs are offered primarily at the master's, specialist's, or professional level, although one or two doctoral programs may also be offered. A *university* offers four years of undergraduate work plus graduate degrees through the doctorate in more than two academic and/or professional fields.

Founding date: This is the year the college came into existence or was chartered, reflecting the period during which it has existed as an educational institution, regardless of subsequent mergers or other organizational changes.

Degree levels: An *associate* degree program may consist of either a college-transfer program, equivalent to the first two years of a bachelor's degree, or a one- to three-year terminal program that provides training for a specific occupation. A *bachelor's* degree program represents a three- to five-year liberal arts, science, professional, or preprofessional program. A *master's* degree is the first graduate degree in the liberal arts and sciences and certain professional fields and usually requires one to two years of full-time study. A *doctoral* degree is the highest degree awarded in research-oriented academic disciplines and usually requires from three to six years of full-time graduate study; the *first professional* degrees in such fields as law and medicine are also at the doctoral level. For colleges that award degrees in one field only, such as art or music, the field of specialization is indicated.

Campus setting: This indicates the size of the campus in acres or hectares and its location.

Academic Information

This paragraph contains information on the following items.

Faculty: The number of full-time and part-time faculty members as of fall 2003 is given, followed by the percentage of the full-time faculty members who hold doctoral, first professional, or terminal degrees and the student-faculty ratio. (Not all colleges calculate the student-faculty ratio in the same way; Peterson's prints the ratio as provided by the college.)

Library holdings: The numbers of books, serials, and audiovisual materials in the college's collections are listed.

Special programs: *Academic remediation for entering students* consists of instructional courses designed for students deficient in the general competencies necessary for a regular postsecondary curriculum and educational setting. *Services for LD students* include special help for learning-disabled students with resolvable difficulties, such as dyslexia. *Honors programs* are any special programs for very able students offering the opportunity for educational enrichment, independent study, acceleration, or some combination of these. *Cooperative (co-op) education programs* are formal arrangements with off-campus employers allowing students to combine work and study in order to gain degree-related experience, usually extending the time required to complete a degree. *Study abroad* is an arrangement by which a student completes part of the academic program studying in another country. A college may operate a campus abroad or it may have a cooperative agreement with other U.S. institutions or institutions in other countries. *Advanced placement* gives credit toward a degree awarded for acceptable scores on College Board Advanced Placement tests. *Accelerated degree programs* allow students to earn a bachelor's degree in three academic years. *Freshmen honors college* is a separate academic program for talented freshmen. *Tutorials* allow undergraduates to arrange for special in-depth academic assignments (not for remediation) working with faculty members one-on-one or in small groups. *English as a second language (ESL)* is a course of study designed specifically for students whose native language is not English. *Double major* consists of a program of study in which a student concurrently completes the requirements of two majors. *Independent study* consists of academic work, usually undertaken outside the regular classroom structure, chosen or designed by the student with the departmental approval and instructor supervision. *Distance learning* consists of credit courses that can be accessed off campus via cable television, the Internet, satellite, videotapes, correspondence courses, or other media. *Self-designed major* is a program of study based on individual interests, designed by the student with the assistance of an adviser. *Summer session for credit* includes summer courses through which students may make up degree work or accelerate their program. *Part-time degree programs* offer students the ability to earn a degree through part-time enrollment in regular session (daytime) classes or evening, weekend, or summer classes. *External degree programs* are programs of study in which students earn credits toward a degree through a combination of independent study, college courses, proficiency examinations, and personal experience. External degree programs require minimal or no classroom attendance. *Adult/continuing education programs* are courses offered for nontraditional students who are currently working or are returning to formal education. *Internships* are any short-term, supervised work experience usually related to a student's major field, for which the student earns academic credit. The work can be full- or part-time, on or off campus, paid or unpaid. *Off-campus study* is a formal arrangement with one or more domestic institutions under which students may take courses at the other institution(s) for credit.

Most popular majors: The most popular field or fields of study at the college, in terms of the number of undergraduate degrees conferred in 2003, are listed.

Student Body Statistics

Enrollment: The total number of students, undergraduates, and freshmen (or entering students for an upper-level institution) enrolled in degree programs as of fall 2003 are given.

With reference to the undergraduate enrollment for fall 2003, the percentages of women and men and the number of states and countries from which students hail are listed. The following percentages are also provided: in-state students, international students, and the percentage of last year's graduating class who went on to graduate and professional schools.

Expenses

Costs are given, as indicated in the head of this paragraph in each profile, in one of three ways according to the most up-to-date figures available from each college: (1) actual expenses for the 2003-04 academic year; (2) estimated expenses for 2003-04; or (3) actual expenses for 2002-03.

Annual expenses may be expressed as comprehensive fee (includes full-time tuition, mandatory fees, and college room and board) or as separate figures for full-time tuition, fees, room and board, and/or room only. For public institutions where tuition differs according to residence, separate figures are given for area and/or state residents and for nonresidents. Part-time tuition and fees are expressed in terms of a per-unit rate (per credit, per semester hour, etc.) as specified by the college.

The tuition structure at some institutions is complex in that freshmen and sophomores may be charged a different rate from that for juniors and seniors. A professional or vocational division may have a different structure from the liberal arts division of the same institution, or part-time tuition may be prorated on a sliding scale according to the number of credit hours taken. In all these cases, the average figures are given along with an explanation of the basis for the variable rate. For colleges that report that room and board costs vary according to type of accommodation and meal plan, the average costs are given. The phrase *no college housing* indicates that the college does not own or operate any housing facilities for undergraduate students.

Financial Aid

This paragraph contains information on the following items.

Forms of financial aid: The categories of college-administered aid available to undergraduates are listed. College-administered means that the college determines the recipient and amount of each award. The types of aid covered are non-need scholarships, need-based scholarships, athletic grants, and part-time jobs.

Financial aid: This item pertains to undergraduates who enrolled full-time in a four-year college in 2002 or 2003. The figures given are the dollar amount of the average financial aid package, including scholarships, grants, loans, and part-time jobs, received by such undergraduates.

Financial aid application deadline: This deadline may be given as a specific date, as continuous processing up to a specific date or until all available aid has been awarded, or as a priority date rather than a strict deadline, meaning that students are encouraged to apply by that date in order to have the best chance of obtaining aid.

Freshman Admission

The supporting data that a student must submit when applying for freshman admission are grouped into three categories: required for all, recommended, and required for some. They may include an essay, a high school transcript, high school course requirements (e.g., three years of math), letters of recommendation, an interview on campus or with local alumni, standardized test scores, and, for certain types of schools or programs, special requirements such as a musical audition or an art portfolio.

The most commonly required standardized tests are the ACT Assessment and the College Board's SAT I and SAT II Subject Tests. TOEFL (Test of English as a Foreign Language) is for international students whose native language is not English.

The application deadline for admission is given as either a specific date or *rolling*. Rolling means that applications are processed as they are received, and qualified students are accepted as long as there are openings. The application deadline for out-of-state students is indicated if it differs from the date for state residents. *Early decision* and *early action* deadlines are also given when applicable. Early decision is a program whereby students may apply early, are notified of acceptance or rejection well in advance of the usual notification date, and agree to accept an offer of admission, the assumption being that only one early application has been made. Early action is the same as early decision except that applicants are not obligated to accept an offer of admission.

Transfer Admission

This paragraph gives the application requirements and application deadline for a student applying for admission as a transfer from another institution. In addition to the requirements for freshman applicants listed above, requirements for transfers may also include a college transcript and a minimum college grade point average (expressed as a number on a scale of 0 to 4.0, where 4.0 equals A, 3.0 equals B, etc.). The name of the person to contact for additional transfer information is also given if it is different from the person listed in **For Further Information**.

Transfer Associate Degree Program Admission

This paragraph may be substituted for the **Freshman Admission** paragraph for two-year colleges that offer a college transfer program. The categories and requirements are listed in the same way as in the **Freshman Admission** paragraph.

Terminal Associate Degree Program Admission

This paragraph may also be substituted for the **Freshman Admission** paragraph for two-year colleges. It contains the requirements for admission to a terminal program that provides specific occupational training. The format for this paragraph also follows that of the **Freshman Admission**.

Entrance Difficulty

This paragraph contains the college's own assessment of its *entrance difficulty level*, including notation of an *open admission policy* where applicable. Open admission means that virtually all applicants are accepted without regard to standardized test scores, grade average, or class rank. A college may indicate that open admission is limited to a certain category of applicants, such as state residents, or does not apply to certain selective programs, often those in the health professions.

The five levels of entrance difficulty are: *most difficult*, *very difficult*, *moderately difficult*, *minimally difficult*, and *noncompetitive*.

The final item in this paragraph is the percentage of applicants accepted for the fall 2003 freshman (or entering) class.

For Further Information

The name, title, and mailing address of the person to contact for more information on application and admission procedures are given at the end of the profile. A telephone number, fax number, e-mail address, and Web site are also included in this paragraph for profiles that do not contain this information in the paragraph on interviews and campus visits.

SPECIAL MESSAGE TO STUDENTS

In addition, a number of college admissions office staff members, as part of a major information-dissemination effort, have supplemented the basic profile with special descriptive information on four topics of particular interest to students. This section appears only for those colleges that submitted supplementary information and covers the following:

Social Life: This paragraph conveys a feeling for life on campus by addressing such questions as: What are the most popular activities? Are there active fraternities and sororities? What is the role of student government? Do most students live on campus or commute? Does the college have a religious orientation?

Academic Highlights: This paragraph describes some of the special features and characteristics of the college's academic program, such as special degree programs and opportunities for study abroad or internships.

Interviews and Campus Visits: Colleges that conduct on-campus admission interviews describe the importance of an interview in their admission process and what they try to learn about a student through the interview. For those colleges that do not interview applicants individually, there is information on how a student interested in the college can visit the campus to meet administrators, faculty members, and currently enrolled students as well as on what the prospective applicant should try to accomplish through such a visit. This paragraph may also include a list of the most noteworthy places or things to see during a campus visit and the location, telephone number (including toll-free numbers if available), and business hours of the office to contact for information about appointments and campus visits. Also included, when available, is travel information, specifically the nearest commercial airport and the nearest interstate highway, with the appropriate exit.

IN-DEPTH DESCRIPTIONS OF COLLEGES IN THE MIDWEST

Two-page narrative descriptions appear in this section, providing an inside look at colleges and universities, shifting the focus to a variety of other factors, some of them intangible, that should also be considered. The descriptions presented in this section provide a wealth of statistics that are crucial components in the college decision-making equation—components such as tuition, financial aid, and major fields of study. Prepared exclusively by college officials, the descriptions are designed to help give students a better sense of the individuality of each institution, in terms that include campus environment, student activities, and lifestyle. Such quality-of-life intangibles can be the deciding factors in the college selection process. The absence from this

section of any college or university does not constitute an editorial decision on the part of Peterson's. In essence, this section is an open forum for colleges and universities, on a voluntary basis, to communicate their particular message to prospective college students. The colleges included have paid a fee to Peterson's to provide this information. The descriptions are edited to provide a consistent format across entries for your ease of comparison and are presented alphabetically by the official name of the institution.

PROFILES AND IN-DEPTH DESCRIPTIONS OF OTHER COLLEGES TO CONSIDER

Do you know that schools sometimes target specific areas of the country for student recruitment, even if those states are not part of a specific region? In this section, you'll find profiles and **In-Depth Descriptions** of schools outside the region of this guide looking to recruit students like you. The format of both the profiles and the **In-Depth Descriptions** in this section matches the format in the previous sections.

INDEXES

Majors and Degrees

This index lists hundreds of undergraduate major fields of study that are currently offered most widely. The majors appear in alphabetical order, each followed by an alphabetical list of the colleges that report offering a program in that field and the degree levels (*A* for associate, *B* for bachelor's) available. The majors represented here are based on the National Center for Education Statistics (NCES) 2000 Classification of Instructional Programs (CIP). The CIP is a taxonomic coding scheme that contains titles and descriptions of instructional programs, primarily at the postsecondary level. CIP was originally developed to facilitate NCES's collection and reporting of postsecondary degree completions, by major field of study, using standard classifications that capture the majority of program activity. The CIP is now the accepted federal government statistical standard for classifying instructional programs. However, although the term "major" is used in this guide, some colleges may use other terms, such as "concentration," "program of study," or "field."

Athletic Programs and Scholarships

This index lists the colleges that report offering intercollegiate athletic programs, listed alphabetically. An *M* or *W* following the college name indicates that the sport is offered for men or women, respectively. An *s* in parentheses following an *M* or *W* indicates that athletic scholarships (or grants-in-aid) are offered by the college for men or women, respectively, in that sport.

ROTC Programs

This index lists the colleges that report offering Reserve Officers' Training Corps programs in one or more branches of the armed services, as indicated by letter codes following the college name: *A* for Army, *N* for Navy, and *AF* for Air Force. A *c* in parentheses following the branch letter code indicates that the program is offered through a cooperative arrangement on another college's campus.

Alphabetical Listing of Colleges and Universities

This index gives the page locations of various entries for all the colleges and universities in this book. The page numbers for the college profiles are printed in regular type, those for profiles with **Special Messages** in *italic* type, and those for **In-Depth Descriptions** in **boldface** type. When there is more than one number in **boldface** type, it indicates that the institution has more than one **In-Depth Description**.

DATA COLLECTION PROCEDURES

The data contained in the College Profiles and Indexes were researched between fall 2003 and spring 2004 through *Thomson Peterson's Annual Survey of Undergraduate Institutions*. Questionnaires were sent to the more than 2,000 colleges and universities that met the outlined inclusion criteria. All data included in this edition have been submitted by officials (usually admissions and financial aid officers, registrars, or institutional research personnel) at the colleges. In addition, many of the institutions that submitted data were contacted directly by the Thomson Peterson's research staff to verify unusual figures, resolve discrepancies, or obtain additional data. All usable information received in time for publication has been included. The omission of any particular item from an index or profile listing signifies that the information is either not applicable to that institution or not available. Because of Thomson Peterson's comprehensive editorial review and because all material comes directly from college officials, we believe that the information presented in this guide is accurate. You should check with a specific college or university at the time of application to verify such figures as tuition and fees, which may have changed since the publication of this volume.

CRITERIA FOR INCLUSION IN THIS BOOK

The term "four-year college" is the commonly used designation for institutions that grant the baccalaureate degree. Four years is the expected amount of time required to earn this degree, although some bachelor's degree programs may be completed in three years, others require five years, and part-time programs may take considerably longer. Upper-level institutions offer only the junior and senior years and accept only students with two years of college-level credit. Therefore, "four-year college" is a conventional term that accurately describes most of the institutions included in this guide, but should not be taken literally in all cases.

To be included in this guide, an institution must have full accreditation or be a candidate for accreditation (preaccreditation) status by an institutional or specialized accrediting body recognized by the U.S. Department of Education or the Council for Higher Education Accreditation (CHEA). Institutional accrediting bodies, which review each institution as a whole, include the six regional associations of schools and colleges (Middle States, New England, North Central, Northwest, Southern, and Western), each of which is responsible for a specified portion of the United States and its territories. Other institutional accrediting bodies are national in scope and accredit specific kinds of institutions (e.g., Bible colleges, independent colleges, and rabbinical and Talmudic schools). Program registration by the New York State Board of Regents is considered to be the equivalent of institutional accreditation, since the board requires that all programs offered by an institution meet its standards before recognition is granted. A Canadian institution must be chartered and authorized to grant degrees by the provincial government, affiliated with a chartered institution, or accredited by a recognized U.S. accrediting body. This guide also includes institutions outside the United States that are accredited by these U.S. accrediting bodies. There are recognized specialized or professional accrediting bodies in more than forty different fields, each of which is authorized to accredit institutions or specific programs in its particular field. For specialized institutions that offer programs in one field only, we designate this to be the equivalent of institutional accreditation. A full explanation of the accrediting process and complete information on recognized, institutional (regional and national) and specialized accrediting bodies can be found online at www.chea.org or at www.ed.gov/admins/finaid/accred/index.html.

Profiles of Colleges
in the Midwest

The Midwest

This map provides a general perspective on the Midwest and shows the major metropolitan areas and capital of each state.

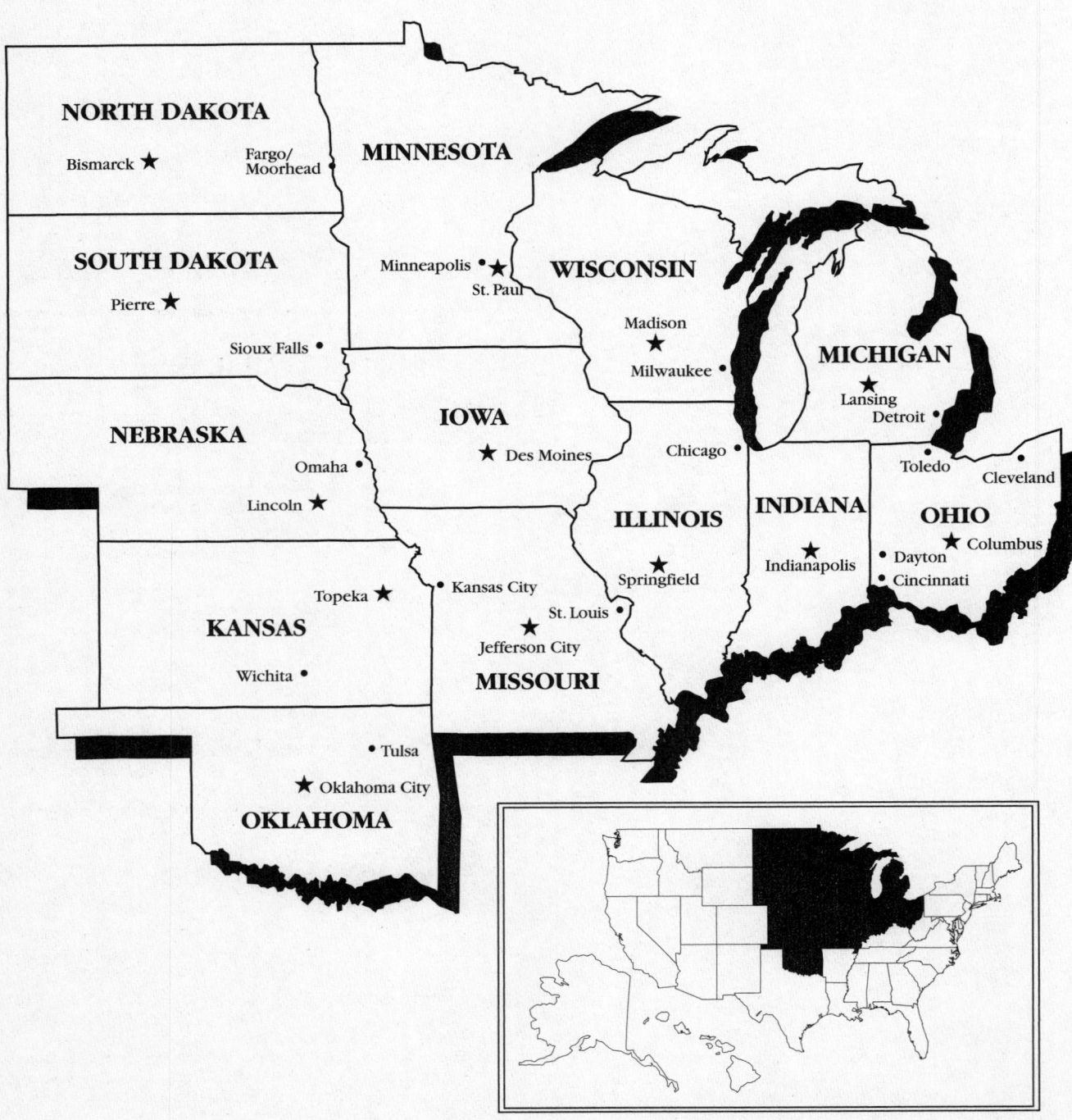

Illinois

AMERICAN ACADEMY OF ART
Chicago, Illinois

American Academy of Art is a coed, proprietary, comprehensive institution, founded in 1923, offering degrees at the bachelor's and master's levels in art.

Academic Information The faculty has 30 members (87% full-time), 73% with terminal degrees. The undergraduate student-faculty ratio is 15:1. The library holds 1,730 titles, 62 serial subscriptions, and 101 audiovisual materials. Special programs include academic remediation, study abroad, accelerated degree programs, independent study, summer session for credit, part-time degree programs (daytime, evenings, summer), adult/continuing education programs, and internships. The most frequently chosen baccalaureate field is visual/performing arts.
Student Body Statistics The student body is made up of 360 undergraduates (87 freshmen). 34 percent are women and 66 percent are men. Students come from 8 states and territories. 98 percent are from Illinois. 0.6 percent are international students.
Expenses for 2003–04 *Application fee:* $25. *Tuition:* $17,780 full-time. Full-time tuition varies according to course load. *Part-time tuition:* varies with course load.
Financial Aid Forms of aid include need-based scholarships and part-time jobs. The application deadline for financial aid is continuous.
Freshman Admission American Academy of Art requires a high school transcript, 2 recommendations, an interview, portfolio review, and TOEFL scores for international students. The application deadline for regular admission is rolling.
Transfer Admission The application deadline for admission is rolling.
Entrance Difficulty American Academy of Art assesses its entrance difficulty level as moderately difficult. For the fall 2003 freshman class, 100 percent of the applicants were accepted.

For Further Information Contact Mr. Stuart Rosenbloom, Director of Admissions, American Academy of Art, 332 South Michigan Avenue, Suite 300, Chicago, IL 60604-4302. *Telephone:* 312-461-0600 Ext. 143. *E-mail:* stuartrnet@comcast.net. *Web site:* http://www.aaart.edu/.

AMERICAN INTERCONTINENTAL UNIVERSITY ONLINE
Hoffman Estates, Illinois

American InterContinental University Online is a coed, proprietary, comprehensive unit of American InterContinental University, founded in 1970, offering degrees at the associate, bachelor's, and master's levels (offers online degree programs only). It has a 1-acre campus in Hoffman Estates.

Freshman Admission American InterContinental University Online requires an interview and documentation of high school graduation or its equivalency. An essay is recommended. The application deadline for regular admission is rolling.
Transfer Admission The application deadline for admission is rolling.

For Further Information Contact Mr. Steve Fireng, Senior Vice President of Admissions and Marketing, American InterContinental University Online, 5550 Prairie Stone Parkway, Suite 400, Hoffman Estates, IL 60192. *Telephone:* 877-701-3800 or 877-701-3800 (toll-free). *Fax:* 847-851-6002. *E-mail:* info@aiu-online.com. *Web site:* http://www.aiuonline.edu/.

ARGOSY UNIVERSITY/CHICAGO
Chicago, Illinois

Argosy University/Chicago is a coed, proprietary, upper-level institution, founded in 1976, offering degrees at the bachelor's, master's, and doctoral levels.

Academic Information The faculty has 4 members. The most frequently chosen baccalaureate field is psychology.
Student Body Statistics The student body totals 731, of whom 23 are undergraduates. 87 percent are women and 13 percent are men.
Expenses for 2003–04 *Application fee:* $50. *Tuition:* $12,000 full-time, $360 per credit part-time. *Mandatory fees:* $120 full-time, $80 per year part-time.
Financial Aid Forms of aid include need-based and non-need-based scholarships and part-time jobs. The average aided 2003–04 undergraduate received an aid package worth an estimated $7745. The application deadline for financial aid is continuous.
Transfer Admission Argosy University/Chicago requires a college transcript.
Entrance Difficulty For the fall 2003 entering class, 65 percent of the applicants were accepted.

For Further Information Contact Ms. Ashley Delaney, Director of Admissions, Argosy University/Chicago, Admissions Department, 20 South Clark Street Third Floor, Chicago, IL 60603. *Telephone:* 800-626-4123 Ext. 3906 or 800-626-4123 (toll-free in-state). *Fax:* 312-201-0200. *E-mail:* chicagoadmissions@argosyu.edu. *Web site:* http://www.argosyu.edu/.

ARGOSY UNIVERSITY/CHICAGO NORTHWEST
Rolling Meadows, Illinois

Argosy University/Chicago Northwest is a coed, proprietary, upper-level institution, founded in 1979, offering degrees at the bachelor's, master's, and doctoral levels and post-master's certificates. It is located in Rolling Meadows near Chicago.

Expenses for 2003–04 *Application fee:* $50. *Tuition:* $360 per credit hour part-time. *Mandatory fees:* $40 per term part-time.
Financial Aid Forms of aid include need-based and non-need-based scholarships and part-time jobs. The average aided 2003–04 undergraduate received an aid package worth an estimated $6617. The application deadline for financial aid is continuous.
Transfer Admission Argosy University/Chicago Northwest requires a college transcript. Standardized test scores are required for some.

For Further Information Contact Mr. Jamal Scott, Director of Admissions, Argosy University/Chicago Northwest, 1000 North Plaza Drive, Suite 100, Schaumburg, IL 60173. *Telephone:* 847-290-7400 or 866-290-2777 (toll-free in-state). *Fax:* 847-290-9977. *E-mail:* jscott@argosyu.edu. *Web site:* http://www.argosyu.edu/.

AUGUSTANA COLLEGE
Rock Island, Illinois

Augie is a coed, private, four-year college, founded in 1860, affiliated with the Evangelical Lutheran Church in America, offering degrees at the bachelor's level. It has a 115-acre campus in Rock Island.

Academic Information The faculty has 223 members (65% full-time), 68% with terminal degrees. The student-faculty ratio is 12:1. The library holds 190,641 titles, 1,705 serial subscriptions, and 2,019 audiovisual materials. Special programs include services for learning-disabled students, an honors program, study abroad, advanced placement credit, accelerated degree programs, double majors, independent study, summer session for credit, part-time degree programs (daytime, evenings), and internships. The most frequently chosen baccalaureate fields are biological/life sciences, business/marketing, social sciences and history.

Augustana College (continued)

Student Body Statistics The student body is made up of 2,309 undergraduates (614 freshmen). 58 percent are women and 42 percent are men. Students come from 26 states and territories and 19 other countries. 87 percent are from Illinois. 0.9 percent are international students. 42 percent of the 2003 graduating class went on to graduate and professional schools.

Expenses for 2003–04 *Application fee:* $25. *Comprehensive fee:* $26,610 includes full-time tuition ($20,397), mandatory fees ($432), and college room and board ($5781). *College room only:* $2928. Full-time tuition and fees vary according to course load. Room and board charges vary according to housing facility. *Part-time tuition:* $855 per credit hour.

Financial Aid Forms of aid include need-based and non-need-based scholarships and part-time jobs. The average aided 2003–04 undergraduate received an aid package worth an estimated $15,207. The priority application deadline for financial aid is April 1.

Freshman Admission Augie requires a high school transcript, SAT I or ACT scores, and TOEFL scores for international students. An essay, 2 recommendations, and an interview are required for some. The application deadline for regular admission is rolling.

Transfer Admission The application deadline for admission is rolling.

Entrance Difficulty Augie assesses its entrance difficulty level as moderately difficult. For the fall 2003 freshman class, 68 percent of the applicants were accepted.

For Further Information Contact Mr. Martin Sauer, Director of Admissions, Augustana College, 639 38th Street, Rock Island, IL 61201-2296. *Telephone:* 309-794-7341 or 800-798-8100 (toll-free). *Fax:* 309-794-7422. *E-mail:* admissions@augustana.edu. *Web site:* http://www.augustana.edu/.

AURORA UNIVERSITY

Aurora, Illinois

AU is a coed, private, comprehensive institution, founded in 1893, offering degrees at the bachelor's, master's, and doctoral levels and post-master's certificates. It has a 26-acre campus in Aurora near Chicago.

Academic Information The faculty has 216 members (45% full-time), 54% with terminal degrees. The undergraduate student-faculty ratio is 19:1. The library holds 115,642 titles, 749 serial subscriptions, and 6,015 audiovisual materials. Special programs include academic remediation, services for learning-disabled students, study abroad, advanced placement credit, double majors, independent study, distance learning, self-designed majors, summer session for credit, part-time degree programs (daytime, evenings, weekends, summer), adult/continuing education programs, internships, and arrangement for off-campus study with 3 members of the Council of West Suburban Colleges. The most frequently chosen baccalaureate fields are business/marketing, education, health professions and related sciences.

Student Body Statistics The student body totals 3,450, of whom 1,646 are undergraduates (333 freshmen). 64 percent are women and 36 percent are men. Students come from 14 states and territories. 95 percent are from Illinois. 0.1 percent are international students. 15 percent of the 2003 graduating class went on to graduate and professional schools.

Expenses for 2004–05 *Application fee:* $25. *Comprehensive fee:* $21,364 includes full-time tuition ($14,750) and college room and board ($6614). *College room only:* $2968. Full-time tuition varies according to course load, location, and program. Room and board charges vary according to board plan and housing facility. *Part-time tuition:* $507 per semester hour. Part-time tuition varies according to location and program.

Financial Aid Forms of aid include need-based and non-need-based scholarships and part-time jobs. The average aided 2003–04 undergraduate received an aid package worth an estimated $15,470. The priority application deadline for financial aid is April 15.

Freshman Admission AU requires a high school transcript, a minimum 2.0 high school GPA, and TOEFL scores for international students. An essay, an interview, and SAT I or ACT scores are recommended. An essay, 2 recommendations, and an interview are required for some. The application deadline for regular admission is rolling.

Transfer Admission The application deadline for admission is rolling.

Entrance Difficulty AU assesses its entrance difficulty level as moderately difficult. For the fall 2003 freshman class, 56 percent of the applicants were accepted.

SPECIAL MESSAGE TO STUDENTS

Social Life Aurora University is a great place to get involved. Students may choose to participate in social clubs, student government, service activities, Campus Ministries, Greek organizations, and intramural sports. Students may also take advantage of the various social activities that are offered in Aurora—the second-largest city in Illinois—and Chicago, 40 miles to the east. Aurora University combines a residential and commuter population.

Academic Highlights The University comprises three colleges: the College of Arts, Sciences, and Business; the College of Education; and the George Williams College of Health and Human Services, which includes the School of Social Work, the School of Nursing, and the School of Human Services. Aurora University offers the YMCA Senior Director Certificate program, indicative of its commitment to human service education.

Interviews and Campus Visits Aurora University encourages campus visits. Fall, winter, and spring open houses are held. Individual visits are always welcome. Students can meet with an admission counselor, faculty members, a financial aid counselor, and coaches as well as take a tour of campus and visit with current students. Campus tours include academic buildings, such as Dunham and Stephens Halls, and four residence halls. Housed in Dunham Hall is the Schingoethe Museum of Native American Culture, which is open to the public. The University is accessible by train and local bus lines. For more information about appointments and campus visits, students should call the Office of Admission and Financial Aid at 630-844-5533 or 800-742-5281 (toll-free). The nearest commercial airport is O'Hare International.

For Further Information Write to the Office of Admission and Financial Aid, Aurora University, Aurora, IL 60506. *Web site:* http://www.aurora.edu.

See page 252 for a narrative description.

BARAT COLLEGE

See DePaul University

BENEDICTINE UNIVERSITY

Lisle, Illinois

Benedictine University is a coed, private, Roman Catholic, comprehensive institution, founded in 1887, offering degrees at the associate, bachelor's, master's, and doctoral levels. It has a 108-acre campus in Lisle near Chicago.

Academic Information The faculty has 313 members (30% full-time). The undergraduate student-faculty ratio is 13:1. The library holds 166,341 titles, 8,900 serial subscriptions, and 9,349 audiovisual materials. Special programs include academic remediation, services for learning-disabled students, an honors program, study abroad, advanced placement credit, accelerated degree programs, ESL programs, double majors, independent study, distance learning, summer session for credit, part-time degree programs, adult/continuing education programs, internships, and arrangement for off-campus study with 3 members of the Council of West Suburban Colleges. The most frequently chosen baccalaureate fields are biological/life sciences, business/marketing, psychology.

Student Body Statistics The student body totals 2,968, of whom 2,114 are undergraduates (303 freshmen). 63 percent are women and 37 percent are men. Students come from 25 states and territories and 8 other countries. 96 percent are from Illinois. 1.9 percent are international students.

Expenses for 2004–05 *Application fee:* $40. *Comprehensive fee:* $23,840 includes full-time tuition ($16,960), mandatory fees ($510), and college room and board ($6370). Full-time tuition and fees vary according to class time and degree level. Room and board charges vary according to board plan and housing facility. *Part-time tuition:* $570 per credit hour. *Part-time mandatory fees:* $15 per credit hour. Part-time tuition and fees vary according to class time and degree level.

Financial Aid   Forms of aid include need-based and non-need-based scholarships and part-time jobs. The average aided 2003–04 undergraduate received an aid package worth an estimated $11,489. The application deadline for financial aid is April 15 with a priority deadline of April 15.

Freshman Admission   Benedictine University requires an essay, a high school transcript, recommendations, ACT scores, and TOEFL scores for international students. Rank in top 50% of high school class, ACT score of 21 is recommended. An interview is required for some. The application deadline for regular admission is rolling.

Transfer Admission   The application deadline for admission is rolling.

Entrance Difficulty   Benedictine University assesses its entrance difficulty level as moderately difficult.

For Further Information   Contact Ms. Kari Gibbons, Dean of Undergraduate Admissions, Benedictine University, 5700 College Road, Lisle, IL 60532-0900. *Telephone:* 630-829-6306 or 888-829-6363 (toll-free out-of-state). *Fax:* 630-960-1126. *E-mail:* admissions@ben.edu. *Web site:* http://www.ben.edu/.

See page 258 for a narrative description.

BLACKBURN COLLEGE
Carlinville, Illinois

Blackburn College is a coed, private, Presbyterian, four-year college, founded in 1837, offering degrees at the bachelor's level. It has an 80-acre campus in Carlinville near St. Louis.

Academic Information   The faculty has 51 members (69% full-time), 53% with terminal degrees. The student-faculty ratio is 16:1. The library holds 87,175 titles, 17,000 serial subscriptions, and 1,940 audiovisual materials. Special programs include an honors program, cooperative (work-study) education, study abroad, advanced placement credit, double majors, independent study, self-designed majors, part-time degree programs (daytime), internships, and arrangement for off-campus study with American University. The most frequently chosen baccalaureate fields are business/marketing, education, psychology.

Student Body Statistics   The student body is made up of 615 undergraduates (176 freshmen). 58 percent are women and 42 percent are men. Students come from 12 states and territories and 8 other countries. 3.1 percent are international students. 18 percent of the 2003 graduating class went on to graduate and professional schools.

Expenses for 2004–05   *Application fee:* $0. *Comprehensive fee:* $15,940 includes full-time tuition ($12,360) and college room and board ($3580). *College room only:* $1680. Full-time tuition varies according to program. *Part-time tuition:* $487 per semester hour.

Financial Aid   Forms of aid include need-based and non-need-based scholarships and part-time jobs. The average aided 2003–04 undergraduate received an aid package worth an estimated $9652. The priority application deadline for financial aid is April 1.

Freshman Admission   Blackburn College requires an essay, a high school transcript, a minimum 2.0 high school GPA, SAT I or ACT scores, and TOEFL scores for international students. 1 recommendation and an interview are required for some. The application deadline for regular admission is rolling.

Transfer Admission   The application deadline for admission is rolling.

Entrance Difficulty   Blackburn College assesses its entrance difficulty level as moderately difficult. For the fall 2003 freshman class, 56 percent of the applicants were accepted.

For Further Information   Contact Mr. John Malin, Dean of Enrollment Management, Blackburn College, 700 College Avenue, Carlinville, IL 62626-1498. *Telephone:* 217-854-3231 Ext. 4252 or 800-233-3550 (toll-free). *Fax:* 217-854-3713. *E-mail:* admit@mail.blackburn.edu. *Web site:* http://www.blackburn.edu/.

BLESSING-RIEMAN COLLEGE OF NURSING
Quincy, Illinois

Blessing-Rieman is a coed, primarily women's, private, four-year college, founded in 1985, offering degrees at the bachelor's level in nursing. It has a 1-acre campus in Quincy.

Academic Information   The faculty has 13 members (100% full-time), 31% with terminal degrees. The student-faculty ratio is 12:1. The library holds 4,275 titles, 123 serial subscriptions, and 570 audiovisual materials. Special programs include academic remediation, an honors program, advanced placement credit, double majors, distance learning, summer session for credit, part-time degree programs (daytime, evenings), adult/continuing education programs, and internships. The most frequently chosen baccalaureate field is health professions and related sciences.

Student Body Statistics   The student body is made up of 178 undergraduates (26 freshmen). 96 percent are women and 4 percent are men. Students come from 8 states and territories. 66 percent are from Illinois.

Expenses for 2003–04   *Application fee:* $0. *Comprehensive fee:* $18,200 includes full-time tuition ($12,400), mandatory fees ($350), and college room and board ($5450). Full-time tuition and fees vary according to course load, location, and student level. Room and board charges vary according to location. *Part-time tuition:* $325 per credit. Part-time tuition varies according to course load, location, and student level.

Financial Aid   Forms of aid include need-based scholarships. The application deadline for financial aid is continuous.

Freshman Admission   Blessing-Rieman requires a high school transcript, a minimum 3.0 high school GPA, SAT I or ACT scores, and TOEFL scores for international students. An essay and an interview are recommended. The application deadline for regular admission is rolling.

Transfer Admission   The application deadline for admission is rolling.

Entrance Difficulty   Blessing-Rieman assesses its entrance difficulty level as moderately difficult. For the fall 2003 freshman class, 70 percent of the applicants were accepted.

For Further Information   Contact Ms. Heather Mutter, Admissions Counselor, Blessing-Rieman College of Nursing, PO Box 7005, Quincy, IL 62305-7005. *Telephone:* 217-228-5520 Ext. 6984 or 800-877-9140 Ext. 6964 (toll-free). *Fax:* 217-223-4661. *E-mail:* admissions@brcn.edu. *Web site:* http://www.brcn.edu/.

BRADLEY UNIVERSITY
Peoria, Illinois

Bradley is a coed, private, comprehensive institution, founded in 1897, offering degrees at the bachelor's and master's levels. It has a 75-acre campus in Peoria near Chicago and St. Louis.

Academic Information   The faculty has 528 members (63% full-time), 52% with terminal degrees. The undergraduate student-faculty ratio is 15:1. The library holds 424,753 titles, 1,996 serial subscriptions, and 9,574 audiovisual materials. Special programs include academic remediation, an honors program, cooperative (work-study) education, study abroad, advanced placement credit, accelerated degree programs, double majors, independent study, distance learning, self-designed majors, summer session for credit, part-time degree programs (daytime, evenings, summer), adult/continuing education programs, internships, and arrangement for off-campus study with Georgetown University. The most frequently chosen baccalaureate fields are business/marketing, communications/communication technologies, engineering/engineering technologies.

Student Body Statistics   The student body totals 6,137, of whom 5,305 are undergraduates (1,105 freshmen). 54 percent are women and 46 percent are men. Students come from 42 states and territories and 55 other countries. 86 percent are from Illinois. 1.3 percent are international students. 18 percent of the 2003 graduating class went on to graduate and professional schools.

Expenses for 2003–04   *Application fee:* $35. *Comprehensive fee:* $22,910 includes full-time tuition ($16,800), mandatory fees ($130), and college room and board ($5980). *College room only:* $3400. Full-time tuition and

Bradley University (continued)

fees vary according to program. Room and board charges vary according to board plan. *Part-time tuition:* $460 per credit. Part-time tuition varies according to course load.

Financial Aid Forms of aid include need-based and non-need-based scholarships, athletic grants, and part-time jobs. The average aided 2003–04 undergraduate received an aid package worth an estimated $12,636. The priority application deadline for financial aid is March 1.

Freshman Admission Bradley requires an essay, a high school transcript, SAT I or ACT scores, and TOEFL scores for international students. A minimum 3.0 high school GPA, recommendations, and an interview are recommended. The application deadline for regular admission is rolling.

Entrance Difficulty Bradley assesses its entrance difficulty level as moderately difficult. For the fall 2003 freshman class, 69 percent of the applicants were accepted.

For Further Information Contact Mr. Thomas Richmond, Director of Admissions, Bradley University, 1501 West Bradley Avenue, 100 Swords Hall, Peoria, IL 61625-0002. *Telephone:* 309-677-3144 or 800-447-6460 (toll-free). *E-mail:* admissions@bradley.edu. *Web site:* http://www.bradley.edu/.

CHICAGO STATE UNIVERSITY
Chicago, Illinois

CSU is a coed, public, comprehensive institution, founded in 1867, offering degrees at the bachelor's and master's levels. It has a 161-acre campus in Chicago.

Academic Information The faculty has 364 members (87% full-time), 59% with terminal degrees. The undergraduate student-faculty ratio is 12:1. The library holds 320,000 titles and 1,539 serial subscriptions. Special programs include academic remediation, services for learning-disabled students, an honors program, cooperative (work-study) education, study abroad, advanced placement credit, accelerated degree programs, ESL programs, double majors, distance learning, self-designed majors, summer session for credit, part-time degree programs (daytime, evenings, weekends, summer), external degree programs, adult/continuing education programs, and internships. The most frequently chosen baccalaureate fields are business/marketing, education, liberal arts/general studies.

Student Body Statistics The student body totals 7,040, of whom 4,904 are undergraduates (542 freshmen). 73 percent are women and 27 percent are men. Students come from 12 states and territories and 8 other countries. 99 percent are from Illinois.

Expenses for 2004–05 *Application fee:* $20. *State resident tuition:* $4830 full-time, $161 per credit hour part-time. *Nonresident tuition:* $9660 full-time, $322 per credit hour part-time. *Mandatory fees:* $1313 full-time, $210 per term part-time. *College room and board:* $6032.

Financial Aid Forms of aid include need-based and non-need-based scholarships and part-time jobs. The priority application deadline for financial aid is March 30.

Freshman Admission CSU requires a high school transcript, SAT I or ACT scores, and TOEFL scores for international students. The application deadline for regular admission is July 15.

Transfer Admission The application deadline for admission is July 15.

Entrance Difficulty CSU assesses its entrance difficulty level as moderately difficult. For the fall 2003 freshman class, 42 percent of the applicants were accepted.

For Further Information Contact Ms. Addie Epps, Director of Admissions, Chicago State University, 95th Street at King Drive, ADM 200, Chicago, IL 60628. *Telephone:* 773-995-2513. *E-mail:* ug-admissions@csu.edu. *Web site:* http://www.csu.edu/.

CHRISTIAN LIFE COLLEGE
Mount Prospect, Illinois

Christian Life College is a coed, private, four-year college, offering degrees at the associate and bachelor's levels.

Expenses for 2003–04 *Tuition:* $6000 full-time, $250 per credit hour part-time. *Mandatory fees:* $700 full-time. *College room only:* $3500.

For Further Information Contact Mr. Jim Spenner, Director of Admissions, Christian Life College, 400 East Gregory Street, Mount Prospect, IL 60056. *Telephone:* 847-259-1840 Ext. 17. *Web site:* http://www.christianlifecollege.edu/.

COLLEGE OF ST. FRANCIS
See University of St. Francis

COLUMBIA COLLEGE CHICAGO
Chicago, Illinois

Columbia is a coed, private, comprehensive institution, founded in 1890, offering degrees at the bachelor's and master's levels and postbachelor's certificates.

Academic Information The faculty has 1,662 members (18% full-time). The undergraduate student-faculty ratio is 11:1. The library holds 219,952 titles and 1,150 serial subscriptions. Special programs include academic remediation, services for learning-disabled students, study abroad, advanced placement credit, ESL programs, independent study, self-designed majors, summer session for credit, part-time degree programs (daytime, evenings, weekends, summer), internships, and arrangement for off-campus study with Adler Planetarium. The most frequently chosen baccalaureate fields are liberal arts/general studies, communications/communication technologies, visual/performing arts.

Student Body Statistics The student body totals 9,915, of whom 9,265 are undergraduates (1,557 freshmen). 52 percent are women and 48 percent are men. Students come from 50 states and territories and 73 other countries. 85 percent are from Illinois. 2.2 percent are international students. 9 percent of the 2003 graduating class went on to graduate and professional schools.

Expenses for 2004–05 *Application fee:* $35. *Comprehensive fee:* $24,144 includes full-time tuition ($14,880), mandatory fees ($390), and college room and board ($8874). *College room only:* $7155. Room and board charges vary according to housing facility. *Part-time tuition:* $575 per semester hour. *Part-time mandatory fees:* $85 per term.

Financial Aid Forms of aid include need-based and non-need-based scholarships and part-time jobs. The priority application deadline for financial aid is August 1.

Freshman Admission Columbia requires an essay, a high school transcript, recommendations, and TOEFL scores for international students. A minimum 2.0 high school GPA, an interview, and SAT I or ACT scores are recommended. The application deadline for regular admission is July 1.

Entrance Difficulty Columbia has an open admission policy.

For Further Information Contact Mr. Murphy Monroe, Director of Admissions and Recruitment, Columbia College Chicago, 600 South Michigan Avenue, Chicago, IL 60605-1996. *Telephone:* 312-663-1600 Ext. 7133 or 312-663-1600 Ext. 7130 (toll-free in-state). *Fax:* 312-344-8024. *E-mail:* admissions@colum.edu. *Web site:* http://www.colum.edu/.

See page 272 for a narrative description.

CONCORDIA UNIVERSITY
River Forest, Illinois

Concordia is a coed, private, comprehensive unit of Concordia University System, founded in 1864, affiliated with the Lutheran Church–Missouri Synod, offering degrees at the bachelor's, master's, and doctoral levels and post-master's and postbachelor's certificates. It has a 40-acre campus in River Forest near Chicago.

Academic Information The faculty has 66 full-time members. The undergraduate student-faculty ratio is 11:1. The library holds 171,510 titles, 256 serial subscriptions, and 6,010 audiovisual materials. Special programs include academic remediation, services for learning-disabled students, an honors program, study abroad, advanced placement credit, accelerated degree programs, double majors, independent study, distance learning, summer session for credit, part-time degree programs (daytime, evenings, summer), adult/continuing education programs, internships, and arrangement for off-campus study with Chicago Consortium of Colleges and Universities, Dominican University. The most frequently chosen baccalaureate fields are business/marketing, education, health professions and related sciences.

Student Body Statistics The student body totals 1,706, of whom 1,203 are undergraduates (227 freshmen). 63 percent are women and 37 percent are men. Students come from 26 states and territories. 65 percent are from Illinois. 0.4 percent are international students. 15 percent of the 2003 graduating class went on to graduate and professional schools.

Expenses for 2003–04 *Application fee:* $100. *Comprehensive fee:* $23,600 includes full-time tuition ($17,900), mandatory fees ($300), and college room and board ($5400). Full-time tuition and fees vary according to program. *Part-time tuition:* $530 per semester hour. *Part-time mandatory fees:* $10 per semester hour. Part-time tuition and fees vary according to program.

Financial Aid Forms of aid include need-based and non-need-based scholarships and part-time jobs. The average aided 2003–04 undergraduate received an aid package worth an estimated $11,333. The priority application deadline for financial aid is April 1.

Freshman Admission Concordia requires a high school transcript, a minimum 2.0 high school GPA, 1 recommendation, minimum ACT score of 20 or SAT I score of 930, SAT I or ACT scores, and TOEFL scores for international students. An essay and an interview are required for some. The application deadline for regular admission is rolling.

Transfer Admission The application deadline for admission is rolling.

Entrance Difficulty Concordia assesses its entrance difficulty level as moderately difficult. For the fall 2003 freshman class, 21 percent of the applicants were accepted.

For Further Information Contact Dr. Evelyn Burdick, Vice President for Enrollment Services, Concordia University, 7400 Augusta Street, River Forest, IL 60305. *Telephone:* 708-209-3100 or 800-285-2668 (toll-free). *Fax:* 708-209-3473. *E-mail:* crfadmis@curf.edu. *Web site:* http://www.curf.edu/.

DEPAUL UNIVERSITY
Chicago, Illinois

DePaul is a coed, private, Roman Catholic university, founded in 1898, offering degrees at the bachelor's, master's, doctoral, and first professional levels and post-master's and postbachelor's certificates. It has a 36-acre campus in Chicago.

Academic Information The faculty has 1,516 members (53% full-time). The undergraduate student-faculty ratio is 17:1. The library holds 1 million titles, 14,585 serial subscriptions, and 96,669 audiovisual materials. Special programs include academic remediation, services for learning-disabled students, an honors program, cooperative (work-study) education, study abroad, advanced placement credit, accelerated degree programs, Freshman Honors College, ESL programs, double majors, independent study, distance learning, summer session for credit, part-time degree programs, adult/continuing education programs, and internships. The most frequently chosen baccalaureate fields are business/marketing, computer/information sciences, liberal arts/general studies.

Student Body Statistics The student body totals 23,610, of whom 14,585 are undergraduates (2,261 freshmen). 58 percent are women and 42 percent are men. Students come from 50 states and territories and 74 other countries. 87 percent are from Illinois. 1.6 percent are international students.

Expenses for 2003–04 *Application fee:* $40. *One-time mandatory fee:* $140. *Comprehensive fee:* $27,580 includes full-time tuition ($18,750), mandatory fees ($40), and college room and board ($8790). *College room only:* $5970. Full-time tuition and fees vary according to program. Room and board charges vary according to board plan and housing facility. *Part-time tuition:* $348 per quarter hour. Part-time tuition varies according to program.

Financial Aid Forms of aid include need-based and non-need-based scholarships, athletic grants, and part-time jobs. The average aided

2002–03 undergraduate received an aid package worth $13,691. The application deadline for financial aid is April 1 with a priority deadline of March 1.

Freshman Admission DePaul requires a high school transcript, a minimum 2.0 high school GPA, 1 recommendation, SAT I or ACT scores, and TOEFL scores for international students. A minimum 3.0 high school GPA is recommended. A minimum 3.0 high school GPA, an interview, and audition are required for some. The application deadline for regular admission is rolling and for early action it is December 15.

Transfer Admission The application deadline for admission is rolling.

Entrance Difficulty DePaul assesses its entrance difficulty level as moderately difficult. For the fall 2003 freshman class, 73 percent of the applicants were accepted.

For Further Information Contact Carlene Klaas, Undergraduate Admissions, DePaul University, 1 East Jackson Boulevard, Suite 9100, Chicago, IL 60604. *Telephone:* 312-362-8650. *Fax:* 312-362-3322. *E-mail:* admitdpu@depaul.edu. *Web site:* http://www.depaul.edu/.

DEVRY UNIVERSITY
Oakbrook Terrace, Illinois

For Information Write to DeVry University, Oakbrook Terrace, IL 60181.

DEVRY UNIVERSITY
Naperville, Illinois

For Information Write to DeVry University, Naperville, IL 60563-2361.

DEVRY UNIVERSITY
Elgin, Illinois

For Information Write to DeVry University, Elgin, IL 60123-9341.

DEVRY UNIVERSITY
Gurnee, Illinois

For Information Write to DeVry University, Gurnee, IL 60031-9126.

DEVRY UNIVERSITY
Addison, Illinois

DeVry is a coed, proprietary, four-year college of DeVry University, founded in 1982, offering degrees at the associate and bachelor's levels and postbachelor's certificates. It has a 14-acre campus in Addison near Chicago.

Academic Information The library holds 18,500 titles, 4,000 serial subscriptions, and 1,000 audiovisual materials. Special programs include academic remediation, services for learning-disabled students, cooperative (work-study) education, advanced placement credit, accelerated degree programs, distance learning, summer session for credit, part-time degree programs (daytime, evenings, weekends, summer), and adult/continuing education programs. The most frequently chosen baccalaureate fields are business/marketing, computer/information sciences, engineering/engineering technologies.

Student Body Statistics The student body is made up of 2,420 undergraduates (444 freshmen). 22 percent are women and 78 percent are men. 1.7 percent are international students.

DeVry University (continued)

Expenses for 2003–04 *Application fee:* $50. *Tuition:* $10,100 full-time, $360 per credit hour part-time. *Mandatory fees:* $165 full-time. Full-time tuition and fees vary according to course load. Part-time tuition varies according to course load.

Financial Aid Forms of aid include need-based and non-need-based scholarships and part-time jobs. The average aided 2002–03 undergraduate received an aid package worth $8431. The application deadline for financial aid is continuous.

Freshman Admission DeVry requires a high school transcript, an interview, and TOEFL scores for international students. SAT I, ACT or CPT is recommended. The application deadline for regular admission is rolling.

Entrance Difficulty DeVry assesses its entrance difficulty level as minimally difficult; moderately difficult for electronics engineering technology program.

For Further Information Contact Ms. Jane Miritello, Assistant New Student Coordinator, DeVry University, 1221 North Swift Road, Addison, IL 60101-6106. *Telephone:* 708-342-3300 or 800-346-5420 (toll-free). *Fax:* 630-953-1236. *E-mail:* mbutler@dpg.devry.edu. *Web site:* http://www.devry.edu/.

DEVRY UNIVERSITY
Chicago, Illinois

DeVry is a coed, proprietary, comprehensive unit of DeVry University, founded in 1931, offering degrees at the associate and bachelor's levels and postbachelor's certificates. It has a 17-acre campus in Chicago.

Academic Information The library holds 16,573 titles, 79 serial subscriptions, and 1,047 audiovisual materials. Special programs include academic remediation, services for learning-disabled students, cooperative (work-study) education, advanced placement credit, accelerated degree programs, ESL programs, distance learning, summer session for credit, part-time degree programs (daytime, evenings, weekends, summer), and adult/continuing education programs. The most frequently chosen baccalaureate fields are business/marketing, computer/information sciences, engineering/engineering technologies.

Student Body Statistics The student body is made up of 3,000 undergraduates. 36 percent are women and 64 percent are men.

Expenses for 2003–04 *Application fee:* $50. *Tuition:* $10,100 full-time, $360 per credit hour part-time. *Mandatory fees:* $165 full-time. Full-time tuition and fees vary according to course load. Part-time tuition varies according to course load.

Financial Aid Forms of aid include need-based and non-need-based scholarships and part-time jobs. The average aided 2002–03 undergraduate received an aid package worth $11,079. The application deadline for financial aid is continuous.

Freshman Admission DeVry requires a high school transcript, an interview, and TOEFL scores for international students. SAT I, ACT or CPT is recommended. The application deadline for regular admission is rolling.

Entrance Difficulty DeVry assesses its entrance difficulty level as minimally difficult; moderately difficult for electronics engineering technology program.

For Further Information Contact Ms. Christine Hierl, Director of Admissions, DeVry University, 3300 North Campbell Avenue, Chicago, IL 60618-5994. *Telephone:* 773-929-6550 or 800-383-3879 (toll-free). *Fax:* 773-697-2710. *E-mail:* admissions2@devry.edu. *Web site:* http://www.devry.edu/.

DEVRY UNIVERSITY
Tinley Park, Illinois

DeVry University is a coed, proprietary, comprehensive unit of DeVry University, founded in 2000, offering degrees at the associate, bachelor's, and master's levels and postbachelor's certificates. It has a 12-acre campus in Tinley Park.

Academic Information The undergraduate student-faculty ratio is 27:1. The library holds 17,500 titles, 82 serial subscriptions, and 476 audiovisual materials. Special programs include academic remediation, services for learning-disabled students, cooperative (work-study) education, advanced placement credit, accelerated degree programs, distance learning, summer session for credit, part-time degree programs (daytime, evenings, weekends, summer), and adult/continuing education programs. The most frequently chosen baccalaureate fields are computer/information sciences, business/marketing, engineering/engineering technologies.

Student Body Statistics The student body totals 1,674, of whom 1,432 are undergraduates (239 freshmen). 29 percent are women and 71 percent are men. 0.8 percent are international students.

Expenses for 2003–04 *Application fee:* $50. *Tuition:* $10,100 full-time, $360 per credit hour part-time. *Mandatory fees:* $165 full-time. Full-time tuition and fees vary according to course load. Part-time tuition varies according to course load.

Financial Aid Forms of aid include need-based and non-need-based scholarships and part-time jobs. The average aided 2002–03 undergraduate received an aid package worth $9695. The application deadline for financial aid is continuous.

Freshman Admission DeVry University requires a high school transcript, an interview, and TOEFL scores for international students. SAT I, ACT or CPT is recommended. The application deadline for regular admission is rolling.

Entrance Difficulty DeVry University assesses its entrance difficulty level as minimally difficult; moderately difficult for electronics engineering technology program.

For Further Information Contact Ms. Kerrie Flynn, Assistant New Student Coordinator, DeVry University, 18624 West Creek Drive, Tinley Park, IL 60477-6243. *Telephone:* 708-342-3300 or 877-305-8184 (toll-free). *Fax:* 708-342-3505. *E-mail:* imccauley@tp.devry.edu. *Web site:* http://www.devry.edu/.

DOMINICAN UNIVERSITY
River Forest, Illinois

Dominican is a coed, private, Roman Catholic, comprehensive institution, founded in 1901, offering degrees at the bachelor's and master's levels and post-master's certificates. It has a 30-acre campus in River Forest near Chicago.

Academic Information The faculty has 251 members (39% full-time), 66% with terminal degrees. The undergraduate student-faculty ratio is 12:1. The library holds 280,475 titles, 4,422 serial subscriptions, and 7,000 audiovisual materials. Special programs include services for learning-disabled students, an honors program, study abroad, advanced placement credit, accelerated degree programs, ESL programs, double majors, independent study, distance learning, self-designed majors, summer session for credit, part-time degree programs (daytime, evenings, weekends, summer), adult/continuing education programs, internships, and arrangement for off-campus study with Concordia University (IL), Illinois Institute of Technology. The most frequently chosen baccalaureate fields are business/marketing, communications/communication technologies, social sciences and history.

Student Body Statistics The student body totals 2,900, of whom 1,211 are undergraduates (241 freshmen). 69 percent are women and 31 percent are men. Students come from 21 states and territories and 18 other countries. 89 percent are from Illinois. 1.9 percent are international students. 15 percent of the 2003 graduating class went on to graduate and professional schools.

Expenses for 2004–05 *Application fee:* $20. *One-time mandatory fee:* $100. *Comprehensive fee:* $24,890 includes full-time tuition ($18,900), mandatory fees ($100), and college room and board ($5890). Room and board charges vary according to board plan and housing facility. *Part-time tuition:* $630 per semester hour. *Part-time mandatory fees:* $10 per course. Part-time tuition and fees vary according to location and program.

Financial Aid Forms of aid include need-based and non-need-based scholarships and part-time jobs. The average aided 2002–03 undergraduate received an aid package worth $11,710. The priority application deadline for financial aid is June 1.

Freshman Admission Dominican requires an essay, a high school transcript, a minimum 2.75 high school GPA, SAT I or ACT scores, and TOEFL scores for international students. Recommendations and an interview are recommended. 2 recommendations and an interview are required for some. The application deadline for regular admission is rolling.

Transfer Admission The application deadline for admission is rolling.

Entrance Difficulty Dominican assesses its entrance difficulty level as moderately difficult. For the fall 2003 freshman class, 82 percent of the applicants were accepted.

For Further Information Contact Mr. Glenn Hamilton, Director of Freshman Admission, Dominican University, 7900 West Division Street, River Forest, IL 60305. *Telephone:* 708-524-6800 or 800-828-8475 (toll-free). *Fax:* 708-366-5360. *E-mail:* domadmis@dom.edu. *Web site:* http://www.dom.edu/.

EASTERN ILLINOIS UNIVERSITY
Charleston, Illinois

Eastern is a coed, public, comprehensive institution, founded in 1895, offering degrees at the bachelor's and master's levels and post-master's and postbachelor's certificates. It has a 320-acre campus in Charleston.

Academic Information The faculty has 682 members (87% full-time), 71% with terminal degrees. The undergraduate student-faculty ratio is 16:1. The library holds 955,245 titles, 3,510 serial subscriptions, and 33,460 audiovisual materials. Special programs include academic remediation, services for learning-disabled students, an honors program, study abroad, advanced placement credit, ESL programs, double majors, independent study, summer session for credit, part-time degree programs (daytime, evenings, summer), external degree programs, adult/continuing education programs, and internships. The most frequently chosen baccalaureate fields are business/marketing, education, English.

Student Body Statistics The student body totals 11,522, of whom 9,845 are undergraduates (1,918 freshmen). 58 percent are women and 42 percent are men. Students come from 38 states and territories and 36 other countries. 97 percent are from Illinois. 0.7 percent are international students. 31 percent of the 2003 graduating class went on to graduate and professional schools.

Expenses for 2003–04 *Application fee:* $30. *Area resident tuition:* $119 per credit hour part-time. *State resident tuition:* $3563 full-time, $119 per credit hour part-time. *Nonresident tuition:* $10,688 full-time, $356 per credit hour part-time. *Mandatory fees:* $1419 full-time, $51.20 per credit hour part-time. Full-time tuition and fees vary according to course load. Part-time tuition and fees vary according to course load. *College room and board:* $6210. Room and board charges vary according to board plan.

Financial Aid Forms of aid include need-based scholarships, athletic grants, and part-time jobs. The average aided 2003–04 undergraduate received an aid package worth an estimated $8766. The priority application deadline for financial aid is April 1.

Freshman Admission Eastern requires a high school transcript, audition for music program, SAT I or ACT scores, and TOEFL scores for international students. An essay and 3 recommendations are required for some. The application deadline for regular admission is rolling.

Transfer Admission The application deadline for admission is rolling.

Entrance Difficulty Eastern assesses its entrance difficulty level as moderately difficult. For the fall 2003 freshman class, 78 percent of the applicants were accepted.

For Further Information Contact Mr. Dale W. Wolf, Director of Admissions, Eastern Illinois University, 600 Lincoln Avenue, Charleston, IL 61920-3099. *Telephone:* 217-581-2223 or 800-252-5711 (toll-free). *Fax:* 217-581-7060. *E-mail:* admissns@eiu.edu. *Web site:* http://www.eiu.edu/.

EAST-WEST UNIVERSITY
Chicago, Illinois

East-West University is a coed, private, four-year college, founded in 1978, offering degrees at the associate and bachelor's levels.

Expenses for 2003–04 *Application fee:* $30. *Tuition:* $9900 full-time, $3300 per term part-time. *Mandatory fees:* $495 full-time, $465 per term part-time. Full-time tuition and fees vary according to course level.

For Further Information Contact Mr. William Link, Director of Admissions, East-West University, 819 South Wabash Avenue, Chicago, IL 60605-2103. *Telephone:* 312-939-0111 Ext. 1830. *Fax:* 312-939-0083. *E-mail:* seeyou@eastwest.edu. *Web site:* http://www.eastwest.edu/.

ELMHURST COLLEGE
Elmhurst, Illinois

Elmhurst is a coed, private, comprehensive institution, founded in 1871, affiliated with the United Church of Christ, offering degrees at the bachelor's and master's levels. It has a 38-acre campus in Elmhurst near Chicago.

Academic Information The faculty has 278 members (40% full-time), 44% with terminal degrees. The undergraduate student-faculty ratio is 13:1. The library holds 222,441 titles, 2,010 serial subscriptions, and 7,537 audiovisual materials. Special programs include academic remediation, services for learning-disabled students, an honors program, cooperative (work-study) education, study abroad, advanced placement credit, accelerated degree programs, double majors, independent study, summer session for credit, part-time degree programs (daytime, evenings, weekends, summer), adult/continuing education programs, internships, and arrangement for off-campus study. The most frequently chosen baccalaureate fields are business/marketing, education, social sciences and history.

Student Body Statistics The student body totals 2,593, of whom 2,396 are undergraduates (366 freshmen). 66 percent are women and 34 percent are men. Students come from 26 states and territories and 21 other countries. 92 percent are from Illinois. 1.1 percent are international students. 17 percent of the 2003 graduating class went on to graduate and professional schools.

Expenses for 2003–04 *Application fee:* $25. *Comprehensive fee:* $24,630 includes full-time tuition ($18,600) and college room and board ($6030). *College room only:* $3460. Room and board charges vary according to board plan and housing facility. *Part-time tuition:* $529 per credit hour.

Financial Aid Forms of aid include need-based and non-need-based scholarships and part-time jobs. The average aided 2003–04 undergraduate received an aid package worth an estimated $15,400. The priority application deadline for financial aid is April 15.

Freshman Admission Elmhurst requires a high school transcript, SAT I or ACT scores, and TOEFL scores for international students. An essay and an interview are recommended. An essay, recommendations, and an interview are required for some. The application deadline for regular admission is July 15.

Elmhurst College (continued)

Entrance Difficulty Elmhurst assesses its entrance difficulty level as moderately difficult. For the fall 2003 freshman class, 73 percent of the applicants were accepted.

For Further Information Contact Mr. Andrew B. Sison, Director of Admission, Elmhurst College, 190 Prospect Avenue, Elmhurst, IL 60126. *Telephone:* 630-617-3400 Ext. 3070 or 800-697-1871 (toll-free out-of-state). *Fax:* 630-617-5501. *E-mail:* admit@elmhurst.edu. *Web site:* http://www.elmhurst.edu/.

EUREKA COLLEGE
Eureka, Illinois

Eureka is a coed, private, four-year college, founded in 1855, affiliated with the Christian Church (Disciples of Christ), offering degrees at the bachelor's level. It has a 112-acre campus in Eureka.

Academic Information The faculty has 69 members (61% full-time), 55% with terminal degrees. The student-faculty ratio is 13:1. The library holds 75,000 titles, 330 serial subscriptions, and 500 audiovisual materials. Special programs include an honors program, cooperative (work-study) education, study abroad, advanced placement credit, ESL programs, double majors, independent study, self-designed majors, summer session for credit, part-time degree programs (daytime, evenings, summer), and internships. The most frequently chosen baccalaureate fields are business/marketing, biological/life sciences, education.

Student Body Statistics The student body is made up of 516 undergraduates (138 freshmen). 56 percent are women and 44 percent are men. Students come from 15 states and territories and 2 other countries. 1.4 percent are international students. 11 percent of the 2003 graduating class went on to graduate and professional schools.

Expenses for 2004–05 *Application fee:* $0. *Comprehensive fee:* $19,280 includes full-time tuition ($13,000), mandatory fees ($400), and college room and board ($5880). *College room only:* $2820. Room and board charges vary according to housing facility. *Part-time tuition:* $375 per semester hour.

Financial Aid Forms of aid include need-based and non-need-based scholarships and part-time jobs. The average aided 2003–04 undergraduate received an aid package worth an estimated $12,677. The priority application deadline for financial aid is April 15.

Freshman Admission Eureka requires a high school transcript, a minimum 2.0 high school GPA, 1 recommendation, SAT I or ACT scores, and TOEFL scores for international students. An interview is recommended. An essay and 3 recommendations are required for some. The application deadline for regular admission is August 15.

Transfer Admission The application deadline for admission is August 15.

Entrance Difficulty Eureka assesses its entrance difficulty level as moderately difficult. For the fall 2003 freshman class, 75 percent of the applicants were accepted.

For Further Information Contact Dr. Brian Sajko, Dean of Admissions and Financial Aid, Eureka College, 300 East College Avenue, Eureka, IL 61530-0128. *Telephone:* 309-467-6350 or 888-4-EUREKA (toll-free). *Fax:* 309-467-6576. *E-mail:* admissions@eureka.edu. *Web site:* http://www.eureka.edu/.

See page 282 for a narrative description.

GOVERNORS STATE UNIVERSITY
University Park, Illinois

Governors State University is a coed, public, upper-level institution, founded in 1969, offering degrees at the bachelor's and master's levels. It has a 750-acre campus in University Park near Chicago.

Academic Information The faculty has 204 members (86% full-time), 71% with terminal degrees. The undergraduate student-faculty ratio is 17:1. The library holds 252,000 titles, 2,200 serial subscriptions, and 2,700 audiovisual materials. Special programs include academic remediation, services for learning-disabled students, an honors program, study abroad, advanced placement credit, independent study, distance learning, self-designed majors, summer session for credit, part-time degree programs (daytime, evenings, weekends, summer), external degree programs, adult/continuing education programs, internships, and arrangement for off-campus study with Chicago State University, Northeastern Illinois University, Western Illinois University, Eastern Illinois University. The most frequently chosen baccalaureate fields are education, health professions and related sciences, liberal arts/general studies.

Student Body Statistics The student body totals 5,317, of whom 2,618 are undergraduates. 71 percent are women and 29 percent are men. Students come from 8 states and territories and 22 other countries. 97 percent are from Illinois. 1.6 percent are international students. 26 percent of the 2003 graduating class went on to graduate and professional schools.

Expenses for 2003–04 *Application fee:* $0. *State resident tuition:* $2832 full-time, $118 per credit part-time. *Nonresident tuition:* $8496 full-time, $354 per credit part-time. *Mandatory fees:* $360 full-time, $225 per term part-time. Full-time tuition and fees vary according to location. Part-time tuition and fees vary according to course load and location.

Financial Aid Forms of aid include need-based and non-need-based scholarships and part-time jobs. The priority application deadline for financial aid is May 1.

Transfer Admission Governors State University requires a college transcript and a minimum 2.0 college GPA. Standardized test scores are required for some. The application deadline for admission is July 15.

Entrance Difficulty Governors State University assesses its entrance difficulty level as moderately difficult.

For Further Information Contact Mr. Larry Polselli, Executive Director of Enrollment Services, Governors State University, One University Parkway, University Park, IL 60466. *Telephone:* 708-534-3148. *Fax:* 708-534-1640. *E-mail:* gsunow@govst.edu. *Web site:* http://www.govst.edu/.

GREENVILLE COLLEGE
Greenville, Illinois

GC is a coed, private, Free Methodist, comprehensive institution, founded in 1892, offering degrees at the bachelor's and master's levels. It has a 12-acre campus in Greenville near St. Louis.

Academic Information The faculty has 133 members (45% full-time), 42% with terminal degrees. The undergraduate student-faculty ratio is 14:1. The library holds 126,210 titles, 490 serial subscriptions, and 4,377 audiovisual materials. Special programs include academic remediation, an honors program, cooperative (work-study) education, study abroad, advanced placement credit, accelerated degree programs, double majors, independent study, self-designed majors, summer session for credit, part-time degree programs (daytime, evenings, summer), adult/continuing education programs, internships, and arrangement for off-campus study with 13 members of the Christian College Consortium; 100 members of the Council for Christian Colleges and Universities. The most frequently chosen baccalaureate fields are business/marketing, communications/communication technologies, education.

Student Body Statistics The student body totals 1,342, of whom 1,188 are undergraduates (263 freshmen). 52 percent are women and 48 percent are men. Students come from 40 states and territories and 14 other countries. 70 percent are from Illinois. 1.2 percent are international students.

Expenses for 2003–04 *Application fee:* $25. *Comprehensive fee:* $21,342 includes full-time tuition ($15,666), mandatory fees ($110), and college room and board ($5566). *College room only:* $2634. Room and board charges vary according to housing facility. *Part-time tuition:* $330 per credit hour. Part-time tuition varies according to course load.

Financial Aid Forms of aid include need-based and non-need-based scholarships and part-time jobs. The average aided 2002–03 undergraduate received an aid package worth $12,660. The application deadline for financial aid is continuous.

Freshman Admission GC requires an essay, a high school transcript, a minimum 2.5 high school GPA, 2 recommendations, agreement to code of conduct, SAT I or ACT scores, and TOEFL scores for international students. An interview is required for some. The application deadline for regular admission is August 1.

Transfer Admission The application deadline for admission is August 1.
Entrance Difficulty GC assesses its entrance difficulty level as moderately difficult. For the fall 2003 freshman class, 95 percent of the applicants were accepted.

For Further Information Contact Dr. R. Pepper Dill, Vice President for Enrollment Management, Greenville College, 315 East College Avenue, Greenville, IL 62246. *Telephone:* 618-664-7100 or 800-345-4440 (toll-free). *Fax:* 618-664-9841. *E-mail:* admissions@greenville.edu. *Web site:* http://www.greenville.edu/.

HARRINGTON COLLEGE OF DESIGN
Chicago, Illinois

Harrington College of Design is a coed, primarily women's, proprietary, four-year college of Career Education Corporation, founded in 1931, offering degrees at the associate and bachelor's levels in interior design.

Academic Information The faculty has 123 members (8% full-time), 36% with terminal degrees. The student-faculty ratio is 11:1. The library holds 22,000 titles, 90 serial subscriptions, and 26,000 audiovisual materials. Special programs include study abroad, part-time degree programs (evenings), adult/continuing education programs, internships, and arrangement for off-campus study with Roosevelt University. The most frequently chosen baccalaureate field is visual/performing arts.
Student Body Statistics The student body is made up of 1,364 undergraduates (203 freshmen). 90 percent are women and 10 percent are men. Students come from 14 states and territories. 91 percent are from Illinois.
Expenses for 2004–05 *Application fee:* $60. *Tuition:* $12,600 full-time, $500 per credit part-time. *Mandatory fees:* $200 full-time. Full-time tuition and fees vary according to course load. Part-time tuition varies according to course load. *College room only:* $4800. Room charges vary according to housing facility.
Financial Aid Forms of aid include need-based and non-need-based scholarships. The average aided 2002–03 undergraduate received an aid package worth $3500. The application deadline for financial aid is continuous.
Freshman Admission Harrington College of Design requires a high school transcript, an interview, and TOEFL scores for international students. An essay and 1 recommendation are recommended. The application deadline for regular admission is rolling.
Entrance Difficulty Harrington College of Design has an open admission policy.

For Further Information Contact Melissa Laurentius, Director of Admissions, Harrington College of Design, 200 West Madison, Chicago, IL 60606. *Telephone:* 877-939-4975 Ext. 1188 or 877-939-4975 (toll-free). *Fax:* 312-939-8032. *E-mail:* barrington@interiordesign.edu. *Web site:* http://www.interiordesign.edu/.

HEBREW THEOLOGICAL COLLEGE
Skokie, Illinois

For Information Write to Hebrew Theological College, Skokie, IL 60077-3263.

ILLINOIS COLLEGE
Jacksonville, Illinois

IC is a coed, private, interdenominational, four-year college, founded in 1829, offering degrees at the bachelor's level. It has a 62-acre campus in Jacksonville near St. Louis.

Academic Information The faculty has 93 members (66% full-time), 62% with terminal degrees. The student-faculty ratio is 14:1. The library holds 143,500 titles and 620 serial subscriptions. Special programs include study abroad, advanced placement credit, accelerated degree programs, double majors, independent study, summer session for credit, and internships. The most frequently chosen baccalaureate fields are business/marketing, education, social sciences and history.
Student Body Statistics The student body is made up of 1,016 undergraduates (318 freshmen). 56 percent are women and 44 percent are men. Students come from 15 states and territories and 7 other countries. 97 percent are from Illinois. 0.9 percent are international students. 27 percent of the 2003 graduating class went on to graduate and professional schools.
Expenses for 2003–04 *Application fee:* $25. *Comprehensive fee:* $19,100 includes full-time tuition ($13,300) and college room and board ($5800). *Part-time tuition:* $555 per credit hour.
Financial Aid Forms of aid include need-based and non-need-based scholarships and part-time jobs. The average aided 2003–04 undergraduate received an aid package worth an estimated $13,273. The priority application deadline for financial aid is March 1.
Freshman Admission IC requires a high school transcript, 1 recommendation, SAT I or ACT scores, and TOEFL scores for international students. An essay, a minimum 2.5 high school GPA, and an interview are recommended. An essay is required for some. The application deadline for regular admission is July 1.
Transfer Admission The application deadline for admission is July 1.
Entrance Difficulty IC assesses its entrance difficulty level as moderately difficult. For the fall 2003 freshman class, 72 percent of the applicants were accepted.

For Further Information Contact Mr. Rick Bystry, Associate Director of Admission, Illinois College, 1101 West College, Jacksonville, IL 62650. *Telephone:* 217-245-3030 or 866-464-5265 (toll-free). *Fax:* 217-245-3034. *E-mail:* admissions@ic.edu. *Web site:* http://www.ic.edu/.

THE ILLINOIS INSTITUTE OF ART
Chicago, Illinois

The Illinois Institute of Art is a coed, proprietary, four-year college of The Art Institutes, founded in 1916, offering degrees at the associate and bachelor's levels. It has a 2-acre campus in Chicago.

Academic Information The faculty has 110 members. The student-faculty ratio is 20:1. The library holds 11,324 titles, 264 serial subscriptions, and 502 audiovisual materials. Special programs include academic remediation, services for learning-disabled students, cooperative (work-study) education, advanced placement credit, accelerated degree programs, independent study, summer session for credit, part-time degree programs (daytime, evenings, weekends, summer), adult/continuing education programs, internships, and arrangement for off-campus study with members of the International Council of Design Schools.
Student Body Statistics The student body is made up of 1,950 undergraduates. Students come from 42 states and territories and 26 other countries. 70 percent are from Illinois. 3 percent of the 2003 graduating class went on to graduate and professional schools.
Expenses for 2004–05 *Application fee:* $50. *Tuition:* $16,848 full-time, $351 per credit part-time. *Mandatory fees:* $100 full-time.
Financial Aid Forms of aid include need-based and non-need-based scholarships and part-time jobs. The application deadline for financial aid is continuous.
Freshman Admission The Illinois Institute of Art requires an essay, a high school transcript, an interview, and TOEFL scores for international students. A minimum 2.0 high school GPA and SAT I or ACT scores are recommended. Recommendations and a portfolio are required for some. The application deadline for regular admission is rolling.
Transfer Admission The application deadline for admission is rolling.

The Illinois Institute of Art (continued)

Entrance Difficulty The Illinois Institute of Art assesses its entrance difficulty level as minimally difficult. For the fall 2003 freshman class, 93 percent of the applicants were accepted.

For Further Information Contact Ms. Janis Anton, Vice President/Director of Admissions, The Illinois Institute of Art, 350 North Orleans Street, Chicago, IL 60654-1510. *Telephone:* 312-280-3500 Ext. 132 or 800-351-3450 (toll-free). *Fax:* 312-280-8562. *E-mail:* janton@aii.edu. *Web site:* http://www.ilic.artinstitutes.edu/.

See page 292 for a narrative description.

THE ILLINOIS INSTITUTE OF ART-SCHAUMBURG
Schaumburg, Illinois

The Illinois Institute of Art-Schaumburg is a coed, proprietary, four-year college of The Arts Institutes International, offering degrees at the bachelor's level.

Academic Information The faculty has 55 members (49% full-time), 18% with terminal degrees. The student-faculty ratio is 16:1. Special programs include services for learning-disabled students, advanced placement credit, accelerated degree programs, double majors, independent study, self-designed majors, summer session for credit, internships, and arrangement for off-campus study. The most frequently chosen baccalaureate field is visual/performing arts.
Student Body Statistics The student body is made up of 1,107 undergraduates (270 freshmen). 45 percent are women and 55 percent are men. Students come from 10 states and territories and 8 other countries. 90 percent are from Illinois. 1.1 percent are international students.
Expenses for 2004–05 *Application fee:* $50. *Tuition:* $16,200 full-time, $360 per credit hour part-time.
Financial Aid Forms of aid include need-based and non-need-based scholarships and part-time jobs. The average aided 2002–03 undergraduate received an aid package worth $10,122. The priority application deadline for financial aid is May 1.
Freshman Admission The Illinois Institute of Art-Schaumburg requires an essay, a high school transcript, a minimum 2.0 high school GPA, and TOEFL scores for international students. SAT I and SAT II or ACT scores are recommended. Recommendations and an interview are required for some. The application deadline for regular admission is rolling.
Transfer Admission The application deadline for admission is rolling.
Entrance Difficulty The Illinois Institute of Art-Schaumburg assesses its entrance difficulty level as minimally difficult. For the fall 2003 freshman class, 75 percent of the applicants were accepted.

For Further Information Contact Mr. Sam Hinojosa, Director of Admissions, The Illinois Institute of Art-Schaumburg, 1000 Plaza Drive, Schaumburg, IL 60173. *Telephone:* 847-619-3450 Ext. 4506 or 800-314-3450 (toll-free). *Fax:* 847-619-3064. *Web site:* http://www.ilis.artinstitutes.edu/.

ILLINOIS INSTITUTE OF TECHNOLOGY
Chicago, Illinois

IIT is a coed, private university, founded in 1890, offering degrees at the bachelor's, master's, doctoral, and first professional levels and postbachelor's certificates. It has a 120-acre campus in Chicago.

Academic Information The faculty has 524 members (58% full-time). The undergraduate student-faculty ratio is 12:1. The library holds 854,771 titles, 773 serial subscriptions, and 52,368 audiovisual materials. Special programs include services for learning-disabled students, cooperative (work-study) education, study abroad, advanced placement credit, accelerated degree programs, double majors, independent study, distance learning, summer session for credit, part-time degree programs, and internships. The most frequently chosen baccalaureate fields are computer/information sciences, architecture, engineering/engineering technologies.

Student Body Statistics The student body totals 6,167, of whom 1,941 are undergraduates (398 freshmen). 25 percent are women and 75 percent are men. Students come from 50 states and territories and 58 other countries. 63 percent are from Illinois. 16.9 percent are international students. 46 percent of the 2003 graduating class went on to graduate and professional schools.
Expenses for 2004–05 *Application fee:* $30. *Comprehensive fee:* $28,288 includes full-time tuition ($20,764), mandatory fees ($578), and college room and board ($6946). Room and board charges vary according to board plan. *Part-time tuition:* $647 per credit hour.
Financial Aid Forms of aid include need-based and non-need-based scholarships, athletic grants, and part-time jobs. The average aided 2002–03 undergraduate received an aid package worth $19,588. The priority application deadline for financial aid is April 15.
Freshman Admission IIT requires an essay, a high school transcript, a minimum 3.0 high school GPA, 1 recommendation, SAT score over 1150; ACT score over 24, SAT I or ACT scores, and TOEFL scores for international students. SAT II: Subject Test scores are recommended. An interview is required for some. The application deadline for regular admission is rolling.
Transfer Admission The application deadline for admission is rolling.
Entrance Difficulty IIT assesses its entrance difficulty level as very difficult. For the fall 2003 freshman class, 59 percent of the applicants were accepted.

For Further Information Contact Mr. Brent Benner, Director of Undergraduate Admission, Illinois Institute of Technology, 10 West 33rd Street PH101, Chicago, IL 60616-3793. *Telephone:* 312-567-3025 or 800-448-2329 (toll-free out-of-state). *Fax:* 312-567-6939. *E-mail:* admission@iit.edu. *Web site:* http://www.iit.edu/.

See page 294 for a narrative description.

ILLINOIS STATE UNIVERSITY
Normal, Illinois

Illinois State is a coed, public university, founded in 1857, offering degrees at the bachelor's, master's, and doctoral levels and post-master's and postbachelor's certificates. It has an 850-acre campus in Normal.

Academic Information The faculty has 1,084 members (78% full-time), 72% with terminal degrees. The undergraduate student-faculty ratio is 19:1. The library holds 2 million titles and 4,873 serial subscriptions. Special programs include academic remediation, services for learning-disabled students, an honors program, cooperative (work-study) education, study abroad, advanced placement credit, accelerated degree programs, ESL programs, double majors, independent study, distance learning, self-designed majors, summer session for credit, part-time degree programs (daytime, evenings, summer), adult/continuing education programs, internships, and arrangement for off-campus study with National Student Exchange. The most frequently chosen baccalaureate fields are business/marketing, education, social sciences and history.
Student Body Statistics The student body totals 20,860, of whom 18,097 are undergraduates (3,097 freshmen). 58 percent are women and 42 percent are men. Students come from 48 states and territories and 55 other countries. 98 percent are from Illinois. 0.8 percent are international students.
Expenses for 2003–04 *Application fee:* $30. *State resident tuition:* $4123 full-time, $137.43 per credit hour part-time. *Nonresident tuition:* $8593 full-time, $286.43 per credit hour part-time. *Mandatory fees:* $1407 full-time, $40.57 per credit hour part-time, $608.55 per term part-time. Full-time tuition and fees vary according to course load. Part-time tuition and fees vary according to course load. *College room and board:* $5414. *College room only:* $2682. Room and board charges vary according to board plan.
Financial Aid Forms of aid include need-based and non-need-based scholarships, athletic grants, and part-time jobs. The average aided 2003–04 undergraduate received an aid package worth an estimated $7801. The priority application deadline for financial aid is March 1.

Freshman Admission Illinois State requires an essay, a high school transcript, SAT I or ACT scores, and TOEFL scores for international students. ACT scores are recommended. The application deadline for regular admission is March 1.
Transfer Admission The application deadline for admission is rolling.
Entrance Difficulty Illinois State assesses its entrance difficulty level as moderately difficult. For the fall 2003 freshman class, 75 percent of the applicants were accepted.

For Further Information Contact Molly Arnold, Acting Director of Admissions, Illinois State University, Campus Box 2200, Normal, IL 61790-2200. *Telephone:* 309-438-2181 or 800-366-2478 (toll-free in-state). *Fax:* 309-438-3932. *E-mail:* ugradadm@ilstu.edu. *Web site:* http://www.ilstu.edu/.

ILLINOIS WESLEYAN UNIVERSITY
Bloomington, Illinois

IWU is a coed, private, four-year college, founded in 1850, offering degrees at the bachelor's level. It has a 79-acre campus in Bloomington.

Academic Information The faculty has 208 members (76% full-time), 82% with terminal degrees. The student-faculty ratio is 12:1. The library holds 307,861 titles, 14,264 serial subscriptions, and 13,833 audiovisual materials. Special programs include an honors program, cooperative (work-study) education, study abroad, advanced placement credit, double majors, independent study, self-designed majors, summer session for credit, internships, and arrangement for off-campus study with Case Western Reserve University, Northwestern University, Washington University, Dartmouth College. The most frequently chosen baccalaureate fields are business/marketing, social sciences and history, visual/performing arts.
Student Body Statistics The student body is made up of 2,106 undergraduates (578 freshmen). 57 percent are women and 43 percent are men. Students come from 36 states and territories and 20 other countries. 87 percent are from Illinois. 2.1 percent are international students. 29 percent of the 2003 graduating class went on to graduate and professional schools.
Expenses for 2004–05 *Application fee:* $0. *Comprehensive fee:* $32,270 includes full-time tuition ($25,980), mandatory fees ($150), and college room and board ($6140). *College room only:* $3680. Room and board charges vary according to board plan and housing facility. *Part-time tuition:* $3250 per course.
Financial Aid Forms of aid include need-based and non-need-based scholarships and part-time jobs. The average aided 2003–04 undergraduate received an aid package worth an estimated $17,044. The application deadline for financial aid is March 1.
Freshman Admission IWU requires an essay, a high school transcript, a minimum 2.0 high school GPA, SAT I or ACT scores, and TOEFL scores for international students. A minimum 3.0 high school GPA, 3 recommendations, and an interview are recommended. The application deadline for regular admission is February 15.
Entrance Difficulty IWU assesses its entrance difficulty level as very difficult. For the fall 2003 freshman class, 43 percent of the applicants were accepted.

For Further Information Contact Mr. Jerry Pope, Dean of Admissions, Illinois Wesleyan University, PO Box 2900, Bloomington, IL 61702-2900. *Telephone:* 309-556-3031 or 800-332-2498 (toll-free). *Fax:* 309-556-3820. *E-mail:* iwuadmit@titan.iwu.edu. *Web site:* http://www.iwu.edu/.

INTERNATIONAL ACADEMY OF DESIGN & TECHNOLOGY
Chicago, Illinois

International Academy is a coed, proprietary, four-year college of Career Education Corporation, founded in 1977, offering degrees at the associate and bachelor's levels. It has a 1-acre campus in Chicago.

Academic Information The faculty has 183 members (11% full-time), 3% with terminal degrees. The student-faculty ratio is 14:1. The library holds 5,000 titles, 90 serial subscriptions, and 500 audiovisual materials. Special programs include academic remediation, study abroad, advanced placement credit, independent study, summer session for credit, part-time degree programs (daytime, evenings, weekends, summer), adult/continuing education programs, and internships. The most frequently chosen baccalaureate fields are business/marketing, visual/performing arts.
Student Body Statistics The student body is made up of 2,769 undergraduates (755 freshmen). 66 percent are women and 34 percent are men. Students come from 28 states and territories and 23 other countries. 94 percent are from Illinois. 0.8 percent are international students.
Expenses for 2004–05 *Application fee:* $50. *Tuition:* $18,400 full-time, $1200 per course part-time. *Mandatory fees:* $300 full-time. Full-time tuition and fees vary according to course load and program. Part-time tuition varies according to program.
Financial Aid Forms of aid include need-based scholarships and part-time jobs. The application deadline for financial aid is continuous.
Freshman Admission International Academy requires a high school transcript and an interview. An essay, a minimum 2.0 high school GPA, SAT I and SAT II or ACT scores, and SAT II: Writing Test scores are recommended. GED is required for some. The application deadline for regular admission is rolling.
Transfer Admission The application deadline for admission is rolling.
Entrance Difficulty International Academy assesses its entrance difficulty level as minimally difficult. For the fall 2003 freshman class, 54 percent of the applicants were accepted.

For Further Information Contact Ms. Laura Wincup, Associate Director of Student Management, International Academy of Design & Technology, One North State Street, Suite 400, Chicago, IL 60602. *Telephone:* 312-980-9200 or 877-ACADEMY (toll-free out-of-state). *Fax:* 312-541-3929. *E-mail:* academy@iadtchicago.com. *Web site:* http://www.iadtchicago.com/.

See page 296 for a narrative description.

ITT TECHNICAL INSTITUTE
Mount Prospect, Illinois

ITT Tech is a coed, proprietary, primarily two-year college of ITT Educational Services, Inc., founded in 1986, offering degrees at the associate and bachelor's levels. It has a 1-acre campus in Mount Prospect near Chicago.

Student Body Statistics The student body is made up of 590 undergraduates.
Expenses for 2003–04 *Application fee:* $100. Total Program Cost varies depending on course of study. Consult school catalog.
Financial Aid Forms of aid include need-based scholarships and part-time jobs. The application deadline for financial aid is continuous.
Freshman Admission ITT Tech requires a high school transcript, an interview, and Wonderlic aptitude test. Recommendations and TOEFL scores for international students are recommended. The application deadline for regular admission is rolling.
Transfer Admission The application deadline for admission is rolling.
Entrance Difficulty ITT Tech assesses its entrance difficulty level as minimally difficult.

For Further Information Contact Mr. Ernest Lloyd, Director of Recruitment, ITT Technical Institute, 1401 Feehanville Drive, Mount Prospect, IL 60056. *Telephone:* 847-375-8800. *Fax:* 847-375-9022. *Web site:* http://www.itt-tech.edu/.

JUDSON COLLEGE
Elgin, Illinois

Judson is a coed, private, Baptist, four-year college, founded in 1963, offering degrees at the bachelor's and master's levels. It has an 80-acre campus in Elgin near Chicago.

Judson College (continued)

Academic Information The faculty has 114 members (47% full-time), 47% with terminal degrees. The undergraduate student-faculty ratio is 16:1. The library holds 104,331 titles, 450 serial subscriptions, and 12,500 audiovisual materials. Special programs include academic remediation, an honors program, study abroad, advanced placement credit, accelerated degree programs, double majors, independent study, distance learning, self-designed majors, part-time degree programs (evenings, weekends), adult/continuing education programs, internships, and arrangement for off-campus study with Christian College Coalition. The most frequently chosen baccalaureate fields are business/marketing, education, protective services/public administration.

Student Body Statistics The student body totals 1,166, of whom 1,123 are undergraduates (132 freshmen). 57 percent are women and 43 percent are men. Students come from 21 states and territories and 18 other countries. 65 percent are from Illinois. 3.8 percent are international students.

Expenses for 2003–04 *Application fee:* $30. *Comprehensive fee:* $22,050 includes full-time tuition ($15,800), mandatory fees ($250), and college room and board ($6000). Room and board charges vary according to board plan. *Part-time tuition:* $515 per term. *Part-time mandatory fees:* $56.25 per term. Part-time tuition and fees vary according to course load.

Financial Aid Forms of aid include need-based and non-need-based scholarships and part-time jobs. The application deadline for financial aid is continuous.

Freshman Admission Judson requires an essay, a high school transcript, a minimum 2.0 high school GPA, SAT I or ACT scores, and TOEFL scores for international students. 2 recommendations and an interview are required for some. The application deadline for regular admission is rolling.

Transfer Admission The application deadline for admission is rolling.

Entrance Difficulty Judson assesses its entrance difficulty level as moderately difficult. For the fall 2003 freshman class, 79 percent of the applicants were accepted.

For Further Information Contact Mr. Billy Dean, Director of Admissions, Judson College, 1151 North State Street, Elgin, IL 60123-1498. *Telephone:* 847-695-2500 Ext. 2315 or 800-839-5376 (toll-free). *Fax:* 847-695-0216. *E-mail:* admission@judsoncollege.edu. *Web site:* http://www.judsoncollege.edu/.

KENDALL COLLEGE
Chicago, Illinois

Kendall is a coed, private, United Methodist, four-year college, founded in 1934, offering degrees at the associate and bachelor's levels. It has a 1-acre campus in Chicago.

Academic Information The faculty has 74 members, 41% with terminal degrees. The student-faculty ratio is 9:1. The library holds 37,000 titles, 215 serial subscriptions, and 150 audiovisual materials. Special programs include academic remediation, cooperative (work-study) education, study abroad, advanced placement credit, accelerated degree programs, ESL programs, independent study, self-designed majors, summer session for credit, part-time degree programs (daytime, evenings, weekends, summer), adult/continuing education programs, and internships.

Student Body Statistics The student body is made up of 628 undergraduates (70 freshmen). 54 percent are women and 46 percent are men. Students come from 20 states and territories and 19 other countries. 62 percent are from Illinois. 4.9 percent are international students.

Expenses for 2003–04 *Application fee:* $30. *Comprehensive fee:* $21,578 includes full-time tuition ($14,445), mandatory fees ($305), and college room and board ($6828). Full-time tuition and fees vary according to program. Room and board charges vary according to housing facility. *Part-time tuition:* $436 per quarter hour. *Part-time mandatory fees:* $127 per term. Part-time tuition and fees vary according to program.

Financial Aid Forms of aid include need-based and non-need-based scholarships, athletic grants, and part-time jobs. The priority application deadline for financial aid is May 1.

Freshman Admission Kendall requires an essay, a high school transcript, minimum ACT score of 18, SAT I or ACT scores, and TOEFL scores for international students. A minimum 2.0 high school GPA and an interview

are recommended. Recommendations and an interview are required for some. The application deadline for regular admission is rolling.

Transfer Admission The application deadline for admission is rolling.

Entrance Difficulty Kendall assesses its entrance difficulty level as minimally difficult. For the fall 2003 freshman class, 79 percent of the applicants were accepted.

For Further Information Contact Carl Goodmonson, Director of Admissions, Kendall College, 900 North Branch Street, Chicago, IL 60622. *Telephone:* 847-448-2304 or 877-588-8860 (toll-free). *Fax:* 847-448-2120. *E-mail:* admissions@kendall.edu. *Web site:* http://www.kendall.edu/.

See page 300 for a narrative description.

KNOX COLLEGE
Galesburg, Illinois

Knox is a coed, private, four-year college, founded in 1837, offering degrees at the bachelor's level. It has an 82-acre campus in Galesburg near Peoria.

Academic Information The faculty has 116 members (79% full-time), 84% with terminal degrees. The student-faculty ratio is 12:1. The library holds 185,923 titles, 1,037 serial subscriptions, and 6,336 audiovisual materials. Special programs include academic remediation, services for learning-disabled students, an honors program, study abroad, advanced placement credit, ESL programs, double majors, independent study, self-designed majors, part-time degree programs (daytime), internships, and arrangement for off-campus study with Associated Colleges of the Midwest, Great Lakes College Association. The most frequently chosen baccalaureate fields are biological/life sciences, social sciences and history, visual/performing arts.

Student Body Statistics The student body is made up of 1,127 undergraduates (268 freshmen). 53 percent are women and 47 percent are men. Students come from 46 states and territories and 50 other countries. 56 percent are from Illinois. 8.7 percent are international students. 35 percent of the 2003 graduating class went on to graduate and professional schools.

Expenses for 2004–05 *Application fee:* $35. *Comprehensive fee:* $31,338 includes full-time tuition ($24,960), mandatory fees ($276), and college room and board ($6102). *College room only:* $2703. Room and board charges vary according to board plan.

Financial Aid Forms of aid include need-based and non-need-based scholarships and part-time jobs. The average aided 2003–04 undergraduate received an aid package worth an estimated $20,770. The priority application deadline for financial aid is March 1.

Freshman Admission Knox requires an essay, a high school transcript, 2 recommendations, SAT I or ACT scores, and TOEFL scores for international students. An interview is recommended. The application deadline for regular admission is February 1 and for early action it is December 1.

Transfer Admission The application deadline for admission is April 1.

Entrance Difficulty Knox assesses its entrance difficulty level as very difficult. For the fall 2003 freshman class, 73 percent of the applicants were accepted.

For Further Information Contact Mr. Paul Steenis, Director of Admissions, Knox College, Box K-148, Galesburg, IL 61401. *Telephone:* 309-341-7100 or 800-678-KNOX (toll-free). *Fax:* 309-341-7070. *E-mail:* admission@knox.edu. *Web site:* http://www.knox.edu/.

LAKE FOREST COLLEGE
Lake Forest, Illinois

Lake Forest is a coed, private, comprehensive institution, founded in 1857, offering degrees at the bachelor's and master's levels. It has a 110-acre campus in Lake Forest near Chicago.

Academic Information The faculty has 151 members (58% full-time), 74% with terminal degrees. The undergraduate student-faculty ratio is 12:1. The library holds 268,760 titles, 886 serial subscriptions, and 12,125 audiovisual materials. Special programs include services for learning-disabled students, an honors program, study abroad, advanced placement credit, accelerated degree programs, Freshman Honors College, double majors, independent study, self-designed majors, summer session for credit, part-time degree programs, adult/continuing education programs, internships, and arrangement for off-campus study with 14 members of the Associated Colleges of the Midwest. The most frequently chosen baccalaureate fields are business/marketing, communications/communication technologies, social sciences and history.

Student Body Statistics The student body totals 1,348, of whom 1,336 are undergraduates (347 freshmen). 57 percent are women and 43 percent are men. Students come from 47 states and territories and 50 other countries. 48 percent are from Illinois. 9.7 percent are international students. 32 percent of the 2003 graduating class went on to graduate and professional schools.

Expenses for 2003–04 *Application fee:* $40. *One-time mandatory fee:* $200. *Comprehensive fee:* $30,170 includes full-time tuition ($24,096), mandatory fees ($310), and college room and board ($5764). *College room only:* $3164. Room and board charges vary according to housing facility. *Part-time tuition:* $3012 per course. *Part-time mandatory fees:* $155 per term.

Financial Aid Forms of aid include need-based and non-need-based scholarships and part-time jobs. The average aided 2003–04 undergraduate received an aid package worth an estimated $19,466. The priority application deadline for financial aid is March 1.

Freshman Admission Lake Forest requires an essay, a high school transcript, 2 recommendations, graded paper, SAT I or ACT scores, and TOEFL scores for international students. An interview is recommended. The application deadline for regular admission is March 1; for early decision it is January 1; and for early action it is December 1.

Transfer Admission The application deadline for admission is rolling.

Entrance Difficulty Lake Forest assesses its entrance difficulty level as very difficult. For the fall 2003 freshman class, 68 percent of the applicants were accepted.

For Further Information Contact Mr. William G. Motzer Jr., Director of Admissions, Lake Forest College, 555 North Sheridan Road, Lake Forest, IL 60045-2399. *Telephone:* 847-735-5000 or 800-828-4751 (toll-free). *Fax:* 847-735-6271. *E-mail:* admissions@lakeforest.edu. *Web site:* http://www.lakeforest.edu/.

See page 304 for a narrative description.

LAKEVIEW COLLEGE OF NURSING
Danville, Illinois

LCON is a coed, private, upper-level unit of Danville Area Community College, founded in 1987, offering degrees at the bachelor's level in nursing. It has a 1-acre campus in Danville.

Expenses for 2003–04 *Application fee:* $50. *Tuition:* $8250 full-time, $275 per credit hour part-time. *Mandatory fees:* $1050 full-time, $35 per credit hour part-time.

For Further Information Contact Kelly M. Holden, MS Ed, Registrar, Lakeview College of Nursing, 903 North Logan Avenue, Danville, IL 61832. *Telephone:* 217-443-5238 Ext. 5385, 217-443-5238 Ext. 5454 (toll-free in-state), or 217-443-5238 (toll-free out-of-state). *Fax:* 217-442-2279. *E-mail:* kholden@lakeviewcol.edu. *Web site:* http://www.lakeviewcol.edu/.

LEWIS UNIVERSITY
Romeoville, Illinois

Lewis is a coed, private, comprehensive institution, founded in 1932, affiliated with the Roman Catholic Church, offering degrees at the associate, bachelor's, and master's levels and postbachelor's certificates. It has a 375-acre campus in Romeoville near Chicago.

Academic Information The faculty has 157 members (92% full-time), 61% with terminal degrees. The undergraduate student-faculty ratio is 13:1. The library holds 149,870 titles, 1,990 serial subscriptions, and 2,281 audiovisual materials. Special programs include academic remediation, an

honors program, study abroad, advanced placement credit, accelerated degree programs, ESL programs, double majors, independent study, distance learning, self-designed majors, summer session for credit, part-time degree programs (daytime, evenings, weekends, summer), adult/continuing education programs, and internships. The most frequently chosen baccalaureate fields are business/marketing, health professions and related sciences, protective services/public administration.

Student Body Statistics The student body totals 4,468, of whom 3,214 are undergraduates (458 freshmen). 59 percent are women and 41 percent are men. Students come from 24 states and territories and 31 other countries. 96 percent are from Illinois. 3.9 percent are international students. 10 percent of the 2003 graduating class went on to graduate and professional schools.

Expenses for 2004–05 *Application fee:* $35. *Comprehensive fee:* $24,106 includes full-time tuition ($16,906) and college room and board ($7200). *College room only:* $4850. Full-time tuition varies according to course load and program. Room and board charges vary according to board plan and housing facility. *Part-time tuition:* $546 per credit. Part-time tuition varies according to course load and program.

Financial Aid Forms of aid include need-based and non-need-based scholarships, athletic grants, and part-time jobs. The average aided 2003–04 undergraduate received an aid package worth an estimated $13,302. The priority application deadline for financial aid is May 1.

Freshman Admission Lewis requires a high school transcript, a minimum 2.0 high school GPA, SAT I or ACT scores, and TOEFL scores for international students. An interview is required for some. The application deadline for regular admission is August 1.

Transfer Admission The application deadline for admission is rolling.

Entrance Difficulty Lewis assesses its entrance difficulty level as moderately difficult; noncompetitive for applicants 24 or over. For the fall 2003 freshman class, 66 percent of the applicants were accepted.

For Further Information Contact Mr. Ryan Cockerill, Admission Counselor, Lewis University, Box 297, One University Parkway, Romeoville, IL 60446. *Telephone:* 815-838-0500 Ext. 5684 or 800-897-9000 (toll-free). *Fax:* 815-836-5002. *E-mail:* admissions@lewisu.edu. *Web site:* http://www.lewisu.edu/.

LEXINGTON COLLEGE
Chicago, Illinois

Lexington College is a women's, private, four-year college, founded in 1977, offering degrees at the associate and bachelor's levels.

Academic Information The faculty has 17 members (24% full-time), 100% with terminal degrees. The student-faculty ratio is 2:1. The library holds 2,000 titles and 40 serial subscriptions. Special programs include academic remediation, cooperative (work-study) education, part-time degree programs (daytime), adult/continuing education programs, and internships.

Student Body Statistics The student body is made up of 41 undergraduates (14 freshmen). Students come from 5 states and territories and 2 other countries. 88 percent are from Illinois. 4.9 percent are international students.

Expenses for 2003–04 *Application fee:* $30. *Tuition:* $12,600 full-time, $450 per credit hour part-time. *Mandatory fees:* $750 full-time.

Financial Aid Forms of aid include need-based scholarships and part-time jobs. The average aided 2003–04 undergraduate received an aid package worth an estimated $10,000. The application deadline for financial aid is October 1 with a priority deadline of May 15.

Freshman Admission Lexington College requires an essay, a high school transcript, a minimum 2.0 high school GPA, and SAT I or ACT scores. An interview is recommended. 2 recommendations are required for some. The application deadline for regular admission is rolling.

Lexington College *(continued)*

Entrance Difficulty Lexington College has an open admission policy. It assesses its entrance difficulty as minimally difficult for out-of-state applicants; minimally difficult for transfers.

For Further Information Contact Ms. Giselle Castillo, Director of Admissions, Lexington College, 310 South Peoria Street, Chicago, IL 60607-3534. *Telephone:* 312-226-6294 Ext. 225. *Fax:* 312-226-6405. *E-mail:* adm@lexingtoncollege.edu. *Web site:* http://www.lexingtoncollege.edu/.

LINCOLN CHRISTIAN COLLEGE
Lincoln, Illinois

Lincoln Christian is a coed, private, four-year college, founded in 1944, affiliated with the Christian Churches and Churches of Christ, offering degrees at the associate and bachelor's levels. It has a 227-acre campus in Lincoln.

Expenses for 2003–04 *Application fee:* $20. *Comprehensive fee:* $13,558 includes full-time tuition ($7890), mandatory fees ($1200), and college room and board ($4468). *Part-time tuition:* $263 per semester hour. *Part-time mandatory fees:* $40 per semester hour. Part-time tuition and fees vary according to course load and program.

For Further Information Contact Mrs. Mary K. Davis, Assistant Director of Admissions, Lincoln Christian College, 100 Campus View Drive, Lincoln, IL 62656. *Telephone:* 217-732-3168 Ext. 2367 or 888-522-5228 (toll-free). *Fax:* 217-732-4199. *E-mail:* coladmis@lccs.edu. *Web site:* http://www.lccs.edu/.

LINCOLN COLLEGE
Normal, Illinois

Lincoln College is a coed, private, primarily two-year college, founded in 1865, offering degrees at the associate and bachelor's levels. It has a 10-acre campus in Normal.

Expenses for 2004–05 *Application fee:* $25. *Comprehensive fee:* $19,170 includes full-time tuition ($13,600), mandatory fees ($570), and college room and board ($5000). *College room only:* $3200. Full-time tuition and fees vary according to program. Room and board charges vary according to board plan. *Part-time tuition:* $453 per credit hour. *Part-time mandatory fees:* $25 per term. Part-time tuition and fees vary according to course load.

For Further Information Contact Mr. Joe Hendrix, Director of Admissions, Lincoln College, 715 West Raab Road, Normal, IL 61761. *Telephone:* 309-452-0500 or 800-569-0558 (toll-free). *Fax:* 309-454-5652. *E-mail:* admissions@lincoln.mclean.il.us. *Web site:* http://www.lincolncollege.edu/normal/.

LINCOLN COLLEGE
Lincoln, Illinois

Lincoln College is a coed, private, two-year college, founded in 1865, offering degrees at the associate level. It has a 42-acre campus in Lincoln.

Academic Information The faculty has 53 members (64% full-time). The student-faculty ratio is 15:1. The library holds 42,500 titles and 380 serial subscriptions. Special programs include academic remediation, an honors program, accelerated degree programs, Freshman Honors College, independent study, summer session for credit, and part-time degree programs (daytime, evenings, summer).

Student Body Statistics The student body is made up of 758 undergraduates (380 freshmen). 46 percent are women and 54 percent are men. Students come from 15 states and territories. 91 percent are from Illinois. 89 percent of the 2003 graduating class went on to four-year colleges.

Expenses for 2004–05 *Application fee:* $25. *Comprehensive fee:* $19,960 includes full-time tuition ($13,600), mandatory fees ($960), and college room and board ($5400). Room and board charges vary according to housing facility.

Financial Aid Forms of aid include need-based scholarships and part-time jobs. The priority application deadline for financial aid is May 1.

Freshman Admission Lincoln College requires a high school transcript, SAT I or ACT scores, and TOEFL scores for international students. An interview is recommended. 1 recommendation is required for some. The application deadline for regular admission is rolling.

Transfer Admission The application deadline for admission is rolling.

Entrance Difficulty Lincoln College assesses its entrance difficulty level as minimally difficult. For the fall 2003 freshman class, 65 percent of the applicants were accepted.

For Further Information Contact Mr. Tony Schilling, Director of Admissions, Lincoln College, 300 Keokuk Street, Lincoln, IL 62656-1699. *Telephone:* 800-569-0556 Ext. 254 or 800-569-0556 (toll-free). *Fax:* 217-732-7715. *E-mail:* information@lincolncollege.com. *Web site:* http://www.lincolncollege.edu/.

LOYOLA UNIVERSITY CHICAGO
Chicago, Illinois

Loyola is a coed, private, Roman Catholic (Jesuit) university, founded in 1870, offering degrees at the bachelor's, master's, doctoral, and first professional levels and post-master's and postbachelor's certificates (also offers adult part-time program with significant enrollment not reflected in profile). It has a 105-acre campus in Chicago.

Academic Information The faculty has 975 members (54% full-time). The undergraduate student-faculty ratio is 13:1. The library holds 1 million titles, 68,886 serial subscriptions, and 35,090 audiovisual materials. Special programs include academic remediation, services for learning-disabled students, an honors program, study abroad, advanced placement credit, accelerated degree programs, ESL programs, double majors, summer session for credit, part-time degree programs (evenings), adult/continuing education programs, internships, and arrangement for off-campus study with School of the Art Institute of Chicago. The most frequently chosen baccalaureate fields are business/marketing, psychology, social sciences and history.

Student Body Statistics The student body totals 13,362, of whom 7,916 are undergraduates (1,915 freshmen). 66 percent are women and 34 percent are men. Students come from 50 states and territories and 60 other countries. 66 percent are from Illinois. 1.7 percent are international students.

Expenses for 2004–05 *Application fee:* $25. *Comprehensive fee:* $31,164 includes full-time tuition ($21,780), mandatory fees ($560), and college room and board ($8824). *College room only:* $5974. Room and board charges vary according to board plan and housing facility. *Part-time tuition:* $429 per semester hour. *Part-time mandatory fees:* $75 per term. Part-time tuition and fees vary according to course load.

Financial Aid Forms of aid include need-based and non-need-based scholarships, athletic grants, and part-time jobs. The average aided 2003–04 undergraduate received an aid package worth an estimated $20,488. The priority application deadline for financial aid is March 1.

Freshman Admission Loyola requires an essay, a high school transcript, SAT I or ACT scores, and TOEFL scores for international students. An interview is recommended. The application deadline for regular admission is April 1.

Transfer Admission The application deadline for admission is August 1.

Entrance Difficulty Loyola assesses its entrance difficulty level as moderately difficult. For the fall 2003 freshman class, 82 percent of the applicants were accepted.

For Further Information Contact Ms. April Hansen, Director of Admissions, Loyola University Chicago, 820 North Michigan Avenue, Suite 613, Chicago, IL 60611-9810. *Telephone:* 773-508-3080 or 800-262-2373 (toll-free). *Fax:* 312-915-7216. *E-mail:* admission@luc.edu. *Web site:* http://www.luc.edu/.

See page 306 for a narrative description.

MACCORMAC COLLEGE
Chicago, Illinois

MacCormac College is a coed, primarily women's, private, two-year college, founded in 1904, offering degrees at the associate level.

Academic Information The faculty has 34 members (12% full-time), 12% with terminal degrees. The student-faculty ratio is 15:1. The library holds 11,000 titles and 140 serial subscriptions. Special programs include academic remediation, an honors program, advanced placement credit, ESL programs, summer session for credit, part-time degree programs (daytime, evenings), adult/continuing education programs, and internships.

Student Body Statistics The student body is made up of 377 undergraduates (227 freshmen). 87 percent are women and 13 percent are men. Students come from 7 states and territories and 8 other countries. 99 percent are from Illinois. 20 percent of the 2003 graduating class went on to four-year colleges.

Expenses for 2004–05 *Application fee:* $20. *Tuition:* $9960 full-time, $350 per credit part-time. *Mandatory fees:* $200 full-time, $10 per credit part-time.

Financial Aid Forms of aid include need-based scholarships and part-time jobs. The application deadline for financial aid is continuous.

Freshman Admission MacCormac College requires a high school transcript, ACT scores, and TOEFL scores for international students. An interview and SAT I scores are recommended. The application deadline for regular admission is rolling.

Transfer Admission The application deadline for admission is rolling.

Entrance Difficulty MacCormac College assesses its entrance difficulty level as moderately difficult.

For Further Information Contact Ms. Rosa Medina, Coordinator of Admissions, MacCormac College, 506 South Wabash Avenue, Chicago, IL 60605-1667. *Telephone:* 312-922-1884 Ext. 106. *Fax:* 630-941-0937. *Web site:* http://www.maccormac.edu/.

MACMURRAY COLLEGE
Jacksonville, Illinois

MacMurray is a coed, private, United Methodist, four-year college, founded in 1846, offering degrees at the associate and bachelor's levels. It has a 60-acre campus in Jacksonville.

Academic Information The faculty has 70 members (57% full-time), 41% with terminal degrees. The student-faculty ratio is 12:1. The library holds 935,000 titles, 235 serial subscriptions, and 936 audiovisual materials. Special programs include academic remediation, services for learning-disabled students, an honors program, advanced placement credit, double majors, independent study, summer session for credit, part-time degree programs (daytime, evenings, summer), internships, and arrangement for off-campus study with 5 members of the Western Illinois Foreign Language Consortium. The most frequently chosen baccalaureate fields are business/marketing, education, health professions and related sciences.

Student Body Statistics The student body is made up of 673 undergraduates (162 freshmen). 59 percent are women and 41 percent are men. Students come from 21 states and territories and 7 other countries. 85 percent are from Illinois. 1 percent are international students. 10 percent of the 2003 graduating class went on to graduate and professional schools.

Expenses for 2004–05 *Application fee:* $0. *Comprehensive fee:* $20,270 includes full-time tuition ($14,500), mandatory fees ($150), and college room and board ($5620). *College room only:* $2850. Room and board charges vary according to board plan and housing facility. *Part-time tuition:* $235 per credit hour.

Financial Aid Forms of aid include need-based and non-need-based scholarships and part-time jobs. The average aided 2003–04 undergraduate received an aid package worth an estimated $16,659. The priority application deadline for financial aid is May 31.

Freshman Admission MacMurray requires a high school transcript, SAT I or ACT scores, and TOEFL scores for international students. An essay, a minimum 2.5 high school GPA, recommendations, and an interview are required for some. The application deadline for regular admission is rolling.

Transfer Admission The application deadline for admission is rolling.

Entrance Difficulty MacMurray assesses its entrance difficulty level as moderately difficult. For the fall 2003 freshman class, 64 percent of the applicants were accepted.

For Further Information Contact Ms. Rhonda Cors, vice President for Enrollment, MacMurray College, 447 East College Avenue, Jacksonville, IL 62650. *Telephone:* 217-479-7056 or 800-252-7485 (toll-free in-state). *Fax:* 217-291-0702. *E-mail:* admiss@mac.edu. *Web site:* http://www.mac.edu/.

MCKENDREE COLLEGE
Lebanon, Illinois

McKendree is a coed, private, four-year college, founded in 1828, affiliated with the United Methodist Church, offering degrees at the bachelor's and master's levels. It has an 80-acre campus in Lebanon near St. Louis.

Academic Information The faculty has 204 members (34% full-time), 38% with terminal degrees. The undergraduate student-faculty ratio is 12:1. The library holds 105,000 titles, 450 serial subscriptions, and 9,500 audiovisual materials. Special programs include academic remediation, services for learning-disabled students, an honors program, study abroad, advanced placement credit, accelerated degree programs, double majors, independent study, self-designed majors, summer session for credit, part-time degree programs (daytime, evenings, summer), internships, and arrangement for off-campus study with University of Evansville. The most frequently chosen baccalaureate fields are business/marketing, education, health professions and related sciences.

Student Body Statistics The student body is made up of 2,115 undergraduates (310 freshmen). 61 percent are women and 39 percent are men. Students come from 23 states and territories and 15 other countries. 69 percent are from Illinois. 1.2 percent are international students. 18 percent of the 2003 graduating class went on to graduate and professional schools.

Expenses for 2003–04 *Application fee:* $40. *One-time mandatory fee:* $50. *Comprehensive fee:* $21,120 includes full-time tuition ($15,200) and college room and board ($5920). Full-time tuition varies according to class time, course load, and location. Room and board charges vary according to board plan and housing facility. *Part-time tuition:* $510 per credit. Part-time tuition varies according to class time, course load, and location.

Financial Aid Forms of aid include need-based and non-need-based scholarships, athletic grants, and part-time jobs. The average aided 2003–04 undergraduate received an aid package worth an estimated $12,400. The priority application deadline for financial aid is May 31.

Freshman Admission McKendree requires an essay, a high school transcript, a minimum 2.5 high school GPA, 1 recommendation, top half of class, ACT of 20 or greater, SAT I or ACT scores, and TOEFL scores for international students. An essay and an interview are required for some. The application deadline for regular admission is rolling.

Transfer Admission The application deadline for admission is rolling.

Entrance Difficulty McKendree assesses its entrance difficulty level as moderately difficult. For the fall 2003 freshman class, 73 percent of the applicants were accepted.

For Further Information Contact Mr. Mark Campbell, Vice President for Admissions and Financial Aid, McKendree College, 701 College Road, Lebanon, IL 62254. *Telephone:* 800-232-7228 Ext. 6835 or 800-232-7228 Ext. 6831 (toll-free). *Fax:* 618-537-6496. *E-mail:* inquiry@mckendree.edu. *Web site:* http://www.mckendree.edu/.

MENNONITE COLLEGE OF NURSING
See Illinois State University

Illinois

MIDSTATE COLLEGE
Peoria, Illinois

Midstate is a coed, primarily women's, proprietary, four-year college, founded in 1888, offering degrees at the associate and bachelor's levels. It has a 1-acre campus in Peoria.

Expenses for 2003–04 *Application fee:* $25. *Tuition:* $11,600 full-time, $775 per course part-time.

For Further Information Contact Ms. Jessica Auer, Director of Admissions, Midstate College, 411 West Northmoor Road, Peoria, IL 61614. *Telephone:* 309-692-4092. *Fax:* 309-692-3893. *Web site:* http://www.midstate.edu/.

MILLIKIN UNIVERSITY
Decatur, Illinois

Millikin is a coed, private, comprehensive institution, founded in 1901, affiliated with the Presbyterian Church (U.S.A.), offering degrees at the bachelor's and master's levels. It has a 70-acre campus in Decatur.

Academic Information The library holds 199,660 titles, 927 serial subscriptions, and 9,017 audiovisual materials. Special programs include services for learning-disabled students, an honors program, study abroad, advanced placement credit, double majors, independent study, self-designed majors, summer session for credit, part-time degree programs (daytime, evenings, summer), internships, and arrangement for off-campus study with Drew University, American University, Urban Life Center. The most frequently chosen baccalaureate fields are communications/communication technologies, engineering/engineering technologies, visual/performing arts.
Student Body Statistics The student body totals 2,633, of whom 2,602 are undergraduates (598 freshmen). 56 percent are women and 44 percent are men. Students come from 33 states and territories. 85 percent are from Illinois. 0.3 percent are international students. 14 percent of the 2003 graduating class went on to graduate and professional schools.
Expenses for 2003–04 *Comprehensive fee:* $25,357 includes full-time tuition ($18,834), mandatory fees ($400), and college room and board ($6123). *College room only:* $3315. Full-time tuition and fees vary according to course load. Room and board charges vary according to board plan and housing facility. *Part-time tuition:* $554 per credit.
Financial Aid Forms of aid include need-based and non-need-based scholarships and part-time jobs. The average aided 2002–03 undergraduate received an aid package worth $16,233. The application deadline for financial aid is June 1 with a priority deadline of April 15.
Freshman Admission Millikin requires a high school transcript, a minimum 2.0 high school GPA, 2 recommendations, SAT I or ACT scores, and TOEFL scores for international students. An interview is recommended. Audition for school of music; portfolio review for art program is required for some. The application deadline for regular admission is rolling.
Entrance Difficulty Millikin assesses its entrance difficulty level as moderately difficult; most difficult for James Millikin Scholars, Presidential Scholars programs. For the fall 2003 freshman class, 74 percent of the applicants were accepted.

For Further Information Contact Mr. Lin Stoner, Dean of Admission, Millikin University, 1184 West Main Street, Decatur, IL 62522-2084. *Telephone:* 217-424-6210 or 800-373-7733 (toll-free). *Fax:* 217-425-4669. *E-mail:* admis@millikin.edu. *Web site:* http://www.millikin.edu/.

MONMOUTH COLLEGE
Monmouth, Illinois

Monmouth is a coed, private, four-year college, founded in 1853, affiliated with the Presbyterian Church, offering degrees at the bachelor's level. It has an 80-acre campus in Monmouth near Peoria.

Academic Information The faculty has 111 members (62% full-time), 61% with terminal degrees. The student-faculty ratio is 14:1. The library holds 176,470 titles, 514 serial subscriptions, and 3,975 audiovisual materials. Special programs include an honors program, study abroad, advanced placement credit, double majors, independent study, self-designed majors, part-time degree programs (daytime), internships, and arrangement for off-campus study with members of the Associated Colleges of the Midwest, Great Lakes Colleges Association. The most frequently chosen baccalaureate fields are business/marketing, education, English.
Student Body Statistics The student body is made up of 1,162 undergraduates (357 freshmen). 52 percent are women and 48 percent are men. Students come from 20 states and territories and 15 other countries. 93 percent are from Illinois. 1.7 percent are international students. 20 percent of the 2003 graduating class went on to graduate and professional schools.
Expenses for 2004–05 *Application fee:* $0. *Comprehensive fee:* $24,800 includes full-time tuition ($19,350) and college room and board ($5450). Room and board charges vary according to board plan and housing facility. *Part-time tuition:* $810 per semester hour.
Financial Aid Forms of aid include need-based and non-need-based scholarships and part-time jobs. The average aided 2003–04 undergraduate received an aid package worth an estimated $15,432. The priority application deadline for financial aid is March 1.
Freshman Admission Monmouth requires a high school transcript, SAT I or ACT scores, and TOEFL scores for international students. An interview is recommended. An essay and 2 recommendations are required for some. The application deadline for regular admission is rolling.
Transfer Admission The application deadline for admission is rolling.
Entrance Difficulty Monmouth assesses its entrance difficulty level as moderately difficult. For the fall 2003 freshman class, 76 percent of the applicants were accepted.

For Further Information Contact Ms. Christine Johnston, Director of New Student Recruitment, Monmouth College, 700 East Broadway, Monmouth, IL 61462-1998. *Telephone:* 309-457-2131 or 800-747-2687 (toll-free). *Fax:* 309-457-2141. *E-mail:* admit@monm.edu. *Web site:* http://www.monm.edu/.

MOODY BIBLE INSTITUTE
Chicago, Illinois

MBI is a coed, private, nondenominational, comprehensive institution, founded in 1886, offering degrees at the bachelor's, master's, and first professional levels. It has a 25-acre campus in Chicago.

Academic Information The faculty has 100 members (84% full-time), 73% with terminal degrees. The undergraduate student-faculty ratio is 20:1. The library holds 135,000 titles and 987 serial subscriptions. Special programs include study abroad, advanced placement credit, ESL programs, double majors, independent study, distance learning, summer session for credit, part-time degree programs (daytime, evenings, weekends, summer), external degree programs, adult/continuing education programs, internships, and arrangement for off-campus study with Roosevelt University, University of Illinois at Chicago, City Colleges of Chicago, Harold Washington College.
Student Body Statistics The student body totals 1,732, of whom 1,431 are undergraduates. 42 percent are women and 58 percent are men. Students come from 48 states and territories and 41 other countries. 31 percent are from Illinois. 6.7 percent are international students.
Expenses for 2003–04 *Application fee:* $35. *Comprehensive fee:* $7741 includes full-time tuition ($0), mandatory fees ($1401), and college room and board ($6340). *College room only:* $3620. All students are awarded full-tuition scholarships.
Financial Aid Forms of aid include need-based scholarships. The application deadline for financial aid is continuous.
Freshman Admission MBI requires an essay, a high school transcript, a minimum 2.3 high school GPA, 4 recommendations, Christian testimony, SAT I and SAT II or ACT scores, and TOEFL scores for international students. An interview is required for some. The application deadline for regular admission is March 1 and for early decision it is December 1.
Transfer Admission The application deadline for admission is March 1.

Entrance Difficulty MBI assesses its entrance difficulty level as moderately difficult. For the fall 2003 freshman class, 50 percent of the applicants were accepted.

For Further Information Contact Mrs. Marthe Campa, Application Coordinator, Moody Bible Institute, 820 North LaSalle Boulevard, Chicago, IL 60610. *Telephone:* 312-329-4267 or 800-967-4MBI (toll-free). *Fax:* 312-329-8987. *E-mail:* admissions@moody.edu. *Web site:* http://www.moody.edu/.

MORRISON INSTITUTE OF TECHNOLOGY
Morrison, Illinois

Morrison is a coed, primarily men's, private, two-year college, founded in 1973, offering degrees at the associate level in engineering technology. It has a 17-acre campus in Morrison.

Academic Information The faculty has 10 members (90% full-time). The student-faculty ratio is 14:1. The library holds 7,946 titles and 39 serial subscriptions. Special programs include academic remediation, double majors, part-time degree programs (daytime), and internships.
Student Body Statistics The student body is made up of 143 undergraduates (62 freshmen). 15 percent are women and 85 percent are men. Students come from 5 states and territories. 94 percent are from Illinois. 20 percent of the 2003 graduating class went on to four-year colleges.
Expenses for 2004–05 *Application fee:* $100. *Tuition:* $11,000 full-time, $458 per credit part-time. *Mandatory fees:* $250 full-time, $250 per year part-time. *College room only:* $2200.
Financial Aid Forms of aid include need-based scholarships and part-time jobs. The priority application deadline for financial aid is June 1.
Freshman Admission Morrison requires a high school transcript and proof of immunization. SAT I or ACT scores are recommended. The application deadline for regular admission is rolling.
Entrance Difficulty Morrison has an open admission policy.

For Further Information Contact Mrs. Tammy Pruis, Admission Secretary, Morrison Institute of Technology, 701 Portland Avenue, Morrison, IL 61270. *Telephone:* 815-772-7218. *Fax:* 815-772-7584. *E-mail:* admissions@morrison.tec.il.us. *Web site:* http://www.morrison.tec.il.us/.

NAES COLLEGE
Chicago, Illinois

For Information Write to NAES College, Chicago, IL 60659-3813.

NATIONAL-LOUIS UNIVERSITY
Chicago, Illinois

NLU is a coed, private university, founded in 1886, offering degrees at the bachelor's, master's, and doctoral levels and post-master's and postbachelor's certificates. It has a 12-acre campus in Chicago.

Academic Information The faculty has 284 members (100% full-time), 17% with terminal degrees. The undergraduate student-faculty ratio is 16:1. The library holds 5,043 audiovisual materials. Special programs include academic remediation, services for learning-disabled students, an honors program, advanced placement credit, accelerated degree programs, ESL programs, independent study, summer session for credit, part-time degree programs (daytime, evenings, weekends, summer), external degree programs, adult/continuing education programs, and internships. The most frequently chosen baccalaureate fields are business/marketing, education, interdisciplinary studies.
Student Body Statistics The student body totals 7,665, of whom 2,534 are undergraduates (67 freshmen). 73 percent are women and 27 percent are men. Students come from 18 states and territories. 99 percent are from Illinois.

Expenses for 2003–04 *Application fee:* $25. *Comprehensive fee:* $23,049 includes full-time tuition ($16,200), mandatory fees ($936), and college room and board ($5913). Room and board charges vary according to board plan. *Part-time tuition:* $360 per quarter hour.
Financial Aid Forms of aid include need-based and non-need-based scholarships and part-time jobs. The average aided 2003–04 undergraduate received an aid package worth an estimated $8314. The application deadline for financial aid is continuous.
Freshman Admission NLU requires a high school transcript and a minimum 2.0 high school GPA. An interview is recommended. 2 recommendations and SAT I or ACT scores are required for some. The application deadline for regular admission is rolling.
Transfer Admission The application deadline for admission is rolling.
Entrance Difficulty NLU assesses its entrance difficulty level as minimally difficult.

For Further Information Contact Ms. Pat Petillo, Director of Admissions, National-Louis University, 122 South Michigan Avenue, Chicago, IL 60603. *Telephone:* 888-NLU-TODAY, 888-NLU-TODAY (toll-free in-state), or 800-443-5522 (toll-free out-of-state). *Fax:* 312-261-3057. *Web site:* http://www.nl.edu/.

NORTH CENTRAL COLLEGE
Naperville, Illinois

North Central is a coed, private, United Methodist, comprehensive institution, founded in 1861, offering degrees at the bachelor's and master's levels. It has a 56-acre campus in Naperville near Chicago.

Academic Information The faculty has 217 members (58% full-time), 60% with terminal degrees. The undergraduate student-faculty ratio is 14:1. The library holds 145,707 titles, 707 serial subscriptions, and 3,367 audiovisual materials. Special programs include academic remediation, services for learning-disabled students, an honors program, cooperative (work-study) education, study abroad, advanced placement credit, accelerated degree programs, ESL programs, double majors, independent study, self-designed majors, summer session for credit, part-time degree programs, adult/continuing education programs, internships, and arrangement for off-campus study with Aurora University, Benedictine University. The most frequently chosen baccalaureate fields are business/marketing, communications/communication technologies, social sciences and history.
Student Body Statistics The student body totals 2,458, of whom 2,086 are undergraduates (408 freshmen). 59 percent are women and 41 percent are men. Students come from 26 states and territories and 18 other countries. 91 percent are from Illinois. 1.5 percent are international students. 10 percent of the 2003 graduating class went on to graduate and professional schools.
Expenses for 2003–04 *Application fee:* $25. *Comprehensive fee:* $25,656 includes full-time tuition ($19,041), mandatory fees ($240), and college room and board ($6375). Room and board charges vary according to housing facility. *Part-time tuition:* $485 per semester hour. *Part-time mandatory fees:* $60 per year.
Financial Aid Forms of aid include need-based and non-need-based scholarships and part-time jobs. The average aided 2003–04 undergraduate received an aid package worth an estimated $18,212. The application deadline for financial aid is continuous.
Freshman Admission North Central requires a high school transcript, a minimum 2.0 high school GPA, and SAT I or ACT scores. An essay, 1 recommendation, and ACT scores are recommended. An interview is required for some. The application deadline for regular admission is rolling.
Transfer Admission The application deadline for admission is rolling.

North Central College (continued)

Entrance Difficulty North Central assesses its entrance difficulty level as moderately difficult. For the fall 2003 freshman class, 71 percent of the applicants were accepted.

For Further Information Contact Mr. Michael Brown, Director of Freshman Admission, North Central College, 30 North Brainard Street, PO Box 3063, Naperville, IL 60566-7063. *Telephone:* 630-637-5802 or 800-411-1861 (toll-free). *Fax:* 630-637-5819. *E-mail:* ncadm@noctrl.edu. *Web site:* http://www.northcentralcollege.edu/.

See page 320 for a narrative description.

NORTHEASTERN ILLINOIS UNIVERSITY
Chicago, Illinois

Northeastern Illinois University is a coed, public, comprehensive institution, founded in 1961, offering degrees at the bachelor's and master's levels. It has a 67-acre campus in Chicago.

Academic Information The faculty has 627 members (63% full-time), 53% with terminal degrees. The undergraduate student-faculty ratio is 18:1. The library holds 441,911 titles, 3,421 serial subscriptions, and 6,034 audiovisual materials. Special programs include academic remediation, services for learning-disabled students, an honors program, cooperative (work-study) education, study abroad, advanced placement credit, ESL programs, double majors, independent study, distance learning, summer session for credit, part-time degree programs (daytime, evenings, summer), external degree programs, adult/continuing education programs, internships, and arrangement for off-campus study with National Student Exchange. The most frequently chosen baccalaureate fields are education, business/marketing, liberal arts/general studies.

Student Body Statistics The student body totals 11,825, of whom 8,985 are undergraduates (1,120 freshmen). 63 percent are women and 37 percent are men. Students come from 18 states and territories and 45 other countries. 99 percent are from Illinois. 3 percent are international students. 32 percent of the 2003 graduating class went on to graduate and professional schools.

Expenses for 2004–05 *Application fee:* $25. *State resident tuition:* $3720 full-time, $124 per credit part-time. *Nonresident tuition:* $7440 full-time, $248 per credit hour part-time. *Mandatory fees:* $515 full-time. Full-time tuition and fees vary according to student level.

Financial Aid Forms of aid include need-based and non-need-based scholarships and part-time jobs. The average aided 2003–04 undergraduate received an aid package worth an estimated $5591. The priority application deadline for financial aid is March 1.

Freshman Admission Northeastern Illinois University requires a high school transcript, ACT scores, and TOEFL scores for international students. The application deadline for regular admission is July 1.

Transfer Admission The application deadline for admission is July 1.

Entrance Difficulty Northeastern Illinois University assesses its entrance difficulty level as minimally difficult; moderately difficult for transfers. For the fall 2003 freshman class, 71 percent of the applicants were accepted.

For Further Information Contact Ms. Kay D. Gulli, Administrative Assistant, Northeastern Illinois University, 5500 North St. Louis Avenue, Chicago, IL 60625. *Telephone:* 773-442-4000. *Fax:* 773-794-6243. *E-mail:* admrec@neiu.edu. *Web site:* http://www.neiu.edu/.

NORTHERN ILLINOIS UNIVERSITY
De Kalb, Illinois

Northern Illinois University is a coed, public university, founded in 1895, offering degrees at the bachelor's, master's, doctoral, and first professional levels. It has a 589-acre campus in De Kalb near Chicago.

Academic Information The faculty has 1,146 members (79% full-time). The undergraduate student-faculty ratio is 17:1. The library holds 2 million titles, 17,000 serial subscriptions, and 50,182 audiovisual materials. Special programs include services for learning-disabled students, an honors program, cooperative (work-study) education, study abroad, advanced placement credit, accelerated degree programs, double majors, independent study, self-designed majors, summer session for credit, part-time degree programs, adult/continuing education programs, internships, and arrangement for off-campus study with Rockford Regional Academic Center, Quad-Cities Graduate Study Center, Hoffman Estate. The most frequently chosen baccalaureate fields are business/marketing, education, social sciences and history.

Student Body Statistics The student body totals 25,260, of whom 18,275 are undergraduates (3,253 freshmen). 53 percent are women and 47 percent are men. Students come from 50 states and territories and 105 other countries. 97 percent are from Illinois. 1.1 percent are international students. 10 percent of the 2003 graduating class went on to graduate and professional schools.

Expenses for 2003–04 *State resident tuition:* $3903 full-time. *Nonresident tuition:* $7815 full-time. *Mandatory fees:* $1261 full-time. Full-time tuition and fees vary according to course load. *College room and board:* $5360. Room and board charges vary according to board plan and housing facility.

Financial Aid Forms of aid include need-based and non-need-based scholarships and part-time jobs. The average aided 2002–03 undergraduate received an aid package worth $8948. The priority application deadline for financial aid is March 1.

Freshman Admission Northern Illinois University requires a high school transcript, high school rank, SAT I or ACT scores, and TOEFL scores for international students. The application deadline for regular admission is August 1.

Transfer Admission The application deadline for admission is August 1.

Entrance Difficulty Northern Illinois University assesses its entrance difficulty level as moderately difficult. For the fall 2003 freshman class, 62 percent of the applicants were accepted.

For Further Information Contact Dr. Robert Burk, Director of Admissions, Northern Illinois University, De Kalb, IL 60115-2854. *Telephone:* 815-753-0446 or 800-892-3050 (toll-free in-state). *E-mail:* admission-info@niu.edu. *Web site:* http://www.niu.edu/.

NORTH PARK UNIVERSITY
Chicago, Illinois

North Park is a coed, private, comprehensive institution, founded in 1891, affiliated with the Evangelical Covenant Church, offering degrees at the bachelor's, master's, doctoral, and first professional levels. It has a 30-acre campus in Chicago.

Academic Information The faculty has 121 members (73% full-time), 64% with terminal degrees. The undergraduate student-faculty ratio is 16:1. The library holds 260,685 titles and 1,178 serial subscriptions. Special programs include academic remediation, an honors program, study abroad, advanced placement credit, accelerated degree programs, Freshman Honors College, ESL programs, self-designed majors, summer session for credit, part-time degree programs, adult/continuing education programs, internships, and arrangement for off-campus study with Christian College Coalition. The most frequently chosen baccalaureate fields are biological/life sciences, education, philosophy, religion, and theology.

Student Body Statistics The student body totals 2,181, of whom 1,573 are undergraduates (320 freshmen). 62 percent are women and 38 percent are men. Students come from 38 states and territories and 32 other countries. 61 percent are from Illinois. 5 percent are international students. 20 percent of the 2003 graduating class went on to graduate and professional schools.

Expenses for 2004–05 *Application fee:* $20. *Comprehensive fee:* $26,860 includes full-time tuition ($20,350) and college room and board ($6510). Full-time tuition varies according to program. Room and board charges vary according to board plan, housing facility, and student level. *Part-time tuition:* varies with program.

Financial Aid Forms of aid include need-based and non-need-based scholarships and part-time jobs. The priority application deadline for financial aid is May 1.

Freshman Admission North Park requires an essay, a high school transcript, a minimum 2.0 high school GPA, 2 recommendations, SAT I or ACT scores, and TOEFL scores for international students. A minimum

3.0 high school GPA is recommended. An interview is required for some. The application deadline for regular admission is rolling.

Transfer Admission The application deadline for admission is rolling.

Entrance Difficulty North Park assesses its entrance difficulty level as moderately difficult. For the fall 2003 freshman class, 74 percent of the applicants were accepted.

For Further Information Contact Mr. Mark Olson, Dean of Enrollment, North Park University, 3225 West Foster Avenue, Chicago, IL 60625-4895. *Telephone:* 773-244-5500 or 800-888-NPC8 (toll-free). *Fax:* 773-583-0858. *E-mail:* afao@northpark.edu. *Web site:* http://www.northpark.edu/.

NORTHWESTERN UNIVERSITY
Evanston, Illinois

Northwestern is a coed, private university, founded in 1851, offering degrees at the bachelor's, master's, doctoral, and first professional levels and post-master's certificates. It has a 250-acre campus in Evanston near Chicago.

Academic Information The faculty has 1,078 members (83% full-time), 100% with terminal degrees. The undergraduate student-faculty ratio is 7:1. The library holds 4 million titles, 39,423 serial subscriptions, and 72,837 audiovisual materials. Special programs include services for learning-disabled students, an honors program, cooperative (work-study) education, study abroad, advanced placement credit, accelerated degree programs, double majors, independent study, self-designed majors, summer session for credit, part-time degree programs (daytime, evenings, summer), adult/continuing education programs, and internships. The most frequently chosen baccalaureate fields are communications/communication technologies, engineering/engineering technologies, social sciences and history.

Student Body Statistics The student body totals 16,266, of whom 8,001 are undergraduates (1,941 freshmen). 53 percent are women and 47 percent are men. Students come from 51 states and territories and 51 other countries. 25 percent are from Illinois. 5.3 percent are international students.

Expenses for 2004–05 *Application fee:* $65. *Comprehensive fee:* $39,478 includes full-time tuition ($29,940), mandatory fees ($145), and college room and board ($9393). *College room only:* $5398. Room and board charges vary according to board plan and housing facility. *Part-time tuition:* $3552 per course.

Financial Aid Forms of aid include need-based scholarships, athletic grants, and part-time jobs. The average aided 2003–04 undergraduate received an aid package worth an estimated $24,508. The priority application deadline for financial aid is February 1.

Freshman Admission Northwestern requires an essay, a high school transcript, 1 recommendation, SAT I or ACT scores, and TOEFL scores for international students. SAT II: Subject Test scores and SAT II: Writing Test scores are recommended. Audition for music program, SAT II: Subject Test scores, and SAT II: Writing Test scores are required for some. The application deadline for regular admission is January 1 and for early decision it is November 1.

Transfer Admission The application deadline for admission is June 1.

Entrance Difficulty Northwestern assesses its entrance difficulty level as most difficult; very difficult for transfers. For the fall 2003 freshman class, 33 percent of the applicants were accepted.

For Further Information Contact Ms. Carol Lunkenheimer, Dean of Undergraduate Admission, Northwestern University, PO Box 3060, Evanston, IL 60204-3060. *Telephone:* 847-491-7271. *E-mail:* ug-admission@northwestern.edu. *Web site:* http://www.northwestern.edu/.

OLIVET NAZARENE UNIVERSITY
Bourbonnais, Illinois

Olivet is a coed, private, comprehensive institution, founded in 1907, affiliated with the Church of the Nazarene, offering degrees at the associate, bachelor's, and master's levels. It has a 200-acre campus in Bourbonnais near Chicago.

Academic Information The faculty has 123 members (70% full-time). The undergraduate student-faculty ratio is 21:1. The library holds 160,039 titles, 925 serial subscriptions, and 6,818 audiovisual materials. Special programs include academic remediation, study abroad, advanced placement credit, double majors, independent study, summer session for credit, part-time degree programs (daytime, evenings, summer), adult/continuing education programs, and internships. The most frequently chosen baccalaureate fields are business/marketing, education, health professions and related sciences.

Student Body Statistics The student body totals 4,314, of whom 2,427 are undergraduates (594 freshmen). 59 percent are women and 41 percent are men. Students come from 41 states and territories and 15 other countries. 49 percent are from Illinois. 1.1 percent are international students. 10 percent of the 2003 graduating class went on to graduate and professional schools.

Expenses for 2004–05 *Application fee:* $0. *Comprehensive fee:* $21,540 includes full-time tuition ($14,900), mandatory fees ($840), and college room and board ($5800). *College room only:* $2900. Full-time tuition and fees vary according to course load. Room and board charges vary according to board plan. *Part-time tuition:* $621 per hour. *Part-time mandatory fees:* $10 per term. Part-time tuition and fees vary according to course load.

Financial Aid Forms of aid include need-based and non-need-based scholarships, athletic grants, and part-time jobs. The average aided 2003–04 undergraduate received an aid package worth an estimated $11,634. The priority application deadline for financial aid is March 1.

Freshman Admission Olivet requires a high school transcript, a minimum 2.0 high school GPA, 2 recommendations, ACT scores, and TOEFL scores for international students. An essay and an interview are recommended. The application deadline for regular admission is rolling.

Transfer Admission The application deadline for admission is rolling.

Entrance Difficulty Olivet assesses its entrance difficulty level as minimally difficult. For the fall 2003 freshman class, 78 percent of the applicants were accepted.

For Further Information Contact Ms. Mary Cary, Applicant Coordinator, Olivet Nazarene University, One University Avenue, Bourbonnais, IL 60914. *Telephone:* 815-939-5203 or 800-648-1463 (toll-free). *Fax:* 815-935-4998. *E-mail:* admissions@olivet.edu. *Web site:* http://www.olivet.edu/.

See page 324 for a narrative description.

PRINCIPIA COLLEGE
Elsah, Illinois

Prin is a coed, private, Christian Science, four-year college, founded in 1910, offering degrees at the bachelor's level. It has a 2,600-acre campus in Elsah near St. Louis.

Academic Information The faculty has 66 members (73% full-time), 70% with terminal degrees. The student-faculty ratio is 9:1. The library holds 208,197 titles, 10,547 serial subscriptions, and 7,273 audiovisual materials. Special programs include an honors program, study abroad, advanced placement credit, accelerated degree programs, ESL programs, double majors, independent study, self-designed majors, and internships. The most frequently chosen baccalaureate fields are business/marketing, social sciences and history, visual/performing arts.

Student Body Statistics The student body is made up of 552 undergraduates (147 freshmen). 55 percent are women and 45 percent are men. Students come from 37 states and territories and 28 other countries. 9 percent are from Illinois. 12.3 percent are international students. 21 percent of the 2003 graduating class went on to graduate and professional schools.

Principia College (continued)

Expenses for 2004–05 *Application fee:* $40. *Comprehensive fee:* $26,286 includes full-time tuition ($19,185), mandatory fees ($270), and college room and board ($6831). *College room only:* $3315. *Part-time tuition:* $426 per quarter hour.

Financial Aid Forms of aid include need-based and non-need-based scholarships and part-time jobs. The average aided 2002–03 undergraduate received an aid package worth $16,787. The application deadline for financial aid is March 1.

Freshman Admission Prin requires an essay, a high school transcript, a minimum 2.0 high school GPA, 4 recommendations, Christian Science commitment, SAT I or ACT scores, and TOEFL scores for international students. An interview is recommended. An interview is required for some. The application deadline for regular admission is March 1.

Transfer Admission The application deadline for admission is March 1.

Entrance Difficulty Prin assesses its entrance difficulty level as moderately difficult. For the fall 2003 freshman class, 85 percent of the applicants were accepted.

For Further Information Contact Mrs. Martha Green Quirk, Dean of Admissions, Principia College, One Maybeck Place, Elsah, IL 62028. *Telephone:* 618-374-5180 or 800-277-4648 Ext. 2802 (toll-free). *Fax:* 618-374-4000. *E-mail:* collegeadmissions@prin.edu. *Web site:* http://www.prin.edu/college/.

QUINCY UNIVERSITY
Quincy, Illinois

Quincy University is a coed, private, Roman Catholic, comprehensive institution, founded in 1860, offering degrees at the associate, bachelor's, and master's levels. It has a 75-acre campus in Quincy.

Academic Information The faculty has 115 members (42% full-time), 50% with terminal degrees. The undergraduate student-faculty ratio is 15:1. The library holds 239,368 titles, 814 serial subscriptions, and 5,640 audiovisual materials. Special programs include academic remediation, an honors program, study abroad, advanced placement credit, accelerated degree programs, ESL programs, double majors, independent study, distance learning, self-designed majors, summer session for credit, part-time degree programs (daytime, evenings, summer), adult/continuing education programs, and internships. The most frequently chosen baccalaureate fields are business/marketing, education, health professions and related sciences.

Student Body Statistics The student body totals 1,269, of whom 1,130 are undergraduates (222 freshmen). 55 percent are women and 45 percent are men. Students come from 22 states and territories and 5 other countries. 74 percent are from Illinois. 0.7 percent are international students. 18 percent of the 2003 graduating class went on to graduate and professional schools.

Expenses for 2003–04 *Application fee:* $25. *Comprehensive fee:* $23,585 includes full-time tuition ($16,400), mandatory fees ($450), and college room and board ($6735). *College room only:* $3265. Room and board charges vary according to board plan and housing facility. *Part-time tuition:* $460 per credit hour.

Financial Aid Forms of aid include need-based and non-need-based scholarships, athletic grants, and part-time jobs. The average aided 2003–04 undergraduate received an aid package worth an estimated $14,835. The priority application deadline for financial aid is March 15.

Freshman Admission Quincy University requires a high school transcript, SAT I or ACT scores, and TOEFL scores for international students. A minimum 2.0 high school GPA and an interview are recommended. The application deadline for regular admission is rolling.

Transfer Admission The application deadline for admission is rolling.

Entrance Difficulty Quincy University assesses its entrance difficulty level as moderately difficult. For the fall 2003 freshman class, 94 percent of the applicants were accepted.

For Further Information Contact Mr. Kevin A. Brown, Director of Admissions, Quincy University, 1800 College Avenue, Quincy, IL 62301-2699. *Telephone:* 217-222-8020 Ext. 5215 or 800-688-4295 (toll-free). *Fax:* 217-228-5479. *E-mail:* admissions@quincy.edu. *Web site:* http://www.quincy.edu/.

See page 328 for a narrative description.

ROBERT MORRIS COLLEGE
Chicago, Illinois

RMC is a coed, private, four-year college, founded in 1913, offering degrees at the associate and bachelor's levels.

Academic Information The faculty has 365 members (34% full-time), 24% with terminal degrees. The student-faculty ratio is 21:1. The library holds 101,130 titles, 709 serial subscriptions, and 9,800 audiovisual materials. Special programs include academic remediation, an honors program, cooperative (work-study) education, study abroad, advanced placement credit, accelerated degree programs, distance learning, summer session for credit, part-time degree programs (evenings), adult/continuing education programs, and internships. The most frequently chosen baccalaureate fields are business/marketing, computer/information sciences, visual/performing arts.

Student Body Statistics The student body is made up of 5,139 undergraduates (1,011 freshmen). 68 percent are women and 32 percent are men. 99 percent are from Illinois. 0.6 percent are international students.

Expenses for 2004–05 *Application fee:* $20. *Tuition:* $14,250 full-time, $1580 per course part-time.

Financial Aid Forms of aid include need-based and non-need-based scholarships, athletic grants, and part-time jobs. The average aided 2003–04 undergraduate received an aid package worth an estimated $10,605. The application deadline for financial aid is continuous.

Freshman Admission RMC requires a high school transcript, a minimum 2.0 high school GPA, an interview, and TOEFL scores for international students. The application deadline for regular admission is rolling.

Transfer Admission The application deadline for admission is rolling.

Entrance Difficulty RMC assesses its entrance difficulty level as minimally difficult. For the fall 2003 freshman class, 76 percent of the applicants were accepted.

For Further Information Contact Candace Goodwin, Senior Vice President for Enrollment, Robert Morris College, 401 South State Street, Chicago, IL 60605. *Telephone:* 312-935-6600 or 800-225-1520 (toll-free). *Fax:* 312-935-6819. *E-mail:* enroll@robertmorris.edu. *Web site:* http://www.robertmorris.edu/.

See page 332 for a narrative description.

ROCKFORD BUSINESS COLLEGE
Rockford, Illinois

RBC is a coed, primarily women's, private, two-year college, founded in 1862, offering degrees at the associate level. It is located in Rockford near Chicago.

For Further Information Contact Ms. Barbara Holliman, Director of Admissions, Rockford Business College, 730 North Church Street, Rockford, IL 61103. *Telephone:* 815-965-8616 Ext. 16. *Fax:* 815-965-0360. *Web site:* http://www.rbcsuccess.com/.

ROCKFORD COLLEGE
Rockford, Illinois

RC is a coed, private, comprehensive institution, founded in 1847, offering degrees at the bachelor's and master's levels. It has a 130-acre campus in Rockford near Chicago.

Academic Information The faculty has 162 members (46% full-time), 43% with terminal degrees. The undergraduate student-faculty ratio is 10:1. The library holds 140,000 titles, 831 serial subscriptions, and 9,723 audiovisual materials. Special programs include academic remediation, an honors program, study abroad, advanced placement credit, ESL programs, double majors, self-designed majors, summer session for credit, part-time degree programs (daytime, evenings, summer), adult/continuing education programs, internships, and arrangement for off-campus study with American University, Central College (IA), Drew University.

Student Body Statistics The student body totals 1,280, of whom 976 are undergraduates (131 freshmen). 63 percent are women and 38 percent are men. Students come from 8 states and territories and 10 other countries. 96 percent are from Illinois. 8 percent of the 2003 graduating class went on to graduate and professional schools.

Expenses for 2004–05 *Application fee:* $35. *Tuition:* $21,200 full-time, $560 per credit hour part-time.

Financial Aid Forms of aid include need-based and non-need-based scholarships and part-time jobs. The priority application deadline for financial aid is March 15.

Freshman Admission RC requires a high school transcript, SAT I or ACT scores, and TOEFL scores for international students. A minimum 2.5 high school GPA, an interview, and campus visit are recommended. An essay, a minimum 2.5 high school GPA, and 2 recommendations are required for some. The application deadline for regular admission is rolling.

Transfer Admission The application deadline for admission is rolling.

Entrance Difficulty RC assesses its entrance difficulty level as moderately difficult. For the fall 2003 freshman class, 59 percent of the applicants were accepted.

For Further Information Contact Mr. William Laffey, Director of Admission, Rockford College, Nelson Hall, Rockford, IL 61108-2393. *Telephone:* 815-226-4050 or 800-892-2984 (toll-free). *Fax:* 815-226-2822. *E-mail:* admission@rockford.edu. *Web site:* http://www.rockford.edu/.

See page 334 for a narrative description.

ROOSEVELT UNIVERSITY
Chicago, Illinois

Roosevelt is a coed, private, comprehensive institution, founded in 1945, offering degrees at the bachelor's, master's, and doctoral levels and postbachelor's certificates.

Academic Information The faculty has 662 members (32% full-time). The undergraduate student-faculty ratio is 11:1. The library holds 233,016 titles, 1,195 serial subscriptions, and 9,897 audiovisual materials. Special programs include academic remediation, services for learning-disabled students, an honors program, advanced placement credit, accelerated degree programs, ESL programs, double majors, independent study, distance learning, self-designed majors, summer session for credit, part-time degree programs (daytime, evenings, weekends, summer), external degree programs, adult/continuing education programs, internships, and arrangement for off-campus study with School of the Art Institute of Chicago. The most frequently chosen baccalaureate fields are business/marketing, computer/information sciences, psychology.

Student Body Statistics The student body totals 7,524, of whom 4,290 are undergraduates (277 freshmen). 67 percent are women and 33 percent are men. Students come from 24 states and territories and 70 other countries. 96 percent are from Illinois. 2.5 percent are international students.

Expenses for 2003–04 *Application fee:* $25. *Comprehensive fee:* $22,580 includes full-time tuition ($15,180), mandatory fees ($250), and college room and board ($7150). *College room only:* $5300. Full-time tuition and fees vary according to program. *Part-time tuition:* varies with program.

Financial Aid Forms of aid include need-based and non-need-based scholarships and part-time jobs. The average aided 2003–04 undergraduate received an aid package worth an estimated $11,600. The priority application deadline for financial aid is April 1.

Freshman Admission Roosevelt requires an essay, a high school transcript, a minimum 2.0 high school GPA, audition for music and theater programs, SAT I or ACT scores, and TOEFL scores for international students. Recommendations and an interview are required for some. The application deadline for regular admission is August 15.

Transfer Admission The application deadline for admission is September 1.

Entrance Difficulty Roosevelt assesses its entrance difficulty level as moderately difficult. For the fall 2003 freshman class, 51 percent of the applicants were accepted.

For Further Information Contact Ms. Gwen Kanelos, Assistant Vice President for Enrollment Services, Roosevelt University, 430 South Michigan Avenue, Room 576, Chicago, IL 60605-1394. *Telephone:* 847-619-8620 or 877-APPLYRU (toll-free). *Fax:* 312-341-3523. *E-mail:* applyru@roosevelt.edu. *Web site:* http://www.roosevelt.edu/.

RUSH UNIVERSITY
Chicago, Illinois

Rush is a coed, private, upper-level institution, founded in 1969, offering degrees at the bachelor's, master's, doctoral, and first professional levels and post-master's certificates. It has a 35-acre campus in Chicago.

Academic Information The faculty has 796 members (100% full-time). The undergraduate student-faculty ratio is 8:1. The library holds 120,042 titles, 1,100 serial subscriptions, and 4,750 audiovisual materials. Special programs include accelerated degree programs, distance learning, and part-time degree programs (daytime). The most frequently chosen baccalaureate field is biological/life sciences.

Student Body Statistics The student body totals 1,252, of whom 186 are undergraduates. 88 percent are women and 12 percent are men. Students come from 13 states and territories and 4 other countries. 88 percent are from Illinois. 0.5 percent are international students. 12 percent of the 2003 graduating class went on to graduate and professional schools.

Expenses for 2003–04 *Application fee:* $40. *Tuition:* $15,600 full-time, $450 per quarter hour part-time. Full-time tuition varies according to program. Part-time tuition varies according to program. *College room only:* $11,970. Room charges vary according to housing facility.

Financial Aid Forms of aid include need-based and non-need-based scholarships and part-time jobs. The average aided 2003–04 undergraduate received an aid package worth an estimated $18,000. The application deadline for financial aid is May 1 with a priority deadline of March 1.

Transfer Admission Rush requires a college transcript. A minimum 2.75 college GPA is recommended. Standardized test scores are required for some. The application deadline for admission is rolling.

Entrance Difficulty Rush assesses its entrance difficulty level as moderately difficult. For the fall 2003 entering class, 55 percent of the applicants were accepted.

For Further Information Contact Ms. Hicela Castruita Woods, Director of College Admission Services, Rush University, 600 South Paulina—Suite 440, College Admissions Services, Chicago, IL 60612-3878. *Telephone:* 312-942-7100. *Fax:* 312-942-2219. *E-mail:* rush_admissions@rush.edu. *Web site:* http://www.rushu.rush.edu/.

SAINT ANTHONY COLLEGE OF NURSING
Rockford, Illinois

SACN is a coed, primarily women's, private, Roman Catholic, upper-level institution, founded in 1915, offering degrees at the bachelor's level in nursing. It has a 17-acre campus in Rockford near Chicago.

Academic Information The faculty has 12 members (92% full-time), 17% with terminal degrees. The student-faculty ratio is 8:1. The library holds 1,394 titles, 3,136 serial subscriptions, and 163 audiovisual materials.

Saint Anthony College of Nursing (continued)

Special programs include services for learning-disabled students, advanced placement credit, accelerated degree programs, independent study, summer session for credit, part-time degree programs (daytime, evenings, summer), internships, and arrangement for off-campus study. The most frequently chosen baccalaureate field is health professions and related sciences.

Student Body Statistics The student body is made up of 95 undergraduates. 91 percent are women and 9 percent are men. Students come from 2 states and territories. 97 percent are from Illinois. 1.1 percent are international students. 2 percent of the 2003 graduating class went on to graduate and professional schools.

Expenses for 2004–05 *Application fee:* $50. *One-time mandatory fee:* $90. *Tuition:* $14,700 full-time, $460 per credit part-time. *Mandatory fees:* $112 full-time, $55.35 per term part-time. Full-time tuition and fees vary according to course load. Part-time tuition and fees vary according to course load.

Financial Aid Forms of aid include need-based scholarships. The average aided 2002–03 undergraduate received an aid package worth $13,145. The priority application deadline for financial aid is May 1.

Transfer Admission SACN requires a college transcript. A minimum 2.5 college GPA is recommended. The application deadline for admission is rolling.

Entrance Difficulty SACN assesses its entrance difficulty level as moderately difficult.

For Further Information Contact Ms. Nancy Sanders, Assistant Dean for Admissions and Student Affairs, Saint Anthony College of Nursing, 5658 East State Street, Rockford, IL 61108-2468. *Telephone:* 815-395-5100. *Fax:* 815-395-2275. *E-mail:* cheryldelgado@sacn.edu. *Web site:* http://www.sacn.edu/.

ST. AUGUSTINE COLLEGE
Chicago, Illinois

St. Augustine College is a coed, private, four-year college, founded in 1980, offering degrees at the associate and bachelor's levels (offers bilingual Spanish/English degree programs). It has a 4-acre campus in Chicago.

Academic Information The faculty has 159 members (18% full-time). The student-faculty ratio is 10:1. The library holds 15,500 titles. Special programs include academic remediation, cooperative (work-study) education, ESL programs, independent study, summer session for credit, part-time degree programs (daytime, evenings, summer), and internships. The most frequently chosen baccalaureate field is social sciences and history.

Student Body Statistics The student body is made up of 1,710 undergraduates (673 freshmen). 78 percent are women and 22 percent are men. Students come from 3 states and territories. 99 percent are from Illinois. 1.4 percent are international students. 32 percent of the 2003 graduating class went on to graduate and professional schools.

Expenses for 2003–04 *Application fee:* $0. *Tuition:* $7128 full-time, $297 per credit part-time.

Financial Aid Forms of aid include need-based and non-need-based scholarships and part-time jobs. The application deadline for financial aid is continuous.

Freshman Admission St. Augustine College requires Ability-To-Benefit Admissions Test. The application deadline for regular admission is rolling.

Transfer Admission The application deadline for admission is rolling.

Entrance Difficulty St. Augustine College has an open admission policy.

For Further Information Contact Ms. Gloria Quiroz, Director of Recruitment, St. Augustine College, 1345 West Argyle Street, Chicago, IL 60604-3501. *Telephone:* 773-878-7989. *E-mail:* info@staugustinecollege.edu. *Web site:* http://www.staugustinecollege.edu/.

SAINT FRANCIS MEDICAL CENTER COLLEGE OF NURSING
Peoria, Illinois

Saint Francis College of Nursing is a coed, primarily women's, private, Roman Catholic, upper-level institution, founded in 1986, offering degrees at the bachelor's and master's levels in nursing.

Academic Information The faculty has 19 members (100% full-time). The undergraduate student-faculty ratio is 8:1. The library holds 6,215 titles and 125 serial subscriptions. Special programs include advanced placement credit, independent study, distance learning, summer session for credit, and part-time degree programs. The most frequently chosen baccalaureate field is health professions and related sciences.

Student Body Statistics The student body totals 221, of whom 183 are undergraduates. 91 percent are women and 9 percent are men. Students come from 2 states and territories.

Expenses for 2003–04 *Application fee:* $50. *Tuition:* $10,088 full-time, $402 per semester hour part-time. *Mandatory fees:* $200 full-time. Full-time tuition and fees vary according to course load. Part-time tuition varies according to course load. *College room only:* $1680.

Financial Aid Forms of aid include need-based and non-need-based scholarships. The average aided 2003–04 undergraduate received an aid package worth an estimated $9398. The priority application deadline for financial aid is March 1.

Transfer Admission Saint Francis College of Nursing requires a college transcript and a minimum 2.5 college GPA. The application deadline for admission is rolling.

Entrance Difficulty Saint Francis College of Nursing assesses its entrance difficulty level as moderately difficult. For the fall 2003 entering class, 100 percent of the applicants were accepted.

For Further Information Contact Mrs. Janice Farquharson, Director of Admissions and Registrar, Saint Francis Medical Center College of Nursing, 511 Greenleaf Street, Peoria, IL 61603-3783. *Telephone:* 309-624-8980. *Fax:* 309-624-8973. *E-mail:* janice.farquharson@osfhealthcare.org. *Web site:* http://www.sfmccon.edu/.

ST. JOHN'S COLLEGE
Springfield, Illinois

St. John's College is a coed, primarily women's, private, Roman Catholic, upper-level institution, founded in 1886, offering degrees at the bachelor's level in nursing.

Academic Information The faculty has 15 members (93% full-time), 7% with terminal degrees. The student-faculty ratio is 4:1. The library holds 7,715 titles, 349 serial subscriptions, and 735 audiovisual materials. Special programs include part-time degree programs (daytime). The most frequently chosen baccalaureate field is health professions and related sciences.

Student Body Statistics The student body is made up of 64 undergraduates. 95 percent are women and 5 percent are men. Students come from 2 states and territories and 1 other country. 99 percent are from Illinois. 1.6 percent are international students.

Expenses for 2003–04 *Application fee:* $25. *Tuition:* $9220 full-time. *Mandatory fees:* $338 full-time. Full-time tuition and fees vary according to course load. *Part-time tuition:* varies with course load.

Financial Aid Forms of aid include need-based scholarships and part-time jobs. The average aided 2002–03 undergraduate received an aid package worth $8943. The priority application deadline for financial aid is May 31.

Transfer Admission St. John's College requires a college transcript and a minimum 2.4 college GPA.

Entrance Difficulty St. John's College assesses its entrance difficulty level as moderately difficult. For the fall 2003 entering class, 100 percent of the applicants were accepted.

For Further Information Contact Ms. Beth Beasley, Student Development Officer, St. John's College, 421 North Ninth Street, Springfield, IL 62702-5317. *Telephone:* 217-525-5628 Ext. 45468. *Fax:* 217-757-6870. *E-mail:* college@st-johns.org. *Web site:* http://www.st-johns.org/education/schools/nursing/.

SAINT JOSEPH COLLEGE OF NURSING

See University of St. Francis

SAINT XAVIER UNIVERSITY

Chicago, Illinois

Saint Xavier is a coed, private, Roman Catholic, comprehensive institution, founded in 1847, offering degrees at the bachelor's and master's levels and post-master's and postbachelor's certificates. It has a 70-acre campus in Chicago.

Academic Information The faculty has 339 members (47% full-time), 51% with terminal degrees. The undergraduate student-faculty ratio is 15:1. The library holds 170,753 titles, 717 serial subscriptions, and 3,112 audiovisual materials. Special programs include academic remediation, services for learning-disabled students, an honors program, cooperative (work-study) education, study abroad, advanced placement credit, accelerated degree programs, ESL programs, double majors, independent study, self-designed majors, summer session for credit, part-time degree programs (daytime, evenings, weekends, summer), adult/continuing education programs, and internships. The most frequently chosen baccalaureate fields are business/marketing, education, health professions and related sciences.

Student Body Statistics The student body totals 5,566, of whom 3,062 are undergraduates (384 freshmen). 71 percent are women and 29 percent are men. Students come from 21 states and territories and 4 other countries. 96 percent are from Illinois. 0.3 percent are international students. 23 percent of the 2003 graduating class went on to graduate and professional schools.

Expenses for 2003–04 *Application fee:* $25. *Comprehensive fee:* $23,144 includes full-time tuition ($16,500), mandatory fees ($180), and college room and board ($6464). *College room only:* $3688. Full-time tuition and fees vary according to course load. Room and board charges vary according to board plan. *Part-time tuition:* $550 per credit hour. Part-time tuition varies according to course load.

Financial Aid Forms of aid include need-based and non-need-based scholarships, athletic grants, and part-time jobs. The average aided 2003–04 undergraduate received an aid package worth an estimated $14,282. The priority application deadline for financial aid is March 1.

Freshman Admission Saint Xavier requires a high school transcript, SAT I or ACT scores, and TOEFL scores for international students. An essay, a minimum 2.5 high school GPA, and an interview are recommended. An interview is required for some. The application deadline for regular admission is rolling.

Transfer Admission The application deadline for admission is rolling.

Entrance Difficulty Saint Xavier assesses its entrance difficulty level as moderately difficult. For the fall 2003 freshman class, 68 percent of the applicants were accepted.

For Further Information Contact Elizabeth A. Gierach, Director of Enrollment Services, Saint Xavier University, 3700 West 103rd Street, Chicago, IL 60655-3105. *Telephone:* 773-298-3121 or 800-462-9288 (toll-free). *Fax:* 773-298-3076. *E-mail:* admissions@sxu.edu. *Web site:* http://www.sxu.edu/.

SCHOOL OF THE ART INSTITUTE OF CHICAGO

Chicago, Illinois

SAIC is a coed, private, comprehensive institution, founded in 1866, offering degrees at the bachelor's and master's levels in art. It has a 1-acre campus in Chicago.

Academic Information The faculty has 468 members (26% full-time). The undergraduate student-faculty ratio is 13:1. The library holds 72,490 titles, 334 serial subscriptions, and 4,067 audiovisual materials. Special programs include academic remediation, services for learning-disabled students, cooperative (work-study) education, study abroad, advanced placement credit, ESL programs, double majors, independent study, self-designed majors, summer session for credit, part-time degree programs (daytime, evenings, weekends, summer), internships, and arrangement for off-campus study with Association of Independent Colleges of Art and Design.

Student Body Statistics The student body totals 2,728, of whom 2,159 are undergraduates (345 freshmen). 66 percent are women and 34 percent are men. Students come from 50 states and territories and 23 other countries. 22 percent are from Illinois. 15 percent are international students.

Expenses for 2003–04 *Application fee:* $65. *Tuition:* $24,000 full-time, $800 per credit hour part-time. *College room only:* $7300.

Financial Aid Forms of aid include need-based and non-need-based scholarships and part-time jobs. The priority application deadline for financial aid is March 15.

Freshman Admission SAIC requires an essay, a high school transcript, 1 recommendation, a portfolio, SAT I or ACT scores, and TOEFL scores for international students. An interview is recommended. The application deadline for regular admission is September 1.

Transfer Admission The application deadline for admission is September 1.

Entrance Difficulty SAIC assesses its entrance difficulty level as moderately difficult. For the fall 2003 freshman class, 83 percent of the applicants were accepted.

For Further Information Contact Ms. Kendra E. Dane, Executive Director of Admissions and Marketing, School of the Art Institute of Chicago, 37 South Wabash, Chicago, IL 60603. *Telephone:* 312-899-5219 or 800-232-SAIC (toll-free). *Fax:* 312-263-0141. *E-mail:* admiss@artic.edu. *Web site:* http://www.artic.edu/saic/.

SHIMER COLLEGE

Waukegan, Illinois

Shimer is a coed, private, four-year college, founded in 1853, offering degrees at the bachelor's level and postbachelor's certificates. It has a 3-acre campus in Waukegan near Chicago and Milwaukee.

Academic Information The faculty has 15 members (87% full-time), 93% with terminal degrees. The student-faculty ratio is 8:1. The library holds 200,000 titles and 200 serial subscriptions. Special programs include cooperative (work-study) education, study abroad, double majors, independent study, distance learning, self-designed majors, summer session for credit, part-time degree programs (daytime, weekends, summer), adult/continuing education programs, internships, and arrangement for off-campus study with Barat College, Northwestern University. The most frequently chosen baccalaureate fields are liberal arts/general studies, physical sciences, social sciences and history.

Student Body Statistics The student body totals 138, of whom 126 are undergraduates (26 freshmen). 33 percent are women and 67 percent are men. Students come from 20 states and territories and 4 other countries. 58 percent are from Illinois. 4 percent are international students.

Expenses for 2003–04 *Application fee:* $25. *Comprehensive fee:* $19,530 includes full-time tuition ($16,100), mandatory fees ($650), and college room and board ($2780). Full-time tuition and fees vary according to class time and course load. Room and board charges vary according to housing

Shimer College (continued)
facility. *Part-time tuition:* $575 per credit hour. *Part-time mandatory fees:* $250 per term. Part-time tuition and fees vary according to class time and course load.

Financial Aid Forms of aid include need-based and non-need-based scholarships and part-time jobs. The average aided 2003–04 undergraduate received an aid package worth an estimated $14,000. The application deadline for financial aid is continuous.

Freshman Admission Shimer requires an essay, a high school transcript, 1 recommendation, an interview, and TOEFL scores for international students. SAT I or ACT scores are recommended. SAT I or ACT scores are required for some. The application deadline for regular admission is August 30.

Transfer Admission The application deadline for admission is August 30.

Entrance Difficulty Shimer has an open admission policy.

For Further Information Contact Mr. Bill Paterson, Associate Director of Admissions, Shimer College, PO Box 500, Waukegan, IL 60079. *Telephone:* 847-249-7173 or 800-215-7173 (toll-free). *Fax:* 847-249-8798. *E-mail:* admissions@shimer.edu. *Web site:* http://www.shimer.edu/.

SOUTHERN ILLINOIS UNIVERSITY CARBONDALE
Carbondale, Illinois

SIUC is a coed, public unit of Southern Illinois University, founded in 1869, offering degrees at the associate, bachelor's, master's, doctoral, and first professional levels and first professional and postbachelor's certificates. It has a 1,133-acre campus in Carbondale near St. Louis.

Academic Information The faculty has 1,116 members (81% full-time), 78% with terminal degrees. The undergraduate student-faculty ratio is 18:1. The library holds 4 million titles, 18,271 serial subscriptions, and 371,180 audiovisual materials. Special programs include academic remediation, services for learning-disabled students, an honors program, cooperative (work-study) education, study abroad, advanced placement credit, accelerated degree programs, ESL programs, double majors, independent study, distance learning, summer session for credit, part-time degree programs, adult/continuing education programs, internships, and arrangement for off-campus study with Southern Illinois University School of Medicine. The most frequently chosen baccalaureate fields are education, business/marketing, engineering/engineering technologies.

Student Body Statistics The student body totals 21,387, of whom 16,366 are undergraduates (2,624 freshmen). 44 percent are women and 56 percent are men. Students come from 50 states and territories and 110 other countries. 88 percent are from Illinois. 3 percent are international students.

Expenses for 2004–05 *Application fee:* $30. *State resident tuition:* $4560 full-time, $164 per semester hour part-time. *Nonresident tuition:* $9120 full-time, $410 per semester hour part-time. *Mandatory fees:* $1421 full-time. Full-time tuition and fees vary according to course load. Part-time tuition varies according to course load. *College room and board:* $5200. *College room only:* $2640. Room and board charges vary according to board plan and housing facility.

Financial Aid Forms of aid include need-based and non-need-based scholarships, athletic grants, and part-time jobs. The average aided 2002–03 undergraduate received an aid package worth $7969. The priority application deadline for financial aid is April 1.

Freshman Admission SIUC requires a high school transcript, SAT I or ACT scores, and TOEFL scores for international students. The application deadline for regular admission is rolling.

Transfer Admission The application deadline for admission is rolling.

Entrance Difficulty SIUC assesses its entrance difficulty level as moderately difficult. For the fall 2003 freshman class, 77 percent of the applicants were accepted.

For Further Information Contact Dr. Anne DeLuca, Assistant Vice Chancellor, Student Affairs and Enrollment Management and Director of Admissions, Southern Illinois University Carbondale, Mail Code 4710, Carbondale, IL 62901-4710. *Telephone:* 618-453-2908. *Fax:* 618-453-3250. *E-mail:* joinsiuc@siu.edu. *Web site:* http://www.siuc.edu/.

See page 340 for a narrative description.

SOUTHERN ILLINOIS UNIVERSITY EDWARDSVILLE
Edwardsville, Illinois

SIUE is a coed, public, comprehensive unit of Southern Illinois University, founded in 1957, offering degrees at the bachelor's, master's, and first professional levels and post-master's, first professional, and postbachelor's certificates. It has a 2,660-acre campus in Edwardsville near St. Louis.

Academic Information The faculty has 763 members (68% full-time). The undergraduate student-faculty ratio is 17:1. The library holds 783,050 titles, 14,807 serial subscriptions, and 29,183 audiovisual materials. Special programs include academic remediation, services for learning-disabled students, an honors program, cooperative (work-study) education, study abroad, advanced placement credit, accelerated degree programs, ESL programs, double majors, independent study, distance learning, self-designed majors, summer session for credit, part-time degree programs (daytime, evenings, weekends, summer), adult/continuing education programs, internships, and arrangement for off-campus study with University of Missouri–St. Louis, International Student Exchange Program. The most frequently chosen baccalaureate fields are business/marketing, education, social sciences and history.

Student Body Statistics The student body totals 13,295, of whom 10,563 are undergraduates (1,743 freshmen). 55 percent are women and 45 percent are men. Students come from 47 states and territories and 53 other countries. 90 percent are from Illinois. 1.2 percent are international students. 31 percent of the 2003 graduating class went on to graduate and professional schools.

Expenses for 2003–04 *Application fee:* $30. *State resident tuition:* $3360 full-time, $112 per semester hour part-time. *Nonresident tuition:* $6720 full-time, $224 per semester hour part-time. *Mandatory fees:* $823 full-time, $234.40 per term part-time. Full-time tuition and fees vary according to course load. Part-time tuition and fees vary according to course load. *College room and board:* $5364. *College room only:* $3077. Room and board charges vary according to board plan and housing facility.

Financial Aid Forms of aid include need-based and non-need-based scholarships, athletic grants, and part-time jobs. The average aided 2003–04 undergraduate received an aid package worth an estimated $7890. The priority application deadline for financial aid is March 1.

Freshman Admission SIUE requires a high school transcript, SAT I or ACT scores, and TOEFL scores for international students. The application deadline for regular admission is May 31.

Transfer Admission The application deadline for admission is July 31.

Entrance Difficulty SIUE assesses its entrance difficulty level as moderately difficult. For the fall 2003 freshman class, 81 percent of the applicants were accepted.

For Further Information Contact Mr. Boyd Bradshaw, Assistant Vice Chancellor for Enrollment Management, Southern Illinois University Edwardsville, Campus Box 1600, Edwardsville, IL 62026-1600. *Telephone:* 618-650-2298 or 800-447-SIUE (toll-free). *Fax:* 618-650-5013. *E-mail:* admis@siue.edu. *Web site:* http://www.siue.edu/.

SPRINGFIELD COLLEGE IN ILLINOIS
Springfield, Illinois

SCI is a coed, private, two-year college, founded in 1929, affiliated with the Roman Catholic Church, offering degrees at the associate level. It has an 8-acre campus in Springfield.

Expenses for 2003–04 *Application fee:* $15. *Tuition:* $7272 full-time. *Mandatory fees:* $112 full-time. *College room only:* $2244.

For Further Information Contact Ms. Kim Fontana, Director of Admissions, Springfield College in Illinois, 1500 North Fifth Street, Springfield, IL 62702-2694. *Telephone:* 217-525-1420 Ext. 241 or 800-635-7289 (toll-free). *Fax:* 217-525-1497. *Web site:* http://www.sci.edu/.

TELSHE YESHIVA–CHICAGO
Chicago, Illinois

For Information Write to Telshe Yeshiva–Chicago, Chicago, IL 60625-5598.

TRINITY CHRISTIAN COLLEGE
Palos Heights, Illinois

Trinity Christian College is a coed, private, Christian Reformed, four-year college, founded in 1959, offering degrees at the bachelor's level. It has a 53-acre campus in Palos Heights near Chicago.

Academic Information The faculty has 124 members (52% full-time), 46% with terminal degrees. The student-faculty ratio is 12:1. The library holds 77,833 titles, 441 serial subscriptions, and 762 audiovisual materials. Special programs include academic remediation, services for learning-disabled students, an honors program, cooperative (work-study) education, study abroad, advanced placement credit, double majors, independent study, part-time degree programs (evenings), adult/continuing education programs, internships, and arrangement for off-campus study with Saint Xavier College, Moraine Valley Community College. The most frequently chosen baccalaureate fields are business/marketing, education, health professions and related sciences.
Student Body Statistics The student body is made up of 1,263 undergraduates (255 freshmen). 63 percent are women and 37 percent are men. Students come from 37 states and territories and 10 other countries. 58 percent are from Illinois. 1.8 percent are international students. 9 percent of the 2003 graduating class went on to graduate and professional schools.
Expenses for 2003–04 *Application fee:* $20. *Comprehensive fee:* $21,490 includes full-time tuition ($15,490) and college room and board ($6000). *College room only:* $3100. Room and board charges vary according to board plan. *Part-time tuition:* $520 per semester hour. Part-time tuition varies according to course load.
Financial Aid Forms of aid include need-based and non-need-based scholarships, athletic grants, and part-time jobs. The average aided 2002–03 undergraduate received an aid package worth $9875. The priority application deadline for financial aid is February 15.
Freshman Admission Trinity Christian College requires an essay, a high school transcript, a minimum 2.0 high school GPA, an interview, SAT I or ACT scores, and TOEFL scores for international students. 1 recommendation is required for some. The application deadline for regular admission is rolling.
Entrance Difficulty Trinity Christian College assesses its entrance difficulty level as moderately difficult. For the fall 2003 freshman class, 93 percent of the applicants were accepted.

For Further Information Contact Mr. Josh Lenarz, Director of Admissions, Trinity Christian College, 6601 West College Drive, Palos Heights, IL 60463. *Telephone:* 708-239-4708 or 800-748-0085 (toll-free). *Fax:* 708-239-4826. *E-mail:* admissions@trnty.edu. *Web site:* http://www.trnty.edu/.

TRINITY COLLEGE OF NURSING AND HEALTH SCIENCES
Rock Island, Illinois

Trinity College of Nursing and Health Sciences is a coed, private, four-year college, founded in 1994, offering degrees at the associate and bachelor's levels in nursing (general education requirements are taken off campus, usually at Black Hawk College, Eastern Iowa Community College District and Western Illinois University). It has a 2-acre campus in Rock Island.

Academic Information The faculty has 14 members (86% full-time). The student-faculty ratio is 10:1. Special programs include academic remediation, services for learning-disabled students, an honors program, independent study, distance learning, summer session for credit, part-time degree programs (daytime, evenings), adult/continuing education programs, and arrangement for off-campus study with Black Hawk College, Western Illinois University. The most frequently chosen baccalaureate field is health professions and related sciences.
Student Body Statistics The student body is made up of 165 undergraduates (5 freshmen). 79 percent are women and 21 percent are men. Students come from 2 states and territories. 72 percent are from Illinois.
Expenses for 2003–04 *Application fee:* $50. *Tuition:* $8780 full-time. *Mandatory fees:* $320 full-time. Full-time tuition and fees vary according to degree level. *Part-time tuition:* varies with degree level.
Financial Aid Forms of aid include need-based scholarships and part-time jobs. The application deadline for financial aid is continuous.
Freshman Admission Trinity College of Nursing and Health Sciences requires a high school transcript, a minimum 2.75 high school GPA, minimum ACT score of 21, SAT I or ACT scores, and TOEFL scores for international students. The application deadline for regular admission is June 1.
Transfer Admission The application deadline for admission is June 1.
Entrance Difficulty Trinity College of Nursing and Health Sciences assesses its entrance difficulty level as most difficult. For the fall 2003 freshman class, 43 percent of the applicants were accepted.

For Further Information Contact Ms. Barbara Kimpe, Admissions Representative, Trinity College of Nursing and Health Sciences, 2122 25th Avenue, Rock Island, IL 61201. *Telephone:* 309-779-7812. *Fax:* 309-779-7748. *E-mail:* con@trinityqc.com. *Web site:* http://www.trinitycollegeqc.edu/.

TRINITY INTERNATIONAL UNIVERSITY
Deerfield, Illinois

Trinity is a coed, private university, founded in 1897, affiliated with the Evangelical Free Church of America, offering degrees at the bachelor's, master's, doctoral, and first professional levels and postbachelor's certificates. It has a 108-acre campus in Deerfield near Chicago.

Academic Information The faculty has 155 members (28% full-time), 32% with terminal degrees. The undergraduate student-faculty ratio is 17:1. The library holds 155,811 titles, 1,332 serial subscriptions, and 4,332 audiovisual materials. Special programs include academic remediation, an honors program, study abroad, advanced placement credit, double majors, independent study, part-time degree programs (daytime, evenings), adult/continuing education programs, internships, and arrangement for off-campus study with 13 members of the Christian College Consortium. The most frequently chosen baccalaureate fields are education, business/marketing, philosophy, religion, and theology.
Student Body Statistics The student body totals 2,863, of whom 1,428 are undergraduates (431 freshmen). 59 percent are women and 41 percent are men. Students come from 33 states and territories and 6 other countries. 48 percent are from Illinois. 0.4 percent are international students. 9 percent of the 2003 graduating class went on to graduate and professional schools.
Expenses for 2003–04 *Application fee:* $25. *Comprehensive fee:* $22,980 includes full-time tuition ($16,900), mandatory fees ($250), and college

Trinity International University (continued)

room and board ($5830). *College room only:* $3060. Full-time tuition and fees vary according to location. Room and board charges vary according to board plan. *Part-time tuition:* $705 per hour. *Part-time mandatory fees:* $125 per term. Part-time tuition and fees vary according to location.

Financial Aid Forms of aid include need-based and non-need-based scholarships, athletic grants, and part-time jobs. The average aided 2003–04 undergraduate received an aid package worth an estimated $12,980. The priority application deadline for financial aid is April 1.

Freshman Admission Trinity requires an essay, a high school transcript, a minimum 2.5 high school GPA, 1 recommendation, SAT I or ACT scores, and TOEFL scores for international students. A minimum 3.0 high school GPA is recommended. An interview is required for some. The application deadline for regular admission is rolling.

Transfer Admission The application deadline for admission is rolling.

Entrance Difficulty Trinity assesses its entrance difficulty level as moderately difficult. For the fall 2003 freshman class, 87 percent of the applicants were accepted.

For Further Information Contact Mr. Matt Yoder, Director of Undergraduate Admissions, Trinity International University, 2065 Half Day Road, Deerfield, IL 60015-1284. *Telephone:* 847-317-7000 or 800-822-3225 (toll-free out-of-state). *Fax:* 847-317-8097. *E-mail:* tcdadm@tiu.edu. *Web site:* http://www.tiu.edu/.

UNIVERSITY OF CHICAGO
Chicago, Illinois

Chicago is a coed, private university, founded in 1891, offering degrees at the bachelor's, master's, doctoral, and first professional levels. It has a 211-acre campus in Chicago.

Academic Information The faculty has 1,934 members (87% full-time). The undergraduate student-faculty ratio is 4:1. The library holds 6 million titles and 47,000 serial subscriptions. Special programs include study abroad, advanced placement credit, accelerated degree programs, double majors, independent study, self-designed majors, summer session for credit, adult/continuing education programs, internships, and arrangement for off-campus study with Committee on Institutional Cooperation, Associated Colleges of the Midwest. The most frequently chosen baccalaureate fields are biological/life sciences, psychology, social sciences and history.

Student Body Statistics The student body totals 13,887, of whom 4,355 are undergraduates (1,155 freshmen). 51 percent are women and 49 percent are men. Students come from 52 states and territories and 59 other countries. 22 percent are from Illinois. 8.1 percent are international students.

Expenses for 2003–04 *Application fee:* $60. *Comprehensive fee:* $38,553 includes full-time tuition ($28,689), mandatory fees ($549), and college room and board ($9315). Full-time tuition and fees vary according to course load. Room and board charges vary according to board plan. *Part-time tuition:* varies with course load.

Financial Aid Forms of aid include need-based and non-need-based scholarships and part-time jobs. The priority application deadline for financial aid is February 1.

Freshman Admission Chicago requires an essay, a high school transcript, 3 recommendations, SAT I or ACT scores, and TOEFL scores for international students. An interview is recommended. The application deadline for regular admission is January 1 and for early action it is November 1.

Transfer Admission The application deadline for admission is April 11.

Entrance Difficulty Chicago assesses its entrance difficulty level as most difficult. For the fall 2003 freshman class, 40 percent of the applicants were accepted.

For Further Information Contact Mr. Theodore O'Neill, Dean of Admissions, University of Chicago, 1116 East 59th Street, Chicago, IL 60637-1513. *Telephone:* 773-702-8650. *Fax:* 773-702-4199. *Web site:* http://www.uchicago.edu/.

UNIVERSITY OF ILLINOIS AT CHICAGO
Chicago, Illinois

UIC is a coed, public unit of University of Illinois System, founded in 1946, offering degrees at the bachelor's, master's, doctoral, and first professional levels and first professional certificates. It has a 240-acre campus in Chicago.

Academic Information The faculty has 1,456 members (82% full-time), 80% with terminal degrees. The undergraduate student-faculty ratio is 16:1. The library holds 2 million titles, 21,571 serial subscriptions, and 28,436 audiovisual materials. Special programs include academic remediation, services for learning-disabled students, an honors program, cooperative (work-study) education, study abroad, advanced placement credit, accelerated degree programs, ESL programs, double majors, independent study, distance learning, self-designed majors, summer session for credit, part-time degree programs (daytime, summer), internships, and arrangement for off-campus study with University Center of Lake County. The most frequently chosen baccalaureate fields are business/marketing, engineering/engineering technologies, psychology.

Student Body Statistics The student body totals 25,763, of whom 16,012 are undergraduates (2,942 freshmen). 55 percent are women and 45 percent are men. Students come from 52 states and territories and 48 other countries. 98 percent are from Illinois. 1.2 percent are international students.

Expenses for 2004–05 *Application fee:* $40. *State resident tuition:* $5682 full-time. *Nonresident tuition:* $16,930 full-time. *Mandatory fees:* $2178 full-time. Full-time tuition and fees vary according to course load and program. *College room and board:* $6884. Room and board charges vary according to board plan and housing facility.

Financial Aid Forms of aid include need-based and non-need-based scholarships, athletic grants, and part-time jobs. The average aided 2003–04 undergraduate received an aid package worth an estimated $11,600. The priority application deadline for financial aid is March 1.

Freshman Admission UIC requires a high school transcript, SAT I or ACT scores, and TOEFL scores for international students. An essay and an interview are required for some. The application deadline for regular admission is January 15.

Transfer Admission The application deadline for admission is March 1.

Entrance Difficulty UIC assesses its entrance difficulty level as moderately difficult; very difficult for honors program, Guaranteed Professional Program. For the fall 2003 freshman class, 61 percent of the applicants were accepted.

For Further Information Contact Mr. Thomas E. Glenn, Executive Director of Admissions, University of Illinois at Chicago, Box 5220, Chicago, IL 60680-5220. *Telephone:* 312-996-4350. *Fax:* 312-413-7628. *E-mail:* uic.admit@uic.edu. *Web site:* http://www.uic.edu/.

UNIVERSITY OF ILLINOIS AT SPRINGFIELD
Springfield, Illinois

UIS is a coed, public, upper-level unit of University of Illinois, founded in 1969, offering degrees at the bachelor's, master's, and doctoral levels. It has a 746-acre campus in Springfield.

Academic Information The faculty has 300 members (57% full-time). The undergraduate student-faculty ratio is 15:1. The library holds 521,389 titles, 2,014 serial subscriptions, and 40,171 audiovisual materials. Special programs include academic remediation, cooperative (work-study) education, self-designed majors, summer session for credit, part-time degree programs (daytime, evenings, weekends, summer), external degree programs, adult/continuing education programs, internships, and arrangement for off-campus study with Springfield College, Illinois College, MacMurray College, Lincoln Land Community College, Western Illinois University, Southern Illinois University, Illinois State University. The most frequently chosen baccalaureate fields are business/marketing, protective services/public administration, psychology.

Student Body Statistics The student body totals 4,569, of whom 2,569 are undergraduates (36 in entering class). 61 percent are women and 39 percent are men. Students come from 26 states and territories. 98 percent are from Illinois. 0.7 percent are international students.

Expenses for 2003–04 *Application fee:* $40. *State resident tuition:* $3450 full-time, $115 per credit part-time. *Nonresident tuition:* $10,350 full-time, $345 per credit part-time. *Mandatory fees:* $860 full-time, $430 per term part-time. *College room and board:* $7000. Room and board charges vary according to housing facility.

Financial Aid Forms of aid include need-based and non-need-based scholarships, athletic grants, and part-time jobs. The average aided 2003–04 undergraduate received an aid package worth an estimated $7226. The application deadline for financial aid is November 15 with a priority deadline of April 1.

Transfer Admission UIS requires a college transcript and a minimum 2.0 college GPA. Standardized test scores are required for some. The application deadline for admission is rolling.

Entrance Difficulty UIS assesses its entrance difficulty level as minimally difficult. For the fall 2003 entering class, 52 percent of the applicants were accepted.

For Further Information Contact Mr. Darren Bush, Director of Admissions and Records, University of Illinois at Springfield, Building SAB. *Telephone:* 217-206-6626 or 888-977-4847 (toll-free). *Fax:* 217-206-6620. *Web site:* http://www.uis.edu/.

UNIVERSITY OF ILLINOIS AT URBANA–CHAMPAIGN

Champaign, Illinois

Illinois is a coed, public unit of University of Illinois System, founded in 1867, offering degrees at the bachelor's, master's, doctoral, and first professional levels and post-master's certificates. It has a 1,470-acre campus in Champaign.

Academic Information The faculty has 2,537 members (86% full-time), 87% with terminal degrees. The undergraduate student-faculty ratio is 12:1. The library holds 10 million titles, 90,707 serial subscriptions, and 1 million audiovisual materials. Special programs include services for learning-disabled students, an honors program, cooperative (work-study) education, study abroad, advanced placement credit, accelerated degree programs, double majors, distance learning, self-designed majors, summer session for credit, internships, and arrangement for off-campus study with members of the Committee on Institutional Cooperation, Midwest Universities Consortium for International Activities. The most frequently chosen baccalaureate fields are business/marketing, engineering/engineering technologies, social sciences and history.

Student Body Statistics The student body totals 40,458, of whom 29,226 are undergraduates (6,811 freshmen). 47 percent are women and 53 percent are men. Students come from 52 states and territories and 70 other countries. 88 percent are from Illinois. 3.2 percent are international students. 56 percent of the 2003 graduating class went on to graduate and professional schools.

Expenses for 2004–05 *Application fee:* $40. *State resident tuition:* $7922 full-time. *Nonresident tuition:* $19,404 full-time. *Mandatory fees:* $1462 full-time. Full-time tuition and fees vary according to course load, program, and student level. *College room and board:* $6848. *College room only:* $2831. Room and board charges vary according to board plan and housing facility.

Financial Aid Forms of aid include need-based scholarships, athletic grants, and part-time jobs. The average aided 2003–04 undergraduate received an aid package worth an estimated $8521. The priority application deadline for financial aid is March 15.

Freshman Admission Illinois requires an essay, a high school transcript, SAT I or ACT scores, and TOEFL scores for international students. Audition, statement of professional interest is required for some. The application deadline for regular admission is January 1.

Transfer Admission The application deadline for admission is March 15.

Entrance Difficulty Illinois assesses its entrance difficulty level as very difficult. For the fall 2003 freshman class, 63 percent of the applicants were accepted.

For Further Information Contact Mr. Abel Montoya, Acting Associate Director, University of Illinois at Urbana–Champaign, 901 West Illinois, Urbana, IL 61801. *Telephone:* 217-333-0302. *Fax:* 217-244-7278. *E-mail:* admissions@oar.uiuc.edu. *Web site:* http://www.uiuc.edu/.

UNIVERSITY OF PHOENIX–CHICAGO CAMPUS

Schaumburg, Illinois

University of Phoenix–Chicago Campus is a coed, proprietary, comprehensive institution, founded in 2002, offering degrees at the associate, bachelor's, master's, and doctoral levels and post-master's and postbachelor's certificates (courses conducted at 121 campuses and learning centers in 25 states).

Academic Information The faculty has 36 members (8% full-time), 25% with terminal degrees. The library holds 27 million titles and 11,648 serial subscriptions. Special programs include advanced placement credit, accelerated degree programs, independent study, distance learning, external degree programs, and adult/continuing education programs. The most frequently chosen baccalaureate fields are business/marketing, computer/information sciences.

Student Body Statistics The student body totals 608, of whom 453 are undergraduates (35 freshmen). 51 percent are women and 49 percent are men. 6.6 percent are international students.

Expenses for 2003–04 *Application fee:* $100. *Tuition:* $9900 full-time, $330 per credit part-time.

Financial Aid Forms of aid include need-based and non-need-based scholarships. The average aided 2002–03 undergraduate received an aid package worth $1171. The application deadline for financial aid is continuous.

Freshman Admission University of Phoenix–Chicago Campus requires 1 recommendation, 2 years of work experience, 23 years of age, and TOEFL scores for international students. A high school transcript is required for some. The application deadline for regular admission is rolling.

Transfer Admission The application deadline for admission is rolling.

Entrance Difficulty University of Phoenix–Chicago Campus has an open admission policy.

For Further Information Contact Ms. Beth Barilla, Director of Admissions, University of Phoenix–Chicago Campus, 4615 East Elwood Street, Mail Stop AA-K101, Phoenix, AZ 85040-1958. *Telephone:* 480-557-1712 or 800-228-7240 (toll-free). *Fax:* 480-594-1758. *E-mail:* beth.barilla@phoenix.edu. *Web site:* http://www.phoenix.edu/.

UNIVERSITY OF ST. FRANCIS

Joliet, Illinois

USF is a coed, private, Roman Catholic, comprehensive institution, founded in 1920, offering degrees at the bachelor's and master's levels and postbachelor's certificates. It has a 17-acre campus in Joliet near Chicago.

Academic Information The faculty has 189 members (36% full-time), 38% with terminal degrees. The undergraduate student-faculty ratio is 14:1. The library holds 105,121 titles, 953 serial subscriptions, and 8,601 audiovisual materials. Special programs include academic remediation, study abroad, advanced placement credit, accelerated degree programs, double majors, independent study, distance learning, self-designed majors, summer session for credit, part-time degree programs (daytime, evenings, weekends, summer), external degree programs, adult/continuing education programs, internships, and arrangement for off-campus study. The most frequently chosen baccalaureate fields are business/marketing, education, health professions and related sciences.

University of St. Francis (continued)

Student Body Statistics The student body totals 1,988, of whom 1,143 are undergraduates (189 freshmen). 67 percent are women and 33 percent are men. Students come from 8 states and territories and 2 other countries. 98 percent are from Illinois. 0.2 percent are international students. 6 percent of the 2003 graduating class went on to graduate and professional schools.

Expenses for 2003–04 *Application fee: $20. Comprehensive fee: $22,870* includes full-time tuition ($16,480), mandatory fees ($360), and college room and board ($6030). *College room only: $2930. Part-time tuition: $480* per semester hour. *Part-time mandatory fees: $15.* Part-time tuition and fees vary according to course load.

Financial Aid Forms of aid include need-based and non-need-based scholarships, athletic grants, and part-time jobs. The average aided 2003–04 undergraduate received an aid package worth an estimated $13,695. The priority application deadline for financial aid is May 1.

Freshman Admission USF requires a high school transcript, a minimum 2.0 high school GPA, SAT I or ACT scores, and TOEFL scores for international students. An essay, 2 recommendations, and an interview are required for some. The application deadline for regular admission is September 1.

Entrance Difficulty USF assesses its entrance difficulty level as moderately difficult. For the fall 2003 freshman class, 58 percent of the applicants were accepted.

For Further Information Contact Ms. Jean Norris, Vice President, Admissions and Enrollment Services, University of St. Francis, 500 North Wilcox Street, Joliet, IL 60435-6188. *Telephone:* 815-740-3366 or 800-735-3500 (toll-free). *Fax:* 815-740-5032. *E-mail:* admissions@ stfrancis.edu. *Web site:* http://www.stfrancis.edu/.

See page 348 for a narrative description.

VANDERCOOK COLLEGE OF MUSIC
Chicago, Illinois

VCM is a coed, private, comprehensive institution, founded in 1909, offering degrees at the bachelor's and master's levels in music education. It has a 1-acre campus in Chicago.

Academic Information The faculty has 28 members (36% full-time), 21% with terminal degrees. The undergraduate student-faculty ratio is 8:1. Special programs include advanced placement credit, independent study, and internships. The most frequently chosen baccalaureate field is education.

Student Body Statistics The student body totals 209, of whom 114 are undergraduates (19 freshmen). 46 percent are women and 54 percent are men. Students come from 12 states and territories and 2 other countries. 67 percent are from Illinois. 2.4 percent are international students.

Expenses for 2004–05 *Application fee: $35. Comprehensive fee: $22,660* includes full-time tuition ($15,130), mandatory fees ($630), and college room and board ($6900). Room and board charges vary according to board plan and housing facility. *Part-time tuition: $635* per semester hour. *Part-time mandatory fees: $315* per term. Part-time tuition and fees vary according to course load.

Financial Aid Forms of aid include need-based and non-need-based scholarships and part-time jobs. The application deadline for financial aid is June 7.

Freshman Admission VCM requires an essay, a high school transcript, 3 recommendations, an interview, audition, SAT I or ACT scores, and TOEFL scores for international students. A minimum 3.0 high school GPA is recommended. A minimum 3.0 high school GPA is required for some. The application deadline for regular admission is May 1.

Transfer Admission The application deadline for admission is May 1.

Entrance Difficulty VCM assesses its entrance difficulty level as moderately difficult. For the fall 2003 freshman class, 81 percent of the applicants were accepted.

For Further Information Contact Ms. Tamara V. Trutwin, Student Recruiter, VanderCook College of Music, 3140 South Federal Street, Chicago, IL 60616. *Telephone:* 800-448-2655 Ext. 241 or 800-448-2655 Ext. 230 (toll-free). *Fax:* 312-225-5211. *E-mail:* admissions@ vandercook.edu. *Web site:* http://www.vandercook.edu/.

See page 350 for a narrative description.

WESTERN ILLINOIS UNIVERSITY
Macomb, Illinois

WIU is a coed, public, comprehensive institution, founded in 1899, offering degrees at the bachelor's and master's levels and post-master's and postbachelor's certificates. It has a 1,050-acre campus in Macomb.

Academic Information The faculty has 685 members (91% full-time), 66% with terminal degrees. The undergraduate student-faculty ratio is 17:1. The library holds 998,041 titles, 3,200 serial subscriptions, and 3,445 audiovisual materials. Special programs include academic remediation, services for learning-disabled students, an honors program, study abroad, advanced placement credit, Freshman Honors College, ESL programs, double majors, independent study, distance learning, self-designed majors, summer session for credit, part-time degree programs (daytime, evenings, weekends, summer), external degree programs, adult/continuing education programs, internships, and arrangement for off-campus study with Western Illinois Education Consortium. The most frequently chosen baccalaureate fields are education, liberal arts/general studies, protective services/public administration.

Student Body Statistics The student body totals 13,469, of whom 11,027 are undergraduates (1,961 freshmen). 49 percent are women and 51 percent are men. Students come from 33 states and territories and 44 other countries. 94 percent are from Illinois. 1.4 percent are international students. 25 percent of the 2003 graduating class went on to graduate and professional schools.

Expenses for 2003–04 *Application fee: $30. State resident tuition: $3915* full-time, $130.50 per credit hour part-time. *Nonresident tuition: $7830* full-time, $261 per credit hour part-time. *Mandatory fees: $1487* full-time, $36.08 per credit hour part-time. Full-time tuition and fees vary according to location. Part-time tuition and fees vary according to location. *College room and board: $5366. College room only: $3122.*

Financial Aid Forms of aid include need-based and non-need-based scholarships, athletic grants, and part-time jobs. The average aided 2003–04 undergraduate received an aid package worth an estimated $7428. The priority application deadline for financial aid is February 15.

Freshman Admission WIU requires a high school transcript, SAT I or ACT scores, and TOEFL scores for international students. The application deadline for regular admission is August 1.

Transfer Admission The application deadline for admission is rolling.

Entrance Difficulty WIU assesses its entrance difficulty level as moderately difficult. For the fall 2003 freshman class, 66 percent of the applicants were accepted.

For Further Information Contact Ms. Karen Helmers, Director of Admissions, Western Illinois University, 1 University Circle, 115 Sherman Hall, Macomb, IL 61455-1390. *Telephone:* 309-298-3157 or 877-742-5948 (toll-free). *Fax:* 309-298-3111. *E-mail:* kl-helmers@wiu. edu. *Web site:* http://www.wiu.edu/.

WEST SUBURBAN COLLEGE OF NURSING
Oak Park, Illinois

West Suburban College of Nursing is a coed, primarily women's, private, upper-level institution, founded in 1982, offering degrees at the bachelor's level in nursing. It has a 10-acre campus in Oak Park near Chicago.

Expenses for 2003–04 *Application fee:* $0. *Tuition:* $17,745 full-time, $600 per semester hour part-time. *Mandatory fees:* $250 full-time, $125 per term part-time.

For Further Information Contact Ms. Cindy Valdez, Director of Admission and Records/Registrar, West Suburban College of Nursing, 3 Erie Court, Oak Park, IL 60302. *Telephone:* 708-763-6530. *Fax:* 708-763-1531. *Web site:* http://www.wscn.edu/.

WESTWOOD COLLEGE–CHICAGO DU PAGE
Woodridge, Illinois

Westwood College–Chicago Du Page is a coed, proprietary, primarily two-year college, offering degrees at the associate and bachelor's levels. It is located in Woodridge near Chicago, IL.

Academic Information The faculty has 46 members, 2% with terminal degrees. The most frequently chosen baccalaureate fields are communications/communication technologies, visual/performing arts.
Student Body Statistics The student body is made up of 470 undergraduates (227 freshmen). 24 percent are women and 76 percent are men. 90 percent are from Illinois. 0.4 percent are international students.
Financial Aid Forms of aid include need-based scholarships and part-time jobs. The application deadline for financial aid is continuous.
Freshman Admission Westwood College–Chicago Du Page requires an interview and entrance exam (SAT, ACT or Accuplacer) and H.S. diploma or GED.
Entrance Difficulty For the fall 2003 freshman class, 40 percent of the applicants were accepted.

For Further Information Contact Mr. Scott Kawall, Director of Admissions, Westwood College–Chicago Du Page, 7155 James Avenue, Woodridge, IL 60517-2321. *Telephone:* 630-434-8244 or 888-721-7646 (toll-free in-state). *Fax:* 630-434-8255. *E-mail:* info@westwood.edu. *Web site:* http://www.westwood.edu/.

WESTWOOD COLLEGE–CHICAGO LOOP CAMPUS
Chicago, Illinois

Westwood College–Chicago Loop Campus is a coed, proprietary, primarily two-year college, founded in 2002, offering degrees at the associate and bachelor's levels.

Academic Information The faculty has 15 members, 7% with terminal degrees.
Student Body Statistics The student body is made up of 106 undergraduates (106 freshmen). 46 percent are women and 54 percent are men.
Freshman Admission Westwood College–Chicago Loop Campus requires an interview and HS diploma or GED, and passing SAT/ACT or Accuplacer scores.
Entrance Difficulty For the fall 2003 freshman class, 68 percent of the applicants were accepted.

For Further Information Contact Gus Pyrolis, Acting Director of Admissions, Westwood College–Chicago Loop Campus, 17 North State Street, Suite 1500, Chicago, IL 60602. *Telephone:* 312-739-0850. *Fax:* 312-739-1004. *E-mail:* info@westwood.edu. *Web site:* http://www.westwood.edu/.

WESTWOOD COLLEGE–CHICAGO O'HARE AIRPORT
Schiller Park, Illinois

Westwood College–Chicago O'Hare Airport is a coed, proprietary, primarily two-year college, offering degrees at the associate and bachelor's levels. It is located in Schiller Park near Chicago.

Academic Information The faculty has 32 members.
Student Body Statistics The student body is made up of 425 undergraduates (367 freshmen). 28 percent are women and 72 percent are men. 90 percent are from Illinois.
Financial Aid Forms of aid include need-based scholarships and part-time jobs. The application deadline for financial aid is continuous.
Freshman Admission Westwood College–Chicago O'Hare Airport requires an essay, an interview, and entrance exam (SAT, ACT or ACCUPLACER) and H.S. diploma/GED.

For Further Information Contact Mr. David Traub, Director of Admissions, Westwood College–Chicago O'Hare Airport, 4825 North Scott Street, Suite 100, Schiller Park, IL 60176-1209. *Telephone:* 847-928-0200 Ext. 100 or 877-877-8857 (toll-free in-state). *Fax:* 847-928-2120. *E-mail:* info@westwood.edu. *Web site:* http://www.westwood.edu/.

WESTWOOD COLLEGE–CHICAGO RIVER OAKS
Calumet City, Illinois

Westwood College–Chicago River Oaks is a coed, proprietary, primarily two-year college, offering degrees at the associate and bachelor's levels. It is located in Calumet City near Chicago.

Academic Information The faculty has 77 members. The most frequently chosen baccalaureate fields are computer/information sciences, visual/performing arts.
Student Body Statistics The student body is made up of 650 undergraduates (92 freshmen). 38 percent are women and 62 percent are men.
Financial Aid Forms of aid include need-based scholarships and part-time jobs. The application deadline for financial aid is continuous.
Freshman Admission Westwood College–Chicago River Oaks requires an interview and HS diploma or GED and passing scores on entrance exam (ACT/SAT or Accuplacer).
Entrance Difficulty For the fall 2003 freshman class, 55 percent of the applicants were accepted.

For Further Information Contact Tash Uray, Director of Admissions, Westwood College–Chicago River Oaks, 80 River Oaks Drive, Suite D-49, Calumet City, IL 60409-5820. *Telephone:* 708-832-1988 or 888-549-6873 (toll-free in-state). *Fax:* 708-832-9617. *E-mail:* info@westwood.edu. *Web site:* http://www.westwood.edu/.

WHEATON COLLEGE
Wheaton, Illinois

Wheaton is a coed, private, nondenominational, comprehensive institution, founded in 1860, offering degrees at the bachelor's, master's, and doctoral levels and postbachelor's certificates. It has an 80-acre campus in Wheaton near Chicago.

Academic Information The faculty has 279 members (68% full-time), 74% with terminal degrees. The undergraduate student-faculty ratio is 11:1. The library holds 429,892 titles, 2,751 serial subscriptions, and 38,591 audiovisual materials. Special programs include services for learning-disabled students, study abroad, advanced placement credit, double majors, independent study, self-designed majors, summer session for credit, internships, and arrangement for off-campus study with members of the Christian College Consortium, Council for Christian Colleges and Universities. The most frequently chosen baccalaureate fields are philosophy, religion, and theology, business/marketing, social sciences and history.
Student Body Statistics The student body totals 2,944, of whom 2,430 are undergraduates (576 freshmen). 51 percent are women and 49 percent are men. Students come from 51 states and territories and 16 other countries. 31 percent are from Illinois. 1.1 percent are international students. 22.4 percent of the 2003 graduating class went on to graduate and professional schools.

Wheaton College (continued)

Expenses for 2004–05 *Application fee:* $50. *Comprehensive fee:* $26,466 includes full-time tuition ($20,000) and college room and board ($6466). *College room only:* $3784. Room and board charges vary according to board plan and housing facility. *Part-time tuition:* varies with course load.

Financial Aid Forms of aid include need-based and non-need-based scholarships and part-time jobs. The average aided 2003–04 undergraduate received an aid package worth an estimated $16,040. The priority application deadline for financial aid is February 15.

Freshman Admission Wheaton requires an essay, a high school transcript, 2 recommendations, SAT I or ACT scores, and TOEFL scores for international students. An interview, SAT II: Writing Test scores, and SAT II Subject Test in French, German, Latin, Spanish or Hebrew are recommended. The application deadline for regular admission is January 15 and for early action it is November 1.

Transfer Admission The application deadline for admission is March 1.

Entrance Difficulty Wheaton assesses its entrance difficulty level as very difficult. For the fall 2003 freshman class, 53 percent of the applicants were accepted.

For Further Information Contact Ms. Shawn Leftwich, Director of Admissions, Wheaton College, 501 College Avenue, Wheaton, IL 60187. *Telephone:* 630-752-5011 or 800-222-2419 (toll-free out-of-state). *Fax:* 630-752-5285. *E-mail:* admissions@wheaton.edu. *Web site:* http://www.wheaton.edu/.

WORSHAM COLLEGE OF MORTUARY SCIENCE

Wheeling, Illinois

Worsham College of Mortuary Science is a coed, private, two-year college, offering degrees at the associate level.

Academic Information The faculty has 12 members. The student-faculty ratio is 10:1.

Student Body Statistics The student body is made up of 115 undergraduates.

Expenses for 2003–04 *Tuition:* $13,300 full-time. *Mandatory fees:* $275 full-time.

Financial Aid Forms of aid include need-based scholarships. The application deadline for financial aid is continuous.

Entrance Difficulty For the fall 2003 freshman class, 100 percent of the applicants were accepted.

For Further Information Contact Ms. Stephanie Kann, President, Worsham College of Mortuary Science, 495 Northgate Parkway, Wheeling, IL 60090-2646. *Telephone:* 847-808-8444. *Fax:* 847-808-8493. *Web site:* http://www.worshamcollege.com/.

Indiana

ANCILLA COLLEGE

Donaldson, Indiana

Ancilla is a coed, private, Roman Catholic, two-year college, founded in 1937, offering degrees at the associate level. It has a 63-acre campus in Donaldson near Chicago.

Academic Information The faculty has 53 members (32% full-time), 11% with terminal degrees. The student-faculty ratio is 15:1. The library holds 28,199 titles, 179 serial subscriptions, and 1,426 audiovisual materials. Special programs include academic remediation, services for learning-disabled students, cooperative (work-study) education, advanced placement credit, double majors, independent study, summer session for credit, part-time degree programs (daytime, evenings, weekends, summer), and adult/continuing education programs.

Student Body Statistics The student body is made up of 602 undergraduates (179 freshmen). 69 percent are women and 31 percent are men. Students come from 2 states and territories and 4 other countries. 99 percent are from Indiana. 0.5 percent are international students. 59 percent of the 2003 graduating class went on to four-year colleges.

Expenses for 2004–05 *Application fee:* $25. *Tuition:* $8700 full-time, $290 per credit hour part-time. *Mandatory fees:* $200 full-time, $50 per term part-time.

Financial Aid Forms of aid include need-based scholarships and part-time jobs. The application deadline for financial aid is March 1.

Freshman Admission Ancilla requires a high school transcript and TOEFL scores for international students. An interview is recommended. The application deadline for regular admission is rolling.

Transfer Admission The application deadline for admission is rolling.

Entrance Difficulty Ancilla has an open admission policy.

For Further Information Contact Mr. Jim Bastis, Executive Director of Enrollment Management, Ancilla College, 9601 Union Road, Donaldson, IN 46513. *Telephone:* 574-936-8898 Ext. 350 or 866-262-4552 Ext. 350 (toll-free in-state). *Fax:* 574-935-1773. *E-mail:* admissions@ancilla.edu. *Web site:* http://www.ancilla.edu/.

ANDERSON UNIVERSITY

Anderson, Indiana

Anderson University is a coed, private, comprehensive institution, founded in 1917, affiliated with the Church of God, offering degrees at the associate, bachelor's, master's, doctoral, and first professional levels. It has a 100-acre campus in Anderson near Indianapolis.

Expenses for 2003–04 *Application fee:* $20. *Comprehensive fee:* $22,610 includes full-time tuition ($17,050) and college room and board ($5560). *College room only:* $3330. Room and board charges vary according to board plan. *Part-time tuition:* varies with course load.

For Further Information Contact Mr. Jim King, Director of Admissions, Anderson University, 1100 East 5th Street, Anderson, IN 46012-3495. *Telephone:* 765-641-4080, 800-421-3014 (toll-free in-state), or 800-428-6414 (toll-free out-of-state). *Fax:* 765-641-3851. *E-mail:* info@anderson.edu. *Web site:* http://www.anderson.edu/.

BALL STATE UNIVERSITY

Muncie, Indiana

Ball State is a coed, public university, founded in 1918, offering degrees at the associate, bachelor's, master's, and doctoral levels and post-master's and postbachelor's certificates. It has a 955-acre campus in Muncie near Indianapolis.

Academic Information The faculty has 1,162 members (77% full-time), 64% with terminal degrees. The undergraduate student-faculty ratio is 17:1. The library holds 1 million titles, 2,937 serial subscriptions, and 506,303 audiovisual materials. Special programs include academic remediation, an honors program, cooperative (work-study) education, study abroad, advanced placement credit, Freshman Honors College, ESL programs, double majors, independent study, distance learning, summer session for credit, part-time degree programs, adult/continuing education programs, and internships. The most frequently chosen baccalaureate fields are business/marketing, communications/communication technologies, education.

Student Body Statistics The student body totals 20,533, of whom 17,641 are undergraduates (3,987 freshmen). 53 percent are women and 47 percent are men. Students come from 49 states and territories. 91 percent are from Indiana.

Expenses for 2003–04 *Application fee:* $25. *State resident tuition:* $5532 full-time. *Nonresident tuition:* $13,950 full-time. *Mandatory fees:* $398 full-time. *College room and board:* $5880. Room and board charges vary according to board plan and housing facility.

Financial Aid Forms of aid include need-based and non-need-based scholarships, athletic grants, and part-time jobs. The average aided 2003–04 undergraduate received an aid package worth an estimated $6836. The priority application deadline for financial aid is March 1.

Freshman Admission Ball State requires a high school transcript and TOEFL scores for international students. An essay, recommendations, an interview, and SAT I or ACT scores are required for some. The application deadline for regular admission is May 1.

Transfer Admission The application deadline for admission is rolling.

Entrance Difficulty Ball State assesses its entrance difficulty level as moderately difficult; very difficult for architecture program. For the fall 2003 freshman class, 76 percent of the applicants were accepted.

SPECIAL MESSAGE TO STUDENTS

Social Life At Ball State, the life lived outside the classroom is important, too. That is why all first-year students must live in residence halls unless they commute from their parents' primary residences. Ball State's thirty-two residence halls are safe, affordable, and convenient. A full-time residence hall director lives in every hall. The amenities in each hall include large-screen televisions, pianos, pool tables, video games, kitchenettes, and on-site computer labs. Residence halls offer a wide range of visitation policies, and there are fitness and aerobic areas and special programs that emphasize positive lifestyle choices. Ball State has everything from lasagna to lattes at its five dining hall locations.

Academic Highlights Ball State is a coed public university that offers degrees at the associate, bachelor's, master's, and doctoral levels. Founded in 1918, the 750-acre residential campus includes more than fifty major buildings with an additional 285 acres of research property. The University brings together the powerful resources of a large research university and the personal learning of a small college. The University operates thirty-four public computer labs and numerous departmental labs, which provide a computer terminal for every 6 students. Ranked as a Doctoral I institution by the Carnegie Foundation, the University has seven academic colleges, an Honors College, University College, and a graduate school. Ball State awards approximately 4,000 degrees each year. There are 868 full-time faculty members; 90 percent of the tenure-track faculty members hold doctoral degrees. Bracken Library, one of the largest and most modern libraries in Indiana, houses 1.5 million volumes and more than 4,000 current periodical titles.

Interviews and Campus Visits Students can experience Ball State during a Cardinal Preview Day, Football Saturday, or by scheduling an individual visit. An individual visit provides opportunities for students and their families to tour the campus, attend an admissions information session, and enjoy a meal in a dining hall. With advance notice of a visit, Ball State can make arrangements for students to meet with faculty members to discuss academic areas of interest. To arrange a campus visit, students should call 866-770-3163. The nearest commercial airport is Indianapolis International.

For Further Information Write to Office of Admissions, Ball State University, Muncie, IN 47306-1099. *Telephone:* 800-482-4BSU (toll-free). *Fax:* 765-285-1632. *Web site:* http://www.bsu.edu/admissions,.

See page 254 for a narrative description.

BETHEL COLLEGE
Mishawaka, Indiana

Bethel is a coed, private, comprehensive institution, founded in 1947, affiliated with the Missionary Church, offering degrees at the associate, bachelor's, and master's levels. It has a 70-acre campus in Mishawaka.

Academic Information The faculty has 149 members (40% full-time), 34% with terminal degrees. The undergraduate student-faculty ratio is 14:1. The library holds 106,584 titles, 450 serial subscriptions, and 3,926 audiovisual materials. Special programs include academic remediation, an honors program, study abroad, advanced placement credit, accelerated degree programs, double majors, independent study, summer session for credit, part-time degree programs (daytime, evenings, summer), adult/continuing education programs, internships, and arrangement for off-campus study with Northern Indiana Consortium for Education, Coalition for Christian Colleges and Universities. The most frequently chosen baccalaureate fields are business/marketing, education, health professions and related sciences.

Student Body Statistics The student body totals 1,847, of whom 1,740 are undergraduates (306 freshmen). 63 percent are women and 37 percent are men. Students come from 32 states and territories and 13 other countries. 67 percent are from Indiana. 2.1 percent are international students. 10 percent of the 2003 graduating class went on to graduate and professional schools.

Expenses for 2003–04 *Application fee:* $25. *Comprehensive fee:* $19,210 includes full-time tuition ($14,390), mandatory fees ($140), and college room and board ($4680). Room and board charges vary according to board plan and housing facility. *Part-time tuition:* $270 per hour. Part-time tuition varies according to course load.

Financial Aid Forms of aid include need-based and non-need-based scholarships, athletic grants, and part-time jobs. The average aided 2003–04 undergraduate received an aid package worth an estimated $12,313. The priority application deadline for financial aid is March 1.

Freshman Admission Bethel requires an essay, a high school transcript, a minimum 2.0 high school GPA, 1 recommendation, SAT I or ACT scores, and TOEFL scores for international students. A minimum 2.5 high school GPA and an interview are recommended. The application deadline for regular admission is August 6.

Transfer Admission The application deadline for admission is August 6.

Entrance Difficulty Bethel assesses its entrance difficulty level as minimally difficult. For the fall 2003 freshman class, 65 percent of the applicants were accepted.

For Further Information Contact Mr. Randy Beachy, Assistant Vice President of Enrollment/Marketing, Bethel College, 1001 West McKinley Avenue, Mishawaka, IN 46545-5591. *Telephone:* 574-257-3319 or 800-422-4101 (toll-free). *Fax:* 574-257-3335. *E-mail:* admissions@bethelcollege.edu. *Web site:* http://www.bethelcollege.edu/.

BUTLER UNIVERSITY
Indianapolis, Indiana

Butler is a coed, private, comprehensive institution, founded in 1855, offering degrees at the associate, bachelor's, master's, and first professional levels and postbachelor's certificates. It has a 290-acre campus in Indianapolis.

Academic Information The faculty has 425 members (63% full-time), 60% with terminal degrees. The undergraduate student-faculty ratio is 13:1. The library holds 308,689 titles, 2,000 serial subscriptions, and 13,091 audiovisual materials. Special programs include an honors program, cooperative (work-study) education, study abroad, advanced placement credit, ESL programs, double majors, independent study, self-designed majors, summer session for credit, part-time degree programs (daytime, evenings, summer), adult/continuing education programs, internships, and arrangement for off-campus study with 6 members of the Consortium for Urban Education. The most frequently chosen baccalaureate fields are business/marketing, education, health professions and related sciences.

Student Body Statistics The student body totals 4,424, of whom 3,657 are undergraduates (976 freshmen). 63 percent are women and 37 percent are men. Students come from 42 states and territories and 51 other countries. 60 percent are from Indiana. 2 percent are international students. 19 percent of the 2003 graduating class went on to graduate and professional schools.

Expenses for 2003–04 *Application fee:* $35. *Comprehensive fee:* $28,250 includes full-time tuition ($20,990), mandatory fees ($220), and college room and board ($7040). *College room only:* $3240. Full-time tuition and fees vary according to program. Room and board charges vary according to housing facility. *Part-time tuition:* $880 per credit. Part-time tuition varies according to program.

Financial Aid Forms of aid include need-based and non-need-based scholarships, athletic grants, and part-time jobs. The average aided 2003–04 undergraduate received an aid package worth an estimated $16,400. The priority application deadline for financial aid is March 1.

Butler University (continued)

Freshman Admission Butler requires an essay, a high school transcript, SAT I or ACT scores, and TOEFL scores for international students. SAT II: Subject Test scores are recommended. An interview and audition are required for some. The application deadline for regular admission is August 15 and for early action it is December 1.

Transfer Admission The application deadline for admission is August 15.

Entrance Difficulty Butler assesses its entrance difficulty level as moderately difficult. For the fall 2003 freshman class, 77 percent of the applicants were accepted.

For Further Information Contact Mr. William Preble, Dean of Admissions, Butler University, 4600 Sunset Avenue, Indianapolis, IN 46208-3485. *Telephone:* 317-940-8100 Ext. 8124 or 888-940-8100 (toll-free). *Fax:* 317-940-8150. *E-mail:* admission@butler.edu. *Web site:* http://www.butler.edu/.

CALUMET COLLEGE OF SAINT JOSEPH

Whiting, Indiana

Calumet College is a coed, private, Roman Catholic, comprehensive institution, founded in 1951, offering degrees at the associate, bachelor's, and master's levels. It has a 25-acre campus in Whiting near Chicago.

Academic Information The faculty has 123 members (24% full-time), 33% with terminal degrees. The undergraduate student-faculty ratio is 14:1. The library holds 93,055 titles, 354 serial subscriptions, and 6,412 audiovisual materials. Special programs include academic remediation, cooperative (work-study) education, advanced placement credit, accelerated degree programs, double majors, independent study, self-designed majors, summer session for credit, part-time degree programs (daytime, evenings, weekends), external degree programs, adult/continuing education programs, and internships. The most frequently chosen baccalaureate fields are business/marketing, health professions and related sciences, protective services/public administration.

Student Body Statistics The student body totals 1,332, of whom 1,214 are undergraduates (108 freshmen). 59 percent are women and 41 percent are men. Students come from 4 states and territories. 71 percent are from Indiana.

Expenses for 2003–04 *Application fee:* $0. *Tuition:* $9000 full-time, $300 per credit hour part-time.

Financial Aid Forms of aid include need-based scholarships and part-time jobs. The priority application deadline for financial aid is March 1.

Freshman Admission Calumet College requires a high school transcript and TOEFL scores for international students. A minimum 2.0 high school GPA, an interview, and SAT I or ACT scores are recommended. An essay and ACT COMPASS are required for some. The application deadline for regular admission is rolling.

Transfer Admission The application deadline for admission is rolling.

Entrance Difficulty Calumet College assesses its entrance difficulty level as minimally difficult. For the fall 2003 freshman class, 73 percent of the applicants were accepted.

For Further Information Contact Mr. Chuck Walz, Director of Admissions, Calumet College of Saint Joseph, 2400 New York Avenue, Whiting, IN 46394. *Telephone:* 219-473-4215 Ext. 379 or 877-700-9100 (toll-free). *Fax:* 219-473-4259. *E-mail:* admissions@ccsj.edu. *Web site:* http://www.ccsj.edu/.

CROSSROADS BIBLE COLLEGE

Indianapolis, Indiana

Crossroads Bible College is a coed, private, Baptist, four-year college, founded in 1980, offering degrees at the associate and bachelor's levels. It has a 6-acre campus in Indianapolis.

Academic Information The faculty has 25 members (20% full-time), 80% with terminal degrees. The student-faculty ratio is 22:1. The most frequently chosen baccalaureate fields are education, philosophy, religion, and theology.

Student Body Statistics The student body is made up of 203 undergraduates (31 freshmen). 39 percent are women and 61 percent are men.

Expenses for 2004–05 *Application fee:* $10. *Tuition:* $6600 full-time, $200 per credit hour part-time. *Mandatory fees:* $140 full-time, $140 per term part-time. *College room only:* $3000.

Financial Aid Forms of aid include need-based scholarships and part-time jobs. The priority application deadline for financial aid is May 31.

Freshman Admission The application deadline for regular admission is August 8.

Entrance Difficulty Crossroads Bible College assesses its entrance difficulty level as noncompetitive. For the fall 2003 freshman class, 84 percent of the applicants were accepted.

For Further Information Contact Ms. Bethanie Holdcroft, Director of Admissions, Crossroads Bible College, 601 North Shortridge Road, Indianapolis, IN 46219. *Telephone:* 317-352-8736 Ext. 230 or 800-273-2224 (toll-free). *Fax:* 317-352-9145. *Web site:* http://www.crossroads.edu/.

DAVENPORT UNIVERSITY

Granger, Indiana

For Information Write to Davenport University, Granger, IN 46530.

DAVENPORT UNIVERSITY

Hammond, Indiana

For Information Write to Davenport University, Hammond, IN 46320.

DAVENPORT UNIVERSITY

Merrillville, Indiana

For Information Write to Davenport University, Merrillville, IN 46410.

DEPAUW UNIVERSITY

Greencastle, Indiana

DePauw is a coed, private, four-year college, founded in 1837, affiliated with the United Methodist Church, offering degrees at the bachelor's level. It has a 655-acre campus in Greencastle near Indianapolis.

Academic Information The faculty has 249 members (84% full-time), 88% with terminal degrees. The student-faculty ratio is 10:1. The library holds 545,736 titles, 2,134 serial subscriptions, and 12,126 audiovisual materials. Special programs include an honors program, study abroad, advanced placement credit, double majors, independent study, self-designed majors, part-time degree programs (daytime, evenings), internships, and arrangement for off-campus study with Great Lakes Colleges Association. The most frequently chosen baccalaureate fields are communications/communication technologies, English, social sciences and history.

Student Body Statistics The student body is made up of 2,365 undergraduates (581 freshmen). 55 percent are women and 45 percent are men. Students come from 41 states and territories and 19 other countries. 51 percent are from Indiana. 1.9 percent are international students. 21.3 percent of the 2003 graduating class went on to graduate and professional schools.

Expenses for 2003–04 *Application fee:* $0. *Comprehensive fee:* $31,500 includes full-time tuition ($24,000), mandatory fees ($450), and college room and board ($7050). *College room only:* $3650. *Part-time tuition:* $764 per semester hour.

Financial Aid Forms of aid include need-based and non-need-based scholarships and part-time jobs. The average aided 2003–04 undergraduate received an aid package worth an estimated $20,208. The application deadline for financial aid is February 15.

Freshman Admission DePauw requires an essay, a high school transcript, 1 recommendation, and SAT I or ACT scores. A minimum 3.25 high school GPA, an interview, and TOEFL scores for international students are recommended. The application deadline for regular admission is February 1; for early decision it is November 1; and for early action it is December 1.

Transfer Admission The application deadline for admission is March 1.

Entrance Difficulty DePauw assesses its entrance difficulty level as moderately difficult. For the fall 2003 freshman class, 63 percent of the applicants were accepted.

For Further Information Contact Ms. Madeleine Eagon, Vice President for Admission and Financial Aid, DePauw University, 101 East Seminary Street, Greencastle, IN 46135-0037. *Telephone:* 765-658-4006 or 800-447-2495 (toll-free). *Fax:* 765-658-4007. *E-mail:* admission@depauw.edu. *Web site:* http://www.depauw.edu/.

See page 278 for a narrative description.

DEVRY UNIVERSITY

Indianapolis, Indiana

DeVry University is a coed, proprietary, comprehensive unit of DeVry University.

Freshman Admission SAT I, ACT or CPT is recommended. The application deadline for regular admission is rolling.

For Further Information Contact DeVry University, 9100 Keystone Crossing, Suite 350, Indianapolis, IN 46240-2158. *Telephone:* 317-581-8854. *E-mail:* ahein@keller.edu. *Web site:* http://www.devry.edu/.

DEVRY UNIVERSITY

Merrillville, Indiana

For Information Write to DeVry University, Merrillville, IN 46410-5673.

EARLHAM COLLEGE

Richmond, Indiana

Earlham is a coed, private, comprehensive institution, founded in 1847, affiliated with the Society of Friends, offering degrees at the bachelor's, master's, and first professional levels. It has an 800-acre campus in Richmond near Cincinnati, Indianapolis, and Dayton.

Academic Information The faculty has 111 members (86% full-time), 77% with terminal degrees. The undergraduate student-faculty ratio is 11:1. The library holds 392,100 titles, 1,660 serial subscriptions, and 53,000 audiovisual materials. Special programs include services for learning-disabled students, study abroad, advanced placement credit, accelerated degree programs, double majors, independent study, self-designed majors, internships, and arrangement for off-campus study with members of the Great Lakes Colleges Association. The most frequently chosen baccalaureate fields are social sciences and history, biological/life sciences, visual/performing arts.

Student Body Statistics The student body totals 1,262, of whom 1,170 are undergraduates (348 freshmen). 56 percent are women and 44 percent are men. Students come from 46 states and territories and 34 other countries. 26 percent are from Indiana. 4.4 percent are international students. 22 percent of the 2003 graduating class went on to graduate and professional schools.

Expenses for 2003–04 *Application fee:* $30. *Comprehensive fee:* $29,976 includes full-time tuition ($23,920), mandatory fees ($640), and college room and board ($5416). *College room only:* $2650. Room and board charges vary according to board plan. *Part-time tuition:* $797 per credit hour.

Financial Aid Forms of aid include need-based and non-need-based scholarships and part-time jobs. The average aided 2003–04 undergraduate received an aid package worth an estimated $21,215. The priority application deadline for financial aid is March 1.

Freshman Admission Earlham requires an essay, a high school transcript, a minimum 3.0 high school GPA, 2 recommendations, SAT I or ACT scores, and TOEFL scores for international students. An interview and SAT I scores are recommended. The application deadline for regular admission is February 15; for early decision it is December 1; and for early action it is January 1.

Transfer Admission The application deadline for admission is April 1.

Entrance Difficulty Earlham assesses its entrance difficulty level as moderately difficult. For the fall 2003 freshman class, 77 percent of the applicants were accepted.

For Further Information Contact Mr. Jeff Rickey, Dean of Admissions and Financial Aid, Earlham College, 801 National Road West, Richmond, IN 47374. *Telephone:* 765-983-1600 or 800-327-5426 (toll-free). *Fax:* 765-983-1560. *E-mail:* admission@earlham.edu. *Web site:* http://www.earlham.edu/.

FRANKLIN COLLEGE

Franklin, Indiana

Franklin is a coed, private, four-year college, founded in 1834, affiliated with the American Baptist Churches in the U.S.A., offering degrees at the bachelor's level. It has a 74-acre campus in Franklin near Indianapolis.

Academic Information The faculty has 111 members (53% full-time), 62% with terminal degrees. The student-faculty ratio is 13:1. The library holds 122,605 titles, 484 serial subscriptions, and 7,388 audiovisual materials. Special programs include academic remediation, services for learning-disabled students, study abroad, advanced placement credit, double majors, independent study, summer session for credit, part-time degree programs (daytime, summer), internships, and arrangement for off-campus study with Marian College, University of Indianapolis, Indiana University-Purdue University at Indianapolis, Butler University, Martin University, Ivy Tech State College. The most frequently chosen baccalaureate fields are education, communications/communication technologies, social sciences and history.

Student Body Statistics The student body is made up of 1,038 undergraduates (277 freshmen). 56 percent are women and 44 percent are men. Students come from 19 states and territories and 7 other countries. 94 percent are from Indiana. 0.9 percent are international students. 14 percent of the 2003 graduating class went on to graduate and professional schools.

Expenses for 2003–04 *Application fee:* $30. *Comprehensive fee:* $22,195 includes full-time tuition ($16,750), mandatory fees ($175), and college room and board ($5270). *College room only:* $3080. Room and board charges vary according to board plan and housing facility. *Part-time tuition:* varies with course load.

Financial Aid Forms of aid include need-based and non-need-based scholarships and part-time jobs. The average aided 2002–03 undergraduate received an aid package worth $12,519. The application deadline for financial aid is March 1.

Freshman Admission Franklin requires an essay, a high school transcript, 1 recommendation, TOEFL for international students, SAT I or ACT scores, and TOEFL scores for international students. An interview is recommended. The application deadline for regular admission is May 1.

Franklin College (continued)

Entrance Difficulty Franklin assesses its entrance difficulty level as moderately difficult. For the fall 2003 freshman class, 86 percent of the applicants were accepted.

For Further Information Contact Ms. Kathryn D. Coffman, Director of Admissions, Franklin College, 501 East Monroe Street, Franklin, IN 46131-2598. *Telephone:* 317-738-8062 or 800-852-0232 (toll-free). *Fax:* 317-738-8274. *E-mail:* admissions@franklincollege.edu. *Web site:* http://www.franklincollege.edu/.

GOSHEN COLLEGE
Goshen, Indiana

Goshen is a coed, private, Mennonite, four-year college, founded in 1894, offering degrees at the bachelor's level. It has a 135-acre campus in Goshen.

Academic Information The faculty has 124 members (56% full-time), 49% with terminal degrees. The student-faculty ratio is 10:1. The library holds 127,028 titles, 750 serial subscriptions, and 3,250 audiovisual materials. Special programs include academic remediation, services for learning-disabled students, an honors program, cooperative (work-study) education, study abroad, advanced placement credit, accelerated degree programs, Freshman Honors College, ESL programs, double majors, independent study, distance learning, self-designed majors, summer session for credit, part-time degree programs, adult/continuing education programs, internships, and arrangement for off-campus study with Northern Indiana Consortium for Education. The most frequently chosen baccalaureate fields are business/marketing, education, health professions and related sciences.

Student Body Statistics The student body is made up of 920 undergraduates (182 freshmen). 62 percent are women and 38 percent are men. Students come from 36 states and territories and 30 other countries. 57 percent are from Indiana. 8.7 percent are international students. 40 percent of the 2003 graduating class went on to graduate and professional schools.

Expenses for 2003–04 *Application fee:* $25. *Comprehensive fee:* $22,450 includes full-time tuition ($16,320), mandatory fees ($330), and college room and board ($5800). *College room only:* $3000. Room and board charges vary according to board plan and student level. *Part-time tuition:* $640 per credit hour. Part-time tuition varies according to course load.

Financial Aid Forms of aid include need-based and non-need-based scholarships, athletic grants, and part-time jobs. The average aided 2003–04 undergraduate received an aid package worth an estimated $15,626. The priority application deadline for financial aid is February 15.

Freshman Admission Goshen requires an essay, a high school transcript, a minimum 2.5 high school GPA, 2 recommendations, rank in upper 50% of high school class, minimum SAT score of 1000, ACT score of 22, SAT I or ACT scores, and TOEFL scores for international students. An interview is recommended. The application deadline for regular admission is August 15 and for early action it is December 15.

Transfer Admission The application deadline for admission is August 15.

Entrance Difficulty Goshen assesses its entrance difficulty level as moderately difficult. For the fall 2003 freshman class, 61 percent of the applicants were accepted.

For Further Information Contact Ms. Karen Lowe Raftus, Director of Admission, Goshen College, 1700 South Main Street, Goshen, IN 46526-4794. *Telephone:* 574-535-7535 or 800-348-7422 (toll-free). *Fax:* 574-535-7609. *E-mail:* admissions@goshen.edu. *Web site:* http://www.goshen.edu/.

See page 284 for a narrative description.

GRACE COLLEGE
Winona Lake, Indiana

Grace is a coed, private, comprehensive institution, founded in 1948, affiliated with the Fellowship of Grace Brethren Churches, offering degrees at the associate, bachelor's, and master's levels. It has a 160-acre campus in Winona Lake.

Academic Information The faculty has 91 members (45% full-time), 44% with terminal degrees. The undergraduate student-faculty ratio is 17:1. The library holds 142,865 titles, 12,500 serial subscriptions, and 3,583 audiovisual materials. Special programs include academic remediation, services for learning-disabled students, study abroad, advanced placement credit, accelerated degree programs, double majors, independent study, distance learning, summer session for credit, part-time degree programs, adult/continuing education programs, internships, and arrangement for off-campus study with Coalition for Christian Colleges and Universities. The most frequently chosen baccalaureate fields are business/marketing, education, psychology.

Student Body Statistics The student body totals 1,208, of whom 1,086 are undergraduates (181 freshmen). 50 percent are women and 50 percent are men. Students come from 35 states and territories and 8 other countries. 62 percent are from Indiana. 1.2 percent are international students.

Expenses for 2003–04 *Application fee:* $20. *Comprehensive fee:* $19,825 includes full-time tuition ($13,690), mandatory fees ($380), and college room and board ($5755). *College room only:* $2865. Room and board charges vary according to board plan and housing facility. *Part-time tuition:* $255 per credit. *Part-time mandatory fees:* $230 per year. Part-time tuition and fees vary according to course load.

Financial Aid Forms of aid include need-based and non-need-based scholarships, athletic grants, and part-time jobs. The average aided 2003–04 undergraduate received an aid package worth an estimated $12,437. The priority application deadline for financial aid is March 1.

Freshman Admission Grace requires a high school transcript, a minimum 2.3 high school GPA, 2 recommendations, personal statement of faith, SAT I or ACT scores, and TOEFL scores for international students. An interview is required for some. The application deadline for regular admission is August 1.

Transfer Admission The application deadline for admission is August 1.

Entrance Difficulty Grace assesses its entrance difficulty level as moderately difficult. For the fall 2003 freshman class, 71 percent of the applicants were accepted.

For Further Information Contact Ms. Lisa Middleton, Assistant Director of Admissions/Registrar, Grace College, 200 Seminary Drive, Winona Lake, IN 46590-1294. *Telephone:* 574-372-5100 Ext. 6411, 800-54-GRACE Ext. 6412 (toll-free in-state), or 800-54 GRACE Ext. 6412 (toll-free out-of-state). *Fax:* 574-372-5114. *E-mail:* enroll@grace.edu. *Web site:* http://www.grace.edu/.

HANOVER COLLEGE
Hanover, Indiana

Hanover is a coed, private, Presbyterian, four-year college, founded in 1827, offering degrees at the bachelor's level. It has a 630-acre campus in Hanover near Louisville.

Academic Information The faculty has 91 members (93% full-time), 96% with terminal degrees. The student-faculty ratio is 10:1. The library holds 224,478 titles, 1,035 serial subscriptions, and 5,080 audiovisual materials. Special programs include study abroad, advanced placement credit, accelerated degree programs, double majors, independent study, internships, and arrangement for off-campus study with 8 members of the Spring Term Consortium. The most frequently chosen baccalaureate fields are education, business/marketing, social sciences and history.

Student Body Statistics The student body is made up of 997 undergraduates (292 freshmen). 54 percent are women and 46 percent are men. Students come from 35 states and territories and 15 other countries. 71 percent are from Indiana. 3.5 percent are international students. 27 percent of the 2003 graduating class went on to graduate and professional schools.

Expenses for 2003–04 *Application fee:* $30. *Comprehensive fee:* $20,600 includes full-time tuition ($14,300), mandatory fees ($400), and college room and board ($5900). *College room only:* $2800. Full-time tuition and fees vary according to reciprocity agreements. Room and board charges vary according to housing facility. *Part-time tuition:* varies with course load, reciprocity agreements.

Financial Aid Forms of aid include need-based and non-need-based scholarships and part-time jobs. The average aided 2003–04 undergraduate received an aid package worth an estimated $14,788. The priority application deadline for financial aid is March 10.

Freshman Admission Hanover requires an essay, a high school transcript, 1 recommendation, SAT I or ACT scores, and TOEFL scores for international students. An interview is recommended. The application deadline for regular admission is March 1 and for early action it is December 1.

Transfer Admission The application deadline for admission is rolling.

Entrance Difficulty Hanover assesses its entrance difficulty level as moderately difficult. For the fall 2003 freshman class, 79 percent of the applicants were accepted.

For Further Information Contact Mr. Kenneth Moyer, Dean of Admission, Hanover College, PO Box 108, Hanover, IN 47243-0108. *Telephone:* 812-866-7021 or 800-213-2178 (toll-free). *Fax:* 812-866-7098. *E-mail:* admission@hanover.edu. *Web site:* http://www.hanover.edu/.

HOLY CROSS COLLEGE

Notre Dame, Indiana

Holy Cross College is a coed, private, Roman Catholic, primarily two-year college, founded in 1966, offering degrees at the associate and bachelor's levels. It has a 150-acre campus in Notre Dame.

Academic Information The faculty has 42 members (60% full-time), 29% with terminal degrees. The student-faculty ratio is 17:1. The library holds 15,000 titles and 160 serial subscriptions. Special programs include academic remediation, advanced placement credit, ESL programs, summer session for credit, part-time degree programs (daytime, summer), and arrangement for off-campus study with members of the Northern Indiana Consortium for Education.

Student Body Statistics The student body is made up of 492 undergraduates (238 freshmen). 37 percent are women and 63 percent are men. 54 percent are from Indiana. 85 percent of the 2003 graduating class went on to four-year colleges.

Expenses for 2004–05 *Application fee:* $50. *Comprehensive fee:* $18,000 includes full-time tuition ($10,500), mandatory fees ($400), and college room and board ($7100). *Part-time tuition:* $345 per semester hour.

Financial Aid Forms of aid include need-based scholarships and part-time jobs. The priority application deadline for financial aid is March 1.

Freshman Admission Holy Cross College requires an essay, a high school transcript, a minimum 2.0 high school GPA, SAT I or ACT scores, and TOEFL scores for international students. An interview is recommended. The application deadline for regular admission is rolling.

Transfer Admission The application deadline for admission is rolling.

Entrance Difficulty Holy Cross College assesses its entrance difficulty level as minimally difficult.

For Further Information Contact Mr. Vincent M. Duke, Director of Admissions, Holy Cross College, PO Box 308, Notre Dame, IN 46556. *Telephone:* 574-239-8400 Ext. 407. *Fax:* 574-233-7427. *E-mail:* vduke@hcc-nd.edu. *Web site:* http://www.hcc-nd.edu/.

HUNTINGTON COLLEGE

Huntington, Indiana

Huntington is a coed, private, comprehensive institution, founded in 1897, affiliated with the Church of the United Brethren in Christ, offering degrees at the associate, bachelor's, and master's levels and postbachelor's certificates. It has a 200-acre campus in Huntington near Fort Wayne.

Academic Information The faculty has 97 members (57% full-time), 53% with terminal degrees. The undergraduate student-faculty ratio is 18:1. The library holds 91,709 titles, 553 serial subscriptions, and 4,323 audiovisual materials. Special programs include academic remediation, study abroad, advanced placement credit, accelerated degree programs, ESL programs, double majors, independent study, distance learning, summer session for credit, part-time degree programs, adult/continuing education programs, internships, and arrangement for off-campus study with Saint Francis College (IN). The most frequently chosen baccalaureate fields are business/marketing, education, philosophy, religion, and theology.

Student Body Statistics The student body totals 976, of whom 923 are undergraduates (192 freshmen). 57 percent are women and 43 percent are men. Students come from 27 states and territories and 15 other countries. 60 percent are from Indiana. 2.6 percent are international students. 10 percent of the 2003 graduating class went on to graduate and professional schools.

Expenses for 2003–04 *Application fee:* $20. *Comprehensive fee:* $23,590 includes full-time tuition ($17,280), mandatory fees ($420), and college room and board ($5890). Room and board charges vary according to board plan. *Part-time tuition:* $500 per semester hour. Part-time tuition varies according to course load.

Financial Aid Forms of aid include need-based and non-need-based scholarships, athletic grants, and part-time jobs. The average aided 2003–04 undergraduate received an aid package worth an estimated $13,794. The priority application deadline for financial aid is March 1.

Freshman Admission Huntington requires an essay, a high school transcript, a minimum 2.3 high school GPA, SAT I or ACT scores, and TOEFL scores for international students. An interview is recommended. The application deadline for regular admission is August 15.

Transfer Admission The application deadline for admission is rolling.

Entrance Difficulty Huntington assesses its entrance difficulty level as moderately difficult. For the fall 2003 freshman class, 92 percent of the applicants were accepted.

For Further Information Contact Mr. Jeff Berggren, Dean of Enrollment, Huntington College, 2303 College Avenue, Huntington, IN 46750-1299. *Telephone:* 260-356-6000 Ext. 4016 or 800-642-6493 (toll-free). *Fax:* 260-356-9448. *E-mail:* admissions@huntington.edu. *Web site:* http://www.huntington.edu/.

INDIANA INSTITUTE OF TECHNOLOGY

Fort Wayne, Indiana

Indiana Tech is a coed, private, comprehensive institution, founded in 1930, offering degrees at the associate, bachelor's, and master's levels. It has a 25-acre campus in Fort Wayne.

Academic Information The faculty has 272 members (15% full-time), 9% with terminal degrees. The undergraduate student-faculty ratio is 17:1. The library holds 35,200 titles, 158 serial subscriptions, and 92 audiovisual materials. Special programs include academic remediation, services for learning-disabled students, advanced placement credit, accelerated degree programs, ESL programs, double majors, independent study, distance learning, self-designed majors, summer session for credit, part-time degree programs, external degree programs, adult/continuing education programs, and internships. The most frequently chosen baccalaureate fields are business/marketing, computer/information sciences, engineering/engineering technologies.

Student Body Statistics The student body totals 3,390, of whom 2,971 are undergraduates (749 freshmen). 56 percent are women and 44 percent are men. 65 percent are from Indiana. 0.8 percent are international students. 11 percent of the 2003 graduating class went on to graduate and professional schools.

Expenses for 2004–05 *Application fee:* $50. *Comprehensive fee:* $22,952 includes full-time tuition ($16,680) and college room and board ($6272). *College room only:* $3136. Full-time tuition varies according to class time, course load, and program. Room and board charges vary according to housing facility and student level. *Part-time tuition:* $556 per credit hour. Part-time tuition varies according to class time, course load, and program.

Financial Aid Forms of aid include need-based and non-need-based scholarships and part-time jobs. The priority application deadline for financial aid is March 1.

Freshman Admission Indiana Tech requires a high school transcript, SAT I or ACT scores, and TOEFL scores for international students. A minimum 3.0 high school GPA, an interview, and 2 references are recommended.

Entrance Difficulty Indiana Tech assesses its entrance difficulty level as moderately difficult. For the fall 2003 freshman class, 92 percent of the applicants were accepted.

For Further Information Contact Ms. Allison Carnahan, Director of Admissions, Indiana Institute of Technology, 1600 East Washington Boulevard, Fort Wayne, IN 46803. *Telephone:* 260-422-5561 Ext. 2251, 800-937-2448 (toll-free in-state), or 888-666-TECH (toll-free out-of-state). *Fax:* 260-422-7696. *E-mail:* admissions@indtech.edu. *Web site:* http://www.indtech.edu/.

INDIANA STATE UNIVERSITY

Terre Haute, Indiana

Indiana State is a coed, public university, founded in 1865, offering degrees at the associate, bachelor's, master's, and doctoral levels and post-master's and postbachelor's certificates. It has a 91-acre campus in Terre Haute near Indianapolis.

Academic Information The faculty has 715 members (78% full-time). The undergraduate student-faculty ratio is 16:1. The library holds 2 million titles and 2,827 serial subscriptions. Special programs include academic remediation, services for learning-disabled students, an honors program, cooperative (work-study) education, study abroad, advanced placement credit, accelerated degree programs, ESL programs, double majors, independent study, distance learning, summer session for credit, part-time degree programs (daytime, evenings, summer), adult/continuing education programs, internships, and arrangement for off-campus study with Saint Mary-of-the-Woods College, Rose-Hulman Institute of Technology. The most frequently chosen baccalaureate fields are business/marketing, education, social sciences and history.

Student Body Statistics The student body totals 11,360, of whom 9,615 are undergraduates (2,016 freshmen). 52 percent are women and 48 percent are men. Students come from 41 states and territories and 41 other countries. 92 percent are from Indiana. 1.8 percent are international students.

Expenses for 2003–04 *Application fee:* $25. *State resident tuition:* $5322 full-time, $192 per credit part-time. *Nonresident tuition:* $11,790 full-time, $416 per credit part-time. *Mandatory fees:* $100 full-time, $50 per term part-time. *College room and board:* $5297. *College room only:* $2790. Room and board charges vary according to board plan, housing facility, and student level.

Financial Aid Forms of aid include need-based and non-need-based scholarships, athletic grants, and part-time jobs. The average aided 2003–04 undergraduate received an aid package worth an estimated $5836. The priority application deadline for financial aid is March 1.

Freshman Admission Indiana State requires a high school transcript, a minimum 2.0 high school GPA, SAT I or ACT scores, and TOEFL scores for international students. Recommendations and an interview are required for some. The application deadline for regular admission is August 1.

Entrance Difficulty Indiana State assesses its entrance difficulty level as moderately difficult. For the fall 2003 freshman class, 86 percent of the applicants were accepted.

For Further Information Contact Mr. Ronald Brown, Director of Admissions, Indiana State University, Tirey Hall 134, 210 North 7th Street, Terre Haute, IN 47809. *Telephone:* 812-237-2121 or 800-742-0891 (toll-free). *Fax:* 812-237-8023. *E-mail:* admissions@indstate.edu. *Web site:* http://www.indstate.edu/.

INDIANA UNIVERSITY BLOOMINGTON

Bloomington, Indiana

IU is a coed, public unit of Indiana University System, founded in 1820, offering degrees at the associate, bachelor's, master's, doctoral, and first professional levels and post-master's and postbachelor's certificates. It has a 1,931-acre campus in Bloomington near Indianapolis.

Academic Information The faculty has 2,071 members (85% full-time), 65% with terminal degrees. The undergraduate student-faculty ratio is 19:1. The library holds 7 million titles, 60,019 serial subscriptions, and 252,801 audiovisual materials. Special programs include academic remediation, services for learning-disabled students, an honors program, cooperative (work-study) education, study abroad, advanced placement credit, accelerated degree programs, Freshman Honors College, ESL programs, double majors, independent study, distance learning, self-designed majors, summer session for credit, part-time degree programs (daytime, evenings, summer), external degree programs, adult/continuing education programs, internships, and arrangement for off-campus study. The most frequently chosen baccalaureate fields are business/marketing, communications/communication technologies, education.

Student Body Statistics The student body totals 38,589, of whom 30,319 are undergraduates (6,784 freshmen). 52 percent are women and 48 percent are men. Students come from 56 states and territories and 135 other countries. 70 percent are from Indiana. 4.3 percent are international students.

Expenses for 2003–04 *Application fee:* $45. *State resident tuition:* $5756 full-time, $148.45 per credit hour part-time. *Nonresident tuition:* $16,791 full-time, $493.50 per credit hour part-time. *Mandatory fees:* $761 full-time. Part-time tuition varies according to course load. *College room and board:* $5872. *College room only:* $3482. Room and board charges vary according to board plan and housing facility.

Financial Aid Forms of aid include need-based and non-need-based scholarships, athletic grants, and part-time jobs. The average aided 2003–04 undergraduate received an aid package worth an estimated $7425. The application deadline for financial aid is continuous.

Freshman Admission IU requires a high school transcript and SAT I or ACT scores. An interview, SAT II: Subject Test scores, and TOEFL scores for international students are recommended. The application deadline for regular admission is April 1.

Transfer Admission The application deadline for admission is rolling.

Entrance Difficulty IU assesses its entrance difficulty level as moderately difficult. For the fall 2003 freshman class, 81 percent of the applicants were accepted.

For Further Information Contact Mr. Don Hossler, Vice Chancellor for Enrollment Services, Indiana University Bloomington, 300 North Jordan Avenue, Bloomington, IN 47405-1106. *Telephone:* 812-855-0661. *Fax:* 812-855-5102. *E-mail:* iuadmit@indiana.edu. *Web site:* http://www.iu.edu/.

INDIANA UNIVERSITY EAST

Richmond, Indiana

IU East is a coed, public, four-year college of Indiana University System, founded in 1971, offering degrees at the associate and bachelor's levels and postbachelor's certificates. It has a 194-acre campus in Richmond near Indianapolis.

Academic Information The faculty has 204 members (38% full-time), 20% with terminal degrees. The student-faculty ratio is 14:1. The library holds 67,036 titles, 435 serial subscriptions, and 2,222 audiovisual materials. Special programs include academic remediation, services for learning-disabled students, cooperative (work-study) education, advanced placement credit, double majors, independent study, distance learning, summer session for credit, part-time degree programs, external degree programs, adult/continuing education programs, internships, and arrangement for off-campus study with Earlham College. The most frequently chosen baccalaureate fields are business/marketing, education, health professions and related sciences.

Student Body Statistics The student body totals 2,568, of whom 2,505 are undergraduates (474 freshmen). 70 percent are women and 30 percent are men. Students come from 7 states and territories. 90 percent are from Indiana. 0.4 percent are international students.

Expenses for 2003–04 *Application fee:* $25. *State resident tuition:* $4118 full-time, $137.25 per credit hour part-time. *Nonresident tuition:* $10,068 full-time, $335.60 per credit hour part-time. *Mandatory fees:* $315 full-time. Full-time tuition and fees vary according to course load. Part-time tuition varies according to course load.

Financial Aid   Forms of aid include need-based and non-need-based scholarships and part-time jobs. The average aided 2003–04 undergraduate received an aid package worth an estimated $5838. The priority application deadline for financial aid is March 1.

Freshman Admission   IU East requires a high school transcript. A minimum 2.0 high school GPA and SAT I or ACT scores are recommended.

Transfer Admission   The application deadline for admission is rolling.

Entrance Difficulty   IU East assesses its entrance difficulty level as moderately difficult. For the fall 2003 freshman class, 79 percent of the applicants were accepted.

For Further Information   Contact Ms. Susanna Tanner, Admissions Counselor, Indiana University East, 2325 Chester Boulevard, WZ 116, Richmond, IN 47374-1289. *Telephone:* 765-973-8208 or 800-959-EAST (toll-free). *Fax:* 765-973-8288. *E-mail:* eaadmit@indiana.edu. *Web site:* http://www.iu.edu/.

INDIANA UNIVERSITY KOKOMO
Kokomo, Indiana

IUK is a coed, public, comprehensive unit of Indiana University System, founded in 1945, offering degrees at the associate, bachelor's, and master's levels and postbachelor's certificates. It has a 51-acre campus in Kokomo near Indianapolis.

Academic Information   The faculty has 177 members (50% full-time), 37% with terminal degrees. The undergraduate student-faculty ratio is 17:1. The library holds 132,424 titles, 1,513 serial subscriptions, and 1,466 audiovisual materials. Special programs include academic remediation, services for learning-disabled students, an honors program, study abroad, advanced placement credit, Freshman Honors College, independent study, distance learning, summer session for credit, part-time degree programs, external degree programs, adult/continuing education programs, and internships. The most frequently chosen baccalaureate fields are education, business/marketing, liberal arts/general studies.

Student Body Statistics   The student body totals 2,954, of whom 2,730 are undergraduates (557 freshmen). 71 percent are women and 29 percent are men. Students come from 3 states and territories. 99 percent are from Indiana. 0.5 percent are international students.

Expenses for 2003–04   *Application fee:* $30. *State resident tuition:* $4118 full-time, $137.25 per credit hour part-time. *Nonresident tuition:* $10,068 full-time, $335.60 per credit hour part-time. *Mandatory fees:* $345 full-time.

Financial Aid   Forms of aid include need-based and non-need-based scholarships and part-time jobs. The average aided 2003–04 undergraduate received an aid package worth an estimated $5654. The priority application deadline for financial aid is March 1.

Freshman Admission   IUK requires a high school transcript, SAT I or ACT scores, and TOEFL scores for international students. The application deadline for regular admission is August 3.

Entrance Difficulty   IUK assesses its entrance difficulty level as minimally difficult. For the fall 2003 freshman class, 86 percent of the applicants were accepted.

For Further Information   Contact Ms. Patty Young, Admissions Director, Indiana University Kokomo, PO Box 9003, Kelley Student Center 230A, Kokomo, IN 46904-9003. *Telephone:* 765-455-9217 or 888-875-4485 (toll-free). *Fax:* 765-455-9537. *E-mail:* iuadmis@iuk.edu. *Web site:* http://www.iu.edu/.

INDIANA UNIVERSITY NORTHWEST
Gary, Indiana

IUN is a coed, public, comprehensive unit of Indiana University System, founded in 1959, offering degrees at the associate, bachelor's, and master's levels and postbachelor's certificates. It has a 38-acre campus in Gary near Chicago.

Academic Information   The faculty has 380 members (49% full-time), 30% with terminal degrees. The undergraduate student-faculty ratio is 13:1. The library holds 251,508 titles, 1,541 serial subscriptions, and 331 audiovisual materials. Special programs include academic remediation, services for learning-disabled students, an honors program, cooperative (work-study) education, study abroad, advanced placement credit, accelerated degree programs, double majors, independent study, distance learning, self-designed majors, summer session for credit, part-time degree programs, external degree programs, adult/continuing education programs, internships, and arrangement for off-campus study. The most frequently chosen baccalaureate fields are business/marketing, liberal arts/general studies, protective services/public administration.

Student Body Statistics   The student body totals 5,097, of whom 4,476 are undergraduates (860 freshmen). 69 percent are women and 31 percent are men. Students come from 6 states and territories. 99 percent are from Indiana. 0.4 percent are international students.

Expenses for 2003–04   *Application fee:* $25. *State resident tuition:* $4118 full-time, $120.60 per credit hour part-time. *Nonresident tuition:* $10,068 full-time, $318.95 per credit hour part-time. *Mandatory fees:* $420 full-time. Full-time tuition and fees vary according to course level. Part-time tuition varies according to course level.

Financial Aid   Forms of aid include need-based and non-need-based scholarships, athletic grants, and part-time jobs. The average aided 2003–04 undergraduate received an aid package worth an estimated $6261. The priority application deadline for financial aid is March 1.

Freshman Admission   IUN requires a high school transcript, a minimum 2.0 high school GPA, and SAT I or ACT scores. TOEFL scores for international students are recommended. The application deadline for regular admission is August 1.

Transfer Admission   The application deadline for admission is rolling.

Entrance Difficulty   IUN assesses its entrance difficulty level as minimally difficult; moderately difficult for out-of-state applicants. For the fall 2003 freshman class, 67 percent of the applicants were accepted.

For Further Information   Contact Dr. Linda B. Templeton, Director of Admissions, Indiana University Northwest, Hawthorne 100, 3400 Broadway, Gary, IN 46408-1197. *Telephone:* 219-980-6767 or 800-968-7486 (toll-free). *Fax:* 219-981-4219. *E-mail:* admit@iun.edu. *Web site:* http://www.iu.edu/.

INDIANA UNIVERSITY–PURDUE UNIVERSITY FORT WAYNE
Fort Wayne, Indiana

IPFW is a coed, public, comprehensive unit of Indiana University System and Purdue University System, founded in 1917, offering degrees at the associate, bachelor's, and master's levels and postbachelor's certificates. It has a 565-acre campus in Fort Wayne.

Academic Information   The faculty has 690 members (49% full-time), 51% with terminal degrees. The undergraduate student-faculty ratio is 17:1. The library holds 479,992 titles, 10,964 serial subscriptions, and 1,000 audiovisual materials. Special programs include academic remediation, services for learning-disabled students, an honors program, cooperative (work-study) education, study abroad, advanced placement credit, accelerated degree programs, ESL programs, double majors, independent study, distance learning, self-designed majors, summer session for credit, part-time degree programs (daytime, evenings, weekends, summer), adult/continuing education programs, internships, and arrangement for off-campus study with National Student Exchange. The most frequently chosen baccalaureate fields are business/marketing, education, liberal arts/general studies.

Student Body Statistics   The student body totals 11,806, of whom 11,068 are undergraduates (1,643 freshmen). 58 percent are women and 42 percent are men. Students come from 41 states and territories and 72 other countries. 94 percent are from Indiana. 1.5 percent are international students. 15 percent of the 2003 graduating class went on to graduate and professional schools.

Expenses for 2003–04   *Application fee:* $30. *State resident tuition:* $4535 full-time, $170.25 per semester hour part-time. *Nonresident tuition:* $10,983 full-time, $385.20 per semester hour part-time. *Mandatory fees:* $573

Indiana University–Purdue University Fort Wayne (continued)
full-time, $19.10 per semester hour part-time. Full-time tuition and fees vary according to course load and student level. Part-time tuition and fees vary according to course load and student level.

Financial Aid Forms of aid include need-based and non-need-based scholarships, athletic grants, and part-time jobs. The average aided 2002–03 undergraduate received an aid package worth $5101. The priority application deadline for financial aid is March 10.

Freshman Admission IPFW requires a high school transcript, SAT I or ACT scores, and TOEFL scores for international students. Rank in upper 50% of high school class is recommended. The application deadline for regular admission is August 1.

Entrance Difficulty IPFW assesses its entrance difficulty level as minimally difficult; moderately difficult for out-of-state applicants; noncompetitive for students graduating high school over 2 years ago. For the fall 2003 freshman class, 97 percent of the applicants were accepted.

For Further Information Contact Ms. Carol Isaacs, Director of Admissions, Indiana University–Purdue University Fort Wayne, 2101 East Coliseum Boulevard, Fort Wayne, IN 46805-1499. *Telephone:* 260-481-6812 or 800-324-4739 (toll-free in-state). *Fax:* 260-481-6880. *E-mail:* ipfwadms@ipfw.edu. *Web site:* http://www.iu.edu/.

INDIANA UNIVERSITY–PURDUE UNIVERSITY INDIANAPOLIS

Indianapolis, Indiana

IUPUI is a coed, public unit of Indiana University System, founded in 1969, offering degrees at the associate, bachelor's, master's, doctoral, and first professional levels and postbachelor's certificates. It has a 511-acre campus in Indianapolis.

Academic Information The faculty has 2,919 members (68% full-time), 65% with terminal degrees. The undergraduate student-faculty ratio is 17:1. The library holds 1 million titles, 14,673 serial subscriptions, and 1,663 audiovisual materials. Special programs include academic remediation, services for learning-disabled students, an honors program, cooperative (work-study) education, study abroad, advanced placement credit, ESL programs, double majors, independent study, distance learning, summer session for credit, part-time degree programs, external degree programs, adult/continuing education programs, internships, and arrangement for off-campus study with 5 members of the Consortium for Urban Education. The most frequently chosen baccalaureate fields are business/marketing, health professions and related sciences, liberal arts/ general studies.

Student Body Statistics The student body totals 29,860, of whom 21,388 are undergraduates (2,826 freshmen). 59 percent are women and 41 percent are men. Students come from 40 states and territories. 98 percent are from Indiana. 2.1 percent are international students.

Expenses for 2003–04 *Application fee:* $45. *State resident tuition:* $5151 full-time, $171.70 per credit hour part-time. *Nonresident tuition:* $14,334 full-time, $477.80 per credit hour part-time. *Mandatory fees:* $552 full-time. Full-time tuition and fees vary according to course load. Part-time tuition varies according to course load. *College room only:* $2554. Room charges vary according to housing facility.

Financial Aid Forms of aid include need-based and non-need-based scholarships, athletic grants, and part-time jobs. The average aided 2003–04 undergraduate received an aid package worth an estimated $6534. The priority application deadline for financial aid is March 1.

Freshman Admission IUPUI requires a high school transcript, SAT I or ACT scores, and TOEFL scores for international students. Portfolio for art program is recommended. An interview is required for some. The application deadline for regular admission is rolling.

Transfer Admission The application deadline for admission is rolling.

Entrance Difficulty IUPUI assesses its entrance difficulty level as moderately difficult. For the fall 2003 freshman class, 77 percent of the applicants were accepted.

For Further Information Contact Michael Donahue, Director of Admissions, Indiana University–Purdue University Indianapolis, 425 North University Boulevard, Cavanaugh Hall Room 129, Indianapolis, IN 46202-5143. *Telephone:* 317-274-4591. *Fax:* 317-278-1862. *E-mail:* apply@iupui.edu. *Web site:* http://www.iu.edu/.

INDIANA UNIVERSITY SOUTH BEND

South Bend, Indiana

IUSB is a coed, public, comprehensive unit of Indiana University System, founded in 1922, offering degrees at the associate, bachelor's, and master's levels and postbachelor's certificates. It has a 73-acre campus in South Bend near Chicago.

Academic Information The faculty has 541 members (49% full-time), 36% with terminal degrees. The undergraduate student-faculty ratio is 14:1. The library holds 300,202 titles, 1,937 serial subscriptions, and 13,001 audiovisual materials. Special programs include an honors program, study abroad, accelerated degree programs, ESL programs, double majors, distance learning, summer session for credit, part-time degree programs, external degree programs, adult/continuing education programs, internships, and arrangement for off-campus study with Bethel College, Saint Mary's College (IN), Holy Cross College, Goshen College. The most frequently chosen baccalaureate fields are business/marketing, education, liberal arts/general studies.

Student Body Statistics The student body totals 7,280, of whom 6,093 are undergraduates (895 freshmen). 63 percent are women and 37 percent are men. Students come from 13 states and territories. 98 percent are from Indiana. 3.1 percent are international students.

Expenses for 2003–04 *Application fee:* $40. *State resident tuition:* $4181 full-time, $122.70 per credit hour part-time. *Nonresident tuition:* $10,773 full-time, $342.45 per credit hour part-time. *Mandatory fees:* $390 full-time. Full-time tuition and fees vary according to course load. Part-time tuition varies according to course load.

Financial Aid Forms of aid include need-based and non-need-based scholarships, athletic grants, and part-time jobs. The average aided 2003–04 undergraduate received an aid package worth an estimated $5320. The priority application deadline for financial aid is March 1.

Freshman Admission IUSB requires a high school transcript, a minimum 2.0 high school GPA, and SAT I or ACT scores. TOEFL scores for international students are recommended. The application deadline for regular admission is July 1.

Transfer Admission The application deadline for admission is June 1.

Entrance Difficulty IUSB assesses its entrance difficulty level as moderately difficult. For the fall 2003 freshman class, 83 percent of the applicants were accepted.

For Further Information Contact Jeff Johnston, Director of Recruitment/Admissions, Indiana University South Bend, 1700 Mishawaka Avenue, Administration Building, Room 169, PO Box 7111, South Bend, IN 46634-7111. *Telephone:* 574-237-4480 or 877-GO-2-IUSB (toll-free). *Fax:* 574-237-4834. *E-mail:* admissio@iusb.edu. *Web site:* http://www.iu.edu/.

INDIANA UNIVERSITY SOUTHEAST

New Albany, Indiana

IU Southeast is a coed, public, comprehensive unit of Indiana University System, founded in 1941, offering degrees at the associate, bachelor's, and master's levels and postbachelor's certificates. It has a 177-acre campus in New Albany near Louisville.

Academic Information The faculty has 446 members (44% full-time), 39% with terminal degrees. The undergraduate student-faculty ratio is 15:1. The library holds 215,429 titles, 962 serial subscriptions, and 9,360 audiovisual materials. Special programs include academic remediation, services for learning-disabled students, study abroad, advanced placement credit, accelerated degree programs, double majors, independent study, summer session for credit, part-time degree programs, external degree programs, adult/continuing education programs, internships, and arrangement for off-campus study with 7 members of the Kentuckiana Metroversity. The most frequently chosen baccalaureate fields are business/marketing, education, liberal arts/general studies.

Student Body Statistics The student body totals 6,408, of whom 5,581 are undergraduates (824 freshmen). 62 percent are women and 38 percent are men. Students come from 3 states and territories. 81 percent are from Indiana. 0.6 percent are international students.

Expenses for 2003–04 *Application fee:* $30. *State resident tuition:* $4118 full-time, $137.25 per credit hour part-time. *Nonresident tuition:* $10,068 full-time, $355.60 per credit hour part-time. *Mandatory fees:* $386 full-time. Full-time tuition and fees vary according to course load. Part-time tuition varies according to course load.

Financial Aid Forms of aid include need-based and non-need-based scholarships, athletic grants, and part-time jobs. The average aided 2003–04 undergraduate received an aid package worth an estimated $5556. The priority application deadline for financial aid is March 1.

Freshman Admission IU Southeast requires a high school transcript, SAT I or ACT scores, and TOEFL scores for international students. An interview is required for some. The application deadline for regular admission is July 15.

Transfer Admission The application deadline for admission is July 1.

Entrance Difficulty IU Southeast assesses its entrance difficulty level as minimally difficult; moderately difficult for out-of-state applicants; moderately difficult for transfers. For the fall 2003 freshman class, 85 percent of the applicants were accepted.

For Further Information Contact Mr. David B. Campbell, Director of Admissions, Indiana University Southeast, University Center Building, Room 100, 4201 Grant Line Road, New Albany, IN 47150. *Telephone:* 812-941-2212 or 800-852-8835 (toll-free in-state). *Fax:* 812-941-2595. *E-mail:* admissions@ius.edu. *Web site:* http://www.iu.edu/.

INDIANA WESLEYAN UNIVERSITY
Marion, Indiana

IWU is a coed, private, Wesleyan, comprehensive institution, founded in 1920, offering degrees at the associate, bachelor's, and master's levels (also offers adult program with significant enrollment not reflected in profile). It has a 132-acre campus in Marion near Indianapolis.

Expenses for 2003–04 *Application fee:* $25. *Comprehensive fee:* $19,900 includes full-time tuition ($14,420) and college room and board ($5480). *College room only:* $2550. Room and board charges vary according to board plan. *Part-time tuition:* $482 per credit hour. Part-time tuition varies according to course load.

For Further Information Contact Ms. Gaytha Holloway, Director of Admissions, Indiana Wesleyan University, 4201 South Washington Street, Marion, IN 46953. *Telephone:* 765-677-2138 or 800-332-6901 (toll-free). *Fax:* 765-677-2333. *E-mail:* admissions@indwes.edu. *Web site:* http://www.indwes.edu/.

INTERNATIONAL BUSINESS COLLEGE
Fort Wayne, Indiana

IBC is a coed, primarily women's, proprietary, primarily two-year college of Bradford Schools, Inc., founded in 1889, offering degrees at the associate and bachelor's levels. It has a 2-acre campus in Fort Wayne.

Expenses for 2003–04 *Application fee:* $50. *Tuition:* $10,100 full-time. *College room only:* $4600.

For Further Information Contact Mr. Steve Kinzer, School Director, International Business College, 5699 Coventry Lane, Fort Wayne, IN 46804. *Telephone:* 219-459-4513 or 800-589-6363 (toll-free). *Fax:* 219-436-1896. *Web site:* http://www.bradfordschools.com/.

ITT TECHNICAL INSTITUTE
Fort Wayne, Indiana

ITT Tech is a coed, proprietary, primarily two-year college of ITT Educational Services, Inc., founded in 1967, offering degrees at the associate and bachelor's levels.

Student Body Statistics The student body is made up of 468 undergraduates.

Expenses for 2003–04 *Application fee:* $100. Total Program Cost varies depending on course of study. Consult school catalog.

Financial Aid Forms of aid include need-based scholarships and part-time jobs. The application deadline for financial aid is continuous.

Freshman Admission ITT Tech requires a high school transcript, an interview, TOEFL scores for international students, and Wonderlic aptitude test. Recommendations are recommended. The application deadline for regular admission is rolling.

Transfer Admission The application deadline for admission is rolling.

Entrance Difficulty ITT Tech assesses its entrance difficulty level as minimally difficult.

For Further Information Contact Ms. Patricia Mozley, Director of Recruitment, ITT Technical Institute, 4919 Coldwater Road, Fort Wayne, IN 46825. *Telephone:* 260-484-4107 Ext. 244 or 800-866-4488 (toll-free). *Fax:* 260-484-0860. *Web site:* http://www.itt-tech.edu/.

ITT TECHNICAL INSTITUTE
Indianapolis, Indiana

ITT Tech is a coed, proprietary, primarily two-year college of ITT Educational Services, Inc., founded in 1966, offering degrees at the associate and bachelor's levels. It has a 10-acre campus in Indianapolis.

Academic Information Special programs include distance learning.

Student Body Statistics The student body is made up of 899 undergraduates.

Expenses for 2003–04 *Application fee:* $100. Total Program Cost varies depending on course of study. Consult school catalog.

Financial Aid Forms of aid include need-based scholarships and part-time jobs. The application deadline for financial aid is continuous.

Freshman Admission ITT Tech requires a high school transcript, an interview, and Wonderlic aptitude test. Recommendations are recommended. The application deadline for regular admission is rolling.

Transfer Admission The application deadline for admission is rolling.

Entrance Difficulty ITT Tech assesses its entrance difficulty level as minimally difficult.

For Further Information Contact Mr. Byron Ratclife, Director of Recruitment, ITT Technical Institute, 9511 Angola Court, Indianapolis, IN 46268. *Telephone:* 317-875-8640 or 800-937-4488 (toll-free). *Fax:* 317-875-8641. *Web site:* http://www.itt-tech.edu/.

ITT TECHNICAL INSTITUTE
Newburgh, Indiana

ITT Tech is a coed, proprietary, primarily two-year college of ITT Educational Services, Inc., founded in 1966, offering degrees at the associate and bachelor's levels.

Student Body Statistics The student body is made up of 400 undergraduates.

Expenses for 2003–04 *Application fee:* $100. Total Program Cost varies depending on course of study. Consult school catalog.

Financial Aid Forms of aid include need-based scholarships and part-time jobs. The application deadline for financial aid is continuous.

Freshman Admission ITT Tech requires a high school transcript, an interview, and Wonderlic aptitude test. Recommendations and TOEFL scores for international students are recommended. The application deadline for regular admission is rolling.

Transfer Admission The application deadline for admission is rolling.

ITT Technical Institute (continued)
Entrance Difficulty ITT Tech assesses its entrance difficulty level as minimally difficult.

For Further Information Contact Mr. Jim Smolinski, Director of Recruitment, ITT Technical Institute, 10999 Stahl Road, Newburgh, IN 47630. *Telephone:* 812-858-1600 or 800-832-4488 (toll-free in-state). *Fax:* 812-858-0646. *Web site:* http://www.itt-tech.edu/.

LUTHERAN COLLEGE OF HEALTH PROFESSIONS

See University of Saint Francis

MANCHESTER COLLEGE

North Manchester, Indiana

MC is a coed, private, comprehensive institution, founded in 1889, affiliated with the Church of the Brethren, offering degrees at the associate, bachelor's, and master's levels. It has a 125-acre campus in North Manchester.

Academic Information The faculty has 92 members (74% full-time), 72% with terminal degrees. The undergraduate student-faculty ratio is 14:1. The library holds 172,822 titles, 733 serial subscriptions, and 5,188 audiovisual materials. Special programs include services for learning-disabled students, an honors program, study abroad, advanced placement credit, double majors, independent study, self-designed majors, summer session for credit, part-time degree programs, adult/continuing education programs, internships, and arrangement for off-campus study. The most frequently chosen baccalaureate fields are business/marketing, education, social sciences and history.
Student Body Statistics The student body totals 1,170, of whom 1,153 are undergraduates (335 freshmen). 55 percent are women and 45 percent are men. Students come from 23 states and territories and 29 other countries. 90 percent are from Indiana. 7.3 percent are international students. 24 percent of the 2003 graduating class went on to graduate and professional schools.
Expenses for 2004–05 *Application fee:* $20. *Comprehensive fee:* $24,710 includes full-time tuition ($17,950), mandatory fees ($110), and college room and board ($6650). *College room only:* $4150. Room and board charges vary according to board plan and housing facility. *Part-time tuition:* $600 per credit hour.
Financial Aid Forms of aid include need-based and non-need-based scholarships and part-time jobs. The average aided 2003–04 undergraduate received an aid package worth an estimated $16,033. The application deadline for financial aid is continuous.
Freshman Admission MC requires a high school transcript, 1 recommendation, rank in upper 50% of high school class, SAT I or ACT scores, and TOEFL scores for international students. A minimum 2.3 high school GPA and an interview are recommended. An essay, a minimum 3.0 high school GPA, and an interview are required for some. The application deadline for regular admission is rolling.
Transfer Admission The application deadline for admission is rolling.
Entrance Difficulty MC assesses its entrance difficulty level as moderately difficult. For the fall 2003 freshman class, 79 percent of the applicants were accepted.

For Further Information Contact Ms. Jolane Rohr, Director of Admissions, Manchester College, 604 East College Avenue, North Manchester, IN 46962. *Telephone:* 260-982-5055 or 800-852-3648 (toll-free). *Fax:* 260-982-5239. *E-mail:* admitinfo@manchester.edu. *Web site:* http://www.manchester.edu/.

See page 308 for a narrative description.

MARIAN COLLEGE

Indianapolis, Indiana

Marian is a coed, private, Roman Catholic, comprehensive institution, founded in 1851, offering degrees at the associate, bachelor's, and master's levels. It has a 114-acre campus in Indianapolis.

Academic Information The faculty has 132 members (49% full-time). The undergraduate student-faculty ratio is 12:1. The library holds 132,000 titles, 300 serial subscriptions, and 100 audiovisual materials. Special programs include academic remediation, services for learning-disabled students, an honors program, cooperative (work-study) education, study abroad, advanced placement credit, accelerated degree programs, double majors, independent study, summer session for credit, part-time degree programs (daytime, evenings, weekends, summer), adult/continuing education programs, internships, and arrangement for off-campus study with Franklin College of Indiana, Indiana University–Purdue University at Indianapolis, University of Indianapolis, Christian Theological Seminary, Butler University. The most frequently chosen baccalaureate fields are business/marketing, education, health professions and related sciences.
Student Body Statistics The student body totals 1,561, of whom 1,547 are undergraduates (471 freshmen). 74 percent are women and 26 percent are men. Students come from 23 states and territories and 16 other countries. 90 percent are from Indiana. 1.6 percent are international students. 12 percent of the 2003 graduating class went on to graduate and professional schools.
Expenses for 2003–04 *Application fee:* $20. *Comprehensive fee:* $23,260 includes full-time tuition ($16,800), mandatory fees ($660), and college room and board ($5800). Room and board charges vary according to board plan and housing facility. *Part-time tuition:* $735 per credit. Part-time tuition varies according to class time and course load.
Financial Aid Forms of aid include need-based and non-need-based scholarships, athletic grants, and part-time jobs. The average aided 2003–04 undergraduate received an aid package worth an estimated $13,717. The priority application deadline for financial aid is March 1.
Freshman Admission Marian requires a high school transcript, a minimum 2.00 high school GPA, SAT I or ACT scores, and TOEFL scores for international students. An essay, recommendations, and an interview are required for some. The application deadline for regular admission is August 15.
Transfer Admission The application deadline for admission is August 1.
Entrance Difficulty Marian assesses its entrance difficulty level as moderately difficult. For the fall 2003 freshman class, 75 percent of the applicants were accepted.

For Further Information Contact Mrs. Karen Full, Director of Admission, Marian College, 3200 Cold Spring Road, Indianapolis, IN 46222-1997. *Telephone:* 317-955-6300 or 800-772-7264 (toll-free in-state). *Web site:* http://www.marian.edu/.

MARTIN UNIVERSITY

Indianapolis, Indiana

Martin University is a coed, private, comprehensive institution, founded in 1977, offering degrees at the bachelor's and master's levels. It has a 5-acre campus in Indianapolis.

Academic Information The faculty has 38 members (84% full-time). The undergraduate student-faculty ratio is 20:1. Special programs include academic remediation, an honors program, advanced placement credit, accelerated degree programs, double majors, independent study, self-designed majors, summer session for credit, part-time degree programs (daytime, evenings, weekends, summer), adult/continuing education programs, internships, and arrangement for off-campus study with Consortium for Urban Education (CUE).
Student Body Statistics The student body totals 571, of whom 465 are undergraduates (49 freshmen). 76 percent are women and 24 percent are men. Students come from 1 state or territory and 6 other countries. 1.3 percent are international students.
Expenses for 2003–04 *Application fee:* $25. *Tuition:* $10,200 full-time, $340 per credit part-time. *Mandatory fees:* $120 full-time, $60 per term part-time.

Financial Aid Forms of aid include need-based scholarships and part-time jobs. The average aided 2003–04 undergraduate received an aid package worth an estimated $8779. The application deadline for financial aid is continuous.

Freshman Admission Martin University requires an essay, a high school transcript, an interview, writing sample, and TOEFL scores for international students. Wonderlic aptitude test, Wide Range Achievement Test is required for some. The application deadline for regular admission is rolling.

Transfer Admission The application deadline for admission is rolling.

Entrance Difficulty Martin University has an open admission policy.

For Further Information Contact Ms. Brenda Shaheed, Director of Enrollment Management, Martin University, PO Box 18567, 2171 Avondale Place, Indianapolis, IN 46218-3867. *Telephone:* 317-543-3237. *Fax:* 317-543-4790. *Web site:* http://www.martin.edu/.

MID-AMERICA COLLEGE OF FUNERAL SERVICE
Jeffersonville, Indiana

Mid-America College of Funeral Service is a coed, primarily men's, private, primarily two-year college, founded in 1905, offering degrees at the associate and bachelor's levels in funeral service. It has a 3-acre campus in Jeffersonville near Louisville.

For Further Information Contact Mr. Richard Nelson, Dean of Students, Mid-America College of Funeral Service, 3111 Hamburg Pike, Jeffersonville, IN 47130-9630. *Telephone:* 812-288-8878 or 800-221-6158 (toll-free). *E-mail:* macfs@mindspring.com. *Web site:* http://www.mid-america.edu/.

OAKLAND CITY UNIVERSITY
Oakland City, Indiana

OCU is a coed, private, General Baptist, comprehensive institution, founded in 1885, offering degrees at the associate, bachelor's, master's, doctoral, and first professional levels. It has a 20-acre campus in Oakland City.

Academic Information The faculty has 168 members (26% full-time), 20% with terminal degrees. The undergraduate student-faculty ratio is 17:1. The library holds 75,000 titles and 350 serial subscriptions. Special programs include academic remediation, services for learning-disabled students, advanced placement credit, accelerated degree programs, summer session for credit, part-time degree programs (daytime, evenings, summer), external degree programs, and adult/continuing education programs. The most frequently chosen baccalaureate fields are business/marketing, education, social sciences and history.

Student Body Statistics The student body totals 1,753, of whom 1,486 are undergraduates (319 freshmen). 53 percent are women and 47 percent are men. Students come from 5 states and territories. 77 percent are from Indiana. 0.1 percent are international students.

Expenses for 2004–05 *Application fee:* $35. *Comprehensive fee:* $17,720 includes full-time tuition ($12,600), mandatory fees ($320), and college room and board ($4800). *College room only:* $1550. Full-time tuition and fees vary according to location and program. Room and board charges vary according to housing facility. *Part-time tuition:* $420 per hour. Part-time tuition varies according to location and program.

Financial Aid Forms of aid include need-based and non-need-based scholarships and part-time jobs. The priority application deadline for financial aid is March 10.

Freshman Admission OCU requires an essay, a high school transcript, a minimum 2.0 high school GPA, 1 recommendation, SAT I or ACT scores, and TOEFL scores for international students. An interview is recommended. The application deadline for regular admission is rolling.

Entrance Difficulty OCU assesses its entrance difficulty level as minimally difficult. For the fall 2003 freshman class, 99 percent of the applicants were accepted.

For Further Information Contact Mr. Buddy Harris, Director of Admissions, Oakland City University, 143 North Lucretia Street, Oakland City, IN 47660-1099. *Telephone:* 812-749-1222 or 800-737-5125 (toll-free). *Fax:* 812-749-1233. *Web site:* http://www.oak.edu/.

PROFESSIONAL CAREERS INSTITUTE
Indianapolis, Indiana

For Information Write to Professional Careers Institute, Indianapolis, IN 46278.

PURDUE UNIVERSITY
West Lafayette, Indiana

Purdue is a coed, public unit of Purdue University System, founded in 1869, offering degrees at the associate, bachelor's, master's, doctoral, and first professional levels. It has a 1,579-acre campus in West Lafayette near Indianapolis.

Academic Information The faculty has 1,977 members (97% full-time), 98% with terminal degrees. The undergraduate student-faculty ratio is 16:1. The library holds 1 million titles, 18,374 serial subscriptions, and 12,733 audiovisual materials. Special programs include services for learning-disabled students, an honors program, cooperative (work-study) education, study abroad, advanced placement credit, Freshman Honors College, double majors, independent study, distance learning, summer session for credit, part-time degree programs, adult/continuing education programs, and internships. The most frequently chosen baccalaureate fields are business/marketing, education, engineering/engineering technologies.

Student Body Statistics The student body totals 38,847, of whom 30,851 are undergraduates (6,371 freshmen). 41 percent are women and 59 percent are men. Students come from 51 states and territories and 96 other countries. 75 percent are from Indiana. 6.4 percent are international students.

Expenses for 2003–04 *Application fee:* $30. *State resident tuition:* $5860 full-time, $210 per credit part-time. *Nonresident tuition:* $17,480 full-time, $600 per credit part-time. Full-time tuition varies according to course load and program. Part-time tuition varies according to course load. *College room and board:* $6700. Room and board charges vary according to board plan and housing facility.

Financial Aid Forms of aid include need-based and non-need-based scholarships, athletic grants, and part-time jobs. The average aided 2003–04 undergraduate received an aid package worth an estimated $8796. The priority application deadline for financial aid is March 1.

Freshman Admission Purdue requires a high school transcript, SAT I or ACT scores, and TOEFL scores for international students. The application deadline for regular admission is March 1.

Transfer Admission The application deadline for admission is rolling.

Entrance Difficulty Purdue assesses its entrance difficulty level as moderately difficult; most difficult for engineering, aviation flight, nursing, veterinary technology, computer related, health related programs. For the fall 2003 freshman class, 79 percent of the applicants were accepted.

For Further Information Contact Dr. Douglas L. Christiansen, Director of Admissions, Purdue University, 1080 Schleman Hall, West Lafayette, IN 47907-1080. *Telephone:* 765-494-1776. *Fax:* 765-494-0544. *E-mail:* admissions@purdue.edu. *Web site:* http://www.purdue.edu/.

Indiana

PURDUE UNIVERSITY CALUMET

Hammond, Indiana

Purdue Cal is a coed, public, comprehensive unit of Purdue University System, founded in 1951, offering degrees at the associate, bachelor's, and master's levels and postbachelor's certificates. It has a 167-acre campus in Hammond near Chicago.

Academic Information The faculty has 295 members (97% full-time), 100% with terminal degrees. The undergraduate student-faculty ratio is 21:1. The library holds 215,830 titles and 1,736 serial subscriptions. Special programs include academic remediation, services for learning-disabled students, an honors program, cooperative (work-study) education, advanced placement credit, summer session for credit, part-time degree programs (daytime, evenings, weekends, summer), adult/continuing education programs, and internships. The most frequently chosen baccalaureate fields are business/marketing, engineering/engineering technologies, social sciences and history.

Student Body Statistics The student body totals 9,128, of whom 8,196 are undergraduates (1,198 freshmen). 56 percent are women and 44 percent are men. 0.8 percent are international students.

Expenses for 2004–05 *State resident tuition:* $4448 full-time, $148.25 per credit hour part-time. *Nonresident tuition:* $9878 full-time, $346.75 per credit hour part-time. *Mandatory fees:* $378 full-time, $13 per credit hour part-time. Part-time tuition and fees vary according to course load.

Financial Aid Forms of aid include need-based and non-need-based scholarships, athletic grants, and part-time jobs. The average aided 2003–04 undergraduate received an aid package worth an estimated $5324. The priority application deadline for financial aid is March 1.

Freshman Admission Purdue Cal requires a high school transcript. SAT I or ACT scores are required for some. The application deadline for regular admission is rolling.

Transfer Admission The application deadline for admission is rolling.

Entrance Difficulty Purdue Cal has an open admission policy.

For Further Information Contact Mr. Paul McGuinness, Director of Admissions, Purdue University Calumet, 173rd and Woodmar Avenue, Hammond, IN 46323-2094. *Telephone:* 219-989-2213 or 800-447-8738 (toll-free in-state). *Fax:* 219-989-2775. *E-mail:* adms@calumet.purdue.edu. *Web site:* http://www.calumet.purdue.edu/.

PURDUE UNIVERSITY NORTH CENTRAL

Westville, Indiana

Purdue University North Central is a coed, public, comprehensive unit of Purdue University System, founded in 1967, offering degrees at the associate, bachelor's, and master's levels. It has a 305-acre campus in Westville near Chicago.

Academic Information The faculty has 244 members (34% full-time), 27% with terminal degrees. The undergraduate student-faculty ratio is 18:1. The library holds 87,675 titles, 403 serial subscriptions, and 602 audiovisual materials. Special programs include academic remediation, services for learning-disabled students, an honors program, cooperative (work-study) education, study abroad, advanced placement credit, double majors, distance learning, self-designed majors, summer session for credit, part-time degree programs (daytime, evenings, summer), adult/continuing education programs, and internships. The most frequently chosen baccalaureate fields are education, business/marketing, liberal arts/general studies.

Student Body Statistics The student body totals 3,467, of whom 3,443 are undergraduates (617 freshmen). 60 percent are women and 40 percent are men. Students come from 5 states and territories. 99 percent are from Indiana. 0.2 percent are international students.

Expenses for 2003–04 *State resident tuition:* $4344 full-time, $145 per credit hour part-time. *Nonresident tuition:* $10,503 full-time, $350 per credit hour part-time. *Mandatory fees:* $368 full-time, $12 per credit hour part-time. Full-time tuition and fees vary according to course load, location, and program. Part-time tuition and fees vary according to course load, location, and program.

Financial Aid Forms of aid include need-based and non-need-based scholarships and part-time jobs. The average aided 2002–03 undergraduate received an aid package worth $4893. The priority application deadline for financial aid is March 1.

Freshman Admission Purdue University North Central requires a high school transcript and TOEFL scores for international students. SAT I scores and ACT scores are recommended. An essay, a minimum 2.0 high school GPA, an interview, and SAT I or ACT scores are required for some. The application deadline for regular admission is August 6.

Transfer Admission The application deadline for admission is August 1.

Entrance Difficulty Purdue University North Central assesses its entrance difficulty level as minimally difficult; moderately difficult for engineering, nursing programs. For the fall 2003 freshman class, 83 percent of the applicants were accepted.

For Further Information Contact Ms. Cathy Buckman, Director of Admissions, Purdue University North Central, 1401 South U.S. Highway 421, Westville, IN 46391. *Telephone:* 219-785-5458 or 800-872-1231 (toll-free in-state). *Fax:* 219-785-5538. *E-mail:* cbuckman@purduenc.edu. *Web site:* http://www.pnc.edu/.

ROSE-HULMAN INSTITUTE OF TECHNOLOGY

Terre Haute, Indiana

Rose-Hulman is a coed, primarily men's, private, comprehensive institution, founded in 1874, offering degrees at the bachelor's and master's levels. It has a 200-acre campus in Terre Haute near Indianapolis.

Academic Information The faculty has 145 members (96% full-time), 95% with terminal degrees. The undergraduate student-faculty ratio is 13:1. The library holds 77,348 titles, 280 serial subscriptions, and 493 audiovisual materials. Special programs include services for learning-disabled students, an honors program, cooperative (work-study) education, study abroad, advanced placement credit, accelerated degree programs, double majors, independent study, summer session for credit, adult/continuing education programs, and arrangement for off-campus study with Indiana State University, St. Mary-of-the-Woods College. The most frequently chosen baccalaureate fields are computer/information sciences, engineering/engineering technologies, physical sciences.

Student Body Statistics The student body totals 1,864, of whom 1,721 are undergraduates (490 freshmen). 18 percent are women and 82 percent are men. Students come from 49 states and territories and 9 other countries. 48 percent are from Indiana. 0.9 percent are international students. 18 percent of the 2003 graduating class went on to graduate and professional schools.

Expenses for 2003–04 *Application fee:* $40. *One-time mandatory fee:* $3125. *Comprehensive fee:* $31,425 includes full-time tuition ($24,255), mandatory fees ($450), and college room and board ($6720). *College room only:* $3840. Full-time tuition and fees vary according to course load and student level. Room and board charges vary according to board plan. *Part-time tuition:* $696 per credit. Part-time tuition varies according to course load.

Financial Aid Forms of aid include need-based scholarships and part-time jobs. The average aided 2003–04 undergraduate received an aid package worth an estimated $15,261. The priority application deadline for financial aid is March 1.

Freshman Admission Rose-Hulman requires a high school transcript, 1 recommendation, SAT I or ACT scores, and TOEFL scores for international students. An essay and an interview are recommended. The application deadline for regular admission is March 1.

Entrance Difficulty Rose-Hulman assesses its entrance difficulty level as very difficult. For the fall 2003 freshman class, 71 percent of the applicants were accepted.

For Further Information Contact Mr. Charles G. Howard, Dean of Admissions/Vice President, Rose-Hulman Institute of Technology, 5500 Wabash Avenue, CM 1, Terre Haute, IN 47803-3920. *Telephone:* 812-877-8213 or 800-248-7448 (toll-free). *Fax:* 812-877-8941. *E-mail:* admis.ofc@rose-hulman.edu. *Web site:* http://www.rose-hulman.edu/.

SAINT FRANCIS COLLEGE

See University of Saint Francis

SAINT JOSEPH'S COLLEGE

Rensselaer, Indiana

Saint Joseph's is a coed, private, Roman Catholic, comprehensive institution, founded in 1889, offering degrees at the associate, bachelor's, and master's levels. It has a 180-acre campus in Rensselaer near Chicago.

Academic Information The faculty has 85 members (64% full-time), 72% with terminal degrees. The undergraduate student-faculty ratio is 14:1. The library holds 157,481 titles, 498 serial subscriptions, and 22,416 audiovisual materials. Special programs include academic remediation, services for learning-disabled students, an honors program, study abroad, advanced placement credit, accelerated degree programs, double majors, independent study, self-designed majors, summer session for credit, part-time degree programs (daytime), and internships. The most frequently chosen baccalaureate fields are business/marketing, education, protective services/public administration.

Student Body Statistics The student body is made up of 998 undergraduates (259 freshmen). 58 percent are women and 42 percent are men. Students come from 20 states and territories and 3 other countries. 71 percent are from Indiana. 0.3 percent are international students. 18 percent of the 2003 graduating class went on to graduate and professional schools.

Expenses for 2004–05 *Application fee:* $25. *Comprehensive fee:* $25,460 includes full-time tuition ($19,000), mandatory fees ($160), and college room and board ($6300). Room and board charges vary according to housing facility. *Part-time tuition:* $640 per credit.

Financial Aid Forms of aid include need-based and non-need-based scholarships, athletic grants, and part-time jobs. The average aided 2002–03 undergraduate received an aid package worth $13,000. The priority application deadline for financial aid is March 1.

Freshman Admission Saint Joseph's requires a high school transcript, a minimum 2.0 high school GPA, SAT I or ACT scores, and TOEFL scores for international students. An essay and recommendations are recommended. An interview is required for some. The application deadline for regular admission is rolling and for early decision it is October 1.

Transfer Admission The application deadline for admission is rolling.

Entrance Difficulty Saint Joseph's assesses its entrance difficulty level as moderately difficult. For the fall 2003 freshman class, 76 percent of the applicants were accepted.

For Further Information Contact Mr. Jeremy Spencer, Director of Admissions, Saint Joseph's College, PO Box 815, Rensselaer, IN 47978-0850. *Telephone:* 219-866-6170 or 800-447-8781 (toll-free out-of-state). *Fax:* 219-866-6122. *E-mail:* admissions@saintjoe.edu. *Web site:* http://www.saintjoe.edu/.

SAINT MARY-OF-THE-WOODS COLLEGE

Saint Mary-of-the-Woods, Indiana

The Woods is a women's, private, Roman Catholic, comprehensive institution, founded in 1840, offering degrees at the associate, bachelor's, and master's levels and post-master's and postbachelor's certificates (also offers external degree program with significant enrollment reflected in profile). It has a 67-acre campus in Saint Mary-of-the-Woods near Indianapolis.

Academic Information The faculty has 67 members (97% full-time), 64% with terminal degrees. The undergraduate student-faculty ratio is 12:1. The library holds 152,162 titles, 301 serial subscriptions, and 522 audiovisual materials. Special programs include academic remediation, study abroad, advanced placement credit, accelerated degree programs, double majors, independent study, distance learning, self-designed majors, summer session for credit, part-time degree programs (evenings, weekends, summer), external degree programs, adult/continuing education programs, internships, and arrangement for off-campus study with Indiana State

University, Rose-Hulman Institute of Technology, DePauw University, Wabash College. The most frequently chosen baccalaureate fields are business/marketing, education, psychology.

Student Body Statistics The student body totals 1,687, of whom 1,565 are undergraduates (282 freshmen). Students come from 26 states and territories and 5 other countries. 70 percent are from Indiana. 0.2 percent are international students. 25 percent of the 2003 graduating class went on to graduate and professional schools.

Expenses for 2003–04 *Application fee:* $30. *Comprehensive fee:* $23,280 includes full-time tuition ($16,530), mandatory fees ($500), and college room and board ($6250). *College room only:* $2440. *Part-time tuition:* $319 per hour. *Part-time mandatory fees:* $25 per term. Part-time tuition and fees vary according to course load and program.

Financial Aid Forms of aid include need-based and non-need-based scholarships and part-time jobs. The application deadline for financial aid is continuous.

Freshman Admission The Woods requires a minimum 2.0 high school GPA, 1 recommendation, and TOEFL scores for international students. An essay, a high school transcript, an interview, and SAT I or ACT scores are required for some. The application deadline for regular admission is August 15.

Transfer Admission The application deadline for admission is August 15.

Entrance Difficulty The Woods assesses its entrance difficulty level as moderately difficult. For the fall 2003 freshman class, 78 percent of the applicants were accepted.

For Further Information Contact Mr. James Malley, Director of Admission, Saint Mary-of-the-Woods College, Guerin Hall, Saint Mary-of-the-Woods, IN 47876. *Telephone:* 812-535-5106 or 800-926-SMWC (toll-free). *Fax:* 812-535-4900. *E-mail:* smwcadms@smwc.edu. *Web site:* http://www.smwc.edu/.

SAINT MARY'S COLLEGE

Notre Dame, Indiana

Saint Mary's is a women's, private, Roman Catholic, four-year college, founded in 1844, offering degrees at the bachelor's level. It has a 275-acre campus in Notre Dame.

Academic Information The faculty has 186 members (61% full-time). The student-faculty ratio is 11:1. The library holds 210,812 titles, 776 serial subscriptions, and 2,471 audiovisual materials. Special programs include academic remediation, services for learning-disabled students, cooperative (work-study) education, study abroad, advanced placement credit, accelerated degree programs, double majors, independent study, self-designed majors, summer session for credit, part-time degree programs (daytime), internships, and arrangement for off-campus study with University of Notre Dame, members of the Northern Indiana Consortium for Education. The most frequently chosen baccalaureate fields are communications/communication technologies, business/marketing, social sciences and history.

Student Body Statistics The student body is made up of 1,475 undergraduates (402 freshmen). Students come from 47 states and territories and 12 other countries. 27 percent are from Indiana. 1 percent are international students. 22 percent of the 2003 graduating class went on to graduate and professional schools.

Expenses for 2003–04 *Application fee:* $30. *Comprehensive fee:* $29,263 includes full-time tuition ($21,624), mandatory fees ($350), and college room and board ($7289). Full-time tuition and fees vary according to location. Room and board charges vary according to housing facility. *Part-time tuition:* $855 per semester hour.

Financial Aid Forms of aid include need-based and non-need-based scholarships and part-time jobs. The average aided 2003–04 undergraduate received an aid package worth an estimated $17,358. The priority application deadline for financial aid is March 1.

Freshman Admission Saint Mary's requires an essay, a high school transcript, 1 recommendation, SAT I or ACT scores, and TOEFL scores for international students. An interview is recommended. The application deadline for regular admission is March 1 and for early decision it is November 15.

Transfer Admission The application deadline for admission is rolling.

Saint Mary's College (continued)

Entrance Difficulty Saint Mary's assesses its entrance difficulty level as moderately difficult. For the fall 2003 freshman class, 82 percent of the applicants were accepted.

For Further Information Contact Ms. Mary Pat Nolan, Director of Admission, Saint Mary's College, Notre Dame, IN 46556. *Telephone:* 574-284-4587 or 800-551-7621 (toll-free). *Fax:* 574-284-4713. *E-mail:* admission@saintmarys.edu. *Web site:* http://www.saintmarys.edu/.

See page 336 for a narrative description.

TAYLOR UNIVERSITY
Upland, Indiana

Taylor is a coed, private, interdenominational, comprehensive institution, founded in 1846, offering degrees at the associate, bachelor's, and master's levels. It has a 250-acre campus in Upland near Indianapolis.

Academic Information The faculty has 162 members (73% full-time), 60% with terminal degrees. The undergraduate student-faculty ratio is 14:1. The library holds 193,343 titles, 902 serial subscriptions, and 6,653 audiovisual materials. Special programs include academic remediation, services for learning-disabled students, an honors program, cooperative (work-study) education, study abroad, advanced placement credit, double majors, independent study, distance learning, self-designed majors, summer session for credit, part-time degree programs, internships, and arrangement for off-campus study with members of the Christian College Coalition and the Christian College Consortium, Bowling Green University, Trinity Christian College. The most frequently chosen baccalaureate fields are business/marketing, education, philosophy, religion, and theology.
Student Body Statistics The student body totals 1,843, of whom 1,834 are undergraduates (470 freshmen). 53 percent are women and 47 percent are men. Students come from 47 states and territories. 33 percent are from Indiana. 0.9 percent are international students. 13 percent of the 2003 graduating class went on to graduate and professional schools.
Expenses for 2003–04 *Application fee:* $25. *Comprehensive fee:* $23,820 includes full-time tuition ($18,306), mandatory fees ($222), and college room and board ($5292). *College room only:* $2572. Room and board charges vary according to housing facility. *Part-time tuition:* $655 per credit. *Part-time mandatory fees:* $30 per term.
Financial Aid Forms of aid include need-based and non-need-based scholarships, athletic grants, and part-time jobs. The average aided 2003–04 undergraduate received an aid package worth an estimated $13,351. The application deadline for financial aid is March 10.
Freshman Admission Taylor requires an essay, a high school transcript, 2 recommendations, an interview, SAT I or ACT scores, and TOEFL scores for international students. A minimum 2.8 high school GPA is recommended. The application deadline for regular admission is January 15 and for early action it is December 1.
Transfer Admission The application deadline for admission is rolling.
Entrance Difficulty Taylor assesses its entrance difficulty level as very difficult. For the fall 2003 freshman class, 84 percent of the applicants were accepted.

For Further Information Contact Mr. Stephen R. Mortland, Director of Admissions, Taylor University, 236 West Reade Avenue, Upland, IN 46989-1001. *Telephone:* 765-998-5134 or 800-882-3456 (toll-free). *Fax:* 765-998-4925. *E-mail:* admissions_u@tayloru.edu. *Web site:* http://www.tayloru.edu/.

TAYLOR UNIVERSITY FORT WAYNE
Fort Wayne, Indiana

Taylor Fort Wayne is a coed, private, interdenominational, comprehensive unit of Taylor University, founded in 1992, offering degrees at the associate, bachelor's, and master's levels and postbachelor's certificates. It has a 32-acre campus in Fort Wayne.

Academic Information The faculty has 52 members (50% full-time), 46% with terminal degrees. The undergraduate student-faculty ratio is 14:1. The library holds 78,662 titles, 670 serial subscriptions, and 4,699 audiovisual materials. Special programs include academic remediation, services for learning-disabled students, cooperative (work-study) education, study abroad, advanced placement credit, accelerated degree programs, double majors, independent study, distance learning, self-designed majors, summer session for credit, part-time degree programs (daytime, evenings, weekends, summer), internships, and arrangement for off-campus study with Christian College Coalition, Christian College Consortium, Wesleyan Urban Coalition. The most frequently chosen baccalaureate fields are philosophy, religion, and theology, communications/communication technologies, protective services/public administration.
Student Body Statistics The student body totals 653, of whom 637 are undergraduates (119 freshmen). 62 percent are women and 38 percent are men. Students come from 24 states and territories and 3 other countries. 77 percent are from Indiana. 0.8 percent are international students. 20 percent of the 2003 graduating class went on to graduate and professional schools.
Expenses for 2003–04 *Application fee:* $20. *Comprehensive fee:* $20,584 includes full-time tuition ($15,790), mandatory fees ($114), and college room and board ($4680). *College room only:* $2040. Room and board charges vary according to board plan. *Part-time tuition:* $180 per hour. *Part-time mandatory fees:* $25 per hour. Part-time tuition and fees vary according to course load.
Financial Aid Forms of aid include need-based and non-need-based scholarships, athletic grants, and part-time jobs. The average aided 2002–03 undergraduate received an aid package worth $15,298. The priority application deadline for financial aid is March 10.
Freshman Admission Taylor Fort Wayne requires an essay, a high school transcript, a minimum 2.0 high school GPA, 2 recommendations, SAT I or ACT scores, and TOEFL scores for international students. A minimum 3.0 high school GPA and an interview are recommended. The application deadline for regular admission is rolling.
Transfer Admission The application deadline for admission is rolling.
Entrance Difficulty Taylor Fort Wayne assesses its entrance difficulty level as moderately difficult. For the fall 2003 freshman class, 83 percent of the applicants were accepted.

For Further Information Contact Mr. Leo Gonot, Associate Vice President for Enrollment Management, Taylor University Fort Wayne, 1025 West Rudisill Boulevard, Fort Wayne, IN 46807-2197. *Telephone:* 219-744-8689 or 800-233-3922 (toll-free). *Fax:* 260-744-8660. *E-mail:* admissions_f@tayloru.edu. *Web site:* http://www.tayloru.edu/fw/.

TRI-STATE UNIVERSITY
Angola, Indiana

Tri-State is a coed, private, comprehensive institution, founded in 1884, offering degrees at the associate, bachelor's, and master's levels. It has a 400-acre campus in Angola.

Academic Information The faculty has 98 members (69% full-time), 46% with terminal degrees. The undergraduate student-faculty ratio is 15:1. The library holds 82,474 titles, 336 serial subscriptions, and 625 audiovisual materials. Special programs include academic remediation, cooperative (work-study) education, study abroad, advanced placement credit, double majors, distance learning, summer session for credit, part-time degree programs (daytime, evenings, summer), adult/continuing education programs, and internships. The most frequently chosen baccalaureate fields are business/marketing, education, engineering/engineering technologies.
Student Body Statistics The student body totals 1,192, of whom 1,186 are undergraduates (335 freshmen). 36 percent are women and 64 percent are men. Students come from 23 states and territories and 15 other countries. 60 percent are from Indiana. 1.9 percent are international students. 25 percent of the 2003 graduating class went on to graduate and professional schools.
Expenses for 2003–04 *Application fee:* $20. *Comprehensive fee:* $23,600 includes full-time tuition ($18,000) and college room and board ($5600). *Part-time tuition:* $562 per semester hour.

Financial Aid Forms of aid include need-based and non-need-based scholarships, athletic grants, and part-time jobs. The average aided 2003–04 undergraduate received an aid package worth an estimated $12,100. The application deadline for financial aid is March 10.

Freshman Admission Tri-State requires a high school transcript, a minimum 2.0 high school GPA, and SAT I or ACT scores. Recommendations, an interview, and TOEFL scores for international students are recommended. The application deadline for regular admission is June 1.

Transfer Admission The application deadline for admission is August 1.

Entrance Difficulty Tri-State assesses its entrance difficulty level as moderately difficult. For the fall 2003 freshman class, 72 percent of the applicants were accepted.

For Further Information Contact Ms. Sara Yarian, Admissions Officer, Tri-State University, 1 University Avenue, Angola, IN 46703. *Telephone:* 260-665-4365 or 800-347-4TSU (toll-free). *Fax:* 260-665-4578. *E-mail:* admit@tristate.edu. *Web site:* http://www.tristate.edu/.

UNIVERSITY OF EVANSVILLE

Evansville, Indiana

UE is a coed, private, comprehensive institution, founded in 1854, affiliated with the United Methodist Church, offering degrees at the associate, bachelor's, and master's levels. It has a 75-acre campus in Evansville.

Academic Information The faculty has 232 members (72% full-time). The undergraduate student-faculty ratio is 13:1. The library holds 275,980 titles, 1,320 serial subscriptions, and 10,094 audiovisual materials. Special programs include services for learning-disabled students, an honors program, cooperative (work-study) education, study abroad, advanced placement credit, accelerated degree programs, Freshman Honors College, ESL programs, double majors, independent study, distance learning, self-designed majors, summer session for credit, part-time degree programs (daytime), external degree programs, adult/continuing education programs, and internships. The most frequently chosen baccalaureate fields are business/marketing, liberal arts/general studies, visual/performing arts.

Student Body Statistics The student body totals 2,650, of whom 2,566 are undergraduates (663 freshmen). 62 percent are women and 38 percent are men. Students come from 44 states and territories and 38 other countries. 66 percent are from Indiana. 5.6 percent are international students. 27 percent of the 2003 graduating class went on to graduate and professional schools.

Expenses for 2003–04 *Application fee:* $35. *Comprehensive fee:* $24,740 includes full-time tuition ($18,900), mandatory fees ($330), and college room and board ($5510). *College room only:* $2600. Room and board charges vary according to board plan and housing facility. *Part-time tuition:* $525 per hour. *Part-time mandatory fees:* $30 per term. Part-time tuition and fees vary according to course load.

Financial Aid Forms of aid include need-based and non-need-based scholarships, athletic grants, and part-time jobs. The average aided 2003–04 undergraduate received an aid package worth an estimated $17,375. The priority application deadline for financial aid is March 1.

Freshman Admission UE requires an essay, a high school transcript, a minimum 2.0 high school GPA, 1 recommendation, SAT I or ACT scores, and TOEFL scores for international students. A minimum 3.0 high school GPA and an interview are recommended. An interview is required for some. The application deadline for regular admission is rolling and for early action it is December 1.

Transfer Admission The application deadline for admission is July 1.

Entrance Difficulty UE assesses its entrance difficulty level as moderately difficult; very difficult for engineering, physical therapy programs. For the fall 2003 freshman class, 86 percent of the applicants were accepted.

For Further Information Contact Dr. Tom Bear, Dean of Admission, University of Evansville, 1800 Lincoln Avenue, Evansville, IN 47722-0002. *Telephone:* 812-479-2683 or 800-423-8633 (toll-free). *Fax:* 812-474-4076. *E-mail:* admission@evansville.edu. *Web site:* http://www.evansville.edu/.

UNIVERSITY OF INDIANAPOLIS

Indianapolis, Indiana

U of I is a coed, private, comprehensive institution, founded in 1902, affiliated with the United Methodist Church, offering degrees at the associate, bachelor's, master's, and doctoral levels. It has a 60-acre campus in Indianapolis.

Academic Information The faculty has 358 members (45% full-time), 59% with terminal degrees. The undergraduate student-faculty ratio is 14:1. The library holds 173,363 titles, 1,015 serial subscriptions, and 5,324 audiovisual materials. Special programs include academic remediation, services for learning-disabled students, an honors program, cooperative (work-study) education, study abroad, advanced placement credit, accelerated degree programs, ESL programs, double majors, independent study, distance learning, self-designed majors, summer session for credit, part-time degree programs (evenings), adult/continuing education programs, internships, and arrangement for off-campus study with 7 members of the Consortium for Urban Education, 10 members of the May Term Consortium. The most frequently chosen baccalaureate fields are business/marketing, education, psychology.

Student Body Statistics The student body totals 3,986, of whom 3,007 are undergraduates (661 freshmen). 66 percent are women and 34 percent are men. Students come from 31 states and territories and 55 other countries. 92 percent are from Indiana. 4.5 percent are international students. 25 percent of the 2003 graduating class went on to graduate and professional schools.

Expenses for 2004–05 *Application fee:* $20. *Comprehensive fee:* $23,350 includes full-time tuition ($17,200) and college room and board ($6150). Full-time tuition varies according to program. Room and board charges vary according to board plan and housing facility. *Part-time tuition:* varies with class time.

Financial Aid Forms of aid include need-based and non-need-based scholarships, athletic grants, and part-time jobs. The average aided 2002–03 undergraduate received an aid package worth $14,721. The priority application deadline for financial aid is March 1.

Freshman Admission U of I requires a high school transcript, a minimum 2.0 high school GPA, SAT I or ACT scores, and TOEFL scores for international students. An interview is required for some. The application deadline for regular admission is rolling.

Transfer Admission The application deadline for admission is rolling.

Entrance Difficulty U of I assesses its entrance difficulty level as moderately difficult. For the fall 2003 freshman class, 74 percent of the applicants were accepted.

For Further Information Contact Mr. Ronald W. Wilks, Director of Admissions, University of Indianapolis, 1400 East Hanna Avenue, Indianapolis, IN 46227-3697. *Telephone:* 317-788-3216 or 800-232-8634 Ext. 3216 (toll-free). *Fax:* 317-778-3300. *E-mail:* admissions@uindy.edu. *Web site:* http://www.uindy.edu/.

UNIVERSITY OF NOTRE DAME

Notre Dame, Indiana

Notre Dame is a coed, private, Roman Catholic university, founded in 1842, offering degrees at the bachelor's, master's, doctoral, and first professional levels. It has a 1,250-acre campus in Notre Dame.

Academic Information The library holds 3 million titles, 19,232 serial subscriptions, and 23,497 audiovisual materials. Special programs include services for learning-disabled students, an honors program, cooperative (work-study) education, study abroad, advanced placement credit, accelerated degree programs, double majors, independent study, distance learning, self-designed majors, summer session for credit, internships, and arrangement for off-campus study with Saint Mary's College (IN), Xavier University of Louisiana, Clark Atlanta University, St. Mary's University of San Antonio. The most frequently chosen baccalaureate fields are business/marketing, engineering/engineering technologies, social sciences and history.

Student Body Statistics The student body totals 11,415, of whom 8,311 are undergraduates (1,996 freshmen). 47 percent are women and 53 percent are men. Students come from 54 states and territories and 65 other

University of Notre Dame (continued)

countries. 13 percent are from Indiana. 3.6 percent are international students. 37 percent of the 2003 graduating class went on to graduate and professional schools.

Expenses for 2003–04 *Application fee:* $50. *Comprehensive fee:* $34,542 includes full-time tuition ($27,170), mandatory fees ($442), and college room and board ($6930). Room and board charges vary according to board plan and housing facility. *Part-time tuition:* $1132 per credit.

Financial Aid Forms of aid include need-based and non-need-based scholarships, athletic grants, and part-time jobs. The average aided 2003–04 undergraduate received an aid package worth an estimated $23,412. The application deadline for financial aid is February 15.

Freshman Admission Notre Dame requires an essay, a high school transcript, 1 recommendation, SAT I or ACT scores, and TOEFL scores for international students. The application deadline for regular admission is January 9 and for early action it is November 1.

Transfer Admission The application deadline for admission is April 15.

Entrance Difficulty Notre Dame assesses its entrance difficulty level as most difficult. For the fall 2003 freshman class, 29 percent of the applicants were accepted.

For Further Information Contact Mr. Daniel J. Saracino, Assistant Provost for Admissions, University of Notre Dame, 220 Main Building, Notre Dame, IN 46556-5612. *Telephone:* 574-631-7505. *Fax:* 574-631-8865. *E-mail:* admissio.1@nd.edu. *Web site:* http://www.nd.edu/.

UNIVERSITY OF PHOENIX–INDIANAPOLIS CAMPUS

Indianapolis, Indiana

For Information Write to University of Phoenix–Indianapolis Campus, Indianapolis, IN 46250.

UNIVERSITY OF SAINT FRANCIS

Fort Wayne, Indiana

University of Saint Francis is a coed, private, Roman Catholic, comprehensive institution, founded in 1890, offering degrees at the associate, bachelor's, and master's levels and postbachelor's certificates. It has a 73-acre campus in Fort Wayne.

Academic Information The faculty has 211 members (44% full-time), 26% with terminal degrees. The undergraduate student-faculty ratio is 11:1. The library holds 47,877 titles and 449 serial subscriptions. Special programs include academic remediation, services for learning-disabled students, an honors program, cooperative (work-study) education, study abroad, advanced placement credit, Freshman Honors College, double majors, independent study, distance learning, summer session for credit, part-time degree programs (daytime, evenings, weekends, summer), adult/continuing education programs, and internships. The most frequently chosen baccalaureate fields are business/marketing, education, health professions and related sciences.

Student Body Statistics The student body totals 1,834, of whom 1,608 are undergraduates (348 freshmen). 71 percent are women and 29 percent are men. Students come from 8 states and territories. 91 percent are from Indiana. 0.2 percent are international students. 13 percent of the 2003 graduating class went on to graduate and professional schools.

Expenses for 2003–04 *Application fee:* $20. *Comprehensive fee:* $20,964 includes full-time tuition ($14,900), mandatory fees ($614), and college room and board ($5450). Full-time tuition and fees vary according to course load. Room and board charges vary according to housing facility. *Part-time tuition:* $470 per semester hour. Part-time tuition varies according to course load.

Financial Aid Forms of aid include need-based and non-need-based scholarships, athletic grants, and part-time jobs. The average aided 2003–04 undergraduate received an aid package worth an estimated $12,668. The application deadline for financial aid is June 30 with a priority deadline of March 1.

Freshman Admission University of Saint Francis requires a high school transcript, a minimum 2.0 high school GPA, and TOEFL scores for international students. An essay and SAT I or ACT scores are recommended. Recommendations and an interview are required for some. The application deadline for regular admission is rolling.

Transfer Admission The application deadline for admission is rolling.

Entrance Difficulty University of Saint Francis assesses its entrance difficulty level as moderately difficult. For the fall 2003 freshman class, 73 percent of the applicants were accepted.

For Further Information Contact Mr. Ron Schumacher, Vice President for Enrollment Management, University of Saint Francis, 2701 Spring Street, Fort Wayne, IN 46808. *Telephone:* 260-434-3279 or 800-729-4732 (toll-free). *E-mail:* admiss@sfc.edu. *Web site:* http://www.sf.edu/.

UNIVERSITY OF SOUTHERN INDIANA

Evansville, Indiana

USI is a coed, public, comprehensive unit of Indiana Commission for Higher Education, founded in 1965, offering degrees at the associate, bachelor's, and master's levels and postbachelor's certificates. It has a 330-acre campus in Evansville.

Academic Information The faculty has 573 members (52% full-time), 40% with terminal degrees. The undergraduate student-faculty ratio is 18:1. The library holds 234,406 titles, 3,035 serial subscriptions, and 7,924 audiovisual materials. Special programs include academic remediation, services for learning-disabled students, an honors program, cooperative (work-study) education, study abroad, advanced placement credit, ESL programs, double majors, independent study, distance learning, summer session for credit, part-time degree programs (daytime, evenings, weekends, summer), adult/continuing education programs, and internships. The most frequently chosen baccalaureate fields are business/marketing, education, health professions and related sciences.

Student Body Statistics The student body totals 9,899, of whom 9,154 are undergraduates (2,079 freshmen). 60 percent are women and 40 percent are men. Students come from 28 states and territories and 34 other countries. 90 percent are from Indiana. 0.6 percent are international students. 18.1 percent of the 2003 graduating class went on to graduate and professional schools.

Expenses for 2003–04 *Application fee:* $25. *State resident tuition:* $3825 full-time, $127.50 per semester hour part-time. *Nonresident tuition:* $9128 full-time, $304.25 per semester hour part-time. *Mandatory fees:* $60 full-time, $22.75 per term part-time. Full-time tuition and fees vary according to course load and reciprocity agreements. Part-time tuition and fees vary according to course load and reciprocity agreements. *College room and board:* $5140. *College room only:* $2740. Room and board charges vary according to board plan and housing facility.

Financial Aid Forms of aid include need-based and non-need-based scholarships, athletic grants, and part-time jobs. The average aided 2003–04 undergraduate received an aid package worth an estimated $5134. The application deadline for financial aid is March 1.

Freshman Admission USI requires a high school transcript, SAT I or ACT scores, and TOEFL scores for international students. An essay and a minimum 2.0 high school GPA are recommended. An interview is required for some. The application deadline for regular admission is August 15.

Entrance Difficulty USI assesses its entrance difficulty level as noncompetitive; minimally difficult for transfers; moderately difficult for allied health, social work programs. For the fall 2003 freshman class, 93 percent of the applicants were accepted.

For Further Information Contact Mr. Eric Otto, Director of Admission, University of Southern Indiana, 8600 University Boulevard, Evansville, IN 47712-3590. *Telephone:* 812-464-1765 or 800-467-1965 (toll-free). *Fax:* 812-465-7154. *E-mail:* enroll@usi.edu. *Web site:* http://www.usi.edu/.

VALPARAISO UNIVERSITY
Valparaiso, Indiana

Valpo is a coed, private, comprehensive institution, founded in 1859, affiliated with the Lutheran Church, offering degrees at the associate, bachelor's, master's, and first professional levels and post-master's and postbachelor's certificates. It has a 310-acre campus in Valparaiso near Chicago.

Academic Information The faculty has 344 members (67% full-time), 75% with terminal degrees. The undergraduate student-faculty ratio is 13:1. The library holds 521,907 titles, 5,282 serial subscriptions, and 13,413 audiovisual materials. Special programs include an honors program, cooperative (work-study) education, study abroad, advanced placement credit, accelerated degree programs, Freshman Honors College, ESL programs, double majors, independent study, distance learning, self-designed majors, summer session for credit, part-time degree programs (daytime, evenings, summer), adult/continuing education programs, internships, and arrangement for off-campus study with Associated Colleges of the Midwest. The most frequently chosen baccalaureate fields are business/marketing, engineering/engineering technologies, social sciences and history.
Student Body Statistics The student body totals 3,850, of whom 3,026 are undergraduates (795 freshmen). 53 percent are women and 47 percent are men. Students come from 47 states and territories and 41 other countries. 33 percent are from Indiana. 1.7 percent are international students. 27 percent of the 2003 graduating class went on to graduate and professional schools.
Expenses for 2003–04 *Application fee:* $30. *Comprehensive fee:* $26,112 includes full-time tuition ($20,000), mandatory fees ($632), and college room and board ($5480). *College room only:* $3480. Room and board charges vary according to housing facility and student level. *Part-time tuition:* $860 per credit hour. *Part-time mandatory fees:* $50 per term. Part-time tuition and fees vary according to course load.
Financial Aid Forms of aid include need-based and non-need-based scholarships, athletic grants, and part-time jobs. The average aided 2003–04 undergraduate received an aid package worth an estimated $17,404. The priority application deadline for financial aid is March 1.
Freshman Admission Valpo requires an essay, a high school transcript, SAT I or ACT scores, and TOEFL scores for international students. 2 recommendations are recommended. An interview is required for some. The application deadline for regular admission is August 15 and for early action it is November 1.
Entrance Difficulty Valpo assesses its entrance difficulty level as moderately difficult. For the fall 2003 freshman class, 82 percent of the applicants were accepted.

For Further Information Contact Ms. Joyce Lantz, Director of Admissions, Valparaiso University, Kretzmann Hall, 1700 Chapel Drive, Valparaiso, IN 46383-6493. *Telephone:* 219-464-5011 or 888-GO-VALPO (toll-free). *Fax:* 219-464-6898. *E-mail:* undergrad.admissions@valpo.edu. *Web site:* http://www.valpo.edu/.

WABASH COLLEGE
Crawfordsville, Indiana

Wabash is a men's, private, four-year college, founded in 1832, offering degrees at the bachelor's level. It has a 50-acre campus in Crawfordsville near Indianapolis.

Academic Information The faculty has 88 members (98% full-time), 92% with terminal degrees. The student-faculty ratio is 10:1. The library holds 420,906 titles, 1,634 serial subscriptions, and 10,557 audiovisual materials. Special programs include services for learning-disabled students, cooperative (work-study) education, study abroad, advanced placement credit, accelerated degree programs, double majors, independent study, internships, and arrangement for off-campus study with members of the Great Lakes Colleges Association. The most frequently chosen baccalaureate fields are English, psychology, social sciences and history.
Student Body Statistics The student body is made up of 863 undergraduates (239 freshmen). Students come from 34 states and territories and 14 other countries. 73 percent are from Indiana. 3.7 percent are international students. 37 percent of the 2003 graduating class went on to graduate and professional schools.
Expenses for 2004–05 *Application fee:* $30. *Comprehensive fee:* $29,328 includes full-time tuition ($21,870), mandatory fees ($405), and college room and board ($7053). *College room only:* $2609. Room and board charges vary according to board plan and housing facility. *Part-time tuition:* $3472 per course. Part-time tuition varies according to course load.
Financial Aid Forms of aid include need-based and non-need-based scholarships and part-time jobs. The average aided 2003–04 undergraduate received an aid package worth an estimated $19,944. The application deadline for financial aid is March 1 with a priority deadline of February 15.
Freshman Admission Wabash requires an essay, a high school transcript, a minimum 2.0 high school GPA, 1 recommendation, SAT I or ACT scores, and TOEFL scores for international students. A minimum 3.0 high school GPA and an interview are recommended. The application deadline for regular admission is March 15; for early decision it is November 15; and for early action it is December 15.
Transfer Admission The application deadline for admission is March 15.
Entrance Difficulty Wabash assesses its entrance difficulty level as moderately difficult. For the fall 2003 freshman class, 50 percent of the applicants were accepted.

For Further Information Contact Mr. Steve Klein, Director of Admissions, Wabash College, PO Box 362, Crawfordsville, IN 47933-0352. *Telephone:* 765-361-6225 or 800-345-5385 (toll-free). *Fax:* 765-361-6437. *E-mail:* admissions@wabash.edu. *Web site:* http://www.wabash.edu/.

Iowa

AIB COLLEGE OF BUSINESS
Des Moines, Iowa

AIB is a coed, private, two-year college, founded in 1921, offering degrees at the associate level. It has a 20-acre campus in Des Moines.

Academic Information The faculty has 67 members (39% full-time), 7% with terminal degrees. The student-faculty ratio is 21:1. The library holds 5,400 titles and 185 serial subscriptions. Special programs include academic remediation, accelerated degree programs, double majors, summer session for credit, part-time degree programs (daytime, evenings, summer), adult/continuing education programs, and internships.
Student Body Statistics The student body is made up of 938 undergraduates (250 freshmen). 69 percent are women and 31 percent are men. Students come from 5 states and territories. 95 percent are from Iowa.
Expenses for 2004–05 *Application fee:* $25. *Tuition:* $8820 full-time, $245 per credit hour part-time. *Mandatory fees:* $240 full-time, $240 per year part-time. *College room only:* $2775.
Financial Aid Forms of aid include need-based scholarships and part-time jobs. The priority application deadline for financial aid is April 1.
Freshman Admission AIB requires a high school transcript and TOEFL scores for international students. An interview and ACT scores are recommended. The application deadline for regular admission is rolling.
Transfer Admission The application deadline for admission is rolling.
Entrance Difficulty AIB assesses its entrance difficulty level as minimally difficult; moderately difficult for Realtime Reporting program. For the fall 2003 freshman class, 74 percent of the applicants were accepted.

For Further Information Contact Ms. Gail Cline, Director of Admissions, AIB College of Business, Keith Fenton Administration Building, 2500 Fleur Drive, Des Moines, IA 50321-1799. *Telephone:* 515-244-4221 Ext. 5634 or 800-444-1921 (toll-free). *Fax:* 515-244-6773. *E-mail:* clineg@aib.edu. *Web site:* http://www.aib.edu/.

ALLEN COLLEGE
Waterloo, Iowa

Allen College is a coed, primarily women's, private, comprehensive institution, founded in 1989, offering degrees at the associate, bachelor's, and master's levels (liberal arts and general education courses are taken at either University of North Iowa or Wartburg College). It has a 20-acre campus in Waterloo.

Academic Information The faculty has 24 members (67% full-time), 8% with terminal degrees. The undergraduate student-faculty ratio is 19:1. The library holds 2,797 titles, 184 serial subscriptions, and 421 audiovisual materials. Special programs include advanced placement credit, independent study, distance learning, part-time degree programs (daytime, evenings), internships, and arrangement for off-campus study. The most frequently chosen baccalaureate field is health professions and related sciences.

Student Body Statistics The student body totals 309, of whom 276 are undergraduates (33 freshmen). 93 percent are women and 7 percent are men. Students come from 1 state or territory. 99 percent are from Iowa.

Expenses for 2003–04 *Application fee:* $50. *One-time mandatory fee:* $300. *Comprehensive fee:* $15,468 includes full-time tuition ($9324), mandatory fees ($1214), and college room and board ($4930). *College room only:* $2465. Full-time tuition and fees vary according to course load, location, program, and student level. Room and board charges vary according to board plan and housing facility. *Part-time tuition:* $356 per credit hour. *Part-time mandatory fees:* $25 per credit hour, $185 per term. Part-time tuition and fees vary according to program.

Financial Aid Forms of aid include need-based and non-need-based scholarships and part-time jobs. The average aided 2003–04 undergraduate received an aid package worth an estimated $7580. The application deadline for financial aid is continuous.

Freshman Admission Allen College requires an essay, a high school transcript, 1 recommendation, SAT I and SAT II or ACT scores, and TOEFL scores for international students. A minimum 2.3 high school GPA is recommended. An interview is required for some. The application deadline for regular admission is August 1.

Transfer Admission The application deadline for admission is August 1.

Entrance Difficulty Allen College assesses its entrance difficulty level as moderately difficult. For the fall 2003 freshman class, 67 percent of the applicants were accepted.

For Further Information Contact Ms. Lois Hagedorn, Student Services Assistant, Allen College, Barrett Forum, 1825 Logan Avenue, Waterloo, IA 50703. *Telephone:* 319-226-2002. *Fax:* 319-226-2051. *E-mail:* hagedole@ihs.org. *Web site:* http://www.allencollege.edu/.

BRIAR CLIFF UNIVERSITY
Sioux City, Iowa

Briar Cliff is a coed, private, Roman Catholic, comprehensive institution, founded in 1930, offering degrees at the associate, bachelor's, and master's levels. It has a 70-acre campus in Sioux City.

Academic Information The faculty has 53 members (89% full-time), 57% with terminal degrees. The undergraduate student-faculty ratio is 12:1. The library holds 83,737 titles, 6,366 serial subscriptions, and 9,791 audiovisual materials. Special programs include academic remediation, services for learning-disabled students, advanced placement credit, accelerated degree programs, ESL programs, double majors, independent study, distance learning, self-designed majors, summer session for credit, part-time degree programs (daytime, evenings, weekends, summer), adult/continuing education programs, internships, and arrangement for off-campus study with Colleges of Mid-America. The most frequently chosen baccalaureate fields are business/marketing, health professions and related sciences, protective services/public administration.

Student Body Statistics The student body is made up of 1,063 undergraduates (258 freshmen). 60 percent are women and 40 percent are men. Students come from 25 states and territories and 1 other country. 68 percent are from Iowa. 0.1 percent are international students. 13 percent of the 2003 graduating class went on to graduate and professional schools.

Expenses for 2003–04 *Application fee:* $20. *Comprehensive fee:* $21,660 includes full-time tuition ($15,960), mandatory fees ($390), and college room and board ($5310). *College room only:* $2655. Room and board charges vary according to board plan and housing facility. *Part-time tuition:* $532 per hour. *Part-time mandatory fees:* $13. Part-time tuition and fees vary according to class time and course load.

Financial Aid Forms of aid include need-based and non-need-based scholarships and part-time jobs. The average aided 2002–03 undergraduate received an aid package worth $15,950. The application deadline for financial aid is March 15.

Freshman Admission Briar Cliff requires a high school transcript, a minimum 2.0 high school GPA, minimum ACT score of 18, and SAT I or ACT scores. An essay and TOEFL scores for international students are recommended. 3 recommendations and an interview are required for some. The application deadline for regular admission is rolling.

Transfer Admission The application deadline for admission is rolling.

Entrance Difficulty Briar Cliff assesses its entrance difficulty level as moderately difficult. For the fall 2003 freshman class, 80 percent of the applicants were accepted.

For Further Information Contact Ms. Tammy Namminga, Applications Specialist, Briar Cliff University, 3303 Rebecca Street, Sioux City, IA 51104. *Telephone:* 712-279-5200 Ext. 1628 or 800-662-3303 Ext. 5200 (toll-free). *Fax:* 712-279-1632. *E-mail:* admissions@briarcliff.edu. *Web site:* http://www.briarcliff.edu/.

BUENA VISTA UNIVERSITY
Storm Lake, Iowa

BVU is a coed, private, comprehensive institution, founded in 1891, affiliated with the Presbyterian Church (U.S.A.), offering degrees at the bachelor's and master's levels. It has a 60-acre campus in Storm Lake.

Academic Information The faculty has 114 members (71% full-time), 55% with terminal degrees. The undergraduate student-faculty ratio is 15:1. The library holds 153,084 titles, 698 serial subscriptions, and 4,158 audiovisual materials. Special programs include academic remediation, services for learning-disabled students, an honors program, study abroad, advanced placement credit, Freshman Honors College, ESL programs, double majors, independent study, distance learning, self-designed majors, summer session for credit, part-time degree programs, adult/continuing education programs, internships, and arrangement for off-campus study with Washington University in St. Louis. The most frequently chosen baccalaureate fields are business/marketing, education, interdisciplinary studies.

Student Body Statistics The student body totals 1,364, of whom 1,288 are undergraduates (378 freshmen). 53 percent are women and 47 percent are men. Students come from 17 states and territories and 4 other countries. 82 percent are from Iowa. 0.3 percent are international students. 17 percent of the 2003 graduating class went on to graduate and professional schools.

Expenses for 2003–04 *Application fee:* $0. *Comprehensive fee:* $25,406 includes full-time tuition ($19,862) and college room and board ($5544). *Part-time tuition:* $668 per semester hour.

Financial Aid Forms of aid include need-based and non-need-based scholarships and part-time jobs. The average aided 2003–04 undergraduate received an aid package worth an estimated $19,049. The priority application deadline for financial aid is June 1.

Freshman Admission BVU requires a high school transcript, recommendations, SAT I or ACT scores, and TOEFL scores for international students. A minimum 3.0 high school GPA is recommended. An essay and an interview are required for some.

Entrance Difficulty BVU assesses its entrance difficulty level as moderately difficult. For the fall 2003 freshman class, 84 percent of the applicants were accepted.

For Further Information Contact Ms. Louise Cummings-Simmons, Director of Admissions, Buena Vista University, 610 West Fourth Street, Storm Lake, IA 50588. *Telephone:* 712-749-2235 or 800-383-9600 (toll-free). *Fax:* 712-749-2037. *E-mail:* admissions@bvu.edu. *Web site:* http://www.bvu.edu/.

CENTRAL COLLEGE
Pella, Iowa

Central is a coed, private, four-year college, founded in 1853, affiliated with the Reformed Church in America, offering degrees at the bachelor's level. It has a 133-acre campus in Pella near Des Moines.

Academic Information The faculty has 153 members (63% full-time), 65% with terminal degrees. The student-faculty ratio is 14:1. The library holds 220,526 titles, 1,161 serial subscriptions, and 13,160 audiovisual materials. Special programs include academic remediation, services for learning-disabled students, an honors program, study abroad, double majors, independent study, self-designed majors, summer session for credit, part-time degree programs (daytime, evenings), internships, and arrangement for off-campus study. The most frequently chosen baccalaureate fields are business/marketing, education, social sciences and history.

Student Body Statistics The student body is made up of 1,698 undergraduates (417 freshmen). 57 percent are women and 43 percent are men. Students come from 33 states and territories and 13 other countries. 81 percent are from Iowa. 1 percent are international students. 15 percent of the 2003 graduating class went on to graduate and professional schools.

Expenses for 2003–04 *Application fee:* $25. *Comprehensive fee:* $23,898 includes full-time tuition ($17,609), mandatory fees ($144), and college room and board ($6145). *College room only:* $3132. Room and board charges vary according to board plan. *Part-time tuition:* $611 per credit hour. Part-time tuition varies according to course load.

Financial Aid Forms of aid include need-based and non-need-based scholarships and part-time jobs. The average aided 2003–04 undergraduate received an aid package worth an estimated $16,020. The priority application deadline for financial aid is March 15.

Freshman Admission Central requires a high school transcript, SAT I or ACT scores, and TOEFL scores for international students. A minimum 2.0 high school GPA and an interview are recommended. An essay, 3 recommendations, and an interview are required for some. The application deadline for regular admission is rolling.

Transfer Admission The application deadline for admission is rolling.

Entrance Difficulty Central assesses its entrance difficulty level as moderately difficult. For the fall 2003 freshman class, 83 percent of the applicants were accepted.

For Further Information Contact Mr. John Olsen, Vice President for Admission and Student Enrollment Services, Central College, 812 University Street, Pella, IA 50219-1999. *Telephone:* 641-628-7600 or 800-458-5503 (toll-free). *Fax:* 641-628-5316. *E-mail:* admissions@central.edu. *Web site:* http://www.central.edu/.

CLARKE COLLEGE
Dubuque, Iowa

Clarke is a coed, private, Roman Catholic, comprehensive institution, founded in 1843, offering degrees at the associate, bachelor's, and master's levels. It has a 55-acre campus in Dubuque.

Academic Information The faculty has 92 members (89% full-time), 63% with terminal degrees. The undergraduate student-faculty ratio is 12:1. The library holds 127,089 titles, 897 serial subscriptions, and 1,504 audiovisual materials. Special programs include an honors program, cooperative (work-study) education, study abroad, advanced placement credit, ESL programs, double majors, independent study, distance learning, self-designed majors, summer session for credit, part-time degree programs (evenings), adult/continuing education programs, internships, and arrangement for off-campus study with Tri-College Cooperative Effort. The most frequently chosen baccalaureate fields are business/marketing, education, health professions and related sciences.

Student Body Statistics The student body totals 1,126, of whom 1,005 are undergraduates (171 freshmen). 70 percent are women and 30 percent are men. Students come from 10 states and territories and 10 other countries. 62 percent are from Iowa. 1.8 percent are international students. 29 percent of the 2003 graduating class went on to graduate and professional schools.

Expenses for 2003–04 *Application fee:* $25. *Comprehensive fee:* $23,165 includes full-time tuition ($16,580), mandatory fees ($510), and college room and board ($6075). *College room only:* $2970. Full-time tuition and fees vary according to class time. Room and board charges vary according to board plan and housing facility. *Part-time tuition:* $422 per credit. Part-time tuition varies according to class time.

Financial Aid Forms of aid include need-based and non-need-based scholarships and part-time jobs. The average aided 2003–04 undergraduate received an aid package worth an estimated $14,654. The priority application deadline for financial aid is April 15.

Freshman Admission Clarke requires a high school transcript, a minimum 2.0 high school GPA, rank in upper 50% of high school class, minimum ACT score of 21 or SAT score of 1000, SAT I or ACT scores, and TOEFL scores for international students. An interview is required for some. The application deadline for regular admission is rolling.

Transfer Admission The application deadline for admission is rolling.

Entrance Difficulty Clarke assesses its entrance difficulty level as moderately difficult; very difficult for physical therapy program. For the fall 2003 freshman class, 56 percent of the applicants were accepted.

For Further Information Contact Mr. Omar G. Correa, Executive Director of Admissions and Financial Aid, Clarke College, 1550 Clarke Drive, Dubuque, IA 52001-3198. *Telephone:* 563-588-6316 or 800-383-2345 (toll-free). *Fax:* 319-588-6789. *E-mail:* admissions@clarke.edu. *Web site:* http://www.clarke.edu/.

COE COLLEGE
Cedar Rapids, Iowa

Coe is a coed, private, comprehensive institution, founded in 1851, affiliated with the Presbyterian Church, offering degrees at the bachelor's and master's levels. It has a 53-acre campus in Cedar Rapids.

Academic Information The faculty has 127 members (58% full-time), 76% with terminal degrees. The undergraduate student-faculty ratio is 12:1. The library holds 213,270 titles, 750 serial subscriptions, and 8,653 audiovisual materials. Special programs include services for learning-disabled students, an honors program, study abroad, advanced placement credit, accelerated degree programs, ESL programs, double majors, independent study, self-designed majors, summer session for credit, part-time degree programs (daytime, evenings, summer), adult/continuing education programs, internships, and arrangement for off-campus study with University of Iowa, Mount Mercy College, Associated Colleges of the Midwest, Washington University in St. Louis. The most frequently chosen baccalaureate fields are business/marketing, psychology, social sciences and history.

Student Body Statistics The student body totals 1,317, of whom 1,290 are undergraduates (322 freshmen). 56 percent are women and 44 percent are men. Students come from 34 states and territories and 16 other countries. 70 percent are from Iowa. 3.4 percent are international students. 26 percent of the 2003 graduating class went on to graduate and professional schools.

Expenses for 2003–04 *Application fee:* $0. *Comprehensive fee:* $27,385 includes full-time tuition ($21,280), mandatory fees ($325), and college room and board ($5780). *College room only:* $2720. Room and board charges vary according to board plan and housing facility. *Part-time tuition:* $1040 per course.

Financial Aid Forms of aid include need-based and non-need-based scholarships and part-time jobs. The average aided 2003–04 undergraduate received an aid package worth an estimated $18,882. The priority application deadline for financial aid is March 1.

Freshman Admission Coe requires an essay, a high school transcript, 1 recommendation, SAT I or ACT scores, and TOEFL scores for international students. A minimum 3.0 high school GPA and an interview are recommended. The application deadline for regular admission is March 1 and for early action it is December 10.

Transfer Admission The application deadline for admission is rolling.

Coe College (continued)

Entrance Difficulty Coe assesses its entrance difficulty level as moderately difficult. For the fall 2003 freshman class, 71 percent of the applicants were accepted.

For Further Information Contact Mr. John Sullivan, Executive Director of Admission and Financial Aid, Coe College, 1220 1st Avenue, NE, Cedar Rapids, IA 52402-5070. *Telephone:* 319-399-8500 or 877-225-5263 (toll-free). *Fax:* 319-399-8816. *E-mail:* admission@coe.edu. *Web site:* http://www.coe.edu/.

CORNELL COLLEGE
Mount Vernon, Iowa

Cornell is a coed, private, Methodist, four-year college, founded in 1853, offering degrees at the bachelor's level. It has a 129-acre campus in Mount Vernon.

Academic Information The faculty has 101 members (84% full-time), 82% with terminal degrees. The student-faculty ratio is 12:1. The library holds 197,780 titles, 1,236 serial subscriptions, and 4,471 audiovisual materials. Special programs include study abroad, advanced placement credit, ESL programs, double majors, independent study, self-designed majors, adult/continuing education programs, internships, and arrangement for off-campus study with Associated Colleges of the Midwest, Fisk University. The most frequently chosen baccalaureate fields are education, psychology, social sciences and history.
Student Body Statistics The student body is made up of 1,117 undergraduates (367 freshmen). 59 percent are women and 41 percent are men. Students come from 42 states and territories and 14 other countries. 31 percent are from Iowa. 1.5 percent are international students. 33 percent of the 2003 graduating class went on to graduate and professional schools.
Expenses for 2003–04 *Application fee:* $25. *Comprehensive fee:* $27,825 includes full-time tuition ($21,630), mandatory fees ($160), and college room and board ($6035). *College room only:* $2825. Full-time tuition and fees vary according to reciprocity agreements. Room and board charges vary according to board plan. *Part-time tuition:* varies with course load.
Financial Aid Forms of aid include need-based and non-need-based scholarships and part-time jobs. The average aided 2003–04 undergraduate received an aid package worth an estimated $19,455. The application deadline for financial aid is March 1.
Freshman Admission Cornell requires an essay, a high school transcript, 1 recommendation, SAT I or ACT scores, and TOEFL scores for international students. A minimum 2.80 high school GPA and an interview are recommended. The application deadline for regular admission is February 1.
Transfer Admission The application deadline for admission is February 1.
Entrance Difficulty Cornell assesses its entrance difficulty level as moderately difficult. For the fall 2003 freshman class, 69 percent of the applicants were accepted.

For Further Information Contact Mr. Jonathan Stroud, Dean of Admissions and Financial Assistance, Cornell College, 600 First Street West, Mount Vernon, IA 52314-1098. *Telephone:* 319-895-4477 or 800-747-1112 (toll-free). *Fax:* 319-895-4451. *E-mail:* admissions@cornellcollege.edu. *Web site:* http://www.cornellcollege.edu/.

See page 274 for a narrative description.

DIVINE WORD COLLEGE
Epworth, Iowa

For Information Write to Divine Word College, Epworth, IA 52045-0380.

DORDT COLLEGE
Sioux Center, Iowa

Dordt is a coed, private, Christian Reformed, comprehensive institution, founded in 1955, offering degrees at the associate, bachelor's, and master's levels. It has a 100-acre campus in Sioux Center.

Academic Information The faculty has 116 members (69% full-time), 53% with terminal degrees. The undergraduate student-faculty ratio is 15:1. The library holds 160,000 titles, 6,597 serial subscriptions, and 1,989 audiovisual materials. Special programs include academic remediation, services for learning-disabled students, study abroad, advanced placement credit, ESL programs, double majors, independent study, distance learning, self-designed majors, part-time degree programs, internships, and arrangement for off-campus study with Christian College Coalition, Chicago Metro Program, American Studies Program, Los Angeles Film Studies Program. The most frequently chosen baccalaureate fields are business/marketing, education, engineering/engineering technologies.
Student Body Statistics The student body totals 1,359, of whom 1,287 are undergraduates (351 freshmen). 54 percent are women and 46 percent are men. Students come from 32 states and territories and 12 other countries. 42 percent are from Iowa. 12.7 percent are international students. 12 percent of the 2003 graduating class went on to graduate and professional schools.
Expenses for 2003–04 *Application fee:* $25. *Comprehensive fee:* $20,170 includes full-time tuition ($15,550), mandatory fees ($220), and college room and board ($4400). *College room only:* $2310. Room and board charges vary according to board plan and housing facility. *Part-time tuition:* $650 per credit hour. *Part-time mandatory fees:* $110 per term.
Financial Aid Forms of aid include need-based and non-need-based scholarships, athletic grants, and part-time jobs. The average aided 2003–04 undergraduate received an aid package worth an estimated $14,665. The priority application deadline for financial aid is April 1.
Freshman Admission Dordt requires a high school transcript, a minimum 2.25 high school GPA, minimum ACT composite score of 19 or combined SAT I score of 920, SAT I or ACT scores, and TOEFL scores for international students. An essay and an interview are required for some.
Transfer Admission The application deadline for admission is August 1.
Entrance Difficulty Dordt assesses its entrance difficulty level as moderately difficult. For the fall 2003 freshman class, 92 percent of the applicants were accepted.

For Further Information Contact Mr. Quentin Van Essen, Executive Director of Admissions, Dordt College, 498 4th Avenue, NE, Sioux Center, IA 51250-1697. *Telephone:* 712-722-6080 or 800-343-6738 (toll-free). *Fax:* 712-722-1967. *E-mail:* admissions@dordt.edu. *Web site:* http://www.dordt.edu/.

DRAKE UNIVERSITY
Des Moines, Iowa

Drake is a coed, private university, founded in 1881, offering degrees at the bachelor's, master's, doctoral, and first professional levels and post-master's certificates. It has a 120-acre campus in Des Moines.

Academic Information The faculty has 362 members (65% full-time). The undergraduate student-faculty ratio is 18:1. The library holds 472,110 titles, 2,000 serial subscriptions, and 858 audiovisual materials. Special programs include services for learning-disabled students, an honors program, cooperative (work-study) education, study abroad, advanced placement credit, accelerated degree programs, ESL programs, double majors, independent study, distance learning, self-designed majors, summer session for credit, part-time degree programs (daytime, evenings, weekends, summer), internships, and arrangement for off-campus study with 2 members of the Des Moines Consortium. The most frequently chosen baccalaureate fields are business/marketing, communications/communication technologies, education.
Student Body Statistics The student body totals 5,164, of whom 3,434 are undergraduates (815 freshmen). 59 percent are women and 41 percent

are men. Students come from 40 states and territories and 53 other countries. 39 percent are from Iowa. 20.7 percent of the 2003 graduating class went on to graduate and professional schools.

Expenses for 2003–04 *Application fee:* $25. *Comprehensive fee:* $25,120 includes full-time tuition ($19,100), mandatory fees ($320), and college room and board ($5700). *College room only:* $2760. Full-time tuition and fees vary according to course load and student level. Room and board charges vary according to board plan. *Part-time tuition:* $387 per hour. *Part-time mandatory fees:* $7 per hour. Part-time tuition and fees vary according to class time.

Financial Aid Forms of aid include need-based and non-need-based scholarships, athletic grants, and part-time jobs. The average aided 2002–03 undergraduate received an aid package worth $16,354. The priority application deadline for financial aid is March 1.

Freshman Admission Drake requires a high school transcript, SAT I or ACT scores, and TOEFL scores for international students. An essay and an interview are recommended. PCAT for pharmacy transfers is required for some. The application deadline for regular admission is March 1.

Transfer Admission The application deadline for admission is rolling.

Entrance Difficulty Drake assesses its entrance difficulty level as moderately difficult; most difficult for transfer students to the College of Pharmacy. For the fall 2003 freshman class, 83 percent of the applicants were accepted.

For Further Information Contact Mr. Thomas F. Willoughby, Vice President for Admission and Financial Aid, Drake University, 2507 University Avenue, Des Moines, IA 50311. *Telephone:* 515-271-3181 or 800-44DRAKE Ext. 3181 (toll-free). *Fax:* 515-271-2831. *E-mail:* admission@drake.edu. *Web site:* http://www.drake.edu/.

EMMAUS BIBLE COLLEGE

Dubuque, Iowa

Emmaus is a coed, private, nondenominational, four-year college, founded in 1941, offering degrees at the associate and bachelor's levels. It has a 22-acre campus in Dubuque.

Expenses for 2003–04 *Application fee:* $25. *Comprehensive fee:* $10,611 includes full-time tuition ($6900), mandatory fees ($231), and college room and board ($3480). *Part-time tuition:* varies with course load.

For Further Information Contact Mr. Steve Schimpf, Enrollment Services Manager, Emmaus Bible College, 2570 Asbury Road, Dubuque, IA 52001. *Telephone:* 563-588-8000 Ext. 1310 or 800-397-2425 (toll-free). *Fax:* 563-557-0573. *E-mail:* admissions@emmaus.edu. *Web site:* http://www.emmaus.edu/.

FAITH BAPTIST BIBLE COLLEGE AND THEOLOGICAL SEMINARY

Ankeny, Iowa

FBBC&TS is a coed, private, comprehensive institution, founded in 1921, affiliated with the General Association of Regular Baptist Churches, offering degrees at the associate, bachelor's, master's, and first professional levels. It has a 52-acre campus in Ankeny.

Academic Information The faculty has 30 members (57% full-time), 47% with terminal degrees. The undergraduate student-faculty ratio is 18:1. The library holds 63,123 titles, 492 serial subscriptions, and 6,629 audiovisual materials. Special programs include academic remediation, advanced placement credit, double majors, independent study, summer session for credit, part-time degree programs (daytime, summer), adult/continuing education programs, and internships. The most frequently chosen baccalaureate fields are education, philosophy, religion, and theology.

Student Body Statistics The student body totals 533, of whom 392 are undergraduates (113 freshmen). 54 percent are women and 46 percent are men. Students come from 29 states and territories. 49 percent are from Iowa. 0.3 percent are international students. 35 percent of the 2003 graduating class went on to graduate and professional schools.

Expenses for 2003–04 *Application fee:* $25. *Comprehensive fee:* $14,424 includes full-time tuition ($10,042), mandatory fees ($376), and college room and board ($4006). *College room only:* $1866. Full-time tuition and fees vary according to course load. *Part-time tuition:* $365 per semester hour. *Part-time mandatory fees:* $188 per term.

Financial Aid Forms of aid include need-based and non-need-based scholarships. The average aided 2002–03 undergraduate received an aid package worth $6417. The priority application deadline for financial aid is March 1.

Freshman Admission FBBC&TS requires 2 recommendations, SAT I or ACT scores, and TOEFL scores for international students. An interview is required for some. The application deadline for regular admission is May 1.

Entrance Difficulty FBBC&TS assesses its entrance difficulty level as minimally difficult. For the fall 2003 freshman class, 50 percent of the applicants were accepted.

For Further Information Contact Mr. Tim Nilius, Vice President of Enrollment and Constituent Services, Faith Baptist Bible College and Theological Seminary, 1900 NW 4th Street, Ankeny, IA 50021. *Telephone:* 515-964-0601 Ext. 238 or 888-FAITH 4U (toll-free). *Fax:* 515-964-1638. *E-mail:* admissions@faith.edu. *Web site:* http://www.faith.edu/.

THE FRANCISCAN UNIVERSITY

Clinton, Iowa

The Franciscan University is a coed, private, Roman Catholic, four-year college, founded in 1918, offering degrees at the bachelor's and master's levels. It has a 24-acre campus in Clinton near Chicago.

Academic Information The faculty has 52 members (52% full-time), 33% with terminal degrees. The undergraduate student-faculty ratio is 12:1. The library holds 80,759 titles, 1,442 serial subscriptions, and 363 audiovisual materials. Special programs include academic remediation, an honors program, study abroad, advanced placement credit, Freshman Honors College, ESL programs, double majors, independent study, distance learning, self-designed majors, summer session for credit, part-time degree programs (daytime, evenings, summer), external degree programs, and internships.

Student Body Statistics The student body totals 518, of whom 426 are undergraduates (54 freshmen). 56 percent are women and 44 percent are men. Students come from 11 states and territories and 10 other countries. 60 percent are from Iowa. 3.1 percent are international students. 28 percent of the 2003 graduating class went on to graduate and professional schools.

Expenses for 2003–04 *Application fee:* $20. *Comprehensive fee:* $19,430 includes full-time tuition ($13,920), mandatory fees ($260), and college room and board ($5250). *College room only:* $2500. Room and board charges vary according to board plan and housing facility.

Financial Aid Forms of aid include need-based and non-need-based scholarships, athletic grants, and part-time jobs. The average aided 2003–04 undergraduate received an aid package worth an estimated $11,041. The application deadline for financial aid is August 1 with a priority deadline of March 1.

Freshman Admission The Franciscan University requires a high school transcript, SAT I or ACT scores, and TOEFL scores for international students. A minimum 2.0 high school GPA and an interview are recommended. Recommendations and an interview are required for some. The application deadline for regular admission is August 15.

Transfer Admission The application deadline for admission is rolling.

Entrance Difficulty The Franciscan University assesses its entrance difficulty level as minimally difficult; moderately difficult for transfers. For the fall 2003 freshman class, 82 percent of the applicants were accepted.

For Further Information Contact Ms. Waunita M. Sullivan, Director of Enrollment, The Franciscan University, 400 North Bluff Boulevard, PO Box 2967, Clinton, IA 52733-2967. *Telephone:* 563-242-4023 Ext. 3401 or 800-242-4153 (toll-free). *Fax:* 563-243-6102. *E-mail:* admissns@tfu.edu. *Web site:* http://www.tfu.edu/.

GRACELAND UNIVERSITY

Lamoni, Iowa

Graceland is a coed, private, Community of Christ, comprehensive institution, founded in 1895, offering degrees at the bachelor's and master's levels and post-master's certificates. It has a 169-acre campus in Lamoni near Des Moines.

Academic Information The faculty has 118 members (80% full-time), 46% with terminal degrees. The undergraduate student-faculty ratio is 14:1. The library holds 143,523 titles, 5,545 serial subscriptions, and 3,500 audiovisual materials. Special programs include academic remediation, services for learning-disabled students, an honors program, cooperative (work-study) education, study abroad, advanced placement credit, accelerated degree programs, ESL programs, double majors, independent study, distance learning, self-designed majors, summer session for credit, part-time degree programs (daytime), external degree programs, adult/continuing education programs, internships, and arrangement for off-campus study with American Institute of Business, Indian Hills Community College, North Central Missouri College. The most frequently chosen baccalaureate fields are business/marketing, education, health professions and related sciences.

Student Body Statistics The student body totals 2,359, of whom 2,033 are undergraduates (254 freshmen). 66 percent are women and 34 percent are men. Students come from 49 states and territories and 37 other countries. 40 percent are from Iowa. 7.2 percent are international students.

Expenses for 2003–04 *Application fee:* $50. *Comprehensive fee:* $19,550 includes full-time tuition ($14,650), mandatory fees ($150), and college room and board ($4750). *College room only:* $1770. Full-time tuition and fees vary according to course load. Room and board charges vary according to board plan, housing facility, and location. *Part-time tuition:* $460 per semester hour. Part-time tuition varies according to location.

Financial Aid Forms of aid include need-based and non-need-based scholarships, athletic grants, and part-time jobs. The average aided 2003–04 undergraduate received an aid package worth an estimated $14,192. The application deadline for financial aid is continuous.

Freshman Admission Graceland requires a high school transcript, a minimum 2.5 high school GPA, SAT I or ACT scores, and TOEFL scores for international students. Minimum SAT score of 960 or ACT score of 21 is recommended. An essay, 2 recommendations, and an interview are required for some. The application deadline for regular admission is rolling.

Transfer Admission The application deadline for admission is rolling.

Entrance Difficulty Graceland assesses its entrance difficulty level as moderately difficult. For the fall 2003 freshman class, 58 percent of the applicants were accepted.

For Further Information Contact Mr. Brian Shantz, Dean of Admissions, Graceland University, 1 University Place, Larnoni, IA 50140. *Telephone:* 641-784-5118 or 866-GRACELAND (toll-free). *Fax:* 641-784-5480. *E-mail:* admissions@graceland.edu. *Web site:* http://www.graceland.edu/.

See page 286 for a narrative description.

GRAND VIEW COLLEGE

Des Moines, Iowa

Grand View is a coed, private, four-year college, founded in 1896, affiliated with the Evangelical Lutheran Church in America, offering degrees at the associate and bachelor's levels and postbachelor's certificates. It has a 25-acre campus in Des Moines.

Academic Information The faculty has 163 members (47% full-time), 37% with terminal degrees. The student-faculty ratio is 13:1. The library holds 103,468 titles, 3,412 serial subscriptions, and 6,360 audiovisual materials. Special programs include academic remediation, services for learning-disabled students, an honors program, cooperative (work-study) education, study abroad, advanced placement credit, accelerated degree programs, Freshman Honors College, double majors, independent study, distance learning, self-designed majors, summer session for credit, part-time degree programs (daytime, evenings, weekends, summer), adult/continuing education programs, internships, and arrangement for off-campus study with Drake University, Des Moines Area Community College. The most frequently chosen baccalaureate fields are business/marketing, education, health professions and related sciences.

Student Body Statistics The student body is made up of 1,630 undergraduates (167 freshmen). 70 percent are women and 30 percent are men. Students come from 27 states and territories and 13 other countries. 92 percent are from Iowa. 1.3 percent are international students.

Expenses for 2003–04 *Application fee:* $0. *Comprehensive fee:* $19,972 includes full-time tuition ($14,460), mandatory fees ($280), and college room and board ($5232). Room and board charges vary according to board plan and housing facility. *Part-time tuition:* $410 per credit hour. Part-time tuition varies according to class time.

Financial Aid Forms of aid include need-based and non-need-based scholarships, athletic grants, and part-time jobs. The average aided 2003–04 undergraduate received an aid package worth an estimated $11,670. The priority application deadline for financial aid is March 1.

Freshman Admission Grand View requires a high school transcript, SAT I or ACT scores, and TOEFL scores for international students. A minimum 2.0 high school GPA is recommended. The application deadline for regular admission is August 15.

Transfer Admission The application deadline for admission is August 15.

Entrance Difficulty Grand View assesses its entrance difficulty level as minimally difficult; very difficult for honors program. For the fall 2003 freshman class, 95 percent of the applicants were accepted.

For Further Information Contact Ms. Diane Johnson Schaefer, Director of Admissions, Grand View College, 1200 Grandview Avenue, Des Moines, IA 50316-1599. *Telephone:* 515-263-2810 or 800-444-6083 (toll-free). *Fax:* 515-263-2974. *E-mail:* admiss@gvc.edu. *Web site:* http://www.gvc.edu/.

GRINNELL COLLEGE

Grinnell, Iowa

Grinnell College is a coed, private, four-year college, founded in 1846, offering degrees at the bachelor's level. It has a 120-acre campus in Grinnell.

Academic Information The faculty has 142 members (98% full-time), 98% with terminal degrees. The student-faculty ratio is 10:1. The library holds 1 million titles, 3,470 serial subscriptions, and 28,368 audiovisual materials. Special programs include services for learning-disabled students, study abroad, advanced placement credit, accelerated degree programs, double majors, independent study, self-designed majors, internships, and arrangement for off-campus study. The most frequently chosen baccalaureate fields are biological/life sciences, foreign language/literature, social sciences and history.

Student Body Statistics The student body is made up of 1,524 undergraduates (404 freshmen). 55 percent are women and 45 percent are men. Students come from 52 states and territories and 52 other countries. 13 percent are from Iowa. 10.3 percent are international students. 33 percent of the 2003 graduating class went on to graduate and professional schools.

Expenses for 2003–04 *Application fee:* $30. *Comprehensive fee:* $31,060 includes full-time tuition ($23,898), mandatory fees ($592), and college room and board ($6570). *College room only:* $3080. Room and board charges vary according to board plan and housing facility. *Part-time tuition:* $747 per credit hour.

Financial Aid Forms of aid include need-based and non-need-based scholarships and part-time jobs. The average aided 2003–04 undergraduate received an aid package worth an estimated $20,298. The application deadline for financial aid is February 1.

Freshman Admission Grinnell College requires an essay, a high school transcript, 3 recommendations, SAT I or ACT scores, and TOEFL scores for international students. An interview is recommended. The application deadline for regular admission is January 20 and for early decision it is November 20.

Transfer Admission The application deadline for admission is May 1.

Entrance Difficulty Grinnell College assesses its entrance difficulty level as very difficult. For the fall 2003 freshman class, 63 percent of the applicants were accepted.

For Further Information Contact Mr. James Sumner, Dean for Admission and Financial Aid, Grinnell College, 1103 Park Street, Grinnell, IA 50112. *Telephone:* 641-269-3600 or 800-247-0113 (toll-free). *Fax:* 641-269-4800. *E-mail:* askgrin@grinnell.edu. *Web site:* http://www.grinnell.edu/.

HAMILTON COLLEGE
Cedar Rapids, Iowa

Hamilton College is a coed, proprietary, primarily two-year college, founded in 1900, offering degrees at the associate and bachelor's levels (branch locations in Des Moines, Mason City, and Cedar Falls with significant enrollment reflected in profile). It has a 4-acre campus in Cedar Rapids.

Expenses for 2003–04 *Application fee:* $25. *Tuition:* $14,160 full-time.

For Further Information Contact Mr. Brad Knudson, Director of Admissions, Hamilton College, 1924 D Street SW, Cedar Rapids, IA 52404. *Telephone:* 319-363-0481 or 800-728-0481 (toll-free out-of-state). *Fax:* 319-363-3812. *Web site:* http://www.hamiltonia.edu/.

HAMILTON TECHNICAL COLLEGE
Davenport, Iowa

Hamilton Technical College is a coed, proprietary, four-year college, founded in 1969, offering degrees at the associate and bachelor's levels.

Academic Information The faculty has 18 members. The student-faculty ratio is 20:1. The library holds 4,500 titles and 30 serial subscriptions. Special programs include accelerated degree programs.

Student Body Statistics The student body is made up of 420 undergraduates.

Expenses for 2003–04 *Application fee:* $25. *Tuition:* $6600 full-time, $220 per credit part-time.

Financial Aid Forms of aid include need-based scholarships. The priority application deadline for financial aid is June 30.

Freshman Admission Hamilton Technical College requires a high school transcript and an interview. The application deadline for regular admission is rolling.

Transfer Admission The application deadline for admission is rolling.

Entrance Difficulty Hamilton Technical College has an open admission policy.

For Further Information Contact Mr. Chad Nelson, Admissions, Hamilton Technical College, 1011 East 53rd Street, Davenport, IA 52807. *Telephone:* 563-386-3570. *Fax:* 563-386-6756. *Web site:* http://www.hamiltontechcollege.com/.

IOWA STATE UNIVERSITY OF SCIENCE AND TECHNOLOGY
Ames, Iowa

Iowa State is a coed, public university, founded in 1858, offering degrees at the bachelor's, master's, doctoral, and first professional levels and post-master's certificates. It has a 1,788-acre campus in Ames.

Academic Information The faculty has 1,659 members (85% full-time), 87% with terminal degrees. The undergraduate student-faculty ratio is 16:1. The library holds 2 million titles, 29,681 serial subscriptions, and 58,055 audiovisual materials. Special programs include academic remediation, services for learning-disabled students, an honors program, cooperative (work-study) education, study abroad, advanced placement credit, accelerated degree programs, Freshman Honors College, ESL programs, double majors, independent study, distance learning, self-designed majors, summer session for credit, part-time degree programs, external degree programs, adult/continuing education programs, internships, and arrangement for off-campus study with Iowa Regents' Universities Student Exchange, National Student Exchange. The most frequently chosen baccalaureate fields are business/marketing, agriculture, engineering/engineering technologies.

Student Body Statistics The student body totals 27,380, of whom 22,230 are undergraduates (3,897 freshmen). 44 percent are women and 56 percent are men. Students come from 54 states and territories and 113 other countries. 81 percent are from Iowa. 3.9 percent are international students. 19 percent of the 2003 graduating class went on to graduate and professional schools.

Expenses for 2004–05 *Application fee:* $30. *State resident tuition:* $4702 full-time, $196 per semester hour part-time. *Nonresident tuition:* $14,404 full-time, $601 per semester hour part-time. *Mandatory fees:* $724 full-time. Full-time tuition and fees vary according to class time, degree level, and program. Part-time tuition varies according to class time, course load, degree level, and program. *College room and board:* $6121. *College room only:* $3350. Room and board charges vary according to board plan and housing facility.

Financial Aid Forms of aid include need-based and non-need-based scholarships, athletic grants, and part-time jobs. The average aided 2003–04 undergraduate received an aid package worth an estimated $7395. The priority application deadline for financial aid is March 1.

Freshman Admission Iowa State requires a high school transcript, rank in upper 50% of high school class, SAT I or ACT scores, and TOEFL scores for international students. The application deadline for regular admission is August 1.

Transfer Admission The application deadline for admission is August 1.

Entrance Difficulty Iowa State assesses its entrance difficulty level as moderately difficult. For the fall 2003 freshman class, 90 percent of the applicants were accepted.

SPECIAL MESSAGE TO STUDENTS

Social Life Campus life is energized by a diverse community of 27,380 students living in a variety of housing arrangements, including eighteen residence halls (7,500 students), 737 apartments for single students, 456 apartments for married students, and fifty fraternities and sororities (2,700 students). The *Daily* student newspaper and the Web are great resources to access information about Iowa State's more than 550 clubs and organizations, fifty intramural sports and forty-eight club sports, four indoor recreation facilities, and Big 12 competition in eighteen Division I men's and women's sports. Students catch all the top acts at the Iowa State Center, an on-campus arts and entertainment complex that houses the 2,700-seat Stephens Auditorium, the 450-seat Fisher Theater, and the 15,000-seat Hilton Coliseum. Ames offers arts groups, recreational facilities, biking and hiking trails, more than eighty restaurants, a great downtown, shopping, and a variety of movie theaters. Des Moines, Iowa's capital, is a 40-minute drive from campus.

Academic Highlights Iowa State, with more than 100 undergraduate degree programs, ranks tenth in the nation among public universities in the enrollment of first-year National Merit Scholars and twelfth among public universities for enrolling first-year National Achievement Scholars; second among universities in the nation for the number of top technologies honored by *R&D Magazine;* and tenth in the nation for patents awarded. Academic options include Soar in Four (a four-year graduation program), the University Honors Program, international exchange programs (more than 100 institutions in forty countries), and the National Student Exchange program (180 reciprocating universities around the country). Computing resources include thousands of workstations, 24-hour availability, and mainframe/Internet access from residence hall rooms.

Interviews and Campus Visits Visitors are always welcome. Visit options include student-guided walking tours, residence hall tours, college advising appointments, and facility tours. Students and parents can participate in a group visit program called "Experience Iowa State." For more information or

Iowa State University of Science and Technology (continued)

to receive a Campus Visit Planner and plan a customized schedule, students should call the Office of Admissions at 800-262-3810 (toll-free). The office is located in Alumni Hall, on campus.

For Further Information Write to the Office of Admissions, Alumni Hall, Iowa State University, Ames, IA 50011-2010. *E-mail:* admissions@iastate.edu. *Web site:* http://www.admissions.iastate.edu/~admis_info/.

See page 298 for a narrative description.

IOWA WESLEYAN COLLEGE
Mount Pleasant, Iowa

Iowa Wesleyan is a coed, private, United Methodist, four-year college, founded in 1842, offering degrees at the bachelor's level. It has a 60-acre campus in Mount Pleasant.

Academic Information The faculty has 63 members (67% full-time), 33% with terminal degrees. The student-faculty ratio is 14:1. The library holds 107,227 titles, 431 serial subscriptions, and 6,553 audiovisual materials. Special programs include academic remediation, services for learning-disabled students, study abroad, advanced placement credit, ESL programs, double majors, independent study, distance learning, self-designed majors, summer session for credit, part-time degree programs (daytime, evenings, summer), adult/continuing education programs, internships, and arrangement for off-campus study with Southeastern Community College, Muscatine Community College. The most frequently chosen baccalaureate fields are business/marketing, education, psychology.
Student Body Statistics The student body is made up of 753 undergraduates (118 freshmen). 60 percent are women and 40 percent are men. Students come from 22 states and territories and 7 other countries. 83 percent are from Iowa. 2.7 percent are international students. 2 percent of the 2003 graduating class went on to graduate and professional schools.
Expenses for 2004–05 *Comprehensive fee:* $20,990 includes full-time tuition ($16,070) and college room and board ($4920). *College room only:* $2050. Room and board charges vary according to board plan and housing facility. *Part-time tuition:* $375 per credit hour. Part-time tuition varies according to class time.
Financial Aid Forms of aid include need-based and non-need-based scholarships, athletic grants, and part-time jobs. The average aided 2002–03 undergraduate received an aid package worth $10,775. The priority application deadline for financial aid is April 1.
Freshman Admission Iowa Wesleyan requires a high school transcript, a minimum 2.0 high school GPA, SAT I or ACT scores, and TOEFL scores for international students. An interview is recommended. An essay and recommendations are required for some. The application deadline for regular admission is August 15.
Transfer Admission The application deadline for admission is August 15.
Entrance Difficulty Iowa Wesleyan assesses its entrance difficulty level as moderately difficult. For the fall 2003 freshman class, 53 percent of the applicants were accepted.

For Further Information Contact Mr. Cary A. Owens, Dean of Enrollment Management, Iowa Wesleyan College, 601 North Main Street, Mount Pleasant, IA 52641-1398. *Telephone:* 319-385-6230 or 800-582-2383 (toll-free). *Fax:* 319-385-6296. *E-mail:* admitrwl@iwc.edu. *Web site:* http://www.iwc.edu/.

KAPLAN COLLEGE
Davenport, Iowa

Kaplan College is a coed, proprietary, primarily two-year college of Kaplan Higher Education, founded in 1937, offering degrees at the associate and bachelor's levels (profile includes both traditional and on-line students).

Academic Information The faculty has 411 members (14% full-time), 23% with terminal degrees. The student-faculty ratio is 11:1. The library holds 7,000 titles, 120 serial subscriptions, and 504 audiovisual materials. Special programs include academic remediation, cooperative (work-study) education, double majors, independent study, distance learning, summer session for credit, part-time degree programs (daytime, evenings), adult/continuing education programs, and internships. The most frequently chosen baccalaureate field is business/marketing.
Student Body Statistics The student body is made up of 9,194 undergraduates (4,635 freshmen). 72 percent are women and 28 percent are men. Students come from 2 states and territories. 9 percent are from Iowa.
Expenses for 2003–04 *Application fee:* $25. *Tuition:* $10,620 full-time, $236 per credit part-time.
Financial Aid Forms of aid include need-based scholarships and part-time jobs. The application deadline for financial aid is continuous.
Freshman Admission Kaplan College requires a high school transcript, an interview, and TOEFL scores for international students. The application deadline for regular admission is rolling.
Transfer Admission The application deadline for admission is rolling.
Entrance Difficulty Kaplan College assesses its entrance difficulty level as minimally difficult. For the fall 2003 freshman class, 94 percent of the applicants were accepted.

For Further Information Contact Mr. Robert Hoffmann, Director of Admissions, Kaplan College, 1801 East Kimberly Road, Suite 1, Davenport, IA 52807. *Telephone:* 563-441-2496 or 800-747-1035 (toll-free in-state). *Fax:* 563-355-1320. *E-mail:* infoke@kaplancollege.edu. *Web site:* http://www.kaplancollegeia.com/.

LORAS COLLEGE
Dubuque, Iowa

Loras is a coed, private, Roman Catholic, comprehensive institution, founded in 1839, offering degrees at the associate, bachelor's, and master's levels. It has a 60-acre campus in Dubuque.

Academic Information The faculty has 173 members (68% full-time), 64% with terminal degrees. The undergraduate student-faculty ratio is 12:1. The library holds 290,517 titles, 912 serial subscriptions, and 1,676 audiovisual materials. Special programs include academic remediation, services for learning-disabled students, an honors program, cooperative (work-study) education, study abroad, advanced placement credit, ESL programs, double majors, independent study, self-designed majors, summer session for credit, part-time degree programs (daytime, evenings, summer), adult/continuing education programs, internships, and arrangement for off-campus study. The most frequently chosen baccalaureate fields are business/marketing, education, protective services/public administration.
Student Body Statistics The student body totals 1,764, of whom 1,613 are undergraduates (414 freshmen). 51 percent are women and 49 percent are men. Students come from 22 states and territories and 10 other countries. 54 percent are from Iowa. 1.3 percent are international students. 16.1 percent of the 2003 graduating class went on to graduate and professional schools.
Expenses for 2003–04 *Application fee:* $25. *Comprehensive fee:* $24,233 includes full-time tuition ($17,370), mandatory fees ($968), and college room and board ($5895). *College room only:* $2900. Full-time tuition and fees vary according to course load and degree level. Room and board charges vary according to board plan and housing facility. *Part-time tuition:* $385 per credit.
Financial Aid Forms of aid include need-based and non-need-based scholarships and part-time jobs. The average aided 2003–04 undergraduate received an aid package worth an estimated $16,479. The priority application deadline for financial aid is April 15.
Freshman Admission Loras requires a high school transcript, a minimum 2.5 high school GPA, SAT I or ACT scores, and TOEFL scores for international students. An essay and 1 recommendation are recommended. An interview is required for some. The application deadline for regular admission is rolling.
Transfer Admission The application deadline for admission is rolling.

Entrance Difficulty Loras assesses its entrance difficulty level as moderately difficult. For the fall 2003 freshman class, 96 percent of the applicants were accepted.

SPECIAL MESSAGE TO STUDENTS

Social Life Loras College students develop a sense of belonging and involvement by choosing from twenty-one men's and women's varsity athletics and more than fifty-five clubs and organizations. In addition, more than 80 percent of students participate in more than ninety intramural sports. World-renowned speakers and performers punctuate the Loras calendar. The scenic Dubuque area has two skiing and snowboarding areas, extensive bike trails, and an abundance of restaurants while also offering a vibrant arts community with a beautiful art museum, a symphony, and theater groups.

Academic Highlights Loras students connect with the campus and the world through its technology-enriched campus, integrated into the academic experience. All full-time students receive multimedia laptop computers with wireless network connections, freeing them from traditional computer labs. Loras students are well-connected to faculty members and other students as well, enjoying the close-knit environment of a 12:1 student-faculty ratio and an average class size of 17. Loras offers a choice of more than forty majors and fifteen preprofessional majors, ranging from biochemistry to English writing. The College's 1,764 students hail from twenty-seven states and thirteen countries. Loras's Center for Experiential Learning offers invaluable learning opportunities with its study-abroad and internship programs.

Interviews and Campus Visits A campus visit helps students make the right college choice by taking them beyond course listings and faculty members' credentials to get the feel of the College. By arranging an individual campus visit or attending an official campus Visit Day, students can choose from two different methods to experience the College firsthand. Visit Days offer an overview of the college and campus tours, introducing students to a wide array of academic departments, student services, and campus life. Individual visits offer students the ability to tailor their visit to suit their interests and needs, including a personal tour of the Loras campus, hosted by a current student. Every visit offers the opportunity to meet with an admissions counselor and tour campus. Like a Loras education, faculty and staff members make the visit an individual experience. To arrange a campus visit, students should call the Admissions Office, Monday through Friday, 9 a.m. to 3 p.m. at 563-588-7236 or 800-245-6727 (toll-free). Dubuque Regional Airport is just 10 minutes from campus. The nearest commercial airport is Dubuque Regional.

For Further Information Write to Mr. Tim Hauber, Director of Admissions, Loras College, 1450 Alta Vista, Dubuque, IA 52004-0178. *E-mail:* admissions@loras.edu. *Web site:* http://www.loras.edu.

LUTHER COLLEGE

Decorah, Iowa

Luther is a coed, private, four-year college, founded in 1861, affiliated with the Evangelical Lutheran Church in America, offering degrees at the bachelor's level. It has an 800-acre campus in Decorah.

Academic Information The faculty has 235 members (75% full-time), 68% with terminal degrees. The student-faculty ratio is 13:1. The library holds 336,605 titles, 1,600 serial subscriptions, and 7,000 audiovisual materials. Special programs include academic remediation, an honors program, study abroad, advanced placement credit, double majors, independent study, self-designed majors, summer session for credit, part-time degree programs, internships, and arrangement for off-campus study. The most frequently chosen baccalaureate fields are biological/life sciences, business/marketing, social sciences and history.

Student Body Statistics The student body is made up of 2,565 undergraduates (668 freshmen). 60 percent are women and 40 percent are men. Students come from 35 states and territories and 32 other countries. 36 percent are from Iowa. 4.4 percent are international students. 23 percent of the 2003 graduating class went on to graduate and professional schools.

Expenses for 2004–05 *Application fee:* $25. *Comprehensive fee:* $27,240 includes full-time tuition ($23,070) and college room and board ($4170).

College room only: $2040. Full-time tuition varies according to course load. Room and board charges vary according to housing facility. *Part-time tuition:* $824 per semester hour. Part-time tuition varies according to course load.

Financial Aid Forms of aid include need-based and non-need-based scholarships and part-time jobs. The average aided 2002–03 undergraduate received an aid package worth $16,612. The priority application deadline for financial aid is March 1.

Freshman Admission Luther requires an essay, a high school transcript, 1 recommendation, SAT I or ACT scores, and TOEFL scores for international students. An interview is recommended.

Entrance Difficulty Luther assesses its entrance difficulty level as moderately difficult. For the fall 2003 freshman class, 77 percent of the applicants were accepted.

For Further Information Contact Mr. Jon Lund, Vice President for Enrollment and Marketing, Luther College, 700 College Drive, Decorah, IA 52101. *Telephone:* 563-387-1287 or 800-458-8437 (toll-free). *Fax:* 563-387-2159. *E-mail:* admissions@luther.edu. *Web site:* http://www.luther.edu/.

MAHARISHI UNIVERSITY OF MANAGEMENT

Fairfield, Iowa

M.U.M. is a coed, private university, founded in 1971, offering degrees at the bachelor's, master's, and doctoral levels and postbachelor's certificates. It has a 272-acre campus in Fairfield.

Academic Information The faculty has 59 members (76% full-time), 59% with terminal degrees. The undergraduate student-faculty ratio is 14:1. The library holds 113,580 titles, 868 serial subscriptions, and 21,850 audiovisual materials. Special programs include academic remediation, services for learning-disabled students, an honors program, cooperative (work-study) education, study abroad, advanced placement credit, ESL programs, double majors, independent study, distance learning, self-designed majors, adult/continuing education programs, and internships. The most frequently chosen baccalaureate fields are business/marketing, computer/information sciences, visual/performing arts.

Student Body Statistics The student body totals 790, of whom 251 are undergraduates (59 freshmen). 47 percent are women and 53 percent are men. Students come from 32 states and territories and 22 other countries. 52 percent are from Iowa. 30.4 percent are international students. 27 percent of the 2003 graduating class went on to graduate and professional schools.

Expenses for 2004–05 *Application fee:* $25. *One-time mandatory fee:* $2500. *Comprehensive fee:* $30,430 includes full-time tuition ($24,000), mandatory fees ($430), and college room and board ($6000). *College room only:* $2800. *Part-time tuition:* $550 per unit. Part-time tuition varies according to course load.

Financial Aid Forms of aid include need-based and non-need-based scholarships and part-time jobs. The average aided 2003–04 undergraduate received an aid package worth an estimated $22,649. The priority application deadline for financial aid is April 15.

Freshman Admission M.U.M. requires an essay, a high school transcript, a minimum 2.5 high school GPA, 2 recommendations, minimum SAT score of 950 or ACT score of 19, SAT I or ACT scores, and TOEFL scores for international students. An interview is recommended. The application deadline for regular admission is August 1.

Transfer Admission The application deadline for admission is August 1.

Entrance Difficulty M.U.M. assesses its entrance difficulty level as moderately difficult. For the fall 2003 freshman class, 69 percent of the applicants were accepted.

For Further Information Contact Mrs. Lois Neate, Associate Director of Admissions, Maharishi University of Management, Office of Admissions, Fairfield, IA 52557. *Telephone:* 641-472-1110 or 800-369-6480 (toll-free). *Fax:* 641-472-1179. *E-mail:* admissions@mum.edu. *Web site:* http://www.mum.edu/.

MERCY COLLEGE OF HEALTH SCIENCES

Des Moines, Iowa

Mercy College of Health Sciences is a coed, primarily women's, private, four-year college, founded in 1995, affiliated with the Roman Catholic Church, offering degrees at the associate and bachelor's levels. It has a 5-acre campus in Des Moines.

Academic Information The faculty has 58 members (52% full-time), 16% with terminal degrees. The student-faculty ratio is 12:1. The most frequently chosen baccalaureate field is health professions and related sciences.
Student Body Statistics The student body is made up of 616 undergraduates (61 freshmen). 90 percent are women and 10 percent are men.
Expenses for 2004–05 *Application fee:* $25. *Tuition:* $11,300 full-time, $375 per semester hour part-time.
Financial Aid Forms of aid include need-based and non-need-based scholarships and part-time jobs. The average aided 2002–03 undergraduate received an aid package worth $6425. The application deadline for financial aid is July 1.
Freshman Admission Mercy College of Health Sciences requires a high school transcript, a minimum 3.2 high school GPA, ACT scores, and TOEFL scores for international students. An interview is required for some. The application deadline for regular admission is rolling.
Entrance Difficulty Mercy College of Health Sciences has an open admission policy.

For Further Information Contact Ms. Susan Rhoades, Dean, Student Services and Enrollment, Mercy College of Health Sciences, IA. *Telephone:* 515-643-3180 or 800-637-2994 (toll-free). *Fax:* 515-643-6698. *Web site:* http://www.mchs.edu/.

MORNINGSIDE COLLEGE

Sioux City, Iowa

Morningside is a coed, private, comprehensive institution, founded in 1894, affiliated with the United Methodist Church, offering degrees at the bachelor's and master's levels. It has a 41-acre campus in Sioux City.

Academic Information The faculty has 111 members (57% full-time), 48% with terminal degrees. The undergraduate student-faculty ratio is 14:1. The library holds 114,250 titles, 571 serial subscriptions, and 5,372 audiovisual materials. Special programs include academic remediation, services for learning-disabled students, an honors program, study abroad, advanced placement credit, ESL programs, double majors, independent study, self-designed majors, summer session for credit, part-time degree programs (daytime, evenings, summer), adult/continuing education programs, internships, and arrangement for off-campus study with American University, Drew University. The most frequently chosen baccalaureate fields are business/marketing, education, visual/performing arts.
Student Body Statistics The student body totals 1,176, of whom 942 are undergraduates (273 freshmen). 57 percent are women and 43 percent are men. Students come from 23 states and territories and 8 other countries. 71 percent are from Iowa. 2.5 percent are international students. 12.4 percent of the 2003 graduating class went on to graduate and professional schools.
Expenses for 2003–04 *Application fee:* $25. *Comprehensive fee:* $21,610 includes full-time tuition ($15,450), mandatory fees ($900), and college room and board ($5260). *College room only:* $2750. Room and board charges vary according to board plan. *Part-time tuition:* $500 per semester hour.
Financial Aid Forms of aid include need-based and non-need-based scholarships, athletic grants, and part-time jobs. The average aided 2003–04 undergraduate received an aid package worth an estimated $15,716. The priority application deadline for financial aid is March 1.
Freshman Admission Morningside requires a high school transcript, minimum SAT score of 930 or ACT score of 20 and rank in top 50% of high school class or achieved GPA of 2.5 or better, SAT I or ACT scores,

and TOEFL scores for international students. An interview is recommended. 2 recommendations are required for some. The application deadline for regular admission is rolling.
Transfer Admission The application deadline for admission is rolling.
Entrance Difficulty Morningside assesses its entrance difficulty level as moderately difficult. For the fall 2003 freshman class, 74 percent of the applicants were accepted.

For Further Information Contact Mr. Joel Weyand, Director of Admissions, Morningside College, 1501 Morningside Avenue, Sioux City, IA 51106. *Telephone:* 712-274-5111 or 800-831-0806 Ext. 5111 (toll-free). *Fax:* 712-274-5101. *E-mail:* mscadm@morningside.edu. *Web site:* http://www.morningside.edu/.

See page 316 for a narrative description.

MOUNT MERCY COLLEGE

Cedar Rapids, Iowa

Mount Mercy is a coed, private, Roman Catholic, four-year college, founded in 1928, offering degrees at the bachelor's level. It has a 40-acre campus in Cedar Rapids.

Academic Information The faculty has 135 members (53% full-time), 43% with terminal degrees. The student-faculty ratio is 13:1. The library holds 118,000 titles, 1,000 serial subscriptions, and 5,000 audiovisual materials. Special programs include academic remediation, services for learning-disabled students, an honors program, advanced placement credit, accelerated degree programs, Freshman Honors College, double majors, independent study, self-designed majors, summer session for credit, part-time degree programs (daytime, evenings, weekends, summer), adult/continuing education programs, internships, and arrangement for off-campus study with Coe College. The most frequently chosen baccalaureate fields are business/marketing, education, health professions and related sciences.
Student Body Statistics The student body is made up of 1,473 undergraduates (196 freshmen). 70 percent are women and 30 percent are men. Students come from 23 states and territories. 87 percent are from Iowa. 0.1 percent are international students. 11 percent of the 2003 graduating class went on to graduate and professional schools.
Expenses for 2003–04 *Application fee:* $20. *Comprehensive fee:* $21,400 includes full-time tuition ($16,070) and college room and board ($5330). *College room only:* $2164. Full-time tuition varies according to course load. Room and board charges vary according to board plan. *Part-time tuition:* $445 per credit hour. Part-time tuition varies according to course load.
Financial Aid Forms of aid include need-based and non-need-based scholarships and part-time jobs. The average aided 2003–04 undergraduate received an aid package worth an estimated $13,649. The priority application deadline for financial aid is March 1.
Freshman Admission Mount Mercy requires a high school transcript, a minimum 2.5 high school GPA, 1 recommendation, SAT I or ACT scores, and TOEFL scores for international students. An essay and a minimum 3.0 high school GPA are recommended. An interview is required for some. The application deadline for regular admission is August 30.
Transfer Admission The application deadline for admission is August 30.
Entrance Difficulty Mount Mercy assesses its entrance difficulty level as moderately difficult. For the fall 2003 freshman class, 84 percent of the applicants were accepted.

SPECIAL MESSAGE TO STUDENTS

Social Life Shows on campus by musicians and comedians on weekend nights, regular "Club Friday" at Lundy Commons, and the activities of more than thirty clubs and organizations, plus an active student government and newspaper, spark the social life on the Mount Mercy campus. When students are in the mood to expand their entertainment horizons, they are also in the right place, just 2 miles in either direction from downtown or a major mall. With city bus stops at the edge of campus, students have easy access to everything the thriving Midwestern city of Cedar Rapids has to offer—a noted symphony, Theater Cedar Rapids, the Paramount Theater, the Cedar Rapids Museum of Art, minor league baseball and hockey, a downtown arena that hosts popular concerts and shows, and the Science Station with an IMAX theater.

Academic Highlights With high academic quality, moderate cost, and generous scholarships, Mount Mercy College offers outstanding educational value. At Mount Mercy, students achieve more than just a credential; they are molded with the intellectual tools to succeed. Mount Mercy students are prepared to be well-rounded critical thinkers and effective communicators. The Freshman Partnership program helps first-time freshmen make a smooth transition to college life; the Honors Program offers accomplished students unique classes that encourage exploration beyond traditional academic boundaries; and the Academic Achievement Center provides academic counseling and assistance to all students. Classes are small and the faculty members are focused on teaching. At Mount Mercy College, an active learning environment helps students gain confidence in discussing their views and opinions—an environment that well prepares students for a job or graduate school.

Interviews and Campus Visits The best way to learn about the College is to visit, sit in on a class, meet with students and faculty members, and learn about scholarships and other forms of financial assistance. Mount Mercy welcomes students on special visit days throughout the year, and the staff members are happy to arrange individual weekday or weekend appointments. For more information about interviews and campus visits, students should call the Mount Mercy College Office of Admission, Monday through Friday, 8 a.m. to 5 p.m. (CST), at 319-368-6460 or 800-248-4504 (toll-free). The nearest commercial airport is Cedar Rapids Municipal.

For Further Information Write to the Dean of Admission, Mount Mercy College, 1330 Elmhurst Drive, NE, Cedar Rapids, IA 52402. *E-mail:* admission@mtmercy.edu. *Web site:* http://www.mtmercy.edu.

See page 318 for a narrative description.

MOUNT ST. CLARE COLLEGE

See The Franciscan University

NORTHWESTERN COLLEGE
Orange City, Iowa

Northwestern is a coed, private, four-year college, founded in 1882, affiliated with the Reformed Church in America, offering degrees at the associate and bachelor's levels. It has a 45-acre campus in Orange City.

Academic Information The faculty has 121 members (64% full-time), 52% with terminal degrees. The student-faculty ratio is 14:1. The library holds 125,000 titles, 615 serial subscriptions, and 5,000 audiovisual materials. Special programs include academic remediation, an honors program, cooperative (work-study) education, study abroad, advanced placement credit, accelerated degree programs, Freshman Honors College, ESL programs, double majors, independent study, self-designed majors, summer session for credit, part-time degree programs, internships, and arrangement for off-campus study with 5 members of the Mid-America States Universities Association, Council for Christian Colleges and Universities. The most frequently chosen baccalaureate fields are business/marketing, education, philosophy, religion, and theology.
Student Body Statistics The student body is made up of 1,285 undergraduates (311 freshmen). 61 percent are women and 39 percent are men. Students come from 29 states and territories and 12 other countries. 59 percent are from Iowa. 2.7 percent are international students. 22 percent of the 2003 graduating class went on to graduate and professional schools.
Expenses for 2003–04 *Application fee:* $25. *Comprehensive fee:* $19,640 includes full-time tuition ($15,290) and college room and board ($4350). *College room only:* $1850. Room and board charges vary according to housing facility. *Part-time tuition:* $320 per credit. Part-time tuition varies according to course load.

Financial Aid Forms of aid include need-based and non-need-based scholarships, athletic grants, and part-time jobs. The average aided 2002–03 undergraduate received an aid package worth $13,738. The priority application deadline for financial aid is April 1.
Freshman Admission Northwestern requires an essay, a high school transcript, a minimum 2.0 high school GPA, 1 recommendation, SAT I or ACT scores, and TOEFL scores for international students. A minimum 2.5 high school GPA and an interview are recommended. The application deadline for regular admission is rolling.
Transfer Admission The application deadline for admission is rolling.
Entrance Difficulty Northwestern assesses its entrance difficulty level as moderately difficult. For the fall 2003 freshman class, 83 percent of the applicants were accepted.

For Further Information Contact Mr. Ronald K. DeJong, Director of Admissions, Northwestern College, 101 College Lane, Orange City, IA 51041-1996. *Telephone:* 712-737-7130 or 800-747-4757 (toll-free). *Fax:* 712-707-7164. *E-mail:* markb@nwciowa.edu. *Web site:* http://www.nwciowa.edu/.

PALMER COLLEGE OF CHIROPRACTIC
Davenport, Iowa

PCC is a coed, private, comprehensive unit of Palmer Chiropractic University System, founded in 1897, offering degrees at the associate, incidental bachelor's, master's, and first professional levels in chiropractic.

Academic Information The faculty has 112 members (100% full-time). The undergraduate student-faculty ratio is 17:1. The library holds 51,445 titles, 894 serial subscriptions, and 22,869 audiovisual materials. Special programs include academic remediation, services for learning-disabled students, summer session for credit, and internships. The most frequently chosen baccalaureate field is health professions and related sciences.
Student Body Statistics The student body totals 1,859, of whom 97 are undergraduates (33 freshmen). 58 percent are women and 42 percent are men.
Expenses for 2003–04 *Application fee:* $50. *Tuition:* $5325 full-time, $126 per credit part-time. *Mandatory fees:* $200 per term part-time.
Financial Aid Forms of aid include need-based and non-need-based scholarships and part-time jobs. The application deadline for financial aid is continuous.
Freshman Admission PCC requires a high school transcript, a minimum 2.0 high school GPA, minimum 2.0 in math, science, and English courses, and TOEFL scores for international students. An essay and an interview are required for some. The application deadline for regular admission is rolling.
Entrance Difficulty PCC assesses its entrance difficulty level as moderately difficult.

For Further Information Contact Ms. Lisa Walden, Interim Director of Admissions, Palmer College of Chiropractic, 1000 Brady Street, Davenport, IA 52803-5287. *Telephone:* 563-884-5656 or 800-722-3648 (toll-free). *Fax:* 563-884-5414. *E-mail:* pcadmit@palmer.edu. *Web site:* http://www.palmer.edu/.

QUEST COLLEGE

See Kaplan College

ST. AMBROSE UNIVERSITY
Davenport, Iowa

St. Ambrose is a coed, private, Roman Catholic, comprehensive institution, founded in 1882, offering degrees at the bachelor's, master's, and doctoral levels and post-master's and postbachelor's certificates. It has an 11-acre campus in Davenport.

Academic Information The faculty has 293 members (55% full-time), 42% with terminal degrees. The undergraduate student-faculty ratio is

St. Ambrose University (continued)

15:1. The library holds 135,920 titles, 735 serial subscriptions, and 2,930 audiovisual materials. Special programs include academic remediation, services for learning-disabled students, cooperative (work-study) education, study abroad, advanced placement credit, accelerated degree programs, double majors, independent study, distance learning, self-designed majors, summer session for credit, part-time degree programs (daytime, evenings, weekends, summer), external degree programs, adult/continuing education programs, internships, and arrangement for off-campus study with Black Hawk College, Eastern Iowa Community Colleges. The most frequently chosen baccalaureate fields are business/marketing, education, psychology.

Student Body Statistics The student body totals 3,447, of whom 2,483 are undergraduates (436 freshmen). 59 percent are women and 41 percent are men. Students come from 23 states and territories and 15 other countries. 62 percent are from Iowa. 25 percent of the 2003 graduating class went on to graduate and professional schools.

Expenses for 2004–05 *Application fee:* $25. *One-time mandatory fee:* $100. *Comprehensive fee:* $24,200 includes full-time tuition ($17,565) and college room and board ($6635). *College room only:* $3380. Full-time tuition varies according to course load and location. Room and board charges vary according to board plan and housing facility. *Part-time tuition:* $547 per semester hour. Part-time tuition varies according to course load and location.

Financial Aid Forms of aid include need-based and non-need-based scholarships, athletic grants, and part-time jobs. The average aided 2003–04 undergraduate received an aid package worth an estimated $12,467. The priority application deadline for financial aid is March 15.

Freshman Admission St. Ambrose requires a high school transcript, a minimum 2.5 high school GPA, minimum ACT score of 20 or rank in top 50% of high school class, SAT I or ACT scores, and TOEFL scores for international students. An interview and ACT scores are recommended. Recommendations and an interview are required for some. The application deadline for regular admission is rolling.

Transfer Admission The application deadline for admission is rolling.

Entrance Difficulty St. Ambrose assesses its entrance difficulty level as moderately difficult. For the fall 2003 freshman class, 87 percent of the applicants were accepted.

For Further Information Contact Ms. Meg Halligan, Director of Admissions, St. Ambrose University, 518 West Locust Street, Davenport, IA 52803-2898. *Telephone:* 563-333-6300 Ext. 6311 or 800-383-2627 (toll-free). *Fax:* 563-333-6297. *E-mail:* halliganmegf@sau.edu. *Web site:* http://www.sau.edu/.

ST. LUKE'S COLLEGE

Sioux City, Iowa

St. Luke's College is a coed, primarily women's, private, two-year college of St. Luke's Regional Medical Center, offering degrees at the associate level.

Academic Information The faculty has 16 members (62% full-time), 31% with terminal degrees. The student-faculty ratio is 7:1. The library holds 115 serial subscriptions and 1,800 audiovisual materials. Special programs include cooperative (work-study) education, advanced placement credit, summer session for credit, and part-time degree programs (daytime, evenings, summer).

Student Body Statistics The student body is made up of 147 undergraduates (27 freshmen). 91 percent are women and 9 percent are men. Students come from 8 states and territories and 1 other country. 75 percent are from Iowa. 0.7 percent are international students. 61 percent of the 2003 graduating class went on to four-year colleges.

Expenses for 2004–05 *Application fee:* $100. *Comprehensive fee:* $14,780 includes full-time tuition ($11,088), mandatory fees ($570), and college room and board ($3122). *College room only:* $2622. Full-time tuition and fees vary according to course load and program. Room and board charges vary according to board plan. *Part-time tuition:* $308 per credit hour. Part-time tuition varies according to course load and program.

Financial Aid Forms of aid include need-based scholarships and part-time jobs. The priority application deadline for financial aid is March 1.

Freshman Admission St. Luke's College requires an essay, a high school transcript, a minimum 2.50 high school GPA, minimum ACT score of 19, and ACT scores. The application deadline for regular admission is August 1.

Entrance Difficulty St. Luke's College assesses its entrance difficulty level as minimally difficult. For the fall 2003 freshman class, 55 percent of the applicants were accepted.

For Further Information Contact Ms. Sherry McCarthy, Admissions Coordinator, St. Luke's College, 2720 Stone Park Boulevard, Sioux City, IA 51104. *Telephone:* 712-279-3149 or 800-352-4660 Ext. 3149 (toll-free). *Fax:* 712-279-3155. *E-mail:* mccartsj@stlukes.org. *Web site:* http://www.stlukes.org/college/.

SIMPSON COLLEGE

Indianola, Iowa

Simpson is a coed, private, United Methodist, four-year college, founded in 1860, offering degrees at the bachelor's level and postbachelor's certificates. It has a 74-acre campus in Indianola.

Academic Information The faculty has 140 members (60% full-time). The student-faculty ratio is 14:1. The library holds 151,359 titles, 599 serial subscriptions, and 5,357 audiovisual materials. Special programs include academic remediation, services for learning-disabled students, an honors program, cooperative (work-study) education, study abroad, advanced placement credit, accelerated degree programs, Freshman Honors College, double majors, independent study, self-designed majors, summer session for credit, part-time degree programs (daytime, evenings, weekends, summer), adult/continuing education programs, internships, and arrangement for off-campus study with Drew University, American University, Washington Center Internships and Symposia. The most frequently chosen baccalaureate fields are business/marketing, communications/communication technologies, education.

Student Body Statistics The student body is made up of 1,937 undergraduates (413 freshmen). 59 percent are women and 41 percent are men. Students come from 27 states and territories and 20 other countries. 88 percent are from Iowa. 1.9 percent are international students. 11 percent of the 2003 graduating class went on to graduate and professional schools.

Expenses for 2003–04 *Application fee:* $0. *Comprehensive fee:* $24,159 includes full-time tuition ($17,908), mandatory fees ($189), and college room and board ($6062). *College room only:* $3170. Room and board charges vary according to board plan and housing facility. *Part-time tuition:* varies with class time, course load.

Financial Aid Forms of aid include need-based and non-need-based scholarships and part-time jobs. The average aided 2003–04 undergraduate received an aid package worth an estimated $17,124. The application deadline for financial aid is continuous.

Freshman Admission Simpson requires a high school transcript, 1 recommendation, SAT I or ACT scores, and TOEFL scores for international students. Rank in upper 50% of high school class is recommended. The application deadline for regular admission is August 15.

Transfer Admission The application deadline for admission is August 15.

Entrance Difficulty Simpson assesses its entrance difficulty level as moderately difficult. For the fall 2003 freshman class, 86 percent of the applicants were accepted.

SPECIAL MESSAGE TO STUDENTS

Social Life One of the characteristics of Simpson is the number of opportunities available on campus. Activities include vocal and instrumental music groups, Theatre Simpson, honor and professional societies, and religious life council. Simpson competes in Division III of the NCAA and offers eighteen intercollegiate teams for men and women. Students annually elect a president and vice president of the Student Government. Each housing unit elects representatives to Student Senate, and the senate appoints student members to appropriate College committees. Simpson is a residential campus with four traditional residence halls, seven apartment-style residences, ten theme houses, three national fraternities, one local fraternity, and four national sororities. Approximately 30 percent of the students participate in the Greek system.

Academic Highlights Simpson's academic program is based on the best traditions of the liberal arts, enhanced by a genuine respect for the career requirements of today. Simpson's professors are dedicated to teaching. With a student-faculty ratio of 14:1, professors get to know students personally. More than forty different majors and career programs are available. Simpson is on a 4-4-1 calendar, with two 4-month semesters and one 3-week term of concentrated study in May. The May-Term course offerings provide an in-depth exploration of a subject and include internships, study abroad, and career observations. Simpson has exchange programs with international and domestic universities and offers study-abroad programs on a regular basis.

Interviews and Campus Visits Simpson College strongly encourages all prospective students to visit the campus. An interview is not required but is considered an excellent opportunity for prospective students and their parents to discuss academic programs, financial assistance, and scholarship opportunities. During the visit, prospective students tour the campus with a Student Ambassador, perhaps meet with a professor or attend a class, and interview with an admissions counselor. Students can take advantage of music or theater productions, athletic events, or other activities during their visit. Simpson blends tradition with practicality, and this is reflected in the architecture on campus. Buildings of interest include the historic College Hall, built in 1869; Carver Science Center, named after George Washington Carver, who attended Simpson College; McNeill Hall for Business, housing a seminar room, conference center, computer labs, and classrooms; Dunn Library; the Amy Robertson Music Center, housing a 250-seat recital hall, studios, and practice rooms; and Cowles Athletic Center, in which a 25-meter swimming pool, physical education facilities, weight rooms, racquetball courts, and a field house are located. For information about appointments and campus visits, students should call the Office of Admissions at 515-961-1624 or 800-362-2454 (toll-free), Monday through Friday, 8 a.m. to 4:30 p.m., or on designated Saturdays, 9 a.m. to noon. Students may also schedule visits online at http://www.simpson.edu. The fax number is 515-961-1870. The office is located in College Hall, first floor, on campus. The nearest commercial airport is Des Moines International.

For Further Information Write to the Office of Admissions, Simpson College, 701 North C Street, Indianola, IA 50125. *E-mail:* admiss@simpson.edu. *Web site:* http://www.simpson.edu.

See page 338 for a narrative description.

UNIVERSITY OF DUBUQUE
Dubuque, Iowa

UD is a coed, private, Presbyterian, comprehensive institution, founded in 1852, offering degrees at the associate, bachelor's, master's, doctoral, and first professional levels. It has a 56-acre campus in Dubuque.

Academic Information The faculty has 148 members (41% full-time), 46% with terminal degrees. The undergraduate student-faculty ratio is 14:1. The library holds 166,331 titles, 565 serial subscriptions, and 525 audiovisual materials. Special programs include academic remediation, services for learning-disabled students, study abroad, advanced placement credit, accelerated degree programs, ESL programs, double majors, independent study, distance learning, self-designed majors, summer session for credit, part-time degree programs (daytime, evenings, weekends, summer), adult/continuing education programs, internships, and arrangement for off-campus study with Loras College, Clarke College (IA). The most frequently chosen baccalaureate fields are business/marketing, education, visual/performing arts.

Student Body Statistics The student body totals 1,253, of whom 990 are undergraduates (313 freshmen). 35 percent are women and 65 percent are men. Students come from 37 states and territories and 2 other countries. 54 percent are from Iowa. 1.4 percent are international students.

Expenses for 2004–05 *Application fee:* $25. *Comprehensive fee:* $21,680 includes full-time tuition ($16,100), mandatory fees ($160), and college

room and board ($5420). *College room only:* $2610. Room and board charges vary according to board plan and housing facility. *Part-time tuition:* $360 per credit.

Financial Aid Forms of aid include need-based and non-need-based scholarships and part-time jobs. The average aided 2003–04 undergraduate received an aid package worth an estimated $15,986. The application deadline for financial aid is continuous.

Freshman Admission UD requires an essay, a high school transcript, a minimum 2.0 high school GPA, 2 recommendations, SAT I or ACT scores, and TOEFL scores for international students. An interview is recommended. The application deadline for regular admission is rolling.

Transfer Admission The application deadline for admission is rolling.

Entrance Difficulty UD assesses its entrance difficulty level as moderately difficult. For the fall 2003 freshman class, 82 percent of the applicants were accepted.

For Further Information Contact Mr. Jesse James, Director of Admissions, University of Dubuque, 2000 University Avenue, Dubuque, IA 52001-5099. *Telephone:* 563-589-3214 or 800-722-5583 (toll-free in-state). *Fax:* 563-589-3690. *E-mail:* admssns@dbq.edu. *Web site:* http://www.dbq.edu/.

THE UNIVERSITY OF IOWA
Iowa City, Iowa

Iowa is a coed, public university, founded in 1847, offering degrees at the bachelor's, master's, doctoral, and first professional levels. It has a 1,900-acre campus in Iowa City.

Academic Information The faculty has 1,705 members (95% full-time), 96% with terminal degrees. The undergraduate student-faculty ratio is 15:1. The library holds 4 million titles, 44,644 serial subscriptions, and 267,192 audiovisual materials. Special programs include academic remediation, services for learning-disabled students, an honors program, cooperative (work-study) education, study abroad, advanced placement credit, accelerated degree programs, ESL programs, double majors, independent study, distance learning, self-designed majors, summer session for credit, part-time degree programs (daytime, evenings, weekends, summer), external degree programs, adult/continuing education programs, internships, and arrangement for off-campus study with Iowa State University of Science and Technology, University of Northern Iowa, Committee on Institutional Cooperation. The most frequently chosen baccalaureate fields are business/marketing, communications/communication technologies, social sciences and history.

Student Body Statistics The student body totals 29,744, of whom 20,233 are undergraduates (4,083 freshmen). 54 percent are women and 46 percent are men. Students come from 52 states and territories and 65 other countries. 67 percent are from Iowa. 1.2 percent are international students.

Expenses for 2004–05 *Application fee:* $30. *State resident tuition:* $4702 full-time, $196 per semester hour part-time. *Nonresident tuition:* $15,354 full-time, $640 per semester hour part-time. *Mandatory fees:* $694 full-time, $347 per term part-time. Full-time tuition and fees vary according to course load and program. Part-time tuition and fees vary according to course load and program. *College room and board:* $6350. Room and board charges vary according to board plan and housing facility.

Financial Aid Forms of aid include need-based and non-need-based scholarships, athletic grants, and part-time jobs. The average aided 2003–04 undergraduate received an aid package worth an estimated $7386. The application deadline for financial aid is continuous.

Freshman Admission Iowa requires a high school transcript, rank in top 50% for residents, rank in top 30% for nonresidents, SAT I or ACT scores, and TOEFL scores for international students. The application deadline for regular admission is April 1.

Transfer Admission The application deadline for admission is April 1.

Iowa

The University of Iowa (continued)

Entrance Difficulty Iowa assesses its entrance difficulty level as moderately difficult; very difficult for engineering programs. For the fall 2003 freshman class, 82 percent of the applicants were accepted.

For Further Information Contact Mr. Michael Barron, Director of Admissions, The University of Iowa, 107 Calvin Hall, Iowa City, IA 52242. *Telephone:* 319-335-3847 or 800-553-4692 (toll-free). *Fax:* 319-335-1535. *E-mail:* admissions@uiowa.edu. *Web site:* http://www.uiowa.edu/.

UNIVERSITY OF NORTHERN IOWA
Cedar Falls, Iowa

UNI is a coed, public, comprehensive unit of Board of Regents, State of Iowa, founded in 1876, offering degrees at the bachelor's, master's, and doctoral levels. It has a 916-acre campus in Cedar Falls.

Academic Information The faculty has 799 members (84% full-time), 74% with terminal degrees. The undergraduate student-faculty ratio is 16:1. The library holds 760,595 titles, 7,226 serial subscriptions, and 22,883 audiovisual materials. Special programs include academic remediation, services for learning-disabled students, an honors program, cooperative (work-study) education, study abroad, advanced placement credit, accelerated degree programs, ESL programs, double majors, independent study, distance learning, self-designed majors, summer session for credit, part-time degree programs (daytime, evenings, summer), adult/continuing education programs, internships, and arrangement for off-campus study with Iowa Regents' Universities Student Exchange, National Student Exchange. The most frequently chosen baccalaureate fields are business/marketing, education, social sciences and history.
Student Body Statistics The student body totals 13,666, of whom 11,910 are undergraduates (1,785 freshmen). 58 percent are women and 42 percent are men. Students come from 44 states and territories and 66 other countries. 96 percent are from Iowa. 1.8 percent are international students. 13 percent of the 2003 graduating class went on to graduate and professional schools.
Expenses for 2003–04 *Application fee:* $30. *State resident tuition:* $4342 full-time, $181 per hour part-time. *Nonresident tuition:* $11,300 full-time, $471 per hour part-time. *Mandatory fees:* $574 full-time. Full-time tuition and fees vary according to course load. Part-time tuition varies according to course load. *College room and board:* $4918. *College room only:* $2272. Room and board charges vary according to board plan and housing facility.
Financial Aid Forms of aid include need-based and non-need-based scholarships, athletic grants, and part-time jobs. The average aided 2003–04 undergraduate received an aid package worth an estimated $6705. The application deadline for financial aid is continuous.
Freshman Admission UNI requires a high school transcript, rank in upper 50% of high school class, SAT I or ACT scores, and TOEFL scores for international students. An interview is required for some. The application deadline for regular admission is August 15.
Transfer Admission The application deadline for admission is August 15.
Entrance Difficulty UNI assesses its entrance difficulty level as moderately difficult. For the fall 2003 freshman class, 80 percent of the applicants were accepted.

For Further Information Contact Mr. Clark Elmer, Director of Enrollment Management and Admissions, University of Northern Iowa, 120 Gilchrist Hall, Cedar Falls, IA 50614-0018. *Telephone:* 319-273-2281 or 800-772-2037 (toll-free). *Fax:* 319-273-2885. *E-mail:* admissions@uni.edu. *Web site:* http://www.uni.edu/.

UPPER IOWA UNIVERSITY
Fayette, Iowa

Upper Iowa is a coed, private, comprehensive institution, founded in 1857, offering degrees at the associate, bachelor's, and master's levels (also offers continuing education program with significant enrollment not reflected in profile). It has an 80-acre campus in Fayette.

Academic Information The faculty has 65 members (88% full-time), 62% with terminal degrees. The undergraduate student-faculty ratio is 14:1. The library holds 64,043 titles, 3,241 serial subscriptions, and 4,031 audiovisual materials. Special programs include academic remediation, study abroad, advanced placement credit, accelerated degree programs, double majors, independent study, distance learning, self-designed majors, summer session for credit, part-time degree programs (daytime, evenings, summer), external degree programs, adult/continuing education programs, and internships. The most frequently chosen baccalaureate fields are business/marketing, education, protective services/public administration.
Student Body Statistics The student body totals 840, of whom 683 are undergraduates (146 freshmen). 40 percent are women and 60 percent are men. Students come from 25 states and territories and 7 other countries. 58 percent are from Iowa. 1.9 percent are international students.
Expenses for 2004–05 *Application fee:* $15. *Comprehensive fee:* $21,828 includes full-time tuition ($16,556) and college room and board ($5272). *College room only:* $2188. Full-time tuition varies according to course load. Room and board charges vary according to board plan and housing facility. *Part-time tuition:* $550 per credit hour.
Financial Aid Forms of aid include need-based and non-need-based scholarships and part-time jobs. The priority application deadline for financial aid is June 1.
Freshman Admission Upper Iowa requires a high school transcript, a minimum 2.0 high school GPA, SAT I or ACT scores, and TOEFL scores for international students. An essay, recommendations, and an interview are required for some. The application deadline for regular admission is rolling.
Transfer Admission The application deadline for admission is rolling.
Entrance Difficulty Upper Iowa assesses its entrance difficulty level as moderately difficult. For the fall 2003 freshman class, 56 percent of the applicants were accepted.

For Further Information Contact Ms. Linda Hoopes, Director of Admissions, Upper Iowa University, Box 1859, 605 Washington Street, Fayette, IA 52142-1857. *Telephone:* 563-425-5281 Ext. 5279 or 800-553-4150 Ext. 2 (toll-free). *Fax:* 563-425-5323. *E-mail:* admission@uiu.edu. *Web site:* http://www.uiu.edu/.

VENNARD COLLEGE
University Park, Iowa

Vennard is a coed, private, interdenominational, four-year college, founded in 1996, offering degrees at the associate and bachelor's levels. It has a 70-acre campus in University Park near Des Moines.

Academic Information The faculty has 12 members (42% full-time), 25% with terminal degrees. The student-faculty ratio is 12:1. The library holds 17,950 titles and 538,323 serial subscriptions. Special programs include academic remediation, services for learning-disabled students, cooperative (work-study) education, advanced placement credit, double majors, independent study, distance learning, self-designed majors, summer session for credit, part-time degree programs (daytime, evenings), external degree programs, internships, and arrangement for off-campus study with William Penn University. The most frequently chosen baccalaureate fields are interdisciplinary studies, philosophy, religion, and theology, psychology.
Student Body Statistics The student body is made up of 109 undergraduates (20 freshmen). 43 percent are women and 57 percent are men. Students come from 22 states and territories and 2 other countries. 35 percent are from Iowa. 3.7 percent are international students. 6 percent of the 2003 graduating class went on to graduate and professional schools.
Expenses for 2003–04 *Application fee:* $20. Full-time (12+hours) tuition is $255 per credit hour.
Financial Aid Forms of aid include need-based scholarships and part-time jobs. The average aided 2003–04 undergraduate received an aid package worth an estimated $7000. The priority application deadline for financial aid is April 1.

Freshman Admission Vennard requires an essay, a high school transcript, a minimum 2.2 high school GPA, and 3 recommendations. SAT I or ACT scores and SAT I and SAT II or ACT scores are required for some.
Entrance Difficulty For the fall 2003 freshman class, 47 percent of the applicants were accepted.

For Further Information Contact Ms. Robyn Chrisman, Director of Admissions, Vennard College, PO Box 29, University Park, IA 52595. *Telephone:* 641-673-8391 Ext. 116 or 800-686-8391 (toll-free). *Fax:* 641-673-8365. *Web site:* http://www.vennard.edu/.

WALDORF COLLEGE
Forest City, Iowa

Waldorf is a coed, private, Lutheran, four-year college, founded in 1903, offering degrees at the bachelor's level. It has a 29-acre campus in Forest City.

Academic Information The faculty has 53 members (68% full-time), 30% with terminal degrees. The student-faculty ratio is 13:1. The library holds 33,422 titles, 55,989 serial subscriptions, and 274 audiovisual materials. Special programs include academic remediation, services for learning-disabled students, an honors program, cooperative (work-study) education, study abroad, advanced placement credit, accelerated degree programs, Freshman Honors College, ESL programs, double majors, summer session for credit, part-time degree programs, adult/continuing education programs, and internships. The most frequently chosen baccalaureate fields are business/marketing, communications/communication technologies, education.
Student Body Statistics The student body is made up of 592 undergraduates (295 freshmen). 50 percent are women and 50 percent are men. Students come from 20 states and territories and 13 other countries. 67 percent are from Iowa. 4.7 percent are international students. 2 percent of the 2003 graduating class went on to graduate and professional schools.
Expenses for 2003–04 *Application fee:* $0. *Comprehensive fee:* $17,862 includes full-time tuition ($13,000), mandatory fees ($662), and college room and board ($4200). *College room only:* $2100. Full-time tuition and fees vary according to class time and course load. Room and board charges vary according to board plan and housing facility. *Part-time tuition:* $180 per credit. *Part-time mandatory fees:* $35 per semester hour.
Financial Aid Forms of aid include need-based and non-need-based scholarships, athletic grants, and part-time jobs. The average aided 2003–04 undergraduate received an aid package worth an estimated $15,752. The priority application deadline for financial aid is March 1.
Freshman Admission Waldorf requires a high school transcript, 1 recommendation, SAT I or ACT scores, and TOEFL scores for international students. A minimum 2.0 high school GPA is recommended. An interview is required for some. The application deadline for regular admission is rolling.
Transfer Admission The application deadline for admission is rolling.
Entrance Difficulty Waldorf assesses its entrance difficulty level as moderately difficult. For the fall 2003 freshman class, 72 percent of the applicants were accepted.

For Further Information Contact Mr. Steve Hall, Assistant Dean of Admission, Waldorf College, 106 South 6th Street, Forest City, IA 50436. *Telephone:* 641-585-8112 or 800-292-1903 (toll-free). *Fax:* 641-585-8125. *E-mail:* admissions@waldorf.edu. *Web site:* http://www.waldorf.edu/.

WARTBURG COLLEGE
Waverly, Iowa

Wartburg is a coed, private, Lutheran, four-year college, founded in 1852, offering degrees at the bachelor's level. It has a 118-acre campus in Waverly.

Academic Information The faculty has 162 members (64% full-time), 60% with terminal degrees. The student-faculty ratio is 14:1. The library holds 171,852 titles, 826 serial subscriptions, and 3,754 audiovisual materials. Special programs include academic remediation, study abroad, advanced placement credit, accelerated degree programs, double majors, independent study, self-designed majors, summer session for credit, part-time degree programs, internships, and arrangement for off-campus study with members of the May Term Consortium. The most frequently chosen baccalaureate fields are business/marketing, communications/communication technologies, education.
Student Body Statistics The student body is made up of 1,775 undergraduates (504 freshmen). 55 percent are women and 45 percent are men. Students come from 23 states and territories and 32 other countries. 81 percent are from Iowa. 4.3 percent are international students.
Expenses for 2003–04 *Application fee:* $20. *Comprehensive fee:* $23,730 includes full-time tuition ($18,150), mandatory fees ($400), and college room and board ($5180). *College room only:* $2530. Room and board charges vary according to board plan and housing facility. *Part-time tuition:* $670 per credit. *Part-time mandatory fees:* $15 per term. Part-time tuition and fees vary according to class time and course load.
Financial Aid Forms of aid include need-based and non-need-based scholarships and part-time jobs. The average aided 2003–04 undergraduate received an aid package worth an estimated $17,031. The priority application deadline for financial aid is March 1.
Freshman Admission Wartburg requires a high school transcript, a minimum 2.0 high school GPA, SAT I or ACT scores, and TOEFL scores for international students. Recommendations and secondary school report are recommended. An interview is required for some.
Entrance Difficulty Wartburg assesses its entrance difficulty level as moderately difficult. For the fall 2003 freshman class, 83 percent of the applicants were accepted.

For Further Information Contact Mr. Doug Bowman, Dean of Admissions/Financial Aid, Wartburg College, 100 Wartburg Boulevard, PO Box 1003, Waverly, IA 50677-0903. *Telephone:* 319-352-8264 or 800-772-2085 (toll-free). *Fax:* 319-352-8579. *E-mail:* admissions@wartburg.edu. *Web site:* http://www.wartburg.edu/.

See page 352 for a narrative description.

WILLIAM PENN UNIVERSITY
Oskaloosa, Iowa

William Penn is a coed, private, four-year college, founded in 1873, affiliated with the Society of Friends, offering degrees at the associate and bachelor's levels. It has a 60-acre campus in Oskaloosa near Des Moines.

Academic Information The faculty has 52 members (67% full-time), 37% with terminal degrees. The student-faculty ratio is 14:1. The library holds 72,907 titles, 354 serial subscriptions, and 738 audiovisual materials. Special programs include academic remediation, services for learning-disabled students, cooperative (work-study) education, study abroad, advanced placement credit, ESL programs, double majors, independent study, self-designed majors, summer session for credit, part-time degree programs (daytime, evenings, summer), adult/continuing education programs, and internships. The most frequently chosen baccalaureate fields are business/marketing, education, psychology.
Student Body Statistics The student body is made up of 1,499 undergraduates (230 freshmen). 48 percent are women and 52 percent are men. Students come from 42 states and territories and 12 other countries. 72 percent are from Iowa. 1.1 percent are international students. 15 percent of the 2003 graduating class went on to graduate and professional schools.
Expenses for 2004–05 *Application fee:* $20. *Comprehensive fee:* $19,350 includes full-time tuition ($14,234), mandatory fees ($370), and college room and board ($4746). *College room only:* $1852. Room and board charges vary according to board plan and housing facility. *Part-time tuition:* varies with course load.
Financial Aid Forms of aid include need-based and non-need-based scholarships and part-time jobs. The priority application deadline for financial aid is April 15.
Freshman Admission William Penn requires a high school transcript, a minimum 2.0 high school GPA, SAT I or ACT scores, and TOEFL scores for international students. An essay, recommendations, and an interview are required for some.

William Penn University (continued)

Entrance Difficulty William Penn assesses its entrance difficulty level as moderately difficult. For the fall 2003 freshman class, 65 percent of the applicants were accepted.

For Further Information Contact Mrs. Mary Boyd, Director of Admissions, William Penn University, 201 Trueblood Avenue, Oskaloosa, IA 52577-1799. *Telephone:* 641-673-1012 or 800-779-7366 (toll-free). *Fax:* 641-673-2113. *E-mail:* admissions@wmpenn.edu. *Web site:* http://www.wmpenn.edu/.

Kansas

BAKER UNIVERSITY
Baldwin City, Kansas

Baker is a coed, private, United Methodist, comprehensive institution, founded in 1858, offering degrees at the bachelor's and master's levels. It has a 26-acre campus in Baldwin City near Kansas City.

Academic Information The faculty has 101 members (62% full-time), 51% with terminal degrees. The undergraduate student-faculty ratio is 12:1. The library holds 84,114 titles, 507 serial subscriptions, and 1,139 audiovisual materials. Special programs include services for learning-disabled students, an honors program, study abroad, advanced placement credit, double majors, independent study, self-designed majors, summer session for credit, and internships. The most frequently chosen baccalaureate fields are business/marketing, education, health professions and related sciences.
Student Body Statistics The student body is made up of 1,015 undergraduates (226 freshmen). 57 percent are women and 43 percent are men. Students come from 21 states and territories and 7 other countries. 73 percent are from Kansas. 0.7 percent are international students.
Expenses for 2003–04 *Application fee:* $20. *One-time mandatory fee:* $80. *Comprehensive fee:* $19,860 includes full-time tuition ($14,210), mandatory fees ($350), and college room and board ($5300). *College room only:* $2400. Full-time tuition and fees vary according to location and program. Room and board charges vary according to board plan and housing facility. *Part-time tuition:* $455 per credit hour. *Part-time mandatory fees:* $15 per credit hour. Part-time tuition and fees vary according to course load.
Financial Aid Forms of aid include need-based and non-need-based scholarships, athletic grants, and part-time jobs. The average aided 2003–04 undergraduate received an aid package worth an estimated $14,534. The priority application deadline for financial aid is March 1.
Freshman Admission Baker requires a high school transcript, 1 recommendation, SAT I or ACT scores, and TOEFL scores for international students. A minimum 3.0 high school GPA and minimum ACT score of 21 are recommended. An essay and an interview are required for some. The application deadline for regular admission is rolling.
Transfer Admission The application deadline for admission is rolling.
Entrance Difficulty Baker assesses its entrance difficulty level as moderately difficult. For the fall 2003 freshman class, 82 percent of the applicants were accepted.

For Further Information Contact Ms. Annette Galluzzi, Vice President for Marketing, Baker University, PO Box 65, Baldwin City, KS 66006-0065. *Telephone:* 785-594-6451 Ext. 344 or 800-873-4282 (toll-free). *Fax:* 785-594-8372. *E-mail:* admission@bakeru.edu. *Web site:* http://www.bakeru.edu/.

BARCLAY COLLEGE
Haviland, Kansas

Barclay is a coed, private, four-year college, founded in 1917, affiliated with the Society of Friends, offering degrees at the associate and bachelor's levels. It has a 13-acre campus in Haviland.

Academic Information The faculty has 38 members (21% full-time), 8% with terminal degrees. The student-faculty ratio is 7:1. The library holds 60,397 titles, 6,959 serial subscriptions, and 2,291 audiovisual materials. Special programs include academic remediation, advanced placement credit, accelerated degree programs, double majors, independent study, distance learning, self-designed majors, part-time degree programs (daytime, evenings), external degree programs, adult/continuing education programs, and internships. The most frequently chosen baccalaureate fields are philosophy, religion, and theology, business/marketing, psychology.
Student Body Statistics The student body is made up of 185 undergraduates (29 freshmen). 50 percent are women and 50 percent are men. Students come from 21 states and territories and 1 other country. 56 percent are from Kansas. 1.1 percent are international students. 15 percent of the 2003 graduating class went on to graduate and professional schools.
Expenses for 2004–05 *Application fee:* $15. *Comprehensive fee:* $14,650 includes full-time tuition ($9250), mandatory fees ($700), and college room and board ($4700). *College room only:* $1850. Room and board charges vary according to board plan. *Part-time tuition:* varies with course load.
Financial Aid Forms of aid include need-based and non-need-based scholarships and part-time jobs. The average aided 2003–04 undergraduate received an aid package worth an estimated $6700. The priority application deadline for financial aid is March 15.
Freshman Admission Barclay requires an essay, a high school transcript, a minimum 2.3 high school GPA, 2 recommendations, SAT I or ACT scores, and TOEFL scores for international students. The application deadline for regular admission is September 1.
Transfer Admission The application deadline for admission is September 1.
Entrance Difficulty Barclay assesses its entrance difficulty level as minimally difficult. For the fall 2003 freshman class, 66 percent of the applicants were accepted.

For Further Information Contact Ryan Haase, Director of Admissions, Barclay College, 607 North Kingman, Haviland, KS 67059. *Telephone:* 620-862-5252 Ext. 41 or 800-862-0226 (toll-free). *Fax:* 620-862-5242. *E-mail:* admissions@barclaycollege.edu. *Web site:* http://www.barclaycollege.edu/.

BENEDICTINE COLLEGE
Atchison, Kansas

Benedictine College is a coed, private, Roman Catholic, comprehensive institution, founded in 1859, offering degrees at the associate, bachelor's, and master's levels. It has a 225-acre campus in Atchison near Kansas City.

Academic Information The faculty has 96 members (56% full-time), 51% with terminal degrees. The undergraduate student-faculty ratio is 16:1. The library holds 366,212 titles, 501 serial subscriptions, and 831 audiovisual materials. Special programs include academic remediation, cooperative (work-study) education, study abroad, advanced placement credit, ESL programs, independent study, self-designed majors, summer session for credit, part-time degree programs (daytime, evenings, summer), internships, and arrangement for off-campus study with 16 members of the Kansas City Regional Council for Higher Education, Kansas State University. The most frequently chosen baccalaureate fields are business/marketing, education, philosophy, religion, and theology.
Student Body Statistics The student body totals 1,330, of whom 1,271 are undergraduates (253 freshmen). 52 percent are women and 48 percent are men. Students come from 38 states and territories and 18 other countries. 47 percent are from Kansas. 3.1 percent are international students. 29 percent of the 2003 graduating class went on to graduate and professional schools.
Expenses for 2003–04 *Application fee:* $25. *Comprehensive fee:* $20,533 includes full-time tuition ($14,083), mandatory fees ($530), and college

room and board ($5920). *College room only:* $2560. Full-time tuition and fees vary according to course load and degree level. Room and board charges vary according to board plan and housing facility. *Part-time tuition:* $300 per credit hour. Part-time tuition varies according to course load and degree level.

Financial Aid Forms of aid include need-based and non-need-based scholarships, athletic grants, and part-time jobs. The average aided 2003–04 undergraduate received an aid package worth an estimated $12,667. The priority application deadline for financial aid is March 15.

Freshman Admission Benedictine College requires a high school transcript, a minimum 2.0 high school GPA, SAT I or ACT scores, and TOEFL scores for international students. An interview is required for some.

Entrance Difficulty Benedictine College assesses its entrance difficulty level as moderately difficult. For the fall 2003 freshman class, 96 percent of the applicants were accepted.

For Further Information Contact Ms. Kelly Vowels, Dean of Enrollment Management, Benedictine College, 1020 North 2nd Street, Atchison, KS 66002. *Telephone:* 913-367-5340 Ext. 2476 or 800-467-5340 (toll-free). *Fax:* 913-367-5462. *E-mail:* bcadmiss@benedictine.edu. *Web site:* http://www.benedictine.edu/.

See page 256 for a narrative description.

BETHANY COLLEGE
Lindsborg, Kansas

Bethany is a coed, private, Lutheran, four-year college, founded in 1881, offering degrees at the bachelor's level. It has an 80-acre campus in Lindsborg.

Academic Information The faculty has 69 members (59% full-time), 38% with terminal degrees. The student-faculty ratio is 13:1. The library holds 609 serial subscriptions and 3,518 audiovisual materials. Special programs include services for learning-disabled students, advanced placement credit, accelerated degree programs, double majors, independent study, self-designed majors, summer session for credit, internships, and arrangement for off-campus study with 6 members of the Associated Colleges of Central Kansas. The most frequently chosen baccalaureate fields are business/marketing, biological/life sciences, education.

Student Body Statistics The student body is made up of 631 undergraduates (172 freshmen). 44 percent are women and 56 percent are men. Students come from 27 states and territories and 10 other countries. 59 percent are from Kansas. 2.3 percent are international students. 17 percent of the 2003 graduating class went on to graduate and professional schools.

Expenses for 2004–05 *Application fee:* $20. *Comprehensive fee:* $19,950 includes full-time tuition ($14,800) and college room and board ($5150). *College room only:* $2800. Full-time tuition varies according to location. Room and board charges vary according to board plan and housing facility. *Part-time tuition:* $265 per credit hour. Part-time tuition varies according to course load.

Financial Aid Forms of aid include need-based and non-need-based scholarships, athletic grants, and part-time jobs. The average aided 2003–04 undergraduate received an aid package worth an estimated $15,310. The application deadline for financial aid is continuous.

Freshman Admission Bethany requires a high school transcript, a minimum 2.5 high school GPA, SAT I or ACT scores, and TOEFL scores for international students. An essay, recommendations, and an interview are required for some. The application deadline for regular admission is July 1.

Transfer Admission The application deadline for admission is rolling.

Entrance Difficulty Bethany assesses its entrance difficulty level as moderately difficult. For the fall 2003 freshman class, 71 percent of the applicants were accepted.

For Further Information Contact Thandabantu Maceo, Enrollment Management, Bethany College, 421 North First Street, Lindsborg, KS 67456. *Telephone:* 785-227-3311 Ext. 8274, 800-826-2281 (toll-free in-state), or 800-826-8993 (toll-free out-of-state). *Fax:* 785-227-2004. *E-mail:* admissions@bethanylb.edu. *Web site:* http://www.bethanylb.edu/.

BETHEL COLLEGE
North Newton, Kansas

Bethel is a coed, private, four-year college, founded in 1887, affiliated with the Mennonite Church USA, offering degrees at the bachelor's level. It has a 60-acre campus in North Newton near Wichita.

Academic Information The faculty has 53 members (85% full-time), 58% with terminal degrees. The student-faculty ratio is 9:1. The library holds 99,287 titles, 560 serial subscriptions, and 161,396 audiovisual materials. Special programs include academic remediation, services for learning-disabled students, cooperative (work-study) education, study abroad, advanced placement credit, double majors, independent study, summer session for credit, part-time degree programs (daytime, evenings, summer), internships, and arrangement for off-campus study with 6 members of the Associated Colleges of Central Kansas, Hesston College. The most frequently chosen baccalaureate fields are business/marketing, health professions and related sciences, visual/performing arts.

Student Body Statistics The student body is made up of 470 undergraduates (98 freshmen). 53 percent are women and 47 percent are men. Students come from 26 states and territories and 15 other countries. 71 percent are from Kansas. 3.6 percent are international students. 7 percent of the 2003 graduating class went on to graduate and professional schools.

Expenses for 2003–04 *Application fee:* $20. *Comprehensive fee:* $19,800 includes full-time tuition ($13,900) and college room and board ($5900). Full-time tuition varies according to course load. Room and board charges vary according to board plan and housing facility. *Part-time tuition:* $495 per credit hour. Part-time tuition varies according to course load.

Financial Aid Forms of aid include need-based and non-need-based scholarships, athletic grants, and part-time jobs. The average aided 2002–03 undergraduate received an aid package worth $14,161. The priority application deadline for financial aid is March 15.

Freshman Admission Bethel requires a high school transcript, a minimum 2.5 high school GPA, SAT I or ACT scores, and TOEFL scores for international students. An interview is recommended. An essay and 2 recommendations are required for some. The application deadline for regular admission is August 1.

Transfer Admission The application deadline for admission is August 1.

Entrance Difficulty Bethel assesses its entrance difficulty level as moderately difficult. For the fall 2003 freshman class, 72 percent of the applicants were accepted.

For Further Information Contact Mr. Allan Bartel, Director of Admissions and Enrollment, Bethel College, 300 East 27th Street, North Newton, KS 67117-0531. *Telephone:* 316-284-5230 or 800-522-1887 Ext. 230 (toll-free). *Fax:* 316-284-5870. *E-mail:* admissions@bethelks.edu. *Web site:* http://www.bethelks.edu/.

See page 260 for a narrative description.

CENTRAL CHRISTIAN COLLEGE OF KANSAS
McPherson, Kansas

Central is a coed, private, Free Methodist, four-year college, founded in 1884, offering degrees at the associate and bachelor's levels. It has a 16-acre campus in McPherson.

Academic Information The faculty has 24 members (67% full-time), 12% with terminal degrees. The student-faculty ratio is 14:1. The library holds 26,700 titles, 95 serial subscriptions, and 988 audiovisual materials. Special programs include academic remediation, services for learning-disabled students, cooperative (work-study) education, study abroad, advanced placement credit, double majors, independent study, self-designed majors, part-time degree programs (daytime, evenings), adult/continuing education programs, internships, and arrangement for off-campus study with McPherson College, Christian Center for Urban Studies. The most frequently chosen baccalaureate fields are business/marketing, liberal arts/general studies, philosophy, religion, and theology.

Student Body Statistics The student body is made up of 320 undergraduates. 52 percent are women and 48 percent are men. Students

Kansas

Central Christian College of Kansas (continued)

come from 28 states and territories and 3 other countries. 38 percent are from Kansas. 2.5 percent are international students. 7 percent of the 2003 graduating class went on to graduate and professional schools.

Expenses for 2004–05 *Application fee:* $20. *Comprehensive fee:* $17,225 includes full-time tuition ($12,625), mandatory fees ($500), and college room and board ($4100). *College room only:* $1900. Full-time tuition and fees vary according to course load. Room and board charges vary according to board plan and gender. *Part-time tuition:* $350 per credit hour. Part-time tuition varies according to course load.

Financial Aid Forms of aid include need-based and non-need-based scholarships, athletic grants, and part-time jobs. The average aided 2003–04 undergraduate received an aid package worth an estimated $10,313. The priority application deadline for financial aid is March 1.

Freshman Admission Central requires a high school transcript, a minimum 2.5 high school GPA, 2 recommendations, SAT I or ACT scores, and TOEFL scores for international students. An essay and an interview are recommended. The application deadline for regular admission is rolling.

Transfer Admission The application deadline for admission is rolling.

Entrance Difficulty Central assesses its entrance difficulty level as moderately difficult. For the fall 2003 freshman class, 98 percent of the applicants were accepted.

For Further Information Contact Dr. David Ferrell, Dean of Admissions, Central Christian College of Kansas, PO Box 1403, McPherson, KS 67460. *Telephone:* 620-241-0723 Ext. 380 or 800-835-0078 Ext. 337 (toll-free). *Fax:* 620-241-6032. *E-mail:* admissions@centralchristian.edu. *Web site:* http://www.centralchristian.edu/.

DONNELLY COLLEGE

Kansas City, Kansas

Donnelly College is a coed, private, Roman Catholic, two-year college, founded in 1949, offering degrees at the associate level. It has a 4-acre campus in Kansas City.

Academic Information The faculty has 46 members (28% full-time), 15% with terminal degrees. The student-faculty ratio is 10:1. The library holds 33,752 titles, 114 serial subscriptions, and 1,020 audiovisual materials. Special programs include academic remediation, services for learning-disabled students, advanced placement credit, ESL programs, double majors, independent study, summer session for credit, part-time degree programs (daytime, evenings, weekends, summer), external degree programs, and internships.

Student Body Statistics The student body is made up of 398 undergraduates (262 freshmen). 70 percent are women and 30 percent are men. Students come from 15 states and territories. 88 percent are from Kansas. 4.3 percent are international students. 90 percent of the 2003 graduating class went on to four-year colleges.

Expenses for 2003–04 *Application fee:* $0. *Tuition:* $3780 full-time, $145 per credit part-time. *Mandatory fees:* $40 full-time. Full-time tuition and fees vary according to course load. Part-time tuition varies according to course load.

Financial Aid Forms of aid include need-based scholarships and part-time jobs. The priority application deadline for financial aid is April 1.

Freshman Admission Donnelly College requires TOEFL scores for international students. A high school transcript is recommended. The application deadline for regular admission is rolling.

Transfer Admission The application deadline for admission is rolling.

Entrance Difficulty Donnelly College has an open admission policy.

For Further Information Contact Mr. Kevin Kelley, Vice President of Enrollment Management, Donnelly College, 608 North 18th Street, Kansas City, KS 66102. *Telephone:* 913-621-8769. *Fax:* 913-621-0354. *E-mail:* bernetta@donnelly.edu. *Web site:* http://www.donnelly.edu/.

EMPORIA STATE UNIVERSITY

Emporia, Kansas

ESU is a coed, public, comprehensive unit of Kansas Board of Regents, founded in 1863, offering degrees at the bachelor's, master's, and doctoral levels and post-master's and postbachelor's certificates. It has a 207-acre campus in Emporia near Wichita.

Academic Information The faculty has 273 members (91% full-time), 77% with terminal degrees. The undergraduate student-faculty ratio is 19:1. The library holds 558,565 titles, 1,416 serial subscriptions, and 7,649 audiovisual materials. Special programs include academic remediation, services for learning-disabled students, an honors program, study abroad, advanced placement credit, accelerated degree programs, ESL programs, double majors, independent study, distance learning, summer session for credit, part-time degree programs (daytime, evenings, weekends, summer), adult/continuing education programs, internships, and arrangement for off-campus study. The most frequently chosen baccalaureate fields are business/marketing, education, social sciences and history.

Student Body Statistics The student body totals 6,278, of whom 4,434 are undergraduates (817 freshmen). 61 percent are women and 39 percent are men. Students come from 41 states and territories and 49 other countries. 96 percent are from Kansas. 1.8 percent are international students. 26 percent of the 2003 graduating class went on to graduate and professional schools.

Expenses for 2003–04 *Application fee:* $30. *State resident tuition:* $2200 full-time, $73 per credit hour part-time. *Nonresident tuition:* $8338 full-time, $278 per credit hour part-time. *Mandatory fees:* $576 full-time, $35 per credit hour part-time. *College room and board:* $4222. *College room only:* $2104. Room and board charges vary according to board plan and housing facility.

Financial Aid Forms of aid include need-based and non-need-based scholarships, athletic grants, and part-time jobs. The average aided 2002–03 undergraduate received an aid package worth $4937. The priority application deadline for financial aid is March 15.

Freshman Admission ESU requires a high school transcript, SAT I or ACT scores, and TOEFL scores for international students. A minimum 2.0 high school GPA is recommended. The application deadline for regular admission is rolling.

Transfer Admission The application deadline for admission is rolling.

Entrance Difficulty ESU assesses its entrance difficulty level as noncompetitive; minimally difficult for transfers. For the fall 2003 freshman class, 74 percent of the applicants were accepted.

For Further Information Contact Ms. Laura Eddy, Director of Admissions (Interim), Emporia State University, 1200 Commercial Street, Campus Box 4034, Plumb Hall Room 106, Emporia, KS 66801-5087. *Telephone:* 620-341-5465, 877-GOTOESU (toll-free in-state), or 877-468-6378 (toll-free out-of-state). *Fax:* 620-341-5599. *E-mail:* go2esu@emporia.edu. *Web site:* http://www.emporia.edu/.

FORT HAYS STATE UNIVERSITY

Hays, Kansas

FHSU is a coed, public, comprehensive unit of Kansas Board of Regents, founded in 1902, offering degrees at the associate, bachelor's, and master's levels and post-master's certificates. It has a 200-acre campus in Hays.

Academic Information The faculty has 291 members (87% full-time), 66% with terminal degrees. The undergraduate student-faculty ratio is 17:1. The library holds 624,637 titles and 1,689 serial subscriptions. Special programs include academic remediation, services for learning-disabled students, study abroad, advanced placement credit, ESL programs, double majors, distance learning, self-designed majors, summer session for credit, part-time degree programs (daytime, evenings, weekends, summer), external degree programs, adult/continuing education programs, internships, and arrangement for off-campus study with members of the National Student Exchange. The most frequently chosen baccalaureate fields are business/marketing, education, liberal arts/general studies.

Student Body Statistics The student body totals 7,373, of whom 5,920 are undergraduates (904 freshmen). 54 percent are women and 46 percent

are men. Students come from 48 states and territories and 15 other countries. 90 percent are from Kansas. 16 percent are international students. 19 percent of the 2003 graduating class went on to graduate and professional schools.

Expenses for 2003–04 *Application fee:* $30. *State resident tuition:* $2032 full-time, $84.65 per credit hour part-time. *Nonresident tuition:* $8165 full-time, $272.15 per credit hour part-time. *Mandatory fees:* $507 full-time. Full-time tuition and fees vary according to course load, location, and reciprocity agreements. Part-time tuition varies according to course load and location. *College room and board:* $4843. *College room only:* $2146. Room and board charges vary according to board plan, housing facility, and student level.

Financial Aid Forms of aid include need-based and non-need-based scholarships, athletic grants, and part-time jobs. The average aided 2002–03 undergraduate received an aid package worth $5542. The priority application deadline for financial aid is March 15.

Freshman Admission FHSU requires a high school transcript, SAT I or ACT scores, and TOEFL scores for international students. The application deadline for regular admission is rolling.

Transfer Admission The application deadline for admission is rolling.

Entrance Difficulty FHSU assesses its entrance difficulty level as noncompetitive; minimally difficult for out-of-state applicants; minimally difficult for transfers; moderately difficult for radiological technology program, School of Nursing. For the fall 2003 freshman class, 94 percent of the applicants were accepted.

For Further Information Contact Ms. Christy Befort, Senior Administrative Assistant, Office of Admissions, Fort Hays State University, 600 Park Street, Hays, KS 67601-4099. *Telephone:* 785-628-5666 or 800-628-FHSU (toll-free). *Fax:* 800-432-0248. *E-mail:* tigers@fhsu.edu. *Web site:* http://www.fhsu.edu/.

FRIENDS UNIVERSITY
Wichita, Kansas

For Information Write to Friends University, Wichita, KS 67213.

HASKELL INDIAN NATIONS UNIVERSITY
Lawrence, Kansas

Haskell is a coed, public, four-year college, founded in 1884, offering degrees at the associate and bachelor's levels. It has a 320-acre campus in Lawrence.

Academic Information The faculty has 48 members (100% full-time). The student-faculty ratio is 15:1. The library holds 50,000 titles and 400 serial subscriptions. Special programs include academic remediation, services for learning-disabled students, advanced placement credit, independent study, distance learning, self-designed majors, summer session for credit, part-time degree programs (daytime, summer), internships, and arrangement for off-campus study with members of the American Indian Higher Education Consortium, Kansas City Regional Council for Higher Education, University of Kansas.

Student Body Statistics The student body is made up of 1,028 undergraduates (350 freshmen). 47 percent are women and 53 percent are men. Students come from 37 states and territories.

Expenses for 2003–04 *Application fee:* $10. *State resident tuition:* $0 full-time. *Nonresident tuition:* $0 full-time. *Mandatory fees:* $210 full-time, $105 per term part-time. *College room and board:* $70.

Financial Aid Forms of aid include need-based scholarships and part-time jobs. The application deadline for financial aid is continuous.

Freshman Admission Haskell requires a high school transcript, a minimum 2.0 high school GPA, and ACT scores. 2 recommendations are required for some. The application deadline for regular admission is July 30.

Transfer Admission The application deadline for admission is July 30.

Entrance Difficulty Haskell assesses its entrance difficulty level as minimally difficult.

For Further Information Contact Ms. Patty Grant, Recruitment Officer, Haskell Indian Nations University, 155 Indian Avenue, #5031, Lawrence, KS 66046. *Telephone:* 785-749-8454 Ext. 456. *Fax:* 785-749-8429. *Web site:* http://www.haskell.edu/.

HESSTON COLLEGE
Hesston, Kansas

Hesston College is a coed, private, Mennonite, two-year college, founded in 1909, offering degrees at the associate level. It has a 50-acre campus in Hesston near Wichita.

Academic Information The faculty has 43 members (65% full-time), 23% with terminal degrees. The student-faculty ratio is 12:1. The library holds 35,000 titles, 234 serial subscriptions, and 2,409 audiovisual materials. Special programs include academic remediation, services for learning-disabled students, cooperative (work-study) education, advanced placement credit, ESL programs, double majors, independent study, summer session for credit, part-time degree programs (daytime, evenings), and internships.

Student Body Statistics The student body is made up of 446 undergraduates (174 freshmen). 55 percent are women and 45 percent are men. Students come from 30 states and territories and 12 other countries. 43 percent are from Kansas. 11.2 percent are international students.

Expenses for 2004–05 *Application fee:* $15. *Comprehensive fee:* $19,998 includes full-time tuition ($14,378), mandatory fees ($220), and college room and board ($5400). *Part-time tuition:* $600 per hour. *Part-time mandatory fees:* $55 per term. Part-time tuition and fees vary according to course load.

Financial Aid Forms of aid include need-based scholarships and part-time jobs. The priority application deadline for financial aid is May 1.

Freshman Admission Hesston College requires a high school transcript, recommendations, and TOEFL scores for international students. SAT I or ACT scores are recommended. An interview is required for some. The application deadline for regular admission is rolling.

Transfer Admission The application deadline for admission is rolling.

Entrance Difficulty Hesston College has an open admission policy except for nursing and pastoral ministries programs. It assesses its entrance difficulty as moderately difficult for nursing program.

For Further Information Contact Mr. Clark Roth, Vice President for Admissions, Hesston College, Box 3000, Hesston, KS 67062. *Telephone:* 620-327-8222 or 800-995-2757 (toll-free). *Fax:* 620-327-8300. *E-mail:* admissions@hesston.edu. *Web site:* http://www.hesston.edu/.

KANSAS NEWMAN COLLEGE
See Newman University

KANSAS STATE UNIVERSITY
Manhattan, Kansas

KSU is a coed, public unit of Kansas Board of Regents, founded in 1863, offering degrees at the associate, bachelor's, master's, doctoral, and first professional levels. It has a 668-acre campus in Manhattan near Kansas City.

Academic Information The faculty has 976 members (87% full-time), 83% with terminal degrees. The undergraduate student-faculty ratio is 12:1. The library holds 2 million titles, 1,365 serial subscriptions, and 5,056 audiovisual materials. Special programs include academic remediation, services for learning-disabled students, an honors program, cooperative (work-study) education, study abroad, advanced placement credit, accelerated degree programs, Freshman Honors College, ESL programs, double majors, independent study, distance learning, summer session for credit, part-time degree programs (daytime, evenings, summer),

Kansas State University (continued)

adult/continuing education programs, internships, and arrangement for off-campus study with Manhattan Christian College, University of Missouri-Kansas City, 19 Kansas community colleges. The most frequently chosen baccalaureate fields are business/marketing, agriculture, engineering/engineering technologies.

Student Body Statistics The student body totals 23,050, of whom 19,083 are undergraduates (3,439 freshmen). 48 percent are women and 52 percent are men. Students come from 50 states and territories and 100 other countries. 90 percent are from Kansas. 1 percent are international students. 18.3 percent of the 2003 graduating class went on to graduate and professional schools.

Expenses for 2003–04 *Application fee:* $30. *State resident tuition:* $3510 full-time, $117 per credit hour part-time. *Nonresident tuition:* $11,400 full-time, $380 per credit hour part-time. *Mandatory fees:* $549 full-time, $19 per credit hour part-time, $66 per term part-time. *College room and board:* $5080. Room and board charges vary according to board plan.

Financial Aid Forms of aid include need-based and non-need-based scholarships, athletic grants, and part-time jobs. The average aided 2002–03 undergraduate received an aid package worth $5512. The priority application deadline for financial aid is March 1.

Freshman Admission KSU requires a high school transcript, a minimum 2.0 high school GPA, SAT I or ACT scores, and TOEFL scores for international students. ACT scores are recommended. The application deadline for regular admission is rolling.

Transfer Admission The application deadline for admission is rolling.

Entrance Difficulty KSU assesses its entrance difficulty level as noncompetitive; moderately difficult for out-of-state applicants; moderately difficult for transfers; very difficult for architecture and design program. For the fall 2003 freshman class, 60 percent of the applicants were accepted.

For Further Information Contact Ms. Christy Crenshaw, Associate Director of Admissions, Kansas State University, 119 Anderson Hall, Manhattan, KS 66506. *Telephone:* 785-532-6250 or 800-432-8270 (toll-free in-state). *Fax:* 785-532-6393. *E-mail:* kstate@ksu.edu. *Web site:* http://www.ksu.edu/.

KANSAS WESLEYAN UNIVERSITY

Salina, Kansas

Kansas Wesleyan is a coed, private, United Methodist, comprehensive institution, founded in 1886, offering degrees at the associate, bachelor's, and master's levels. It has a 28-acre campus in Salina.

Academic Information The faculty has 59 members (71% full-time), 54% with terminal degrees. The undergraduate student-faculty ratio is 18:1. The library holds 370 serial subscriptions and 1,055 audiovisual materials. Special programs include academic remediation, study abroad, advanced placement credit, ESL programs, double majors, independent study, distance learning, self-designed majors, summer session for credit, part-time degree programs (daytime, evenings, summer), external degree programs, adult/continuing education programs, internships, and arrangement for off-campus study with Associated Colleges of Central Kansas. The most frequently chosen baccalaureate fields are business/ marketing, education, protective services/public administration.

Student Body Statistics The student body totals 805, of whom 768 are undergraduates (147 freshmen). 59 percent are women and 41 percent are men. Students come from 24 states and territories and 4 other countries. 61 percent are from Kansas. 0.4 percent are international students.

Expenses for 2004–05 *Application fee:* $20. *Comprehensive fee:* $20,400 includes full-time tuition ($15,000) and college room and board ($5400). *College room only:* $2400. *Part-time tuition:* $200 per credit hour. Part-time tuition varies according to course load.

Financial Aid Forms of aid include need-based and non-need-based scholarships and part-time jobs. The priority application deadline for financial aid is March 15.

Freshman Admission Kansas Wesleyan requires a high school transcript, a minimum 2.5 high school GPA, minimum ACT composite score of 18, SAT I or ACT scores, and TOEFL scores for international students. SAT I scores and ACT scores are recommended. The application deadline for regular admission is rolling.

Transfer Admission The application deadline for admission is rolling.
Entrance Difficulty Kansas Wesleyan assesses its entrance difficulty level as moderately difficult. For the fall 2003 freshman class, 53 percent of the applicants were accepted.

For Further Information Contact Ms. Tina Thayer, Director of Admissions, Kansas Wesleyan University, 100 East Claflin Avenue, Salina, KS 67401-6196. *Telephone:* 785-829-5541 Ext. 1283 or 800-874-1154 Ext. 1285 (toll-free). *Fax:* 785-827-0927. *E-mail:* admissions@kwu.edu. *Web site:* http://www.kwu.edu/.

MANHATTAN CHRISTIAN COLLEGE

Manhattan, Kansas

MCC is a coed, private, four-year college, founded in 1927, affiliated with the Christian Churches and Churches of Christ, offering degrees at the associate and bachelor's levels. It has a 10-acre campus in Manhattan.

Academic Information The faculty has 31 members (32% full-time), 26% with terminal degrees. The student-faculty ratio is 17:1. The library holds 2,500 titles and 45 serial subscriptions. Special programs include academic remediation, advanced placement credit, double majors, independent study, distance learning, summer session for credit, adult/ continuing education programs, internships, and arrangement for off-campus study with Kansas State University. The most frequently chosen baccalaureate fields are business/marketing, philosophy, religion, and theology.

Student Body Statistics The student body is made up of 336 undergraduates (76 freshmen). 49 percent are women and 51 percent are men. Students come from 13 states and territories and 2 other countries. 72 percent are from Kansas. 0.6 percent are international students. 1 percent of the 2003 graduating class went on to graduate and professional schools.

Expenses for 2003–04 *Application fee:* $25. *Comprehensive fee:* $13,356 includes full-time tuition ($8332), mandatory fees ($30), and college room and board ($4994). Room and board charges vary according to board plan. *Part-time tuition:* $347 per hour. Part-time tuition varies according to course load.

Financial Aid Forms of aid include need-based and non-need-based scholarships and part-time jobs. The average aided 2002–03 undergraduate received an aid package worth $7420. The priority application deadline for financial aid is March 15.

Freshman Admission MCC requires an essay, a high school transcript, a minimum 2.0 high school GPA, 3 recommendations, SAT I or ACT scores, and TOEFL scores for international students. An interview is required for some. The application deadline for regular admission is August 1.

Transfer Admission The application deadline for admission is August 1.
Entrance Difficulty MCC assesses its entrance difficulty level as minimally difficult. For the fall 2003 freshman class, 84 percent of the applicants were accepted.

For Further Information Contact Mr. Scott Jenkins, Director of Admissions, Manhattan Christian College, 1415 Anderson Avenue, Manhattan, KS 66502-4081. *Telephone:* 785-539-3571 Ext. 323 or 877-246-4622 (toll-free). *Fax:* 785-776-9251. *E-mail:* admit@mccks.edu. *Web site:* http://www.mccks.edu/.

MCPHERSON COLLEGE

McPherson, Kansas

McPherson College is a coed, private, four-year college, founded in 1887, affiliated with the Church of the Brethren, offering degrees at the associate and bachelor's levels. It has a 26-acre campus in McPherson.

Academic Information The faculty has 54 members (74% full-time), 52% with terminal degrees. The student-faculty ratio is 10:1. The library holds 89,946 titles, 345 serial subscriptions, and 4,465 audiovisual materials. Special programs include academic remediation, services for

learning-disabled students, study abroad, advanced placement credit, double majors, independent study, self-designed majors, summer session for credit, part-time degree programs (daytime, evenings, summer), adult/continuing education programs, internships, and arrangement for off-campus study with 6 members of the Associated Colleges of Central Kansas. The most frequently chosen baccalaureate fields are business/marketing, education, psychology.
Student Body Statistics The student body is made up of 436 undergraduates (133 freshmen). 39 percent are women and 61 percent are men. Students come from 30 states and territories. 1 percent are international students.
Expenses for 2004–05 *Application fee:* $25. *Comprehensive fee:* $20,265 includes full-time tuition ($14,385), mandatory fees ($260), and college room and board ($5620). *College room only:* $2345. Room and board charges vary according to board plan. *Part-time tuition:* $450 per credit hour. Part-time tuition varies according to course load.
Financial Aid Forms of aid include need-based and non-need-based scholarships, athletic grants, and part-time jobs. The average aided 2003–04 undergraduate received an aid package worth an estimated $16,475. The priority application deadline for financial aid is April 1.
Freshman Admission McPherson College requires a high school transcript, a minimum 2.0 high school GPA, SAT I or ACT scores, and TOEFL scores for international students. ACT scores are recommended. The application deadline for regular admission is rolling.
Transfer Admission The application deadline for admission is rolling.
Entrance Difficulty McPherson College assesses its entrance difficulty level as moderately difficult. For the fall 2003 freshman class, 73 percent of the applicants were accepted.

For Further Information Contact Mr. Fred Schmidt, Dean of Enrollment, McPherson College, 1600 East Euclid, McPherson, KS 67460. *Telephone:* 620-241-0731 Ext. 1270 or 800-365-7402 (toll-free). *Fax:* 620-241-8443. *E-mail:* admiss@mcpherson.edu. *Web site:* http://www.mcpherson.edu/.

MIDAMERICA NAZARENE UNIVERSITY
Olathe, Kansas

MNU is a coed, private, comprehensive institution, founded in 1966, affiliated with the Church of the Nazarene, offering degrees at the associate, bachelor's, and master's levels. It has a 105-acre campus in Olathe near Kansas City.

Academic Information The faculty has 163 members (47% full-time), 25% with terminal degrees. The undergraduate student-faculty ratio is 19:1. The library holds 428,450 titles, 1,225 serial subscriptions, and 7,391 audiovisual materials. Special programs include academic remediation, services for learning-disabled students, study abroad, advanced placement credit, accelerated degree programs, double majors, independent study, summer session for credit, part-time degree programs (daytime, summer), adult/continuing education programs, internships, and arrangement for off-campus study with Coalition for Christian Colleges and Universities. The most frequently chosen baccalaureate fields are business/marketing, communications/communication technologies, education.
Student Body Statistics The student body totals 1,952, of whom 1,438 are undergraduates (260 freshmen). 54 percent are women and 46 percent are men. Students come from 40 states and territories and 11 other countries. 61 percent are from Kansas. 1.7 percent are international students.
Expenses for 2003–04 *Application fee:* $15. *Comprehensive fee:* $18,738 includes full-time tuition ($11,910), mandatory fees ($1000), and college room and board ($5828). Full-time tuition and fees vary according to course load. Room and board charges vary according to board plan and housing facility. *Part-time tuition:* $397 per semester hour. *Part-time mandatory fees:* $500 per term. Part-time tuition and fees vary according to course load.
Financial Aid Forms of aid include need-based and non-need-based scholarships, athletic grants, and part-time jobs. The average aided 2003–04 undergraduate received an aid package worth an estimated $11,189. The priority application deadline for financial aid is March 1.

Freshman Admission MNU requires a high school transcript, a minimum 2.0 high school GPA, 1 recommendation, SAT I or ACT scores, and TOEFL scores for international students. The application deadline for regular admission is August 1.
Transfer Admission The application deadline for admission is August 1.
Entrance Difficulty MNU assesses its entrance difficulty level as minimally difficult. For the fall 2003 freshman class, 41 percent of the applicants were accepted.

For Further Information Contact Mr. Mike Redwine, Vice President for Enrollment Development, MidAmerica Nazarene University, 2030 East College Way, Olathe, KS 66062-1899. *Telephone:* 913-791-3380 Ext. 481 or 800-800-8887 (toll-free). *Fax:* 913-791-3481. *E-mail:* admissions@mnu.edu. *Web site:* http://www.mnu.edu/.

NEWMAN UNIVERSITY
Wichita, Kansas

Newman is a coed, private, Roman Catholic, comprehensive institution, founded in 1933, offering degrees at the associate, bachelor's, and master's levels. It has a 61-acre campus in Wichita.

Academic Information The faculty has 192 members (35% full-time). The undergraduate student-faculty ratio is 14:1. The library holds 107,911 titles, 478 serial subscriptions, and 2,042 audiovisual materials. Special programs include academic remediation, services for learning-disabled students, cooperative (work-study) education, study abroad, advanced placement credit, accelerated degree programs, double majors, independent study, distance learning, summer session for credit, part-time degree programs (daytime, evenings, weekends, summer), external degree programs, adult/continuing education programs, internships, and arrangement for off-campus study with Friends University.
Student Body Statistics The student body totals 2,063, of whom 1,757 are undergraduates. 64 percent are women and 36 percent are men. Students come from 34 states and territories. 89 percent are from Kansas.
Expenses for 2003–04 *Application fee:* $20. *Comprehensive fee:* $18,168 includes full-time tuition ($13,198), mandatory fees ($150), and college room and board ($4820). Full-time tuition and fees vary according to location. Room and board charges vary according to housing facility. *Part-time tuition:* $365 per credit hour. *Part-time mandatory fees:* $5 per credit hour. Part-time tuition and fees vary according to location.
Financial Aid Forms of aid include need-based and non-need-based scholarships, athletic grants, and part-time jobs. The average aided 2002–03 undergraduate received an aid package worth $9191. The priority application deadline for financial aid is March 1.
Freshman Admission Newman requires a high school transcript, a minimum 2.0 high school GPA, SAT I or ACT scores, and TOEFL scores for international students. An interview is recommended. The application deadline for regular admission is rolling.
Transfer Admission The application deadline for admission is rolling.
Entrance Difficulty Newman assesses its entrance difficulty level as minimally difficult; moderately difficult for nursing, occupational therapy programs.

For Further Information Contact Mrs. Marla Sexson, Dean of Admissions, Newman University, 3100 McCormick Avenue, Wichita, KS 67213. *Telephone:* 316-942-4291 Ext. 2144 or 877-NEWMANU Ext. 2144 (toll-free). *Fax:* 316-942-4483. *E-mail:* admissions@newmanu.edu. *Web site:* http://www.newmanu.edu/.

OTTAWA UNIVERSITY
Ottawa, Kansas

OU is a coed, private, American Baptist Churches in the USA, comprehensive institution, founded in 1865, offering degrees at the bachelor's level (also offers master's, adult, international and on-line education programs with significant enrollment not reflected in profile). It has a 60-acre campus in Ottawa near Kansas City.

Academic Information The faculty has 37 members (51% full-time), 27% with terminal degrees. The student-faculty ratio is 19:1. The library

Ottawa University (continued)

holds 80,500 titles and 310 serial subscriptions. Special programs include advanced placement credit, ESL programs, double majors, independent study, self-designed majors, summer session for credit, part-time degree programs (daytime), and internships. The most frequently chosen baccalaureate fields are business/marketing, education, parks and recreation.
Student Body Statistics The student body is made up of 530 undergraduates (116 freshmen). 45 percent are women and 55 percent are men. Students come from 25 states and territories and 4 other countries. 67 percent are from Kansas. 6.8 percent are international students. 20 percent of the 2003 graduating class went on to graduate and professional schools.
Expenses for 2004–05 *Application fee:* $15. *Comprehensive fee:* $19,600 includes full-time tuition ($13,850), mandatory fees ($300), and college room and board ($5450). *College room only:* $2400. Full-time tuition and fees vary according to course load. Room and board charges vary according to board plan and housing facility. *Part-time tuition:* varies with course load.
Financial Aid Forms of aid include need-based and non-need-based scholarships and part-time jobs. The priority application deadline for financial aid is March 15.
Freshman Admission OU requires a high school transcript, a minimum 2.5 high school GPA, SAT I or ACT scores, and TOEFL scores for international students. 2 recommendations and an interview are recommended. An essay is required for some. The application deadline for regular admission is rolling.
Transfer Admission The application deadline for admission is rolling.
Entrance Difficulty OU assesses its entrance difficulty level as moderately difficult. For the fall 2003 freshman class, 44 percent of the applicants were accepted.

For Further Information Contact Ms. Ina Agnew, Dean of Student Affairs, Ottawa University, 1001 South Cedar #17, Ottawa, KS 66067-3399. *Telephone:* 785-242-5200 Ext. 5561 or 800-755-5200 (toll-free). *Fax:* 785-242-7429. *E-mail:* admiss@ottawa.edu. *Web site:* http://www.ottawa.edu/.

PITTSBURG STATE UNIVERSITY
Pittsburg, Kansas

Pitt State is a coed, public, comprehensive unit of Kansas Board of Regents, founded in 1903, offering degrees at the associate, bachelor's, and master's levels. It has a 233-acre campus in Pittsburg.

Academic Information The faculty has 288 full-time members. The undergraduate student-faculty ratio is 18:1. The library holds 290,798 titles and 1,368 serial subscriptions. Special programs include academic remediation, services for learning-disabled students, an honors program, cooperative (work-study) education, study abroad, advanced placement credit, Freshman Honors College, ESL programs, double majors, independent study, self-designed majors, summer session for credit, part-time degree programs (daytime, evenings, summer), external degree programs, adult/continuing education programs, internships, and arrangement for off-campus study with Southside Education Center, Wichita, KS, Kansas City Metro Center, Lenexa, KS. The most frequently chosen baccalaureate fields are business/marketing, education, psychology.
Student Body Statistics The student body totals 6,731, of whom 5,531 are undergraduates. 50 percent are women and 50 percent are men. Students come from 50 states and territories and 47 other countries. 81 percent are from Kansas. 4.2 percent are international students.
Expenses for 2003–04 *Application fee:* $30. *State resident tuition:* $2962 full-time, $105 per credit hour part-time. *Nonresident tuition:* $8784 full-time, $299 per credit hour part-time. *College room and board:* $4166. Room and board charges vary according to board plan.
Financial Aid Forms of aid include need-based and non-need-based scholarships, athletic grants, and part-time jobs. The average aided 2003–04 undergraduate received an aid package worth an estimated $6666. The priority application deadline for financial aid is March 1.
Freshman Admission Pitt State requires a high school transcript, ACT scores, and TOEFL scores for international students. A minimum 2.0 high school GPA is required for some. The application deadline for regular admission is rolling.

Transfer Admission The application deadline for admission is rolling.
Entrance Difficulty Pitt State has an open admission policy for state residents. It assesses its entrance difficulty as moderately difficult for out-of-state applicants; moderately difficult for transfers; very difficult for international students.

For Further Information Contact Ms. Ange Peterson, Director of Admission and Retention, Pittsburg State University, Pittsburg, KS 66762. *Telephone:* 620-235-4251 or 800-854-7488 Ext. 1 (toll-free). *Fax:* 316-235-6003. *E-mail:* psuadmit@pittstate.edu. *Web site:* http://www.pittstate.edu/.

SOUTHWESTERN COLLEGE
Winfield, Kansas

Southwestern is a coed, private, United Methodist, comprehensive institution, founded in 1885, offering degrees at the bachelor's and master's levels. It has a 70-acre campus in Winfield near Wichita.

Academic Information The faculty has 173 members (29% full-time), 16% with terminal degrees. The undergraduate student-faculty ratio is 10:1. The library holds 77,000 titles, 320 serial subscriptions, and 320 audiovisual materials. Special programs include academic remediation, an honors program, study abroad, advanced placement credit, double majors, independent study, self-designed majors, summer session for credit, part-time degree programs (daytime, evenings, weekends, summer), external degree programs, adult/continuing education programs, internships, and arrangement for off-campus study with Urban Life Center, Chicago. The most frequently chosen baccalaureate fields are business/marketing, computer/information sciences, health professions and related sciences.
Student Body Statistics The student body totals 1,405, of whom 1,218 are undergraduates (177 freshmen). 47 percent are women and 53 percent are men. Students come from 23 states and territories and 7 other countries. 80 percent are from Kansas. 2.2 percent are international students.
Expenses for 2004–05 *Application fee:* $20. *Comprehensive fee:* $20,447 includes full-time tuition ($15,349) and college room and board ($5098). *College room only:* $2288. Full-time tuition varies according to degree level and location. Room and board charges vary according to board plan, housing facility, and location. *Part-time tuition:* $638 per semester hour. Part-time tuition varies according to degree level and location.
Financial Aid Forms of aid include need-based and non-need-based scholarships, athletic grants, and part-time jobs. The average aided 2003–04 undergraduate received an aid package worth an estimated $12,287. The priority application deadline for financial aid is April 1.
Freshman Admission Southwestern requires an essay, a high school transcript, a minimum 2.25 high school GPA, SAT I or ACT scores, and TOEFL scores for international students. An interview is required for some. The application deadline for regular admission is March 1.
Transfer Admission The application deadline for admission is August 15.
Entrance Difficulty Southwestern assesses its entrance difficulty level as moderately difficult. For the fall 2003 freshman class, 71 percent of the applicants were accepted.

For Further Information Contact Mr. Todd Moore, Director of Admission, Southwestern College, 100 College Street, Winfield, KS 67156. *Telephone:* 620-229-6236 or 800-846-1543 (toll-free). *Fax:* 620-229-6344. *E-mail:* scadmit@sckans.edu. *Web site:* http://www.sckans.edu/.

STERLING COLLEGE
Sterling, Kansas

Sterling College is a coed, private, Presbyterian, four-year college, founded in 1887, offering degrees at the bachelor's level. It has a 46-acre campus in Sterling.

Academic Information The faculty has 64 members (61% full-time), 39% with terminal degrees. The student-faculty ratio is 12:1. The library holds 76,637 titles, 350 serial subscriptions, and 2,159 audiovisual materials. Special programs include services for learning-disabled students, an honors program, study abroad, advanced placement credit, double majors, independent study, self-designed majors, internships, and arrangement for off-campus study with 6 members of the Associated Colleges of Central Kansas. The most frequently chosen baccalaureate fields are business/marketing, biological/life sciences, education.

Student Body Statistics The student body is made up of 495 undergraduates (126 freshmen). 51 percent are women and 49 percent are men. Students come from 28 states and territories and 14 other countries. 58 percent are from Kansas. 2.8 percent are international students.

Expenses for 2003–04 *Application fee:* $25. *Comprehensive fee:* $19,033 includes full-time tuition ($13,150), mandatory fees ($370), and college room and board ($5513). *College room only:* $2170. Room and board charges vary according to board plan and housing facility. *Part-time tuition:* varies with course load.

Financial Aid Forms of aid include need-based and non-need-based scholarships, athletic grants, and part-time jobs. The average aided 2002–03 undergraduate received an aid package worth $13,719. The priority application deadline for financial aid is March 15.

Freshman Admission Sterling College requires a high school transcript, a minimum 2.2 high school GPA, SAT I or ACT scores, and TOEFL scores for international students. An essay and an interview are recommended. 2 recommendations and audition required for fine arts majors are required for some. The application deadline for regular admission is July 1 and for early action it is November 15.

Transfer Admission The application deadline for admission is rolling.

Entrance Difficulty Sterling College assesses its entrance difficulty level as moderately difficult. For the fall 2003 freshman class, 57 percent of the applicants were accepted.

For Further Information Contact Mr. Dennis Dutton, Vice President for Enrollment Services, Sterling College, PO Box 98, Administration Building, 125 West Cooper, Sterling, KS 67579-0098. *Telephone:* 620-278-4364 Ext. 364 or 800-346-1017 (toll-free). *Fax:* 620-278-4416. *E-mail:* admissions@sterling.edu. *Web site:* http://www.sterling.edu/.

TABOR COLLEGE
Hillsboro, Kansas

Tabor is a coed, private, Mennonite Brethren, comprehensive institution, founded in 1908, offering degrees at the associate, bachelor's, and master's levels. It has a 26-acre campus in Hillsboro near Wichita.

Academic Information The faculty has 43 members (74% full-time), 44% with terminal degrees. The undergraduate student-faculty ratio is 10:1. The library holds 80,754 titles, 265 serial subscriptions, and 945 audiovisual materials. Special programs include academic remediation, services for learning-disabled students, an honors program, cooperative (work-study) education, study abroad, advanced placement credit, accelerated degree programs, double majors, independent study, distance learning, self-designed majors, summer session for credit, part-time degree programs (evenings, weekends, summer), adult/continuing education programs, internships, and arrangement for off-campus study with Associated Colleges of Central Kansas.

Student Body Statistics The student body totals 543, of whom 522 are undergraduates (86 freshmen). 48 percent are women and 52 percent are men. Students come from 27 states and territories and 4 other countries. 70 percent are from Kansas. 1.1 percent are international students.

Expenses for 2003–04 *Application fee:* $20. *Comprehensive fee:* $19,500 includes full-time tuition ($13,990), mandatory fees ($360), and college room and board ($5150). *College room only:* $2000. Full-time tuition and fees vary according to course load. Room and board charges vary according to board plan, housing facility, and location. *Part-time tuition:* varies with course load.

Financial Aid Forms of aid include need-based and non-need-based scholarships, athletic grants, and part-time jobs. The average aided 2002–03 undergraduate received an aid package worth $13,837. The application deadline for financial aid is August 15 with a priority deadline of March 1.

Freshman Admission Tabor requires an essay, a high school transcript, a minimum 2.0 high school GPA, 2 recommendations, minimum ACT score

of 18, SAT I or ACT scores, and TOEFL scores for international students. A minimum 3.0 high school GPA and an interview are recommended. The application deadline for regular admission is August 1.

Transfer Admission The application deadline for admission is August 1.

Entrance Difficulty Tabor assesses its entrance difficulty level as moderately difficult. For the fall 2003 freshman class, 40 percent of the applicants were accepted.

For Further Information Contact Mr. Rusty Allen, Director of Admissions, Tabor College, 400 South Jefferson, Hillsboro, KS 67063. *Telephone:* 620-947-3121 Ext. 1727 or 800-822-6799 (toll-free). *Fax:* 620-947-2607. *E-mail:* admissions@tabor.edu. *Web site:* http://www.tabor.edu/.

UNIVERSITY OF KANSAS
Lawrence, Kansas

KU is a coed, public university, founded in 1866, offering degrees at the bachelor's, master's, doctoral, and first professional levels and post-master's certificates (University of Kansas is a single institution with academic programs and facilities at two primary locations: Lawrence and Kansas City. Undergraduate, graduate, and professional education are the principal missions of the Lawrence campus, with medicine and related professional education the focus of the Kansas City campus). It has a 1,100-acre campus in Lawrence near Kansas City.

Academic Information The faculty has 1,332 members (90% full-time), 86% with terminal degrees. The undergraduate student-faculty ratio is 19:1. The library holds 5 million titles, 33,874 serial subscriptions, and 51,153 audiovisual materials. Special programs include academic remediation, services for learning-disabled students, an honors program, cooperative (work-study) education, study abroad, advanced placement credit, accelerated degree programs, ESL programs, double majors, independent study, distance learning, summer session for credit, part-time degree programs (daytime, summer), adult/continuing education programs, and internships. The most frequently chosen baccalaureate fields are business/marketing, English, social sciences and history.

Student Body Statistics The student body totals 28,580, of whom 20,866 are undergraduates (4,066 freshmen). 52 percent are women and 48 percent are men. Students come from 53 states and territories and 111 other countries. 76 percent are from Kansas. 3.1 percent are international students. 28 percent of the 2003 graduating class went on to graduate and professional schools.

Expenses for 2003–04 *Application fee:* $30. *State resident tuition:* $3527 full-time, $117.55 per credit hour part-time. *Nonresident tuition:* $11,003 full-time, $366.75 per credit hour part-time. *Mandatory fees:* $574 full-time, $48 per credit hour part-time. Full-time tuition and fees vary according to program and reciprocity agreements. Part-time tuition and fees vary according to program and reciprocity agreements. *College room and board:* $4822. *College room only:* $2498. Room and board charges vary according to board plan and housing facility.

Financial Aid Forms of aid include need-based and non-need-based scholarships, athletic grants, and part-time jobs. The average aided 2002–03 undergraduate received an aid package worth $6445. The priority application deadline for financial aid is March 1.

Freshman Admission KU requires a high school transcript, a minimum 2.0 high school GPA, Kansas Board of Regents admissions criteria with GPA of 2.0/2.5; top third of high school class; minimum ACT score of 24 or minimum SAT score of 1090, and SAT I or ACT scores. TOEFL scores for international students are recommended. A minimum 2.5 high school GPA is required for some. The application deadline for regular admission is April 1.

Transfer Admission The application deadline for admission is May 1.

University of Kansas (continued)

Entrance Difficulty KU assesses its entrance difficulty level as moderately difficult; very difficult for architecture, architectural engineering programs. For the fall 2003 freshman class, 67 percent of the applicants were accepted.

For Further Information Contact Ms. Lisa Pinamonti, Director of Admissions and Scholarships, University of Kansas, KU Visitor Center, 1502 Iowa Street, Lawrence, KS 66045-7576. *Telephone:* 785-864-3911 or 888-686-7323 (toll-free in-state). *Fax:* 785-864-5006. *E-mail:* adm@ku.edu. *Web site:* http://www.ku.edu/.

UNIVERSITY OF PHOENIX–WICHITA CAMPUS

Wichita, Kansas

For Information Write to University of Phoenix–Wichita Campus, Wichita, KS 67226.

UNIVERSITY OF SAINT MARY

Leavenworth, Kansas

Saint Mary is a coed, private, Roman Catholic, comprehensive institution, founded in 1923, offering degrees at the associate, bachelor's, and master's levels. It has a 240-acre campus in Leavenworth near Kansas City.

Academic Information The faculty has 94 members (44% full-time), 35% with terminal degrees. The undergraduate student-faculty ratio is 12:1. The library holds 117,070 titles, 223 serial subscriptions, and 1,907 audiovisual materials. Special programs include an honors program, cooperative (work-study) education, study abroad, advanced placement credit, double majors, independent study, distance learning, self-designed majors, summer session for credit, part-time degree programs (daytime, evenings, summer), adult/continuing education programs, internships, and arrangement for off-campus study with University of Kansas, members of the Council of Independent Colleges. The most frequently chosen baccalaureate fields are business/marketing, education, social sciences and history.

Student Body Statistics The student body totals 881, of whom 580 are undergraduates (91 freshmen). 54 percent are women and 46 percent are men. Students come from 24 states and territories and 4 other countries. 70 percent are from Kansas. 0.9 percent are international students.

Expenses for 2003–04 *Application fee:* $25. *Comprehensive fee:* $19,028 includes full-time tuition ($13,574), mandatory fees ($160), and college room and board ($5294). *College room only:* $2300. Room and board charges vary according to student level. *Part-time tuition:* $254 per credit. *Part-time mandatory fees:* $55 per term. Part-time tuition and fees vary according to course load.

Financial Aid Forms of aid include need-based and non-need-based scholarships and part-time jobs. The application deadline for financial aid is continuous.

Freshman Admission Saint Mary requires a high school transcript, a minimum 2.5 high school GPA, 1 recommendation, SAT I or ACT scores, and TOEFL scores for international students. An interview is recommended. The application deadline for regular admission is rolling.

Transfer Admission The application deadline for admission is rolling.

Entrance Difficulty Saint Mary assesses its entrance difficulty level as moderately difficult. For the fall 2003 freshman class, 47 percent of the applicants were accepted.

For Further Information Contact Ms. Judy Wiedower, Director of Admissions and Financial Aid, University of Saint Mary, 4100 South Fourth Street, Leavenworth, KS 66048. *Telephone:* 913-682-5151 Ext. 6118 or 800-752-7043 (toll-free out-of-state). *Fax:* 913-758-6140. *E-mail:* admiss@stmary.edu. *Web site:* http://www.stmary.edu/.

WASHBURN UNIVERSITY

Topeka, Kansas

Washburn is a coed, public, comprehensive institution, founded in 1865, offering degrees at the associate, bachelor's, master's, and first professional levels. It has a 160-acre campus in Topeka near Kansas City.

Academic Information The faculty has 497 members (51% full-time). The undergraduate student-faculty ratio is 15:1. The library holds 2 million titles and 14,000 serial subscriptions. Special programs include academic remediation, services for learning-disabled students, an honors program, cooperative (work-study) education, study abroad, advanced placement credit, ESL programs, double majors, independent study, distance learning, self-designed majors, summer session for credit, part-time degree programs, adult/continuing education programs, internships, and arrangement for off-campus study with Kansas City Kansas Community College, Johnson County Community College. The most frequently chosen baccalaureate fields are business/marketing, health professions and related sciences, protective services/public administration.

Student Body Statistics The student body totals 7,002, of whom 6,045 are undergraduates. 63 percent are women and 37 percent are men. Students come from 49 states and territories and 45 other countries. 96 percent are from Kansas. 25 percent of the 2003 graduating class went on to graduate and professional schools.

Expenses for 2004–05 *Application fee:* $20.

Financial Aid Forms of aid include need-based and non-need-based scholarships, athletic grants, and part-time jobs. The average aided 2002–03 undergraduate received an aid package worth $4300. The priority application deadline for financial aid is March 1.

Freshman Admission Washburn requires a high school transcript, ACT scores, and TOEFL scores for international students. The application deadline for regular admission is rolling.

Transfer Admission The application deadline for admission is August 1.

Entrance Difficulty Washburn has an open admission policy except for nursing program. It assesses its entrance difficulty as moderately difficult for out-of-state applicants; minimally difficult for transfers; moderately difficult for nursing program.

For Further Information Contact Kirk R. Haskins, Director of Admission, Washburn University, 1700 SW College Avenue, Topeka, KS 66621. *Telephone:* 785-231-1010 Ext. 1812 or 800-332-0291 (toll-free in-state). *Fax:* 785-231-1089. *E-mail:* zzhansen@acc.washburn.edu. *Web site:* http://www.washburn.edu/.

WICHITA STATE UNIVERSITY

Wichita, Kansas

WSU is a coed, public unit of Kansas Board of Regents, founded in 1895, offering degrees at the associate, bachelor's, master's, and doctoral levels and post-master's and postbachelor's certificates. It has a 335-acre campus in Wichita.

Academic Information The faculty has 540 members (86% full-time), 72% with terminal degrees. The undergraduate student-faculty ratio is 18:1. The library holds 2 million titles, 15,169 serial subscriptions, and 47,558 audiovisual materials. Special programs include academic remediation, services for learning-disabled students, an honors program, cooperative (work-study) education, study abroad, advanced placement credit, accelerated degree programs, Freshman Honors College, ESL programs, double majors, independent study, distance learning, self-designed majors, summer session for credit, part-time degree programs (daytime, evenings, weekends, summer), internships, and arrangement for off-campus study with National Student Exchange, Midwest Student Exchange. The most frequently chosen baccalaureate fields are business/marketing, education, health professions and related sciences.

Student Body Statistics The student body totals 14,896, of whom 11,692 are undergraduates (1,211 freshmen). 56 percent are women and 44 percent are men. Students come from 45 states and territories and 83 other countries. 97 percent are from Kansas. 4.8 percent are international students.

Expenses for 2003–04 *Application fee:* $30. *State resident tuition:* $2866 full-time, $95.55 per credit hour part-time. *Nonresident tuition:* $10,320 full-time, $344 per credit hour part-time. *Mandatory fees:* $640 full-time, $20.20 per credit hour part-time, $17 per term part-time. Full-time tuition and fees vary according to course load. *College room and board:* $4620. Room and board charges vary according to board plan and housing facility.
Financial Aid Forms of aid include need-based and non-need-based scholarships, athletic grants, and part-time jobs. The average aided 2002–03 undergraduate received an aid package worth $5344. The priority application deadline for financial aid is March 15.
Freshman Admission WSU requires a high school transcript and TOEFL scores for international students. A minimum 2.0 high school GPA and ACT scores are required for some. The application deadline for regular admission is rolling.
Transfer Admission The application deadline for admission is rolling.
Entrance Difficulty WSU has an open admission policy for state residents who graduated from a Kansas high school before May 2001. It assesses its entrance difficulty as moderately difficult for out-of-state applicants; moderately difficult for transfers; very difficult for physical therapy, dental hygiene, nursing, physician assistant programs.

For Further Information Contact Ms. Gina Crabtree, Director of Admissions, Wichita State University, 1845 North Fairmount, Wichita, KS 67260-0124. *Telephone:* 316-978-3085 or 800-362-2594 (toll-free). *Fax:* 316-978-3174. *E-mail:* admissions@wichita.edu. *Web site:* http://www.wichita.edu/.

Michigan

ADRIAN COLLEGE
Adrian, Michigan

Adrian is a coed, private, four-year college, founded in 1859, affiliated with the United Methodist Church, offering degrees at the associate and bachelor's levels. It has a 100-acre campus in Adrian near Detroit and Toledo.

Academic Information The faculty has 107 members (61% full-time), 58% with terminal degrees. The student-faculty ratio is 13:1. The library holds 143,484 titles, 610 serial subscriptions, and 1,178 audiovisual materials. Special programs include academic remediation, services for learning-disabled students, an honors program, cooperative (work-study) education, study abroad, ESL programs, double majors, independent study, self-designed majors, summer session for credit, part-time degree programs (daytime), adult/continuing education programs, internships, and arrangement for off-campus study with Urban Life Center (Chicago), The Washington Center. The most frequently chosen baccalaureate fields are business/marketing, social sciences and history, visual/performing arts.
Student Body Statistics The student body is made up of 1,028 undergraduates (307 freshmen). 56 percent are women and 44 percent are men. Students come from 18 states and territories and 8 other countries. 79 percent are from Michigan. 1.3 percent are international students.
Expenses for 2003–04 *Application fee:* $20. *Comprehensive fee:* $22,330 includes full-time tuition ($16,470), mandatory fees ($100), and college room and board ($5760). *College room only:* $2460. Room and board charges vary according to board plan.
Financial Aid Forms of aid include need-based and non-need-based scholarships and part-time jobs. The average aided 2003–04 undergraduate received an aid package worth an estimated $15,434. The priority application deadline for financial aid is March 1.
Freshman Admission Adrian requires a high school transcript, SAT I or ACT scores, and TOEFL scores for international students. An interview and ACT scores are recommended. An essay is required for some. The application deadline for regular admission is August 15.
Transfer Admission The application deadline for admission is August 15.

Entrance Difficulty Adrian assesses its entrance difficulty level as moderately difficult. For the fall 2003 freshman class, 88 percent of the applicants were accepted.

For Further Information Contact Ms. Janel Sutkus, Director of Admissions, Adrian College, 110 South Madison Street, Adrian, MI 49221. *Telephone:* 517-265-5161 Ext. 4326 or 800-877-2246 (toll-free). *Fax:* 517-264-3331. *E-mail:* admissions@adrian.edu. *Web site:* http://www.adrian.edu/.

ALBION COLLEGE
Albion, Michigan

Albion is a coed, private, Methodist, four-year college, founded in 1835, offering degrees at the bachelor's level. It has a 565-acre campus in Albion near Detroit.

Academic Information The faculty has 157 members (78% full-time), 83% with terminal degrees. The student-faculty ratio is 13:1. The library holds 363,000 titles, 2,016 serial subscriptions, and 6,540 audiovisual materials. Special programs include services for learning-disabled students, an honors program, study abroad, advanced placement credit, double majors, independent study, self-designed majors, summer session for credit, part-time degree programs (daytime, evenings, summer), internships, and arrangement for off-campus study with Great Lakes Colleges Association. The most frequently chosen baccalaureate fields are English, psychology, social sciences and history.
Student Body Statistics The student body is made up of 1,732 undergraduates (487 freshmen). 57 percent are women and 43 percent are men. Students come from 32 states and territories and 19 other countries. 94 percent are from Michigan. 1.3 percent are international students.
Expenses for 2003–04 *Application fee:* $20. *Comprehensive fee:* $28,210 includes full-time tuition ($21,692), mandatory fees ($256), and college room and board ($6262). *College room only:* $3062. Room and board charges vary according to housing facility.
Financial Aid Forms of aid include need-based and non-need-based scholarships and part-time jobs. The average aided 2003–04 undergraduate received an aid package worth an estimated $18,706. The priority application deadline for financial aid is February 15.
Freshman Admission Albion requires an essay, a high school transcript, 1 recommendation, SAT I or ACT scores, and TOEFL scores for international students. A minimum 3.0 high school GPA is recommended. An interview, SAT II: Subject Test scores, and SAT II: Writing Test scores are required for some. The application deadline for regular admission is July 1.
Transfer Admission The application deadline for admission is rolling.
Entrance Difficulty Albion assesses its entrance difficulty level as moderately difficult. For the fall 2003 freshman class, 87 percent of the applicants were accepted.

For Further Information Contact Mr. Doug Kellar, Associate Vice President for Enrollment, Albion College, 611 East Porter Street, Albion, MI 49224. *Telephone:* 517-629-0600 or 800-858-6770 (toll-free). *Fax:* 517-629-0569. *E-mail:* admissions@albion.edu. *Web site:* http://www.albion.edu/.

See page 248 for a narrative description.

ALMA COLLEGE
Alma, Michigan

Alma is a coed, private, Presbyterian, four-year college, founded in 1886, offering degrees at the bachelor's level. It has a 125-acre campus in Alma.

Academic Information The faculty has 135 members (62% full-time), 67% with terminal degrees. The student-faculty ratio is 12:1. The library holds 246,649 titles, 1,157 serial subscriptions, and 7,962 audiovisual materials. Special programs include academic remediation, services for learning-disabled students, study abroad, advanced placement credit, double majors, independent study, self-designed majors, summer session

Alma College (continued)

for credit, internships, and arrangement for off-campus study. The most frequently chosen baccalaureate fields are business/marketing, education, social sciences and history.

Student Body Statistics The student body is made up of 1,291 undergraduates (322 freshmen). 58 percent are women and 42 percent are men. Students come from 20 states and territories. 96 percent are from Michigan. 0.1 percent are international students. 30 percent of the 2003 graduating class went on to graduate and professional schools.

Expenses for 2003–04 *Application fee:* $25. *Comprehensive fee:* $25,566 includes full-time tuition ($18,684), mandatory fees ($170), and college room and board ($6712). *College room only:* $3324. Room and board charges vary according to board plan and housing facility. *Part-time tuition:* $716 per credit. *Part-time mandatory fees:* $716 per credit. Part-time tuition and fees vary according to course load.

Financial Aid Forms of aid include need-based and non-need-based scholarships and part-time jobs. The average aided 2003–04 undergraduate received an aid package worth an estimated $16,461. The priority application deadline for financial aid is March 1.

Freshman Admission Alma requires a high school transcript, a minimum 3.0 high school GPA, minimum SAT score of 1030 or ACT score of 22, SAT I or ACT scores, and TOEFL scores for international students. An essay and an interview are recommended. The application deadline for regular admission is rolling and for early action it is November 1.

Transfer Admission The application deadline for admission is rolling.

Entrance Difficulty Alma assesses its entrance difficulty level as moderately difficult. For the fall 2003 freshman class, 77 percent of the applicants were accepted.

For Further Information Contact Mr. Paul Pollatz, Director of Admissions, Alma College, Admissions Office, Alma, MI 48801-1599. *Telephone:* 989-463-7139 or 800-321-ALMA (toll-free). *Fax:* 989-463-7057. *E-mail:* admissions@alma.edu. *Web site:* http://www.alma.edu/.

ANDREWS UNIVERSITY
Berrien Springs, Michigan

Andrews is a coed, private, Seventh-day Adventist university, founded in 1874, offering degrees at the associate, bachelor's, master's, doctoral, and first professional levels and post-master's certificates. It has a 1,650-acre campus in Berrien Springs.

Academic Information The faculty has 234 members (94% full-time), 66% with terminal degrees. The undergraduate student-faculty ratio is 12:1. The library holds 512,100 titles, 3,032 serial subscriptions, and 41,503 audiovisual materials. Special programs include academic remediation, an honors program, cooperative (work-study) education, study abroad, advanced placement credit, accelerated degree programs, Freshman Honors College, ESL programs, double majors, distance learning, self-designed majors, summer session for credit, part-time degree programs (daytime, evenings), external degree programs, adult/continuing education programs, internships, and arrangement for off-campus study. The most frequently chosen baccalaureate fields are biological/life sciences, health professions and related sciences, visual/performing arts.

Student Body Statistics The student body totals 2,995, of whom 1,687 are undergraduates (325 freshmen). 53 percent are women and 47 percent are men. Students come from 48 states and territories and 49 other countries. 48 percent are from Michigan. 11.9 percent are international students.

Expenses for 2004–05 *Application fee:* $30. *Comprehensive fee:* $20,566 includes full-time tuition ($15,050), mandatory fees ($396), and college room and board ($5120). *College room only:* $2430. Full-time tuition and fees vary according to course load. Room and board charges vary according to board plan. *Part-time tuition:* $630 per credit hour. Part-time tuition varies according to course load.

Financial Aid Forms of aid include need-based and non-need-based scholarships and part-time jobs. The average aided 2002–03 undergraduate received an aid package worth $17,675. The application deadline for financial aid is continuous.

Freshman Admission Andrews requires an essay, a high school transcript, a minimum 2.25 high school GPA, 2 recommendations, and SAT I or ACT scores. ACT scores are recommended. The application deadline for regular admission is rolling.

Transfer Admission The application deadline for admission is rolling.

Entrance Difficulty Andrews assesses its entrance difficulty level as moderately difficult. For the fall 2003 freshman class, 58 percent of the applicants were accepted.

For Further Information Contact Ms. Charlotte Coy, Admissions Supervisor, Andrews University, Berrien Springs, MI 49104. *Telephone:* 269-471-7771 or 800-253-2874 (toll-free). *Fax:* 269-471-3228. *E-mail:* enroll@andrews.edu. *Web site:* http://www.andrews.edu/.

AQUINAS COLLEGE
Grand Rapids, Michigan

Aquinas College is a coed, private, Roman Catholic, comprehensive institution, founded in 1886, offering degrees at the associate, bachelor's, and master's levels. It has a 107-acre campus in Grand Rapids near Detroit.

Academic Information The faculty has 218 members (45% full-time), 34% with terminal degrees. The undergraduate student-faculty ratio is 16:1. The library holds 112,458 titles, 14,725 serial subscriptions, and 4,907 audiovisual materials. Special programs include academic remediation, services for learning-disabled students, an honors program, cooperative (work-study) education, study abroad, advanced placement credit, accelerated degree programs, double majors, independent study, distance learning, self-designed majors, summer session for credit, part-time degree programs, adult/continuing education programs, internships, and arrangement for off-campus study with members of the Dominican College Interchange. The most frequently chosen baccalaureate fields are business/marketing, education, psychology.

Student Body Statistics The student body totals 2,338, of whom 1,828 are undergraduates (284 freshmen). 66 percent are women and 34 percent are men. Students come from 20 states and territories and 11 other countries. 94 percent are from Michigan. 0.7 percent are international students. 8.8 percent of the 2003 graduating class went on to graduate and professional schools.

Expenses for 2003–04 *Application fee:* $0. *Comprehensive fee:* $21,894 includes full-time tuition ($16,400) and college room and board ($5494). *College room only:* $2510. Full-time tuition varies according to course load. Room and board charges vary according to board plan and housing facility. *Part-time tuition:* $330 per credit. Part-time tuition varies according to course load.

Financial Aid Forms of aid include need-based and non-need-based scholarships, athletic grants, and part-time jobs. The average aided 2003–04 undergraduate received an aid package worth an estimated $15,461. The application deadline for financial aid is August 15 with a priority deadline of March 1.

Freshman Admission Aquinas College requires a high school transcript, a minimum 2.5 high school GPA, ACT scores, and TOEFL scores for international students. An essay and an interview are required for some. The application deadline for regular admission is rolling.

Transfer Admission The application deadline for admission is rolling.

Entrance Difficulty Aquinas College assesses its entrance difficulty level as moderately difficult. For the fall 2003 freshman class, 79 percent of the applicants were accepted.

SPECIAL MESSAGE TO STUDENTS

Social Life Aquinas College, located in Grand Rapids, Michigan, has the advantages of a city that is the cultural, medical, business, and commercial center of western Michigan. Students involve themselves in the Community Senate, intramural and intercollegiate athletics, music performance groups, volunteer and service groups, and campus ministry. Some campus sponsored events include white-water rafting, Spring Fling, Homecoming, dinner nightclubs, a Jazz Festival, a cultural series, Welcome Week, movie nights,

Winterfest, a film series, dances, and lectures. Off-campus events include theater, concerts and musical performances by nationally known performers, and a local IHL hockey team as well as minor league baseball.

Academic Highlights Aquinas offers more than forty different majors. The College has three schools within this structure: the School of Education, the School of Liberal Arts and Sciences, and the School of Management. The study program in Ireland provides a semester abroad for 30 students during the second semester of each academic year. The curriculum centers on Irish studies and culture and provides independent travel opportunities to the British Isles and the Continent. Other cultural immersion programs include Costa Rica, France, Germany, Japan, and Spain. A revised general education plan ensures that the student is equipped with the skills necessary for both life and a career. Aquinas also offers a semester of field experience in career-related employment through which the student earns college credit and a salary. The location of the College in Grand Rapids provides myriad experiences for students in medical, business, and commercial fields. More than 200 internships with leading firms and organizations are available.

Interviews and Campus Visits While the admission interview is not a requirement, campus visits are highly recommended. Aquinas provides three Campus Days throughout the year. This program gives the student the opportunity to tour the campus, meet with faculty members, participate in financial aid workshops, and enjoy a complimentary lunch. Parents are also welcome. Individual appointments with the Admissions Office are available. Students are encouraged to see the Holmdene Mansion, part of the original estate on which Aquinas is built, and the Art and Music Center, which houses recital halls, an art gallery, a sculpture studio, a photography lab, and a darkroom. The Albertus Magnus Hall of Science houses laboratories, a greenhouse, and an observatory. For information about appointments and campus visits, students should call the Admissions Office at 616-732-4460 or 800-678-9593 (toll-free), Monday through Friday, 8:30 a.m. to 5 p.m., and Saturdays, 9 a.m. to 1 p.m. The office is located in Hruby Hall, 1760 Fulton Street, on campus. The nearest commercial airport is Kent County International.

For Further Information Write to Paula Meehan, Dean of Admissions, Aquinas College, 1607 Robinson Road, SE, Grand Rapids, MI 49506-1799. *E-mail:* admissions@aquinas.edu. *Web site:* http://www.aquinas.edu.

AVE MARIA COLLEGE
Ypsilanti, Michigan

Ave Maria College is a coed, private, Roman Catholic, four-year college, founded in 1998, offering degrees at the bachelor's level. It is located in Ypsilanti near Detroit.

Academic Information The faculty has 27 members (63% full-time). The student-faculty ratio is 15:1. Special programs include study abroad.
Student Body Statistics The student body is made up of 308 undergraduates. Students come from 39 states and territories and 13 other countries. 28 percent are from Michigan. 12.3 percent are international students.
Expenses for 2003–04 *Application fee:* $25. *Comprehensive fee:* $15,000 includes full-time tuition ($9650), mandatory fees ($350), and college room and board ($5000). Full-time tuition and fees vary according to program. *Part-time tuition:* $300 per credit. *Part-time mandatory fees:* $10 per credit. Part-time tuition and fees vary according to program.
Financial Aid Forms of aid include need-based and non-need-based scholarships. The average aided 2002–03 undergraduate received an aid package worth $6992. The priority application deadline for financial aid is April 15.
Freshman Admission Ave Maria College requires an essay, a high school transcript, a minimum 2.4 high school GPA, 2 recommendations, SAT I or ACT scores, and TOEFL scores for international students. An interview is recommended. Minimum SAT score of 1000 or ACT score of 21 is required for some.

Entrance Difficulty Ave Maria College assesses its entrance difficulty level as very difficult. For the fall 2003 freshman class, 78 percent of the applicants were accepted.

For Further Information Contact Ms. Nicole Myshak, Admissions Counselor, Ave Maria College, 300 West Forest Avenue, Ypsilanti, MI 48197. *Telephone:* 734-337-4528 or 866-866-3030 (toll-free). *Fax:* 734-337-4140. *E-mail:* admissions@avemaria.edu. *Web site:* http://www.avemaria.edu/.

BAKER COLLEGE OF ALLEN PARK
Allen Park, Michigan

Baker College of Allen Park is a coed, primarily women's, private, four-year college of Baker College System, founded in 2003, offering degrees at the bachelor's level. It has a 13-acre campus in Allen Park near Detroit.

Student Body Statistics The student body is made up of 397 undergraduates. 78 percent are women and 22 percent are men. Students come from 1 state or territory.
Expenses for 2003–04 *Tuition:* $5940 full-time, $165 per quarter hour part-time. Full-time tuition varies according to program.
Freshman Admission Baker College of Allen Park requires a high school transcript and an interview. The application deadline for regular admission is September 24.
Entrance Difficulty For the fall 2003 freshman class, 100 percent of the applicants were accepted.

For Further Information Contact Mr. Steve Peterson, Director of Admissions, Baker College of Allen Park, 4500 Enterprise Drive, Allen Park, MI 48101. *Telephone:* 313-425-3700 or 313-425-3700 (toll-free). *E-mail:* steve.peterson@baker.edu. *Web site:* http://www.baker.edu/.

BAKER COLLEGE OF AUBURN HILLS
Auburn Hills, Michigan

Baker is a coed, private, four-year college of Baker College System, founded in 1911, offering degrees at the associate and bachelor's levels and postbachelor's certificates. It has a 7-acre campus in Auburn Hills near Detroit.

Academic Information The faculty has 115 members (8% full-time), 10% with terminal degrees. The student-faculty ratio is 22:1. The library holds 5,400 titles and 95 serial subscriptions. Special programs include academic remediation, services for learning-disabled students, cooperative (work-study) education, advanced placement credit, accelerated degree programs, double majors, independent study, distance learning, summer session for credit, part-time degree programs (daytime, evenings, summer), external degree programs, and internships.
Student Body Statistics The student body is made up of 3,177 undergraduates. Students come from 1 state or territory.
Expenses for 2003–04 *Application fee:* $20. *Tuition:* $5940 full-time, $165 per quarter hour part-time.
Freshman Admission Baker requires a high school transcript and TOEFL scores for international students. SAT I or ACT scores are recommended. The application deadline for regular admission is rolling.
Transfer Admission The application deadline for admission is rolling.
Entrance Difficulty Baker has an open admission policy.

For Further Information Contact Ms. Jan Bohlen, Vice President for Admissions, Baker College of Auburn Hills, 1500 University Drive, Auburn Hills, MI 48326-1586. *Telephone:* 248-340-0600 or 888-429-0410 (toll-free in-state). *Fax:* 248-340-0608. *E-mail:* jan.bohlen@baker.edu. *Web site:* http://www.baker.edu/.

BAKER COLLEGE OF CADILLAC

Cadillac, Michigan

Baker is a coed, private, four-year college of Baker College System, founded in 1986, offering degrees at the associate and bachelor's levels. It has a 40-acre campus in Cadillac.

Academic Information   The faculty has 73 members (5% full-time). The student-faculty ratio is 16:1. The library holds 4,000 titles and 78 serial subscriptions. Special programs include academic remediation, services for learning-disabled students, cooperative (work-study) education, advanced placement credit, double majors, independent study, distance learning, summer session for credit, part-time degree programs (daytime, evenings, weekends, summer), external degree programs, and internships.
Student Body Statistics   The student body is made up of 1,386 undergraduates. 77 percent are women and 23 percent are men. Students come from 4 states and territories.
Expenses for 2003–04   *Application fee:* $20. *Tuition:* $5940 full-time, $165 per quarter hour part-time. Full-time tuition varies according to program. Part-time tuition varies according to program.
Freshman Admission   Baker requires a high school transcript and TOEFL scores for international students. An interview and SAT I or ACT scores are recommended. The application deadline for regular admission is rolling.
Transfer Admission   The application deadline for admission is rolling.
Entrance Difficulty   Baker has an open admission policy.

For Further Information   Contact Mr. Mike Tisdale, Director of Admissions, Baker College of Cadillac, 9600 East 13th Street, Cadillac, MI 49601. *Telephone:* 616-775-8458, 888-313-3463 (toll-free in-state), or 231-876-3100 (toll-free out-of-state). *Fax:* 231-775-8505. *E-mail:* mike.tisdale@baker.edu. *Web site:* http://www.baker.edu/.

BAKER COLLEGE OF CLINTON TOWNSHIP

Clinton Township, Michigan

Baker is a coed, private, four-year college of Baker College System, founded in 1990, offering degrees at the associate and bachelor's levels. It has a 25-acre campus in Clinton Township near Detroit.

Academic Information   The faculty has 147 members (8% full-time). The student-faculty ratio is 19:1. The library holds 8,000 titles and 97 serial subscriptions. Special programs include academic remediation, services for learning-disabled students, cooperative (work-study) education, advanced placement credit, summer session for credit, part-time degree programs (daytime, evenings, weekends, summer), external degree programs, and internships.
Student Body Statistics   The student body is made up of 4,510 undergraduates. 79 percent are women and 21 percent are men. Students come from 2 states and territories.
Expenses for 2003–04   *Application fee:* $20. *Tuition:* $5940 full-time, $165 per quarter hour part-time. Full-time tuition varies according to program. Part-time tuition varies according to program.
Freshman Admission   Baker requires a high school transcript and TOEFL scores for international students. SAT I or ACT scores are recommended. The application deadline for regular admission is rolling.
Transfer Admission   The application deadline for admission is rolling.
Entrance Difficulty   Baker has an open admission policy.

For Further Information   Contact Ms. Annette M. Looser, Vice President for Admissions, Baker College of Clinton Township, 34950 Little Mack Avenue, Clinton Township, MI 48035. *Telephone:* 810-791-6610 or 888-272-2842 (toll-free). *Fax:* 810-791-6611. *E-mail:* annette.looser@baker.edu. *Web site:* http://www.baker.edu/.

BAKER COLLEGE OF FLINT

Flint, Michigan

Baker is a coed, private, four-year college of Baker College System, founded in 1911, offering degrees at the associate and bachelor's levels. It has a 30-acre campus in Flint near Detroit.

Academic Information   The faculty has 173 members (15% full-time), 10% with terminal degrees. The student-faculty ratio is 37:1. The library holds 168,700 titles. Special programs include academic remediation, services for learning-disabled students, cooperative (work-study) education, advanced placement credit, accelerated degree programs, double majors, independent study, distance learning, summer session for credit, part-time degree programs, external degree programs, and internships.
Student Body Statistics   The student body is made up of 5,639 undergraduates. 69 percent are women and 31 percent are men. Students come from 5 states and territories. 99 percent are from Michigan.
Expenses for 2003–04   *Application fee:* $20. *Tuition:* $5940 full-time, $165 per quarter hour part-time. Full-time tuition varies according to program. Part-time tuition varies according to program. *College room only:* $2600.
Freshman Admission   Baker requires a high school transcript and TOEFL scores for international students. SAT I or ACT scores are recommended. The application deadline for regular admission is September 20.
Transfer Admission   The application deadline for admission is September 20.
Entrance Difficulty   Baker has an open admission policy.

For Further Information   Contact Mr. Troy Crowe, Vice President for Admissions, Baker College of Flint, 1050 West Bristol Road, Flint, MI 48507-5508. *Telephone:* 810-766-4015 or 800-964-4299 (toll-free). *Fax:* 810-766-4049. *E-mail:* troy.crowe@baker.edu. *Web site:* http://www.baker.edu/.

BAKER COLLEGE OF JACKSON

Jackson, Michigan

Baker is a coed, private, four-year college of Baker College System, founded in 1994, offering degrees at the associate and bachelor's levels. It has a 42-acre campus in Jackson near Lansing.

Academic Information   The faculty has 90 members (10% full-time), 10% with terminal degrees. The student-faculty ratio is 13:1. The library holds 7,000 titles and 150 serial subscriptions. Special programs include academic remediation, services for learning-disabled students, cooperative (work-study) education, advanced placement credit, accelerated degree programs, double majors, independent study, distance learning, summer session for credit, part-time degree programs (daytime, evenings, weekends, summer), external degree programs, and internships.
Student Body Statistics   The student body is made up of 1,593 undergraduates. 77 percent are women and 23 percent are men. Students come from 2 states and territories. 99 percent are from Michigan.
Expenses for 2003–04   *Application fee:* $20. *Tuition:* $5940 full-time, $165 per quarter hour part-time. Full-time tuition varies according to program. Part-time tuition varies according to program.
Freshman Admission   Baker requires a high school transcript. SAT I or ACT scores are recommended. The application deadline for regular admission is September 19.
Transfer Admission   The application deadline for admission is rolling.
Entrance Difficulty   Baker has an open admission policy.

For Further Information   Contact Ms. Kelli Stepka, Director of Admissions, Baker College of Jackson, 2800 Springport Road, Jackson, MI 49202. *Telephone:* 517-788-7800 or 888-343-3683 (toll-free). *Fax:* 517-789-7331. *E-mail:* kelli.stepka@baker.edu. *Web site:* http://www.baker.edu/.

BAKER COLLEGE OF MUSKEGON

Muskegon, Michigan

Baker is a coed, private, four-year college of Baker College System, founded in 1888, offering degrees at the associate and bachelor's levels. It has a 40-acre campus in Muskegon near Grand Rapids.

Academic Information   The faculty has 145 members (10% full-time), 6% with terminal degrees. The student-faculty ratio is 30:1. The library holds 32,000 titles and 140 serial subscriptions. Special programs include academic remediation, services for learning-disabled students, cooperative (work-study) education, advanced placement credit, accelerated degree programs, double majors, independent study, distance learning, summer session for credit, part-time degree programs (daytime, evenings, weekends), external degree programs, adult/continuing education programs, and internships.

Student Body Statistics The student body is made up of 4,076 undergraduates. 69 percent are women and 31 percent are men. Students come from 13 states and territories. 99 percent are from Michigan. 1 percent of the 2003 graduating class went on to graduate and professional schools.

Expenses for 2003–04 *Application fee:* $20. *Tuition:* $5940 full-time, $165 per quarter hour part-time. Full-time tuition varies according to program. Part-time tuition varies according to program. *College room only:* $2400.

Freshman Admission Baker requires a high school transcript and TOEFL scores for international students. SAT I or ACT scores are recommended. The application deadline for regular admission is September 24.

Transfer Admission The application deadline for admission is rolling.

Entrance Difficulty Baker has an open admission policy.

For Further Information Contact Ms. Kathy Jacobson, Vice President of Admissions, Baker College of Muskegon, 1903 Marquette Avenue, Muskegon, MI 49442-3497. *Telephone:* 231-777-5207 or 800-937-0337 (toll-free in-state). *Fax:* 231-777-5201. *E-mail:* kathy.jacobson@baker.edu. *Web site:* http://www.baker.edu/.

BAKER COLLEGE OF OWOSSO
Owosso, Michigan

Baker is a coed, private, four-year college of Baker College System, founded in 1984, offering degrees at the associate and bachelor's levels. It has a 32-acre campus in Owosso.

Academic Information The faculty has 103 members (5% full-time), 11% with terminal degrees. The student-faculty ratio is 38:1. The library holds 35,424 titles, 215 serial subscriptions, and 344 audiovisual materials. Special programs include academic remediation, services for learning-disabled students, cooperative (work-study) education, advanced placement credit, accelerated degree programs, summer session for credit, part-time degree programs, external degree programs, adult/continuing education programs, and internships.

Student Body Statistics The student body is made up of 2,538 undergraduates. 68 percent are women and 32 percent are men. Students come from 4 states and territories. 100 percent are from Michigan.

Expenses for 2003–04 *Application fee:* $20. *Tuition:* $5940 full-time, $165 per quarter hour part-time. Full-time tuition varies according to program. *College room only:* $2175.

Freshman Admission Baker requires a high school transcript and TOEFL scores for international students. SAT I or ACT scores are recommended. The application deadline for regular admission is rolling.

Transfer Admission The application deadline for admission is rolling.

Entrance Difficulty Baker has an open admission policy.

For Further Information Contact Mr. Michael Konopacke, Vice President for Admissions, Baker College of Owosso, Owosso, MI 48867. *Telephone:* 517-729-3353 or 800-879-3797 (toll-free). *Fax:* 517-729-3359. *E-mail:* mike.konopacke@baker.edu. *Web site:* http://www.baker.edu/.

BAKER COLLEGE OF PORT HURON
Port Huron, Michigan

Baker is a coed, private, four-year college of Baker College System, founded in 1990, offering degrees at the associate and bachelor's levels. It has a 10-acre campus in Port Huron near Detroit.

Academic Information The faculty has 95 members (11% full-time), 9% with terminal degrees. The student-faculty ratio is 14:1. The library holds 16,823 titles, 181 serial subscriptions, and 135 audiovisual materials.

Special programs include academic remediation, services for learning-disabled students, cooperative (work-study) education, advanced placement credit, accelerated degree programs, double majors, independent study, distance learning, summer session for credit, part-time degree programs (daytime, evenings, weekends, summer), external degree programs, and internships.

Student Body Statistics The student body is made up of 1,477 undergraduates. 78 percent are women and 22 percent are men. 90 percent are from Michigan.

Expenses for 2003–04 *Application fee:* $20. *Tuition:* $5940 full-time, $165 per quarter hour part-time. Full-time tuition varies according to program.

Freshman Admission Baker requires a high school transcript, an interview, and TOEFL scores for international students. The application deadline for regular admission is September 24.

Transfer Admission The application deadline for admission is rolling.

Entrance Difficulty Baker has an open admission policy.

For Further Information Contact Mr. Daniel Kenny, Director of Admissions, Baker College of Port Huron, 3403 Lapeer Road, Port Huron, MI 48060-2597. *Telephone:* 810-985-7000 or 888-262-2442 (toll-free). *Fax:* 810-985-7066. *E-mail:* kenny_d@porthuron.baker.edu. *Web site:* http://www.baker.edu/.

CALVIN COLLEGE
Grand Rapids, Michigan

Calvin is a coed, private, comprehensive institution, founded in 1876, affiliated with the Christian Reformed Church, offering degrees at the bachelor's and master's levels and postbachelor's certificates. It has a 370-acre campus in Grand Rapids.

Academic Information The faculty has 382 members (80% full-time), 70% with terminal degrees. The undergraduate student-faculty ratio is 13:1. The library holds 801,802 titles, 2,658 serial subscriptions, and 22,394 audiovisual materials. Special programs include academic remediation, services for learning-disabled students, an honors program, study abroad, advanced placement credit, accelerated degree programs, double majors, independent study, self-designed majors, summer session for credit, part-time degree programs (daytime, evenings, summer), adult/continuing education programs, internships, and arrangement for off-campus study with Council for Christian Colleges and Universities, Central College, Trinity Christian College, Au Sable Institute. The most frequently chosen baccalaureate fields are business/marketing, education, social sciences and history.

Student Body Statistics The student body totals 4,323, of whom 4,289 are undergraduates (1,042 freshmen). 56 percent are women and 44 percent are men. Students come from 48 states and territories and 44 other countries. 61 percent are from Michigan. 8 percent are international students. 20 percent of the 2003 graduating class went on to graduate and professional schools.

Expenses for 2003–04 *Application fee:* $50. *Comprehensive fee:* $22,615 includes full-time tuition ($16,775) and college room and board ($5840). *College room only:* $3180. Room and board charges vary according to board plan. *Part-time tuition:* $410 per credit hour. Part-time tuition varies according to course load.

Financial Aid Forms of aid include need-based and non-need-based scholarships and part-time jobs. The average aided 2002–03 undergraduate received an aid package worth $12,252. The priority application deadline for financial aid is February 15.

Freshman Admission Calvin requires an essay, a high school transcript, a minimum 2.5 high school GPA, 1 recommendation, SAT I or ACT scores, and TOEFL scores for international students. An interview is recommended. The application deadline for regular admission is August 15.

Transfer Admission The application deadline for admission is rolling.

Calvin College (continued)

Entrance Difficulty Calvin assesses its entrance difficulty level as moderately difficult. For the fall 2003 freshman class, 99 percent of the applicants were accepted.

For Further Information Contact Mr. Dale D. Kuiper, Director of Admissions, Calvin College, 3201 Burton Street, SE, Grand Rapids, MI 49546-4388. *Telephone:* 616-526-6106 or 800-688-0122 (toll-free). *Fax:* 616-526-6777. *E-mail:* admissions@calvin.edu. *Web site:* http://www.calvin.edu/.

CENTER FOR CREATIVE STUDIES-COLLEGE OF ART AND DESIGN

See College for Creative Studies

CENTRAL MICHIGAN UNIVERSITY
Mount Pleasant, Michigan

Central Michigan is a coed, public university, founded in 1892, offering degrees at the bachelor's, master's, and doctoral levels and post-master's and postbachelor's certificates. It has an 854-acre campus in Mount Pleasant.

Academic Information The faculty has 1,118 members (60% full-time), 57% with terminal degrees. The undergraduate student-faculty ratio is 22:1. The library holds 998,460 titles, 4,634 serial subscriptions, and 24,630 audiovisual materials. Special programs include academic remediation, an honors program, study abroad, advanced placement credit, accelerated degree programs, Freshman Honors College, ESL programs, double majors, distance learning, self-designed majors, summer session for credit, part-time degree programs, external degree programs, adult/continuing education programs, and internships. The most frequently chosen baccalaureate fields are business/marketing, education, social sciences and history.

Student Body Statistics The student body totals 27,758, of whom 19,642 are undergraduates (3,680 freshmen). 59 percent are women and 41 percent are men. Students come from 45 states and territories and 40 other countries. 97 percent are from Michigan. 0.6 percent are international students. 14 percent of the 2003 graduating class went on to graduate and professional schools.

Expenses for 2003–04 *Application fee:* $35. *State resident tuition:* $4463 full-time, $148.75 per credit part-time. *Nonresident tuition:* $11,393 full-time, $379.75 per credit part-time. *Mandatory fees:* $755 full-time, $212.50 per term part-time. *College room and board:* $5924. *College room only:* $2962. Room and board charges vary according to board plan and housing facility.

Financial Aid Forms of aid include need-based and non-need-based scholarships, athletic grants, and part-time jobs. The average aided 2003–04 undergraduate received an aid package worth an estimated $8539. The priority application deadline for financial aid is March 1.

Freshman Admission Central Michigan requires a high school transcript, SAT I or ACT scores, and TOEFL scores for international students. A minimum 3.0 high school GPA is recommended. An essay, recommendations, and an interview are required for some. The application deadline for regular admission is rolling.

Transfer Admission The application deadline for admission is rolling.

Entrance Difficulty Central Michigan assesses its entrance difficulty level as moderately difficult. For the fall 2003 freshman class, 70 percent of the applicants were accepted.

For Further Information Contact Mrs. Betty J. Wagner, Director of Admissions, Central Michigan University, 105 Warriner Hall, Mt. Pleasant, MI 48859. *Telephone:* 989-774-3076. *Fax:* 989-774-7267. *E-mail:* cmuadmit@cmich.edu. *Web site:* http://www.cmich.edu/.

CLEARY UNIVERSITY
Ann Arbor, Michigan

Cleary is a coed, private, comprehensive institution, founded in 1883, offering degrees at the associate, bachelor's, and master's levels in business. It has a 32-acre campus in Ann Arbor near Detroit and Lansing.

Academic Information The faculty has 112 members (10% full-time), 18% with terminal degrees. The undergraduate student-faculty ratio is 10:1. The library holds 4,500 titles, 22 serial subscriptions, and 100 audiovisual materials. Special programs include cooperative (work-study) education, advanced placement credit, accelerated degree programs, independent study, distance learning, summer session for credit, adult/continuing education programs, and internships. The most frequently chosen baccalaureate field is business/marketing.

Student Body Statistics The student body totals 968, of whom 908 are undergraduates. 58 percent are women and 42 percent are men. Students come from 2 states and territories and 4 other countries. 99 percent are from Michigan. 1 percent are international students. 35 percent of the 2003 graduating class went on to graduate and professional schools.

Expenses for 2004–05 *Application fee:* $25. *Tuition:* $11,760 full-time, $245 per quarter hour part-time. Full-time tuition varies according to degree level.

Financial Aid Forms of aid include need-based and non-need-based scholarships and part-time jobs. The average aided 2002–03 undergraduate received an aid package worth $8568. The priority application deadline for financial aid is March 1.

Freshman Admission Cleary requires a high school transcript, a minimum 2.5 high school GPA, and complete the Technology Skills Inventory (TSI). An interview is recommended. An essay, 2 recommendations, SAT I or ACT scores, and SAT I and SAT II or ACT scores are required for some. The application deadline for regular admission is August 15.

Transfer Admission The application deadline for admission is August 15.

Entrance Difficulty Cleary assesses its entrance difficulty level as moderately difficult. For the fall 2003 freshman class, 97 percent of the applicants were accepted.

For Further Information Contact Ms. Charlotte Paquette, Admissions Representative, Cleary University, 3750 Cleary Drive, Howell, MI 48843. *Telephone:* 517-548-3670 Ext. 2213 or 888-5-CLEARY Ext. 2249 (toll-free). *Fax:* 517-552-7805. *E-mail:* admissions@cleary.edu. *Web site:* http://www.cleary.edu/.

COLLEGE FOR CREATIVE STUDIES
Detroit, Michigan

CCS is a coed, private, four-year college, founded in 1926, offering degrees at the bachelor's level in art. It has an 11-acre campus in Detroit.

Academic Information The faculty has 217 members (20% full-time). The student-faculty ratio is 10:1. The library holds 24,000 titles and 75 serial subscriptions. Special programs include academic remediation, services for learning-disabled students, cooperative (work-study) education, advanced placement credit, ESL programs, double majors, independent study, summer session for credit, part-time degree programs (daytime, evenings, weekends, summer), internships, and arrangement for off-campus study with Association of Independent Colleges of Art and Design. The most frequently chosen baccalaureate field is visual/performing arts.

Student Body Statistics The student body is made up of 1,218 undergraduates (190 freshmen). 42 percent are women and 58 percent are men. Students come from 35 states and territories and 18 other countries. 83 percent are from Michigan. 4.3 percent are international students.

Expenses for 2004–05 *Application fee:* $35. *Tuition:* $20,250 full-time, $675 per credit hour part-time. *Mandatory fees:* $1126 full-time, $563 per term part-time. Part-time tuition and fees vary according to course load. *College room only:* $3500. Room charges vary according to housing facility.

Financial Aid Forms of aid include need-based and non-need-based scholarships and part-time jobs. The priority application deadline for financial aid is February 21.

Freshman Admission CCS requires an essay, a high school transcript, a portfolio, SAT I or ACT scores, and TOEFL scores for international students. A minimum 2.5 high school GPA is recommended. Recommendations and an interview are required for some. The application deadline for regular admission is rolling.

Transfer Admission The application deadline for admission is rolling.

Entrance Difficulty CCS assesses its entrance difficulty level as moderately difficult. For the fall 2003 freshman class, 74 percent of the applicants were accepted.

For Further Information Contact College for Creative Studies, 201 East Kirby, Detroit, MI 48202-4034. *Telephone:* 313-664-7425 or 800-952-ARTS (toll-free). *Fax:* 313-872-2739. *E-mail:* admissions@ccscad.edu. *Web site:* http://www.ccscad.edu/.

CONCORDIA UNIVERSITY
Ann Arbor, Michigan

Concordia is a coed, private, comprehensive unit of Concordia University System, founded in 1963, affiliated with the Lutheran Church–Missouri Synod, offering degrees at the associate, bachelor's, and master's levels. It has a 234-acre campus in Ann Arbor near Detroit.

Academic Information The faculty has 91 members (44% full-time). The undergraduate student-faculty ratio is 9:1. The library holds 120,000 titles, 3,950 serial subscriptions, and 10,500 audiovisual materials. Special programs include academic remediation, services for learning-disabled students, study abroad, advanced placement credit, accelerated degree programs, double majors, independent study, distance learning, self-designed majors, summer session for credit, part-time degree programs (daytime, evenings, weekends, summer), adult/continuing education programs, internships, and arrangement for off-campus study with Concordia University System. The most frequently chosen baccalaureate fields are English, business/marketing, visual/performing arts.

Student Body Statistics The student body totals 477, of whom 438 are undergraduates (72 freshmen). 57 percent are women and 43 percent are men. Students come from 14 states and territories and 3 other countries. 81 percent are from Michigan. 1 percent are international students.

Expenses for 2003–04 *Application fee:* $25. *Comprehensive fee:* $23,995 includes full-time tuition ($16,900), mandatory fees ($350), and college room and board ($6745). *Part-time tuition:* $565 per semester hour.

Financial Aid Forms of aid include need-based and non-need-based scholarships, athletic grants, and part-time jobs. The average aided 2003–04 undergraduate received an aid package worth an estimated $14,769. The priority application deadline for financial aid is March 1.

Freshman Admission Concordia requires a high school transcript, a minimum 2.5 high school GPA, and SAT I or ACT scores. 1 recommendation and ACT scores are recommended. An essay and an interview are required for some. The application deadline for regular admission is rolling.

Transfer Admission The application deadline for admission is rolling.

Entrance Difficulty Concordia assesses its entrance difficulty level as moderately difficult. For the fall 2003 freshman class, 75 percent of the applicants were accepted.

For Further Information Contact Ms. Sydney Wolf, Director of Admissions, Concordia University, 4090 Geddes Road, Ann Arbor, MI 48105. *Telephone:* 734-995-7322 Ext. 7311 or 800-253-0680 (toll-free). *Fax:* 734-995-7455. *E-mail:* admissions@cuaa.edu. *Web site:* http://www.cuaa.edu/.

CORNERSTONE UNIVERSITY
Grand Rapids, Michigan

Cornerstone University is a coed, private, nondenominational, comprehensive institution, founded in 1941, offering degrees at the associate, bachelor's, master's, and first professional levels. It has a 132-acre campus in Grand Rapids.

Academic Information The faculty has 143 members (58% full-time), 27% with terminal degrees. The undergraduate student-faculty ratio is 16:1. The library holds 109,376 titles, 1,073 serial subscriptions, and 19,702 audiovisual materials. Special programs include academic remediation, advanced placement credit, accelerated degree programs, double majors, independent study, summer session for credit, part-time degree programs, adult/continuing education programs, internships, and arrangement for off-campus study with Calvin College, Reformed Bible College, Grace Bible College. The most frequently chosen baccalaureate fields are business/marketing, English, philosophy, religion, and theology.

Student Body Statistics The student body totals 2,353, of whom 2,074 are undergraduates (359 freshmen). 62 percent are women and 38 percent are men. Students come from 31 states and territories and 1 other country. 80 percent are from Michigan. 1.2 percent are international students. 14 percent of the 2003 graduating class went on to graduate and professional schools.

Expenses for 2003–04 *Application fee:* $25. *Comprehensive fee:* $19,846 includes full-time tuition ($14,420) and college room and board ($5426). *College room only:* $2476. Room and board charges vary according to board plan. *Part-time tuition:* $555 per credit. Part-time tuition varies according to course load.

Financial Aid Forms of aid include need-based and non-need-based scholarships, athletic grants, and part-time jobs. The average aided 2003–04 undergraduate received an aid package worth an estimated $12,302. The application deadline for financial aid is February 1.

Freshman Admission Cornerstone University requires an essay, a high school transcript, a minimum 2.5 high school GPA, 1 recommendation, SAT I or ACT scores, and TOEFL scores for international students. An interview is recommended. The application deadline for regular admission is rolling.

Transfer Admission The application deadline for admission is rolling.

Entrance Difficulty Cornerstone University assesses its entrance difficulty level as moderately difficult. For the fall 2003 freshman class, 76 percent of the applicants were accepted.

For Further Information Contact Mr. Brent Rudin, Director of Admissions, Cornerstone University, 1001 East Beltline Avenue, NE, Grand Rapids, MI 49525. *Telephone:* 616-222-1426 or 800-787-9778 (toll-free). *Fax:* 616-222-1400. *E-mail:* admissions@cornerstone.edu. *Web site:* http://www.cornerstone.edu/.

DAVENPORT UNIVERSITY
Alma, Michigan

For Information Write to Davenport University, Alma, MI 48801.

DAVENPORT UNIVERSITY
Bad Axe, Michigan

For Information Write to Davenport University, Bad Axe, MI 48413.

DAVENPORT UNIVERSITY
Bay City, Michigan

For Information Write to Davenport University, Bay City, MI 48706.

DAVENPORT UNIVERSITY
Caro, Michigan

For Information Write to Davenport University, Caro, MI 48723.

DAVENPORT UNIVERSITY
Dearborn, Michigan

Davenport University is a coed, private, comprehensive institution, founded in 1985, offering degrees at the associate, bachelor's, and master's levels. It has a 17-acre campus in Dearborn near Detroit.

Academic Information The faculty has 170 members (12% full-time), 13% with terminal degrees. The undergraduate student-faculty ratio is 23:1. The library holds 33,560 titles, 224 serial subscriptions, and 299 audiovisual materials. Special programs include academic remediation, cooperative (work-study) education, advanced placement credit, double majors, independent study, summer session for credit, part-time degree programs, and internships. The most frequently chosen baccalaureate fields are business/marketing, health professions and related sciences.
Student Body Statistics The student body totals 2,512, of whom 2,185 are undergraduates (202 freshmen). 75 percent are women and 25 percent are men. Students come from 16 states and territories. 99 percent are from Michigan. 0.6 percent are international students.
Expenses for 2003–04 *Application fee:* $25. *Tuition:* $10,170 full-time, $339 per credit hour part-time. *Mandatory fees:* $100 full-time. *College room only:* $3400.
Financial Aid Forms of aid include need-based and non-need-based scholarships and part-time jobs. The average aided 2002–03 undergraduate received an aid package worth $12,200. The application deadline for financial aid is continuous.
Freshman Admission Davenport University requires a high school transcript and TOEFL scores for international students. An interview is recommended. The application deadline for regular admission is rolling.
Transfer Admission The application deadline for admission is rolling.
Entrance Difficulty Davenport University has an open admission policy.

For Further Information Contact Ms. Elizabeth Aitken, Director of Admissions, Davenport University, 4801 Oakman Boulevard, Dearborn, MI 48126-3799. *Telephone:* 313-581-4400 or 800-815-8023 (toll-free). *Fax:* 313-581-1985. *E-mail:* jennifer.salloum@davenport.edu. *Web site:* http://www.davenport.edu/.

DAVENPORT UNIVERSITY
Gaylord, Michigan

Davenport University is a coed, private, four-year college, founded in 1977, offering degrees at the associate and bachelor's levels.

Academic Information The faculty has 12 members (8% full-time). The student-faculty ratio is 17:1.
Student Body Statistics The student body is made up of 126 undergraduates (9 freshmen). 71 percent are women and 29 percent are men. Students come from 2 states and territories.
Expenses for 2003–04 *Application fee:* $25. *Tuition:* $10,170 full-time, $339 per credit hour part-time. *Mandatory fees:* $100 full-time. *College room only:* $3400.
Financial Aid Forms of aid include need-based scholarships and part-time jobs. The priority application deadline for financial aid is February 21.
Freshman Admission The application deadline for regular admission is rolling.

For Further Information Contact Ms. Sheila Simpson, Career and Education Specialist, Davenport University, 80 Livingston Boulevard, Gaylord, MI 49735. *Telephone:* 989-731-2966 or 888-352-5791 (toll-free). *Fax:* 989-705-3727. *Web site:* http://www.davenport.edu/.

DAVENPORT UNIVERSITY
Grand Rapids, Michigan

Davenport is a coed, private, comprehensive unit of Davenport University, founded in 1866, offering degrees at the associate, bachelor's, and master's levels and post-master's and postbachelor's certificates.

Academic Information The faculty has 104 members (25% full-time), 17% with terminal degrees. The undergraduate student-faculty ratio is 25:1. The library holds 40,810 titles and 1,500 serial subscriptions. Special programs include academic remediation, cooperative (work-study) education, study abroad, advanced placement credit, accelerated degree programs, ESL programs, independent study, distance learning, summer session for credit, part-time degree programs (daytime, evenings, weekends, summer), external degree programs, adult/continuing education programs, and internships.
Student Body Statistics The student body totals 1,868, of whom 1,751 are undergraduates (156 freshmen). 63 percent are women and 37 percent are men. Students come from 15 states and territories. 0.6 percent are international students. 1.7 percent of the 2003 graduating class went on to graduate and professional schools.
Expenses for 2003–04 *Application fee:* $25. *Tuition:* $10,170 full-time, $339 per credit hour part-time. *Mandatory fees:* $100 full-time. *College room only:* $3400.
Financial Aid Forms of aid include need-based and non-need-based scholarships and part-time jobs. The priority application deadline for financial aid is March 15.
Freshman Admission Davenport requires a high school transcript. An essay, an interview, ACT scores, and TOEFL scores for international students are recommended. The application deadline for regular admission is rolling and for nonresidents it is September 15.
Transfer Admission The application deadline for admission is rolling.
Entrance Difficulty Davenport has an open admission policy.

For Further Information Contact Davenport University, 415 East Fulton Street, Administration Building, Fulton and Prospect, Grand Rapids, MI 49503. *Telephone:* 616-451-3511 or 800-724-7708 (toll-free). *Fax:* 616-732-1142. *Web site:* http://www.davenport.edu/.

DAVENPORT UNIVERSITY
Holland, Michigan

Davenport University is a coed, private, comprehensive institution, founded in 1977.

Academic Information The faculty has 45 members (11% full-time), 7% with terminal degrees. The student-faculty ratio is 23:1.
Student Body Statistics The student body totals 747, of whom 706 are undergraduates (50 freshmen). 64 percent are women and 36 percent are men. Students come from 3 states and territories and 1 other country. 0.1 percent are international students.
Expenses for 2003–04 *Application fee:* $25. *Tuition:* $10,170 full-time, $339 per credit hour part-time. *Mandatory fees:* $100 full-time. *College room only:* $3400.
Financial Aid Forms of aid include need-based scholarships and part-time jobs. The priority application deadline for financial aid is February 21.

For Further Information Contact Mr. Ken Moored, Financial Aid Coordinator, Davenport University, 643 Waverly Road, Holland, MI 49423. *Telephone:* 616-395-4600 or 800-643-4630 (toll-free). *Fax:* 616-395-4698. *Web site:* http://www.davenport.edu/.

DAVENPORT UNIVERSITY
Kalamazoo, Michigan

Davenport University is a coed, private, four-year college of Davenport Educational System, founded in 1977, offering degrees at the associate and bachelor's levels and postbachelor's certificates. It has a 5-acre campus in Kalamazoo.

Academic Information The faculty has 56 members (14% full-time), 12% with terminal degrees. The student-faculty ratio is 16:1. The library holds 10,257 titles and 949 audiovisual materials. Special programs include academic remediation, cooperative (work-study) education, study abroad, ESL programs, independent study, distance learning, summer session for credit, part-time degree programs (daytime, evenings, weekends, summer), adult/continuing education programs, internships, and arrangement for off-campus study with Kalamazoo Consortium.

Student Body Statistics The student body is made up of 549 undergraduates (43 freshmen). 72 percent are women and 28 percent are men. Students come from 8 states and territories. 0.4 percent are international students.

Expenses for 2003–04 *Application fee:* $25. *Tuition:* $10,170 full-time, $339 per credit hour part-time. *Mandatory fees:* $100 full-time. *College room only:* $3400.

Financial Aid Forms of aid include need-based scholarships and part-time jobs. The priority application deadline for financial aid is February 21.

Freshman Admission Davenport University requires an essay and a high school transcript. TOEFL scores for international students are recommended. The application deadline for regular admission is rolling.

Transfer Admission The application deadline for admission is rolling.

Entrance Difficulty Davenport University has an open admission policy.

For Further Information Contact Ms. Dawn Vander Ploeg, Director of Career and Education Advising, Davenport University, 4123 West Main Street, Kalamazoo, MI 49006-2791. *Telephone:* 269-382-2835 or 800-632-8928 (toll-free). *Fax:* 616-382-2661. *Web site:* http://www.davenport.edu/.

DAVENPORT UNIVERSITY
Lansing, Michigan

Davenport University is a coed, private, four-year college of Davenport Educational System, founded in 1977, offering degrees at the associate, bachelor's, and master's levels. It has a 2-acre campus in Lansing near Detroit.

Academic Information The faculty has 53 members (11% full-time), 15% with terminal degrees. The undergraduate student-faculty ratio is 30:1. The library holds 10,680 titles and 850 serial subscriptions. Special programs include academic remediation, services for learning-disabled students, cooperative (work-study) education, advanced placement credit, accelerated degree programs, independent study, distance learning, self-designed majors, summer session for credit, part-time degree programs, external degree programs, adult/continuing education programs, and internships.

Student Body Statistics The student body totals 781, of whom 718 are undergraduates (85 freshmen). 70 percent are women and 30 percent are men. Students come from 11 states and territories and 5 other countries. 0.8 percent are international students. 3 percent of the 2003 graduating class went on to graduate and professional schools.

Expenses for 2003–04 *Application fee:* $25. *Tuition:* $10,170 full-time, $339 per credit hour part-time. *Mandatory fees:* $100 full-time. *College room only:* $3400.

Financial Aid Forms of aid include need-based and non-need-based scholarships and part-time jobs. The priority application deadline for financial aid is March 15.

Freshman Admission Davenport University requires a high school transcript. An interview is recommended. ACT scores are required for some. The application deadline for regular admission is rolling.

Transfer Admission The application deadline for admission is September 15.

Entrance Difficulty Davenport University has an open admission policy.

For Further Information Contact Tonna Winks, Enrollment Manager, Davenport University, 220 East Kalamazoo, Lansing, MI 48933-2197. *Telephone:* 517-484-2600 or 800-686-1600 (toll-free). *Fax:* 517-484-9719. *E-mail:* laadmissions@davenport.edu. *Web site:* http://www.davenport.edu/.

DAVENPORT UNIVERSITY
Lapeer, Michigan

Davenport University is a coed, private, four-year college, founded in 1985, offering degrees at the associate and bachelor's levels.

Academic Information The faculty has 25 members, 4% with terminal degrees. The student-faculty ratio is 14:1.

Student Body Statistics The student body is made up of 145 undergraduates (25 freshmen). 81 percent are women and 19 percent are men. Students come from 1 state or territory.

Expenses for 2003–04 *Application fee:* $25. *Tuition:* $10,170 full-time, $339 per credit hour part-time. *Mandatory fees:* $100 full-time. *College room only:* $3400.

Financial Aid Forms of aid include need-based scholarships and part-time jobs. The priority application deadline for financial aid is February 21.

Freshman Admission The application deadline for regular admission is rolling.

For Further Information Contact Mr. Jim Block, Executive Director, Davenport University, 550 Lake Drive, Lapeer, MI 48446. *Telephone:* 810-664-9655. *Fax:* 810-664-1912. *Web site:* http://www.davenport.edu/.

DAVENPORT UNIVERSITY
Midland, Michigan

For Information Write to Davenport University, Midland, MI 48642.

DAVENPORT UNIVERSITY
Romeo, Michigan

For Information Write to Davenport University, Romeo, MI 48065.

DAVENPORT UNIVERSITY
Saginaw, Michigan

For Information Write to Davenport University, Saginaw, MI 48604.

DAVENPORT UNIVERSITY
Traverse City, Michigan

Davenport University is a coed, private, comprehensive institution, founded in 1977.

Academic Information The faculty has 13 members (8% full-time). The student-faculty ratio is 13:1.

Student Body Statistics The student body totals 133, of whom 86 are undergraduates (10 freshmen). 62 percent are women and 38 percent are men. Students come from 6 states and territories.

Expenses for 2003–04 *Application fee:* $25. *Tuition:* $10,170 full-time, $339 per credit hour part-time. *Mandatory fees:* $100 full-time. *College room only:* $3400.

Financial Aid Forms of aid include need-based scholarships and part-time jobs. The priority application deadline for financial aid is February 21.

Freshman Admission The application deadline for regular admission is rolling.

For Further Information Contact Davenport University, 2200 Dendrinos Drive, Suite 110, Traverse City, MI 49684. *Telephone:* 213-995-1740 or 231-995-1740 (toll-free). *Fax:* 231-995-1743. *Web site:* http://www.davenport.edu/.

DAVENPORT UNIVERSITY
Warren, Michigan

Davenport University is a coed, private, comprehensive institution, founded in 1985, offering degrees at the associate, bachelor's, and master's levels. It has a 9-acre campus in Warren near Detroit.

Academic Information The faculty has 86 members (17% full-time), 19% with terminal degrees. The undergraduate student-faculty ratio is 23:1. The library holds 95,000 titles, 185 serial subscriptions, and 237 audiovisual materials. Special programs include academic remediation, cooperative (work-study) education, advanced placement credit, double majors, summer session for credit, part-time degree programs, and internships. The most frequently chosen baccalaureate fields are business/marketing, health professions and related sciences.
Student Body Statistics The student body totals 1,407, of whom 1,250 are undergraduates (90 freshmen). 77 percent are women and 23 percent are men. Students come from 8 states and territories and 3 other countries. 99 percent are from Michigan. 0.2 percent are international students.
Expenses for 2003–04 *Application fee:* $25. *Tuition:* $10,170 full-time, $339 per credit hour part-time. *Mandatory fees:* $100 full-time. *College room only:* $3400.
Financial Aid Forms of aid include need-based and non-need-based scholarships and part-time jobs. The priority application deadline for financial aid is March 21.
Freshman Admission Davenport University requires a high school transcript. TOEFL scores for international students are recommended. The application deadline for regular admission is rolling.
Transfer Admission The application deadline for admission is rolling.
Entrance Difficulty Davenport University has an open admission policy.

For Further Information Contact Kash Richmonds, Assistant Director of Registration, Davenport University, 27650 Dequindre Road, Warren, MI 48092-5209. *Telephone:* 586-558-8700 or 800-724-7708 (toll-free). *Fax:* 810-558-7868. *Web site:* http://www.davenport.edu/.

EASTERN MICHIGAN UNIVERSITY
Ypsilanti, Michigan

EMU is a coed, public, comprehensive institution, founded in 1849, offering degrees at the bachelor's, master's, and doctoral levels and post-master's and postbachelor's certificates. It has a 460-acre campus in Ypsilanti near Detroit.

Academic Information The faculty has 1,223 members (62% full-time), 47% with terminal degrees. The undergraduate student-faculty ratio is 19:1. The library holds 658,648 titles, 4,457 serial subscriptions, and 11,524 audiovisual materials. Special programs include academic remediation, services for learning-disabled students, an honors program, cooperative (work-study) education, study abroad, advanced placement credit, accelerated degree programs, ESL programs, double majors, independent study, distance learning, self-designed majors, summer session for credit, part-time degree programs (daytime, evenings, weekends, summer), adult/continuing education programs, and internships. The most frequently chosen baccalaureate fields are business/marketing, education, social sciences and history.
Student Body Statistics The student body totals 24,129, of whom 19,577 are undergraduates (2,577 freshmen). 61 percent are women and 39 percent are men. Students come from 47 states and territories and 77 other countries. 94 percent are from Michigan. 1.6 percent are international students. 20 percent of the 2003 graduating class went on to graduate and professional schools.
Expenses for 2003–04 *Application fee:* $30. *State resident tuition:* $4595 full-time, $153.15 per credit hour part-time. *Nonresident tuition:* $14,013 full-time, $467.10 per credit hour part-time. *Mandatory fees:* $1032 full-time, $31.75 per credit hour part-time, $40 per term part-time. Full-time tuition and fees vary according to reciprocity agreements. Part-time tuition and fees vary according to reciprocity agreements. *College room and board:* $5850. *College room only:* $2748. Room and board charges vary according to housing facility and location.

Financial Aid Forms of aid include need-based and non-need-based scholarships, athletic grants, and part-time jobs. The average aided 2002–03 undergraduate received an aid package worth $9504. The priority application deadline for financial aid is March 15.
Freshman Admission EMU requires a high school transcript, a minimum 2.0 high school GPA, SAT I or ACT scores, and TOEFL scores for international students. ACT scores are recommended. 1 recommendation and an interview are required for some. The application deadline for regular admission is June 30.
Transfer Admission The application deadline for admission is rolling.
Entrance Difficulty EMU assesses its entrance difficulty level as moderately difficult. For the fall 2003 freshman class, 79 percent of the applicants were accepted.

For Further Information Contact Ms. Judy Benfield-Tatum, Director of Admissions, Eastern Michigan University, 400 Pierce Hall, Ypsilanti, MI 48197. *Telephone:* 734-487-3060 or 800-GO TO EMU (toll-free). *Fax:* 734-487-1484. *E-mail:* admissions@emich.edu. *Web site:* http://www.emich.edu/.

FERRIS STATE UNIVERSITY
Big Rapids, Michigan

Ferris is a coed, public, comprehensive institution, founded in 1884, offering degrees at the associate, bachelor's, master's, and first professional levels. It has an 850-acre campus in Big Rapids near Grand Rapids.

Academic Information The faculty has 1,023 members (51% full-time), 92% with terminal degrees. The undergraduate student-faculty ratio is 16:1. The library holds 340,048 titles, 9,809 serial subscriptions, and 10,199 audiovisual materials. Special programs include academic remediation, an honors program, cooperative (work-study) education, study abroad, advanced placement credit, accelerated degree programs, Freshman Honors College, ESL programs, double majors, distance learning, summer session for credit, part-time degree programs (daytime, evenings, weekends, summer), external degree programs, adult/continuing education programs, internships, and arrangement for off-campus study. The most frequently chosen baccalaureate fields are business/marketing, engineering/engineering technologies, protective services/public administration.
Student Body Statistics The student body totals 11,821, of whom 10,767 are undergraduates (2,248 freshmen). 47 percent are women and 53 percent are men. Students come from 43 states and territories and 55 other countries. 95 percent are from Michigan. 1.8 percent are international students. 6 percent of the 2003 graduating class went on to graduate and professional schools.
Expenses for 2003–04 *Application fee:* $30. *State resident tuition:* $6044 full-time, $250 per credit hour part-time. *Nonresident tuition:* $12,088 full-time, $500 per credit hour part-time. *Mandatory fees:* $142 full-time, $71 per term part-time. Full-time tuition and fees vary according to program and reciprocity agreements. Part-time tuition and fees vary according to course load. *College room and board:* $6326. *College room only:* $3118. Room and board charges vary according to board plan and housing facility.
Financial Aid Forms of aid include need-based and non-need-based scholarships, athletic grants, and part-time jobs. The average aided 2002–03 undergraduate received an aid package worth $7900. The priority application deadline for financial aid is March 15.
Freshman Admission Ferris requires a high school transcript, a minimum 2.25 high school GPA, SAT I or ACT scores, and TOEFL scores for international students. An interview is recommended. 3 recommendations and an interview are required for some. The application deadline for regular admission is August 1.
Transfer Admission The application deadline for admission is August 1.
Entrance Difficulty Ferris assesses its entrance difficulty level as minimally difficult; moderately difficult for transfers; very difficult for

Michigan

pharmacy, dental hygiene, nursing, optometry programs. For the fall 2003 freshman class, 73 percent of the applicants were accepted.

For Further Information   Contact Dr. Craig Westmann, Director Admissions Records/Associate Dean of Enrollment Services, Ferris State University, 1201 South State Street, CSS201, Big Rapids, MI 49307-2742. *Telephone:* 231-591-2100 or 800-433-7747 (toll-free). *Fax:* 616-592-2978. *E-mail:* admissions@ferris.edu. *Web site:* http://www.ferris.edu/.

FINLANDIA UNIVERSITY
Hancock, Michigan

Finlandia University is a coed, private, four-year college, founded in 1896, affiliated with the Evangelical Lutheran Church in America, offering degrees at the associate and bachelor's levels. It has a 25-acre campus in Hancock.

Expenses for 2003–04   *Application fee:* $30. *One-time mandatory fee:* $75. *Comprehensive fee:* $18,620 includes full-time tuition ($13,750) and college room and board ($4870). Full-time tuition varies according to degree level. Room and board charges vary according to housing facility. *Part-time tuition:* $460 per credit. Part-time tuition varies according to course load and reciprocity agreements.

For Further Information   Contact Mr. Ben Larson, Executive Director of Admissions, Finlandia University, 601 Quincy Street, Hancock, MI 49930. *Telephone:* 906-487-7324 or 877-202-5491 (toll-free). *Fax:* 906-487-7383. *E-mail:* admissions@finlandia.edu. *Web site:* http://www.finlandia.edu/.

GMI ENGINEERING & MANAGEMENT INSTITUTE
See Kettering University

GRACE BIBLE COLLEGE
Grand Rapids, Michigan

Grace is a coed, private, four-year college, founded in 1945, affiliated with the Grace Gospel Fellowship, offering degrees at the associate and bachelor's levels. It has a 16-acre campus in Grand Rapids.

Academic Information   The faculty has 29 members (24% full-time), 14% with terminal degrees. The student-faculty ratio is 11:1. The library holds 32,291 titles, 192 serial subscriptions, and 2,121 audiovisual materials. Special programs include academic remediation, advanced placement credit, ESL programs, independent study, internships, and arrangement for off-campus study with Grand Rapids Community College, Davenport University, Cornerstone University. The most frequently chosen baccalaureate fields are education, philosophy, religion, and theology, protective services/public administration.
Student Body Statistics   The student body is made up of 153 undergraduates (32 freshmen). 51 percent are women and 49 percent are men. Students come from 17 states and territories and 1 other country. 69 percent are from Michigan. 2.7 percent are international students.
Expenses for 2003–04   *Application fee:* $0. *Comprehensive fee:* $15,890 includes full-time tuition ($9300), mandatory fees ($430), and college room and board ($6160). Room and board charges vary according to housing facility. *Part-time tuition:* $395 per semester hour. Part-time tuition varies according to course load.
Financial Aid   Forms of aid include need-based and non-need-based scholarships and part-time jobs. The average aided 2002–03 undergraduate received an aid package worth $9169. The priority application deadline for financial aid is February 15.
Freshman Admission   Grace requires a high school transcript, 2 recommendations, ACT scores, and TOEFL scores for international

students. A minimum 2.5 high school GPA is recommended. An interview is required for some. The application deadline for regular admission is July 15.
Entrance Difficulty   Grace assesses its entrance difficulty level as minimally difficult. For the fall 2003 freshman class, 48 percent of the applicants were accepted.

For Further Information   Contact Mr. Kevin Gilliam, Director of Enrollment, Grace Bible College, 1101 Aldon Street, SW, PO Box 910, Grand Rapids, MI 49509. *Telephone:* 616-538-2330 Ext. 239 or 800-968-1887 (toll-free). *Fax:* 616-538-0599. *E-mail:* gbc@gbcol.edu. *Web site:* http://www.gbcol.edu/.

GRAND VALLEY STATE UNIVERSITY
Allendale, Michigan

GVSU is a coed, public, comprehensive institution, founded in 1960, offering degrees at the bachelor's and master's levels and post-master's and postbachelor's certificates. It has a 900-acre campus in Allendale near Grand Rapids.

Academic Information   The faculty has 1,259 members (68% full-time), 47% with terminal degrees. The undergraduate student-faculty ratio is 17:1. The library holds 620,000 titles and 3,207 serial subscriptions. Special programs include academic remediation, services for learning-disabled students, an honors program, cooperative (work-study) education, study abroad, advanced placement credit, accelerated degree programs, Freshman Honors College, ESL programs, double majors, independent study, distance learning, summer session for credit, part-time degree programs (daytime, evenings, weekends, summer), adult/continuing education programs, and internships. The most frequently chosen baccalaureate fields are business/marketing, English, health professions and related sciences.
Student Body Statistics   The student body totals 21,429, of whom 17,807 are undergraduates (3,288 freshmen). 60 percent are women and 40 percent are men. Students come from 53 states and territories and 53 other countries. 96 percent are from Michigan. 0.6 percent are international students. 35 percent of the 2003 graduating class went on to graduate and professional schools.
Expenses for 2003–04   *Application fee:* $30. *State resident tuition:* $5648 full-time, $246 per semester hour part-time. *Nonresident tuition:* $12,216 full-time, $520 per semester hour part-time. Full-time tuition varies according to student level. Part-time tuition varies according to course load and student level. *College room and board:* $5768. Room and board charges vary according to board plan, housing facility, and location.
Financial Aid   Forms of aid include need-based and non-need-based scholarships, athletic grants, and part-time jobs. The average aided 2002–03 undergraduate received an aid package worth $6614. The priority application deadline for financial aid is February 15.
Freshman Admission   GVSU requires a high school transcript, SAT I or ACT scores, and TOEFL scores for international students. An essay and an interview are required for some. The application deadline for regular admission is May 1.
Transfer Admission   The application deadline for admission is July 25.
Entrance Difficulty   GVSU assesses its entrance difficulty level as moderately difficult. For the fall 2003 freshman class, 73 percent of the applicants were accepted.

For Further Information   Contact Ms. Jodi Chycinski, Director of Admissions, Grand Valley State University, 1 Campus Drive, Allendale, MI 49401. *Telephone:* 616-331-2025 or 800-748-0246 (toll-free). *Fax:* 616-331-2000. *E-mail:* go2gvsu@gvsu.edu. *Web site:* http://www.gvsu.edu/.

GREAT LAKES CHRISTIAN COLLEGE
Lansing, Michigan

GLCC is a coed, private, four-year college, founded in 1949, affiliated with the Christian Churches and Churches of Christ, offering degrees at the associate and bachelor's levels. It has a 50-acre campus in Lansing.

Great Lakes Christian College (continued)

Expenses for 2003–04 *Application fee: $30. Comprehensive fee: $14,080* includes full-time tuition ($7680), mandatory fees ($1600), and college room and board ($4800). *Part-time tuition: $240 per hour.*

For Further Information Contact Mr. Mike Klauka, Dean of Student Affairs, Great Lakes Christian College, 6211 West Willow Highway, Lansing, MI 48917-1299. *Telephone:* 517-321-0242 Ext. 221 or 800-YES-GLCC (toll-free). *Fax:* 517-321-5902. *Web site:* http://www.glcc.edu/.

HILLSDALE COLLEGE
Hillsdale, Michigan

Hillsdale is a coed, private, four-year college, founded in 1844, offering degrees at the bachelor's level. It has a 200-acre campus in Hillsdale.

Academic Information The faculty has 130 members (74% full-time), 78% with terminal degrees. The student-faculty ratio is 11:1. The library holds 205,000 titles, 1,625 serial subscriptions, and 7,950 audiovisual materials. Special programs include an honors program, study abroad, advanced placement credit, accelerated degree programs, double majors, independent study, summer session for credit, part-time degree programs (daytime, summer), and internships. The most frequently chosen baccalaureate fields are business/marketing, biological/life sciences, social sciences and history.
Student Body Statistics The student body is made up of 1,230 undergraduates (360 freshmen). 53 percent are women and 47 percent are men. Students come from 47 states and territories and 14 other countries. 47 percent are from Michigan.
Expenses for 2003–04 *Application fee: $15. Comprehensive fee: $22,450* includes full-time tuition ($15,750), mandatory fees ($300), and college room and board ($6400). *College room only: $3140.* Room and board charges vary according to board plan. *Part-time tuition: $610 per semester hour.*
Financial Aid Forms of aid include need-based and non-need-based scholarships and athletic grants. The average aided 2002–03 undergraduate received an aid package worth $12,714. The priority application deadline for financial aid is February 15.
Freshman Admission Hillsdale requires an essay, a high school transcript, a minimum 3.15 high school GPA, 1 recommendation, SAT I or ACT scores, and TOEFL scores for international students. 2 recommendations, an interview, SAT II: Subject Test scores, and SAT II: Writing Test scores are recommended. 2 recommendations and an interview are required for some. The application deadline for regular admission is rolling.
Transfer Admission The application deadline for admission is rolling.
Entrance Difficulty Hillsdale assesses its entrance difficulty level as very difficult. For the fall 2003 freshman class, 77 percent of the applicants were accepted.

For Further Information Contact Mr. Jeffrey S. Lantis, Director of Admissions, Hillsdale College, 33 East College Street, Hillsdale, MI 49242-1298. *Telephone:* 517-607-2327 Ext. 2327. *Fax:* 517-607-2223. *E-mail:* admissions@hillsdale.edu. *Web site:* http://www.hillsdale.edu/.

HOPE COLLEGE
Holland, Michigan

Hope is a coed, private, four-year college, founded in 1866, affiliated with the Reformed Church in America, offering degrees at the bachelor's level. It has a 45-acre campus in Holland near Grand Rapids.

Academic Information The faculty has 293 members (69% full-time), 61% with terminal degrees. The student-faculty ratio is 13:1. The library holds 343,865 titles, 2,250 serial subscriptions, and 11,970 audiovisual materials. Special programs include services for learning-disabled students, study abroad, advanced placement credit, ESL programs, double majors, independent study, self-designed majors, summer session for credit, part-time degree programs (daytime), internships, and arrangement for off-campus study with members of the Great Lakes Colleges Association, Associated Colleges of the Midwest, Institute of European Studies, Council for International Educational Exchange. The most frequently chosen baccalaureate fields are business/marketing, education, social sciences and history.
Student Body Statistics The student body is made up of 3,068 undergraduates (811 freshmen). 62 percent are women and 38 percent are men. Students come from 45 states and territories and 32 other countries. 76 percent are from Michigan. 1.4 percent are international students. 20 percent of the 2003 graduating class went on to graduate and professional schools.
Expenses for 2003–04 *Application fee: $35. Comprehensive fee: $25,340* includes full-time tuition ($19,212), mandatory fees ($110), and college room and board ($6018). *College room only: $2744.* Full-time tuition and fees vary according to course load. Room and board charges vary according to board plan.
Financial Aid Forms of aid include need-based and non-need-based scholarships and part-time jobs. The average aided 2002–03 undergraduate received an aid package worth $16,860. The priority application deadline for financial aid is March 1.
Freshman Admission Hope requires an essay, a high school transcript, SAT I or ACT scores, and TOEFL scores for international students. An interview is recommended. 1 recommendation is required for some. The application deadline for regular admission is rolling.
Transfer Admission The application deadline for admission is rolling.
Entrance Difficulty Hope assesses its entrance difficulty level as moderately difficult. For the fall 2003 freshman class, 83 percent of the applicants were accepted.

For Further Information Contact Dr. James R. Bekkering, Vice President for Admissions, Hope College, 69 East 10th Street, PO Box 9000, Holland, MI 49422-9000. *Telephone:* 616-395-7955 or 800-968-7850 (toll-free). *Fax:* 616-395-7130. *E-mail:* admissions@hope.edu. *Web site:* http://www.hope.edu/.

KALAMAZOO COLLEGE
Kalamazoo, Michigan

K-College is a coed, private, four-year college, founded in 1833, affiliated with the American Baptist Churches in the U.S.A., offering degrees at the bachelor's level. It has a 60-acre campus in Kalamazoo.

Academic Information The faculty has 117 members (88% full-time), 85% with terminal degrees. The student-faculty ratio is 12:1. The library holds 342,939 titles, 1,495 serial subscriptions, and 6,967 audiovisual materials. Special programs include services for learning-disabled students, cooperative (work-study) education, study abroad, advanced placement credit, ESL programs, double majors, independent study, internships, and arrangement for off-campus study with Western Michigan University. The most frequently chosen baccalaureate fields are psychology, English, social sciences and history.
Student Body Statistics The student body is made up of 1,280 undergraduates (383 freshmen). 56 percent are women and 44 percent are men. Students come from 35 states and territories and 14 other countries. 74 percent are from Michigan. 1.9 percent are international students. 33 percent of the 2003 graduating class went on to graduate and professional schools.
Expenses for 2003–04 *Comprehensive fee: $29,388* includes full-time tuition ($22,908) and college room and board ($6480). *College room only: $3210.*
Financial Aid Forms of aid include need-based and non-need-based scholarships and part-time jobs. The average aided 2003–04 undergraduate received an aid package worth an estimated $19,556. The priority application deadline for financial aid is February 15.
Freshman Admission K-College requires an essay, a high school transcript, 2 recommendations, SAT I or ACT scores, and TOEFL scores for international students. A minimum 3.0 high school GPA and an interview are recommended. The application deadline for regular admission is February 15; for early decision it is November 15; and for early action it is December 1.

Transfer Admission The application deadline for admission is February 15.

Entrance Difficulty K-College assesses its entrance difficulty level as very difficult. For the fall 2003 freshman class, 70 percent of the applicants were accepted.

For Further Information Contact Mrs. Linda Wirgau, Records Manager, Kalamazoo College, Mandelle Hall, 1200 Academy Street, Kalamazoo, MI 49006-3295. *Telephone:* 269-337-7166 or 800-253-3602 (toll-free). *Fax:* 269-337-7251. *E-mail:* admission@kzoo.edu. *Web site:* http://www.kzoo.edu/.

KETTERING UNIVERSITY
Flint, Michigan

Kettering/GMI is a coed, private, comprehensive institution, founded in 1919, offering degrees at the bachelor's and master's levels. It has an 85-acre campus in Flint near Detroit.

Academic Information The faculty has 153 members (91% full-time), 86% with terminal degrees. The undergraduate student-faculty ratio is 12:1. The library holds 115,000 titles, 1,200 serial subscriptions, and 778 audiovisual materials. Special programs include services for learning-disabled students, cooperative (work-study) education, study abroad, advanced placement credit, accelerated degree programs, double majors, independent study, distance learning, and internships. The most frequently chosen baccalaureate fields are business/marketing, computer/information sciences, engineering/engineering technologies.

Student Body Statistics The student body totals 3,126, of whom 2,558 are undergraduates (561 freshmen). 17 percent are women and 83 percent are men. Students come from 52 states and territories and 24 other countries. 63 percent are from Michigan. 2.3 percent are international students. 33 percent of the 2003 graduating class went on to graduate and professional schools.

Expenses for 2003–04 *Application fee:* $35. *Comprehensive fee:* $26,478 includes full-time tuition ($21,184), mandatory fees ($370), and college room and board ($4924). *College room only:* $3174. Room and board charges vary according to student level. *Part-time tuition:* $662 per credit.

Financial Aid Forms of aid include need-based and non-need-based scholarships and part-time jobs. The average aided 2003–04 undergraduate received an aid package worth an estimated $10,740. The priority application deadline for financial aid is February 14.

Freshman Admission Kettering/GMI requires a high school transcript, SAT I or ACT scores, and TOEFL scores for international students. A minimum 3.0 high school GPA, an interview, and SAT II: Subject Test scores are recommended. An essay is required for some. The application deadline for regular admission is rolling.

Transfer Admission The application deadline for admission is rolling.

Entrance Difficulty Kettering/GMI assesses its entrance difficulty level as very difficult. For the fall 2003 freshman class, 71 percent of the applicants were accepted.

For Further Information Contact Ms. Barbara Sosin, Director of Admissions, Kettering University, 1700 West Third Avenue, Flint, MI 48504-4898. *Telephone:* 810-762-7865, 800-955-4464 Ext. 7865 (toll-free in-state), or 800-955-4464 (toll-free out-of-state). *Fax:* 810-762-9837. *E-mail:* admissions@kettering.edu. *Web site:* http://www.kettering.edu/.

See page 302 for a narrative description.

LAKE SUPERIOR STATE UNIVERSITY
Sault Sainte Marie, Michigan

LSSU is a coed, public, four-year college, founded in 1946, offering degrees at the associate and bachelor's levels. It has a 121-acre campus in Sault Sainte Marie.

Academic Information The faculty has 232 members (48% full-time). The student-faculty ratio is 17:1. The library holds 112,920 titles and 714 serial subscriptions. Special programs include academic remediation, services for learning-disabled students, an honors program, cooperative

(work-study) education, advanced placement credit, Freshman Honors College, double majors, independent study, distance learning, self-designed majors, summer session for credit, part-time degree programs, adult/continuing education programs, and internships. The most frequently chosen baccalaureate fields are business/marketing, education, protective services/public administration.

Student Body Statistics The student body is made up of 3,258 undergraduates (541 freshmen). 49 percent are women and 51 percent are men. Students come from 20 states and territories and 12 other countries. 96 percent are from Michigan. 11.3 percent are international students. 10 percent of the 2003 graduating class went on to graduate and professional schools.

Expenses for 2003–04 *Application fee:* $20. *State resident tuition:* $5136 full-time, $214 per credit hour part-time. *Nonresident tuition:* $10,062 full-time, $419.25 per credit hour part-time. *Mandatory fees:* $318 full-time. Full-time tuition and fees vary according to reciprocity agreements. Part-time tuition varies according to reciprocity agreements. *College room and board:* $5993. *College room only:* $5334. Room and board charges vary according to board plan.

Financial Aid Forms of aid include need-based and non-need-based scholarships, athletic grants, and part-time jobs. The average aided 2002–03 undergraduate received an aid package worth $6700. The priority application deadline for financial aid is February 21.

Freshman Admission LSSU requires a high school transcript, ACT scores, and TOEFL scores for international students. A minimum 2.0 high school GPA is required for some. The application deadline for regular admission is August 15.

Transfer Admission The application deadline for admission is rolling.

Entrance Difficulty LSSU assesses its entrance difficulty level as moderately difficult. For the fall 2003 freshman class, 89 percent of the applicants were accepted.

For Further Information Contact Mr. Kevin Pollock, Director of Admissions, Lake Superior State University, 650 West Easterday Avenue, Sault Saint Marie, MI 49783-1699. *Telephone:* 906-635-2670 or 888-800-LSSU Ext. 2231 (toll-free). *Fax:* 906-635-6669. *E-mail:* admissions@gw.lssu.edu. *Web site:* http://www.lssu.edu/.

LAWRENCE TECHNOLOGICAL UNIVERSITY
Southfield, Michigan

Lawrence Tech is a coed, private university, founded in 1932, offering degrees at the associate, bachelor's, and master's levels. It has a 115-acre campus in Southfield near Detroit.

Academic Information The faculty has 424 members (27% full-time), 50% with terminal degrees. The undergraduate student-faculty ratio is 13:1. The library holds 110,250 titles, 700 serial subscriptions, and 420 audiovisual materials. Special programs include academic remediation, services for learning-disabled students, cooperative (work-study) education, study abroad, advanced placement credit, ESL programs, double majors, independent study, distance learning, summer session for credit, part-time degree programs (daytime, evenings, weekends, summer), adult/continuing education programs, internships, and arrangement for off-campus study with Macomb University Center, Oakland Technical Center. The most frequently chosen baccalaureate fields are architecture, computer/information sciences, engineering/engineering technologies.

Student Body Statistics The student body totals 4,241, of whom 2,958 are undergraduates (470 freshmen). 24 percent are women and 76 percent are men. Students come from 16 states and territories and 16 other countries. 99 percent are from Michigan. 4.4 percent are international students.

Expenses for 2003–04 *Application fee:* $30. *Comprehensive fee:* $20,487 includes full-time tuition ($14,112), mandatory fees ($250), and college room and board ($6125). *College room only:* $4306. Full-time tuition and fees vary according to degree level, program, and student level. Room and board charges vary according to board plan and housing facility. *Part-time tuition:* $484 per hour. *Part-time mandatory fees:* $125 per term. Part-time tuition and fees vary according to degree level, program, and student level.

Lawrence Technological University (continued)

Financial Aid   Forms of aid include need-based and non-need-based scholarships and part-time jobs. The average aided 2002–03 undergraduate received an aid package worth $11,137. The priority application deadline for financial aid is April 1.

Freshman Admission   Lawrence Tech requires a high school transcript, a minimum 2.5 high school GPA, ACT scores, and SAT I or ACT scores. SAT I scores and TOEFL scores for international students are recommended. An essay, recommendations, and an interview are required for some. The application deadline for regular admission is August 15.

Transfer Admission   The application deadline for admission is August 15.

Entrance Difficulty   Lawrence Tech assesses its entrance difficulty level as moderately difficult. For the fall 2003 freshman class, 76 percent of the applicants were accepted.

For Further Information   Contact Ms. Jane Rohrback, Director of Admissions, Lawrence Technological University, 21000 West Ten Mile Road, Southfield, MI 48075. *Telephone:* 248-204-3180 or 800-225-5588 (toll-free). *Fax:* 248-204-3188. *E-mail:* admissions@ltu.edu. *Web site:* http://www.ltu.edu/.

LEWIS COLLEGE OF BUSINESS
Detroit, Michigan

Lewis College is a coed, private, two-year college, founded in 1929, offering degrees at the associate level. It has an 11-acre campus in Detroit.

For Further Information   Contact Ms. Frances Ambrose, Admissions Secretary, Lewis College of Business, 17370 Meyers Road, Detroit, MI 48235-1423. *Telephone:* 313-862-6300 Ext. 230. *Fax:* 313-862-1027. *Web site:* http://www.lewiscollege.edu/.

MADONNA UNIVERSITY
Livonia, Michigan

Madonna University is a coed, private, Roman Catholic, comprehensive institution, founded in 1947, offering degrees at the associate, bachelor's, and master's levels and post-master's and postbachelor's certificates. It has a 49-acre campus in Livonia near Detroit.

Academic Information   The faculty has 324 members (33% full-time), 32% with terminal degrees. The undergraduate student-faculty ratio is 17:1. The library holds 199,144 titles and 1,679 serial subscriptions. Special programs include academic remediation, services for learning-disabled students, cooperative (work-study) education, study abroad, advanced placement credit, accelerated degree programs, ESL programs, double majors, independent study, distance learning, summer session for credit, part-time degree programs (daytime, evenings, weekends, summer), adult/continuing education programs, internships, and arrangement for off-campus study with 5 members of the Detroit Area Consortium of Catholic Colleges. The most frequently chosen baccalaureate fields are business/marketing, health professions and related sciences, protective services/public administration.

Student Body Statistics   The student body totals 4,276, of whom 3,243 are undergraduates (241 freshmen). 74 percent are women and 26 percent are men. Students come from 32 states and territories and 31 other countries. 96 percent are from Michigan. 4.7 percent are international students. 40 percent of the 2003 graduating class went on to graduate and professional schools.

Expenses for 2004–05   *Application fee:* $25. *Comprehensive fee:* $15,412 includes full-time tuition ($9700), mandatory fees ($100), and college room and board ($5612). *College room only:* $2550. Room and board charges vary according to board plan.

Financial Aid   Forms of aid include need-based and non-need-based scholarships, athletic grants, and part-time jobs. The priority application deadline for financial aid is February 21.

Freshman Admission   Madonna University requires a high school transcript, a minimum 2.75 high school GPA, ACT scores, and TOEFL scores for international students. 2 recommendations are required for some. The application deadline for regular admission is rolling.

Transfer Admission   The application deadline for admission is rolling.

Entrance Difficulty   Madonna University assesses its entrance difficulty level as moderately difficult. For the fall 2003 freshman class, 86 percent of the applicants were accepted.

For Further Information   Contact Mr. Frank J. Hribar, Director of Enrollment Management, Madonna University, 36600 Schoolcraft Road, Livonia, MI 48150-1173. *Telephone:* 734-432-5317 or 800-852-4951 (toll-free). *Fax:* 734-432-5393. *E-mail:* muinfo@smtp.munet.edu. *Web site:* http://www.munet.edu/.

MARYGROVE COLLEGE
Detroit, Michigan

Marygrove is a coed, primarily women's, private, Roman Catholic, comprehensive institution, founded in 1905, offering degrees at the associate, bachelor's, and master's levels and postbachelor's certificates. It has a 50-acre campus in Detroit.

Academic Information   The faculty has 74 members (91% full-time), 58% with terminal degrees. The undergraduate student-faculty ratio is 14:1. The library holds 98,817 titles, 500 serial subscriptions, and 1,559 audiovisual materials. Special programs include academic remediation, cooperative (work-study) education, advanced placement credit, double majors, distance learning, self-designed majors, summer session for credit, part-time degree programs (daytime, evenings, weekends, summer), internships, and arrangement for off-campus study with Detroit Area Consortium of Catholic Colleges. The most frequently chosen baccalaureate fields are business/marketing, education, social sciences and history.

Student Body Statistics   The student body totals 5,584, of whom 858 are undergraduates (60 freshmen). 80 percent are women and 20 percent are men. Students come from 2 states and territories and 3 other countries. 99 percent are from Michigan. 2 percent are international students. 36 percent of the 2003 graduating class went on to graduate and professional schools.

Expenses for 2003–04   *Application fee:* $25. *Comprehensive fee:* $17,550 includes full-time tuition ($11,500), mandatory fees ($250), and college room and board ($5800). *Part-time tuition:* $418 per credit. *Part-time mandatory fees:* $10 per credit.

Financial Aid   Forms of aid include non-need-based scholarships and part-time jobs.

Freshman Admission   Marygrove requires a high school transcript, a minimum 2.7 high school GPA, ACT scores, and TOEFL scores for international students. Recommendations and an interview are required for some. The application deadline for regular admission is August 15.

Transfer Admission   The application deadline for admission is August 15.

Entrance Difficulty   Marygrove assesses its entrance difficulty level as moderately difficult. For the fall 2003 freshman class, 60 percent of the applicants were accepted.

For Further Information   Contact Mr. John Ambrose, Admission Counselor, Freshman, Marygrove College, Office of Admissions, Detroit, MI 48221-2599. *Telephone:* 313-927-1243 or 866-313-1297 (toll-free). *Fax:* 313-927-1345. *E-mail:* info@marygrove.edu. *Web site:* http://www.marygrove.edu/.

MICHIGAN CHRISTIAN COLLEGE
See Rochester College

MICHIGAN JEWISH INSTITUTE
Oak Park, Michigan

For Information Write to Michigan Jewish Institute, Oak Park, MI 48237-1304.

MICHIGAN STATE UNIVERSITY
East Lansing, Michigan

Michigan State is a coed, public university, founded in 1855, offering degrees at the bachelor's, master's, doctoral, and first professional levels and post-master's certificates. It has a 5,192-acre campus in East Lansing near Detroit.

Academic Information The faculty has 2,653 members (87% full-time), 89% with terminal degrees. The undergraduate student-faculty ratio is 18:1. The library holds 4 million titles, 29,470 serial subscriptions, and 290,206 audiovisual materials. Special programs include academic remediation, services for learning-disabled students, an honors program, cooperative (work-study) education, study abroad, advanced placement credit, accelerated degree programs, Freshman Honors College, ESL programs, double majors, independent study, distance learning, self-designed majors, summer session for credit, part-time degree programs, adult/continuing education programs, internships, and arrangement for off-campus study with Committee on Institutional Cooperation. The most frequently chosen baccalaureate fields are business/marketing, communications/communication technologies, social sciences and history.
Student Body Statistics The student body totals 44,542, of whom 34,853 are undergraduates (7,122 freshmen). 54 percent are women and 46 percent are men. Students come from 54 states and territories and 120 other countries. 93 percent are from Michigan. 2.8 percent are international students.
Expenses for 2003–04 *Application fee:* $35. *State resident tuition:* $5925 full-time, $197.50 per semester hour part-time. *Nonresident tuition:* $15,885 full-time, $529.50 per semester hour part-time. *Mandatory fees:* $778 full-time, $778 per year part-time. Full-time tuition and fees vary according to course load, degree level, program, and student level. Part-time tuition and fees vary according to course load, degree level, program, and student level. *College room and board:* $5230. *College room only:* $2250. Room and board charges vary according to housing facility.
Financial Aid Forms of aid include need-based and non-need-based scholarships, athletic grants, and part-time jobs. The average aided 2003–04 undergraduate received an aid package worth an estimated $8487. The application deadline for financial aid is June 30 with a priority deadline of February 21.
Freshman Admission Michigan State requires a high school transcript, SAT I or ACT scores, and TOEFL scores for international students. The application deadline for regular admission is rolling and for early action it is October 1.
Entrance Difficulty Michigan State assesses its entrance difficulty level as moderately difficult. For the fall 2003 freshman class, 71 percent of the applicants were accepted.

For Further Information Contact Ms. Pamela Horne, Assistant to the Provost for Enrollment and Director of Admissions, Michigan State University, 250 Administration Building, East Lansing, MI 48824. *Telephone:* 517-355-8332. *Fax:* 517-353-1647. *E-mail:* admis@msu.edu. *Web site:* http://www.msu.edu/.

MICHIGAN TECHNOLOGICAL UNIVERSITY
Houghton, Michigan

Michigan Tech is a coed, public university, founded in 1885, offering degrees at the associate, bachelor's, master's, and doctoral levels. It has a 240-acre campus in Houghton.

Academic Information The faculty has 394 members (88% full-time), 83% with terminal degrees. The undergraduate student-faculty ratio is 12:1. The library holds 820,414 titles, 10,369 serial subscriptions, and 4,529 audiovisual materials. Special programs include services for learning-disabled students, cooperative (work-study) education, study abroad, advanced placement credit, ESL programs, double majors, distance learning, self-designed majors, summer session for credit, part-time degree programs, internships, and arrangement for off-campus study with National Student Exchange. The most frequently chosen baccalaureate fields are business/marketing, computer/information sciences, engineering/engineering technologies.
Student Body Statistics The student body totals 6,565, of whom 5,765 are undergraduates (1,187 freshmen). 24 percent are women and 76 percent are men. Students come from 45 states and territories and 80 other countries. 79 percent are from Michigan. 5.8 percent are international students. 20 percent of the 2003 graduating class went on to graduate and professional schools.
Expenses for 2003–04 *Application fee:* $40. *State resident tuition:* $6810 full-time, $227 per credit hour part-time. *Nonresident tuition:* $17,700 full-time, $590 per credit hour part-time. *Mandatory fees:* $630 full-time. Full-time tuition and fees vary according to course load and student level. Part-time tuition varies according to course load and student level. *College room and board:* $5795. *College room only:* $2759. Room and board charges vary according to board plan and housing facility.
Financial Aid Forms of aid include need-based and non-need-based scholarships, athletic grants, and part-time jobs. The average aided 2003–04 undergraduate received an aid package worth an estimated $8213. The priority application deadline for financial aid is February 21.
Freshman Admission Michigan Tech requires a high school transcript, SAT I or ACT scores, and TOEFL scores for international students. An interview is recommended. The application deadline for regular admission is rolling.
Transfer Admission The application deadline for admission is rolling.
Entrance Difficulty Michigan Tech assesses its entrance difficulty level as moderately difficult; noncompetitive for transfers. For the fall 2003 freshman class, 93 percent of the applicants were accepted.

For Further Information Contact Ms. Nancy Rehling, Director of Undergraduate Admissions, Michigan Technological University, 1400 Townsend Drive, Houghton, MI 49931-1295. *Telephone:* 906-487-2335 or 888-MTU-1885 (toll-free). *Fax:* 906-487-2125. *E-mail:* mtu4u@mtu.edu. *Web site:* http://www.mtu.edu/.

NORTHERN MICHIGAN UNIVERSITY
Marquette, Michigan

NMU is a coed, public, comprehensive unit of Autonomous, founded in 1899, offering degrees at the associate, bachelor's, and master's levels and post-master's and postbachelor's certificates. It has a 300-acre campus in Marquette near Sawyer International.

Academic Information The faculty has 428 members (73% full-time), 64% with terminal degrees. The undergraduate student-faculty ratio is 21:1. The library holds 1 million titles, 1,711 serial subscriptions, and 19,167 audiovisual materials. Special programs include academic remediation, services for learning-disabled students, an honors program, study abroad, advanced placement credit, accelerated degree programs, double majors, independent study, distance learning, self-designed majors, summer session for credit, part-time degree programs (daytime, evenings, weekends, summer), adult/continuing education programs, internships, and arrangement for off-campus study with other public institutions in Michigan. The most frequently chosen baccalaureate fields are business/marketing, education, social sciences and history.
Student Body Statistics The student body totals 9,326, of whom 8,536 are undergraduates. 52 percent are women and 48 percent are men. 84 percent are from Michigan. 18 percent of the 2003 graduating class went on to graduate and professional schools.
Expenses for 2003–04 *Application fee:* $25. *One-time mandatory fee:* $100. *State resident tuition:* $4632 full-time, $193 per credit hour part-time. *Nonresident tuition:* $7920 full-time, $330 per credit hour part-time. *Mandatory fees:* $738 full-time, $30 per term part-time. Full-time tuition and fees vary according to program. Part-time tuition and fees vary according to location. *College room and board:* $5724. Room and board charges vary according to board plan and housing facility.

Northern Michigan University (continued)

Financial Aid Forms of aid include need-based and non-need-based scholarships, athletic grants, and part-time jobs. The average aided 2002–03 undergraduate received an aid package worth $7054. The priority application deadline for financial aid is February 20.

Freshman Admission NMU requires a high school transcript, SAT I or ACT scores, and TOEFL scores for international students. A minimum 2.25 high school GPA is required for some. The application deadline for regular admission is rolling.

Transfer Admission The application deadline for admission is rolling.

Entrance Difficulty NMU assesses its entrance difficulty level as minimally difficult. For the fall 2003 freshman class, 84 percent of the applicants were accepted.

For Further Information Contact Ms. Gerri Daniels, Director of Admissions, Northern Michigan University, 1401 Presque Isle Avenue, Marquette, MI 49855. *Telephone:* 906-227-2650, 800-682-9797 Ext. 1 (toll-free in-state), or 800-682-9797 (toll-free out-of-state). *Fax:* 906-227-1747. *E-mail:* admiss@nmu.edu. *Web site:* http://www.nmu.edu/.

NORTHWOOD UNIVERSITY

Midland, Michigan

Northwood is a coed, private, comprehensive institution, founded in 1959, offering degrees at the associate, bachelor's, and master's levels. It has a 434-acre campus in Midland.

Academic Information The faculty has 75 members (59% full-time), 21% with terminal degrees. The undergraduate student-faculty ratio is 32:1. The library holds 40,140 titles and 402 serial subscriptions. Special programs include academic remediation, an honors program, cooperative (work-study) education, study abroad, advanced placement credit, accelerated degree programs, ESL programs, double majors, independent study, distance learning, summer session for credit, part-time degree programs (daytime, evenings, weekends, summer), external degree programs, adult/continuing education programs, internships, and arrangement for off-campus study with Lansing Community College, Delta College. The most frequently chosen baccalaureate fields are business/marketing, communications/communication technologies, computer/information sciences.

Student Body Statistics The student body totals 3,770, of whom 3,472 are undergraduates (394 freshmen). 46 percent are women and 54 percent are men. Students come from 35 states and territories and 27 other countries. 87 percent are from Michigan. 9.8 percent are international students. 4 percent of the 2003 graduating class went on to graduate and professional schools.

Expenses for 2003–04 *Application fee:* $25. *Comprehensive fee:* $20,265 includes full-time tuition ($13,485), mandatory fees ($510), and college room and board ($6270). Room and board charges vary according to board plan and location. *Part-time tuition:* $281 per credit.

Financial Aid Forms of aid include need-based and non-need-based scholarships, athletic grants, and part-time jobs. The average aided 2003–04 undergraduate received an aid package worth an estimated $11,175. The application deadline for financial aid is continuous.

Freshman Admission Northwood requires an essay, a high school transcript, SAT I or ACT scores, and TOEFL scores for international students. A minimum 2.0 high school GPA, 1 recommendation, and an interview are recommended. The application deadline for regular admission is rolling.

Transfer Admission The application deadline for admission is rolling.

Entrance Difficulty Northwood assesses its entrance difficulty level as moderately difficult. For the fall 2003 freshman class, 87 percent of the applicants were accepted.

For Further Information Contact Mr. Daniel F. Toland, Director of Admission, Northwood University, 4000 Whiting Drive, Midland, MI 48640. *Telephone:* 989-837-4367 or 800-457-7878 (toll-free). *Fax:* 989-837-4490. *E-mail:* admissions@northwood.edu. *Web site:* http://www.northwood.edu/.

OAKLAND UNIVERSITY

Rochester, Michigan

Oakland is a coed, public university, founded in 1957, offering degrees at the bachelor's, master's, and doctoral levels and post-master's and postbachelor's certificates. It has a 1,444-acre campus in Rochester near Detroit.

Academic Information The faculty has 786 members (54% full-time), 65% with terminal degrees. The undergraduate student-faculty ratio is 19:1. The library holds 738,420 titles, 1,660 serial subscriptions, and 5,340 audiovisual materials. Special programs include academic remediation, services for learning-disabled students, an honors program, cooperative (work-study) education, study abroad, advanced placement credit, accelerated degree programs, ESL programs, double majors, independent study, distance learning, self-designed majors, summer session for credit, part-time degree programs (daytime, evenings, weekends, summer), internships, and arrangement for off-campus study with Macomb Community College, Beaumont Hospital-Troy. The most frequently chosen baccalaureate fields are business/marketing, communications/communication technologies, education.

Student Body Statistics The student body totals 16,575, of whom 12,958 are undergraduates (2,101 freshmen). 62 percent are women and 38 percent are men. Students come from 35 states and territories and 28 other countries. 99 percent are from Michigan. 0.8 percent are international students. 19.76 percent of the 2003 graduating class went on to graduate and professional schools.

Expenses for 2003–04 *Application fee:* $35. *State resident tuition:* $4774 full-time, $159.13 per credit hour part-time. *Nonresident tuition:* $11,468 full-time, $382.25 per credit hour part-time. *Mandatory fees:* $486 full-time, $243 per term part-time. Full-time tuition and fees vary according to program and student level. Part-time tuition and fees vary according to program and student level. *College room and board:* $5540. Room and board charges vary according to housing facility.

Financial Aid Forms of aid include need-based and non-need-based scholarships, athletic grants, and part-time jobs. The average aided 2003–04 undergraduate received an aid package worth an estimated $5556. The priority application deadline for financial aid is February 15.

Freshman Admission Oakland requires a high school transcript, a minimum 2.5 high school GPA, ACT scores, and TOEFL scores for international students. A minimum 3.0 high school GPA, recommendations, an interview, and audition are required for some. The application deadline for regular admission is rolling.

Transfer Admission The application deadline for admission is rolling.

Entrance Difficulty Oakland assesses its entrance difficulty level as moderately difficult. For the fall 2003 freshman class, 80 percent of the applicants were accepted.

For Further Information Contact Mr. Robert E. Johnson, Vice Provost for Enrollment Management, Oakland University, 101 North Foundation Hall, Rochester, MI 48309-4401. *Telephone:* 248-370-3360 or 800-OAK-UNIV (toll-free). *Fax:* 248-370-4462. *E-mail:* ouinfo@oakland.edu. *Web site:* http://www.oakland.edu/.

OLIVET COLLEGE

Olivet, Michigan

Olivet is a coed, private, comprehensive institution, founded in 1844, affiliated with the Congregational Christian Church, offering degrees at the bachelor's and master's levels. It has a 92-acre campus in Olivet.

Academic Information The faculty has 79 members (58% full-time), 51% with terminal degrees. The undergraduate student-faculty ratio is 15:1. The library holds 90,000 titles and 415 serial subscriptions. Special programs include services for learning-disabled students, an honors program, cooperative (work-study) education, study abroad, advanced placement credit, accelerated degree programs, double majors, independent study, self-designed majors, summer session for credit, part-time degree programs (daytime, evenings, summer), and internships. The most frequently chosen baccalaureate fields are business/marketing, biological/life sciences, education.

Student Body Statistics The student body totals 1,070, of whom 1,042 are undergraduates (297 freshmen). 43 percent are women and 57 percent are men. Students come from 15 states and territories and 16 other countries. 84 percent are from Michigan. 3.6 percent are international students. 22 percent of the 2003 graduating class went on to graduate and professional schools.

Expenses for 2004–05 *Application fee:* $25. *Comprehensive fee:* $21,271 includes full-time tuition ($15,521), mandatory fees ($420), and college room and board ($5330). *College room only:* $2901. Room and board charges vary according to board plan and housing facility. *Part-time tuition:* $500 per credit. Part-time tuition varies according to course load.

Financial Aid Forms of aid include need-based and non-need-based scholarships and part-time jobs. The average aided 2002–03 undergraduate received an aid package worth $12,230. The application deadline for financial aid is continuous.

Freshman Admission Olivet requires a high school transcript, SAT I or ACT scores, and TOEFL scores for international students. A minimum 2.6 high school GPA is recommended. An essay, recommendations, and an interview are required for some. The application deadline for regular admission is rolling.

Transfer Admission The application deadline for admission is rolling.

Entrance Difficulty Olivet assesses its entrance difficulty level as minimally difficult. For the fall 2003 freshman class, 59 percent of the applicants were accepted.

For Further Information Contact Mr. Bernie McConnell, Director of Admissions, Olivet College, 320 South Main Street, Olivet, MI 49076. *Telephone:* 800-456-7189 Ext. 7161 or 800-456-7189 (toll-free). *Fax:* 269-749-6617. *E-mail:* admissions@olivetcollege.edu. *Web site:* http://www.olivetcollege.edu/.

REFORMED BIBLE COLLEGE

Grand Rapids, Michigan

RBC is a coed, private, four-year college, founded in 1939, offering degrees at the associate and bachelor's levels and postbachelor's certificates in Christian ministries. It has a 34-acre campus in Grand Rapids.

Academic Information The faculty has 40 members (42% full-time), 32% with terminal degrees. The student-faculty ratio is 17:1. The library holds 55,760 titles, 234 serial subscriptions, and 3,855 audiovisual materials. Special programs include academic remediation, services for learning-disabled students, cooperative (work-study) education, study abroad, advanced placement credit, ESL programs, double majors, independent study, summer session for credit, part-time degree programs (daytime, evenings), adult/continuing education programs, internships, and arrangement for off-campus study with Grand Rapids Community College, Cornerstone University. The most frequently chosen baccalaureate fields are philosophy, religion, and theology, education, protective services/public administration.

Student Body Statistics The student body is made up of 298 undergraduates (56 freshmen). 52 percent are women and 48 percent are men. Students come from 14 states and territories and 8 other countries. 92 percent are from Michigan. 6.4 percent are international students.

Expenses for 2003–04 *Application fee:* $25. *Comprehensive fee:* $15,240 includes full-time tuition ($9670), mandatory fees ($470), and college room and board ($5100). *College room only:* $2300. Room and board charges vary according to board plan, housing facility, and student level. *Part-time tuition:* $405 per credit hour. *Part-time mandatory fees:* $80 per term. Part-time tuition and fees vary according to course load.

Financial Aid Forms of aid include need-based and non-need-based scholarships and part-time jobs. The average aided 2003–04 undergraduate received an aid package worth an estimated $9581. The priority application deadline for financial aid is March 1.

Freshman Admission RBC requires an essay, a high school transcript, a minimum 2.5 high school GPA, 2 recommendations, SAT I or ACT scores, and TOEFL scores for international students. An interview is recommended. The application deadline for regular admission is rolling.

Entrance Difficulty RBC assesses its entrance difficulty level as moderately difficult. For the fall 2003 freshman class, 41 percent of the applicants were accepted.

For Further Information Contact Ms. Jeanine Kopaska Broek, Director of Admissions, Reformed Bible College, 3333 East Beltline North East, Grand Rapids, MI 49525. *Telephone:* 616-222-3000 Ext. 695 or 800-511-3749 (toll-free). *Fax:* 616-222-3045. *E-mail:* admissions@reformed.edu. *Web site:* http://www.reformed.edu/.

ROCHESTER COLLEGE

Rochester Hills, Michigan

Rochester College is a coed, private, four-year college, founded in 1959, affiliated with the Church of Christ, offering degrees at the associate and bachelor's levels. It has an 83-acre campus in Rochester Hills near Detroit.

Academic Information The faculty has 106 members (36% full-time), 42% with terminal degrees. The student-faculty ratio is 13:1. The library holds 45,000 titles, 325 serial subscriptions, and 1,000 audiovisual materials. Special programs include academic remediation, study abroad, advanced placement credit, accelerated degree programs, double majors, independent study, distance learning, summer session for credit, part-time degree programs (daytime, evenings, weekends, summer), external degree programs, adult/continuing education programs, internships, and arrangement for off-campus study with Madonna University, Macomb Community College, Oakland Community College, Mott Community College. The most frequently chosen baccalaureate fields are business/marketing, education, psychology.

Student Body Statistics The student body is made up of 1,001 undergraduates (119 freshmen). 59 percent are women and 41 percent are men. Students come from 22 states and territories and 12 other countries. 87 percent are from Michigan. 2.4 percent are international students.

Expenses for 2003–04 *Application fee:* $25. *Comprehensive fee:* $16,718 includes full-time tuition ($10,272), mandatory fees ($822), and college room and board ($5624). *Part-time tuition:* $321 per credit hour. *Part-time mandatory fees:* $142. Part-time tuition and fees vary according to course load.

Financial Aid Forms of aid include need-based and non-need-based scholarships, athletic grants, and part-time jobs. The average aided 2002–03 undergraduate received an aid package worth $8221. The priority application deadline for financial aid is March 15.

Freshman Admission Rochester College requires a high school transcript, SAT I or ACT scores, and TOEFL scores for international students. An essay, a minimum 2.25 high school GPA, and 1 recommendation are recommended. An interview is required for some. The application deadline for regular admission is rolling.

Transfer Admission The application deadline for admission is rolling.

Entrance Difficulty Rochester College assesses its entrance difficulty level as minimally difficult; moderately difficult for early admission applicants. For the fall 2003 freshman class, 42 percent of the applicants were accepted.

For Further Information Contact Mr. Larry Norman, Vice President for Enrollment Management, Rochester College, 800 West Avon Road, Rochester Hills, MI 48307-2764. *Telephone:* 248-218-2032 or 800-521-6010 (toll-free). *Fax:* 248-218-2005. *E-mail:* admissions@rc.edu. *Web site:* http://www.rc.edu/.

SACRED HEART MAJOR SEMINARY

Detroit, Michigan

Sacred Heart Major Seminary is a coed, private, Roman Catholic, comprehensive institution, founded in 1919, offering degrees at the associate, bachelor's, master's, and first professional levels and postbachelor's certificates in philosophy. It has a 24-acre campus in Detroit.

Academic Information The faculty has 42 members (50% full-time), 79% with terminal degrees. The undergraduate student-faculty ratio is 9:1.

Sacred Heart Major Seminary (continued)

The library holds 160,000 titles and 510 serial subscriptions. Special programs include academic remediation, services for learning-disabled students, advanced placement credit, independent study, part-time degree programs (daytime, evenings), and arrangement for off-campus study with Detroit Area Catholic Higher Education Consortium. The most frequently chosen baccalaureate fields are liberal arts/general studies, philosophy, religion, and theology.

Student Body Statistics The student body totals 382, of whom 260 are undergraduates (3 freshmen). 41 percent are women and 59 percent are men. Students come from 3 states and territories and 1 other country. 83 percent are from Michigan. 60 percent of the 2003 graduating class went on to graduate and professional schools.

Expenses for 2003–04 *Application fee:* $30. *One-time mandatory fee:* $100. *Comprehensive fee:* $14,380 includes full-time tuition ($8330), mandatory fees ($60), and college room and board ($5990). Full-time tuition and fees vary according to course load. *Part-time tuition:* $213 per credit hour. Part-time tuition varies according to course load.

Financial Aid Forms of aid include need-based and non-need-based scholarships and part-time jobs. The average aided 2002–03 undergraduate received an aid package worth $3000. The application deadline for financial aid is continuous.

Freshman Admission Sacred Heart Major Seminary requires an essay, a high school transcript, a minimum 2.0 high school GPA, 1 recommendation, an interview, and SAT I or ACT scores. The application deadline for regular admission is July 31.

Transfer Admission The application deadline for admission is July 31.

Entrance Difficulty Sacred Heart Major Seminary assesses its entrance difficulty level as moderately difficult. For the fall 2003 freshman class, 100 percent of the applicants were accepted.

For Further Information Contact Fr. Michael Byrnes, Vice Rector, Sacred Heart Major Seminary, 2701 Chicago Boulevard, Detroit, MI 48206. *Telephone:* 313-883-8552. *Web site:* http://www.archdioceseofdetroit.org/shms/shms.htm.

SAGINAW CHIPPEWA TRIBAL COLLEGE
Mount Pleasant, Michigan

For Information Write to Saginaw Chippewa Tribal College, Mount Pleasant, MI 48858.

SAGINAW VALLEY STATE UNIVERSITY
University Center, Michigan

SVSU is a coed, public, comprehensive institution, founded in 1963, offering degrees at the bachelor's and master's levels and post-master's certificates. It has a 782-acre campus in University Center.

Academic Information The faculty has 243 members (97% full-time). The undergraduate student-faculty ratio is 28:1. The library holds 631,455 titles, 1,113 serial subscriptions, and 22,713 audiovisual materials. Special programs include academic remediation, services for learning-disabled students, an honors program, cooperative (work-study) education, study abroad, advanced placement credit, accelerated degree programs, ESL programs, double majors, independent study, distance learning, self-designed majors, summer session for credit, part-time degree programs (daytime, evenings, summer), adult/continuing education programs, and internships. The most frequently chosen baccalaureate fields are business/marketing, education, social sciences and history.

Student Body Statistics The student body totals 9,168, of whom 7,580 are undergraduates (1,181 freshmen). 60 percent are women and 40 percent are men. Students come from 18 states and territories and 41 other countries. 100 percent are from Michigan. 4 percent are international students.

Expenses for 2003–04 *Application fee:* $25. *Area resident tuition:* $139.60 per credit hour part-time. *State resident tuition:* $4799 full-time, $139.60 per credit hour part-time. *Nonresident tuition:* $10,398 full-time, $325.95 per credit hour part-time. *Mandatory fees:* $611 full-time, $20.35 per credit hour part-time. Full-time tuition and fees vary according to course load,

location, and program. Part-time tuition and fees vary according to course load, location, and program. *College room and board:* $5645. *College room only:* $3530. Room and board charges vary according to board plan and housing facility.

Financial Aid Forms of aid include need-based and non-need-based scholarships, athletic grants, and part-time jobs. The average aided 2002–03 undergraduate received an aid package worth $5382. The priority application deadline for financial aid is February 14.

Freshman Admission SVSU requires a high school transcript, ACT scores, and TOEFL scores for international students. A minimum 2.5 high school GPA is recommended. SAT II: Subject Test scores are required for some. The application deadline for regular admission is rolling.

Transfer Admission The application deadline for admission is rolling.

Entrance Difficulty SVSU assesses its entrance difficulty level as moderately difficult. For the fall 2003 freshman class, 90 percent of the applicants were accepted.

For Further Information Contact Mr. James P. Dwyer, Director of Admissions, Saginaw Valley State University, 7400 Bay Road, University Center, MI 48710-0001. *Telephone:* 989-964-4200 or 800-968-9500 (toll-free). *Fax:* 517-790-0180. *E-mail:* admissions@svsu.edu. *Web site:* http://www.svsu.edu/.

SIENA HEIGHTS UNIVERSITY
Adrian, Michigan

Siena is a coed, private, Roman Catholic, comprehensive institution, founded in 1919, offering degrees at the associate, bachelor's, and master's levels. It has a 140-acre campus in Adrian near Detroit.

Academic Information The faculty has 65 full-time members. The undergraduate student-faculty ratio is 14:1. The library holds 120,407 titles and 451 serial subscriptions. Special programs include academic remediation, services for learning-disabled students, cooperative (work-study) education, study abroad, advanced placement credit, accelerated degree programs, double majors, independent study, self-designed majors, summer session for credit, part-time degree programs, external degree programs, adult/continuing education programs, internships, and arrangement for off-campus study with Adrian College. The most frequently chosen baccalaureate field is philosophy, religion, and theology.

Student Body Statistics The student body totals 2,153, of whom 1,886 are undergraduates. Students come from 8 states and territories. 0.7 percent are international students. 9 percent of the 2003 graduating class went on to graduate and professional schools.

Expenses for 2004–05 *Application fee:* $25. *Comprehensive fee:* $20,975 includes full-time tuition ($15,020), mandatory fees ($500), and college room and board ($5455). *Part-time tuition:* $415 per hour. *Part-time mandatory fees:* $100 per term.

Financial Aid Forms of aid include need-based and non-need-based scholarships and part-time jobs. The average aided 2002–03 undergraduate received an aid package worth $12,200. The priority application deadline for financial aid is March 15.

Freshman Admission Siena requires a high school transcript, SAT I or ACT scores, and TOEFL scores for international students. A minimum 2.3 high school GPA and an interview are recommended. An essay, recommendations, and an interview are required for some. The application deadline for regular admission is rolling.

Transfer Admission The application deadline for admission is rolling.

Entrance Difficulty Siena assesses its entrance difficulty level as moderately difficult. For the fall 2003 freshman class, 64 percent of the applicants were accepted.

For Further Information Contact Mr. Kevin Kucera, Dean of Admissions and Enrollment Services, Siena Heights University, 1247 East Siena Heights Drive, Adrian, MI 49221-1796. *Telephone:* 517-264-7180 or 800-521-0009 (toll-free). *Fax:* 517-264-7745. *E-mail:* admissions@sienahts.edu. *Web site:* http://www.sienahts.edu/.

SPRING ARBOR UNIVERSITY
Spring Arbor, Michigan

Spring Arbor is a coed, private, Free Methodist, comprehensive institution, founded in 1873, offering degrees at the associate, bachelor's, and master's levels. It has a 123-acre campus in Spring Arbor.

Academic Information The faculty has 118 members (58% full-time), 33% with terminal degrees. The undergraduate student-faculty ratio is 15:1. The library holds 90,042 titles, 667 serial subscriptions, and 2,025 audiovisual materials. Special programs include academic remediation, services for learning-disabled students, an honors program, advanced placement credit, accelerated degree programs, ESL programs, double majors, independent study, self-designed majors, summer session for credit, part-time degree programs (daytime, evenings, weekends, summer), external degree programs, adult/continuing education programs, internships, and arrangement for off-campus study with Christian College Consortium. The most frequently chosen baccalaureate fields are business/marketing, education, home economics/vocational home economics.
Student Body Statistics The student body totals 3,531, of whom 2,623 are undergraduates (312 freshmen). 69 percent are women and 31 percent are men. Students come from 26 states and territories and 10 other countries. 87 percent are from Michigan. 1 percent are international students. 27 percent of the 2003 graduating class went on to graduate and professional schools.
Expenses for 2003–04 *Application fee:* $30. *Comprehensive fee:* $20,206 includes full-time tuition ($14,700), mandatory fees ($216), and college room and board ($5290). *College room only:* $2420. Room and board charges vary according to board plan, housing facility, and location. *Part-time tuition:* $290 per credit. Part-time tuition varies according to course load.
Financial Aid Forms of aid include need-based and non-need-based scholarships and part-time jobs. The average aided 2003–04 undergraduate received an aid package worth an estimated $11,773. The priority application deadline for financial aid is March 1.
Freshman Admission Spring Arbor requires a high school transcript, a minimum 2.0 high school GPA, SAT I or ACT scores, and TOEFL scores for international students. An essay, an interview, guidance counselor's evaluation form, and ACT scores are recommended. Recommendations are required for some. The application deadline for regular admission is August 1.
Transfer Admission The application deadline for admission is rolling.
Entrance Difficulty Spring Arbor assesses its entrance difficulty level as moderately difficult. For the fall 2003 freshman class, 86 percent of the applicants were accepted.

For Further Information Contact Mr. Randy Comfort, Director of Admissions, Spring Arbor University, 106 East Main Street, Spring Arbor, MI 49283-9799. *Telephone:* 517-750-1200 Ext. 1475 or 800-968-0011 (toll-free). *Fax:* 517-750-6620. *E-mail:* admissions@arbor.edu. *Web site:* http://www.arbor.edu/.

UNIVERSITY OF DETROIT MERCY
Detroit, Michigan

U of D Mercy is a coed, private, Roman Catholic (Jesuit) university, founded in 1877, offering degrees at the associate, bachelor's, master's, doctoral, and first professional levels and post-master's, first professional, and postbachelor's certificates. It has a 70-acre campus in Detroit.

Academic Information The faculty has 655 members (41% full-time). The undergraduate student-faculty ratio is 15:1. The library holds 9,340 serial subscriptions and 32,053 audiovisual materials. Special programs include academic remediation, an honors program, cooperative (work-study) education, study abroad, advanced placement credit, accelerated degree programs, ESL programs, double majors, independent study, summer session for credit, part-time degree programs (daytime, evenings, weekends, summer), adult/continuing education programs, internships, and arrangement for off-campus study with 4 members of the Detroit Area

Consortium of Catholic Colleges. The most frequently chosen baccalaureate fields are business/marketing, engineering/engineering technologies, health professions and related sciences.
Student Body Statistics The student body totals 5,571, of whom 3,383 are undergraduates (486 freshmen). 66 percent are women and 34 percent are men. Students come from 27 states and territories and 19 other countries. 95 percent are from Michigan. 2.6 percent are international students. 20 percent of the 2003 graduating class went on to graduate and professional schools.
Expenses for 2004–05 *Application fee:* $25. *Comprehensive fee:* $28,010 includes full-time tuition ($20,400), mandatory fees ($570), and college room and board ($7040). *College room only:* $4128. Room and board charges vary according to housing facility. *Part-time tuition:* $500 per credit hour. *Part-time mandatory fees:* $185 per term.
Financial Aid Forms of aid include need-based and non-need-based scholarships, athletic grants, and part-time jobs. The average aided 2003–04 undergraduate received an aid package worth an estimated $18,195. The priority application deadline for financial aid is March 1.
Freshman Admission U of D Mercy requires a high school transcript, a minimum 2.50 high school GPA, and SAT I or ACT scores. An essay, recommendations, and an interview are recommended. 1 recommendation and an interview are required for some. The application deadline for regular admission is July 1.
Transfer Admission The application deadline for admission is August 15.
Entrance Difficulty U of D Mercy assesses its entrance difficulty level as moderately difficult. For the fall 2003 freshman class, 81 percent of the applicants were accepted.

For Further Information Contact Ms. Denise Williams, Dean of Admissions, University of Detroit Mercy, PO Box 19900, Detroit, MI 48219-0900. *Telephone:* 313-993-1245 or 800-635-5020 (toll-free out-of-state). *Fax:* 313-993-3326. *E-mail:* admissions@udmercy.edu. *Web site:* http://www.udmercy.edu/.

UNIVERSITY OF MICHIGAN
Ann Arbor, Michigan

Michigan is a coed, public university, founded in 1817, offering degrees at the bachelor's, master's, doctoral, and first professional levels and post-master's and postbachelor's certificates. It has an 8,070-acre campus in Ann Arbor near Detroit.

Academic Information The faculty has 2,835 members (78% full-time), 88% with terminal degrees. The undergraduate student-faculty ratio is 15:1. The library holds 7 million titles, 69,849 serial subscriptions, and 73,568 audiovisual materials. Special programs include services for learning-disabled students, an honors program, cooperative (work-study) education, study abroad, advanced placement credit, accelerated degree programs, ESL programs, double majors, independent study, distance learning, self-designed majors, summer session for credit, part-time degree programs, adult/continuing education programs, internships, and arrangement for off-campus study with Committee on Institutional Cooperation. The most frequently chosen baccalaureate fields are engineering/engineering technologies, psychology, social sciences and history.
Student Body Statistics The student body totals 39,031, of whom 24,517 are undergraduates (5,551 freshmen). 51 percent are women and 49 percent are men. Students come from 54 states and territories and 87 other countries. 68 percent are from Michigan. 4.6 percent are international students. 34 percent of the 2003 graduating class went on to graduate and professional schools.
Expenses for 2003–04 *Application fee:* $40. *State resident tuition:* $7788 full-time, $299 per credit part-time. *Nonresident tuition:* $24,590 full-time, $999 per credit part-time. *Mandatory fees:* $187 full-time. *College room and board:* $6704.
Financial Aid Forms of aid include need-based and non-need-based scholarships, athletic grants, and part-time jobs. The average aided 2002–03 undergraduate received an aid package worth $11,375. The application deadline for financial aid is April 30 with a priority deadline of February 15.

University of Michigan (continued)

Freshman Admission Michigan requires an essay, a high school transcript, SAT I or ACT scores, and TOEFL scores for international students. Recommendations, an interview, SAT II: Subject Test scores, and SAT II: Writing Test scores are required for some. The application deadline for regular admission is February 1.

Transfer Admission The application deadline for admission is February 1.

Entrance Difficulty Michigan assesses its entrance difficulty level as very difficult. For the fall 2003 freshman class, 53 percent of the applicants were accepted.

For Further Information Contact Mr. Ted Spencer, Director of Undergraduate Admissions, University of Michigan, 1220 Student Activities Building, 515 East Jefferson, Ann Arbor, MI 48109-1316. *Telephone:* 734-764-7433. *Fax:* 734-936-0740. *E-mail:* ugadmiss@umich.edu. *Web site:* http://www.umich.edu/.

UNIVERSITY OF MICHIGAN–DEARBORN

Dearborn, Michigan

UM-D is a coed, public, comprehensive unit of University of Michigan System, founded in 1959, offering degrees at the bachelor's and master's levels and postbachelor's certificates. It has a 210-acre campus in Dearborn near Detroit.

Academic Information The faculty has 502 members (53% full-time), 66% with terminal degrees. The undergraduate student-faculty ratio is 16:1. The library holds 340,897 titles, 1,099 serial subscriptions, and 4,734 audiovisual materials. Special programs include academic remediation, services for learning-disabled students, an honors program, cooperative (work-study) education, study abroad, accelerated degree programs, double majors, independent study, self-designed majors, summer session for credit, part-time degree programs (daytime, evenings, weekends, summer), adult/continuing education programs, internships, and arrangement for off-campus study with University of Michigan. The most frequently chosen baccalaureate fields are business/marketing, education, engineering/engineering technologies.

Student Body Statistics The student body totals 9,021, of whom 6,646 are undergraduates (767 freshmen). 53 percent are women and 47 percent are men. Students come from 25 states and territories and 22 other countries. 97 percent are from Michigan. 1.9 percent are international students. 22.8 percent of the 2003 graduating class went on to graduate and professional schools.

Expenses for 2003–04 *Application fee:* $30. *State resident tuition:* $5839 full-time. *Nonresident tuition:* $12,911 full-time. *Mandatory fees:* $107 full-time. Full-time tuition and fees vary according to course level, course load, program, and student level.

Financial Aid Forms of aid include need-based and non-need-based scholarships, athletic grants, and part-time jobs. The average aided 2002–03 undergraduate received an aid package worth $7513. The application deadline for financial aid is continuous.

Freshman Admission UM-D requires a high school transcript, a minimum 3.0 high school GPA, SAT I or ACT scores, and TOEFL scores for international students. ACT scores are recommended. An interview is required for some. The application deadline for regular admission is rolling.

Transfer Admission The application deadline for admission is rolling.

Entrance Difficulty UM-D assesses its entrance difficulty level as moderately difficult. For the fall 2003 freshman class, 67 percent of the applicants were accepted.

For Further Information Contact Mr. David Placey, Director of Admissions, University of Michigan–Dearborn, 4901 Evergreen Road, Dearborn, MI 48128-1491. *Telephone:* 313-593-5100. *Fax:* 313-436-9167. *E-mail:* admissions@umd.umich.edu. *Web site:* http://www.umd.umich.edu/.

UNIVERSITY OF MICHIGAN–FLINT

Flint, Michigan

UM-Flint is a coed, public, comprehensive unit of University of Michigan System, founded in 1956, offering degrees at the bachelor's, master's, and first professional levels. It has a 72-acre campus in Flint near Detroit.

Academic Information The faculty has 367 members (58% full-time), 49% with terminal degrees. The undergraduate student-faculty ratio is 16:1. The library holds 267,062 titles, 1,111 serial subscriptions, and 18,063 audiovisual materials. Special programs include academic remediation, services for learning-disabled students, an honors program, cooperative (work-study) education, study abroad, advanced placement credit, double majors, independent study, distance learning, self-designed majors, summer session for credit, part-time degree programs (daytime, evenings, weekends, summer), and internships. The most frequently chosen baccalaureate fields are business/marketing, education, health professions and related sciences.

Student Body Statistics The student body totals 6,152, of whom 5,578 are undergraduates (474 freshmen). 64 percent are women and 36 percent are men. Students come from 23 states and territories and 17 other countries. 99 percent are from Michigan. 0.5 percent are international students. 9 percent of the 2003 graduating class went on to graduate and professional schools.

Expenses for 2003–04 *Application fee:* $30. *State resident tuition:* $5274 full-time, $208.35 per credit part-time. *Nonresident tuition:* $10,274 full-time, $416.70 per credit part-time. *Mandatory fees:* $274 full-time, $137 per term part-time. Full-time tuition and fees vary according to program and student level. Part-time tuition and fees vary according to program and student level.

Financial Aid Forms of aid include need-based and non-need-based scholarships and part-time jobs. The average aided 2002–03 undergraduate received an aid package worth $6325. The priority application deadline for financial aid is March 1.

Freshman Admission UM-Flint requires a high school transcript and TOEFL scores for international students. An essay and SAT I or ACT scores are recommended. The application deadline for regular admission is September 2.

Transfer Admission The application deadline for admission is August 19.

Entrance Difficulty UM-Flint assesses its entrance difficulty level as moderately difficult. For the fall 2003 freshman class, 81 percent of the applicants were accepted.

For Further Information Contact Dr. Mary Jo Sekelsky, Assistant Vice Chancellor for Student Services and Enrollment, University of Michigan–Flint, 303 East Kearsley Street, 245 UPAV, Flint, MI 48502-1950. *Telephone:* 810-762-3434 or 800-942-5636 (toll-free in-state). *Fax:* 810-762-3272. *E-mail:* admissions@umflint.edu. *Web site:* http://www.umflint.edu/.

UNIVERSITY OF PHOENIX–METRO DETROIT CAMPUS

Troy, Michigan

University of Phoenix–Metro Detroit Campus is a coed, proprietary, comprehensive institution, offering degrees at the associate, bachelor's, master's, and doctoral levels and post-master's and postbachelor's certificates (courses conducted at 121 campuses and learning centers in 25 states).

Academic Information The faculty has 653 members (1% full-time), 28% with terminal degrees. The undergraduate student-faculty ratio is 11:1. The library holds 27 million titles and 11,648 serial subscriptions. Special programs include advanced placement credit, accelerated degree programs, independent study, distance learning, and external degree programs. The most frequently chosen baccalaureate fields are business/marketing, computer/information sciences, health professions and related sciences.

Student Body Statistics The student body totals 3,102, of whom 2,255 are undergraduates (107 freshmen). 64 percent are women and 36 percent are men. 2.4 percent are international students.

Expenses for 2003–04 *Application fee:* $100. *Tuition:* $10,110 full-time, $337 per credit part-time.

Financial Aid Forms of aid include need-based and non-need-based scholarships. The average aided 2002–03 undergraduate received an aid package worth $1246. The application deadline for financial aid is continuous.

Freshman Admission University of Phoenix–Metro Detroit Campus requires 1 recommendation, 2 years of work experience, 23 years of age, and TOEFL scores for international students. A high school transcript is required for some. The application deadline for regular admission is rolling.

Transfer Admission The application deadline for admission is rolling.

Entrance Difficulty University of Phoenix–Metro Detroit Campus has an open admission policy.

For Further Information Contact Ms. Beth Barilla, Director of Admissions, University of Phoenix–Metro Detroit Campus, 4615 East Elwood Street, Mail Stop AA-K101, Phoenix, AZ 85040-1958. *Telephone:* 480-557-1712 or 800-834-2438 (toll-free). *Fax:* 480-594-1758. *E-mail:* beth.barilla@phoenix.edu. *Web site:* http://www.phoenix.edu/.

UNIVERSITY OF PHOENIX–WEST MICHIGAN CAMPUS

Grand Rapids, Michigan

University of Phoenix–West Michigan Campus is a coed, proprietary, comprehensive institution, founded in 2000, offering degrees at the associate, bachelor's, master's, and doctoral levels and post-master's and postbachelor's certificates (courses conducted at 121 campuses and learning centers in 25 states).

Academic Information The faculty has 99 members (4% full-time), 14% with terminal degrees. The undergraduate student-faculty ratio is 7:1. The library holds 27 million titles and 11,648 serial subscriptions. Special programs include advanced placement credit, accelerated degree programs, independent study, distance learning, external degree programs, and adult/continuing education programs. The most frequently chosen baccalaureate fields are business/marketing, computer/information sciences, health professions and related sciences.

Student Body Statistics The student body totals 581, of whom 436 are undergraduates (18 freshmen). 53 percent are women and 47 percent are men. 3.2 percent are international students.

Expenses for 2003–04 *Application fee:* $85. *Tuition:* $9870 full-time, $329 per credit part-time.

Financial Aid Forms of aid include need-based and non-need-based scholarships. The average aided 2002–03 undergraduate received an aid package worth $1355. The application deadline for financial aid is continuous.

Freshman Admission University of Phoenix–West Michigan Campus requires 1 recommendation, 2 years of work experience, 23 years of age, and TOEFL scores for international students. A high school transcript is required for some. The application deadline for regular admission is rolling.

Transfer Admission The application deadline for admission is rolling.

Entrance Difficulty University of Phoenix–West Michigan Campus has an open admission policy.

For Further Information Contact Ms. Beth Barilla, Director of Admissions, University of Phoenix–West Michigan Campus, 4615 East Elwood Street, Mail Stop AA-K101, Phoenix, AZ 85040-1958. *Telephone:* 480-557-1712 or 800-228-7240 (toll-free). *E-mail:* beth.barilla@phoenix.edu. *Web site:* http://www.phoenix.edu/.

WALSH COLLEGE OF ACCOUNTANCY AND BUSINESS ADMINISTRATION

Troy, Michigan

Walsh College is a coed, private, upper-level institution, founded in 1922, offering degrees at the bachelor's and master's levels. It has a 29-acre campus in Troy near Detroit.

Academic Information The faculty has 128 members (11% full-time), 29% with terminal degrees. The undergraduate student-faculty ratio is 20:1. The library holds 26,180 titles, 437 serial subscriptions, and 121 audiovisual materials. Special programs include services for learning-disabled students, advanced placement credit, double majors, independent study, distance learning, summer session for credit, part-time degree programs, adult/continuing education programs, internships, and arrangement for off-campus study. The most frequently chosen baccalaureate field is business/marketing.

Student Body Statistics The student body totals 3,111, of whom 942 are undergraduates. 61 percent are women and 39 percent are men. Students come from 1 state or territory. 5.8 percent are international students.

Expenses for 2003–04 *Application fee:* $25. *Tuition:* $7170 full-time, $239 per credit part-time. *Mandatory fees:* $230 full-time, $115 per term part-time.

Financial Aid Forms of aid include need-based and non-need-based scholarships and part-time jobs. The average aided 2003–04 undergraduate received an aid package worth an estimated $10,012. The application deadline for financial aid is continuous.

Transfer Admission Walsh College requires a college transcript and a minimum 2.0 college GPA. Standardized test scores are required for some. The application deadline for admission is rolling.

Entrance Difficulty Walsh College has an open admission policy.

For Further Information Contact Ms. Karen Mahaffy, Director of Admissions, Walsh College of Accountancy and Business Administration, 3838 Livernois Road, PO Box 7006, Troy, MI 48007-7006. *Telephone:* 248-823-1610 or 800-925-7401 (toll-free in-state). *Fax:* 248-524-2520. *E-mail:* admissions@walshcollege.edu. *Web site:* http://www.walshcollege.edu/.

WAYNE STATE UNIVERSITY

Detroit, Michigan

Wayne State is a coed, public university, founded in 1868, offering degrees at the bachelor's, master's, doctoral, and first professional levels and post-master's and postbachelor's certificates. It has a 203-acre campus in Detroit.

Academic Information The faculty has 1,805 members (53% full-time). The undergraduate student-faculty ratio is 11:1. The library holds 2 million titles, 18,645 serial subscriptions, and 70,131 audiovisual materials. Special programs include academic remediation, services for learning-disabled students, an honors program, cooperative (work-study) education, study abroad, advanced placement credit, accelerated degree programs, ESL programs, double majors, independent study, distance learning, self-designed majors, summer session for credit, part-time degree programs (daytime, evenings, weekends, summer), adult/continuing education programs, internships, and arrangement for off-campus study with University of Michigan, University of Windsor. The most frequently chosen baccalaureate fields are business/marketing, education, health professions and related sciences.

Student Body Statistics The student body totals 33,091, of whom 20,150 are undergraduates. 60 percent are women and 40 percent are men. Students come from 42 states and territories and 107 other countries. 99 percent are from Michigan. 5.1 percent are international students.

Expenses for 2003–04 *Application fee:* $30. *State resident tuition:* $4662 full-time, $155 per semester hour part-time. *Nonresident tuition:* $10,683 full-time, $356 per semester hour part-time. *Mandatory fees:* $528 full-time, $14 per semester hour part-time, $96.20 per term part-time. Full-time tuition and fees vary according to course level and student level. Part-time

Wayne State University (continued)

tuition and fees vary according to course level and student level. *College room and board:* $6500. Room and board charges vary according to housing facility.

Financial Aid Forms of aid include need-based and non-need-based scholarships, athletic grants, and part-time jobs. The average aided 2002–03 undergraduate received an aid package worth $6251. The priority application deadline for financial aid is March 1.

Freshman Admission Wayne State requires a high school transcript, a minimum 2.0 high school GPA, SAT I or ACT scores, and TOEFL scores for international students. Recommendations, an interview, and a portfolio are required for some. The application deadline for regular admission is August 1.

Transfer Admission The application deadline for admission is August 1.

Entrance Difficulty Wayne State assesses its entrance difficulty level as moderately difficult. For the fall 2003 freshman class, 68 percent of the applicants were accepted.

For Further Information Contact Ms. Susan Zwieg, Director of University Admissions, Wayne State University, 3E HNJ, Detroit, MI 48202. *Telephone:* 313-577-3581. *Fax:* 313-577-7536. *E-mail:* admissions@wayne.edu. *Web site:* http://www.wayne.edu/.

WESTERN MICHIGAN UNIVERSITY
Kalamazoo, Michigan

WMU is a coed, public university, founded in 1903, offering degrees at the bachelor's, master's, and doctoral levels and post-master's certificates. It has a 1,200-acre campus in Kalamazoo.

Academic Information The faculty has 1,189 members (83% full-time). The undergraduate student-faculty ratio is 16:1. The library holds 4 million titles, 6,707 serial subscriptions, and 32,535 audiovisual materials. Special programs include academic remediation, services for learning-disabled students, an honors program, cooperative (work-study) education, study abroad, advanced placement credit, accelerated degree programs, Freshman Honors College, ESL programs, double majors, independent study, distance learning, self-designed majors, summer session for credit, part-time degree programs (daytime, evenings, weekends, summer), adult/continuing education programs, internships, and arrangement for off-campus study with Kalamazoo College, Kalamazoo Valley Community College, Davenport College of Business. The most frequently chosen baccalaureate fields are business/marketing, communications/communication technologies, education.

Student Body Statistics The student body totals 29,178, of whom 23,309 are undergraduates (4,258 freshmen). 51 percent are women and 49 percent are men. Students come from 54 states and territories and 110 other countries. 93 percent are from Michigan. 3.1 percent are international students.

Expenses for 2003–04 *Application fee:* $25. *State resident tuition:* $4934 full-time, $164.43 per credit hour part-time. *Nonresident tuition:* $12,446 full-time, $414.88 per credit hour part-time. *Mandatory fees:* $602 full-time, $162 per term part-time. Full-time tuition and fees vary according to course load. Part-time tuition and fees vary according to course load. *College room and board:* $6496. *College room only:* $3350. Room and board charges vary according to board plan.

Financial Aid Forms of aid include need-based and non-need-based scholarships, athletic grants, and part-time jobs. The average aided 2003–04 undergraduate received an aid package worth an estimated $7300. The application deadline for financial aid is continuous.

Freshman Admission WMU requires a high school transcript, SAT I or ACT scores, and TOEFL scores for international students. An interview is required for some. The application deadline for regular admission is rolling.

Transfer Admission The application deadline for admission is August 1.

Entrance Difficulty WMU assesses its entrance difficulty level as moderately difficult. For the fall 2003 freshman class, 86 percent of the applicants were accepted.

For Further Information Contact Mr. John Fraire, Dean, Office of Admissions and Orientation, Western Michigan University, 1903 West Michigan Avenue, Kalamazoo, MI 49008. *Telephone:* 269-387-2000 or 800-400-4968 (toll-free in-state). *Fax:* 269-387-2096. *E-mail:* ask-wmu@wmich.edu. *Web site:* http://www.wmich.edu/.

See page 354 for a narrative description.

WILLIAM TYNDALE COLLEGE
Farmington Hills, Michigan

Tyndale is a coed, private, nondenominational, four-year college, founded in 1945, offering degrees at the associate and bachelor's levels. It has a 28-acre campus in Farmington Hills near Detroit.

Academic Information The faculty has 74 members (5% full-time), 23% with terminal degrees. The student-faculty ratio is 8:1. The library holds 63,500 titles, 230 serial subscriptions, and 3,300 audiovisual materials. Special programs include academic remediation, advanced placement credit, accelerated degree programs, double majors, independent study, summer session for credit, part-time degree programs (daytime, evenings, weekends, summer), adult/continuing education programs, and internships. The most frequently chosen baccalaureate fields are business/marketing, philosophy, religion, and theology, psychology.

Student Body Statistics The student body is made up of 292 undergraduates (16 freshmen). 46 percent are women and 54 percent are men. Students come from 3 states and territories and 6 other countries. 93 percent are from Michigan. 2.4 percent are international students.

Expenses for 2003–04 *Application fee:* $0. *Comprehensive fee:* $12,170 includes full-time tuition ($8550), mandatory fees ($100), and college room and board ($3520). Room and board charges vary according to housing facility. *Part-time tuition:* $285 per credit.

Financial Aid Forms of aid include need-based and non-need-based scholarships and part-time jobs. The average aided 2002–03 undergraduate received an aid package worth $9500. The application deadline for financial aid is June 1 with a priority deadline of February 15.

Freshman Admission Tyndale requires a high school transcript, a minimum 2.25 high school GPA, SAT I or ACT scores, and TOEFL scores for international students. A minimum 3.0 high school GPA is recommended. An essay, recommendations, and an interview are required for some. The application deadline for regular admission is rolling.

Transfer Admission The application deadline for admission is rolling.

Entrance Difficulty Tyndale assesses its entrance difficulty level as minimally difficult. For the fall 2003 freshman class, 50 percent of the applicants were accepted.

For Further Information Contact Mr. Fred A. Schebor, Vice President for Enrollment Management, William Tyndale College, 37500 West Twelve Mile Road, Farmington Hills, MI 48331. *Telephone:* 248-553-7200 Ext. 301 or 800-483-0707 (toll-free). *Fax:* 248-553-5963. *E-mail:* admissions@williamtyndale.edu. *Web site:* http://www.williamtyndale.edu/.

YESHIVA GEDDOLAH OF GREATER DETROIT RABBINICAL COLLEGE
Oak Park, Michigan

For Information Write to Yeshiva Geddolah of Greater Detroit Rabbinical College, Oak Park, MI 48237-1544.

Minnesota

ACADEMY COLLEGE

Minneapolis, Minnesota

Academy College is a coed, proprietary, primarily two-year college, offering degrees at the associate and bachelor's levels.

Academic Information The faculty has 55 members (11% full-time). The student-faculty ratio is 8:1. Special programs include academic remediation, services for learning-disabled students, an honors program, cooperative (work-study) education, accelerated degree programs, ESL programs, double majors, summer session for credit, part-time degree programs (daytime, evenings, weekends, summer), adult/continuing education programs, and internships.
Student Body Statistics The student body is made up of 320 undergraduates (35 freshmen). 20 percent are women and 80 percent are men.
Expenses for 2003–04 *Tuition:* $13,618 full-time, $270 per credit part-time. *Mandatory fees:* $275 full-time. Full-time tuition and fees vary according to course level. Part-time tuition varies according to course level.
Financial Aid Forms of aid include need-based scholarships and part-time jobs. The application deadline for financial aid is continuous.
Freshman Admission Academy College requires a high school transcript and an interview.
Entrance Difficulty Academy College has an open admission policy.

For Further Information Contact Mary Erickson, Director of Administration, Academy College, 1101 East 78th Street, Suite e100, Minneapolis, MN 55420. *Telephone:* 952-851-0066 or 800-292-9149 (toll-free). *Fax:* 952-851-0094. *E-mail:* admissions@academycollege.edu. *Web site:* http://www.academycollege.edu/.

ARGOSY UNIVERSITY/TWIN CITIES

Eagan, Minnesota

Argosy University/Twin Cities is a coed, primarily women's, proprietary, upper-level unit of Education Management Corporation, founded in 1987, offering degrees at the bachelor's, master's, and doctoral levels and post-master's certificates. It is located in Eagan near Minneapolis and St. Paul.

Academic Information The faculty has 140 members (38% full-time), 38% with terminal degrees. The undergraduate student-faculty ratio is 12:1. The most frequently chosen baccalaureate field is psychology.
Student Body Statistics The student body totals 1,334, of whom 919 are undergraduates. 85 percent are women and 15 percent are men. Students come from 20 states and territories.
Expenses for 2003–04 *Application fee:* $50. *Tuition:* $360 per credit hour part-time. *Mandatory fees:* $4 per term part-time.
Financial Aid Forms of aid include need-based and non-need-based scholarships and part-time jobs. The application deadline for financial aid is continuous.
Transfer Admission Argosy University/Twin Cities requires a college transcript. Standardized test scores are required for some.
Entrance Difficulty For the fall 2003 entering class, 86 percent of the applicants were accepted.

For Further Information Contact Jeanne Stoneking, Vice President of Enrollment Services, Argosy University/Twin Cities, 1515 Central Parkway, Eagan, MN 55121. *Telephone:* 651-846-3331 or 888-844-2004 (toll-free out-of-state). *Fax:* 651-994-7956. *E-mail:* tcadmissions@argosyu.edu. *Web site:* http://www.argosyu.edu/.

ARGOSY UNIVERSITY/TWIN CITIES

Eagan, Minnesota

Argosy University/Twin Cities is a coed, proprietary unit of Education Management Corporation, Pittsburgh, PA, founded in 1961, offering degrees at the associate, bachelor's, master's, and doctoral levels and post-master's certificates in health sciences. It is located in Eagan near Minneapolis–St. Paul, MN.

Academic Information The faculty has 140 members (38% full-time), 38% with terminal degrees. The undergraduate student-faculty ratio is 12:1. The library holds 2,000 titles and 15 serial subscriptions. Special programs include academic remediation, services for learning-disabled students, double majors, summer session for credit, part-time degree programs (daytime, evenings), and internships. The most frequently chosen baccalaureate field is psychology.
Student Body Statistics The student body totals 1,334, of whom 919 are undergraduates. 85 percent are women and 15 percent are men. Students come from 20 states and territories and 1 other country. 90 percent are from Minnesota.
Expenses for 2003–04 *Application fee:* $50. *Tuition:* $10,867 full-time, $360 per semester hour part-time. *Mandatory fees:* $365 full-time. Full-time tuition and fees vary according to course load and program.
Financial Aid Forms of aid include need-based scholarships and part-time jobs. The application deadline for financial aid is continuous.
Freshman Admission Argosy University/Twin Cities requires a high school transcript, an interview, SAT I or ACT scores, TOEFL scores for international students, and Wonderlic Scholastic Level Exam. SAT I or ACT scores are recommended. An essay and recommendations are required for some. The application deadline for regular admission is rolling and for nonresidents it is rolling.
Transfer Admission Argosy University/Twin Cities requires a college transcript. Standardized test scores are required for some. The application deadline for admission is rolling.
Entrance Difficulty Argosy University/Twin Cities assesses its entrance difficulty level as moderately difficult. For the fall 2003 freshman class, 86 percent of the applicants were accepted.

For Further Information Contact Ms. Jeanne Stoneking, Director of Admissions, Argosy University/Twin Cities, 1515 Central Parkway, Eagan, MN 55121. *Telephone:* 651-846-3331, 651-846-3300 (toll-free in-state), or 888-844-2004 (toll-free out-of-state). *Fax:* 651-994-7956. *E-mail:* tcadmissions@argosyu.edu. *Web site:* http://www.argosyu.edu/.

THE ART INSTITUTES INTERNATIONAL MINNESOTA

Minneapolis, Minnesota

The Art Institutes International Minnesota is a coed, proprietary, primarily two-year college of The Art Institute, founded in 1964, offering degrees at the associate and bachelor's levels.

Academic Information The faculty has 66 members (38% full-time). The student-faculty ratio is 20:1. The library holds 1,450 titles and 25 serial subscriptions. Special programs include academic remediation, services for learning-disabled students, cooperative (work-study) education, advanced placement credit, summer session for credit, part-time degree programs (daytime, evenings), and internships. The most frequently chosen baccalaureate field is visual/performing arts.
Student Body Statistics The student body is made up of 1,162 undergraduates. Students come from 35 states and territories and 8 other countries. 94 percent are from Minnesota. 1 percent are international students. 2.8 percent of the 2003 graduating class went on to four-year colleges.
Expenses for 2003–04 *Application fee:* $50. *Tuition:* $16,128 full-time, $336 per credit part-time. Full-time tuition varies according to course load, degree level, and program. Part-time tuition varies according to course load, degree level, and program. *College room only:* $6550.
Financial Aid Forms of aid include need-based scholarships and part-time jobs. The application deadline for financial aid is continuous.

The Art Institutes International Minnesota (continued)

Freshman Admission The Art Institutes International Minnesota requires an essay, a high school transcript, an interview, TOEFL scores for international students, and Thurston Mental Alertness Test. ACT scores are recommended. The application deadline for regular admission is rolling.

Transfer Admission The application deadline for admission is rolling.

Entrance Difficulty The Art Institutes International Minnesota assesses its entrance difficulty level as minimally difficult. For the fall 2003 freshman class, 51 percent of the applicants were accepted.

For Further Information Contact Mr. Russ Gill, Director of Admissions, The Art Institutes International Minnesota, 15 South 9th Street, Minneapolis, MN 55402. *Telephone:* 612-332-3361 Ext. 6820 or 800-777-3643 (toll-free). *Fax:* 612-332-3934. *E-mail:* kozela@aii.edu. *Web site:* http://www.aim.artinstitutes.edu/.

AUGSBURG COLLEGE

Minneapolis, Minnesota

Augsburg is a coed, private, Lutheran, comprehensive institution, founded in 1869, offering degrees at the bachelor's and master's levels and post-master's and postbachelor's certificates. It has a 23-acre campus in Minneapolis.

Academic Information The faculty has 289 members (54% full-time), 64% with terminal degrees. The undergraduate student-faculty ratio is 15:1. The library holds 146,166 titles, 754 serial subscriptions, and 2,908 audiovisual materials. Special programs include academic remediation, services for learning-disabled students, an honors program, cooperative (work-study) education, study abroad, advanced placement credit, Freshman Honors College, ESL programs, double majors, independent study, self-designed majors, summer session for credit, part-time degree programs (daytime, weekends, summer), adult/continuing education programs, internships, and arrangement for off-campus study with Associated Colleges of the Twin Cities. The most frequently chosen baccalaureate fields are business/marketing, education, social sciences and history.

Student Body Statistics The student body totals 3,172, of whom 2,861 are undergraduates (377 freshmen). 58 percent are women and 42 percent are men. Students come from 45 states and territories and 29 other countries. 89 percent are from Minnesota. 1.3 percent are international students. 17 percent of the 2003 graduating class went on to graduate and professional schools.

Expenses for 2003–04 *Application fee:* $25. *Comprehensive fee:* $25,298 includes full-time tuition ($18,900), mandatory fees ($498), and college room and board ($5900). *College room only:* $3010. Full-time tuition and fees vary according to location. Room and board charges vary according to board plan and housing facility. *Part-time tuition:* $2300 per course. *Part-time mandatory fees:* $66.25 per course. Part-time tuition and fees vary according to course load and location.

Financial Aid Forms of aid include need-based and non-need-based scholarships and part-time jobs. The average aided 2002–03 undergraduate received an aid package worth $12,491. The application deadline for financial aid is April 15.

Freshman Admission Augsburg requires an essay, a high school transcript, a minimum 2.5 high school GPA, an interview, SAT I or ACT scores, and TOEFL scores for international students. 2 recommendations are required for some. The application deadline for regular admission is August 15.

Transfer Admission The application deadline for admission is August 10.

Entrance Difficulty Augsburg assesses its entrance difficulty level as moderately difficult. For the fall 2003 freshman class, 82 percent of the applicants were accepted.

For Further Information Contact Ms. Sally Daniels, Director of Undergraduate Day Admissions, Augsburg College, 2211 Riverside Avenue, Minneapolis, MN 55454-1351. *Telephone:* 612-330-1001 or 800-788-5678 (toll-free). *Fax:* 612-330-1590. *E-mail:* admissions@ augsburg.edu. *Web site:* http://www.augsburg.edu/.

BEMIDJI STATE UNIVERSITY

Bemidji, Minnesota

Bemidji State University is a coed, public, comprehensive unit of Minnesota State Colleges and Universities System, founded in 1919, offering degrees at the associate, bachelor's, and master's levels. It has an 89-acre campus in Bemidji.

Academic Information The faculty has 401 members (53% full-time), 44% with terminal degrees. The undergraduate student-faculty ratio is 19:1. The library holds 554,087 titles, 991 serial subscriptions, and 5,521 audiovisual materials. Special programs include academic remediation, services for learning-disabled students, an honors program, cooperative (work-study) education, study abroad, advanced placement credit, ESL programs, double majors, independent study, distance learning, summer session for credit, part-time degree programs (daytime, evenings, summer), external degree programs, adult/continuing education programs, internships, and arrangement for off-campus study with other colleges in the Minnesota State College and University System. The most frequently chosen baccalaureate fields are business/marketing, education, protective services/public administration.

Student Body Statistics The student body totals 5,024, of whom 4,660 are undergraduates (692 freshmen). 53 percent are women and 47 percent are men. Students come from 28 states and territories and 47 other countries. 95 percent are from Minnesota. 5.6 percent are international students.

Expenses for 2003–04 *Application fee:* $20. *State resident tuition:* $4338 full-time, $212 per credit part-time. *Nonresident tuition:* $9200 full-time, $307 per credit part-time. *Mandatory fees:* $710 full-time, $78.16 per credit part-time. Full-time tuition and fees vary according to reciprocity agreements. Part-time tuition and fees vary according to course load and reciprocity agreements. *College room and board:* $4597. *College room only:* $2448. Room and board charges vary according to board plan and housing facility.

Financial Aid Forms of aid include need-based and non-need-based scholarships, athletic grants, and part-time jobs. The average aided 2003–04 undergraduate received an aid package worth an estimated $7072. The priority application deadline for financial aid is May 15.

Freshman Admission Bemidji State University requires a high school transcript, ACT scores, and TOEFL scores for international students. An essay, recommendations, and an interview are required for some. The application deadline for regular admission is rolling.

Transfer Admission The application deadline for admission is rolling.

Entrance Difficulty Bemidji State University assesses its entrance difficulty level as moderately difficult. For the fall 2003 freshman class, 74 percent of the applicants were accepted.

For Further Information Contact Mr. Paul Muller, Director of Admissions, Bemidji State University, Deputy-102, Bemidji, MN 56601. *Telephone:* 218-755-2040, 800-475-2001 (toll-free in-state), or 800-652-9747 (toll-free out-of-state). *Fax:* 218-755-2074. *E-mail:* admissions@bemidjistate.edu. *Web site:* http://www.bemidjistate.edu/.

BETHANY LUTHERAN COLLEGE

Mankato, Minnesota

Bethany is a coed, private, Lutheran, four-year college, founded in 1927, offering degrees at the associate and bachelor's levels. It has a 50-acre campus in Mankato near Minneapolis–St. Paul.

Academic Information The faculty has 64 members (58% full-time), 30% with terminal degrees. The student-faculty ratio is 8:1. The library holds 63,436 titles, 237 serial subscriptions, and 4,002 audiovisual materials. Special programs include academic remediation, services for learning-disabled students, an honors program, advanced placement credit, and ESL programs. The most frequently chosen baccalaureate fields are communications/communication technologies, business/marketing, liberal arts/general studies.

Student Body Statistics The student body is made up of 504 undergraduates (226 freshmen). 57 percent are women and 43 percent are men. Students come from 25 states and territories and 14 other countries.

70 percent are from Minnesota. 5 percent are international students. 5 percent of the 2003 graduating class went on to graduate and professional schools.

Expenses for 2004–05 *Application fee:* $20. *Comprehensive fee:* $19,724 includes full-time tuition ($14,482), mandatory fees ($260), and college room and board ($4982). *College room only:* $1852. Room and board charges vary according to board plan. *Part-time tuition:* $660 per credit. *Part-time mandatory fees:* $130 per term.

Financial Aid Forms of aid include need-based and non-need-based scholarships, athletic grants, and part-time jobs. The average aided 2002–03 undergraduate received an aid package worth $11,699. The priority application deadline for financial aid is April 15.

Freshman Admission Bethany requires an essay, a high school transcript, a minimum 2.4 high school GPA, SAT I or ACT scores, and TOEFL scores for international students. A minimum 3.2 high school GPA and an interview are recommended. An interview is required for some. The application deadline for regular admission is July 15.

Entrance Difficulty Bethany assesses its entrance difficulty level as moderately difficult; minimally difficult for transfers. For the fall 2003 freshman class, 83 percent of the applicants were accepted.

For Further Information Contact Mr. Donald Westphal, Dean of Admissions, Bethany Lutheran College, 700 Luther Drive, Mankato, MN 56001. *Telephone:* 507-344-7320 or 800-944-3066 (toll-free). *Fax:* 507-344-7376. *E-mail:* admiss@blc.edu. *Web site:* http://www.blc.edu/.

BETHEL UNIVERSITY

St. Paul, Minnesota

Bethel is a coed, private, comprehensive institution, founded in 1871, affiliated with the Baptist General Conference, offering degrees at the associate, bachelor's, and master's levels. It has a 231-acre campus in St. Paul near Twin Cities.

Academic Information The faculty has 255 members (65% full-time), 54% with terminal degrees. The undergraduate student-faculty ratio is 15:1. The library holds 173,000 titles, 14,678 serial subscriptions, and 12,204 audiovisual materials. Special programs include services for learning-disabled students, an honors program, study abroad, advanced placement credit, accelerated degree programs, Freshman Honors College, ESL programs, double majors, independent study, self-designed majors, summer session for credit, part-time degree programs (daytime, evenings, summer), external degree programs, adult/continuing education programs, internships, and arrangement for off-campus study with members of the Christian College Consortium, Au Sable Institute, Coalition for Christian Colleges and Universities. The most frequently chosen baccalaureate fields are business/marketing, education, health professions and related sciences.

Student Body Statistics The student body totals 3,303, of whom 2,911 are undergraduates (658 freshmen). 61 percent are women and 39 percent are men. Students come from 41 states and territories. 73 percent are from Minnesota. 0.1 percent are international students.

Expenses for 2004–05 *Application fee:* $25. *Comprehensive fee:* $26,560 includes full-time tuition ($19,880), mandatory fees ($110), and college room and board ($6570). *College room only:* $3900. Room and board charges vary according to board plan. *Part-time tuition:* $755 per credit. Part-time tuition varies according to course load.

Financial Aid Forms of aid include need-based and non-need-based scholarships and part-time jobs. The average aided 2003–04 undergraduate received an aid package worth an estimated $14,810. The priority application deadline for financial aid is April 15.

Freshman Admission Bethel requires an essay, a high school transcript, 2 recommendations, TOEFL scores for international students, An interview is recommended. An interview is required for some. The application deadline for regular admission is March 1 and for early action it is December 1.

Transfer Admission The application deadline for admission is March 1.

Entrance Difficulty Bethel assesses its entrance difficulty level as moderately difficult. For the fall 2003 freshman class, 91 percent of the applicants were accepted.

SPECIAL MESSAGE TO STUDENTS

Social Life The social atmosphere at Bethel is exciting, with many student-run campus activities. Bethel has excellent music performance groups, varsity and intramural sports, student government, theater productions, and a wide variety of student clubs and spiritual growth groups. Spiritual life is a priority at Bethel. Community chapel services, residence hall Bible studies, and discipleship programs offer opportunities for Christian growth. There are also many opportunities for students to get involved in ministry through campus outreach events, Habitat for Humanity, community service programs, inner-city projects, and missions trips.

Academic Highlights With sixty-four majors within seventy-six areas of study, Bethel ranks in the top Midwestern Universities category of the *U.S. News & World Report* "America's Best Colleges." Bethel's general education curriculum has become a model for many other liberal arts colleges nationwide. General education courses give students a broad view of the world and their role as Christians in it. The courses are grouped around the following themes: Bible and theology, Western culture, world citizenship, self-understanding, math, science, technology, health and wholeness, and final integration. Bethel strongly encourages and provides students with the opportunity to participate in a number of off-campus study programs, such as the Latin American Studies Program in Costa Rica, Los Angeles Film Studies Program, American Studies Program in Washington, D.C., AuSable Institute for Environmental Studies in Michigan, England Term, Jerusalem University College, Australia Term, and Daystar University in Kenya.

Interviews and Campus Visits On-campus interviews are strongly encouraged but not required. An interview gives the prospective student the opportunity to learn more about the University, ask questions, and better determine if the University is a good fit. A campus visit at Bethel gives students opportunities to stay in a residence hall, attend classes and chapel, meet with professors and coaches, enjoy free meals with Bethel students, and attend on-campus events. Bethel's beautiful wooded campus is located on the shores of Lake Valentine in Arden Hills, Minnesota—just 15 minutes from downtown St. Paul and Minneapolis. The Bethel campus offers modern academic, housing, and recreation facilities. The Community Life Center houses the 1,700-seat Benson Great Hall, hailed as one of the best music performance halls in the upper Midwest. For more information about Bethel University or to arrange a campus visit, students can call the Office of Admissions at 651-638-6242 or 800-255-8706 (toll-free), Monday through Friday, 8:30 a.m. to 4:30 p.m. The fax number is 651-635-1490. The Office of Admissions is located on campus in RC 341, Robertson Center building. The nearest commercial airport is Minneapolis-St. Paul International.

For Further Information Write to Office of Admissions, Bethel University, 3900 Bethel Drive, St. Paul, MN 55112. *E-mail:* bcoll-admit@bethel.edu. *Web site:* http://www.bethel.edu.

BROWN COLLEGE

Mendota Heights, Minnesota

Brown College is a coed, proprietary, primarily two-year college of Career Education Corporation, founded in 1946, offering degrees at the associate and bachelor's levels. It has a 20-acre campus in Mendota Heights near Minneapolis–St. Paul.

Expenses for 2003–04 *Application fee:* $50. *Tuition:* $16,800 full-time. *Mandatory fees:* $50 full-time.

For Further Information Contact Mr. Mike Price, Director of Admissions, Brown College, 1440 Northland Drive, Mendota Heights, MN 55120. *Telephone:* 651-905-3400 or 800-6BROWN6 (toll-free). *Fax:* 651-905-3510. *Web site:* http://www.browncollege.edu/.

CAPELLA UNIVERSITY

Minneapolis, Minnesota

Capella University is a coed, proprietary, upper-level institution, founded in 1993, offering degrees at the bachelor's, master's, doctoral,

Capella University (continued)
and first professional levels and first professional and postbachelor's certificates (offers only distance learning degree programs).

Academic Information The faculty has 372 members. The undergraduate student-faculty ratio is 20:1. Special programs include services for learning-disabled students, double majors, independent study, distance learning, self-designed majors, summer session for credit, part-time degree programs, external degree programs, adult/continuing education programs, internships, and arrangement for off-campus study.
Student Body Statistics The student body totals 8,406. 15 percent are from Minnesota.
Expenses for 2003–04 *Application fee:* $50. *Tuition:* $12,000 full-time. Full-time tuition varies according to degree level and program. *Part-time tuition:* varies with degree level, program.
Financial Aid Forms of aid include need-based scholarships. The average aided 2002–03 undergraduate received an aid package worth $10,500. The application deadline for financial aid is continuous.
Transfer Admission Capella University requires a college transcript and a minimum 2.0 college GPA. The application deadline for admission is rolling.
Entrance Difficulty Capella University assesses its entrance difficulty level as moderately difficult.

For Further Information Contact Ms. Liz Hinz, Associate Director, Enrollment Services, Capella University, 222 South 9th Street, 20th Floor, Minneapolis, MN 55402. *Telephone:* 612-659-5871 or 888-CAPELLA (toll-free). *Fax:* 612-339-8022. *E-mail:* info@capella.edu. *Web site:* http://www.capellauniversity.edu/.

CARLETON COLLEGE
Northfield, Minnesota

Carleton is a coed, private, four-year college, founded in 1866, offering degrees at the bachelor's level. It has a 955-acre campus in Northfield near Minneapolis–St. Paul.

Academic Information The faculty has 220 members (89% full-time), 91% with terminal degrees. The student-faculty ratio is 9:1. The library holds 662,871 titles, 10,964 serial subscriptions, and 778 audiovisual materials. Special programs include services for learning-disabled students, study abroad, advanced placement credit, accelerated degree programs, double majors, independent study, self-designed majors, internships, and arrangement for off-campus study with St. Olaf College, Associated Colleges of the Midwest, Higher Education Consortium for Urban Affairs. The most frequently chosen baccalaureate fields are biological/life sciences, physical sciences, social sciences and history.
Student Body Statistics The student body is made up of 1,943 undergraduates (488 freshmen). 52 percent are women and 48 percent are men. Students come from 49 states and territories and 30 other countries. 24 percent are from Minnesota. 4.7 percent are international students. 20 percent of the 2003 graduating class went on to graduate and professional schools.
Expenses for 2003–04 *Application fee:* $30. *Comprehensive fee:* $34,395 includes full-time tuition ($28,362), mandatory fees ($165), and college room and board ($5868). *College room only:* $2547.
Financial Aid Forms of aid include need-based and non-need-based scholarships and part-time jobs. The average aided 2002–03 undergraduate received an aid package worth $19,933. The priority application deadline for financial aid is February 15.
Freshman Admission Carleton requires an essay, a high school transcript, 2 recommendations, SAT I or ACT scores, and TOEFL scores for international students. An interview, SAT II: Subject Test scores, and SAT II: Writing Test scores are recommended. The application deadline for regular admission is January 15; for early decision plan 1 it is November 15; and for early decision plan 2 it is January 15.
Transfer Admission The application deadline for admission is March 31.

Entrance Difficulty Carleton assesses its entrance difficulty level as very difficult; most difficult for transfers. For the fall 2003 freshman class, 30 percent of the applicants were accepted.

For Further Information Contact Mr. Paul Thiboutot, Dean of Admissions, Carleton College, 100 South College Street, Northfield, MN 55057. *Telephone:* 507-646-4190 or 800-995-2275 (toll-free). *Fax:* 507-646-4526. *E-mail:* admissions@acs.carleton.edu. *Web site:* http://www.carleton.edu/.

COLLEGE OF SAINT BENEDICT
Saint Joseph, Minnesota

St. Ben's is a coed, primarily women's, private, Roman Catholic, four-year college, founded in 1887, coordinate with Saint John's University (MN), offering degrees at the bachelor's level (coordinate with Saint John's University for men). It has a 315-acre campus in Saint Joseph near Minneapolis–St. Paul.

Academic Information The faculty has 174 members (85% full-time), 66% with terminal degrees. The student-faculty ratio is 13:1. The library holds 805,376 titles, 5,735 serial subscriptions, and 22,452 audiovisual materials. Special programs include services for learning-disabled students, an honors program, study abroad, advanced placement credit, accelerated degree programs, ESL programs, double majors, independent study, self-designed majors, internships, and arrangement for off-campus study with Tri-College Exchange Program (MN), Saint John's University (MN). The most frequently chosen baccalaureate fields are business/marketing, English, social sciences and history.
Student Body Statistics The student body is made up of 2,054 undergraduates (502 freshmen). 100 percent are women and 100 percent are men. Students come from 31 states and territories and 24 other countries. 86 percent are from Minnesota. 3.5 percent are international students. 13 percent of the 2003 graduating class went on to graduate and professional schools.
Expenses for 2003–04 *Application fee:* $30. *Comprehensive fee:* $26,672 includes full-time tuition ($20,335), mandatory fees ($350), and college room and board ($5987). *College room only:* $3169. Room and board charges vary according to board plan and housing facility. *Part-time tuition:* $847 per credit. *Part-time mandatory fees:* $175 per term. Part-time tuition and fees vary according to course load.
Financial Aid Forms of aid include need-based and non-need-based scholarships and part-time jobs. The average aided 2003–04 undergraduate received an aid package worth an estimated $17,223. The priority application deadline for financial aid is March 15.
Freshman Admission St. Ben's requires an essay, a high school transcript, 1 recommendation, SAT I or ACT scores, and TOEFL scores for international students. A minimum 3.0 high school GPA and an interview are recommended. The application deadline for regular admission is January 15 and for early action it is December 1.
Transfer Admission The application deadline for admission is rolling.
Entrance Difficulty St. Ben's assesses its entrance difficulty level as moderately difficult. For the fall 2003 freshman class, 90 percent of the applicants were accepted.

For Further Information Contact Ms. Karen Backes, Associate Dean of Admissions, College of Saint Benedict, PO Box 7155, Collegeville, MN 56321. *Telephone:* 320-363-2196 or 800-544-1489 (toll-free). *Fax:* 320-363-2750. *E-mail:* admissions@csbsju.edu. *Web site:* http://www.csbsju.edu/.

COLLEGE OF ST. CATHERINE
St. Paul, Minnesota

CSC is a women's, private, Roman Catholic, comprehensive institution, founded in 1905, offering degrees at the associate, bachelor's, master's, and doctoral levels and post-master's and postbachelor's certificates. It has a 110-acre campus in St. Paul near Minneapolis.

Academic Information The faculty has 528 members (42% full-time), 42% with terminal degrees. The undergraduate student-faculty ratio is 11:1. The library holds 263,495 titles, 1,141 serial subscriptions, and 13,627 audiovisual materials. Special programs include academic remediation, services for learning-disabled students, an honors program, study abroad, advanced placement credit, ESL programs, double majors, independent study, distance learning, self-designed majors, summer session for credit, part-time degree programs (daytime, weekends, summer), external degree programs, adult/continuing education programs, internships, and arrangement for off-campus study with Associated Colleges of the Twin Cities, Sisters of St. Joseph College Consortium, Higher Education Consortium for Urban Affairs. The most frequently chosen baccalaureate fields are business/marketing, education, health professions and related sciences.

Student Body Statistics The student body totals 4,807, of whom 3,681 are undergraduates (407 freshmen). Students come from 31 states and territories and 30 other countries. 90 percent are from Minnesota. 2.3 percent are international students. 19 percent of the 2003 graduating class went on to graduate and professional schools.

Expenses for 2003–04 *Application fee:* $20. *Comprehensive fee:* $25,230 includes full-time tuition ($19,520), mandatory fees ($250), and college room and board ($5460). *College room only:* $3060. Full-time tuition and fees vary according to class time. Room and board charges vary according to board plan and housing facility. *Part-time tuition:* $610 per credit. Part-time tuition varies according to class time.

Financial Aid Forms of aid include need-based and non-need-based scholarships and part-time jobs. The average aided 2003–04 undergraduate received an aid package worth an estimated $18,319. The priority application deadline for financial aid is April 15.

Freshman Admission CSC requires a high school transcript, 1 recommendation, SAT I or ACT scores, and TOEFL scores for international students. An interview is recommended. An essay and an interview are required for some. The application deadline for regular admission is August 15.

Transfer Admission The application deadline for admission is rolling.

Entrance Difficulty CSC assesses its entrance difficulty level as moderately difficult. For the fall 2003 freshman class, 77 percent of the applicants were accepted.

For Further Information Contact Ms. Cory Piper-Hauswirth, Associate Director of Admission and Financial Aid, College of St. Catherine, 2004 Randolph Avenue, F-02, St. Paul, MN 55105. *Telephone:* 651-690-6505 or 800-945-4599 (toll-free in-state). *Fax:* 651-690-8824. *E-mail:* admissions@stkate.edu. *Web site:* http://www.stkate.edu/.

COLLEGE OF ST. CATHERINE–MINNEAPOLIS
Minneapolis, Minnesota

College of St. Catherine–Minneapolis is a coed, primarily women's, private, Roman Catholic, comprehensive institution, founded in 1964, offering degrees at the associate level. It has a 1-acre campus in Minneapolis.

Academic Information The faculty has 519 members (43% full-time), 52% with terminal degrees. The student-faculty ratio is 11:1. The library holds 267,558 titles, 1,141 serial subscriptions, and 13,627 audiovisual materials. Special programs include academic remediation, services for learning-disabled students, ESL programs, independent study, summer session for credit, part-time degree programs (daytime, evenings, weekends, summer), adult/continuing education programs, and internships.

Student Body Statistics The student body totals 4,807, of whom 3,681 are undergraduates (407 freshmen). 97 percent are women and 3 percent are men. Students come from 18 states and territories. 96 percent are from Minnesota. 2.3 percent are international students.

Expenses for 2004–05 *Application fee:* $20. *Comprehensive fee:* $20,078 includes full-time tuition ($14,240), mandatory fees ($30), and college room and board ($5808). *College room only:* $3258. Room and board charges vary according to board plan and housing facility. *Part-time tuition:* $445 per credit. *Part-time mandatory fees:* $15 per term.

Financial Aid Forms of aid include need-based scholarships and part-time jobs. The priority application deadline for financial aid is June 1.

Freshman Admission College of St. Catherine–Minneapolis requires an essay, a high school transcript, and 2 recommendations. A minimum 2.0 high school GPA, an interview, and ACT scores are recommended. A minimum 3.0 high school GPA is required for some. The application deadline for regular admission is rolling.

Transfer Admission The application deadline for admission is rolling.

Entrance Difficulty College of St. Catherine–Minneapolis assesses its entrance difficulty level as minimally difficult; moderately difficult for transfers. For the fall 2003 freshman class, 77 percent of the applicants were accepted.

For Further Information Contact Mr. Cal Mosley, Assistant to the President for Admission, College of St. Catherine–Minneapolis, 601 25th Avenue South, Minneapolis, MN 55454-1494. *Telephone:* 651-690-8600 or 800-945-4599 Ext. 7800 (toll-free). *Fax:* 651-690-8119. *E-mail:* career-info@stkate.edu. *Web site:* http://www.stkate.edu/.

THE COLLEGE OF ST. SCHOLASTICA
Duluth, Minnesota

St. Scholastica is a coed, private, comprehensive institution, founded in 1912, affiliated with the Roman Catholic Church, offering degrees at the bachelor's and master's levels and post-master's and postbachelor's certificates. It has a 186-acre campus in Duluth.

Academic Information The faculty has 209 members (59% full-time), 45% with terminal degrees. The undergraduate student-faculty ratio is 13:1. The library holds 125,091 titles, 1,135 serial subscriptions, and 15,262 audiovisual materials. Special programs include academic remediation, services for learning-disabled students, an honors program, study abroad, advanced placement credit, accelerated degree programs, double majors, independent study, distance learning, self-designed majors, summer session for credit, part-time degree programs (evenings), external degree programs, adult/continuing education programs, internships, and arrangement for off-campus study with University of Wisconsin-Superior, University of Minnesota, Duluth. The most frequently chosen baccalaureate fields are business/marketing, computer/information sciences, health professions and related sciences.

Student Body Statistics The student body totals 2,838, of whom 2,308 are undergraduates (437 freshmen). 70 percent are women and 30 percent are men. Students come from 19 states and territories and 10 other countries. 89 percent are from Minnesota. 1.5 percent are international students. 30 percent of the 2003 graduating class went on to graduate and professional schools.

Expenses for 2003–04 *Application fee:* $25. *Comprehensive fee:* $24,970 includes full-time tuition ($19,192), mandatory fees ($110), and college room and board ($5668). *College room only:* $3228. Full-time tuition and fees vary according to class time. Room and board charges vary according to board plan. *Part-time tuition:* $601 per credit hour. Part-time tuition varies according to class time and course load.

Financial Aid Forms of aid include need-based and non-need-based scholarships and part-time jobs. The average aided 2003–04 undergraduate received an aid package worth an estimated $15,945. The priority application deadline for financial aid is March 15.

Freshman Admission St. Scholastica requires a high school transcript, SAT I or ACT scores, and TOEFL scores for international students. An essay, recommendations, an interview, and PSAT are recommended. A minimum 2.0 high school GPA and an interview are required for some. The application deadline for regular admission is rolling.

Transfer Admission The application deadline for admission is rolling.

Entrance Difficulty St. Scholastica assesses its entrance difficulty level as moderately difficult. For the fall 2003 freshman class, 88 percent of the applicants were accepted.

For Further Information Contact Mr. Brian Dalton, Vice President for Enrollment Management, The College of St. Scholastica, 1200 Kenwood Avenue, Duluth, MN 55811-4199. *Telephone:* 218-723-6053 or 800-249-6412 (toll-free). *Fax:* 218-723-5991. *E-mail:* admissions@css.edu. *Web site:* http://www.css.edu/.

COLLEGE OF VISUAL ARTS
St. Paul, Minnesota

CVA is a coed, private, four-year college, founded in 1924, offering degrees at the bachelor's level in art and design. It has a 2-acre campus in St. Paul near Minneapolis.

Academic Information The faculty has 54 members (17% full-time), 74% with terminal degrees. The student-faculty ratio is 8:1. The library holds 7,100 titles, 55 serial subscriptions, and 30,370 audiovisual materials. Special programs include academic remediation, an honors program, study abroad, advanced placement credit, double majors, independent study, summer session for credit, part-time degree programs (daytime, evenings, summer), and internships. The most frequently chosen baccalaureate field is visual/performing arts.
Student Body Statistics The student body is made up of 219 undergraduates (37 freshmen). 55 percent are women and 45 percent are men. Students come from 13 states and territories. 90 percent are from Minnesota. 0.5 percent are international students.
Expenses for 2003–04 *Application fee:* $40. *Tuition:* $15,576 full-time, $780 per credit part-time. *Mandatory fees:* $530 full-time, $53 per course part-time. Full-time tuition and fees vary according to course load. Part-time tuition and fees vary according to course load.
Financial Aid Forms of aid include need-based and non-need-based scholarships and part-time jobs. The average aided 2003–04 undergraduate received an aid package worth an estimated $7956. The application deadline for financial aid is continuous.
Freshman Admission CVA requires an essay, a high school transcript, a minimum 2.7 high school GPA, an interview, a portfolio, SAT I or ACT scores, and TOEFL scores for international students. A minimum 3.0 high school GPA and recommendations are recommended. The application deadline for regular admission is rolling.
Transfer Admission The application deadline for admission is rolling.
Entrance Difficulty CVA assesses its entrance difficulty level as moderately difficult. For the fall 2003 freshman class, 50 percent of the applicants were accepted.

For Further Information Contact Ms. Elizabeth Catron, Associate Director of Admissions, College of Visual Arts, 344 Summit Avenue, St. Paul, MN 55102-2124. *Telephone:* 651-224-3416 or 800-224-1536 (toll-free). *Fax:* 651-224-8854. *E-mail:* info@cva.edu. *Web site:* http://www.cva.edu/.

CONCORDIA COLLEGE
Moorhead, Minnesota

Concordia is a coed, private, four-year college, founded in 1891, affiliated with the Evangelical Lutheran Church in America, offering degrees at the bachelor's level. It has a 120-acre campus in Moorhead.

Academic Information The faculty has 268 members (65% full-time), 57% with terminal degrees. The student-faculty ratio is 14:1. The library holds 299,808 titles, 1,433 serial subscriptions, and 20,778 audiovisual materials. Special programs include services for learning-disabled students, an honors program, cooperative (work-study) education, study abroad, advanced placement credit, ESL programs, double majors, independent study, summer session for credit, part-time degree programs (daytime, summer), adult/continuing education programs, internships, and arrangement for off-campus study with Tri-College University. The most frequently chosen baccalaureate fields are biological/life sciences, business/marketing, education.
Student Body Statistics The student body is made up of 2,856 undergraduates (783 freshmen). 63 percent are women and 37 percent are men. Students come from 39 states and territories and 42 other countries. 63 percent are from Minnesota. 6 percent are international students. 23 percent of the 2003 graduating class went on to graduate and professional schools.
Expenses for 2003–04 *Application fee:* $20. *Comprehensive fee:* $21,100 includes full-time tuition ($16,420), mandatory fees ($140), and college room and board ($4540). *College room only:* $2040. Room and board

charges vary according to board plan and housing facility. *Part-time tuition:* $2580 per course. Part-time tuition varies according to course load.
Financial Aid Forms of aid include need-based and non-need-based scholarships and part-time jobs. The average aided 2002–03 undergraduate received an aid package worth $12,737. The application deadline for financial aid is continuous.
Freshman Admission Concordia requires a high school transcript, 2 recommendations, SAT I or ACT scores, and TOEFL scores for international students. ACT scores are recommended. The application deadline for regular admission is rolling.
Transfer Admission The application deadline for admission is rolling.
Entrance Difficulty Concordia assesses its entrance difficulty level as moderately difficult. For the fall 2003 freshman class, 86 percent of the applicants were accepted.

For Further Information Contact Mr. Scott E. Ellingson, Director of Admissions, Concordia College, 901 8th Street South, Moorhead, MN 56562. *Telephone:* 218-299-3004 or 800-699-9897 (toll-free). *Fax:* 218-299-3947. *E-mail:* admissions@cord.edu. *Web site:* http://www.concordiacollege.edu/.

CONCORDIA UNIVERSITY, ST. PAUL
St. Paul, Minnesota

Concordia-St. Paul is a coed, private, comprehensive unit of Concordia University System, founded in 1893, affiliated with the Lutheran Church–Missouri Synod, offering degrees at the associate, bachelor's, and master's levels and postbachelor's certificates. It has a 37-acre campus in St. Paul.

Academic Information The faculty has 382 members (21% full-time). The undergraduate student-faculty ratio is 11:1. The library holds 131,242 titles, 1,400 serial subscriptions, and 6,843 audiovisual materials. Special programs include academic remediation, services for learning-disabled students, cooperative (work-study) education, study abroad, advanced placement credit, accelerated degree programs, ESL programs, double majors, independent study, distance learning, self-designed majors, summer session for credit, part-time degree programs (daytime, evenings, summer), external degree programs, adult/continuing education programs, internships, and arrangement for off-campus study with University of Minnesota–Twin Cities Campus. The most frequently chosen baccalaureate fields are business/marketing, education, philosophy, religion, and theology.
Student Body Statistics The student body totals 2,051, of whom 1,741 are undergraduates (167 freshmen). 59 percent are women and 41 percent are men. Students come from 39 states and territories and 6 other countries. 78 percent are from Minnesota. 0.7 percent are international students.
Expenses for 2004–05 *Application fee:* $30. *Comprehensive fee:* $26,084 includes full-time tuition ($19,928) and college room and board ($6156). Full-time tuition varies according to program. *Part-time tuition:* varies with course load.
Financial Aid Forms of aid include need-based and non-need-based scholarships, athletic grants, and part-time jobs. The average aided 2003–04 undergraduate received an aid package worth an estimated $11,339. The application deadline for financial aid is continuous.
Freshman Admission Concordia-St. Paul requires a high school transcript, 2 recommendations, and ACT scores. A minimum 2.0 high school GPA and an interview are recommended. An essay is required for some. The application deadline for regular admission is August 1.
Transfer Admission The application deadline for admission is August 1.
Entrance Difficulty Concordia-St. Paul assesses its entrance difficulty level as minimally difficult. For the fall 2003 freshman class, 64 percent of the applicants were accepted.

For Further Information Contact Concordia University, St. Paul, 275 Syndicate North, St. Paul, MN 55104-5494. *Telephone:* 651-641-8230 or 800-333-4705 (toll-free). *Fax:* 651-659-0207. *E-mail:* admiss@csp.edu. *Web site:* http://www.csp.edu/.

CROSSROADS COLLEGE
Rochester, Minnesota

Crossroads College is a coed, private, four-year college, founded in 1913, affiliated with the Christian Churches and Churches of Christ, offering degrees at the associate and bachelor's levels. It has a 40-acre campus in Rochester near Minneapolis–St. Paul.

Academic Information   The faculty has 22 members (36% full-time), 27% with terminal degrees. The student-faculty ratio is 10:1. The library holds 31,059 titles, 300 serial subscriptions, and 1,532 audiovisual materials. Special programs include academic remediation, advanced placement credit, double majors, independent study, self-designed majors, and internships. The most frequently chosen baccalaureate fields are liberal arts/general studies, philosophy, religion, and theology.

Student Body Statistics   The student body is made up of 133 undergraduates (31 freshmen). 47 percent are women and 53 percent are men. Students come from 11 states and territories and 6 other countries. 74 percent are from Minnesota. 4.5 percent are international students. 21 percent of the 2003 graduating class went on to graduate and professional schools.

Expenses for 2004–05   *Application fee:* $30. *Tuition:* $8310 full-time, $277 per semester hour part-time. *Mandatory fees:* $130 full-time. Full-time tuition and fees vary according to course load. Part-time tuition varies according to course load. *College room only:* $2158. Room charges vary according to housing facility.

Financial Aid   Forms of aid include need-based and non-need-based scholarships and part-time jobs. The average aided 2002–03 undergraduate received an aid package worth $7124. The priority application deadline for financial aid is May 1.

Freshman Admission   Crossroads College requires an essay, a high school transcript, 3 recommendations, SAT I or ACT scores, and TOEFL scores for international students. An interview is required for some. The application deadline for regular admission is August 15.

Transfer Admission   The application deadline for admission is August 15.

Entrance Difficulty   Crossroads College assesses its entrance difficulty level as noncompetitive. For the fall 2003 freshman class, 67 percent of the applicants were accepted.

For Further Information   Contact Mr. Michael Golembiesky, Director of Admissions, Crossroads College, 920 Mayowood Road, SW, Rochester, MN 55902-2382. *Telephone:* 507-288-4563 Ext. 313 or 800-456-7651 (toll-free). *Fax:* 507-288-9046. *E-mail:* admissions@crossroadscollege.edu. *Web site:* http://www.crossroadscollege.edu/.

CROWN COLLEGE
St. Bonifacius, Minnesota

Crown College is a coed, private, comprehensive institution, founded in 1916, affiliated with The Christian and Missionary Alliance, offering degrees at the associate, bachelor's, and master's levels. It has a 215-acre campus in St. Bonifacius near Minneapolis–St. Paul.

Academic Information   The faculty has 69 members (48% full-time), 35% with terminal degrees. The undergraduate student-faculty ratio is 22:1. The library holds 78,000 titles, 1,780 serial subscriptions, and 2,400 audiovisual materials. Special programs include academic remediation, services for learning-disabled students, an honors program, study abroad, advanced placement credit, ESL programs, double majors, independent study, distance learning, summer session for credit, part-time degree programs (daytime, evenings, weekends, summer), adult/continuing education programs, and internships. The most frequently chosen baccalaureate fields are education, business/marketing, philosophy, religion, and theology.

Student Body Statistics   The student body totals 1,031, of whom 986 are undergraduates (118 freshmen). 57 percent are women and 43 percent are men. Students come from 39 states and territories. 75 percent are from Minnesota.

Expenses for 2003–04   *Application fee:* $35. *Comprehensive fee:* $18,720 includes full-time tuition ($13,168) and college room and board ($5552).

College room only: $2528. Room and board charges vary according to board plan. *Part-time tuition:* $550 per credit. Part-time tuition varies according to course load.

Financial Aid   Forms of aid include need-based and non-need-based scholarships and part-time jobs. The average aided 2003–04 undergraduate received an aid package worth an estimated $10,054. The priority application deadline for financial aid is April 1.

Freshman Admission   Crown College requires an essay, a high school transcript, a minimum 2.0 high school GPA, 2 recommendations, SAT I or ACT scores, and TOEFL scores for international students. An interview is required for some. The application deadline for regular admission is rolling.

Transfer Admission   The application deadline for admission is rolling.

Entrance Difficulty   Crown College assesses its entrance difficulty level as minimally difficult. For the fall 2003 freshman class, 82 percent of the applicants were accepted.

For Further Information   Contact Mr. Mitch Fisk, Director of Admissions, Crown College, 6425 County Road 30, St. Bonifacius, MN 55375-9001. *Telephone:* 952-446-4144 or 800-68-CROWN (toll-free). *Fax:* 952-446-4149. *E-mail:* info@crown.edu. *Web site:* http://www.crown.edu/.

DUNWOODY COLLEGE OF TECHNOLOGY
Minneapolis, Minnesota

Dunwoody is a coed, primarily men's, private, two-year college, founded in 1914, offering degrees at the associate level. It has a 12-acre campus in Minneapolis.

Academic Information   The faculty has 105 members (77% full-time), 4% with terminal degrees. The student-faculty ratio is 15:1. The library holds 8,000 titles, 115 serial subscriptions, and 250 audiovisual materials. Special programs include academic remediation, ESL programs, independent study, summer session for credit, and internships.

Student Body Statistics   The student body is made up of 1,611 undergraduates (397 freshmen). 10 percent are women and 90 percent are men. Students come from 12 states and territories and 3 other countries. 95 percent are from Minnesota. 0.3 percent are international students.

Expenses for 2004–05   *Application fee:* $50. *Tuition:* $20,742 full-time, $227 per credit part-time. *Mandatory fees:* $1155 full-time, $1155 per year part-time.

Financial Aid   Forms of aid include need-based scholarships and part-time jobs. The priority application deadline for financial aid is April 15.

Freshman Admission   Dunwoody requires a high school transcript, an interview, institutional entrance test, and TOEFL scores for international students. The application deadline for regular admission is rolling.

Entrance Difficulty   Dunwoody assesses its entrance difficulty level as noncompetitive. For the fall 2003 freshman class, 62 percent of the applicants were accepted.

For Further Information   Contact Ms. Yun-bok Christenson, Records Coordinator, Dunwoody College of Technology, 818 Dunwoody Boulevard, Minneapolis, MN 55403. *Telephone:* 612-374-5800 Ext. 2014 or 800-292-4625 (toll-free). *Fax:* 612-374-4128. *E-mail:* aylreb@dunwoody.tec.mn.us. *Web site:* http://www.dunwoody.edu/.

GLOBE COLLEGE
Oakdale, Minnesota

Globe College is a coed, private, primarily two-year college, founded in 1885, offering degrees at the associate, bachelor's, and master's levels.

Academic Information   The undergraduate student-faculty ratio is 15:1. The library holds 1,700 titles, 85 serial subscriptions, and 100 audiovisual materials. Special programs include academic remediation, advanced placement credit, independent study, distance learning, part-time degree programs (daytime, evenings, weekends, summer), external degree programs, adult/continuing education programs, and internships.

Globe College (continued)

Student Body Statistics The student body is made up of 997 undergraduates. 92 percent are from Minnesota.

Expenses for 2003–04 *Tuition:* $11,340 full-time, $315 per credit part-time. Full-time tuition varies according to course load. Part-time tuition varies according to course load.

Financial Aid Forms of aid include need-based scholarships. The application deadline for financial aid is continuous.

Freshman Admission Globe College requires an interview. SAT I or ACT scores are recommended.

Entrance Difficulty Globe College has an open admission policy.

For Further Information Contact Mr. Rob Harker, Director of Admissions, Globe College, 7166 10th Street North, Oakdale, MN 55128. *Telephone:* 651-714-7313. *Fax:* 651-730-5151. *E-mail:* admissions@globecollege.edu. *Web site:* http://www.globecollege.com/.

GUSTAVUS ADOLPHUS COLLEGE

St. Peter, Minnesota

Gustavus is a coed, private, four-year college, founded in 1862, affiliated with the Evangelical Lutheran Church in America, offering degrees at the bachelor's level. It has a 330-acre campus in St. Peter near Minneapolis–St. Paul.

Academic Information The faculty has 247 members (72% full-time), 66% with terminal degrees. The student-faculty ratio is 13:1. The library holds 287,761 titles, 1,001 serial subscriptions, and 16,063 audiovisual materials. Special programs include services for learning-disabled students, an honors program, cooperative (work-study) education, study abroad, advanced placement credit, accelerated degree programs, double majors, independent study, self-designed majors, summer session for credit, internships, and arrangement for off-campus study with Minnesota State University, Mankato. The most frequently chosen baccalaureate fields are business/marketing, biological/life sciences, social sciences and history.

Student Body Statistics The student body is made up of 2,574 undergraduates (688 freshmen). 57 percent are women and 43 percent are men. Students come from 38 states and territories and 18 other countries. 81 percent are from Minnesota. 1.2 percent are international students. 36 percent of the 2003 graduating class went on to graduate and professional schools.

Expenses for 2003–04 *Application fee:* $0. *Comprehensive fee:* $27,120 includes full-time tuition ($21,300), mandatory fees ($360), and college room and board ($5460). *College room only:* $3060. Full-time tuition and fees vary according to student level. Room and board charges vary according to board plan, housing facility, and student level. *Part-time tuition:* $3000 per course. *Part-time mandatory fees:* $100.

Financial Aid Forms of aid include need-based and non-need-based scholarships and part-time jobs. The average aided 2002–03 undergraduate received an aid package worth $14,765. The priority application deadline for financial aid is February 15.

Freshman Admission Gustavus requires an essay, a high school transcript, 2 recommendations, SAT I or ACT scores, and TOEFL scores for international students. An interview is recommended. The application deadline for regular admission is April 1 and for early action it is November 1.

Transfer Admission The application deadline for admission is April 1.

Entrance Difficulty Gustavus assesses its entrance difficulty level as very difficult. For the fall 2003 freshman class, 77 percent of the applicants were accepted.

For Further Information Contact Mr. Mark H. Anderson, Dean of Admission, Gustavus Adolphus College, 800 West College Avenue, St. Peter, MN 56082-1498. *Telephone:* 507-933-7676 or 800-GUSTAVU(S) (toll-free). *Fax:* 507-933-7474. *E-mail:* admission@gac.edu. *Web site:* http://www.gustavus.edu/.

HAMLINE UNIVERSITY

St. Paul, Minnesota

Hamline is a coed, private, comprehensive institution, founded in 1854, affiliated with the United Methodist Church, offering degrees at the bachelor's, master's, doctoral, and first professional levels and post-master's, first professional, and postbachelor's certificates. It has a 50-acre campus in St. Paul.

Academic Information The faculty has 344 members (51% full-time), 77% with terminal degrees. The undergraduate student-faculty ratio is 13:1. The library holds 556,450 titles, 3,858 serial subscriptions, and 2,642 audiovisual materials. Special programs include academic remediation, services for learning-disabled students, an honors program, cooperative (work-study) education, study abroad, advanced placement credit, ESL programs, double majors, independent study, self-designed majors, summer session for credit, part-time degree programs, adult/continuing education programs, internships, and arrangement for off-campus study with members of the Associated Colleges of the Twin Cities, American University, Southern College Student Exchange Program, Higher Education Consortium for Urban Affairs, Drew University. The most frequently chosen baccalaureate fields are business/marketing, psychology, social sciences and history.

Student Body Statistics The student body totals 4,469, of whom 1,980 are undergraduates (455 freshmen). 63 percent are women and 37 percent are men. Students come from 27 states and territories and 21 other countries. 29 percent are from Minnesota. 3.4 percent are international students. 25 percent of the 2003 graduating class went on to graduate and professional schools.

Expenses for 2003–04 *Application fee:* $0. *One-time mandatory fee:* $100. *Comprehensive fee:* $27,052 includes full-time tuition ($20,582), mandatory fees ($250), and college room and board ($6220). *College room only:* $3208. Full-time tuition and fees vary according to student level. Room and board charges vary according to board plan and housing facility. *Part-time tuition:* $643 per credit. *Part-time mandatory fees:* $200 per term. Part-time tuition and fees vary according to course load and student level.

Financial Aid Forms of aid include need-based and non-need-based scholarships and part-time jobs. The average aided 2003–04 undergraduate received an aid package worth an estimated $21,606. The priority application deadline for financial aid is May 1.

Freshman Admission Hamline requires an essay, a high school transcript, 2 recommendations, SAT I or ACT scores, and TOEFL scores for international students. An interview and activity resume are recommended. The application deadline for regular admission is rolling and for early action it is December 1.

Transfer Admission The application deadline for admission is rolling.

Entrance Difficulty Hamline assesses its entrance difficulty level as moderately difficult. For the fall 2003 freshman class, 75 percent of the applicants were accepted.

For Further Information Contact Mr. Steven Bjork, Director of Undergraduate Admission, Hamline University, 1536 Hewitt Avenue C1930, St. Paul, MN 55104-1284. *Telephone:* 651-523-2207 or 800-753-9753 (toll-free). *Fax:* 651-523-2458. *E-mail:* cla-admis@gw.hamline.edu. *Web site:* http://www.hamline.edu/.

HERZING COLLEGE, MINNEAPOLIS DRAFTING SCHOOL DIVISION

Minneapolis, Minnesota

Herzing College, Minneapolis Drafting School Division is a coed, primarily women's, proprietary, primarily two-year college of Herzing College, offering degrees at the associate and bachelor's levels. It has a 1-acre campus in Minneapolis.

Academic Information The faculty has 32 members (66% full-time), 25% with terminal degrees. The student-faculty ratio is 14:1. Special programs include part-time degree programs (daytime, evenings) and adult/continuing education programs.

Student Body Statistics The student body is made up of 346 undergraduates (96 freshmen). 79 percent are women and 21 percent are men. Students come from 3 states and territories. 99 percent are from Minnesota.

Expenses for 2004–05 *Application fee:* $0. *Tuition:* $9680 full-time, $303 per credit part-time. *Mandatory fees:* $25 full-time. Full-time tuition and fees vary according to course load and program. Part-time tuition varies according to course load and program.

Freshman Admission Herzing College, Minneapolis Drafting School Division requires a high school transcript, an interview, and ACCUPLACER. SAT I and SAT II or ACT scores and SAT II: Writing Test scores are recommended.

Entrance Difficulty Herzing College, Minneapolis Drafting School Division has an open admission policy.

For Further Information Contact Mr. James Decker, Director of Admissions, Herzing College, Minneapolis Drafting School Division, 5700 West Broadway, Minneapolis, MN 55428. *Telephone:* 763-231-3152 or 800-878-DRAW (toll-free). *Fax:* 763-535-9205. *E-mail:* info@mpls.herzing.edu. *Web site:* http://www.herzing.edu/.

LEECH LAKE TRIBAL COLLEGE
Cass Lake, Minnesota

For Information Write to Leech Lake Tribal College, Cass Lake, MN 56633-0180.

LOWTHIAN COLLEGE
See The Art Institutes International Minnesota

MACALESTER COLLEGE
St. Paul, Minnesota

Mac is a coed, private, Presbyterian, four-year college, founded in 1874, offering degrees at the bachelor's level. It has a 53-acre campus in St. Paul.

Academic Information The faculty has 215 members (69% full-time), 83% with terminal degrees. The student-faculty ratio is 11:1. The library holds 407,321 titles, 2,119 serial subscriptions, and 9,288 audiovisual materials. Special programs include an honors program, study abroad, double majors, independent study, self-designed majors, part-time degree programs, internships, and arrangement for off-campus study with College of St. Catherine, University of St. Thomas, Augsburg College, Hamline University, Minneapolis College of Art and Design. The most frequently chosen baccalaureate fields are English, psychology, social sciences and history.

Student Body Statistics The student body is made up of 1,884 undergraduates (513 freshmen). 58 percent are women and 42 percent are men. Students come from 50 states and 86 other countries. 25 percent are from Minnesota. 14 percent are international students.

Expenses for 2004–05 *Application fee:* $40. *Comprehensive fee:* $34,156 includes full-time tuition ($26,638), mandatory fees ($168), and college room and board ($7350). *College room only:* $3820. Room and board charges vary according to housing facility.

Financial Aid Forms of aid include need-based and non-need-based scholarships and part-time jobs. The average aided 2003–04 undergraduate received an aid package worth an estimated $21,386. The priority application deadline for financial aid is February 9.

Freshman Admission Mac requires an essay, a high school transcript, 3 recommendations, SAT I or ACT scores, and TOEFL scores for international students. An interview is recommended. The application deadline for regular admission is January 15; for early decision plan 1 it is November 15; and for early decision plan 2 it is January 15.

Transfer Admission The application deadline for admission is April 1.

Entrance Difficulty Mac assesses its entrance difficulty level as very difficult. For the fall 2003 freshman class, 44 percent of the applicants were accepted.

For Further Information Contact Mr. Lorne T. Robinson, Dean of Admissions and Financial Aid, Macalester College, 1600 Grand Avenue, St. Paul, MN 55105-1899. *Telephone:* 651-696-6357 or 800-231-7974 (toll-free). *Fax:* 651-696-6724. *E-mail:* admissions@macalester.edu. *Web site:* http://www.macalester.edu/.

MANKATO STATE UNIVERSITY
See Minnesota State University Mankato

MARTIN LUTHER COLLEGE
New Ulm, Minnesota

MLC is a coed, private, four-year college, founded in 1995, affiliated with the Wisconsin Evangelical Lutheran Synod, offering degrees at the bachelor's level. It has a 50-acre campus in New Ulm.

Academic Information The faculty has 88 members (86% full-time), 44% with terminal degrees. The student-faculty ratio is 14:1. The library holds 115,309 titles, 519 serial subscriptions, and 5,786 audiovisual materials. Special programs include academic remediation, advanced placement credit, ESL programs, double majors, independent study, summer session for credit, and internships. The most frequently chosen baccalaureate fields are education, philosophy, religion, and theology.

Student Body Statistics The student body is made up of 1,020 undergraduates (222 freshmen). 49 percent are women and 51 percent are men. Students come from 35 states and territories and 9 other countries. 14 percent are from Minnesota. 1.1 percent are international students.

Expenses for 2004–05 *Application fee:* $25. *Comprehensive fee:* $11,800 includes full-time tuition ($8500) and college room and board ($3300). *Part-time tuition:* $190 per credit hour.

Financial Aid Forms of aid include need-based and non-need-based scholarships and part-time jobs. The average aided 2002–03 undergraduate received an aid package worth $5324. The application deadline for financial aid is April 15.

Freshman Admission MLC requires a high school transcript, a minimum 2.0 high school GPA, recommendations, ACT scores, and TOEFL scores for international students. The application deadline for regular admission is April 15.

Entrance Difficulty MLC assesses its entrance difficulty level as moderately difficult. For the fall 2003 freshman class, 98 percent of the applicants were accepted.

For Further Information Contact Prof. Ronald B. Brutlag, Associate Director of Admissions, Martin Luther College, 1995 Luther Court, New Ulm, MN 56073. *Telephone:* 507-354-8221 Ext. 211. *Fax:* 507-354-8225. *E-mail:* mlcadmit@mlc-wels.edu. *Web site:* http://www.mlc-wels.edu/.

MEDICAL INSTITUTE OF MINNESOTA
See Argosy University/Twin Cities

METROPOLITAN STATE UNIVERSITY
St. Paul, Minnesota

Metro State is a coed, public, comprehensive unit of Minnesota State Colleges and Universities System, founded in 1971, offering degrees at the bachelor's and master's levels (offers primarily part-time evening degree programs).

Academic Information The faculty has 439 members (26% full-time), 49% with terminal degrees. The undergraduate student-faculty ratio is 16:1. The library holds 9,856 titles, 235 serial subscriptions, and 507 audiovisual materials. Special programs include ESL programs, double

Minnesota

Metropolitan State University (continued)

majors, independent study, self-designed majors, summer session for credit, part-time degree programs (daytime, evenings, weekends, summer), external degree programs, adult/continuing education programs, internships, and arrangement for off-campus study with other colleges in the Minnesota State College and University System. The most frequently chosen baccalaureate fields are business/marketing, interdisciplinary studies, protective services/public administration.

Student Body Statistics The student body totals 6,467, of whom 5,936 are undergraduates (88 freshmen). 59 percent are women and 41 percent are men. Students come from 15 states and territories and 53 other countries. 98 percent are from Minnesota. 3.1 percent are international students. 23 percent of the 2003 graduating class went on to graduate and professional schools.

Expenses for 2003–04 *Application fee:* $20. *State resident tuition:* $3600 full-time, $120 per credit part-time. *Nonresident tuition:* $7980 full-time, $266 per credit part-time. *Mandatory fees:* $252 full-time, $8.39 per credit part-time. Full-time tuition and fees vary according to reciprocity agreements. Part-time tuition and fees vary according to course load and reciprocity agreements.

Financial Aid Forms of aid include need-based and non-need-based scholarships and part-time jobs. The average aided 2002–03 undergraduate received an aid package worth $8671. The priority application deadline for financial aid is June 1.

Freshman Admission Metro State requires a high school transcript, a minimum 2.0 high school GPA, and TOEFL scores for international students. SAT I or ACT scores are required for some. The application deadline for regular admission is June 28.

Transfer Admission The application deadline for admission is June 28.

Entrance Difficulty Metro State assesses its entrance difficulty level as minimally difficult. For the fall 2003 freshman class, 67 percent of the applicants were accepted.

For Further Information Contact Ms. Rosa Rodriguez, Interim Director, Metropolitan State University, 700 East 7th Street, St. Paul, MN 55106-5000. *Telephone:* 651-793-1303. *Fax:* 651-793-1310. *E-mail:* admissionsmetro@metrostate.edu. *Web site:* http://www.metrostate.edu/.

MINNEAPOLIS COLLEGE OF ART AND DESIGN

Minneapolis, Minnesota

MCAD is a coed, private, comprehensive institution, founded in 1886, offering degrees at the bachelor's and master's levels and postbachelor's certificates in art. It has a 7-acre campus in Minneapolis.

Academic Information The faculty has 95 members (42% full-time), 24% with terminal degrees. The undergraduate student-faculty ratio is 15:1. The library holds 47,166 titles, 196 serial subscriptions, and 139,245 audiovisual materials. Special programs include services for learning-disabled students, cooperative (work-study) education, study abroad, advanced placement credit, independent study, distance learning, summer session for credit, part-time degree programs, adult/continuing education programs, internships, and arrangement for off-campus study with members of the Association of Independent Colleges of Art and Design, Macalester College. The most frequently chosen baccalaureate field is visual/performing arts.

Student Body Statistics The student body totals 673, of whom 615 are undergraduates (117 freshmen). 46 percent are women and 54 percent are men. Students come from 37 states and territories. 10 percent of the 2003 graduating class went on to graduate and professional schools.

Expenses for 2003–04 *Application fee:* $35. *Comprehensive fee:* $28,170 includes full-time tuition ($22,400), mandatory fees ($370), and college room and board ($5400). *College room only:* $3600. Full-time tuition and fees vary according to student level. Room and board charges vary according to housing facility. *Part-time tuition:* $747 per credit. *Part-time mandatory fees:* $185 per term. Part-time tuition and fees vary according to course load and student level.

Financial Aid Forms of aid include need-based and non-need-based scholarships and part-time jobs. The average aided 2003–04 undergraduate received an aid package worth an estimated $11,794. The priority application deadline for financial aid is March 15.

Freshman Admission MCAD requires an essay, a high school transcript, 1 recommendation, SAT I or ACT scores, and TOEFL scores for international students. An interview is recommended. A portfolio is required for some. The application deadline for regular admission is rolling.

Transfer Admission The application deadline for admission is rolling.

Entrance Difficulty MCAD assesses its entrance difficulty level as moderately difficult. For the fall 2003 freshman class, 71 percent of the applicants were accepted.

For Further Information Contact Mr. William Mullen, Director of Admissions, Minneapolis College of Art and Design, 2501 Stevens Avenue South, Minneapolis, MN 55404. *Telephone:* 612-874-3762 or 800-874-6223 (toll-free). *Fax:* 612-874-3704. *E-mail:* admissions@mn.mcad.edu. *Web site:* http://www.mcad.edu/.

MINNESOTA BIBLE COLLEGE

See Crossroads College

MINNESOTA SCHOOL OF BUSINESS–BROOKLYN CENTER

Brooklyn Center, Minnesota

Minnesota School of Business–Brooklyn Center is a coed, proprietary, primarily two-year college, founded in 1989, offering degrees at the associate, bachelor's, and master's levels.

Academic Information The undergraduate student-faculty ratio is 16:1.

Student Body Statistics The student body is made up of 809 undergraduates.

Expenses for 2003–04 *Tuition:* $11,340 full-time, $315 per credit part-time.

For Further Information Contact Mr. Jeffrey Georgeson, Director of Admissions, Minnesota School of Business–Brooklyn Center, 5910 Shingle Creek Parkway, Brooklyn Center, MN 55430. *Telephone:* 763-585-7777. *Fax:* 763-566-7030. *Web site:* http://www.msbcollege.com/.

MINNESOTA SCHOOL OF BUSINESS-PLYMOUTH

Minneapolis, Minnesota

Minnesota School of Business-Plymouth is a coed, proprietary, primarily two-year college, founded in 2002, offering degrees at the associate, bachelor's, and master's levels. It has a 3-acre campus in Minneapolis.

Academic Information The undergraduate student-faculty ratio is 10:1.

Student Body Statistics The student body is made up of 500 undergraduates.

Expenses for 2003–04 *Tuition:* $11,340 full-time, $315 per credit part-time.

For Further Information Contact Mr. Don Baker, Director of Admissions, Minnesota School of Business-Plymouth, 1455 Country Road 101 North, Minneapolis, MN 55447. *Telephone:* 763-476-2000. *Web site:* http://www.msbcollege.edu/.

MINNESOTA SCHOOL OF BUSINESS-RICHFIELD

Richfield, Minnesota

MSB is a coed, proprietary, primarily two-year college, founded in 1877, offering degrees at the associate, bachelor's, and master's levels. It has a 3-acre campus in Richfield near Minneapolis–St. Paul.

Academic Information The undergraduate student-faculty ratio is 15:1. The library holds 3,000 titles and 5 serial subscriptions. Special programs include academic remediation, cooperative (work-study) education, accelerated degree programs, distance learning, adult/continuing education programs, and internships.
Student Body Statistics The student body is made up of 944 undergraduates. Students come from 5 states and territories.
Expenses for 2003–04 *Application fee:* $50. *Tuition:* $11,340 full-time, $315 per credit part-time.
Financial Aid Forms of aid include need-based scholarships. The application deadline for financial aid is continuous.
Freshman Admission MSB requires a high school transcript, an interview, and CPAt. An essay is required for some. The application deadline for regular admission is October 6.
Entrance Difficulty MSB has an open admission policy.

For Further Information Contact Ms. Patricia Murray, Director of Admissions, Minnesota School of Business-Richfield, 1401 West 76th Street, Richfield, MN 55430. *Telephone:* 612-861-2000 Ext. 720 or 800-752-4223 (toll-free in-state). *Fax:* 612-861-5548. *E-mail:* rkuhl@msbcollege.com. *Web site:* http://www.msbcollege.edu/.

MINNESOTA STATE UNIVERSITY MANKATO

Mankato, Minnesota

Mankato State is a coed, public, comprehensive unit of Minnesota State Colleges and Universities System, founded in 1868, offering degrees at the associate, bachelor's, and master's levels and post-master's certificates. It has a 303-acre campus in Mankato near Minneapolis–St. Paul.

Academic Information The faculty has 633 members (72% full-time), 57% with terminal degrees. The undergraduate student-faculty ratio is 24:1. The library holds 468,567 titles, 3,275 serial subscriptions, and 31,078 audiovisual materials. Special programs include academic remediation, services for learning-disabled students, an honors program, study abroad, advanced placement credit, ESL programs, double majors, independent study, distance learning, self-designed majors, summer session for credit, part-time degree programs (daytime, evenings, weekends, summer), adult/continuing education programs, internships, and arrangement for off-campus study with other colleges in the Minnesota State College and University System. The most frequently chosen baccalaureate fields are business/marketing, education, health professions and related sciences.
Student Body Statistics The student body totals 14,065, of whom 12,390 are undergraduates (2,287 freshmen). 53 percent are women and 47 percent are men. Students come from 44 states and territories and 65 other countries. 87 percent are from Minnesota. 3.6 percent are international students. 8 percent of the 2003 graduating class went on to graduate and professional schools.
Expenses for 2003–04 *Application fee:* $20. *State resident tuition:* $3806 full-time, $152 per credit part-time. *Nonresident tuition:* $8075 full-time, $322 per credit part-time. *Mandatory fees:* $700 full-time, $29.09 per credit part-time. Full-time tuition and fees vary according to course load and reciprocity agreements. Part-time tuition and fees vary according to course load and reciprocity agreements. *College room and board:* $4297. Room and board charges vary according to board plan.
Financial Aid Forms of aid include need-based and non-need-based scholarships, athletic grants, and part-time jobs. The average aided 2003–04 undergraduate received an aid package worth an estimated $6417. The priority application deadline for financial aid is March 15.

Freshman Admission Mankato State requires a high school transcript, ACT scores, and TOEFL scores for international students. An essay and 3 recommendations are required for some. The application deadline for regular admission is rolling.
Transfer Admission The application deadline for admission is rolling.
Entrance Difficulty Mankato State assesses its entrance difficulty level as moderately difficult. For the fall 2003 freshman class, 88 percent of the applicants were accepted.

For Further Information Contact Mr. Walt Wolff, Director of Admissions, Minnesota State University Mankato, 122 Taylor Center, Mankato, MN 56001. *Telephone:* 507-389-6670 or 800-722-0544 (toll-free). *Fax:* 507-389-1511. *E-mail:* admissions@mnsu.edu. *Web site:* http://www.mnsu.edu/.

MINNESOTA STATE UNIVERSITY MOORHEAD

Moorhead, Minnesota

Minnesota State University Moorhead is a coed, public, comprehensive unit of Minnesota State Colleges and Universities System, founded in 1885, offering degrees at the associate, bachelor's, and master's levels and post-master's certificates. It has a 118-acre campus in Moorhead.

Academic Information The faculty has 315 members, 79% with terminal degrees. The undergraduate student-faculty ratio is 23:1. The library holds 367,334 titles and 1,539 serial subscriptions. Special programs include academic remediation, services for learning-disabled students, an honors program, study abroad, advanced placement credit, Freshman Honors College, double majors, independent study, distance learning, self-designed majors, summer session for credit, part-time degree programs (daytime, evenings, weekends, summer), external degree programs, adult/continuing education programs, internships, and arrangement for off-campus study with North Dakota State University, Concordia College (Moorhead, MN), other colleges of the Minnesota State Colleges and Universities System. The most frequently chosen baccalaureate fields are business/marketing, education, protective services/public administration.
Student Body Statistics The student body totals 7,695, of whom 7,282 are undergraduates (1,291 freshmen). 61 percent are women and 39 percent are men. Students come from 34 states and territories and 32 other countries. 62 percent are from Minnesota. 2.6 percent are international students. 6.9 percent of the 2003 graduating class went on to graduate and professional schools.
Expenses for 2003–04 *Application fee:* $20. *State resident tuition:* $3628 full-time, $120.92 per credit hour part-time. *Nonresident tuition:* $3628 full-time, $120.92 per credit hour part-time. *Mandatory fees:* $626 full-time, $25.99 per credit part-time. *College room and board:* $4340. *College room only:* $2560.
Financial Aid Forms of aid include need-based and non-need-based scholarships, athletic grants, and part-time jobs. The average aided 2003–04 undergraduate received an aid package worth an estimated $4193. The priority application deadline for financial aid is March 1.
Freshman Admission Minnesota State University Moorhead requires a high school transcript, SAT I or ACT scores, TOEFL scores for international students, and PSAT. The application deadline for regular admission is August 7.
Transfer Admission The application deadline for admission is August 7.
Entrance Difficulty Minnesota State University Moorhead assesses its entrance difficulty level as moderately difficult. For the fall 2003 freshman class, 86 percent of the applicants were accepted.

For Further Information Contact Ms. Gina Monson, Director of Admissions, Minnesota State University Moorhead, Owens Hall, Moorhead, MN 56563-0002. *Telephone:* 218-477-2161 or 800-593-7246 (toll-free). *Fax:* 218-236-2168. *Web site:* http://www.mnstate.edu/.

NATIONAL AMERICAN UNIVERSITY

Roseville, Minnesota

For Information Write to National American University, Roseville, MN 55113-4035.

NORTH CENTRAL UNIVERSITY

Minneapolis, Minnesota

North Central is a coed, private, four-year college, founded in 1930, affiliated with the Assemblies of God, offering degrees at the associate and bachelor's levels. It has a 9-acre campus in Minneapolis.

Academic Information The faculty has 97 members (41% full-time). The student-faculty ratio is 18:1. The library holds 70,041 titles and 384 serial subscriptions. Special programs include academic remediation, services for learning-disabled students, cooperative (work-study) education, study abroad, advanced placement credit, self-designed majors, summer session for credit, part-time degree programs (daytime, evenings, weekends, summer), external degree programs, adult/continuing education programs, internships, and arrangement for off-campus study. The most frequently chosen baccalaureate fields are philosophy, religion, and theology, education, psychology.
Student Body Statistics The student body is made up of 1,227 undergraduates (275 freshmen). 50 percent are women and 50 percent are men. Students come from 40 states and territories and 11 other countries. 50 percent are from Minnesota. 1.3 percent are international students.
Expenses for 2003–04 *Application fee:* $25. *Comprehensive fee:* $15,274 includes full-time tuition ($9840), mandatory fees ($754), and college room and board ($4680). *College room only:* $1950. Room and board charges vary according to board plan and housing facility.
Financial Aid Forms of aid include need-based and non-need-based scholarships and part-time jobs. The application deadline for financial aid is continuous.
Freshman Admission North Central requires an essay, a high school transcript, a minimum 2.2 high school GPA, recommendations, Christian testimony, SAT I or ACT scores, and TOEFL scores for international students. The application deadline for regular admission is June 1.
Transfer Admission The application deadline for admission is June 1.
Entrance Difficulty North Central assesses its entrance difficulty level as noncompetitive. For the fall 2003 freshman class, 55 percent of the applicants were accepted.

For Further Information Contact Ms. Linda Kammerer, Admissions Secretary, North Central University, 910 Elliot Avenue, Minneapolis, MN 55404. *Telephone:* 612-343-4480 or 800-289-6222 (toll-free). *Fax:* 612-343-4146. *E-mail:* admissions@northcentral.edu. *Web site:* http://www.northcentral.edu/.

NORTHWESTERN COLLEGE

St. Paul, Minnesota

Northwestern is a coed, private, nondenominational, four-year college, founded in 1902, offering degrees at the associate and bachelor's levels. It has a 100-acre campus in St. Paul.

Academic Information The faculty has 156 members (54% full-time), 46% with terminal degrees. The student-faculty ratio is 16:1. The library holds 75,082 titles, 560 serial subscriptions, and 3,716 audiovisual materials. Special programs include academic remediation, an honors program, study abroad, advanced placement credit, ESL programs, double majors, independent study, distance learning, summer session for credit, part-time degree programs (evenings, weekends), adult/continuing education programs, internships, and arrangement for off-campus study with Coalition for Christian Colleges and Universities, Focus on the Family Institute, William Mitchell College of Law. The most frequently chosen baccalaureate fields are business/marketing, education, philosophy, religion, and theology.
Student Body Statistics The student body is made up of 2,592 undergraduates (459 freshmen). 63 percent are women and 37 percent are men. Students come from 32 states and territories. 72 percent are from Minnesota. 0.4 percent are international students. 8 percent of the 2003 graduating class went on to graduate and professional schools.
Expenses for 2004–05 *Application fee:* $25. *Comprehensive fee:* $24,390 includes full-time tuition ($18,370) and college room and board ($6020). *College room only:* $3300. Full-time tuition varies according to course load. Room and board charges vary according to board plan. *Part-time tuition:* $775 per credit. Part-time tuition varies according to course load.
Financial Aid Forms of aid include need-based and non-need-based scholarships and part-time jobs. The average aided 2002–03 undergraduate received an aid package worth $13,037. The application deadline for financial aid is June 1 with a priority deadline of March 1.
Freshman Admission Northwestern requires an essay, a high school transcript, a minimum 2.0 high school GPA, 2 recommendations, lifestyle agreement, statement of Christian faith, SAT I or ACT scores, and TOEFL scores for international students. A minimum 3.0 high school GPA is recommended. An interview is required for some. The application deadline for regular admission is August 1.
Transfer Admission The application deadline for admission is August 1.
Entrance Difficulty Northwestern assesses its entrance difficulty level as moderately difficult. For the fall 2003 freshman class, 94 percent of the applicants were accepted.

For Further Information Contact Mr. Kenneth K. Faffler, Director of Admissions, Northwestern College, 3003 Snelling Avenue North, Nazareth Hall, Room 2122, St. Paul, MN 55113-1598. *Telephone:* 651-631-5492 or 800-827-6827 (toll-free). *Fax:* 651-631-5680. *E-mail:* admissions@nwc.edu. *Web site:* http://www.nwc.edu/.

OAK HILLS CHRISTIAN COLLEGE

Bemidji, Minnesota

Oak Hills is a coed, private, interdenominational, four-year college, founded in 1946, offering degrees at the associate and bachelor's levels. It has a 180-acre campus in Bemidji.

Academic Information The faculty has 19 members (37% full-time), 21% with terminal degrees. The student-faculty ratio is 18:1. The library holds 25,079 titles, 99 serial subscriptions, and 1,338 audiovisual materials. Special programs include academic remediation, services for learning-disabled students, an honors program, advanced placement credit, double majors, independent study, part-time degree programs (daytime, evenings), internships, and arrangement for off-campus study with Bemidji State University, Crown College.
Student Body Statistics The student body is made up of 168 undergraduates (31 freshmen). 48 percent are women and 52 percent are men. Students come from 12 states and territories. 75 percent are from Minnesota.
Expenses for 2003–04 *Application fee:* $20. *Comprehensive fee:* $13,990 includes full-time tuition ($10,180) and college room and board ($3810). *College room only:* $1830. Full-time tuition varies according to course load. Room and board charges vary according to board plan and housing facility. *Part-time tuition:* $125 per semester hour. Part-time tuition varies according to course load.
Financial Aid Forms of aid include need-based and non-need-based scholarships and part-time jobs. The average aided 2002–03 undergraduate received an aid package worth $9306. The application deadline for financial aid is continuous.
Freshman Admission Oak Hills requires an essay, a high school transcript, 2 recommendations, and ACT scores. A minimum 2.0 high school GPA is required for some. The application deadline for regular admission is rolling.
Transfer Admission The application deadline for admission is rolling.
Entrance Difficulty Oak Hills assesses its entrance difficulty level as minimally difficult. For the fall 2003 freshman class, 90 percent of the applicants were accepted.

For Further Information Contact Mr. Dan Hovestol, Admissions Director, Oak Hills Christian College, Bemidji, MN 56601. *Telephone:* 218-751-8670 Ext. 1285 or 888-751-8670 Ext. 285 (toll-free). *Fax:* 218-751-8825. *E-mail:* admissions@oakhills.edu. *Web site:* http://www.oakhills.edu/.

PILLSBURY BAPTIST BIBLE COLLEGE
Owatonna, Minnesota

Pillsbury is a coed, private, Baptist, four-year college, founded in 1957, offering degrees at the associate and bachelor's levels. It has a 14-acre campus in Owatonna near Minneapolis–St. Paul.

Academic Information The faculty has 27 members (70% full-time), 4% with terminal degrees. The student-faculty ratio is 8:1. The library holds 52,340 titles, 245 serial subscriptions, and 817 audiovisual materials. Special programs include academic remediation, services for learning-disabled students, advanced placement credit, accelerated degree programs, double majors, independent study, summer session for credit, part-time degree programs (daytime, evenings, summer), and internships. The most frequently chosen baccalaureate fields are education, business/marketing, philosophy, religion, and theology.
Student Body Statistics The student body is made up of 191 undergraduates (45 freshmen). 55 percent are women and 45 percent are men. Students come from 20 states and territories. 72 percent are from Minnesota.
Expenses for 2003–04 *Application fee:* $25. *Comprehensive fee:* $11,720 includes full-time tuition ($6560), mandatory fees ($1560), and college room and board ($3600). *Part-time tuition:* $205 per credit hour. *Part-time mandatory fees:* $896 per year. Part-time tuition and fees vary according to course load.
Financial Aid Forms of aid include need-based and non-need-based scholarships. The application deadline for financial aid is continuous.
Freshman Admission Pillsbury requires an essay, a high school transcript, 2 recommendations, 2 photographs, ACT scores, and TOEFL scores for international students. An interview is recommended. The application deadline for regular admission is August 20.
Transfer Admission The application deadline for admission is August 20.
Entrance Difficulty Pillsbury has an open admission policy.

For Further Information Contact Mr. Steve Seidler, Director of Admissions, Pillsbury Baptist Bible College, 315 South Grove Avenue, Owatonna, MN 55060-3097. *Telephone:* 507-451-2710 Ext. 279 or 800-747-4557 (toll-free). *Fax:* 507-451-6459. *E-mail:* pbbc@pillsbury.edu. *Web site:* http://www.pillsbury.edu/.

ROCHESTER COMMUNITY AND TECHNICAL COLLEGE
Rochester, Minnesota

RCTC is a coed, public, primarily two-year college of Minnesota State Colleges and Universities System, founded in 1915, offering degrees at the associate and bachelor's levels (also offers 13 programs that lead to a bachelor's degree with Winona State University or University of Minnesota). It has a 460-acre campus in Rochester.

Academic Information The faculty has 225 members (41% full-time). The library holds 62,000 titles and 600 serial subscriptions. Special programs include academic remediation, services for learning-disabled students, an honors program, advanced placement credit, ESL programs, independent study, distance learning, summer session for credit, part-time degree programs (daytime, evenings, weekends, summer), internships, and arrangement for off-campus study with other colleges in the Minnesota State Colleges and Universities System, Winona State University–Rochester Center.
Student Body Statistics The student body is made up of 5,862 undergraduates. Students come from 39 states and territories and 36 other countries. 90 percent are from Minnesota.
Expenses for 2003–04 *Application fee:* $20. *State resident tuition:* $2823 full-time, $117 per credit part-time. *Nonresident tuition:* $5257 full-time, $219.03 per credit part-time.
Financial Aid Forms of aid include need-based scholarships and part-time jobs. The application deadline for financial aid is continuous.
Freshman Admission RCTC requires a high school transcript and TOEFL scores for international students. The application deadline for regular admission is August 24.

Transfer Admission The application deadline for admission is August 24.
Entrance Difficulty RCTC has an open admission policy except for allied health, technology programs. It assesses its entrance difficulty as moderately difficult for allied health programs.

For Further Information Contact Mr. Troy Tynsky, Director of Admissions, Rochester Community and Technical College, 851 30th Avenue, SE, Rochester, MN 55904-4999. *Telephone:* 507-280-3509. *Fax:* 507-285-7496. *Web site:* http://www.roch.edu/.

ST. CLOUD STATE UNIVERSITY
St. Cloud, Minnesota

SCSU is a coed, public, comprehensive unit of Minnesota State Colleges and Universities System, founded in 1869, offering degrees at the associate, bachelor's, and master's levels and first professional and postbachelor's certificates. It has a 922-acre campus in St. Cloud near Minneapolis–St. Paul.

Academic Information The faculty has 793 members (79% full-time), 69% with terminal degrees. The undergraduate student-faculty ratio is 19:1. The library holds 560,251 titles, 1,487 serial subscriptions, and 33,900 audiovisual materials. Special programs include academic remediation, services for learning-disabled students, an honors program, study abroad, advanced placement credit, accelerated degree programs, ESL programs, double majors, independent study, distance learning, self-designed majors, summer session for credit, part-time degree programs (daytime, evenings, weekends, summer), adult/continuing education programs, internships, and arrangement for off-campus study with members of the Tri-College Exchange Program, other colleges in the Minnesota State Colleges and University System. The most frequently chosen baccalaureate fields are business/marketing, education, social sciences and history.
Student Body Statistics The student body totals 15,925, of whom 14,483 are undergraduates (2,298 freshmen). 55 percent are women and 45 percent are men. Students come from 50 states and territories and 85 other countries. 91 percent are from Minnesota. 5 percent are international students.
Expenses for 2003–04 *Application fee:* $20. *State resident tuition:* $3980 full-time, $132.65 per credit part-time. *Nonresident tuition:* $8639 full-time, $287.95 per credit part-time. *Mandatory fees:* $570 full-time, $23.77 per credit part-time. Full-time tuition and fees vary according to course load and reciprocity agreements. Part-time tuition and fees vary according to course load and reciprocity agreements. *College room and board:* $3812. *College room only:* $2548. Room and board charges vary according to board plan and housing facility.
Financial Aid Forms of aid include need-based and non-need-based scholarships, athletic grants, and part-time jobs. The average aided 2003–04 undergraduate received an aid package worth an estimated $6590. The priority application deadline for financial aid is May 1.
Freshman Admission SCSU requires a high school transcript, SAT I or ACT scores, and TOEFL scores for international students. Recommendations are required for some. The application deadline for regular admission is June 1.
Transfer Admission The application deadline for admission is July 11.
Entrance Difficulty SCSU assesses its entrance difficulty level as moderately difficult; most difficult for honors program. For the fall 2003 freshman class, 76 percent of the applicants were accepted.

For Further Information Contact Pat Krueger, Associate Director of Admissions, St. Cloud State University, 115 AS Building, 720 4th Avenue South, St. Cloud, MN 56301-4498. *Telephone:* 320-308-2244 or 877-654-7278 (toll-free). *Fax:* 320-308-2243. *E-mail:* scsu4u@stcloudstate.edu. *Web site:* http://www.stcloudstate.edu/.

SAINT JOHN'S UNIVERSITY
Collegeville, Minnesota

St. John's is a coed, primarily men's, private, Roman Catholic, comprehensive institution, founded in 1857, coordinate with College of Saint Benedict, offering degrees at the bachelor's, master's, and first professional levels (coordinate with College of Saint Benedict for women). It has a 2,400-acre campus in Collegeville near Minneapolis–St. Paul.

Academic Information The faculty has 167 members (89% full-time), 83% with terminal degrees. The undergraduate student-faculty ratio is 13:1. The library holds 805,376 titles, 5,735 serial subscriptions, and 22,452 audiovisual materials. Special programs include services for learning-disabled students, an honors program, study abroad, advanced placement credit, accelerated degree programs, ESL programs, double majors, independent study, self-designed majors, internships, and arrangement for off-campus study with College of Saint Benedict, Tri-College Exchange Program. The most frequently chosen baccalaureate fields are business/marketing, English, social sciences and history.
Student Body Statistics The student body totals 2,067, of whom 1,940 are undergraduates (490 freshmen). 100 percent are men. Students come from 34 states and territories and 25 other countries. 86 percent are from Minnesota. 3.5 percent are international students. 16 percent of the 2003 graduating class went on to graduate and professional schools.
Expenses for 2003–04 *Application fee:* $30. *Comprehensive fee:* $26,473 includes full-time tuition ($20,335), mandatory fees ($350), and college room and board ($5788). *College room only:* $2900. Room and board charges vary according to board plan and housing facility. *Part-time tuition:* $847 per credit. *Part-time mandatory fees:* $175 per term. Part-time tuition and fees vary according to course load.
Financial Aid Forms of aid include need-based and non-need-based scholarships and part-time jobs. The average aided 2003–04 undergraduate received an aid package worth an estimated $17,585. The priority application deadline for financial aid is March 15.
Freshman Admission St. John's requires an essay, a high school transcript, 1 recommendation, SAT I or ACT scores, and TOEFL scores for international students. A minimum 3.0 high school GPA and an interview are recommended. The application deadline for regular admission is January 15 and for early action it is December 1.
Transfer Admission The application deadline for admission is rolling.
Entrance Difficulty St. John's assesses its entrance difficulty level as moderately difficult. For the fall 2003 freshman class, 89 percent of the applicants were accepted.

For Further Information Contact Ms. Renee Miller, Director of Admission, Saint John's University, PO Box 7155, Collegeville, MN 56321-7155. *Telephone:* 320-363-2196 or 800-544-1489 (toll-free). *Fax:* 320-363-2750. *E-mail:* admissions@csbsju.edu. *Web site:* http://www.csbsju.edu/.

SAINT MARY'S UNIVERSITY OF MINNESOTA
Winona, Minnesota

Saint Mary's is a coed, private, Roman Catholic, comprehensive institution, founded in 1912, offering degrees at the bachelor's, master's, and doctoral levels and post-master's and postbachelor's certificates. It has a 350-acre campus in Winona.

Academic Information The faculty has 553 members (20% full-time), 69% with terminal degrees. The undergraduate student-faculty ratio is 13:1. The library holds 130,944 titles, 708 serial subscriptions, and 8,281 audiovisual materials. Special programs include academic remediation, services for learning-disabled students, an honors program, study abroad, advanced placement credit, accelerated degree programs, ESL programs, double majors, independent study, self-designed majors, summer session for credit, part-time degree programs (daytime, evenings, summer), adult/continuing education programs, internships, and arrangement for off-campus study with Winona State University. The most frequently chosen baccalaureate fields are biological/life sciences, business/marketing, communications/communication technologies.
Student Body Statistics The student body totals 4,996, of whom 1,704 are undergraduates (369 freshmen). 55 percent are women and 45 percent are men. Students come from 25 states and territories. 61 percent are from Minnesota. 0.6 percent are international students. 36 percent of the 2003 graduating class went on to graduate and professional schools.
Expenses for 2004–05 *Application fee:* $25. *Comprehensive fee:* $23,375 includes full-time tuition ($17,480), mandatory fees ($445), and college room and board ($5450). *College room only:* $3050. Full-time tuition and fees vary according to course load and program. Room and board charges vary according to housing facility. *Part-time tuition:* $580 per credit. Part-time tuition varies according to course load and program.
Financial Aid Forms of aid include need-based and non-need-based scholarships and part-time jobs. The average aided 2003–04 undergraduate received an aid package worth an estimated $13,719. The priority application deadline for financial aid is March 15.
Freshman Admission Saint Mary's requires an essay, a high school transcript, a minimum 2.5 high school GPA, SAT I or ACT scores, and TOEFL scores for international students. 2 recommendations are recommended. An interview is required for some. The application deadline for regular admission is May 1.
Transfer Admission The application deadline for admission is rolling.
Entrance Difficulty Saint Mary's assesses its entrance difficulty level as moderately difficult. For the fall 2003 freshman class, 75 percent of the applicants were accepted.

For Further Information Contact Mr. Anthony M. Piscitiello, Vice President for Admission, Saint Mary's University of Minnesota, Admissions, 700 Terrace Heights, Winona, MN 55987-1399. *Telephone:* 507-457-1700 or 800-635-5987 (toll-free). *Fax:* 507-457-1722. *E-mail:* admissions@smumn.edu. *Web site:* http://www.smumn.edu/.

ST. OLAF COLLEGE
Northfield, Minnesota

St. Olaf is a coed, private, Lutheran, four-year college, founded in 1874, offering degrees at the bachelor's level. It has a 300-acre campus in Northfield near Minneapolis-St. Paul.

Academic Information The faculty has 334 members (62% full-time), 76% with terminal degrees. The student-faculty ratio is 12:1. The library holds 654,950 titles, 1,616 serial subscriptions, and 16,194 audiovisual materials. Special programs include services for learning-disabled students, study abroad, advanced placement credit, double majors, independent study, self-designed majors, summer session for credit, part-time degree programs (daytime), internships, and arrangement for off-campus study with Carleton College, Augsburg College, Minnesota Intercollegiate Nursing Consortium, Washington University. The most frequently chosen baccalaureate fields are social sciences and history, biological/life sciences, visual/performing arts.
Student Body Statistics The student body is made up of 2,994 undergraduates (720 freshmen). 59 percent are women and 41 percent are men. Students come from 49 states and territories and 22 other countries. 55 percent are from Minnesota. 1 percent are international students. 27 percent of the 2003 graduating class went on to graduate and professional schools.
Expenses for 2004–05 *Application fee:* $35. *Comprehensive fee:* $30,950 includes full-time tuition ($25,150) and college room and board ($5800). *College room only:* $2750. Room and board charges vary according to board plan. *Part-time tuition:* $785 per credit hour.
Financial Aid Forms of aid include need-based and non-need-based scholarships and part-time jobs. The average aided 2003–04 undergraduate received an aid package worth an estimated $18,172. The priority application deadline for financial aid is February 15.
Freshman Admission St. Olaf requires an essay, a high school transcript, 2 recommendations, SAT I or ACT scores, and TOEFL scores for international students. An interview is recommended. The application deadline for regular admission is rolling; for early decision it is November 15; and for early action it is December 15.

Entrance Difficulty St. Olaf assesses its entrance difficulty level as very difficult. For the fall 2003 freshman class, 75 percent of the applicants were accepted.

For Further Information Contact Mr. Jeff McLaughlin, Director of Admissions, St. Olaf College, 1520 St. Olaf Avenue, Northfield, MN 55057. *Telephone:* 507-646-3025 or 800-800-3025 (toll-free). *Fax:* 507-646-3832. *E-mail:* admiss@stolaf.edu. *Web site:* http://www.stolaf.edu/.

SOUTHWEST MINNESOTA STATE UNIVERSITY

Marshall, Minnesota

SSU is a coed, public, comprehensive unit of Minnesota State Colleges and Universities System, founded in 1963, offering degrees at the associate, bachelor's, and master's levels. It has a 216-acre campus in Marshall.

Expenses for 2003–04 *Application fee:* $20. *State resident tuition:* $3945 full-time. *Nonresident tuition:* $3945 full-time. *Mandatory fees:* $670 full-time. *College room and board:* $4491.

For Further Information Contact Richard Shearer, Director of Enrollment Services, Southwest Minnesota State University, 1501 State Street, Marshall, MN 56258-1598. *Telephone:* 507-537-6286 or 800-642-0684 (toll-free). *Fax:* 507-537-7154. *E-mail:* shearerr@southwest.msus.edu. *Web site:* http://www.southwest.msus.edu/.

UNIVERSITY OF MINNESOTA, CROOKSTON

Crookston, Minnesota

UMC is a coed, public, four-year college of University of Minnesota System, founded in 1966, offering degrees at the associate and bachelor's levels. It has a 95-acre campus in Crookston.

Academic Information The faculty has 100 members (55% full-time), 42% with terminal degrees. The student-faculty ratio is 15:1. The library holds 30,000 titles and 700 serial subscriptions. Special programs include academic remediation, services for learning-disabled students, study abroad, advanced placement credit, double majors, independent study, distance learning, summer session for credit, part-time degree programs, adult/continuing education programs, and internships. The most frequently chosen baccalaureate fields are agriculture, business/marketing, computer/information sciences.

Student Body Statistics The student body is made up of 2,320 undergraduates (247 freshmen). 52 percent are women and 48 percent are men. Students come from 38 states and territories and 13 other countries. 72 percent are from Minnesota. 2.9 percent are international students.

Expenses for 2003–04 *Application fee:* $25. *State resident tuition:* $5471 full-time, $162.38 per credit part-time. *Nonresident tuition:* $5471 full-time, $162.38 per credit part-time. *Mandatory fees:* $1309 full-time. Full-time tuition and fees vary according to reciprocity agreements. Part-time tuition varies according to course load. *College room and board:* $4684. Room and board charges vary according to board plan and housing facility.

Financial Aid Forms of aid include need-based and non-need-based scholarships, athletic grants, and part-time jobs. The average aided 2002–03 undergraduate received an aid package worth $8856. The priority application deadline for financial aid is March 31.

Freshman Admission UMC requires a high school transcript, ACT scores, and TOEFL scores for international students. The application deadline for regular admission is July 15.

Transfer Admission The application deadline for admission is July 15.

Entrance Difficulty UMC assesses its entrance difficulty level as moderately difficult. For the fall 2003 freshman class, 89 percent of the applicants were accepted.

For Further Information Contact Mr. Russell L. Kreager, Director of Admissions, University of Minnesota, Crookston, 2900 University Avenue, 170 Owen Hall, Crookston, MN 56716-5001. *Telephone:* 218-281-8569 or 800-862-6466 (toll-free). *Fax:* 218-281-8575. *E-mail:* info@mail.crk.umn.edu. *Web site:* http://www.crk.umn.edu/.

UNIVERSITY OF MINNESOTA, DULUTH

Duluth, Minnesota

UMD is a coed, public, comprehensive unit of University of Minnesota System, founded in 1947, offering degrees at the bachelor's, master's, and first professional levels. It has a 250-acre campus in Duluth.

Academic Information The faculty has 467 members (78% full-time), 76% with terminal degrees. The undergraduate student-faculty ratio is 22:1. The library holds 709,145 titles, 4,500 serial subscriptions, and 15,245 audiovisual materials. Special programs include academic remediation, services for learning-disabled students, an honors program, study abroad, advanced placement credit, ESL programs, double majors, independent study, distance learning, self-designed majors, summer session for credit, part-time degree programs (daytime, evenings, summer), adult/continuing education programs, internships, and arrangement for off-campus study with University of Wisconsin-Superior, College of St. Scholastica. The most frequently chosen baccalaureate fields are biological/life sciences, business/marketing, education.

Student Body Statistics The student body totals 10,114, of whom 9,288 are undergraduates (2,194 freshmen). 49 percent are women and 51 percent are men. Students come from 36 states and territories and 32 other countries. 88 percent are from Minnesota. 2.5 percent are international students. 20 percent of the 2003 graduating class went on to graduate and professional schools.

Expenses for 2003–04 *Application fee:* $35. *State resident tuition:* $6047 full-time, $201 per credit part-time. *Nonresident tuition:* $16,412 full-time, $547 per credit part-time. *Mandatory fees:* $1323 full-time, $661 per term part-time. Full-time tuition and fees vary according to course load, degree level, program, and reciprocity agreements. Part-time tuition and fees vary according to course load, degree level, program, and reciprocity agreements. *College room and board:* $5100.

Financial Aid Forms of aid include need-based scholarships, athletic grants, and part-time jobs. The average aided 2003–04 undergraduate received an aid package worth an estimated $7662. The priority application deadline for financial aid is March 1.

Freshman Admission UMD requires a high school transcript, SAT I or ACT scores, and TOEFL scores for international students. The application deadline for regular admission is February 1.

Transfer Admission The application deadline for admission is August 1.

Entrance Difficulty UMD assesses its entrance difficulty level as moderately difficult. For the fall 2003 freshman class, 74 percent of the applicants were accepted.

For Further Information Contact Ms. Beth Esselstrom, Director of Admissions, University of Minnesota, Duluth, 23 Solon Campus Center, 1117 University Drive, Duluth, MN 55812-3000. *Telephone:* 218-726-7171 or 800-232-1339 (toll-free). *Fax:* 218-726-7040. *E-mail:* umdadmis@d.umn.edu. *Web site:* http://www.d.umn.edu/.

UNIVERSITY OF MINNESOTA, MORRIS

Morris, Minnesota

UMM is a coed, public, four-year college of University of Minnesota System, founded in 1959, offering degrees at the bachelor's level. It has a 130-acre campus in Morris.

Academic Information The faculty has 132 members, 94% with terminal degrees. The student-faculty ratio is 14:1. The library holds 191,469 titles, 9,042 serial subscriptions, and 2,140 audiovisual materials. Special programs include services for learning-disabled students, an honors

University of Minnesota, Morris (continued)

program, study abroad, advanced placement credit, accelerated degree programs, Freshman Honors College, ESL programs, double majors, distance learning, self-designed majors, summer session for credit, part-time degree programs (daytime, summer), external degree programs, adult/continuing education programs, internships, and arrangement for off-campus study with other units of the University of Minnesota System. The most frequently chosen baccalaureate fields are education, biological/life sciences, psychology.

Student Body Statistics The student body is made up of 1,861 undergraduates (412 freshmen). 60 percent are women and 40 percent are men. Students come from 31 states and territories and 18 other countries. 83 percent are from Minnesota. 1.1 percent are international students. 30 percent of the 2003 graduating class went on to graduate and professional schools.

Expenses for 2003–04 *Application fee:* $35. *State resident tuition:* $6908 full-time, $230.25 per credit part-time. *Nonresident tuition:* $6908 full-time, $230.25 per credit part-time. *Mandatory fees:* $1188 full-time. Full-time tuition and fees vary according to reciprocity agreements. Part-time tuition varies according to course load and reciprocity agreements. *College room and board:* $4800. *College room only:* $2260. Room and board charges vary according to board plan and housing facility.

Financial Aid Forms of aid include need-based and non-need-based scholarships, athletic grants, and part-time jobs. The average aided 2002–03 undergraduate received an aid package worth $9754. The priority application deadline for financial aid is March 1.

Freshman Admission UMM requires an essay, a high school transcript, SAT I or ACT scores, and TOEFL scores for international students. A minimum 3.0 high school GPA is recommended. An interview is required for some. The application deadline for regular admission is March 15 and for early action it is December 1.

Transfer Admission The application deadline for admission is May 1.

Entrance Difficulty UMM assesses its entrance difficulty level as moderately difficult. For the fall 2003 freshman class, 83 percent of the applicants were accepted.

For Further Information Contact Dr. James Mootz, Associate Vice Chancellor for Enrollment, University of Minnesota, Morris, 600 East 4th Street, Morris, MN 56267-2199. *Telephone:* 320-539-6035 or 800-992-8863 (toll-free). *Fax:* 320-589-1673. *E-mail:* admissions@mrs.umn.edu. *Web site:* http://www.mrs.umn.edu/.

UNIVERSITY OF MINNESOTA, TWIN CITIES CAMPUS

Minneapolis, Minnesota

U of M-Twin Cities Campus is a coed, public unit of University of Minnesota System, founded in 1851, offering degrees at the bachelor's, master's, doctoral, and first professional levels and post-master's and postbachelor's certificates. It has a 2,000-acre campus in Minneapolis.

Academic Information The faculty has 3,079 members (88% full-time), 95% with terminal degrees. The undergraduate student-faculty ratio is 22:1. The library holds 6 million titles, 45,000 serial subscriptions, and 1 million audiovisual materials. Special programs include academic remediation, services for learning-disabled students, an honors program, cooperative (work-study) education, study abroad, advanced placement credit, accelerated degree programs, Freshman Honors College, ESL programs, double majors, independent study, distance learning, self-designed majors, summer session for credit, part-time degree programs, external degree programs, adult/continuing education programs, internships, and arrangement for off-campus study with National Student Exchange, Minnesota Community College System. The most frequently chosen baccalaureate fields are business/marketing, engineering/engineering technologies, social sciences and history.

Student Body Statistics The student body totals 49,474, of whom 32,474 are undergraduates (5,186 freshmen). 53 percent are women and 47 percent are men. Students come from 55 states and territories and 85 other countries. 74 percent are from Minnesota. 2 percent are international students.

Expenses for 2003–04 *Application fee:* $35. *State resident tuition:* $5962 full-time. *Nonresident tuition:* $17,592 full-time. *Mandatory fees:* $1154 full-time. Full-time tuition and fees vary according to program. *College room and board:* $6044. Room and board charges vary according to board plan, housing facility, and location.

Financial Aid Forms of aid include need-based and non-need-based scholarships, athletic grants, and part-time jobs. The average aided 2003–04 undergraduate received an aid package worth an estimated $9027. The priority application deadline for financial aid is January 15.

Freshman Admission U of M-Twin Cities Campus requires a high school transcript, SAT I or ACT scores, and TOEFL scores for international students. A minimum 2.0 high school GPA is recommended. The application deadline for regular admission is rolling.

Transfer Admission The application deadline for admission is March 1.

Entrance Difficulty U of M-Twin Cities Campus assesses its entrance difficulty level as moderately difficult; very difficult for Institute of Technology, management, biological science programs. For the fall 2003 freshman class, 76 percent of the applicants were accepted.

For Further Information Contact Ms. Patricia Jones Whyte, Associate Director of Admissions, University of Minnesota, Twin Cities Campus, 240 Williamson Hall, Minneapolis, MN 55455-0115. *Telephone:* 612-625-2008 or 800-752-1000 (toll-free). *Fax:* 612-626-1693. *E-mail:* admissions@tc.umn.edu. *Web site:* http://www1.umn.edu/twincities/index.php.

UNIVERSITY OF ST. THOMAS

St. Paul, Minnesota

St. Thomas is a coed, private, Roman Catholic university, founded in 1885, offering degrees at the bachelor's, master's, doctoral, and first professional levels and post-master's and postbachelor's certificates. It has a 78-acre campus in St. Paul near Minneapolis.

Academic Information The faculty has 800 members (50% full-time), 60% with terminal degrees. The undergraduate student-faculty ratio is 14:1. The library holds 440,023 titles, 4,168 serial subscriptions, and 3,516 audiovisual materials. Special programs include services for learning-disabled students, an honors program, study abroad, advanced placement credit, ESL programs, double majors, independent study, self-designed majors, summer session for credit, part-time degree programs (daytime, evenings, weekends, summer), adult/continuing education programs, internships, and arrangement for off-campus study with 5 members of the Associated Colleges of the Twin Cities. The most frequently chosen baccalaureate fields are business/marketing, communications/communication technologies, social sciences and history.

Student Body Statistics The student body totals 11,037, of whom 5,236 are undergraduates (1,039 freshmen). 51 percent are women and 49 percent are men. Students come from 44 states and territories and 36 other countries. 82 percent are from Minnesota. 1.1 percent are international students. 15 percent of the 2003 graduating class went on to graduate and professional schools.

Expenses for 2003–04 *Application fee:* $0. *Comprehensive fee:* $25,827 includes full-time tuition ($18,975), mandatory fees ($368), and college room and board ($6484). *College room only:* $3774. Full-time tuition and fees vary according to course load. Room and board charges vary according to board plan and housing facility. *Part-time tuition:* varies with course load.

Financial Aid Forms of aid include need-based and non-need-based scholarships and part-time jobs. The average aided 2003–04 undergraduate received an aid package worth an estimated $15,688. The priority application deadline for financial aid is April 1.

Freshman Admission St. Thomas requires an essay, a high school transcript, SAT I or ACT scores, and TOEFL scores for international students. Recommendations, an interview, and ACT scores are recommended. The application deadline for regular admission is rolling.

Transfer Admission The application deadline for admission is August 1.

Entrance Difficulty St. Thomas assesses its entrance difficulty level as moderately difficult. For the fall 2003 freshman class, 87 percent of the applicants were accepted.

For Further Information Contact Ms. Marla Friederichs, Associate Vice President of Enrollment Management, University of St. Thomas, 2115 Summit Avenue, Mail #32F-1, St. Paul, MN 55105-1096. *Telephone:* 651-962-6150 or 800-328-6819 Ext. 26150 (toll-free). *Fax:* 651-962-6160. *E-mail:* admissions@stthomas.edu. *Web site:* http://www.stthomas.edu/.

WALDEN UNIVERSITY
Minneapolis, Minnesota

For Information Write to Walden University, Minneapolis, MN 55401.

WINONA STATE UNIVERSITY
Winona, Minnesota

Winona State is a coed, public, comprehensive unit of Minnesota State Colleges and Universities System, founded in 1858, offering degrees at the associate, bachelor's, and master's levels and post-master's certificates. It has a 40-acre campus in Winona.

Academic Information The faculty has 357 members (88% full-time), 62% with terminal degrees. The undergraduate student-faculty ratio is 19:1. The library holds 243,500 titles and 1,950 serial subscriptions. Special programs include academic remediation, services for learning-disabled students, an honors program, study abroad, advanced placement credit, accelerated degree programs, ESL programs, double majors, independent study, distance learning, self-designed majors, summer session for credit, part-time degree programs (daytime, evenings, weekends, summer), external degree programs, adult/continuing education programs, internships, and arrangement for off-campus study with Saint Mary's University of Minnesota, other colleges in the Minnesota State Colleges and Universities System. The most frequently chosen baccalaureate fields are business/marketing, education, health professions and related sciences.
Student Body Statistics The student body totals 8,236, of whom 7,569 are undergraduates (1,552 freshmen). 63 percent are women and 37 percent are men. Students come from 21 states and territories and 48 other countries. 66 percent are from Minnesota. 3.7 percent are international students. 25 percent of the 2003 graduating class went on to graduate and professional schools.
Expenses for 2003-04 *Application fee:* $20. *One-time mandatory fee:* $1000. *State resident tuition:* $4800 full-time. *Nonresident tuition:* $9260 full-time. *College room and board:* $4640. Room and board charges vary according to board plan and housing facility.
Financial Aid Forms of aid include need-based and non-need-based scholarships, athletic grants, and part-time jobs. The average aided 2002-03 undergraduate received an aid package worth $5236. The application deadline for financial aid is continuous.
Freshman Admission Winona State requires a high school transcript, class rank, SAT I or ACT scores, and TOEFL scores for international students. An essay, recommendations, and an interview are required for some. The application deadline for regular admission is rolling.
Transfer Admission The application deadline for admission is August 1.
Entrance Difficulty Winona State assesses its entrance difficulty level as moderately difficult; minimally difficult for adult students. For the fall 2003 freshman class, 79 percent of the applicants were accepted.

For Further Information Contact Mr. Douglas Schacke, Director of Admissions, Winona State University, PO Box 5838, Winona, MN 55987. *Telephone:* 507-457-5100 or 800-DIAL WSU (toll-free). *Fax:* 507-457-5620. *E-mail:* admissions@winona.edu. *Web site:* http://www.winona.edu/.

Missouri

AVILA UNIVERSITY
Kansas City, Missouri

Avila is a coed, private, Roman Catholic, comprehensive institution, founded in 1916, offering degrees at the bachelor's and master's levels. It has a 50-acre campus in Kansas City.

Academic Information The faculty has 202 members (31% full-time), 40% with terminal degrees. The undergraduate student-faculty ratio is 12:1. The library holds 80,865 titles, 7,179 serial subscriptions, and 3,265 audiovisual materials. Special programs include academic remediation, services for learning-disabled students, cooperative (work-study) education, study abroad, advanced placement credit, accelerated degree programs, ESL programs, double majors, independent study, distance learning, summer session for credit, part-time degree programs (daytime, evenings, weekends, summer), adult/continuing education programs, internships, and arrangement for off-campus study with Sisters of St. Joseph Consortium, Council of Independent Colleges Exchange Program. The most frequently chosen baccalaureate fields are business/marketing, health professions and related sciences, psychology.
Student Body Statistics The student body totals 1,683, of whom 1,160 are undergraduates (152 freshmen). 62 percent are women and 38 percent are men. Students come from 23 states and territories and 26 other countries. 68 percent are from Missouri.
Expenses for 2004-05 *Application fee:* $0. *Comprehensive fee:* $21,270 includes full-time tuition ($15,500), mandatory fees ($370), and college room and board ($5400). Full-time tuition and fees vary according to course load. Room and board charges vary according to board plan and housing facility. *Part-time tuition:* $365 per credit hour. *Part-time mandatory fees:* $12.25 per credit hour. Part-time tuition and fees vary according to course load.
Financial Aid Forms of aid include need-based and non-need-based scholarships, athletic grants, and part-time jobs. The application deadline for financial aid is continuous.
Freshman Admission Avila requires a high school transcript, a minimum 2.5 high school GPA, SAT I or ACT scores, and TOEFL scores for international students. An interview is recommended. An essay and recommendations are required for some. The application deadline for regular admission is rolling.
Transfer Admission The application deadline for admission is rolling.
Entrance Difficulty Avila assesses its entrance difficulty level as minimally difficult. For the fall 2003 freshman class, 42 percent of the applicants were accepted.

For Further Information Contact Ms. Paige Illum, Director of Admissions, Avila University, 11901 Wornall Rd, Kansas City, MO 64145. *Telephone:* 816-501-3773 or 800-GO-AVILA (toll-free). *Fax:* 816-501-2453. *E-mail:* admissions@mail.avila.edu. *Web site:* http://www.avila.edu/.

BAPTIST BIBLE COLLEGE
Springfield, Missouri

Baptist Bible College is a coed, private, Baptist, comprehensive institution, founded in 1950, offering degrees at the associate, bachelor's, master's, and first professional levels. It has a 38-acre campus in Springfield.

Academic Information The faculty has 37 members (73% full-time). The library holds 36,844 titles and 226 serial subscriptions. Special programs include academic remediation, summer session for credit, part-time degree programs (daytime, summer), and internships.
Student Body Statistics The student body is made up of 653 undergraduates. Students come from 46 states and territories and 5 other countries. 20 percent are from Missouri. 1.5 percent are international students.

Baptist Bible College (continued)

Expenses for 2003–04 *Application fee:* $40. *Comprehensive fee:* $8860 includes full-time tuition ($3562), mandatory fees ($574), and college room and board ($4724). Full-time tuition and fees vary according to program.

Financial Aid Forms of aid include need-based scholarships. The application deadline for financial aid is continuous.

Freshman Admission Baptist Bible College requires a high school transcript, 1 recommendation, and ACT scores. The application deadline for regular admission is rolling.

Transfer Admission The application deadline for admission is rolling.

Entrance Difficulty Baptist Bible College has an open admission policy.

For Further Information Contact Dr. Joseph Gleason, Director of Admissions, Baptist Bible College, 628 East Kearney, Springfield, MO 65803-3498. *Telephone:* 417-268-6000 Ext. 6013. *Fax:* 417-268-6694. *Web site:* http://www.bbcnet.edu/.

CALVARY BIBLE COLLEGE AND THEOLOGICAL SEMINARY
Kansas City, Missouri

Calvary is a coed, private, nondenominational, comprehensive institution, founded in 1932, offering degrees at the associate, bachelor's, master's, and first professional levels. It has a 55-acre campus in Kansas City.

Academic Information The faculty has 34 members (24% full-time), 32% with terminal degrees. The undergraduate student-faculty ratio is 12:1. The library holds 59,000 titles and 307 serial subscriptions. Special programs include academic remediation, advanced placement credit, accelerated degree programs, double majors, independent study, distance learning, summer session for credit, part-time degree programs, adult/continuing education programs, and arrangement for off-campus study. The most frequently chosen baccalaureate fields are education, library science, philosophy, religion, and theology.

Student Body Statistics The student body totals 316, of whom 266 are undergraduates (44 freshmen). 42 percent are women and 58 percent are men. Students come from 22 states and territories and 4 other countries. 44 percent are from Missouri. 1.9 percent are international students.

Expenses for 2004–05 *Application fee:* $25. *Comprehensive fee:* $10,312 includes full-time tuition ($6180), mandatory fees ($432), and college room and board ($3700). Full-time tuition and fees vary according to course load. Room and board charges vary according to housing facility. *Part-time tuition:* $230 per credit. *Part-time mandatory fees:* $18 per credit. Part-time tuition and fees vary according to course load.

Financial Aid Forms of aid include need-based and non-need-based scholarships and part-time jobs. The application deadline for financial aid is April 1 with a priority deadline of March 1.

Freshman Admission Calvary requires an essay, a high school transcript, 2 recommendations, statement of faith, SAT I or ACT scores, and TOEFL scores for international students. An interview is required for some. The application deadline for regular admission is August 11.

Transfer Admission The application deadline for admission is August 11.

Entrance Difficulty Calvary assesses its entrance difficulty level as minimally difficult. For the fall 2003 freshman class, 76 percent of the applicants were accepted.

For Further Information Contact Mr. Robert E. Crank, Director of Admissions and Financial Aid, Calvary Bible College and Theological Seminary, 15800 Calvary Road, Kansas City, MO 64147-1341. *Telephone:* 816-322-0110 Ext. 1326 or 800-326-3960 (toll-free). *Fax:* 816-331-4474. *E-mail:* admissions@calvary.edu. *Web site:* http://www.calvary.edu/.

CENTRAL BIBLE COLLEGE
Springfield, Missouri

CBC is a coed, private, Assemblies of God, four-year college, founded in 1922, offering degrees at the associate and bachelor's levels in religious studies. It has a 108-acre campus in Springfield.

Expenses for 2003–04 *Application fee:* $25. *Comprehensive fee:* $11,478 includes full-time tuition ($6942), mandatory fees ($594), and college room and board ($3942).

For Further Information Contact Mrs. Eunice A. Bruegman, Director of Admissions and Records, Central Bible College, 3000 North Grant Avenue, Springfield, MO 65803-1096. *Telephone:* 417-833-2551 Ext. 1184 or 800-831-4222 Ext. 1184 (toll-free). *Fax:* 417-833-5141. *E-mail:* info@cbcag.edu. *Web site:* http://www.cbcag.edu/.

CENTRAL CHRISTIAN COLLEGE OF THE BIBLE
Moberly, Missouri

For Information Write to Central Christian College of the Bible, Moberly, MO 65270-1997.

CENTRAL METHODIST COLLEGE
Fayette, Missouri

CMC is a coed, private, Methodist, comprehensive institution, founded in 1854, offering degrees at the associate, bachelor's, and master's levels. It has an 80-acre campus in Fayette.

Academic Information The faculty has 71 members (76% full-time), 55% with terminal degrees. The undergraduate student-faculty ratio is 14:1. The library holds 97,793 titles, 316 serial subscriptions, and 379 audiovisual materials. Special programs include academic remediation, services for learning-disabled students, an honors program, study abroad, advanced placement credit, accelerated degree programs, double majors, independent study, distance learning, self-designed majors, summer session for credit, part-time degree programs (daytime, evenings, summer), internships, and arrangement for off-campus study with Mineral Area College, East Central College. The most frequently chosen baccalaureate fields are business/marketing, education, protective services/public administration.

Student Body Statistics The student body totals 932, of whom 850 are undergraduates (224 freshmen). 52 percent are women and 48 percent are men. Students come from 17 states and territories. 90 percent are from Missouri. 2.4 percent are international students.

Expenses for 2003–04 *Application fee:* $0. *Comprehensive fee:* $18,680 includes full-time tuition ($13,160), mandatory fees ($600), and college room and board ($4920). *College room only:* $2420. *Part-time tuition:* $140 per credit hour. *Part-time mandatory fees:* $26 per credit hour. Part-time tuition and fees vary according to course load.

Financial Aid Forms of aid include need-based and non-need-based scholarships, athletic grants, and part-time jobs. The average aided 2003–04 undergraduate received an aid package worth an estimated $10,109. The priority application deadline for financial aid is March 15.

Freshman Admission CMC requires a high school transcript, a minimum 2.0 high school GPA, SAT I or ACT scores, and TOEFL scores for international students. ACT scores are recommended. 2 recommendations are required for some. The application deadline for regular admission is August 1.

Transfer Admission The application deadline for admission is August 15.

Entrance Difficulty CMC assesses its entrance difficulty level as moderately difficult. For the fall 2003 freshman class, 73 percent of the applicants were accepted.

For Further Information Contact Mr. Edward J Lamm, Director of Admissions, Central Methodist College, 411 Central Methodist Square, Fayette, MO 65248-1198. *Telephone:* 660-248-6247 or 888-CMC-1854 (toll-free in-state). *Fax:* 660-248-1872. *E-mail:* admissions@cmc.edu. *Web site:* http://www.cmc.edu/.

CENTRAL MISSOURI STATE UNIVERSITY
Warrensburg, Missouri

Central is a coed, public, comprehensive institution, founded in 1871, offering degrees at the associate, bachelor's, and master's levels and post-master's and postbachelor's certificates. It has a 1,561-acre campus in Warrensburg near Kansas City.

Academic Information The faculty has 551 members (78% full-time), 63% with terminal degrees. The undergraduate student-faculty ratio is 18:1. The library holds 567,934 titles, 3,582 serial subscriptions, and 23,690 audiovisual materials. Special programs include academic remediation, services for learning-disabled students, an honors program, cooperative (work-study) education, study abroad, advanced placement credit, ESL programs, double majors, distance learning, self-designed majors, summer session for credit, part-time degree programs (daytime, evenings, weekends, summer), adult/continuing education programs, internships, and arrangement for off-campus study. The most frequently chosen baccalaureate fields are business/marketing, education, protective services/public administration.

Student Body Statistics The student body totals 10,351, of whom 8,707 are undergraduates (1,438 freshmen). 54 percent are women and 46 percent are men. Students come from 44 states and territories and 59 other countries. 93 percent are from Missouri. 3.2 percent are international students. 19 percent of the 2003 graduating class went on to graduate and professional schools.

Expenses for 2003–04 *Application fee:* $25. *State resident tuition:* $4980 full-time, $154 per credit part-time. *Nonresident tuition:* $9600 full-time, $308 per credit part-time. *Mandatory fees:* $360 full-time, $12 per credit part-time. Full-time tuition and fees vary according to course load and location. *College room and board:* $4796. *College room only:* $2998. Room and board charges vary according to board plan and housing facility.

Financial Aid Forms of aid include need-based and non-need-based scholarships, athletic grants, and part-time jobs. The average aided 2002–03 undergraduate received an aid package worth $6752. The priority application deadline for financial aid is March 1.

Freshman Admission Central requires a high school transcript, rank in upper two-thirds of high school class, minimum ACT score of 20, ACT scores, and TOEFL scores for international students. Recommendations are required for some. The application deadline for regular admission is rolling.

Transfer Admission The application deadline for admission is rolling.

Entrance Difficulty Central assesses its entrance difficulty level as moderately difficult; very difficult for business, teacher education, nursing programs. For the fall 2003 freshman class, 76 percent of the applicants were accepted.

For Further Information Contact Mr. Matt Melvin, Assistant Provost, Enrollment Management, Central Missouri State University, 1401 Ward Edwards, Warrensburg, MO 64093. *Telephone:* 660-543-4290 or 800-729-2678 (toll-free in-state). *Fax:* 660-543-8517. *E-mail:* admit@cmsuvmb.cmsu.edu. *Web site:* http://www.cmsu.edu/.

CLEVELAND CHIROPRACTIC COLLEGE-KANSAS CITY CAMPUS
Kansas City, Missouri

Cleveland Chiropractic College-Kansas City Campus is a coed, private, upper-level institution, founded in 1922, offering degrees at the bachelor's and first professional levels.

Academic Information The faculty has 45 full-time members. The undergraduate student-faculty ratio is 15:1. The library holds 14,000 titles, 268 serial subscriptions, and 12,320 audiovisual materials. Special programs include academic remediation, services for learning-disabled students, cooperative (work-study) education, accelerated degree programs, summer session for credit, and internships.

Student Body Statistics The student body totals 459, of whom 71 are undergraduates. 37 percent are women and 63 percent are men. Students come from 18 states and territories and 1 other country. 57 percent are from Missouri. 1.4 percent are international students.

Expenses for 2003–04 *Application fee:* $35. *Tuition:* $3670 full-time. *Mandatory fees:* $150 full-time.

Transfer Admission Cleveland Chiropractic College-Kansas City Campus requires a college transcript and a minimum 2.5 college GPA.

Entrance Difficulty Cleveland Chiropractic College-Kansas City Campus has an open admission policy except cumulative college GPA of 2.0 or 2.0 high school GPA required to enter BS degree program.

For Further Information Contact Ms. Melissa Denton, Director of Admissions, Cleveland Chiropractic College-Kansas City Campus, 6401 Rockhill Road, Kansas City, MO 64131. *Telephone:* 816-501-0100 or 800-467-2252 (toll-free). *Fax:* 816-501-0205. *E-mail:* kc.admissions@cleveland.edu. *Web site:* http://www.cleveland.edu/.

COLLEGE OF THE OZARKS
Point Lookout, Missouri

C of O is a coed, private, Presbyterian, four-year college, founded in 1906, offering degrees at the bachelor's level. It has a 1,000-acre campus in Point Lookout.

Academic Information The faculty has 119 members (73% full-time), 46% with terminal degrees. The student-faculty ratio is 15:1. The library holds 118,235 titles, 503 serial subscriptions, and 5,193 audiovisual materials. Special programs include academic remediation, an honors program, cooperative (work-study) education, study abroad, advanced placement credit, accelerated degree programs, self-designed majors, summer session for credit, part-time degree programs, and internships. The most frequently chosen baccalaureate fields are business/marketing, agriculture, education.

Student Body Statistics The student body is made up of 1,348 undergraduates (254 freshmen). 56 percent are women and 44 percent are men. Students come from 26 states and territories and 22 other countries. 67 percent are from Missouri. 2.1 percent are international students. 8 percent of the 2003 graduating class went on to graduate and professional schools.

Expenses for 2004–05 *Application fee:* $0. *Comprehensive fee:* $3800 includes full-time tuition ($0), mandatory fees ($250), and college room and board ($3550). *College room only:* $1800. *Part-time tuition:* $275 per credit. *Part-time mandatory fees:* $125 per term.

Financial Aid Forms of aid include need-based and non-need-based scholarships, athletic grants, and part-time jobs. The average aided 2002–03 undergraduate received an aid package worth $12,446. The priority application deadline for financial aid is March 15.

Freshman Admission C of O requires a high school transcript, 2 recommendations, an interview, medical history, financial statement, SAT I or ACT scores, and TOEFL scores for international students. A minimum 2.0 high school GPA is recommended. The application deadline for regular admission is February 15.

Transfer Admission The application deadline for admission is February 1.

Entrance Difficulty C of O assesses its entrance difficulty level as moderately difficult. For the fall 2003 freshman class, 14 percent of the applicants were accepted.

For Further Information Contact Mrs. Gayle Groves, Admissions Secretary, College of the Ozarks, PO Box 17, Point Lookout, MO 65726. *Telephone:* 417-334-6411 Ext. 4218 or 800-222-0525 (toll-free). *Fax:* 417-335-2618. *E-mail:* admiss4@cofo.edu. *Web site:* http://www.cofo.edu/.

COLUMBIA COLLEGE
Columbia, Missouri

Columbia College is a coed, private, comprehensive institution, founded in 1851, affiliated with the Christian Church (Disciples of Christ), offering degrees at the associate, bachelor's, and master's levels (offers continuing education program with significant enrollment not reflected in profile). It has a 29-acre campus in Columbia.

Academic Information The faculty has 88 members (67% full-time), 57% with terminal degrees. The undergraduate student-faculty ratio is 11:1. The library holds 62,265 titles, 382 serial subscriptions, and 3,613 audiovisual materials. Special programs include academic remediation, an honors program, cooperative (work-study) education, study abroad, advanced placement credit, accelerated degree programs, ESL programs, double majors, independent study, distance learning, self-designed majors, summer session for credit, part-time degree programs (daytime, evenings, summer), adult/continuing education programs, internships, and arrangement for off-campus study with 6 members of the Mid-Missouri Associated Colleges and Universities. The most frequently chosen baccalaureate fields are business/marketing, education, protective services/public administration.

Student Body Statistics The student body totals 1,068, of whom 916 are undergraduates (157 freshmen). 62 percent are women and 38 percent are men. Students come from 20 states and territories and 28 other countries. 95 percent are from Missouri. 5.4 percent are international students.

Expenses for 2004–05 *Application fee:* $25. *Comprehensive fee:* $16,502 includes full-time tuition ($11,589) and college room and board ($4913). *College room only:* $3090. Full-time tuition varies according to class time and course load. Room and board charges vary according to board plan. *Part-time tuition:* $248 per credit hour. Part-time tuition varies according to class time, course load, and location.

Financial Aid Forms of aid include need-based and non-need-based scholarships, athletic grants, and part-time jobs. The average aided 2003–04 undergraduate received an aid package worth an estimated $7426. The priority application deadline for financial aid is March 1.

Freshman Admission Columbia College requires a high school transcript, a minimum 2.0 high school GPA, ACT scores, and TOEFL scores for international students. Rank in upper 50% of high school class and SAT I scores are recommended. An essay, recommendations, and an interview are required for some. The application deadline for regular admission is rolling.

Transfer Admission The application deadline for admission is rolling.

Entrance Difficulty Columbia College assesses its entrance difficulty level as minimally difficult. For the fall 2003 freshman class, 59 percent of the applicants were accepted.

SPECIAL MESSAGE TO STUDENTS

Social Life A strong Student Government Association plans and organizes social activities. There are more than thirty clubs and organizations, ranging from academic associations to special interest groups, providing myriad choices for students to get involved and experience leadership opportunities. Strong athletics are a tradition at Columbia College with a history of nationally ranked NAIA Division I teams. One of three institutions of higher education in town, Columbia College provides a vibrant small campus environment within a larger college community.

Academic Highlights Columbia College is known for its excellence in teaching and learning. Among the nearly thirty programs offered, those in criminal justice, art, education, and business are quite distinctive. The Writing and Math Centers build upon quality teaching in the classroom to provide opportunities for students to enhance their learning experience. INCC 111, Introduction to Columbia College, is a popular freshman orientation course team-taught by a full-time professor and an upperclass student. Study-abroad opportunities are available, and internships can be obtained for a more hands-on experience in any field.

Interviews and Campus Visits Located in a small city consistently recognized by national magazines as an exceptional place to live, Columbia College welcomes visitors to its beautiful historic campus. The campus dates from 1851 and has several distinct architectural features in its older buildings. Williams Hall is the oldest building west of the Mississippi still in continuous use for education purposes. Visitors have the opportunity to sit in on a class and meet faculty members and students as well as financial aid officials. Campus visits may be arranged weekdays from 8 a.m. to 5 p.m. by calling the Admissions Office at 573-875-7352 or 800-231-2391 Ext. 7352 (toll-free). The nearest commercial airport is Columbia Regional.

For Further Information Write to Ms. Regina M. Morin, Director of Admissions, Columbia College, 1001 Rogers Street, Columbia, MO 65216. *E-mail:* admissions@ccis.edu. *Web site:* http://www.ccis.edu.

See page 270 for a narrative description.

CONCEPTION SEMINARY COLLEGE
Conception, Missouri

Conception Seminary College is a men's, private, Roman Catholic, four-year college, founded in 1886, offering degrees at the bachelor's level. It has a 30-acre campus in Conception.

Academic Information The faculty has 26 members (92% full-time), 77% with terminal degrees. The student-faculty ratio is 4:1. The library holds 115,000 titles, 300 serial subscriptions, and 5,000 audiovisual materials. Special programs include academic remediation, advanced placement credit, ESL programs, double majors, independent study, and arrangement for off-campus study with Northwest Missouri State University. The most frequently chosen baccalaureate field is liberal arts/general studies.

Student Body Statistics The student body is made up of 100 undergraduates (10 freshmen). Students come from 18 states and territories and 5 other countries. 33 percent are from Missouri. 8 percent are international students.

Expenses for 2004–05 *Application fee:* $0. *Comprehensive fee:* $18,406 includes full-time tuition ($11,432), mandatory fees ($180), and college room and board ($6794). *College room only:* $2874. Room and board charges vary according to board plan. *Part-time tuition:* $150 per credit.

Financial Aid Forms of aid include need-based and non-need-based scholarships and part-time jobs. The average aided 2003–04 undergraduate received an aid package worth an estimated $16,464. The application deadline for financial aid is continuous.

Freshman Admission Conception Seminary College requires an essay, a high school transcript, a minimum 2.0 high school GPA, 2 recommendations, church certificate, medical history, and ACT scores. The application deadline for regular admission is July 31.

Transfer Admission The application deadline for admission is July 31.

Entrance Difficulty Conception Seminary College assesses its entrance difficulty level as noncompetitive. For the fall 2003 freshman class, 100 percent of the applicants were accepted.

For Further Information Contact Mr. Vincent Casper, Director of Recruitment and Admissions, Conception Seminary College, PO Box 502, Highway 136 & VV, 37174 State Highway VV, Conception, MO 64433. *Telephone:* 660-944-2886. *Fax:* 660-944-2829. *E-mail:* vocations@conception.edu. *Web site:* http://www.conceptionabbey.org/.

COTTEY COLLEGE
Nevada, Missouri

Cottey is a women's, private, two-year college, founded in 1884, offering degrees at the associate level. It has a 51-acre campus in Nevada.

Expenses for 2004–05 *Application fee:* $20. *Comprehensive fee:* $16,380 includes full-time tuition ($10,800), mandatory fees ($580), and college room and board ($5000).

For Further Information Contact Ms. Marjorie J. Cooke, Dean of Enrollment Management, Cottey College, 1000 West Austin, Nevada, MO 64772. *Telephone:* 417-667-8181 or 888-526-8839 (toll-free). *Fax:* 417-667-8103. *E-mail:* enrollmgt@cottey.edu. *Web site:* http://www.cottey.edu/.

CULVER-STOCKTON COLLEGE
Canton, Missouri

Culver-Stockton is a coed, private, four-year college, founded in 1853, affiliated with the Christian Church (Disciples of Christ), offering degrees at the bachelor's level. It has a 143-acre campus in Canton.

Academic Information The faculty has 77 members (74% full-time), 52% with terminal degrees. The student-faculty ratio is 12:1. The library holds 155,487 titles, 777 serial subscriptions, and 4,327 audiovisual materials. Special programs include an honors program, study abroad, advanced placement credit, double majors, independent study, self-designed majors, summer session for credit, part-time degree programs, internships, and arrangement for off-campus study with Central College. The most frequently chosen baccalaureate fields are business/marketing, education, health professions and related sciences.

Student Body Statistics The student body is made up of 835 undergraduates (219 freshmen). 57 percent are women and 43 percent are men. Students come from 21 states and territories and 6 other countries. 55 percent are from Missouri. 0.8 percent are international students. 12 percent of the 2003 graduating class went on to graduate and professional schools.

Expenses for 2003–04 *Application fee:* $25. *Comprehensive fee:* $17,850 includes full-time tuition ($12,400) and college room and board ($5450). *College room only:* $2525. Room and board charges vary according to board plan. *Part-time tuition:* $340 per credit hour.

Financial Aid Forms of aid include need-based and non-need-based scholarships, athletic grants, and part-time jobs. The average aided 2003–04 undergraduate received an aid package worth an estimated $11,676. The application deadline for financial aid is June 15.

Freshman Admission Culver-Stockton requires a high school transcript, a minimum 2.0 high school GPA, rank in top 50% of high school class, SAT I or ACT scores, and TOEFL scores for international students. An essay, recommendations, and an interview are recommended. An interview is required for some.

Transfer Admission The application deadline for admission is rolling.

Entrance Difficulty Culver-Stockton assesses its entrance difficulty level as moderately difficult. For the fall 2003 freshman class, 72 percent of the applicants were accepted.

For Further Information Contact Ms. Karyn Bishoff, Director of Enrollment Services, Culver-Stockton College, One College Hill, Canton, MO 63435-1299. *Telephone:* 800-537-1883 or 800-537-1883 (toll-free). *Fax:* 217-231-6618. *E-mail:* enrollment@culver.edu. *Web site:* http://www.culver.edu/.

See page 276 for a narrative description.

DEACONESS COLLEGE OF NURSING
St. Louis, Missouri

Deaconess is a coed, primarily women's, proprietary, four-year college, founded in 1889, offering degrees at the associate and bachelor's levels in nursing. It has a 15-acre campus in St. Louis.

Expenses for 2003–04 *Application fee:* $30. *Comprehensive fee:* $16,000 includes full-time tuition ($10,550), mandatory fees ($250), and college room and board ($5200).

For Further Information Contact Ms. Lisa Mancini, Dean of Enrollment and Student Services, Deaconess College of Nursing, 6150 Oakland Avenue, St. Louis, MO 63139-3215. *Telephone:* 314-768-3179 or 800-942-4310 (toll-free). *Fax:* 314-768-5673. *Web site:* http://www.deaconess.edu/.

DEVRY UNIVERSITY
Kansas City, Missouri

For Information Write to DeVry University, Kansas City, MO 64105-2112.

DEVRY UNIVERSITY
St. Louis, Missouri

For Information Write to DeVry University, St. Louis, MO 63146-4020.

DEVRY UNIVERSITY
Kansas City, Missouri

DeVry is a coed, proprietary, four-year college of DeVry University, founded in 1931, offering degrees at the associate and bachelor's levels and postbachelor's certificates. It has a 12-acre campus in Kansas City.

Academic Information The student-faculty ratio is 23:1. The library holds 15,000 titles, 68 serial subscriptions, and 457 audiovisual materials. Special programs include academic remediation, services for learning-disabled students, cooperative (work-study) education, advanced placement credit, accelerated degree programs, distance learning, summer session for credit, part-time degree programs (daytime, evenings, weekends, summer), and adult/continuing education programs. The most frequently chosen baccalaureate fields are business/marketing, computer/information sciences, engineering/engineering technologies.

Student Body Statistics The student body is made up of 1,931 undergraduates (299 freshmen). 26 percent are women and 74 percent are men. 0.7 percent are international students.

Expenses for 2003–04 *Application fee:* $50. *Tuition:* $9990 full-time, $355 per credit hour part-time. *Mandatory fees:* $165 full-time. Full-time tuition and fees vary according to course load. Part-time tuition varies according to course load.

Financial Aid Forms of aid include need-based and non-need-based scholarships and part-time jobs. The average aided 2002–03 undergraduate received an aid package worth $8714. The application deadline for financial aid is continuous.

Freshman Admission DeVry requires a high school transcript, an interview, and TOEFL scores for international students. SAT I, ACT or CPT is recommended. The application deadline for regular admission is rolling.

Entrance Difficulty DeVry assesses its entrance difficulty level as minimally difficult; moderately difficult for electronics engineering technology program.

For Further Information Contact Ms. Anna Diamond, New Student Coordinator, DeVry University, 11224 Holmes Road, Kansas City, MO 64131-3626. *Telephone:* 816-941-2810 or 800-821-3766 (toll-free). *Fax:* 816-941-0896. *E-mail:* ssmeed@kc.devry.edu. *Web site:* http://www.devry.edu/.

DRURY UNIVERSITY

Springfield, Missouri

Drury is a coed, private, comprehensive institution, founded in 1873, offering degrees at the bachelor's level (also offers evening program with significant enrollment not reflected in profile). It has an 80-acre campus in Springfield.

Academic Information The faculty has 179 members (67% full-time), 74% with terminal degrees. The student-faculty ratio is 11:1. The library holds 177,794 titles, 868 serial subscriptions, and 60,098 audiovisual materials. Special programs include services for learning-disabled students, an honors program, cooperative (work-study) education, study abroad, advanced placement credit, accelerated degree programs, ESL programs, double majors, independent study, distance learning, self-designed majors, summer session for credit, part-time degree programs (daytime, evenings, summer), adult/continuing education programs, internships, and arrangement for off-campus study.
Student Body Statistics The student body totals 1,933, of whom 1,541 are undergraduates (365 freshmen). 56 percent are women and 44 percent are men. Students come from 35 states and territories and 50 other countries. 81 percent are from Missouri. 4.6 percent are international students. 36 percent of the 2003 graduating class went on to graduate and professional schools.
Expenses for 2004–05 *Application fee:* $25. *Comprehensive fee:* $19,032 includes full-time tuition ($13,600), mandatory fees ($304), and college room and board ($5128). Room and board charges vary according to board plan and housing facility. *Part-time tuition:* $448 per semester hour.
Financial Aid Forms of aid include need-based and non-need-based scholarships, athletic grants, and part-time jobs. The average aided 2003–04 undergraduate received an aid package worth an estimated $7695. The priority application deadline for financial aid is March 15.
Freshman Admission Drury requires an essay, a high school transcript, a minimum 2.7 high school GPA, 1 recommendation, minimum ACT score of 21, SAT I or ACT scores, and TOEFL scores for international students. An interview is recommended. The application deadline for regular admission is March 15.
Transfer Admission The application deadline for admission is rolling.
Entrance Difficulty Drury assesses its entrance difficulty level as moderately difficult. For the fall 2003 freshman class, 77 percent of the applicants were accepted.

For Further Information Contact Mr. Chip Parker, Director of Admission, Drury University, 900 North Benton, Bay Hall, Springfield, MO 65802. *Telephone:* 417-873-7205 or 800-922-2274 (toll-free). *Fax:* 417-866-3873. *E-mail:* druryad@drury.edu. *Web site:* http://www.drury.edu/.

EVANGEL UNIVERSITY

Springfield, Missouri

Evangel University is a coed, private, comprehensive institution, founded in 1955, affiliated with the Assemblies of God, offering degrees at the associate, bachelor's, and master's levels. It has an 80-acre campus in Springfield.

Academic Information The faculty has 147 members (64% full-time), 41% with terminal degrees. The undergraduate student-faculty ratio is 18:1. The library holds 100,691 titles, 1,060 serial subscriptions, and 6,962 audiovisual materials. Special programs include academic remediation, services for learning-disabled students, advanced placement credit, accelerated degree programs, double majors, summer session for credit, part-time degree programs (daytime, summer), adult/continuing education programs, and internships. The most frequently chosen baccalaureate fields are business/marketing, education, philosophy, religion, and theology.
Student Body Statistics The student body totals 1,852, of whom 1,811 are undergraduates (442 freshmen). 59 percent are women and 41 percent are men. Students come from 49 states and territories. 41 percent are from Missouri. 0.2 percent are international students.
Expenses for 2004–05 *Application fee:* $25. *Comprehensive fee:* $16,305 includes full-time tuition ($11,250), mandatory fees ($695), and college room and board ($4360). *College room only:* $2100. Full-time tuition and

fees vary according to course load. Room and board charges vary according to board plan. *Part-time tuition:* $438 per credit hour. *Part-time mandatory fees:* $273.50 per term.
Financial Aid Forms of aid include need-based and non-need-based scholarships, athletic grants, and part-time jobs. The average aided 2002–03 undergraduate received an aid package worth $8091. The priority application deadline for financial aid is March 1.
Freshman Admission Evangel University requires a high school transcript, SAT I or ACT scores, and TOEFL scores for international students. A minimum 2.0 high school GPA is recommended. The application deadline for regular admission is August 1.
Transfer Admission The application deadline for admission is August 1.
Entrance Difficulty Evangel University assesses its entrance difficulty level as moderately difficult. For the fall 2003 freshman class, 81 percent of the applicants were accepted.

For Further Information Contact Ms. Charity Waltner, Director of Admissions, Evangel University, 1111 North Glenstone, Springfield, MO 65802. *Telephone:* 417-865-2811 Ext. 7262 or 800-382-6435 (toll-free in-state). *Fax:* 417-865-9599. *E-mail:* admissions@evangel.edu. *Web site:* http://www.evangel.edu/.

FONTBONNE UNIVERSITY

St. Louis, Missouri

Fontbonne University is a coed, private, Roman Catholic, comprehensive institution, founded in 1917, offering degrees at the bachelor's and master's levels and postbachelor's certificates. It has a 13-acre campus in St. Louis.

Academic Information The faculty has 294 members (22% full-time), 38% with terminal degrees. The undergraduate student-faculty ratio is 12:1. The library holds 102,552 titles, 333 serial subscriptions, and 14,983 audiovisual materials. Special programs include academic remediation, services for learning-disabled students, an honors program, cooperative (work-study) education, advanced placement credit, accelerated degree programs, ESL programs, double majors, independent study, distance learning, self-designed majors, summer session for credit, adult/continuing education programs, internships, and arrangement for off-campus study with Webster University, Maryville College, Lindenwood College, Missouri Baptist College. The most frequently chosen baccalaureate fields are business/marketing, education, visual/performing arts.
Student Body Statistics The student body totals 2,538, of whom 1,767 are undergraduates (205 freshmen). 77 percent are women and 23 percent are men. Students come from 23 states and territories and 1 other country. 86 percent are from Missouri. 0.8 percent are international students. 15 percent of the 2003 graduating class went on to graduate and professional schools.
Expenses for 2004–05 *Application fee:* $25. *Comprehensive fee:* $22,408 includes full-time tuition ($15,100), mandatory fees ($320), and college room and board ($6988). Full-time tuition and fees vary according to program and reciprocity agreements. Room and board charges vary according to board plan and housing facility. *Part-time tuition:* $410 per credit hour. *Part-time mandatory fees:* $16 per credit hour. Part-time tuition and fees vary according to course load, program, and reciprocity agreements.
Financial Aid Forms of aid include need-based and non-need-based scholarships and part-time jobs. The average aided 2003–04 undergraduate received an aid package worth an estimated $15,600. The priority application deadline for financial aid is April 30.
Freshman Admission Fontbonne University requires an essay, a high school transcript, a minimum 2.5 high school GPA, SAT I or ACT scores, and TOEFL scores for international students. 2 recommendations and an interview are recommended. The application deadline for regular admission is August 1.
Transfer Admission The application deadline for admission is rolling.

Entrance Difficulty Fontbonne University assesses its entrance difficulty level as moderately difficult. For the fall 2003 freshman class, 81 percent of the applicants were accepted.

For Further Information Contact Ms. Peggy Musen, Associate Dean for Enrollment Management, Fontbonne University, 6800 Wydown Boulevard, St. Louis, MO 63105-3098. *Telephone:* 314-889-1400. *Fax:* 314-719-8021. *E-mail:* pmusen@fontbonne.edu. *Web site:* http://www.fontbonne.edu/.

GLOBAL UNIVERSITY OF THE ASSEMBLIES OF GOD

Springfield, Missouri

Global University of the Assemblies of God is a coed, private, comprehensive institution, founded in 1948, affiliated with the Assemblies of God, offering degrees at the associate, bachelor's, and master's levels and postbachelor's certificates in biblical studies (offers only external degree programs).

Academic Information The faculty has 498 members (12% full-time), 46% with terminal degrees. The library holds 180 serial subscriptions. Special programs include academic remediation, an honors program, cooperative (work-study) education, advanced placement credit, accelerated degree programs, independent study, distance learning, part-time degree programs, external degree programs, adult/continuing education programs, and internships. The most frequently chosen baccalaureate field is philosophy, religion, and theology.

Student Body Statistics The student body totals 6,748, of whom 6,503 are undergraduates. 35 percent are women and 65 percent are men. Students come from 50 states and territories and 127 other countries. 3 percent are from Missouri.

Expenses for 2003–04 *Application fee:* $35. *Tuition:* $2160 full-time, $90 per credit hour part-time. Full-time tuition varies according to reciprocity agreements. Part-time tuition varies according to course load and reciprocity agreements.

Freshman Admission Global University of the Assemblies of God requires a high school transcript. An essay is recommended. 1 recommendation is required for some. The application deadline for regular admission is rolling.

Transfer Admission The application deadline for admission is rolling.

Entrance Difficulty Global University of the Assemblies of God has an open admission policy.

For Further Information Contact Ms. Jessica Dorn, Director of US Enrollments, Global University of the Assemblies of God, 1211 South Glenstone Avenue, Springfield, MO 65804. *Telephone:* 800-443-1083 or 800-443-1083 (toll-free). *Fax:* 417-862-5318. *E-mail:* studentinfo@globaluniversity.edu. *Web site:* http://www.globaluniversity.edu/.

HANNIBAL-LAGRANGE COLLEGE

Hannibal, Missouri

HLG is a coed, private, Southern Baptist, four-year college, founded in 1858, offering degrees at the associate and bachelor's levels. It has a 110-acre campus in Hannibal.

Academic Information The faculty has 92 members (58% full-time), 34% with terminal degrees. The student-faculty ratio is 14:1. The library holds 71,680 titles, 516 serial subscriptions, and 6,605 audiovisual materials. Special programs include academic remediation, services for learning-disabled students, an honors program, cooperative (work-study) education, study abroad, advanced placement credit, accelerated degree programs, Freshman Honors College, double majors, independent study, self-designed majors, summer session for credit, part-time degree programs, adult/continuing education programs, and internships.

Student Body Statistics The student body is made up of 1,133 undergraduates. 62 percent are women and 38 percent are men. Students come from 24 states and territories. 83 percent are from Missouri.

Expenses for 2003–04 *Application fee:* $25. *Comprehensive fee:* $13,940 includes full-time tuition ($9840), mandatory fees ($320), and college room and board ($3780). Full-time tuition and fees vary according to course load. Room and board charges vary according to board plan and housing facility. *Part-time tuition:* $328 per credit hour. *Part-time mandatory fees:* $70 per term. Part-time tuition and fees vary according to course load.

Financial Aid Forms of aid include need-based and non-need-based scholarships, athletic grants, and part-time jobs. The average aided 2003–04 undergraduate received an aid package worth an estimated $8918. The application deadline for financial aid is continuous.

Freshman Admission HLG requires a high school transcript, a minimum 2.0 high school GPA, 2 recommendations, SAT I or ACT scores, and TOEFL scores for international students. The application deadline for regular admission is August 26.

Transfer Admission The application deadline for admission is rolling.

Entrance Difficulty HLG assesses its entrance difficulty level as moderately difficult. For the fall 2003 freshman class, 94 percent of the applicants were accepted.

For Further Information Contact Mr. Raymond Carty, Dean of Enrollment Management, Hannibal-LaGrange College, 2800 Palmyra Road, Hannibal, MO 63401-1999. *Telephone:* 573-221-3113 or 800-HLG-1119 (toll-free). *Fax:* 573-221-6594. *E-mail:* admissio@hlg.edu. *Web site:* http://www.hlg.edu/.

HARRIS-STOWE STATE COLLEGE

St. Louis, Missouri

Harris-Stowe State College is a coed, public, four-year college of Missouri Coordinating Board for Higher Education, founded in 1857, offering degrees at the bachelor's level. It has a 22-acre campus in St. Louis.

Academic Information The faculty has 145 members (38% full-time), 17% with terminal degrees. The student-faculty ratio is 17:1. The library holds 60,000 titles, 340 serial subscriptions, and 15 audiovisual materials. Special programs include academic remediation, services for learning-disabled students, cooperative (work-study) education, advanced placement credit, self-designed majors, summer session for credit, part-time degree programs (daytime, evenings, weekends, summer), internships, and arrangement for off-campus study with Saint Louis University, University of Missouri–St. Louis. The most frequently chosen baccalaureate fields are education, business/marketing, interdisciplinary studies.

Student Body Statistics The student body is made up of 1,911 undergraduates (128 freshmen). 77 percent are women and 23 percent are men. Students come from 3 states and territories and 13 other countries. 91 percent are from Missouri.

Expenses for 2003–04 *Application fee:* $15. *State resident tuition:* $3120 full-time, $130 per credit hour part-time. *Nonresident tuition:* $6146 full-time, $256.10 per credit hour part-time. *Mandatory fees:* $160 full-time, $80 per term part-time. Full-time tuition and fees vary according to course load. Part-time tuition and fees vary according to course load.

Financial Aid Forms of aid include need-based and non-need-based scholarships, athletic grants, and part-time jobs. The average aided 2002–03 undergraduate received an aid package worth $2890. The priority application deadline for financial aid is April 1.

Freshman Admission Harris-Stowe State College requires a high school transcript, a minimum 2.0 high school GPA, SAT I or ACT scores, and TOEFL scores for international students. The application deadline for regular admission is rolling.

Transfer Admission The application deadline for admission is rolling.

Entrance Difficulty Harris-Stowe State College assesses its entrance difficulty level as moderately difficult. For the fall 2003 freshman class, 47 percent of the applicants were accepted.

For Further Information Contact Ms. LaShanda Boone, Director of Admissions, Harris-Stowe State College, 3026 Laclede Avenue, St. Louis, MO 63103. *Telephone:* 314-340-3301. *Fax:* 314-340-3555. *E-mail:* admissions@hssc.edu. *Web site:* http://www.hssc.edu/.

HICKEY COLLEGE

St. Louis, Missouri

Hickey College is a coed, proprietary, primarily two-year college, founded in 1933, offering degrees at the associate and bachelor's levels.

Academic Information The faculty has 18 members (67% full-time). The student-faculty ratio is 30:1. Special programs include accelerated degree programs.
Student Body Statistics The student body is made up of 500 undergraduates.
Expenses for 2004–05 *Application fee:* $50. *Tuition:* $10,480 full-time, $300 per credit hour part-time. *College room only:* $4800.
Freshman Admission Hickey College requires a high school transcript and an interview. The application deadline for regular admission is rolling.
Transfer Admission The application deadline for admission is rolling.
Entrance Difficulty Hickey College assesses its entrance difficulty level as minimally difficult.

For Further Information Contact Ms. Michelle Hayes, Director of Admissions, Hickey College, 940 West Port Plaza Drive, St. Louis, MO 63146. *Telephone:* 314-434-2212 Ext. 136 or 800-777-1544 (toll-free). *Fax:* 314-434-1974. *E-mail:* admin@hickeycollege.com. *Web site:* http://www.hickeycollege.com/.

IHM HEALTH STUDIES CENTER

St. Louis, Missouri

IHM Health Studies Center is a coed, private, two-year college, founded in 1977, offering degrees at the associate level.

Academic Information The faculty has 7 members (57% full-time).
Student Body Statistics The student body is made up of 136 undergraduates. 40 percent are women and 60 percent are men.

For Further Information Contact Mr. Taz A. Meyer, Director of Education, IHM Health Studies Center, 2500 Abbott Place, St. Louis, MO 63143-2636. *Telephone:* 314-768-1234 Ext. 1128. *Fax:* 314-768-1595. *Web site:* http://www.ihmhealthstudies.com/.

ITT TECHNICAL INSTITUTE

Arnold, Missouri

ITT Technical Institute is a coed, proprietary, primarily two-year college of ITT Educational Services, Inc., offering degrees at the associate and bachelor's levels.

Student Body Statistics The student body is made up of 483 undergraduates.
Expenses for 2003–04 *Application fee:* $100. Total Program Cost varies depending on course of study. Consult school catalog.
Financial Aid Forms of aid include need-based scholarships and part-time jobs. The application deadline for financial aid is continuous.
Freshman Admission ITT Technical Institute requires a high school transcript, an interview, and Wonderlic aptitude test. Recommendations are recommended. The application deadline for regular admission is rolling.
Transfer Admission The application deadline for admission is rolling.
Entrance Difficulty ITT Technical Institute assesses its entrance difficulty level as minimally difficult.

For Further Information Contact Mr. James R. Rowe, Director of Recruitment, ITT Technical Institute, 1930 Meyer Drury Drive, Arnold, MO 63010. *Telephone:* 636-464-6600 or 888-488-1082 (toll-free). *Fax:* 636-464-6611. *Web site:* http://www.itt-tech.edu/.

ITT TECHNICAL INSTITUTE

Earth City, Missouri

ITT Tech is a coed, proprietary, primarily two-year college of ITT Educational Services, Inc., founded in 1936, offering degrees at the associate and bachelor's levels. It has a 2-acre campus in Earth City near St. Louis.

Student Body Statistics The student body is made up of 603 undergraduates.
Expenses for 2003–04 *Application fee:* $100. Total Program Cost varies depending on course of study. Consult school catalog.
Financial Aid Forms of aid include need-based scholarships and part-time jobs. The application deadline for financial aid is continuous.
Freshman Admission ITT Tech requires a high school transcript, an interview, TOEFL scores for international students, and Wonderlic aptitude test. Recommendations are recommended. The application deadline for regular admission is rolling.
Transfer Admission The application deadline for admission is rolling.
Entrance Difficulty ITT Tech assesses its entrance difficulty level as minimally difficult.

For Further Information Contact Ms. Karen Finkenkeller, Director, ITT Technical Institute, 13505 Lakefront Drive, Earth City, MO 63045. *Telephone:* 314-298-7800 or 800-235-5488 (toll-free). *Fax:* 314-298-0559. *Web site:* http://www.itt-tech.edu/.

JEWISH HOSPITAL COLLEGE OF NURSING AND ALLIED HEALTH

St. Louis, Missouri

Jewish Hospital College is a coed, primarily women's, private, comprehensive institution, founded in 1902, offering degrees at the associate, bachelor's, and master's levels and post-master's and postbachelor's certificates.

Academic Information The faculty has 43 members (77% full-time), 40% with terminal degrees. The undergraduate student-faculty ratio is 10:1. The library holds 3,765 titles, 232 serial subscriptions, and 400 audiovisual materials. Special programs include services for learning-disabled students, advanced placement credit, double majors, independent study, summer session for credit, part-time degree programs (daytime, evenings, weekends, summer), and arrangement for off-campus study with Washington University in St. Louis. The most frequently chosen baccalaureate field is health professions and related sciences.
Student Body Statistics The student body totals 781, of whom 686 are undergraduates (42 freshmen). 89 percent are women and 11 percent are men. Students come from 7 states and territories. 86 percent are from Missouri. 10 percent of the 2003 graduating class went on to graduate and professional schools.
Expenses for 2004–05 *Application fee:* $25. *Tuition:* $8808 full-time. *Mandatory fees:* $300 full-time. Full-time tuition and fees vary according to course load. *Part-time tuition:* varies with course load. *College room only:* $2550.
Financial Aid Forms of aid include need-based and non-need-based scholarships and part-time jobs. The average aided 2003–04 undergraduate received an aid package worth an estimated $16,000. The priority application deadline for financial aid is April 1.
Freshman Admission Jewish Hospital College requires a high school transcript, a minimum 2.0 high school GPA, 2 recommendations, and SAT I or ACT scores. The application deadline for regular admission is rolling.
Transfer Admission The application deadline for admission is rolling.
Entrance Difficulty Jewish Hospital College assesses its entrance difficulty level as moderately difficult. For the fall 2003 freshman class, 91 percent of the applicants were accepted.

For Further Information Contact Ms. Christie Schneider, Chief Admissions Officer, Jewish Hospital College of Nursing and Allied Health, 306 South Kingshighway Boulevard, St. Louis, MO 63110. *Telephone:* 314-454-7538 or 800-832-9009 (toll-free in-state). *Fax:* 314-454-5239. *E-mail:* jhcollegeinquiry@bjc.org. *Web site:* http://www.jhconah.edu/.

KANSAS CITY ART INSTITUTE
Kansas City, Missouri

KCAI is a coed, private, four-year college, founded in 1885, offering degrees at the bachelor's level in art. It has an 18-acre campus in Kansas City.

Academic Information The faculty has 79 members (53% full-time), 71% with terminal degrees. The student-faculty ratio is 9:1. The library holds 30,000 titles and 125 serial subscriptions. Special programs include academic remediation, services for learning-disabled students, cooperative (work-study) education, study abroad, advanced placement credit, ESL programs, double majors, independent study, summer session for credit, adult/continuing education programs, internships, and arrangement for off-campus study with New York Studio Program, AICAD School Exchange. The most frequently chosen baccalaureate field is visual/performing arts.
Student Body Statistics The student body totals 602, of whom 571 are undergraduates (114 freshmen). 53 percent are women and 47 percent are men. Students come from 37 states and territories. 64 percent are from Missouri. 1.5 percent are international students. 20 percent of the 2003 graduating class went on to graduate and professional schools.
Expenses for 2004–05 *Application fee:* $35. *Comprehensive fee:* $28,126 includes full-time tuition ($21,326) and college room and board ($6800). Room and board charges vary according to board plan and housing facility. *Part-time tuition:* $850 per credit hour.
Financial Aid Forms of aid include need-based and non-need-based scholarships and part-time jobs. The average aided 2003–04 undergraduate received an aid package worth an estimated $16,260. The priority application deadline for financial aid is March 15.
Freshman Admission KCAI requires an essay, a high school transcript, a minimum 2.5 high school GPA, 2 recommendations, portfolio, statement of purpose, SAT I or ACT scores, and TOEFL scores for international students. An interview is recommended. The application deadline for regular admission is rolling.
Transfer Admission The application deadline for admission is rolling.
Entrance Difficulty KCAI assesses its entrance difficulty level as moderately difficult. For the fall 2003 freshman class, 81 percent of the applicants were accepted.

For Further Information Contact Mr. Gerald Valet, Director of Admission Technology, Kansas City Art Institute, 4415 Warwick Boulevard, Kansas City, MO 64111-1874. *Telephone:* 816-474-5224 or 800-522-5224 (toll-free). *Fax:* 816-802-3309. *E-mail:* admiss@kcai.edu. *Web site:* http://www.kcai.edu/.

KANSAS CITY COLLEGE OF LEGAL STUDIES
Kansas City, Missouri

For Information Write to Kansas City College of Legal Studies, Kansas City, MO 64131.

LESTER L. COX COLLEGE OF NURSING AND HEALTH SCIENCES
Springfield, Missouri

Lester L. Cox College of Nursing and Health Sciences is a coed, primarily women's, private, four-year college, founded in 1994, offering degrees at the associate and bachelor's levels.

Academic Information The faculty has 47 members (45% full-time), 23% with terminal degrees. The student-faculty ratio is 9:1. Special programs include academic remediation, accelerated degree programs, summer session for credit, and part-time degree programs (daytime, evenings). The most frequently chosen baccalaureate field is health professions and related sciences.

Student Body Statistics The student body is made up of 529 undergraduates (53 freshmen). 92 percent are women and 8 percent are men. Students come from 4 states and territories. 99 percent are from Missouri.
Expenses for 2004–05 *Application fee:* $30. *One-time mandatory fee:* $100. *Tuition:* $8910 full-time, $297 per credit hour part-time. *Mandatory fees:* $1050 full-time, $35 per credit hour part-time. Full-time tuition and fees vary according to course load and program. Part-time tuition and fees vary according to course load and program. *College room only:* $2000.
Financial Aid Forms of aid include need-based and non-need-based scholarships and part-time jobs. The average aided 2002–03 undergraduate received an aid package worth $8500. The priority application deadline for financial aid is April 1.
Freshman Admission Lester L. Cox College of Nursing and Health Sciences requires a high school transcript, a minimum 2.5 high school GPA, and ACT scores. ACT scores, SAT I or ACT scores, and SAT I and SAT II or ACT scores are recommended. The application deadline for regular admission is February 1 and for early decision it is November 1.
Transfer Admission The application deadline for admission is August 1.
Entrance Difficulty For the fall 2003 freshman class, 81 percent of the applicants were accepted.

For Further Information Contact Ms. Jennifer Plimmer, Admission Coordinator, Lester L. Cox College of Nursing and Health Sciences, 1423 North Jefferson, Springfield, MO 65802. *Telephone:* 417-269-3038 or 866-898-5355 (toll-free in-state). *Fax:* 417-269-3581. *E-mail:* admissions@coxcollege.edu. *Web site:* http://www.coxcollege.edu/.

LINCOLN UNIVERSITY
Jefferson City, Missouri

LU is a coed, public, comprehensive unit of Missouri Coordinating Board for Higher Education, founded in 1866, offering degrees at the associate, bachelor's, and master's levels and first professional certificates. It has a 152-acre campus in Jefferson City.

Academic Information The faculty has 224 members (61% full-time), 36% with terminal degrees. The undergraduate student-faculty ratio is 16:1. The library holds 151,595 titles and 761 serial subscriptions. Special programs include academic remediation, services for learning-disabled students, an honors program, cooperative (work-study) education, advanced placement credit, accelerated degree programs, Freshman Honors College, self-designed majors, summer session for credit, part-time degree programs (daytime, evenings, weekends, summer), adult/continuing education programs, and internships. The most frequently chosen baccalaureate fields are business/marketing, computer/information sciences, education.
Student Body Statistics The student body totals 3,128, of whom 2,910 are undergraduates (533 freshmen). 61 percent are women and 39 percent are men. 82 percent are from Missouri. 5.8 percent are international students.
Expenses for 2003–04 *Application fee:* $17. *State resident tuition:* $3894 full-time, $134.80 per credit hour part-time. *Nonresident tuition:* $7434 full-time, $252.80 per credit hour part-time. *Mandatory fees:* $668 full-time. *College room and board:* $3790. *College room only:* $1850.
Financial Aid Forms of aid include need-based and non-need-based scholarships, athletic grants, and part-time jobs. The average aided 2002–03 undergraduate received an aid package worth $6000. The priority application deadline for financial aid is March 1.
Freshman Admission LU requires a high school transcript, 1 recommendation, and TOEFL scores for international students. The application deadline for regular admission is August 1.
Entrance Difficulty LU has an open admission policy for state residents. It assesses its entrance difficulty as minimally difficult for out-of-state applicants; minimally difficult for transfers.

For Further Information Contact Mr. Mohammad Khaleel, Associate Director of Admissions, Lincoln University, 820 Chestnut Street, PO Box 29, Jefferson City, MO 62102-0029. *Telephone:* 573-681-5599 or 800-521-5052 (toll-free). *Fax:* 573-681-5889. *Web site:* http://www.lincolnu.edu/.

LINDENWOOD UNIVERSITY

St. Charles, Missouri

Lindenwood is a coed, private, Presbyterian, comprehensive institution, founded in 1827, offering degrees at the bachelor's and master's levels and post-master's certificates. It has a 420-acre campus in St. Charles near St. Louis.

Academic Information   The faculty has 426 members (41% full-time). The undergraduate student-faculty ratio is 17:1. The library holds 130,412 titles, 3,789 serial subscriptions, and 2,748 audiovisual materials. Special programs include academic remediation, services for learning-disabled students, an honors program, cooperative (work-study) education, study abroad, advanced placement credit, accelerated degree programs, Freshman Honors College, double majors, independent study, self-designed majors, summer session for credit, part-time degree programs (daytime, evenings, weekends, summer), external degree programs, adult/continuing education programs, internships, and arrangement for off-campus study with St. Louis Private College Consortium, Washington University in St. Louis, University of Missouri–Columbia. The most frequently chosen baccalaureate fields are business/marketing, communications/communication technologies, education.

Student Body Statistics   The student body totals 7,838, of whom 4,923 are undergraduates (784 freshmen). 56 percent are women and 44 percent are men. Students come from 38 states and territories and 61 other countries. 82 percent are from Missouri. 8 percent are international students. 14 percent of the 2003 graduating class went on to graduate and professional schools.

Expenses for 2004–05   *Application fee:* $25. *Comprehensive fee:* $17,050 includes full-time tuition ($11,200), mandatory fees ($450), and college room and board ($5400). *College room only:* $2700. *Part-time tuition:* $300 per credit hour. Part-time tuition varies according to course load.

Financial Aid   Forms of aid include need-based and non-need-based scholarships and part-time jobs. The priority application deadline for financial aid is March 15.

Freshman Admission   Lindenwood requires a high school transcript, minimum ACT score of 20 or minimum SAT score of 900, SAT I or ACT scores, and TOEFL scores for international students. An interview is recommended. An essay, recommendations, and an interview are required for some. The application deadline for regular admission is rolling.

Transfer Admission   The application deadline for admission is rolling.

Entrance Difficulty   Lindenwood assesses its entrance difficulty level as moderately difficult. For the fall 2003 freshman class, 46 percent of the applicants were accepted.

For Further Information   Contact Ms. Kammie Kobyleski, Associate Director of Admissions, Lindenwood University, 209 South Kingshighway, St. Charles, MO 63301-1695. *Telephone:* 636-949-4934 or 636-949-4949 (toll-free). *Fax:* 636-949-4989. *Web site:* http://www.lindenwood.edu/.

LOGAN UNIVERSITY-COLLEGE OF CHIROPRACTIC

Chesterfield, Missouri

Logan is a coed, private, upper-level institution, founded in 1935, offering degrees at the bachelor's and first professional levels in health sciences. It has a 111-acre campus in Chesterfield near St. Louis.

Academic Information   The faculty has 90 members (56% full-time), 94% with terminal degrees. The undergraduate student-faculty ratio is 12:1. The library holds 12,838 titles, 225 serial subscriptions, and 2,078 audiovisual materials. Special programs include services for learning-disabled students, advanced placement credit, independent study, distance learning, adult/continuing education programs, and internships. The most frequently chosen baccalaureate field is biological/life sciences.

Student Body Statistics   The student body totals 1,118, of whom 115 are undergraduates. 34 percent are women and 66 percent are men. Students come from 26 states and territories and 1 other country. 43 percent are from Missouri. 0.9 percent are international students.

Expenses for 2004–05   *Application fee:* $50. *Tuition:* $3090 full-time, $95 per credit hour part-time. *Mandatory fees:* $220 full-time, $110. Full-time tuition and fees vary according to program. Part-time tuition and fees vary according to program.

Financial Aid   Forms of aid include need-based and non-need-based scholarships and part-time jobs. The priority application deadline for financial aid is April 30.

Transfer Admission   Logan requires a minimum 2.5 college GPA and a college transcript. The application deadline for admission is rolling.

Entrance Difficulty   Logan assesses its entrance difficulty level as moderately difficult.

For Further Information   Contact Dr. Patrick Browne, Vice President of Enrollment, Logan University-College of Chiropractic, 1851 Schoettler Road, Chesterfield, MO 63006-1065. *Telephone:* 636-227-2100 Ext. 149 or 800-533-9210 (toll-free). *Fax:* 636-207-2425. *E-mail:* loganadm@logan.edu. *Web site:* http://www.logan.edu/.

MARYVILLE UNIVERSITY OF SAINT LOUIS

St. Louis, Missouri

Maryville is a coed, private, comprehensive institution, founded in 1872, offering degrees at the bachelor's and master's levels. It has a 130-acre campus in St. Louis.

Academic Information   The faculty has 342 members (26% full-time), 58% with terminal degrees. The undergraduate student-faculty ratio is 13:1. The library holds 205,512 titles, 9,004 serial subscriptions, and 10,933 audiovisual materials. Special programs include services for learning-disabled students, an honors program, cooperative (work-study) education, study abroad, advanced placement credit, accelerated degree programs, Freshman Honors College, ESL programs, double majors, independent study, distance learning, self-designed majors, summer session for credit, part-time degree programs (daytime, evenings, weekends, summer), adult/continuing education programs, internships, and arrangement for off-campus study with Fontbonne University, Lindenwood University, Webster University, Missouri Baptist University. The most frequently chosen baccalaureate fields are business/marketing, health professions and related sciences, psychology.

Student Body Statistics   The student body totals 3,301, of whom 2,705 are undergraduates (335 freshmen). 76 percent are women and 24 percent are men. Students come from 17 states and territories and 20 other countries. 91 percent are from Missouri. 1.7 percent are international students.

Expenses for 2004–05   *Application fee:* $25. *Comprehensive fee:* $23,300 includes full-time tuition ($16,000), mandatory fees ($300), and college room and board ($7000). Room and board charges vary according to housing facility. *Part-time tuition:* $485 per credit hour. *Part-time mandatory fees:* $75 per term. Part-time tuition and fees vary according to class time.

Financial Aid   Forms of aid include need-based and non-need-based scholarships and part-time jobs. The average aided 2003–04 undergraduate received an aid package worth an estimated $10,822. The priority application deadline for financial aid is April 1.

Freshman Admission   Maryville requires a high school transcript, a minimum 2.5 high school GPA, SAT I or ACT scores, and TOEFL scores for international students. An essay, recommendations, an interview, and audition, portfolio are required for some. The application deadline for regular admission is August 15.

Transfer Admission   The application deadline for admission is rolling.

Entrance Difficulty   Maryville assesses its entrance difficulty level as moderately difficult; very difficult for physical therapy, occupational therapy, education, actuarial science programs. For the fall 2003 freshman class, 73 percent of the applicants were accepted.

For Further Information   Contact Ms. Lynn Jackson, Admissions Director, Maryville University of Saint Louis, 13550 Conway Road, St. Louis, MO 63141-7299. *Telephone:* 314-529-9350 or 800-627-9855 (toll-free). *Fax:* 314-529-9927. *E-mail:* admissions@maryville.edu. *Web site:* http://www.maryville.edu/.

MESSENGER COLLEGE
Joplin, Missouri

Messenger College is a coed, private, Pentecostal, four-year college, founded in 1987, offering degrees at the associate and bachelor's levels. It has a 16-acre campus in Joplin near Springfield.

Academic Information The faculty has 14 members (29% full-time), 29% with terminal degrees. The student-faculty ratio is 8:1. The library holds 28,874 titles, 114 serial subscriptions, and 326 audiovisual materials. Special programs include academic remediation, an honors program, cooperative (work-study) education, double majors, independent study, distance learning, part-time degree programs (daytime, evenings), external degree programs, and internships. The most frequently chosen baccalaureate fields are education, philosophy, religion, and theology, visual/performing arts.
Student Body Statistics The student body is made up of 100 undergraduates (31 freshmen). 47 percent are women and 53 percent are men. Students come from 17 states and territories. 51 percent are from Missouri. 13 percent of the 2003 graduating class went on to graduate and professional schools.
Expenses for 2003–04 *Application fee:* $35. *Comprehensive fee:* $7970 includes full-time tuition ($4500), mandatory fees ($370), and college room and board ($3100). Room and board charges vary according to housing facility. *Part-time tuition:* $150 per credit hour.
Financial Aid Forms of aid include need-based and non-need-based scholarships and part-time jobs. The average aided 2002–03 undergraduate received an aid package worth $7000. The application deadline for financial aid is continuous.
Freshman Admission Messenger College requires an essay, a high school transcript, a minimum 2.0 high school GPA, 3 recommendations, a health form, SAT I or ACT scores, and TOEFL scores for international students. An interview is required for some. The application deadline for regular admission is August 1.
Transfer Admission The application deadline for admission is August 1.
Entrance Difficulty Messenger College assesses its entrance difficulty level as moderately difficult. For the fall 2003 freshman class, 87 percent of the applicants were accepted.

For Further Information Contact Tiffany Stump, Director of Admissions, Messenger College, 300 East 50th, Joplin, MO 64804. *Telephone:* 417-624-7070 Ext. 108 or 800-385-8940 (toll-free in-state). *Fax:* 417-624-5070. *E-mail:* info@messengercollege.edu. *Web site:* http://www.messengercollege.edu/.

METRO BUSINESS COLLEGE
Cape Girardeau, Missouri

Metro Business College is a coed, proprietary, primarily two-year college, offering degrees at the associate and bachelor's levels.

For Further Information Contact Ms. Kyla Evans, Admissions Director, Metro Business College, 1732 North Kings Highway, Cape Girardeau, MO 63701. *Telephone:* 573-334-9181. *Fax:* 573-334-0617. *Web site:* http://www.metrobusinesscollege.edu/.

MISSOURI BAPTIST UNIVERSITY
St. Louis, Missouri

Missouri Baptist University is a coed, private, Southern Baptist, comprehensive institution, founded in 1964, offering degrees at the associate, bachelor's, and master's levels and postbachelor's certificates. It has a 65-acre campus in St. Louis.

Academic Information The faculty has 157 members (29% full-time). The undergraduate student-faculty ratio is 18:1. The library holds 90,387 titles, 610 serial subscriptions, and 4,181 audiovisual materials. Special programs include services for learning-disabled students, study abroad, advanced placement credit, accelerated degree programs, double majors, independent study, distance learning, self-designed majors, summer session

for credit, part-time degree programs (daytime, evenings, summer), adult/continuing education programs, internships, and arrangement for off-campus study with Maryville University of Saint Louis, Lindenwood University, Fontbonne College, Webster University. The most frequently chosen baccalaureate fields are business/marketing, education, philosophy, religion, and theology.
Student Body Statistics The student body totals 3,656, of whom 2,947 are undergraduates (210 freshmen). 61 percent are women and 39 percent are men. Students come from 22 states and territories and 21 other countries. 89 percent are from Missouri. 2.6 percent are international students.
Expenses for 2003–04 *Application fee:* $25. *Comprehensive fee:* $18,080 includes full-time tuition ($11,770), mandatory fees ($510), and college room and board ($5800). Full-time tuition and fees vary according to course load and location. Room and board charges vary according to housing facility. *Part-time tuition:* $410 per credit. Part-time tuition varies according to course load and location.
Financial Aid Forms of aid include need-based and non-need-based scholarships, athletic grants, and part-time jobs. The average aided 2002–03 undergraduate received an aid package worth $7400. The priority application deadline for financial aid is April 1.
Freshman Admission Missouri Baptist University requires a high school transcript, a minimum 2.0 high school GPA, recommendations, an interview, and TOEFL scores for international students. SAT I or ACT scores are required for some. The application deadline for regular admission is rolling.
Transfer Admission The application deadline for admission is rolling.
Entrance Difficulty Missouri Baptist University assesses its entrance difficulty level as moderately difficult. For the fall 2003 freshman class, 71 percent of the applicants were accepted.

For Further Information Contact Mr. Robert Cornwell, Director of Admissions, Missouri Baptist University, One College Park Drive, St. Louis, MO 63141-8660. *Telephone:* 314-392-2296 or 877-434-1115 Ext. 2290 (toll-free). *Fax:* 314-434-7596. *E-mail:* admissions@mobap.edu. *Web site:* http://www.mobap.edu/.

MISSOURI SOUTHERN STATE UNIVERSITY
Joplin, Missouri

Missouri Southern State is a coed, public, four-year college, founded in 1937, offering degrees at the associate and bachelor's levels. It has a 350-acre campus in Joplin.

Academic Information The faculty has 286 members (69% full-time), 47% with terminal degrees. The student-faculty ratio is 18:1. The library holds 157,362 titles, 1,574 serial subscriptions, and 10,417 audiovisual materials. Special programs include academic remediation, services for learning-disabled students, an honors program, cooperative (work-study) education, study abroad, advanced placement credit, accelerated degree programs, ESL programs, double majors, independent study, distance learning, summer session for credit, part-time degree programs (daytime, evenings, weekends, summer), external degree programs, adult/continuing education programs, internships, and arrangement for off-campus study with Crowder College and Nevada Telecenter. The most frequently chosen baccalaureate fields are business/marketing, education, protective services/public administration.
Student Body Statistics The student body is made up of 5,410 undergraduates (692 freshmen). 59 percent are women and 41 percent are men. Students come from 28 states and territories and 35 other countries. 87 percent are from Missouri. 1.7 percent are international students.
Expenses for 2004–05 *Application fee:* $15. *State resident tuition:* $3810 full-time, $127 per credit part-time. *Nonresident tuition:* $7620 full-time, $254 per credit part-time. *Mandatory fees:* $166 full-time, $83 per term part-time. *College room and board:* $4770.
Financial Aid Forms of aid include need-based and non-need-based scholarships, athletic grants, and part-time jobs. The average aided 2003–04 undergraduate received an aid package worth an estimated $6722. The priority application deadline for financial aid is February 15.
Freshman Admission Missouri Southern State requires a high school transcript, SAT I or ACT scores, and TOEFL scores for international

Missouri Southern State University (continued)

students. ACT scores are recommended. ACT scores and Michigan Test of English Language Proficiency are required for some. The application deadline for regular admission is August 3.

Transfer Admission The application deadline for admission is August 3.

Entrance Difficulty Missouri Southern State assesses its entrance difficulty level as moderately difficult; noncompetitive for transfers. For the fall 2003 freshman class, 74 percent of the applicants were accepted.

For Further Information Contact Mr. Derek Skaggs, Director of Enrollment Services, Missouri Southern State University, 3950 East Newman Road, Joplin, MO 64801-1595. *Telephone:* 417-625-9537 or 866-818-MSSU (toll-free). *Fax:* 417-659-4429. *E-mail:* admissions@mssu.edu. *Web site:* http://www.mssu.edu/.

See page 312 for a narrative description.

MISSOURI TECH

St. Louis, Missouri

Missouri Tech is a coed, primarily men's, proprietary, four-year college, founded in 1932, offering degrees at the associate and bachelor's levels in electronics engineering technology.

Academic Information The faculty has 11 members (64% full-time), 9% with terminal degrees. The student-faculty ratio is 10:1. Special programs include advanced placement credit, accelerated degree programs, summer session for credit, part-time degree programs (daytime, evenings), adult/continuing education programs, and internships. The most frequently chosen baccalaureate field is engineering/engineering technologies.

Student Body Statistics The student body is made up of 201 undergraduates (11 freshmen). 11 percent are women and 89 percent are men. Students come from 4 states and territories. 80 percent are from Missouri. 3.5 percent are international students. 10 percent of the 2003 graduating class went on to graduate and professional schools.

Expenses for 2004–05 *Tuition:* $11,560 full-time, $370 per semester hour part-time. *Mandatory fees:* $380 full-time. Full-time tuition and fees vary according to course load. Part-time tuition varies according to course load. *College room only:* $3265.

Financial Aid Forms of aid include need-based and non-need-based scholarships. The application deadline for financial aid is continuous.

Freshman Admission Missouri Tech requires a high school transcript and TOEFL scores for international students. ACT scores are recommended. An interview and minimum ACT score of 20 are required for some. The application deadline for regular admission is rolling.

Entrance Difficulty Missouri Tech assesses its entrance difficulty level as moderately difficult. For the fall 2003 freshman class, 56 percent of the applicants were accepted.

For Further Information Contact Mr. Bob Honaker, Director of Admissions, Missouri Tech, 1167 Corporate Lake Drive, St. Louis, MO 63132. *Telephone:* 314-569-3600 Ext. 363. *Fax:* 314-569-1167. *Web site:* http://www.motech.edu/.

MISSOURI VALLEY COLLEGE

Marshall, Missouri

Missouri Valley is a coed, private, four-year college, founded in 1889, affiliated with the Presbyterian Church, offering degrees at the associate and bachelor's levels. It has a 140-acre campus in Marshall near Kansas City.

Academic Information The faculty has 113 members (58% full-time), 43% with terminal degrees. The student-faculty ratio is 18:1. The library holds 61,907 titles, 391 serial subscriptions, and 1,399 audiovisual materials. Special programs include services for learning-disabled students, cooperative (work-study) education, advanced placement credit, ESL programs, double majors, independent study, summer session for credit, part-time degree programs (daytime, evenings), adult/continuing education

programs, and internships. The most frequently chosen baccalaureate fields are business/marketing, education, protective services/public administration.

Student Body Statistics The student body is made up of 1,623 undergraduates (405 freshmen). 47 percent are women and 53 percent are men. Students come from 40 states and territories and 29 other countries. 66 percent are from Missouri. 7.5 percent are international students.

Expenses for 2004–05 *Application fee:* $15. *Comprehensive fee:* $18,700 includes full-time tuition ($13,000), mandatory fees ($500), and college room and board ($5200). *Part-time tuition:* $350 per credit hour.

Financial Aid Forms of aid include need-based and non-need-based scholarships and part-time jobs. The average aided 2002–03 undergraduate received an aid package worth $12,141. The application deadline for financial aid is September 15 with a priority deadline of March 20.

Freshman Admission Missouri Valley requires a high school transcript, SAT I or ACT scores, and TOEFL scores for international students. A minimum 2.0 high school GPA, an interview, and SAT II: Writing Test scores are recommended. An essay, 3 recommendations, and an interview are required for some. The application deadline for regular admission is rolling.

Transfer Admission The application deadline for admission is rolling.

Entrance Difficulty Missouri Valley assesses its entrance difficulty level as minimally difficult. For the fall 2003 freshman class, 67 percent of the applicants were accepted.

For Further Information Contact Ms. Debi Bultmann, Admissions, Missouri Valley College, Admissions Office, 500 East College, Marshall, MO 65340. *Telephone:* 660-831-4157. *Fax:* 660-831-4233. *E-mail:* admissions@moval.edu. *Web site:* http://www.moval.edu/.

See page 314 for a narrative description.

MISSOURI WESTERN STATE COLLEGE

St. Joseph, Missouri

MWSC is a coed, public, four-year college, founded in 1915, offering degrees at the associate and bachelor's levels. It has a 744-acre campus in St. Joseph near Kansas City.

Academic Information The faculty has 318 members (57% full-time), 49% with terminal degrees. The student-faculty ratio is 18:1. The library holds 147,509 titles, 1,068 serial subscriptions, and 13,705 audiovisual materials. Special programs include academic remediation, an honors program, advanced placement credit, accelerated degree programs, Freshman Honors College, double majors, distance learning, summer session for credit, part-time degree programs (daytime, evenings, weekends, summer), and internships. The most frequently chosen baccalaureate fields are business/marketing, education, protective services/public administration.

Student Body Statistics The student body is made up of 4,928 undergraduates (1,045 freshmen). 60 percent are women and 40 percent are men. Students come from 31 states and territories and 7 other countries. 93 percent are from Missouri. 0.3 percent are international students. 22 percent of the 2003 graduating class went on to graduate and professional schools.

Expenses for 2003–04 *Application fee:* $15. *State resident tuition:* $4098 full-time, $146 per credit part-time. *Nonresident tuition:* $7674 full-time, $267 per credit part-time. *Mandatory fees:* $366 full-time, $11 per credit part-time, $30 per term part-time. *College room and board:* $4058. Room and board charges vary according to board plan and housing facility.

Financial Aid Forms of aid include need-based and non-need-based scholarships and part-time jobs. The priority application deadline for financial aid is April 1.

Freshman Admission MWSC requires a high school transcript, ACT scores, and TOEFL scores for international students. The application deadline for regular admission is July 30.

Transfer Admission The application deadline for admission is July 30.

Entrance Difficulty MWSC has an open admission policy. It assesses its entrance difficulty as moderately difficult for nursing, computer science, education, criminal justice, leisure management, math, history, political science, social work programs.

For Further Information Contact Mr. Howard McCauley, Director of Admissions, Missouri Western State College, 4525 Downs Drive, St. Joseph, MO 64507-2294. *Telephone:* 816-271-4267 or 800-662-7041 Ext. 60 (toll-free). *Fax:* 816-271-5833. *E-mail:* admissn@mwsc.edu. *Web site:* http://www.mwsc.edu/.

NATIONAL AMERICAN UNIVERSITY

Kansas City, Missouri

For Information Write to National American University, Kansas City, MO 64133-1612.

NORTHWEST MISSOURI STATE UNIVERSITY

Maryville, Missouri

Northwest is a coed, public, comprehensive unit of Missouri Coordinating Board for Higher Education, founded in 1905, offering degrees at the bachelor's and master's levels. It has a 240-acre campus in Maryville near Kansas City.

Expenses for 2003–04 *Application fee:* $15. *State resident tuition:* $4845 full-time. *Nonresident tuition:* $8355 full-time. *Mandatory fees:* $180 full-time. Full-time tuition and fees vary according to course load. *College room and board:* $5042. Room and board charges vary according to board plan.

For Further Information Contact Ms. Deb Powers, Associate Director of Admission, Northwest Missouri State University, Office of Admissions, 800 University Drive, Maryville, MO 64468. *Telephone:* 660-562-1587 or 800-633-1175 (toll-free). *Fax:* 660-562-1121. *E-mail:* admissions@acad.nwmissouri.edu. *Web site:* http://www.nwmissouri.edu/.

OZARK CHRISTIAN COLLEGE

Joplin, Missouri

OCC is a coed, private, Christian, four-year college, founded in 1942, offering degrees at the associate and bachelor's levels. It has a 110-acre campus in Joplin.

Expenses for 2003–04 *Application fee:* $30. *Comprehensive fee:* $10,265 includes full-time tuition ($5760), mandatory fees ($535), and college room and board ($3970). *College room only:* $990. Room and board charges vary according to board plan.

For Further Information Contact Mr. Troy B. Nelson, Executive Director of Admissions, Ozark Christian College, 1111 North Main Street, Joplin, MO 64801-4804. *Telephone:* 417-624-2518 Ext. 2006 or 800-299-4622 (toll-free). *Fax:* 417-624-0090. *E-mail:* occadmin@occ.edu. *Web site:* http://www.occ.edu/.

PARK UNIVERSITY

Parkville, Missouri

Park is a coed, private, comprehensive institution, founded in 1875, offering degrees at the associate, bachelor's, and master's levels. It has an 800-acre campus in Parkville near Kansas City.

Academic Information The faculty has 805 members (12% full-time). The undergraduate student-faculty ratio is 14:1. The library holds 144,870 titles, 775 serial subscriptions, and 850 audiovisual materials. Special programs include academic remediation, services for learning-disabled students, an honors program, advanced placement credit, ESL programs, double majors, independent study, distance learning, self-designed majors, summer session for credit, part-time degree programs, external degree programs, adult/continuing education programs, internships, and arrangement for off-campus study with members of the Kansas City Professional Development Council. The most frequently chosen baccalaureate fields are business/marketing, education, psychology.

Student Body Statistics The student body totals 11,868, of whom 11,520 are undergraduates (100 freshmen). 48 percent are women and 52 percent are men. Students come from 49 states and territories and 90 other countries. 18 percent are from Missouri. 1.9 percent are international students. 7 percent of the 2003 graduating class went on to graduate and professional schools.

Expenses for 2003–04 *Application fee:* $25. *Comprehensive fee:* $10,780 includes full-time tuition ($5600) and college room and board ($5180). Room and board charges vary according to board plan and housing facility. *Part-time tuition:* $200 per credit hour.

Financial Aid Forms of aid include need-based and non-need-based scholarships, athletic grants, and part-time jobs. The average aided 2002–03 undergraduate received an aid package worth $4800. The priority application deadline for financial aid is April 1.

Freshman Admission Park requires a high school transcript, a minimum 2.0 high school GPA, SAT I or ACT scores, and TOEFL scores for international students. An essay is recommended. 2 recommendations and an interview are required for some. The application deadline for regular admission is August 1.

Transfer Admission The application deadline for admission is August 1.

Entrance Difficulty Park assesses its entrance difficulty level as moderately difficult.

For Further Information Contact Jo Grove Henderson, Office of Admissions, Park University, 8700 NW River Park Drive, Campus Box 1, Parkville, MO 64152. *Telephone:* 816-584-6215 or 800-745-7275 (toll-free). *Fax:* 816-741-4462. *E-mail:* admissions@mail.park.edu. *Web site:* http://www.park.edu/.

RANKEN TECHNICAL COLLEGE

St. Louis, Missouri

Ranken is a coed, primarily men's, private, primarily two-year college, founded in 1907, offering degrees at the associate and bachelor's levels. It has a 10-acre campus in St. Louis.

Academic Information The faculty has 67 members (88% full-time). The student-faculty ratio is 15:1. The library holds 11,000 titles and 182 serial subscriptions. Special programs include academic remediation, services for learning-disabled students, cooperative (work-study) education, advanced placement credit, independent study, distance learning, summer session for credit, part-time degree programs (daytime, evenings, weekends, summer), adult/continuing education programs, and internships.

Student Body Statistics The student body is made up of 1,423 undergraduates (321 freshmen). 4 percent are women and 96 percent are men. Students come from 3 states and territories. 60 percent are from Missouri. 5 percent of the 2003 graduating class went on to four-year colleges.

Expenses for 2004–05 *Application fee:* $95. *Tuition:* $9500 full-time, $695 per term part-time. *Mandatory fees:* $140 full-time, $95 per term part-time.

Financial Aid Forms of aid include need-based scholarships and part-time jobs. The application deadline for financial aid is continuous.

Freshman Admission Ranken requires an essay, a high school transcript, an interview, and SAT I or ACT scores. TOEFL scores for international students are recommended. The application deadline for regular admission is rolling.

Ranken Technical College (continued)

Entrance Difficulty Ranken assesses its entrance difficulty level as moderately difficult. For the fall 2003 freshman class, 92 percent of the applicants were accepted.

For Further Information Contact Ms. Elizabeth Keserauskis, Director of Admissions, Ranken Technical College, 4431 Finney Avenue, St. Louis, MO 63113. *Telephone:* 314-371-0233 Ext. 4811 or 866-4RANKEN (toll-free out-of-state). *Fax:* 314-371-0241. *E-mail:* admissions@ranken.edu. *Web site:* http://www.ranken.edu/.

RESEARCH COLLEGE OF NURSING
Kansas City, Missouri

Research College of Nursing is a coed, primarily women's, private, comprehensive unit of Rockhurst University, founded in 1980, offering degrees at the bachelor's and master's levels in nursing (bachelor's degree offered jointly with Rockhurst College). It has a 66-acre campus in Kansas City.

Academic Information The faculty has 35 members (71% full-time). The undergraduate student-faculty ratio is 7:1. The library holds 150,000 titles and 675 serial subscriptions. Special programs include services for learning-disabled students, an honors program, study abroad, advanced placement credit, accelerated degree programs, double majors, independent study, and summer session for credit. The most frequently chosen baccalaureate field is health professions and related sciences.
Student Body Statistics The student body totals 219, of whom 197 are undergraduates (35 freshmen). 88 percent are women and 12 percent are men. Students come from 7 states and territories.
Expenses for 2003–04 *Application fee:* $25. *Comprehensive fee:* $22,850 includes full-time tuition ($16,950), mandatory fees ($450), and college room and board ($5450). Full-time tuition and fees vary according to program. Room and board charges vary according to board plan, housing facility, and location. *Part-time tuition:* $575 per credit hour. *Part-time mandatory fees:* $25 per term. Part-time tuition and fees vary according to class time and program.
Financial Aid Forms of aid include need-based and non-need-based scholarships. The average aided 2003–04 undergraduate received an aid package worth an estimated $18,933. The priority application deadline for financial aid is March 15.
Freshman Admission Research College of Nursing requires a high school transcript, 1 recommendation, SAT I or ACT scores, and TOEFL scores for international students. A minimum 2.8 high school GPA, an interview, and minimum ACT score of 20 are recommended. The application deadline for regular admission is June 30.
Transfer Admission The application deadline for admission is January 31.
Entrance Difficulty Research College of Nursing assesses its entrance difficulty level as moderately difficult. For the fall 2003 freshman class, 77 percent of the applicants were accepted.

For Further Information Contact Ms. Amy Johnson, Rockhurst College Admission Office, Research College of Nursing, 1100 Rockhurst Road, Kansas City, MO 64110. *Telephone:* 816-276-4733 or 800-842-6776 (toll-free). *Fax:* 816-501-4588. *E-mail:* mendenhall@vax2.rockhurst.edu. *Web site:* http://www.researchcollege.edu/.

ROCKHURST UNIVERSITY
Kansas City, Missouri

Rockhurst is a coed, private, Roman Catholic (Jesuit), comprehensive institution, founded in 1910, offering degrees at the bachelor's and master's levels and postbachelor's certificates. It has a 35-acre campus in Kansas City.

Academic Information The faculty has 208 members (62% full-time), 63% with terminal degrees. The undergraduate student-faculty ratio is 10:1. The library holds 597,800 titles, 750 serial subscriptions, and 3,339 audiovisual materials. Special programs include academic remediation, services for learning-disabled students, an honors program, cooperative

(work-study) education, study abroad, advanced placement credit, accelerated degree programs, Freshman Honors College, double majors, independent study, distance learning, summer session for credit, part-time degree programs (daytime, evenings, weekends, summer), adult/continuing education programs, internships, and arrangement for off-campus study with Kansas City Area Student Exchange. The most frequently chosen baccalaureate fields are business/marketing, health professions and related sciences, psychology.
Student Body Statistics The student body totals 2,764, of whom 1,957 are undergraduates (245 freshmen). 57 percent are women and 43 percent are men. Students come from 24 states and territories and 10 other countries. 69 percent are from Missouri. 1.3 percent are international students. 37 percent of the 2003 graduating class went on to graduate and professional schools.
Expenses for 2003–04 *Application fee:* $25. *Comprehensive fee:* $23,160 includes full-time tuition ($16,950), mandatory fees ($460), and college room and board ($5750). Full-time tuition and fees vary according to course load. Room and board vary according to board plan and housing facility. *Part-time tuition:* $575 per semester hour. *Part-time mandatory fees:* $25 per term. Part-time tuition and fees vary according to class time and course load.
Financial Aid Forms of aid include need-based and non-need-based scholarships, athletic grants, and part-time jobs. The average aided 2002–03 undergraduate received an aid package worth $16,299. The priority application deadline for financial aid is March 1.
Freshman Admission Rockhurst requires a high school transcript, a minimum 2.0 high school GPA, 1 recommendation, SAT I or ACT scores, and TOEFL scores for international students. An essay and an interview are required for some. The application deadline for regular admission is June 30.
Transfer Admission The application deadline for admission is rolling.
Entrance Difficulty Rockhurst assesses its entrance difficulty level as moderately difficult. For the fall 2003 freshman class, 80 percent of the applicants were accepted.

For Further Information Contact Mr. Lane Ramey, Director of Freshman Admissions, Rockhurst University, 1100 Rockhurst Road, Kansas City, MO 64110-2561. *Telephone:* 816-501-4100 or 800-842-6776 (toll-free). *Fax:* 816-501-4142. *E-mail:* admission@rockhurst.edu. *Web site:* http://www.rockhurst.edu/.

ST. LOUIS CHRISTIAN COLLEGE
Florissant, Missouri

SLCC is a coed, private, Christian, four-year college, founded in 1956, offering degrees at the associate and bachelor's levels. It has a 20-acre campus in Florissant near St. Louis.

Academic Information The faculty has 33 members (27% full-time), 24% with terminal degrees. The student-faculty ratio is 12:1. The library holds 39,728 titles and 144 serial subscriptions. Special programs include academic remediation, services for learning-disabled students, advanced placement credit, accelerated degree programs, part-time degree programs (daytime), adult/continuing education programs, and internships. The most frequently chosen baccalaureate field is philosophy, religion, and theology.
Student Body Statistics The student body is made up of 213 undergraduates (26 freshmen). 46 percent are women and 54 percent are men. Students come from 11 states and territories and 3 other countries. 63 percent are from Missouri. 0.9 percent are international students. 21 percent of the 2003 graduating class went on to graduate and professional schools.
Expenses for 2004–05 *Application fee:* $0. *Comprehensive fee:* $12,860 includes full-time tuition ($7680) and college room and board ($5180). Room and board charges vary according to housing facility. *Part-time tuition:* $240 per hour.
Financial Aid Forms of aid include need-based and non-need-based scholarships and part-time jobs. The average aided 2003–04 undergraduate received an aid package worth an estimated $5104. The priority application deadline for financial aid is May 1.
Freshman Admission SLCC requires an essay, a high school transcript, 2 recommendations, ACT scores, and TOEFL scores for international

students. A minimum 2.0 high school GPA is recommended. An interview is required for some. The application deadline for regular admission is August 15.

Transfer Admission The application deadline for admission is August 15.

Entrance Difficulty SLCC assesses its entrance difficulty level as minimally difficult. For the fall 2003 freshman class, 76 percent of the applicants were accepted.

For Further Information Contact Mr. Richard Fordyce, Registrar, St. Louis Christian College, 1360 Grandview Drive, Florissant, MO 63033-6499. *Telephone:* 314-837-6777 Ext. 1500 or 800-887-SLCC (toll-free). *Fax:* 314-837-8291. *E-mail:* questions@slcc4ministry.edu. *Web site:* http://www.slcc4ministry.edu/.

ST. LOUIS COLLEGE OF PHARMACY
St. Louis, Missouri

St. Louis College of Pharmacy is a coed, private, comprehensive institution, founded in 1864, offering degrees at the bachelor's, master's, and first professional levels (bachelor of science degree program in pharmaceutical studies cannot be applied to directly; students have the option to transfer in after their second year in the PharmD program. Bachelor's degree candidates are not eligible to take the pharmacist's licensing examination). It has a 5-acre campus in St. Louis.

Academic Information The faculty has 125 members (54% full-time). The undergraduate student-faculty ratio is 12:1. The library holds 59,012 titles, 234 serial subscriptions, and 802 audiovisual materials. Special programs include advanced placement credit, summer session for credit, adult/continuing education programs, and internships. The most frequently chosen baccalaureate field is health professions and related sciences.

Student Body Statistics The student body totals 927, of whom 170 are undergraduates. 65 percent are women and 35 percent are men. Students come from 10 states and territories. 52 percent are from Missouri. 0.6 percent are international students. 6 percent of the 2003 graduating class went on to graduate and professional schools.

Expenses for 2004–05 *Application fee:* $35. *Comprehensive fee:* $24,610 includes full-time tuition ($17,010), mandatory fees ($250), and college room and board ($7350). Full-time tuition and fees vary according to student level. Room and board charges vary according to housing facility. *Part-time tuition:* $708 per credit.

Financial Aid Forms of aid include need-based and non-need-based scholarships and part-time jobs. The application deadline for financial aid is November 15 with a priority deadline of April 1.

Freshman Admission St. Louis College of Pharmacy requires an essay, a high school transcript, a minimum 3.0 high school GPA, 2 recommendations, SAT I or ACT scores, and TOEFL scores for international students. An interview is required for some. The application deadline for regular admission is rolling.

Transfer Admission The application deadline for admission is March 1.

Entrance Difficulty St. Louis College of Pharmacy assesses its entrance difficulty level as moderately difficult; most difficult for transfers. For the fall 2003 freshman class, 44 percent of the applicants were accepted.

For Further Information Contact Ms. Patty Kulage, Admissions and Financial Aid Coordinator, St. Louis College of Pharmacy, 4588 Parkview Place, St. Louis, MO 63110-1088. *Telephone:* 314-446-8313 or 800-278-5267 (toll-free in-state). *Fax:* 314-446-8310. *E-mail:* pkulage@stlcop.edu. *Web site:* http://www.stlcop.edu/.

SAINT LOUIS UNIVERSITY
St. Louis, Missouri

SLU is a coed, private, Roman Catholic (Jesuit) university, founded in 1818, offering degrees at the associate, bachelor's, master's, doctoral, and first professional levels and post-master's and postbachelor's certificates. It has a 373-acre campus in St. Louis.

Academic Information The faculty has 933 members (67% full-time), 75% with terminal degrees. The undergraduate student-faculty ratio is 12:1. The library holds 1 million titles, 12,881 serial subscriptions, and 195,651 audiovisual materials. Special programs include academic remediation, services for learning-disabled students, an honors program, cooperative (work-study) education, study abroad, advanced placement credit, accelerated degree programs, ESL programs, double majors, independent study, distance learning, self-designed majors, summer session for credit, part-time degree programs (daytime, evenings, weekends, summer), adult/continuing education programs, internships, and arrangement for off-campus study with Washington University in St. Louis. The most frequently chosen baccalaureate fields are business/marketing, communications/communication technologies, health professions and related sciences.

Student Body Statistics The student body totals 11,217, of whom 7,091 are undergraduates (1,526 freshmen). 55 percent are women and 45 percent are men. Students come from 48 states and territories and 78 other countries. 51 percent are from Missouri. 2.3 percent are international students. 28 percent of the 2003 graduating class went on to graduate and professional schools.

Expenses for 2003–04 *Application fee:* $25. *Comprehensive fee:* $29,958 includes full-time tuition ($22,050), mandatory fees ($168), and college room and board ($7740). *College room only:* $4240. Full-time tuition and fees vary according to location. Room and board charges vary according to board plan, housing facility, and location. *Part-time tuition:* $770 per credit hour. *Part-time mandatory fees:* $55 per term. Part-time tuition and fees vary according to class time, location, and program.

Financial Aid Forms of aid include need-based and non-need-based scholarships, athletic grants, and part-time jobs. The average aided 2003–04 undergraduate received an aid package worth an estimated $18,526. The priority application deadline for financial aid is March 1.

Freshman Admission SLU requires an essay, a high school transcript, secondary school report form, and SAT I or ACT scores. A minimum 2.5 high school GPA, 2 recommendations, an interview, and TOEFL scores for international students are recommended. The application deadline for regular admission is rolling.

Entrance Difficulty SLU assesses its entrance difficulty level as moderately difficult. For the fall 2003 freshman class, 70 percent of the applicants were accepted.

For Further Information Contact Ms. Shani Lenore, Director, Saint Louis University, 221 North Grand Boulevard, St. Louis, MO 63103-2097. *Telephone:* 314-977-3415 or 800-758-3678 (toll-free out-of-state). *Fax:* 314-977-7136. *E-mail:* admitme@slu.edu. *Web site:* http://www.slu.edu/.

SAINT LUKE'S COLLEGE
Kansas City, Missouri

Saint Luke's College is a coed, primarily women's, private, Episcopal, upper-level institution, founded in 1903, offering degrees at the bachelor's level in nursing. It has a 3-acre campus in Kansas City.

Academic Information The faculty has 16 members (100% full-time), 12% with terminal degrees. The student-faculty ratio is 7:1. Special programs include cooperative (work-study) education and summer session for credit. The most frequently chosen baccalaureate field is health professions and related sciences.

Student Body Statistics The student body is made up of 110 undergraduates. 92 percent are women and 8 percent are men. Students come from 5 states and territories.

Expenses for 2004–05 *Application fee:* $35. *Tuition:* $8250 full-time, $275 per credit hour part-time. *Mandatory fees:* $510 full-time.

Financial Aid Forms of aid include need-based and non-need-based scholarships and part-time jobs. The average aided 2003–04 undergraduate received an aid package worth an estimated $6600. The application deadline for financial aid is continuous.

Transfer Admission Saint Luke's College requires a college transcript and a minimum 2.5 college GPA. Standardized test scores are required for some. The application deadline for admission is December 31.

Saint Luke's College (continued)
Entrance Difficulty Saint Luke's College assesses its entrance difficulty level as very difficult.

For Further Information Contact Ms. Christina Wood, Director of Admissions, Saint Luke's College, 8320 Wand parkway, Suite 300, Kansas City, MO 64114. *Telephone:* 816-932-2073. *E-mail:* slc-admissions@saint-lukes.org. *Web site:* http://www.saintlukescollege.edu/.

SANFORD-BROWN COLLEGE
Fenton, Missouri

Sanford-Brown is a coed, proprietary, primarily two-year college, founded in 1868, offering degrees at the associate and bachelor's levels. It has a 6-acre campus in Fenton near St. Louis.

For Further Information Contact Ms. Judy Wilga, Director of Admissions, Sanford-Brown College, 1203 Smizer Mill Road, Fenton, MO 63026. *Telephone:* 636-349-4900 Ext. 102 or 800-456-7222 (toll-free). *Fax:* 636-349-9170. *Web site:* http://www.sanford-brown.edu/.

SOUTHEAST MISSOURI HOSPITAL COLLEGE OF NURSING AND HEALTH SCIENCES
Cape Girardeau, Missouri

For Information Write to Southeast Missouri Hospital College of Nursing and Health Sciences, Cape Girardeau, MO 63701.

SOUTHEAST MISSOURI STATE UNIVERSITY
Cape Girardeau, Missouri

Southeast is a coed, public, comprehensive unit of Missouri Coordinating Board for Higher Education, founded in 1873, offering degrees at the associate, bachelor's, and master's levels and post-master's certificates. It has a 693-acre campus in Cape Girardeau near St. Louis.

Academic Information The faculty has 524 members (74% full-time), 63% with terminal degrees. The undergraduate student-faculty ratio is 18:1. The library holds 411,992 titles, 2,781 serial subscriptions, and 9,400 audiovisual materials. Special programs include academic remediation, services for learning-disabled students, an honors program, cooperative (work-study) education, study abroad, advanced placement credit, ESL programs, double majors, independent study, distance learning, self-designed majors, summer session for credit, part-time degree programs, adult/continuing education programs, and internships. The most frequently chosen baccalaureate fields are business/marketing, education, protective services/public administration.
Student Body Statistics The student body totals 9,570, of whom 8,483 are undergraduates (1,495 freshmen). 58 percent are women and 42 percent are men. Students come from 40 states and territories and 37 other countries. 87 percent are from Missouri. 1.8 percent are international students.
Expenses for 2003–04 *Application fee:* $20. *State resident tuition:* $4254 full-time, $152.50 per credit part-time. *Nonresident tuition:* $7839 full-time, $272 per credit part-time. *Mandatory fees:* $321 full-time, $10.70 per credit part-time. *College room and board:* $5450. *College room only:* $3505. Room and board charges vary according to board plan and housing facility.
Financial Aid Forms of aid include need-based and non-need-based scholarships, athletic grants, and part-time jobs. The average aided 2002–03 undergraduate received an aid package worth $6109. The priority application deadline for financial aid is March 1.

Freshman Admission Southeast requires a high school transcript, a minimum 2.0 high school GPA, SAT I or ACT scores, and TOEFL scores for international students. The application deadline for regular admission is August 1.
Entrance Difficulty Southeast assesses its entrance difficulty level as moderately difficult; minimally difficult for transfers. For the fall 2003 freshman class, 83 percent of the applicants were accepted.

For Further Information Contact Ms. Deborah Below, Director of Admissions, Southeast Missouri State University, MS 3550, Cape Girardeau, MO 63701. *Telephone:* 573-651-2590. *Fax:* 573-651-5936. *E-mail:* admissions@semo.edu. *Web site:* http://www.semo.edu/.

SOUTHWEST BAPTIST UNIVERSITY
Bolivar, Missouri

SBU is a coed, private, Southern Baptist, comprehensive institution, founded in 1878, offering degrees at the associate, bachelor's, and master's levels and post-master's certificates. It has a 152-acre campus in Bolivar.

Academic Information The faculty has 295 members (35% full-time), 41% with terminal degrees. The undergraduate student-faculty ratio is 21:1. The library holds 108,128 titles, 2,518 serial subscriptions, and 9,370 audiovisual materials. Special programs include academic remediation, an honors program, cooperative (work-study) education, study abroad, advanced placement credit, accelerated degree programs, ESL programs, double majors, independent study, summer session for credit, part-time degree programs (daytime, evenings, summer), and internships. The most frequently chosen baccalaureate fields are education, health professions and related sciences, psychology.
Student Body Statistics The student body totals 3,563, of whom 2,746 are undergraduates (470 freshmen). 66 percent are women and 34 percent are men. Students come from 40 states and territories and 11 other countries. 49 percent are from Missouri. 0.7 percent are international students.
Expenses for 2004–05 *Application fee:* $25. *Comprehensive fee:* $16,220 includes full-time tuition ($11,800), mandatory fees ($532), and college room and board ($3888). *College room only:* $2088. Room and board charges vary according to board plan and housing facility. *Part-time tuition:* $500 per hour. *Part-time mandatory fees:* $8 per hour, $95 per term. Part-time tuition and fees vary according to course load.
Financial Aid Forms of aid include need-based and non-need-based scholarships, athletic grants, and part-time jobs. The average aided 2003–04 undergraduate received an aid package worth an estimated $9976. The priority application deadline for financial aid is March 15.
Freshman Admission SBU requires an essay, a high school transcript, SAT I or ACT scores, and TOEFL scores for international students. An interview is recommended. 3 recommendations are required for some. The application deadline for regular admission is rolling.
Transfer Admission The application deadline for admission is rolling.
Entrance Difficulty SBU assesses its entrance difficulty level as moderately difficult. For the fall 2003 freshman class, 86 percent of the applicants were accepted.

For Further Information Contact Mr. Rob Harris, Director of Admissions, Southwest Baptist University, 1600 University Avenue, Bolivar, MO 65613-2597. *Telephone:* 417-328-1809 or 800-526-5859 (toll-free). *Fax:* 417-328-1514. *E-mail:* rharris@sbuniv.edu. *Web site:* http://www.sbuniv.edu/.

SOUTHWEST MISSOURI STATE UNIVERSITY
Springfield, Missouri

SMSU is a coed, public, comprehensive institution, founded in 1905, offering degrees at the bachelor's and master's levels and postbachelor's certificates. It has a 225-acre campus in Springfield.

Academic Information The faculty has 1,000 members (73% full-time), 64% with terminal degrees. The undergraduate student-faculty ratio is 18:1. The library holds 2 million titles, 4,238 serial subscriptions, and 33,547 audiovisual materials. Special programs include services for learning-disabled students, an honors program, cooperative (work-study) education, study abroad, advanced placement credit, accelerated degree programs, Freshman Honors College, ESL programs, double majors, independent study, distance learning, self-designed majors, summer session for credit, part-time degree programs, adult/continuing education programs, internships, and arrangement for off-campus study with National Student Exchange. The most frequently chosen baccalaureate fields are business/marketing, communications/communication technologies, education.

Student Body Statistics The student body totals 18,930, of whom 15,771 are undergraduates (2,695 freshmen). 56 percent are women and 44 percent are men. Students come from 48 states and territories and 80 other countries. 92 percent are from Missouri. 1.9 percent are international students. 20 percent of the 2003 graduating class went on to graduate and professional schools.

Expenses for 2003–04 *Application fee:* $25. *State resident tuition:* $4636 full-time, $138 per credit hour part-time. *Nonresident tuition:* $8776 full-time, $276 per credit hour part-time. Full-time tuition varies according to course load and degree level. Part-time tuition varies according to course load and degree level. *College room and board:* $4282. *College room only:* $2982. Room and board charges vary according to board plan and housing facility.

Financial Aid Forms of aid include need-based and non-need-based scholarships, athletic grants, and part-time jobs. The average aided 2003–04 undergraduate received an aid package worth an estimated $7253. The priority application deadline for financial aid is March 30.

Freshman Admission SMSU requires a high school transcript, SAT I or ACT scores, and TOEFL scores for international students. ACT scores are recommended. An essay and an interview are required for some. The application deadline for regular admission is June 20.

Transfer Admission The application deadline for admission is December 20.

Entrance Difficulty SMSU assesses its entrance difficulty level as moderately difficult. For the fall 2003 freshman class, 86 percent of the applicants were accepted.

For Further Information Contact Ms. Jill Duncan, Associate Director of Admissions, Southwest Missouri State University, 901 South National, Springfield, MO 65804. *Telephone:* 417-836-5521 or 800-492-7900 (toll-free). *Fax:* 417-836-6334. *E-mail:* smsuinfo@smsu.edu. *Web site:* http://www.smsu.edu/.

STEPHENS COLLEGE
Columbia, Missouri

Stephens is a women's, private, comprehensive institution, founded in 1833, offering degrees at the bachelor's and master's levels and postbachelor's certificates. It has an 86-acre campus in Columbia.

Academic Information The faculty has 77 members (61% full-time), 69% with terminal degrees. The undergraduate student-faculty ratio is 10:1. The library holds 121,084 titles, 534 serial subscriptions, and 4,764 audiovisual materials. Special programs include academic remediation, services for learning-disabled students, an honors program, cooperative (work-study) education, study abroad, advanced placement credit, accelerated degree programs, Freshman Honors College, ESL programs, double majors, independent study, distance learning, self-designed majors, part-time degree programs (daytime, weekends), external degree programs, adult/continuing education programs, internships, and arrangement for off-campus study with University of Missouri, Columbia College (MO). The most frequently chosen baccalaureate fields are communications/communication technologies, psychology, visual/performing arts.

Student Body Statistics The student body totals 647, of whom 577 are undergraduates (139 freshmen). Students come from 41 states and territories and 3 other countries. 45 percent are from Missouri. 0.5 percent are international students.

Expenses for 2003–04 *Application fee:* $25. *Comprehensive fee:* $24,260 includes full-time tuition ($17,360) and college room and board ($6900). *College room only:* $3050. Room and board charges vary according to board plan.

Financial Aid Forms of aid include need-based and non-need-based scholarships and part-time jobs. The average aided 2003–04 undergraduate received an aid package worth an estimated $16,576. The priority application deadline for financial aid is March 15.

Freshman Admission Stephens requires an essay, a high school transcript, a minimum 2.5 high school GPA, 1 recommendation, SAT I or ACT scores, and TOEFL scores for international students. An interview is recommended. The application deadline for regular admission is July 31.

Entrance Difficulty Stephens assesses its entrance difficulty level as moderately difficult. For the fall 2003 freshman class, 79 percent of the applicants were accepted.

For Further Information Contact Ms. Amy Shaver, Director of Enrollment Services, Stephens College, 1200 East Broadway, Box 2121, Columbia, MO 65215-0002. *Telephone:* 573-876-7207 or 800-876-7207 (toll-free). *Fax:* 573-876-7237. *E-mail:* apply@stephens.edu. *Web site:* http://www.stephens.edu/.

See page 342 for a narrative description.

TRUMAN STATE UNIVERSITY
Kirksville, Missouri

Truman is a coed, public, comprehensive institution, founded in 1867, offering degrees at the bachelor's and master's levels. It has a 140-acre campus in Kirksville.

Academic Information The faculty has 377 members (94% full-time), 82% with terminal degrees. The undergraduate student-faculty ratio is 15:1. The library holds 481,424 titles, 3,197 serial subscriptions, and 36,724 audiovisual materials. Special programs include services for learning-disabled students, an honors program, study abroad, advanced placement credit, accelerated degree programs, ESL programs, double majors, summer session for credit, part-time degree programs (daytime, summer), internships, and arrangement for off-campus study with Gulf Coast Research Laboratory, Reis Biological Station, Kirksville College of Osteopathic Medicine. The most frequently chosen baccalaureate fields are business/marketing, biological/life sciences, English.

Student Body Statistics The student body totals 5,833, of whom 5,479 are undergraduates (1,317 freshmen). 59 percent are women and 41 percent are men. Students come from 37 states and territories and 48 other countries. 76 percent are from Missouri. 4.7 percent are international students. 41.3 percent of the 2003 graduating class went on to graduate and professional schools.

Expenses for 2003–04 *Application fee:* $0. *State resident tuition:* $4600 full-time, $191.50 per credit hour part-time. *Nonresident tuition:* $8400 full-time, $350 per credit hour part-time. *Mandatory fees:* $56 full-time. Part-time tuition varies according to course load. *College room and board:* $5072. Room and board charges vary according to housing facility.

Financial Aid Forms of aid include need-based and non-need-based scholarships, athletic grants, and part-time jobs. The average aided 2002–03 undergraduate received an aid package worth $5774. The priority application deadline for financial aid is April 1.

Freshman Admission Truman requires an essay, a high school transcript, SAT I or ACT scores, and TOEFL scores for international students. A minimum 3.0 high school GPA, an interview, and ACT scores are recommended. The application deadline for regular admission is March 1 and for early action it is November 15.

Entrance Difficulty Truman assesses its entrance difficulty level as moderately difficult. For the fall 2003 freshman class, 84 percent of the applicants were accepted.

For Further Information Contact Mr. Brad Chambers, Co-Director of Admissions, Truman State University, 205 McClain Hall, Kirksville, MO 63501-4221. *Telephone:* 660-785-4114 or 800-892-7792 (toll-free in-state). *Fax:* 660-785-7456. *E-mail:* admissions@truman.edu. *Web site:* http://www.truman.edu/.

See page 344 for a narrative description.

UNIVERSITY OF MISSOURI–COLUMBIA
Columbia, Missouri

MU is a coed, public unit of University of Missouri System, founded in 1839, offering degrees at the bachelor's, master's, doctoral, and first professional levels and post-master's certificates. It has a 1,358-acre campus in Columbia.

Academic Information The faculty has 1,545 members (96% full-time), 94% with terminal degrees. The undergraduate student-faculty ratio is 18:1. The library holds 3 million titles, 16,073 serial subscriptions, and 19,383 audiovisual materials. Special programs include academic remediation, services for learning-disabled students, an honors program, cooperative (work-study) education, study abroad, advanced placement credit, accelerated degree programs, Freshman Honors College, ESL programs, double majors, independent study, distance learning, self-designed majors, summer session for credit, part-time degree programs (daytime, evenings), external degree programs, adult/continuing education programs, internships, and arrangement for off-campus study with Mid-Missouri Associated Colleges and Universities, National Student Exchange. The most frequently chosen baccalaureate fields are business/marketing, communications/communication technologies, social sciences and history.

Student Body Statistics The student body totals 26,805, of whom 20,441 are undergraduates (4,669 freshmen). 52 percent are women and 48 percent are men. Students come from 51 states and territories and 85 other countries. 88 percent are from Missouri. 1.4 percent are international students.

Expenses for 2003–04 *Application fee:* $35. *State resident tuition:* $5838 full-time, $194.60 per credit hour part-time. *Nonresident tuition:* $15,285 full-time, $509.50 per credit hour part-time. *Mandatory fees:* $720 full-time, $21.62 per credit hour part-time. *College room and board:* $5770. Room and board charges vary according to board plan and housing facility.

Financial Aid Forms of aid include need-based and non-need-based scholarships, athletic grants, and part-time jobs. The average aided 2003–04 undergraduate received an aid package worth an estimated $9278. The priority application deadline for financial aid is March 1.

Freshman Admission MU requires a high school transcript, specific high school curriculum, SAT I or ACT scores, and TOEFL scores for international students. The application deadline for regular admission is rolling.

Transfer Admission The application deadline for admission is rolling.

Entrance Difficulty MU assesses its entrance difficulty level as moderately difficult. For the fall 2003 freshman class, 89 percent of the applicants were accepted.

For Further Information Contact Ms. Georgeanne Porter, Director of Admissions, University of Missouri–Columbia, 230 Jesse Hall, Columbia, MO 65211. *Telephone:* 573-882-7786 or 800-225-6075 (toll-free in-state). *Fax:* 573-882-7887. *E-mail:* mu4u@missouri.edu. *Web site:* http://www.missouri.edu/.

UNIVERSITY OF MISSOURI–KANSAS CITY
Kansas City, Missouri

UMKC is a coed, public unit of University of Missouri System, founded in 1929, offering degrees at the bachelor's, master's, doctoral, and first professional levels and post-master's and first professional certificates. It has a 191-acre campus in Kansas City.

Academic Information The faculty has 910 members (58% full-time), 65% with terminal degrees. The undergraduate student-faculty ratio is 9:1. The library holds 1 million titles, 6,951 serial subscriptions, and 449,074 audiovisual materials. Special programs include services for learning-disabled students, an honors program, cooperative (work-study) education, study abroad, advanced placement credit, accelerated degree programs, ESL programs, self-designed majors, summer session for credit, part-time degree programs (daytime, evenings, weekends, summer), adult/continuing education programs, internships, and arrangement for off-campus study with other campuses of the University of Missouri System. The most frequently chosen baccalaureate fields are business/marketing, education, liberal arts/general studies.

Student Body Statistics The student body totals 14,226, of whom 9,167 are undergraduates (785 freshmen). 60 percent are women and 40 percent are men. Students come from 42 states and territories and 105 other countries. 77 percent are from Missouri. 4.5 percent are international students.

Expenses for 2003–04 *Application fee:* $35. *State resident tuition:* $5448 full-time. *Nonresident tuition:* $14,266 full-time. *Mandatory fees:* $698 full-time. Full-time tuition and fees vary according to course load, program, and student level. *College room and board:* $7270. *College room only:* $3170. Room and board charges vary according to board plan and housing facility.

Financial Aid Forms of aid include need-based and non-need-based scholarships, athletic grants, and part-time jobs. The average aided 2003–04 undergraduate received an aid package worth an estimated $11,547. The priority application deadline for financial aid is March 1.

Freshman Admission UMKC requires a high school transcript, ACT scores, and TOEFL scores for international students. The application deadline for regular admission is rolling.

Transfer Admission The application deadline for admission is rolling.

Entrance Difficulty UMKC assesses its entrance difficulty level as moderately difficult; most difficult for medicine programs. For the fall 2003 freshman class, 93 percent of the applicants were accepted.

For Further Information Contact Ms. Jennifer DeHaemers, Director of Admissions, University of Missouri–Kansas City, Office of Admissions, 5100 Rockhill Road, Kansas City, MO 64110-2499. *Telephone:* 816-235-1111 or 800-775-8652 (toll-free out-of-state). *Fax:* 816-235-5544. *E-mail:* admit@umkc.edu. *Web site:* http://www.umkc.edu/.

UNIVERSITY OF MISSOURI–ROLLA
Rolla, Missouri

UMR is a coed, public unit of University of Missouri System, founded in 1870, offering degrees at the bachelor's, master's, and doctoral levels and postbachelor's certificates. It has a 284-acre campus in Rolla.

Academic Information The faculty has 392 members (78% full-time), 85% with terminal degrees. The undergraduate student-faculty ratio is 14:1. The library holds 255,768 titles, 1,495 serial subscriptions, and 6,353 audiovisual materials. Special programs include academic remediation, services for learning-disabled students, an honors program, cooperative (work-study) education, study abroad, advanced placement credit, accelerated degree programs, Freshman Honors College, ESL programs, double majors, independent study, distance learning, summer session for credit, part-time degree programs, adult/continuing education programs, internships, and arrangement for off-campus study with University of Missouri–Columbia. The most frequently chosen baccalaureate fields are computer/information sciences, engineering/engineering technologies, physical sciences.

Student Body Statistics The student body totals 5,459, of whom 4,089 are undergraduates (878 freshmen). 23 percent are women and 77 percent are men. Students come from 45 states and territories and 34 other countries. 79 percent are from Missouri. 2.5 percent are international students. 17 percent of the 2003 graduating class went on to graduate and professional schools.

Expenses for 2003–04 *Application fee:* $35. *State resident tuition:* $5838 full-time, $194.60 per credit hour part-time. *Nonresident tuition:* $15,285 full-time, $509.50 per credit hour part-time. *Mandatory fees:* $1001 full-time, $112.15 per credit hour part-time. *College room and board:* $5453.

Financial Aid Forms of aid include need-based and non-need-based scholarships, and part-time jobs. The average aided 2003–04 undergraduate received an aid package worth an estimated $9550. The priority application deadline for financial aid is March 1.

Freshman Admission UMR requires a high school transcript and SAT I or ACT scores. TOEFL scores for international students are recommended. The application deadline for regular admission is July 1.

Transfer Admission The application deadline for admission is July 1.

Entrance Difficulty UMR assesses its entrance difficulty level as very difficult; moderately difficult for transfers. For the fall 2003 freshman class, 90 percent of the applicants were accepted.

For Further Information Contact Ms. Lynn Stichnote, Director of Admissions, University of Missouri–Rolla, 106 Parker Hall, Rolla, MO 65409. *Telephone:* 573-341-4164 or 800-522-0938 (toll-free). *Fax:* 573-341-4082. *E-mail:* umrolla@umr.edu. *Web site:* http://www.umr.edu/.

UNIVERSITY OF MISSOURI–ST. LOUIS

St. Louis, Missouri

UM-St. Louis is a coed, public unit of University of Missouri System, founded in 1963, offering degrees at the bachelor's, master's, doctoral, and first professional levels and postbachelor's certificates. It has a 350-acre campus in St. Louis.

Academic Information The faculty has 679 members (53% full-time), 55% with terminal degrees. The undergraduate student-faculty ratio is 20:1. The library holds 782,431 titles, 3,570 serial subscriptions, and 3,878 audiovisual materials. Special programs include services for learning-disabled students, an honors program, cooperative (work-study) education, study abroad, advanced placement credit, accelerated degree programs, Freshman Honors College, ESL programs, double majors, independent study, distance learning, self-designed majors, summer session for credit, part-time degree programs (daytime, evenings, weekends, summer), adult/continuing education programs, internships, and arrangement for off-campus study with Southern Illinois University, Saint Louis University, Washington University in St. Louis, St. Charles Community College, Mineral Area Community College, East Central Community College, Jefferson Community College. The most frequently chosen baccalaureate fields are business/marketing, education, social sciences and history.

Student Body Statistics The student body totals 15,605, of whom 12,630 are undergraduates (534 freshmen). 61 percent are women and 39 percent are men. Students come from 38 states and territories and 63 other countries. 95 percent are from Missouri. 2.2 percent are international students. 13 percent of the 2003 graduating class went on to graduate and professional schools.

Expenses for 2003–04 *Application fee:* $25. *State resident tuition:* $5838 full-time, $194.60 per credit hour part-time. *Nonresident tuition:* $15,285 full-time, $509.50 per credit hour part-time. *Mandatory fees:* $1028 full-time, $39.54 per credit hour part-time. Full-time tuition and fees vary according to program and reciprocity agreements. Part-time tuition and fees vary according to course load and program. *College room and board:* $5600. *College room only:* $4300. Room and board charges vary according to board plan and housing facility.

Financial Aid Forms of aid include need-based and non-need-based scholarships, athletic grants, and part-time jobs. The average aided 2003–04 undergraduate received an aid package worth an estimated $9103. The priority application deadline for financial aid is April 1.

Freshman Admission UM-St. Louis requires a high school transcript, CBHE Core Requirements, SAT I or ACT scores, and TOEFL scores for international students. The application deadline for regular admission is rolling.

Transfer Admission The application deadline for admission is August 1.

Entrance Difficulty UM-St. Louis assesses its entrance difficulty level as moderately difficult. For the fall 2003 freshman class, 48 percent of the applicants were accepted.

For Further Information Contact Ms. Melissa Hattman, Director of Admissions, University of Missouri–St. Louis, 351 Millennuim Student Center, 8001 National Bridge Road, St. Louis, MO 63121-4499. *Telephone:* 314-516-5460 or 888-GO2-UMSL (toll-free). *Fax:* 314-516-5310. *E-mail:* admissions@umsl.edu. *Web site:* http://www.umsl.edu/.

UNIVERSITY OF PHOENIX–KANSAS CITY CAMPUS

Kansas City, Missouri

University of Phoenix–Kansas City Campus is a coed, proprietary, comprehensive institution, founded in 2002, offering degrees at the associate, bachelor's, master's, and doctoral levels and post-master's and postbachelor's certificates (courses conducted at 121 campuses and learning centers in 25 states).

Academic Information The faculty has 25 members (12% full-time), 20% with terminal degrees. The undergraduate student-faculty ratio is 7:1. The library holds 27 million titles and 11,648 serial subscriptions. Special programs include advanced placement credit, accelerated degree programs, independent study, distance learning, external degree programs, and adult/continuing education programs.

Student Body Statistics The student body totals 571, of whom 405 are undergraduates (29 freshmen). 52 percent are women and 48 percent are men. 7.7 percent are international students.

Expenses for 2003–04 *Application fee:* $100. *Tuition:* $9990 full-time, $333 per credit part-time.

Financial Aid Forms of aid include need-based and non-need-based scholarships. The average aided 2002–03 undergraduate received an aid package worth $1314. The application deadline for financial aid is continuous.

Freshman Admission University of Phoenix–Kansas City Campus requires 1 recommendation, 2 years of work experience, 23 years of age, and TOEFL scores for international students. A high school transcript is required for some. The application deadline for regular admission is rolling.

Transfer Admission The application deadline for admission is rolling.

Entrance Difficulty University of Phoenix–Kansas City Campus has an open admission policy.

For Further Information Contact Ms. Beth Barilla, Director of Admissions, University of Phoenix–Kansas City Campus, 4615 East Elwood Street, Mail Stop AA-K101, Phoenix, AZ 85040-1958. *Telephone:* 480-557-1712 or 800-228-7240 (toll-free). *Fax:* 480-594-1758. *E-mail:* beth.barilla@phoenix.edu. *Web site:* http://www.phoenix.edu/.

UNIVERSITY OF PHOENIX–ST. LOUIS CAMPUS

St. Louis, Missouri

University of Phoenix–St. Louis Campus is a coed, proprietary, comprehensive institution, founded in 2000, offering degrees at the associate, bachelor's, master's, and doctoral levels and post-master's and postbachelor's certificates (courses conducted at 121 campuses and learning centers in 25 states).

Academic Information The faculty has 43 members (9% full-time), 19% with terminal degrees. The undergraduate student-faculty ratio is 7:1. The library holds 27 million titles and 11,648 serial subscriptions. Special programs include advanced placement credit, accelerated degree programs, independent study, distance learning, external degree programs, and adult/continuing education programs. The most frequently chosen baccalaureate fields are business/marketing, computer/information sciences.

Student Body Statistics The student body totals 1,711, of whom 1,327 are undergraduates (27 freshmen). 59 percent are women and 41 percent are men. 24 percent are international students.

Expenses for 2003–04 *Application fee:* $85. *Tuition:* $10,500 full-time, $350 per credit part-time.

Financial Aid Forms of aid include need-based and non-need-based scholarships. The average aided 2002–03 undergraduate received an aid package worth $1271. The application deadline for financial aid is continuous.

Freshman Admission University of Phoenix–St. Louis Campus requires 1 recommendation, 2 years of work experience, 23 years of age, and

University of Phoenix–St. Louis Campus (continued)

TOEFL scores for international students. A high school transcript is required for some. The application deadline for regular admission is rolling.

Transfer Admission The application deadline for admission is rolling.
Entrance Difficulty University of Phoenix–St. Louis Campus has an open admission policy.

For Further Information Contact Ms. Beth Barilla, Director of Admissions, University of Phoenix–St. Louis Campus, 4615 East Elwood Street, Mail Stop AA-K101, Phoenix, AZ 85040-1958. *Telephone:* 480-557-1712, 888-326-7737 (toll-free in-state), or 800-228-7240 (toll-free out-of-state). *Fax:* 480-594-1758. *E-mail:* beth.barilla@phoenix.edu. *Web site:* http://www.phoenix.edu/.

VATTEROTT COLLEGE
St. Ann, Missouri

Vatterott College is a coed, proprietary, primarily two-year college, founded in 1969, offering degrees at the associate and bachelor's levels. It has a 5-acre campus in St. Ann near St. Louis.

Academic Information The faculty has 24 full-time members. The student-faculty ratio is 25:1. The most frequently chosen baccalaureate field is computer/information sciences.
Student Body Statistics The student body is made up of 580 undergraduates (126 freshmen). 19 percent are women and 81 percent are men.
Financial Aid Forms of aid include need-based scholarships. The application deadline for financial aid is continuous.

For Further Information Contact Mrs. Shari H. Cobb, Director of Admissions, Vatterott College, 3925 Industrial Drive, St. Ann, MO 63074-1807. *Telephone:* 314-428-5900 Ext. 215 or 800-345-6018 (toll-free). *Fax:* 314-428-5956. *Web site:* http://www.vatterott-college.edu/.

VATTEROTT COLLEGE
Sunset Hills, Missouri

Vatterott College is a coed, proprietary, primarily two-year college, offering degrees at the associate and bachelor's levels.

For Further Information Contact Ms. Michelle Tinsley, Director of Admission, Vatterott College, 12970 Maurer Industrial Drive, Sunset Hills, MO 63127. *Telephone:* 314-843-4200. *Fax:* 314-843-1709. *E-mail:* sunsethills@vatterott-college.edu. *Web site:* http://www. vatterott-college.edu/.

WASHINGTON UNIVERSITY IN ST. LOUIS
St. Louis, Missouri

Washington is a coed, private university, founded in 1853, offering degrees at the bachelor's, master's, doctoral, and first professional levels and postbachelor's certificates. It has a 169-acre campus in St. Louis.

Academic Information The faculty has 1,100 members (76% full-time), 75% with terminal degrees. The undergraduate student-faculty ratio is 7:1. The library holds 2 million titles, 18,316 serial subscriptions, and 69,422 audiovisual materials. Special programs include services for learning-disabled students, cooperative (work-study) education, study abroad, advanced placement credit, accelerated degree programs, ESL programs, double majors, independent study, self-designed majors, summer session for credit, part-time degree programs, adult/continuing education programs, internships, and arrangement for off-campus study with Consortium on Financing Higher Education. The most frequently chosen baccalaureate fields are business/marketing, engineering/engineering technologies, social sciences and history.

Student Body Statistics The student body totals 13,020, of whom 7,188 are undergraduates (1,367 freshmen). 53 percent are women and 47 percent are men. Students come from 53 states and territories and 88 other countries. 11 percent are from Missouri. 4.2 percent are international students. 33 percent of the 2003 graduating class went on to graduate and professional schools.
Expenses for 2004–05 *Application fee:* $55. *Comprehensive fee:* $40,186 includes full-time tuition ($29,700), mandatory fees ($846), and college room and board ($9640). *College room only:* $5750. Room and board charges vary according to board plan and housing facility. *Part-time tuition:* varies with class time.
Financial Aid Forms of aid include need-based and non-need-based scholarships and part-time jobs. The average aided 2003–04 undergraduate received an aid package worth an estimated $24,461. The application deadline for financial aid is February 15.
Freshman Admission Washington requires an essay, a high school transcript, 2 recommendations, SAT I or ACT scores, and TOEFL scores for international students. A minimum 3.0 high school GPA and portfolio for art and architecture programs are recommended. The application deadline for regular admission is January 15; for early decision plan 1 it is November 15; and for early decision plan 2 it is January 1.
Transfer Admission The application deadline for admission is April 15.
Entrance Difficulty Washington assesses its entrance difficulty level as most difficult. For the fall 2003 freshman class, 20 percent of the applicants were accepted.

For Further Information Contact Ms. Nanette Tarbouni, Director of Admissions, Washington University in St. Louis, Campus Box 1089, One Brookings Drive, St. Louis, MO 63130-4899. *Telephone:* 314-935-6000 or 800-638-0700 (toll-free). *Fax:* 314-935-4290. *E-mail:* admissions@wustl.edu. *Web site:* http://www.wustl.edu/.

WEBSTER UNIVERSITY
St. Louis, Missouri

Webster is a coed, private, comprehensive institution, founded in 1915, offering degrees at the bachelor's, master's, and doctoral levels and post-master's and postbachelor's certificates. It has a 47-acre campus in St. Louis.

Academic Information The faculty has 842 members (19% full-time), 37% with terminal degrees. The undergraduate student-faculty ratio is 12:1. The library holds 268,000 titles, 1,480 serial subscriptions, and 14,800 audiovisual materials. Special programs include academic remediation, services for learning-disabled students, cooperative (work-study) education, study abroad, advanced placement credit, accelerated degree programs, ESL programs, double majors, independent study, distance learning, self-designed majors, summer session for credit, part-time degree programs (daytime, evenings, summer), adult/continuing education programs, internships, and arrangement for off-campus study with Fontbonne College, Lindenwood College, Maryville University of Saint Louis, Eden Theological Seminary, Missouri Baptist College. The most frequently chosen baccalaureate fields are business/marketing, communications/communication technologies, computer/information sciences.
Student Body Statistics The student body totals 7,250, of whom 3,559 are undergraduates (453 freshmen). 63 percent are women and 37 percent are men. Students come from 44 states and territories and 46 other countries. 79 percent are from Missouri. 3.2 percent are international students.
Expenses for 2003–04 *Application fee:* $25. *Comprehensive fee:* $21,848 includes full-time tuition ($15,480) and college room and board ($6368). *College room only:* $3140. Full-time tuition varies according to program. Room and board charges vary according to board plan and housing facility. *Part-time tuition:* $430 per credit hour. Part-time tuition varies according to location.
Financial Aid Forms of aid include need-based and non-need-based scholarships and part-time jobs. The average aided 2003–04 undergraduate received an aid package worth an estimated $15,845. The priority application deadline for financial aid is April 1.
Freshman Admission Webster requires an essay, a high school transcript, a minimum 2.5 high school GPA, 1 recommendation, SAT I or

ACT scores, and TOEFL scores for international students. A minimum 3.0 high school GPA and an interview are recommended. Audition is required for some. The application deadline for regular admission is June 1.

Transfer Admission   The application deadline for admission is August 1.

Entrance Difficulty   Webster assesses its entrance difficulty level as moderately difficult. For the fall 2003 freshman class, 58 percent of the applicants were accepted.

For Further Information   Contact Mr. Andrew Laue, Associate Director of Undergraduate Admission, Webster University, 470 East Lockwood Avenue, St. Louis, MO 63119-3194. *Telephone:* 314-968-6991 or 800-75-ENROL (toll-free). *Fax:* 314-968-7115. *E-mail:* admit@webster.edu. *Web site:* http://www.webster.edu/.

WENTWORTH MILITARY ACADEMY AND JUNIOR COLLEGE
Lexington, Missouri

WMA is a coed, private, two-year college, founded in 1880, offering degrees at the associate level. It has a 130-acre campus in Lexington near Kansas City.

For Further Information   Contact Maj. Todd Kitchen, Dean of Admissions, Wentworth Military Academy and Junior College, 1880 Washington Avenue, Lexington, MO 64067. *Telephone:* 660-259-2221. *Fax:* 660-259-2677. *E-mail:* admissions@wma1880.org. *Web site:* http://www.wma1880.org/.

WESTMINSTER COLLEGE
Fulton, Missouri

Westminster is a coed, private, four-year college, founded in 1851, affiliated with the Presbyterian Church, offering degrees at the bachelor's level. It has a 65-acre campus in Fulton.

Academic Information   The faculty has 75 members (69% full-time), 67% with terminal degrees. The student-faculty ratio is 14:1. The library holds 111,922 titles, 3,081 serial subscriptions, and 9,082 audiovisual materials. Special programs include academic remediation, services for learning-disabled students, an honors program, cooperative (work-study) education, study abroad, advanced placement credit, double majors, independent study, self-designed majors, summer session for credit, part-time degree programs (daytime), internships, and arrangement for off-campus study with Chicago Urban Studies Semester, American University, Beaver College. The most frequently chosen baccalaureate fields are business/marketing, education, social sciences and history.

Student Body Statistics   The student body is made up of 821 undergraduates (240 freshmen). 42 percent are women and 58 percent are men. Students come from 24 states and territories and 16 other countries. 73 percent are from Missouri. 6 percent are international students. 20 percent of the 2003 graduating class went on to graduate and professional schools.

Expenses for 2004–05   *Application fee:* $0. *Comprehensive fee:* $19,060 includes full-time tuition ($12,990), mandatory fees ($420), and college room and board ($5650). *College room only:* $2880. Room and board charges vary according to board plan and housing facility. *Part-time tuition:* $710 per credit hour. *Part-time mandatory fees:* $210 per term.

Financial Aid   Forms of aid include need-based and non-need-based scholarships and part-time jobs. The average aided 2003–04 undergraduate received an aid package worth an estimated $14,689. The priority application deadline for financial aid is February 15.

Freshman Admission   Westminster requires a high school transcript, 1 recommendation, a minimum ACT score of 21 or minimum SAT score of 970, and SAT I or ACT scores. An essay and a minimum 2.5 high school GPA are recommended. An interview is required for some.

Entrance Difficulty   Westminster assesses its entrance difficulty level as moderately difficult. For the fall 2003 freshman class, 75 percent of the applicants were accepted.

For Further Information   Contact Dr. Patrick Kirby, Dean of Enrollment Services, Westminster College, 501 Westminster Avenue, Fulton, MO 65251-1299. *Telephone:* 573-592-5251 or 800-475-3361 (toll-free). *Fax:* 573-592-5255. *E-mail:* admissions@jaynet.wcmo.edu. *Web site:* http://www.westminster-mo.edu/.

WILLIAM JEWELL COLLEGE
Liberty, Missouri

William Jewell is a coed, private, Baptist, four-year college, founded in 1849, offering degrees at the bachelor's level (also offers evening program with significant enrollment not reflected in profile). It has a 200-acre campus in Liberty near Kansas City.

Academic Information   The faculty has 134 members (56% full-time). The student-faculty ratio is 13:1. The library holds 260,119 titles, 868 serial subscriptions, and 27,617 audiovisual materials. Special programs include academic remediation, an honors program, cooperative (work-study) education, study abroad, advanced placement credit, double majors, independent study, self-designed majors, summer session for credit, part-time degree programs (daytime, evenings, weekends, summer), adult/continuing education programs, and internships. The most frequently chosen baccalaureate fields are business/marketing, communications/communication technologies, psychology.

Student Body Statistics   The student body is made up of 1,274 undergraduates (358 freshmen). 59 percent are women and 41 percent are men. Students come from 32 states and territories and 12 other countries. 78 percent are from Missouri. 1 percent are international students. 24 percent of the 2003 graduating class went on to graduate and professional schools.

Expenses for 2003–04   *Application fee:* $25. *Comprehensive fee:* $21,320 includes full-time tuition ($16,500) and college room and board ($4820). Full-time tuition varies according to class time and course load. Room and board charges vary according to board plan and housing facility. *Part-time tuition:* varies with class time.

Financial Aid   Forms of aid include need-based and non-need-based scholarships, athletic grants, and part-time jobs. The average aided 2003–04 undergraduate received an aid package worth an estimated $13,859. The priority application deadline for financial aid is March 1.

Freshman Admission   William Jewell requires a high school transcript, a minimum 2.0 high school GPA, SAT I or ACT scores, and TOEFL scores for international students. An essay, a minimum 2.5 high school GPA, 2 recommendations, and an interview are recommended. The application deadline for regular admission is August 25 and for early action it is November 15.

Transfer Admission   The application deadline for admission is rolling.

Entrance Difficulty   William Jewell assesses its entrance difficulty level as moderately difficult. For the fall 2003 freshman class, 95 percent of the applicants were accepted.

For Further Information   Contact Mr. Chad Jolly, Dean of Enrollment Development, William Jewell College, 500 College Hill, Liberty, MO 64068. *Telephone:* 816-781-7700 or 800-753-7009 (toll-free). *Fax:* 816-415-5027. *E-mail:* admission@william.jewell.edu. *Web site:* http://www.jewell.edu/.

WILLIAM WOODS UNIVERSITY
Fulton, Missouri

William Woods is a coed, private, comprehensive institution, founded in 1870, affiliated with the Christian Church (Disciples of Christ), offering degrees at the associate, bachelor's, and master's levels. It has a 170-acre campus in Fulton near St. Louis.

Academic Information   The faculty has 92 members (61% full-time). The undergraduate student-faculty ratio is 12:1. The library holds 93,917 titles and 26,773 audiovisual materials. Special programs include academic

William Woods University (continued)

remediation, an honors program, study abroad, advanced placement credit, accelerated degree programs, double majors, independent study, self-designed majors, summer session for credit, part-time degree programs (evenings, weekends), adult/continuing education programs, internships, and arrangement for off-campus study with University of Missouri–Columbia, Westminster College (MO), Stephens College, Lincoln University (MO). The most frequently chosen baccalaureate fields are business/marketing, computer/information sciences, visual/performing arts.

Student Body Statistics The student body totals 2,670, of whom 1,132 are undergraduates (254 freshmen). 72 percent are women and 28 percent are men. Students come from 39 states and territories and 14 other countries. 71 percent are from Missouri. 5.2 percent are international students.

Expenses for 2004–05 *Application fee:* $25. *Comprehensive fee:* $20,120 includes full-time tuition ($14,000), mandatory fees ($420), and college room and board ($5700). Full-time tuition and fees vary according to program. Room and board charges vary according to board plan. *Part-time tuition:* $465 per credit hour. *Part-time mandatory fees:* $15 per term.

Financial Aid Forms of aid include need-based and non-need-based scholarships, athletic grants, and part-time jobs. The average aided 2003–04 undergraduate received an aid package worth an estimated $13,532. The priority application deadline for financial aid is March 1.

Freshman Admission William Woods requires a high school transcript, SAT I or ACT scores, and TOEFL scores for international students. An interview is recommended. An essay and 2 recommendations are required for some. The application deadline for regular admission is rolling.

Transfer Admission The application deadline for admission is rolling.

Entrance Difficulty William Woods assesses its entrance difficulty level as moderately difficult.

For Further Information Contact Mr. Jimmy Clay, Executive Director of Enrollment Services, William Woods University, One University Avenue, Fulton, MO 65251. *Telephone:* 573-592-4221 or 800-995-3159 Ext. 4221 (toll-free). *Fax:* 573-592-1146. *E-mail:* admissions@williamwoods.edu. *Web site:* http://www.williamwoods.edu/.

See page 356 for a narrative description.

Nebraska

BELLEVUE UNIVERSITY

Bellevue, Nebraska

Bellevue University is a coed, private, comprehensive institution, founded in 1965, offering degrees at the bachelor's and master's levels. It has a 35-acre campus in Bellevue near Omaha.

Academic Information The faculty has 264 members (24% full-time), 25% with terminal degrees. The undergraduate student-faculty ratio is 17:1. The library holds 87,000 titles, 7,564 serial subscriptions, and 3,955 audiovisual materials. Special programs include academic remediation, cooperative (work-study) education, advanced placement credit, accelerated degree programs, ESL programs, double majors, independent study, distance learning, summer session for credit, part-time degree programs, external degree programs, adult/continuing education programs, and internships. The most frequently chosen baccalaureate fields are business/marketing, computer/information sciences, health professions and related sciences.

Student Body Statistics The student body totals 5,110, of whom 3,933 are undergraduates (327 freshmen). 50 percent are women and 50 percent are men. Students come from 42 states and territories and 69 other countries. 80 percent are from Nebraska. 8.5 percent are international students.

Expenses for 2004–05 *Application fee:* $25. *Tuition:* $4650 full-time, $155 per credit hour part-time. *Mandatory fees:* $90 full-time, $45 per term part-time. Full-time tuition and fees vary according to program. Part-time tuition and fees vary according to program.

Financial Aid Forms of aid include need-based and non-need-based scholarships, athletic grants, and part-time jobs. The application deadline for financial aid is continuous.

Freshman Admission Bellevue University requires a high school transcript, ACT scores, and TOEFL scores for international students. 3 recommendations and SAT I or ACT scores are required for some. The application deadline for regular admission is rolling.

Transfer Admission The application deadline for admission is rolling.

Entrance Difficulty Bellevue University has an open admission policy.

For Further Information Contact Melinda Cruz, Associate Vice President of Enrollment Management, Bellevue University, 1000 Galvin Road South, Bellevue, NE 68005-3098. *Telephone:* 402-293-2026 or 800-756-7920 (toll-free). *Fax:* 402-293-3730. *E-mail:* set@scholars.bellevue.edu. *Web site:* http://www.bellevue.edu/.

CHADRON STATE COLLEGE

Chadron, Nebraska

Chadron State is a coed, public, comprehensive unit of Nebraska State College System, founded in 1911, offering degrees at the bachelor's and master's levels. It has a 281-acre campus in Chadron.

Academic Information The faculty has 118 members (81% full-time), 53% with terminal degrees. The undergraduate student-faculty ratio is 22:1. The library holds 213,231 titles, 720 serial subscriptions, and 5,596 audiovisual materials. Special programs include services for learning-disabled students, an honors program, cooperative (work-study) education, study abroad, advanced placement credit, Freshman Honors College, double majors, independent study, distance learning, self-designed majors, summer session for credit, part-time degree programs (daytime, evenings, summer), adult/continuing education programs, and internships. The most frequently chosen baccalaureate fields are business/marketing, education, protective services/public administration.

Student Body Statistics The student body totals 2,711, of whom 2,294 are undergraduates (503 freshmen). 60 percent are women and 40 percent are men. Students come from 31 states and territories and 10 other countries. 74 percent are from Nebraska. 1 percent are international students.

Expenses for 2003–04 *Application fee:* $15. *State resident tuition:* $2610 full-time. *Nonresident tuition:* $5220 full-time. *Mandatory fees:* $631 full-time. *College room and board:* $3862. *College room only:* $1778.

Financial Aid Forms of aid include need-based scholarships and part-time jobs. The average aided 2003–04 undergraduate received an aid package worth an estimated $2615. The priority application deadline for financial aid is June 1.

Freshman Admission Chadron State requires a high school transcript, health forms, and TOEFL scores for international students. SAT I or ACT scores are recommended. The application deadline for regular admission is rolling.

Transfer Admission The application deadline for admission is rolling.

Entrance Difficulty Chadron State has an open admission policy. It assesses its entrance difficulty as minimally difficult for transfers.

For Further Information Contact Ms. Tena Cook Gould, Director of Admissions, Chadron State College, 1000 Main Street, Chadron, NE 69337-2690. *Telephone:* 308-432-6263 or 800-242-3766 (toll-free in-state). *Fax:* 308-432-6229. *E-mail:* inquire@csc1.csc.edu. *Web site:* http://www.csc.edu/.

CLARKSON COLLEGE

Omaha, Nebraska

Clarkson is a coed, primarily women's, private, comprehensive unit of Nebraska Health System, founded in 1888, offering degrees at the associate, bachelor's, and master's levels. It has a 3-acre campus in Omaha.

Expenses for 2003–04 *Application fee:* $15. *Comprehensive fee:* $12,662 includes full-time tuition ($9300), mandatory fees ($462), and college room and board ($2900). Room and board charges vary according to housing facility and location. *Part-time tuition:* $310 per credit hour. *Part-time mandatory fees:* $18 per credit hour, $15 per term.

For Further Information Contact Ms. Nicole Wegenast, Dean of Enrollment Services, Clarkson College, 101 South 42nd Street, Omaha, NE 68131-2739. *Telephone:* 402-552-3100 or 800-647-5500 (toll-free). *Fax:* 402-552-6057. *E-mail:* admiss@clarksoncollege.edu. *Web site:* http://www.clarksoncollege.edu/.

COLLEGE OF SAINT MARY
Omaha, Nebraska

CSM is a women's, private, Roman Catholic, four-year college, founded in 1923, offering degrees at the associate and bachelor's levels. It has a 25-acre campus in Omaha.

Academic Information The faculty has 51 members (100% full-time), 37% with terminal degrees. The student-faculty ratio is 10:1. The library holds 70,514 titles, 12,675 serial subscriptions, and 1,300 audiovisual materials. Special programs include academic remediation, services for learning-disabled students, study abroad, advanced placement credit, accelerated degree programs, double majors, independent study, summer session for credit, part-time degree programs, adult/continuing education programs, and internships. The most frequently chosen baccalaureate fields are business/marketing, education, health professions and related sciences.
Student Body Statistics The student body is made up of 915 undergraduates (78 freshmen). Students come from 16 states and territories and 7 other countries. 87 percent are from Nebraska. 1 percent are international students. 13 percent of the 2003 graduating class went on to graduate and professional schools.
Expenses for 2004–05 *Application fee:* $30. *Comprehensive fee:* $22,577 includes full-time tuition ($16,637), mandatory fees ($240), and college room and board ($5700). Room and board charges vary according to housing facility. *Part-time tuition:* varies with class time.
Financial Aid Forms of aid include need-based and non-need-based scholarships, athletic grants, and part-time jobs. The average aided 2003–04 undergraduate received an aid package worth an estimated $11,763. The priority application deadline for financial aid is March 1.
Freshman Admission CSM requires a high school transcript, a minimum 2.0 high school GPA, SAT I or ACT scores, and TOEFL scores for international students. An essay is recommended. A minimum 3.0 high school GPA, 2 recommendations, and an interview are required for some. The application deadline for regular admission is rolling.
Transfer Admission The application deadline for admission is rolling.
Entrance Difficulty CSM assesses its entrance difficulty level as minimally difficult. For the fall 2003 freshman class, 70 percent of the applicants were accepted.

For Further Information Contact Ms. Natalie Vrbka, Senior Admissions Counselor, College of Saint Mary, 1901 South 72nd Street, Omaha, NE 68124-2377. *Telephone:* 402-399-2407 or 800-926-5534 (toll-free). *Fax:* 402-399-2412. *E-mail:* enroll@csm.edu. *Web site:* http://www.csm.edu/.

CONCORDIA UNIVERSITY
Seward, Nebraska

Concordia University is a coed, private, comprehensive unit of Concordia University System, founded in 1894, affiliated with the Lutheran Church–Missouri Synod, offering degrees at the bachelor's and master's levels. It has a 120-acre campus in Seward near Omaha.

Academic Information The faculty has 120 members (52% full-time), 59% with terminal degrees. The undergraduate student-faculty ratio is 14:1. The library holds 171,688 titles, 575 serial subscriptions, and 12,068 audiovisual materials. Special programs include academic remediation, services for learning-disabled students, an honors program, cooperative (work-study) education, study abroad, advanced placement credit, accelerated degree programs, ESL programs, double majors, independent study, distance learning, summer session for credit, part-time degree

programs (daytime, evenings, summer), adult/continuing education programs, internships, and arrangement for off-campus study with University of Nebraska–Lincoln. The most frequently chosen baccalaureate fields are business/marketing, education, philosophy, religion, and theology.
Student Body Statistics The student body totals 1,317, of whom 1,202 are undergraduates (222 freshmen). 57 percent are women and 43 percent are men. Students come from 38 states and territories. 41 percent are from Nebraska.
Expenses for 2003–04 *Application fee:* $25. *Comprehensive fee:* $20,480 includes full-time tuition ($16,000) and college room and board ($4480). *College room only:* $1980. Room and board charges vary according to board plan. *Part-time tuition:* $500 per credit. Part-time tuition varies according to course load.
Financial Aid Forms of aid include need-based and non-need-based scholarships, athletic grants, and part-time jobs. The average aided 2003–04 undergraduate received an aid package worth an estimated $14,099. The application deadline for financial aid is May 1 with a priority deadline of March 1.
Freshman Admission Concordia University requires a high school transcript, SAT I or ACT scores, and TOEFL scores for international students. A minimum 2.0 high school GPA and an interview are recommended. Recommendations are required for some. The application deadline for regular admission is July 31.
Transfer Admission The application deadline for admission is August 1.
Entrance Difficulty Concordia University assesses its entrance difficulty level as moderately difficult. For the fall 2003 freshman class, 89 percent of the applicants were accepted.

For Further Information Contact Mr. Pete Kenow, Director of Admissions, Concordia University, 800 North Columbia Avenue, Seward, NE 68434-1599. *Telephone:* 402-643-7233 or 800-535-5494 (toll-free). *Fax:* 402-643-4073. *E-mail:* admiss@cune.edu. *Web site:* http://www.cune.edu/.

CREIGHTON UNIVERSITY
Omaha, Nebraska

Creighton is a coed, private, Roman Catholic (Jesuit) university, founded in 1878, offering degrees at the associate, bachelor's, master's, doctoral, and first professional levels. It has a 110-acre campus in Omaha.

Academic Information The faculty has 860 members (72% full-time), 92% with terminal degrees. The undergraduate student-faculty ratio is 14:1. The library holds 481,848 titles, 1,666 serial subscriptions, and 2,500 audiovisual materials. Special programs include academic remediation, services for learning-disabled students, an honors program, study abroad, advanced placement credit, accelerated degree programs, ESL programs, double majors, independent study, summer session for credit, part-time degree programs (daytime, evenings, weekends, summer), adult/continuing education programs, internships, and arrangement for off-campus study with Creighton University; West Omaha Campus. The most frequently chosen baccalaureate fields are business/marketing, biological/life sciences, health professions and related sciences.
Student Body Statistics The student body totals 6,537, of whom 3,736 are undergraduates (933 freshmen). 61 percent are women and 39 percent are men. Students come from 44 states and territories and 52 other countries. 51 percent are from Nebraska. 1.5 percent are international students.
Expenses for 2003–04 *Application fee:* $40. *Comprehensive fee:* $26,748 includes full-time tuition ($19,202), mandatory fees ($720), and college room and board ($6826). *College room only:* $3870. Room and board charges vary according to board plan and housing facility. *Part-time tuition:* $600 per credit hour. *Part-time mandatory fees:* $120.
Financial Aid Forms of aid include need-based and non-need-based scholarships, athletic grants, and part-time jobs. The average aided 2002–03 undergraduate received an aid package worth $17,937. The priority application deadline for financial aid is May 15.
Freshman Admission Creighton requires an essay, a high school transcript, a minimum 2.75 high school GPA, 1 recommendation, SAT I or ACT scores, and TOEFL scores for international students. The application deadline for regular admission is August 1.

Creighton University (continued)

Transfer Admission The application deadline for admission is rolling.
Entrance Difficulty Creighton assesses its entrance difficulty level as moderately difficult. For the fall 2003 freshman class, 88 percent of the applicants were accepted.

For Further Information Contact Ms. Mary Chase, Director of Admissions-Scholarships, Creighton University, 2500 California Plaza, Omaha, NE 68178-0001. *Telephone:* 402-280-2703 Ext. 2162 or 800-282-5835 (toll-free). *Fax:* 402-280-2685. *E-mail:* admissions@creighton.edu. *Web site:* http://www.creighton.edu/.

DANA COLLEGE
Blair, Nebraska

Dana is a coed, private, four-year college, founded in 1884, affiliated with the Evangelical Lutheran Church in America, offering degrees at the bachelor's level. It has a 150-acre campus in Blair near Omaha.

Academic Information The faculty has 71 members (62% full-time), 41% with terminal degrees. The student-faculty ratio is 12:1. The library holds 157,860 titles, 27,150 serial subscriptions, and 4,092 audiovisual materials. Special programs include services for learning-disabled students, an honors program, study abroad, advanced placement credit, accelerated degree programs, ESL programs, double majors, independent study, self-designed majors, summer session for credit, part-time degree programs (daytime), adult/continuing education programs, internships, and arrangement for off-campus study with Consortium of Eastern Nebraska Colleges. The most frequently chosen baccalaureate fields are business/marketing, biological/life sciences, education.
Student Body Statistics The student body is made up of 581 undergraduates (164 freshmen). 41 percent are women and 59 percent are men. Students come from 38 states and territories and 2 other countries. 51 percent are from Nebraska. 0.5 percent are international students.
Expenses for 2003–04 *Application fee:* $0. *Comprehensive fee:* $20,630 includes full-time tuition ($15,200), mandatory fees ($550), and college room and board ($4880). *College room only:* $1900. Room and board charges vary according to board plan and housing facility. *Part-time tuition:* $465 per semester hour. *Part-time mandatory fees:* $30 per term. Part-time tuition and fees vary according to course load.
Financial Aid Forms of aid include need-based and non-need-based scholarships, athletic grants, and part-time jobs. The average aided 2003–04 undergraduate received an aid package worth an estimated $14,622. The priority application deadline for financial aid is March 15.
Freshman Admission Dana requires a high school transcript, a minimum 2.0 high school GPA, SAT I or ACT scores, and TOEFL scores for international students. ACT scores are recommended. An essay, 1 recommendation, and an interview are required for some. The application deadline for regular admission is rolling.
Entrance Difficulty Dana assesses its entrance difficulty level as moderately difficult. For the fall 2003 freshman class, 98 percent of the applicants were accepted.

For Further Information Contact Mr. James Lynes, Director of Admissions, Dana College, 2848 College Drive, Blair, NE 68008-1099. *Telephone:* 402-426-7220 or 800-444-3262 (toll-free). *Fax:* 402-426-7386. *E-mail:* admissions@acad2.dana.edu. *Web site:* http://www.dana.edu/.

DOANE COLLEGE
Crete, Nebraska

Doane is a coed, private, comprehensive institution, founded in 1872, affiliated with the United Church of Christ, offering degrees at the bachelor's and master's levels (nontraditional undergraduate programs and graduate programs offered at Lincoln campus). It has a 300-acre campus in Crete near Omaha.

Academic Information The faculty has 127 members (57% full-time), 39% with terminal degrees. The undergraduate student-faculty ratio is 12:1. The library holds 257,560 titles, 3,500 serial subscriptions, and 1,313 audiovisual materials. Special programs include academic remediation, an honors program, cooperative (work-study) education, study abroad, advanced placement credit, accelerated degree programs, ESL programs, double majors, independent study, self-designed majors, summer session for credit, part-time degree programs (daytime, evenings), adult/continuing education programs, internships, and arrangement for off-campus study with Association of Nebraska Interterm Colleges. The most frequently chosen baccalaureate fields are business/marketing, education, social sciences and history.
Student Body Statistics The student body totals 2,273, of whom 1,610 are undergraduates (291 freshmen). 56 percent are women and 44 percent are men. Students come from 23 states and territories and 7 other countries. 80 percent are from Nebraska.
Expenses for 2004–05 *Application fee:* $15. *Comprehensive fee:* $20,690 includes full-time tuition ($15,620), mandatory fees ($350), and college room and board ($4720). Full-time tuition and fees vary according to location. Room and board charges vary according to board plan, housing facility, and location. *Part-time tuition:* varies with course load, location.
Financial Aid Forms of aid include need-based and non-need-based scholarships, athletic grants, and part-time jobs. The average aided 2003–04 undergraduate received an aid package worth an estimated $12,953. The priority application deadline for financial aid is March 1.
Freshman Admission Doane requires a high school transcript, 2 recommendations, SAT I or ACT scores, and TOEFL scores for international students. A minimum 2.0 high school GPA is recommended. An interview is required for some. The application deadline for regular admission is rolling.
Transfer Admission The application deadline for admission is rolling.
Entrance Difficulty Doane assesses its entrance difficulty level as moderately difficult. For the fall 2003 freshman class, 84 percent of the applicants were accepted.

For Further Information Contact Mr. Dan Kunzman, Dean of Admissions, Doane College, Crete, NE 68333. *Telephone:* 402-826-8222 or 800-333-6263 (toll-free). *Fax:* 402-826-8600. *E-mail:* admissions@doane.edu. *Web site:* http://www.doane.edu/.

GRACE UNIVERSITY
Omaha, Nebraska

Grace is a coed, private, interdenominational, comprehensive institution, founded in 1943, offering degrees at the associate, bachelor's, and master's levels. It has a 15-acre campus in Omaha.

Academic Information The faculty has 50 members (50% full-time), 90% with terminal degrees. The undergraduate student-faculty ratio is 18:1. The library holds 46,736 titles, 3,721 serial subscriptions, and 3,882 audiovisual materials. Special programs include services for learning-disabled students, cooperative (work-study) education, study abroad, advanced placement credit, accelerated degree programs, double majors, independent study, distance learning, self-designed majors, summer session for credit, part-time degree programs, external degree programs, adult/continuing education programs, internships, and arrangement for off-campus study with Iowa Western Community College, Metropolitan Community College (NE), University of Nebraska at Omaha, Bellevue University, Clarkson College.
Student Body Statistics The student body totals 513, of whom 427 are undergraduates (122 freshmen). 57 percent are women and 43 percent are men. Students come from 30 states and territories and 4 other countries. 64 percent are from Nebraska.
Expenses for 2003–04 *Application fee:* $35. *Comprehensive fee:* $15,680 includes full-time tuition ($10,500), mandatory fees ($180), and college room and board ($5000). Room and board charges vary according to board plan and housing facility. *Part-time tuition:* $350 per credit hour. Part-time tuition varies according to course load.
Financial Aid Forms of aid include need-based and non-need-based scholarships and part-time jobs. The average aided 2002–03 undergraduate received an aid package worth $6479. The priority application deadline for financial aid is February 1.
Freshman Admission Grace requires an essay, a high school transcript, a minimum 2.0 high school GPA, 3 recommendations, ACT scores, and

TOEFL scores for international students. An interview is required for some. The application deadline for regular admission is rolling.
Transfer Admission The application deadline for admission is rolling.
Entrance Difficulty Grace assesses its entrance difficulty level as moderately difficult. For the fall 2003 freshman class, 46 percent of the applicants were accepted.

For Further Information Contact Ms. Diane V. Lee, Director of Admissions, Grace University, 1311 South Ninth Street, Omaha, NE 68108. *Telephone:* 402-449-2831 or 800-383-1422 (toll-free). *Fax:* 402-341-9587. *E-mail:* admissions@graceuniversity.com. *Web site:* http://www.graceuniversity.edu/.

HAMILTON COLLEGE
Omaha, Nebraska

NCB is a coed, proprietary, primarily two-year college of Educational Medical, Inc, founded in 1891, offering degrees at the associate and bachelor's levels. It has a 3-acre campus in Omaha.

Academic Information The faculty has 35 members (49% full-time). The student-faculty ratio is 20:1. The library holds 4,800 titles and 50 serial subscriptions. Special programs include academic remediation, cooperative (work-study) education, advanced placement credit, summer session for credit, part-time degree programs (daytime, evenings), adult/continuing education programs, and internships.
Student Body Statistics The student body is made up of 700 undergraduates (700 freshmen). 64 percent are women and 36 percent are men. Students come from 5 states and territories.
Financial Aid Forms of aid include part-time jobs.
Freshman Admission NCB requires a high school transcript, an interview, and CPAt. TOEFL scores for international students are recommended. The application deadline for regular admission is rolling.
Transfer Admission The application deadline for admission is rolling.
Entrance Difficulty NCB assesses its entrance difficulty level as minimally difficult.

For Further Information Contact Mr. Mark Stoltenberger, Director of Admissions, Hamilton College, 3350 North 90 Street, Omaha, NE 68134. *Telephone:* 402-572-8500 or 800-642-1456 (toll-free). *Fax:* 402-573-1341. *Web site:* http://www.hamiltonomaha.edu/.

HASTINGS COLLEGE
Hastings, Nebraska

Hastings is a coed, private, Presbyterian, comprehensive institution, founded in 1882, offering degrees at the bachelor's and master's levels. It has a 109-acre campus in Hastings.

Academic Information The faculty has 117 members (68% full-time), 56% with terminal degrees. The undergraduate student-faculty ratio is 13:1. The library holds 101,000 titles, 607 serial subscriptions, and 714 audiovisual materials. Special programs include services for learning-disabled students, study abroad, advanced placement credit, double majors, independent study, self-designed majors, summer session for credit, part-time degree programs (daytime, summer), adult/continuing education programs, internships, and arrangement for off-campus study. The most frequently chosen baccalaureate fields are business/marketing, education, psychology.
Student Body Statistics The student body totals 1,113, of whom 1,074 are undergraduates (339 freshmen). 48 percent are women and 52 percent are men. Students come from 25 states and territories and 5 other countries. 78 percent are from Nebraska. 1 percent are international students. 16 percent of the 2003 graduating class went on to graduate and professional schools.
Expenses for 2003–04 *Application fee:* $20. *Comprehensive fee:* $19,928 includes full-time tuition ($14,782), mandatory fees ($616), and college room and board ($4530). *College room only:* $1910. Full-time tuition and fees vary according to degree level and program. Room and board charges

vary according to board plan. *Part-time tuition:* $612 per semester hour. *Part-time mandatory fees:* $162 per term. Part-time tuition and fees vary according to course load, degree level, and program.
Financial Aid Forms of aid include need-based and non-need-based scholarships, athletic grants, and part-time jobs. The average aided 2003–04 undergraduate received an aid package worth an estimated $11,464. The application deadline for financial aid is September 1 with a priority deadline of May 1.
Freshman Admission Hastings requires a high school transcript, a minimum 2.0 high school GPA, counselor's recommendation, SAT I or ACT scores, and TOEFL scores for international students. An essay, 2 recommendations, and an interview are required for some. The application deadline for regular admission is August 1.
Transfer Admission The application deadline for admission is August 1.
Entrance Difficulty Hastings assesses its entrance difficulty level as moderately difficult. For the fall 2003 freshman class, 80 percent of the applicants were accepted.

For Further Information Contact Ms. Mary Molliconi, Director of Admissions, Hastings College, 800 Turner Avenue, Hastings, NE 68901-7696. *Telephone:* 402-461-7320 or 800-532-7642 (toll-free). *Fax:* 402-461-7490. *E-mail:* mmolliconi@hastings.edu. *Web site:* http://www.hastings.edu/.

ITT TECHNICAL INSTITUTE
Omaha, Nebraska

ITT Tech is a coed, proprietary, primarily two-year college of ITT Educational Services, Inc, founded in 1991, offering degrees at the associate and bachelor's levels. It has a 1-acre campus in Omaha.

Student Body Statistics The student body is made up of 382 undergraduates.
Expenses for 2003–04 *Application fee:* $100. Total Program Cost varies depending on course of study. Consult school catalog.
Financial Aid Forms of aid include need-based scholarships. The application deadline for financial aid is continuous.
Freshman Admission ITT Tech requires a high school transcript, an interview, TOEFL scores for international students, and Wonderlic aptitude test. Recommendations are recommended. The application deadline for regular admission is rolling.
Transfer Admission The application deadline for admission is rolling.
Entrance Difficulty ITT Tech assesses its entrance difficulty level as minimally difficult.

For Further Information Contact Ms. Jacqueline M. Hawthorne, Director of Recruitment, ITT Technical Institute, 9814 M Street, Omaha, NE 68127. *Telephone:* 402-331-2900 or 800-677-9260 (toll-free). *Fax:* 402-331-9495. *Web site:* http://www.itt-tech.edu/.

LITTLE PRIEST TRIBAL COLLEGE
Winnebago, Nebraska

Little Priest Tribal College is a private, two-year college, offering degrees at the associate level.

Academic Information The faculty has 16 members (25% full-time). The student-faculty ratio is 11:1.
Student Body Statistics The student body is made up of 130 undergraduates (21 freshmen).
Expenses for 2003–04 *Tuition:* $2220 full-time, $74 per credit part-time. *Mandatory fees:* $575 full-time, $18.20 per credit part-time.
Financial Aid Forms of aid include need-based scholarships and part-time jobs. The application deadline for financial aid is continuous.
Freshman Admission Little Priest Tribal College requires TOEFL scores for international students.

Little Priest Tribal College (continued)

Entrance Difficulty For the fall 2003 freshman class, 100 percent of the applicants were accepted.

For Further Information Contact Ms. Karen Kemling, Director of Admissions and Records, Little Priest Tribal College, PO Box 270, Winnebago, NE 68071. *Telephone:* 402-878-2380. *Fax:* 402-878-2355. *Web site:* http://www.lptc.bia.edu/.

MIDLAND LUTHERAN COLLEGE
Fremont, Nebraska

Midland is a coed, private, Lutheran, four-year college, founded in 1883, offering degrees at the associate and bachelor's levels. It has a 27-acre campus in Fremont near Omaha.

Expenses for 2003–04 *Application fee:* $30. *Comprehensive fee:* $20,730 includes full-time tuition ($16,310) and college room and board ($4420). *College room only:* $1950.

For Further Information Contact Ms. Stacy Poggendorf, Assistant Vice President for Admissions, Midland Lutheran College, Admissions Office, Fremont, NE 68025-4200. *Telephone:* 402-941-6508 or 800-642-8382 Ext. 6501 (toll-free). *Fax:* 402-941-6513. *E-mail:* admissions@admin.mlc.edu. *Web site:* http://www.mlc.edu/.

NEBRASKA CHRISTIAN COLLEGE
Norfolk, Nebraska

Nebraska Christian College is a coed, private, four-year college, founded in 1944, affiliated with the Christian Churches and Churches of Christ, offering degrees at the associate and bachelor's levels. It has an 85-acre campus in Norfolk.

Expenses for 2003–04 *Application fee:* $25. *Comprehensive fee:* $9660 includes full-time tuition ($5380), mandatory fees ($580), and college room and board ($3700). *Part-time tuition:* $180 per credit.

For Further Information Contact Mr. Jason Epperson, Associate Director of Admissions, Nebraska Christian College, 1800 Syracuse Avenue, Norfolk, NE 68701. *Telephone:* 402-379-5000 Ext. 411. *Fax:* 402-379-5100. *E-mail:* admissions@nechristian.edu. *Web site:* http://www.nechristian.edu/.

NEBRASKA COLLEGE OF BUSINESS
See Hamilton College

NEBRASKA METHODIST COLLEGE
Omaha, Nebraska

Nebraska Methodist College is a coed, primarily women's, private, comprehensive institution, founded in 1891, affiliated with the United Methodist Church, offering degrees at the associate, bachelor's, and master's levels and post-master's certificates. It has a 5-acre campus in Omaha.

Academic Information The faculty has 57 members (58% full-time), 23% with terminal degrees. The undergraduate student-faculty ratio is 10:1. The library holds 8,656 titles, 475 serial subscriptions, and 985 audiovisual materials. Special programs include academic remediation, services for learning-disabled students, advanced placement credit, accelerated degree programs, independent study, distance learning, summer session for credit, and internships. The most frequently chosen baccalaureate field is health professions and related sciences.

Student Body Statistics The student body totals 422, of whom 390 are undergraduates (37 freshmen). 87 percent are women and 13 percent are men. Students come from 3 states and territories and 2 other countries. 80 percent are from Nebraska. 0.5 percent are international students. 3 percent of the 2003 graduating class went on to graduate and professional schools.

Expenses for 2003–04 *Application fee:* $25. *Tuition:* $9600 full-time, $320 per credit hour part-time. *Mandatory fees:* $600 full-time, $20 per credit hour part-time, $10 per term part-time. *College room only:* $1700. Room charges vary according to housing facility and location.

Financial Aid Forms of aid include need-based and non-need-based scholarships and part-time jobs. The average aided 2003–04 undergraduate received an aid package worth an estimated $8229. The priority application deadline for financial aid is May 1.

Freshman Admission Nebraska Methodist College requires an essay, a high school transcript, a minimum 2.0 high school GPA, 3 recommendations, an interview, SAT I or ACT scores, and TOEFL scores for international students. The application deadline for regular admission is April 1.

Transfer Admission The application deadline for admission is April 1.

Entrance Difficulty Nebraska Methodist College assesses its entrance difficulty level as moderately difficult. For the fall 2003 freshman class, 81 percent of the applicants were accepted.

For Further Information Contact Ms. Deann Sterner, Director of Admissions, Nebraska Methodist College, Omaha, NE 68114. *Telephone:* 402-354-4922 or 800-335-5510 (toll-free). *Fax:* 402-354-8875. *E-mail:* dsterne@methodistcollege.edu. *Web site:* http://www.methodistcollege.edu/.

NEBRASKA WESLEYAN UNIVERSITY
Lincoln, Nebraska

NWU is a coed, private, United Methodist, comprehensive institution, founded in 1887, offering degrees at the bachelor's and master's levels. It has a 50-acre campus in Lincoln near Omaha.

Academic Information The faculty has 168 members (60% full-time), 62% with terminal degrees. The undergraduate student-faculty ratio is 14:1. The library holds 178,531 titles, 743 serial subscriptions, and 7,951 audiovisual materials. Special programs include services for learning-disabled students, study abroad, advanced placement credit, double majors, independent study, summer session for credit, part-time degree programs (evenings, summer), adult/continuing education programs, internships, and arrangement for off-campus study with Chicago Urban Life Center. The most frequently chosen baccalaureate fields are business/marketing, parks and recreation, psychology.

Student Body Statistics The student body totals 1,840, of whom 1,687 are undergraduates (420 freshmen). 56 percent are women and 44 percent are men. Students come from 25 states and territories and 8 other countries. 94 percent are from Nebraska. 0.8 percent are international students. 30 percent of the 2003 graduating class went on to graduate and professional schools.

Expenses for 2003–04 *Application fee:* $20. *Comprehensive fee:* $20,960 includes full-time tuition ($16,140), mandatory fees ($290), and college room and board ($4530). Room and board charges vary according to board plan and housing facility. *Part-time tuition:* $609 per hour. Part-time tuition varies according to class time and course load.

Financial Aid Forms of aid include need-based and non-need-based scholarships and part-time jobs. The average aided 2003–04 undergraduate received an aid package worth an estimated $12,708. The application deadline for financial aid is continuous.

Freshman Admission NWU requires a minimum 2.0 high school GPA, SAT I or ACT scores, and TOEFL scores for international students. An interview is recommended. An essay and resume of activities are required for some. The application deadline for regular admission is August 15 and for early decision it is November 15.

Transfer Admission The application deadline for admission is August 15.

Entrance Difficulty NWU assesses its entrance difficulty level as moderately difficult. For the fall 2003 freshman class, 93 percent of the applicants were accepted.

For Further Information Contact Ms. Patty Karthauser, Vice President for Enrollment and Marketing, Nebraska Wesleyan University, 5000 Saint Paul Avenue, Lincoln, NE 68504. *Telephone:* 402-465-2218 or 800-541-3818 (toll-free). *Fax:* 402-465-2179. *E-mail:* admissions@nebrwesleyan.edu. *Web site:* http://www.nebrwesleyan.edu/.

PERU STATE COLLEGE

Peru, Nebraska

PSC is a coed, public, comprehensive unit of Nebraska State College System, founded in 1867, offering degrees at the bachelor's and master's levels. It has a 104-acre campus in Peru.

Academic Information The faculty has 123 members (32% full-time), 41% with terminal degrees. The undergraduate student-faculty ratio is 17:1. The library holds 177,373 titles and 232 serial subscriptions. Special programs include academic remediation, services for learning-disabled students, an honors program, cooperative (work-study) education, advanced placement credit, Freshman Honors College, summer session for credit, part-time degree programs (daytime, evenings, summer), external degree programs, adult/continuing education programs, internships, and arrangement for off-campus study with Southeast Community College, Beatrice Campus; Metropolitan Community College.

Student Body Statistics The student body totals 1,671, of whom 1,467 are undergraduates (188 freshmen). 55 percent are women and 45 percent are men. Students come from 27 states and territories and 3 other countries. 90 percent are from Nebraska. 0.9 percent are international students. 13 percent of the 2003 graduating class went on to graduate and professional schools.

Expenses for 2003–04 *State resident tuition:* $2610 full-time. *Nonresident tuition:* $5220 full-time. *Mandatory fees:* $674 full-time. Full-time tuition and fees vary according to course load, location, and reciprocity agreements. *College room and board:* $4911. *College room only:* $2361. Room and board charges vary according to board plan and housing facility.

Financial Aid Forms of aid include need-based and non-need-based scholarships and part-time jobs. The priority application deadline for financial aid is March 1.

Freshman Admission PSC requires a high school transcript and TOEFL scores for international students. A minimum 2.0 high school GPA, recommendations, and SAT I or ACT scores are required for some. The application deadline for regular admission is rolling.

Transfer Admission The application deadline for admission is rolling.

Entrance Difficulty PSC has an open admission policy. It assesses its entrance difficulty as minimally difficult for out-of-state applicants.

For Further Information Contact Ms. Janelle Moran, Director of Recruitment and Admissions, Peru State College, PO Box 10, Peru, NE 68421. *Telephone:* 402-872-2221 or 800-742-4412 (toll-free in-state). *Fax:* 402-872-2296. *E-mail:* jmoran@oakmail.peru.edu. *Web site:* http://www.peru.edu/.

UNION COLLEGE

Lincoln, Nebraska

Union is a coed, private, Seventh-day Adventist, four-year college, founded in 1891, offering degrees at the associate and bachelor's levels. It has a 26-acre campus in Lincoln near Omaha.

Academic Information The faculty has 92 members (57% full-time). The student-faculty ratio is 14:1. The library holds 147,813 titles, 1,357 serial subscriptions, and 3,278 audiovisual materials. Special programs include services for learning-disabled students, an honors program, cooperative (work-study) education, study abroad, advanced placement credit, accelerated degree programs, ESL programs, double majors, independent study, self-designed majors, summer session for credit, part-time degree programs (daytime, summer), adult/continuing education

programs, internships, and arrangement for off-campus study with University of Nebraska, Southeast Community College. The most frequently chosen baccalaureate fields are business/marketing, education, health professions and related sciences.

Student Body Statistics The student body is made up of 903 undergraduates (165 freshmen). 59 percent are women and 41 percent are men. Students come from 41 states and territories and 34 other countries. 23 percent are from Nebraska. 12.3 percent are international students.

Expenses for 2004–05 *Application fee:* $0. *Comprehensive fee:* $18,246 includes full-time tuition ($13,380), mandatory fees ($500), and college room and board ($4366). *College room only:* $2576.

Financial Aid Forms of aid include need-based and non-need-based scholarships and part-time jobs. The average aided 2003–04 undergraduate received an aid package worth an estimated $8376. The priority application deadline for financial aid is May 1.

Freshman Admission Union requires a high school transcript, a minimum 2.5 high school GPA, 3 recommendations, and ACT scores. An essay is recommended. An interview is required for some. The application deadline for regular admission is rolling.

Transfer Admission The application deadline for admission is rolling.

Entrance Difficulty Union has an open admission policy except for nursing, elementary education, physician assistant programs.

For Further Information Contact Huda McClelland, Director of Admissions, Union College, 3800 South 48th Street, Lincoln, NE 68506. *Telephone:* 402-486-2504 or 800-228-4600 (toll-free out-of-state). *Fax:* 402-486-2895. *E-mail:* ucenrol@ucollege.edu. *Web site:* http://www.ucollege.edu/.

UNIVERSITY OF NEBRASKA AT KEARNEY

Kearney, Nebraska

UNK is a coed, public, comprehensive unit of University of Nebraska System, founded in 1903, offering degrees at the bachelor's and master's levels. It has a 235-acre campus in Kearney.

Expenses for 2003–04 *Application fee:* $45. *State resident tuition:* $3120 full-time. *Nonresident tuition:* $6382 full-time. *Mandatory fees:* $765 full-time. *College room and board:* $4436.

For Further Information Contact Mr. John Kundel, Director of Admissions, University of Nebraska at Kearney, 905 West 25th Street, Kearney, NE 68849-0001. *Telephone:* 308-865-8702 or 800-532-7639 (toll-free). *Fax:* 308-865-8987. *E-mail:* admissionsug@unk.edu. *Web site:* http://www.unk.edu/.

UNIVERSITY OF NEBRASKA AT OMAHA

Omaha, Nebraska

UNO is a coed, public unit of University of Nebraska System, founded in 1908, offering degrees at the bachelor's, master's, and doctoral levels and post-master's and postbachelor's certificates. It has a 158-acre campus in Omaha.

Academic Information The faculty has 781 members (60% full-time), 61% with terminal degrees. The undergraduate student-faculty ratio is 18:1. The library holds 750,000 titles, 3,000 serial subscriptions, and 7,000 audiovisual materials. Special programs include services for learning-disabled students, an honors program, cooperative (work-study) education, study abroad, advanced placement credit, ESL programs, double majors, distance learning, self-designed majors, summer session for credit, part-time degree programs (daytime, evenings, summer), adult/continuing education programs, internships, and arrangement for off-campus study with other units of the University of Nebraska System. The most frequently chosen baccalaureate fields are business/marketing, education, protective services/public administration.

Student Body Statistics The student body totals 13,997, of whom 11,102 are undergraduates (1,537 freshmen). 53 percent are women and 47 percent are men. Students come from 48 states and territories and 70 other countries. 89 percent are from Nebraska. 2.4 percent are international students.

University of Nebraska at Omaha (continued)

Expenses for 2003–04 *Application fee: $45. State resident tuition: $3518* full-time, $117.25 per semester hour part-time. *Nonresident tuition: $10,358* full-time, $345.25 per semester hour part-time. *Mandatory fees: $564* full-time, $15.50 per semester hour part-time, $72 per term part-time. Full-time tuition and fees vary according to course load and student level. Part-time tuition and fees vary according to course load and student level. *College room and board: $3998. College room only: $3078.* Room and board charges vary according to board plan.
Financial Aid Forms of aid include need-based and non-need-based scholarships, athletic grants, and part-time jobs. The priority application deadline for financial aid is March 1.
Freshman Admission UNO requires a high school transcript, minimum ACT score of 20 or rank in upper 50% of high school class, SAT I or ACT scores, and TOEFL scores for international students. The application deadline for regular admission is August 1.
Transfer Admission The application deadline for admission is August 1.
Entrance Difficulty UNO assesses its entrance difficulty level as minimally difficult; moderately difficult for engineering program; noncompetitive for nontraditional, adult applicants. For the fall 2003 freshman class, 85 percent of the applicants were accepted.

For Further Information Contact Ms. Jolene Adams, Associate Director of Admissions, University of Nebraska at Omaha, 6001 Dodge Street, Omaha, NE 68182. *Telephone:* 402-554-2416 or 800-858-8648 (toll-free in-state). *Fax:* 402-554-3472. *Web site:* http://www.unomaha.edu/.

UNIVERSITY OF NEBRASKA–LINCOLN
Lincoln, Nebraska

UNL is a coed, public unit of University of Nebraska System, founded in 1869, offering degrees at the associate, bachelor's, master's, doctoral, and first professional levels and post-master's certificates. It has a 623-acre campus in Lincoln near Omaha.

Academic Information The faculty has 1,022 members (99% full-time), 96% with terminal degrees. The undergraduate student-faculty ratio is 17:1. The library holds 1 million titles, 21,309 serial subscriptions, and 73,405 audiovisual materials. Special programs include services for learning-disabled students, an honors program, cooperative (work-study) education, study abroad, advanced placement credit, accelerated degree programs, ESL programs, double majors, independent study, distance learning, self-designed majors, summer session for credit, part-time degree programs (daytime, evenings, summer), adult/continuing education programs, internships, and arrangement for off-campus study with University of Missouri, Kansas State University, University of South Dakota. The most frequently chosen baccalaureate fields are business/marketing, communications/communication technologies, engineering/engineering technologies.
Student Body Statistics The student body totals 22,559, of whom 17,851 are undergraduates (3,679 freshmen). 48 percent are women and 52 percent are men. Students come from 51 states and territories and 80 other countries. 88 percent are from Nebraska. 2.6 percent are international students.
Expenses for 2003–04 *Application fee: $25. State resident tuition: $3848* full-time, $128.25 per credit hour part-time. *Nonresident tuition: $11,430* full-time, $381 per credit hour part-time. *Mandatory fees: $863 full-time, $6* per credit hour part-time, $174.50 per term part-time. Full-time tuition and fees vary according to course load. Part-time tuition and fees vary according to course load. *College room and board: $5204. College room only: $2404.* Room and board charges vary according to board plan and housing facility.
Financial Aid Forms of aid include need-based and non-need-based scholarships, athletic grants, and part-time jobs. The average aided 2002–03 undergraduate received an aid package worth $6947. The application deadline for financial aid is continuous.
Freshman Admission UNL requires a high school transcript, SAT I or ACT scores, and TOEFL scores for international students. Rank in upper 50% of high school class is required for some. The application deadline for regular admission is June 30.
Transfer Admission The application deadline for admission is June 30.

Entrance Difficulty UNL assesses its entrance difficulty level as moderately difficult; very difficult for architecture, engineering programs. For the fall 2003 freshman class, 76 percent of the applicants were accepted.

For Further Information Contact Pat McBride, Director, New Student Enrollment, University of Nebraska–Lincoln, 313 North 13th Street, Ross Van Brunt Building, Lincoln, NE 68588-0256. *Telephone:* 402-472-2030 or 800-742-8800 (toll-free). *Fax:* 402-472-0670. *E-mail:* nuhusker@unl.edu. *Web site:* http://www.unl.edu/.

UNIVERSITY OF NEBRASKA MEDICAL CENTER
Omaha, Nebraska

UNMC is a coed, public, upper-level unit of University of Nebraska System, founded in 1869, offering degrees at the bachelor's, master's, doctoral, and first professional levels and post-master's, first professional, and postbachelor's certificates. It has a 51-acre campus in Omaha.

Academic Information The faculty has 883 members (80% full-time), 71% with terminal degrees. The library holds 247,434 titles, 1,741 serial subscriptions, and 849 audiovisual materials. Special programs include services for learning-disabled students, an honors program, distance learning, summer session for credit, part-time degree programs (daytime, summer), internships, and arrangement for off-campus study with University of Nebraska–Lincoln, University of Nebraska at Omaha, University of Nebraska at Kearney. The most frequently chosen baccalaureate field is health professions and related sciences.
Student Body Statistics The student body totals 2,865, of whom 742 are undergraduates. 93 percent are women and 7 percent are men. Students come from 14 states and territories and 6 other countries. 91 percent are from Nebraska. 0.9 percent are international students.
Expenses for 2003–04 *Application fee: $45. State resident tuition: $4875* full-time, $162.50 per semester hour part-time. *Nonresident tuition: $14,280* full-time, $476 per semester hour part-time. *Mandatory fees: $353 full-time.* Full-time tuition and fees vary according to program. Part-time tuition varies according to program.
Financial Aid Forms of aid include need-based scholarships and part-time jobs. The priority application deadline for financial aid is February 1.
Transfer Admission UNMC requires a college transcript and a minimum 2.0 college GPA. Standardized test scores and a minimum 3.0 college GPA are required for some. The application deadline for admission is rolling.
Entrance Difficulty UNMC assesses its entrance difficulty level as moderately difficult. For the fall 2003 entering class, 33 percent of the applicants were accepted.

For Further Information Contact Ms. Crystal Oldham, Administrative Technician, University of Nebraska Medical Center, 984265 Nebraska Medical Center, Omaha, NE 68198-4230. *Telephone:* 402-559-6409 or 800-626-8431 Ext. 6468 (toll-free). *Fax:* 402-559-6796. *E-mail:* thorton@unmc.edu. *Web site:* http://www.unmc.edu/.

WAYNE STATE COLLEGE
Wayne, Nebraska

WSC is a coed, public, comprehensive unit of Nebraska State College System, founded in 1910, offering degrees at the bachelor's and master's levels and post-master's certificates. It has a 128-acre campus in Wayne.

Academic Information The faculty has 191 members (66% full-time), 57% with terminal degrees. The undergraduate student-faculty ratio is 19:1. The library holds 147,205 titles, 656 serial subscriptions, and 5,300 audiovisual materials. Special programs include services for learning-disabled students, an honors program, cooperative (work-study) education, double majors, independent study, distance learning, self-designed majors, summer session for credit, part-time degree programs (daytime, evenings, weekends, summer), adult/continuing education programs, internships, and arrangement for off-campus study with Northeast Community College, Central Community College. The most frequently chosen baccalaureate fields are business/marketing, education, psychology.

Student Body Statistics The student body totals 3,317, of whom 2,769 are undergraduates (610 freshmen). 56 percent are women and 44 percent are men. Students come from 25 states and territories and 22 other countries. 85 percent are from Nebraska. 0.8 percent are international students.

Expenses for 2003–04 *Application fee:* $30. *State resident tuition:* $2610 full-time. *Nonresident tuition:* $5220 full-time. *Mandatory fees:* $822 full-time. *College room and board:* $3920. *College room only:* $1860. Room and board charges vary according to board plan and housing facility.

Financial Aid Forms of aid include need-based and non-need-based scholarships, athletic grants, and part-time jobs. The average aided 2002–03 undergraduate received an aid package worth $3615. The priority application deadline for financial aid is May 1.

Freshman Admission WSC requires a high school transcript and TOEFL scores for international students. SAT I or ACT scores are recommended. The application deadline for regular admission is rolling.

Transfer Admission The application deadline for admission is rolling.

Entrance Difficulty WSC has an open admission policy for state residents. It assesses its entrance difficulty as minimally difficult for transfers.

For Further Information Contact R. Lincoln Morris, Director of Admissions, Wayne State College, 1111 Main Street, Wayne, NE 68787. *Telephone:* 402-375-7234 or 800-228-9972 (toll-free in-state). *Fax:* 402-375-7204. *E-mail:* admit1@wsc.edu. *Web site:* http://www.wsc.edu/.

YORK COLLEGE
York, Nebraska

York is a coed, private, four-year college, founded in 1890, affiliated with the Church of Christ, offering degrees at the associate and bachelor's levels. It has a 44-acre campus in York.

Academic Information The faculty has 51 members (67% full-time), 25% with terminal degrees. The student-faculty ratio is 12:1. The library holds 49,891 titles, 339 serial subscriptions, and 5,867 audiovisual materials. Special programs include academic remediation, services for learning-disabled students, an honors program, cooperative (work-study) education, study abroad, advanced placement credit, double majors, independent study, summer session for credit, part-time degree programs, external degree programs, adult/continuing education programs, and internships. The most frequently chosen baccalaureate fields are business/marketing, education, psychology.

Student Body Statistics The student body is made up of 461 undergraduates (116 freshmen). 52 percent are women and 48 percent are men. Students come from 30 states and territories and 16 other countries. 29 percent are from Nebraska. 0.7 percent are international students. 4 percent of the 2003 graduating class went on to graduate and professional schools.

Expenses for 2003–04 *Application fee:* $20. *Comprehensive fee:* $14,975 includes full-time tuition ($10,400), mandatory fees ($1000), and college room and board ($3575). *College room only:* $1375. Full-time tuition and fees vary according to course load. Room and board charges vary according to board plan and housing facility. *Part-time tuition:* $325 per credit hour. *Part-time mandatory fees:* $50 per hour. Part-time tuition and fees vary according to course load.

Financial Aid Forms of aid include need-based and non-need-based scholarships and part-time jobs. The priority application deadline for financial aid is April 30.

Freshman Admission York requires a high school transcript, 2 recommendations, SAT I or ACT scores, and TOEFL scores for international students. A minimum 2.0 high school GPA is recommended. A minimum 2.0 high school GPA is required for some. The application deadline for regular admission is rolling.

Transfer Admission The application deadline for admission is rolling.

Entrance Difficulty York assesses its entrance difficulty level as moderately difficult. For the fall 2003 freshman class, 63 percent of the applicants were accepted.

For Further Information Contact Ms. Kristin Mathews, Associate Director of Admissions, York College, 1125 East 8th Street, York, NE 68467-2699. *Telephone:* 402-363-5608 or 800-950-9675 (toll-free). *Fax:* 402-363-5623. *E-mail:* enroll@york.edu. *Web site:* http://www.york.edu/.

North Dakota

DICKINSON STATE UNIVERSITY
Dickinson, North Dakota

Dickinson State University is a coed, public, four-year college of North Dakota University System, founded in 1918, offering degrees at the associate and bachelor's levels. It has a 100-acre campus in Dickinson.

Academic Information The faculty has 146 members (51% full-time), 30% with terminal degrees. The student-faculty ratio is 19:1. The library holds 87,324 titles, 5,450 serial subscriptions, and 4,668 audiovisual materials. Special programs include academic remediation, services for learning-disabled students, an honors program, cooperative (work-study) education, study abroad, advanced placement credit, accelerated degree programs, double majors, independent study, distance learning, self-designed majors, summer session for credit, part-time degree programs (daytime, evenings, weekends, summer), external degree programs, adult/continuing education programs, internships, and arrangement for off-campus study. The most frequently chosen baccalaureate fields are business/marketing, education, liberal arts/general studies.

Student Body Statistics The student body is made up of 2,461 undergraduates (684 freshmen). 57 percent are women and 43 percent are men. Students come from 26 states and territories and 28 other countries. 72 percent are from North Dakota. 4.6 percent are international students. 10 percent of the 2003 graduating class went on to graduate and professional schools.

Expenses for 2003–04 *Application fee:* $35. *State resident tuition:* $3139 full-time. *Nonresident tuition:* $7406 full-time. Full-time tuition varies according to location, program, and reciprocity agreements. *College room and board:* $3350. *College room only:* $1200. Room and board charges vary according to board plan.

Financial Aid Forms of aid include need-based and non-need-based scholarships, athletic grants, and part-time jobs. The priority application deadline for financial aid is March 15.

Freshman Admission Dickinson State University requires a high school transcript, medical history, proof of measles-rubella shot, SAT I or ACT scores, and TOEFL scores for international students. The application deadline for regular admission is rolling.

Transfer Admission The application deadline for admission is rolling.

Entrance Difficulty Dickinson State University has an open admission policy for all United States students. It assesses its entrance difficulty as minimally difficult for out-of-state applicants; minimally difficult for transfers; moderately difficult for nursing program.

For Further Information Contact Ms. Deb Dazell, Director of Student Recruitment, Dickinson State University, Campus Box 169, Dickinson, ND 58601. *Telephone:* 701-483-2331 or 800-279-4295 (toll-free). *Fax:* 701-483-2409. *E-mail:* dsu.hawks@dsu.nodak.edu. *Web site:* http://www.dsu.nodak.edu/.

See page 280 for a narrative description.

FORT BERTHOLD COMMUNITY COLLEGE

New Town, North Dakota

For Information Write to Fort Berthold Community College, New Town, ND 58763-0490.

JAMESTOWN COLLEGE

Jamestown, North Dakota

Jamestown College is a coed, private, Presbyterian, four-year college, founded in 1883, offering degrees at the bachelor's level. It has a 107-acre campus in Jamestown.

Academic Information The faculty has 70 members (83% full-time), 44% with terminal degrees. The student-faculty ratio is 18:1. The library holds 128,915 titles, 675 serial subscriptions, and 5,219 audiovisual materials. Special programs include services for learning-disabled students, an honors program, cooperative (work-study) education, study abroad, advanced placement credit, double majors, independent study, self-designed majors, summer session for credit, part-time degree programs (daytime, evenings), internships, and arrangement for off-campus study. The most frequently chosen baccalaureate fields are business/marketing, education, health professions and related sciences.

Student Body Statistics The student body is made up of 1,152 undergraduates (293 freshmen). 55 percent are women and 45 percent are men. Students come from 30 states and territories and 16 other countries. 62 percent are from North Dakota. 4.1 percent are international students. 11 percent of the 2003 graduating class went on to graduate and professional schools.

Expenses for 2004–05 *Application fee:* $20. *One-time mandatory fee:* $50. *Comprehensive fee:* $13,370 includes full-time tuition ($9400) and college room and board ($3970). *College room only:* $1700. Room and board charges vary according to board plan. *Part-time tuition:* $270 per credit hour. Part-time tuition varies according to course load and program.

Financial Aid Forms of aid include need-based and non-need-based scholarships, athletic grants, and part-time jobs. The average aided 2003–04 undergraduate received an aid package worth an estimated $7775. The application deadline for financial aid is continuous.

Freshman Admission Jamestown College requires a high school transcript and TOEFL scores for international students. A minimum 2.5 high school GPA, minimum ACT score of 18 or minimum SAT score of 850, and SAT I or ACT scores are recommended. Recommendations, minimum ACT score of 18 or minimum SAT score of 850, and SAT I or ACT scores are required for some. The application deadline for regular admission is rolling.

Transfer Admission The application deadline for admission is rolling.

Entrance Difficulty Jamestown College assesses its entrance difficulty level as minimally difficult. For the fall 2003 freshman class, 98 percent of the applicants were accepted.

For Further Information Contact Ms. Judy Erickson, Director of Admissions, Jamestown College, 6081 College Lane, Jamestown, ND 58405. *Telephone:* 701-252-3467 Ext. 2548 or 800-336-2554 (toll-free). *Fax:* 701-253-4318. *E-mail:* admissions@jc.edu. *Web site:* http://www.jc.edu/.

MAYVILLE STATE UNIVERSITY

Mayville, North Dakota

Mayville State University is a coed, public, four-year college of North Dakota University System, founded in 1889, offering degrees at the associate and bachelor's levels. It has a 60-acre campus in Mayville.

Academic Information The faculty has 62 members (56% full-time), 31% with terminal degrees. The student-faculty ratio is 15:1. The library holds 71,595 titles, 599 serial subscriptions, and 20,679 audiovisual materials. Special programs include academic remediation, services for learning-disabled students, cooperative (work-study) education, advanced placement credit, accelerated degree programs, double majors, distance learning, self-designed majors, summer session for credit, part-time degree programs (daytime, evenings, summer), adult/continuing education programs, and internships. The most frequently chosen baccalaureate fields are business/marketing, computer/information sciences, education.

Student Body Statistics The student body is made up of 817 undergraduates (222 freshmen). 57 percent are women and 43 percent are men. Students come from 21 states and territories and 9 other countries. 72 percent are from North Dakota. 3.1 percent are international students. 6 percent of the 2003 graduating class went on to graduate and professional schools.

Expenses for 2004–05 *Application fee:* $35. *State resident tuition:* $3014 full-time. *Nonresident tuition:* $7535 full-time. *Mandatory fees:* $1342 full-time. Full-time tuition and fees vary according to reciprocity agreements. *College room and board:* $3508. *College room only:* $1452. Room and board charges vary according to board plan and housing facility.

Financial Aid Forms of aid include need-based and non-need-based scholarships, athletic grants, and part-time jobs. The average aided 2002–03 undergraduate received an aid package worth $5782. The priority application deadline for financial aid is March 15.

Freshman Admission Mayville State University requires a high school transcript, SAT I or ACT scores, and TOEFL scores for international students. An interview is recommended. The application deadline for regular admission is rolling.

Transfer Admission The application deadline for admission is rolling.

Entrance Difficulty Mayville State University has an open admission policy. It assesses its entrance difficulty as minimally difficult for transfers.

For Further Information Contact Mr. Brian Larson, Director of Enrollment Services, Mayville State University, 330 3rd Street, NE, Mayville, ND 58257-1299. *Telephone:* 701-788-4773 Ext. 34773 or 800-437-4104 (toll-free). *Fax:* 701-788-4748. *E-mail:* admit@mail.masu.nodak.edu. *Web site:* http://www.mayvillestate.edu/.

MEDCENTER ONE COLLEGE OF NURSING

Bismarck, North Dakota

Medcenter One College of Nursing is a coed, primarily women's, private, upper-level institution, founded in 1988, offering degrees at the bachelor's level in nursing. It has a 15-acre campus in Bismarck.

Academic Information The faculty has 12 members (83% full-time). The student-faculty ratio is 9:1. The library holds 28,470 titles, 331 serial subscriptions, and 1,467 audiovisual materials. Special programs include an honors program, independent study, and internships. The most frequently chosen baccalaureate field is health professions and related sciences.

Student Body Statistics The student body is made up of 83 undergraduates. 96 percent are women and 4 percent are men. Students come from 6 states and territories. 93 percent are from North Dakota.

Expenses for 2003–04 *Application fee:* $40. *Tuition:* $8000 full-time, $334 per credit part-time. *Mandatory fees:* $620 full-time, $5 per credit part-time, $190 per term part-time. Full-time tuition and fees vary according to student level. Part-time tuition and fees vary according to course load and student level. *College room only:* $900.

Financial Aid Forms of aid include need-based and non-need-based scholarships and part-time jobs. The average aided 2003–04 undergraduate received an aid package worth an estimated $8405. The priority application deadline for financial aid is May 1.

Transfer Admission Medcenter One College of Nursing requires a college transcript and a minimum 2.5 college GPA. The application deadline for admission is November 7.

Entrance Difficulty Medcenter One College of Nursing assesses its entrance difficulty level as moderately difficult. For the fall 2003 entering class, 51 percent of the applicants were accepted.

For Further Information Contact Ms. Mary Smith, Director of Student Services, Medcenter One College of Nursing, 512 North 7th Street, Bismarck, ND 58501-4494. *Telephone:* 701-323-6271. *Fax:* 701-323-6967. *Web site:* http://www.medcenterone.com/nursing/nursing.htm.

MINOT STATE UNIVERSITY
Minot, North Dakota

Minot State is a coed, public, comprehensive unit of North Dakota University System, founded in 1913, offering degrees at the associate, bachelor's, and master's levels and post-master's certificates. It has a 103-acre campus in Minot.

Academic Information The faculty has 221 members (72% full-time), 46% with terminal degrees. The undergraduate student-faculty ratio is 16:1. The library holds 240,395 titles, 805 serial subscriptions, and 11,073 audiovisual materials. Special programs include academic remediation, services for learning-disabled students, an honors program, cooperative (work-study) education, study abroad, advanced placement credit, accelerated degree programs, double majors, independent study, distance learning, self-designed majors, summer session for credit, part-time degree programs (daytime, evenings, summer), adult/continuing education programs, and internships. The most frequently chosen baccalaureate fields are business/marketing, education, health professions and related sciences.
Student Body Statistics The student body totals 3,825, of whom 3,594 are undergraduates (568 freshmen). 62 percent are women and 38 percent are men. Students come from 44 states and territories and 18 other countries. 88 percent are from North Dakota. 5.2 percent are international students. 11 percent of the 2003 graduating class went on to graduate and professional schools.
Expenses for 2003–04 *Application fee:* $35. *State resident tuition:* $2730 full-time, $113.75 per semester hour part-time. *Nonresident tuition:* $7289 full-time, $303.71 per semester hour part-time. *Mandatory fees:* $498 full-time, $20.75 per semester hour part-time. Full-time tuition and fees vary according to course load, location, and reciprocity agreements. Part-time tuition and fees vary according to location and reciprocity agreements. *College room and board:* $3274. *College room only:* $1200. Room and board charges vary according to board plan and housing facility.
Financial Aid Forms of aid include need-based and non-need-based scholarships, athletic grants, and part-time jobs. The average aided 2003–04 undergraduate received an aid package worth an estimated $6372. The priority application deadline for financial aid is March 15.
Freshman Admission Minot State requires a high school transcript, SAT I or ACT scores, and TOEFL scores for international students. A minimum 2.75 high school GPA is required for some. The application deadline for regular admission is rolling.
Transfer Admission The application deadline for admission is rolling.
Entrance Difficulty Minot State assesses its entrance difficulty level as minimally difficult. For the fall 2003 freshman class, 86 percent of the applicants were accepted.

For Further Information Contact Ms. Mariah Huizenga, Admissions Specialist, Minot State University, 500 University Avenue West, Minot, ND 58707-0002. *Telephone:* 701-858-3350 or 800-777-0750 Ext. 3350 (toll-free). *Fax:* 701-839-6933. *E-mail:* askmsu@misu.nodak.edu. *Web site:* http://www.minotstateu.edu/.

NORTH DAKOTA STATE COLLEGE OF SCIENCE
Wahpeton, North Dakota

NDSCS is a coed, public, primarily two-year college of North Dakota University System, founded in 1903, offering degrees at the bachelor's, master's, doctoral, and first professional levels. It has a 125-acre campus in Wahpeton.

Academic Information The faculty has 140 members (91% full-time), 1% with terminal degrees. The undergraduate student-faculty ratio is 15:1. The library holds 124,508 titles, 852 serial subscriptions, and 4,178 audiovisual materials. Special programs include academic remediation, services for learning-disabled students, cooperative (work-study) education, advanced placement credit, accelerated degree programs, ESL programs, distance learning, self-designed majors, summer session for credit, part-time degree programs (daytime, evenings, summer), adult/continuing education programs, and internships.
Student Body Statistics The student body is made up of 2,398 undergraduates. Students come from 21 states and territories and 8 other countries. 73 percent are from North Dakota. 1.1 percent are international students. 81 percent of the 2003 graduating class went on to four-year colleges.
Expenses for 2003–04 *Application fee:* $35. *State resident tuition:* $2052 full-time. *Nonresident tuition:* $5478 full-time. *Mandatory fees:* $450 full-time. Full-time tuition and fees vary according to reciprocity agreements. *College room and board:* $4066. *College room only:* $1269.
Financial Aid Forms of aid include need-based scholarships and part-time jobs. The priority application deadline for financial aid is March 1.
Freshman Admission NDSCS requires a high school transcript and ACT scores. The application deadline for regular admission is rolling.
Transfer Admission The application deadline for admission is rolling.
Entrance Difficulty NDSCS has an open admission policy.

For Further Information Contact Mr. Keath Borchert, Director of Enrollment Services, North Dakota State College of Science, 800 North 6th Street, Wahpeton, ND 58076. *Telephone:* 701-671-2202 or 800-342-4325 Ext. 2202 (toll-free). *Fax:* 701-671-2332. *Web site:* http://www.ndscs.nodak.edu/.

NORTH DAKOTA STATE UNIVERSITY
Fargo, North Dakota

NDSU is a coed, public unit of North Dakota University System, founded in 1890, offering degrees at the bachelor's, master's, doctoral, and first professional levels and post-master's certificates. It has a 2,100-acre campus in Fargo.

Academic Information The faculty has 596 members (84% full-time), 85% with terminal degrees. The undergraduate student-faculty ratio is 19:1. The library holds 303,274 titles, 4,497 serial subscriptions, and 2,757 audiovisual materials. Special programs include academic remediation, services for learning-disabled students, an honors program, cooperative (work-study) education, study abroad, advanced placement credit, ESL programs, double majors, independent study, distance learning, self-designed majors, summer session for credit, part-time degree programs (daytime, evenings, summer), internships, and arrangement for off-campus study with members of the Tri-College University-Concordia College, Moorhead, MN, Minnesota State University Moorhead. The most frequently chosen baccalaureate fields are business/marketing, architecture, engineering/engineering technologies.
Student Body Statistics The student body totals 11,623, of whom 10,148 are undergraduates (1,974 freshmen). 44 percent are women and 56 percent are men. Students come from 36 states and territories and 62 other countries. 60 percent are from North Dakota. 1.1 percent are international students. 18.4 percent of the 2003 graduating class went on to graduate and professional schools.
Expenses for 2003–04 *Application fee:* $35. *One-time mandatory fee:* $45. *Area resident tuition:* $3374 full-time. *State resident tuition:* $3600 full-time, $140.58 per credit part-time. *Nonresident tuition:* $9009 full-time, $375.36 per credit part-time. *Mandatory fees:* $590 full-time, $24.61 per credit part-time. Full-time tuition and fees vary according to reciprocity agreements. Part-time tuition and fees vary according to course load and reciprocity agreements. *College room and board:* $4471. *College room only:* $1711. Room and board charges vary according to board plan and housing facility.
Financial Aid Forms of aid include need-based and non-need-based scholarships, athletic grants, and part-time jobs. The average aided 2002–03 undergraduate received an aid package worth $5367. The priority application deadline for financial aid is March 15.
Freshman Admission NDSU requires a high school transcript, a minimum 2.5 high school GPA, SAT I or ACT scores, and TOEFL scores for international students. The application deadline for regular admission is August 15.
Transfer Admission The application deadline for admission is August 15.

North Dakota State University (continued)

Entrance Difficulty NDSU assesses its entrance difficulty level as moderately difficult. For the fall 2003 freshman class, 61 percent of the applicants were accepted.

For Further Information Contact Dr. Kate Haugen, Director of Admission, North Dakota State University, PO Box 5454, Fargo, ND 58105-5454. *Telephone:* 701-231-8643 or 800-488-NDSU (toll-free). *Fax:* 701-231-8802. *E-mail:* ndsu.admission@ndsu.nodak.edu. *Web site:* http://www.ndsu.edu/.

SITTING BULL COLLEGE
Fort Yates, North Dakota

Sitting Bull College is a coed, private, two-year college, founded in 1973, offering degrees at the associate level.

For Further Information Contact Ms. Melody Silk, Director of Registration and Admissions, Sitting Bull College, 1341 92nd Street, Fort Yates, ND 58538-9701. *Telephone:* 701-854-3864. *Fax:* 701-854-3403. *Web site:* http://www.sittingbull.edu/.

TRINITY BIBLE COLLEGE
Ellendale, North Dakota

TBC is a coed, private, Assemblies of God, four-year college, founded in 1948, offering degrees at the associate and bachelor's levels. It has a 28-acre campus in Ellendale.

Academic Information The faculty has 38 members (76% full-time), 13% with terminal degrees. The student-faculty ratio is 8:1. The library holds 67,868 titles, 227 serial subscriptions, and 2,258 audiovisual materials. Special programs include academic remediation, advanced placement credit, accelerated degree programs, double majors, distance learning, summer session for credit, part-time degree programs (evenings), and internships. The most frequently chosen baccalaureate fields are education, philosophy, religion, and theology.
Student Body Statistics The student body is made up of 307 undergraduates (73 freshmen). 54 percent are women and 46 percent are men. Students come from 29 states and territories. 23 percent are from North Dakota. 5 percent of the 2003 graduating class went on to graduate and professional schools.
Expenses for 2004–05 *Application fee:* $25. *Comprehensive fee:* $15,280 includes full-time tuition ($8880), mandatory fees ($2178), and college room and board ($4222). *College room only:* $1986. Full-time tuition and fees vary according to course load. Room and board charges vary according to housing facility. *Part-time tuition:* $296 per credit. *Part-time mandatory fees:* $350 per term. Part-time tuition and fees vary according to course load.
Financial Aid Forms of aid include need-based and non-need-based scholarships and part-time jobs. The application deadline for financial aid is September 1 with a priority deadline of March 1.
Freshman Admission TBC requires an essay, a high school transcript, a minimum 2.0 high school GPA, 2 recommendations, health form, evidence of Christian conversion, and ACT scores. TOEFL scores for international students are recommended. An interview and SAT I scores are required for some. The application deadline for regular admission is rolling.
Transfer Admission The application deadline for admission is rolling.
Entrance Difficulty TBC assesses its entrance difficulty level as noncompetitive. For the fall 2003 freshman class, 50 percent of the applicants were accepted.

For Further Information Contact Rev. Steve Tvedt, Vice President of College Relations, Trinity Bible College, 50 South Sixth Avenue, Ellendale, ND 58436. *Telephone:* 701-349-3621 Ext. 2045 or 888-TBC-2DAY (toll-free). *Fax:* 701-349-5443. *E-mail:* admissions@trinitybiblecollege.edu. *Web site:* http://www.trinitybiblecollege.edu/.

TURTLE MOUNTAIN COMMUNITY COLLEGE
Belcourt, North Dakota

For Information Write to Turtle Mountain Community College, Belcourt, ND 58316-0340.

UNIVERSITY OF MARY
Bismarck, North Dakota

Mary is a coed, private, Roman Catholic, comprehensive institution, founded in 1959, offering degrees at the associate, bachelor's, and master's levels. It has a 107-acre campus in Bismarck.

Academic Information The faculty has 218 members (43% full-time), 31% with terminal degrees. The undergraduate student-faculty ratio is 16:1. The library holds 74,205 titles, 597 serial subscriptions, and 5,382 audiovisual materials. Special programs include academic remediation, services for learning-disabled students, cooperative (work-study) education, study abroad, advanced placement credit, accelerated degree programs, double majors, independent study, distance learning, summer session for credit, part-time degree programs (daytime, evenings, weekends, summer), external degree programs, adult/continuing education programs, internships, and arrangement for off-campus study. The most frequently chosen baccalaureate fields are business/marketing, education, health professions and related sciences.
Student Body Statistics The student body totals 2,619, of whom 2,152 are undergraduates (391 freshmen). 61 percent are women and 39 percent are men. Students come from 25 states and territories and 21 other countries. 73 percent are from North Dakota. 1.7 percent are international students. 28 percent of the 2003 graduating class went on to graduate and professional schools.
Expenses for 2004–05 *Application fee:* $25. *Comprehensive fee:* $14,370 includes full-time tuition ($9990), mandatory fees ($300), and college room and board ($4080). *College room only:* $1940. Full-time tuition and fees vary according to course load and program. Room and board charges vary according to board plan, housing facility, and location. *Part-time tuition:* varies with degree level.
Financial Aid Forms of aid include need-based and non-need-based scholarships and part-time jobs. The priority application deadline for financial aid is May 1.
Freshman Admission Mary requires a high school transcript, 1 recommendation, SAT I and SAT II or ACT scores, and TOEFL scores for international students. A minimum 2.5 high school GPA is recommended. An essay and an interview are required for some. The application deadline for regular admission is rolling.
Transfer Admission The application deadline for admission is rolling.
Entrance Difficulty Mary assesses its entrance difficulty level as moderately difficult. For the fall 2003 freshman class, 90 percent of the applicants were accepted.

For Further Information Contact Dr. Dave Hebinger, Vice President for Enrollment Services, University of Mary, 7500 University Drive, Bismarck, ND 58504-9652. *Telephone:* 701-355-81910 or 800-288-6279 (toll-free). *Fax:* 701-255-7687. *E-mail:* marauder@umary.edu. *Web site:* http://www.umary.edu/.

UNIVERSITY OF NORTH DAKOTA
Grand Forks, North Dakota

UND is a coed, public unit of North Dakota University System, founded in 1883, offering degrees at the bachelor's, master's, doctoral, and first professional levels and post-master's certificates. It has a 543-acre campus in Grand Forks.

Academic Information The faculty has 897 members (64% full-time). The undergraduate student-faculty ratio is 18:1. The library holds 658,957 titles, 10,438 serial subscriptions, and 14,306 audiovisual materials. Special programs include services for learning-disabled students, an honors program, cooperative (work-study) education, study abroad, advanced placement credit, accelerated degree programs, double majors, independent study, distance learning, self-designed majors, summer session for credit, part-time degree programs, adult/continuing education programs, internships, and arrangement for off-campus study. The most frequently chosen baccalaureate fields are business/marketing, education, trade and industry.

Student Body Statistics The student body totals 13,034, of whom 10,711 are undergraduates (2,233 freshmen). 47 percent are women and 53 percent are men. Students come from 54 states and territories and 32 other countries. 53 percent are from North Dakota. 2.2 percent are international students. 13 percent of the 2003 graduating class went on to graduate and professional schools.

Expenses for 2003–04 *Application fee:* $35. *State resident tuition:* $3441 full-time, $143.38 per credit hour part-time. *Nonresident tuition:* $9187 full-time, $382.78 per credit hour part-time. *Mandatory fees:* $715 full-time. Full-time tuition and fees vary according to degree level, program, and reciprocity agreements. Part-time tuition varies according to course load, degree level, program, and reciprocity agreements. *College room and board:* $4234. *College room only:* $1706. Room and board charges vary according to board plan and housing facility.

Financial Aid Forms of aid include need-based and non-need-based scholarships, athletic grants, and part-time jobs. The average aided 2003–04 undergraduate received an aid package worth an estimated $8150. The priority application deadline for financial aid is March 15.

Freshman Admission UND requires a high school transcript, SAT I or ACT scores, and TOEFL scores for international students. A minimum 2.25 high school GPA and ACT scores are recommended. The application deadline for regular admission is July 1.

Transfer Admission The application deadline for admission is rolling.

Entrance Difficulty UND assesses its entrance difficulty level as minimally difficult; moderately difficult for transfers. For the fall 2003 freshman class, 76 percent of the applicants were accepted.

For Further Information Contact Ms. Heidi Kippenhan, Director of Admissions, University of North Dakota, PO Box 8135, Grand Forks, ND 58202. *Telephone:* 701-777-4463 or 800-CALL UND (toll-free). *Fax:* 701-777-4857. *E-mail:* enrolser@sage.und.nodak.edu. *Web site:* http://www.und.edu/.

VALLEY CITY STATE UNIVERSITY
Valley City, North Dakota

VCSU is a coed, public, four-year college of North Dakota University System, founded in 1890, offering degrees at the bachelor's level. It has a 55-acre campus in Valley City.

Academic Information The faculty has 86 members (71% full-time), 31% with terminal degrees. The student-faculty ratio is 12:1. The library holds 94,236 titles, 392 serial subscriptions, and 15,305 audiovisual materials. Special programs include academic remediation, services for learning-disabled students, cooperative (work-study) education, double majors, distance learning, self-designed majors, summer session for credit, part-time degree programs (daytime, evenings, summer), internships, and arrangement for off-campus study with North Dakota State University, Mayville State University. The most frequently chosen baccalaureate fields are business/marketing, computer/information sciences, education.

Student Body Statistics The student body is made up of 998 undergraduates (166 freshmen). 55 percent are women and 45 percent are men. Students come from 22 states and territories and 7 other countries. 75 percent are from North Dakota. 4.4 percent are international students. 13 percent of the 2003 graduating class went on to graduate and professional schools.

Expenses for 2003–04 *Application fee:* $35. *State resident tuition:* $2652 full-time, $110.50 per semester hour part-time. *Nonresident tuition:* $7080 full-time, $295 per semester hour part-time. *Mandatory fees:* $597 full-time, $57.25 per semester hour part-time. *College room and board:* $3254. *College room only:* $1230. Room and board charges vary according to board plan.

Financial Aid Forms of aid include need-based and non-need-based scholarships, athletic grants, and part-time jobs. The average aided 2002–03 undergraduate received an aid package worth $5838. The priority application deadline for financial aid is March 15.

Freshman Admission VCSU requires a high school transcript, SAT I or ACT scores, and TOEFL scores for international students. The application deadline for regular admission is rolling.

Transfer Admission The application deadline for admission is rolling.

Entrance Difficulty VCSU has an open admission policy.

For Further Information Contact Mr. Dan Klein, Director of Enrollment Services, Valley City State University, 101 College Street Southwest, Valley City, ND 58072. *Telephone:* 701-845-7101 Ext. 37204 or 800-532-8641 Ext. 37101 (toll-free). *Fax:* 701-845-7299. *E-mail:* enrollment.services@vcsu.edu. *Web site:* http://www.vcsu.edu/.

Ohio

ALLEGHENY WESLEYAN COLLEGE
Salem, Ohio

Allegheny Wesleyan College is a coed, private, four-year college, offering degrees at the bachelor's level.

Expenses for 2003–04 *Tuition:* $6060 full-time.

For Further Information Contact Allegheny Wesleyan College, 2161 Woodsdale Road, Salem, OH 44460. *Telephone:* 330-337-6403 or 800-292-3153 (toll-free). *Fax:* 330-337-6255. *Web site:* http://www.awc.edu/.

ANTIOCH COLLEGE
Yellow Springs, Ohio

Antioch is a coed, private, four-year college of Antioch University, founded in 1852, offering degrees at the bachelor's level. It has a 100-acre campus in Yellow Springs near Dayton.

Academic Information The faculty has 60 members (95% full-time), 100% with terminal degrees. The student-faculty ratio is 10:1. The library holds 300,000 titles, 10,504 serial subscriptions, and 6,259 audiovisual materials. Special programs include academic remediation, services for learning-disabled students, cooperative (work-study) education, study abroad, advanced placement credit, double majors, independent study, self-designed majors, summer session for credit, internships, and arrangement for off-campus study with members of the Great Lakes Colleges Association, Southwestern Ohio Council for Higher Education. The most frequently chosen baccalaureate fields are area/ethnic studies, foreign language/literature, interdisciplinary studies.

Student Body Statistics The student body totals 589, of whom 571 are undergraduates (142 freshmen). 62 percent are women and 38 percent are men. Students come from 43 states and territories and 2 other countries. 24 percent are from Ohio. 0.3 percent are international students.

Expenses for 2003–04 *Application fee:* $35. *Comprehensive fee:* $29,589 includes full-time tuition ($22,673), mandatory fees ($922), and college room and board ($5994). *College room only:* $2932. Room and board charges vary according to board plan. *Part-time tuition:* $400 per credit hour.

Financial Aid Forms of aid include need-based and non-need-based scholarships and part-time jobs. The average aided 2003–04 undergraduate received an aid package worth an estimated $19,214. The priority application deadline for financial aid is March 1.

Freshman Admission Antioch requires an essay, a high school transcript, a minimum 2.5 high school GPA, and 2 recommendations. An interview is recommended. The application deadline for regular admission is February 1 and for early action it is November 15.

Transfer Admission The application deadline for admission is rolling.

Ohio

Antioch College (continued)

Entrance Difficulty Antioch assesses its entrance difficulty level as moderately difficult. For the fall 2003 freshman class, 75 percent of the applicants were accepted.

For Further Information Contact Ms. Cathy Paige, Information Manager, Antioch College, 795 Livermore Street, Yellow Springs, OH 45387-1697. *Telephone:* 937-769-1100 Ext. 1107 or 800-543-9436 (toll-free). *Fax:* 937-769-1111. *E-mail:* admissions@antioch-college.edu. *Web site:* http://www.antioch-college.edu/.

ANTIOCH UNIVERSITY MCGREGOR
Yellow Springs, Ohio

Antioch University McGregor is a coed, private, upper-level unit of Antioch University, founded in 1988, offering degrees at the bachelor's and master's levels. It has a 100-acre campus in Yellow Springs near Dayton.

Expenses for 2003–04 *Application fee:* $45. *Tuition:* $10,755 full-time. *Mandatory fees:* $225 full-time.

For Further Information Contact Mr. Oscar Robinson, Enrollment Services Manager, Antioch University McGregor, Student and Alumni Services Division, Enrollment Services, 800 Livermore Street, Yellow Springs, OH 45387. *Telephone:* 937-769-1823 or 937-769-1818 (toll-free). *Fax:* 937-769-1805. *E-mail:* sas@mcgregor.edu. *Web site:* http://www.mcgregor.edu/.

ART ACADEMY OF CINCINNATI
Cincinnati, Ohio

Art Academy of Cincinnati is a coed, private, comprehensive institution, founded in 1887, offering degrees at the associate, bachelor's, and master's levels in art. It has a 184-acre campus in Cincinnati.

Academic Information The faculty has 51 members (33% full-time), 84% with terminal degrees. The undergraduate student-faculty ratio is 12:1. The library holds 66,404 titles, 150 serial subscriptions, and 588 audiovisual materials. Special programs include services for learning-disabled students, study abroad, advanced placement credit, double majors, independent study, self-designed majors, summer session for credit, part-time degree programs (daytime, evenings, summer), adult/continuing education programs, internships, and arrangement for off-campus study with members of the Greater Cincinnati Consortium of Colleges and Universities, Association of Independent Colleges of Art and Design. The most frequently chosen baccalaureate field is visual/performing arts.
Student Body Statistics The student body totals 194, of whom 193 are undergraduates (43 freshmen). 53 percent are women and 47 percent are men. Students come from 14 states and territories and 3 other countries. 75 percent are from Ohio. 1.6 percent are international students. 5 percent of the 2003 graduating class went on to graduate and professional schools.
Expenses for 2004–05 *Application fee:* $25. *Tuition:* $17,700 full-time, $740 per credit hour part-time. *Mandatory fees:* $350 full-time, $175 per term part-time. Part-time tuition and fees vary according to course load.
Financial Aid Forms of aid include need-based and non-need-based scholarships and part-time jobs. The average aided 2003–04 undergraduate received an aid package worth an estimated $10,735. The priority application deadline for financial aid is March 1.
Freshman Admission Art Academy of Cincinnati requires an essay, a high school transcript, a minimum 2.0 high school GPA, 1 recommendation, a portfolio, SAT I or ACT scores, and TOEFL scores for international students. The application deadline for regular admission is June 30.
Transfer Admission The application deadline for admission is June 30.

Entrance Difficulty Art Academy of Cincinnati assesses its entrance difficulty level as moderately difficult. For the fall 2003 freshman class, 69 percent of the applicants were accepted.

For Further Information Contact Ms. Mary Jane Zumwalde, Director of Admissions, Art Academy of Cincinnati, 1125 Saint Gregory Street, Cincinnati, OH 45202. *Telephone:* 513-562-8744 or 800-323-5692 (toll-free in-state). *Fax:* 513-562-8778. *E-mail:* admissions@artacademy.edu. *Web site:* http://www.artacademy.edu/.

ASHLAND UNIVERSITY
Ashland, Ohio

AU is a coed, private, comprehensive institution, founded in 1878, affiliated with the Brethren Church, offering degrees at the associate, bachelor's, master's, doctoral, and first professional levels. It has a 98-acre campus in Ashland near Cleveland.

Academic Information The faculty has 553 members (39% full-time), 51% with terminal degrees. The undergraduate student-faculty ratio is 15:1. The library holds 205,200 titles, 1,625 serial subscriptions, and 3,550 audiovisual materials. Special programs include academic remediation, services for learning-disabled students, an honors program, study abroad, advanced placement credit, ESL programs, double majors, independent study, self-designed majors, summer session for credit, part-time degree programs (daytime, evenings, weekends, summer), adult/continuing education programs, internships, and arrangement for off-campus study with Case Western Reserve University, Art Institute of Pittsburgh, Purdue University, Drew University, American University, Merrill-Palmer Institute, Hunter College of the City University of New York. The most frequently chosen baccalaureate fields are business/marketing, communications/communication technologies, education.
Student Body Statistics The student body totals 6,835, of whom 2,782 are undergraduates (610 freshmen). 61 percent are women and 39 percent are men. Students come from 27 states and territories and 14 other countries. 95 percent are from Ohio. 1.5 percent are international students. 9.5 percent of the 2003 graduating class went on to graduate and professional schools.
Expenses for 2004–05 *Application fee:* $25. *Comprehensive fee:* $25,822 includes full-time tuition ($18,394), mandatory fees ($464), and college room and board ($6964). *College room only:* $3740. Full-time tuition and fees vary according to location and reciprocity agreements. Room and board charges vary according to board plan and housing facility. *Part-time tuition:* $565 per credit hour. *Part-time mandatory fees:* $14 per credit hour. Part-time tuition and fees vary according to location and program.
Financial Aid Forms of aid include need-based and non-need-based scholarships, athletic grants, and part-time jobs. The average aided 2003–04 undergraduate received an aid package worth an estimated $16,446. The application deadline for financial aid is March 15.
Freshman Admission AU requires an essay, a high school transcript, a minimum 2.5 high school GPA, SAT I or ACT scores, and TOEFL scores for international students. An interview is recommended. Recommendations and an interview are required for some. The application deadline for regular admission is rolling.
Transfer Admission The application deadline for admission is rolling.
Entrance Difficulty AU assesses its entrance difficulty level as moderately difficult. For the fall 2003 freshman class, 86 percent of the applicants were accepted.

For Further Information Contact Mr. Thomas Mansperger, Director of Admission, Ashland University, 401 College Avenue, Ashland, OH 44805. *Telephone:* 419-289-5052 or 800-882-1548 (toll-free). *Fax:* 419-289-5999. *E-mail:* auadmsn@ashland.edu. *Web site:* http://www.ashland.edu/.

BALDWIN-WALLACE COLLEGE

Berea, Ohio

B-W is a coed, private, Methodist, comprehensive institution, founded in 1845, offering degrees at the bachelor's and master's levels. It has a 100-acre campus in Berea near Cleveland.

Academic Information The faculty has 389 members (42% full-time), 44% with terminal degrees. The undergraduate student-faculty ratio is 14:1. The library holds 200,000 titles and 883 serial subscriptions. Special programs include academic remediation, services for learning-disabled students, an honors program, study abroad, advanced placement credit, accelerated degree programs, ESL programs, double majors, independent study, distance learning, self-designed majors, summer session for credit, part-time degree programs (daytime, evenings, weekends, summer), adult/continuing education programs, internships, and arrangement for off-campus study with Drew University, American University. The most frequently chosen baccalaureate fields are business/marketing, education, social sciences and history.

Student Body Statistics The student body totals 4,692, of whom 3,862 are undergraduates (702 freshmen). 61 percent are women and 39 percent are men. Students come from 30 states and territories and 14 other countries. 91 percent are from Ohio. 1.4 percent are international students. 33 percent of the 2003 graduating class went on to graduate and professional schools.

Expenses for 2003–04 *Application fee:* $15. *Comprehensive fee:* $23,880 includes full-time tuition ($18,478) and college room and board ($5402). *College room only:* $3042. *Part-time tuition:* $588 per hour. Part-time tuition varies according to class time.

Financial Aid Forms of aid include need-based and non-need-based scholarships and part-time jobs. The average aided 2003–04 undergraduate received an aid package worth an estimated $13,257. The application deadline for financial aid is September 1 with a priority deadline of May 1.

Freshman Admission B-W requires an essay, a high school transcript, a minimum 2.6 high school GPA, 1 recommendation, SAT I or ACT scores, and TOEFL scores for international students. A minimum 3.2 high school GPA and an interview are recommended. The application deadline for regular admission is rolling.

Transfer Admission The application deadline for admission is rolling.

Entrance Difficulty B-W assesses its entrance difficulty level as moderately difficult. For the fall 2003 freshman class, 82 percent of the applicants were accepted.

For Further Information Contact Ms. Grace B. Chalker, Interim Associate Director of Admissions, Baldwin-Wallace College, 275 Eastland Road, Berea, OH 44017-2088. *Telephone:* 440-826-2222 or 877-BWAPPLY (toll-free in-state). *Fax:* 440-826-3830. *E-mail:* admission@bw.edu. *Web site:* http://www.bw.edu/.

BLUFFTON COLLEGE

Bluffton, Ohio

Bluffton College is a coed, private, Mennonite, comprehensive institution, founded in 1899, offering degrees at the bachelor's and master's levels. It has a 65-acre campus in Bluffton near Toledo.

Academic Information The faculty has 117 members (54% full-time), 44% with terminal degrees. The undergraduate student-faculty ratio is 14:1. The library holds 163,448 titles, 385 serial subscriptions, and 1,259 audiovisual materials. Special programs include academic remediation, an honors program, study abroad, advanced placement credit, independent study, self-designed majors, summer session for credit, part-time degree programs, adult/continuing education programs, internships, and arrangement for off-campus study with Christian College Coalition, Council of Independent Colleges. The most frequently chosen baccalaureate fields are business/marketing, education, parks and recreation.

Student Body Statistics The student body totals 1,121, of whom 1,056 are undergraduates (236 freshmen). 60 percent are women and 40 percent are men. Students come from 21 states and territories and 16 other countries. 89 percent are from Ohio. 2.2 percent are international students.

Expenses for 2004–05 *Application fee:* $20. *Comprehensive fee:* $24,620 includes full-time tuition ($17,950), mandatory fees ($400), and college room and board ($6270). *College room only:* $2868. Full-time tuition and fees vary according to course load and program. Room and board charges vary according to board plan and housing facility. *Part-time tuition:* $748 per credit hour. Part-time tuition varies according to course load and program.

Financial Aid Forms of aid include need-based and non-need-based scholarships and part-time jobs. The average aided 2003–04 undergraduate received an aid package worth an estimated $16,776. The application deadline for financial aid is October 1 with a priority deadline of May 1.

Freshman Admission Bluffton College requires a high school transcript, 2 recommendations, rank in upper 50% of high school class or 2.3 high school GPA, SAT I or ACT scores, and TOEFL scores for international students. An interview is recommended. An essay is required for some. The application deadline for regular admission is May 31.

Transfer Admission The application deadline for admission is rolling.

Entrance Difficulty Bluffton College assesses its entrance difficulty level as moderately difficult. For the fall 2003 freshman class, 77 percent of the applicants were accepted.

For Further Information Contact Mr. Eric Fulcomer, Director of Admissions, Vice President for Enrollment Management, Bluffton College, 280 West College Avenue, Bluffton, OH 45817. *Telephone:* 419-358-3254 or 800-488-3257 (toll-free). *Fax:* 419-358-3232. *E-mail:* admissions@bluffton.edu. *Web site:* http://www.bluffton.edu/.

See page 262 for a narrative description.

BOHECKER'S BUSINESS COLLEGE

Ravenna, Ohio

For Information Write to Bohecker's Business College, Ravenna, OH 44266.

BOWLING GREEN STATE UNIVERSITY

Bowling Green, Ohio

BGSU is a coed, public university, founded in 1910, offering degrees at the bachelor's, master's, and doctoral levels and post-master's certificates. It has a 1,230-acre campus in Bowling Green near Toledo.

Academic Information The faculty has 1,026 members (80% full-time). The undergraduate student-faculty ratio is 19:1. The library holds 2 million titles, 4,833 serial subscriptions, and 718,734 audiovisual materials. Special programs include academic remediation, services for learning-disabled students, an honors program, cooperative (work-study) education, study abroad, advanced placement credit, accelerated degree programs, ESL programs, double majors, independent study, distance learning, self-designed majors, summer session for credit, part-time degree programs (daytime, evenings, summer), adult/continuing education programs, internships, and arrangement for off-campus study with University of Toledo, Medical College of Ohio. The most frequently chosen baccalaureate fields are business/marketing, education, visual/performing arts.

Student Body Statistics The student body totals 18,534, of whom 15,481 are undergraduates (3,541 freshmen). 56 percent are women and 44 percent are men. Students come from 47 states and territories and 41 other countries. 93 percent are from Ohio. 0.7 percent are international students.

Expenses for 2003–04 *Application fee:* $35. *State resident tuition:* $5940 full-time, $292 per credit hour part-time. *Nonresident tuition:* $12,900 full-time, $624 per credit hour part-time. *Mandatory fees:* $1204 full-time, $60 per credit hour part-time. Part-time tuition and fees vary according to course load. *College room and board:* $5892. *College room only:* $3642. Room and board charges vary according to board plan and housing facility.

Financial Aid Forms of aid include need-based and non-need-based scholarships, athletic grants, and part-time jobs. The average aided 2002–03 undergraduate received an aid package worth $8536. The application deadline for financial aid is continuous.

Bowling Green State University (continued)

Freshman Admission BGSU requires a high school transcript, a minimum 2.5 high school GPA, SAT I or ACT scores, and TOEFL scores for international students. An interview is recommended. The application deadline for regular admission is July 15.

Transfer Admission The application deadline for admission is July 15.

Entrance Difficulty BGSU assesses its entrance difficulty level as moderately difficult. For the fall 2003 freshman class, 90 percent of the applicants were accepted.

For Further Information Contact Mr. Gary Swegan, Director of Admissions, Bowling Green State University, 110 McFall, Bowling Green, OH 43403. *Telephone:* 419-372-2086. *Fax:* 419-372-6955. *E-mail:* admissions@bgnet.bgsu.edu. *Web site:* http://www.bgsu.edu/.

BRYANT AND STRATTON COLLEGE
Cleveland, Ohio

Bryant and Stratton is a coed, proprietary, four-year college of Bryant and Stratton Business Institute, Inc., founded in 1929, offering degrees at the associate and bachelor's levels.

Expenses for 2003–04 *Application fee:* $25. *Tuition:* $10,410 full-time, $347 per credit hour part-time. *Mandatory fees:* $200 full-time. *College room only:* $3887.

For Further Information Contact Ms. Marilyn Scheaffer, Director of Admissions, Bryant and Stratton College, 1700 East 13th Street, Cleveland, OH 44114-3203. *Telephone:* 216-771-1700. *Fax:* 216-771-7787. *Web site:* http://www.bryantstratton.edu/.

CAPITAL UNIVERSITY
Columbus, Ohio

Capital is a coed, private, comprehensive institution, founded in 1830, affiliated with the Evangelical Lutheran Church in America, offering degrees at the bachelor's, master's, and first professional levels. It has a 48-acre campus in Columbus.

Academic Information The faculty has 445 members (47% full-time), 60% with terminal degrees. The undergraduate student-faculty ratio is 9:1. The library holds 187,281 titles, 3,741 serial subscriptions, and 6,048 audiovisual materials. Special programs include services for learning-disabled students, study abroad, advanced placement credit, Freshman Honors College, ESL programs, double majors, independent study, self-designed majors, summer session for credit, part-time degree programs (evenings, weekends, summer), adult/continuing education programs, internships, and arrangement for off-campus study with members of the Higher Education Council of Columbus. The most frequently chosen baccalaureate fields are business/marketing, interdisciplinary studies, social sciences and history.

Student Body Statistics The student body totals 3,959, of whom 2,830 are undergraduates (577 freshmen). 64 percent are women and 36 percent are men. Students come from 24 states and territories and 10 other countries. 99 percent are from Ohio. 0.5 percent are international students.

Expenses for 2003–04 *Application fee:* $25. *One-time mandatory fee:* $200. *Comprehensive fee:* $26,550 includes full-time tuition ($20,500) and college room and board ($6050). Full-time tuition varies according to program. Room and board charges vary according to board plan and housing facility.

Financial Aid Forms of aid include need-based and non-need-based scholarships and part-time jobs. The average aided 2003–04 undergraduate received an aid package worth an estimated $16,856. The priority application deadline for financial aid is February 28.

Freshman Admission Capital requires a high school transcript, a minimum 2.6 high school GPA, SAT I or ACT scores, and TOEFL scores for international students. An interview is recommended. 1 recommendation and audition are required for some. The application deadline for regular admission is April 15 and for early action it is September 22.

Transfer Admission The application deadline for admission is rolling.

Entrance Difficulty Capital assesses its entrance difficulty level as moderately difficult. For the fall 2003 freshman class, 84 percent of the applicants were accepted.

For Further Information Contact Mrs. Kimberly V. Ebbrecht, Director of Admission, Capital University, 2199 East Main Street, Columbus, OH 43209. *Telephone:* 614-236-6101 or 800-289-6289 (toll-free). *Fax:* 614-236-6926. *E-mail:* admissions@capital.edu. *Web site:* http://www.capital.edu/.

CASE WESTERN RESERVE UNIVERSITY
Cleveland, Ohio

CWRU is a coed, private university, founded in 1826, offering degrees at the bachelor's, master's, doctoral, and first professional levels and postbachelor's certificates. It has a 150-acre campus in Cleveland.

Academic Information The faculty has 600 members (100% full-time), 96% with terminal degrees. The undergraduate student-faculty ratio is 8:1. The library holds 2 million titles, 17,506 serial subscriptions, and 49,889 audiovisual materials. Special programs include services for learning-disabled students, an honors program, cooperative (work-study) education, study abroad, advanced placement credit, accelerated degree programs, ESL programs, double majors, independent study, self-designed majors, summer session for credit, part-time degree programs (daytime, evenings), adult/continuing education programs, internships, and arrangement for off-campus study with Cleveland Institute of Art, Cleveland Institute of Music, 11 other Cleveland area institutions. The most frequently chosen baccalaureate fields are biological/life sciences, engineering/engineering technologies, social sciences and history.

Student Body Statistics The student body totals 9,186, of whom 3,587 are undergraduates (878 freshmen). 39 percent are women and 61 percent are men. Students come from 50 states and territories and 24 other countries. 55 percent are from Ohio. 4.5 percent are international students. 41 percent of the 2003 graduating class went on to graduate and professional schools.

Expenses for 2003–04 *Application fee:* $35. *Comprehensive fee:* $32,002 includes full-time tuition ($24,100), mandatory fees ($242), and college room and board ($7660). *College room only:* $4770. Room and board charges vary according to board plan and housing facility. *Part-time tuition:* varies with course load.

Financial Aid Forms of aid include need-based and non-need-based scholarships and part-time jobs. The average aided 2003–04 undergraduate received an aid package worth an estimated $23,571. The priority application deadline for financial aid is February 15.

Freshman Admission CWRU requires an essay, a high school transcript, 1 recommendation, SAT I or ACT scores, and TOEFL scores for international students. An interview and SAT II: Subject Test scores are recommended. The application deadline for regular admission is January 15 and for early action it is November 15.

Transfer Admission The application deadline for admission is May 15.

Entrance Difficulty CWRU assesses its entrance difficulty level as very difficult. For the fall 2003 freshman class, 75 percent of the applicants were accepted.

For Further Information Contact Ms. Elizabeth H. Woyczynski, Director of Undergraduate Admission, Case Western Reserve University, 10900 Euclid Avenue, Cleveland, OH 44106. *Telephone:* 216-368-4450. *Fax:* 216-368-5111. *E-mail:* admission@case.edu. *Web site:* http://www.case.edu/.

See page 264 for a narrative description.

CEDARVILLE UNIVERSITY
Cedarville, Ohio

Cedarville is a coed, private, Baptist, comprehensive institution, founded in 1887, offering degrees at the bachelor's and master's levels. It has a 400-acre campus in Cedarville near Columbus and Dayton.

Academic Information The faculty has 271 members (74% full-time), 49% with terminal degrees. The undergraduate student-faculty ratio is 14:1. The library holds 149,164 titles, 4,932 serial subscriptions, and 15,452 audiovisual materials. Special programs include academic remediation, services for learning-disabled students, an honors program, study abroad, advanced placement credit, accelerated degree programs, double majors, independent study, distance learning, summer session for credit, part-time degree programs (daytime), internships, and arrangement for off-campus study with Au Sable Institute. The most frequently chosen baccalaureate fields are business/marketing, communications/communication technologies, education.

Student Body Statistics The student body totals 2,997, of whom 2,996 are undergraduates (787 freshmen). 54 percent are women and 46 percent are men. Students come from 49 states and territories and 16 other countries. 33 percent are from Ohio. 0.5 percent are international students.

Expenses for 2003–04 *Application fee:* $30. *Comprehensive fee:* $19,954 includes full-time tuition ($14,944) and college room and board ($5010). *College room only:* $2684. Room and board charges vary according to board plan. *Part-time tuition:* $467 per semester hour. Part-time tuition varies according to course load.

Financial Aid Forms of aid include need-based and non-need-based scholarships, athletic grants, and part-time jobs. The average aided 2002–03 undergraduate received an aid package worth $12,738. The priority application deadline for financial aid is March 1.

Freshman Admission Cedarville requires an essay, a high school transcript, a minimum 3.0 high school GPA, 2 recommendations, SAT I or ACT scores, and TOEFL scores for international students. An interview is required for some. The application deadline for regular admission is rolling.

Entrance Difficulty Cedarville assesses its entrance difficulty level as moderately difficult. For the fall 2003 freshman class, 81 percent of the applicants were accepted.

For Further Information Contact Mr. Roscoe Smith, Director of Admissions, Cedarville University, 251 North Main Street, Cedarville, OH 45314-0601. *Telephone:* 937-766-7700 or 800-CEDARVILLE (toll-free). *Fax:* 937-766-7575. *E-mail:* admiss@cedarville.edu. *Web site:* http://www.cedarville.edu/.

CENTRAL STATE UNIVERSITY
Wilberforce, Ohio

Central is a coed, public, comprehensive unit of Ohio Board of Regents, founded in 1887, offering degrees at the bachelor's and master's levels and postbachelor's certificates. It has a 60-acre campus in Wilberforce near Dayton.

Academic Information The faculty has 143 members (61% full-time), 38% with terminal degrees. The undergraduate student-faculty ratio is 14:1. The library holds 280,470 titles, 26,066 serial subscriptions, and 497 audiovisual materials. Special programs include services for learning-disabled students, an honors program, cooperative (work-study) education, study abroad, double majors, independent study, summer session for credit, part-time degree programs (daytime, evenings, weekends, summer), adult/continuing education programs, internships, and arrangement for off-campus study with members of the Southwestern Ohio Council for Higher Education. The most frequently chosen baccalaureate fields are business/marketing, education, social sciences and history.

Student Body Statistics The student body totals 1,621, of whom 1,611 are undergraduates (550 freshmen). 54 percent are women and 46 percent are men. Students come from 26 states and territories and 5 other countries. 75 percent are from Ohio. 0.7 percent are international students. 37 percent of the 2003 graduating class went on to graduate and professional schools.

Expenses for 2003–04 *Application fee:* $20. *State resident tuition:* $2340 full-time. *Nonresident tuition:* $7335 full-time. *Mandatory fees:* $1947 full-time. Full-time tuition and fees vary according to course load. *College room and board:* $6069. *College room only:* $3198.

Financial Aid Forms of aid include need-based and non-need-based scholarships and part-time jobs. The priority application deadline for financial aid is March 31.

Freshman Admission Central requires a high school transcript, SAT I or ACT scores, and TOEFL scores for international students. An interview and ACT scores are recommended. A minimum 2.0 high school GPA, 2 recommendations, and 2.5 high school GPA for nonresidents are required for some. The application deadline for regular admission is June 15.

Transfer Admission The application deadline for admission is June 15.

Entrance Difficulty Central has an open admission policy for state residents. It assesses its entrance difficulty as moderately difficult for out-of-state applicants; moderately difficult for transfers.

For Further Information Contact Dr. Eric V. Hilton, Director, Admissions, Central State University, PO Box 1004, 1400 Blush Row Road, Wilberforce, OH 45384. *Telephone:* 937-376-6348 or 800-388-CSU1 (toll-free in-state). *Fax:* 937-376-6648. *E-mail:* admissions@csu.ces.edu. *Web site:* http://www.centralstate.edu/.

CHATFIELD COLLEGE
St. Martin, Ohio

Chatfield is a coed, primarily women's, private, two-year college, founded in 1970, affiliated with the Roman Catholic Church, offering degrees at the associate level. It has a 200-acre campus in St. Martin near Cincinnati and Dayton.

Academic Information The faculty has 43 members (7% full-time). The student-faculty ratio is 12:1. The library holds 15,000 titles and 30 serial subscriptions. Special programs include academic remediation, advanced placement credit, summer session for credit, part-time degree programs (daytime, evenings, summer), adult/continuing education programs, internships, and arrangement for off-campus study with 14 members of the Greater Cincinnati Consortium of Colleges and Universities.

Student Body Statistics The student body is made up of 230 undergraduates. Students come from 1 state or territory. 39 percent of the 2003 graduating class went on to four-year colleges.

Expenses for 2004–05 *Application fee:* $10. *Tuition:* $235 per credit hour part-time. *Mandatory fees:* $130 per term part-time.

Financial Aid Forms of aid include need-based scholarships and part-time jobs. The application deadline for financial aid is August 1 with a priority deadline of April 26.

Freshman Admission Chatfield requires a high school transcript. TOEFL scores for international students are recommended. The application deadline for regular admission is rolling.

Transfer Admission The application deadline for admission is rolling.

Entrance Difficulty Chatfield has an open admission policy.

For Further Information Contact Mr. Bill F. Balzano, PhD, Director of Admissions, Chatfield College, St. Martin, OH 45118. *Telephone:* 513-875-3344. *Fax:* 513-875-3912. *E-mail:* chatfield@chatfield.edu. *Web site:* http://www.chatfield.edu/.

CINCINNATI BIBLE COLLEGE AND SEMINARY
Cincinnati, Ohio

Cincinnati Bible College is a coed, private, comprehensive institution, founded in 1924, affiliated with the Church of Christ, offering degrees at the associate, bachelor's, master's, and first professional levels. It has a 40-acre campus in Cincinnati.

Cincinnati Bible College and Seminary (continued)

Expenses for 2003–04 *Application fee:* $35. *Comprehensive fee:* $13,730 includes full-time tuition ($8320), mandatory fees ($570), and college room and board ($4840).

For Further Information Contact Mr. Alex Eady, Director of Undergraduate Admissions, Cincinnati Bible College and Seminary, 2700 Glenway Avenue, Cincinnati, OH 45204-1799. *Telephone:* 800-949-4222 Ext. 8610 or 800-949-4CBC (toll-free). *Fax:* 513-244-8140. *E-mail:* admissions@cincybible.edu. *Web site:* http://www.cincybible.edu/.

CINCINNATI COLLEGE OF MORTUARY SCIENCE
Cincinnati, Ohio

Cincinnati Mortuary College is a coed, private, primarily two-year college, founded in 1882, offering degrees at the associate and bachelor's levels in funeral service. It has a 10-acre campus in Cincinnati.

Academic Information The faculty has 12 members (58% full-time). The student-faculty ratio is 5:1. The library holds 5,000 titles and 30 serial subscriptions. Special programs include academic remediation, advanced placement credit, summer session for credit, and adult/continuing education programs.
Student Body Statistics The student body is made up of 121 undergraduates (14 freshmen). 37 percent are women and 63 percent are men. Students come from 17 states and territories.
Expenses for 2004–05 *Application fee:* $25. *Tuition:* $12,900 full-time, $172 per credit hour part-time. *Mandatory fees:* $120 full-time, $60 per term part-time.
Financial Aid Forms of aid include need-based scholarships. The application deadline for financial aid is continuous.
Freshman Admission Cincinnati Mortuary College requires a high school transcript. Recommendations and TOEFL scores for international students are recommended. The application deadline for regular admission is rolling.
Transfer Admission The application deadline for admission is rolling.
Entrance Difficulty Cincinnati Mortuary College assesses its entrance difficulty level as minimally difficult. For the fall 2003 freshman class, 47 percent of the applicants were accepted.

For Further Information Contact Ms. Pat Leon, Director of Financial Aid, Cincinnati College of Mortuary Science, 645 West North Bend Road, Cincinnati, OH 45224-1462. *Telephone:* 513-761-2020. *Fax:* 513-761-3333. *Web site:* http://www.ccms.edu/.

CIRCLEVILLE BIBLE COLLEGE
Circleville, Ohio

CBC is a coed, private, four-year college, founded in 1948, affiliated with the Churches of Christ in Christian Union, offering degrees at the associate and bachelor's levels. It has a 40-acre campus in Circleville near Columbus.

Expenses for 2003–04 *Application fee:* $25. *Comprehensive fee:* $14,394 includes full-time tuition ($8460), mandatory fees ($844), and college room and board ($5090). Full-time tuition and fees vary according to course load, location, and reciprocity agreements. Room and board charges vary according to board plan. *Part-time tuition:* varies with course load, location, reciprocity agreements.

For Further Information Contact Rev. James Schroeder, Acting Director of Enrollment, Circleville Bible College, PO Box 458, Circleville, OH 43113-9487. *Telephone:* 740-477-7741 or 800-701-0222 (toll-free). *Fax:* 740-477-7755. *E-mail:* enroll@biblecollege.edu. *Web site:* http://www.biblecollege.edu/.

CLEVELAND COLLEGE OF JEWISH STUDIES

See Laura and Alvin Siegal College of Judaic Studies

THE CLEVELAND INSTITUTE OF ART
Cleveland, Ohio

CIA is a coed, private, comprehensive institution, founded in 1882, offering degrees at the bachelor's and master's levels in art. It has a 488-acre campus in Cleveland.

Academic Information The faculty has 99 members (47% full-time), 62% with terminal degrees. The undergraduate student-faculty ratio is 10:1. The library holds 42,000 titles, 250 serial subscriptions, and 95,000 audiovisual materials. Special programs include academic remediation, services for learning-disabled students, an honors program, study abroad, advanced placement credit, independent study, part-time degree programs (daytime), internships, and arrangement for off-campus study with Case Western Reserve University, Northeast Ohio Commission on Higher Education, Association of Independent Colleges of Art and Design. The most frequently chosen baccalaureate field is visual/performing arts.
Student Body Statistics The student body totals 624, of whom 618 are undergraduates (92 freshmen). 50 percent are women and 50 percent are men. Students come from 30 states and territories and 9 other countries. 69 percent are from Ohio. 2.9 percent are international students. 17 percent of the 2003 graduating class went on to graduate and professional schools.
Expenses for 2003–04 *Application fee:* $30. *Comprehensive fee:* $30,875 includes full-time tuition ($21,975), mandatory fees ($1360), and college room and board ($7540). *College room only:* $4600. Room and board charges vary according to board plan and housing facility. *Part-time tuition:* $920 per credit. *Part-time mandatory fees:* $80 per credit. Part-time tuition and fees vary according to course load.
Financial Aid Forms of aid include need-based and non-need-based scholarships and part-time jobs. The average aided 2003–04 undergraduate received an aid package worth an estimated $23,429. The priority application deadline for financial aid is March 15.
Freshman Admission CIA requires an essay, a high school transcript, a minimum 2.0 high school GPA, 2 recommendations, a portfolio, SAT I or ACT scores, and TOEFL scores for international students. An interview is recommended. The application deadline for regular admission is rolling.
Transfer Admission The application deadline for admission is rolling.
Entrance Difficulty CIA assesses its entrance difficulty level as moderately difficult. For the fall 2003 freshman class, 65 percent of the applicants were accepted.

For Further Information Contact Ms. Catherine Redhead, Director of Admissions, The Cleveland Institute of Art, 11141 East Boulevard, Cleveland, OH 44106. *Telephone:* 216-421-7418 or 800-223-4700 (toll-free). *Fax:* 216-754-3634. *E-mail:* admiss@gate.cia.edu. *Web site:* http://www.cia.edu/.

CLEVELAND INSTITUTE OF MUSIC
Cleveland, Ohio

Cleveland Institute of Music is a coed, private, comprehensive institution, founded in 1920, offering degrees at the bachelor's, master's, and doctoral levels and postbachelor's certificates. It has a 488-acre campus in Cleveland.

Academic Information The faculty has 96 members (33% full-time), 4% with terminal degrees. The undergraduate student-faculty ratio is 7:1. The library holds 48,128 titles, 115 serial subscriptions, and 19,633 audiovisual materials. Special programs include academic remediation, advanced placement credit, accelerated degree programs, ESL programs, summer session for credit, internships, and arrangement for off-campus study with Case Western Reserve University. The most frequently chosen baccalaureate field is visual/performing arts.

Student Body Statistics The student body totals 413, of whom 245 are undergraduates (67 freshmen). 59 percent are women and 41 percent are men. Students come from 38 states and territories and 15 other countries. 18 percent are from Ohio. 11.8 percent are international students. 90 percent of the 2003 graduating class went on to graduate and professional schools.

Expenses for 2003–04 *Application fee:* $100. *Comprehensive fee:* $30,028 includes full-time tuition ($21,866), mandatory fees ($902), and college room and board ($7260). *College room only:* $4370. Room and board charges vary according to board plan. *Part-time tuition:* $1004 per credit hour. *Part-time mandatory fees:* $610 per term.

Financial Aid Forms of aid include need-based and non-need-based scholarships and part-time jobs. The average aided 2002–03 undergraduate received an aid package worth $15,299. The application deadline for financial aid is February 15.

Freshman Admission Cleveland Institute of Music requires an essay, a high school transcript, 2 recommendations, audition, SAT I or ACT scores, and TOEFL scores for international students. An interview is recommended. The application deadline for regular admission is December 1.

Transfer Admission The application deadline for admission is December 1.

Entrance Difficulty Cleveland Institute of Music assesses its entrance difficulty level as very difficult. For the fall 2003 freshman class, 40 percent of the applicants were accepted.

For Further Information Contact Mr. William Fay, Director of Admission, Cleveland Institute of Music, 11021 East Boulevard, Cleveland, OH 44106-1776. *Telephone:* 216-795-3107. *Fax:* 216-791-1530. *E-mail:* cimadmission@po.cwru.edu. *Web site:* http://www.cim.edu/.

CLEVELAND STATE UNIVERSITY
Cleveland, Ohio

Cleveland State is a coed, public university, founded in 1964, offering degrees at the bachelor's, master's, doctoral, and first professional levels and post-master's, first professional, and postbachelor's certificates. It has a 70-acre campus in Cleveland near Akron.

Academic Information The faculty has 920 members (59% full-time), 58% with terminal degrees. The undergraduate student-faculty ratio is 16:1. The library holds 484,914 titles, 6,186 serial subscriptions, and 101,376 audiovisual materials. Special programs include academic remediation, an honors program, cooperative (work-study) education, study abroad, advanced placement credit, accelerated degree programs, Freshman Honors College, ESL programs, independent study, self-designed majors, summer session for credit, part-time degree programs, adult/continuing education programs, internships, and arrangement for off-campus study with 7 members of the Cleveland Commission on Higher Education, University of Akron, Baldwin-Wallace College, University of Toledo. The most frequently chosen baccalaureate fields are business/marketing, education, social sciences and history.

Student Body Statistics The student body totals 16,014, of whom 10,054 are undergraduates (987 freshmen). 54 percent are women and 46 percent are men. Students come from 21 states and territories and 63 other countries. 99 percent are from Ohio. 2 percent are international students.

Expenses for 2003–04 *Application fee:* $30. *State resident tuition:* $6072 full-time, $253 per semester hour part-time. *Nonresident tuition:* $11,940 full-time, $498 per semester hour part-time. Full-time tuition varies according to program and student level. Part-time tuition varies according to program and student level. *College room and board:* $7805. *College room only:* $5316. Room and board charges vary according to board plan and housing facility.

Financial Aid Forms of aid include need-based and non-need-based scholarships, athletic grants, and part-time jobs. The average aided 2003–04 undergraduate received an aid package worth an estimated $6893. The priority application deadline for financial aid is February 15.

Freshman Admission Cleveland State requires a high school transcript, SAT I or ACT scores, and TOEFL scores for international students. The application deadline for regular admission is rolling.

Transfer Admission The application deadline for admission is July 15.

Entrance Difficulty Cleveland State has an open admission policy for state residents. It assesses its entrance difficulty as moderately difficult for out-of-state applicants; moderately difficult for transfers; moderately difficult for engineering, education, health science programs.

For Further Information Contact Ms. Bonnie Jones, Office of Admissions, Cleveland State University, Rhodes Tower West, Room 204, 1983 East 24th Street, Cleveland, OH 44115. *Telephone:* 216-523-5139 or 888-CSU-OHIO (toll-free). *Fax:* 216-687-9210. *E-mail:* admissions@csuohio.edu. *Web site:* http://www.csuohio.edu/.

COLLEGE OF MOUNT ST. JOSEPH
Cincinnati, Ohio

The Mount is a coed, private, Roman Catholic, comprehensive institution, founded in 1920, offering degrees at the associate, bachelor's, and master's levels and postbachelor's certificates. It has an 88-acre campus in Cincinnati.

Academic Information The faculty has 193 members (60% full-time), 49% with terminal degrees. The undergraduate student-faculty ratio is 12:1. The library holds 98,849 titles, 429 serial subscriptions, and 3,109 audiovisual materials. Special programs include academic remediation, services for learning-disabled students, an honors program, cooperative (work-study) education, study abroad, advanced placement credit, accelerated degree programs, Freshman Honors College, ESL programs, double majors, independent study, distance learning, summer session for credit, part-time degree programs (daytime, evenings, weekends, summer), external degree programs, adult/continuing education programs, internships, and arrangement for off-campus study with Greater Cincinnati Consortium of Colleges and Universities. The most frequently chosen baccalaureate fields are business/marketing, education, health professions and related sciences.

Student Body Statistics The student body totals 2,110, of whom 1,876 are undergraduates (309 freshmen). 69 percent are women and 31 percent are men. Students come from 17 states and territories. 89 percent are from Ohio. 0.1 percent are international students. 13 percent of the 2003 graduating class went on to graduate and professional schools.

Expenses for 2004–05 *Application fee:* $25. *Comprehensive fee:* $24,285 includes full-time tuition ($17,200), mandatory fees ($1240), and college room and board ($5845). *College room only:* $2875. Full-time tuition and fees vary according to course load, program, reciprocity agreements, and student level. Room and board charges vary according to board plan and housing facility. *Part-time tuition:* $420 per semester hour. *Part-time mandatory fees:* $65 per term. Part-time tuition and fees vary according to course load, location, and reciprocity agreements.

Financial Aid Forms of aid include need-based and non-need-based scholarships and part-time jobs. The average aided 2002–03 undergraduate received an aid package worth $13,332. The priority application deadline for financial aid is March 1.

Freshman Admission The Mount requires a high school transcript, a minimum 2.25 high school GPA, minimum SAT score of 960 or ACT score of 19, SAT I or ACT scores, and TOEFL scores for international students. An essay, 1 recommendation, and an interview are required for some. The application deadline for regular admission is August 15.

Transfer Admission The application deadline for admission is August 15.

Entrance Difficulty The Mount assesses its entrance difficulty level as moderately difficult; minimally difficult for transfers; very difficult for physical therapy. For the fall 2003 freshman class, 76 percent of the applicants were accepted.

For Further Information Contact Ms. Peggy Minnich, Director of Admission, College of Mount St. Joseph, 5701 Delhi Road, Cincinnati, OH 45233-1672. *Telephone:* 513-244-4814 or 800-654-9314 (toll-free). *Fax:* 513-244-4629. *E-mail:* peggy_minnich@mail.msj.edu. *Web site:* http://www.msj.edu/.

See page 266 for a narrative description.

Ohio

THE COLLEGE OF WOOSTER
Wooster, Ohio

Wooster is a coed, private, four-year college, founded in 1866, affiliated with the Presbyterian Church (U.S.A.), offering degrees at the bachelor's level. It has a 240-acre campus in Wooster near Cleveland.

Academic Information The faculty has 179 members (75% full-time), 91% with terminal degrees. The student-faculty ratio is 12:1. The library holds 581,518 titles and 12,416 audiovisual materials. Special programs include services for learning-disabled students, study abroad, advanced placement credit, double majors, independent study, self-designed majors, summer session for credit, internships, and arrangement for off-campus study. The most frequently chosen baccalaureate fields are English, social sciences and history, visual/performing arts.
Student Body Statistics The student body is made up of 1,871 undergraduates (552 freshmen). 53 percent are women and 47 percent are men. Students come from 39 states and territories and 21 other countries. 58 percent are from Ohio. 6.7 percent are international students.
Expenses for 2003–04 *Application fee:* $40. *Comprehensive fee:* $31,300 includes full-time tuition ($25,040) and college room and board ($6260). *College room only:* $2850. Full-time tuition varies according to course load and reciprocity agreements. *Part-time tuition:* varies with course load.
Financial Aid Forms of aid include need-based and non-need-based scholarships and part-time jobs. The average aided 2003–04 undergraduate received an aid package worth an estimated $21,812. The priority application deadline for financial aid is February 15.
Freshman Admission Wooster requires an essay, a high school transcript, 2 recommendations, SAT I or ACT scores, and TOEFL scores for international students. An interview is recommended. The application deadline for regular admission is February 15; for early decision plan 1 it is December 1; and for early decision plan 2 it is January 15.
Transfer Admission The application deadline for admission is June 1.
Entrance Difficulty Wooster assesses its entrance difficulty level as moderately difficult. For the fall 2003 freshman class, 70 percent of the applicants were accepted.

For Further Information Contact Mr. Paul Deutsch, Dean of Admissions, The College of Wooster, 847 College Avenue, Wooster, OH 44691. *Telephone:* 330-263-2270 Ext. 2118 or 800-877-9905 (toll-free). *Fax:* 330-263-2621. *E-mail:* admissions@wooster.edu. *Web site:* http://www.wooster.edu/.

See page 268 for a narrative description.

COLUMBUS COLLEGE OF ART & DESIGN
Columbus, Ohio

CCAD is a coed, private, four-year college, founded in 1879, offering degrees at the bachelor's level in art. It has a 10-acre campus in Columbus.

Academic Information The faculty has 187 members (43% full-time), 40% with terminal degrees. The student-faculty ratio is 12:1. The library holds 45,257 titles, 275 serial subscriptions, and 126,726 audiovisual materials. Special programs include academic remediation, services for learning-disabled students, advanced placement credit, ESL programs, double majors, independent study, summer session for credit, part-time degree programs (daytime, evenings, summer), internships, and arrangement for off-campus study with members of the Higher Education Council of Columbus. The most frequently chosen baccalaureate field is visual/performing arts.
Student Body Statistics The student body is made up of 1,634 undergraduates (186 freshmen). 51 percent are women and 49 percent are men. Students come from 41 states and territories and 31 other countries. 78 percent are from Ohio. 7.3 percent are international students. 10 percent of the 2003 graduating class went on to graduate and professional schools.
Expenses for 2003–04 *Application fee:* $25. *Comprehensive fee:* $24,720 includes full-time tuition ($17,880), mandatory fees ($540), and college room and board ($6300). Room and board charges vary according to

housing facility and student level. *Part-time tuition:* $745 per credit. *Part-time mandatory fees:* $180 per term. Part-time tuition and fees vary according to course load.
Financial Aid Forms of aid include need-based and non-need-based scholarships and part-time jobs. The average aided 2003–04 undergraduate received an aid package worth an estimated $12,897. The priority application deadline for financial aid is March 3.
Freshman Admission CCAD requires an essay, a high school transcript, a minimum 2.0 high school GPA, a portfolio, SAT I or ACT scores, and TOEFL scores for international students. An interview is recommended. Recommendations are required for some. The application deadline for regular admission is rolling.
Transfer Admission The application deadline for admission is rolling.
Entrance Difficulty CCAD assesses its entrance difficulty level as moderately difficult. For the fall 2003 freshman class, 64 percent of the applicants were accepted.

For Further Information Contact Mr. Thomas E. Green, Director of Admissions, Columbus College of Art & Design, 107 North Ninth Street, Columbus, OH 43215-1758. *Telephone:* 614-224-9101 or 877-997-2223 (toll-free). *Fax:* 614-232-8344. *E-mail:* admissions@ccad. edu. *Web site:* http://www.ccad.edu/.

DAVID N. MYERS UNIVERSITY
Cleveland, Ohio

For Information Write to David N. Myers University, Cleveland, OH 44115-1096.

DEFIANCE COLLEGE
Defiance, Ohio

Defiance College is a coed, private, comprehensive institution, founded in 1850, affiliated with the United Church of Christ, offering degrees at the associate, bachelor's, and master's levels. It has a 150-acre campus in Defiance near Toledo.

Academic Information The faculty has 93 members (48% full-time), 27% with terminal degrees. The undergraduate student-faculty ratio is 14:1. The library holds 88,000 titles, 424 serial subscriptions, and 25,000 audiovisual materials. Special programs include academic remediation, an honors program, cooperative (work-study) education, study abroad, advanced placement credit, double majors, independent study, distance learning, self-designed majors, summer session for credit, part-time degree programs (daytime, evenings, weekends, summer), external degree programs, adult/continuing education programs, internships, and arrangement for off-campus study with Bowling Green State University. The most frequently chosen baccalaureate fields are business/marketing, education, health professions and related sciences.
Student Body Statistics The student body totals 1,036, of whom 938 are undergraduates (216 freshmen). 57 percent are women and 43 percent are men. Students come from 11 states and territories and 4 other countries. 85 percent are from Ohio. 0.4 percent are international students.
Expenses for 2003–04 *Application fee:* $25. *Comprehensive fee:* $22,615 includes full-time tuition ($16,950), mandatory fees ($415), and college room and board ($5250). *College room only:* $2650. Room and board charges vary according to board plan and housing facility. *Part-time tuition:* $300 per credit hour.
Financial Aid Forms of aid include need-based and non-need-based scholarships and part-time jobs. The average aided 2002–03 undergraduate received an aid package worth $13,294. The priority application deadline for financial aid is March 1.
Freshman Admission Defiance College requires a high school transcript, a minimum 2.25 high school GPA, SAT I or ACT scores, and TOEFL scores for international students. Recommendations and an interview are recommended. An essay and an interview are required for some. The application deadline for regular admission is August 15.
Transfer Admission The application deadline for admission is August 15.

Entrance Difficulty Defiance College assesses its entrance difficulty level as moderately difficult. For the fall 2003 freshman class, 75 percent of the applicants were accepted.

For Further Information Contact Mr. Mark Thompson, Dean of Admissions, Defiance College, 701 North Clinton Street, Defiance, OH 43512-1610. *Telephone:* 419-783-2361 or 800-520-4632 Ext. 2359 (toll-free). *Fax:* 419-783-2468. *E-mail:* admissions@defiance.edu. *Web site:* http://www.defiance.edu/.

DENISON UNIVERSITY
Granville, Ohio

Denison is a coed, private, four-year college, founded in 1831, offering degrees at the bachelor's level. It has a 1,200-acre campus in Granville near Columbus.

Academic Information The faculty has 191 members (94% full-time), 92% with terminal degrees. The student-faculty ratio is 11:1. The library holds 728,949 titles, 4,445 serial subscriptions, and 25,452 audiovisual materials. Special programs include services for learning-disabled students, an honors program, cooperative (work-study) education, study abroad, advanced placement credit, double majors, independent study, self-designed majors, part-time degree programs (daytime), internships, and arrangement for off-campus study with American University, Great Lakes Colleges Association, Marine Science Consortium. The most frequently chosen baccalaureate fields are communications/communication technologies, English, social sciences and history.

Student Body Statistics The student body is made up of 2,232 undergraduates (629 freshmen). 56 percent are women and 44 percent are men. Students come from 48 states and territories and 31 other countries. 45 percent are from Ohio. 4.3 percent are international students. 21 percent of the 2003 graduating class went on to graduate and professional schools.

Expenses for 2003–04 *Application fee:* $40. *Comprehensive fee:* $33,050 includes full-time tuition ($25,090), mandatory fees ($670), and college room and board ($7290). *College room only:* $3980. Room and board charges vary according to housing facility. *Part-time tuition:* varies with course load.

Financial Aid Forms of aid include need-based and non-need-based scholarships and part-time jobs. The average aided 2002–03 undergraduate received an aid package worth $22,756. The priority application deadline for financial aid is February 15.

Freshman Admission Denison requires an essay, a high school transcript, 2 recommendations, and SAT I or ACT scores. An interview, SAT II: Subject Test scores, and TOEFL scores for international students are recommended. The application deadline for regular admission is February 1; for early decision plan 1 it is November 15; and for early decision plan 2 it is January 15.

Transfer Admission The application deadline for admission is July 1.

Entrance Difficulty Denison assesses its entrance difficulty level as moderately difficult. For the fall 2003 freshman class, 68 percent of the applicants were accepted.

For Further Information Contact Mr. Perry Robinson, Director of Admissions, Denison University, Box H, Granville, OH 43023. *Telephone:* 740-587-6276 or 800-DENISON (toll-free). *Fax:* 740-587-6306. *E-mail:* admissions@denison.edu. *Web site:* http://www.denison.edu/.

DEVRY UNIVERSITY
Cleveland, Ohio

For Information Write to DeVry University, Cleveland, OH 44114-2301.

DEVRY UNIVERSITY
Seven Hills, Ohio

For Information Write to DeVry University, Seven Hills, OH 44131-6907.

DEVRY UNIVERSITY
Columbus, Ohio

DeVry is a coed, proprietary, comprehensive unit of DeVry University, founded in 1952, offering degrees at the associate, bachelor's, and master's levels and postbachelor's certificates. It has a 21-acre campus in Columbus.

Academic Information The library holds 30,000 titles, 5,892 serial subscriptions, and 1,050 audiovisual materials. Special programs include academic remediation, services for learning-disabled students, cooperative (work-study) education, advanced placement credit, accelerated degree programs, distance learning, summer session for credit, part-time degree programs (daytime, evenings, weekends, summer), and adult/continuing education programs. The most frequently chosen baccalaureate fields are business/marketing, computer/information sciences, engineering/engineering technologies.

Student Body Statistics The student body totals 3,335, of whom 3,158 are undergraduates (698 freshmen). 25 percent are women and 75 percent are men. 0.9 percent are international students.

Expenses for 2003–04 *Application fee:* $50. *Tuition:* $9990 full-time, $355 per credit hour part-time. *Mandatory fees:* $165 full-time. Full-time tuition and fees vary according to course load. Part-time tuition varies according to course load.

Financial Aid Forms of aid include need-based and non-need-based scholarships and part-time jobs. The average aided 2002–03 undergraduate received an aid package worth $9184. The application deadline for financial aid is continuous.

Freshman Admission DeVry requires a high school transcript, an interview, and TOEFL scores for international students. SAT I, ACT or CPT is recommended. The application deadline for regular admission is rolling.

Entrance Difficulty DeVry assesses its entrance difficulty level as minimally difficult; moderately difficult for electronics engineering technology program.

For Further Information Contact Ms. Shelia Brown, New Student Coordinator, DeVry University, 1350 Alum Creek Drive, Columbus, OH 43209-2705. *Telephone:* 614-253-7291 Ext. 700 or 800-426-2206 (toll-free). *Fax:* 614-253-0843. *E-mail:* admissions@devry.edu. *Web site:* http://www.devry.edu/.

FRANCISCAN UNIVERSITY OF STEUBENVILLE
Steubenville, Ohio

Franciscan University of Steubenville is a coed, private, Roman Catholic, comprehensive institution, founded in 1946, offering degrees at the associate, bachelor's, and master's levels. It has a 124-acre campus in Steubenville near Pittsburgh.

Academic Information The faculty has 172 members (60% full-time), 48% with terminal degrees. The undergraduate student-faculty ratio is 16:1. The library holds 231,176 titles, 578 serial subscriptions, and 1,260 audiovisual materials. Special programs include services for learning-disabled students, an honors program, study abroad, advanced placement credit, accelerated degree programs, double majors, independent study, distance learning, summer session for credit, part-time degree programs (daytime, evenings, summer), adult/continuing education programs, and internships. The most frequently chosen baccalaureate fields are business/marketing, education, philosophy, religion, and theology.

Student Body Statistics The student body totals 2,281, of whom 1,844 are undergraduates (357 freshmen). 60 percent are women and 40 percent

Franciscan University of Steubenville (continued)

are men. Students come from 52 states and territories and 24 other countries. 24 percent are from Ohio. 1.5 percent are international students. 13 percent of the 2003 graduating class went on to graduate and professional schools.

Expenses for 2003–04 *Application fee:* $20. *Comprehensive fee:* $20,300 includes full-time tuition ($14,670), mandatory fees ($380), and college room and board ($5250). Room and board charges vary according to board plan. *Part-time tuition:* $485 per credit. *Part-time mandatory fees:* $10 per credit. Part-time tuition and fees vary according to class time.

Financial Aid Forms of aid include need-based and non-need-based scholarships and part-time jobs. The average aided 2003–04 undergraduate received an aid package worth an estimated $10,631. The priority application deadline for financial aid is April 15.

Freshman Admission Franciscan University of Steubenville requires an essay, a high school transcript, a minimum 2.4 high school GPA, recommendations, SAT I or ACT scores, and TOEFL scores for international students. An interview is recommended. The application deadline for regular admission is May 1.

Transfer Admission The application deadline for admission is May 1.

Entrance Difficulty Franciscan University of Steubenville assesses its entrance difficulty level as moderately difficult. For the fall 2003 freshman class, 84 percent of the applicants were accepted.

For Further Information Contact Mrs. Margaret Weber, Director of Admissions, Franciscan University of Steubenville, 1235 University Boulevard, Steubenville, OH 43952-1763. *Telephone:* 740-283-6226 or 800-783-6220 (toll-free). *Fax:* 740-284-5456. *E-mail:* admissions@franciscan.edu. *Web site:* http://www.franciscan.edu/.

FRANKLIN UNIVERSITY
Columbus, Ohio

Franklin University is a coed, private, comprehensive institution, founded in 1902, offering degrees at the associate, bachelor's, and master's levels. It has a 14-acre campus in Columbus.

Academic Information The faculty has 429 members (9% full-time), 21% with terminal degrees. The undergraduate student-faculty ratio is 19:1. The library holds 73,702 titles, 432 serial subscriptions, and 220 audiovisual materials. Special programs include academic remediation, services for learning-disabled students, cooperative (work-study) education, study abroad, advanced placement credit, accelerated degree programs, ESL programs, independent study, distance learning, self-designed majors, summer session for credit, part-time degree programs (daytime, evenings, weekends, summer), adult/continuing education programs, internships, and arrangement for off-campus study with members of the Higher Education Council of Columbus. The most frequently chosen baccalaureate fields are business/marketing, computer/information sciences, health professions and related sciences.

Student Body Statistics The student body totals 6,286, of whom 5,318 are undergraduates (92 freshmen). 55 percent are women and 45 percent are men. Students come from 42 states and territories and 94 other countries. 78 percent are from Ohio. 7 percent are international students.

Expenses for 2003–04 *Application fee:* $0. *Tuition:* $6720 full-time, $224 per credit hour part-time. Full-time tuition varies according to program. Part-time tuition varies according to program.

Financial Aid Forms of aid include need-based and non-need-based scholarships and part-time jobs. The priority application deadline for financial aid is June 15.

Freshman Admission Franklin University requires TOEFL scores for international students. A high school transcript is required for some. The application deadline for regular admission is rolling.

Transfer Admission The application deadline for admission is rolling.

Entrance Difficulty Franklin University has an open admission policy except for international students. It assesses its entrance difficulty as moderately difficult for international students.

For Further Information Contact Ms. Tracy Austin, Director of Student Services, Franklin University, 201 South Grant Avenue, Columbus, OH 43215. *Telephone:* 614-797-4700 Ext. 7501 or 877-341-6300 (toll-free). *Fax:* 614-224-8027. *E-mail:* info@franklin.edu. *Web site:* http://www.franklin.edu/.

GALLIPOLIS CAREER COLLEGE
Gallipolis, Ohio

Gallipolis Career College is a coed, primarily women's, private, two-year college, founded in 1962, offering degrees at the associate level.

Academic Information The faculty has 16 members (12% full-time). The student-faculty ratio is 8:1. The library holds 94 audiovisual materials. Special programs include academic remediation, double majors, independent study, summer session for credit, part-time degree programs (daytime, evenings, summer), adult/continuing education programs, and internships.

Student Body Statistics The student body is made up of 161 undergraduates (34 freshmen). 86 percent are women and 14 percent are men. Students come from 2 states and territories.

Expenses for 2004–05 *Application fee:* $50. *Tuition:* $8160 full-time, $170 per credit hour part-time. *Mandatory fees:* $100 full-time.

Freshman Admission Gallipolis Career College requires a high school transcript, an interview, and Wonderlic aptitude test. The application deadline for regular admission is rolling.

Transfer Admission The application deadline for admission is rolling.

Entrance Difficulty Gallipolis Career College assesses its entrance difficulty level as minimally difficult.

For Further Information Contact Mr. Jack Henson, Director of Admissions, Gallipolis Career College, 1176 Jackson Pike, Suite 312, Gallipolis, OH 45631. *Telephone:* 740-446-4124 Ext. 12 or 800-214-0452 (toll-free). *Fax:* 740-446-4124. *E-mail:* admissions@gallipoliscareercollege.com. *Web site:* http://www.gallipoliscareercollege.com/.

GOD'S BIBLE SCHOOL AND COLLEGE
Cincinnati, Ohio

God's Bible College is a coed, private, interdenominational, four-year college, founded in 1900, offering degrees at the associate and bachelor's levels. It has a 14-acre campus in Cincinnati.

Academic Information The faculty has 20 members (55% full-time), 30% with terminal degrees. The student-faculty ratio is 14:1. The library holds 28,452 titles and 240 serial subscriptions. Special programs include academic remediation, advanced placement credit, independent study, summer session for credit, part-time degree programs (daytime), and internships. The most frequently chosen baccalaureate fields are education, philosophy, religion, and theology, visual/performing arts.

Student Body Statistics The student body is made up of 252 undergraduates (59 freshmen). 49 percent are women and 51 percent are men. Students come from 25 states and territories and 13 other countries. 8.9 percent are international students. 14 percent of the 2003 graduating class went on to graduate and professional schools.

Expenses for 2004–05 *Application fee:* $50. *Comprehensive fee:* $7780 includes full-time tuition ($4030), mandatory fees ($600), and college room and board ($3150). *College room only:* $1300. *Part-time tuition:* $155 per credit.

Financial Aid Forms of aid include need-based and non-need-based scholarships. The application deadline for financial aid is continuous.

Freshman Admission God's Bible College requires a high school transcript, 3 recommendations, an interview, SAT I or ACT scores, and TOEFL scores for international students. The application deadline for regular admission is August 18.

Transfer Admission The application deadline for admission is rolling.
Entrance Difficulty God's Bible College assesses its entrance difficulty level as minimally difficult. For the fall 2003 freshman class, 100 percent of the applicants were accepted.

For Further Information Contact Mrs. Lori Waggoner, Director of Admissions, God's Bible School and College, 1810 Young Street, Cincinnati, OH 45202-6838. *Telephone:* 513-721-7944 Ext. 205 or 800-486-4637 (toll-free). *Fax:* 513-721-3971. *E-mail:* admissions@gbs.edu. *Web site:* http://www.gbs.edu/.

HEIDELBERG COLLEGE
Tiffin, Ohio

Heidelberg is a coed, private, comprehensive institution, founded in 1850, affiliated with the United Church of Christ, offering degrees at the bachelor's and master's levels. It has a 110-acre campus in Tiffin.

Academic Information The faculty has 118 members (56% full-time), 54% with terminal degrees. The undergraduate student-faculty ratio is 12:1. The library holds 260,055 titles and 829 serial subscriptions. Special programs include academic remediation, services for learning-disabled students, an honors program, study abroad, advanced placement credit, accelerated degree programs, ESL programs, double majors, summer session for credit, part-time degree programs (daytime, evenings, weekends, summer), adult/continuing education programs, internships, and arrangement for off-campus study with members of the East Central College Consortium. The most frequently chosen baccalaureate fields are business/marketing, biological/life sciences, education.
Student Body Statistics The student body totals 1,243, of whom 1,054 are undergraduates (319 freshmen). 52 percent are women and 48 percent are men. Students come from 22 states and territories and 10 other countries. 80 percent are from Ohio. 18 percent of the 2003 graduating class went on to graduate and professional schools.
Expenses for 2004–05 *Application fee:* $25. *Comprehensive fee:* $21,610 includes full-time tuition ($14,575), mandatory fees ($325), and college room and board ($6710). Full-time tuition and fees vary according to course load and location. Room and board charges vary according to board plan.
Financial Aid Forms of aid include need-based and non-need-based scholarships and part-time jobs. The average aided 2003–04 undergraduate received an aid package worth an estimated $16,974. The priority application deadline for financial aid is March 1.
Freshman Admission Heidelberg requires a high school transcript, a minimum 2.0 high school GPA, and SAT I or ACT scores. 2 recommendations, an interview, and TOEFL scores for international students are recommended.
Entrance Difficulty Heidelberg assesses its entrance difficulty level as moderately difficult. For the fall 2003 freshman class, 98 percent of the applicants were accepted.

For Further Information Contact Lindsay Sooy, Director of Admission, Heidelberg College, 310 East Market Street, Tiffin, OH 44883. *Telephone:* 419-448-2342 or 800-434-3352 (toll-free). *Fax:* 419-448-2334. *E-mail:* adminfo@heidelberg.edu. *Web site:* http://www.heidelberg.edu/.

See page 288 for a narrative description.

HIRAM COLLEGE
Hiram, Ohio

Hiram is a coed, private, four-year college, founded in 1850, affiliated with the Christian Church (Disciples of Christ), offering degrees at the bachelor's level. It has a 110-acre campus in Hiram near Cleveland.

Academic Information The faculty has 121 members (60% full-time), 64% with terminal degrees. The student-faculty ratio is 11:1. The library holds 187,451 titles, 3,993 serial subscriptions, and 10,351 audiovisual materials. Special programs include services for learning-disabled students, study abroad, advanced placement credit, accelerated degree programs, ESL programs, double majors, independent study, self-designed majors,

summer session for credit, part-time degree programs (weekends), adult/continuing education programs, internships, and arrangement for off-campus study. The most frequently chosen baccalaureate fields are business/marketing, computer/information sciences, social sciences and history.
Student Body Statistics The student body is made up of 1,110 undergraduates (236 freshmen). 58 percent are women and 42 percent are men. Students come from 31 states and territories and 20 other countries. 80 percent are from Ohio. 2.9 percent are international students.
Expenses for 2003–04 *Application fee:* $35. *Comprehensive fee:* $28,234 includes full-time tuition ($20,440), mandatory fees ($694), and college room and board ($7100). *College room only:* $3160. *Part-time tuition:* $682 per credit hour.
Financial Aid Forms of aid include need-based and non-need-based scholarships and part-time jobs. The average aided 2002–03 undergraduate received an aid package worth $21,218. The priority application deadline for financial aid is February 15.
Freshman Admission Hiram requires an essay, a high school transcript, 2 recommendations, SAT I or ACT scores, and TOEFL scores for international students. 3 recommendations and an interview are recommended. An interview is required for some. The application deadline for regular admission is February 1 and for early decision it is December 1.
Transfer Admission The application deadline for admission is July 15.
Entrance Difficulty Hiram assesses its entrance difficulty level as very difficult. For the fall 2003 freshman class, 88 percent of the applicants were accepted.

For Further Information Contact Ms. Brenda Swihart Meyer, Director of Admission, Hiram College, PO Box 96, Hiram, OH 44234. *Telephone:* 330-569-5169 or 800-362-5280 (toll-free). *Fax:* 330-569-5944. *E-mail:* admission@hiram.edu. *Web site:* http://www.hiram.edu/.

See page 290 for a narrative description.

JOHN CARROLL UNIVERSITY
University Heights, Ohio

John Carroll is a coed, private, Roman Catholic (Jesuit), comprehensive institution, founded in 1886, offering degrees at the bachelor's and master's levels. It has a 60-acre campus in University Heights near Cleveland.

Academic Information The faculty has 411 members (59% full-time). The undergraduate student-faculty ratio is 15:1. The library holds 620,000 titles, 2,198 serial subscriptions, and 5,820 audiovisual materials. Special programs include an honors program, cooperative (work-study) education, study abroad, advanced placement credit, accelerated degree programs, double majors, independent study, self-designed majors, summer session for credit, part-time degree programs, adult/continuing education programs, internships, and arrangement for off-campus study with Northeast Ohio Commission on Higher Education. The most frequently chosen baccalaureate fields are business/marketing, communications/communication technologies, social sciences and history.
Student Body Statistics The student body totals 4,242, of whom 3,279 are undergraduates. Students come from 35 states and territories. 73 percent are from Ohio. 22 percent of the 2003 graduating class went on to graduate and professional schools.
Expenses for 2003–04 *Application fee:* $25. *Comprehensive fee:* $27,658 includes full-time tuition ($20,566), mandatory fees ($200), and college room and board ($6892). Room and board charges vary according to board plan. *Part-time tuition:* varies with course load.
Financial Aid Forms of aid include need-based and non-need-based scholarships and part-time jobs. The priority application deadline for financial aid is March 1.
Freshman Admission John Carroll requires a high school transcript, 1 recommendation, SAT I or ACT scores, and TOEFL scores for international students. An essay and an interview are recommended. An interview is required for some. The application deadline for regular admission is February 1.
Transfer Admission The application deadline for admission is rolling.

John Carroll University (continued)

Entrance Difficulty John Carroll assesses its entrance difficulty level as moderately difficult. For the fall 2003 freshman class, 86 percent of the applicants were accepted.

For Further Information Contact Mr. Thomas P. Fanning, Director of Admission, John Carroll University, 20700 North Park Boulevard, University Heights, OH 44118. *Telephone:* 216-397-4294. *Fax:* 216-397-4981. *E-mail:* admission@jcu.edu. *Web site:* http://www.jcu.edu/.

KENT STATE UNIVERSITY
Kent, Ohio

Kent is a coed, public unit of Kent State University System, founded in 1910, offering degrees at the associate, bachelor's, master's, and doctoral levels and post-master's and postbachelor's certificates. It has a 1,347-acre campus in Kent near Cleveland.

Academic Information The faculty has 1,335 members (61% full-time), 47% with terminal degrees. The undergraduate student-faculty ratio is 20:1. The library holds 1 million titles, 8,771 serial subscriptions, and 27,447 audiovisual materials. Special programs include academic remediation, services for learning-disabled students, an honors program, cooperative (work-study) education, study abroad, advanced placement credit, accelerated degree programs, Freshman Honors College, ESL programs, double majors, independent study, distance learning, self-designed majors, summer session for credit, part-time degree programs (daytime, evenings, weekends, summer), adult/continuing education programs, internships, and arrangement for off-campus study with Cuyahoga Community College, Lorain County Community College, Lakeland Community College. The most frequently chosen baccalaureate fields are business/marketing, education, visual/performing arts.

Student Body Statistics The student body totals 23,536, of whom 19,173 are undergraduates (3,822 freshmen). 59 percent are women and 41 percent are men. Students come from 51 states and territories and 61 other countries. 92 percent are from Ohio. 0.9 percent are international students.

Expenses for 2003–04 *Application fee:* $30. *One-time mandatory fee:* $100. *State resident tuition:* $6882 full-time, $314 per credit hour part-time. *Nonresident tuition:* $13,314 full-time, $607 per credit hour part-time. Full-time tuition varies according to course level, course load, degree level, location, reciprocity agreements, and student level. Part-time tuition varies according to course level, course load, degree level, location, program, reciprocity agreements, and student level. *College room and board:* $7920. *College room only:* $3540. Room and board charges vary according to board plan and housing facility.

Financial Aid Forms of aid include need-based and non-need-based scholarships, athletic grants, and part-time jobs. The average aided 2003–04 undergraduate received an aid package worth an estimated $7151. The priority application deadline for financial aid is March 1.

Freshman Admission Kent requires a high school transcript, a minimum 2.5 high school GPA, SAT I or ACT scores, and TOEFL scores for international students. The application deadline for regular admission is May 1.

Entrance Difficulty Kent assesses its entrance difficulty level as moderately difficult; minimally difficult for transfers; very difficult for architecture, 6-year medical programs. For the fall 2003 freshman class, 89 percent of the applicants were accepted.

For Further Information Contact Mr. Christopher Buttenschon, Assistant Director of Admissions, Kent State University, 161 Michael Schwartz Center, Kent, OH 44242-0001. *Telephone:* 330-672-2444 or 800-988-KENT (toll-free). *Fax:* 330-672-2499. *E-mail:* admissions@kent.edu. *Web site:* http://www.kent.edu/.

KENT STATE UNIVERSITY, ASHTABULA CAMPUS
Ashtabula, Ohio

Kent Ashtabula is a coed, public, primarily two-year college of Kent State University System, founded in 1958, offering degrees at the associate and bachelor's levels (also offers some upper-level and graduate courses). It has a 120-acre campus in Ashtabula near Cleveland.

Expenses for 2004–05 *State resident tuition:* $4326 full-time. *Nonresident tuition:* $11,338 full-time.

For Further Information Contact Ms. Kelly Sanford, Director, Enrollment Management and Student Services, Kent State University, Ashtabula Campus, 3325 West 13th Street, Ashtabula, OH 44004-2299. *Telephone:* 440-964-4217. *Fax:* 440-964-4269. *E-mail:* robinson@ashtabula.kent.edu. *Web site:* http://www.ashtabula.kent.edu/.

KENT STATE UNIVERSITY, GEAUGA CAMPUS
Burton, Ohio

Kent State Geauga is a coed, public, primarily two-year college of Kent State University System, founded in 1964, offering degrees at the associate, bachelor's, and master's levels. It has an 87-acre campus in Burton near Cleveland.

Expenses for 2003–04 *Application fee:* $30. *State resident tuition:* $3968 full-time. *Nonresident tuition:* $10,400 full-time.

For Further Information Contact Ms. Betty Landrus, Admissions and Records Secretary, Kent State University, Geauga Campus, 14111 Claridon-Troy Road, Burton, OH 44021. *Telephone:* 440-834-4187. *Fax:* 440-834-8846. *E-mail:* cbaker@geauga.kent.edu. *Web site:* http://www.geauga.kent.edu/.

KENT STATE UNIVERSITY, SALEM CAMPUS
Salem, Ohio

Kent Salem is a coed, public, primarily two-year college of Kent State University System, founded in 1966, offering degrees at the associate and bachelor's levels (also offers some upper-level and graduate courses). It has a 98-acre campus in Salem.

Academic Information The faculty has 106 members (47% full-time). The student-faculty ratio is 13:1. The library holds 19,000 titles, 163 serial subscriptions, and 158 audiovisual materials. Special programs include academic remediation, services for learning-disabled students, an honors program, advanced placement credit, Freshman Honors College, distance learning, summer session for credit, part-time degree programs (daytime, evenings, weekends), adult/continuing education programs, and internships.

Student Body Statistics The student body totals 1,332, of whom 1,320 are undergraduates. Students come from 2 states and territories and 2 other countries.

Expenses for 2003–04 *Application fee:* $30. *State resident tuition:* $3968 full-time, $181 per credit part-time. *Nonresident tuition:* $10,400 full-time, $474 per credit part-time. Full-time tuition varies according to course level. Part-time tuition varies according to course level.

Financial Aid Forms of aid include need-based scholarships and part-time jobs. The priority application deadline for financial aid is March 1.

Freshman Admission Kent Salem requires a high school transcript and TOEFL scores for international students. SAT I or ACT scores are recommended. An essay, a minimum X high school GPA, recommendations, ACT scores, and SAT I or ACT scores are required for some. The application deadline for regular admission is rolling.

Transfer Admission The application deadline for admission is rolling.
Entrance Difficulty Kent Salem has an open admission policy except for radiological technology, human services programs, and honors program. It assesses its entrance difficulty as very difficult for radiological technology, human services programs.

For Further Information Contact Mrs. Judy Heisler, Admissions Secretary, Kent State University, Salem Campus, 2491 State Route 45 South, Salem, OH 44460-9412. *Telephone:* 330-332-0361. *Fax:* 330-332-9256. *Web site:* http://www.salem.kent.edu/.

KENT STATE UNIVERSITY, STARK CAMPUS

Canton, Ohio

Kent Stark is a coed, public, primarily two-year college of Kent State University System, founded in 1967, offering degrees at the associate and bachelor's levels (also offers some graduate courses). It has a 200-acre campus in Canton near Cleveland.

Academic Information The faculty has 200 members (42% full-time). The student-faculty ratio is 19:1. The library holds 72,807 titles and 313 serial subscriptions. Special programs include academic remediation, services for learning-disabled students, an honors program, study abroad, advanced placement credit, Freshman Honors College, ESL programs, independent study, self-designed majors, summer session for credit, part-time degree programs (daytime, evenings, weekends, summer), adult/continuing education programs, internships, and arrangement for off-campus study with Stark State College of Technology.
Student Body Statistics The student body is made up of 3,736 undergraduates. Students come from 2 states and territories.
Expenses for 2003–04 *Application fee:* $30. *State resident tuition:* $3968 full-time, $181 per hour part-time. *Nonresident tuition:* $10,400 full-time, $474 per hour part-time.
Financial Aid Forms of aid include need-based scholarships and part-time jobs. The priority application deadline for financial aid is March 1.
Freshman Admission Kent Stark requires a high school transcript and TOEFL scores for international students. An interview and SAT I or ACT scores are required for some. The application deadline for regular admission is rolling.
Transfer Admission The application deadline for admission is rolling.
Entrance Difficulty Kent Stark has an open admission policy.

For Further Information Contact Ms. Deborah Ann Speck, Director of Admissions, Kent State University, Stark Campus, 6000 Frank Avenue NW, Canton, OH 44720-7599. *Telephone:* 330-244-3259. *Fax:* 330-499-0301. *E-mail:* aspeck@stark.kent.edu. *Web site:* http://www.stark.kent.edu/.

KENT STATE UNIVERSITY, TUSCARAWAS CAMPUS

New Philadelphia, Ohio

Kent Tuscarawas is a coed, public, primarily two-year college of Kent State University System, founded in 1962, offering degrees at the associate, bachelor's, and master's levels (also offers some upper-level and graduate courses). It has a 172-acre campus in New Philadelphia near Cleveland.

Academic Information The faculty has 144 members (31% full-time), 24% with terminal degrees. The undergraduate student-faculty ratio is 16:1. The library holds 58,946 titles, 400 serial subscriptions, and 520 audiovisual materials. Special programs include academic remediation, services for learning-disabled students, an honors program, advanced placement credit, accelerated degree programs, Freshman Honors College, double majors, distance learning, self-designed majors, summer session for credit, part-time degree programs (daytime, evenings, weekends, summer), adult/continuing education programs, and internships. The most frequently chosen baccalaureate fields are business/marketing, engineering/engineering technologies, health professions and related sciences.
Student Body Statistics The student body totals 2,019, of whom 2,008 are undergraduates.
Expenses for 2003–04 *Application fee:* $30. *State resident tuition:* $3968 full-time, $181 per credit part-time. *Nonresident tuition:* $10,400 full-time, $474 per credit part-time. Full-time tuition varies according to course level, course load, and location. Part-time tuition varies according to course level, course load, and location.
Financial Aid Forms of aid include need-based scholarships and part-time jobs. The priority application deadline for financial aid is March 1.
Freshman Admission Kent Tuscarawas requires a high school transcript and TOEFL scores for international students. SAT I or ACT scores are required for some. The application deadline for regular admission is September 1.
Transfer Admission The application deadline for admission is September 1.
Entrance Difficulty Kent Tuscarawas has an open admission policy except for business administration, education, nursing, fine and performing arts programs. It assesses its entrance difficulty as moderately difficult for nursing, education, business administration, fine and performing arts programs.

For Further Information Contact Ms. Denise L. Testa, Director of Admissions, Kent State University, Tuscarawas Campus, 330 University Drive NE, New Philadelphia, OH 44663-9403. *Telephone:* 330-339-3391 Ext. 47425. *Fax:* 330-339-3321. *Web site:* http://www.tusc.kent.edu/.

KENYON COLLEGE

Gambier, Ohio

Kenyon is a coed, private, four-year college, founded in 1824, offering degrees at the bachelor's level. It has a 1,200-acre campus in Gambier near Columbus.

Academic Information The faculty has 168 members (86% full-time), 93% with terminal degrees. The student-faculty ratio is 10:1. The library holds 858,000 titles, 5,300 serial subscriptions, and 171,230 audiovisual materials. Special programs include services for learning-disabled students, an honors program, study abroad, advanced placement credit, accelerated degree programs, double majors, independent study, self-designed majors, internships, and arrangement for off-campus study. The most frequently chosen baccalaureate fields are English, social sciences and history, visual/performing arts.
Student Body Statistics The student body is made up of 1,612 undergraduates (454 freshmen). 55 percent are women and 45 percent are men. 22 percent are from Ohio. 2.4 percent are international students. 25 percent of the 2003 graduating class went on to graduate and professional schools.
Expenses for 2003–04 *Application fee:* $45. *Comprehensive fee:* $35,370 includes full-time tuition ($29,500), mandatory fees ($830), and college room and board ($5040). *College room only:* $2340. Room and board charges vary according to housing facility.
Financial Aid Forms of aid include need-based and non-need-based scholarships and part-time jobs. The average aided 2003–04 undergraduate received an aid package worth an estimated $22,151. The priority application deadline for financial aid is February 15.
Freshman Admission Kenyon requires an essay, a high school transcript, a minimum 2.0 high school GPA, 1 recommendation, SAT I or ACT scores, and TOEFL scores for international students. A minimum 3.0 high school GPA, 2 recommendations, and an interview are recommended. The application deadline for regular admission is February 1; for early decision plan 1 it is December 1; and for early decision plan 2 it is January 15.
Transfer Admission The application deadline for admission is June 1.

Kenyon College (continued)

Entrance Difficulty Kenyon assesses its entrance difficulty level as very difficult. For the fall 2003 freshman class, 46 percent of the applicants were accepted.

For Further Information Contact Ms. Jennifer Britz, Dean of Admissions, Kenyon College, Ransom Hall, Gambier, OH 43022. *Telephone:* 740-427-5776 or 800-848-2468 (toll-free). *Fax:* 740-427-5770. *E-mail:* admissions@kenyon.edu. *Web site:* http://www.kenyon.edu/.

KETTERING COLLEGE OF MEDICAL ARTS
Kettering, Ohio

KCMA is a coed, primarily women's, private, Seventh-day Adventist, primarily two-year college, founded in 1967, offering degrees at the associate and bachelor's levels and postbachelor's certificates. It has a 35-acre campus in Kettering.

Academic Information The faculty has 51 members (49% full-time), 22% with terminal degrees. The library holds 29,390 titles and 266 serial subscriptions. Special programs include advanced placement credit, summer session for credit, part-time degree programs (daytime, evenings), internships, and arrangement for off-campus study with members of the Southwestern Ohio Council for Higher Education.

Student Body Statistics The student body is made up of 653 undergraduates. Students come from 29 states and territories and 3 other countries. 0.5 percent are international students.

Expenses for 2004–05 *Application fee:* $25. *Comprehensive fee:* $18,138 includes full-time tuition ($10,824), mandatory fees ($960), and college room and board ($6354). *College room only:* $2994. *Part-time tuition:* $260 per credit hour. *Part-time mandatory fees:* $110.

Financial Aid Forms of aid include need-based scholarships and part-time jobs. The priority application deadline for financial aid is March 31.

Freshman Admission KCMA requires a high school transcript, a minimum 2.0 high school GPA, 3 recommendations, ACT scores, and TOEFL scores for international students. A minimum 3.0 high school GPA, an interview, and SAT I scores are recommended. The application deadline for regular admission is rolling.

Transfer Admission The application deadline for admission is rolling.

Entrance Difficulty KCMA assesses its entrance difficulty level as moderately difficult; most difficult for physician's assistant program.

For Further Information Contact Mr. David Lofthouse, Director of Enrollment Services, Kettering College of Medical Arts, 3737 Southern Boulevard, Kettering, OH 45429-1299. *Telephone:* 937-296-7228 or 800-433-5262 (toll-free). *Fax:* 937-296-4238. *Web site:* http://www.kcma.edu/.

LAKE ERIE COLLEGE
Painesville, Ohio

Lake Erie is a coed, private, comprehensive institution, founded in 1856, offering degrees at the bachelor's and master's levels. It has a 57-acre campus in Painesville near Cleveland.

Academic Information The faculty has 81 members (37% full-time), 43% with terminal degrees. The undergraduate student-faculty ratio is 12:1. The library holds 86,600 titles, 6,020 serial subscriptions, and 1,093 audiovisual materials. Special programs include academic remediation, services for learning-disabled students, cooperative (work-study) education, study abroad, advanced placement credit, accelerated degree programs, double majors, independent study, self-designed majors, summer session for credit, part-time degree programs (daytime, evenings, weekends, summer), external degree programs, adult/continuing education programs, internships, and arrangement for off-campus study with Northeast Ohio Commission on Higher Education.

Student Body Statistics The student body totals 859, of whom 720 are undergraduates (121 freshmen). 76 percent are women and 24 percent are men. Students come from 22 states and territories and 5 other countries. 84 percent are from Ohio.

Expenses for 2003–04 *Application fee:* $25. *Comprehensive fee:* $23,550 includes full-time tuition ($16,880), mandatory fees ($840), and college room and board ($5830). *College room only:* $3120. Full-time tuition and fees vary according to course load and program. Room and board charges vary according to board plan. *Part-time tuition:* $460 per credit hour. *Part-time mandatory fees:* $25 per credit hour.

Financial Aid Forms of aid include need-based and non-need-based scholarships and part-time jobs. The application deadline for financial aid is continuous.

Freshman Admission Lake Erie requires a high school transcript, a minimum 2.0 high school GPA, SAT I or ACT scores, and TOEFL scores for international students. An interview is recommended.

Entrance Difficulty Lake Erie assesses its entrance difficulty level as minimally difficult. For the fall 2003 freshman class, 55 percent of the applicants were accepted.

For Further Information Contact Jennifer Calhoun, Director of Admissions, Lake Erie College, 391 West Washington Street, Painesville, OH 44077-3389. *Telephone:* 440-375-7055 or 800-916-0904 (toll-free). *Fax:* 440-375-7005. *E-mail:* admissions@lec.edu. *Web site:* http://www.lec.edu/.

LAURA AND ALVIN SIEGAL COLLEGE OF JUDAIC STUDIES
Beachwood, Ohio

Siegal College is a coed, private, comprehensive institution, founded in 1963, offering degrees at the bachelor's and master's levels. It has a 2-acre campus in Beachwood near Cleveland.

Academic Information The faculty has 40 members (28% full-time), 52% with terminal degrees. The undergraduate student-faculty ratio is 8:1. The library holds 28,000 titles and 100 serial subscriptions. Special programs include cooperative (work-study) education, double majors, independent study, distance learning, summer session for credit, part-time degree programs, external degree programs, adult/continuing education programs, internships, and arrangement for off-campus study with John Carroll University, Ursuline College, Case Western Reserve University.

Student Body Statistics The student body totals 160, of whom 17 are undergraduates (4 freshmen). 88 percent are women and 12 percent are men. Students come from 1 state or territory.

Expenses for 2003–04 *Application fee:* $50. *Tuition:* $9750 full-time, $325 per credit part-time. *Mandatory fees:* $25 full-time, $25 per year part-time. Full-time tuition and fees vary according to course load. Part-time tuition and fees vary according to course load.

Financial Aid Forms of aid include need-based and non-need-based scholarships. The average aided 2003–04 undergraduate received an aid package worth an estimated $500. The application deadline for financial aid is continuous.

Freshman Admission Siegal College requires an essay, a high school transcript, 2 recommendations, and an interview. The application deadline for regular admission is rolling.

Transfer Admission The application deadline for admission is rolling.

Entrance Difficulty Siegal College has an open admission policy.

For Further Information Contact Ms. Linda L. Rosen, Director of Student Services, Laura and Alvin Siegal College of Judaic Studies, 26500 Shaker Boulevard, Beachwood, OH 44122-7116. *Telephone:* 216-464-4050 Ext. 101 or 888-336-2257 (toll-free). *Fax:* 216-464-5827. *E-mail:* admissions@siegalcollege.edu. *Web site:* http://www.siegalcollege.edu/.

LOURDES COLLEGE
Sylvania, Ohio

Lourdes is a coed, private, Roman Catholic, comprehensive institution, founded in 1958, offering degrees at the associate, bachelor's, and master's levels. It has a 90-acre campus in Sylvania near Toledo.

Academic Information The faculty has 125 members (48% full-time), 26% with terminal degrees. The undergraduate student-faculty ratio is 14:1. The library holds 57,730 titles, 448 serial subscriptions, and 1,571 audiovisual materials. Special programs include academic remediation, services for learning-disabled students, cooperative (work-study) education, study abroad, advanced placement credit, accelerated degree programs, double majors, independent study, self-designed majors, summer session for credit, part-time degree programs (daytime, evenings, weekends, summer), adult/continuing education programs, and internships. The most frequently chosen baccalaureate fields are business/marketing, education, health professions and related sciences.

Student Body Statistics The student body totals 1,249, of whom 1,202 are undergraduates (62 freshmen). 84 percent are women and 16 percent are men. Students come from 2 states and territories and 1 other country. 91 percent are from Ohio. 0.1 percent are international students. 24 percent of the 2003 graduating class went on to graduate and professional schools.

Expenses for 2003–04 *Application fee:* $25. *Tuition:* $14,200 full-time, $330 per credit hour part-time. *Mandatory fees:* $900 full-time, $40 per credit hour part-time. Full-time tuition and fees vary according to course load and program. Part-time tuition and fees vary according to course load and program.

Financial Aid Forms of aid include need-based and non-need-based scholarships and part-time jobs. The average aided 2003–04 undergraduate received an aid package worth an estimated $13,596. The priority application deadline for financial aid is March 7.

Freshman Admission Lourdes requires a high school transcript, SAT I or ACT scores, and TOEFL scores for international students. An interview is required for some. The application deadline for regular admission is rolling.

Transfer Admission The application deadline for admission is rolling.

Entrance Difficulty Lourdes assesses its entrance difficulty level as moderately difficult; minimally difficult for transfers. For the fall 2003 freshman class, 25 percent of the applicants were accepted.

For Further Information Contact Ms. Amy Mergen, Office of Admissions, Lourdes College, 6832 Convent Boulevard, Sylvania, OH 43560. *Telephone:* 419-885-5291 or 800-878-3210 Ext. 1299 (toll-free). *Fax:* 419-882-3987. *E-mail:* lcadmits@lourdes.edu. *Web site:* http://www.lourdes.edu/.

MALONE COLLEGE
Canton, Ohio

Malone is a coed, private, comprehensive institution, founded in 1892, affiliated with the Evangelical Friends Church–Eastern Region, offering degrees at the bachelor's and master's levels. It has a 78-acre campus in Canton near Cleveland.

Academic Information The faculty has 199 members (50% full-time), 39% with terminal degrees. The undergraduate student-faculty ratio is 14:1. The library holds 158,974 titles, 1,517 serial subscriptions, and 9,693 audiovisual materials. Special programs include academic remediation, services for learning-disabled students, an honors program, cooperative (work-study) education, study abroad, advanced placement credit, accelerated degree programs, double majors, independent study, distance learning, self-designed majors, summer session for credit, part-time degree programs (daytime, evenings, summer), adult/continuing education programs, internships, and arrangement for off-campus study with members of the Christian College Consortium, Council for Christian Colleges and Universities. The most frequently chosen baccalaureate fields are business/marketing, education, health professions and related sciences.

Student Body Statistics The student body totals 2,206, of whom 1,937 are undergraduates (401 freshmen). 61 percent are women and 39 percent are men. Students come from 24 states and territories and 12 other countries. 90 percent are from Ohio. 0.7 percent are international students. 39 percent of the 2003 graduating class went on to graduate and professional schools.

Expenses for 2003–04 *Application fee:* $20. *Comprehensive fee:* $20,995 includes full-time tuition ($14,745), mandatory fees ($250), and college room and board ($6000). *College room only:* $3200. Room and board charges vary according to board plan. *Part-time tuition:* $315 per semester hour. *Part-time mandatory fees:* $62.50 per term. Part-time tuition and fees vary according to course load.

Financial Aid Forms of aid include need-based and non-need-based scholarships, athletic grants, and part-time jobs. The average aided 2003–04 undergraduate received an aid package worth an estimated $11,365. The application deadline for financial aid is July 31 with a priority deadline of March 1.

Freshman Admission Malone requires an essay, a high school transcript, a minimum 2.5 high school GPA, SAT I or ACT scores, and TOEFL scores for international students. An interview is required for some. The application deadline for regular admission is July 1.

Transfer Admission The application deadline for admission is July 1.

Entrance Difficulty Malone assesses its entrance difficulty level as moderately difficult. For the fall 2003 freshman class, 85 percent of the applicants were accepted.

For Further Information Contact Mr. John Russell, Director of Admissions, Malone College, 515 25th Street, NW, Canton, OH 44709-3897. *Telephone:* 330-471-8145 or 800-521-1146 (toll-free). *Fax:* 330-471-8149. *E-mail:* admissions@malone.edu. *Web site:* http://www.malone.edu/.

MARIETTA COLLEGE
Marietta, Ohio

Marietta is a coed, private, comprehensive institution, founded in 1835, offering degrees at the associate, bachelor's, and master's levels. It has a 120-acre campus in Marietta.

Academic Information The faculty has 116 members (67% full-time), 66% with terminal degrees. The undergraduate student-faculty ratio is 12:1. The library holds 250,000 titles, 7,100 serial subscriptions, and 5,800 audiovisual materials. Special programs include academic remediation, services for learning-disabled students, an honors program, study abroad, advanced placement credit, accelerated degree programs, ESL programs, double majors, independent study, self-designed majors, summer session for credit, part-time degree programs (daytime, evenings, summer), adult/continuing education programs, internships, and arrangement for off-campus study with American University, Stillman College, Central College, Institute of European Studies, Institute of Asian Studies. The most frequently chosen baccalaureate fields are business/marketing, education, social sciences and history.

Student Body Statistics The student body totals 1,341, of whom 1,222 are undergraduates (378 freshmen). 49 percent are women and 51 percent are men. Students come from 42 states and territories and 13 other countries. 50 percent are from Ohio. 5.7 percent are international students. 30 percent of the 2003 graduating class went on to graduate and professional schools.

Expenses for 2003–04 *Application fee:* $25. *Comprehensive fee:* $26,838 includes full-time tuition ($20,356), mandatory fees ($536), and college room and board ($5946). *College room only:* $3176. Room and board charges vary according to board plan. *Part-time tuition:* $676 per credit. Part-time tuition varies according to class time.

Financial Aid Forms of aid include need-based and non-need-based scholarships and part-time jobs. The average aided 2003–04 undergraduate received an aid package worth an estimated $17,671. The priority application deadline for financial aid is March 1.

Freshman Admission Marietta requires an essay, a high school transcript, a minimum 2.0 high school GPA, 2 recommendations, SAT I or ACT scores, and TOEFL scores for international students. A minimum 3.0 high school GPA, an interview, and SAT II: Subject Test scores are recommended. The application deadline for regular admission is April 15.

Transfer Admission The application deadline for admission is rolling.

Entrance Difficulty Marietta assesses its entrance difficulty level as moderately difficult. For the fall 2003 freshman class, 78 percent of the applicants were accepted.

For Further Information Contact Ms. Marke Vickers, Director of Admission, Marietta College, 215 Fifth Street, Marietta, OH 45750. *Telephone:* 740-376-4600 or 800-331-7896 (toll-free). *Fax:* 740-376-8888. *E-mail:* admit@marietta.edu. *Web site:* http://www.marietta.edu/.

THE MCGREGOR SCHOOL OF ANTIOCH UNIVERSITY

See Antioch University McGregor

MEDCENTRAL COLLEGE OF NURSING
Mansfield, Ohio

MedCentral College of Nursing is a coed, primarily women's, private, four-year college, founded in 1996, offering degrees at the bachelor's level. It is located in Mansfield near Cleveland Ohio.

Academic Information The faculty has 8 members (88% full-time). The student-faculty ratio is 15:1.
Student Body Statistics The student body is made up of 153 undergraduates (59 freshmen). 90 percent are women and 10 percent are men. Students come from 1 state or territory.
Expenses for 2003–04 *Application fee:* $50. *Tuition:* $6658 full-time.
Freshman Admission MedCentral College of Nursing requires a high school transcript, a minimum 2.6 high school GPA, and SAT I or ACT scores. A minimum 3.0 high school GPA is recommended. An essay and an interview are required for some. The application deadline for regular admission is August 1.
Transfer Admission The application deadline for admission is August 1.
Entrance Difficulty For the fall 2003 freshman class, 58 percent of the applicants were accepted.

For Further Information Contact Mr. Mark A. Fegley, Associate Director for Enrollment Services, MedCentral College of Nursing, 335 Glessner Avenue, Mansfield, OH 44903. *Telephone:* 877-656-4360 or 877-656-4360 (toll-free). *Fax:* 419-520-2610. *E-mail:* mfegley@medcentral.edu. *Web site:* http://www.medcentral.edu/.

MERCY COLLEGE OF NORTHWEST OHIO
Toledo, Ohio

Mercy College of Northwest Ohio is a coed, primarily women's, private, primarily two-year college, founded in 1993, affiliated with the Roman Catholic Church, offering degrees at the associate and bachelor's levels. It is located in Toledo near Detroit.

Academic Information The faculty has 43 members (100% full-time), 21% with terminal degrees. The student-faculty ratio is 13:1. The library holds 5,900 titles, 171 serial subscriptions, and 331 audiovisual materials. Special programs include academic remediation, services for learning-disabled students, advanced placement credit, independent study, summer session for credit, part-time degree programs (daytime, evenings, summer), and internships. The most frequently chosen baccalaureate field is health professions and related sciences.
Student Body Statistics The student body is made up of 565 undergraduates (66 freshmen). 91 percent are women and 9 percent are men. Students come from 5 states and territories. 88 percent are from Ohio.
Expenses for 2003–04 *Application fee:* $25. *One-time mandatory fee:* $60. *Tuition:* $6234 full-time, $242 per credit hour part-time. *Mandatory fees:* $160 full-time, $5 per credit hour part-time. Full-time tuition and fees vary according to course load. Part-time tuition and fees vary according to course load. *College room only:* $2800. Room charges vary according to housing facility.
Financial Aid Forms of aid include need-based scholarships and part-time jobs. The application deadline for financial aid is continuous.
Freshman Admission Mercy College of Northwest Ohio requires a high school transcript. SAT I or ACT scores are recommended. A minimum 2.3 high school GPA and SAT I or ACT scores are required for some. The application deadline for regular admission is rolling.
Transfer Admission The application deadline for admission is rolling.

Entrance Difficulty Mercy College of Northwest Ohio assesses its entrance difficulty level as moderately difficult. For the fall 2003 freshman class, 79 percent of the applicants were accepted.

For Further Information Contact Ms. Janice Bernard, Secretary, Mercy College of Northwest Ohio, 2221 Madison Avenue, Toledo, OH 43624-1197. *Telephone:* 419-251-1313 Ext. 11203 or 888-80-Mercy (toll-free). *Fax:* 419-251-1462. *E-mail:* admissions@mercycollege.edu. *Web site:* http://www.mercycollege.edu/.

MIAMI UNIVERSITY
Oxford, Ohio

Miami University is a coed, public unit of Miami University System, founded in 1809, offering degrees at the associate, bachelor's, master's, and doctoral levels and post-master's certificates. It has a 2,000-acre campus in Oxford near Cincinnati.

Academic Information The faculty has 1,137 members (73% full-time), 73% with terminal degrees. The undergraduate student-faculty ratio is 18:1. The library holds 3 million titles, 14,089 serial subscriptions, and 143,868 audiovisual materials. Special programs include services for learning-disabled students, an honors program, cooperative (work-study) education, study abroad, advanced placement credit, double majors, independent study, self-designed majors, summer session for credit, adult/continuing education programs, internships, and arrangement for off-campus study with Greater Cincinnati Consortium of Colleges and Universities. The most frequently chosen baccalaureate fields are business/marketing, education, social sciences and history.
Student Body Statistics The student body totals 16,795, of whom 15,174 are undergraduates (3,309 freshmen). 54 percent are women and 46 percent are men. Students come from 48 states and territories and 59 other countries. 72 percent are from Ohio. 0.8 percent are international students.
Expenses for 2003–04 *Application fee:* $45. *State resident tuition:* $7019 full-time. *Nonresident tuition:* $16,789 full-time. *Mandatory fees:* $1334 full-time. *College room and board:* $6680. *College room only:* $3340.
Financial Aid Forms of aid include need-based and non-need-based scholarships, athletic grants, and part-time jobs. The average aided 2003–04 undergraduate received an aid package worth an estimated $7090. The priority application deadline for financial aid is February 15.
Freshman Admission Miami University requires a high school transcript, SAT I or ACT scores, and TOEFL scores for international students. An essay and 1 recommendation are recommended. The application deadline for regular admission is January 31 and for early decision it is November 1.
Transfer Admission The application deadline for admission is May 1.
Entrance Difficulty Miami University assesses its entrance difficulty level as moderately difficult; noncompetitive for district residents. For the fall 2003 freshman class, 71 percent of the applicants were accepted.

For Further Information Contact Mr. Michael E. Mills, Director of Undergraduate Admissions, Miami University, 301 South Campus Avenue, Oxford, OH 45056. *Telephone:* 513-529-5040. *Fax:* 513-529-1550. *E-mail:* admission@muohio.edu. *Web site:* http://www.muohio.edu/.

MIAMI UNIVERSITY HAMILTON
Hamilton, Ohio

Miami University Hamilton is a coed, public, primarily two-year college of Miami University System, founded in 1968, offering degrees at the associate, bachelor's, and master's levels (degrees awarded by Miami University main campus). It has a 78-acre campus in Hamilton near Cincinnati.

Academic Information The faculty has 222 members (41% full-time). The undergraduate student-faculty ratio is 15:1. The library holds 68,000 titles and 400 serial subscriptions. Special programs include academic remediation, services for learning-disabled students, an honors program, cooperative (work-study) education, study abroad, advanced placement credit, ESL programs, double majors, self-designed majors, summer session for credit, part-time degree programs (daytime, evenings, weekends, summer), adult/continuing education programs, and internships.

Student Body Statistics The student body totals 3,405, of whom 3,322 are undergraduates (649 freshmen). 57 percent are women and 43 percent are men.

Expenses for 2003–04 *Application fee:* $25. *State resident tuition:* $3150 full-time, $131.25 per credit part-time. *Nonresident tuition:* $12,901 full-time, $537.54 per credit part-time. *Mandatory fees:* $382 full-time, $14.50 per credit part-time, $17 per term part-time.

Financial Aid Forms of aid include need-based scholarships and part-time jobs. The application deadline for financial aid is continuous.

Freshman Admission Miami University Hamilton requires a high school transcript and TOEFL scores for international students. SAT I or ACT scores are required for some. The application deadline for regular admission is rolling.

Entrance Difficulty Miami University Hamilton has an open admission policy except for nursing program, transfer students. It assesses its entrance difficulty as minimally difficult for transfers; moderately difficult for nursing program.

For Further Information Contact Ms. Triana Adlon, Director of Admission and Financial Aid, Miami University Hamilton, 1601 Peck Boulevard, Hamilton, OH 45011-3399. *Telephone:* 513-785-3111. *Fax:* 513-785-3148. *E-mail:* adlontm@muohio.edu. *Web site:* http://www.ham.muohio.edu/.

MIAMI UNIVERSITY–MIDDLETOWN CAMPUS
Middletown, Ohio

Miami University–Middletown Campus is a coed, public, primarily two-year college of Miami University System, founded in 1966, offering degrees at the associate and bachelor's levels (also offers up to 2 years of most bachelor's degree programs offered at Miami University main campus). It has a 141-acre campus in Middletown near Cincinnati and Dayton.

Expenses for 2003–04 *Application fee:* $25. *State resident tuition:* $3498 full-time, $145.75 per credit hour part-time. *Nonresident tuition:* $13,248 full-time, $552 per credit hour part-time. *Mandatory fees:* $201 full-time. Full-time tuition and fees vary according to student level. Part-time tuition varies according to student level.

For Further Information Contact Mrs. Mary Lou Flynn, Director of Enrollment Services, Miami University–Middletown Campus, 4200 East University Boulevard, Middletown, OH 45042. *Telephone:* 513-727-3346 or 800-622-2262 (toll-free in-state). *Fax:* 513-727-3223. *E-mail:* flynnml@muohio.edu. *Web site:* http://www.mid.muohio.edu/.

MOUNT CARMEL COLLEGE OF NURSING
Columbus, Ohio

Mount Carmel College of Nursing is a coed, primarily women's, private, comprehensive institution, offering degrees at the bachelor's and master's levels.

Expenses for 2004–05 *Application fee:* $30. *Tuition:* $14,520 full-time. *Mandatory fees:* $292 full-time. *College room only:* $1870.

For Further Information Contact Ms. Merchel Menefield, Director of Admissions, Mount Carmel College of Nursing, 127 South Davis Avenue, Columbus, OH 43222. *Telephone:* 614-234-5800. *Web site:* http://www.mccn.edu/.

MOUNT UNION COLLEGE
Alliance, Ohio

Mount Union is a coed, private, United Methodist, four-year college, founded in 1846, offering degrees at the bachelor's level. It has a 105-acre campus in Alliance near Cleveland.

Academic Information The faculty has 211 members (60% full-time), 55% with terminal degrees. The student-faculty ratio is 14:1. The library holds 228,850 titles, 972 serial subscriptions, and 500 audiovisual materials. Special programs include services for learning-disabled students, an honors program, cooperative (work-study) education, study abroad, advanced placement credit, accelerated degree programs, ESL programs, double majors, independent study, self-designed majors, summer session for credit, part-time degree programs (daytime, evenings, summer), external degree programs, adult/continuing education programs, internships, and arrangement for off-campus study with 6 members of the East Central College Consortium. The most frequently chosen baccalaureate fields are business/marketing, education, social sciences and history.

Student Body Statistics The student body is made up of 2,425 undergraduates (586 freshmen). 55 percent are women and 45 percent are men. Students come from 26 states and territories and 12 other countries. 91 percent are from Ohio. 1.1 percent are international students. 29.4 percent of the 2003 graduating class went on to graduate and professional schools.

Expenses for 2004–05 *Application fee:* $20. *Comprehensive fee:* $24,440 includes full-time tuition ($18,560), mandatory fees ($250), and college room and board ($5630). *College room only:* $2360. Room and board charges vary according to housing facility. *Part-time tuition:* $775 per semester hour. *Part-time mandatory fees:* $50 per term.

Financial Aid Forms of aid include need-based and non-need-based scholarships and part-time jobs. The average aided 2003–04 undergraduate received an aid package worth an estimated $15,324. The application deadline for financial aid is continuous.

Freshman Admission Mount Union requires an essay, a high school transcript, a minimum 2.0 high school GPA, 1 recommendation, SAT I or ACT scores, and TOEFL scores for international students. An interview is recommended. The application deadline for regular admission is rolling.

Transfer Admission The application deadline for admission is rolling.

Entrance Difficulty Mount Union assesses its entrance difficulty level as moderately difficult. For the fall 2003 freshman class, 75 percent of the applicants were accepted.

For Further Information Contact Mr. Vince Heslop, Director of Admissions, Mount Union College, 1972 Clark Avenue, Alliance, OH 44601. *Telephone:* 330-823-2590, 800-334-6682 (toll-free in-state), or 800-992-6682 (toll-free out-of-state). *Fax:* 330-823-3487. *E-mail:* admissn@muc.edu. *Web site:* http://www.muc.edu/.

MOUNT VERNON NAZARENE UNIVERSITY
Mount Vernon, Ohio

MVNU is a coed, private, Nazarene, comprehensive institution, founded in 1964, offering degrees at the associate, bachelor's, and master's levels. It has a 401-acre campus in Mount Vernon near Columbus.

Academic Information The faculty has 214 members (41% full-time), 40% with terminal degrees. The undergraduate student-faculty ratio is 17:1. The library holds 92,169 titles, 586 serial subscriptions, and 4,744 audiovisual materials. Special programs include academic remediation, services for learning-disabled students, an honors program, study abroad, advanced placement credit, Freshman Honors College, double majors, independent study, summer session for credit, part-time degree programs (evenings), adult/continuing education programs, internships, and arrangement for off-campus study with Kenyon College, Capital University, Coalition for Christian Colleges and Universities. The most frequently chosen baccalaureate fields are business/marketing, education, philosophy, religion, and theology.

Student Body Statistics The student body totals 2,392, of whom 2,206 are undergraduates (375 freshmen). 57 percent are women and 43 percent are men. Students come from 24 states and territories. 90 percent are from

Mount Vernon Nazarene University (continued)

Ohio. 0.2 percent are international students. 26 percent of the 2003 graduating class went on to graduate and professional schools.

Expenses for 2004–05 *Application fee:* $25. *Comprehensive fee:* $19,710 includes full-time tuition ($14,482), mandatory fees ($494), and college room and board ($4734). *College room only:* $2619. Full-time tuition and fees vary according to course load and program. Room and board charges vary according to board plan and housing facility. *Part-time tuition:* varies with course load, program.

Financial Aid Forms of aid include need-based and non-need-based scholarships, athletic grants, and part-time jobs. The average aided 2003–04 undergraduate received an aid package worth an estimated $10,581. The priority application deadline for financial aid is March 15.

Freshman Admission MVNU requires an essay, a high school transcript, a minimum 2.5 high school GPA, 2 recommendations, SAT I or ACT scores, and TOEFL scores for international students. An interview is recommended. The application deadline for regular admission is May 31.

Entrance Difficulty MVNU assesses its entrance difficulty level as moderately difficult. For the fall 2003 freshman class, 86 percent of the applicants were accepted.

For Further Information Contact Mr. Tim Eades, Director of Admissions and Student Recruitment, Mount Vernon Nazarene University, 800 Martinsburg Road, Mount Vernon, OH 43050. *Telephone:* 740-392-6868 Ext. 4511 or 866-462-6868 (toll-free). *Fax:* 740-393-0511. *E-mail:* admissions@mvnu.edu. *Web site:* http://www.mvnu.edu/.

MUSKINGUM COLLEGE

New Concord, Ohio

Muskingum is a coed, private, comprehensive institution, founded in 1837, affiliated with the Presbyterian Church (U.S.A.), offering degrees at the bachelor's and master's levels. It has a 215-acre campus in New Concord near Columbus.

Academic Information The faculty has 129 members (74% full-time), 71% with terminal degrees. The undergraduate student-faculty ratio is 16:1. The library holds 233,000 titles, 900 serial subscriptions, and 6,000 audiovisual materials. Special programs include services for learning-disabled students, study abroad, advanced placement credit, accelerated degree programs, ESL programs, double majors, independent study, self-designed majors, summer session for credit, part-time degree programs (daytime, evenings, summer), external degree programs, internships, and arrangement for off-campus study with Case Western Reserve University. The most frequently chosen baccalaureate fields are business/marketing, education, social sciences and history.

Student Body Statistics The student body totals 2,142, of whom 1,622 are undergraduates (386 freshmen). 50 percent are women and 50 percent are men. Students come from 26 states and territories and 19 other countries. 88 percent are from Ohio. 2.3 percent are international students.

Expenses for 2004–05 *Application fee:* $0. *Comprehensive fee:* $21,830 includes full-time tuition ($14,920), mandatory fees ($710), and college room and board ($6200). Room and board charges vary according to board plan and housing facility. *Part-time tuition:* $280 per credit hour. Part-time tuition varies according to course load.

Financial Aid Forms of aid include need-based and non-need-based scholarships and part-time jobs. The average aided 2003–04 undergraduate received an aid package worth an estimated $13,767. The priority application deadline for financial aid is March 15.

Freshman Admission Muskingum requires a high school transcript, a minimum 2.0 high school GPA, 1 recommendation, SAT I or ACT scores, and TOEFL scores for international students. An essay, a minimum 3.0 high school GPA, and an interview are recommended. The application deadline for regular admission is June 1.

Transfer Admission The application deadline for admission is August 1.

Entrance Difficulty Muskingum assesses its entrance difficulty level as moderately difficult. For the fall 2003 freshman class, 80 percent of the applicants were accepted.

For Further Information Contact Mrs. Beth DaLonzo, Director of Admission, Muskingum College, 163 Stormont Street, New Concord, OH 43762. *Telephone:* 740-826-8137 or 800-752-6082 (toll-free). *Fax:* 740-826-8100. *E-mail:* adminfo@muskingum.edu. *Web site:* http://www.muskingum.edu/.

NORTHWESTERN COLLEGE

See University of Northwestern Ohio

NOTRE DAME COLLEGE

South Euclid, Ohio

Notre Dame College is a coed, private, Roman Catholic, comprehensive institution, founded in 1922, offering degrees at the associate, bachelor's, and master's levels and postbachelor's certificates. It has a 53-acre campus in South Euclid near Cleveland.

Academic Information The faculty has 84 members (29% full-time). The undergraduate student-faculty ratio is 14:1. The library holds 9,983 audiovisual materials. Special programs include academic remediation, cooperative (work-study) education, study abroad, advanced placement credit, accelerated degree programs, double majors, independent study, self-designed majors, summer session for credit, part-time degree programs (daytime, evenings, weekends, summer), adult/continuing education programs, internships, and arrangement for off-campus study with members of the Northeast Ohio Commission on Higher Education. The most frequently chosen baccalaureate fields are business/marketing, education, psychology.

Student Body Statistics The student body totals 943, of whom 766 are undergraduates (64 freshmen). 76 percent are women and 24 percent are men. Students come from 4 states and territories and 17 other countries. 90 percent are from Ohio. 5.1 percent are international students. 7 percent of the 2003 graduating class went on to graduate and professional schools.

Expenses for 2003–04 *Application fee:* $30. *Comprehensive fee:* $23,690 includes full-time tuition ($16,990), mandatory fees ($500), and college room and board ($6200). *College room only:* $3114. Full-time tuition and fees vary according to class time. Room and board charges vary according to board plan. *Part-time tuition:* $405 per credit. Part-time tuition varies according to class time.

Financial Aid Forms of aid include need-based and non-need-based scholarships, athletic grants, and part-time jobs. The average aided 2002–03 undergraduate received an aid package worth $15,336. The application deadline for financial aid is continuous.

Freshman Admission Notre Dame College requires an essay, a high school transcript, a minimum 2.0 high school GPA, an interview, SAT I or ACT scores, and TOEFL scores for international students. A minimum 2.5 high school GPA and an interview are recommended. The application deadline for regular admission is rolling.

Transfer Admission The application deadline for admission is rolling.

Entrance Difficulty Notre Dame College assesses its entrance difficulty level as moderately difficult. For the fall 2003 freshman class, 47 percent of the applicants were accepted.

For Further Information Contact Mr. David Armstrong, Esq., Dean of Admissions, Notre Dame College, 4545 College Road, South Euclid, OH 44121-4293. *Telephone:* 216-373-5214 or 800-632-1680 (toll-free). *Fax:* 216-381-3802. *E-mail:* admissions@ndc.edu. *Web site:* http://www.notredamecollege.edu/.

Ohio

OBERLIN COLLEGE
Oberlin, Ohio

Oberlin is a coed, private, comprehensive institution, founded in 1833, offering degrees at the bachelor's and master's levels and postbachelor's certificates. It has a 440-acre campus in Oberlin near Cleveland.

Academic Information The faculty has 292 members (93% full-time). The undergraduate student-faculty ratio is 10:1. The library holds 2 million titles, 4,560 serial subscriptions, and 59,186 audiovisual materials. Special programs include services for learning-disabled students, an honors program, study abroad, advanced placement credit, ESL programs, double majors, independent study, self-designed majors, part-time degree programs (daytime), internships, and arrangement for off-campus study with Great Lakes Colleges Association. The most frequently chosen baccalaureate fields are social sciences and history, English, visual/performing arts.

Student Body Statistics The student body totals 2,898, of whom 2,883 are undergraduates (764 freshmen). 55 percent are women and 45 percent are men. Students come from 50 states and territories and 44 other countries. 10 percent are from Ohio. 6.2 percent are international students. 22 percent of the 2003 graduating class went on to graduate and professional schools.

Expenses for 2003–04 *Application fee:* $35. *Comprehensive fee:* $36,938 includes full-time tuition ($29,500), mandatory fees ($188), and college room and board ($7250). *College room only:* $3800. Room and board charges vary according to housing facility. *Part-time tuition:* $1230 per credit. Part-time tuition varies according to course load.

Financial Aid Forms of aid include need-based and non-need-based scholarships and part-time jobs. The average aided 2003–04 undergraduate received an aid package worth an estimated $22,576. The priority application deadline for financial aid is February 1.

Freshman Admission Oberlin requires an essay, a high school transcript, 2 recommendations, SAT I or ACT scores, and TOEFL scores for international students. SAT II: Subject Test scores and SAT II: Writing Test scores are recommended. An interview is required for some. The application deadline for regular admission is January 15; for early decision plan 1 it is November 15; and for early decision plan 2 it is January 2.

Transfer Admission The application deadline for admission is March 15.

Entrance Difficulty Oberlin assesses its entrance difficulty level as very difficult. For the fall 2003 freshman class, 36 percent of the applicants were accepted.

For Further Information Contact Ms. Debra Chermonte, Dean of Admissions and Financial Aid, Oberlin College, Admissions Office, Carnegie Building, Oberlin, OH 44074-1090. *Telephone:* 440-775-8411 or 800-622-OBIE (toll-free). *Fax:* 440-775-6905. *E-mail:* college.admissions@oberlin.edu. *Web site:* http://www.oberlin.edu/.

OHIO COLLEGE OF MASSOTHERAPY
Akron, Ohio

For Information Write to Ohio College of Massotherapy, Akron, OH 44321.

OHIO DOMINICAN UNIVERSITY
Columbus, Ohio

ODU is a coed, private, Roman Catholic, comprehensive institution, founded in 1911, offering degrees at the associate, bachelor's, and master's levels. It has a 62-acre campus in Columbus.

Academic Information The faculty has 160 members (38% full-time), 51% with terminal degrees. The undergraduate student-faculty ratio is 16:1. The library holds 110,953 titles, 553 serial subscriptions, and 4,302 audiovisual materials. Special programs include academic remediation, an honors program, study abroad, advanced placement credit, ESL programs, independent study, self-designed majors, summer session for credit,

part-time degree programs (daytime, evenings, weekends, summer), adult/continuing education programs, internships, and arrangement for off-campus study with members of the Higher Education Council of Columbus. The most frequently chosen baccalaureate fields are business/marketing, computer/information sciences, education.

Student Body Statistics The student body totals 2,566, of whom 2,308 are undergraduates (312 freshmen). 70 percent are women and 30 percent are men. Students come from 15 states and territories and 16 other countries. 99 percent are from Ohio. 1.3 percent are international students.

Expenses for 2004–05 *Application fee:* $25. *Comprehensive fee:* $23,900 includes full-time tuition ($18,000) and college room and board ($5900). Room and board charges vary according to housing facility. *Part-time tuition:* $370 per credit hour. *Part-time mandatory fees:* $100 per term.

Financial Aid Forms of aid include need-based and non-need-based scholarships, athletic grants, and part-time jobs. The average aided 2002–03 undergraduate received an aid package worth $12,467. The priority application deadline for financial aid is April 1.

Freshman Admission ODU requires an essay, a high school transcript, a minimum 2.0 high school GPA, and an interview. TOEFL scores for international students are recommended. Recommendations and SAT I and SAT II or ACT scores are required for some. The application deadline for regular admission is rolling.

Transfer Admission The application deadline for admission is rolling.

Entrance Difficulty ODU assesses its entrance difficulty level as moderately difficult. For the fall 2003 freshman class, 76 percent of the applicants were accepted.

For Further Information Contact Ms. Vicki Thompson-Campbell, Director of Admissions, Ohio Dominican University, 1216 Sunbury Road, Columbus, OH 43219-2099. *Telephone:* 614-251-4588 or 800-854-2670 (toll-free). *Fax:* 614-251-0156. *E-mail:* admissions@ohiodominican.edu. *Web site:* http://www.ohiodominican.edu/.

OHIO NORTHERN UNIVERSITY
Ada, Ohio

Ohio Northern is a coed, private, comprehensive institution, founded in 1871, affiliated with the United Methodist Church, offering degrees at the bachelor's, master's, and first professional levels and postbachelor's certificates. It has a 285-acre campus in Ada.

Academic Information The faculty has 275 members (75% full-time), 72% with terminal degrees. The undergraduate student-faculty ratio is 13:1. The library holds 250,231 titles, 9,220 serial subscriptions, and 9,776 audiovisual materials. Special programs include academic remediation, services for learning-disabled students, an honors program, cooperative (work-study) education, study abroad, advanced placement credit, double majors, independent study, distance learning, summer session for credit, part-time degree programs (daytime, evenings), internships, and arrangement for off-campus study. The most frequently chosen baccalaureate fields are business/marketing, engineering/engineering technologies, health professions and related sciences.

Student Body Statistics The student body totals 3,451, of whom 2,214 are undergraduates (554 freshmen). 47 percent are women and 53 percent are men. Students come from 37 states and territories. 87 percent are from Ohio. 0.6 percent are international students. 26 percent of the 2003 graduating class went on to graduate and professional schools.

Expenses for 2003–04 *Application fee:* $30. *Comprehensive fee:* $30,675 includes full-time tuition ($24,435), mandatory fees ($210), and college room and board ($6030). *College room only:* $3015. Full-time tuition and fees vary according to program and student level. Room and board charges vary according to board plan and housing facility. *Part-time tuition:* $679 per quarter hour. *Part-time mandatory fees:* $210 per term. Part-time tuition and fees vary according to course load, program, and student level.

Financial Aid Forms of aid include need-based and non-need-based scholarships and part-time jobs. The average aided 2003–04 undergraduate received an aid package worth an estimated $20,347. The application deadline for financial aid is June 1 with a priority deadline of April 15.

Peterson's Colleges in the Midwest 2005   *www.petersons.com* **205**

Ohio Northern University (continued)

Freshman Admission Ohio Northern requires a high school transcript, SAT I or ACT scores, and TOEFL scores for international students. An essay, a minimum 2.5 high school GPA, and an interview are recommended. 2 recommendations are required for some. The application deadline for regular admission is August 15.

Transfer Admission The application deadline for admission is September 1.

Entrance Difficulty Ohio Northern assesses its entrance difficulty level as moderately difficult. For the fall 2003 freshman class, 80 percent of the applicants were accepted.

SPECIAL MESSAGE TO STUDENTS

Social Life More than 150 campus organizations make life outside the classroom a rewarding, learning experience. Weekend activities are geared for students on a residential campus and include sporting events, concerts, plays, and a variety of entertainment. Ohio Northern University (ONU) students also become active in Greek life and religious groups. A strong student government is also in place.

Academic Highlights Internships, externships, and cooperative education programs are available in each of the four undergraduate colleges. These real-life work experiences provide an invaluable asset to those entering the professional workplace after graduation. Ohio Northern's academic programs begin with a liberal arts philosophy and are strengthened by professional training in the Colleges of Business Administration, Engineering, and Pharmacy. It is this combination of the liberal arts with professional and/or preprofessional programs that helps make Ohio Northern unique. The beautiful and well-maintained 285-acre campus includes many exceptional facilities such as the Freed Center for the Performing Arts, home to a magnificent theater/concert hall, and the new James F. Dicke Hall, which houses the College of Business Administration and is completely equipped with state-of-the-art technology.

Interviews and Campus Visits While interviews are not required for admission to Ohio Northern, they are encouraged. Depending upon a student's preference, there are opportunities to attend class, tour campus, speak to a professor about a specific area of interest, meet an athletic coach, and meet with an admissions or financial aid representative. Among the many modern facilities at Ohio Northern, the ONU Sports Center, home to varsity athletics, is both impressive and functional. It has been the site of three NCAA Division III Indoor Track and Field Championships and three NCAA Division III Wrestling Championships. Students have recreational use of three gymnasiums, a wrestling room, a six-lane swimming pool, three racquetball courts, and gymnastics rooms. The center also includes a 200-meter indoor running track, two weight-training rooms, and modern athletic training and fitness areas. For information about appointments and campus visits, students should call the Office of Admissions at 888-408-4onu (4668) (toll-free), Monday through Friday, 8 a.m. to 4:30 p.m., or Saturday, 8 a.m. to noon. The fax number is 419-772-2313. The nearest commercial airport is Port Columbus International.

For Further Information Write to Mrs. Karen P. Condeni, Vice President and Dean of Admissions and Financial Aid, Admissions Office, Ohio Northern University, Ada, OH 45810. *E-mail:* admissions-ug@onu.edu. *Web site:* http://www.onu.edu.

THE OHIO STATE UNIVERSITY
Columbus, Ohio

Ohio State is a coed, public university, founded in 1870, offering degrees at the associate, bachelor's, master's, doctoral, and first professional levels and post-master's and postbachelor's certificates. It has a 3,117-acre campus in Columbus.

Academic Information The faculty has 3,657 members (75% full-time). The undergraduate student-faculty ratio is 14:1. The library holds 6 million titles, 43,086 serial subscriptions, and 46,705 audiovisual materials. Special programs include academic remediation, services for learning-disabled students, an honors program, cooperative (work-study) education, study abroad, advanced placement credit, accelerated degree programs,

Freshman Honors College, ESL programs, double majors, independent study, distance learning, self-designed majors, summer session for credit, part-time degree programs (daytime, evenings, weekends, summer), adult/continuing education programs, internships, and arrangement for off-campus study with Higher Education Council of Columbus. The most frequently chosen baccalaureate fields are business/marketing, home economics/vocational home economics, social sciences and history.

Student Body Statistics The student body totals 50,731, of whom 37,605 are undergraduates (6,390 freshmen). 48 percent are women and 52 percent are men. Students come from 53 states and territories and 85 other countries. 89 percent are from Ohio. 3.9 percent are international students. 10 percent of the 2003 graduating class went on to graduate and professional schools.

Expenses for 2003–04 *Application fee:* $40. *State resident tuition:* $6651 full-time. *Nonresident tuition:* $16,638 full-time. Full-time tuition varies according to course load, program, and reciprocity agreements. *College room and board:* $6429. Room and board charges vary according to board plan and housing facility.

Financial Aid Forms of aid include need-based and non-need-based scholarships, athletic grants, and part-time jobs. The average aided 2003–04 undergraduate received an aid package worth an estimated $8897. The priority application deadline for financial aid is March 1.

Freshman Admission Ohio State requires an essay, a high school transcript, SAT I or ACT scores, and TOEFL scores for international students. The application deadline for regular admission is February 1.

Transfer Admission The application deadline for admission is June 25.

Entrance Difficulty Ohio State assesses its entrance difficulty level as moderately difficult. For the fall 2003 freshman class, 72 percent of the applicants were accepted.

For Further Information Contact Dr. Mabel G. Freeman, Assistant Vice President for Undergraduate Admissions and First Year Experience, The Ohio State University, Enarson Hall, 154 West 12th Avenue, Columbus, OH 43210. *Telephone:* 614-247-6281. *Fax:* 614-292-4818. *E-mail:* askabuckeye@osu.edu. *Web site:* http://www.osu.edu/.

THE OHIO STATE UNIVERSITY AT LIMA
Lima, Ohio

OSU-Lima is a coed, public, comprehensive unit of Ohio State University, founded in 1960, offering degrees at the associate, bachelor's, and master's levels. It has a 565-acre campus in Lima.

Academic Information The faculty has 83 members (47% full-time). The undergraduate student-faculty ratio is 15:1. The library holds 74,619 titles and 592 serial subscriptions. Special programs include academic remediation, services for learning-disabled students, an honors program, advanced placement credit, accelerated degree programs, ESL programs, summer session for credit, part-time degree programs, and adult/continuing education programs.

Student Body Statistics The student body totals 1,338, of whom 1,248 are undergraduates (364 freshmen). 57 percent are women and 43 percent are men. Students come from 1 state or territory. 99 percent are from Ohio.

Expenses for 2003–04 *Application fee:* $40. *State resident tuition:* $4443 full-time. *Nonresident tuition:* $14,430 full-time. Full-time tuition varies according to course load and student level.

Freshman Admission OSU-Lima requires an essay, a high school transcript, and SAT I or ACT scores.

Transfer Admission The application deadline for admission is July 1.

Entrance Difficulty OSU-Lima has an open admission policy for state residents. It assesses its entrance difficulty as moderately difficult for out-of-state applicants; moderately difficult for transfers.

For Further Information Contact Ms. Marissa Christoff Snyder, Admissions Counselor, The Ohio State University at Lima, 4240 Campus Drive, Lima, OH 45804. *Telephone:* 419-995-8220. *Fax:* 419-995-8483. *E-mail:* admissions@lima.ohio-state.edu. *Web site:* http://www.lima.ohio-state.edu/.

THE OHIO STATE UNIVERSITY AT MARION
Marion, Ohio

OSU-Marion is a coed, public, comprehensive unit of Ohio State University, founded in 1958, offering degrees at the associate, bachelor's, and master's levels. It has a 180-acre campus in Marion near Columbus.

Academic Information   The faculty has 106 members (29% full-time). The undergraduate student-faculty ratio is 12:1. The library holds 38,858 titles and 413 serial subscriptions. Special programs include academic remediation, services for learning-disabled students, an honors program, advanced placement credit, accelerated degree programs, ESL programs, summer session for credit, part-time degree programs (daytime, evenings, summer), and adult/continuing education programs.
Student Body Statistics   The student body totals 1,567, of whom 1,471 are undergraduates (435 freshmen). 61 percent are women and 39 percent are men. Students come from 6 states and territories. 0.1 percent are international students.
Expenses for 2003–04   *Application fee:* $40. *State resident tuition:* $4443 full-time. *Nonresident tuition:* $14,430 full-time. Full-time tuition varies according to course load and student level.
Freshman Admission   OSU-Marion requires an essay, a high school transcript, SAT I or ACT scores, and TOEFL scores for international students.
Transfer Admission   The application deadline for admission is July 1.
Entrance Difficulty   OSU-Marion has an open admission policy for state residents. It assesses its entrance difficulty as minimally difficult for transfers.

For Further Information   Contact Mr. Mathrey Moreau, Admissions Coordinator, The Ohio State University at Marion, 1465 Mount Vernon Avenue, Marion, OH 43302. *Telephone:* 740-389-6786 Ext. 6337. *E-mail:* moreau.1@osu.edu. *Web site:* http://www.marion.ohio-state.edu/.

THE OHIO STATE UNIVERSITY–MANSFIELD CAMPUS
Mansfield, Ohio

OSU-Mansfield is a coed, public, comprehensive unit of Ohio State University, founded in 1958, offering degrees at the associate, bachelor's, and master's levels. It has a 644-acre campus in Mansfield near Columbus and Cleveland.

Academic Information   The faculty has 82 members (55% full-time). The library holds 45,977 titles and 453 serial subscriptions. Special programs include academic remediation, services for learning-disabled students, an honors program, advanced placement credit, accelerated degree programs, ESL programs, summer session for credit, part-time degree programs (daytime, evenings, summer), and adult/continuing education programs.
Student Body Statistics   The student body totals 1,640, of whom 1,550 are undergraduates (494 freshmen). 62 percent are women and 38 percent are men. Students come from 10 states and territories.
Expenses for 2003–04   *Application fee:* $40. *State resident tuition:* $4443 full-time. *Nonresident tuition:* $14,430 full-time. Full-time tuition varies according to course load and student level.
Freshman Admission   OSU-Mansfield requires an essay, a high school transcript, and SAT I or ACT scores.
Transfer Admission   The application deadline for admission is July 1.
Entrance Difficulty   OSU-Mansfield has an open admission policy for state residents. It assesses its entrance difficulty as moderately difficult for out-of-state applicants; moderately difficult for transfers.

For Further Information   Contact Mr. Henry D. Thomas, Coordinator of Admissions and Financial Aid, The Ohio State University–Mansfield Campus, 1680 University Drive, Mansfield, OH 44906. *Telephone:* 419-755-4226. *Fax:* 419-755-4241. *E-mail:* admissions@mansfield.ohio-state.edu. *Web site:* http://www.mansfield.ohio-state.edu/.

THE OHIO STATE UNIVERSITY–NEWARK CAMPUS
Newark, Ohio

OSU-Newark is a coed, public, comprehensive unit of Ohio State University, founded in 1957, offering degrees at the associate, bachelor's, and master's levels. It has a 101-acre campus in Newark near Columbus.

Academic Information   The faculty has 124 members (35% full-time). The undergraduate student-faculty ratio is 23:1. The library holds 49,232 titles and 423 serial subscriptions. Special programs include academic remediation, services for learning-disabled students, an honors program, advanced placement credit, accelerated degree programs, ESL programs, summer session for credit, part-time degree programs (daytime, evenings, summer), and adult/continuing education programs.
Student Body Statistics   The student body totals 2,148, of whom 2,016 are undergraduates (730 freshmen). 59 percent are women and 41 percent are men. Students come from 14 states and territories and 1 other country. 0.1 percent are international students.
Expenses for 2003–04   *Application fee:* $40. *State resident tuition:* $4443 full-time. *Nonresident tuition:* $14,430 full-time. Full-time tuition varies according to course load and student level.
Freshman Admission   OSU-Newark requires an essay, a high school transcript, and SAT I or ACT scores.
Transfer Admission   The application deadline for admission is July 1.
Entrance Difficulty   OSU-Newark has an open admission policy for state residents. It assesses its entrance difficulty as moderately difficult for out-of-state applicants; moderately difficult for transfers.

For Further Information   Contact Ms. Ann Donahue, Director of Enrollment, The Ohio State University–Newark Campus, 1179 University Drive, Newark, OH 43055. *Telephone:* 614-366-9333. *Fax:* 740-364-9645. *E-mail:* vogelmeier.1@osu.edu. *Web site:* http://www.newark.osu.edu/.

OHIO UNIVERSITY
Athens, Ohio

Ohio is a coed, public unit of Ohio Board of Regents, founded in 1804, offering degrees at the associate, bachelor's, master's, doctoral, and first professional levels. It has a 1,700-acre campus in Athens.

Academic Information   The faculty has 1,163 members (74% full-time), 82% with terminal degrees. The undergraduate student-faculty ratio is 18:1. The library holds 2 million titles, 15,906 serial subscriptions, and 111,579 audiovisual materials. Special programs include academic remediation, services for learning-disabled students, an honors program, cooperative (work-study) education, study abroad, advanced placement credit, accelerated degree programs, ESL programs, double majors, independent study, distance learning, self-designed majors, summer session for credit, part-time degree programs, external degree programs, adult/continuing education programs, internships, and arrangement for off-campus study. The most frequently chosen baccalaureate fields are business/marketing, communications/communication technologies, education.
Student Body Statistics   The student body totals 20,394, of whom 17,192 are undergraduates (3,673 freshmen). 54 percent are women and 46 percent are men. Students come from 52 states and territories and 52 other countries. 91 percent are from Ohio. 1.7 percent are international students. 28 percent of the 2003 graduating class went on to graduate and professional schools.
Expenses for 2003–04   *Application fee:* $45. *State resident tuition:* $7128 full-time, $288 per quarter hour part-time. *Nonresident tuition:* $15,351 full-time, $499 per quarter hour part-time. *College room and board:* $7320. *College room only:* $3600. Room and board charges vary according to board plan.
Financial Aid   Forms of aid include need-based and non-need-based scholarships, athletic grants, and part-time jobs. The average aided 2003–04 undergraduate received an aid package worth an estimated $6823. The priority application deadline for financial aid is March 15.

Ohio University (continued)

Freshman Admission Ohio requires a high school transcript and SAT I or ACT scores. 2 recommendations are recommended. An essay and an interview are required for some. The application deadline for regular admission is February 1.

Transfer Admission The application deadline for admission is May 15.

Entrance Difficulty Ohio assesses its entrance difficulty level as moderately difficult; very difficult for transfers; very difficult for business, engineering, journalism, radio-television programs, Honors Tutorial College. For the fall 2003 freshman class, 79 percent of the applicants were accepted.

For Further Information Contact Mr. N. Kip Howard Jr., Director of Admissions, Ohio University, Athens, OH 45701-2979. *Telephone:* 740-593-4100. *Fax:* 740-593-4229. *E-mail:* admissions.freshmen@ohiou.edu. *Web site:* http://www.ohio.edu/.

OHIO UNIVERSITY–CHILLICOTHE

Chillicothe, Ohio

Ohio University–Chillicothe is a coed, public, four-year college of Ohio Board of Regents, founded in 1946, offering degrees at the associate, bachelor's, and master's levels (offers first 2 years of most bachelor's degree programs available at the main campus in Athens; also offers several bachelor's degree programs that can be completed at this campus and several programs exclusive to this campus; also offers some graduate programs). It has a 124-acre campus in Chillicothe near Columbus.

Academic Information The faculty has 106 members (39% full-time). The library holds 47,900 titles and 418 serial subscriptions. Special programs include academic remediation, services for learning-disabled students, advanced placement credit, accelerated degree programs, double majors, independent study, distance learning, self-designed majors, summer session for credit, part-time degree programs (daytime, evenings, summer), adult/continuing education programs, and internships.

Student Body Statistics The student body totals 2,000, of whom 1,960 are undergraduates. Students come from 2 states and territories. 0.2 percent are international students. 10 percent of the 2003 graduating class went on to graduate and professional schools.

Expenses for 2003–04 *Application fee:* $20. *State resident tuition:* $4008 full-time, $121 per hour part-time. *Nonresident tuition:* $10,146 full-time, $325 per hour part-time.

Financial Aid Forms of aid include need-based and non-need-based scholarships and part-time jobs. The average aided 2003–04 undergraduate received an aid package worth an estimated $6689. The priority application deadline for financial aid is March 15.

Freshman Admission Ohio University–Chillicothe requires a high school transcript and SAT I or ACT scores. The application deadline for regular admission is September 1.

Transfer Admission The application deadline for admission is September 1.

Entrance Difficulty Ohio University–Chillicothe has an open admission policy for state residents. It assesses its entrance difficulty as minimally difficult for transfers.

For Further Information Contact Mr. Doug Henning, Coordinator, Admissions Office, Ohio University–Chillicothe, 571 West Fifth Street, Chillicothe, OH 45601. *Telephone:* 740-774-7200 Ext. 242 or 877-462-6824 (toll-free in-state). *Fax:* 740-774-7295. *Web site:* http://www.ohio.edu/chillicothe/.

OHIO UNIVERSITY–EASTERN

St. Clairsville, Ohio

For Information Write to Ohio University–Eastern, St. Clairsville, OH 43950-9724.

OHIO UNIVERSITY–LANCASTER

Lancaster, Ohio

Ohio University–Lancaster is a coed, public, comprehensive unit of Ohio Board of Regents, founded in 1968, offering degrees at the associate, bachelor's, and master's levels. It has a 360-acre campus in Lancaster near Columbus.

Expenses for 2003–04 *Application fee:* $20. *State resident tuition:* $4008 full-time. *Nonresident tuition:* $10,146 full-time.

For Further Information Contact Mr. Nathan Thomas, Admissions Officer, Ohio University–Lancaster, 1570 Granville Pike, Lancaster, OH 43130-1097. *Telephone:* 740-654-6711 Ext. 215 or 888-446-4468 Ext. 215 (toll-free). *Fax:* 740-687-9497. *E-mail:* fox@ohio.edu. *Web site:* http://www.ohiou.edu/lancaster/.

OHIO UNIVERSITY–SOUTHERN CAMPUS

Ironton, Ohio

Ohio University–Southern Campus is a coed, public, comprehensive unit of Ohio Board of Regents, founded in 1956, offering degrees at the associate, bachelor's, and master's levels. It has a 9-acre campus in Ironton.

Academic Information The faculty has 155 members (10% full-time). The library holds 26,000 titles, 275 serial subscriptions, and 524 audiovisual materials. Special programs include academic remediation, self-designed majors, summer session for credit, part-time degree programs (daytime, evenings, weekends, summer), and adult/continuing education programs.

Student Body Statistics The student body totals 1,746, of whom 1,630 are undergraduates (348 freshmen). 63 percent are women and 37 percent are men. Students come from 4 states and territories. 86 percent are from Ohio. 0.1 percent are international students.

Expenses for 2003–04 *Application fee:* $20. *State resident tuition:* $3693 full-time. *Nonresident tuition:* $5013 full-time. Full-time tuition varies according to student level.

Financial Aid Forms of aid include need-based and non-need-based scholarships and part-time jobs. The average aided 2003–04 undergraduate received an aid package worth an estimated $6807. The priority application deadline for financial aid is April 1.

Freshman Admission SAT I or ACT scores are recommended. A high school transcript is required for some. The application deadline for regular admission is rolling.

Transfer Admission The application deadline for admission is rolling.

Entrance Difficulty Ohio University–Southern Campus has an open admission policy.

For Further Information Contact Dr. Kim K. Lawson, Coordinator of Admissions, Ohio University–Southern Campus, 1804 Liberty Avenue, Ironton, OH 45638. *Telephone:* 740-533-4612 or 800-626-0513 (toll-free). *Fax:* 740-593-4632. *Web site:* http://www.ohiou.edu/.

OHIO UNIVERSITY–ZANESVILLE

Zanesville, Ohio

OUZ is a coed, public, comprehensive unit of Ohio Board of Regents, founded in 1946, offering degrees at the associate, bachelor's, and master's levels (offers first 2 years of most bachelor's degree programs available at the main campus in Athens; also offers several bachelor's degree programs that can be completed at this campus; also offers some graduate courses). It has a 179-acre campus in Zanesville near Columbus.

Academic Information The faculty has 130 members (24% full-time), 25% with terminal degrees. The undergraduate student-faculty ratio is 23:1. The library holds 64,227 titles and 489 serial subscriptions. Special programs include academic remediation, services for learning-disabled students, advanced placement credit, self-designed majors, summer session for credit, part-time degree programs, external degree programs, adult/ continuing education programs, and arrangement for off-campus study with Muskingum Area Technical College.

Student Body Statistics The student body totals 1,826, of whom 1,709 are undergraduates (388 freshmen). 69 percent are women and 31 percent are men. Students come from 4 states and territories. 99 percent are from Ohio. 0.1 percent are international students.

Expenses for 2003–04 *Application fee:* $20. *State resident tuition:* $4008 full-time. *Nonresident tuition:* $10,146 full-time.

Financial Aid Forms of aid include need-based and non-need-based scholarships and part-time jobs. The average aided 2003–04 undergraduate received an aid package worth an estimated $6417. The priority application deadline for financial aid is April 1.

Freshman Admission OUZ requires a high school transcript. SAT I or ACT scores and nursing exam are required for some. The application deadline for regular admission is rolling.

Transfer Admission The application deadline for admission is rolling.

Entrance Difficulty OUZ has an open admission policy except for nursing, engineering, business, communications programs. It assesses its entrance difficulty as moderately difficult for nursing, business, engineering, communications programs.

For Further Information Contact Mrs. Karen Ragsdale, Student Services Secretary, Ohio University–Zanesville, 1425 Newark Road, Zanesville, OH 43701-2695. *Telephone:* 740-588-1439 Ext. 1446. *Fax:* 740-453-6161. *Web site:* http://www.zanesville.ohiou.edu/.

OHIO WESLEYAN UNIVERSITY
Delaware, Ohio

Ohio Wesleyan is a coed, private, United Methodist, four-year college, founded in 1842, offering degrees at the bachelor's level. It has a 200-acre campus in Delaware near Columbus.

Academic Information The faculty has 188 members (69% full-time), 81% with terminal degrees. The student-faculty ratio is 13:1. The library holds 420,936 titles, 1,084 serial subscriptions, and 2,980 audiovisual materials. Special programs include services for learning-disabled students, an honors program, study abroad, advanced placement credit, Freshman Honors College, double majors, independent study, self-designed majors, summer session for credit, part-time degree programs (daytime, summer), internships, and arrangement for off-campus study with Great Lakes Colleges Association, New York City Arts Program. The most frequently chosen baccalaureate fields are business/marketing, psychology, social sciences and history.

Student Body Statistics The student body is made up of 1,929 undergraduates (567 freshmen). 54 percent are women and 46 percent are men. Students come from 44 states and territories and 45 other countries. 59 percent are from Ohio. 10 percent are international students. 32 percent of the 2003 graduating class went on to graduate and professional schools.

Expenses for 2003–04 *Application fee:* $35. *Comprehensive fee:* $32,550 includes full-time tuition ($25,080), mandatory fees ($360), and college room and board ($7110). *College room only:* $3530. Room and board charges vary according to board plan. *Part-time tuition:* $2730 per course.

Financial Aid Forms of aid include need-based and non-need-based scholarships and part-time jobs. The average aided 2003–04 undergraduate received an aid package worth an estimated $22,149. The application deadline for financial aid is May 15 with a priority deadline of March 15.

Freshman Admission Ohio Wesleyan requires an essay, a high school transcript, 1 recommendation, SAT I or ACT scores, and TOEFL scores for international students. A minimum 2.5 high school GPA, 2 recommendations, an interview, and SAT II: Subject Test scores are recommended. The application deadline for regular admission is March 1; for early decision it is December 1; and for early action it is December 15.

Transfer Admission The application deadline for admission is May 15.

Entrance Difficulty Ohio Wesleyan assesses its entrance difficulty level as very difficult; most difficult for honors program. For the fall 2003 freshman class, 74 percent of the applicants were accepted.

For Further Information Contact Ms. Carol Wheatley, Director of Admission, Ohio Wesleyan University, 61 South Sandusky Street, Delaware, OH 43015. *Telephone:* 740-368-3020 or 800-922-8953 (toll-free). *Fax:* 740-368-3314. *E-mail:* owuadmit@owu.edu. *Web site:* http://web.owu.edu/.

See page 322 for a narrative description.

OTTERBEIN COLLEGE
Westerville, Ohio

Otterbein is a coed, private, United Methodist, comprehensive institution, founded in 1847, offering degrees at the bachelor's and master's levels. It has a 142-acre campus in Westerville near Columbus.

Academic Information The faculty has 249 members (58% full-time). The undergraduate student-faculty ratio is 13:1. The library holds 182,629 titles, 1,012 serial subscriptions, and 8,971 audiovisual materials. Special programs include academic remediation, services for learning-disabled students, an honors program, study abroad, advanced placement credit, double majors, self-designed majors, summer session for credit, part-time degree programs (daytime, evenings, weekends, summer), adult/continuing education programs, internships, and arrangement for off-campus study with American University, University of Pittsburgh (Semester at Sea), members of the Higher Education Council of Columbus. The most frequently chosen baccalaureate fields are communications/communication technologies, business/marketing, education.

Student Body Statistics The student body totals 3,031, of whom 2,673 are undergraduates (632 freshmen). 63 percent are women and 37 percent are men. Students come from 34 states and territories. 92 percent are from Ohio.

Expenses for 2003–04 *Application fee:* $25. *Comprehensive fee:* $26,085 includes full-time tuition ($20,133) and college room and board ($5952). *College room only:* $2712. Full-time tuition varies according to course load and program. Room and board charges vary according to housing facility. *Part-time tuition:* $242 per credit hour. Part-time tuition varies according to course load and program.

Financial Aid Forms of aid include need-based and non-need-based scholarships and part-time jobs. The priority application deadline for financial aid is April 1.

Freshman Admission Otterbein requires a high school transcript, SAT I or ACT scores, and TOEFL scores for international students. A minimum 2.5 high school GPA and an interview are recommended. The application deadline for regular admission is March 1.

Transfer Admission The application deadline for admission is rolling.

Entrance Difficulty Otterbein assesses its entrance difficulty level as moderately difficult. For the fall 2003 freshman class, 84 percent of the applicants were accepted.

SPECIAL MESSAGE TO STUDENTS

Social Life Students participate in more than 100 campus organizations, from music performance groups, such as the marching band, concert choir, and orchestra, to student government to student-run radio and television studios to intramural sports. Twenty-seven percent join one of the five fraternities and six sororities. Many students are involved in campus service organizations, such as Habitat for Humanity. Religious activities are also available for students in most denominations. Cultural activities on campus include a Professional Artist Series, the Otterbein College Theatre, and musical performances. Off-campus activities in nearby Columbus include many social, sports, and cultural offerings.

Academic Highlights The curriculum revolves around Otterbein's nationally recognized liberal arts curriculum, Integrative Studies, combined with professional and career preparation. Otterbein offers forty-nine majors and

Otterbein College (continued)
seven baccalaureate and four graduate degrees. Internships are encouraged in order to give students hands-on work experience to complement their course work. Programs in theater and equine science have each achieved national recognition.

Interviews and Campus Visits Individual interviews are not required of all applicants, but campus visits are strongly recommended for all accepted students. The visit is structured so that students can gain a thorough understanding of the campus from a variety of perspectives. Faculty conferences, student-conducted tours, admission and financial aid conferences, and classroom observation are part of each campus visit. Roush Hall, the multipurpose, state-of-the-art classroom building; Battelle Fine Arts Center; the Rike Physical Education Building; the Science Hall–Observatory; the campus center; residence halls; Towers Hall; the computer center; Courtright Memorial Library; and the new Clements Recreation Center should not be missed. For information about appointments and campus visits, students should call the Office of Admission at 614-823-1500 (collect) or 800-488-8144 (toll-free), Monday through Friday, 8:30 a.m. to 5 p.m., or Saturday, 9:30 a.m. to 1 p.m. The office is located in the Clippinger Administration Building on campus. The nearest commercial airport is Port Columbus International.

For Further Information Write to Dr. Cass Johnson, Director of Admission, Otterbein College, Westerville, OH 43081.

See page 326 for a narrative description.

PONTIFICAL COLLEGE JOSEPHINUM
Columbus, Ohio

Josephinum is a coed, primarily men's, private, Roman Catholic, comprehensive institution, founded in 1888, offering degrees at the bachelor's, master's, and first professional levels. It has a 100-acre campus in Columbus.

Academic Information The faculty has 19 members (47% full-time). The undergraduate student-faculty ratio is 6:1. The library holds 124,742 titles and 520 serial subscriptions. Special programs include academic remediation, services for learning-disabled students, an honors program, advanced placement credit, ESL programs, double majors, internships, and arrangement for off-campus study with 2 members of the Theological Cluster. The most frequently chosen baccalaureate fields are area/ethnic studies, English, philosophy, religion, and theology.
Student Body Statistics The student body totals 149, of whom 80 are undergraduates (8 freshmen). 100 percent are men. Students come from 19 states and territories and 3 other countries. 51 percent are from Ohio. 6.8 percent are international students. 90 percent of the 2003 graduating class went on to graduate and professional schools.
Expenses for 2003–04 *Application fee:* $25. *Comprehensive fee:* $16,320 includes full-time tuition ($10,220), mandatory fees ($100), and college room and board ($6000).
Financial Aid Forms of aid include need-based and non-need-based scholarships and part-time jobs. The average aided 2003–04 undergraduate received an aid package worth an estimated $14,084. The priority application deadline for financial aid is September 2.
Freshman Admission Josephinum requires an essay, a high school transcript, 3 recommendations, and TOEFL scores for international students. An interview and SAT I and SAT II or ACT scores are recommended. The application deadline for regular admission is July 31.
Transfer Admission The application deadline for admission is rolling.
Entrance Difficulty Josephinum assesses its entrance difficulty level as minimally difficult. For the fall 2003 freshman class, 90 percent of the applicants were accepted.

For Further Information Contact Arminda Crawford, Secretary for Admissions, Pontifical College Josephinum, Columbus, OH 43235. *Telephone:* 614-985-2241 or 888-252-5812 (toll-free). *Fax:* 614-885-2307. *E-mail:* acrawford@pcj.edu. *Web site:* http://www.pcj.edu/.

RABBINICAL COLLEGE OF TELSHE
Wickliffe, Ohio

For Information Write to Rabbinical College of Telshe, Wickliffe, OH 44092-2523.

ROSEDALE BIBLE COLLEGE
Irwin, Ohio

For Information Write to Rosedale Bible College, Irwin, OH 43029-9501.

SHAWNEE STATE UNIVERSITY
Portsmouth, Ohio

Shawnee State is a coed, public, four-year college of Ohio Board of Regents, founded in 1986, offering degrees at the associate and bachelor's levels. It has a 52-acre campus in Portsmouth.

Academic Information The faculty has 276 members (45% full-time). The student-faculty ratio is 18:1. The library holds 152,961 titles, 6,909 serial subscriptions, and 19,316 audiovisual materials. Special programs include academic remediation, services for learning-disabled students, an honors program, study abroad, advanced placement credit, double majors, independent study, distance learning, summer session for credit, part-time degree programs, adult/continuing education programs, internships, and arrangement for off-campus study. The most frequently chosen baccalaureate fields are business/marketing, education, social sciences and history.
Student Body Statistics The student body is made up of 3,693 undergraduates (709 freshmen). 60 percent are women and 40 percent are men. Students come from 13 states and territories and 10 other countries. 91 percent are from Ohio. 0.7 percent are international students.
Expenses for 2003–04 *Application fee:* $0. *State resident tuition:* $4212 full-time, $117 per credit hour part-time. *Nonresident tuition:* $7497 full-time, $208.25 per credit hour part-time. *Mandatory fees:* $522 full-time, $14.50 per credit hour part-time. Full-time tuition and fees vary according to reciprocity agreements and student level. Part-time tuition and fees vary according to reciprocity agreements and student level. *College room and board:* $6297. *College room only:* $4155. Room and board charges vary according to board plan and housing facility.
Financial Aid Forms of aid include need-based and non-need-based scholarships, athletic grants, and part-time jobs. The priority application deadline for financial aid is April 1.
Freshman Admission Shawnee State requires a high school transcript and TOEFL scores for international students. ACT scores are recommended. Recommendations and an interview are required for some. The application deadline for regular admission is rolling.
Transfer Admission The application deadline for admission is rolling.
Entrance Difficulty Shawnee State has an open admission policy except for allied health programs, nonresident aliens. It assesses its entrance difficulty as moderately difficult for allied health programs.

For Further Information Contact Mr. Bob Trusz, Director of Admission, Shawnee State University, 940 Second Street, Commons Building, Portsmouth, OH 45662. *Telephone:* 740-351-3610 Ext. 610 or 800-959-2SSU (toll-free). *Fax:* 740-351-3111. *E-mail:* to_ssu@shawnee.edu. *Web site:* http://www.shawnee.edu/.

SOUTHEASTERN BUSINESS COLLEGE
See Gallipolis Career College

TEMPLE BAPTIST COLLEGE
Cincinnati, Ohio

For Information Write to Temple Baptist College, Cincinnati, OH 45240.

TIFFIN UNIVERSITY
Tiffin, Ohio

Tiffin is a coed, private, comprehensive institution, founded in 1888, offering degrees at the associate, bachelor's, and master's levels. It has a 110-acre campus in Tiffin near Toledo.

Academic Information The faculty has 147 members (33% full-time), 39% with terminal degrees. The undergraduate student-faculty ratio is 10:1. The library holds 29,779 titles, 250 serial subscriptions, and 544 audiovisual materials. Special programs include study abroad, advanced placement credit, accelerated degree programs, double majors, independent study, distance learning, summer session for credit, adult/continuing education programs, and internships. The most frequently chosen baccalaureate fields are business/marketing, computer/information sciences, protective services/public administration.

Student Body Statistics The student body totals 1,407, of whom 1,026 are undergraduates (262 freshmen). 54 percent are women and 46 percent are men. Students come from 14 states and territories and 10 other countries. 91 percent are from Ohio. 2.6 percent are international students. 18 percent of the 2003 graduating class went on to graduate and professional schools.

Expenses for 2004–05 *Application fee:* $20. *Comprehensive fee:* $20,365 includes full-time tuition ($14,290) and college room and board ($6075). *College room only:* $3075. Room and board charges vary according to board plan and housing facility. *Part-time tuition:* $473.33 per credit hour.

Financial Aid Forms of aid include need-based and non-need-based scholarships and part-time jobs. The average aided 2002–03 undergraduate received an aid package worth $10,415. The application deadline for financial aid is continuous.

Freshman Admission Tiffin requires an essay, a high school transcript, SAT I or ACT scores, and TOEFL scores for international students. A minimum 3.00 high school GPA, an interview, and 19 on ACT or 890 on SAT are recommended. An essay, recommendations, and an interview are required for some. The application deadline for regular admission is rolling.

Entrance Difficulty Tiffin assesses its entrance difficulty level as minimally difficult. For the fall 2003 freshman class, 91 percent of the applicants were accepted.

For Further Information Contact Mr. Cameron Cruickshank, Director of Admissions, Tiffin University, 155 Miami Street, Tiffin, OH 44883. *Telephone:* 419-448-3368 or 800-968-6446 (toll-free). *Fax:* 419-443-5006. *E-mail:* admiss@tiffin.edu. *Web site:* http://www.tiffin.edu/.

TRI-STATE BIBLE COLLEGE
South Point, Ohio

For Information Write to Tri-State Bible College, South Point, OH 45680-8402.

UNION INSTITUTE & UNIVERSITY
Cincinnati, Ohio

Union is a coed, private university, founded in 1969, offering degrees at the bachelor's, master's, and doctoral levels and post-master's certificates. It has a 5-acre campus in Cincinnati.

Academic Information The faculty has 240 members (47% full-time), 77% with terminal degrees. The undergraduate student-faculty ratio is 15:1. The library holds 50,000 titles and 300 audiovisual materials. Special programs include services for learning-disabled students, advanced placement credit, accelerated degree programs, double majors, independent study, distance learning, self-designed majors, summer session for credit, part-time degree programs (daytime, evenings, weekends, summer), external degree programs, and adult/continuing education programs. The most frequently chosen baccalaureate fields are education, liberal arts/general studies, protective services/public administration.

Student Body Statistics The student body totals 2,910, of whom 1,288 are undergraduates (38 freshmen). 71 percent are women and 29 percent are men. Students come from 45 states and territories and 6 other countries. 77 percent are from Ohio. 0.5 percent are international students. 40 percent of the 2003 graduating class went on to graduate and professional schools.

Expenses for 2003–04 *Application fee:* $50. *Tuition:* $7776 full-time, $324 per semester hour part-time. *Mandatory fees:* $72 full-time, $36 per term part-time. Full-time tuition and fees vary according to course load and program.

Financial Aid Forms of aid include need-based and non-need-based scholarships and part-time jobs. The priority application deadline for financial aid is April 15.

Freshman Admission Union requires an essay, a high school transcript, 2 recommendations, and an interview.

Entrance Difficulty Union assesses its entrance difficulty level as moderately difficult.

For Further Information Contact Dr. Emily Harbold, Associate Vice President-Academic Affairs, Union Institute & University, 440 East McMillan Street, Cincinnati, OH 45206. *Telephone:* 800-486-3116 or 800-486-3116 (toll-free). *Fax:* 513-861-0779. *E-mail:* admissions@tui.edu. *Web site:* http://www.tui.edu/.

THE UNIVERSITY OF AKRON
Akron, Ohio

Akron is a coed, public university, founded in 1870, offering degrees at the associate, bachelor's, master's, doctoral, and first professional levels. It has a 170-acre campus in Akron near Cleveland.

Academic Information The faculty has 1,721 members (47% full-time), 56% with terminal degrees. The undergraduate student-faculty ratio is 19:1. The library holds 1 million titles, 12,849 serial subscriptions, and 43,448 audiovisual materials. Special programs include academic remediation, services for learning-disabled students, an honors program, cooperative (work-study) education, study abroad, advanced placement credit, accelerated degree programs, ESL programs, double majors, independent study, distance learning, self-designed majors, summer session for credit, part-time degree programs (daytime, evenings, weekends, summer), adult/continuing education programs, and internships. The most frequently chosen baccalaureate fields are business/marketing, education, protective services/public administration.

Student Body Statistics The student body totals 24,335, of whom 20,111 are undergraduates (3,715 freshmen). 54 percent are women and 46 percent are men. Students come from 42 states and territories and 86 other countries. 98 percent are from Ohio. 0.8 percent are international students.

Expenses for 2004–05 *Application fee:* $30. *One-time mandatory fee:* $300. *State resident tuition:* $6425 full-time, $268 per credit part-time. *Nonresident tuition:* $14,094 full-time, $587 per credit part-time. *Mandatory fees:* $1085 full-time, $45 per credit part-time. Full-time tuition and fees vary according to course load, degree level, location, and student level. Part-time tuition and fees vary according to course load, degree level, location, and student level. *College room and board:* $6660. *College room only:* $4240. Room and board charges vary according to board plan and housing facility.

Financial Aid Forms of aid include need-based and non-need-based scholarships, athletic grants, and part-time jobs. The average aided 2003–04 undergraduate received an aid package worth an estimated $1988. The application deadline for financial aid is March 1 with a priority deadline of February 1.

Freshman Admission Akron requires a high school transcript, SAT I or ACT scores, and TOEFL scores for international students. An essay, 3 recommendations, and an interview are required for some. The application deadline for regular admission is August 15 and for early action it is February 1.

The University of Akron (continued)

Transfer Admission The application deadline for admission is August 15.

Entrance Difficulty Akron assesses its entrance difficulty level as minimally difficult; moderately difficult for transfers; noncompetitive for Community and Technical College. For the fall 2003 freshman class, 87 percent of the applicants were accepted.

For Further Information Contact Ms. Diane Raybuck, Director of Admissions, The University of Akron, 381 Buchtel Common, Akron, OH 44325-2001. *Telephone:* 330-972-6425 or 800-655-4884 (toll-free). *Fax:* 330-972-7676. *E-mail:* admissions@uakron.edu. *Web site:* http://www.uakron.edu/.

UNIVERSITY OF CINCINNATI

Cincinnati, Ohio

UC is a coed, public unit of University of Cincinnati System, founded in 1819, offering degrees at the associate, bachelor's, master's, doctoral, and first professional levels and postbachelor's certificates. It has a 137-acre campus in Cincinnati.

Academic Information The faculty has 1,173 members (95% full-time), 62% with terminal degrees. The undergraduate student-faculty ratio is 15:1. The library holds 16,560 serial subscriptions and 51,224 audiovisual materials. Special programs include academic remediation, services for learning-disabled students, an honors program, cooperative (work-study) education, study abroad, advanced placement credit, accelerated degree programs, ESL programs, double majors, independent study, distance learning, summer session for credit, part-time degree programs, adult/continuing education programs, internships, and arrangement for off-campus study with Greater Cincinnati Consortium of Colleges and Universities. The most frequently chosen baccalaureate fields are business/marketing, engineering/engineering technologies, visual/performing arts.

Student Body Statistics The student body totals 26,817, of whom 19,159 are undergraduates (3,820 freshmen). 48 percent are women and 52 percent are men. Students come from 48 states and territories and 93 other countries. 93 percent are from Ohio. 1 percent are international students. 36 percent of the 2003 graduating class went on to graduate and professional schools.

Expenses for 2003–04 *Application fee:* $35. *State resident tuition:* $6336 full-time, $212 per credit hour part-time. *Nonresident tuition:* $17,943 full-time, $535 per credit hour part-time. *Mandatory fees:* $1287 full-time. Full-time tuition and fees vary according to location. Part-time tuition varies according to location. *College room and board:* $7113. Room and board charges vary according to board plan and housing facility.

Financial Aid Forms of aid include need-based and non-need-based scholarships, athletic grants, and part-time jobs. The average aided 2003–04 undergraduate received an aid package worth an estimated $7524. The application deadline for financial aid is continuous.

Freshman Admission UC requires a high school transcript, SAT I scores, SAT II: Subject Test scores, and TOEFL scores for international students. An interview is recommended. 2 recommendations and audition are required for some. The application deadline for regular admission is rolling.

Transfer Admission The application deadline for admission is rolling.

Entrance Difficulty UC assesses its entrance difficulty level as moderately difficult; most difficult for engineering, architecture programs. For the fall 2003 freshman class, 88 percent of the applicants were accepted.

For Further Information Contact Mr. James Williams, Director of Enrollment Services, University of Cincinnati, 340 University Pavillion, Cincinnati, OH 45221-0091. *Telephone:* 513-556-6999 or 513-556-4100 (toll-free out-of-state). *Fax:* 513-556-1105. *E-mail:* admissions@uc.edu. *Web site:* http://www.uc.edu/.

UNIVERSITY OF DAYTON

Dayton, Ohio

UD is a coed, private, Roman Catholic university, founded in 1850, offering degrees at the bachelor's, master's, doctoral, and first professional levels and post-master's certificates. It has a 110-acre campus in Dayton near Cincinnati.

Academic Information The faculty has 822 members (49% full-time). The undergraduate student-faculty ratio is 15:1. The library holds 849,244 titles, 7,318 serial subscriptions, and 1,763 audiovisual materials. Special programs include academic remediation, services for learning-disabled students, an honors program, cooperative (work-study) education, study abroad, advanced placement credit, accelerated degree programs, ESL programs, double majors, independent study, summer session for credit, part-time degree programs (daytime, evenings, summer), adult/continuing education programs, internships, and arrangement for off-campus study with Southwestern Ohio Council for Higher Education, Chaminade University of Honolulu, St. Mary's University. The most frequently chosen baccalaureate fields are business/marketing, education, engineering/engineering technologies.

Student Body Statistics The student body totals 10,284, of whom 7,103 are undergraduates (1,858 freshmen). 50 percent are women and 50 percent are men. Students come from 48 states and territories and 29 other countries. 66 percent are from Ohio. 0.6 percent are international students.

Expenses for 2004–05 *Application fee:* $0. *Comprehensive fee:* $26,930 includes full-time tuition ($19,950), mandatory fees ($680), and college room and board ($6300). *College room only:* $2700. Full-time tuition and fees vary according to program. Room and board charges vary according to board plan, housing facility, and student level. *Part-time tuition:* $652 per credit hour. Part-time tuition varies according to course load and program.

Financial Aid Forms of aid include need-based and non-need-based scholarships, athletic grants, and part-time jobs. The average aided 2002–03 undergraduate received an aid package worth $13,258. The priority application deadline for financial aid is March 31.

Freshman Admission UD requires a high school transcript, 1 recommendation, SAT I or ACT scores, and TOEFL scores for international students. An essay and an interview are recommended. Audition required for music, music therapy, music education programs is required for some. The application deadline for regular admission is rolling.

Transfer Admission The application deadline for admission is June 15.

Entrance Difficulty UD assesses its entrance difficulty level as moderately difficult. For the fall 2003 freshman class, 97 percent of the applicants were accepted.

SPECIAL MESSAGE TO STUDENTS

Social Life The residential character of the University of Dayton (UD) campus supports a stimulating academic and extracurricular life for approximately 6,500 full-time undergraduate students, of whom more than 95 percent choose to live on campus. Participation in clubs and organizations—whether athletic, performance, professional, service, or social—is a distinguishing characteristic of the active UD student body. More than 190 clubs and organizations are active on campus. One of the most notable interests of students, however, is service to others. Virtually every organization offers some type of service.

Academic Highlights The University of Dayton is a place where students are encouraged and challenged to reach their full potential in and out of the classroom. Students are the most important part of UD, and teaching and advising are the University's highest priorities. The University of Dayton provides cooperative education, internships, study abroad, and the University Honors and John W. Berry Sr. Scholars programs as well as opportunities in undergraduate research to supplement academic course work. UD's campus is completely wired, providing 24-hour access to the library, the Internet, and administrative services such as course registration. All University-owned housing is fully wired for the Internet, and a wireless network covers several academic buildings, the library, residential buildings, the student union, and outdoor plazas, and it expands each year to include more areas.

Interviews and Campus Visits The campus interview is not required for admission but is recommended as a means of sharing information. Campus visits include an appointment with an admission counselor, a campus tour, and a residence hall tour. An appointment with a financial aid counselor, meeting with a faculty member, attending class, or accompanying a UD student through his or her day can also be arranged. The University of Dayton urges visitors to see new and renovated campus facilities, including ArtStreet, an innovative living and learning center in the heart of the south student neighborhood; Marianist Hall, a 400-bed residential facility for first- and second-year students; the Science Center, home to the University's science and mathematics programs; and the Arena Sports Complex, including the recently renovated University of Dayton Arena. Construction is underway on a new fitness and recreation complex, the RecPlex, which is scheduled for completion in January 2006. Visitors are also encouraged to visit Roesch Library, which holds more than 1.2 million volumes; the Ryan C. Harris Learning Teaching Center; and the Davis Center for Portfolio Management. More information about appointments and campus visits can be found online at http://admission.udayton.edu/visitud/ or by calling the Office of Admission at 937-229-4411 or 800-837-7433 (toll-free), Monday through Friday, 8:30 a.m. to 4:30 p.m. Open house programs are available in the fall, and individual appointments may be scheduled on Saturday mornings from January through May. The nearest commercial airport is Dayton International.

For Further Information Write to Mr. Robert Durkle, Director of Admission, University of Dayton, 300 College Park, Dayton, OH 45469-1300. *E-mail:* admission@udayton.edu. *Web site:* http://admission.udayton.edu.

THE UNIVERSITY OF FINDLAY
Findlay, Ohio

Findlay is a coed, private, comprehensive institution, founded in 1882, affiliated with the Church of God, offering degrees at the associate, bachelor's, and master's levels. It has a 200-acre campus in Findlay near Toledo.

Academic Information The faculty has 336 members (46% full-time). The undergraduate student-faculty ratio is 19:1. The library holds 135,000 titles, 1,050 serial subscriptions, and 2,000 audiovisual materials. Special programs include academic remediation, services for learning-disabled students, an honors program, cooperative (work-study) education, study abroad, advanced placement credit, accelerated degree programs, ESL programs, double majors, independent study, distance learning, self-designed majors, summer session for credit, part-time degree programs (daytime, evenings, weekends, summer), adult/continuing education programs, internships, and arrangement for off-campus study. The most frequently chosen baccalaureate fields are business/marketing, education, health professions and related sciences.
Student Body Statistics The student body totals 4,712, of whom 3,432 are undergraduates (998 freshmen). 58 percent are women and 42 percent are men. Students come from 45 states and territories and 34 other countries. 86 percent are from Ohio. 2.3 percent are international students. 16 percent of the 2003 graduating class went on to graduate and professional schools.
Expenses for 2003–04 *Application fee:* $0. *Comprehensive fee:* $27,014 includes full-time tuition ($19,052), mandatory fees ($900), and college room and board ($7062). *College room only:* $3540. Full-time tuition and fees vary according to location and program. Room and board charges vary according to housing facility. *Part-time tuition:* varies with location, program.
Financial Aid Forms of aid include need-based and non-need-based scholarships, athletic grants, and part-time jobs. The average aided 2003–04 undergraduate received an aid package worth an estimated $14,150. The application deadline for financial aid is continuous.
Freshman Admission Findlay requires a high school transcript, a minimum 2.3 high school GPA, and SAT I or ACT scores. TOEFL scores for international students are recommended. An essay, recommendations, and an interview are required for some. The application deadline for regular admission is rolling.
Transfer Admission The application deadline for admission is August 1.

Entrance Difficulty Findlay assesses its entrance difficulty level as moderately difficult. For the fall 2003 freshman class, 74 percent of the applicants were accepted.

For Further Information Contact Mr. Michael Momany, Executive Director of Enrollment Services, The University of Findlay, 1000 North Main Street, Findlay, OH 45840-3653. *Telephone:* 419-434-4732 or 800-548-0932 (toll-free). *Fax:* 419-434-4898. *E-mail:* admissions@findlay.edu. *Web site:* http://www.findlay.edu/.

See page 346 for a narrative description.

UNIVERSITY OF NORTHWESTERN OHIO
Lima, Ohio

University of Northwestern Ohio is a coed, private, primarily two-year college, founded in 1920, offering degrees at the associate and bachelor's levels. It has a 35-acre campus in Lima near Dayton and Toledo.

Academic Information The faculty has 95 members (72% full-time), 9% with terminal degrees. The student-faculty ratio is 24:1. The library holds 8,857 titles, 117 serial subscriptions, and 10 audiovisual materials. Special programs include academic remediation, cooperative (work-study) education, advanced placement credit, accelerated degree programs, double majors, distance learning, summer session for credit, part-time degree programs, and adult/continuing education programs. The most frequently chosen baccalaureate field is health professions and related sciences.
Student Body Statistics The student body is made up of 2,665 undergraduates (1,875 freshmen). 22 percent are women and 78 percent are men. Students come from 37 states and territories. 85 percent are from Ohio. 40 percent of the 2003 graduating class went on to four-year colleges.
Expenses for 2003–04 *Application fee:* $50. *Tuition:* $10,200 full-time, $175 per credit part-time. *College room only:* $2520.
Financial Aid Forms of aid include need-based scholarships and part-time jobs. The priority application deadline for financial aid is April 1.
Freshman Admission University of Northwestern Ohio requires a high school transcript and TOEFL scores for international students. The application deadline for regular admission is rolling.
Transfer Admission The application deadline for admission is rolling.
Entrance Difficulty University of Northwestern Ohio has an open admission policy.

For Further Information Contact Mr. Dan Klopp, Vice President for Enrollment Management, University of Northwestern Ohio, 1441 North Cable Road, Lima, OH 45805-1498. *Telephone:* 419-227-3141. *Fax:* 419-229-6926. *E-mail:* info@nc.edu. *Web site:* http://www.unoh.edu/.

UNIVERSITY OF PHOENIX–CINCINNATI CAMPUS
Cincinnati, Ohio

For Information Write to University of Phoenix–Cincinnati Campus, Cincinnati, OH 45246.

UNIVERSITY OF PHOENIX–CLEVELAND CAMPUS
Independence, Ohio

University of Phoenix–Cleveland Campus is a coed, proprietary, comprehensive institution, founded in 2000, offering degrees at the associate, bachelor's, master's, and doctoral levels and post-master's and postbachelor's certificates (courses conducted at 121 campuses and learning centers in 25 states).

Academic Information The faculty has 44 members (7% full-time), 14% with terminal degrees. The undergraduate student-faculty ratio is 5:1.

University of Phoenix–Cleveland Campus (continued)
The library holds 27 million titles and 11,648 serial subscriptions. Special programs include advanced placement credit, accelerated degree programs, independent study, distance learning, external degree programs, and adult/continuing education programs. The most frequently chosen baccalaureate fields are business/marketing, computer/information sciences.
Student Body Statistics The student body totals 673, of whom 457 are undergraduates (32 freshmen). 56 percent are women and 44 percent are men. 4.6 percent are international students.
Expenses for 2003–04 *Application fee:* $100. *Tuition:* $11,250 full-time, $375 per credit part-time.
Financial Aid Forms of aid include need-based and non-need-based scholarships. The average aided 2002–03 undergraduate received an aid package worth $1473. The application deadline for financial aid is continuous.
Freshman Admission University of Phoenix–Cleveland Campus requires 1 recommendation, 2 years of work experience, 23 years of age, and TOEFL scores for international students. A high school transcript is required for some. The application deadline for regular admission is rolling.
Transfer Admission The application deadline for admission is rolling.
Entrance Difficulty University of Phoenix–Cleveland Campus has an open admission policy.

For Further Information Contact Ms. Beth Barilla, Director of Admissions, University of Phoenix–Cleveland Campus, 4615 East Elwood Street, Mail Stop AA-K101, Phoenix, AZ 85040-1958. *Telephone:* 480-557-1712. *Fax:* 480-594-1758. *E-mail:* beth.barilla@phoenix.edu. *Web site:* http://www.phoenix.edu/.

UNIVERSITY OF PHOENIX–COLUMBUS OHIO CAMPUS
Columbus, Ohio

For Information Write to University of Phoenix–Columbus Ohio Campus, Columbus, OH 43240.

UNIVERSITY OF RIO GRANDE
Rio Grande, Ohio

Rio Grande is a coed, private, comprehensive institution, founded in 1876, offering degrees at the associate, bachelor's, and master's levels. It has a 170-acre campus in Rio Grande.

Academic Information The faculty has 146 members (58% full-time). The undergraduate student-faculty ratio is 18:1. The library holds 96,731 titles and 850 serial subscriptions. Special programs include academic remediation, services for learning-disabled students, an honors program, cooperative (work-study) education, advanced placement credit, accelerated degree programs, Freshman Honors College, ESL programs, independent study, self-designed majors, summer session for credit, part-time degree programs (daytime, evenings), adult/continuing education programs, and internships. The most frequently chosen baccalaureate fields are business/marketing, communications/communication technologies, education.
Student Body Statistics The student body totals 2,076, of whom 1,932 are undergraduates (343 freshmen). 59 percent are women and 41 percent are men. Students come from 11 states and territories and 15 other countries. 95 percent are from Ohio.
Expenses for 2003–04 *Application fee:* $15. *Area resident tuition:* $9514 full-time. *State resident tuition:* $9718 full-time. *Nonresident tuition:* $10,532 full-time. *Mandatory fees:* $520 full-time. *College room and board:* $5768. Room and board charges vary according to board plan.
Financial Aid Forms of aid include need-based and non-need-based scholarships, athletic grants, and part-time jobs. The average aided 2002–03 undergraduate received an aid package worth $7835. The application deadline for financial aid is continuous.
Freshman Admission Rio Grande requires a high school transcript, medical history, ACT scores, and TOEFL scores for international students. The application deadline for regular admission is rolling.

Transfer Admission The application deadline for admission is rolling.
Entrance Difficulty Rio Grande has an open admission policy.

For Further Information Contact Mr. Mark F. Abell, Executive Director of Admissions, University of Rio Grande, PO Box 500, Rio Grande, OH 45674. *Telephone:* 740-245-7208 or 800-282-7201 (toll-free in-state). *Fax:* 740-245-7260. *E-mail:* elambert@rio.edu. *Web site:* http://www.rio.edu/.

UNIVERSITY OF TOLEDO
Toledo, Ohio

UT is a coed, public university, founded in 1872, offering degrees at the associate, bachelor's, master's, doctoral, and first professional levels and post-master's and postbachelor's certificates. It has a 407-acre campus in Toledo near Detroit.

Academic Information The faculty has 1,180 members (58% full-time), 57% with terminal degrees. The undergraduate student-faculty ratio is 18:1. The library holds 1 million titles, 4,754 serial subscriptions, and 4,695 audiovisual materials. Special programs include academic remediation, services for learning-disabled students, an honors program, cooperative (work-study) education, study abroad, advanced placement credit, double majors, independent study, distance learning, self-designed majors, summer session for credit, part-time degree programs (daytime, evenings, weekends, summer), adult/continuing education programs, internships, and arrangement for off-campus study with Bowling Green State University, Medical College of Ohio, Consortium for Health Education, The Central States Universities, Inc. The most frequently chosen baccalaureate fields are business/marketing, education, engineering/engineering technologies.
Student Body Statistics The student body totals 20,594, of whom 17,388 are undergraduates (3,884 freshmen). 51 percent are women and 49 percent are men. Students come from 36 states and territories and 93 other countries. 92 percent are from Ohio. 2.3 percent are international students.
Expenses for 2003–04 *Application fee:* $40. *State resident tuition:* $5410 full-time, $267 per semester hour part-time. *Nonresident tuition:* $14,048 full-time, $627 per semester hour part-time. *Mandatory fees:* $1004 full-time. *College room and board:* $6834. Room and board charges vary according to board plan, housing facility, and location.
Financial Aid Forms of aid include need-based and non-need-based scholarships, athletic grants, and part-time jobs. The average aided 2003–04 undergraduate received an aid package worth an estimated $6881. The priority application deadline for financial aid is April 1.
Freshman Admission UT requires a high school transcript. SAT I scores, ACT scores, and TOEFL scores for international students are recommended. A minimum 2.0 high school GPA and SAT I or ACT scores are required for some. The application deadline for regular admission is rolling.
Transfer Admission The application deadline for admission is rolling.
Entrance Difficulty UT has an open admission policy for state residents. It assesses its entrance difficulty as moderately difficult for out-of-state applicants; moderately difficult for transfers; very difficult for physical therapy, engineering, pharmacy, legal assisting technology, pre-medicine, pre-dentistry programs.

For Further Information Contact Ms. Nancy Hintz, Assistant Director, University of Toledo, 2801 West Bancroft, Toledo, OH 43606-3398. *Telephone:* 419-530-5737 or 800-5TOLEDO (toll-free in-state). *Fax:* 419-530-5872. *E-mail:* enroll@utnet.utoledo.edu. *Web site:* http://www.utoledo.edu/.

URBANA UNIVERSITY
Urbana, Ohio

Urbana is a coed, private, comprehensive institution, founded in 1850, affiliated with the Church of the New Jerusalem, offering degrees at the associate, bachelor's, and master's levels. It has a 128-acre campus in Urbana near Columbus and Dayton.

Academic Information The faculty has 115 members (43% full-time), 39% with terminal degrees. The undergraduate student-faculty ratio is 16:1. The library holds 61,600 titles, 800 serial subscriptions, and 22,036 audiovisual materials. Special programs include academic remediation, services for learning-disabled students, an honors program, cooperative (work-study) education, advanced placement credit, accelerated degree programs, double majors, independent study, self-designed majors, summer session for credit, part-time degree programs (daytime, evenings, summer), adult/continuing education programs, internships, and arrangement for off-campus study with members of the Southwestern Ohio Council for Higher Education. The most frequently chosen baccalaureate fields are business/marketing, education, protective services/public administration.

Student Body Statistics The student body totals 1,527, of whom 1,441 are undergraduates (261 freshmen). 55 percent are women and 45 percent are men. 0.1 percent are international students.

Expenses for 2004–05 *Application fee: $25. Comprehensive fee: $19,900* includes full-time tuition ($14,220) and college room and board ($5680). *College room only: $1920.* Full-time tuition varies according to location. Room and board charges vary according to board plan, housing facility, location, and student level. *Part-time tuition:* $295 per semester hour. *Part-time mandatory fees:* $90 per term. Part-time tuition and fees vary according to location.

Financial Aid Forms of aid include need-based and non-need-based scholarships, athletic grants, and part-time jobs. The average aided 2003–04 undergraduate received an aid package worth an estimated $13,121. The priority application deadline for financial aid is April 1.

Freshman Admission Urbana requires an essay, a high school transcript, a minimum 2.0 high school GPA, SAT I or ACT scores, and TOEFL scores for international students. An interview is recommended. 2 recommendations and an interview are required for some. The application deadline for regular admission is rolling.

Transfer Admission The application deadline for admission is rolling.

Entrance Difficulty Urbana assesses its entrance difficulty level as moderately difficult. For the fall 2003 freshman class, 58 percent of the applicants were accepted.

For Further Information Contact Ms. Melissa Tolle, Associate Director of Admissions, Urbana University, 579 College Way, Urbana, OH 93078. *Telephone:* 937-484-1356 or 800-7-URBANA (toll-free). *Fax:* 937-484-1389. *E-mail:* admiss@urbana.edu. *Web site:* http://www.urbana.edu/.

URSULINE COLLEGE
Pepper Pike, Ohio

Ursuline is a women's, private, Roman Catholic, comprehensive institution, founded in 1871, offering degrees at the bachelor's and master's levels and post-master's certificates (applications from men are also accepted). It has a 112-acre campus in Pepper Pike near Cleveland.

Academic Information The faculty has 185 members (32% full-time), 39% with terminal degrees. The undergraduate student-faculty ratio is 10:1. The library holds 126,491 titles, 332 serial subscriptions, and 6,926 audiovisual materials. Special programs include academic remediation, services for learning-disabled students, cooperative (work-study) education, advanced placement credit, accelerated degree programs, double majors, independent study, distance learning, summer session for credit, part-time degree programs (daytime, evenings, weekends, summer), adult/continuing education programs, internships, and arrangement for off-campus study with Baldwin-Wallace College, Case Western Reserve University, Cleveland State University, Cuyahoga Community College, David N. Myers College, Notre Dame College of Ohio, John Carroll University. The most frequently chosen baccalaureate fields are business/marketing, health professions and related sciences, visual/performing arts.

Student Body Statistics The student body totals 1,409, of whom 1,095 are undergraduates (118 freshmen). Students come from 9 states and territories and 7 other countries. 99 percent are from Ohio. 1 percent are international students.

Expenses for 2003–04 *Application fee: $25. Comprehensive fee: $22,728* includes full-time tuition ($17,100), mandatory fees ($170), and college room and board ($5458). Room and board charges vary according to board plan.

Financial Aid Forms of aid include need-based and non-need-based scholarships, athletic grants, and part-time jobs. The average aided 2003–04 undergraduate received an aid package worth an estimated $15,872. The priority application deadline for financial aid is March 1.

Freshman Admission Ursuline requires a high school transcript, SAT I or ACT scores, and TOEFL scores for international students. An essay, a minimum 2.0 high school GPA, recommendations, and an interview are recommended. The application deadline for regular admission is rolling and for early action it is November 15.

Transfer Admission The application deadline for admission is rolling.

Entrance Difficulty Ursuline assesses its entrance difficulty level as minimally difficult. For the fall 2003 freshman class, 70 percent of the applicants were accepted.

For Further Information Contact Ms. Sarah Carr, Director of Admissions, Ursuline College, 2550 Lander Road, Pepper Pike, OH 44124. *Telephone:* 440-449-4203 or 888-URSULINE (toll-free). *Fax:* 440-684-6138. *E-mail:* admission@ursuline.edu. *Web site:* http://www.ursuline.edu/.

WALSH UNIVERSITY
North Canton, Ohio

Walsh is a coed, private, Roman Catholic, comprehensive institution, founded in 1958, offering degrees at the associate, bachelor's, and master's levels. It has a 107-acre campus in North Canton near Cleveland.

Academic Information The faculty has 196 members (37% full-time), 40% with terminal degrees. The undergraduate student-faculty ratio is 14:1. The library holds 132,957 titles, 663 serial subscriptions, and 1,434 audiovisual materials. Special programs include academic remediation, services for learning-disabled students, an honors program, advanced placement credit, accelerated degree programs, Freshman Honors College, ESL programs, double majors, self-designed majors, summer session for credit, part-time degree programs (daytime, evenings, weekends, summer), adult/continuing education programs, internships, and arrangement for off-campus study with University of Michigan, Case Western Reserve University, Stark State College of Technology. The most frequently chosen baccalaureate fields are business/marketing, communications/communication technologies, education.

Student Body Statistics The student body totals 1,801, of whom 1,573 are undergraduates (294 freshmen). 60 percent are women and 40 percent are men. Students come from 20 states and territories and 16 other countries. 99 percent are from Ohio. 1.7 percent are international students. 24.3 percent of the 2003 graduating class went on to graduate and professional schools.

Expenses for 2004–05 *Application fee: $25. One-time mandatory fee: $165. Comprehensive fee: $23,310* includes full-time tuition ($15,100), mandatory fees ($510), and college room and board ($7700). *College room only: $4500.* Full-time tuition and fees vary according to course load. Room and board charges vary according to board plan and housing facility. *Part-time tuition:* $500 per credit. *Part-time mandatory fees:* $17 per credit.

Financial Aid Forms of aid include need-based and non-need-based scholarships, athletic grants, and part-time jobs. The average aided 2003–04 undergraduate received an aid package worth an estimated $10,364. The application deadline for financial aid is continuous.

Freshman Admission Walsh requires a high school transcript, a minimum 2.1 high school GPA, SAT I or ACT scores, and TOEFL scores for international students. An interview is recommended. An essay, a minimum 3.0 high school GPA, and 2 recommendations are required for some. The application deadline for regular admission is rolling.

Transfer Admission The application deadline for admission is rolling.

Walsh University (continued)

Entrance Difficulty Walsh assesses its entrance difficulty level as moderately difficult. For the fall 2003 freshman class, 82 percent of the applicants were accepted.

For Further Information Contact Mr. Brett Freshour, Dean of Enrollment Management, Walsh University, 2020 East Maple. *Telephone:* 330-490-7171, 800-362-9846 (toll-free in-state), or 800-362-8846 (toll-free out-of-state). *Fax:* 330-490-7165. *E-mail:* admissions@walsh.edu. *Web site:* http://www.walsh.edu/.

WILBERFORCE UNIVERSITY
Wilberforce, Ohio

Wilberforce University is a coed, private, four-year college, founded in 1856, affiliated with the African Methodist Episcopal Church, offering degrees at the bachelor's level. It has a 125-acre campus in Wilberforce near Dayton.

Academic Information The faculty has 74 members (66% full-time). The student-faculty ratio is 17:1. The library holds 63,000 titles, 650 serial subscriptions, and 500 audiovisual materials. Special programs include academic remediation, an honors program, cooperative (work-study) education, study abroad, advanced placement credit, Freshman Honors College, external degree programs, and arrangement for off-campus study with 18 members of the Southwestern Ohio Council for Higher Education. The most frequently chosen baccalaureate fields are business/marketing, communications/communication technologies, computer/information sciences.

Student Body Statistics The student body is made up of 1,180 undergraduates (190 freshmen). 60 percent are women and 40 percent are men. Students come from 30 states and territories and 3 other countries. 62 percent are from Ohio. 0.3 percent are international students.

Expenses for 2003–04 *Application fee:* $20. *Comprehensive fee:* $16,090 includes full-time tuition ($9720), mandatory fees ($1050), and college room and board ($5320). *College room only:* $2820. *Part-time tuition:* $376 per credit hour.

Financial Aid Forms of aid include need-based and non-need-based scholarships and part-time jobs. The application deadline for financial aid is June 1 with a priority deadline of April 30.

Freshman Admission Wilberforce University requires an essay, a high school transcript, a minimum 2.0 high school GPA, 2 recommendations, SAT I or ACT scores, and TOEFL scores for international students. An interview is recommended. The application deadline for regular admission is July 1.

Transfer Admission The application deadline for admission is July 1.

Entrance Difficulty Wilberforce University assesses its entrance difficulty level as minimally difficult. For the fall 2003 freshman class, 22 percent of the applicants were accepted.

For Further Information Contact Mr. Kenneth C. Christmon, Director of Admissions, Wilberforce University, PO Box 1001, Wilberforce, OH 45384-1001. *Telephone:* 937-708-5789 or 800-367-8568 (toll-free). *Fax:* 937-376-4751. *E-mail:* kchristm@wilberforce.edu. *Web site:* http://www.wilberforce.edu/.

WILMINGTON COLLEGE
Wilmington, Ohio

Wilmington College is a coed, private, Friends, comprehensive institution, founded in 1870, offering degrees at the bachelor's and master's levels. It has a 1,465-acre campus in Wilmington near Cincinnati and Columbus.

Expenses for 2003–04 *Application fee:* $25. *Comprehensive fee:* $24,172 includes full-time tuition ($17,256), mandatory fees ($426), and college room and board ($6490). *College room only:* $3080. Room and board charges vary according to board plan and housing facility. *Part-time tuition:* varies with course load.

For Further Information Contact Ms. Tina Garland, Interim Director of Admission and Financial Aid, Wilmington College, Pyle Center Box 1325, 251 Ludovic Street, Wilmington, OH 45177. *Telephone:* 937-382-6661 Ext. 260 or 800-341-9318 Ext. 260 (toll-free). *Fax:* 937-382-7077. *E-mail:* admission@wilmington.edu. *Web site:* http://www.wilmington.edu/.

WITTENBERG UNIVERSITY
Springfield, Ohio

Wittenberg University is a coed, private, comprehensive institution, founded in 1845, affiliated with the Evangelical Lutheran Church, offering degrees at the bachelor's and master's levels. It has a 71-acre campus in Springfield near Columbus and Dayton.

Academic Information The faculty has 200 members (74% full-time), 78% with terminal degrees. The undergraduate student-faculty ratio is 14:1. The library holds 350,000 titles and 1,300 serial subscriptions. Special programs include academic remediation, an honors program, cooperative (work-study) education, study abroad, advanced placement credit, accelerated degree programs, Freshman Honors College, ESL programs, double majors, independent study, self-designed majors, summer session for credit, part-time degree programs (daytime, evenings, summer), external degree programs, adult/continuing education programs, internships, and arrangement for off-campus study with 21 members of the Southwestern Ohio Council for Higher Education. The most frequently chosen baccalaureate fields are biological/life sciences, business/marketing, English.

Student Body Statistics The student body totals 2,189, of whom 2,152 are undergraduates (549 freshmen). 58 percent are women and 42 percent are men. Students come from 40 states and territories and 23 other countries. 54 percent are from Ohio. 2.5 percent are international students. 28 percent of the 2003 graduating class went on to graduate and professional schools.

Expenses for 2004–05 *Application fee:* $40. *Comprehensive fee:* $32,882 includes full-time tuition ($26,040), mandatory fees ($156), and college room and board ($6686). *College room only:* $3454. Room and board charges vary according to board plan. *Part-time tuition:* $826 per hour. Part-time tuition varies according to course load.

Financial Aid Forms of aid include need-based and non-need-based scholarships and part-time jobs. The average aided 2002–03 undergraduate received an aid package worth $21,286. The application deadline for financial aid is March 15 with a priority deadline of February 15.

Freshman Admission Wittenberg University requires an essay, a high school transcript, SAT I or ACT scores, and TOEFL scores for international students. Recommendations and an interview are recommended. The application deadline for for early decision it is November 15 and for early action it is December 1.

Transfer Admission The application deadline for admission is rolling.

Entrance Difficulty Wittenberg University assesses its entrance difficulty level as moderately difficult; very difficult for International United Nations Scholars Program, Institute of International Education Program. For the fall 2003 freshman class, 74 percent of the applicants were accepted.

For Further Information Contact Mr. Kenneth G. Benne, Dean of Admissions and Financial Aid, Wittenberg University, PO Box 720, Springfield, OH 45501-0720. *Telephone:* 937-327-6314 Ext. 6366 or 800-677-7558 Ext. 6314 (toll-free). *Fax:* 937-327-6379. *E-mail:* admission@wittenberg.edu. *Web site:* http://www.wittenberg.edu/.

WRIGHT STATE UNIVERSITY
Dayton, Ohio

Wright State is a coed, public university, founded in 1964, offering degrees at the associate, bachelor's, master's, doctoral, and first professional levels and post-master's certificates. It has a 557-acre campus in Dayton near Cincinnati.

Academic Information The faculty has 864 members (61% full-time). The undergraduate student-faculty ratio is 20:1. The library holds 695,805 titles and 5,312 serial subscriptions. Special programs include academic remediation, services for learning-disabled students, an honors program, cooperative (work-study) education, study abroad, advanced placement credit, ESL programs, self-designed majors, summer session for credit, part-time degree programs, adult/continuing education programs, internships, and arrangement for off-campus study with members of the Southwestern Ohio Council for Higher Education. The most frequently chosen baccalaureate fields are business/marketing, education, social sciences and history.

Student Body Statistics The student body totals 15,694, of whom 11,787 are undergraduates (2,282 freshmen). 57 percent are women and 43 percent are men. Students come from 49 states and territories and 60 other countries. 97 percent are from Ohio. 1.2 percent are international students.

Expenses for 2003–04 *Application fee:* $30. *State resident tuition:* $5892 full-time, $170 per hour part-time. *Nonresident tuition:* $10,524 full-time, $340 per hour part-time. *College room and board:* $6019. Room and board charges vary according to board plan and housing facility.

Financial Aid Forms of aid include need-based and non-need-based scholarships and part-time jobs. The average aided 2002–03 undergraduate received an aid package worth $7857. The priority application deadline for financial aid is February 15.

Freshman Admission Wright State requires a high school transcript, SAT I or ACT scores, and TOEFL scores for international students. A minimum 2.0 high school GPA is recommended. The application deadline for regular admission is rolling.

Transfer Admission The application deadline for admission is rolling.

Entrance Difficulty Wright State assesses its entrance difficulty level as minimally difficult; moderately difficult for out-of-state applicants. For the fall 2003 freshman class, 91 percent of the applicants were accepted.

For Further Information Contact Ms. Cathy Davis, Director of Undergraduate Admissions, Wright State University, 3640 Colonel Glenn Highway, Dayton, OH 45435. *Telephone:* 937-775-5700 or 800-247-1770 (toll-free). *Fax:* 937-775-5795. *E-mail:* admissions@wright.edu. *Web site:* http://www.wright.edu/.

XAVIER UNIVERSITY
Cincinnati, Ohio

Xavier is a coed, private, Roman Catholic, comprehensive institution, founded in 1831, offering degrees at the associate, bachelor's, master's, and doctoral levels and post-master's and postbachelor's certificates. It has a 130-acre campus in Cincinnati.

Academic Information The faculty has 591 members (47% full-time), 52% with terminal degrees. The undergraduate student-faculty ratio is 13:1. The library holds 191,923 titles, 1,633 serial subscriptions, and 8,371 audiovisual materials. Special programs include academic remediation, services for learning-disabled students, an honors program, cooperative (work-study) education, study abroad, advanced placement credit, ESL programs, double majors, independent study, summer session for credit, part-time degree programs (daytime, evenings, weekends, summer), adult/continuing education programs, internships, and arrangement for off-campus study with 13 members of the Greater Cincinnati Consortium of Colleges and Universities. The most frequently chosen baccalaureate fields are business/marketing, communications/communication technologies, liberal arts/general studies.

Student Body Statistics The student body totals 6,626, of whom 3,915 are undergraduates (786 freshmen). 56 percent are women and 44 percent are men. Students come from 46 states and territories and 53 other countries. 66 percent are from Ohio. 2.6 percent are international students. 23 percent of the 2003 graduating class went on to graduate and professional schools.

Expenses for 2003–04 *Application fee:* $35. *Comprehensive fee:* $27,150 includes full-time tuition ($18,850), mandatory fees ($300), and college room and board ($8000). *College room only:* $4400. Full-time tuition and fees vary according to program. Room and board charges vary according to board plan and housing facility. *Part-time tuition:* $395 per credit hour. Part-time tuition varies according to course load.

Financial Aid Forms of aid include need-based and non-need-based scholarships, athletic grants, and part-time jobs. The average aided 2003–04 undergraduate received an aid package worth an estimated $13,616. The priority application deadline for financial aid is February 15.

Freshman Admission Xavier requires an essay, a high school transcript, 1 recommendation, SAT I or ACT scores, and TOEFL scores for international students. An interview is recommended. The application deadline for regular admission is February 1.

Transfer Admission The application deadline for admission is rolling.

Entrance Difficulty Xavier assesses its entrance difficulty level as moderately difficult; very difficult for occupational therapy program; dual enrollment medical program with University of Cincinnati. For the fall 2003 freshman class, 78 percent of the applicants were accepted.

For Further Information Contact Mr. Marc Camille, Dean of Admission, Xavier University, 3800 Victory Parkway, Cincinnati, OH 45207-5311. *Telephone:* 513-745-3301 or 800-344-4698 (toll-free). *Fax:* 513-745-4319. *E-mail:* xuadmit@xavier.edu. *Web site:* http://www.xavier.edu/.

YOUNGSTOWN STATE UNIVERSITY
Youngstown, Ohio

YSU is a coed, public, comprehensive institution, founded in 1908, offering degrees at the associate, bachelor's, master's, and doctoral levels and postbachelor's certificates. It has a 200-acre campus in Youngstown near Cleveland and Pittsburgh.

Academic Information The faculty has 951 members (43% full-time), 49% with terminal degrees. The undergraduate student-faculty ratio is 18:1. The library holds 991,501 titles, 2,908 serial subscriptions, and 16,976 audiovisual materials. Special programs include academic remediation, services for learning-disabled students, an honors program, cooperative (work-study) education, study abroad, advanced placement credit, accelerated degree programs, ESL programs, double majors, distance learning, self-designed majors, summer session for credit, part-time degree programs (daytime, evenings, weekends, summer), adult/continuing education programs, internships, and arrangement for off-campus study with Lorain County Community College. The most frequently chosen baccalaureate fields are business/marketing, education, protective services/public administration.

Student Body Statistics The student body totals 12,850, of whom 11,592 are undergraduates (2,029 freshmen). 55 percent are women and 45 percent are men. Students come from 39 states and territories and 52 other countries. 91 percent are from Ohio. 0.7 percent are international students.

Expenses for 2003–04 *Application fee:* $30. *State resident tuition:* $5328 full-time, $180 per credit part-time. *Nonresident tuition:* $10,536 full-time, $397 per credit part-time. *Mandatory fees:* $150 full-time, $5 per credit part-time. Full-time tuition and fees vary according to course load. Part-time tuition and fees vary according to course load. *College room and board:* $5700. Room and board charges vary according to board plan and housing facility.

Financial Aid Forms of aid include need-based and non-need-based scholarships, athletic grants, and part-time jobs. The priority application deadline for financial aid is February 15.

Freshman Admission YSU requires a high school transcript, SAT I or ACT scores, and TOEFL scores for international students. An interview is required for some. The application deadline for regular admission is August 15 and for early action it is February 15.

Transfer Admission The application deadline for admission is August 15.

Entrance Difficulty YSU has an open admission policy for state residents, students from Mercer and Lawrence Counties in Pennsylvania. It

Ohio

Youngstown State University (continued)

assesses its entrance difficulty as minimally difficult for out-of-state applicants; minimally difficult for transfers; moderately difficult for nursing, engineering, engineering technology, health occupations programs.

For Further Information Contact Ms. Sue Davis, Director of Undergraduate Admissions, Youngstown State University, One University Plaza, Youngstown, OH 44555-0001. *Telephone:* 330-941-2000, 877-468-6978 (toll-free in-state), or 877-466-6978 (toll-free out-of-state). *Fax:* 330-941-3674. *E-mail:* enroll@ysu.edu. *Web site:* http://www.ysu.edu/.

See page 358 for a narrative description.

Oklahoma

BACONE COLLEGE
Muskogee, Oklahoma

Bacone is a coed, private, four-year college, founded in 1880, affiliated with the American Baptist Churches in the U.S.A., offering degrees at the associate and bachelor's levels. It has a 220-acre campus in Muskogee near Tulsa.

Academic Information The faculty has 32 full-time members. The library holds 34,564 titles, 121 serial subscriptions, and 185 audiovisual materials. Special programs include academic remediation, services for learning-disabled students, cooperative (work-study) education, advanced placement credit, accelerated degree programs, self-designed majors, summer session for credit, part-time degree programs (daytime, evenings, weekends, summer), adult/continuing education programs, and internships. The most frequently chosen baccalaureate fields are business/marketing, health professions and related sciences.
Student Body Statistics The student body is made up of 914 undergraduates (231 freshmen). 54 percent are women and 46 percent are men. Students come from 24 states and territories and 10 other countries. 85 percent are from Oklahoma. 3 percent are international students.
Expenses for 2004–05 *Application fee:* $25. *Comprehensive fee:* $14,230 includes full-time tuition ($7900), mandatory fees ($630), and college room and board ($5700). *College room only:* $3000. *Part-time tuition:* $350 per credit hour. *Part-time mandatory fees:* $240 per term. Part-time tuition and fees vary according to course load.
Financial Aid Forms of aid include need-based scholarships and part-time jobs. The priority application deadline for financial aid is March 31.
Freshman Admission Bacone requires a high school transcript, a minimum 2.0 high school GPA, minimum ACT score of 14, SAT I or ACT scores, and TOEFL scores for international students. ACT scores are recommended. The application deadline for regular admission is rolling.
Transfer Admission The application deadline for admission is rolling.
Entrance Difficulty Bacone assesses its entrance difficulty level as minimally difficult; moderately difficult for nursing, radiological technology programs. For the fall 2003 freshman class, 58 percent of the applicants were accepted.

For Further Information Contact Ms. Carla Green, Admissions Counselor, Bacone College, 2299 Old Bacone Road, Muskogee, OK 74403. *Telephone:* 918-781-7349 or 888-682-5514 Ext. 7340 (toll-free). *Fax:* 918-682-5514. *E-mail:* admissions@bacone.edu. *Web site:* http://www.bacone.edu/.

BARTLESVILLE WESLEYAN COLLEGE
See Oklahoma Wesleyan University

CAMERON UNIVERSITY
Lawton, Oklahoma

Cameron is a coed, public, comprehensive unit of Oklahoma State Regents for Higher Education, founded in 1908, offering degrees at the bachelor's and master's levels. It has a 160-acre campus in Lawton.

Academic Information The faculty has 267 members (69% full-time), 42% with terminal degrees. The undergraduate student-faculty ratio is 23:1. The library holds 258,000 titles, 3,840 serial subscriptions, and 7,053 audiovisual materials. Special programs include academic remediation, services for learning-disabled students, an honors program, advanced placement credit, accelerated degree programs, double majors, independent study, distance learning, summer session for credit, part-time degree programs (daytime, evenings, weekends, summer), adult/continuing education programs, and arrangement for off-campus study with University of Oklahoma, East Central University, Oklahoma State University. The most frequently chosen baccalaureate fields are business/marketing, computer/information sciences, education.
Student Body Statistics The student body totals 5,632, of whom 5,193 are undergraduates (888 freshmen). 57 percent are women and 43 percent are men. Students come from 22 states and territories and 21 other countries. 98 percent are from Oklahoma. 2.9 percent are international students.
Expenses for 2004–05 *Application fee:* $15. *State resident tuition:* $2778 full-time, $92.60 per semester hour part-time. *Nonresident tuition:* $6678 full-time, $222.60 per semester hour part-time. *Mandatory fees:* $165 full-time, $80 per term part-time. Full-time tuition and fees vary according to course level, course load, degree level, and student level. Part-time tuition and fees vary according to course level, course load, degree level, and student level. *College room and board:* $2854. Room and board charges vary according to board plan.
Financial Aid Forms of aid include need-based and non-need-based scholarships, athletic grants, and part-time jobs. The application deadline for financial aid is continuous.
Freshman Admission Cameron requires a high school transcript, SAT I or ACT scores, and TOEFL scores for international students. The application deadline for regular admission is rolling.
Transfer Admission The application deadline for admission is rolling.
Entrance Difficulty Cameron assesses its entrance difficulty level as minimally difficult. For the fall 2003 freshman class, 100 percent of the applicants were accepted.

For Further Information Contact Ms. Brenda Dally, Coordinator of Student Recruitment, Cameron University, Cameron University, Attention: Admissions, 2800 West Gore Boulevard, Lawton, OK 73505. *Telephone:* 580-581-2289 or 888-454-7600 (toll-free). *Fax:* 580-581-5514. *E-mail:* admiss@cua.cameron.edu. *Web site:* http://www.cameron.edu/.

EAST CENTRAL UNIVERSITY
Ada, Oklahoma

East Central is a coed, public, comprehensive unit of Oklahoma State Regents for Higher Education, founded in 1909, offering degrees at the bachelor's and master's levels. It has a 140-acre campus in Ada near Oklahoma City.

Academic Information The faculty has 265 members (72% full-time). The undergraduate student-faculty ratio is 19:1. The library holds 213,000 titles and 800 serial subscriptions. Special programs include academic remediation, services for learning-disabled students, an honors program, advanced placement credit, accelerated degree programs, double majors, distance learning, summer session for credit, part-time degree programs, adult/continuing education programs, internships, and arrangement for off-campus study with Ardmore Higher Education Center. The most frequently chosen baccalaureate fields are business/marketing, education, personal/miscellaneous services.

Student Body Statistics The student body totals 4,442, of whom 3,685 are undergraduates (704 freshmen). 59 percent are women and 41 percent are men. Students come from 19 states and territories and 32 other countries. 97 percent are from Oklahoma.

Expenses for 2003–04 *Application fee:* $0. *State resident tuition:* $2685 full-time, $89.45 per semester hour part-time. *Nonresident tuition:* $6585 full-time, $219.45 per semester hour part-time. *Mandatory fees:* $773 full-time. Full-time tuition and fees vary according to course level, course load, and student level. Part-time tuition varies according to course level, course load, and student level. *College room and board:* $2774. *College room only:* $960. Room and board charges vary according to board plan and housing facility.

Financial Aid Forms of aid include need-based and non-need-based scholarships, athletic grants, and part-time jobs. The average aided 2003–04 undergraduate received an aid package worth an estimated $7444. The priority application deadline for financial aid is March 1.

Freshman Admission East Central requires a high school transcript, SAT I or ACT scores, and TOEFL scores for international students. ACT scores are recommended. A minimum 2.7 high school GPA and rank in upper 50% of high school class are required for some. The application deadline for regular admission is September 1.

Transfer Admission The application deadline for admission is September 1.

Entrance Difficulty East Central assesses its entrance difficulty level as moderately difficult; minimally difficult for transfers.

For Further Information Contact Pam Denny, Freshman Admissions Officer, East Central University, PMBJ8, 1100 East 14th Street, Ada, OK 74820-6999. *Telephone:* 580-332-8000 Ext. 239. *Fax:* 580-310-5432. *E-mail:* parmstro@mailclerk.ecok.edu. *Web site:* http://www.ecok.edu/.

HILLSDALE FREE WILL BAPTIST COLLEGE
Moore, Oklahoma

Hillsdale is a coed, private, Free Will Baptist, comprehensive institution, founded in 1959, offering degrees at the associate, bachelor's, and master's levels. It has a 41-acre campus in Moore near Oklahoma City.

Academic Information The faculty has 48 members (38% full-time), 33% with terminal degrees. The undergraduate student-faculty ratio is 9:1. The library holds 20,102 titles, 363 serial subscriptions, and 1,800 audiovisual materials. Special programs include academic remediation, advanced placement credit, accelerated degree programs, ESL programs, double majors, independent study, summer session for credit, part-time degree programs (daytime, evenings, summer), adult/continuing education programs, and internships. The most frequently chosen baccalaureate fields are business/marketing, interdisciplinary studies, philosophy, religion, and theology.

Student Body Statistics The student body totals 276, of whom 265 are undergraduates (71 freshmen). 45 percent are women and 55 percent are men. Students come from 15 states and territories and 13 other countries. 81 percent are from Oklahoma. 7.2 percent are international students. 17 percent of the 2003 graduating class went on to graduate and professional schools.

Expenses for 2004–05 *Application fee:* $20. *Comprehensive fee:* $11,490 includes full-time tuition ($6400), mandatory fees ($890), and college room and board ($4200). *Part-time tuition:* $240 per credit hour.

Financial Aid Forms of aid include need-based and non-need-based scholarships and part-time jobs. The application deadline for financial aid is continuous.

Freshman Admission Hillsdale requires an essay, a high school transcript, 1 recommendation, Biblical foundation statement, student conduct pledge; medical form required for some, SAT I or ACT scores, and TOEFL scores for international students. A minimum 2.0 high school GPA and 2 recommendations are recommended. 1 recommendation and an interview are required for some. The application deadline for regular admission is rolling.

Transfer Admission The application deadline for admission is rolling.

Entrance Difficulty Hillsdale assesses its entrance difficulty level as noncompetitive. For the fall 2003 freshman class, 100 percent of the applicants were accepted.

For Further Information Contact Ms. Sue Chaffin, Registrar/Assistant Director of Admissions, Hillsdale Free Will Baptist College, PO Box 7208, Moore, OK 73153-1208. *Telephone:* 405-912-9006. *Fax:* 405-912-9050. *E-mail:* hillsdale@hc.edu. *Web site:* http://www.hc.edu/.

LANGSTON UNIVERSITY
Langston, Oklahoma

Langston University is a coed, public, comprehensive unit of Oklahoma State Regents for Higher Education, founded in 1897, offering degrees at the associate, bachelor's, and master's levels. It has a 40-acre campus in Langston near Oklahoma City.

Expenses for 2003–04 *State resident tuition:* $1818 full-time. *Nonresident tuition:* $5430 full-time. *Mandatory fees:* $969 full-time. *College room and board:* $4380. *College room only:* $2400.

For Further Information Contact Brent Russell, Assistant Director of Admission, Langston University, Langston University, PO Box 728, Langston, OK 73120. *Telephone:* 405-466-2980 or 405-466-3428 (toll-free). *Fax:* 405-466-3391. *Web site:* http://www.lunet.edu/.

METROPOLITAN COLLEGE
Oklahoma City, Oklahoma

Metropolitan College is a coed, primarily women's, proprietary, four-year college of Wyandotte Collegiate Systems, offering degrees at the associate and bachelor's levels.

Expenses for 2003–04 *Application fee:* $50. *Tuition:* $7710 full-time.

For Further Information Contact Ms. Pamela Picken, Admissions Director, Metropolitan College, 1900 NW Expressway R-302, Oklahoma City, OK 73118. *Telephone:* 405-843-1000. *Fax:* 405-528-0320. *Web site:* http://www.metropolitancollege.edu/.

METROPOLITAN COLLEGE
Tulsa, Oklahoma

Metropolitan College is a coed, primarily women's, proprietary, four-year college, offering degrees at the associate and bachelor's levels.

Academic Information The faculty has 16 members (25% full-time), 50% with terminal degrees. The student-faculty ratio is 15:1. Special programs include academic remediation, accelerated degree programs, part-time degree programs (daytime, evenings), adult/continuing education programs, and internships.

Student Body Statistics The student body is made up of 223 undergraduates (87 freshmen). 91 percent are women and 9 percent are men. Students come from 3 states and territories. 99 percent are from Oklahoma.

Expenses for 2004–05 *Application fee:* $50. *Tuition:* $6535 full-time. *Mandatory fees:* $1200 full-time. Full-time tuition and fees vary according to course load and program.

Financial Aid The application deadline for financial aid is continuous.

Freshman Admission Metropolitan College requires a high school transcript, an interview, and Wonderlic aptitude test.

Entrance Difficulty Metropolitan College has an open admission policy.

For Further Information Contact Ms. Vicki Angelo, Admissions Director, Metropolitan College, 4528 South Sheridan Road, Suite 105, Tulsa, OK 74145-1011. *Telephone:* 918-627-9300 Ext. 213. *Fax:* 918-627-2122. *Web site:* http://www.metropolitancollege.edu/.

MID-AMERICA CHRISTIAN UNIVERSITY

Oklahoma City, Oklahoma

For Information Write to Mid-America Christian University, Oklahoma City, OK 73170-4504.

NORTHEASTERN STATE UNIVERSITY

Tahlequah, Oklahoma

NSU is a coed, public, comprehensive unit of Oklahoma State Regents for Higher Education, founded in 1846, offering degrees at the bachelor's, master's, and first professional levels. It has a 160-acre campus in Tahlequah near Tulsa.

Academic Information The faculty has 446 members. The undergraduate student-faculty ratio is 24:1. The library holds 424,818 titles, 3,983 serial subscriptions, and 6,804 audiovisual materials. Special programs include academic remediation, services for learning-disabled students, an honors program, advanced placement credit, ESL programs, double majors, distance learning, summer session for credit, part-time degree programs, adult/continuing education programs, and internships. The most frequently chosen baccalaureate fields are business/marketing, education, protective services/public administration.
Student Body Statistics The student body totals 9,297, of whom 8,313 are undergraduates (1,294 freshmen). 59 percent are women and 41 percent are men. Students come from 27 states and territories and 44 other countries. 100 percent are from Oklahoma.
Expenses for 2003–04 *Application fee:* $0. *State resident tuition:* $2664 full-time, $88.80 per credit hour part-time. *Nonresident tuition:* $6564 full-time, $218.80 per credit hour part-time. *Mandatory fees:* $36 full-time. Full-time tuition and fees vary according to course level, course load, location, and student level. Part-time tuition varies according to course level, course load, and student level. *College room and board:* $3080. Room and board charges vary according to board plan and housing facility.
Financial Aid Forms of aid include need-based and non-need-based scholarships, athletic grants, and part-time jobs. The average aided 2002–03 undergraduate received an aid package worth $8100. The priority application deadline for financial aid is April 1.
Freshman Admission NSU requires a high school transcript, ACT scores, and TOEFL scores for international students. Recommendations and an interview are required for some. The application deadline for regular admission is August 5.
Transfer Admission The application deadline for admission is August 5.
Entrance Difficulty NSU assesses its entrance difficulty level as moderately difficult; minimally difficult for transfers. For the fall 2003 freshman class, 89 percent of the applicants were accepted.

For Further Information Contact Mr. Todd Essary, Director of High School and College Relations, Northeastern State University, 601 North Grand, Tahlequah, OK 74464. *Telephone:* 918-456-5511 Ext. 2200 or 800-722-9614 (toll-free in-state). *Fax:* 918-458-2342. *E-mail:* nsuadmis@nsuok.edu. *Web site:* http://www.nsuok.edu/.

NORTHWESTERN OKLAHOMA STATE UNIVERSITY

Alva, Oklahoma

NWOSU is a coed, public, comprehensive unit of Oklahoma State Regents for Higher Education, founded in 1897, offering degrees at the bachelor's and master's levels and post-master's and postbachelor's certificates. It has a 70-acre campus in Alva.

Academic Information The faculty has 142 members (49% full-time), 35% with terminal degrees. The undergraduate student-faculty ratio is 16:1. The library holds 299,974 titles, 1,411 serial subscriptions, and 3,466 audiovisual materials. Special programs include academic remediation, services for learning-disabled students, study abroad, advanced placement credit, double majors, independent study, distance learning, summer session for credit, part-time degree programs (daytime, evenings, weekends,

summer), adult/continuing education programs, internships, and arrangement for off-campus study with Northern Oklahoma College, Southwestern Oklahoma State University. The most frequently chosen baccalaureate fields are business/marketing, education, health professions and related sciences.
Student Body Statistics The student body totals 2,126, of whom 1,874 are undergraduates (313 freshmen). 54 percent are women and 46 percent are men. Students come from 33 states and territories and 28 other countries. 83 percent are from Oklahoma. 2.4 percent are international students.
Expenses for 2003–04 *Application fee:* $15. *State resident tuition:* $2697 full-time, $89.90 per credit hour part-time. *Nonresident tuition:* $6597 full-time, $219 per credit hour part-time. *Mandatory fees:* $31 full-time, $16 per term part-time. Full-time tuition and fees vary according to course load, location, and student level. Part-time tuition and fees vary according to course load, location, and student level. *College room and board:* $2720. *College room only:* $860. Room and board charges vary according to board plan.
Financial Aid Forms of aid include need-based and non-need-based scholarships, athletic grants, and part-time jobs. The average aided 2002–03 undergraduate received an aid package worth $4660. The priority application deadline for financial aid is March 1.
Freshman Admission NWOSU requires a high school transcript, SAT I or ACT scores, and TOEFL scores for international students. An essay, a minimum 2.7 high school GPA, and 3 recommendations are required for some. The application deadline for regular admission is rolling.
Transfer Admission The application deadline for admission is rolling.
Entrance Difficulty NWOSU assesses its entrance difficulty level as moderately difficult. For the fall 2003 freshman class, 99 percent of the applicants were accepted.

For Further Information Contact Mrs. Shirley Murrow, Registrar, Northwestern Oklahoma State University, 709 Oklahoma Boulevard, Alva, OK 73717-2799. *Telephone:* 580-327-8550. *Fax:* 580-327-8699. *E-mail:* smmurrow@nwosu.edu. *Web site:* http://www.nwosu.edu/.

OKLAHOMA BAPTIST UNIVERSITY

Shawnee, Oklahoma

OBU is a coed, private, Southern Baptist, comprehensive institution, founded in 1910, offering degrees at the bachelor's and master's levels. It has a 125-acre campus in Shawnee near Oklahoma City.

Academic Information The faculty has 119 members. The undergraduate student-faculty ratio is 15:1. The library holds 230,000 titles, 1,800 serial subscriptions, and 1,600 audiovisual materials. Special programs include academic remediation, services for learning-disabled students, an honors program, cooperative (work-study) education, study abroad, advanced placement credit, double majors, independent study, self-designed majors, summer session for credit, part-time degree programs (daytime, summer), internships, and arrangement for off-campus study with St. Gregory's University. The most frequently chosen baccalaureate fields are education, business/marketing, health professions and related sciences.
Student Body Statistics The student body totals 1,883, of whom 1,866 are undergraduates (411 freshmen). 56 percent are women and 44 percent are men. Students come from 42 states and territories and 17 other countries. 61 percent are from Oklahoma.
Expenses for 2003–04 *Application fee:* $25. *Comprehensive fee:* $15,220 includes full-time tuition ($10,800), mandatory fees ($780), and college room and board ($3640). *College room only:* $1690. Full-time tuition and fees vary according to course load. Room and board charges vary according to board plan and housing facility. *Part-time tuition:* $340 per credit hour. Part-time tuition varies according to course load.
Financial Aid Forms of aid include need-based and non-need-based scholarships, athletic grants, and part-time jobs. The average aided 2003–04 undergraduate received an aid package worth an estimated $10,644. The priority application deadline for financial aid is March 1.
Freshman Admission OBU requires a high school transcript, a minimum 2.5 high school GPA, SAT I or ACT scores, and TOEFL scores for international students. An essay, recommendations, and an interview are required for some. The application deadline for regular admission is rolling.

Transfer Admission The application deadline for admission is August 1.
Entrance Difficulty OBU assesses its entrance difficulty level as moderately difficult. For the fall 2003 freshman class, 85 percent of the applicants were accepted.

For Further Information Contact Mr. Trent Argo, Dean of Enrollment Management, Oklahoma Baptist University, Box 61174, Shawnee, OK 74804. *Telephone:* 405-878-2033 or 800-654-3285 (toll-free). *Fax:* 405-878-2046. *E-mail:* admissions@mail.okbu.edu. *Web site:* http://www.okbu.edu/.

OKLAHOMA CHRISTIAN UNIVERSITY
Oklahoma City, Oklahoma

Oklahoma Christian is a coed, private, comprehensive institution, founded in 1950, affiliated with the Church of Christ, offering degrees at the bachelor's and master's levels. It has a 200-acre campus in Oklahoma City.

Academic Information The faculty has 153 members (58% full-time), 49% with terminal degrees. The undergraduate student-faculty ratio is 14:1. The library holds 99,916 titles, 990 serial subscriptions, and 10,232 audiovisual materials. Special programs include academic remediation, services for learning-disabled students, an honors program, study abroad, advanced placement credit, accelerated degree programs, ESL programs, double majors, distance learning, summer session for credit, adult/continuing education programs, internships, and arrangement for off-campus study with University of Central Oklahoma. The most frequently chosen baccalaureate fields are business/marketing, education, liberal arts/general studies.
Student Body Statistics The student body totals 1,684, of whom 1,553 are undergraduates (386 freshmen). 55 percent are women and 45 percent are men. 48 percent are from Oklahoma.
Expenses for 2004–05 *Application fee:* $25. *Comprehensive fee:* $17,980 includes full-time tuition ($11,780), mandatory fees ($1380), and college room and board ($4820). Full-time tuition and fees vary according to course load. Room and board charges vary according to housing facility. *Part-time tuition:* varies with course load.
Financial Aid Forms of aid include need-based and non-need-based scholarships, athletic grants, and part-time jobs. The average aided 2003–04 undergraduate received an aid package worth an estimated $11,748. The application deadline for financial aid is August 31 with a priority deadline of March 15.
Freshman Admission Oklahoma Christian requires a high school transcript, SAT I or ACT scores, and TOEFL scores for international students. The application deadline for regular admission is rolling.
Transfer Admission The application deadline for admission is rolling.
Entrance Difficulty Oklahoma Christian has an open admission policy.

For Further Information Contact Ms. Risa Forrester, Director of Admissions, Oklahoma Christian University, Box 11000, Oklahoma City, OK 73136-1100. *Telephone:* 405-425-5050 or 800-877-5010 (toll-free in-state). *Fax:* 405-425-5208. *E-mail:* info@oc.edu. *Web site:* http://www.oc.edu/.

OKLAHOMA CITY UNIVERSITY
Oklahoma City, Oklahoma

OCU is a coed, private, United Methodist, comprehensive institution, founded in 1904, offering degrees at the bachelor's, master's, and first professional levels. It has a 68-acre campus in Oklahoma City.

Academic Information The faculty has 270 members (56% full-time). The undergraduate student-faculty ratio is 11:1. The library holds 321,093 titles, 5,498 serial subscriptions, and 10,132 audiovisual materials. Special programs include academic remediation, services for learning-disabled students, an honors program, cooperative (work-study) education, study abroad, advanced placement credit, accelerated degree programs, ESL programs, double majors, independent study, self-designed majors, summer session for credit, part-time degree programs (daytime, evenings, summer), external degree programs, adult/continuing education programs,

internships, and arrangement for off-campus study with American University. The most frequently chosen baccalaureate fields are liberal arts/general studies, business/marketing, visual/performing arts.
Student Body Statistics The student body totals 3,668, of whom 1,793 are undergraduates (319 freshmen). 62 percent are women and 38 percent are men. Students come from 48 states and territories and 67 other countries. 69 percent are from Oklahoma. 22.9 percent are international students.
Expenses for 2003–04 *Application fee:* $30. *Comprehensive fee:* $19,580 includes full-time tuition ($13,340), mandatory fees ($690), and college room and board ($5550). Full-time tuition and fees vary according to program. Room and board charges vary according to board plan and housing facility. *Part-time tuition:* $455 per semester hour. *Part-time mandatory fees:* $100 per term. Part-time tuition and fees vary according to program.
Financial Aid Forms of aid include need-based and non-need-based scholarships, athletic grants, and part-time jobs. The average aided 2002–03 undergraduate received an aid package worth $10,680. The priority application deadline for financial aid is March 1.
Freshman Admission OCU requires a high school transcript, a minimum 3.0 high school GPA, SAT I or ACT scores, and TOEFL scores for international students. An interview and audition for music and dance programs are required for some. The application deadline for regular admission is August 20.
Transfer Admission The application deadline for admission is rolling.
Entrance Difficulty OCU assesses its entrance difficulty level as moderately difficult. For the fall 2003 freshman class, 78 percent of the applicants were accepted.

For Further Information Contact Ms. Shery Boyles, Director of Admissions, Oklahoma City University, 2501 North Blackwelder, Oklahoma City, OK 73106. *Telephone:* 405-521-5050 or 800-633-7242 (toll-free). *Fax:* 405-521-5916. *E-mail:* uadmissions@okcu.edu. *Web site:* http://www.okcu.edu/.

OKLAHOMA PANHANDLE STATE UNIVERSITY
Goodwell, Oklahoma

OPSU is a coed, public, four-year college of Oklahoma State Regents for Higher Education, founded in 1909, offering degrees at the associate and bachelor's levels. It has a 40-acre campus in Goodwell.

Academic Information The faculty has 65 members (82% full-time), 31% with terminal degrees. The student-faculty ratio is 22:1. The library holds 106,000 titles, 308 serial subscriptions, and 2,079 audiovisual materials. Special programs include academic remediation, cooperative (work-study) education, advanced placement credit, accelerated degree programs, ESL programs, double majors, distance learning, summer session for credit, part-time degree programs (daytime, evenings, summer), adult/continuing education programs, and internships.
Student Body Statistics The student body is made up of 1,226 undergraduates (222 freshmen). 53 percent are women and 47 percent are men. Students come from 36 states and territories and 26 other countries. 48 percent are from Oklahoma. 5 percent are international students.
Expenses for 2004–05 *Application fee:* $0. *State resident tuition:* $1800 full-time. *Nonresident tuition:* $3300 full-time. *Mandatory fees:* $1170 full-time. Full-time tuition and fees vary according to course level. *College room and board:* $2810. *College room only:* $930. Room and board charges vary according to board plan, housing facility, and student level.
Financial Aid Forms of aid include need-based and non-need-based scholarships and part-time jobs. The average aided 2002–03 undergraduate received an aid package worth $9200. The priority application deadline for financial aid is January 1.
Freshman Admission OPSU requires a high school transcript, SAT I or ACT scores, and TOEFL scores for international students. The application deadline for regular admission is rolling.
Transfer Admission The application deadline for admission is rolling.

Oklahoma

Oklahoma Panhandle State University (continued)
Entrance Difficulty OPSU has an open admission policy.

For Further Information Contact Mr. Vic Shrock, Registrar and Director of Admissions, Oklahoma Panhandle State University, PO Box 430, 323 Eagle Boulevard, Goodwell, OK 73939-0430. *Telephone:* 580-349-1376 or 800-664-6778 (toll-free). *Fax:* 580-349-2302. *E-mail:* opsu@opsu.edu. *Web site:* http://www.opsu.edu/.

OKLAHOMA STATE UNIVERSITY
Stillwater, Oklahoma

OSU is a coed, public unit of Oklahoma State University, founded in 1890, offering degrees at the bachelor's, master's, doctoral, and first professional levels. It has an 840-acre campus in Stillwater near Oklahoma City and Tulsa.

Academic Information The faculty has 1,060 members (85% full-time), 82% with terminal degrees. The undergraduate student-faculty ratio is 21:1. The library holds 2 million titles, 24,806 serial subscriptions, and 510,548 audiovisual materials. Special programs include academic remediation, services for learning-disabled students, an honors program, cooperative (work-study) education, study abroad, advanced placement credit, accelerated degree programs, Freshman Honors College, ESL programs, double majors, independent study, distance learning, self-designed majors, summer session for credit, part-time degree programs (daytime, evenings, weekends, summer), adult/continuing education programs, internships, and arrangement for off-campus study with National Student Exchange. The most frequently chosen baccalaureate fields are business/marketing, education, engineering/engineering technologies.
Student Body Statistics The student body totals 23,577, of whom 18,689 are undergraduates (3,490 freshmen). 49 percent are women and 51 percent are men. Students come from 50 states and territories and 122 other countries. 87 percent are from Oklahoma. 4.5 percent are international students.
Expenses for 2003–04 *Application fee:* $25. *State resident tuition:* $2513 full-time, $83.75 per credit hour part-time. *Nonresident tuition:* $8459 full-time, $281.95 per credit hour part-time. *Mandatory fees:* $1152 full-time, $40.23 per credit part-time, $115 per term part-time. Full-time tuition and fees vary according to course level. Part-time tuition and fees vary according to course level. *College room and board:* $5468. *College room only:* $2468. Room and board charges vary according to board plan, housing facility, and location.
Financial Aid Forms of aid include need-based and non-need-based scholarships, athletic grants, and part-time jobs. The average aided 2002–03 undergraduate received an aid package worth $7671. The application deadline for financial aid is continuous.
Freshman Admission OSU requires a high school transcript, a minimum 3.0 high school GPA, class rank, SAT I or ACT scores, and TOEFL scores for international students. ACT scores are recommended. An interview is required for some. The application deadline for regular admission is rolling.
Transfer Admission The application deadline for admission is rolling.
Entrance Difficulty OSU assesses its entrance difficulty level as moderately difficult. For the fall 2003 freshman class, 89 percent of the applicants were accepted.

For Further Information Contact Ms. Paulette Cundiff, Coordinator of Admissions Processing, Oklahoma State University, 324 Student Union, Stillwater, OK 74078. *Telephone:* 405-744-7275, 800-233-5019 (toll-free in-state), or 800-852-1255 (toll-free out-of-state). *Fax:* 405-744-5285. *E-mail:* admit@okstate.edu. *Web site:* http://www.okstate.edu/.

OKLAHOMA WESLEYAN UNIVERSITY
Bartlesville, Oklahoma

Oklahoma Wesleyan University is a coed, private, comprehensive institution, founded in 1909, affiliated with the Wesleyan Church, offering degrees at the associate, bachelor's, and master's levels. It has a 127-acre campus in Bartlesville near Tulsa.

Expenses for 2003–04 *Application fee:* $25. *Comprehensive fee:* $16,850 includes full-time tuition ($11,550), mandatory fees ($700), and college room and board ($4600). *College room only:* $2300. Room and board charges vary according to board plan and housing facility.

For Further Information Contact Mr. Jim Weidman, Director of Enrollment Services, Oklahoma Wesleyan University, 2201 Silver Lake Road, Bartlesville, OK 74006-6299. *Telephone:* 800-468-6292 or 800-468-6292 (toll-free in-state). *Fax:* 918-335-6229. *E-mail:* admissions@okwu.edu. *Web site:* http://www.okwu.edu/.

ORAL ROBERTS UNIVERSITY
Tulsa, Oklahoma

ORU is a coed, private, interdenominational, comprehensive institution, founded in 1963, offering degrees at the bachelor's, master's, doctoral, and first professional levels. It has a 263-acre campus in Tulsa.

Academic Information The faculty has 282 members (70% full-time), 47% with terminal degrees. The undergraduate student-faculty ratio is 16:1. The library holds 216,691 titles, 600 serial subscriptions, and 25,445 audiovisual materials. Special programs include academic remediation, services for learning-disabled students, an honors program, study abroad, advanced placement credit, Freshman Honors College, ESL programs, double majors, independent study, distance learning, self-designed majors, summer session for credit, part-time degree programs, external degree programs, adult/continuing education programs, internships, and arrangement for off-campus study with Christian College Coalition. The most frequently chosen baccalaureate fields are business/marketing, communications/communication technologies, philosophy, religion, and theology.
Student Body Statistics The student body totals 4,117, of whom 3,363 are undergraduates (644 freshmen). 61 percent are women and 39 percent are men. 36 percent are from Oklahoma. 3.2 percent are international students.
Expenses for 2003–04 *Application fee:* $35. *Comprehensive fee:* $19,870 includes full-time tuition ($13,550), mandatory fees ($420), and college room and board ($5900). *College room only:* $2880. Room and board charges vary according to board plan. *Part-time tuition:* $565 per credit hour.
Financial Aid Forms of aid include need-based and non-need-based scholarships, athletic grants, and part-time jobs. The average aided 2002–03 undergraduate received an aid package worth $13,998. The priority application deadline for financial aid is March 15.
Freshman Admission ORU requires an essay, a high school transcript, a minimum 2.0 high school GPA, 1 recommendation, proof of immunization, SAT I or ACT scores, and TOEFL scores for international students. An interview is required for some. The application deadline for regular admission is rolling and for early action it is September 1.
Transfer Admission The application deadline for admission is rolling.
Entrance Difficulty ORU assesses its entrance difficulty level as moderately difficult; noncompetitive for transfers. For the fall 2003 freshman class, 64 percent of the applicants were accepted.

For Further Information Contact Chris Miller, Director of Undergraduate Admissions, Oral Roberts University, 7777 South Lewis Avenue, Tulsa, OK 74171. *Telephone:* 918-495-6518 or 800-678-8876 (toll-free). *Fax:* 918-495-6222. *E-mail:* admissions@oru.edu. *Web site:* http://www.oru.edu/.

ROGERS STATE UNIVERSITY
Claremore, Oklahoma

Rogers State University is a coed, public, four-year college of Oklahoma State Regents for Higher Education, founded in 1909, offering degrees at the associate and bachelor's levels. It has a 40-acre campus in Claremore near Tulsa.

Expenses for 2003–04 *Application fee:* $0. *State resident tuition:* $2140 full-time, $89.20 per credit part-time. *Nonresident tuition:* $5261 full-time, $219.20 per credit part-time. *Mandatory fees:* $30 full-time, $15 per term part-time. *College room and board:* $5481. *College room only:* $3321.

For Further Information Contact Ms. Becky Noah, Director of Enrollment Management, Rogers State University, Roger's State University, Office of Admissions, 1701 West Will Rogers Boulevard, Claremore, OK 74017. *Telephone:* 918-343-7545 or 800-256-7511 (toll-free). *Fax:* 918-343-7595. *E-mail:* shunter@rsu.edu. *Web site:* http://www.rsu.edu/.

ST. GREGORY'S UNIVERSITY
Shawnee, Oklahoma

St. Gregory's University is a coed, private, Roman Catholic, four-year college, founded in 1875, offering degrees at the associate and bachelor's levels. It has a 640-acre campus in Shawnee near Oklahoma City.

Academic Information The faculty has 60 members (48% full-time), 33% with terminal degrees. The student-faculty ratio is 10:1. The library holds 55,500 titles and 284 serial subscriptions. Special programs include academic remediation, services for learning-disabled students, an honors program, study abroad, advanced placement credit, ESL programs, double majors, independent study, self-designed majors, summer session for credit, part-time degree programs (daytime, evenings, summer), external degree programs, adult/continuing education programs, internships, and arrangement for off-campus study with Oklahoma Baptist University; Edge Hill College, England. The most frequently chosen baccalaureate fields are business/marketing, communications/communication technologies, social sciences and history.

Student Body Statistics The student body is made up of 705 undergraduates (120 freshmen). 54 percent are women and 46 percent are men. Students come from 15 states and territories and 22 other countries. 82 percent are from Oklahoma. 9.6 percent are international students. 20 percent of the 2003 graduating class went on to graduate and professional schools.

Expenses for 2004–05 *Application fee:* $25. *Comprehensive fee:* $15,964 includes full-time tuition ($10,260), mandatory fees ($816), and college room and board ($4888). *Part-time tuition:* $342 per hour.

Financial Aid Forms of aid include need-based and non-need-based scholarships, athletic grants, and part-time jobs. The average aided 2002–03 undergraduate received an aid package worth $9652. The application deadline for financial aid is continuous.

Freshman Admission St. Gregory's University requires a high school transcript, a minimum 2.0 high school GPA, SAT I or ACT scores, and TOEFL scores for international students. An essay, recommendations, and an interview are required for some. The application deadline for regular admission is rolling.

Transfer Admission The application deadline for admission is rolling.

Entrance Difficulty St. Gregory's University assesses its entrance difficulty level as minimally difficult. For the fall 2003 freshman class, 62 percent of the applicants were accepted.

For Further Information Contact Mrs. Kay Stith, Director of Admissions, St. Gregory's University, 1900 West MacArthur Drive, Shawnee, OK 74804. *Telephone:* 405-878-5447 or 888-STGREGS (toll-free). *Fax:* 405-878-5198. *E-mail:* admissions@stgregorys.edu. *Web site:* http://www.stgregorys.edu/.

SOUTHEASTERN OKLAHOMA STATE UNIVERSITY
Durant, Oklahoma

SOSU is a coed, public, comprehensive unit of Oklahoma State Regents for Higher Education, founded in 1909, offering degrees at the bachelor's and master's levels and post-master's certificates. It has a 177-acre campus in Durant.

Academic Information The faculty has 223 members (69% full-time), 54% with terminal degrees. The undergraduate student-faculty ratio is 20:1. The library holds 187,971 titles, 671 serial subscriptions, and 5,291 audiovisual materials. Special programs include academic remediation, services for learning-disabled students, an honors program, advanced placement credit, accelerated degree programs, double majors, independent study, distance learning, summer session for credit, part-time degree programs (daytime, evenings), adult/continuing education programs, internships, and arrangement for off-campus study with Ardmore Higher Education Center, E.T. Dunlap Higher Education Center. The most frequently chosen baccalaureate fields are business/marketing, education, engineering/engineering technologies.

Student Body Statistics The student body totals 4,203, of whom 3,738 are undergraduates (646 freshmen). 54 percent are women and 46 percent are men. Students come from 34 states and territories and 25 other countries. 78 percent are from Oklahoma. 1.7 percent are international students.

Expenses for 2003–04 *Application fee:* $20. *State resident tuition:* $1950 full-time, $65 per credit hour part-time. *Nonresident tuition:* $5850 full-time, $195 per credit hour part-time. *Mandatory fees:* $997 full-time, $20.70 per semester hour part-time, $50.50 per term part-time. Full-time tuition and fees vary according to course level. Part-time tuition and fees vary according to course level and course load. *College room and board:* $3200. *College room only:* $1400. Room and board charges vary according to board plan and housing facility.

Financial Aid Forms of aid include need-based and non-need-based scholarships, athletic grants, and part-time jobs. The average aided 2002–03 undergraduate received an aid package worth $3631. The priority application deadline for financial aid is March 1.

Freshman Admission SOSU requires a high school transcript and TOEFL scores for international students. An interview, ACT scores, and SAT II: Subject Test scores are required for some. The application deadline for regular admission is rolling.

Transfer Admission The application deadline for admission is rolling.

Entrance Difficulty SOSU has an open admission policy for adults over 21. It assesses its entrance difficulty as minimally difficult for transfers; very difficult for honors program.

For Further Information Contact Mr. Kyle Stafford, Director of Admissions and Enrollment Services, Southeastern Oklahoma State University, 1405 North 4th Avenue PMB 4225, Durant, OK 74701-0609. *Telephone:* 580-745-2060 or 800-435-1327 (toll-free). *Fax:* 580-745-4502. *E-mail:* admissions@sosu.edu. *Web site:* http://www.sosu.edu/.

SOUTHERN NAZARENE UNIVERSITY
Bethany, Oklahoma

SNU is a coed, private, Nazarene, comprehensive institution, founded in 1899, offering degrees at the associate, bachelor's, and master's levels. It has a 40-acre campus in Bethany near Oklahoma City.

Academic Information The faculty has 204 members (34% full-time), 48% with terminal degrees. The undergraduate student-faculty ratio is 18:1. The library holds 115,564 titles and 2,748 audiovisual materials. Special programs include academic remediation, services for learning-disabled students, an honors program, study abroad, advanced placement credit, accelerated degree programs, double majors, self-designed majors, summer session for credit, part-time degree programs (daytime, evenings, summer), external degree programs, adult/continuing education programs, internships, and arrangement for off-campus study with Christian College Coalition Council for Christian Colleges and Universities. The most

Southern Nazarene University (continued)

frequently chosen baccalaureate fields are business/marketing, health professions and related sciences, home economics/vocational home economics.

Student Body Statistics The student body totals 2,199, of whom 1,803 are undergraduates (304 freshmen). 53 percent are women and 47 percent are men. Students come from 34 states and territories. 53 percent are from Oklahoma. 0.3 percent are international students. 22 percent of the 2003 graduating class went on to graduate and professional schools.

Expenses for 2004–05 *Application fee:* $25. *Comprehensive fee:* $17,944 includes full-time tuition ($12,090), mandatory fees ($744), and college room and board ($5110). *College room only:* $2410. Room and board charges vary according to board plan and housing facility. *Part-time tuition:* $403 per credit hour. *Part-time mandatory fees:* $21 per credit hour. Part-time tuition and fees vary according to course load.

Financial Aid Forms of aid include need-based and non-need-based scholarships and part-time jobs. The priority application deadline for financial aid is March 1.

Freshman Admission SNU requires a high school transcript, 2 recommendations, SAT I or ACT scores, and TOEFL scores for international students. An interview and ACT scores are recommended. The application deadline for regular admission is August 15.

Transfer Admission The application deadline for admission is August 15.

Entrance Difficulty SNU has an open admission policy.

For Further Information Contact Mr. Larry Hess, Director of Admissions, Southern Nazarene University, 6729 Northwest 39th Expressway, Bethany, OK 73008. *Telephone:* 405-491-6324 or 800-648-9899 (toll-free). *Fax:* 405-491-6320. *E-mail:* admiss@snu.edu. *Web site:* http://www.snu.edu/.

SOUTHWESTERN CHRISTIAN UNIVERSITY
Bethany, Oklahoma

For Information Write to Southwestern Christian University, Bethany, OK 73008-0340.

SOUTHWESTERN OKLAHOMA STATE UNIVERSITY
Weatherford, Oklahoma

Southwestern is a coed, public, comprehensive unit of Southwestern Oklahoma State University, founded in 1901, offering degrees at the bachelor's, master's, and first professional levels. It has a 73-acre campus in Weatherford near Oklahoma City.

Academic Information The faculty has 229 members (86% full-time), 58% with terminal degrees. The undergraduate student-faculty ratio is 20:1. The library holds 217,051 titles, 1,230 serial subscriptions, and 6,718 audiovisual materials. Special programs include academic remediation, services for learning-disabled students, cooperative (work-study) education, advanced placement credit, accelerated degree programs, double majors, independent study, distance learning, self-designed majors, summer session for credit, part-time degree programs (daytime, evenings, summer), adult/continuing education programs, internships, and arrangement for off-campus study with Academic Common Market. The most frequently chosen baccalaureate fields are business/marketing, education, health professions and related sciences.

Student Body Statistics The student body totals 4,741, of whom 4,181 are undergraduates (964 freshmen). 54 percent are women and 46 percent are men. Students come from 32 states and territories and 32 other countries. 90 percent are from Oklahoma. 3.3 percent are international students.

Expenses for 2003–04 *Application fee:* $15. *State resident tuition:* $1950 full-time, $65 per hour part-time. *Nonresident tuition:* $5850 full-time, $195 per hour part-time. *Mandatory fees:* $808 full-time, $31 per hour part-time, $16.50 per term part-time. *College room and board:* $2910. *College room only:* $1230. Room and board charges vary according to board plan.

Financial Aid Forms of aid include need-based and non-need-based scholarships, athletic grants, and part-time jobs. The average aided 2002–03 undergraduate received an aid package worth $3377. The application deadline for financial aid is March 1.

Freshman Admission Southwestern requires a high school transcript, a minimum 2.0 high school GPA, ACT scores, and TOEFL scores for international students.

Entrance Difficulty Southwestern assesses its entrance difficulty level as moderately difficult. For the fall 2003 freshman class, 93 percent of the applicants were accepted.

For Further Information Contact Ms. Connie Phillips, Admission Counselor, Southwestern Oklahoma State University, 100 Campus Drive, Weatherford, OK 73096. *Telephone:* 580-774-3782. *Fax:* 580-774-3795. *E-mail:* phillic@swosu.edu. *Web site:* http://www.swosu.edu/.

SPARTAN SCHOOL OF AERONAUTICS
Tulsa, Oklahoma

Spartan School of Aeronautics is a coed, primarily men's, proprietary, primarily two-year college, founded in 1928, offering degrees at the associate and bachelor's levels. It has a 26-acre campus in Tulsa.

Expenses for 2003–04 *Application fee:* $100. Full-time tuition varies with program. Single student housing available from $290 to $350 per month.

For Further Information Contact Mr. Mark Fowler, Vice President of Student Records and Finance, Spartan School of Aeronautics, 8820 East Pine Street, PO Box 582833, Tulsa, OK 74158-2833. *Telephone:* 918-836-6886 Ext. 231. *Web site:* http://www.spartan.edu/.

UNIVERSITY OF CENTRAL OKLAHOMA
Edmond, Oklahoma

UCO is a coed, public, comprehensive unit of Oklahoma State Regents for Higher Education, founded in 1890, offering degrees at the bachelor's and master's levels. It has a 200-acre campus in Edmond near Oklahoma City.

Academic Information The faculty has 773 members (49% full-time), 44% with terminal degrees. The undergraduate student-faculty ratio is 23:1. The library holds 254,478 titles, 3,707 serial subscriptions, and 37,484 audiovisual materials. Special programs include services for learning-disabled students, an honors program, advanced placement credit, accelerated degree programs, ESL programs, double majors, independent study, distance learning, summer session for credit, part-time degree programs (daytime, evenings, weekends, summer), adult/continuing education programs, and internships. The most frequently chosen baccalaureate fields are business/marketing, education, liberal arts/general studies.

Student Body Statistics The student body totals 15,246, of whom 13,566 are undergraduates (2,049 freshmen). 58 percent are women and 42 percent are men. Students come from 38 states and territories and 108 other countries. 98 percent are from Oklahoma. 9.2 percent are international students.

Expenses for 2003–04 *Application fee:* $25. *State resident tuition:* $1950 full-time, $90 per semester hour part-time. *Nonresident tuition:* $5850 full-time, $220 per semester hour part-time. *Mandatory fees:* $699 full-time. Full-time tuition and fees vary according to course level, course load, program, and student level. Part-time tuition varies according to course level, course load, program, and student level. *College room and board:* $3670. Room and board charges vary according to board plan and housing facility.

Financial Aid Forms of aid include need-based and non-need-based scholarships, athletic grants, and part-time jobs. The application deadline for financial aid is continuous.

Freshman Admission UCO requires a high school transcript, a minimum 2.7 high school GPA, rank in upper 50% of high school class,

SAT I or ACT scores, and TOEFL scores for international students. ACT scores are recommended. The application deadline for regular admission is rolling.

Entrance Difficulty UCO assesses its entrance difficulty level as minimally difficult. For the fall 2003 freshman class, 88 percent of the applicants were accepted.

For Further Information Contact Ms. Linda Lofton, Director, Admissions and Records Processing, University of Central Oklahoma, Office of Enrollment Services, 100 North University Drive, Box 151, Edmond, OK 73034-5209. *Telephone:* 405-974-2338 Ext. 2338 or 800-254-4215 (toll-free). *Fax:* 405-341-4964. *E-mail:* admituco@ucok.edu. *Web site:* http://www.ucok.edu/.

UNIVERSITY OF OKLAHOMA
Norman, Oklahoma

OU is a coed, public university, founded in 1890, offering degrees at the bachelor's, master's, doctoral, and first professional levels and post-master's certificates. It has a 3,500-acre campus in Norman near Oklahoma City.

Academic Information The faculty has 1,191 members (82% full-time), 80% with terminal degrees. The undergraduate student-faculty ratio is 21:1. The library holds 4 million titles, 26,696 serial subscriptions, and 7,647 audiovisual materials. Special programs include academic remediation, services for learning-disabled students, an honors program, cooperative (work-study) education, study abroad, advanced placement credit, accelerated degree programs, Freshman Honors College, ESL programs, double majors, independent study, distance learning, self-designed majors, summer session for credit, part-time degree programs (daytime, evenings, weekends, summer), external degree programs, adult/continuing education programs, internships, and arrangement for off-campus study with Oklahoma State University, Langston University, Northeastern State University, Rose State College, Oklahoma City Community College, Rogers University, Cameron University. The most frequently chosen baccalaureate fields are business/marketing, communications/communication technologies, social sciences and history.

Student Body Statistics The student body totals 24,483, of whom 20,254 are undergraduates (3,808 freshmen). 49 percent are women and 51 percent are men. Students come from 50 states and territories and 85 other countries. 81 percent are from Oklahoma. 2.6 percent are international students.

Expenses for 2003–04 *Application fee:* $25. *State resident tuition:* $2541 full-time, $85 per credit hour part-time. *Nonresident tuition:* $9054 full-time, $302 per credit hour part-time. *Mandatory fees:* $1200 full-time, $32.90 per credit hour part-time, $106.50 per term part-time. Full-time tuition and fees vary according to course level, course load, location, program, and reciprocity agreements. Part-time tuition and fees vary according to course level, course load, location, program, and reciprocity agreements. *College room and board:* $5485. *College room only:* $2797. Room and board charges vary according to board plan and housing facility.

Financial Aid Forms of aid include need-based and non-need-based scholarships, athletic grants, and part-time jobs. The average aided 2002–03 undergraduate received an aid package worth $7421. The application deadline for financial aid is continuous.

Freshman Admission OU requires a high school transcript, a minimum 3.0 high school GPA, SAT I or ACT scores, and TOEFL scores for international students. An essay is required for some. The application deadline for regular admission is June 1.

Entrance Difficulty OU assesses its entrance difficulty level as moderately difficult; most difficult for honors college program. For the fall 2003 freshman class, 82 percent of the applicants were accepted.

For Further Information Contact Ms. Karen Renfroe, Executive Director of Recruitment Services, University of Oklahoma, 1000 Asp Avenue, Norman, OK 73019. *Telephone:* 405-325-4521 or 800-234-6868 (toll-free). *Fax:* 405-325-7124. *E-mail:* admrec@ou.edu. *Web site:* http://www.ou.edu/.

UNIVERSITY OF OKLAHOMA HEALTH SCIENCES CENTER
Oklahoma City, Oklahoma

OU Health Sciences Center is a coed, public, upper-level unit of University of Oklahoma, founded in 1890, offering degrees at the bachelor's, master's, doctoral, and first professional levels and post-master's, first professional, and postbachelor's certificates. It has a 200-acre campus in Oklahoma City near Oklahoma City.

Academic Information The faculty has 361 members (68% full-time), 82% with terminal degrees. The library holds 234,000 titles and 2,658 serial subscriptions. Special programs include an honors program, advanced placement credit, distance learning, summer session for credit, part-time degree programs (daytime, evenings, summer), and internships. The most frequently chosen baccalaureate field is health professions and related sciences.

Student Body Statistics The student body totals 3,129, of whom 712 are undergraduates. 89 percent are women and 11 percent are men. Students come from 14 states and territories and 11 other countries. 93 percent are from Oklahoma. 0.9 percent are international students.

Expenses for 2003–04 *Application fee:* $25. *State resident tuition:* $2098 full-time, $87 per credit part-time. *Nonresident tuition:* $7615 full-time, $317 per credit part-time. *Mandatory fees:* $959 full-time, $40 per credit part-time. Full-time tuition and fees vary according to program. Part-time tuition and fees vary according to program.

Financial Aid Forms of aid include non-need-based scholarships.

Entrance Difficulty OU Health Sciences Center assesses its entrance difficulty level as moderately difficult.

For Further Information Contact Ms. Leslie Wilbourn, Director of Admissions and Records, University of Oklahoma Health Sciences Center, BSE-200, PO Box 26901, 941 S. L. Young Boulevard, Oklahoma City, OK 73190. *Telephone:* 405-271-2359 Ext. 48902. *Fax:* 405-271-2480. *E-mail:* admissions@ouhsc.edu. *Web site:* http://www.ouhsc.edu/.

UNIVERSITY OF PHOENIX–OKLAHOMA CITY CAMPUS
Oklahoma City, Oklahoma

University of Phoenix–Oklahoma City Campus is a coed, proprietary, comprehensive institution, founded in 1976, offering degrees at the associate, bachelor's, master's, and doctoral levels and post-master's and postbachelor's certificates (courses conducted at 121 campuses and learning centers in 25 states).

Academic Information The faculty has 103 members (3% full-time), 20% with terminal degrees. The undergraduate student-faculty ratio is 6:1. The library holds 27 million titles and 11,648 serial subscriptions. Special programs include advanced placement credit, accelerated degree programs, independent study, distance learning, external degree programs, and adult/continuing education programs. The most frequently chosen baccalaureate field is business/marketing.

Student Body Statistics The student body totals 855, of whom 659 are undergraduates (51 freshmen). 56 percent are women and 44 percent are men. 1.2 percent are international students.

Expenses for 2003–04 *Application fee:* $85. *Tuition:* $8550 full-time, $285 per credit part-time.

Financial Aid Forms of aid include need-based and non-need-based scholarships. The average aided 2002–03 undergraduate received an aid package worth $1392. The application deadline for financial aid is continuous.

Freshman Admission University of Phoenix–Oklahoma City Campus requires 1 recommendation, 2 years of work experience, 23 years of age, and TOEFL scores for international students. A high school transcript is required for some. The application deadline for regular admission is rolling.

Transfer Admission The application deadline for admission is rolling.

University of Phoenix–Oklahoma City Campus (continued)

Entrance Difficulty University of Phoenix–Oklahoma City Campus has an open admission policy.

For Further Information Contact Ms. Beth Barilla, Director of Admissions, University of Phoenix–Oklahoma City Campus, 4615 East Elwood Street, Mail Stop AA-K101, Phoenix, AZ 85040-1958. *Telephone:* 480-557-1712 or 800-228-7240 (toll-free). *Fax:* 480-594-1758. *E-mail:* beth.barilla@phoenix.edu. *Web site:* http://www.phoenix.edu/.

UNIVERSITY OF PHOENIX–TULSA CAMPUS
Tulsa, Oklahoma

University of Phoenix–Tulsa Campus is a coed, proprietary, comprehensive institution, founded in 1998, offering degrees at the associate, bachelor's, master's, and doctoral levels and post-master's and postbachelor's certificates (courses conducted at 121 campuses and learning centers in 25 states).

Academic Information The faculty has 93 members (5% full-time), 15% with terminal degrees. The undergraduate student-faculty ratio is 8:1. The library holds 27 million titles and 11,648 serial subscriptions. Special programs include advanced placement credit, accelerated degree programs, independent study, distance learning, external degree programs, and adult/continuing education programs. The most frequently chosen baccalaureate fields are business/marketing, computer/information sciences.
Student Body Statistics The student body totals 767, of whom 610 are undergraduates (26 freshmen). 58 percent are women and 42 percent are men. 37.7 percent are international students.
Expenses for 2003–04 *Application fee:* $85. *Tuition:* $8550 full-time, $285 per credit part-time.
Financial Aid Forms of aid include need-based and non-need-based scholarships. The average aided 2002–03 undergraduate received an aid package worth $1343. The application deadline for financial aid is continuous.
Freshman Admission University of Phoenix–Tulsa Campus requires 1 recommendation, 2 years of work experience, 23 years of age, and TOEFL scores for international students. A high school transcript is required for some. The application deadline for regular admission is rolling.
Transfer Admission The application deadline for admission is rolling.
Entrance Difficulty University of Phoenix–Tulsa Campus has an open admission policy.

For Further Information Contact Ms. Beth Barilla, Director of Admissions, University of Phoenix–Tulsa Campus, 4615 East Elwood Street, Mail Stop AA-K101, Phoenix, AZ 85040-1958. *Telephone:* 480-557-1712 or 800-228-7240 (toll-free). *Fax:* 480-594-1758. *E-mail:* beth.barilla@phoenix.edu. *Web site:* http://www.phoenix.edu/.

UNIVERSITY OF SCIENCE AND ARTS OF OKLAHOMA
Chickasha, Oklahoma

USAO is a coed, public, four-year college of Oklahoma State Regents for Higher Education, founded in 1908, offering degrees at the bachelor's level. It has a 75-acre campus in Chickasha near Oklahoma City.

Academic Information The faculty has 91 members (53% full-time), 57% with terminal degrees. The student-faculty ratio is 19:1. The library holds 72,395 titles, 137 serial subscriptions, and 4,187 audiovisual materials. Special programs include academic remediation, services for learning-disabled students, advanced placement credit, accelerated degree programs, double majors, independent study, distance learning, self-designed majors, summer session for credit, part-time degree programs (daytime, evenings, summer), adult/continuing education programs, internships, and arrangement for off-campus study. The most frequently chosen baccalaureate fields are business/marketing, education, social sciences and history.

Student Body Statistics The student body is made up of 1,449 undergraduates (296 freshmen). 64 percent are women and 36 percent are men. Students come from 16 states and territories and 14 other countries. 95 percent are from Oklahoma. 1.6 percent are international students.
Expenses for 2003–04 *Application fee:* $15. *State resident tuition:* $2100 full-time, $70 per hour part-time. *Nonresident tuition:* $6000 full-time, $200 per hour part-time. *Mandatory fees:* $790 full-time, $26.35 per hour part-time. Full-time tuition and fees vary according to course load. Part-time tuition and fees vary according to course load. *College room and board:* $3530. Room and board charges vary according to board plan and housing facility.
Financial Aid Forms of aid include need-based and non-need-based scholarships, athletic grants, and part-time jobs. The average aided 2003–04 undergraduate received an aid package worth an estimated $6413. The priority application deadline for financial aid is March 15.
Freshman Admission USAO requires a high school transcript, SAT I or ACT scores, and TOEFL scores for international students. A minimum 2.7 high school GPA and graduated in top half of high school class are recommended. The application deadline for regular admission is September 3.
Transfer Admission The application deadline for admission is June 1.
Entrance Difficulty USAO assesses its entrance difficulty level as moderately difficult. For the fall 2003 freshman class, 86 percent of the applicants were accepted.

For Further Information Contact Mr. Joseph Evans, Registrar and Director of Admissions and Records, University of Science and Arts of Oklahoma, 1727 West Alabama, Chickasha, OK 73018-5322. *Telephone:* 405-574-1204 or 800-933-8726 Ext. 1204 (toll-free). *Fax:* 405-574-1220. *E-mail:* jwevans@usao.edu. *Web site:* http://www.usao.edu/.

UNIVERSITY OF TULSA
Tulsa, Oklahoma

TU is a coed, private university, founded in 1894, affiliated with the Presbyterian Church (U.S.A.), offering degrees at the bachelor's, master's, doctoral, and first professional levels and first professional and postbachelor's certificates. It has a 200-acre campus in Tulsa near Tulsa.

Academic Information The faculty has 412 members (74% full-time), 96% with terminal degrees. The undergraduate student-faculty ratio is 11:1. The library holds 940,105 titles, 6,317 serial subscriptions, and 13,320 audiovisual materials. Special programs include services for learning-disabled students, an honors program, study abroad, advanced placement credit, accelerated degree programs, ESL programs, double majors, independent study, self-designed majors, summer session for credit, part-time degree programs (daytime, evenings, summer), adult/continuing education programs, and internships. The most frequently chosen baccalaureate fields are business/marketing, engineering/engineering technologies, visual/performing arts.
Student Body Statistics The student body totals 4,072, of whom 2,672 are undergraduates (590 freshmen). 50 percent are women and 50 percent are men. Students come from 37 states and territories and 48 other countries. 72 percent are from Oklahoma. 10.3 percent are international students. 27 percent of the 2003 graduating class went on to graduate and professional schools.
Expenses for 2003–04 *Application fee:* $35. *Comprehensive fee:* $21,346 includes full-time tuition ($15,656), mandatory fees ($80), and college room and board ($5610). *College room only:* $3060. Room and board charges vary according to board plan and housing facility. *Part-time tuition:* $562 per credit hour. *Part-time mandatory fees:* $3 per credit hour.
Financial Aid Forms of aid include need-based and non-need-based scholarships, athletic grants, and part-time jobs. The average aided 2003–04 undergraduate received an aid package worth an estimated $13,737. The priority application deadline for financial aid is April 1.
Freshman Admission TU requires a high school transcript, 1 recommendation, SAT I or ACT scores, and TOEFL scores for international students. An essay, a minimum 3.0 high school GPA, and an interview are recommended. The application deadline for regular admission is rolling.

Transfer Admission The application deadline for admission is rolling.
Entrance Difficulty TU assesses its entrance difficulty level as very difficult; moderately difficult for transfers. For the fall 2003 freshman class, 76 percent of the applicants were accepted.

For Further Information Contact Mr. John C. Corso, Associate Vice President for Administration/Dean of Admission, University of Tulsa, 600 South College Avenue, Tulsa, OK 74104. *Telephone:* 918-631-2307 or 800-331-3050 (toll-free). *Fax:* 918-631-5003. *E-mail:* admission@utulsa.edu. *Web site:* http://www.utulsa.edu/.

South Dakota

AUGUSTANA COLLEGE
Sioux Falls, South Dakota

Augustana is a coed, private, comprehensive institution, founded in 1860, affiliated with the Evangelical Lutheran Church in America, offering degrees at the bachelor's and master's levels. It has a 100-acre campus in Sioux Falls.

Academic Information The faculty has 166 members (64% full-time), 60% with terminal degrees. The undergraduate student-faculty ratio is 13:1. The library holds 268,645 titles, 1,418 serial subscriptions, and 7,280 audiovisual materials. Special programs include academic remediation, services for learning-disabled students, an honors program, cooperative (work-study) education, study abroad, advanced placement credit, accelerated degree programs, double majors, independent study, self-designed majors, summer session for credit, part-time degree programs (daytime, evenings, summer), adult/continuing education programs, internships, and arrangement for off-campus study with 10 other colleges in the upper Midwest. The most frequently chosen baccalaureate fields are business/marketing, education, health professions and related sciences.
Student Body Statistics The student body totals 1,848, of whom 1,810 are undergraduates (438 freshmen). 63 percent are women and 37 percent are men. Students come from 35 states and territories and 12 other countries. 45 percent are from South Dakota. 2.1 percent are international students. 23 percent of the 2003 graduating class went on to graduate and professional schools.
Expenses for 2003–04 *Application fee:* $0. *Comprehensive fee:* $21,998 includes full-time tuition ($16,766), mandatory fees ($206), and college room and board ($5026). *College room only:* $2600. Room and board charges vary according to board plan and housing facility. *Part-time tuition:* $247 per credit. Part-time tuition varies according to course load.
Financial Aid Forms of aid include need-based and non-need-based scholarships, athletic grants, and part-time jobs. The average aided 2003–04 undergraduate received an aid package worth an estimated $14,299. The priority application deadline for financial aid is March 1.
Freshman Admission Augustana requires a high school transcript, a minimum 2.5 high school GPA, 1 recommendation, minimum ACT score of 20, SAT I or ACT scores, and TOEFL scores for international students. An interview is recommended. An essay is required for some. The application deadline for regular admission is August 1.
Transfer Admission The application deadline for admission is rolling.
Entrance Difficulty Augustana assesses its entrance difficulty level as moderately difficult; minimally difficult for transfers. For the fall 2003 freshman class, 79 percent of the applicants were accepted.

For Further Information Contact Mr. Robert Preloger, Vice President for Enrollment, Augustana College, 2001 South Summit Avenue, Sioux Falls, SD 57197. *Telephone:* 605-274-5516 Ext. 5504, 800-727-2844 Ext. 5516 (toll-free in-state), or 800-727-2844 (toll-free out-of-state). *Fax:* 605-274-5518. *E-mail:* info@augie.edu. *Web site:* http://www.augie.edu/.

BLACK HILLS STATE UNIVERSITY
Spearfish, South Dakota

Black Hills State University is a coed, public, comprehensive unit of South Dakota University System, founded in 1883, offering degrees at the associate, bachelor's, and master's levels and post-master's and postbachelor's certificates. It has a 123-acre campus in Spearfish.

Academic Information The faculty has 194 members (57% full-time). The undergraduate student-faculty ratio is 23:1. The library holds 209,738 titles, 4,481 serial subscriptions, and 23,901 audiovisual materials. Special programs include academic remediation, services for learning-disabled students, cooperative (work-study) education, advanced placement credit, accelerated degree programs, double majors, independent study, distance learning, summer session for credit, part-time degree programs (daytime, evenings, summer), internships, and arrangement for off-campus study with South Dakota State University. The most frequently chosen baccalaureate fields are business/marketing, education, parks and recreation.
Student Body Statistics The student body totals 3,873, of whom 3,671 are undergraduates (707 freshmen). 64 percent are women and 36 percent are men. Students come from 33 states and territories and 6 other countries. 81 percent are from South Dakota. 0.2 percent are international students.
Expenses for 2003–04 *Application fee:* $20. *State resident tuition:* $2308 full-time, $142.15 per credit part-time. *Nonresident tuition:* $7333 full-time, $299.20 per credit part-time. *Mandatory fees:* $3196 full-time. Full-time tuition and fees vary according to course load and reciprocity agreements. Part-time tuition varies according to course load and reciprocity agreements. *College room and board:* $3196. *College room only:* $1716. Room and board charges vary according to board plan and housing facility.
Financial Aid Forms of aid include need-based and non-need-based scholarships, athletic grants, and part-time jobs. The average aided 2002–03 undergraduate received an aid package worth $4638. The priority application deadline for financial aid is March 1.
Freshman Admission Black Hills State University requires a high school transcript, minimum 2.0 high school GPA in core curriculum, SAT I or ACT scores, and TOEFL scores for international students. The application deadline for regular admission is July 1.
Transfer Admission The application deadline for admission is rolling.
Entrance Difficulty Black Hills State University assesses its entrance difficulty level as minimally difficult. For the fall 2003 freshman class, 99 percent of the applicants were accepted.

For Further Information Contact Mr. Steve Ochsner, Dean of Admissions, Black Hills State University, University Street Box 9502, Spearfish, SD 57799-9502. *Telephone:* 605-642-6343 or 800-255-2478 (toll-free). *E-mail:* admissions@bhsu.edu. *Web site:* http://www.bhsu.edu/.

COLORADO TECHNICAL UNIVERSITY SIOUX FALLS CAMPUS
Sioux Falls, South Dakota

Colorado Technical University Sioux Falls Campus is a coed, proprietary, comprehensive unit of Colorado Technical University—Main Campus Colorado Springs, CO, founded in 1965, offering degrees at the associate, bachelor's, and master's levels. It has a 3-acre campus in Sioux Falls.

Academic Information The faculty has 61 members (15% full-time), 13% with terminal degrees. The undergraduate student-faculty ratio is 18:1. The library holds 5,787 titles, 25 serial subscriptions, and 280 audiovisual materials. Special programs include cooperative (work-study) education, accelerated degree programs, double majors, distance learning, summer session for credit, part-time degree programs (daytime, evenings, weekends, summer), adult/continuing education programs, and internships. The most frequently chosen baccalaureate fields are business/marketing, computer/information sciences, protective services/public administration.

South Dakota

Colorado Technical University Sioux Falls Campus (continued)

Student Body Statistics The student body totals 1,036, of whom 912 are undergraduates (209 freshmen). 59 percent are women and 41 percent are men. Students come from 3 states and territories. 95 percent are from South Dakota.

Expenses for 2003–04 *Application fee:* $50. *Tuition:* $9450 full-time, $195 per credit hour part-time. *Mandatory fees:* $513 full-time, $50 per term part-time. Full-time tuition and fees vary according to course load. Part-time tuition and fees vary according to course load.

Financial Aid Forms of aid include need-based scholarships and part-time jobs. The application deadline for financial aid is continuous.

Freshman Admission Colorado Technical University Sioux Falls Campus requires a high school transcript, an interview, and TOEFL scores for international students. ACT scores are recommended. The application deadline for regular admission is rolling.

Transfer Admission The application deadline for admission is rolling.

Entrance Difficulty Colorado Technical University Sioux Falls Campus has an open admission policy. It assesses its entrance difficulty as noncompetitive for transfers.

For Further Information Contact Elizabeth Carlson, Regional High School Representative, Colorado Technical University Sioux Falls Campus, 3901 West 59th Street, Sioux Falls, SD 57108. *Telephone:* 605-361-0200 Ext. 103. *Fax:* 605-361-5954. *E-mail:* callen@sf.coloradotech.edu. *Web site:* http://www.ctu-siouxfalls.com/.

DAKOTA STATE UNIVERSITY
Madison, South Dakota

Dakota State is a coed, public, comprehensive institution, founded in 1881, offering degrees at the associate, bachelor's, and master's levels. It has a 40-acre campus in Madison near Sioux Falls.

Academic Information The faculty has 98 members (74% full-time), 48% with terminal degrees. The undergraduate student-faculty ratio is 24:1. The library holds 98,156 titles, 350 serial subscriptions, and 2,435 audiovisual materials. Special programs include academic remediation, services for learning-disabled students, an honors program, cooperative (work-study) education, study abroad, advanced placement credit, ESL programs, double majors, independent study, distance learning, summer session for credit, part-time degree programs (daytime, evenings, summer), external degree programs, adult/continuing education programs, internships, and arrangement for off-campus study with South Dakota State University, University of Sioux Falls, University of South Dakota. The most frequently chosen baccalaureate fields are computer/information sciences, business/marketing, education.

Student Body Statistics The student body totals 2,291, of whom 2,098 are undergraduates (320 freshmen). 53 percent are women and 47 percent are men. Students come from 12 states and territories and 6 other countries. 83 percent are from South Dakota. 0.7 percent are international students. 2 percent of the 2003 graduating class went on to graduate and professional schools.

Expenses for 2003–04 *Application fee:* $20. *State resident tuition:* $4378 full-time, $134 per credit hour part-time. *Nonresident tuition:* $9090 full-time, $276 per credit hour part-time. *College room and board:* $3089.

Financial Aid Forms of aid include need-based and non-need-based scholarships, athletic grants, and part-time jobs. The average aided 2002–03 undergraduate received an aid package worth $5593. The priority application deadline for financial aid is March 1.

Freshman Admission Dakota State requires a high school transcript, rank in upper two-thirds of high school class, and ACT scores. TOEFL scores for international students are recommended. The application deadline for regular admission is rolling.

Transfer Admission The application deadline for admission is rolling.

Entrance Difficulty Dakota State assesses its entrance difficulty level as minimally difficult; moderately difficult for out-of-state applicants; moderately difficult for transfers. For the fall 2003 freshman class, 93 percent of the applicants were accepted.

For Further Information Contact Ms. Katy O'Hara, Admissions Secretary, Dakota State University, 820 North Washington, Madison, SD 57042-1799. *Telephone:* 605-256-5696 or 888-DSU-9988 (toll-free). *Fax:* 605-256-5316. *E-mail:* yourfuture@dsu.edu. *Web site:* http://www.dsu.edu/.

DAKOTA WESLEYAN UNIVERSITY
Mitchell, South Dakota

DWU is a coed, private, United Methodist, comprehensive institution, founded in 1885, offering degrees at the associate, bachelor's, and master's levels. It has a 50-acre campus in Mitchell.

Academic Information The faculty has 70 members (60% full-time), 39% with terminal degrees. The undergraduate student-faculty ratio is 17:1. The library holds 61,000 titles, 404 serial subscriptions, and 7,600 audiovisual materials. Special programs include academic remediation, services for learning-disabled students, an honors program, study abroad, advanced placement credit, ESL programs, double majors, independent study, distance learning, self-designed majors, summer session for credit, part-time degree programs (daytime, evenings, summer), adult/continuing education programs, and internships. The most frequently chosen baccalaureate fields are business/marketing, education, protective services/public administration.

Student Body Statistics The student body totals 751, of whom 738 are undergraduates (162 freshmen). 58 percent are women and 42 percent are men. Students come from 29 states and territories. 72 percent are from South Dakota. 0.9 percent are international students. 10 percent of the 2003 graduating class went on to graduate and professional schools.

Expenses for 2004–05 *Application fee:* $25. *Comprehensive fee:* $18,820 includes full-time tuition ($14,158), mandatory fees ($400), and college room and board ($4262). *College room only:* $1802. Full-time tuition and fees vary according to program. Room and board charges vary according to board plan and student level. *Part-time tuition:* $280 per credit. *Part-time mandatory fees:* $15 per credit. Part-time tuition and fees vary according to course load and program.

Financial Aid Forms of aid include need-based and non-need-based scholarships, athletic grants, and part-time jobs. The average aided 2003–04 undergraduate received an aid package worth an estimated $11,061. The priority application deadline for financial aid is April 1.

Freshman Admission DWU requires a high school transcript, SAT I or ACT scores, and TOEFL scores for international students. A minimum 2.0 high school GPA is recommended. The application deadline for regular admission is August 25.

Transfer Admission The application deadline for admission is August 25.

Entrance Difficulty DWU assesses its entrance difficulty level as moderately difficult. For the fall 2003 freshman class, 77 percent of the applicants were accepted.

For Further Information Contact Ms. Laura Miller, Director of Admissions Operations and Outreach Programming, Dakota Wesleyan University, 1200 West University Avenue, Mitchell, SD 57301-4398. *Telephone:* 605-995-2650 Ext. 2651 or 800-333-8506 (toll-free). *Fax:* 605-995-2699. *E-mail:* admissions@dwu.edu. *Web site:* http://www.dwu.edu/.

HURON UNIVERSITY
See Si Tanka Huron University

KILIAN COMMUNITY COLLEGE
Sioux Falls, South Dakota

Kilian is a coed, private, two-year college, founded in 1977, offering degrees at the associate level. It has a 2-acre campus in Sioux Falls.

Academic Information The faculty has 71 members (8% full-time). The student-faculty ratio is 8:1. The library holds 78,000 titles and 395 serial subscriptions. Special programs include academic remediation, services for learning-disabled students, cooperative (work-study) education, double majors, independent study, summer session for credit, part-time degree programs (daytime, evenings, summer), and internships.
Student Body Statistics The student body is made up of 444 undergraduates. Students come from 3 states and territories. 94 percent are from South Dakota.
Expenses for 2004–05 *Application fee:* $25. *Tuition:* $6660 full-time, $185 per credit part-time. *Mandatory fees:* $150 full-time.
Financial Aid Forms of aid include need-based scholarships and part-time jobs. The application deadline for financial aid is continuous.
Freshman Admission Kilian requires a high school transcript and TOEFL scores for international students. ACT ASSET is required for some. The application deadline for regular admission is rolling.
Transfer Admission The application deadline for admission is rolling.
Entrance Difficulty Kilian has an open admission policy.

For Further Information Contact Ms. Jacque Danielson, Director of Admissions, Kilian Community College, 224 North Phillips Avenue, Sioux Falls, SD 57104-6014. *Telephone:* 605-221-3100 or 800-888-1147 (toll-free). *Fax:* 605-336-2606. *E-mail:* info@kilian.edu. *Web site:* http://www.kilian.edu/.

MOUNT MARTY COLLEGE
Yankton, South Dakota

Mount Marty is a coed, private, Roman Catholic, comprehensive institution, founded in 1936, offering degrees at the associate, bachelor's, and master's levels and postbachelor's certificates. It has an 80-acre campus in Yankton.

Academic Information The faculty has 107 members (39% full-time), 30% with terminal degrees. The undergraduate student-faculty ratio is 13:1. The library holds 79,167 titles, 439 serial subscriptions, and 8,537 audiovisual materials. Special programs include academic remediation, services for learning-disabled students, an honors program, cooperative (work-study) education, advanced placement credit, accelerated degree programs, double majors, independent study, self-designed majors, summer session for credit, part-time degree programs (daytime, evenings), adult/continuing education programs, internships, and arrangement for off-campus study with members of the Colleges of Mid-America. The most frequently chosen baccalaureate fields are business/marketing, education, health professions and related sciences.
Student Body Statistics The student body totals 1,185, of whom 1,095 are undergraduates (184 freshmen). 69 percent are women and 31 percent are men. Students come from 18 states and territories and 3 other countries. 78 percent are from South Dakota. 0.7 percent are international students.
Expenses for 2003–04 *Application fee:* $35. *Comprehensive fee:* $18,856 includes full-time tuition ($12,506), mandatory fees ($1680), and college room and board ($4670). Full-time tuition and fees vary according to location. *Part-time tuition:* $205 per credit. Part-time tuition varies according to location.
Financial Aid Forms of aid include need-based and non-need-based scholarships, athletic grants, and part-time jobs. The average aided 2003–04 undergraduate received an aid package worth an estimated $12,417. The priority application deadline for financial aid is March 1.
Freshman Admission Mount Marty requires a high school transcript, a minimum 2.0 high school GPA, ACT scores, and TOEFL scores for international students. An interview is recommended. Recommendations are required for some. The application deadline for regular admission is rolling.
Transfer Admission The application deadline for admission is rolling.

Entrance Difficulty Mount Marty assesses its entrance difficulty level as moderately difficult. For the fall 2003 freshman class, 80 percent of the applicants were accepted.

For Further Information Contact Ms. Brandi Tschumper, Vice President for Enrollment Management, Mount Marty College, 1105 West 8th Street, Yankton, SD 57078. *Telephone:* 605-668-1545 or 800-658-4552 (toll-free). *Fax:* 605-668-1607. *E-mail:* mmcadmit@mtmc.edu. *Web site:* http://www.mtmc.edu/.

NATIONAL AMERICAN UNIVERSITY
Rapid City, South Dakota

National American University is a coed, proprietary, comprehensive unit of National College, founded in 1941, offering degrees at the associate, bachelor's, and master's levels. It has an 8-acre campus in Rapid City.

Academic Information The undergraduate student-faculty ratio is 15:1. The library holds 31,018 titles and 268 serial subscriptions. Special programs include academic remediation, services for learning-disabled students, cooperative (work-study) education, advanced placement credit, accelerated degree programs, ESL programs, independent study, distance learning, summer session for credit, part-time degree programs (daytime, evenings, summer), external degree programs, adult/continuing education programs, and internships.
Student Body Statistics The student body totals 749, of whom 714 are undergraduates (166 freshmen). 48 percent are women and 52 percent are men. Students come from 25 states and territories. 79 percent are from South Dakota. 0.7 percent are international students.
Expenses for 2003–04 *Application fee:* $25. *Comprehensive fee:* $13,710 includes full-time tuition ($9675), mandatory fees ($315), and college room and board ($3720). *College room only:* $1725. Room and board charges vary according to board plan.
Financial Aid Forms of aid include need-based and non-need-based scholarships and part-time jobs. The application deadline for financial aid is continuous.
Freshman Admission National American University requires a high school transcript and TOEFL scores for international students. An interview and ACT scores are recommended. The application deadline for regular admission is rolling.
Transfer Admission The application deadline for admission is rolling.
Entrance Difficulty National American University has an open admission policy.

For Further Information Contact Mr. Tom Shea, Vice President of Enrollment Management, National American University, 321 Kansas City Street, Rapid City, SD 57701. *Telephone:* 605-394-4902 or 800-843-8892 (toll-free). *Fax:* 605-394-4871. *Web site:* http://www.national.edu/.

NATIONAL AMERICAN UNIVERSITY–SIOUX FALLS BRANCH
Sioux Falls, South Dakota

National American University–Sioux Falls Branch is a coed, primarily women's, proprietary, four-year college of National College, founded in 1941, offering degrees at the associate, bachelor's, and master's levels.

Academic Information The faculty has 35 members. The library holds 1,580 titles and 57 serial subscriptions. Special programs include academic remediation, cooperative (work-study) education, advanced placement credit, accelerated degree programs, ESL programs, double majors, distance learning, summer session for credit, part-time degree programs (daytime, evenings, summer), adult/continuing education programs, and internships. The most frequently chosen baccalaureate fields are business/marketing, computer/information sciences.

National American University–Sioux Falls Branch (continued)

Student Body Statistics The student body is made up of 350 undergraduates. Students come from 5 states and territories. 10 percent of the 2003 graduating class went on to graduate and professional schools.

Expenses for 2004–05 *Application fee:* $25. *Tuition:* $7740 full-time, $215 per credit part-time.

Financial Aid Forms of aid include need-based and non-need-based scholarships and part-time jobs. The application deadline for financial aid is continuous.

Freshman Admission National American University–Sioux Falls Branch requires a high school transcript, an interview, and TOEFL scores for international students. The application deadline for regular admission is rolling.

Transfer Admission The application deadline for admission is rolling.

Entrance Difficulty National American University–Sioux Falls Branch has an open admission policy.

For Further Information Contact Ms. Lisa Houtsma, Director of Admissions, National American University–Sioux Falls Branch, 2801 South Kiwanis Avenue, Suite 100, Sioux Falls, SD 57105. *Telephone:* 605-334-5430 or 800-358-5430 (toll-free out-of-state). *Fax:* 605-334-1575. *E-mail:* lhautsma@national.edu. *Web site:* http://www.national.edu/.

NORTHERN STATE UNIVERSITY
Aberdeen, South Dakota

NSU is a coed, public, comprehensive unit of South Dakota Board of Regents, founded in 1901, offering degrees at the associate, bachelor's, and master's levels and postbachelor's certificates. It has a 52-acre campus in Aberdeen.

Academic Information The faculty has 111 members (100% full-time), 73% with terminal degrees. The undergraduate student-faculty ratio is 20:1. The library holds 187,961 titles and 880 serial subscriptions. Special programs include academic remediation, services for learning-disabled students, an honors program, cooperative (work-study) education, study abroad, advanced placement credit, accelerated degree programs, ESL programs, distance learning, self-designed majors, summer session for credit, part-time degree programs, adult/continuing education programs, internships, and arrangement for off-campus study with National Student Exchange. The most frequently chosen baccalaureate fields are business/marketing, education, social sciences and history.

Student Body Statistics The student body totals 3,083, of whom 2,842 are undergraduates (434 freshmen). 59 percent are women and 41 percent are men. Students come from 29 states and territories and 16 other countries. 85 percent are from South Dakota.

Expenses for 2003–04 *Application fee:* $15. *State resident tuition:* $2163 full-time, $72 per credit hour part-time. *Nonresident tuition:* $6875 full-time, $229 per credit hour part-time. *Mandatory fees:* $2,044 full-time, $68.15 per credit hour part-time. Full-time tuition and fees vary according to course level, course load, and reciprocity agreements. Part-time tuition and fees vary according to course level, course load, and reciprocity agreements. *College room and board:* $3306. *College room only:* $1478. Room and board charges vary according to board plan.

Financial Aid Forms of aid include need-based and non-need-based scholarships, athletic grants, and part-time jobs. The average aided 2002–03 undergraduate received an aid package worth $5041. The priority application deadline for financial aid is March 1.

Freshman Admission NSU requires a high school transcript, a minimum X high school GPA, SAT I or ACT scores, and TOEFL scores for international students. Recommendations are required for some. The application deadline for regular admission is September 1.

Transfer Admission The application deadline for admission is September 1.

Entrance Difficulty NSU assesses its entrance difficulty level as minimally difficult; moderately difficult for transfers. For the fall 2003 freshman class, 92 percent of the applicants were accepted.

For Further Information Contact Ms. Sara Hanson, Interim Director of Admissions-Campus, Northern State University, 1200 South Jay Street, Aberdeen, SD 57401. *Telephone:* 605-626-2544 or 800-678-5330 (toll-free). *Fax:* 605-626-2587. *E-mail:* admissions1@northern.edu. *Web site:* http://www.northern.edu/.

OGLALA LAKOTA COLLEGE
Kyle, South Dakota

For Information Write to Oglala Lakota College, Kyle, SD 57752-0490.

PRESENTATION COLLEGE
Aberdeen, South Dakota

Presentation College is a coed, private, Roman Catholic, four-year college, founded in 1951, offering degrees at the associate and bachelor's levels. It has a 100-acre campus in Aberdeen.

Academic Information The faculty has 68 members (43% full-time), 10% with terminal degrees. The student-faculty ratio is 12:1. The library holds 40,000 titles, 430 serial subscriptions, and 2,900 audiovisual materials. Special programs include academic remediation, cooperative (work-study) education, advanced placement credit, accelerated degree programs, double majors, distance learning, summer session for credit, part-time degree programs (daytime, evenings, summer), external degree programs, adult/continuing education programs, and internships.

Student Body Statistics The student body is made up of 618 undergraduates (162 freshmen). 88 percent are women and 12 percent are men. Students come from 1 state or territory and 1 other country. 76 percent are from South Dakota. 0.7 percent are international students.

Expenses for 2003–04 *Application fee:* $0. *Comprehensive fee:* $14,200 includes full-time tuition ($10,050) and college room and board ($4150). *College room only:* $3400. Full-time tuition varies according to course load, location, and program. Room and board charges vary according to board plan, housing facility, and student level. *Part-time tuition:* $354 per credit. Part-time tuition varies according to course load, location, and program.

Financial Aid Forms of aid include need-based and non-need-based scholarships and part-time jobs. The average aided 2002–03 undergraduate received an aid package worth $6845. The application deadline for financial aid is April 1.

Freshman Admission Presentation College requires a high school transcript, TOEFL scores for international students, and ACT ASSET. A minimum 2.0 high school GPA and ACT scores are recommended. 2 recommendations and ACT scores are required for some. The application deadline for regular admission is rolling.

Transfer Admission The application deadline for admission is rolling.

Entrance Difficulty Presentation College has an open admission policy except for allied health programs, nursing. It assesses its entrance difficulty as minimally difficult for allied health programs.

For Further Information Contact Ms. Jo Ellen Lindner, Director of Admissions, Presentation College, 1500 North Main Street, Aberdeen, SD 57401. *Telephone:* 605-229-8493 Ext. 492 or 800-437-6060 (toll-free). *Fax:* 605-229-8518. *E-mail:* admit@presentation.edu. *Web site:* http://www.presentation.edu/.

SINTE GLESKA UNIVERSITY
Rosebud, South Dakota

For Information Write to Sinte Gleska University, Rosebud, SD 57570-0490.

SI TANKA HURON UNIVERSITY
Huron, South Dakota

Si Tanka Huron University is a coed, proprietary, four-year college, founded in 1883, offering degrees at the associate and bachelor's levels. It has a 15-acre campus in Huron.

For Further Information   Contact Mr. Tyler Fisher, Director of Admissions, Si Tanka Huron University, 333 9th Street Southwest, Huron, SD 57350. *Telephone:* 605-352-8721 Ext. 41 or 800-710-7159 (toll-free). *Fax:* 605-352-7421. *E-mail:* admissions@huron.edu. *Web site:* http://www.sitanka.net/1.5/.

SOUTH DAKOTA SCHOOL OF MINES AND TECHNOLOGY
Rapid City, South Dakota

SDSM&T is a coed, public unit of South Dakota State University System, founded in 1885, offering degrees at the associate, bachelor's, master's, and doctoral levels. It has a 120-acre campus in Rapid City.

Academic Information   The faculty has 133 members (78% full-time), 78% with terminal degrees. The undergraduate student-faculty ratio is 18:1. The library holds 219,961 titles, 496 serial subscriptions, and 1,610 audiovisual materials. Special programs include academic remediation, services for learning-disabled students, cooperative (work-study) education, study abroad, advanced placement credit, ESL programs, double majors, independent study, distance learning, summer session for credit, part-time degree programs (daytime, evenings), adult/continuing education programs, and internships. The most frequently chosen baccalaureate fields are engineering/engineering technologies, interdisciplinary studies, physical sciences.

Student Body Statistics   The student body totals 2,454, of whom 2,112 are undergraduates (420 freshmen). 31 percent are women and 69 percent are men. Students come from 34 states and territories and 8 other countries. 73 percent are from South Dakota. 0.8 percent are international students.

Expenses for 2003–04   *Application fee:* $20. *State resident tuition:* $2163 full-time, $72.10 per credit hour part-time. *Nonresident tuition:* $6875 full-time, $229.15 per credit hour part-time. *Mandatory fees:* $2130 full-time, $71 per credit hour part-time. Full-time tuition and fees vary according to course load, program, and reciprocity agreements. Part-time tuition and fees vary according to course load, program, and reciprocity agreements. *College room and board:* $3561. *College room only:* $1625. Room and board charges vary according to board plan and housing facility.

Financial Aid   Forms of aid include need-based and non-need-based scholarships, athletic grants, and part-time jobs. The average aided 2003–04 undergraduate received an aid package worth an estimated $6048. The priority application deadline for financial aid is March 15.

Freshman Admission   SDSM&T requires a high school transcript, SAT I or ACT scores, and TOEFL scores for international students. A minimum 2.6 high school GPA is recommended. ACT scores and are required for some. The application deadline for regular admission is rolling.

Transfer Admission   The application deadline for admission is rolling.

Entrance Difficulty   SDSM&T assesses its entrance difficulty level as moderately difficult. For the fall 2003 freshman class, 94 percent of the applicants were accepted.

For Further Information   Contact Mr. Joseph Mueller, Director of Admissions, South Dakota School of Mines and Technology, 501 East Saint Joseph, Rapid City, SD 57701-3995. *Telephone:* 605-394-2414 Ext. 1266 or 800-544-8162 Ext. 2414 (toll-free). *Fax:* 605-394-1268. *E-mail:* admissions@sdsmt.edu. *Web site:* http://www.sdsmt.edu/.

SOUTH DAKOTA STATE UNIVERSITY
Brookings, South Dakota

SDSU is a coed, public university, founded in 1881, offering degrees at the associate, bachelor's, master's, doctoral, and first professional levels. It has a 272-acre campus in Brookings.

Academic Information   The faculty has 638 members (79% full-time), 60% with terminal degrees. The undergraduate student-faculty ratio is 18:1. The library holds 555,523 titles, 6,023 serial subscriptions, and 2,504 audiovisual materials. Special programs include academic remediation, services for learning-disabled students, an honors program, cooperative (work-study) education, study abroad, advanced placement credit, accelerated degree programs, Freshman Honors College, ESL programs, double majors, independent study, distance learning, summer session for credit, part-time degree programs (daytime, evenings, summer), adult/continuing education programs, internships, and arrangement for off-campus study with National Student Exchange. The most frequently chosen baccalaureate fields are agriculture, engineering/engineering technologies, health professions and related sciences.

Student Body Statistics   The student body totals 10,642, of whom 9,284 are undergraduates (2,073 freshmen). 53 percent are women and 47 percent are men. Students come from 39 states and territories and 19 other countries. 74 percent are from South Dakota. 0.2 percent are international students.

Expenses for 2003–04   *Application fee:* $20. *State resident tuition:* $2308 full-time, $72.10 per credit part-time. *Nonresident tuition:* $7332 full-time, $229.15 per credit part-time. *Mandatory fees:* $2228 full-time, $69.70 per credit part-time. Full-time tuition and fees vary according to course load and program. Part-time tuition and fees vary according to course load and program. *College room and board:* $3586. *College room only:* $1862. Room and board charges vary according to board plan and housing facility.

Financial Aid   Forms of aid include need-based and non-need-based scholarships, athletic grants, and part-time jobs. The average aided 2003–04 undergraduate received an aid package worth an estimated $7126. The priority application deadline for financial aid is March 7.

Freshman Admission   SDSU requires a high school transcript, a minimum 2.6 high school GPA, minimum ACT score of 18, ACT scores, and TOEFL scores for international students. The application deadline for regular admission is rolling.

Transfer Admission   The application deadline for admission is rolling.

Entrance Difficulty   SDSU assesses its entrance difficulty level as moderately difficult. For the fall 2003 freshman class, 96 percent of the applicants were accepted.

For Further Information   Contact Ms. Michelle Kuebler, Assistant Director of Admissions, South Dakota State University, PO Box 2201, Brookings, SD 57007. *Telephone:* 605-688-4121 or 800-952-3541 (toll-free). *Fax:* 605-688-6891. *E-mail:* sdsu_admissions@sdstate.edu. *Web site:* http://www.sdstate.edu/.

UNIVERSITY OF SIOUX FALLS
Sioux Falls, South Dakota

USF is a coed, private, American Baptist Churches in the USA, comprehensive institution, founded in 1883, offering degrees at the associate, bachelor's, master's, and doctoral levels. It has a 22-acre campus in Sioux Falls.

Academic Information   The faculty has 128 members (41% full-time), 29% with terminal degrees. The undergraduate student-faculty ratio is 17:1. The library holds 57,750 titles, 382 serial subscriptions, and 4,480 audiovisual materials. Special programs include academic remediation, services for learning-disabled students, an honors program, cooperative (work-study) education, study abroad, advanced placement credit, accelerated degree programs, double majors, independent study, distance learning, self-designed majors, summer session for credit, part-time degree programs (daytime, evenings, weekends, summer), external degree programs, adult/continuing education programs, internships, and arrangement for off-campus study with Colleges of Mid-America,

University of Sioux Falls (continued)

Augustana College (SD), North American Baptist Seminary, Christian College Coalition. The most frequently chosen baccalaureate fields are biological/life sciences, business/marketing, education.
Student Body Statistics The student body totals 1,485, of whom 1,260 are undergraduates (236 freshmen). 56 percent are women and 44 percent are men. Students come from 20 states and territories and 3 other countries. 66 percent are from South Dakota. 0.8 percent are international students. 14 percent of the 2003 graduating class went on to graduate and professional schools.
Expenses for 2004–05 *Application fee:* $25. *Comprehensive fee:* $19,100 includes full-time tuition ($14,900) and college room and board ($4200). *College room only:* $1830. Room and board charges vary according to board plan and housing facility. *Part-time tuition:* $240 per semester hour.
Financial Aid Forms of aid include need-based and non-need-based scholarships, athletic grants, and part-time jobs. The priority application deadline for financial aid is March 1.
Freshman Admission USF requires a high school transcript, SAT I and SAT II or ACT scores, and TOEFL scores for international students. An essay and a minimum 2.0 high school GPA are recommended. 2 recommendations and an interview are required for some. The application deadline for regular admission is rolling.
Transfer Admission The application deadline for admission is rolling.
Entrance Difficulty USF assesses its entrance difficulty level as moderately difficult. For the fall 2003 freshman class, 95 percent of the applicants were accepted.

For Further Information Contact Ms. Patti Klinkhammer, Office Manager, University of Sioux Falls, 1101 West 22nd Street, Sioux Falls, SD 57105. *Telephone:* 605-331-6600 Ext. 6602 or 800-888-1047 (toll-free). *Fax:* 605-331-6615. *E-mail:* admissions@usiouxfalls.edu. *Web site:* http://www.usiouxfalls.edu/.

THE UNIVERSITY OF SOUTH DAKOTA
Vermillion, South Dakota

USD is a coed, public university, founded in 1862, offering degrees at the associate, bachelor's, master's, doctoral, and first professional levels and post-master's and postbachelor's certificates. It has a 216-acre campus in Vermillion.

Academic Information The faculty has 297 members (97% full-time), 77% with terminal degrees. The undergraduate student-faculty ratio is 15:1. The library holds 335,757 titles, 2,852 serial subscriptions, and 30,885 audiovisual materials. Special programs include services for learning-disabled students, an honors program, study abroad, advanced placement credit, ESL programs, double majors, independent study, distance learning, summer session for credit, part-time degree programs, internships, and arrangement for off-campus study with National Student Exchange. The most frequently chosen baccalaureate fields are business/marketing, education, health professions and related sciences.
Student Body Statistics The student body totals 8,093, of whom 5,851 are undergraduates (1,078 freshmen). 61 percent are women and 39 percent are men. Students come from 34 states and territories and 23 other countries. 77 percent are from South Dakota. 1.8 percent are international students. 33 percent of the 2003 graduating class went on to graduate and professional schools.
Expenses for 2003–04 *Application fee:* $20. *State resident tuition:* $2163 full-time, $72.10 per credit hour part-time. *Nonresident tuition:* $6875 full-time, $229.15 per credit hour part-time. *Mandatory fees:* $2042 full-time, $68.05 per credit hour part-time. Full-time tuition and fees vary according to course load and reciprocity agreements. Part-time tuition and fees vary according to course load and reciprocity agreements. *College room and board:* $3504. *College room only:* $1777. Room and board charges vary according to board plan and housing facility.
Financial Aid Forms of aid include need-based and non-need-based scholarships, athletic grants, and part-time jobs. The average aided 2003–04 undergraduate received an aid package worth an estimated $5644. The priority application deadline for financial aid is March 15.
Freshman Admission USD requires a high school transcript, SAT I or ACT scores, and TOEFL scores for international students. A minimum

2.6 high school GPA is recommended. Recommendations are required for some. The application deadline for regular admission is September 4.
Transfer Admission The application deadline for admission is rolling.
Entrance Difficulty USD assesses its entrance difficulty level as moderately difficult. For the fall 2003 freshman class, 83 percent of the applicants were accepted.

For Further Information Contact Ms. Paula Tacke, Director of Admissions, The University of South Dakota, 414 East Clark Street, Vermillion, SD 57069. *Telephone:* 605-677-5434 or 877-269-6837 (toll-free). *Fax:* 605-677-6753. *E-mail:* admiss@usd.edu. *Web site:* http://www.usd.edu/.

Wisconsin

ALVERNO COLLEGE
Milwaukee, Wisconsin

Alverno is a women's, private, Roman Catholic, comprehensive institution, founded in 1887, offering degrees at the associate, bachelor's, and master's levels (also offers weekend program with significant enrollment not reflected in profile). It has a 46-acre campus in Milwaukee.

Academic Information The faculty has 205 members (51% full-time), 46% with terminal degrees. The undergraduate student-faculty ratio is 14:1. The library holds 92,076 titles, 1,001 serial subscriptions, and 34,795 audiovisual materials. Special programs include academic remediation, services for learning-disabled students, study abroad, advanced placement credit, double majors, summer session for credit, part-time degree programs (daytime, evenings, weekends, summer), adult/continuing education programs, and internships. The most frequently chosen baccalaureate fields are communications/communication technologies, business/marketing, health professions and related sciences.
Student Body Statistics The student body totals 2,160, of whom 1,951 are undergraduates (279 freshmen). Students come from 8 states and territories and 9 other countries. 97 percent are from Wisconsin. 0.9 percent are international students. 10 percent of the 2003 graduating class went on to graduate and professional schools.
Expenses for 2003–04 *Application fee:* $20. *Comprehensive fee:* $18,898 includes full-time tuition ($13,488), mandatory fees ($150), and college room and board ($5260). Full-time tuition and fees vary according to class time and program. Room and board charges vary according to board plan. *Part-time tuition:* $562 per credit hour. *Part-time mandatory fees:* $75 per term. Part-time tuition and fees vary according to class time and program.
Financial Aid Forms of aid include need-based and non-need-based scholarships and part-time jobs. The priority application deadline for financial aid is April 1.
Freshman Admission Alverno requires an essay, a high school transcript, SAT I or ACT scores, and TOEFL scores for international students. An interview and ACT scores are recommended. Recommendations are required for some. The application deadline for regular admission is rolling.
Transfer Admission The application deadline for admission is rolling.
Entrance Difficulty Alverno assesses its entrance difficulty level as moderately difficult. For the fall 2003 freshman class, 56 percent of the applicants were accepted.

For Further Information Contact Ms. Mary Kay Farrell, Director of Admissions, Alverno College, 3400 South 43 Street, PO Box 343922, Milwaukee, WI 53234-3922. *Telephone:* 414-382-6113 or 800-933-3401 (toll-free). *Fax:* 414-382-6354. *E-mail:* admissions@alverno.edu. *Web site:* http://www.alverno.edu/.

See page 250 for a narrative description.

BELLIN COLLEGE OF NURSING

Green Bay, Wisconsin

Bellin College is a coed, primarily women's, private, four-year college, founded in 1909, offering degrees at the bachelor's level in nursing.

Academic Information The faculty has 18 members (89% full-time), 17% with terminal degrees. The student-faculty ratio is 10:1. The library holds 7,000 titles, 225 serial subscriptions, and 600 audiovisual materials. Special programs include advanced placement credit, accelerated degree programs, independent study, summer session for credit, and arrangement for off-campus study with University of Wisconsin-Green Bay. The most frequently chosen baccalaureate field is health professions and related sciences.

Student Body Statistics The student body is made up of 206 undergraduates (36 freshmen). 95 percent are women and 5 percent are men. Students come from 2 states and territories. 100 percent are from Wisconsin. 2 percent of the 2003 graduating class went on to graduate and professional schools.

Expenses for 2003–04 *Application fee:* $20. *Tuition:* $12,672 full-time, $610 per credit hour part-time. *Mandatory fees:* $279 full-time, $279 per year part-time. Full-time tuition and fees vary according to student level.

Financial Aid Forms of aid include need-based and non-need-based scholarships and part-time jobs. The average aided 2003–04 undergraduate received an aid package worth an estimated $12,996. The priority application deadline for financial aid is March 1.

Freshman Admission Bellin College requires a high school transcript, 3 recommendations, an interview, and ACT scores. A minimum 3.0 high school GPA is recommended. The application deadline for regular admission is rolling.

Transfer Admission The application deadline for admission is rolling.

Entrance Difficulty Bellin College assesses its entrance difficulty level as moderately difficult. For the fall 2003 freshman class, 84 percent of the applicants were accepted.

For Further Information Contact Dr. Penny Croghan, Admissions Director, Bellin College of Nursing, 725 South Webster Avenue, Green Bay, WI 54301. *Telephone:* 920-433-5803 or 800-236-8707 (toll-free in-state). *Fax:* 920-433-7416. *E-mail:* admissio@bcon.edu. *Web site:* http://www.bcon.edu/.

BELOIT COLLEGE

Beloit, Wisconsin

Beloit is a coed, private, four-year college, founded in 1846, offering degrees at the bachelor's level. It has a 65-acre campus in Beloit near Chicago and Milwaukee.

Academic Information The faculty has 126 members (82% full-time), 93% with terminal degrees. The student-faculty ratio is 11:1. The library holds 183,736 titles, 946 serial subscriptions, and 7,285 audiovisual materials. Special programs include services for learning-disabled students, study abroad, advanced placement credit, ESL programs, double majors, independent study, self-designed majors, summer session for credit, adult/continuing education programs, internships, and arrangement for off-campus study with University of Wisconsin-Madison, University of Chicago, Spelman College, Morehouse College, Associated Colleges of the Midwest. The most frequently chosen baccalaureate fields are biological/life sciences, English, social sciences and history.

Student Body Statistics The student body is made up of 1,332 undergraduates (346 freshmen). 61 percent are women and 39 percent are men. Students come from 47 states and territories and 40 other countries. 18 percent are from Wisconsin. 5.5 percent are international students. 29 percent of the 2003 graduating class went on to graduate and professional schools.

Expenses for 2003–04 *Application fee:* $30. *Comprehensive fee:* $29,864 includes full-time tuition ($24,166), mandatory fees ($220), and college room and board ($5478). *College room only:* $2672. Room and board charges vary according to board plan.

Financial Aid Forms of aid include need-based and non-need-based scholarships and part-time jobs. The average aided 2003–04 undergraduate received an aid package worth an estimated $18,635. The priority application deadline for financial aid is March 1.

Freshman Admission Beloit requires an essay, a high school transcript, 1 recommendation, SAT I or ACT scores, and TOEFL scores for international students. An interview is recommended. An interview is required for some. The application deadline for regular admission is January 15 and for early action it is December 15.

Transfer Admission The application deadline for admission is rolling.

Entrance Difficulty Beloit assesses its entrance difficulty level as very difficult. For the fall 2003 freshman class, 69 percent of the applicants were accepted.

For Further Information Contact Mr. James S. Zielinski, Director of Admissions, Beloit College, 700 College Street, Beloit, WI 53511-5596. *Telephone:* 608-363-2380 or 800-9-BELOIT (toll-free). *Fax:* 608-363-2075. *E-mail:* admiss@beloit.edu. *Web site:* http://www.beloit.edu/.

BRYANT AND STRATTON COLLEGE

Milwaukee, Wisconsin

Bryant & Stratton is a coed, proprietary, primarily two-year college of Bryant and Stratton Business Institute, Inc., founded in 1863, offering degrees at the associate and bachelor's levels. It has a 2-acre campus in Milwaukee.

Academic Information The faculty has 69 members (12% full-time). The student-faculty ratio is 14:1. The library holds 120 serial subscriptions and 100 audiovisual materials. Special programs include academic remediation, cooperative (work-study) education, advanced placement credit, double majors, independent study, distance learning, summer session for credit, part-time degree programs (daytime, evenings), adult/continuing education programs, and internships.

Student Body Statistics The student body is made up of 656 undergraduates. 76 percent are women and 24 percent are men. Students come from 1 state or territory. 9 percent of the 2003 graduating class went on to four-year colleges.

Expenses for 2003–04 *Application fee:* $25. *One-time mandatory fee:* $25. *Tuition:* $10,440 full-time, $350 per credit hour part-time. *Mandatory fees:* $200 full-time, $100 per term part-time. Full-time tuition and fees vary according to class time and course load. Part-time tuition and fees vary according to class time and course load.

Financial Aid Forms of aid include need-based scholarships and part-time jobs. The application deadline for financial aid is continuous.

Freshman Admission Bryant & Stratton requires a high school transcript, TOEFL scores for international students, and TABE. A minimum 2.0 high school GPA and SAT I or ACT scores are recommended. Recommendations and an interview are required for some. The application deadline for regular admission is rolling.

Transfer Admission The application deadline for admission is rolling.

Entrance Difficulty Bryant & Stratton assesses its entrance difficulty level as minimally difficult. For the fall 2003 freshman class, 82 percent of the applicants were accepted.

For Further Information Contact Ms. Kathryn Cotey, Director of Admissions, Bryant and Stratton College, 310 West Wisconsin Avenue, Milwaukee, WI 53203-2214. *Telephone:* 414-276-5200. *Web site:* http://www.bryantstratton.edu/.

CARDINAL STRITCH UNIVERSITY

Milwaukee, Wisconsin

Stritch is a coed, private, Roman Catholic, comprehensive institution, founded in 1937, offering degrees at the associate, bachelor's, master's, and doctoral levels and postbachelor's certificates. It has a 40-acre campus in Milwaukee.

Academic Information The faculty has 880 members (12% full-time). The undergraduate student-faculty ratio is 18:1. The library holds 124,897 titles, 667 serial subscriptions, and 6,250 audiovisual materials. Special

Cardinal Stritch University (continued)

programs include academic remediation, services for learning-disabled students, an honors program, cooperative (work-study) education, advanced placement credit, accelerated degree programs, ESL programs, double majors, independent study, distance learning, self-designed majors, summer session for credit, part-time degree programs (daytime, evenings, weekends, summer), external degree programs, adult/continuing education programs, internships, and arrangement for off-campus study with Concordia University Wisconsin, Saint Francis Seminary, Sacred Heart School of Theology. The most frequently chosen baccalaureate fields are business/marketing, computer/information sciences, education.

Student Body Statistics The student body totals 6,785, of whom 3,251 are undergraduates (241 freshmen). 68 percent are women and 32 percent are men. Students come from 16 states and territories and 27 other countries. 2.1 percent are international students.

Expenses for 2003–04 *Application fee:* $25. *Comprehensive fee:* $19,700 includes full-time tuition ($14,240), mandatory fees ($300), and college room and board ($5160). Full-time tuition and fees vary according to program. Room and board charges vary according to board plan. *Part-time tuition:* $445 per credit. *Part-time mandatory fees:* $100 per term. Part-time tuition and fees vary according to course load and program.

Financial Aid Forms of aid include need-based and non-need-based scholarships and part-time jobs. The average aided 2002–03 undergraduate received an aid package worth $7843. The application deadline for financial aid is continuous.

Freshman Admission Stritch requires an essay, a high school transcript, a minimum 2.0 high school GPA, SAT I or ACT scores, and TOEFL scores for international students. An interview and ACT scores are recommended. Recommendations are required for some. The application deadline for regular admission is rolling.

Transfer Admission The application deadline for admission is rolling.

Entrance Difficulty Stritch assesses its entrance difficulty level as moderately difficult. For the fall 2003 freshman class, 93 percent of the applicants were accepted.

For Further Information Contact Mr. David Wegener, Director of Admissions, Cardinal Stritch University, 6801 North Yates Road, Milwaukee, WI 53217-3985. *Telephone:* 414-410-4040 or 800-347-8822 Ext. 4040 (toll-free). *Fax:* 414-410-4058. *E-mail:* admityou@stritch.edu. *Web site:* http://www.stritch.edu/.

CARROLL COLLEGE

Waukesha, Wisconsin

Carroll is a coed, private, Presbyterian, comprehensive institution, founded in 1846, offering degrees at the bachelor's and master's levels. It has a 52-acre campus in Waukesha near Milwaukee.

Academic Information The faculty has 243 members (40% full-time), 37% with terminal degrees. The undergraduate student-faculty ratio is 16:1. The library holds 200,000 titles, 520 serial subscriptions, and 362 audiovisual materials. Special programs include academic remediation, services for learning-disabled students, an honors program, study abroad, advanced placement credit, double majors, independent study, distance learning, self-designed majors, summer session for credit, part-time degree programs (daytime, evenings, weekends, summer), adult/continuing education programs, and internships. The most frequently chosen baccalaureate fields are business/marketing, education, visual/performing arts.

Student Body Statistics The student body totals 2,953, of whom 2,699 are undergraduates (513 freshmen). 67 percent are women and 33 percent are men. Students come from 28 states and territories and 27 other countries. 77 percent are from Wisconsin. 2.2 percent are international students.

Expenses for 2004–05 *Application fee:* $0. *Comprehensive fee:* $23,770 includes full-time tuition ($17,800), mandatory fees ($370), and college room and board ($5600). *College room only:* $3030. Full-time tuition and fees vary according to program. Room and board charges vary according to board plan and housing facility. *Part-time tuition:* $220 per credit. Part-time tuition varies according to course load and program.

Financial Aid Forms of aid include need-based and non-need-based scholarships and part-time jobs. The average aided 2002–03 undergraduate received an aid package worth $12,999. The application deadline for financial aid is continuous.

Freshman Admission Carroll requires a high school transcript, a minimum 2.0 high school GPA, 1 recommendation, SAT I and SAT II or ACT scores, and TOEFL scores for international students. An interview is recommended. An essay is required for some. The application deadline for regular admission is rolling.

Transfer Admission The application deadline for admission is rolling.

Entrance Difficulty Carroll assesses its entrance difficulty level as moderately difficult. For the fall 2003 freshman class, 78 percent of the applicants were accepted.

For Further Information Contact Mr. James V. Wiseman III, Vice President of Enrollment, Carroll College, 100 North East Avenue, Waukesha, WI 53186-5593. *Telephone:* 262-524-7221 or 800-CARROLL (toll-free). *Fax:* 262-524-7139. *E-mail:* cc.info@ccadmin.cc.edu. *Web site:* http://www.cc.edu/.

CARTHAGE COLLEGE

Kenosha, Wisconsin

Carthage is a coed, private, comprehensive institution, founded in 1847, affiliated with the Evangelical Lutheran Church in America, offering degrees at the bachelor's and master's levels. It has a 72-acre campus in Kenosha near Chicago and Milwaukee.

Academic Information The faculty has 170 members (64% full-time), 61% with terminal degrees. The undergraduate student-faculty ratio is 17:1. The library holds 128,551 titles, 425 serial subscriptions, and 4,361 audiovisual materials. Special programs include services for learning-disabled students, an honors program, cooperative (work-study) education, study abroad, advanced placement credit, accelerated degree programs, double majors, independent study, self-designed majors, summer session for credit, part-time degree programs, adult/continuing education programs, internships, and arrangement for off-campus study with University of Wisconsin-Parkside, Marquette University. The most frequently chosen baccalaureate fields are business/marketing, education, social sciences and history.

Student Body Statistics The student body totals 2,632, of whom 2,508 are undergraduates (582 freshmen). 58 percent are women and 42 percent are men. Students come from 25 states and territories and 12 other countries. 46 percent are from Wisconsin. 0.7 percent are international students. 14 percent of the 2003 graduating class went on to graduate and professional schools.

Expenses for 2004–05 *Application fee:* $25. *Comprehensive fee:* $27,500 includes full-time tuition ($21,250) and college room and board ($6250). Full-time tuition varies according to reciprocity agreements. Room and board charges vary according to board plan. *Part-time tuition:* $315 per credit hour. Part-time tuition varies according to class time and course load.

Financial Aid Forms of aid include need-based and non-need-based scholarships and part-time jobs. The average aided 2002–03 undergraduate received an aid package worth $8222. The priority application deadline for financial aid is February 15.

Freshman Admission Carthage requires a high school transcript, a minimum 2.0 high school GPA, SAT I or ACT scores, and TOEFL scores for international students. An essay, a minimum 3.0 high school GPA, and an interview are recommended. An essay and 2 recommendations are required for some. The application deadline for regular admission is rolling and for early action it is July 1.

Transfer Admission The application deadline for admission is rolling.

Entrance Difficulty Carthage assesses its entrance difficulty level as moderately difficult. For the fall 2003 freshman class, 73 percent of the applicants were accepted.

For Further Information Contact Ms. Brenda Poggendorf, Vice President for Enrollment, Carthage College, 2001 Alford Park Drive, Kenosha, WI 53140-1994. *Telephone:* 262-551-5850 or 800-351-4058 (toll-free). *Fax:* 262-551-5762. *E-mail:* admissions@carthage.edu. *Web site:* http://www.carthage.edu/.

COLLEGE OF MENOMINEE NATION

Keshena, Wisconsin

College of Menominee Nation is a coed, private, two-year college, offering degrees at the associate level.

Expenses for 2003–04 *Application fee:* $10. *State resident tuition:* $3584 full-time, $148.50 per credit part-time.

For Further Information Contact Ms. Cynthia Norton, Admissions Representative, College of Menominee Nation, PO Box 1179, Keshena, WI 54135. *Telephone:* 715-799-5600 Ext. 3053. *Fax:* 715-799-1326. *Web site:* http://www.menominee.edu/.

COLUMBIA COLLEGE OF NURSING

Milwaukee, Wisconsin

Columbia College of Nursing is a coed, primarily women's, private, four-year college, founded in 1901, offering degrees at the bachelor's level in nursing (nursing degree is awarded in conjunction with Mount Mary College).

Academic Information The faculty has 18 members (61% full-time), 28% with terminal degrees. The student-faculty ratio is 15:1. The library holds 9,060 titles, 253 serial subscriptions, and 508 audiovisual materials. Special programs include an honors program, advanced placement credit, double majors, independent study, summer session for credit, part-time degree programs (daytime, evenings, summer), and arrangement for off-campus study with Carroll College. The most frequently chosen baccalaureate field is health professions and related sciences.
Student Body Statistics The student body is made up of 190 undergraduates (185 freshmen). 97 percent are women and 3 percent are men. 87 percent are from Wisconsin. 21 percent of the 2003 graduating class went on to graduate and professional schools.
Expenses for 2004–05 *Application fee:* $25. *Comprehensive fee:* $19,770 includes full-time tuition ($15,100), mandatory fees ($670), and college room and board ($4000). *College room only:* $3000. Room and board charges vary according to board plan, housing facility, location, and student level. *Part-time tuition:* $420 per credit hour. *Part-time mandatory fees:* $500 per term. Part-time tuition and fees vary according to program.
Financial Aid Forms of aid include need-based and non-need-based scholarships and part-time jobs. The application deadline for financial aid is continuous.
Freshman Admission Columbia College of Nursing requires a high school transcript, SAT I or ACT scores, and TOEFL scores for international students. An essay, 1 recommendation, and an interview are recommended. An essay is required for some. The application deadline for regular admission is August 1.
Transfer Admission The application deadline for admission is rolling.
Entrance Difficulty Columbia College of Nursing assesses its entrance difficulty level as moderately difficult.

For Further Information Contact Ms. Amy Dobson, Dean of Admissions, Columbia College of Nursing, 2900 North Menomonee River Parkway, Milwaukee, WI 53222-4597. *Telephone:* 414-256-1219 or 800-321-6265 (toll-free out-of-state). *Fax:* 414-256-0180. *E-mail:* admiss@mtmary.edu. *Web site:* http://www.ccon.edu/.

CONCORDIA UNIVERSITY WISCONSIN

Mequon, Wisconsin

CUW is a coed, private, comprehensive institution, founded in 1881, affiliated with the Lutheran Church–Missouri Synod, offering degrees at the associate, bachelor's, master's, and doctoral levels. It has a 155-acre campus in Mequon near Milwaukee.

Academic Information The faculty has 191 members (49% full-time), 40% with terminal degrees. The undergraduate student-faculty ratio is 11:1. The library holds 110,929 titles, 1,411 serial subscriptions, and 4,645 audiovisual materials. Special programs include academic remediation, services for learning-disabled students, an honors program, study abroad, advanced placement credit, accelerated degree programs, ESL programs, double majors, independent study, distance learning, self-designed majors, summer session for credit, part-time degree programs, adult/continuing education programs, internships, and arrangement for off-campus study with Milwaukee Area Technical College, Milwaukee Institute of Art and Design, Cardinal Stritch University, Mount Mary College. The most frequently chosen baccalaureate fields are business/marketing, education, health professions and related sciences.
Student Body Statistics The student body totals 5,152, of whom 3,990 are undergraduates (362 freshmen). 63 percent are women and 37 percent are men. Students come from 35 states and territories and 21 other countries. 63 percent are from Wisconsin. 0.6 percent are international students.
Expenses for 2003–04 *Application fee:* $35. *Comprehensive fee:* $21,365 includes full-time tuition ($15,515), mandatory fees ($60), and college room and board ($5790). Room and board charges vary according to board plan. *Part-time tuition:* $645 per credit hour. Part-time tuition varies according to class time and program.
Financial Aid Forms of aid include need-based and non-need-based scholarships and part-time jobs. The average aided 2002–03 undergraduate received an aid package worth $14,124. The priority application deadline for financial aid is May 1.
Freshman Admission CUW requires a high school transcript, a minimum 2.0 high school GPA, SAT I or ACT scores, and TOEFL scores for international students. An interview is recommended. An essay, a minimum 3.0 high school GPA, and 3 recommendations are required for some. The application deadline for regular admission is August 15.
Transfer Admission The application deadline for admission is August 15.
Entrance Difficulty CUW assesses its entrance difficulty level as moderately difficult; minimally difficult for transfers. For the fall 2003 freshman class, 80 percent of the applicants were accepted.

For Further Information Contact Mr. Ken Gaschk, Director of Admissions, Concordia University Wisconsin, 12800 North Lake Shore Drive, Mequon, WI 53097. *Telephone:* 262-243-4305 Ext. 4305 or 888-628-9472 (toll-free). *Fax:* 262-243-4351. *E-mail:* admissions@cuw.edu. *Web site:* http://www.cuw.edu/.

DEVRY UNIVERSITY

Milwaukee, Wisconsin

DeVry University is a coed, proprietary, comprehensive unit of DeVry University, offering degrees at the bachelor's and master's levels and postbachelor's certificates.

Student Body Statistics The student body totals 210, of whom 23 are undergraduates (10 freshmen). 61 percent are women and 39 percent are men.
Freshman Admission The application deadline for regular admission is rolling.

For Further Information Contact DeVry University, 100 East Wisconsin Avenue, Suite 2550, Milwaukee, WI 53202-4107. *Telephone:* 414-278-7677. *Fax:* 414-278-0137. *E-mail:* ejohnson@keller.edu. *Web site:* http://www.devry.edu/.

DEVRY UNIVERSITY

Waukesha, Wisconsin

For Information Write to DeVry University, Waukesha, WI 53186-4047.

EDGEWOOD COLLEGE
Madison, Wisconsin

Edgewood is a coed, private, Roman Catholic, comprehensive institution, founded in 1927, offering degrees at the associate, bachelor's, and master's levels. It has a 55-acre campus in Madison.

Academic Information The faculty has 235 members (39% full-time), 48% with terminal degrees. The undergraduate student-faculty ratio is 13:1. The library holds 90,253 titles, 447 serial subscriptions, and 4,359 audiovisual materials. Special programs include academic remediation, services for learning-disabled students, advanced placement credit, independent study, summer session for credit, part-time degree programs (daytime, evenings, weekends, summer), adult/continuing education programs, and arrangement for off-campus study with University of Wisconsin–Madison. The most frequently chosen baccalaureate fields are business/marketing, education, health professions and related sciences.

Student Body Statistics The student body totals 2,422, of whom 1,909 are undergraduates (314 freshmen). 73 percent are women and 27 percent are men. Students come from 16 states and territories and 22 other countries. 92 percent are from Wisconsin. 2.3 percent are international students. 8 percent of the 2003 graduating class went on to graduate and professional schools.

Expenses for 2003–04 *Application fee:* $25. *Comprehensive fee:* $20,450 includes full-time tuition ($15,100) and college room and board ($5350). *College room only:* $2708. Full-time tuition varies according to program. Room and board charges vary according to housing facility and location. *Part-time tuition:* $457 per credit. Part-time tuition varies according to course load and program.

Financial Aid Forms of aid include need-based and non-need-based scholarships and part-time jobs. The average aided 2002–03 undergraduate received an aid package worth $10,888. The priority application deadline for financial aid is March 15.

Freshman Admission Edgewood requires a high school transcript, a minimum 2.5 high school GPA, SAT I or ACT scores, and TOEFL scores for international students. An essay, 2 recommendations, and an interview are required for some. The application deadline for regular admission is rolling.

Transfer Admission The application deadline for admission is rolling.

Entrance Difficulty Edgewood assesses its entrance difficulty level as moderately difficult. For the fall 2003 freshman class, 80 percent of the applicants were accepted.

For Further Information Contact Mr. Jim Krystofiak, Associate Director of Admissions, Edgewood College, 1000 Edgewood College Drive, Madison, WI 53711-1997. *Telephone:* 608-663-2254 or 800-444-4861 Ext. 2294 (toll-free). *Fax:* 608-663-3291. *E-mail:* admissions@edgewood.edu. *Web site:* http://www.edgewood.edu/.

HERZING COLLEGE
Madison, Wisconsin

Herzing College is a coed, primarily men's, proprietary, primarily two-year college of Herzing Institutes, Inc., founded in 1948, offering degrees at the associate and bachelor's levels. It is located in Madison near Milwaukee.

Expenses for 2003–04 *Application fee:* $0. *Tuition:* $10,000 full-time. *Mandatory fees:* $100 full-time. Full-time tuition and fees vary according to course level and program. *Part-time tuition:* varies with course level, program.

For Further Information Contact Ms. Renee Herzing, Admissions Director, Herzing College, 5218 East Terrace Drive, Madison, WI 53718. *Telephone:* 608-249-6611 or 800-582-1227 (toll-free). *Fax:* 608-249-8593. *E-mail:* mailbag@msn.herzing.edu. *Web site:* http://www.herzing.edu/.

ITT TECHNICAL INSTITUTE
Green Bay, Wisconsin

ITT Tech is a coed, proprietary, primarily two-year college of ITT Educational Services, Inc., founded in 2000, offering degrees at the associate and bachelor's levels.

Student Body Statistics The student body is made up of 419 undergraduates.

Expenses for 2003–04 *Application fee:* $100. Total Program Cost varies depending on course of study. Consult school catalog.

Financial Aid Forms of aid include need-based scholarships and part-time jobs. The application deadline for financial aid is continuous.

Freshman Admission ITT Tech requires a high school transcript, an interview, Recommendations are recommended. The application deadline for regular admission is rolling.

Transfer Admission The application deadline for admission is rolling.

Entrance Difficulty ITT Tech assesses its entrance difficulty level as minimally difficult.

For Further Information Contact Ms. Judi Hughes, Director, ITT Technical Institute, 470 Security Boulevard, Green Bay, WI 54313. *Telephone:* 920-662-9000 or 888-884-3626 (toll-free out-of-state). *Fax:* 920-662-9384. *Web site:* http://www.itt-tech.edu/.

ITT TECHNICAL INSTITUTE
Greenfield, Wisconsin

ITT Tech is a coed, proprietary, primarily two-year college of ITT Educational Services, Inc., founded in 1968, offering degrees at the associate and bachelor's levels. It is located in Greenfield near Milwaukee.

Student Body Statistics The student body is made up of 548 undergraduates.

Expenses for 2003–04 *Application fee:* $100. Total Program Cost varies depending on course of study. Consult school catalog.

Financial Aid Forms of aid include need-based scholarships and part-time jobs. The application deadline for financial aid is continuous.

Freshman Admission ITT Tech requires a high school transcript, an interview, and Wonderlic aptitude test. Recommendations are recommended. The application deadline for regular admission is rolling.

Transfer Admission The application deadline for admission is rolling.

Entrance Difficulty ITT Tech assesses its entrance difficulty level as minimally difficult.

For Further Information Contact Mr. Al Hedin, Director of Recruitment, ITT Technical Institute, 6300 West Layton Avenue, Greenfield, WI 53220. *Telephone:* 414-282-9494. *Fax:* 414-282-9698. *Web site:* http://www.itt-tech.edu/.

LAKELAND COLLEGE
Sheboygan, Wisconsin

Lakeland is a coed, private, comprehensive institution, founded in 1862, affiliated with the United Church of Christ, offering degrees at the bachelor's and master's levels. It has a 240-acre campus in Sheboygan near Milwaukee.

Academic Information The faculty has 65 members (74% full-time), 55% with terminal degrees. The undergraduate student-faculty ratio is 19:1. The library holds 64,970 titles, 317 serial subscriptions, and 647 audiovisual materials. Special programs include academic remediation, services for learning-disabled students, an honors program, study abroad, advanced placement credit, ESL programs, independent study, distance learning, summer session for credit, part-time degree programs (evenings, summer), adult/continuing education programs, internships, and arrangement for off-campus study. The most frequently chosen baccalaureate fields are business/marketing, computer/information sciences, education.

Student Body Statistics The student body totals 3,829, of whom 3,399 are undergraduates (155 freshmen). 61 percent are women and 39 percent are men. Students come from 42 states and territories and 40 other countries. 91 percent are from Wisconsin. 5.1 percent are international students. 10 percent of the 2003 graduating class went on to graduate and professional schools.

Expenses for 2004–05 *Application fee: $20. Comprehensive fee: $20,555* includes full-time tuition ($14,265), mandatory fees ($635), and college room and board ($5655). *College room only: $2655.* Full-time tuition and fees vary according to location. Room and board charges vary according to board plan and housing facility. *Part-time tuition: $1585* per course. Part-time tuition varies according to class time and location.

Financial Aid Forms of aid include need-based and non-need-based scholarships and part-time jobs. The average aided 2002–03 undergraduate received an aid package worth $9976. The application deadline for financial aid is July 1 with a priority deadline of May 1.

Freshman Admission Lakeland requires an essay, a high school transcript, a minimum 2.0 high school GPA, SAT I or ACT scores, and TOEFL scores for international students. Recommendations are recommended. An interview is required for some. The application deadline for regular admission is September 1.

Entrance Difficulty Lakeland assesses its entrance difficulty level as minimally difficult. For the fall 2003 freshman class, 68 percent of the applicants were accepted.

For Further Information Contact Mr. Nathan Dehne, Director of Admissions, Lakeland College, PO Box 359, Nash Visitors Center, Sheboygan, WI 53082-0359. *Telephone:* 920-565-1588 or 800-242-3347 (toll-free in-state). *Fax:* 920-565-1206. *E-mail:* admissions@lakeland.edu. *Web site:* http://www.lakeland.edu/.

LAWRENCE UNIVERSITY
Appleton, Wisconsin

Lawrence is a coed, private, four-year college, founded in 1847, offering degrees at the bachelor's level. It has an 84-acre campus in Appleton.

Academic Information The faculty has 166 members (78% full-time), 79% with terminal degrees. The student-faculty ratio is 11:1. The library holds 376,814 titles, 1,586 serial subscriptions, and 21,086 audiovisual materials. Special programs include services for learning-disabled students, study abroad, advanced placement credit, double majors, independent study, self-designed majors, internships, and arrangement for off-campus study with Associated Colleges of the Midwest, Great Lakes Colleges Association. The most frequently chosen baccalaureate fields are social sciences and history, interdisciplinary studies, visual/performing arts.

Student Body Statistics The student body is made up of 1,407 undergraduates (356 freshmen). 53 percent are women and 47 percent are men. Students come from 49 states and territories and 51 other countries. 42 percent are from Wisconsin. 11.4 percent are international students. 30 percent of the 2003 graduating class went on to graduate and professional schools.

Expenses for 2003–04 *Application fee: $30. Comprehensive fee: $30,741* includes full-time tuition ($24,900), mandatory fees ($189), and college room and board ($5652). Room and board charges vary according to board plan.

Financial Aid Forms of aid include need-based and non-need-based scholarships and part-time jobs. The average aided 2003–04 undergraduate received an aid package worth an estimated $21,596. The priority application deadline for financial aid is March 15.

Freshman Admission Lawrence requires an essay, a high school transcript, 2 recommendations, audition for music program, and SAT I or ACT scores. A minimum 3.0 high school GPA, an interview, and TOEFL scores for international students are recommended. The application deadline for regular admission is January 15; for early decision it is November 15; and for early action it is December 1.

Transfer Admission The application deadline for admission is rolling.

Entrance Difficulty Lawrence assesses its entrance difficulty level as very difficult. For the fall 2003 freshman class, 58 percent of the applicants were accepted.

For Further Information Contact Mr. Steven T. Syverson, Dean of Admissions and Financial Aid, Lawrence University, PO Box 599, Appleton, WI 54912-0599. *Telephone:* 920-832-6500 or 800-227-0982 (toll-free). *Fax:* 920-832-6782. *E-mail:* excel@lawrence.edu. *Web site:* http://www.lawrence.edu/.

MARANATHA BAPTIST BIBLE COLLEGE
Watertown, Wisconsin

Maranatha is a coed, private, Baptist, comprehensive institution, founded in 1968, offering degrees at the associate, bachelor's, and master's levels. It has a 60-acre campus in Watertown near Milwaukee.

Expenses for 2003–04 *Application fee: $40. Comprehensive fee: $12,300* includes full-time tuition ($7040), mandatory fees ($740), and college room and board ($4520). *Part-time tuition: $220* per semester hour.

For Further Information Contact Mr. James H. Harrison, Director of Admissions, Maranatha Baptist Bible College, 745 West Main Street, Watertown, WI 53094. *Telephone:* 920-206-2327 or 800-622-2947 (toll-free). *Fax:* 920-261-9109. *E-mail:* admissions@mbbc.edu. *Web site:* http://www.mbbc.edu/.

MARIAN COLLEGE OF FOND DU LAC
Fond du Lac, Wisconsin

Marian College is a coed, private, Roman Catholic, comprehensive institution, founded in 1936, offering degrees at the bachelor's and master's levels. It has a 77-acre campus in Fond du Lac near Milwaukee.

Academic Information The faculty has 151 members (50% full-time), 35% with terminal degrees. The undergraduate student-faculty ratio is 15:1. The library holds 91,708 titles, 698 serial subscriptions, and 397 audiovisual materials. Special programs include academic remediation, services for learning-disabled students, an honors program, cooperative (work-study) education, study abroad, advanced placement credit, accelerated degree programs, double majors, independent study, distance learning, self-designed majors, summer session for credit, part-time degree programs (daytime, evenings, weekends, summer), external degree programs, adult/continuing education programs, and internships. The most frequently chosen baccalaureate fields are business/marketing, education, health professions and related sciences.

Student Body Statistics The student body totals 2,777, of whom 1,856 are undergraduates (251 freshmen). 70 percent are women and 30 percent are men. Students come from 17 states and territories and 8 other countries. 94 percent are from Wisconsin. 1.7 percent are international students.

Expenses for 2003–04 *Application fee: $20. Comprehensive fee: $19,625* includes full-time tuition ($14,700), mandatory fees ($325), and college room and board ($4600). *College room only: $2600.* Room and board charges vary according to board plan and housing facility. *Part-time tuition: $270* per credit. Part-time tuition varies according to class time, course load, and program.

Financial Aid Forms of aid include need-based and non-need-based scholarships and part-time jobs. The average aided 2003–04 undergraduate received an aid package worth an estimated $13,560. The priority application deadline for financial aid is March 1.

Freshman Admission Marian College requires a high school transcript, SAT I or ACT scores, and TOEFL scores for international students. A minimum 2.0 high school GPA and recommendations are recommended. An interview is required for some. The application deadline for regular admission is rolling.

Transfer Admission The application deadline for admission is rolling.

Marian College of Fond du Lac (continued)

Entrance Difficulty Marian College assesses its entrance difficulty level as moderately difficult. For the fall 2003 freshman class, 77 percent of the applicants were accepted.

For Further Information Contact Stacey L. Akey, Dean of Admissions, Marian College of Fond du Lac, 45 South National Avenue, Fond du Lac, WI 54935. *Telephone:* 920-923-7652 or 800-2-MARIAN Ext. 7652 (toll-free in-state). *Fax:* 920-923-8755. *E-mail:* admit@ mariancollege.edu. *Web site:* http://www.mariancollege.edu/.

MARQUETTE UNIVERSITY
Milwaukee, Wisconsin

Marquette is a coed, private, Roman Catholic (Jesuit) university, founded in 1881, offering degrees at the associate, bachelor's, master's, doctoral, and first professional levels and post-master's and postbachelor's certificates. It has an 80-acre campus in Milwaukee.

Academic Information The faculty has 1,018 members (57% full-time), 67% with terminal degrees. The undergraduate student-faculty ratio is 15:1. The library holds 1 million titles, 5,894 serial subscriptions, and 9,332 audiovisual materials. Special programs include services for learning-disabled students, an honors program, cooperative (work-study) education, study abroad, advanced placement credit, ESL programs, double majors, summer session for credit, part-time degree programs (daytime, evenings, weekends, summer), adult/continuing education programs, internships, and arrangement for off-campus study with Milwaukee Institute of Art and Design, Les Aspin Center for Government, Washington, DC. The most frequently chosen baccalaureate fields are business/marketing, communications/communication technologies, health professions and related sciences.
Student Body Statistics The student body totals 11,355, of whom 7,775 are undergraduates (1,889 freshmen). 55 percent are women and 45 percent are men. Students come from 54 states and territories and 80 other countries. 42 percent are from Wisconsin. 2 percent are international students. 26 percent of the 2003 graduating class went on to graduate and professional schools.
Expenses for 2003–04 *Application fee:* $30. *Comprehensive fee:* $27,710 includes full-time tuition ($20,350), mandatory fees ($360), and college room and board ($7000). *College room only:* $4550. Full-time tuition and fees vary according to course load, program, and reciprocity agreements. Room and board charges vary according to board plan, housing facility, and location. *Part-time tuition:* $600 per credit. Part-time tuition varies according to program.
Financial Aid Forms of aid include need-based and non-need-based scholarships, athletic grants, and part-time jobs. The average aided 2003–04 undergraduate received an aid package worth an estimated $16,853. The application deadline for financial aid is continuous.
Freshman Admission Marquette requires an essay, a high school transcript, a minimum 2.5 high school GPA, 1 recommendation, SAT I or ACT scores, and TOEFL scores for international students. A minimum 3.4 high school GPA is recommended. The application deadline for regular admission is rolling.
Transfer Admission The application deadline for admission is rolling.
Entrance Difficulty Marquette assesses its entrance difficulty level as moderately difficult; very difficult for physical therapy and athletic training. For the fall 2003 freshman class, 83 percent of the applicants were accepted.

For Further Information Contact Mr. Robert Blust, Dean of Undergraduate Admissions, Marquette University, PO Box 1881, Milwaukee, WI 53201-1881. *Telephone:* 414-288-7004 or 800-222-6544 (toll-free). *Fax:* 414-288-3764. *E-mail:* admissions@marquette. edu. *Web site:* http://www.marquette.edu/.

MILWAUKEE INSTITUTE OF ART AND DESIGN
Milwaukee, Wisconsin

MIAD is a coed, private, four-year college, founded in 1974, offering degrees at the bachelor's level in art and design.

Academic Information The faculty has 93 members (35% full-time). The student-faculty ratio is 12:1. The library holds 23,000 titles, 84 serial subscriptions, and 360 audiovisual materials. Special programs include academic remediation, services for learning-disabled students, cooperative (work-study) education, study abroad, advanced placement credit, double majors, independent study, summer session for credit, adult/continuing education programs, internships, and arrangement for off-campus study with Marquette University, Association of Independent Colleges of Art and Design. The most frequently chosen baccalaureate field is visual/performing arts.
Student Body Statistics The student body is made up of 629 undergraduates (161 freshmen). 54 percent are women and 46 percent are men. Students come from 16 states and territories and 5 other countries. 72 percent are from Wisconsin. 2.1 percent are international students. 1 percent of the 2003 graduating class went on to graduate and professional schools.
Expenses for 2003–04 *Application fee:* $25. *Comprehensive fee:* $26,701 includes full-time tuition ($19,900), mandatory fees ($130), and college room and board ($6671). Room and board charges vary according to board plan. *Part-time tuition:* varies with course load.
Financial Aid Forms of aid include need-based and non-need-based scholarships and part-time jobs. The average aided 2002–03 undergraduate received an aid package worth $16,857. The application deadline for financial aid is March 1.
Freshman Admission MIAD requires an essay, a high school transcript, an interview, a portfolio, and TOEFL scores for international students. A minimum 2.0 high school GPA and SAT I or ACT scores are recommended. Recommendations are required for some. The application deadline for regular admission is rolling.
Transfer Admission The application deadline for admission is rolling.
Entrance Difficulty MIAD assesses its entrance difficulty level as moderately difficult. For the fall 2003 freshman class, 83 percent of the applicants were accepted.

For Further Information Contact Mr. Mark Fetherston, Director of Admissions, Milwaukee Institute of Art and Design, 273 East Erie Street, Milwaukee, WI 53202. *Telephone:* 414-847-3259 or 888-749-MIAD (toll-free). *Fax:* 414-291-8077. *E-mail:* admissions@miad.edu. *Web site:* http://www.miad.edu/.

MILWAUKEE SCHOOL OF ENGINEERING
Milwaukee, Wisconsin

MSOE is a coed, primarily men's, private, comprehensive institution, founded in 1903, offering degrees at the bachelor's and master's levels. It has a 15-acre campus in Milwaukee.

Academic Information The faculty has 294 members (43% full-time), 38% with terminal degrees. The undergraduate student-faculty ratio is 11:1. The library holds 56,044 titles, 416 serial subscriptions, and 852 audiovisual materials. Special programs include academic remediation, services for learning-disabled students, study abroad, advanced placement credit, accelerated degree programs, double majors, independent study, distance learning, summer session for credit, part-time degree programs (daytime, evenings, weekends, summer), adult/continuing education programs, and internships. The most frequently chosen baccalaureate fields are business/marketing, engineering/engineering technologies, health professions and related sciences.
Student Body Statistics The student body totals 2,383, of whom 2,101 are undergraduates (439 freshmen). 17 percent are women and 83 percent are men. Students come from 31 states and territories and 24 other countries. 69 percent are from Wisconsin. 2.5 percent are international students. 7 percent of the 2003 graduating class went on to graduate and professional schools.

Expenses for 2003–04 *Application fee:* $25. *Comprehensive fee:* $28,479 includes full-time tuition ($23,034) and college room and board ($5445). *College room only:* $3500. Full-time tuition varies according to student level. Room and board charges vary according to board plan and housing facility. *Part-time tuition:* $402 per quarter hour. Part-time tuition varies according to course load.

Financial Aid Forms of aid include need-based and non-need-based scholarships and part-time jobs. The average aided 2002–03 undergraduate received an aid package worth $13,375. The priority application deadline for financial aid is March 15.

Freshman Admission MSOE requires a high school transcript, a minimum 2.5 high school GPA, SAT I or ACT scores, and TOEFL scores for international students. An essay and an interview are required for some. The application deadline for regular admission is rolling.

Transfer Admission The application deadline for admission is rolling.

Entrance Difficulty MSOE assesses its entrance difficulty level as moderately difficult. For the fall 2003 freshman class, 65 percent of the applicants were accepted.

For Further Information Contact Mr. Paul Borens, Director, Admission, Milwaukee School of Engineering, 1025 North Broadway, Milwaukee, WI 53202-3109. *Telephone:* 414-277-6763 or 800-332-6763 (toll-free). *Fax:* 414-277-7475. *E-mail:* explore@msoe.edu. *Web site:* http://www.msoe.edu/.

See page 310 for a narrative description.

MOUNT MARY COLLEGE
Milwaukee, Wisconsin

MMC is a women's, private, Roman Catholic, comprehensive institution, founded in 1913, offering degrees at the bachelor's and master's levels and postbachelor's certificates. It has an 80-acre campus in Milwaukee.

Academic Information The faculty has 192 members (35% full-time), 39% with terminal degrees. The undergraduate student-faculty ratio is 14:1. The library holds 113,006 titles, 500 serial subscriptions, and 9,832 audiovisual materials. Special programs include academic remediation, services for learning-disabled students, an honors program, study abroad, advanced placement credit, accelerated degree programs, double majors, independent study, self-designed majors, summer session for credit, part-time degree programs (daytime, evenings, weekends, summer), adult/continuing education programs, and internships. The most frequently chosen baccalaureate fields are business/marketing, health professions and related sciences, visual/performing arts.

Student Body Statistics The student body totals 1,600, of whom 1,371 are undergraduates (108 freshmen). Students come from 7 states and territories and 6 other countries. 97 percent are from Wisconsin. 0.5 percent are international students. 19 percent of the 2003 graduating class went on to graduate and professional schools.

Expenses for 2003–04 *Application fee:* $25. *Comprehensive fee:* $20,370 includes full-time tuition ($15,100), mandatory fees ($170), and college room and board ($5100). Room and board charges vary according to board plan. *Part-time tuition:* $440 per credit. *Part-time mandatory fees:* $42.50 per term. Part-time tuition and fees vary according to course load.

Financial Aid Forms of aid include need-based and non-need-based scholarships and part-time jobs. The average aided 2003–04 undergraduate received an aid package worth an estimated $11,347. The priority application deadline for financial aid is March 1.

Freshman Admission MMC requires a high school transcript, a minimum 2.5 high school GPA, SAT I or ACT scores, and TOEFL scores for international students. An interview is recommended. An essay and 2 recommendations are required for some. The application deadline for regular admission is rolling.

Transfer Admission The application deadline for admission is rolling.

Entrance Difficulty MMC assesses its entrance difficulty level as moderately difficult. For the fall 2003 freshman class, 78 percent of the applicants were accepted.

SPECIAL MESSAGE TO STUDENTS

Social Life Students can immerse themselves in Mount Mary's dynamic community. They can join a campus club; study abroad in France or Peru; put their heart into volunteering; explore the new Science, Technology, and Campus Center; or venture off campus. Close proximity to downtown Milwaukee provides numerous field work, internship, and employment opportunities, where Mount Mary students take what they learn in the classroom and get real-world experience.

Academic Highlights Founded by the School Sisters of Notre Dame in 1913, Mount Mary College is fully accredited and provides specialized programs taught by caring, dedicated, and talented faculty members. The parklike, 80-acre campus of Mount Mary is home to a diverse community of approximately 1,600 undergraduate and graduate students.

Interviews and Campus Visits Students can visit any time throughout the year, take a tour, and meet with admissions counselors, financial aid officers, faculty members, and current students. To schedule a visit or for more information, those interested should call 414-256-1219 or 800-321-6265 (toll-free). The nearest commercial airport is Mitchell International.

For Further Information Write to Enrollment Office, Mount Mary College, 2900 North Menomonee River Parkway, Milwaukee, WI 53222-4597. *E-mail:* admiss@mtmary.edu. *Web site:* http://www.mtmary.edu.

NORTHLAND COLLEGE
Ashland, Wisconsin

Northland is a coed, private, four-year college, founded in 1892, affiliated with the United Church of Christ, offering degrees at the bachelor's level. It has a 130-acre campus in Ashland.

Academic Information The faculty has 80 members (54% full-time), 58% with terminal degrees. The student-faculty ratio is 13:1. The library holds 75,000 titles and 260 serial subscriptions. Special programs include services for learning-disabled students, an honors program, cooperative (work-study) education, study abroad, advanced placement credit, accelerated degree programs, double majors, independent study, distance learning, self-designed majors, summer session for credit, part-time degree programs (daytime, evenings, summer), adult/continuing education programs, internships, and arrangement for off-campus study with members of the May Term Consortium, Allegheny College, Beloit College. The most frequently chosen baccalaureate fields are biological/life sciences, education, natural resources/environmental science.

Student Body Statistics The student body is made up of 750 undergraduates (115 freshmen). 54 percent are women and 46 percent are men. Students come from 43 states and territories and 11 other countries. 35 percent are from Wisconsin. 2.9 percent are international students. 25 percent of the 2003 graduating class went on to graduate and professional schools.

Expenses for 2004–05 *Application fee:* $0. *Comprehensive fee:* $24,105 includes full-time tuition ($18,135), mandatory fees ($580), and college room and board ($5390). *College room only:* $2170. Room and board charges vary according to board plan and housing facility. *Part-time tuition:* $330 per credit. Part-time tuition varies according to course load.

Financial Aid Forms of aid include need-based and non-need-based scholarships and part-time jobs. The average aided 2003–04 undergraduate received an aid package worth an estimated $14,321. The priority application deadline for financial aid is April 15.

Freshman Admission Northland requires an essay, a high school transcript, 1 recommendation, SAT I or ACT scores, and TOEFL scores for international students. A minimum 2.0 high school GPA and an interview are recommended. The application deadline for regular admission is August 1.

Transfer Admission The application deadline for admission is August 1.

Wisconsin

Northland College (continued)

Entrance Difficulty Northland assesses its entrance difficulty level as moderately difficult. For the fall 2003 freshman class, 73 percent of the applicants were accepted.

For Further Information Contact Mr. Eric Peterson, Director of Admission, Northland College, 1411 Ellis Avenue, Ashland, WI 54806. *Telephone:* 715-682-1224, 800-753-1840 (toll-free in-state), or 800-753-1040 (toll-free out-of-state). *Fax:* 715-682-1258. *E-mail:* admit@northland.edu. *Web site:* http://www.northland.edu/.

RIPON COLLEGE
Ripon, Wisconsin

Ripon is a coed, private, four-year college, founded in 1851, offering degrees at the bachelor's level. It has a 250-acre campus in Ripon near Milwaukee.

Academic Information The faculty has 75 members (67% full-time), 80% with terminal degrees. The student-faculty ratio is 15:1. The library holds 169,523 titles, 985 serial subscriptions, and 662 audiovisual materials. Special programs include services for learning-disabled students, study abroad, advanced placement credit, accelerated degree programs, double majors, self-designed majors, part-time degree programs (daytime), internships, and arrangement for off-campus study with American University, Newberry Library, Oak Ridge National Laboratory, University of Chicago, Associated Colleges of the Midwest Wilderness Field Station. The most frequently chosen baccalaureate fields are education, psychology, social sciences and history.

Student Body Statistics The student body is made up of 998 undergraduates (259 freshmen). 52 percent are women and 48 percent are men. Students come from 33 states and territories and 14 other countries. 69 percent are from Wisconsin. 1.8 percent are international students. 22 percent of the 2003 graduating class went on to graduate and professional schools.

Expenses for 2004–05 *Application fee:* $30. *Comprehensive fee:* $26,090 includes full-time tuition ($20,490), mandatory fees ($240), and college room and board ($5360). *College room only:* $2530. *Part-time tuition:* $825 per credit.

Financial Aid Forms of aid include need-based and non-need-based scholarships and part-time jobs. The average aided 2003–04 undergraduate received an aid package worth an estimated $17,108. The priority application deadline for financial aid is March 1.

Freshman Admission Ripon requires a high school transcript, a minimum 2.0 high school GPA, 1 recommendation, SAT I or ACT scores, and TOEFL scores for international students. An essay and an interview are recommended. The application deadline for regular admission is rolling.

Transfer Admission The application deadline for admission is rolling.

Entrance Difficulty Ripon assesses its entrance difficulty level as moderately difficult. For the fall 2003 freshman class, 84 percent of the applicants were accepted.

For Further Information Contact Mr. Scott J. Goplin, Vice President and Dean of Admission and Financial Aid, Ripon College, 300 Seward Street, PO Box 248, Ripon, WI 54971. *Telephone:* 920-748-8185 or 800-947-4766 (toll-free). *Fax:* 920-748-8335. *E-mail:* adminfo@ripon.edu. *Web site:* http://www.ripon.edu/.

See page 330 for a narrative description.

ST. NORBERT COLLEGE
De Pere, Wisconsin

St. Norbert is a coed, private, Roman Catholic, comprehensive institution, founded in 1898, offering degrees at the bachelor's and master's levels. It has a 92-acre campus in De Pere.

Academic Information The faculty has 164 members (74% full-time), 73% with terminal degrees. The undergraduate student-faculty ratio is 15:1. The library holds 115,553 titles, 690 serial subscriptions, and 7,625 audiovisual materials. Special programs include academic remediation, services for learning-disabled students, an honors program, cooperative (work-study) education, study abroad, advanced placement credit, ESL programs, double majors, independent study, distance learning, self-designed majors, summer session for credit, part-time degree programs (daytime, summer), internships, and arrangement for off-campus study with Higher Education Consortium for Urban Affairs, American University. The most frequently chosen baccalaureate fields are business/marketing, communications/communication technologies, social sciences and history.

Student Body Statistics The student body totals 2,155, of whom 2,086 are undergraduates (529 freshmen). 57 percent are women and 43 percent are men. Students come from 26 states and territories and 15 other countries. 71 percent are from Wisconsin. 2.5 percent are international students. 19.5 percent of the 2003 graduating class went on to graduate and professional schools.

Expenses for 2004–05 *Application fee:* $25. *Comprehensive fee:* $27,490 includes full-time tuition ($21,210), mandatory fees ($300), and college room and board ($5980). *College room only:* $3160. Full-time tuition and fees vary according to course load. Room and board charges vary according to board plan, housing facility, and student level. *Part-time tuition:* $2651 per course. Part-time tuition varies according to course load.

Financial Aid Forms of aid include need-based and non-need-based scholarships and part-time jobs. The average aided 2003–04 undergraduate received an aid package worth an estimated $15,507. The priority application deadline for financial aid is March 1.

Freshman Admission St. Norbert requires an essay, a high school transcript, 1 recommendation, SAT I or ACT scores, and TOEFL scores for international students. An interview is recommended. The application deadline for regular admission is rolling and for early decision it is December 1.

Transfer Admission The application deadline for admission is rolling.

Entrance Difficulty St. Norbert assesses its entrance difficulty level as moderately difficult. For the fall 2003 freshman class, 86 percent of the applicants were accepted.

For Further Information Contact Mr. Daniel L. Meyer, Dean of Admission and Enrollment Management, St. Norbert College, 100 Grant Street, De Pere, WI 54115-2099. *Telephone:* 920-403-3005 or 800-236-4878 (toll-free). *Fax:* 920-403-4072. *E-mail:* admit@snc.edu. *Web site:* http://www.snc.edu/.

SILVER LAKE COLLEGE
Manitowoc, Wisconsin

SLC is a coed, private, Roman Catholic, comprehensive institution, founded in 1869, offering degrees at the associate, bachelor's, and master's levels and postbachelor's certificates. It has a 30-acre campus in Manitowoc near Milwaukee.

Academic Information The faculty has 162 members (27% full-time), 26% with terminal degrees. The undergraduate student-faculty ratio is 8:1. The library holds 60,466 titles, 296 serial subscriptions, and 11,458 audiovisual materials. Special programs include academic remediation, cooperative (work-study) education, advanced placement credit, accelerated degree programs, ESL programs, double majors, independent study, distance learning, self-designed majors, summer session for credit, part-time degree programs (daytime, evenings, weekends, summer), adult/continuing education programs, and internships. The most frequently chosen baccalaureate fields are business/marketing, education, engineering/engineering technologies.

Student Body Statistics The student body totals 1,104, of whom 780 are undergraduates (27 freshmen). 68 percent are women and 32 percent are men. Students come from 3 states and territories. 98 percent are from Wisconsin. 10 percent of the 2003 graduating class went on to graduate and professional schools.

Expenses for 2003–04 *Application fee:* $35. *Tuition:* $14,350 full-time, $360 per credit part-time. Full-time tuition varies according to location and program. Part-time tuition varies according to course load, location, and program. *College room only:* $4100.

Financial Aid Forms of aid include need-based and non-need-based scholarships, athletic grants, and part-time jobs. The average aided 2002–03 undergraduate received an aid package worth $11,276. The priority application deadline for financial aid is April 15.

Freshman Admission SLC requires a high school transcript, a minimum 2.0 high school GPA, SAT I or ACT scores, and TOEFL scores for international students. An interview and audition are required for some. The application deadline for regular admission is August 31.

Transfer Admission The application deadline for admission is August 31.

Entrance Difficulty SLC assesses its entrance difficulty level as minimally difficult. For the fall 2003 freshman class, 77 percent of the applicants were accepted.

For Further Information Contact Ms. Janis Algozine, Vice President, Dean of Students, Silver Lake College, 2406 South Alverno Road, Manitowoc, WI. *Telephone:* 920-684-5955 Ext. 175 or 800-236-4752 Ext. 175 (toll-free in-state). *Fax:* 920-684-7082. *E-mail:* admslc@silver.sl.edu. *Web site:* http://www.sl.edu/.

STRATTON COLLEGE

See Bryant and Stratton College

UNIVERSITY OF PHOENIX–WISCONSIN CAMPUS

Brookfield, Wisconsin

University of Phoenix–Wisconsin Campus is a coed, proprietary, comprehensive institution, founded in 2001, offering degrees at the associate, bachelor's, master's, and doctoral levels and post-master's and postbachelor's certificates (courses conducted at 121 campuses and learning centers in 25 states).

Academic Information The faculty has 56 members (7% full-time), 16% with terminal degrees. The undergraduate student-faculty ratio is 7:1. The library holds 27 million titles and 11,648 serial subscriptions. Special programs include advanced placement credit, accelerated degree programs, independent study, distance learning, external degree programs, and adult/continuing education programs. The most frequently chosen baccalaureate fields are business/marketing, computer/information sciences.

Student Body Statistics The student body totals 747, of whom 502 are undergraduates (41 freshmen). 59 percent are women and 41 percent are men. 3.4 percent are international students.

Expenses for 2003–04 *Tuition:* $9600 full-time, $320 per credit part-time.

Financial Aid Forms of aid include need-based scholarships. The average aided 2002–03 undergraduate received an aid package worth $1301. The application deadline for financial aid is continuous.

Freshman Admission University of Phoenix–Wisconsin Campus requires 1 recommendation, 2 years of work experience, 23 years of age, and TOEFL scores for international students. A high school transcript is required for some. The application deadline for regular admission is rolling.

Transfer Admission The application deadline for admission is rolling.

Entrance Difficulty University of Phoenix–Wisconsin Campus has an open admission policy.

For Further Information Contact Ms. Beth Barilla, Director of Admissions, University of Phoenix–Wisconsin Campus, 4615 East Elwood Street, Mail Stop AA-K101, Phoenix, AZ 85040-1958. *Telephone:* 480-557-1712 or 800-228-7240 (toll-free). *Fax:* 262-785-0608. *E-mail:* beth.barilla@phoenix.edu. *Web site:* http://www.phoenix.edu/.

UNIVERSITY OF WISCONSIN–EAU CLAIRE

Eau Claire, Wisconsin

UWEC is a coed, public, comprehensive unit of University of Wisconsin System, founded in 1916, offering degrees at the associate, bachelor's, and master's levels and post-master's and postbachelor's certificates. It has a 333-acre campus in Eau Claire.

Academic Information The faculty has 479 members (85% full-time), 78% with terminal degrees. The undergraduate student-faculty ratio is 22:1. The library holds 605,639 titles, 2,570 serial subscriptions, and 14,545 audiovisual materials. Special programs include academic remediation, services for learning-disabled students, an honors program, cooperative (work-study) education, study abroad, advanced placement credit, ESL programs, double majors, independent study, distance learning, summer session for credit, part-time degree programs (daytime, evenings, summer), adult/continuing education programs, internships, and arrangement for off-campus study with National Student Exchange. The most frequently chosen baccalaureate fields are business/marketing, education, health professions and related sciences.

Student Body Statistics The student body totals 10,594, of whom 10,059 are undergraduates (1,879 freshmen). 60 percent are women and 40 percent are men. Students come from 26 states and territories and 43 other countries. 78 percent are from Wisconsin. 1.1 percent are international students. 9 percent of the 2003 graduating class went on to graduate and professional schools.

Expenses for 2003–04 *Application fee:* $35. *State resident tuition:* $4313 full-time, $179.85 per credit part-time. *Nonresident tuition:* $14,360 full-time, $598.45 per credit part-time. Full-time tuition varies according to reciprocity agreements. Part-time tuition varies according to reciprocity agreements. *College room and board:* $4150. *College room only:* $2410. Room and board charges vary according to board plan.

Financial Aid Forms of aid include need-based and non-need-based scholarships and part-time jobs. The average aided 2002–03 undergraduate received an aid package worth $6083. The priority application deadline for financial aid is April 15.

Freshman Admission UWEC requires a high school transcript, rank in upper 50% of high school class, SAT I or ACT scores, and TOEFL scores for international students. The application deadline for regular admission is rolling.

Transfer Admission The application deadline for admission is July 1.

Entrance Difficulty UWEC assesses its entrance difficulty level as moderately difficult. For the fall 2003 freshman class, 60 percent of the applicants were accepted.

For Further Information Contact Ms. Kristina Anderson, Interim Executive Director of Enrollment Management and Director of Admissions, University of Wisconsin–Eau Claire, PO Box 4004, Eau Claire, WI 54702-4004. *Telephone:* 715-836-5415. *Fax:* 715-836-2409. *E-mail:* admissions@uwec.edu. *Web site:* http://www.uwec.edu/.

UNIVERSITY OF WISCONSIN–GREEN BAY

Green Bay, Wisconsin

UW-Green Bay is a coed, public, comprehensive unit of University of Wisconsin System, founded in 1968, offering degrees at the associate, bachelor's, and master's levels and postbachelor's certificates. It has a 700-acre campus in Green Bay.

Academic Information The faculty has 274 members (61% full-time). The undergraduate student-faculty ratio is 23:1. The library holds 333,482 titles, 5,512 serial subscriptions, and 45,396 audiovisual materials. Special programs include academic remediation, services for learning-disabled students, cooperative (work-study) education, study abroad, advanced placement credit, accelerated degree programs, ESL programs, double majors, independent study, distance learning, self-designed majors, summer session for credit, part-time degree programs (daytime, evenings, weekends, summer), external degree programs, adult/continuing education programs, internships, and arrangement for off-campus study with National Student Exchange. The most frequently chosen baccalaureate fields are business/marketing, communications/communication technologies, psychology.

Wisconsin

University of Wisconsin–Green Bay (continued)

Student Body Statistics The student body totals 5,420, of whom 5,256 are undergraduates (964 freshmen). 66 percent are women and 34 percent are men. Students come from 30 states and territories and 28 other countries. 96 percent are from Wisconsin. 0.9 percent are international students. 20 percent of the 2003 graduating class went on to graduate and professional schools.

Expenses for 2003–04 *Application fee:* $35. *State resident tuition:* $3500 full-time, $149 per credit part-time. *Nonresident tuition:* $13,547 full-time, $564 per credit part-time. *Mandatory fees:* $1154 full-time, $38 per credit part-time. Full-time tuition and fees vary according to reciprocity agreements. Part-time tuition and fees vary according to reciprocity agreements. *College room and board:* $4500. *College room only:* $2500. Room and board charges vary according to board plan and housing facility.

Financial Aid Forms of aid include need-based and non-need-based scholarships, athletic grants, and part-time jobs. The average aided 2003–04 undergraduate received an aid package worth an estimated $6831. The priority application deadline for financial aid is April 15.

Freshman Admission UW-Green Bay requires an essay, a high school transcript, minimum ACT score of 17, SAT I or ACT scores, and TOEFL scores for international students. A minimum 2.25 high school GPA is recommended. Recommendations and an interview are required for some.

Entrance Difficulty UW-Green Bay assesses its entrance difficulty level as moderately difficult. For the fall 2003 freshman class, 78 percent of the applicants were accepted.

For Further Information Contact Ms. Pam Harvey-Jacobs, Director of Admissions, University of Wisconsin–Green Bay, 2420 Nicolet Drive, Green Bay, WI 54311-7001. *Telephone:* 920-465-2111 or 888-367-8942 (toll-free out-of-state). *Fax:* 920-465-5754. *E-mail:* admissions@uwgb.edu. *Web site:* http://www.uwgb.edu/.

UNIVERSITY OF WISCONSIN–LA CROSSE
La Crosse, Wisconsin

UW-La Crosse is a coed, public, comprehensive unit of University of Wisconsin System, founded in 1909, offering degrees at the associate, bachelor's, and master's levels. It has a 121-acre campus in La Crosse.

Academic Information The faculty has 410 members (80% full-time), 70% with terminal degrees. The undergraduate student-faculty ratio is 22:1. The library holds 660,159 titles, 1,603 serial subscriptions, and 1,648 audiovisual materials. Special programs include academic remediation, services for learning-disabled students, an honors program, study abroad, advanced placement credit, Freshman Honors College, ESL programs, double majors, distance learning, summer session for credit, part-time degree programs, adult/continuing education programs, internships, and arrangement for off-campus study with Viterbo College. The most frequently chosen baccalaureate fields are business/marketing, parks and recreation, social sciences and history.

Student Body Statistics The student body totals 8,746, of whom 8,100 are undergraduates (1,509 freshmen). 60 percent are women and 40 percent are men. Students come from 33 states and territories and 43 other countries. 82 percent are from Wisconsin. 1.2 percent are international students. 24 percent of the 2003 graduating class went on to graduate and professional schools.

Expenses for 2003–04 *Application fee:* $35. *Area resident tuition:* $182 per credit part-time. *State resident tuition:* $4741 full-time, $198 per credit part-time. *Nonresident tuition:* $14,404 full-time, $600 per credit part-time. Full-time tuition varies according to program and reciprocity agreements. Part-time tuition varies according to course load, program, and reciprocity agreements. *College room and board:* $4050. *College room only:* $2200.

Financial Aid Forms of aid include need-based and non-need-based scholarships and part-time jobs. The average aided 2002–03 undergraduate received an aid package worth $5499. The priority application deadline for financial aid is March 15.

Freshman Admission UW-La Crosse requires a high school transcript and SAT I or ACT scores. An essay, ACT scores, and TOEFL scores for international students are recommended. An interview is required for some. The application deadline for regular admission is rolling.

Transfer Admission The application deadline for admission is rolling.

Entrance Difficulty UW-La Crosse assesses its entrance difficulty level as moderately difficult. For the fall 2003 freshman class, 53 percent of the applicants were accepted.

For Further Information Contact Mr. Tim Lewis, Director of Admissions, University of Wisconsin–La Crosse, 1725 State Street, LaCrosse, WI 54601. *Telephone:* 608-785-8939. *Fax:* 608-785-8940. *E-mail:* admissions@uwlax.edu. *Web site:* http://www.uwlax.edu/.

UNIVERSITY OF WISCONSIN–MADISON
Madison, Wisconsin

Wisconsin is a coed, public unit of University of Wisconsin System, founded in 1848, offering degrees at the bachelor's, master's, doctoral, and first professional levels and post-master's and postbachelor's certificates. It has a 1,050-acre campus in Madison near Milwaukee.

Academic Information The faculty has 2,225 members (100% full-time), 100% with terminal degrees. The undergraduate student-faculty ratio is 14:1. The library holds 6 million titles and 66,000 serial subscriptions. Special programs include services for learning-disabled students, an honors program, cooperative (work-study) education, study abroad, advanced placement credit, Freshman Honors College, ESL programs, double majors, independent study, distance learning, self-designed majors, summer session for credit, part-time degree programs (daytime), adult/continuing education programs, and internships.

Student Body Statistics The student body totals 41,588, of whom 28,583 are undergraduates. Students come from 54 states and territories and 131 other countries. 62 percent are from Wisconsin. 69 percent of the 2003 graduating class went on to graduate and professional schools.

Expenses for 2003–04 *Application fee:* $35. *State resident tuition:* $5140 full-time. *Nonresident tuition:* $19,150 full-time. *College room and board:* $6130.

Financial Aid Forms of aid include need-based and non-need-based scholarships, athletic grants, and part-time jobs. The average aided 2003–04 undergraduate received an aid package worth an estimated $10,305. The application deadline for financial aid is continuous.

Freshman Admission Wisconsin requires an essay, a high school transcript, SAT I or ACT scores, and TOEFL scores for international students. An interview and SAT II: Subject Test scores are recommended. SAT II: Subject Test scores are required for some. The application deadline for regular admission is February 1.

Transfer Admission The application deadline for admission is February 1.

Entrance Difficulty Wisconsin assesses its entrance difficulty level as very difficult. For the fall 2003 freshman class, 61 percent of the applicants were accepted.

For Further Information Contact Mr. Keith White, Associate Director of Admission, University of Wisconsin–Madison, 716 Langdon Street, Madison, WI 53706-1481. *Telephone:* 608-262-3961. *Fax:* 608-262-7706. *E-mail:* on.wisconsin@admissions.wisc.edu. *Web site:* http://www.wisc.edu/.

UNIVERSITY OF WISCONSIN–MILWAUKEE
Milwaukee, Wisconsin

UWM is a coed, public unit of University of Wisconsin System, founded in 1956, offering degrees at the bachelor's, master's, and doctoral levels and post-master's and postbachelor's certificates. It has a 90-acre campus in Milwaukee.

Academic Information The library holds 1 million titles, 8,240 serial subscriptions, and 37,376 audiovisual materials. Special programs include academic remediation, services for learning-disabled students, an honors program, cooperative (work-study) education, study abroad, advanced placement credit, accelerated degree programs, ESL programs, double majors, independent study, distance learning, self-designed majors, summer session for credit, part-time degree programs, adult/continuing education programs, internships, and arrangement for off-campus study with

University of Wisconsin-Parkside. The most frequently chosen baccalaureate fields are business/marketing, social sciences and history, visual/performing arts.

Student Body Statistics The student body totals 25,440, of whom 21,052 are undergraduates (3,855 freshmen). 55 percent are women and 45 percent are men. Students come from 53 states and territories. 99 percent are from Wisconsin. 0.7 percent are international students.

Expenses for 2003–04 *Application fee:* $35. *State resident tuition:* $4439 full-time, $184.95 per credit part-time. *Nonresident tuition:* $17,190 full-time, $716.25 per credit part-time. *Mandatory fees:* $668 full-time. Full-time tuition and fees vary according to location, program, and reciprocity agreements. Part-time tuition varies according to course load, location, program, and reciprocity agreements. *College room and board:* $4320. *College room only:* $2540. Room and board charges vary according to board plan.

Financial Aid Forms of aid include need-based and non-need-based scholarships, athletic grants, and part-time jobs. The average aided 2002–03 undergraduate received an aid package worth $7300. The priority application deadline for financial aid is March 1.

Freshman Admission UWM requires a high school transcript, SAT I or ACT scores, TOEFL scores for international students, and ACT for state residents. SAT I scores are recommended. The application deadline for regular admission is August 1.

Transfer Admission The application deadline for admission is rolling.

Entrance Difficulty UWM assesses its entrance difficulty level as moderately difficult. For the fall 2003 freshman class, 79 percent of the applicants were accepted.

For Further Information Contact Ms. Jan Ford, Director, Recruitment and Outreach, University of Wisconsin–Milwaukee, PO Box 749, Milwaukee, WI 53201. *Telephone:* 414-229-3800. *Fax:* 414-229-6940. *E-mail:* uwmlook@uwm.edu. *Web site:* http://www.uwm.edu/.

UNIVERSITY OF WISCONSIN–OSHKOSH
Oshkosh, Wisconsin

UW Oshkosh is a coed, public, comprehensive unit of University of Wisconsin System, founded in 1871, offering degrees at the associate, bachelor's, and master's levels. It has a 192-acre campus in Oshkosh near Milwaukee.

Academic Information The faculty has 575 members (73% full-time), 99% with terminal degrees. The undergraduate student-faculty ratio is 20:1. The library holds 446,774 titles, 5,219 serial subscriptions, and 9,102 audiovisual materials. Special programs include academic remediation, services for learning-disabled students, an honors program, cooperative (work-study) education, study abroad, advanced placement credit, accelerated degree programs, ESL programs, double majors, independent study, distance learning, self-designed majors, summer session for credit, part-time degree programs (daytime, evenings, weekends, summer), adult/continuing education programs, and internships. The most frequently chosen baccalaureate fields are business/marketing, education, health professions and related sciences.

Student Body Statistics The student body totals 11,155, of whom 9,804 are undergraduates (1,780 freshmen). 60 percent are women and 40 percent are men. Students come from 30 states and territories and 32 other countries. 98 percent are from Wisconsin. 0.7 percent are international students.

Expenses for 2004–05 *Application fee:* $35. *State resident tuition:* $4044 full-time, $168 per credit hour part-time. *Nonresident tuition:* $14,320 full-time, $587 per credit hour part-time. *College room and board:* $4100. *College room only:* $2278.

Financial Aid Forms of aid include need-based and non-need-based scholarships and part-time jobs. The average aided 2002–03 undergraduate received an aid package worth $5000. The priority application deadline for financial aid is March 15.

Freshman Admission UW Oshkosh requires a high school transcript, rank in upper 50% of high school class or ACT composite score of 23 or above, TOEFL scores for international students, and SAT I or ACT for nonresidents, ACT for state residents. An essay is recommended. The application deadline for regular admission is August 1.

Transfer Admission The application deadline for admission is August 1.

Entrance Difficulty UW Oshkosh assesses its entrance difficulty level as moderately difficult. For the fall 2003 freshman class, 47 percent of the applicants were accepted.

For Further Information Contact Mr. Richard Hillman, Associate Director of Admissions, University of Wisconsin–Oshkosh, Oshkosh, WI 54901-8602. *Telephone:* 920-424-0202. *Fax:* 920-424-1098. *E-mail:* oshadmuw@uwosh.edu. *Web site:* http://www.uwosh.edu/.

UNIVERSITY OF WISCONSIN–PARKSIDE
Kenosha, Wisconsin

University of Wisconsin–Parkside is a coed, public, comprehensive unit of University of Wisconsin System, founded in 1968, offering degrees at the bachelor's and master's levels. It has a 700-acre campus in Kenosha near Chicago and Milwaukee.

Academic Information The faculty has 282 members (62% full-time), 54% with terminal degrees. The undergraduate student-faculty ratio is 19:1. The library holds 400,000 titles, 1,590 serial subscriptions, and 21,220 audiovisual materials. Special programs include academic remediation, services for learning-disabled students, advanced placement credit, accelerated degree programs, ESL programs, double majors, independent study, distance learning, summer session for credit, part-time degree programs, external degree programs, internships, and arrangement for off-campus study with Carthage College. The most frequently chosen baccalaureate fields are business/marketing, biological/life sciences, social sciences and history.

Student Body Statistics The student body totals 5,072, of whom 4,939 are undergraduates (975 freshmen). 57 percent are women and 43 percent are men. Students come from 24 states and territories and 27 other countries. 92 percent are from Wisconsin. 1.5 percent are international students. 14 percent of the 2003 graduating class went on to graduate and professional schools.

Expenses for 2004–05 *Application fee:* $35. *One-time mandatory fee:* $87. *State resident tuition:* $3532 full-time, $180.35 per credit hour part-time. *Nonresident tuition:* $13,578 full-time, $598.35 per credit hour part-time. Full-time tuition varies according to course load and reciprocity agreements. Part-time tuition varies according to course load. *College room and board:* $5056. *College room only:* $3156. Room and board charges vary according to board plan and housing facility.

Financial Aid Forms of aid include need-based and non-need-based scholarships, athletic grants, and part-time jobs. The average aided 2003–04 undergraduate received an aid package worth an estimated $5953. The priority application deadline for financial aid is March 15.

Freshman Admission University of Wisconsin–Parkside requires a high school transcript, minimum of 17 high school units distributed as specified in the UW-Parkside catalog, and TOEFL scores for international students. SAT I or ACT scores are required for some. The application deadline for regular admission is August 1.

Transfer Admission The application deadline for admission is August 1.

Entrance Difficulty University of Wisconsin–Parkside assesses its entrance difficulty level as moderately difficult; very difficult for international students. For the fall 2003 freshman class, 60 percent of the applicants were accepted.

For Further Information Contact Mr. Matthew Jensen, Director of Admissions, University of Wisconsin–Parkside, PO Box 2000, 900 Wood Road, Kenosha, WI 53141-2000. *Telephone:* 262-595-2757 or 877-633-3897 (toll-free in-state). *Fax:* 262-595-2008. *E-mail:* matthew.jensen@uwp.edu. *Web site:* http://www.uwp.edu/.

UNIVERSITY OF WISCONSIN–PLATTEVILLE
Platteville, Wisconsin

UW Platteville is a coed, public, comprehensive unit of University of Wisconsin System, founded in 1866, offering degrees at the associate, bachelor's, and master's levels. It has a 380-acre campus in Platteville.

University of Wisconsin–Platteville (continued)

Academic Information The faculty has 306 members (76% full-time), 67% with terminal degrees. The undergraduate student-faculty ratio is 19:1. The library holds 321,456 titles, 1,280 serial subscriptions, and 13,879 audiovisual materials. Special programs include academic remediation, services for learning-disabled students, an honors program, cooperative (work-study) education, study abroad, advanced placement credit, double majors, independent study, distance learning, self-designed majors, summer session for credit, part-time degree programs (daytime, evenings), external degree programs, adult/continuing education programs, internships, and arrangement for off-campus study with Westfield State College. The most frequently chosen baccalaureate fields are education, business/marketing, engineering/engineering technologies.

Student Body Statistics The student body totals 6,077, of whom 5,541 are undergraduates (1,103 freshmen). 39 percent are women and 61 percent are men. Students come from 34 states and territories. 89 percent are from Wisconsin. 0.6 percent are international students.

Expenses for 2003–04 *Application fee: $35. Area resident tuition:* $145.85 per credit part-time. *State resident tuition:* $3500 full-time. *Nonresident tuition:* $13,546 full-time, $564.45 per credit part-time. *Mandatory fees:* $754 full-time. *College room and board:* $4196. *College room only:* $2120.

Financial Aid Forms of aid include need-based and non-need-based scholarships and part-time jobs. The average aided 2002–03 undergraduate received an aid package worth $6161. The priority application deadline for financial aid is March 15.

Freshman Admission UW Platteville requires a high school transcript, SAT I or ACT scores, and TOEFL scores for international students. ACT scores are recommended. Recommendations are required for some. The application deadline for regular admission is rolling.

Transfer Admission The application deadline for admission is rolling.

Entrance Difficulty UW Platteville assesses its entrance difficulty level as moderately difficult. For the fall 2003 freshman class, 80 percent of the applicants were accepted.

For Further Information Contact Dr. Richard Schumacher, Dean of Admissions and Enrollment Management, University of Wisconsin–Platteville, 1 University Plaza, Platteville, WI 53818-3099. *Telephone:* 608-342-1125 or 800-362-5515 (toll-free). *Fax:* 608-342-1122. *E-mail:* admissions@uwplatt.edu. *Web site:* http://www.uwplatt.edu/.

UNIVERSITY OF WISCONSIN–RIVER FALLS
River Falls, Wisconsin

UW River Falls is a coed, public, comprehensive unit of University of Wisconsin System, founded in 1874, offering degrees at the bachelor's and master's levels and post-master's certificates. It has a 225-acre campus in River Falls near Minneapolis–St. Paul.

Academic Information The faculty has 337 members (69% full-time). The undergraduate student-faculty ratio is 20:1. The library holds 448,088 titles, 1,660 serial subscriptions, and 7,500 audiovisual materials. Special programs include academic remediation, services for learning-disabled students, an honors program, cooperative (work-study) education, study abroad, advanced placement credit, accelerated degree programs, double majors, independent study, distance learning, self-designed majors, summer session for credit, part-time degree programs (daytime, summer), external degree programs, adult/continuing education programs, internships, and arrangement for off-campus study with National Student Exchange. The most frequently chosen baccalaureate fields are business/marketing, agriculture, education.

Student Body Statistics The student body totals 5,893, of whom 5,413 are undergraduates (1,227 freshmen). 61 percent are women and 39 percent are men. Students come from 26 states and territories and 12 other countries. 52 percent are from Wisconsin. 0.9 percent are international students. 22 percent of the 2003 graduating class went on to graduate and professional schools.

Expenses for 2003–04 *Application fee: $35. State resident tuition:* $4450 full-time. *Nonresident tuition:* $14,496 full-time. Full-time tuition varies according to course load and reciprocity agreements. *College room and board:* $3968. *College room only:* $2248. Room and board charges vary according to board plan.

Financial Aid Forms of aid include need-based and non-need-based scholarships and part-time jobs. The average aided 2003–04 undergraduate received an aid package worth an estimated $4429. The priority application deadline for financial aid is March 15.

Freshman Admission UW River Falls requires a high school transcript, ACT scores, and TOEFL scores for international students. Rank in upper 40% of high school class is recommended. The application deadline for regular admission is rolling.

Transfer Admission The application deadline for admission is rolling.

Entrance Difficulty UW River Falls assesses its entrance difficulty level as moderately difficult; very difficult for elementary education majors. For the fall 2003 freshman class, 76 percent of the applicants were accepted.

For Further Information Contact Mr. Alan Tuchtenhagen, Director of Admissions, University of Wisconsin–River Falls, 410 South Third Street, 112 South Hall, River Falls, WI 54022-5001. *Telephone:* 715-425-3500. *Fax:* 715-425-0676. *E-mail:* admit@uwrf.edu. *Web site:* http://www.uwrf.edu/.

UNIVERSITY OF WISCONSIN–STEVENS POINT
Stevens Point, Wisconsin

UWSP is a coed, public, comprehensive unit of University of Wisconsin System, founded in 1894, offering degrees at the associate, bachelor's, and master's levels. It has a 335-acre campus in Stevens Point.

Academic Information The faculty has 424 members (85% full-time), 79% with terminal degrees. The undergraduate student-faculty ratio is 20:1. The library holds 978,112 titles, 8,470 serial subscriptions, and 32,916 audiovisual materials. Special programs include academic remediation, services for learning-disabled students, cooperative (work-study) education, study abroad, advanced placement credit, accelerated degree programs, ESL programs, double majors, independent study, distance learning, self-designed majors, summer session for credit, part-time degree programs (daytime, evenings, summer), adult/continuing education programs, internships, and arrangement for off-campus study with University of Wisconsin-Oshkosh, University of Wisconsin-Eau Claire. The most frequently chosen baccalaureate fields are natural resources/environmental science, business/marketing, social sciences and history.

Student Body Statistics The student body totals 9,029, of whom 8,503 are undergraduates (1,506 freshmen). 56 percent are women and 44 percent are men. Students come from 29 states and territories and 27 other countries. 94 percent are from Wisconsin. 1.6 percent are international students. 16 percent of the 2003 graduating class went on to graduate and professional schools.

Expenses for 2003–04 *Application fee: $50. State resident tuition:* $3500 full-time, $146 per credit part-time. *Nonresident tuition:* $13,547 full-time, $564 per credit part-time. *Mandatory fees:* $648 full-time, $58 per credit part-time. Full-time tuition and fees vary according to course load and reciprocity agreements. Part-time tuition and fees vary according to course load and reciprocity agreements. *College room and board:* $3964. *College room only:* $2324.

Financial Aid Forms of aid include need-based and non-need-based scholarships and part-time jobs. The average aided 2002–03 undergraduate received an aid package worth $6047. The priority application deadline for financial aid is June 15.

Freshman Admission UWSP requires a high school transcript, SAT I or ACT scores, and TOEFL scores for international students. Campus visit is recommended. The application deadline for regular admission is rolling.

Transfer Admission The application deadline for admission is rolling.

Entrance Difficulty UWSP assesses its entrance difficulty level as moderately difficult. For the fall 2003 freshman class, 75 percent of the applicants were accepted.

For Further Information Contact Ms. Catherine Glennon, Director of Admissions, University of Wisconsin–Stevens Point, 2100 Main Street, Stevens Point, WI 54481. *Telephone:* 715-346-2441. *Fax:* 715-346-3296. *E-mail:* admiss@uwsp.edu. *Web site:* http://www.uwsp.edu/.

UNIVERSITY OF WISCONSIN–STOUT
Menomonie, Wisconsin

UW Stout is a coed, public, comprehensive unit of University of Wisconsin System, founded in 1891, offering degrees at the bachelor's and master's levels and post-master's certificates. It has a 120-acre campus in Menomonie near Minneapolis–St. Paul.

Academic Information The faculty has 389 members (75% full-time), 63% with terminal degrees. The undergraduate student-faculty ratio is 19:1. The library holds 229,986 titles, 1,784 serial subscriptions, and 16,142 audiovisual materials. Special programs include academic remediation, services for learning-disabled students, an honors program, cooperative (work-study) education, study abroad, advanced placement credit, accelerated degree programs, double majors, independent study, distance learning, summer session for credit, part-time degree programs, external degree programs, adult/continuing education programs, internships, and arrangement for off-campus study with Fashion Institute of Technology, University of Wisconsin–Eau Claire. The most frequently chosen baccalaureate fields are business/marketing, education, visual/performing arts.

Student Body Statistics The student body totals 7,708, of whom 7,101 are undergraduates (1,275 freshmen). 49 percent are women and 51 percent are men. Students come from 26 states and territories. 71 percent are from Wisconsin. 0.4 percent are international students. 8 percent of the 2003 graduating class went on to graduate and professional schools.

Expenses for 2003–04 *Application fee:* $35. *State resident tuition:* $5024 full-time. *Nonresident tuition:* $15,360 full-time. *Mandatory fees:* $656 full-time. Full-time tuition and fees vary according to reciprocity agreements. *College room and board:* $4038. *College room only:* $2292. Room and board charges vary according to board plan.

Financial Aid Forms of aid include need-based and non-need-based scholarships and part-time jobs. The average aided 2003–04 undergraduate received an aid package worth an estimated $6746. The priority application deadline for financial aid is April 1.

Freshman Admission UW Stout requires a high school transcript, SAT I or ACT scores, and TOEFL scores for international students. ACT scores are recommended. A minimum 2.75 high school GPA is required for some. The application deadline for regular admission is rolling.

Transfer Admission The application deadline for admission is rolling.

Entrance Difficulty UW Stout assesses its entrance difficulty level as moderately difficult. For the fall 2003 freshman class, 66 percent of the applicants were accepted.

For Further Information Contact Ms. Cynthia Jenkins, Director of Admissions, University of Wisconsin–Stout, Admissions UW-Stout, Bowman Hall, Menomonie, WI 54751. *Telephone:* 715-232-2639 or 800-HI-STOUT (toll-free in-state). *Fax:* 715-232-1667. *E-mail:* admissions@uwstout.edu. *Web site:* http://www.uwstout.edu/.

UNIVERSITY OF WISCONSIN–SUPERIOR
Superior, Wisconsin

UW-Superior is a coed, public, comprehensive unit of University of Wisconsin System, founded in 1893, offering degrees at the associate, bachelor's, master's, and first professional levels and postbachelor's certificates. It has a 230-acre campus in Superior.

Academic Information The faculty has 198 members (57% full-time), 52% with terminal degrees. The undergraduate student-faculty ratio is 17:1. The library holds 467,700 titles, 753 serial subscriptions, and 5,467 audiovisual materials. Special programs include academic remediation, services for learning-disabled students, an honors program, cooperative (work-study) education, study abroad, advanced placement credit, Freshman Honors College, ESL programs, double majors, independent study, distance learning, self-designed majors, summer session for credit, part-time degree programs (daytime, evenings, weekends, summer), external degree programs, adult/continuing education programs, internships, and arrangement for off-campus study with College of St. Scholastica, Northland College, University of Minnesota, Duluth. The most frequently chosen baccalaureate fields are business/marketing, education, interdisciplinary studies.

Student Body Statistics The student body totals 2,874, of whom 2,530 are undergraduates (352 freshmen). 59 percent are women and 41 percent are men. Students come from 17 states and territories and 32 other countries. 60 percent are from Wisconsin. 6.2 percent are international students. 13 percent of the 2003 graduating class went on to graduate and professional schools.

Expenses for 2003–04 *Application fee:* $35. *State resident tuition:* $4276 full-time. *Nonresident tuition:* $14,322 full-time. Full-time tuition varies according to course load and reciprocity agreements. *College room and board:* $4246. *College room only:* $2406. Room and board charges vary according to housing facility.

Financial Aid Forms of aid include need-based and non-need-based scholarships and part-time jobs. The average aided 2003–04 undergraduate received an aid package worth an estimated $8274. The priority application deadline for financial aid is April 15.

Freshman Admission UW-Superior requires a high school transcript, SAT I or ACT scores, and TOEFL scores for international students. An interview and ACT scores are recommended. A minimum 2.6 high school GPA and recommendations are required for some. The application deadline for regular admission is April 1.

Transfer Admission The application deadline for admission is rolling.

Entrance Difficulty UW-Superior assesses its entrance difficulty level as moderately difficult. For the fall 2003 freshman class, 77 percent of the applicants were accepted.

For Further Information Contact Lee Parker, Admissions Advisor, University of Wisconsin–Superior, Belknap and Catlin, PO Box 2000, Superior, WI 54880-4500. *Telephone:* 715-394-8298 or 715-394-8230 (toll-free in-state). *Fax:* 715-394-8407. *E-mail:* admissions@uwsuper.edu. *Web site:* http://www.uwsuper.edu/.

UNIVERSITY OF WISCONSIN–WHITEWATER
Whitewater, Wisconsin

UW-Whitewater is a coed, public, comprehensive unit of University of Wisconsin System, founded in 1868, offering degrees at the associate, bachelor's, and master's levels. It has a 385-acre campus in Whitewater near Milwaukee.

Academic Information The faculty has 506 members (74% full-time), 65% with terminal degrees. The undergraduate student-faculty ratio is 20:1. The library holds 647,029 titles, 3,358 serial subscriptions, and 15,974 audiovisual materials. Special programs include academic remediation, services for learning-disabled students, an honors program, cooperative (work-study) education, study abroad, advanced placement credit, accelerated degree programs, double majors, independent study, distance learning, self-designed majors, summer session for credit, part-time degree programs, external degree programs, adult/continuing education programs, and internships. The most frequently chosen baccalaureate fields are business/marketing, communications/communication technologies, education.

Student Body Statistics The student body totals 10,817, of whom 9,429 are undergraduates (1,832 freshmen). 53 percent are women and 47 percent are men. Students come from 29 states and territories and 37 other countries. 96 percent are from Wisconsin. 0.8 percent are international students. 10 percent of the 2003 graduating class went on to graduate and professional schools.

Expenses for 2003–04 *Application fee:* $35. *State resident tuition:* $4278 full-time, $178 per credit part-time. *Nonresident tuition:* $14,324 full-time,

University of Wisconsin–Whitewater (continued)
$597 per credit part-time. *Mandatory fees:* $656 full-time. *College room and board:* $3742. *College room only:* $2232. Room and board charges vary according to board plan.

Financial Aid Forms of aid include need-based and non-need-based scholarships and part-time jobs. The average aided 2003–04 undergraduate received an aid package worth an estimated $5970. The priority application deadline for financial aid is March 15.

Freshman Admission UW-Whitewater requires a high school transcript and TOEFL scores for international students. SAT I or ACT scores are recommended. Recommendations and SAT I or ACT scores are required for some. The application deadline for regular admission is rolling.

Transfer Admission The application deadline for admission is rolling.

Entrance Difficulty UW-Whitewater assesses its entrance difficulty level as moderately difficult. For the fall 2003 freshman class, 68 percent of the applicants were accepted.

For Further Information Contact Dr. Tori A. Erickson, Executive Director of Admissions, University of Wisconsin–Whitewater, 800 West Main Street, Whitewater, WI 53190-1790. *Telephone:* 262-472-1440 Ext. 1512. *Fax:* 262-472-1515. *E-mail:* uwwadmit@uww.edu. *Web site:* http://www.uww.edu/.

VITERBO UNIVERSITY
La Crosse, Wisconsin

Viterbo is a coed, private, Roman Catholic, comprehensive institution, founded in 1890, offering degrees at the bachelor's and master's levels. It has a 72-acre campus in La Crosse.

Academic Information The faculty has 169 members (59% full-time), 49% with terminal degrees. The undergraduate student-faculty ratio is 13:1. The library holds 1 million titles, 3,541 serial subscriptions, and 6,181 audiovisual materials. Special programs include academic remediation, cooperative (work-study) education, study abroad, advanced placement credit, accelerated degree programs, double majors, independent study, distance learning, self-designed majors, summer session for credit, part-time degree programs (evenings, weekends, summer), adult/continuing education programs, internships, and arrangement for off-campus study with University of Wisconsin-La Crosse, Western Wisconsin Technical College. The most frequently chosen baccalaureate fields are business/marketing, education, health professions and related sciences.

Student Body Statistics The student body totals 2,549, of whom 1,862 are undergraduates (356 freshmen). 75 percent are women and 25 percent are men. Students come from 22 states and territories and 11 other countries. 81 percent are from Wisconsin. 0.9 percent are international students. 10.1 percent of the 2003 graduating class went on to graduate and professional schools.

Expenses for 2004–05 *Application fee:* $25. *Comprehensive fee:* $21,210 includes full-time tuition ($15,570), mandatory fees ($420), and college room and board ($5220). *College room only:* $2250. Room and board charges vary according to board plan and housing facility. *Part-time tuition:* $455 per credit. *Part-time mandatory fees:* $120. Part-time tuition and fees vary according to course load.

Financial Aid Forms of aid include need-based and non-need-based scholarships, athletic grants, and part-time jobs. The average aided 2003–04 undergraduate received an aid package worth an estimated $13,534. The priority application deadline for financial aid is March 15.

Freshman Admission Viterbo requires a high school transcript, a minimum 2.0 high school GPA, ACT scores, and TOEFL scores for international students. An essay, 1 recommendation, an interview, and audition for theater and music; portfolio for art are required for some. The application deadline for regular admission is rolling.

Transfer Admission The application deadline for admission is rolling.

Entrance Difficulty Viterbo assesses its entrance difficulty level as moderately difficult. For the fall 2003 freshman class, 88 percent of the applicants were accepted.

For Further Information Contact Dr. Roland Nelson, Vice President of Enrollment, Viterbo University, 900 Viterbo Drive, LaCrosse, WI 54601. *Telephone:* 608-796-3010 Ext. 3010 or 800-VITERBO Ext. 3010 (toll-free). *Fax:* 608-796-3020. *E-mail:* admission@viterbo.edu. *Web site:* http://www.viterbo.edu/.

WISCONSIN LUTHERAN COLLEGE
Milwaukee, Wisconsin

Wisconsin Lutheran is a coed, private, four-year college, founded in 1973, affiliated with the Wisconsin Evangelical Lutheran Synod, offering degrees at the bachelor's level. It has a 21-acre campus in Milwaukee.

Academic Information The faculty has 88 members (53% full-time), 40% with terminal degrees. The student-faculty ratio is 11:1. The library holds 71,731 titles, 614 serial subscriptions, and 4,409 audiovisual materials. Special programs include services for learning-disabled students, study abroad, advanced placement credit, double majors, independent study, self-designed majors, summer session for credit, part-time degree programs (daytime, evenings), and internships. The most frequently chosen baccalaureate fields are biological/life sciences, communications/communication technologies, visual/performing arts.

Student Body Statistics The student body is made up of 706 undergraduates (207 freshmen). 60 percent are women and 40 percent are men. Students come from 28 states and territories and 6 other countries. 81 percent are from Wisconsin. 1.5 percent are international students.

Expenses for 2003–04 *Application fee:* $20. *Comprehensive fee:* $21,175 includes full-time tuition ($15,720), mandatory fees ($130), and college room and board ($5325). *College room only:* $2775. Room and board charges vary according to board plan and housing facility. *Part-time tuition:* $480 per credit. *Part-time mandatory fees:* $50 per year.

Financial Aid Forms of aid include need-based and non-need-based scholarships and part-time jobs. The average aided 2003–04 undergraduate received an aid package worth an estimated $13,342. The priority application deadline for financial aid is March 1.

Freshman Admission Wisconsin Lutheran requires a high school transcript, a minimum 2.70 high school GPA, 1 recommendation, minimum ACT score of 21, SAT I or ACT scores, and TOEFL scores for international students. An interview is required for some.

Entrance Difficulty Wisconsin Lutheran assesses its entrance difficulty level as moderately difficult. For the fall 2003 freshman class, 84 percent of the applicants were accepted.

For Further Information Contact Mr. Craig Swiontek, Director of Admissions, Wisconsin Lutheran College, 8800 West Bluemound Road, Milwaukee, WI 53226-9942. *Telephone:* 414-443-8811 or 888-WIS LUTH (toll-free). *Fax:* 414-443-8514. *E-mail:* admissions@wlc.edu. *Web site:* http://www.wlc.edu/.

In-Depth Descriptions of Colleges in the Midwest

ALBION COLLEGE
ALBION, MICHIGAN

The College

Albion College offers the powerful combination of a traditional liberal arts curriculum coupled with a strong professional focus. "Liberal Arts at Work" aptly characterizes Albion's commitment to preparing students for admission into top graduate schools and their first career assignments in medicine, law, teaching, business, the arts, and many other areas. All students have an opportunity to enhance their education through value-added programming in one or more academic institutes, including the Gerald R. Ford Institute for Public Service, the Carl A. Gerstacker Liberal Arts Program in Professional Management, the Pre-Med/Allied Health Institute, the Honors Institute, the Fritz Shurmur Education Institute, and the Institute for the Study of the Environment.

Albion is a national leader for the percentage of students involved in undergraduate research. It is ranked seventh in *Yahoo! Internet Life*'s Most Wired Colleges in the U.S.A., and first among colleges and universities in Michigan. In addition, 52 percent of Albion's alumni regularly support the College, the highest percentage among schools in Michigan and among the top twenty in the nation. Albion is among the top eighty-five private, liberal arts colleges for the number of alumni who are corporate executives, including top executives and CEOs of *Newsweek*, the Lahey Clinic (MA), PricewaterhouseCoopers, Dow Corning, the NCAA, Avon, and the Financial Accounting Standards Board (FASB). Albion's 2003 graduate school placement was 100 percent for law, 96 percent for dental, and 94 percent for medical schools, including Harvard, Michigan, Columbia, Northwestern, Notre Dame, Vanderbilt, and Wisconsin.

Albion's 2003 fall enrollment was 1,743 students. Approximately 87 percent of Albion's students are from Michigan; the rest come from twenty-eight states and nineteen countries. Albion is a residential college and campus life is important for every student. Campus lecturers and other recent performers and speakers include James Earl Jones, Salman Rushdie, Kurt Vonnegut, Duke University basketball coach Mike Krzyzewski, Gloria Steinem, Three Doors Down, Shawn Colvin, and various federal and state legislators. The Kellogg Center, completed in 1996, provides space for concerts and dances, meeting rooms and offices for student organizations, the College bookstore, and a snack bar. The more than 100 student organizations include clubs in academic departments, student publications, a campus radio station, religious fellowship groups, the Black Student Alliance, intercollegiate and intramural athletics, and national fraternities and sororities.

Ninety-six percent of students live on campus. Residence halls, located within walking distance of other campus buildings, are coed, with separate sections for men and women. A comprehensive student services program includes a career development office that assists students in exploring career options and arranges on-campus interviews with employers and graduate schools. More than 40 percent of Albion graduates go directly to graduate or professional school each year; virtually everyone seeking immediate employment has found a position within six months of graduation. Within five years of graduation, more than 75 percent of Albion alumni have enrolled for graduate work.

Location

A 1½-hour drive west of Detroit and a 3-hour drive east of Chicago, the College is located on I-94 in the small city of Albion (population 10,000). Eight other colleges and universities, including Michigan State and the University of Michigan, are located within an hour's drive. The 225-acre main campus is a few blocks from the downtown business section. Students and faculty members are very involved in community activities and regional volunteer efforts and internships.

Majors and Degrees

Albion College awards the Bachelor of Arts and Bachelor of Fine Arts degrees. Majors include American studies, anthropology and sociology, art, art history, athletic training, biology, chemistry, computer science, earth sciences, economics and management, English, French, geological sciences, German, history, human services, international studies, mathematics, music, philosophy, physical education, physics, political science, psychology, public policy, religious studies, Spanish, and speech communication and theater. Individually designed majors, created with faculty approval, are also offered. Students may be certified in secondary education and for grades K–12 in art, music, and physical education.

Preprofessional programs include business management, dentistry, law, medicine, and the ministry. Combined three-year preprofessional programs, involving three years of study at Albion and additional work at other institutions, are available in engineering, health services and nursing, natural resources management, and public policy. Students in these programs are awarded the bachelor's degree from Albion after completing one additional year of study at the participating institutions.

Academic Programs

Albion expects its students to gain a broad knowledge in the arts and sciences while also developing an area of specialization. To graduate with the Bachelor of Arts degree, students must complete 32 units (128 semester hours); to earn the Bachelor of Fine Arts degree, art majors must complete 34 units (136 semester hours). All students must pass a writing examination.

To introduce students to important areas of knowledge, Albion has a core curriculum requirement for study in the natural sciences and mathematics, the social sciences, the humanities, interdisciplinary studies, and the fine arts, together with additional studies in environmental science, ethnic studies, neuroscience, and prelaw. The core curriculum and the requirements for a major total about one half to two thirds of a student's program at Albion. The remainder can be used for electives, to complete a second major, or for a six- to eight-course sequence in business management, computer science, human services, mass communication, public service, or women's studies. Independent study and on-the-job internships for academic credit are also available. College credit can be obtained through Advanced Placement exams, College-Level Examination Program (CLEP) tests, or Albion departmental exams.

Off-Campus Programs

Albion College, together with other leading educational institutions, offers off-campus study in Australia, China, Costa Rica, the Dominican Republic, France, Germany, Great Britain, India, Ireland, Israel, Italy, Japan, Mexico, New Zealand, Russia, Spain, and several African countries. Semester-long programs are available in the United States through the Washington (D.C.) Center for Learning Alternatives, the New York City Arts Program, the Philadelphia Center, the Chicago Urban Life Center, the Newberry Library Program in the Humanities (Chicago), and the Oak Ridge National Laboratory (Tennessee). All arrangements are supervised by the director of off-campus programs.

Academic Facilities

Olin Hall, the $4.5-million home of the biology and psychology departments, features excellent laboratory equipment, including scanning and transmission electron microscopes. In the Stockwell/Mudd Libraries, researchers are helped by an online catalog of the College's book and periodical collections and by access to national databases in many different academic areas. Other prominent campus facilities include the Herrick Center for Speech and

Theatre; the 144-acre Whitehouse Nature Center, used for both science instruction and recreation; and the Nancy G. Held Equestrian Center, featuring indoor and outdoor arenas, boarding in College stables, and 340 acres of pasture and trails. The Dow Recreation and Wellness Center offers a 1/9-mile indoor track, canoe and kayak livery, multipurpose court space, indoor tennis courts, a swimming pool, weight-training facilities for physical education courses, intramural sports, individual conditioning, and wellness programs. Albion students also have access to Digital Equipment Corporation VAX 4000-200 computers and to the Internet through PCs located throughout the campus and in individual rooms. More than 500 microcomputers are available for various research activities. Albion is a leader in Michigan for wireless networking across campus, digital imaging and digital video editing capabilities, and satellite downlink services and is a member of the Internet2 group, the fastest computing and transmission system in the nation, restricted to use by the higher education and nonprofit community.

Costs

Projected costs for the 2004–05 academic year are $22,650 for tuition, $6536 for room and board, and a $268 student activity fee. Laboratory fees and music lessons are additional, as are personal expenses and travel. Costs are the same for both in-state and out-of-state students.

Financial Aid

Every student admitted to Albion College receives financial assistance if need is determined from the Free Application for Federal Student Aid (FAFSA). Families should file the FAFSA as soon as possible after January 1 so that the College receives the analysis from the federal government by February 15. For each student, Albion builds a financial aid package using federal grants and loans and College aid funds. Many Michigan residents are eligible for state scholarships and grants of more than $2000 that are reserved for people attending private colleges and universities in the state. More than 50 percent of Albion students also have jobs on campus. Students must apply for admission and be accepted before a financial aid package is prepared. Students with strong academic records are also eligible for academic scholarships. These range from a few thousand dollars to full tuition. The scholarship application deadline is February 1. Students with special talent in art, music, and theater may qualify for scholarships in these areas of up to $5000.

Faculty

Ninety-two percent of Albion's faculty members hold the doctorate or terminal degree in their field. There are 121 full-time faculty members. Courses and laboratories are taught by regular faculty members and not by graduate teaching assistants. The average class size is 19. First- and second-year courses have average enrollments of 24 students, with the exception of special First Year Experience courses, which limit enrollment to 16 students. Upper-level courses average 15 students.

Albion's faculty members are dedicated to teaching at a liberal arts college. Faculty members know their students personally and are available outside class hours for discussion and counseling. They are also active scholars and researchers, as shown by the grants that they receive from the National Science Foundation, the National Endowment for the Humanities, and many other sources.

Student Government

An elected Student Senate oversees the operation of campus organizations and disburses student activity fee funds to these groups. The Board of Trustees invites Student Senate members to sit on its committees for academic and student affairs, institutional advancement, and buildings and grounds. Student representatives also sit on the faculty's Educational Policies Committee, which reviews the College curriculum.

Admission Requirements

Albion is a selective national liberal arts college, and admission is mainly based on the applicant's academic record in high school with special attention to the college-preparatory courses completed. Standard test scores from either the ACT or SAT are also an important factor, as are personal qualifications and accomplishments outside the classroom. The College seeks a diverse enrollment without regard to race, religion, or national origin. In 2004, entering freshmen have an average GPA of 3.6, with an average ACT score of 26 and SAT score of 1160. Prospective freshmen can take either the SAT I or ACT. The new College Board–sponsored SAT Essay is not required, but is accepted as part of the total application package and can be used in place of the College's own essay if desired. These exams are not required of transfer students who have earned at least a semester of college credit. Candidates for admission are expected to be graduates of an accredited high school or preparatory school and have at least 15 acceptable credit units. Applicants should have a strong background in English, mathematics, and the laboratory and social sciences. Home-schooled applicants are reviewed on an individual basis and need to complete either the SAT I or ACT. International applicants are welcome and must have a minimum TOEFL score of 550 and submit a Declaration of Finances form to show adequate financial resources. An interview may be required. Arrangements for a personal campus visit should be made in advance in writing, by phone, or by e-mail.

Application and Information

Applications for admission are accepted at any time, but most students apply after September 1 of their senior year in high school. Before a decision is made, applicants must submit an application form and $20 application fee (there is no fee for Web applications), high school transcripts, test score results, and recommendations. Students should submit all materials by April 1. Albion is also a member of the Common Application and accepts applications completed on its Web site. Students who wish to receive an admission decision before Albion's regular decision candidates may apply under the early action program.

Applications need to be completed by December 1, and notification of an admission decision is mailed prior to January 1. Students do not have to make a final commitment to Albion until May 1, when the $300 enrollment deposit is required to reserve a place in the class. The deposit may be refunded if the admissions office receives a written request before May 1. Students who apply after December 1 are considered for regular decision. Notification of an admission decision is made on a regular basis beginning February 1. All applicants are encouraged to submit their application for admission prior to March 1, as students who apply after this date are considered for admission on a space-available basis. For further information, students should contact:

Albion College
611 East Porter Street
Albion, Michigan 49224

Telephone: 800-858-6770 (toll-free)
Fax: 517-629-0569
E-mail: admissions@albion.edu
World Wide Web: http://www.albion.edu

Robinson Hall.

ALVERNO COLLEGE
MILWAUKEE, WISCONSIN

The College

Alverno College is an internationally acclaimed, award-winning four-year liberal arts college for women known for an innovative, abilities-based, assessment-as-learning approach to education. Founded in 1887 by the School Sisters of St. Francis, Alverno College has one of the most diverse student bodies in the nation, both culturally and religiously. Currently, there are more than 2,100 students enrolled.

Alverno's mission is to promote the personal and professional development of women through four areas: creating a community of learning, creating a curriculum, creating ties to the community, and creating relationships with higher education. Alverno sets out to accomplish this by remaining focused on the student and higher education. The National Survey of Student Engagement (NSSE), an independent study that asks students to gauge the performance of their college or university and their own outcomes, placed Alverno in the 98th percentile overall nationally. This indicates that Alverno students are actually learning what they set out to learn at Alverno.

Alverno achieves a high level of success in its teaching through a comprehensive curriculum of abilities-based programs and an assessment process that provides each student with continuing evaluation of her performance, allowing her to make the adjustments necessary to succeed in her education. In every class, students learn by doing: they are participants and active learners. In addition, students are able to track their progress through Alverno's patented Diagnostic Digital Portfolio. This first-of-its-kind, Web-based system enables each Alverno student—anyplace, anytime—to follow her learning progress throughout her years of study. It helps the student process the feedback she receives from faculty members, external assessors, and peers. It also enables her to look for patterns in her academic work so she can take more control of her own development and become a more autonomous learner.

Faculty members have worked to create a more comprehensive approach to learning that places lessons into a framework that is relevant to today's changing world. The need to approach situations from a variety of perspectives, to weigh decisions, to engage in meaningful discussion, and to apply creative solutions in problem solving are all abilities women need for success.

Preparing students for real life, not just finals, is the hallmark of an Alverno education. *U.S. News & World Report* consistently ranks Alverno College as a top liberal arts college. At Alverno, each student is required to complete one off-campus professional internship. These internships are designed to complement the classroom experience, exposing each student to real-life work situations and providing insight into career options in each field of study. Alverno's Career Education Center is fully integrated into the learning process, providing students with numerous services, resources, training opportunities, and tools to assist them with their career planning. Within one year of graduation, 90 percent of Alverno College alumnae are working within their chosen field.

Students take advantage of a wide variety of social, athletic, cultural, and cocurricular academic activities on and off campus. Alverno Presents is one of the longest-running performing arts series in the Midwest, offering students the opportunity to see such top-notch performers as Wynton Marsalis, the Waifs, Kate and Anna McGarrigle, Baaba Maal, and many others.

The College's NCAA Division III athletics program provides students with five competitive sports, including basketball, cross-country, soccer, softball, and volleyball. Intramural sports are also available. The student center features the Mug Coffeehouse, run by students for students, as a place to relax and study with a latte or enjoy live music or lively discussions along with a variety of entertainment options, including large screen TVs and movie nights. There are more than thirty student organizations ranging from women's advocacy groups to professional business networking associations, including award-winning chapters of the Association of Women in Communications, Circle K, and Students in Free Enterprise.

Location

Alverno's 40-acre campus is nestled in the residential Jackson Park area of Milwaukee, just 10 minutes from downtown and beautiful Lake Michigan. Students are only minutes away from the world-famous Milwaukee Art Museum and the Calatrava addition as well as the Marcus Center for the Performing Arts and Summerfest grounds, the gallery and theater districts, and Miller Park, home of the Milwaukee Brewers. The city offers a mix of trendy nightspots and chic coffee bars and has a highly eclectic dining scene.

Internships and other cooperative programs with business, industry, and special-interest groups within the community give each student a variety of learning experiences off campus, enabling her to make a contribution through service projects in her areas of interest.

Majors and Degrees

Alverno College is a fully accredited four-year baccalaureate institution conferring Bachelor of Arts, Bachelor of Science, and Master of Education degrees. Alverno offers more than sixty majors and minors, including accounting, art, art therapy, behavioral science, biology, business, chemistry, professional communications, computer science, education, English, environmental studies, global studies, history, international business, Spanish, liberal studies, management, marketing, mathematics, music therapy, natural science, nursing, philosophy, political science, psychology, religious studies, secondary education, social science, and a host of preprofessional training programs. Alverno also offers educational licensure programs and a new licensure-to-master's degree program.

Alverno is also home to Wisconsin's original Weekend College program, one of the first in the nation. The program, which began in 1977, allows students to earn their degrees in professional communications, communication management and technology, community leadership and development, international business, management, management accounting, marketing management, and nursing (RN to B.S.N.) by attending class only twice per month.

Academic Programs

Alverno's learning process prepares students for success. The curriculum includes academic course work as well as external experiences such as internships and develops the student's abilities in eight specific core areas: communication, analysis, problem solving, value judgments, social interaction, decision making, developing a global perspective, and aesthetic engagement. Each student acquires the necessary knowledge to demonstrate learning in each of these areas, tying her studies into her personal and professional life.

Off-Campus Programs

The student's learning experience is enhanced by opportunities in the community and abroad through cutting-edge internship and international studies programs. Students are able to apply their knowledge to real-life situations in Alverno's internship program, working with mentors on job sites in business, industry, politics, nonprofits, and community organizations. Sites that regularly participate include Harley-Davidson, Miller Brewing, Milwaukee Art Museum, the mayor's office, and many others. Alverno's travel-abroad program provides students the opportunity to study for a semester or for a shorter term in such places as England, France, and Japan. In addition, travel courses, which culminate in a trip, are also available.

Academic Facilities

Alverno College remains one of the most technologically advanced campuses in the region, featuring SMART classrooms, a state-of-the-art Center for Instructional Communication, a video conferencing center that allows for long-distance learning, several computer labs, and many other multimedia capabilities. Even the residence hall features high-speed Internet access and cable television capability in each room. Alverno's library provides on-site and remote access to its print, audiovisual, and electronic holdings of more than 250,000 items as well as access to worldwide resources available through technology. The library's resources and services are further enhanced through a consortium of seven local college and university libraries.

The Teaching, Learning, and Technology Center is a 73,000-square-foot facility that features cutting-edge science labs, computer centers, and multimedia centers, including an on-campus digital production facility. The facility houses hundreds of networked, high-tech computers plus writing devices, the latest software, digital cameras, scanners, laptops, and more. The production facility houses nonlinear digital editing equipment, allowing students to produce and edit their own projects. All of these service areas are fully supported, so students have a resource on staff.

The Nursing Education Building provides resources dedicated to meet the needs of nursing students preparing for careers, including a library and a clinical nursing resource center. The center allows students to practice their nursing therapeutic skills and to participate in simulated clinical experiences. Computers are equipped with interactive nursing software. Registered nurses serve as mentors and assessors as they staff the resource center.

Alverno College also features several extra and cocurricular facilities on campus. Pitman Theatre is a beautiful art deco–style theater with seating for 930. The theater is the home of the Alverno Presents performing arts series and numerous concerts and functions each season. Wehr Hall, with seating for 375, is a state-of-the-art presentation hall designed for multimedia presentations as well as smaller performances. Alverno's Conference Center can accommodate seated dinners for up to 300 and is host to countless alumnae weddings and other celebrations each year.

Costs

For 2004–05, the tuition is $7080 per semester ($7452 for nursing), and room and board rates are $2700 per semester for first-year students. Books vary by course load but average $400 per semester for full-time students. Personal expenses vary greatly.

Financial Aid

Financial aid is readily available based on student need, academic performance, and other criteria. Aid can take the form of scholarships, grants, loans, and campus work-study programs. Approximately 85 percent of Alverno students receive some form of financial assistance, with an average award of $9494 per student per year.

Faculty

Alverno's coed faculty is made up of 104 full-time members, more than 90 percent of whom have earned the highest degree available in their fields. Faculty members also serve as academic advisers to students in their major areas of concentration. Class sizes are extremely small, averaging 20 per class.

Student Government

Students can join one of more than thirty student organizations and interest groups, including the Student Activities Planning Team.

This gives students an active voice and leadership role in what happens on campus. Programming opportunities include events such as the Metropolitan Milwaukee Leadership Conference and the National Collegiate Alcohol Awareness Week. Some groups or activities, such as food and clothing drives, are also student initiated and supported by the professional staff.

Admission Requirements

Candidates applying for admission to Alverno College directly after high school must have completed at least 17 academic units. These units should include at least 4 units in English, with the rest distributed among foreign languages, history and the social sciences, mathematics, and natural sciences.

All students must complete an evaluation of their abilities through the Communication Placement Assessment before beginning classes.

Application and Information

Students who wish to apply for admission can apply online or they can write, call, or e-mail the Admission Office for the necessary forms. An application is considered complete on receipt of the application form, the application fee (waived if students apply online), a high school transcript, and ACT scores. Students may submit any additional evidence that they believe might help the College determine their capacity to benefit from an Alverno education.

Alverno's admission policy permits notification of acceptance within three weeks of receipt of all credentials. Acceptance is contingent upon satisfactory completion of the secondary school courses.

For more information about Alverno College, interested students should contact:

Admission Office
Alverno College
3400 South 43rd Street
P.O. Box 343922
Milwaukee, Wisconsin 53234-3922
Telephone: 414-382-6100
        800-933-3401 (toll-free)
E-mail: admissions@alverno.edu
World Wide Web: http://www.alverno.edu

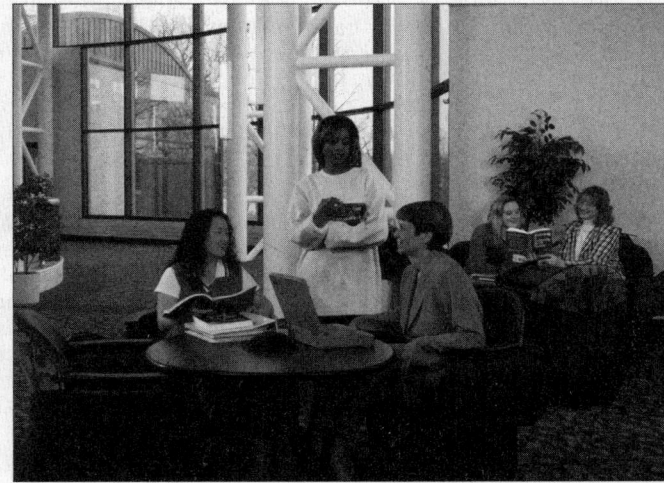

Studying on the campus of Alverno College.

AURORA UNIVERSITY
AURORA, ILLINOIS

The University

Aurora University was founded in 1893. The school has grown substantially over the years and has taken on many new challenges. In 1938, it was one of the first small colleges to achieve regional accreditation. In 1947, the college's evening program was instituted—one of the nation's first adult education programs at a liberal arts college. In 1985, Aurora College was reorganized as Aurora University, reflecting both the increased size of the institution and the needs associated with its many new programs. In addition to the College of Arts, Science, and Business, the University comprises the College of Education and George Williams College of Health and Human Services (social work, nursing, and human services). Today, the University enrolls 4,000 students in more than forty undergraduate programs and four graduate programs in business, recreation administration, social work, and education. An Ed.D. is offered in educational leadership. Courses are offered at other sites in Illinois, Iowa, and Wisconsin, in addition to the Aurora campus.

The University's student body includes 600 on-campus, traditional-age students; 1,000 undergraduate commuters; 1,800 graduate students; and more than 1,600 students at off-campus sites. The majority of Aurora's students come from the upper-Midwest region, but twenty states and five countries are also represented.

Social life is based on campus, and most activities are campuswide. Aurora has more than thirty musical, literary, religious, social, and service clubs and organizations. There are also three fraternities and sororities for students interested in Greek life. Aurora University has a long history of excellence in both intercollegiate and intramural athletics. A member of the NCAA Division III, Aurora fields intercollegiate teams in baseball, basketball, cross country, football, golf, soccer, softball, tennis, track, and volleyball, often with championship results.

Aurora University is accredited at the bachelor's, master's, and doctoral degree levels by the Commission on Institutions of Higher Education of the North Central Association of Colleges and Schools, and its programs are accredited by the Commission on Collegiate Nursing Education, National League for Nursing Accrediting Commission, Illinois Department of Professional Regulation, Council on Social Work Education, National Recreation and Park Association/American Association of Leisure and Recreation, and Association of Collegiate Business Schools and Programs.

Location

Aurora University is located in an attractive residential neighborhood on the southwest side of Aurora, Illinois, which has a population of more than 153,000 and is the state's second-largest city. The 27-acre main campus is located only minutes from the Illinois Research and Development Corridor, the site of dozens of nationally and internationally based businesses and industries. Located within an hour's drive or train ride is Chicago, one of the most vibrant cities in the world.

Majors and Degrees

The Bachelor of Arts degree is awarded in accounting, biology, business administration, communication (media studies and professional practice), computer science, computer science/business information systems, computer science/electronics, criminal justice, elementary education, English, history, management and innovation, marketing, physical education (K–12 teacher certification), political science, psychology, and sociology. The Bachelor of Science degree is awarded in accounting, biology, biology–environmental science, business administration, computer science, health science (predentistry, premedicine, pre–physical therapy, and pre–veterinary studies), management and innovation, marketing and mathematics, and physical education (athletic training and fitness and health promotion). The Bachelor of Science in human services is awarded in youth development, programming, and management. The Bachelor of Science in Nursing and the Bachelor of Science in Social Work are also offered. The University offers supplemental majors in prelaw and secondary education as well as the YMCA Senior Director Certificate Program.

Academic Programs

Aurora University offers academic programs combining a liberal arts foundation with majors emphasizing career preparation and selected concentrations. Graduates are educated to be purposeful, ethical, and proficient—equipped for worthwhile careers and productive lives and for venturing out into a changing world.

To earn a bachelor's degree, students are required to fulfill the general degree requirements of the University and the major requirements for an approved major; complete at least 120 semester hours with a GPA of at least 2.0 on a 4.0 scale, including at least 52 semester hours at a senior college; and complete at least 30 semester hours, including the last 24 for the degree and at least 18 semester hours in the major, at Aurora University.

Aurora University accepts credits earned through the CLEP, DANTES, ACT-PREP, and NLN Mobility testing programs. In addition, credit based on portfolio assessment is available to students who have significant prior learning from career experience or individual study.

The University observes a semester calendar (two sixteen-week semesters), with classes beginning in late August and concluding in early May.

Off-Campus Programs

Aurora University offers travel-study programs in Mexico and England. The University also has off-campus classes in various locations in Illinois and Wisconsin and several degree programs at the University's Lake Geneva campus in Williams Bay, Wisconsin.

Academic Facilities

The major buildings at Aurora are marked by the distinctive, red-tiled roofs specified by Charles Eckhart in his donation for the original campus. Dunham Hall houses state-of-the-art computer facilities as well as the Schingoethe Center for Native American Cultures. Other facilities include the fully equipped Perry Theatre, science labs, flora-fauna complex, and the College Commons. Music practice rooms, piano labs, and a spacious art studio are also available. Charles B. Phillips Library has more than 112,000 volumes, 190,000 microform units, and approximately 700 current periodical subscriptions. In addition, the library provides access to approximately 3,700 journals in electronic full text.

Costs

Tuition for the 2004–05 school year is $14,750 for full-time students (24 to 34 semester hours per year), while yearly room and board costs average $6100.

Financial Aid

Aurora University's financial aid program has been designed to make it possible for any academically qualified student to afford the benefits of a private education. The University works with students to determine the amount of their costs and to identify all available resources so that students can meet these expenses. Financial aid is awarded based on financial need as reported on the FAFSA. In addition to need-based financial aid, Aurora University offers academic scholarships, including the Board of Trustees Scholarship, Crimi Scholarship, Deans' Scholarship, Solon B. Cousins Scholarship, Aurora University Opportunity Grant, and transfer scholarships.

Faculty

The favorable student-faculty ratio of 15:1 ensures that students receive plenty of individual attention in class. Instructors also make time for students outside of class, acting as mentors, advisers, and friends who are eager to answer questions and to join students in sports and social activities.

Student Government

The student body is represented by the AUSA (Aurora University Student Association), which provides funding for various student groups on campus. Students are also active members of committees ranging from faculty searches to academic standards and are provided with certain voting privileges.

Admission Requirements

The Aurora University Committee on Admissions considers the complete record of a candidate for admission. The University seeks qualified students from varied geographical, cultural, economic, racial, and religious backgrounds. No single, inflexible set of admission standards is applied. Two general qualities are considered in each candidate: academic ability, enabling the student to benefit from a high-quality academic program, and a diversity of talents and interests that can contribute to making the campus community a better and more interesting place for learning. An application for admission to Aurora University is considered on the basis of the academic ability, achievements, activities, and motivation of the student. Transfer students with fewer than 30 semester hours of credit should apply in the same manner as freshman applicants. Transfer students with more than 15 semester hours may be admitted to Aurora University if they have a transferable overall GPA of 2.0 or higher. Aurora accepts a maximum of 90 semester hours of transfer credits from a combination of two- and four-year schools. A maximum of 68 semester hours may be transferred from two-year schools. For further information, students should contact a transfer counselor in the Office of Admission and Financial Aid.

Application and Information

To apply for admission to Aurora University, the following items should be sent to the Office of Admission and Financial Aid: a completed application form, an official transcript from the guidance counselor, and official ACT or SAT I scores. Transfer students should submit official transcripts from each college or university attended, along with the completed application.

For applications and further information, students may contact:

Office of Admission and Financial Aid
Aurora University
347 South Gladstone Avenue
Aurora, Illinois 60506
Telephone: 630-844-5533
            800-742-5281 (toll-free)
E-mail: admission@aurora.edu
World Wide Web: http://www.aurora.edu

An aerial view of Aurora University in Aurora, Illinois.

BALL STATE UNIVERSITY
MUNCIE, INDIANA

The University

Ball State University was founded as a state institution in 1918, but its antecedents date from the late nineteenth century when the Ball family, prominent industrialists, purchased and donated to the state of Indiana the campus and buildings of the Muncie Normal Institute. In 1922 the Board of Trustees gave the school the name of Ball Teachers College, and in 1929 the school became Ball State Teachers College. In 1965 the Indiana General Assembly renamed the institution Ball State University in recognition of its phenomenal growth in enrollment, in physical facilities, and in the variety and quality of its educational programs and services. The buildings on the campus reflect the changing architectural styles of the twentieth century.

The total University enrollment stands at 18,059. In fall 2002, undergraduate enrollment was 47 percent men and 53 percent women. The majority of entering freshmen were 18 to 19 years old and single and from cities of moderate to large size; 7 percent belonged to a minority group. About 10 percent of Ball State freshmen came from outside the state of Indiana. There were 416 students from seventy-seven countries other than the United States.

There are more than 300 student organizations that provide extracurricular activities. These include leadership programs, departmental organizations, honorary societies, music groups, religious organizations, fraternities, sororities, governing groups, special-interest organizations, and service groups. The University Health Service staff members offer health education, provide care in cases of acute illness and injury while a student is in attendance, and serve as medical advisers for the University.

Location

The Ball State campus is in a pleasant, residential area of Muncie, an industrial city of 70,000 people in east-central Indiana, 56 miles northeast of Indianapolis. The city's cultural features include the Muncie Symphony Orchestra, the Civic Theater, and the Artists Series and Concert Series presented in the John R. Emens University–Community Auditorium located on the Ball State campus.

Majors and Degrees

Degrees are offered in the fields of administrative information technology (two-year), advertising, anthropology, architecture and planning (architecture, environmental design, landscape architecture, urban planning and development), art (ceramics, drawing, general, metals, painting, photography, printmaking, sculpture, visual arts education, visual communication (graphic design)), athletic training, biology (aquatic biology and fisheries, botany, cellular and molecular ecology, genetics, general, microbiology, wildlife, zoology), business (accounting, business administration, business information technology, business and marketing education, economics (business, liberal arts), finance (corporate finance management, financial institutions, financial planning), management (entrepreneurship and small business management, general management, human resource management, information systems, operations and manufacturing management), marketing, risk management and insurance), business administration (two-year), chemical technology (two-year), chemistry (biochemistry), classical

culture, classical languages, communication studies, computer science (cooperative education, hardware systems, information systems), criminal justice and criminology, criminal justice and criminology (two-year), dance, dietetics, dietetic technology (two-year), early childhood education, earth science, earth/space science education, elementary education, English, English/language arts education, exercise science (aquatics, sport administration), family and consumer sciences (apparel design, family and child, family and consumer sciences education, general fashion merchandising, hospitality and food management, hospitality and food management (two-year), interior design, residential property management), French, French education, general studies, geography (comprehensive, geographic information processing and mapping, operational meteorology and climatology, travel and tourism), geology, German, German education, graphic arts management, health science, health education, history, industrial supervision (two-year), industrial technology (career and technical education, technology education), Japanese, Japanese education, journalism (graphics, journalism education, magazine, news-editorial, photojournalism), Latin American studies, Latin, Latin education, legal assistance (two-year), legal studies (business, public law), library media and computer education, life science education, manufacturing engineering technology, manufacturing technology (two-year), mathematical economics, mathematical sciences (actuarial science, applied mathematics, financial mathematics, mathematics, mathematics education, physics, statistics), mechanical engineering technology (two-year cooperative program with Purdue University), medical technology, military science (minor only), music (guitar, music composition, music education, instrumental and general music, music engineering technology, organ, piano, symphonic instruments, vocal and general music, voice), natural resources and environmental management (environmental communication/interpretation, environmental management, land management, natural resource studies, occupational/industrial hygiene, park and recreation management), nuclear medicine technology (two-year), nursing, philosophy, physical education, physical science education, physics, political science, printing technology (two-year), psychology, public relations, public service (two-year), radiation therapy (two-year), radiography (two-year), religious studies, social studies education, social work (B.S.W.), sociology, Spanish, Spanish education, special education (early childhood special education, exceptional needs, hearing impaired/deaf, mild interventions, severe interventions), speech-language pathology, telecommunications (media studies, news, production, sales and promotion), and theater (acting, design and technology, musical theater, theater education, theatrical studies).

Ball State also offers preprofessional programs in audiology, dental hygiene, dentistry, engineering (general, chemical, and metallurgical), law, medicine, optometry, pharmacy, physical therapy, physician's assistant, and veterinary medicine.

Academic Programs

Undergraduate programs combine general studies with majors and minors. Most degrees require 126 semester hours, at least a 2.0 grade point average, and the last year in residence. The academic calendar consists of fall and spring semesters and two summer terms.

The Honors College, a four-year University-wide program featuring special course offerings, colloquia, seminars, and independent study, is especially designed to challenge the talented student. University College is organized to provide support services to students undecided about their majors. The Learning Center provides free peer tutoring, small-group study sessions, and academic workshops to all Ball State students. Each year, more than 4,000 students, from freshmen through graduate students, use the Learning Centers service. Freshmen who attend tutoring or study groups earn higher grade point averages than those who do not.

The University, recognizing that there are other ways to obtain an education than through regular enrollment in a class, grants credit through any combination of credit for successful scores on Advanced Placement (AP) tests, IB and College-Level Examination Program tests, credit for military service, credit by departmental examination, and credit by departmental authorization.

Off-Campus Programs

Study-abroad programs are open to all Ball State students. It gives students the opportunity to explore intercultural issues outside the classroom. Programs vary in length, location, and cost, and credit is offered for most programs, so that students who participate are not required to delay graduation.

Summer programs are a popular option for students seeking short-term international experiences. The center works in coordination with the various colleges to develop discipline-specific field studies and special tours in all price ranges that appeal to students in all majors. Students receive course credit for most programs, and financial aid is applicable. Programs range in focus from ethnographic studies in British Columbia, student teaching in England, and business in Turkey or England, to architecture and urban planning in Germany and Italy.

Academic Facilities

Bracken library is one of the largest libraries in the state, with more than 1.5 million volumes. Professional collections are housed in the Architecture Library and the Science–Health Science Library. A K–12 school library is maintained at the Burris Laboratory School. Separate materials in the main library are the music collection, special collections, archives, government publications, maps, and educational resources.

Facilities on the campus also include an art museum, an observatory and planetarium, outdoor laboratories, a solar-energy research center, fully equipped science laboratories, a human-performance laboratory, state-of-the-art teaching classrooms, and music laboratories. University Computing Services provides a full range of computing and systems services for students, faculty members, and the administration.

Costs

Expenses for 2003–04 were $5532 for tuition for Indiana residents or $13,590 for tuition for nonresident (out-of-state) students, $5880 for room and board, and $800 (average) for books and supplies. Between $1800 and $2100 is considered reasonable for personal expenses and transportation.

Financial Aid

Through a program of scholarships, grants, loans, and employment, Ball State's Office of Scholarships and Financial Aid provides aid for deserving students. The Free Application for Federal Student Aid (FAFSA), obtainable from a high school guidance counselor, should be filed no later than March 10.

Faculty

Ball State's instructional programs are carried out by 868 full-time faculty members, 90 percent of whom hold earned doctoral degrees. Faculty members serve on the University Senate and on numerous senate and campus committees. Full-time academic advisers work with freshmen. Seven advising centers around campus work with departments and their faculty advisers.

Student Government

The all-campus student governing group is the Ball State University Student Association, composed of executive, legislative, and judicial branches. All students are encouraged to participate in such activities as proposing changes in University policy, working for expanded and improved educational programs at Ball State, and lobbying at the city and state levels. One student is appointed to serve on the University's Board of Trustees. In addition, representatives from the Student Association are appointed to serve on numerous boards, committees, and councils on campus, including the University Senate and its committees.

Admission Requirements

Undergraduate applicants are considered for admission to Ball State University after the Office of Admissions has received the application for admission, the $25 nonrefundable application fee, the secondary school record (official transcript) or GED high school equivalency scores and certificate, and scores on either the SAT I or ACT.

Transfer students must, in addition, submit an official transcript from each vocational or advanced educational institution attended beyond high school. The transcripts must be forwarded to Ball State directly from the institutions attended.

It is suggested that prospective applicants visit the campus and talk with a member of the admission staff.

Application and Information

High school students should complete an application in the fall of their senior year. Application materials must be submitted by March 1 for priority consideration for the autumn semester and by December 1 for the spring semester. Requests for appointments and information should be addressed to:

Dean of Admissions and Enrollment Services
Ball State University
Muncie, Indiana 47306
Telephone: 765-285-8300
          800-482-4BSU (toll-free)
          765-285-2205 (TDD users only)
E-mail: visitus@bsu.edu
World Wide Web: http://www.bsu.edu/admissions

BENEDICTINE COLLEGE
ATCHISON, KANSAS

The College

Benedictine College (BC) is a four-year, Catholic, Benedictine, residential, coeducational college that provides an outstanding liberal arts education for students of all backgrounds and faiths. Benedictine is distinguished by its unique Discovery College program that offers students exceptional opportunities for research and personal growth.

The College was established as the result of the 1971 merger of Mount St. Scholastica College (founded in 1924) and St. Benedict's College (founded in 1858). The sponsoring monastic communities of Mount St. Scholastica and St. Benedict's Abbey set the tone for the campus, where the dignity of all individuals is respected. Benedictine College fosters scholarship, independent research, and performance in its students and faculty members as a means of participating in and contributing to the broader world of learning.

Benedictine College, America's Discovery College, offers students—even freshmen and sophomores—the chance to collaborate with their professors on projects within the Discovery College program. On campus, discovery is a process; it's not a single idea, but a way of life. Students have the opportunity to discover important aspects of themselves and the world around them. This approach to education prepares students to be leaders in their careers and the community.

Every major offers unique, challenging opportunities to pursue outside of the classroom. Biology students may participate in Benedictine's nationally respected Wetlands and Wildlife Restoration Project, where they conduct field studies in a restoration area along the nearby Missouri River. History, business, chemistry, education, political science, and sociology faculty members, as well as others, have authored numerous books and articles, and many faculty members have received major grant funding for their research. The business administration program offers students a rare opportunity to learn to manage and take ownership of small businesses. These and other experiences lead students to become the next generation of managers, teachers, scientists, artists, and caregivers.

Benedictine College is fully accredited by the North Central Association of Colleges and Schools.

The College's ethnically diverse student population exceeds 1,300 students, including students from thirty-four states and fourteen other countries. Benedictine College does not discriminate on the basis of sex, race, color, religion, or national origin.

At Benedictine College, 3 out of 4 students live on campus. Students find the inviting, spacious residence halls offer convenient on-campus living with friendly, supportive staff members in a secure environment. Benedictine offers many different clubs and student organizations—more than thirty-five—to meet just about every interest, including student government, Students in Free Enterprise (SIFE), departmental clubs, Amnesty International, Hunger Coalition, Knights of Columbus, Chamber Singers, African-American Club, *Loomings* literary magazine, *The Raven* yearbook, and *The Circuit* student newspaper.

The Ravens compete in sixteen varsity intercollegiate sports (NAIA and Heart of America Athletic Conference), with men's teams in baseball, basketball, cross-country, football, golf, soccer, tennis, and track and women's teams in basketball, cross-country, golf, soccer, softball, tennis, track, and volleyball. Benedictine's cheerleading and spirit squads have been recognized nationally.

Both varsity and nonvarsity athletes can benefit by participating in fifteen intramural activities, including competition in men's and women's corecreational basketball, flag football, soccer, softball, and volleyball. All students are welcome to exercise their bodies and minds at the Student Union, with a gymnasium, athletic training rooms, and plenty of fitness-oriented equipment.

The Student Union features a comfortable 500-seat auditorium for concerts, plays, and lectures and also houses a gymnasium, coffee shop, snack and pizza bar, training and exercise rooms, TV room, student government and campus life offices, a Career Development Center, and plenty of space to relax and meet friends. Benedictine's Career Development Center offers students a variety of information and services to assist them in career preparation. Services include individual counseling, career testing, workshops, and seminars, as well as assistance with graduate and professional school applications, resume writing, interviewing skills, cover-letter writing, and job search strategies. In the natural sciences, 75 percent of graduates continue their education in graduate or professional schools, which is nearly double the national average for liberal arts college graduates. The College's record of acceptance into medical colleges is among the best in the Midwest. The Raven network of Benedictine alumni is a valuable resource for current BC students and new graduates. BC alumni can be found working in such prestigious places as the Federal Reserve Bank, Hallmark Cards, and the Mayo Clinic.

Location

Benedictine College is located on a peaceful, wooded campus in Atchison, Kansas, a picturesque town of 12,000 overlooking the Missouri River. The College is less than 1 hour's drive northwest of Kansas City and only 35 minutes from the Kansas City International Airport. Atchison offers shopping, beautiful parks, and a modern regional hospital across the street from the campus.

Majors and Degrees

Benedictine currently offers the following accredited degrees: Associate of Arts (business administration), Bachelor of Arts, Bachelor of Science, and Bachelor of Music Education. Every field of study at Benedictine College includes the opportunity for collaborative, hands-on training, a dynamic curriculum, internships, and a supportive faculty. The College offers four-year majors in accounting, astronomy, biochemistry, biology, business administration, chemistry, computer science, economics, education (certification, elementary, secondary, special education), English, French, history, mass communications, mathematics, music, music education, music marketing, natural science, philosophy, physical education, physics, political science, psychology, religious studies, sociology, social science, Spanish, theater arts, theater arts management, and youth ministry. In addition, the College offers preprofessional study programs in dentistry, 3-2 engineering, law, medical technology, medicine, nursing, occupational therapy, optometry, pharmacy, physical therapy, and veterinary studies. The College also offers certifications in athletic training and coaching. For those students who want or need the freedom to design a major to their unique interests, the College offers a liberal studies major.

Academic Programs

Benedictine College divides its academic year into two semesters and one summer session. The semesters are approximately sixteen weeks long. To earn a bachelor's degree from Benedictine College, a student is required to successfully complete 128 semester credit hours of courses numbered above 100. These courses must include courses specified by the student's major department, a total of 40 credit hours numbered 300 or above, and the general education requirements of the College.

Students must also achieve a minimum final grade point average of 2.0 in both the major and overall course work at Benedictine, successfully complete a comprehensive or standardized examination in his or her major at a level designated by the faculty, and finish the last two semesters of work in residence. The general education requirements for a bachelor's degree are divided into three categories: core requirements, disciplinary requirements, and proficiency requirements. Benedictine College offers opportunities for advanced placement, the College-Level Examination Program (CLEP), and credit for experiential learning to nontraditional students at least 23 years of age. The College also has a cross-enrollment agreement with Missouri Western State College and its Reserve Officers' Training Corps (ROTC).

Off-Campus Programs

Benedictine College sponsors a study-abroad program for students of Spanish in Cuernavaca, Mexico. For French students, the affiliation is with the Catholic University of the West at Angers, France. Benedictine students also can study at the Sorbonne in Paris and at the University of Granada in Spain. Students also may opt to study in China, England, Germany, Ireland, the Netherlands, and Wales.

Academic Facilities

The College enhances every student's educational experience with comprehensive facilities, including modern classrooms, nine science laboratories, and a modern computer network with Internet and e-mail access. The BC library is the designated federal depository for the area's congressional district and houses many rare books, including works on monastic history dating from the fifteenth century. The College also is a member of several library consortia, providing students with access to academic and public libraries locally and around the world. The College's Kansas area network (KANRAN) is one of the most sophisticated in America.

Costs

For 2004–05, tuition and fees are approximately $14,576, room is $2650, and board is $3478. Other estimated expenses are books, $550; personal expenses, $1200; and travel, $800.

Financial Aid

More than 90 percent of Benedictine students receive some form of financial assistance. Benedictine College annually awards more than $5.3 million in institutional aid and offers a generous number of scholarships based on academic achievement, athletic ability, and other achievements and merits. The College participates in the federal grant, work-study, and loan programs, as well as ROTC and state of Kansas

financial aid programs. Benedictine's priority deadline for financial aid consideration is March 1.

Faculty

More than 75 percent of Benedictine College faculty members hold terminal degrees, the highest degree in their fields. With a student-faculty ratio of 16:1, students have greater access to professors, who go out of their way to serve students on a personal level. Students are supported by instructors who are not only respected for their professional achievement but also for their commitment to student development. All Benedictine courses are taught by professors, not graduate or teaching assistants.

Student Government

The Student Government is designed to promote the general welfare of the student body in its academic, social, cultural, and religious needs. The executive officers of the student government and class officers are responsible for formulating and executing student government administrative policy.

Admission Requirements

Applicants must submit scores on the SAT I or ACT and all official high school and/or college transcripts. Sixteen units of college-preparatory work are recommended, including 4 units of English, 3 to 4 units of math, 2 to 4 units of foreign language, 2 to 4 units of natural science, 2 units of social science, and 1 unit of history.

Application and Information

The College employs a rolling admission policy. There is a $25 application fee. For further information or to request an application, students should contact:

Kelly J. Vowels
Dean of Enrollment Management
Benedictine College
1020 North Second Street
Atchison, Kansas 66002
Telephone: 913-367-5340
              800-467-5340 (toll-free)
E-mail: bcadmiss@benedictine.edu
World Wide Web: http://www.benedictine.edu

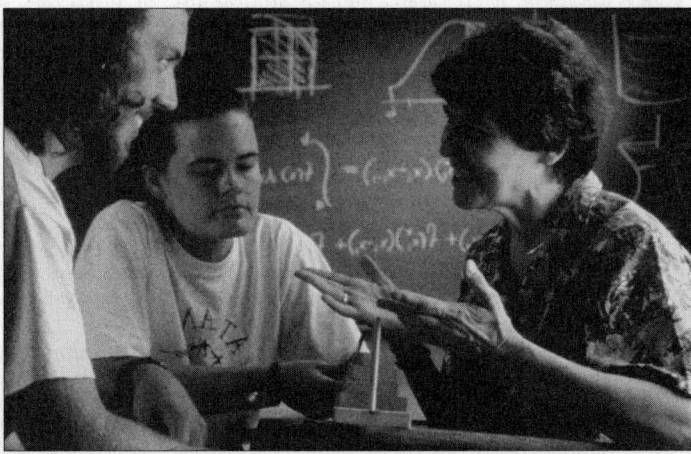

Benedictine College faculty members understand the importance of a personalized education and are committed to lifelong learning. They prove their concern for students by relating to them on a personal level and collaborating with students in research and curriculum design.

BENEDICTINE UNIVERSITY
LISLE, ILLINOIS

The University

Benedictine University was founded in 1887 as St. Procopius College. One hundred sixteen years later, the University remains committed to providing a high-quality, Catholic, liberal education for men and women. The undergraduate enrollment is nearly 2,000 students. The student body comprises students of diverse ages, religions, races, and national origins. Twenty-eight percent of the full-time students reside on campus.

Benedictine University is situated on a rolling, tree-covered 108-acre campus of ten major buildings with air-conditioned classrooms and modern, well-equipped laboratories. A student athletic center features three full-size basketball courts, a competition-size swimming pool, three tennis courts, and training facilities. All of the residence halls are comfortable and spacious and have access to the Internet. On-campus apartments offer one-, two-, and four-bedroom residences. Other features include a scenic lake, spacious and well-kept athletic fields, and a student center with dining halls, lounges, a chapel, a bookstore, and meeting rooms.

At Benedictine University, the environment is strengthened by success, not size. Renowned faculty members know students by name and care as much about each student's progress as they do about their own research. Those personal relationships have produced superb results. Benedictine graduates are accepted into some of the most prestigious graduate programs in the country. Approximately two thirds of Benedictine graduates who apply to medical school are accepted, in addition to similar ratios for other health-related professional schools (optometry, pharmacy, physical therapy, and podiatry). The liberal arts curriculum has helped place the University among some of the finest small private schools in the nation.

U.S. News & World Report's 2004 rankings listed Benedictine University as one of the top schools in the Midwest. The magazine also ranked the school sixth in the region for campus diversity.

Benedictine University is highly competitive in varsity sports. Men's varsity sports are baseball, basketball, cross-country, football, golf, soccer, swimming, and track. Women's varsity sports are basketball, cross-country, golf, soccer, softball, swimming, tennis, track, and volleyball. Aside from varsity and intramural athletic programs, a variety of organizations exist, including student government, a student newspaper, an orchestra, a jazz group, an African-American Student Union, an Indian Student Union, the Coalition of Latin American Students, campus ministry, a drama club, and various other extracurricular and academic organizations.

The graduate division offers the following graduate degrees in the business, education, and health-care areas: the Doctor of Philosophy (Ph.D.) degree in organization development; the Master of Business Administration (M.B.A.); the Master of Arts in Education (M.A.Ed.); the Master of Education (M.Ed.); the Master of Science (M.S.) in clinical psychology, clinical exercise physiology, management and organizational behavior, and management information systems; and the Master of Public Health (M.P.H.).

Adult undergraduate accelerated programs, taught by distinguished faculty members, are available in the following areas: accounting (B.B.A.), business and economics (B.A.), computer information systems (B.S.), computer science (B.S.), health administration (B.B.A.), management and organizational behavior (B.B.A.), nursing and health (degree completion for B.S.N.), organizational leadership (B.A.), and psychology (B.A.). The University also offers an Associate of Arts degree in business administration in an accelerated format.

Location

Benedictine University is 25 miles west of Chicago, in suburban Lisle near Naperville, and is easily accessible from the city and suburbs via the interstate highway system. Metra trains stop in Lisle, and O'Hare International Airport is only a 30-minute drive away. In addition to the many social and cultural offerings of the Chicago metropolitan area, the University enjoys the proximity and use of Argonne National Laboratory, Fermi National Accelerator Laboratory, the Morton Arboretum, a ski hill, a riding stable, and several golf courses. The University's location in the high-tech East-West Tollway corridor gives students opportunities for internships and employment.

Majors and Degrees

Benedictine University offers programs leading to the Bachelor of Arts, Bachelor of Business Administration, and Bachelor of Science degrees. Programs are offered in accounting, arts administration, biochemistry, biology, business and economics, chemistry (concentrations in chemical business and marketing and forensic chemistry), clinical laboratory science, communication arts (concentrations in advertising and public relations, broadcasting and cable, journalism, and mass media), computer science, economics, elementary education, engineering science, English language and literature, environmental science, finance, health administration, health science, history, information systems, international business and economics, international studies, management and organizational behavior, marketing, mathematics (concentration in actuarial science), molecular biology, music (concentrations in instrumental and vocal), nuclear medicine technology, nursing (completion), nutrition (concentrations in dietetics and management), organizational leadership, philosophy, physics (concentrations in engineering physics and physics), political science (concentration in prelaw), prenursing, psychology (concentrations in pre–occupational therapy and pre–physical therapy), radiation therapy, social science, sociology (concentrations in criminal justice and social work), Spanish, special education (concentrations in learning disabilities and social-emotional disorders), studio art, world literature, and writing and publishing.

In education, the University partners with the Golden Apple Foundation. Students selected as a Golden Apple Scholar of Illinois have the opportunity to study elementary, secondary, or special education at Benedictine while receiving the $5000 scholarship through the foundation.

In many areas of study, students may opt for a double major. Preprofessional programs include chiropractic, dentistry, engineering, law, medicine, nursing, occupational therapy, optometry, pharmacy, physical therapy, podiatry, and veterinary medicine. Combined professional programs are available with cooperating institutions in clinical laboratory science, nuclear medicine technology, and engineering. A joint engineering program is offered with the Illinois Institute of Technology. A nursing program is offered in cooperation with Rush University in Chicago and the University of St. Francis; a registered nurse may earn a Bachelor of Science degree in nursing. Secondary education certification is available in the following majors: biology, business and economics, chemistry, English, mathematics, music education, physics, and social science.

Academic Programs

For graduation, a student must earn at least 120 semester hours, 55 of which must be completed at a four-year regionally accredited college. At least the final 45 semester hours must be completed at Benedictine University. The University makes selective exceptions to the normal academic residency requirement of 45 semester hours for adults who are eligible for the Degree Completion Program. Eligibility is limited to those who have nearly completed their undergraduate studies but who, for reasons of employment, career change, or family situation, found it necessary to interrupt their studies.

The Second Major Program is designed for people who already have a degree in one area and would like to gain expertise in another. This program allows the student to concentrate on courses that fulfill the requirements of a second major. The student receives a certificate upon completion.

Each year, a select number of talented and motivated prospective students are invited to participate in the Scholars Program. The program is designed to enhance the college experience by developing students' international awareness and strengthening their leadership ability.

Off-Campus Programs

Benedictine University is a member of a three-school consortium in the west suburban Chicago area through which students are able to take classes at the other member colleges. Study abroad and internships abroad are encouraged to complement a liberal education.

Academic Facilities

The Kindlon Hall of Learning and the Birck Hall of Science bring science and technology to new levels. The Birck Hall of Science houses state-of-the art computer labs, specialized science labs, a research center, and the Jurica Nature Museum.

The Kindlon Hall of Learning houses computer labs, classrooms, multimedia labs, offices, and student lounges. It is also home to the Benedictine Library, which houses more than 160,000 volumes and can be found in the building's impressive four-story tower. The library is also equipped with eleven group study rooms, a computer lab, and an instruction room.

Benedictine University has distance education classrooms that provide students with the capability to interact globally with other colleges and universities in a classroom setting. Scholl Hall was recently renovated and houses classrooms and faculty and administrative offices.

Costs

The cost of tuition for the 2003–04 academic year was $16,960. The average cost of room and board was $6145. Mandatory fees totaled $510 and included health, technology, and student activity fees.

Financial Aid

In 2002–03, Benedictine University freshmen received assistance totaling $3.88 million from sources that included loans, scholarships and grants, tuition remission, and employment opportunities. Ninety-eight percent of the freshman class received financial aid. The average package was $12,567. Benedictine University has dedicated more than $7 million of the annual budget to providing grants and scholarships to its students. Students who wish to apply for aid must complete the Free Application for Federal Student Aid (FAFSA), the Benedictine University application for financial aid, and the Benedictine University application for admission.

Faculty

The 13:1 student-faculty ratio allows for close interaction between students and faculty members. Of the 84 full-time faculty members, 86 percent hold a Ph.D. or the terminal professional degree in their respective fields. All students are assigned a faculty member as an adviser to help plan programs of study.

Student Government

All full-time enrolled students are automatically members of the student government. The Student Government Association (SGA) is a representative body elected annually by the students to represent their interests. The SGA is responsible for the annual allocation of the student activity fee.

Admission Requirements

The Benedictine University admission philosophy is to select students who are expected to perform successfully in the University's academic programs and become active members of the University community. Typically, Benedictine University's freshman students are in the top third of their high school graduating class, with about 50 percent in the top quarter, and report better-than-average ACT or SAT I scores. A minimum of 16 units in academic subjects is required, including 4 units of English, 1 unit of algebra, 1 unit of geometry, 1 unit of history, 1 unit of laboratory science, and 2 units of foreign language. Benedictine University does admit some students who fall below these standards. These applicants receive individual consideration by the Committee on Admission. When appropriate, the committee will place conditions and/or restrictions upon students to help them reach their academic potential.

Students interested in transferring to Benedictine University must have a minimum cumulative average of C (2.0 on a 4.0 scale) or better from all colleges previously attended. Official transcripts from high school and all colleges attended must be submitted directly to the Office of Admissions for evaluation. If fewer than 20 semester hours of transfer credit are submitted, an official high school transcript and SAT I or ACT scores are required, and the general admission high school curriculum requirements must also be satisfied. High school information is not required with A.A. or A.S. degrees. Credits transferred from other institutions are evaluated on the basis of their equivalent at Benedictine University. Grades of D are accepted as transfer credit but do not satisfy Benedictine University requirements, which demand a minimum grade of C.

Requests for admission are considered without regard to the applicant's race, religion, gender, age, or disability.

Application and Information

Applications are reviewed on a rolling basis. Students are encouraged to apply for admission at any time after completing their junior year of high school. Transfer students may apply for admission during their last semester or quarter before anticipated transfer to Benedictine University. Earlier applications are encouraged for scholarship and financial aid opportunities.

For further information, students should contact:

Enrollment Center
Benedictine University
5700 College Road
Lisle, Illinois 60532
Telephone: 630-829-6300
         888-829-6363 (toll-free ouside Illinois)
Fax: 630-829-6301
E-mail: admissions@ben.edu
World Wide Web: http://www.ben.edu

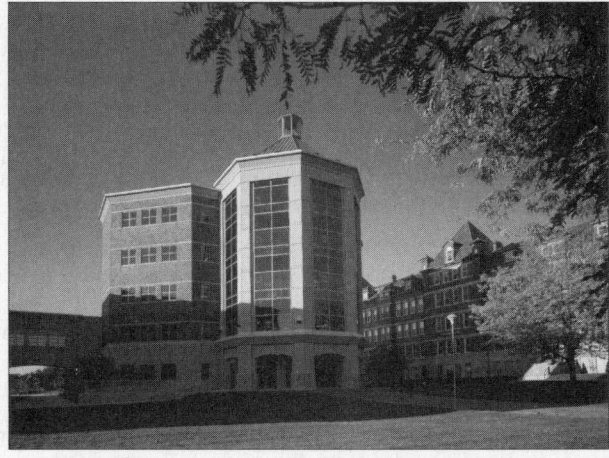

The Kindlon Hall of Learning houses computer labs, classrooms, multimedia labs, offices, and student lounges.

BETHEL COLLEGE
NORTH NEWTON, KANSAS

The College

Founded in 1887, Bethel College is a liberal arts and sciences undergraduate college affiliated with the Mennonite Church USA. Students are encouraged to live and work together and become the kind of leaders who blend faith and learning. To these ends, Bethel maintains a residential environment designed to foster integrative learning experiences, including student organizations, campus worship services, public lectures, symposia, and cultural events. At Bethel, 85 percent of the freshmen and two thirds of the entire student body of more than 500 students live on campus. The sense of community afforded by the residential nature of the campus is invigorating.

Bethel's curriculum is founded on a general education program in the liberal arts and sciences and is geared toward students of moderate to high academic ability who want to be leaders. Distinctive elements include requirements in the study of religion and global issues. The College offers twenty-seven majors and ten specialized programs in traditional liberal arts and selected career areas. Bethel is a diverse community of learners, with students from twenty-three states, seventeen countries, and more than thirty religious denominations.

Bethel's programs are informed by four central values of the mission statement: discipleship, scholarship, service, and integrity. Bethel emphasizes faith, learning, and leadership.

The Bethel campus includes the historic Administration Building, two libraries, a performing arts center, a science center, a student center, two gymnasiums, a natural history museum, an art center, athletic fields, and three residence halls.

The Administration Building is the dominating landmark of the College. Home to the campus Chapel and its Dobson pipe organ, the Administration Building was built in 1888 and is listed in the National Register of Historic Places. Thresher Gymnasium (seating capacity of 2,000) is home to varsity women's volleyball and men's and women's basketball. The Schultz Student Center is a hub of student activity, with a cafeteria, snack bar, game room, bookstore, and meeting rooms. The campus facilities are clustered around an open, grassy area referred to as The Green. The Green, with its benches and fountain, is a gathering place for students.

More than two thirds of Bethel students live on campus in one of three residence halls: Voth Hall, Haury Hall, and Warkentin Court. Each residence hall is supervised by an on-site staff and offers recreational and lounge areas and laundry and vending facilities.

Location

The 90-acre, tree-lined Bethel College campus is in North Newton, which is adjacent to the city of Newton (population 20,000). Located in the rich agricultural and industrial region of south-central Kansas, Bethel borders Interstate 135 and Kansas Highway 15. Wichita, the largest city in Kansas, lies 30 minutes to the south, and Hutchinson is 30 minutes west of the campus. Between Newton, Wichita, and Hutchinson, a wide variety of services and attractions are available to students. These include the Kansas Cosmosphere and Space Center, a world-renowned space museum; several art museums; music theater; opera; symphonies; professional baseball, hockey, and soccer; an ice sports center; and multiple malls and shopping centers. Wichita is served by eleven major airlines, and Amtrak train service is available in Newton.

Majors and Degrees

Bethel College grants Bachelor of Arts and Bachelor of Science degrees. Majors include art, athletic training, Bible and religion, biology, business administration, chemistry, communication studies, computer science, computer system administration, elementary education, English, fine arts, German, global peace and justice, health management, history, history and social sciences, management information systems, mathematical sciences, music, natural science, nursing, physics, psychology, restorative community justice, social work, Spanish, and theater. Within these majors, students may concentrate in the following specialized areas: accounting, economics, environmental studies, finance, general management, marketing, mass media, software development, and speech. Preprofessional programs are offered in engineering, law, and medicine.

Academic Programs

Bethel operates on a 4-1-4 academic calendar. Four-month semesters in the spring and fall are supported by the one-month Interterm in January. Interterm allows for a time of focused study in one selected class, either on campus or through several off-campus options. Interterm study-travel options have included English literature in London, biology in the jungle of Belize, theater in New York, history in Russia, religion in Jerusalem, and art in a snowbound cabin in the Colorado Rockies. Through this multifaceted learning environment, Bethel is committed to the diverse educational goals of its students. Courses facilitate intellectual, cultural, and spiritual learning in the Bethel community. The general education requirement of 55 credit hours ensures development of academic skills and disciplines and of integrative learning. Graduation from Bethel requires at least 124 credit hours with a minimum grade point average of 2.0.

Off-Campus Programs

Bethel offers a wide variety of formal study-abroad programs. Students enrolled in these programs are considered to be enrolled as full-time Bethel students living off campus. Academic progress and financial aid are generally the same as for on-campus programs. Bethel students may participate in study-abroad programs at sixteen colleges and universities in thirteen countries.

Academic Facilities

The Mantz Library has a collection of 130,000 volumes and more than 500 periodical subscriptions. The library also houses the Career Development Office and the Center for Academic Development, which provides academic support in the form of tutoring and supplemental instruction. Additional support is available for postbaccalaureate placement exams, including the GRE, MCAT, and LSAT. Adjacent to the Mantz Library is the Mennonite Library and Archives, which houses more than 45,000 volumes of Mennonite historical and genealogical information.

The Fine Arts Center includes Krehbiel Auditorium, which is used for theater, concerts, and lectures. The Fine Arts Center also houses an art gallery; music rehearsal areas; a computerized music composition lab; studios of KBCU, the campus radio station; and offices of the *Collegian*, the student newspaper.

Krehbiel Science Center, opened in 2002, provides classrooms and laboratories for biology, chemistry, physics, and psychology. Two networked computer laboratories are available in the Academic Center.

Memorial Hall houses the nursing department (classrooms, labs, and research computers), the Wellness Center (exercise and weight rooms), the Academic Health Center (student clinic), Harms Sports Medicine Center (athletic training), and an auditorium and intramural gymnasium (seating capacity of 2,000).

The Franz Art Center has multiple art studios for painting, drawing, ceramics, and photography.

Costs

Tuition and fees for a full-time student for the 2003–04 academic year were $13,900; room and board costs totaled $5900. Interterm is included in these costs if a student is enrolled full-time for either the spring or fall term.

Financial Aid

Bethel College administers a broad spectrum of financial aid intended to make the educational experience affordable for qualified students. Through merit-based financial aid (academic and performance), students may receive assistance ranging from $2500 to $7400 per year. For qualified students, need-based aid is available in the form of Bethel, state, and federal grant and loan programs. More than 94 percent of Bethel students receive some form of financial assistance.

Faculty

Bethel has 44 full-time and 9 part-time faculty members. Of the full-time faculty members, 85 percent have terminal degrees. Faculty members of all ranks teach first-year students in addition to upperclassmen. Bethel faculty members are active in scholarly research and regularly enlist students as collaborators in their research. No classes at Bethel are taught by teaching assistants or graduate assistants. The student-faculty ratio is 11:1. As is consistent with the emphasis Bethel places on global awareness and service, more than half of Bethel faculty members have been engaged in overseas service and travel.

Student Government

Student government at Bethel is based on the federal model and consists of twenty-seven elected offices and several appointed positions. The executive branch comprises the Student Body President and Vice-President. The Senate has 5 senators from each class, 3 commuter senators, one senator from the International Club, and one from the multicultural organization. Bethel's active student government provides an opportunity for student advocacy and leadership development.

Admission Requirements

Bethel seeks to enroll a broad range of students with a demonstrated desire and ability to learn. Admission is competitive, and applicants must provide school transcripts and standardized test scores. Freshman applicants should present a minimum GPA of 2.5 and a minimum ACT score of 19 or SAT I score of 890. Transfer applicants should present a minimum college GPA of 2.0 on 24 hours or more of credit accepted in

transfer. International applicants are required to present a minimum TOEFL score of 540 on the paper-based version or 207 on the computer-based version. All prospective students are encouraged to visit campus, either during a group-visit event or an individual campus visit. The College admits students without regard to race, color, sex, disability, or national or ethnic origin.

Application and Information

Interested students are invited to request an application for admission from the Admissions Office or to complete the application online at http://www.bethelks.edu/admissions/application.html. Although admission is granted on a rolling basis through the beginning of each semester, early application is encouraged for priority consideration for financial aid, class selection, and housing.

For more information, students should contact:

Office of Admissions
Bethel College
300 East 27th Street
North Newton, Kansas 67117
Telephone: 316-283-2500
           800-522-1887 (toll-free)
Fax: 316-284-5870
E-mail: admissions@bethelks.edu
World Wide Web: http://www.bethelks.edu

Bethel College students in front of Memorial Hall.

BLUFFTON COLLEGE

BLUFFTON, OHIO

The College

Bluffton College is a fully accredited, four-year Christian liberal arts college in northwestern Ohio. Founded in 1899 by regional leaders of the General Conference Mennonite Church, it is today affiliated with the Mennonite Church USA. Shaped by the historic peace church tradition and coupled with its desire for excellence in all programs, Bluffton College seeks to prepare students of all backgrounds for life as well as vocation, for responsible citizenship, for service to all peoples, and ultimately for the purposes of God's universal kingdom.

More than 1,100 students from twenty states and eighteen countries study at Bluffton College, which is accredited by the North Central Association of Colleges and Schools (30 North LaSalle Street, Suite 2400, Chicago, Illinois 60602; 800-621-7440, toll-free). The College continues to receive national recognition in *Barron's Best Buys in College Education* for providing outstanding quality at a reasonable price. Bluffton is one of only a handful of Ohio colleges to be included in the prestigious *John Templeton Foundation Honor Roll of Character-Building Colleges.*

The student life program is rich with opportunities for personal and spiritual growth. Weekly chapel services and biweekly Sunday morning worship services provide a community context for joint worship. Examples of the many groups in which students participate include BASIC (Brothers And Sisters In Christ), Diakonia (Christian service/outreach groups), Habitat for Humanity, and PALS Drug Awareness programs. The Honor System, practiced in all classes and throughout campus life, promotes honest, open communication between all members of the campus community.

Students participate in many organizations and activities, including vocal and instrumental music, departmental and preprofessional clubs, student newspaper, student government, and many others. As a member of the NCAA Division III and the Heartland Collegiate Athletic Conference, Bluffton fields varsity athletic teams for both men and women. Men's sports include baseball, basketball, cross-country, football, golf, soccer, tennis, and track. Varsity teams for women include basketball, cross-country, golf, soccer, softball, tennis, track, and volleyball. Bluffton is the first NCAA Division III college in the nation to be selected for the NCAA Life Skills program, which helps prepare student athletes for life after college.

Residence life is integral to the campus community. All students are required to live in campus housing unless they are married or commuting from home. No self-selective fraternities or sororities are permitted, and students are expected to adhere to campus standards of conduct, which prohibit the use of tobacco, alcohol, and drugs. A satisfaction guarantee is offered to new residential students.

In addition to its undergraduate degrees, Bluffton offers a Master of Arts in Education and a Master of Organizational Management.

Location

Bluffton College is located just off Interstate 75, midway between Lima and Findlay, Ohio, in the Allen County village of Bluffton (population 3,900). Several restaurants and a movie theater are within walking distance of campus, and easy access to I-75 provides many additional opportunities in Findlay, Lima, Toledo, Dayton, and Columbus.

The campus is situated on 60 beautifully wooded acres and is adjacent to the 130-acre Bluffton College Nature Preserve.

Majors and Degrees

Bluffton College offers Bachelor of Arts degrees. Bachelor's degrees are available in accounting; adolescent/young adult, multiage, and vocational education; apparel/textiles merchandising and design; art; biology; business administration; chemistry; child development; communication; computer science; criminal justice; dietetics; early childhood education; economics; English; family and consumer sciences; food and nutrition–dietetics; food and nutrition–wellness, health, physical education, and recreation (HPER); history; information systems; information technology; intervention specialist studies (special education); mathematics; middle childhood education; music; music education; physics; premedicine; psychology; recreation management; religion; social studies; social work; sociology; Spanish; Spanish/economics; sport management; writing; and youth ministries and recreation. In addition, a number of minors, preprofessional programs, and special programs are available, including graphic design, prelaw, peace and conflict studies, TESOL studies, women's studies, and self-designed majors.

Academic Programs

The Bluffton College curriculum is centered on a liberal arts and sciences general education program. The strength of this program lies in the many integrated courses in social science, humanities, fine arts, and natural sciences that build upon one another as students advance toward earning their degree. Courses in Bible and theology, an integrated cross-cultural course, and a capstone course titled Christian Values in a Global Community complete the general education program. Key components of the general education curriculum include the First Year Seminar for new students and the cross-cultural requirement. Students seeking a bachelor's degree must complete a minimum of 122 semester hours of academic work and maintain a minimum overall grade point average of 2.0.

Off-Campus Programs

Bluffton College offers several semester-long international and cross-cultural opportunities. Current programs include study in Central America, Mexico, Northern Ireland, and Vietnam. Bluffton is also a member of the Council for Christian Colleges and Universities, which offers study programs at various U.S. locations, including Washington, D.C., as well as international programs in the Middle East, Russia, and Central America. Many Bluffton students participate in short-term off-campus projects with organizations such as Habitat for Humanity, Witness for Peace, and the Urban Life Center in Chicago. In addition, Bluffton students may complete up to four supervised independent study courses, which may be used for off-campus study.

Academic Facilities

The Musselman Library, a 1930 building of Georgian colonial architecture, was the gift of Mr. and Mrs. C. H. Musselman. It holds approximately 150,000 volumes, 116,000 microfilm units, approximately 4,000 current periodicals, and more than 350 CD-ROMs. The library has about 4,500 maps and receives many important U.S. government publications as a selective depository library. The library is a member of both the OPAL (Ohio Private Academic Libraries) and the OhioLINK consortia. Through OhioLINK, Bluffton College students and faculty and staff members have access to more than 24 million library items held at more than seventy college and university libraries throughout the state, to more than 60 separate databases, and to hundreds of full-text periodicals.

One of the newest facilities on campus is the Centennial Hall academic center. The academic center is a multilevel building at the center of the campus and contains state-of-the-art computer facilities, a new media center, technology-enhanced classrooms, and faculty offices.

Completed in 1991, the Sauder Visual Arts Center contains an art gallery and classroom and offers studio facilities for printing, painting, drawing, sculpture, ceramics, woodworking, welding, and photography. Shoker Science Center is a unique underground science facility that houses integrated laboratories for all the sciences, a science library, and instructional computers. Historic College Hall serves as the main administrative building. Marbeck Center, with its new Bob's Place gathering area, is the student union.

Founders Hall is a complete physical education facility, containing a main gymnasium, a newly renovated auxiliary gymnasium, and a weight room. Other recent additions to campus include Salzman Stadium and Neufeld Hall, a suite-style residence hall for 109 students.

The Al and Marie Yoder Recital Hall provides a state-of-the-art performance facility for student recitals and guest artists. Weekly forums and chapel services are also held in Yoder Hall.

Primary student computer access is provided through the microcomputer center located in Centennial Hall. All students may have e-mail addresses, and Internet access is provided in the lab. In addition, computers are located in residence halls, academic departments, and other locations on campus. All residence halls are equipped for students who wish to bring their own computer.

Costs

Tuition for the 2003–04 school year (based on 24 to 34 semester hours per year) was $17,260. Board was $3272 and room was $2758, for a total of $23,290. There is also a $400 technology fee. Books and personal expenses are additional.

Financial Aid

Nearly 100 percent of Bluffton College students receive some form of financial aid. Some awards are based solely on financial need, such as the Bluffton College Grant, while others are tied to academic achievement or demonstrated leadership and service to others. Scholarships and grants unique to Bluffton include the Presidential Scholarship Competition; the Academic Honors Scholarship; the Academic Merit Scholarship; the Tuition Equalization Scholarship Program, for students scoring at least 23 on the ACT or 1050 on the SAT I and ranking in the top 25 percent of their class or achieving at least a 3.0 grade point average; the Bluffton College Incentive Scholarship, for students with at least a 2.8 grade point average and 21 on the ACT or 970 on the SAT I; Leadership/Service Grants, which are available to students who demonstrate significant contributions outside the classroom in school, church, and community activities; and Church Matching Scholarships to students whose church has awarded them a scholarship to attend Bluffton. Additional College awards include scholarships for music and art and need-based grants to dependents of ministers and those serving in foreign missions. The Learn and Earn program provides an opportunity for many students to work on campus to help with expenses and gain valuable work experience.

Faculty

A high-quality program depends on a superior faculty. Students at Bluffton are taught by 64 full-time faculty members and 37 part-time faculty members. More than 70 percent of the full-time faculty members have earned the doctorate or appropriate terminal degree, and all faculty members teach on a regular basis. Many faculty members continue to research and write yet remain committed to teaching. The faculty members are very approachable and work together with students to create a unique learning environment based on mutual trust and respect.

Student Government

A democratic atmosphere prevails in the Bluffton College campus community. The Student Senate is a very important part of the campus community and actively represents the interests of the student body to the administration. Composed of students elected from each of the four classes, the Senate has primary responsibility in the areas of cocurricular activities. Hall associations are organized for the purpose of self-government and social activities.

Admission Requirements

Requirements for admission to the first-year class include graduation from a secondary school or a GED certificate; satisfactory secondary school work, with preference given to students ranking in the top half of their class and who have taken the recommended secondary preparation of 4 units of English, 3 units of mathematics, and 3 units each of social sciences, science, and a foreign language; and satisfactory performance on either the ACT or SAT I. Also considered are participation in cocurricular activities, moral character, purpose for college study, and recommendations.

Application and Information

Application for admission should be made at the end of the junior year or early in the senior year of high school. The deadline for submitting the application for the fall term is May 31. For all other terms the deadline is fifteen days prior to the intended date of enrollment.

Applicants must complete and return the application with a $20 fee along with recommendations from the school guidance counselor and a teacher, a high school transcript, and scores from either the ACT or the SAT I. A personal campus visit and interview are strongly encouraged.

The Office of Admissions operates on a rolling basis and makes its decision and notifies the applicant soon after receiving the required items. Students wishing to receive additional information may contact:

Office of Admissions
Bluffton College
280 West College Avenue
Bluffton, Ohio 45817-1196
Telephone: 419-358-3257
        800-488-3257 (toll-free)
Fax: 419-358-3081
E-mail: admissions@bluffton.edu
World Wide Web: http://www.bluffton.edu

Students enjoy Bluffton College's wooded campus.

CASE WESTERN RESERVE UNIVERSITY

CLEVELAND, OHIO

The University

Formed in 1967 by the federation of Case Institute of Technology and Western Reserve University, Case Western Reserve University is today one of the nation's major independent universities. Currently, 3,587 undergraduates (2,172 men and 1,415 women) are enrolled in programs in engineering, science, management, nursing, the arts, humanities, and the social and behavioral sciences. Students have access to the facilities of a comprehensive university, including graduate and professional schools in applied social sciences, dental medicine, graduate studies (humanities, the social and natural sciences, and engineering), nursing, medicine, law, and management. Several undergraduate programs and majors combine the resources of the undergraduate colleges and the graduate and professional schools. Examples include biochemistry and biomedical engineering (Case School of Medicine) and accounting and management (Weatherhead School of Management). In addition, collaborative arrangements with neighboring cultural and health-care institutions enable the University to provide special opportunities in other fields. A six-year dental program leading to the D.M.D. degree is also available.

There are numerous college activities, including those of dozens of professional, religious, political, social, and academic organizations. Nearly every type of interest group, from political organizations to a film society, is represented on campus, and sports are offered at both the varsity and intramural levels. There are nineteen national fraternities and six sororities; approximately 30 percent of the students participate. Residence halls are coeducational, and 75 percent of the students reside on campus. Automobiles and motorcycles are permitted.

Students at Case Western Reserve enjoy an especially close interaction with the faculty.

Location

The University is located in University Circle, a cultural extension of the campus, which comprises 500 acres of parks, gardens, museums, schools, hospitals, churches, and human service institutions. The Cleveland Museum of Art, the Cleveland Museum of Natural History, and Severance Hall, home of the Cleveland Orchestra, are within walking distance; downtown Cleveland is 10 minutes away by RTA rapid transit. Partnerships in education and research among University Circle institutions enable students to make full use of resources beyond those of the University itself.

Majors and Degrees

Programs of study leading to the Bachelor of Arts degree comprise the following: American studies, anthropology, art history (joint program with the Cleveland Museum of Art), Asian studies, astronomy, biochemistry, biology, chemistry, classics (Greek and Latin), communication sciences (collaborative program with Cleveland Hearing and Speech Center), comparative literature, computer science, economics, English, environmental geology, environmental studies, evolutionary biology, French, French studies, geological sciences, German, German studies, gerontological studies, history, history and philosophy of science, international studies, Japanese studies, mathematics, music (joint program with the Cleveland Institute of Music), natural sciences, nutrition, nutritional biochemistry and metabolism, philosophy, physics, political science, prearchitecture, psychology, religion, sociology, Spanish, statistics, theater (dance and drama), and women's studies. Minor areas

of concentration within the B.A. curriculum include artificial intelligence, art studio, childhood studies, Chinese, electronics, entrepreneurial studies, ethnic studies, history of science and technology, human development, Italian, Japanese, Judaic studies, management information and decision systems, public policy, Russian, and sports medicine.

Bachelor of Science degrees are offered in the following fields: accounting, aerospace engineering, applied mathematics, art education (joint program with the Cleveland Institute of Art), astronomy, biochemistry, biology, biomedical engineering, chemical engineering, chemistry, civil engineering, computer engineering, computer science, electrical engineering, engineering physics, fluid and thermal engineering sciences, geological sciences, management (business), materials science and engineering, mathematics, mathematics and physics (combined major), mechanical engineering, music education, nursing, nutrition, nutritional biochemistry and metabolism, physics, polymer science, statistics, systems and control engineering, and an undesignated engineering major. Course sequences emphasizing architecture, energy, environmental/ water resources studies, and power are offered in conjunction with some engineering and science fields.

High school seniors who are exceptionally well qualified in some fields are eligible for the Pre-Professional Scholars Program offered in association with the Schools of Applied Social Sciences, Dental Medicine, Law, and Medicine. In addition to being admitted into the program, each student selected is also awarded conditional admission to the appropriate professional school upon completion of the entrance requirements set by each school.

Students may work toward a combined B.A./B.S. degree or integrate undergraduate and graduate studies to complete both the bachelor's and master's degrees in five years or less. Combined B.A./B.S. (3-2) programs in astronomy, biochemistry, and engineering are offered in conjunction with a number of four-year liberal arts colleges.

Academic Programs

Through a combination of core curricula, major requirements, and minors or approved course sequences, all undergraduates receive a broad educational base as well as specialized knowledge in their chosen fields.

The University offers students opportunities for independent research and internships or professional practicums in business, health-care, government, arts, or service fields. A five-year co-op option providing two 7-month work periods in industry or government is available for majors in engineering, science, management, accounting, and computer science.

The Undergraduate Scholars Program allows a small number of highly motivated and responsible students to pursue individually tailored baccalaureate programs without the normal credit-hour and course requirements. The program, administered by a faculty committee, must be one that cannot be accomplished within the regular curricula.

Candidates for the B.A. who have been accepted at a school of medicine or dentistry other than one of those at Case may exercise the Senior Year in Absentia Privilege, which permits them to substitute the first year of professional studies at an approved school for the final year at Case Western Reserve. The Senior Year in Professional Studies option allows B.A. candidates who are admitted during their junior year to Case's School of Applied Social Sciences, Dental Medicine, Management, Medicine, or Nursing to substitute the first year of professional school for the final undergraduate year.

The Minority Engineers Industrial Opportunity Program offers a special orientation and support to minority students in secondary schools and academic and financial support to minority undergraduates in engineering.

The University has two 4-month semesters and one 8-week summer program.

Off-Campus Programs

Selected students may enroll as juniors and seniors in the Washington Semester, which is conducted each spring at the American University. Students with a B average or higher may participate in the Junior Year Abroad program. Up to 36 hours of credit may be granted for study at a foreign university. Students may also cross-register at other Cleveland-area colleges and universities for one course per semester.

Academic Facilities

The $30-million Kelvin Smith Library opened in 1997. Through reciprocal borrowing arrangements, Case students have access to the holdings of the Cleveland Public Library, as well as the libraries of five University Circle institutions; the members of OhioLINK, a network that includes state colleges and universities; the State Library of Ohio; and several private institutions. In addition to more traditional departmental research facilities, the University operates two astronomical observatories, a biological field station, and nearly 100 designated research centers and laboratories, many of them interdisciplinary. CWRUnet, the University's high-speed fiber-optic communications network with the switched gigabit to the desktop standard, links every residence hall room with computing centers, libraries, and databases on and off campus. Other computer facilities on campus offer various models of microcomputers and a wide variety of software programs.

Costs

For 2004–05, tuition and compulsory health and laboratory fees total $26,500. The student activity fee is $212. Room and board cost an average of $7800. Books and supplies come to about $1000, and incidental expenses are estimated at $1255. The approximate total cost for the year is $36,770.

Financial Aid

Financial aid consisting of grants, loans, and work assistance is awarded on the basis of a student's need. Last year, all students demonstrating need received financial aid. Applicants must file the Free Application for Federal Student Aid (FAFSA) and the Financial Aid PROFILE of the College Scholarship Service by February 1. A signed copy of the most recent federal tax return (Form 1040) is also required. The University also awards merit-based scholarships ranging from $500 to full tuition. These awards are based solely on the student's academic, creative, or leadership ability.

Faculty

The full-time instructional staff of 2,341, of whom 95 percent hold the Ph.D. or equivalent, is shared by all University students: graduate, undergraduate, and professional. The undergraduate student-faculty ratio is 8:1. Each college provides counselors who are always available for both academic and personal advice. Once a major has been chosen, a member of the department in which the student is majoring acts as his or her academic adviser.

Student Government

The Undergraduate Student Government of Case Western Reserve University represents all undergraduate students. The assembly acts as a liaison between undergraduate students and the faculty, administration, and other groups; grants recognition to undergraduate organizations; and has the responsibility and authority to allocate funds from student activity fees to student organizations.

Admission Requirements

The University requires at least 16 units of full-credit high school work in solid academic subjects, including 4 years of English or its equivalent. All applicants are expected to have completed 3 years of high school mathematics, and students interested in mathematics, science, or engineering majors should have 4. At least 2 years of laboratory science are required of all applicants, and prospective mathematics and science majors must present 3 years. For all engineering candidates, physics and chemistry are required. Two years of foreign language study are recommended for students considering majors in the humanities, arts, and social and behavioral sciences. An interview is not a required part of the admission process, but it is strongly recommended as the best way to learn about the University. Applicants should take the ACT or the SAT I not later than January of their senior year in secondary school. For candidates submitting the SAT I, three SAT II Subject Tests are strongly recommended, including the Writing Test for all students, the Level I or II mathematics test and physics or chemistry for engineering candidates, and two tests of their choice for others.

Application and Information

Freshmen matriculate in August. Students who wish to receive early notification of their admission status may apply for early action by November 15; they are notified by January 15. The final application deadline is January 15 for March notification. Application deadlines for transfer students are June 30 for fall admission and October 15 for spring admission. The application deadline for the Pre-Professional Scholars Program (medicine, dentistry, or law) is November 15. In addition to its own application form, Case Western Reserve University accepts the Common Application and offers online application options.

To obtain an application form and financial aid information, students should contact:

Office of Undergraduate Admission
Case Western Reserve University
10900 Euclid Avenue
Cleveland, Ohio 44106-7055

Telephone: 216-368-4450
E-mail: admission@case.edu
World Wide Web: http://admission.case.edu

Students at Case Western Reserve University in Cleveland, Ohio.

THE COLLEGE OF MOUNT ST. JOSEPH
CINCINNATI, OHIO

The College

As a private liberal arts college founded in 1920, the College of Mount St. Joseph has a rich history of preparing students for the future. Today, the Mount is a coeducational college with more than 2,000 students, offering an outstanding liberal arts curriculum that emphasizes values, integrity, and social responsibility, as well as practical career preparation. Required courses in humanities, science, and the arts are complemented by opportunities for cooperative work experience, a universal computing requirement, specialized and professionally oriented courses, and extracurricular opportunities, which give students the broad-based background that is in high demand among employers.

Catholic in tradition, the Mount emphasizes a value-centered education and supports the personal growth of each student. A warm, close-knit campus community encourages students to exercise their talents to their fullest potential in academic, athletic, and leadership activities. Mount students come primarily from the Midwest, but many other regions of the United States and nearly fifteen countries are also represented. Spacious rooms are available in Seton Center Residence Hall. Resident students may keep cars on campus.

The College is accredited by the North Central Association of Colleges and Schools.

Campus organizations include the student government, student newspaper, academic honor societies, international club, departmental clubs, marching and concert band, chamber singers, and intramural athletics. The Mount offers a full intercollegiate athletics program in the NCAA Division III for men and women and is a member of the Heartland Collegiate Athletic Conference (HCAC). Women's programs include basketball, cross-country, golf, soccer, softball, tennis, track and field, and volleyball. For men, there are baseball, basketball, cross-country, football, golf, tennis, track and field, and wrestling.

Location

Located just 10 minutes from downtown Cincinnati, the College sits on a beautiful, 75-acre suburban campus overlooking the Ohio River. The campus is easily accessible from the airport, bus terminal, railway station, and interstate. Well known for its scenic and rolling hills, greater Cincinnati offers numerous parks, cultural and arts events, professional athletics, shopping areas, and a wide assortment of fine restaurants. In addition to their own on-campus activities, Mount students frequently participate in social and service activities with students from other area colleges.

Majors and Degrees

The College of Mount St. Joseph awards bachelor's degrees in the following areas: accounting, art, art education, athletic training, biological chemistry, biology, business administration, chemistry, chemistry/mathematics, communication studies, computer information systems, computer science with minor in math, education (early childhood, middle childhood, physical education, and special education), English, fine arts, gerontological studies, graphic design, history, interior design, liberal arts and sciences, mathematics, mathematics/chemistry, medical technology, music, natural history, natural science with biology or chemistry concentration, nursing, paralegal studies, paralegal studies for nurses, psychology, recreational therapy, rehabilitation science, religious education, religious pastoral ministry, religious studies, social work, and sociology.

Associate degrees are offered in accounting, art, business administration, communication arts, computer information systems, gerontological studies, graphic design, interior design, and paralegal studies.

Certificate programs are offered in gerontological studies, graphic design, interior design, paralegal studies, paralegal studies for nurses, and parish nurse/health ministries.

For state of Ohio licensure in education, the Mount offers programs in inclusive early childhood, middle childhood, adolescent and young adults, multiage, and intervention specialist/special education. Licensure programs in other states are also available.

Preprofessional programs are available in allied medical professions, law, and medicine.

Academic Programs

All majors are backed by a strong liberal arts curriculum that encourages students to develop skills in analytical thinking, problem solving, decision making, and communication. Students must earn 128 credit hours for a bachelor's degree, with 52 of those credits from the liberal arts and science core. For an associate degree, students must earn 64 credit hours, with 27–28 of those credits from the liberal arts and science core.

The academic year consists of fall and spring semesters and three summer terms, with classes offered in day, evening, or weekend time frames.

The Mount offers a highly respected Cooperative Education program, making available to students the benefits of hands-on work experience within their field of study as early as the second semester of their sophomore year. In addition to the financial advantage of being able to work through college, a student can also make the personal contacts that are so important in professional experiences. Students can also gain practical experience and career development before graduation through participation in programs such as the Kaleidoscope of Careers, Career Advising, e-recruiting, and on-campus recruiting.

Project EXCEL is a special program that offers tutorial services, audiotapes of textbooks, and self-instructional materials for students with learning disabilities. Students learn skills that facilitate success in the college environment. Project EXCEL carries an additional fee for testing and for services while in the program. Interested students must apply for admission through Project EXCEL.

The Mount's Academic Performance Center is a centralized system of support for the enhancement of students' academic skills. It encompasses a Math Center, Peer Tutoring Program, COMPASS testing, makeup testing, Skills and Reading Center, Listening Lab, instructional software, courses in basic academic skills, and academic support for students with disabilities.

Off-Campus Programs

Opportunities are available to study abroad in Heidelberg, Germany, through the Congress/Bundestag program; in London, England, at Thames Valley College and through the Mount's affiliation with Huron University; and in Seville, Spain, through the Spanish American Institute.

Academic Facilities

The Mount's campus features modern buildings with state-of-the-art learning facilities. The Computer Learning Center offers all students access to IBM and Macintosh systems, supporting more than 500 different software packages. Students in the nursing department have access to on-campus laboratories and benefit from the department's relationship with nearby hospitals of outstanding quality and reputation.

The Harrington Center offers space for clubs and organizations and is home to the campus bookstore, food court, and entertainment center. Other recreation facilities include a running track, racquetball courts, a fitness center, a 2,000-seat gymnasium, and an athletic training center. A beautiful College theater seats more than 1,000 people.

Costs

For the 2003–04 academic year, tuition was $16,000 and room and board were $5990 (based on a semiprivate room and the fifteen-meals-per-week plan, with $150 flex dollars to use at the food court). The College offers private and semiprivate housing accommodations and a variety of meal plans. There are a $70 activities fee per semester and a technology fee of $450 per semester, which provides students with a wireless laptop/learning environment to use during their years at the Mount. The cost of books varies depending on course load and major.

Financial Aid

The College of Mount St. Joseph assists as many students as possible who require financial aid. About 94 percent of full-time undergraduate students receive some form of assistance, usually as federal, state, or College grants; work-study awards; and loans. In addition, part-time employment may be available in the metropolitan area for those students with transportation. The Mount offers academic scholarship programs in the areas of scholastic achievement and leadership based on merit or on a combination of merit and need.

Students who wish to apply for financial aid must complete, by April 15, the Free Application for Federal Student Aid (FAFSA). Most scholarships are awarded on a rolling basis. Interested students should inquire as early in their senior year as possible.

Faculty

Because the Mount is a small liberal arts college, the faculty's focus is on teaching. Many faculty members have been recognized regionally and nationally for their research and expertise outside the classroom as well as for their contributions as teachers, particularly in the fields of art, science, math, sociology, and education. The student-faculty ratio of 15:1 encourages personal interaction between students and professors.

Student Government

All matriculated students at the College of Mount St. Joseph are members of the Student Government Association (SGA). The SGA represents and serves as the voice of the entire student body. It strives to help students understand their rights, privileges, and responsibilities and to maintain effective communication among the students, faculty and staff members, and administration.

One of the functions of the SGA is that of appointing students to serve on various College committees to represent the common values of the Mount students and to participate in College government. The SGA works toward avoiding conflict by assisting with developing campus policies that directly affect student life.

The SGA supports and monitors all student club activities and functions through the Fiscal Committee. There are many opportunities for interested students to participate in SGA-sponsored programs and activities, including Campus Fair, movies, dances, fund-raising events, and community service activities.

A Student Affairs staff member serves as the adviser to the SGA.

Admission Requirements

Admission decisions are based on high school course selection, ACT or SAT scores, class rank, and grade point average. The College requires 4 units of English, 2 of math (algebra and geometry), 2 of social studies, 2 of science, 2 of foreign language, and 1 of fine arts. Two electives from the areas listed above may be substituted for foreign language. Students are encouraged to submit recommendation letters and personal essays.

Application and Information

Decisions on offers of admission are generally made within two weeks of the date the file is complete. The application fee is $25; the Project EXCEL fee is $60. Application fees are nonrefundable and do not apply toward tuition. Students who want to know more about the Mount may arrange a visit by contacting the Office of Admission. In addition to scheduling individual appointments, the College holds Get Acquainted Days throughout the year, giving students the opportunity to visit the campus, explore academic programs, and take a tour.

Office of Admission
College of Mount St. Joseph
5701 Delhi Road
Cincinnati, Ohio 45233-1672
Telephone: 513-244-4531
          800-654-9314 (toll-free)
World Wide Web: http://www.msj.edu/admissions

The College of Mount St. Joseph provides a liberal arts and professional education that integrates life and learning while embracing excellence, respect, diversity, and service.

THE COLLEGE OF WOOSTER
WOOSTER, OHIO

The College

One of the first coeducational colleges in the country, the College of Wooster was founded in 1866 by Presbyterians who wanted to do "their proper part in the great work of educating those who are to mold society and give shape to all its institutions." Today it is a fully independent, privately endowed liberal arts college with a rich tradition of academic excellence. That tradition defines student life at Wooster, beginning with the First-Year Seminar in Critical Inquiry and culminating in the Independent Study program.

The current enrollment is about 1,800 men and women. Almost all students live on campus, selecting from a variety of housing options. These include Babcock International House for students interested in international studies, Andrews Hall for students with an interest in the humanities and sciences, and Kenarden Lodge, a modern facility arranged in living suites. There are also thirty-three houses on the edge of campus, many of which serve as living-learning centers for those in community service and volunteer programs.

Wooster's 240-acre campus has forty major buildings. With its distinctive arch, Kauke Hall is instantly recognizable as an icon for Wooster. Kauke is home to many academic departments, classrooms, and faculty offices. Wooster has excellent facilities for physical education, including a fully equipped fitness center, a nine-hole golf course, an all-weather track, and eight hard-surfaced tennis courts. Wooster's newest structure, Bornhuetter Residence Hall, an $8.9-million structure, will house 185 students beginning in fall 2004. The 46,650-square-foot, four-story building is composed of two separate residential wings with double-loaded corridors scaled to house 21–31 students each. Student rooms are double occupancy with adjustable furniture, high-speed data lines for each occupant, and outlets for telephone and cable television. Three new buildings opened in 2002, beginning in March with the $2-million, 10,000-square-foot Longbrake Student Wellness Center. The Student Wellness Center is a state-of-the-art student facility that includes six treatment rooms, eight in-patient beds, and a pharmacy. The Gault Center for Admissions opened in June 2002, and the $8-million, 44,000-square-foot Burton D. Morgan Hall opened in fall 2002. Morgan Hall houses the Departments of Economics (including Business Economics), Psychology, and Education, and is the future home of the College's Information Technology Center. Other facilities include Severance Chemistry Building; Scheide Music Center; the Flo K. Gault Library for Independent Study, which adjoins the Andrews Library; the Ebert Art Center, which contains an art gallery and substantial facilities for studio art and art history; and the Timken Science Library.

Most of the social life at Wooster originates from Lowry Center, the student union. The Student Activities Board organizes dances, concerts, films, off-campus outings, and many other activities. The music and theater departments and local social clubs also contribute to the activities on campus. The student entertainment center (The Underground) hosts live bands, comedians, dance parties, and folksingers, and sometimes serves as a dinner theater.

Location

The College is located in Wooster, Ohio, a city of approximately 26,000. Wooster is 55 miles south of Cleveland and 30 miles west of Akron. An unusually close relationship exists between the College and the community. College-community activities include the Wooster Symphony, a college-community theatrical production, and a variety of volunteer and internship experiences.

Majors and Degrees

The College of Wooster offers the degrees of Bachelor of Arts, Bachelor of Music, and Bachelor of Music Education. A student may choose from thirty-seven possible majors, including seven interdepartmental majors: anthropology, archaeology, art history, art/studio, biochemistry and molecular biology, biology, black studies, business economics, chemical physics, chemistry, classical studies, communication sciences and disorders, communication studies, comparative literature, computer science, cultural area studies, economics, English, French, geology, German, history, international relations, mathematics, music, philosophy, physics, political science, psychology, religious studies, Russian studies, sociology, Spanish, theater, theater/dance, urban studies, and women's studies. In addition, minors are available in many of the areas above as well as physical education. Students also have the option of designing their own major, contingent upon the approval of the Upperclass Programs Committee. The Department of Education offers all courses necessary for either elementary or secondary teaching licensure.

Wooster offers combined-degree opportunities in cooperation with other institutions; such programs lead to either two bachelor's degrees (one from each institution) or a bachelor's from Wooster and a master's from the cooperating institution. Specific programs are in operation with Columbia University (law), Dartmouth College (business administration), the University of Michigan (economics, mathematics, and physics), Duke University (forestry and environmental management), Washington University (engineering), and Case Western Reserve University (dentistry, engineering, nursing, and social work).

Academic Programs

Wooster's academic program is designed to provide a liberal education that prepares undergraduates for a lifetime of inquiry, discovery, and responsible citizenship. In fall 2001, Wooster instituted a curriculum that focuses directly on these curricular goals. To be eligible for a Bachelor of Arts degree, a student must successfully complete thirty-two courses, including a First-Year Seminar in Critical Inquiry and three courses of Independent Study (IS). IS, as it is universally known on campus, gives each Wooster senior the opportunity to create an original research project, written scholarly work, exhibit of artwork or performance in a yearlong project, supported one-on-one by a faculty mentor. An overall grade point average of at least 2.0 (on a 4.0 scale) is required for graduation. Students may receive credit for work done at other colleges and for scores of 4 or better on the Advanced Placement tests offered by the College Board. Courses are graded A–D or No Credit unless the student exercises an option to take certain courses on a Satisfactory/No Credit basis.

Off-Campus Programs

Students who wish to enrich their undergraduate experience by overseas study may choose from a variety of fully accredited programs. Wooster sponsors a number of off-campus programs in the United States and abroad, and, as a member of the Great Lakes Colleges Association, offers off-campus study opportunities in thirteen countries on four continents. There are also programs available through the Institute of European Studies in seven university centers throughout Europe.

A variety of off-campus opportunities within the United States provide both academic and internship experiences. The Washington Semester and the Semester at the United Nations offer extensive possibilities in national and international government. Urban studies centers in Birmingham, Philadelphia, Portland, St. Louis, and San Diego provide many different experiential options. There is also a fine-arts semester in New York City. Other internship possibilities exist in business, the humanities, the natural sciences, and psychology.

Academic Facilities

The College libraries consist of the Andrews Library, the adjacent Flo K. Gault Library for Independent Study, and the nearby Timken Science Library in Frick Hall. Together, the libraries contain more than 1 million books, periodicals, microforms, electronic journals, videotapes, and audio recordings. As a member of CONSORT and OhioLINK, the libraries can provide almost any book from Ohio's academic libraries within two to three days. The libraries subscribe to a wide variety of electronic databases and to some 5,000 periodicals in electronic form, all available campuswide via the computing network. The libraries house more than 300 study carrels, each of which is equipped with electrical and data connections.

Computing is an important part of Wooster's academic environment. All academic buildings and every residence hall room are connected in an interactive computing network. The Taylor Hall computer center houses fifty-two terminals for student use while the Wired Scot, a cyber café that opened in fall 2003, features twenty-two PC workstations with Internet access, two large plasma-screen TVs, and wireless Internet access throughout the building to anyone with wireless capability.

The College's science facilities contain the most up-to-date laboratory equipment, libraries, computer terminals, and instrumentation, including ultraviolet, visible, fluorescence, and infrared spectrometers; a scanning electron microscope; an atomic force microscope; a nuclear magnetic resonance spectrometer; a mass spectrometer; an X-ray diffractometer; and various chromatographs.

Wooster's Learning Center provides academic support for students, and priority is given to students with identified learning disabilities. Adult tutors work with individual students on time management, organization skills, and effective study strategies. Wooster's Writing Center provides writing assistance through one-to-one tutorial sessions and group workshops covering all aspects of the writing process.

The Freedlander Theatre complex contains excellent technical equipment and a separate theater for students' experimental productions. The speech facility itself houses a radio station and a speech and hearing clinic that also serves the community.

The Scheide Music Center, a 35,000-square-foot complex, contains five classrooms, eleven teaching studios, twenty-three soundproof practice rooms, a music library, and a listening lab. The Timken Rehearsal Hall and the acoustically balanced Gault Recital Hall are "tunable" so that the halls can be rendered "live" to greater or lesser degrees.

The Ebert Art Center has expansive space for studio art and art history. The building includes classrooms, individual studios for senior studio art majors, and the Sussel Art Gallery.

Costs

The comprehensive fee (room, board, tuition, and fees) for 2004–05 is $33,200.

Financial Aid

Almost all financial assistance is awarded on the basis of need, as determined by the Free Application for Federal Student Aid (FAFSA). Aid is allocated when students are admitted to the College. Financial assistance information and forms should be requested at the time of application. Applications for aid should be submitted by February 15.

The College of Wooster believes in recognizing individual talent and hard work. Thus, Wooster offers merit-based scholarships that range from $2000 to $18,000 in a number of academic, leadership, and performance areas. All scholarship awards are applicable toward tuition only and are renewable for four years. Each year, the College awards about $16.5 million in competitive scholarship funds to the nations' top students. Students should call the Office of Admissions to request detailed information about scholarship opportunities.

Faculty

The faculty members and administration, 97 percent of whom (excluding those in performance areas) hold a doctoral degree or terminal degree in their field, are dedicated to meeting the educational needs of individual students; they strive to help them realize their inherent potential. The student-faculty ratio is 12:1.

Student Government

The Campus Council, which consists of representatives from the student body, faculty, and administration, is the main legislative body in the areas of student life and cocurricular affairs. The Student Government Association, the Black Students Association, and the International Student Association also contribute to policymaking at Wooster. Students may attend open meetings of the faculty and are represented on virtually all faculty committees; they may also send representatives to observe meetings of the Board of Trustees.

Admission Requirements

A candidate for admission to the College should have earned a minimum of 16 academic units in high school, with emphases in English, foreign language, mathematics, natural science, and social studies. The student must present satisfactory scores on either the SAT I or the ACT. No College Board Subject Test scores are required.

The deadline for regular admission is February 15. Students are notified of the decision by April 1 and must reply by May 1. Early Decision I applicants must apply by December 1 and are notified on December 15. Early Decision II candidates must apply by January 15 and are notified by February 1. Deferred admission is available, as is admission at the end of the junior year of high school. Students are encouraged to visit the campus and have a personal interview.

The College of Wooster does not discriminate on the basis of age, sex, race, creed, national origin, handicap, sexual orientation, or political affiliation in the admission of students or in their participation in College educational programs, activities, financial aid, or employment.

Application and Information

Dean of Admissions
The College of Wooster
Wooster, Ohio 44691
Telephone: 330-263-2000 Ext. 2270 or 2322
        800-877-9905 (toll-free)
Fax: 330-263-2621
E-mail: admissions@wooster.edu
World Wide Web: http://www.wooster.edu

COLUMBIA COLLEGE
COLUMBIA, MISSOURI

COLUMBIA
COLLEGE

The College

Columbia College is a four-year, private, coeducational college offering master's, bachelor's, and associate degrees. It was founded in 1851 as Christian College and is affiliated with the Disciples of Christ. The institution is accredited by the North Central Association of Colleges and Schools. Today, 920 students representing fifteen states and twenty-five other countries attend the College.

The College's 29-acre wireless campus, located four blocks from the downtown area of Columbia, Missouri, has twenty buildings, ranging from Williams Hall, constructed in 1851, through administration and classroom buildings erected in the early 1900s, to more modern residence halls and classroom facilities completed in the 1960s and 1970s. A gymnasium was erected in 1988, the Stafford Library was erected in 1989, and the Cultural Arts Center was remodeled in 1992. Brown Hall, the arts and humanities building, became operational in 1995. A new contemporary Student Commons is scheduled to open in August 2004.

Three spacious residence halls provide housing for students who live on campus. Miller Hall and Banks Hall offer coeducational housing. Banks Hall features a popular Wellness Floor. Every residence hall provides a computer lab, cooking and laundry facilities, individual phone lines, and cable TV and Internet access. Student academic programmers enhance the academic environment within the residence hall system through specialized programming, peer academic counseling, and research and referral information sharing. Every student is entitled to have an automobile, motorcycle, or bicycle on campus. Student service facilities include a Student Center, a central dining facility, a health center, a counseling center, and a career planning and placement center.

Recreational and athletic opportunities are furnished through the College's Southwell Complex, a remodeled fitness center, a gymnasium, a softball field, a soccer field, tennis courts, and also a large back-campus area for intramural sports programs, which are quite popular. The College is a member of the NAIA Division I and the American Midwest Conference, and its teams compete in men's basketball and soccer and women's basketball, softball, and volleyball.

Graduate degrees are available in business, criminal justice, and teaching.

Location

Columbia, Missouri (population 75,000 plus 25,000 college students), is situated halfway between St. Louis and Kansas City. Five hospitals, a major mental health center, social service agencies of all kinds, a large network of parks, and a well-educated populace accustomed to a rich cultural life make Columbia a pleasant place to live, work, and study. *Money* magazine has often ranked it as one of the top twenty cities in the nation.

Majors and Degrees

Columbia College awards the Bachelor of Arts and Bachelor of Science degrees with majors in accounting, art, biology, business administration, chemistry, computer information systems, computer science, criminal justice administration, English, financial services, forensic science, general studies, history, interdisciplinary studies, international business, management, marketing, mathematics, natural sciences, political science, psychology, social work, and sociology. Preprofessional programs in dentistry, law, medicine, and veterinary science are available. The BEACON and DAYSTAR are new, innovative programs in teacher education. The College also confers the Bachelor of Fine Arts and Bachelor of Social Work degrees. Students can choose minors in art history, ethics/philosophy/ religion, music, geology, physics, Spanish, and studio art. Columbia College also awards the associate degree with majors in business administration, computer information systems, criminal justice administration, and fire service administration.

Academic Programs

The academic curriculum supports the mission of the College to provide career degree programs based on a solid background in the liberal arts and sciences. Each of the degree programs can include an internship, enabling students to obtain practical experience in addition to the more theoretical classroom instruction.

The College follows a two-semester plan with an eight-week summer session. Each degree program sets its own sequence of requirements. To be eligible for graduation, students pursuing an associate degree must complete 60 semester hours with a cumulative grade point average of 2.0 (C) or better. Each associate degree program has a general education component. To receive a bachelor's degree, students must complete 120 semester hours of credit with a cumulative grade point average of 2.0 (C) or better. Students pursuing a baccalaureate degree must complete a series of general education courses, including 6 semester hours of English composition and an ethics course, and earn at least 39 semester hours of credit in junior- or senior-level courses.

Off-Campus Programs

Full-time Columbia College students may enroll, at no extra cost, in courses at two neighboring institutions through a cooperative arrangement. ROTC programs (all branches) are available through this arrangement as well. Study-abroad opportunities are also offered.

Academic Facilities

Stafford Library is fully automated and contains more than 70,000 volumes, 500 periodicals, 6,000 audiovisual materials, and innumerable electronic resources. Students also have access to materials through the College's interlibrary loan and exchange program with neighboring institutions and the statewide electronic MOBIUS system.

An art and humanities facility, completed in 1995, provides resources for the art degree programs and a public gallery for promoting cultural growth. The College has a large computer and Internet laboratory; science and psychology lab facilities; an educational curriculum/materials library; the Writing Center and Math Center, which have a variety of individual assistance and tutorial programs; and major classroom buildings for traditional instruction as well as numerous multimedia classrooms.

Costs

For 2003–04, student fees included $11,362 for tuition and $4777 for room and board. Students should plan to spend about $400 per semester for books, supplies, and incidentals. *The Student Guide to America's Best College Scholarships* has rated Columbia College as one of the top colleges with the lowest costs.

Financial Aid

Most Columbia College students receive some type of financial assistance. The College awards to students more than $4 million annually in federal, state, and institutional funds. Financial aid packages may include need-based and merit-based scholarships, grants, loans, and work-study opportunities in a variety of combinations. The most prestigious awards are the Columbia College Scholarship (full tuition, room, and board) and the Presidential Scholarship (full tuition). Five each are awarded annually. Many other competitive scholarships are available. Some awards and scholarships are automatic if certain criteria are met. Talent awards in athletics, art, and music are also available. Half-tuition scholarships are awarded automatically to upperclassmen who earn a 3.4 grade point average (GPA) with 30 hours earned annually. Renewal requires a 3.2 GPA with 24 Columbia College hours earned.

To be considered for financial assistance, students must complete the Free Application for Federal Student Aid (FAFSA) and submit the Columbia College financial assistance application.

Faculty

Excellence in teaching has been a common goal throughout the history of the College. Teaching is the faculty's primary responsibility. The faculty-student ratio of 1:14 fosters personal attention and animated discussion in the classroom. Faculty members also serve as advisers to students. The relatively small size of the student body promotes excellent communication and rapport among students and faculty members. Nearly 80 percent of the faculty members have terminal degrees.

Student Government

All students at Columbia College are members of the Student Government Association (SGA). The SGA Cabinet, elected from this body, serves as a formal liaison between students and the administration. One branch of SGA, the Student Activities Commission, plans and organizes social activities on campus, from programs of interest to specialized groups to campuswide recreational activities. Each residence hall has representation to SGA through its Hall Council, which is composed of elected students.

Admission Requirements

Columbia College evaluates each applicant individually on the basis of the total application, including academic records, ACT/SAT scores, activities, references, goals, and recommendations of high school counselors. A high school diploma or equivalent certification is required for admission. English and math tests are given on campus to appropriately place students. English and math ACT/SAT subscores are also used for placement. Admission requirements at Columbia College are moderately selective.

Transfer students must submit transcripts of all college work attempted and may need to submit high school academic transcripts. There are no restrictions on the number of transfer students accepted each semester.

Application and Information

Descriptive brochures and application forms are available from the Office of Admissions. A campus visit is highly recommended. The completed application should be returned along with a $25 nonrefundable application fee. There is no fee if the application is submitted before January 1 for the fall semester. Notification of the admission decision is made on a rolling basis following the fulfillment of all admission requirements.

For more information and application materials, students should contact:

Director of Admissions
Columbia College
1001 Rogers Street
Columbia, Missouri 65216
Telephone: 573-875-7352
          800-231-2391 (toll-free in the U.S. and
          Canada)
E-mail: admissions@ccis.edu
World Wide Web: http://www.ccis.edu

Rogers Gates at the entrance of the historic Columbia College campus.

COLUMBIA COLLEGE CHICAGO
CHICAGO, ILLINOIS

The College

Columbia College was established during the World's Columbian Exposition of 1893. The College's original emphasis on communication arts has expanded to include media arts, applied and fine arts, theatrical and performing arts, and management and marketing arts. Today, Columbia College Chicago is the nation's premier visual, performing, and media arts college. The foundation of a Columbia education continues to include small class sizes that ensure close interaction with a faculty of working professionals, abundant internship opportunities with major employers in the Chicago marketplace, and outstanding professional facilities that foster learning by doing. All students are encouraged to begin course work in their chosen fields during their freshman year, allowing them four full years in which to master their craft and build professional portfolios, audition tapes, resumes, and clip books. The College provides a strong liberal arts background for the developing artist or communicator and supports student employment goals through a full range of career services.

Columbia's enrollment of more than 9,250 students is drawn from Chicago and its suburbs, the Midwest, across the United States, and more than forty-five other countries. The student body is almost equally divided between men and women. Creative students who enjoy a supportive but challenging environment thrive at Columbia.

Columbia College Chicago's residence halls extend the supportive philosophy of the College. There are a wide variety of available housing options, all with access to computer and study rooms, drawing and painting studio space, a fitness room, and a laundry room. Apartments, suites, and rooms are fully furnished. All facilities are conveniently located steps away from the main campus buildings and close to public transportation, all in the heart of downtown Chicago. Students have access to a wide range of services, including the student health center, counseling, and a variety of local and academic events. Columbia College students are immersed in a creative environment both in and out of the classroom.

Outside the classroom, students participate in activities that include the College's award-winning student newspaper, radio station, electronic newsletter, two student magazines, cable television soap opera, three theaters, dance center, photography and art museums, and film and video festival. Many of the fifty student clubs on campus are linked to an academic discipline and offer opportunities to expand social and professional networking experiences. The Hermann D. Conaway Multicultural Center and the Myron Hokin Center provide gallery/café environments in which students can relax or study between classes. These centers feature a variety of activities, including art exhibits, film screenings, lectures, and live performances of music, comedy, readings, or dance. The 11th Street and Glass Curtain Galleries and the Narrative Arts Center provide additional exhibition spaces for students, faculty members, and others.

At the graduate level, Columbia awards the Master of Arts (M.A.) in arts, entertainment, and media management; creative writing and writing instruction; dance/movement therapy; interdisciplinary arts; journalism; photography; photography–museum studies; and writing instruction. The College awards the Master of Fine Arts (M.F.A.) in architectural studies; creative writing; creative writing and writing instruction; film and video; interdisciplinary book and paper arts; interior architecture; and photography. The Master of Arts in Teaching (M.A.T.) is also offered in elementary education (K–9), interdisciplinary arts education (K–12), and urban teaching.

Location

Columbia's campus is set in Chicago's dynamic South Loop neighborhood, across from Grant Park and Lake Michigan. Close to the Art Institute, Navy Pier, the Adler Planetarium, the Field Museum, the Chicago Symphony, and several other colleges and universities, Columbia's faculty members and students utilize the city of Chicago as a social, educational, and professional resource. Convenient public transportation makes all cultural and educational opportunities easily accessible.

Majors and Degrees

Columbia College grants the Bachelor of Arts (B.A.) and the Bachelor of Fine Arts (B.F.A.) degrees and the Bachelor of Music (B.M.) degree in composition. The School of Fine and Performing Arts offers majors in art and design (advertising art direction, fashion design, fine arts, graphic design, illustration, interior architecture, and product design); arts, entertainment, and media management (arts entrepreneurship and small business, fashion/retail, media, music business, performing arts, and visual arts); dance (choreography, musical theater performance, and teaching); fiction writing; music (contemporary music, including composition, instrumental performance, and vocal performance, and jazz studies, including instrumental and vocal); photography; and theater (acting, directing, playwriting, technical theater, and theater design). The School of Media Arts offers majors in academic computing (digital media technology), audio arts and acoustics (recording, sound contracting, sound reinforcement, and sound technology), film and video (alternative forms, audio, cinematography, computer animation, critical studies, directing, documentary, editing, producing, screenwriting, and traditional animation), interactive multimedia (animation, graphic design, photography, programming, project management, sound design, video, and writing), interdisciplinary (self-designed major), journalism (broadcast, magazine program, news reporting and writing, radio broadcast, and reporting on health, science, and the environment), marketing communication (advertising, creative sports marketing, marketing, and public relations), radio (business and talent/production), and television (interactive, postproduction/effects, production/directing, and writing/producing). The School of Liberal Arts and Sciences offers majors in American Sign Language–English interpretation, early childhood education (center director, infant–toddler studies, language and culture, performing arts, and visual arts), English (poetry), and liberal education (cultural studies).

Academic Programs

Columbia supports creative and integrated approaches to education and encourages interdisciplinary study. The B.A. degree is awarded to students who successfully complete 120 semester hours, and the B.F.A. degree is awarded to students who successfully complete 128 semester hours of study in designated programs. Of the required hours, 48 are distributed among courses in the humanities and literature, science and mathematics, English composition, oral communications, social sciences, and computer applications.

The College continues to expand its extensive internship program. Columbia's location allows students to intern with major employers in Chicago. Chicago provides professional settings, classrooms, and internship opportunities for Columbia students.

The Career Center for Arts and Media offers a full range of services designed to help students launch their careers. Services include career counseling; seminars on interviewing, resume writing, and job-search strategies; internships; placement assistance; job fairs; and alumni activities and assistance.

Off-Campus Programs

Columbia has an affiliation agreement with the American Institute for Foreign Study, which enables students to participate in study-abroad programs in numerous countries. Columbia also sponsors and participates in a variety of its own study-abroad programs. These programs include trips to Moscow and Prague. Summer programs are also offered with Dartington College in Dartington, England; the Santa Reparata International School of Art in Florence, Italy; and the University of Guadalajara in Mexico. Open to all Columbia students, the Semester in Los Angeles program is a five-week immersion program in which the student maintains full-time status while gaining invaluable real-world experience. Located in Bungalow 25 on the CBS Studio Lot in Culver City, Columbia is the only institution of higher learning permanently located on a studio lot. Students are given Lot ID badges and enter the gates of the lot everyday just like working producers, directors, stars, and craft personnel.

Academic Facilities

Columbia College consists of thirteen campus buildings located primarily in the historic South Loop neighborhood of downtown Chicago. Advanced facilities for radio, television, art, computer graphics, photography, interactive multimedia, fashion design, and film are state-of-the-industry and include professionally equipped color and black-and-white darkrooms, digital imaging computer facilities, photography and film stages, film and video editing suites, and studios for painting, drawing, and 3-D design. The campus also includes the Museum of Contemporary Photography, one of only a few such facilities in the United States, and the Audio Technology Center, a recording production and research facility. In addition, Columbia has extensive computer facilities used by basic computer classes as well as dedicated computer facilities utilized by the departments. The centers for dance, music, and theater are separate but conveniently located and are designed for their specific performance needs, including individual and group rehearsal and specialized performance spaces.

The College's 200,000-volume library and instructional service center provides comprehensive information and study facilities. Reading/study rooms and special audiovisual equipment are available for use in individual projects and research. As a member of a statewide online computer catalog and resource-sharing network, Columbia's library provides students with access to the resources of forty-five academic institutions in Illinois, effectively creating an information base of several million volumes. The library also houses special collections, such as the George S. Lurie Memorial collection of books and resource materials on art, photography, and film; the Black Music Resource Center of books and sound recordings; the Screenwriters' Collection of film and television manuscripts; the History of Photography microfilm collection of books and periodicals; and a nonprint collection of 100,000 slides and more than 7,300 videotapes and films. The latest addition to the library is the Albert P. Weisman Center for the Study of Contemporary Issues in Chicago Journalism. The center includes a print and audiovisual collection and a learning center that explores the development of Chicago's political and social history.

Costs

For the 2003–04 academic year, full tuition (12 to 16 credit hours) averaged $7440 per each fifteen-week semester, or $14,880 per year. Part-time tuition (up to 11 credit hours) was $515 per credit hour. Summer school tuition was $400 per credit hour. Some courses require additional service or laboratory fees. Required nonrefundable fees charged each semester include the registration fee, $50; the student activity fee, $50 ($25 for part-time students); the U-Pass, $70 (for unlimited access to the public transportation system); and a health center fee, $25 ($15 for part-time students). There is also a one-time $30 library deposit that is refunded when the student leaves the College.

Financial Aid

Columbia College makes every effort to help students obtain financial assistance, including grants, on-campus work, and loans. The Office of Student Financial Services administers federal and state grant and loan programs. The College also provides information for students seeking part-time employment both on- and off-campus. On-campus jobs are available in technical, clerical, secretarial, and food service areas. Columbia offers institution-based scholarships, such as Presidential Scholarships for freshmen,

scholarships for transfer students, academic excellence awards, leadership awards, and housing grants. The Fischetti Scholarships support the efforts of outstanding Columbia journalism students, and the Weisman Scholarships support special communication-related projects. Appropriate scholarship and applications forms for financial aid are available through the Office of Undergraduate Admissions.

Faculty

Many of Columbia's 1,267 full- and part-time faculty members are working professionals (artists, writers, filmmakers, dancers, etc.) with national reputations. The College is constantly seeking individuals who are both gifted teachers and talented professionals. Many faculty members work nearby in the disciplines in which they teach and share practical expertise with students in informal workshop settings and in the classroom. Interaction with faculty members who are practicing professionals provides students with invaluable access to the latest information in their fields. Students also begin developing their own professional network as faculty members share contacts and information on how to break into the market.

Student Government

Through the Student Government Association (SGA) and the Student Organization Council (SOC), students are able to address college-wide and departmental issues and sponsor services and activities. SGA and SOC work closely with the Office of Student Affairs and serve as liaisons to the administration and departments. The fifty campus clubs and organizations reflect the interests and the diversity of Columbia's student body. Film screenings, student-produced television shows, dance recitals, poetry readings, plays, campus radio, music concerts, and a national award-winning newspaper are just some of the campus events and activities available to students.

Admission Requirements

Columbia College invites applications from all students with creative ability in or inclination to the arts, media, and communication disciplines in which the College specializes. To apply for admissions, students must submit high school transcripts, college transcripts (if applicable), a letter of recommendation, a personal essay, and a $25 application fee. ACT Assessment or SAT I scores are not required but are strongly encouraged. Graduation from high school or an earned GED is required prior to enrollment. Freshmen applicants whose application materials suggest they are likely to be underprepared to meet the College's standards are required to successfully complete the Bridge Program to be admitted to the College. Columbia has a liberal transfer policy.

Application and Information

Students are strongly advised to apply early. The priority date is July 1 for the fall semester, December 1 for the spring semester, and May 1 for the summer term. Applicants are notified within two to four weeks after the College receives all the required information and documents. Students who want to live in campus housing are strongly advised to apply early. Housing assignments are offered on a first-come, first-served basis until full occupancy is achieved.

All students are invited to tour the College and meet with an admissions counselor. To arrange for a tour and an appointment with an admissions counselor, students should call the telephone number below.

For more information, students should contact:

Office of Undergraduate Admissions
Columbia College Chicago
600 South Michigan Avenue
Chicago, Illinois 60605
Telephone: 312-344-7130
Fax: 312-344-8024
E-mail: admissions@colum.edu
World Wide Web: http://www.colum.edu

CORNELL COLLEGE
MOUNT VERNON, IOWA

The College

Cornell College is unique in U.S. higher education in that it offers the combination of liberal arts study within the One-Course-At-A-Time framework, an active residential community, an emphasis on service and leadership, and an ideal, wooded-hilltop setting that is one of only two campuses listed on the National Register of Historic Places.

Cornell College is a leader in educational innovation. A private, independent college founded in 1853, Cornell employs the One-Course-At-A-Time academic calendar; it is one of only four colleges in the United States to implement this advancement in postsecondary teaching and learning. Cornell is historically a place of "firsts": the first coeducational college west of the Mississippi, the first college in Iowa to grant a baccalaureate degree to a woman, the first college in the United States to confer upon a woman a full professorship with the same salary received by the male professors, and the first college in the nation to have its entire campus listed on the National Register of Historic Places. The College was among the first schools in the nation to offer its students a choice of degree programs, establish a teacher-education program, and introduce sociology into its curriculum. Cornell offers a strong leadership-training program and actively promotes community service opportunities. Nearly 70 percent of the student body take part in volunteer projects.

In 2003–04, 1,100 students from forty states and eleven other countries were enrolled at this residential college, which is situated atop a high hill overlooking the Cedar River valley. Centered on a pedestrian mall, the campus covers 129 acres and has more than forty buildings, including nine residence halls. A student center, the Commons, houses central dining rooms, a bookstore, meeting rooms, and recreation rooms. Cornell's sports and recreation center has facilities for wellness and fitness programs as well as year-round recreation and athletics space for practice and play. Cornell has 25 NCAA Postgraduate Scholars, ranking ninth in the nation among NCAA Division III schools. It competes in the Iowa Intercollegiate Athletic Conference in nineteen sports. Nearly 60 percent of students participate in sixty-six intramural sports. More than 100 clubs and organizations offer a wide range of activities, from participation in the KRNL-FM radio station to Habitat for Humanity to Greek social groups.

Location

Mount Vernon provides the best of both worlds—a classically beautiful campus in a small college town minutes from Cedar Rapids and Iowa City. These two metropolitan areas contain three additional colleges and universities and 350,000 people. Chicago, St. Louis, and Minneapolis can be reached in about 5 hours by automobile or in less than an hour by air from Cedar Rapids. Palisades–Kepler State Park, site of the annual Pal Day picnic, is 5 miles away. Cornell is 15 minutes from Cedar Rapids (airport, movies, malls) and 20 minutes from Iowa City and Hancher Auditorium, a regular concert and theater tour stop.

Majors and Degrees

Cornell College awards the Bachelor of Arts, Bachelor of Music, Bachelor of Philosophy, and Bachelor of Special Studies degrees. Majors are offered in art, biochemistry and molecular biology, biology, chemistry, classical studies, computer science, economics and business, elementary and secondary education, English, environmental studies, French, geology, German, history, international business, international relations, Latin American studies, mathematics, medieval and Renaissance studies, music education (general, instrumental, and vocal), music performance,

philosophy, physical education, physics, politics, psychology, religion, Russian, Russian studies, sociology, sociology and anthropology, Spanish, theater, theater and speech, and women's studies. Prelaw and premedicine programs are available, as are programs to prepare for graduate study in social work/human services and theology. Students may design their own interdisciplinary majors.

Combined-degree programs include a 3-2 program in forestry and environmental management offered in cooperation with Duke University, 3-2 programs in engineering and occupational therapy, and a 3-4 program in architecture with Washington University in St. Louis. The College also offers cooperative professional programs in nursing and allied health sciences with Rush University in Chicago and in medical technology with St. Luke's Hospital in Cedar Rapids. For students interested in dentistry, the University of Iowa College of Dentistry offers early acceptance into its program.

Academic Programs

Cornell encourages the creative structuring of students' educational experiences by offering a choice of four degree programs within the framework of a liberal education. Programs range from a traditional curriculum, with course requirements designed to ensure both breadth and depth, to a nontraditional combination of courses, independent studies, and internships that meet specific goals. For the Bachelor of Arts, Bachelor of Music, and Bachelor of Philosophy degree programs, faculty members set the goals. The Bachelor of Special Studies degree program permits students to define their own educational objectives and design a curriculum to meet those objectives.

To increase the quality and intensity of a Cornell education, the College's academic calendar incorporates the One-Course-At-A-Time schedule. Cornell divides the traditional September–May academic year into nine 3½-week terms. During each term, students concentrate on one course chosen from the more than sixty offered and take one final examination. After a four-day break, the next term begins. Students take eight terms per year, which leaves a ninth term free for internships, off-campus programs, international study, travel, independent study, rest and relaxation, or another course.

The College's emphasis on One-Course-At-A-Time enhances the quality of liberal education offered by allowing students increased contact with faculty members, no interference from competing courses, and greater efficiency of study. It also provides rapid feedback to students about their progress. The work assigned on one day is discussed on the following day, when the material is fresh for both students and instructor. In addition, the pressure of having to prepare for several courses and examinations at the same time is eliminated.

Another liberalizing feature of One-Course-At-A-Time is the possibility of having classes meet for periods longer or shorter than the typical 50-minute period. Professors may opt to divide the day into a series of short meetings, with work assignments given and completed from one session to the next. Laboratories are not necessarily limited to one afternoon. Faculty members are also able to take students on daylong field trips or teach their courses off campus, either in the United States or abroad.

Recent Cornell College graduates are studying public health at Harvard, architecture at Washington University (St. Louis), medicine at Iowa, law at Loyola Chicago, and studio art at the Art Institute of Chicago, to name a few. Among the employers of recent graduates are the Peace Corps; Houston Grand Opera; Cheetah Outreach; Visa International; Wells Fargo; AT&T Wireless;

U.S. Agency for International Development; New York Life Insurance; RBC Dain Rauscher, Inc.; and the Red Cross.

Off-Campus Programs

Student internship experiences can be central to understanding the realities, demands, and rewards of the workplace. Internships arranged within Cornell's One-Course-At-A-Time academic calendar are distinctly different from those arranged within a semester system. Students are able to become immersed in the experience every day for an entire month without the distractions of other course demands. Employers/mentors can count on a full-time commitment. This availability earns the attention of many nearby Cedar Rapids businesses and corporations that have offered opportunities from engineering to telecommunications, health-related fields, and art history. More distant internships have also been completed. The intensive internship learning experience makes Cornell students very appealing to prospective employers.

Through Cornell courses abroad and College-affiliated off-campus programs, students may work and travel in other countries and become acquainted with other cultures. Recent classes have journeyed to Mexico to observe local potters, to Montreal to study French, to Mexico and Spain to study Hispanic and Spanish social development, to London for courses in English literature and drama, and to Brazil and Guatemala to experience firsthand the politics of revolutionary movements.

Cornell students have done tropical field research in Costa Rica, studied Chinese culture in Hong Kong, worked with Hispanic communities in urban Chicago, and visited Europe's great cultural centers through off-campus programs administered by the Associated Colleges of the Midwest, of which Cornell is a charter member, and the School for International Training.

Academic Facilities

Cornell's entire campus has been designated a National Historic District, and its carefully restored nineteenth-century academic architecture is combined with contemporary facilities on a fully wired campus, with Internet access in every residence hall room. King Chapel is the historic landmark of the campus and has a 130-foot clock tower. Armstrong Hall and McWethy Hall have recently been renovated and expanded for art, music, and theater. Law Hall Technology Center opened in 2000, and Cole Library was renovated recently.

Costs

The cost for 2003–04 was $27,825, including tuition, fees, and room and board. Students generally enroll for eight courses a year, but, at no extra cost, they may accelerate or broaden their studies by taking nine courses.

Financial Aid

Cornell is committed to making higher education available for all students. The majority of Cornell's students receive financial assistance, and the average aid package exceeds $18,000. A competitive scholarship program recognizes students with strong academic records or special talents. Federal aid programs include Federal Pell Grants, Federal Supplemental Educational Opportunity Grants (FSEOG), and student loans. Federal Work-Study Program awards can provide additional income through part-time, on-campus employment. Additional funds are available through the Iowa Tuition Grant Program and State of Iowa Scholarships. Need is determined by the FAFSA. An early financial aid evaluation is available from the College upon request. Students applying for Cornell-funded scholarships must complete their scholarship applications by March 1.

Faculty

The College's faculty members are distinguished by their desire to teach undergraduates in a small, informal environment. Classes are capped at 25 students. Faculty members outside the department of physical education are required to have a Ph.D. or other terminal degree and are appointed, retained, and promoted based on their ability to teach. Many also distinguish themselves through scholarly and creative activities. The faculty-student ratio is 1:11, and only faculty members, not teaching assistants, teach classes.

Student Government

Student life at Cornell complements the academic program and provides a feeling of community at the College. Students participate actively in the governance of the College, serving on faculty-student committees, the Student Senate, the Residence Hall Council, and the Performing Arts and Activities Council.

Admission Requirements

The courses and degree programs offered at Cornell are intended for students who have been well prepared at the secondary school level, have obvious motivation and a desire to learn, and have the ability and potential to complete a carefully planned degree program and graduate from Cornell College. Admission to Cornell is selective. Applicants are judged on their high school records, test scores, interests, and achievements in such cocurricular activities as debate, student government, music, theater, athletics, and school publications as well as through personal recommendations and, in some cases, interviews. These are not exclusive criteria. Motivation, energy, and persistence are basic to Cornell. Students with the desire to succeed at Cornell and the motivation to benefit from a Cornell education may apply with confidence, knowing that these are important factors in the admission decision.

Application and Information

Cornell College follows a program of rolling admissions, and applicants are notified of admission decisions soon after their files are complete. Special consideration is given to students who apply by December 1. After March 1, applications are accepted on a space-available basis. To apply for admission to Cornell, prospective students should obtain an application form online or from the Office of Admissions, complete and file the application with Cornell with a $25 application fee, have their high school forward an official transcript and a school recommendation, and have their ACT or SAT I scores sent to Cornell. Cornell welcomes transfer students from accredited two- and four-year institutions.

Additional information, catalogs, application forms, and financial aid forms are available from:

Office of Admissions
Cornell College
600 First Street West
Mount Vernon, Iowa 52314-1098

Telephone: 319-895-4477
        800-747-1112 (toll-free)
E-mail: admissions@cornellcollege.edu
World Wide Web: http://www.cornellcollege.edu

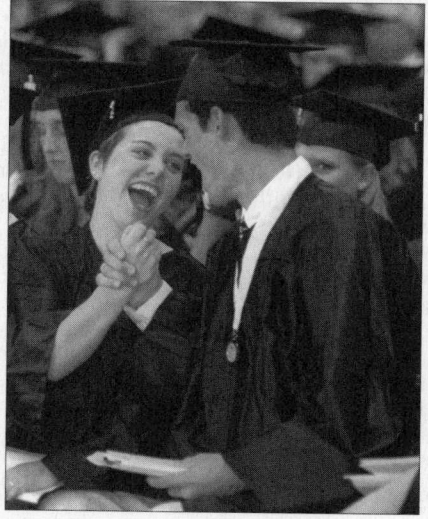

Graduation time at Cornell College.

CULVER–STOCKTON COLLEGE
CANTON, MISSOURI

The College

Culver-Stockton College (C-SC) was founded in 1853 as the first institution of higher learning west of the Mississippi River chartered expressly for coeducation. Affiliated with the Christian Church (Disciples of Christ), the College is personal (850 students) and provides a strong career-oriented education within a liberal arts setting. The College has one of the most attractive campuses in the Midwest and is home to one of the finest science center facilities in the region, which opened in fall 2002.

Principally residential in character, the College presents a full array of cocurricular activities, including course-related clubs and organizations, an active fraternity and sorority system, a fine intramural program, and a strong intercollegiate athletics program highlighted by baseball, basketball, football, golf, soccer, softball, and volleyball.

Culver-Stockton College has more than 9,000 living alumni, many of whom have achieved distinction in the arts, government, medicine, law, education, and other professional fields. With 150 years of history, Culver-Stockton College moves into the twenty-first century as one of the truly distinctive small liberal arts colleges of the Midwest.

Location

Canton, Missouri, a small Mississippi River town of 2,600, is surrounded by the rolling farmland of northeast Missouri. Culver-Stockton is statistically one of the safest college campuses in the United States. The College has close ties with Quincy, Illinois, a progressive, arts-oriented community of approximately 45,000, and is just north of historic Hannibal, the boyhood home of the famous American author Mark Twain. St. Louis is within a 2½-hour drive, and Chicago and Kansas City are close enough to be significant factors in the cultural life of the College. Culver-Stockton sits atop a hill from which three states can be seen and overlooks the city and the Mississippi River.

Majors and Degrees

Culver-Stockton offers Bachelor of Arts and Bachelor of Science degrees in twenty-four areas; the Bachelor of Fine Arts in art, arts management, and theater; the Bachelor of Music Education; and the Bachelor of Science in Nursing. Study areas include accounting, art, art education, arts management, athletic training, biology, business administration, chemistry, communication, criminal justice, early childhood development, elementary education, English, finance, history and political science, management, mathematics, medical technology, music, music education, nursing, physical education, psychology, recreation management, religion and philosophy, middle school education, secondary education, sociology, speech and theater education, and theater. Preprofessional programs are available in dentistry, engineering, law, medicine, ministry, optometry, pharmacy, physical therapy, and veterinary medicine. The College has cooperative arrangements with Washington University in occupational therapy. The College also has a pre-engineering program agreement with the University of Missouri–Rolla.

Academic Programs

The Culver-Stockton emphasis on career preparation is enhanced by the liberal arts. The development of student skills in writing, speaking, critical thinking, and problem solving is a critical element in the liberal arts emphasis. In addition, core courses in composition, speech, and Christian heritage combine with student choices from among five distribution areas to ensure a wide breadth of study. Students must complete 124 credit hours for the bachelor's degree. Major programs require from 28 to 62 credits. Double majors and minors are encouraged, adding further diversity and breadth to graduates' qualifications as they approach the job market.

The College has committed itself to academic distinction. Students are challenged to achieve their maximum potential in learned skills, breadth and depth of knowledge, and understanding their own values. Students are assigned an academic adviser who is prepared to assist students in achieving their educational goals. An individualized plan is developed and then updated each semester until graduation.

For able and highly motivated students, including freshmen, the College Honors Program provides the opportunity to participate in certain specially designated courses and events, culminating in an opportunity for independent study or research in an area of the student's special interest. The program is especially helpful for students planning for graduate programs.

Exploratory and professional internships are available in all majors and are viewed as an important part of the career selection process. Combined with an active career counseling and placement service that includes computerized interest and preference testing, on- and off-campus internships are a key element in the Culver-Stockton approach to preparing students for employment after graduation.

Work completed at other colleges and universities is transferable toward Culver-Stockton graduation requirements, and various testing procedures (e.g., CLEP, AP, CPEP) allow credit for equivalent knowledge or experience. Individualized learning options are plentiful; they range from individually negotiated independent study to specially designed degree programs.

The College operates on a two-semester calendar, with the first semester concluding before Christmas and the spring semester ending in early to mid-May. Summer sessions of varying lengths are available to students who wish to overcome deficiencies or accelerate their programs. All programs and classes are characterized by individual attention to the needs and interests of the student.

Off-Campus Programs

Culver-Stockton students have continuing opportunities for international experience through an agreement with the Central College at Pella (Iowa) International Program. In addition, off-campus and international study experiences, as well as individually designed internship opportunities, are available. Groups of students have traveled with Culver-Stockton faculty members to Eastern Europe, Western Europe, Canada, the Dominican Republic, and Israel. The Concert Choir and the Wind Ensemble tour each year.

Academic Facilities

Culver-Stockton is one of only a handful of colleges its size to put computers at the fingertips of every student. Computer network outlets are available for each student in every residence hall room and provide connections for students' personal computers for continuous access to the Internet, the World Wide Web, e-mail, the College network, laser printers, and library holdings. Culver-Stockton offers Pentium computer clusters in every residence hall and maintains three computer labs with Pentium workstations, the Windows operating system, and Microsoft Office as well as four specialized labs. Faculty members have integrated computers into the classroom in almost every field, using dedicated computer labs equipped with major-specific software.

The computerized Johann Memorial Library has a collection of 151,979 volumes and also presents comprehensive collections of periodicals, journals, and other materials in both hard copy and microform. Extensive interlibrary loan and electronic bibliographical search capabilities are available to both students and the faculty. C-SC students have access to more than 6 million volumes through the College's link to a statewide library database.

The Robert W. Brown Performing Arts Center and Mabee Art Gallery house professional-quality art and performance studios, computer laboratories, and three performance stages where 200 to nearly 1,000 guests can attend theater and music performances.

The new $8-million Science Center is home to the departments of biology, chemistry, physics, mathematics, and computer information systems. Students can benefit from its state-of-the-art labs and technology, classrooms with full multimedia capabilities, and facilities designed specifically for student research.

Costs

The 2004–05 school year costs at Culver-Stockton College were $13,200 for tuition, $6775 for room and board, and approximately $600 for books and supplies. With the exception of students who are married or living with parents, all students receiving college financial aid are required to take room and board contracts. Variable board plans are available for the dining hall and "Cats Pause," the student restaurant.

Financial Aid

Culver-Stockton College has one of the best student financial planning programs available among colleges of comparable size and purpose. The College participates in all federal and state financial aid programs, presenting aid packages that are based on need and merit. The latter include performance— theater, music, art, leadership, and athletics—awards as well as those based on academic achievement. The College accepts the Free Application for Federal Student Aid (FAFSA). Several Pillars for Excellence full tuition scholarships are awarded on a competitive basis each year, and other academic scholarships are available to applicants who meet certain GPA and ACT criteria. Other awards are available for students in various other circumstances. All scholarships are renewable with minimum requirements. Application procedures are detailed in all admission materials and are subject to certain deadlines.

Faculty

Faculty members with diverse backgrounds, preparation, and interests provide instruction of high quality and individualized attention to students. Faculty members are active in scholarship, professional activity, and service and use College programs to maintain a keen interest and the highest competencies in their fields. Faculty members also take an active role in the advising and sponsorship of student organizations.

Student Government

An active Student Government Association regularly plans campuswide student events and, most importantly, deals with significant issues of student interest and communicates information about them to the faculty and administration. Students have voting representation on key faculty committees such as the Academic Council, the Student Services Council, the Academic and Cultural Events Committee, and others that have a direct impact upon the nature and quality of student life.

Admission Requirements

Prospective students are expected to have completed a college-preparatory course of study of 15 units at an accredited secondary school. A proper foundation to facilitate success in college studies includes 4 units of English, 3 units of history, at least 2 units of mathematics (algebra and geometry), and 2 to 4 units of science. Students who intend to major in the science disciplines may wish to select additional high school courses in science and mathematics, and those interested in the humanities and social studies areas typically present additional course work in literature, foreign language, and history. Applicants must submit ACT or SAT scores. Each applicant for admission is given personal attention and considered on the basis of academic performance, test scores, and personal attributes. An electronic application is available on the College's Web site at the address below.

Application and Information

Early application is recommended, as residence halls and classroom space may be limited. For further information, students should contact:

Enrollment Services
One College Hill
Culver-Stockton College
Canton, Missouri 63435
Telephone: 800-537-1883 (toll-free)
E-mail: enrollment@culver.edu
World Wide Web: http://www.culver.edu

Weldon Residence Hall, Culver-Stockton College.

DEPAUW UNIVERSITY
GREENCASTLE, INDIANA

The University

"DePauw is not a spectator sport" is the way one graduate described the DePauw experience. Indeed, DePauw students expect and seek a challenge. In small classes, students are challenged by professors who are leading scholars with a passion for teaching. There are countless opportunities to excel in more than forty programs of study, five honors programs, numerous leadership positions with student organizations and living units, athletic programs, and more. DePauw students have a tradition of volunteerism, as demonstrated by the fact that three fourths of the student body of 2,300 participate in community service each year. In the first annual *Guide to Campuses Where You Can Make a Difference*, DePauw ranked among the top fifteen colleges where students are truly making a difference in terms of service, both on campus and in the community. In brief, DePauw provides a broad, liberal arts education that is intended to serve as a foundation for the student's lifetime of learning and growth.

At DePauw, the traditional liberal arts curriculum is complemented by perhaps the largest per capita student internship program in the country. Eighty-five percent of DePauw students complete at least one internship during a semester, Winter Term, or summer, and many students complete at least two internships. As a result, DePauw offers a unique opportunity for students to explore various interests and career possibilities, which have a significant impact for students following graduation. More than 95 percent of DePauw graduates are employed or enrolled in graduate/professional school within nine months of graduation. The figure increases to more than 99 percent after one year. Of those students obtaining employment after graduation, approximately 1 out of 4 students accept jobs at companies and organizations where they served a student internship.

Much of DePauw's reputation for excellence can be attributed to the uncommon success of its alumni. DePauw ranked eleventh in the nation in terms of the likelihood that its graduates will become chief executive officers of major American companies, according to *Fortune* magazine in 1990. DePauw ranked eighth in the nation and first in the Midwest as the undergraduate origin of the nation's top executives, according to a 1994 study by Standard & Poor's Corp. DePauw also ranked sixteenth as a baccalaureate source for Ph.D. degree recipients in all fields, according to a 1998 survey by Franklin and Marshall College.

DePauw guarantees graduation in four years for students in forty standard programs, or the University waives tuition and fees for any subsequent course work necessary for graduation.

Location

DePauw is located in a town of 10,000 people set amid the gently rolling hills of west-central Indiana. The campus is exceptionally well maintained, blending new, state-of-the-art facilities with buildings, such as the historic East College, that exemplify the University's heritage. DePauw students are very active in the community, as indicated by the fact that about three fourths of the student body volunteers each year for public service in twenty-five community organizations. Greencastle is 45 miles west of Indianapolis and within a 3-hour drive of Chicago, St. Louis, Louisville, Cincinnati, and Columbus.

Majors and Degrees

DePauw offers the Bachelor of Arts (B.A.), Bachelor of Music (B.Mus.), Bachelor of Musical Arts (B.M.A.), and Bachelor of Music Education (B.M.E.).

DePauw offers majors in more than forty areas, including anthropology, art (history), art (studio), biochemistry, biology, black studies, chemistry, classical civilization, communication, computer science, conflict studies, earth science, East Asian studies, economics, elementary education, English (literature), English (writing), environmental geoscience, French, geography, geology, German, Greek, history, interdisciplinary, kinesiology (athletic training, sports medicine and exerise, and sports medicine), Latin, mathematics, music, music/business, music performance, music education, philosophy, physics, political science, psychology, religious studies, Romance languages, Russian studies, sociology, sociology and anthropology, Spanish, and women's studies. Preprofessional programs are available in dentistry, law, medicine, and secondary education. In addition, DePauw offers a 3-2 program in engineering.

Academic Programs

DePauw is committed to providing its students with a traditional, liberal arts education complemented by internship opportunities, and degree requirements reflect this approach. The University follows a 4-1-4 calendar, with four-month fall and spring semesters and a January Winter Term. The normal course load in a semester is four courses, but course loads may vary from three to 4½ courses. During the January Winter Term, first-year students study on campus, and upperclass students participate in research, internships, and travel abroad. DePauw's distinctive honors programs include Honor Scholars, Information Technology Associates Program, Management Fellows, Media Fellows, and Science Research Fellows.

During the 1999–2000 academic year, DePauw began a new first-year experience program, called depauw.year1, that is designed to build a sense of community among first-year students. The program includes special seminars, speakers, programs, and other activities.

Thirty-one courses are required for students earning a Bachelor of Arts, Bachelor of Music, or Bachelor of Musical Arts degree. The Bachelor of Music Education degree requires thirty-two courses. Each student must complete a major, achieve at least a 2.0 GPA (on a 4.0 scale) in that major, and satisfy the senior major requirement. Students must attain a minimum cumulative GPA of 2.0, while students in the B.M.A. and B.M.E. programs need a minimum 2.5 GPA. Fifteen courses leading to a bachelor's degree, including six of the last eight courses, must be completed in residence at DePauw or in a University-approved program. Students in the College of Liberal Arts must achieve certification in writing (W), quantitative reasoning (Q), and oral communication skills (S). Students must complete three Winter Term projects with satisfactory grades, including an on-campus Winter Term for first-year students. A maximum of 3 internship course credits and five internship experiences (including Winter Terms) may be applied toward the bachelor's degree.

Off-Campus Programs

DePauw offers extensive off-campus study programs. Domestic programs include the Washington Semester, United Nations Semester, Sea Semester, New York Arts Program, Newberry Library Program, Oak Ridge Science Semester, and Philadelphia Urban Semester. Study abroad is available in Africa, Asia-Pacific, Australia, Austria, Belgium, Canada, the Caribbean, China, the Czech Republic, Denmark, England, France, Germany, Greece, Hungary, India, Indonesia, Ireland, Italy, Japan, Latin America, Mexico, the Middle East, the Netherlands, Poland, Russia, Scotland, Singapore, Spain, Switzerland, Vietnam, and Wales. Many students also participate in off-campus Winter Term projects. More than 40 percent of students study off-campus as part of their DePauw experience. In order to receive course credit, a student must have approval from the International Center; other restrictions may apply.

Academic Facilities

The new blends with the old on DePauw's 175-acre campus, which features thirty-nine major buildings and a nearby 40-acre nature preserve. DePauw's facilities provide an excellent environment for teaching and learning. The physical plant is equal to or superior to that of other liberal arts universities.

The centerpiece of the campus is historic East College, built in 1877 and listed on the Register of Historic Landmarks. New buildings on campus include the Indoor Tennis and Track Center, which opened in 2001 and was recognized by the United States Tennis Association as an outstanding public tennis facility for 2002. The Julian Science and Math Center is currently undergoing a $38 million expansion and renovation project, adding 110,000 square feet of new classroom and laboratory space, including the 361 degrees Technology Center. The new Peeler Art Center gives students a state-of-the-art space optimal to the teaching, creation, and presentation of art. The Pulliam Center for Contemporary Media has superb facilities and equipment for *The DePauw,* the oldest student newspaper in the state; student-operated WGRE-FM radio; and a television unit in which students produce programs for broadcast statewide and nationwide. The Performing Arts Center is home to the School of Music and features outstanding performance halls.

Costs

Expenses for the 2003–04 academic year included $24,000 for tuition, $7050 for room and board, and $530 in fees for health services and activities. Books and supplies are approximately $600 per year, and personal expenses are approximately $1000 per year.

Financial Aid

Admission to DePauw is need-blind. Ninety-five percent of all DePauw students receive scholarships, grants, loans, or work-study assistance. The average financial aid package covers slightly more than half of total costs. DePauw's financial aid program is designed to recognize achievement and potential and to assist students who otherwise would be unable to attend the University due to financial constraints. DePauw maintains its own scholarship, work, and loan programs and participates in all traditional forms of state and federal financial aid.

February 15 is the priority filing date for applications for fall financial aid. FAFSA and institutional financial aid applications are required. Scholarships/grants available include federal and state scholarships/grants, University scholarships/grants, private scholarships/grants, ROTC scholarships and academic merit scholarships. Approximately 40 percent of students work on campus during the academic year. DePauw participates in the Federal Work-Study Program, and 45 percent of students who receive financial aid participate in work-study.

Faculty

DePauw professors are devoted to teaching students. The University has 223 full-time faculty members, and 92 percent have the terminal degree in their field. The student-faculty ratio is 10:1. All classes at DePauw are taught by professors and not by graduate assistants. Ninety-seven percent of full-time faculty members serve as academic advisers to students.

Student Government

Leadership opportunities in a wide variety of organizations are an integral part of the DePauw experience. Students have numerous opportunities to be involved in student government as well as committees and councils representing student concerns. The president of the student body presides over the many committees of the Student Congress; each committee has several student representatives as members. Sororities, fraternities, and residence halls all have annual elections of officers and representatives to various campus organizations.

Admission Requirements

DePauw does not conduct admission by the numbers. Along with grades and SAT I or ACT scores, the University looks at the required student essays, record of other achievements, and examples of any special talent a student may have. Also considered are the quality of courses selected in the high school; the high school attended; the

recommendations of high school counselors, teachers, coaches, and employers; and the personal interview. DePauw examines each individual's application carefully.

To be admitted to the first-year class at DePauw, students must have graduated from an accredited secondary school or offer evidence of equivalent education. Students should have completed the following work in a college-preparatory program: 4 units of English, 4 units of mathematics, 3-4 units of a foreign language, 3-4 units of social science, and 3-4 units of science (2 or more laboratory sciences). In addition, School of Music candidates must audition.

Application and Information

Prospective students can apply online or obtain an application for admission by calling or writing the Office of Admission. DePauw also is a member of the Common Application Group and gives the common application the same consideration as the University's application.

Students interested in early decision must submit applications by November 1, students interested in early notification must submit applications by December 1, and students interested in regular decision must submit applications by February 1. Admission decisions are mailed by mid-December for early decision applicants and by February 15 for early notification applicants. Regular decision applicants are notified by April 1. Early decision applicants who are admitted must respond by February 1; other admitted applicants who decide to enroll must submit an enrollment deposit by May 1. Students should contact:

Madeleine R. Eagon
Vice President for Admission and Financial Aid
DePauw University
P.O. Box 37
Greencastle, Indiana 46135-0037
Telephone: 765-658-4006
　　　　　800-447-2495 (toll-free)
Fax: 765-658-4007
E-mail: admission@depauw.edu
World Wide Web: http://www.depauw.edu

Historic East College is the centerpiece of DePauw University's campus. The East College bell summons students to class and also signals victories in football.

DICKINSON STATE UNIVERSITY
DICKINSON, NORTH DAKOTA

The University

Student success, both inside and outside the classroom, has been the focus of Dickinson State University since 1918 when the University was established as Dickinson Normal School and Model High. The tradition continues today, allowing easy access and meaningful relationships with qualified professors, supportive and comfortable living arrangements on campus, and with student activities, providing something for everyone.

Dickinson State, with an enrollment of approximately 2,000 students, is the only comprehensive, four-year public university in West River North Dakota. The University is proud of its safe campus. Its location offers students a secure environment in which to pursue their educational and social interests.

The University's mission, as dictated by the North Dakota University System, is to provide high-quality, accessible programs; to promote excellence in teaching and learning; to support scholarly and creative activities; and to provide service relevant to the economy, health, and quality of life of the citizens of North Dakota. With a wide range of academic programs, Dickinson State University prepares students to live, learn, and lead in the twenty-first century.

Dickinson State University is accredited by the North Central Association of Colleges and Schools (NCA), the North Central Association for Teacher Education (NCATE), and the National League for Nursing Accrediting Commission (NLNAC).

At Dickinson State, there are approximately forty-five different organizations to help every student find a niche. Students choose from intramural sports, band, chorus, drama, art, forensics, student government, honorary societies, academic clubs, and cheerleading, to name just a few.

Living in a residence hall at Dickinson State offers many conveniences and countless opportunities to build friendships in an exciting environment close to classes and University activities. Meal plans are available on campus for five or seven days per week. For added ease, students can also opt to purchase meals at the snack bar. Rooms have free access to the campus computer network and cable television. Features in each hall include game room, exercise equipment, computer stations, laundry facilities, and kitchenette. Students can select to live in women's, men's, or coed halls, or student apartments. Family student housing complexes provide apartments at reasonable housing rates to nontraditional students.

Location

Dickinson State is located in Dickinson, North Dakota, near the rugged and beautiful Badlands. With a population of more than 17,000, Dickinson is the hub of West River North Dakota. The community lies only 30 miles from Theodore Roosevelt National Park, and it is just one hour's drive south of Lake Sakakawea. Dickinson is served by both commercial air and bus transportation.

Dickinson's location provides abundant opportunities for people to enjoy outdoor recreational activities year-round. The area's picturesque rivers, lakes, and Badlands are ideal for hiking, fishing, boating, hunting, cross-country skiing, and much more.

As the state's fifth-largest community, Dickinson offers a wide array of restaurants, shopping malls, specialty stores, historic landmarks, museums, movie theaters, and other entertainment outlets. The region offers abundant dinosaur fossils and geological phenomena for explorers of all ages. Many of these treasures are displayed in Dickinson's impressive Dakota Dinosaur Museum.

Health-care services are provided by a 109-bed acute-care hospital, two major clinics, and numerous specialty clinics. The University's Student Health Service provides prompt care on campus for routine health concerns.

Majors and Degrees

Programs offered at Dickinson State University include liberal arts along with specialized programs in education, business, health services, agriculture, and computer science. There are opportunities for preprofessional study and vocational training in selected areas as well.

Dickinson State offers Bachelor of Arts and Bachelor of Science degrees in ten departments, including majors and/or minors (indicated with a *) in accounting, agriculture (with options in natural resource management, integrated ranch management, and business/marketing), art, biology, business administration (with concentrations in accounting, agribusiness, banking and finance, business management, management information systems, manufacturing technology, marketing, office administration, and organizational psychology), business education, chemistry, coaching*, computer science, earth science*, elementary education, English, environmental health, geography*, graphic design*, history, journalism*, mathematics, music, music education, nursing, physical education, political science, psychology, science composite, secondary education, social science composite, social science (elementary education)*, sociology*, social work (linked with University of North Dakota), Spanish, theater and communication, university studies, and writing.

Associate degree and certificate programs include agriculture with specialty areas in agriculture sales and service (with options in agriculture business management and equine management) or farm and ranch management, nursing, office administration (with concentrations in accounting, agribusiness, computer science, legal, management, and medical studies), and university studies.

Preprofessional programs include athletic training, chiropractic, dentistry, dental hygiene, engineering, forestry, law, medicine, medical/lab technology, mortuary science, optometry, physics, seminary, social work, veterinary, and wildlife management.

Academic Programs

While many of the majors that Dickinson State University offers have unique academic requirements, the basic baccalaureate degree academic curriculum consists of approximately 39 semester hours of general education courses from the areas of communications, scientific inquiry, expression of human civilization, understanding human civilization, multicultural studies, and physical education; a specific major core curriculum of 32 to 60 or more semester hours; approximately 24 semester hours of credit in a minor field of study (when a minor is required); and professional education course work for those students entering the teaching profession. Students seeking a Bachelor of Arts degree must also complete a minimum of 16 semester hours of a foreign language. A minimum of 128 semester hours is required for graduation in a baccalaureate degree program. Associate degree programs require 64 credit hours for graduation.

Academic Facilities

The commitment to technology at Dickinson State is evident in the number of cutting-edge computers provided for student use. There is an outstanding student-to-personal computer ratio, resulting in easy access to the type of technology students need to excel. Computer labs are located in academic areas, the library, and all residence halls. Students also have free access to e-mail and the Internet, including the World Wide Web.

Stoxen Library is proud of its highly sophisticated automated library. The On-line Dakota Information Network allows students to access resources from across the United States.

Costs

In 2003–04, tuition and fees were $1570 per semester for North Dakota residents; $1774 per semester for Minnesota residents; $1889 per semester for residents of Montana, South Dakota, Manitoba (Canada), and Saskatchewan (Canada); $2208 per semester for residents of Alaska, Arizona, California, Colorado, Hawaii, Idaho, Kansas, Michigan, Missouri, Nebraska, Nevada, New Mexico, Oregon, Utah, Washington, and Wyoming; and for residents of other states, tuition and fees were $3703 per semester. Room and board costs averaged $1675 per semester. Books were approximately $350 per semester. These figures reflect current costs, which are subject to change.

Financial Aid

College is a valuable investment in the future, and Dickinson State realizes financing it can be challenging. One of the best college buys in the region, Dickinson State's tuition and housing rates are among the lowest in the upper Midwest. In addition, attractive tuition rates are offered for students living in states and provinces bordering on North Dakota. Special rates also exist for students who live in those states participating in the Western Undergraduate Exchange (WUE) and the Midwest Student Exchange Program (MSEP). These include Alaska, Arizona, California, Colorado, Hawaii, Idaho, Kansas, Michigan, Missouri, Nebraska, Nevada, New Mexico, Oregon, Utah, Washington, and Wyoming.

The Office of Financial Aid is ready to help ease the cost of a college education through a number of financial aid programs, including scholarships, grants, loans, student employment opportunities, cultural diversity awards, and international awards. More than 85 percent of Dickinson State's students received financial assistance last year.

Faculty

Dickinson State University has 75 full-time and 70 part-time faculty members. Students develop close relationships with their teachers since three fourths of classes have fewer than 30 students.

Student Government

The Student Senate is the governing body and official voice of Dickinson State University students. The Senate is composed of a cross-section of students elected by the campus community. The Campus Activity Board (CAB) offers a broad range of social and recreational activities, including dances, films, comedians, and other special events. The Campus Programming Committee

(CPC) provides a variety of educational, instructional, and cultural programs. Residence Hall Councils are made up of elected student residents and deal with matters relating to campus housing. The Student Policies Council is composed of students, faculty, and staff members. The Council recommends policies and programs related to student affairs.

Admission Requirements

Dickinson State's admission policy allows students to enroll if they are high school graduates or have successfully completed the GED examination along with completion of the ACT or SAT. The completion of a high school college-preparatory course core curriculum is also required for admission into a baccalaureate program.

The nursing program has special enrollment and admissions requirements. Students should apply early for this program.

All students under the age of 21 who have not completed 60 credit hours are required to live on campus. Exceptions to this policy include married students; students living locally with parents, grandparents, or a legal guardian; students who live with a brother or sister who is a head of a household; and single parents with one or more dependents.

Application and Information

The admissions staff is anxious to discuss the variety of programs the University has to offer and give a tour of the beautiful campus, its classrooms, facilities, and residence halls. When students are on campus, they should meet with the financial aid staff to discuss concerns about financing an education. Admissions representatives are available Monday through Friday, 8 a.m. to 4 p.m., Mountain Time. Students should contact:

Office of Student Recruitment
Dickinson State University
Dickinson, North Dakota 58601-4896
Telephone: 701-483-2175
            800-279-HAWK Ext. 2175 (toll-free)
E-mail: dsu.hawks@dsu.nodak.edu
World Wide Web: http://www.dickinsonstate.com

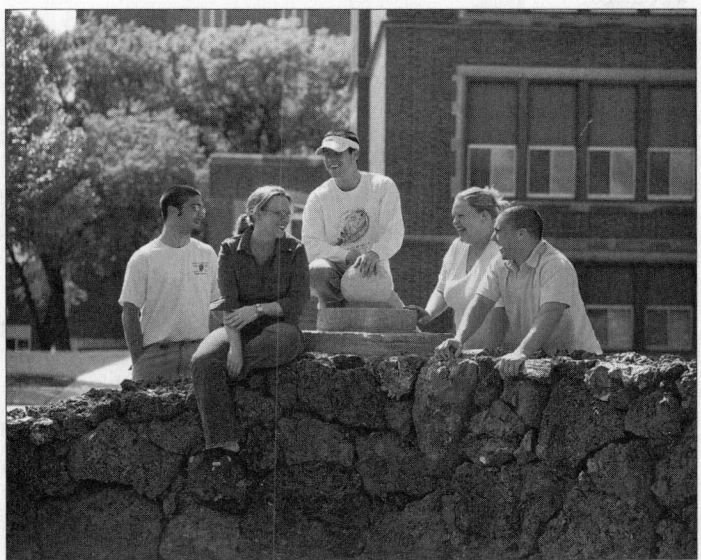

Dickinson State University ensures student success with flexible schedules and by providing numerous group activities for students to live, learn, and lead as they grow together at Dickinson State University.

EUREKA COLLEGE
EUREKA, ILLINOIS

The College

Chartered in 1855, Eureka College was the first existing college in Illinois—and the third in the nation—to offer education on an equal basis to both men and women. In the years since its founding, Eureka has continued to be an innovative leader in coeducational liberal arts education. The College is fully accredited by the North Central Association of Schools and Colleges and is approved for teacher preparation by the Department of Public Faculty Instruction of the State of Illinois and the Illinois State Teacher Certification Board.

Eureka's campus is a wooded 112 acres at the southwest edge of Eureka, Illinois. In addition to the academic buildings, there are seven residence halls in which 91 percent of the students live; the Dickinson Commons food center; facilities for football, baseball, and tennis; the Cerf Center; and the Reagan Physical Education Center, which houses three basketball courts, a swimming pool, a weight room, and faculty offices. The College's stately Administration Building was built in 1858, and its Old Chapel was built in 1869. These two buildings are listed on the National Register of Historic Places.

Students come to the Eureka campus from a variety of areas: rural, urban, small town, and suburban. There is a rich mix of ethnic and racial backgrounds among the students, and a number of them come from other countries. A diverse student body on a small residential campus inevitably creates a community spirit that calls for cooperation, involvement, and interaction. This is a deliberate part of the Eureka program, providing opportunities for students to develop the potential for community leadership in their postcollege life.

Location

Eureka, in the heart of Illinois' fertile farmland, enjoys the best of two worlds. With tree-lined streets and a small population (4,500), the town is peaceful and secure. Yet, as a county seat with a large proportion of young residents, the town is every bit a part of the mainstream of American culture. The cities of Bloomington and Normal lie 20 minutes to the southeast, and the city of Peoria is 20 minutes to the west. Chicago is 140 miles to the northeast, and St. Louis, Missouri, is 190 miles to the southwest.

Majors and Degrees

Eureka College offers programs leading to the Bachelor of Arts and Bachelor of Science degrees. Major fields of study are accounting, art, arts and letters, biology, business administration, business information systems, chemistry, communication, computer science, elementary education, English, environmental sciences, history, mathematics, music, music education, philosophy and religion, physical education, physical science, political science and history, psychology, secondary education, social science, sociology, and theater arts and drama.

Academic Programs

The academic program at Eureka College seeks to maintain a balance between requirements that all students must meet and freedom for students to select those courses that best match and further their interests, skills, and life plan. The structure of the curriculum has been designed to reflect this balance.

The College believes that there are certain basic skills and a common core of knowledge that educated students must possess. Therefore, the College requires that each student acquire and display skills in composition, oral communication, and mathematics. The College also requires that each student devote a portion of time to the study of those disciplines in humanities, fine and performing arts, natural sciences, and social sciences. These distributional requirements insure that each student has the opportunity to explore the body of knowledge that is our common cultural heritage.

The College's academic program represents more than the accumulation of knowledge. Thus the College intends that students and faculty alike engage not only in the search for knowledge but also in the search for the higher goal of how to use that knowledge for the benefit of mankind.

The program at Eureka is rigorous both in its goals and in the efforts it demands, but the College believes that it is also exciting and satisfying.

Actual work experience—one of the most valuable educational tools of all—is normally available through internships and practicums in all fields. Independent study and pass/fail grading are available for qualified students in certain courses. The College also provides assistance to students, upon request, in determining vocational goals and finding employment after graduation.

Off-Campus Programs

A student may enroll for credit in travel-study projects sponsored by or acceptable to the College. Approval of registration for credit must be secured through the Dean of the College and the appropriate division chairman. Travel-study projects may be in this country or overseas, and must include readings, discussion, and a paper.

Academic Facilities

Most of the College's academic buildings are grouped together on the western half of the campus, including the Melick Library, completed in 1967; Vennum/Binkley Hall; Pritchard Performing Arts Center; and Burgess Hall, a classroom building that contains a newly developed "smart classroom." Located in the midst of the campus residence halls is a Learning Center available for students to receive assistance with class work or study skills or have a quiet place to study. Nestled in the wooded back-campus are the Rinker Amphitheater and the Lilac Arboretum.

Costs

The Eureka Idea has resulted in a 30 percent tuition reduction. For the 2003–04 academic year, tuition was $13,000, and room and board were $5880, for a total cost of $18,880 per year. *U.S. News and World Report* found Eureka College to be a best value among comprehensive colleges in the Midwest offering only bachelor's degrees.

Financial Aid

Eureka College administers an extensive financial aid program and encourages those who could not attend the College without financial assistance to apply for aid. Approximately 90 percent of Eureka's students receive some form of financial assistance, often as a package of scholarships, grants, awards, loans, and employment. Students can calculate their scholarship level by using Eureka's simple formula. If students wish to be considered for financial aid, they must submit the Free Application for Federal Student Aid (FAFSA) complete with the Eureka College school code of 001678. Federal and state aid make Eureka less expensive than the flagship state university.

Durward Sandifer Mentorships are available for entering freshman. If at the end of their sophomore year they have at least a 3.5 cumulative GPA and an established record of leadership and service at Eureka College, they will receive a mentorship anywhere in the world, paid for by the College.

Faculty

During the 2003–04 academic year, Eureka College's student-teacher ratio was 13:1. Sixty-three percent of the full-time faculty members of the College have a terminal degree in their field. The Eureka College faculty members are renowned for their excellence in teaching. However, they also recognize that the learning experience extends beyond the classroom. The faculty members play an active role in working toward the success of each student.

Student Government

Eureka College's Student Senate, which makes recommendations on administrative policy and oversees campus activities, comprises 8 senators-at-large and the presidents of the four classes. The senators elect the Chancellor from their own membership. Most campus events are directly sponsored by the Campus Activities Board, which is composed of students appointed by the senate. Student Residence Hall Councils, whose members are elected, control living regulations for individual dormitories.

Admission Requirements

Any person who feels that he or she has both the ability and desire to take advantage of Eureka College's small-campus, liberal arts education is encouraged to seek admission. Applications are welcome at any time after students have completed their junior year of high school. Admission is determined on the basis of prior performance in high school and on either the ACT or SAT I. Admission of applicants transferring from community colleges or other four-year colleges or universities is determined based on prior performance at the school from which they are transferring.

Application and Information

To obtain an application for admission, prospective students may visit the College Web site and either apply online or download the application. Students who wish to receive an application in the mail should write, call, or e-mail the address listed below.

The applicant must complete and return the application form and arrange for high school transcripts and ACT or SAT I scores to be forwarded directly to the College. Transfer students should have transcripts forwarded directly to the Admissions Office from each college or university attended. The applicant is notified of the decision as early as possible after all of the admission materials have been received. The application deadline for the fall is August 15.

Admissions Office
Eureka College
300 East College Avenue
Eureka, Illinois 61530
Telephone: 309-467-6530
         888-4-EUREKA (toll-free)
E-mail: admissions@eureka.edu
World Wide Web: http://www.eureka.edu

GOSHEN COLLEGE
GOSHEN, INDIANA

The College

Goshen College (GC) is a fully accredited national liberal arts college that is known for leadership in international education, service-learning, and peace and justice issues in the Anabaptist-Mennonite tradition. Founded in 1894 by the Mennonite Church, one of the historic peace churches, GC serves more than 1,000 students and encourages dialogue between students with different perspectives, backgrounds, and beliefs. While students from Mennonite backgrounds represent more than half of the student body, about sixteen denominations are represented. Students come from more than forty states, Canadian provinces, and more than thirty-five countries. Goshen College was recognized in *U.S. News & World Report*'s 2004 "America's Best Colleges" rankings as a "least debt college" for its graduates, for enrolling a high percentage of international students, and for adding to the sense of an international campus with its unique study/serve abroad program. Goshen's track record of sustained excellence has attracted national attention. Goshen is one of 300 schools included in *Barron's Best Buys in College Education* for offering a high-quality education at below-average prices. *Money* magazine listed GC fourteenth in the nation for educational value when financial aid is taken into account. For 2002, a study by *U.S. News & World Report* includes GC among the top 113 national liberal arts colleges. Ernest L. Boyer, in *Smart Parents' Guide to College*, praises GC's Study-Service Term (SST) program. GC ranks among the 100 Most Wired Colleges in *Yahoo! Internet Life* and was named one of *The 100 Best Colleges for African-American Students* in a book by Erlene B. Wilson. A study by Franklin and Marshall ranked GC in the top sixth of liberal arts colleges in the number of its graduates who go on to complete doctoral degrees. Among the top 100 schools in its category, GC has the lowest cost among national colleges in the Great Lakes region. Peterson's lists GC among its 190 *Top Colleges for Science*.

In a highly energetic, Christ-centered environment, students have plenty of opportunities to cultivate leadership skills and assume responsibility. Students edit a weekly newspaper and a yearbook, operate a radio station, produce a campus television program, serve on campus publishing editorial boards, and work and perform in theater and musical groups. Representatives of the student body are elected to serve on the Student Senate and Campus Activities Council. Campus groups also include the Student Women's Association, Black Student Union, Campus Ministries team, PAX, Latino Student Union, Nursing Students Association, Eco-PAX, Fellowship of Christian Athletes, Social Work Action Association, International Students Club, Business Club, and Pre-Med Club. GC belongs to the National Association of Intercollegiate Athletics and the Mid-Central College Conference and competes intercollegiately in men's and women's basketball, cross-country, soccer, tennis, and track and field; men's baseball and golf; and women's softball and volleyball. More than 60 percent of GC students participate in intramural athletics. All students have free access to the Roman Gingerich Recreation-Fitness Center.

Most Goshen students live in one of the College's five residence halls, which were made accessible, one port per pillow, to the campus computer network in 1997. Small-group housing is available to upper-level students. College-owned houses are available for married students and families.

With a long history of emphasis on experiential learning, Goshen College's programs encourage partnerships between the College and the community by placing students in practicum, internship, and service experiences. In addition, the College holds an annual Celebrate Service Day; classes are suspended so that students and faculty and staff members can participate in community service projects. Students also benefit from Multicultural Education Office programs that emphasize meaningful ways to address issues of diversity in order to prepare students for life in an increasingly interconnected, multicultural world.

Location

The campus is on the south side of Goshen, a city of 30,000 in north-central Indiana, 2 hours east of Chicago and 45 minutes east of South Bend. Known as the Maple City for its many maple trees, Goshen is part of Elkhart County, one of the fastest-growing counties in the nation during the 1980s and 1990s. The county enjoys its rich Mennonite and Amish heritage while serving as home to major corporations, with proximity to Chicago and Indianapolis.

Majors and Degrees

Goshen College offers seventy programs of study. The Bachelor of Arts is awarded in accounting; American sign language interpreting; art; Bible and religion; biology; business; business information systems; chemistry; communication; computer science; computer science and applied mathematics; early childhood education; economics; environmental studies; elementary education; English; environmental science; family life; French; German; Hispanic ministries; history; history and investigative skills; management information systems; mathematics; molecular biology; music; natural science; peace, justice, and conflict studies; physical education; physics; psychology; social work; sociology/anthropology; Spanish; special education; teaching English to speakers of other languages (TESOL); and theater. A Bachelor of Science in nursing or a Bachelor of Science in organizational management is also awarded. Interdisciplinary majors usually combine work in three different departments and allow students to tailor their studies to individual interests. Preprofessional programs in engineering, law, medicine, occupational therapy, physical therapy, seminary, and veterinary medicine are available as well. The College also offers minors in more than thirty areas.

Academic Programs

The College calendar consists of two 15-week semesters and a 3½-week May term. A total of 120 semester hours (124 for nursing majors) is required for graduation. One third are usually in general studies courses, including art, Bible and religion, history, literature, philosophy, physical education, science, and social science; another third are courses in the student's major. Most majors require a practicum for graduation. All students must complete a course of international study. Most students choose to participate in the Study-Service Term (SST) program abroad, a thirteen-week term, including course work and field experience in a service assignment, in a significantly different country. Students also can fulfill the requirement by taking courses on campus or by participating in other study-abroad programs.

Off-Campus Programs

Goshen is one of the very few U.S. colleges that requires international education. Most students complete this requirement by going on SST, while others choose to take classes with an international emphasis on campus. GC's international education program ranks in the top sixteen both for quality and participation, according to *U.S. News & World Report*. Since the SST program began in 1968, more than 6,500 GC students have benefited from it tremendously, both academically and personally. The program has served as the model for international education programs across the country. In the SST program, students spend six weeks together focusing on the study of one country while immersed in its language and culture. The six-week SST field experience gives students a chance to develop interpersonal skills and to work alongside native residents in service to others. The field experience often relates to the students' major areas of study. During both parts of the program, students live with host families. Most SST units cost the same as a semester on campus. GC students earn 13–14 hours of credit for SST; however, the benefits continue for a lifetime. SST gives students a broader context for living their lives while helping them set an appropriate individual direction. The growing internationalization of U.S. business and culture amplifies SST's benefits; now, more than ever, foreign language skills and knowledge of other cultures are advantages in the job market.

Other off-campus programs include spring term courses in marine biology at the College's center in the Florida Keys and courses in Europe in theater history, art history, and literature.

Academic Facilities

On its 135-acre campus, Goshen College has eighteen major buildings and laboratories. The Roman Gingerich Recreation-Fitness Center features a swimming pool, running track, and gymnasium and houses the physical education department, student health center, and intramural and intercollegiate athletics. The 68,000-square-foot Music Center, which opened in 2002, features 1,000- and 300-seat performance halls, with some of the best acoustics in the nation. The building also holds a community music school, an art gallery and classrooms, and offices and practice rooms.

Another recent addition to the campus is an annex to the Science Building, which contains modern science classrooms, laboratories, and equipment. It also contains the Turner Precision X-Ray Measurements Laboratory and the Biological Research Laboratory. The Turner Laboratory gives physics majors a rare opportunity to assist in basic research on crystals. The Biological Research Laboratory, equipped with an electron microscope, Geiger system, climate chambers, incubators, and microtechnique systems, is also open to qualified students. The College regularly does research for larger universities and major industries.

The Harold and Wilma Good Library houses a collection of 120,000 volumes and 800 periodicals, the Mennonite Historical Library, and the Art Gallery.

At the GC Laboratory Kindergarten, psychology and education majors can observe and participate in activities. The Merry Lea Environmental Learning Center, an 1,150-acre nature preserve, offers internships in environmental and elementary education and is a key site for the College's environmental studies major and minor.

Goshen College has a progressive attitude concerning technology in an effort to encourage students to learn how to use technology intelligently and effectively. Computer facilities include three modern student labs, with one computer for every 7.6 students, as well as printers, scanners, digital cameras, wireless Internet access, and other equipment. Computers in student labs are upgraded annually. Multimedia classrooms feature integrated technology as well as media production facilities. All residence hall rooms are connected to the campus network and the Internet; account and course information is available on the College intranet.

The John S. Umble Center for the Performing Arts is recognized internationally for its exceptional theater acoustics. The Music Center, opened in 2002, has received awards for its design and acoustics in its 1,000 Sauder Performance Hall and 300-seat Rieth Recital Hall. The building also houses a Community School of the Arts.

Costs

Costs for 2003–04 included tuition, $16,320; room $3000; board, $2800; and tech fee, $330. The total for a residential student was $22,450. Costs included two 15-week semesters and one 3½-week May term.

Financial Aid

Ninety percent of the College's students receive some type of financial assistance through federal, state, and Goshen College programs. The average award exceeds $12,000. GC offers more than 130 different scholarships. College aid includes the President's Leadership Award, $10,000; Menno Simons Scholarship, up to $7000, Wens Honors Scholarship, up to $5500; Yoder Honors Scholarship, up to $4000, Grebel Honors Scholarship, up to $2500, and the Kratz Honors Scholarship, up to $1000. About 60 percent of incoming students receive renewable academic scholarships. Work-study jobs and other on-campus jobs are available.

Faculty

The faculty includes about 80 full-time and 30 part-time members. Most have lived or worked abroad. The student-faculty ratio is 13:1.

Student Government

The Student Senate acts as an advocate of student concerns and corresponding policy changes and works with the administration. The Campus Activity Council plans student activities. Most College committees include 1 or 2 voting student members.

Admission Requirements

Applicants should rank in the upper half of their high school graduating class and may apply for admission at any time after the junior year and up to one month before they wish to begin college. ACT or SAT I scores are required. Recommended high school work includes 4 years of English, 2 years of science, 2 years of social science, 2 years of mathematics, and 2 to 4 years of a foreign language. Prospective students are encouraged to visit the campus and meet with faculty members, students, and administrators. Special campus open houses scheduled throughout the year provide excellent opportunities for visits.

Application and Information

Students who would like more information may contact:

Office of Admission
Goshen College
1700 South Main Street
Goshen, Indiana 46526
Telephone: 574-535-7535
          866-566-2637 (toll-free)
Fax: 574-535-7609
E-mail: admissions@goshen.edu
World Wide Web: http://www.goshen.edu

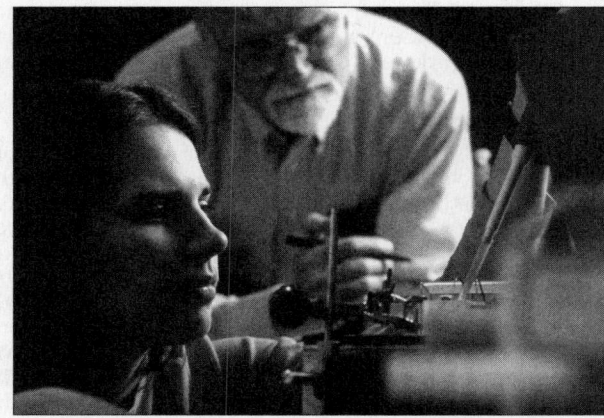

Research and hands-on learning serve students well, especially those who go on to graduate school.

GRACELAND UNIVERSITY
LAMONI, IOWA

GRACELAND
UNIVERSITY

The University

Graceland University offers a strong academic program firmly rooted in the liberal arts tradition with an emphasis on career preparation. Since its founding in 1895 as a private, coeducational university, Graceland has maintained a tradition of academic excellence based on a commitment to the Christian view of the wholeness, worth, and dignity of every person. The University, sponsored by the Community of Christ, is nonsectarian and offers a varied religious life program for those who wish to participate. Thirty-one percent of Graceland students come from Iowa, and the remaining 69 percent represent forty-nine states and twenty-six nations.

Graceland believes that an important part of a student's learning experience is achieved through association with other students in residence hall living. This belief is supported by an on-campus housing system that provides students with the camaraderie of a fraternity or sorority without the competition. Within the residence halls, there are men's and women's houses. Members of each house elect a house council to plan social, intramural athletic, religious, and academic support activities. Residence halls are equipped with voice mail, e-mail, Internet connections, and cable TV.

The North Central Association of Colleges and Schools accredits Graceland as a bachelor's and master's degree–granting institution. Graceland's teacher-education program has been approved by the Iowa Department of Education and is accredited by the National Council for Accreditation of Teacher Education (NCATE). The nursing program is accredited by the National League for Nursing Accrediting Commission and is approved by the Missouri Board of Nursing and the Iowa Board of Nursing.

In addition to its undergraduate programs, Graceland offers a Master of Science in Nursing and an RN to M.S.N. course of study through the Outreach Program. The M.S.N. program has three tracks: family nurse practitioner studies, clinical nurse specialist studies, and health-care administration. Graceland also offers Master of Education, Master of Arts in religion, and Master of Arts in Christian ministries degree programs.

Location

Lamoni, in south-central Iowa, is on Interstate 35, 3 miles north of the Missouri border. It is 1 hour from Des Moines, 2 hours from Kansas City, and 3 hours from Omaha. Lamoni is the home of Liberty Hall Historic Center and antique shops. A county lake, Slip Bluff County Park, and Nine Eagles State Park are within 10 miles.

Majors and Degrees

Graceland awards the degrees of Bachelor of Arts, Bachelor of Science, and Bachelor of Science in Nursing. These degrees represent study in liberal arts with a concentration of courses in a major. The majors and concentrations offered in the Bachelor of Arts programs are accounting, art, athletic training, business administration, chemistry, cinema studies, communication, criminal justice, economics, elementary education, English literature, English writing, entrepreneurship and free enterprise, finance, German, health, history, human services, information technology, international business, international studies, management, management of information systems, marketing, mathematics, modern foreign language, music, music education, peace studies, philosophy and religion, physical education and health, political science, psychology, publications design, recreation, religion, secondary education, social science, sociology, Spanish, speech communication, theater, visual communications,

and wellness program management. Bachelor of Science programs and majors are addiction studies, basic science, biology, chemistry, clinical laboratory science/medical technology, computer science, nursing, pre-engineering, premedicine/predentistry, and pre–veterinary medicine. In addition, a special liberal studies program is offered at Graceland allowing individualized program design by students. Nursing majors complete their last two years at the Graceland Independence Campus in Independence, Missouri.

Graceland offers four undergraduate Outreach Programs: a Bachelor of Science in addiction studies, a Bachelor of Arts in liberal studies (with emphases in health-care administration and health-care psychology), and an RN to B.S.N. program. (Applicants for the B.S.N. must be registered nurses.) These programs allow individuals to complete their degrees through a combination of directed independent study, preceptor-guided practicums, and short residences. For more information, students interested in the addiction studies major should call 800-585-6310 (toll-free); those interested in the nursing and health-care programs should call 877-471-1456 (toll-free).

Academic Programs

Graceland is committed to helping develop the lives of its students—intellectually, socially, physically, and ethically—through a curriculum that is strongly rooted in the liberal arts. General education requirements are based on ten core competencies and can be satisfied by course selections, internships, portfolios, proficiency exams, work experience, independent studies, and performance and achievement. Graceland offers majors that foster conceptual thinking, encourage team building, develop communication skills, and accommodate growth and enrichment.

Two programs at Graceland give attention to the special needs of students. The honors program is designed for highly motivated students who want to expand their learning beyond the regular academic curriculum. Honors students are required to develop and complete an honors thesis or project. Chance is a program for bright students who have the aptitude for university education but have experienced learning difficulties. The Lindamood and Bell clinical models are used for remediation in reading, spelling, and language comprehension.

The University operates on a 4-1-4 academic calendar. The regular semesters are separated by a one-month winter term in January. Full tuition for either the fall or the spring semester includes the winter term. This program is geared toward innovative and exceptional approaches and action-oriented learning experiences. On-campus programs vary from dance basics to science fiction to philosophy. Off-campus winter term experiences range from scuba diving in Grand Cayman to touring Italy. Winter term is also the ideal time to explore career interests through an internship.

Off-Campus Programs

Many students see the world during the winter term by visiting such places as Australia, China, England, France, Grand Cayman Island in the British West Indies, Hungary, Italy, India, Israel, Japan, and Mexico. Students who major in a foreign language may study abroad during their junior or senior year under the auspices of a recognized study program.

Academic Facilities

The Shaw Center for the Performing Arts includes an 800-seat auditorium, a 150-seat studio theater, a 40-foot proscenium stage with orchestra pit, a Casavant pipe organ, a full fly gallery, a spacious scene shop, an art gallery, classrooms, rehearsal rooms, and faculty offices. The Helene Center for the Visual Arts, which opened in January 2004, includes 29,000 square feet for classrooms, studios, and exhibits. The large north-facing windows, an important feature, provide optimum light for artists.

Computer facilities include three primary microcomputer laboratories with Macintosh and IBM-compatible computers. Students have access to equipment of commercial quality for desktop publishing and graphics design and to a music laboratory that provides computer-assisted tutoring, synthesis, and composition as well as professional-quality manuscript printing. The centerpiece of this laboratory is the Kurzweil synthesizer. Graceland's Enter.Net.C@fe provides 24-hour Internet access for student research and recreation.

The Frederick Madison Smith Library uses the latest technologies to provide the information services that students need. Ten fully networked computer workstations offer access to the Internet and many research databases, including 2 databases that provide full-text newspaper articles and periodicals for online reading. Access to LIBBIE, the computerized library catalog, is available from residence hall rooms. Articles and books may be ordered from a worldwide network of research libraries. Students log on to the library's home page to ask reference questions. Holdings include 119,615 books and bound journals, 3,383 audiovisual materials, 77,371 government documents, 569 magazine and newspaper subscriptions, and 5,322 items in the Teacher Curriculum Lab. Three microcomputer labs and the Iowa Communications Network (ICN) classroom are located in the library. Students across the state take classes from Graceland via the ICN.

Students have the opportunity to use the ABT 52 scanning electron microscope, nuclear magnetic resonance spectroscope, Fourier-transform infrared spectroscope, and a computer lab with PCs that provide access to a multiple-operating system environment.

The Eugene E. Closson Physical Education Center includes an indoor junior Olympic-size pool; an indoor track; a weight room; basketball, tennis, and volleyball courts; and a racquetball court. The Bruce Jenner Sports Complex contains the outdoor track, the football stadium, three soccer fields, five intramural fields, and eight tennis courts. The campus borders on a nine-hole golf course and two small ponds for fishing and canoeing.

Costs

Full-time tuition for 2004–05 is $15,000. All freshmen and sophomores are required to live on campus.

Financial Aid

Graceland's financial aid program is designed to assist qualified students attending the University. Ninety-three percent of Graceland's students receive financial aid such as academic scholarships, performance grants, work-study, federal and state grants, and government loans. Academic scholarships are based on the high school GPA and composite ACT or combined SAT I scores for entering freshmen and on cumulative GPA for transfer and continuing students. Grants are available for achievement in athletics and performing arts and for international students. The University matches a grant up to $1000 annually for a contribution made by a church and designated for a student attending Graceland.

Faculty

The majority of faculty members have earned a doctorate or the highest degree in their field. Faculty members are active in their professional fields, but consider teaching their primary responsibility. The student-faculty ratio is 14:1.

Student Government

Students are actively involved in the decision-making process of the University. Executive members of the Graceland Student Government attend faculty meetings and participate with voice and vote. Each academic department has student representatives who participate in business sessions and serve on faculty search committees. Students provide leadership for the housing system and for the campus social program. There are many avenues through which students can gain practical leadership experience.

Admission Requirements

Admission to Graceland is competitive. To be considered, high school graduates must qualify in two of the following three areas: (1) rank in the upper 50 percent of their class; (2) have a minimum 2.5 GPA, based on a 4.0 system; and (3) have either a minimum composite ACT Assessment score of 21 or a minimum combined SAT I score of 960. No one is denied admission to the University on the basis of race, color, religion, age, sex, national origin, disability, or sexual orientation. Prospective students and their families are encouraged to visit the campus.

Application and Information

Students are encouraged to apply as early as possible. For more information and application materials, students should contact:

Brian Shantz
Dean of Admissions
Graceland University
1 University Place
Lamoni, Iowa 50140
Telephone: 641-784-5196 (local)
    866-GRACELAND (toll-free in the United States and Canada)
Fax: 641-784-5480
E-mail: admissions@graceland.edu
World Wide Web: http://www.admissions.graceland.edu

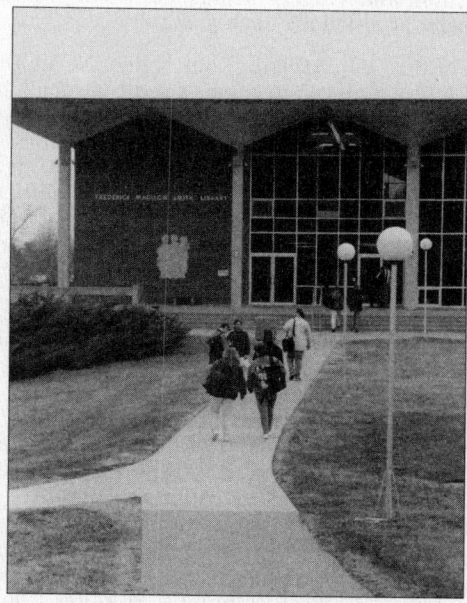

From computer labs with Internet access to thousands of books, journals, and periodicals, the Frederick Madison Smith Library provides students with free access to a world of information.

HEIDELBERG COLLEGE

TIFFIN, OHIO

The College

Heidelberg College, founded in 1850, is a selective, private coeducational liberal arts college that is affiliated with the United Church of Christ. Believing that a liberal education is the best career preparation a person can have to confront the challenges of the future creatively, Heidelberg College offers students a solid base on which to grow in their professional and personal lives. Heidelberg's dynamic community maintains a touch of its Old World heritage yet continually brings innovative ideas into the classroom.

The current undergraduate enrollment is about 1,200 men and women. Students come to Heidelberg from twenty-two states and nine other countries. This cross-cultural mix helps to keep the campus diverse and to broaden students' knowledge and understanding of ethnic and cultural differences.

Heidelberg has more than sixty campus organizations that offer opportunities for leadership, service, and fellowship. Included in these organizations are thirteen departmental clubs and fifteen departmental honorary societies that sponsor discussions, lectures, and field trips. Other cocurricular activities include a student-edited and student-managed newspaper, a television station that broadcasts daily news, forensic programs, choral and instrumental groups, and intramural sports. The Communication and Theatre Arts Department presents four or more dramatic productions each year.

A member of the Ohio Athletic Conference, NCAA Division III, Heidelberg offers nine varsity men's sports: baseball, basketball, cross-country, football, golf, soccer, tennis, track, and wrestling. The women's varsity sports program, among the first in Ohio to be affiliated with the NCAA Division III, fields eight intercollegiate teams: basketball, cross-country, golf, soccer, softball, tennis, track, and volleyball. Athletic facilities include a weight room, handball/racquetball courts, locker rooms, and an eight-lane, all-weather track, which is considered one of the finest in Ohio.

Heidelberg College also offers Master of Arts degree programs in counseling and education as well as a Master of Business Administration (M.B.A.) degree program.

Location

Heidelberg's 110-acre campus is located in Tiffin, Ohio, a town of 20,000. It is the center of a prosperous agricultural and business area. Downtown Tiffin, within half a mile of campus, is traditional in appearance; its charming brickwork stores and large lampposts trimmed in wrought iron resemble an old German town. Four metropolitan areas are within easy driving distance: Toledo, 50 miles; Columbus, 86 miles; Cleveland, 92 miles; and Detroit, 103 miles.

Majors and Degrees

Heidelberg offers a wide variety of undergraduate majors and several preprofessional programs within nineteen academic departments. It awards the Bachelor of Arts, Bachelor of Science, and Bachelor of Music degrees. Majors are available in accounting, anthropology, athletic training, biology, business administration, chemistry, communication and theater arts (communication/media, theater), computer information systems, computer science, economics, education (early childhood, middle childhood, adolescence to young adult, intervention specialist studies, multiage German, multiage Spanish, multiage health and physical education, multiage music education), English (literature, writing), environmental biology, German, health–physical education and recreation, history, international studies (international relations, cross-cultural studies), management science, mathematics, music, music education, music industry, music performance, music performance pedagogy, music theory/composition, philosophy, physics, political science, psychology (child and adolescent, mental health, biopsychology, general), public relations, religion, Spanish, sports management, and water resources (biology, chemistry, geology). Preprofessional and cooperative degree programs include dentistry, engineering, environmental management, law, medical technology, medicine, nursing, occupational therapy, optometry, osteopathy, physical therapy, physician assistant studies, podiatry, and veterinary science.

Academic Programs

To graduate, a student must complete 120 academic semester hours, comprising 36–45 semester hours of general education, 40 semester hours in a selected major, and 35–44 hours of electives. Two credits in health and physical education and 1 credit for Total Student Development (TSD) are also required.

Off-Campus Programs

To supplement their course work, students may choose from a variety of off-campus study programs that provide practical, career-related experience. For example, students interested in studying habitats not found in northwestern Ohio may do on-site field research in Caribbean biogeography in Belize and on-site field research in the Appalachian mountains of West Virginia. Students may also participate in the excavation of an archaeological site.

Opportunities for practical experience in research are also available through Heidelberg's nationally recognized Water Quality Laboratory, which has ongoing research in water-quality studies involving both northern Ohio streams and Lake Erie. Heidelberg's internship program also enables students to participate in on-the-job internships in several area businesses and industries.

Students interested in studying in Washington, D.C., may take part in the Washington Semester at American University; those interested in studying abroad may participate in Heidelberg's own programs in Germany (at Heidelberg University) and Spain or may participate in programs arranged cooperatively with other colleges and universities in such locations as England, Latin America, Africa, and the Far East.

Heidelberg also has cooperative degree programs in engineering with Case Western Reserve University and in forestry with Duke University.

Academic Facilities

Beeghly Library, containing 154,000 volumes, is the intellectual heart of Heidelberg College. The three-story circular library holds a seventy-seat audiovisual room, a seminar and computer room, the Rickard-Mayer Rare Books Room, and the Besse Collection of Letters. Bareis Hall of Science has excellent laboratories and facilities where students may observe demonstrations and experiments. Also located in Bareis Hall are the computer center and the Heidelberg Water Quality Laboratory. The computer center provides access to Macintosh and PC-compatible computers. All of these systems are connected to a campuswide network providing e-mail, file transfer, World Wide Web, and full access to the Internet. The high number of computers and terminals available for student use in addition to the convenience of the computer center hours are outstanding strengths of the College. Additional computer facilities are located in Brenneman Music Hall, the Pfleiderer Center for Religion and the Humanities, and the Aigler Alumni Building. Founders Hall houses a 250-seat performance theater and a rehearsal theater; an FM radio station, WHEI; television studio WHEI-TV; video taping rooms; costume rooms; a dance studio; and offices and classrooms for the Departments of Communication and Theatre Arts and the Languages.

Costs

For the academic year 2003–04, new student tuition and fees were $13,672; room and board were approximately $6275.

Financial Aid

More than 95 percent of the undergraduate student body at Heidelberg receive financial aid. College and government programs—including scholarships, grants, loans, and jobs—total about $14 million annually. Government assistance includes the Federal Pell Grant, direct loan programs, the Federal Supplemental Educational Opportunity Grant, and the Federal Work-Study Program. Heidelberg offers students who meet various academic requirements a number of grants and scholarships that are renewable if eligibility is maintained.

Faculty

Close personal interaction between students and professors is one of Heidelberg's primary strengths. Seventy-nine full-time professors serve the student body, and the student-faculty ratio is 13:1. More than 70 percent of the faculty members hold doctoral degrees in their disciplines. Heidelberg's faculty members are readily available to answer questions and meet with students outside of the classroom.

Student Government

Because students are voting members of 90 percent of the faculty committees, their concerns are heard and have an impact on academic standards, athletics, educational policies, and religious life. Heidelberg's Student Senate is made up of 25 students and a Student Affairs adviser.

Admission Requirements

Heidelberg's selective admission policy seeks to admit those students who will benefit from the educational offerings of the College and who will contribute to the shared life of the campus community. The Admission Committee considers each applicant individually to determine if the student will be able to successfully fulfill the academic responsibilities of a Heidelberg student. The applicant's high school achievement record is the single most important factor considered. Other factors considered are ACT or SAT I scores, cocurricular involvement, character, talent, and teacher recommendations.

Application and Information

Although Heidelberg follows a rolling admission policy, applicants are strongly encouraged to complete this process before January 1. Once all admission credentials are received, applicants are notified of the College's admission decision within two weeks.

For additional information, students should contact:

Office of Admission
Heidelberg College
310 East Market Street
Tiffin, Ohio 44883
Telephone: 419-448-2330
         800-HEIDELBERG (toll-free)
Fax: 419-448-2334
E-mail: adminfo@heidelberg.edu
World Wide Web: http://www.heidelberg.edu

Founders Hall (1851), the oldest building on the Heidelberg campus, is one of ten listed on the National Register of Historic Places.

HIRAM COLLEGE

HIRAM, OHIO

The College

Founded in 1850, Hiram College cherishes its heritage as an institution of academic excellence and rare distinction. Hiram's 900 students come from twenty-six states and twenty-three countries and represent more than twenty-five different religions. SAT I and ACT scores of Hiram's entering freshmen exceed national norms: in 2003, SAT I medians were 570 (verbal) and 570 (math); the ACT composite median was 24. Between 50 and 60 percent of the College's graduates go on to graduate school or professional school within five years. The College was awarded a Phi Beta Kappa chapter in 1971.

Ninety-five percent of Hiram's students live in the eleven residence halls and eat their meals on campus. Newer College buildings are designed to complement Hiram's old, distinguished Western Reserve architecture. Student services include a health center, a fitness center, a sports medicine clinic, a career placement office, professional counseling on a wide range of personal and academic concerns, optional religious services and activities, and sports for everyone. There are honorary societies, social clubs, music and drama groups, student publications, religious groups, and student government and political and social-action groups. The campus radio station, TV station, and student publications are directed by the students themselves.

Location

Hiram's campus is in the scenic, rural Western Reserve area of northeastern Ohio. Located in Portage County, the campus is about 35 miles southeast of Cleveland. The area is served by excellent state and federal highway systems, which make the College easily accessible. Cleveland Hopkins Airport and the Canton Akron Airport are a 45-minute drive from Hiram. The campus is a day's drive or less from New England and northern East Coast cities, about a 6-hour drive from Baltimore, Chicago, and Washington, D.C., and less than 2 hours from Pittsburgh, Pennsylvania.

Majors and Degrees

Hiram College awards the Bachelor of Arts (B.A.). Areas of major concentration are: art, art history, biology, biochemistry, biomedical humanities, chemistry, classical studies, communication, computer science, economics, elementary and secondary education, English, English with a creative writing emphasis, environmental studies, French, history, integrated language arts, integrated social studies, management, mathematics, music, philosophy, physics, political science, psychobiology, psychology, religious studies, social science, sociology/anthropology, Spanish, and theater arts. Minors are available in most areas of study as well as in exercise and sport science, gender studies, Greek, international studies, Latin, and urban studies.

Preprofessional programs offer preparation for study in a wide variety of fields, including dentistry, engineering, law, medicine, physical therapy, and veterinary medicine.

Hiram also offers a cooperative, dual-degree program in engineering with Case Western Reserve University and Washington University, leading to a Bachelor of Arts degree from Hiram in a field of science or mathematics and a Bachelor of Science in engineering from the cooperating engineering school.

Academic Programs

Hiram's academic calendar, the Hiram Plan, is unique among colleges and universities. Each fifteen-week semester is divided into a twelve-week and a three-week session. During the three-week session, students take only one intensive course. The plan provides two formats for learning, which increases opportunity for small group study with faculty, study in special topics, hands-on learning through field trips and internships, and study abroad.

Hiram College's commitment to the liberal arts is manifested in a core curriculum required of all students. Required courses include the Freshman Colloquium, a small, seminar course on a special topic taught by a student's adviser; First Year Seminar, emphasizing critical thinking, effective writing, and speaking; and a sequence of interdisciplinary courses.

The course of study in most areas of major concentration is specified by the departments and divisions. Students generally take ten courses from within a department, as well as two or three courses from related or supporting departments. Alternatively, a student, with the assistance of the adviser, may develop an area of concentration that consists of related courses from different academic areas, crossing departmental lines to focus on particular needs or interests. A student may also submit a proposal for an individually designed program to the Area of Concentration Board.

Off-Campus Programs

A number of domestic and international off-campus programs and study opportunities are available. Programs in Australia, England, France, Germany, Italy, Japan, Mexico, Turkey, and other locations are conducted by the College's own teaching staff. Study-abroad programs are available to students regardless of their major discipline, and more than 40 percent of the College's graduates have participated. Hiram students may also spend a semester at the School of Social Sciences and Public Affairs of the American University in Washington, D.C. Another facet of Hiram's off-campus opportunities is study at John Cabot University, a Hiram affiliate, which is the major American university in Rome. Students may also take advantage of exchange programs with Mithibai College of the University of Bombay, India, and Kansai University of Foreign Studies in Osaka, Japan. Other opportunities are offered through the College's affiliation with the Institute for European Studies and the Institute for Asian Studies.

Internships with corporations and agencies are also available in all academic departments, and arrangements are made for students on an individual basis.

Other opportunities for off-campus study in marine science are described in the section below.

Academic Facilities

The Esther and Carl Gerstacker Science Hall opened in 2000. This state-of-the-art facility includes modern chemical laboratories specially designed for undergraduate instruction and research, plus a substantial amount of new chemical instrumentation. A $12-million addition to the Student Recreation Center is scheduled to open in August 2005. Plans for this addition include new classrooms, offices, and recreation areas. The five-level library contains nearly 180,000 volumes in open stacks and features a reference area that includes recent government documents (the library is one of only 1,400 federal depositories in the U.S.); a media center featuring a listening library, a videotape collection, and a video production room; a computer area equipped with CD-ROM and printers, with access to the Internet and other resources on the information superhighway; and an archival pavilion that houses a number of special collections relating to the history of the Western Reserve, including the papers of notable Hiram alumni James A. Garfield, twentieth president of the United States, and poet Vachel Lindsay.

Other resources include the Stephens Memorial Observatory; the Center for International Studies; the Center for Literature, Medicine, and the Health Care Professions; the Writing Center; InterVIEW™, a PC-based video conferencing and interview system; and SIGI Career Guidance System.

The computer facilities at Hiram include midrange Unix servers for administrative use as well as workstations and servers for academic use and general office work. Personal computers are available for student use in several computer labs located in the library, residence halls, and other locations throughout the campus. These computers are networked via fast Ethernet and wireless technologies to all campus buildings and offices, including the residence halls. Wireless laptop and PDA users are able to access the Internet from most campus locations. Hiram's connection to the Internet consists of a high-capacity, fractional DS3 line (12 megabits per second of bandwidth). The College is a member of the Internet2 initiative, which provides even greater network capacity among member academic institutions for applications such as real-time video conferencing.

Northwoods Field Station in upper Michigan, a day's drive from Hiram, offers an additional facility for field trips, summer course work, and research activities. Many independent and/or team research projects involving students and faculty members from a variety of disciplines take place at the Field Station and on campus.

Students interested in marine science have opportunities for advanced work at Shoals Marine Laboratory off the coast of New Hampshire and at the Gulf Coast Research Laboratory in Mississippi. The College's affiliations with these facilities provide students with field experience in Hiram courses and the opportunity to enroll in any of more than twenty specialized summer courses.

Costs

Hiram has instituted a new Tuition Guarantee program for incoming students beginning in fall 2004. Costs for 2004–05 are $21,970 for tuition and $7525 for room and board. There is also a general fee of $625.

Financial Aid

More than 80 percent of Hiram's students receive financial aid based on need. All financial aid awards are made on a one-year basis, and each year a new Free Application for Federal Student Aid (FAFSA) must be submitted to determine eligibility. Most financial aid at Hiram is a combination of grant-in-aid, scholarships, and work-study. Scholarships awarded on the basis of merit are also available and range from $3000 to full tuition per year. Aid includes Federal Pell Grants, Federal Supplemental Educational Opportunity Grants, Federal Perkins Loans, Federal Stafford Student Loans, state grants, Federal Work-Study awards, and veterans' benefits. Campus employment is available regardless of aid eligibility.

Faculty

Ninety-five percent of Hiram's faculty members hold earned doctorates or the appropriate terminal degree. The student-faculty ratio is 11:1. The ideal of a "community of scholars" thrives at Hiram, where students engage in research side by side with their professors, enjoy extracurricular activities with their teachers, and reach out with the faculty to serve the community. Faculty concern and guidance begin even before the formal opening of the academic year. One week prior to opening,

faculty members work with their advisees, groups of about 15 freshmen, as part of the first-year orientation program. This one-week program, the New Student Institute, is followed by a semester-long seminar in which the freshmen continue to meet as a group. Seminar topics introduce students to scholarship in the liberal arts tradition. Approximately twenty seminars are offered each year.

Student Government

The student governing body, or Student Senate, composed in part of members elected from the academic departments and residence halls, is very active at Hiram. The Senate administers a $150,000 student activities budget and is involved in almost all aspects of college policymaking and governance. It holds seats with faculty, staff, and administrators on most College committees, the College Executive Committee, and the Student Life Subcommittee of Hiram's Board of Trustees. The Kennedy Center Programming Board, an arm of the student government, plans recreational and cultural activities for the campus community.

Admission Requirements

Admission to Hiram College is competitive. The admission process attempts to bring to Hiram students who have the ability and desire to benefit from the College's educational programs. Candidates should have pursued a strong secondary school program of college preparation in the humanities, sciences, and social sciences. All applicants are required to submit SAT I or ACT scores.

Application and Information

Application materials include the completed application form; a secondary school report, which must be completed and returned to Hiram directly by the high school guidance counselor; the results of the SAT I or ACT; and an essay. Teacher recommendations are also required. Hiram employs a rolling admission plan, but for maximum scholarship consideration, applications should be submitted by February 1. An early decision option is also available. Applicants are encouraged to visit the campus. The Office of Admission, located in Teachout-Price Hall, is open year-round for interviews from 9 a.m. to 4 p.m. on weekdays and from 9 a.m. to noon on most Saturdays.

Prospective students should address questions to:

Director of Admission
Hiram College
P.O. Box 96
Hiram, Ohio 44234
Telephone: 330-569-5169
    800-362-5280 (toll-free)
E-mail: admission@hiram.edu
World Wide Web: http://www.hiram.edu

Esther and Carl Gerstacker Science Hall.

THE ILLINOIS INSTITUTE OF ART–CHICAGO
CHICAGO, ILLINOIS

The Institute

The Illinois Institute of Art–Chicago is a leading institution for career preparation in the visual and practical arts, fashion, and culinary arts fields. It is a member of the Art Institutes, which also has several other locations throughout the United States. Founded in 1916 as the Commercial Art School, the Institute was one of the first applied art and design schools in the United States. The Institute became widely known in the 1930s as Ray Vogue School in recognition of its professional programs in fashion, art, and design. Renamed Ray College of Design in 1981 and joining the Art Institutes in 1995, the Institute offers the Bachelor of Fine Arts, Bachelor of Arts, and Associate of Applied Science degrees.

Students attend the Institute to prepare for and begin careers in creative industries. A strong faculty of working professionals strengthens students' skills and cultivates their talents through curricula that are reviewed often to meet the needs of a changing marketplace and qualify graduates for entry-level positions in their chosen fields. Programs are designed with the support and contributions of leading members of the professional community.

Chicago offers students an abundance of sporting, recreational, and cultural events that are world-class. When not in class, many Institute students participate in on-campus clubs such as the Student Animators Club, Fashion Focus, the American Institute of Graphic Artists, and the American Society of Interior Designers.

The Institute is dedicated to providing its students with safe, comfortable housing. Many students live in Pavillion Suites, school-sponsored apartments just a short train ride from the campus.

Location

Chicago, a world center of business, communication, and art, is located on the shores of Lake Michigan. The Institute is located downtown in the art and fashion center of River North in the heart of the city. City transportation is available nearby and also serves suburban locations, including Midway and O'Hare airports.

Majors and Degrees

The Illinois Institute of Art–Chicago offers eleven bachelor's degree programs in advertising, culinary management, digital media production, fashion design, fashion marketing and management, game art and design, interactive media design, interior design, media arts and animation, visual communications, and visual effects and motion graphics. Associate of Applied Science degrees are offered in culinary arts, fashion merchandising, fashion production, graphic design, and multimedia production.

Academic Programs

The bachelor's degree programs require 180 quarter credit hours, which can be earned in three years of full-time study, while the associate degree programs require 96 quarter credit hours, which can be earned in eighteen months of full-time study. There are required core courses, depending on the program, which introduce students to the fundamentals and foundations of their chosen field, followed by hands-on projects providing real-world experience. The curricula offer a challenging blend of textbook study and actual on-the-scene training. All programs are offered on a year-round basis, allowing students to work toward their degrees in an uninterrupted fashion.

Academic Facilities

The Illinois Institute of Art–Chicago occupies approximately 70,000 square feet of space in the Apparel Center/Merchandise Mart complex in downtown Chicago. Classrooms, studios, computer labs with Internet access, administrative and student services offices, galleries, and the Resource Center are available for study and research. In addition, the fashion department contains a full complement of special equipment, such as power sewing machines and large cutting tables and steamers. Fashion merchandising classes utilize a walk-in window, props, mannequins, and other display materials. The Interior Design Resource Center has an extensive collection of fabric and wall- and floor-covering samples.

Located eight blocks from the Mart Center campus, the Loop campus includes the culinary facility occupying approximately 35,000 square feet. The facility contains kitchens, classrooms, and a full-service restaurant and dining lab, which serves lunch to the public. The Loop campus also has multiple computer labs and studios for recording, video shooting, and audio development.

Costs

Tuition is $351 per credit hour and $5616 per quarter for full-time study for all programs, not including a starting kit (with cost ranging from $185 to $660, depending on the program) and various monthly fees for books and supplies, which may range from $50 to $180 per month. Housing costs vary.

Financial Aid

The Illinois Institute of Art–Chicago offers several scholarship programs. Some are awarded by the Art Institutes to winners of various competitions. Six half-tuition scholarships are awarded to high school competition winners. Two scholarships are awarded to recipients of a Regional Portfolio Competition for high school seniors. The Institute also makes available a limited number of scholarships to international students and has a family assistance plan available when two or more family members are currently enrolled.

Various private and government loan programs and grant programs are also available. The Financial Services Department helps students and families develop individual financial plans to meet expenses, including tuition, fees, starting kit, and the cost of living.

Faculty

The Institute has 110 faculty members, the majority of whom hold a master's degree in their field. Many are professionals who have real-world experience in the subjects they are teaching.

Admission Requirements

A prospective student seeking admission to the Institute must be a high school graduate, hold a General Educational Development (GED) certificate, or have earned a bachelor's degree from an accredited college or university to be considered for admission. Each applicant is interviewed, either in person or by telephone. Exams such as the SAT and ACT are considered, but are not required. High school transcripts are required, and each applicant must write an essay (300 words if applying to a bachelor's program, 150 if applying to an associate program). A $50 application fee and a $100 registration fee are required. All applicants for whom English is not the native language must either score 480 or above on the TOEFL, successfully complete a Level 108 ELS course, or have graduated from a high school or university where the primary language of instruction is English.

Application and Information

For the 2004–05 academic year, start dates are July 12, 2004; October 4, 2004; January 10, 2005; and April 4, 2005. Applications should be made in advance of the quarter in which the student wishes to enroll. The Institute has an Early Acceptance program for high school seniors.

Students may request additional information from:

Janis K. Anton
Vice President/Director of Admissions
The Illinois Institute of Art–Chicago
350 North Orleans Street
Chicago, Illinois 60654-1510
Telephone: 312-280-3500
             800-351-3450 (toll-free)
Fax: 312-280-8562
E-mail: janton@aii.edu
World Wide Web: http://www.ilic.artinstitutes.edu

ILLINOIS INSTITUTE OF TECHNOLOGY

CHICAGO, ILLINOIS

The Institute

Illinois Institute of Technology (IIT) is a private, Ph.D.-granting research university with undergraduate programs in architecture, engineering, humanities, psychology, and science. One of the seventeen institutions in the Association of Independent Technological Universities (AITU), IIT offers exceptional preparation for professions that require technological sophistication. Through a committed faculty and close personal attention, IIT provides a challenging academic program focused on the rigor of the real world. The internationally famous main campus is based on a master plan developed by the late Ludwig Mies van der Rohe, one of the most influential architects of the century, who served for twenty years as director of IIT's College of Architecture. An independent university, the Institute includes the College of Architecture, the Armour College of Engineering and Science, the Institute of Psychology, the Stuart School of Business, the Institute of Design, and the Chicago-Kent College of Law.

The more than 6,000 students at IIT (more than 1,500 of whom are undergraduates) are encouraged to participate in the many social, cultural, and athletic opportunities available. Student activities include the campus newspaper, the radio station, special interest clubs, theater and music groups, intramural and varsity athletics, fraternities and sororities, honor societies, professional societies, student government, residence hall organizations, and the student-run Union Board. Campus facilities include the new McCormick Tribune Campus Center, a convenience store and campus book store, a gymnasium, seven residence halls, six new residence halls, one resident sorority house, and seven resident fraternity houses. Counseling, job placement, and student health services are included in the various campus services.

Location

IIT stands in the midst of a developing urban area. It is 1 mile west of Lake Michigan and one block from the White Sox ballpark. The campus is located approximately 3 miles south of the Chicago Loop, offering students unlimited opportunities to enjoy art, music, drama, films, museums, and other entertainment. Also convenient to the campus are a number of recreational areas, including McCormick Place exhibition hall, Soldier Field, Grant Park, Lincoln Park Zoo, various bicycle paths, and lakefront beaches. IIT is easily accessible to the rest of Chicago via two major expressways. Bus and elevated train lines have stops on the campus, and the IIT shuttle bus provides free transportation between the campus and the university's Downtown Campus in Chicago's West Loop area.

Majors and Degrees

The Armour College of Engineering and Science offers the Bachelor of Science in Engineering with specializations in aerospace, architectural, biomedical, chemical, civil, computer, electrical, mechanical, and metallurgical and materials engineering as well as a Bachelor of Science degree in applied mathematics, biology, business administration, chemistry, computer information systems, computer science, humanities, Internet communication, molecular biochemistry and biophysics, physics, political science, professional and technical communication, and psychology.

The College of Architecture awards the Bachelor of Architecture degree through its five-year professional degree program.

There are various options and minors available within each curriculum, such as artificial intelligence, bioengineering, business, computer-aided drafting, law, management, manufacturing technology, military science, psychology, public administration, and technical communications. Other individualized specializations may be arranged with approval of the dean. Combined undergraduate/graduate degrees include those offered in conjunction with business administration (B.S./M.B.A.), law (B.S./J.D.), and public administration (B.S./M.P.A.).

Along with its traditional premed program, IIT has also established an honors combined program in engineering and medicine (B.S./M.D.) with the Finch University of Health Sciences/Chicago Medical School and Rush Medical College and an honors research program. IIT also offers an honors combined program in law (B.S./J.D.) with the Chicago-Kent College of Law and in pharmacy (B.S./Pharm.D.) with Midwestern University/Chicago College of Pharmacy. Students interested in an honors program must submit an undergraduate application and a supplemental application for the graduate portion of the program. All application materials are available online.

Academic Programs

While requirements vary according to the major, all IIT students complete a general education core, which includes a minimum of 7 semester hours in mathematics and computer science, 11 semester hours in natural science or engineering, 12 semester hours in the humanities, and 12 semester hours in the social sciences. Students pursuing a Bachelor of Science in Engineering or in the physical sciences take, in addition, a program that includes further study in mathematics and computer science, chemistry, and physics.

IIT's mission is to educate students for complex professional roles in a changing world and to advance knowledge through research and scholarship. The Institute is committed to the educational ideal of small undergraduate classes and individual mentoring. IIT's unique Introduction to the Professions program brings students and senior faculty members together each week in small groups, where students interact with their advisers as both teachers and mentors. Throughout the curricula, the IIT interprofessional projects provide a learning environment in which interdisciplinary teams of students apply theoretical knowledge gained in the classroom and laboratory to real-world projects sponsored by industry and government. Many IIT students further enhance their education through a wide variety of research and entrepreneurial projects.

Cooperative education is encouraged. This career development program begins with a freshman year of full-time study and then alternates semesters of study and employment in industry for approximately four additional years. Placement services are provided by the university. Ninety-two percent of recent graduates were placed in jobs in the fields of their majors or went on to graduate or professional schools.

Study abroad is available in several academic disciplines.

Academic Facilities

As the central library, the Paul V. Galvin Library provides a broad range of services, including information on engineering, business, science, mathematics, the humanities, architecture, and design via the Internet; numerous electronic and paper-based databases; a document delivery service; interlibrary loan; and special collections. The main campus operates DEC minicomputers, a Silicon Graphics "Challenge" UNIX multiprocessor, and local UNIX servers. Terminals and microcomputers are located in most academic buildings across the campus, in residence halls, and in Galvin Library. Seminars, tutorials, and computer lab work are conducted in microcomputer classrooms. Among IIT's thirty-two research centers are the Center for Synchrotron Radiation Research, the Fluid Dynamics Research Center, and the Research Laboratory in Human Biomechanics. Most research centers offer undergraduates opportunities to participate on their projects.

Costs

Annual tuition for 2003–04 was $19,775. Other expenses are $6282 for room and board and approximately $1000 for books, $1200 for transportation costs, and $2100 for personal expenses. Additional fees are $100. The estimated annual total for freshmen is $29,482. Annual tuition covers the fall and spring semesters.

Financial Aid

Most full-time undergraduates at IIT receive financial aid from a variety of sources. IIT participates in the Federal Perkins Loan, Federal Work-Study, Federal Pell Grant, Federal Supplemental Educational Opportunity Grant, federally insured student loan, Illinois State Scholarship Commission Monetary Award, Illinois Guaranteed Loan, and Federal PLUS loan programs and similar programs. In addition, IIT provides generous merit-based and need-based scholarships and loans from its own funds and from those supported by a number of companies and other organizations. The Camras Scholarships range from $59,000 to $91,000 for the study of any major. A supplemental application is required for Camras Scholarships. All admitted students are automatically reviewed for tuition scholarships. More than 500 are awarded each year. Athletic scholarships are also available for qualified students. Two other programs may be utilized by students working to supplement their financial aid: on-campus employment and the cooperative education program. IIT requires the Free Application for Federal Student Aid (FAFSA). No additional applications or forms are required.

Army, Naval, and Air Force ROTC programs are offered. ROTC scholarship winners receive supplemental scholarships from IIT.

Faculty

There are 339 full-time faculty members and 196 industry professionals as part-time faculty members. The student-faculty ratio is approximately 12:1. All members of the senior teaching faculty instruct in both upper- and lower-division courses. Ninety-eight percent hold doctoral degrees or the highest professional degree in their area.

Student Government

The Student Government Association (SGA) is a vital force in the IIT community. It acts as the students' official voice in communications with faculty and administration, and it plans, develops, and supervises most of the activities pertaining to campus life. In addition to having its own standing committees, SGA is represented on seven of the ten institutional committees pertaining to undergraduates.

Admission Requirements

Admission evaluation is a thorough, personal process. Of paramount consideration is the student's academic performance in high school, specifically in areas that are vital to the student's major at IIT. Minimum high school preparation includes 16 units of credit, including at least 4 units in English, 4 units in mathematics through pre-calculus, and 3 units of science with 2 lab sciences. Calculus is encouraged but not required. Chemistry and physics are strongly recommended.

A completed application, recommendations, test scores—either SAT I or ACT—and an official high school transcript are required for admission. Interviews are not required. Supplemental applications and materials are required for the Honors Program in Engineering and Medicine, the Honors Law Program, the Honors Pharmacy Program, and for the Camras Scholarship Program. Special deadlines apply to these programs. All materials are available online.

Application and Information

Applications are reviewed on a rolling basis. Students are encouraged to apply as early as possible; an online application is available at http://www.iit.edu/~apply. In general, applicants can expect notification within two weeks after their completed applications are received.

For further information, students should contact:

Office of Admission
Illinois Institute of Technology
10 West 33rd Street
Chicago, Illinois 60616-3793
Telephone: 312-567-3025 (from Chicago)
              800-448-2329 (toll-free outside Chicago)
Fax: 312-567-6939
E-mail: admission@iit.edu
World Wide Web: http://www.iit.edu

INTERNATIONAL ACADEMY OF DESIGN & TECHNOLOGY

CHICAGO, ILLINOIS

The Academy

The International Academy of Design & Technology–Chicago is a postsecondary degree-granting institution with career-based curricula and professional staff members who contribute to students' development in their chosen fields. The Academy provides a high-quality education, prepares students for positions in fields related to their area of study, provides students with a professional environment that fosters cultural enrichment and personal development, maintains high-quality curricula that are sensitive to industry needs as defined by the Academy's advisory board, and offers career-planning services leading to employment opportunities for graduates to allow them to utilize their knowledge, skills, and talents.

The International Academy of Design & Technology was founded in 1977 by Clem Stein Jr. as a private coeducational institution. In 1983, the Academy opened a campus in Toronto, Canada. The Tampa, Florida, campus was opened in 1984, and in 1987, the fourth campus was opened in Montreal, Canada. In 1997, Career Education Corporation acquired the Academy. Career Education Corporation operates postsecondary institutions throughout the U.S. and abroad. In 2001, the Academy changed its name from the International Academy of Merchandising & Design to the International Academy of Design & Technology, which better reflects the infusion of technology into all of the program curricula.

The Academy sponsors a student chapter of the American Society of Interior Designers (ASID) and offers student memberships in the American Marketing Association (AMA) and the Fashion Group International Chicago, Inc. These student groups introduce students to the standards set by professional organizations and provide access to professional seminars and workshops. The Student Ambassador Program assists new students through their transition to the Academy and college life.

Other forms of student involvement include the Fashion Council, clubs organized by and for multimedia and information technology students, the International Students Organization, and the student-produced magazine *Mixed Media*.

The Academy is approved by the Illinois State Board of Education and authorized by the Illinois Board of Higher Education to grant the Bachelor of Arts degree in merchandising management; the Bachelor of Fine Arts degree in advertising and design, fashion design, interior design, and multimedia production and design; and the Associate of Applied Science degree in advertising and design, computer graphics, fashion design, interactive media, merchandising management, and PC/LAN.

The Academy is incorporated under the laws of the state of Illinois and accredited by the Accrediting Council for Independent Colleges and Schools (ACICS). The interior design program is accredited by the Foundation for Interior Design Education Research (FIDER).

Location

The Academy is located in Chicago's Loop at historic One North State Street. The campus is close to some of Chicago's famous and world-renowned landmarks. Within walking distance of the campus are the Merchandise Mart and Apparel Center complex in historic River North and the retail shops of North Michigan Avenue. Along the revitalized State Street are Marshall Field's, Carson Pirie Scott, and a multitude of nationally advertised retail outlets. More importantly, IADT Chicago is conveniently located in a region known for its internationally prominent advertising, graphic design, and interior design firms.

Nearby cultural and educational resources include the Art Institute of Chicago, the Harold Washington Library, the Chicago Cultural Center, the Athenaeum Museum of Architecture and Design, the Chicago Architecture Foundation, and the Goodman Theatre.

The natural beauty of Grant Park and the numerous public art works that are located throughout the Loop are the ideal complement to IADT Chicago's exciting urban location.

Majors and Degrees

All degree programs provide students with the opportunity for in-depth career preparation and a firm foundation in general education studies. In the bachelor's degree program, students benefit from advanced career courses and have the option of choosing elective courses to complete their general education requirements.

The International Academy of Design & Technology offers bachelor's degrees in advertising and design, fashion design, interior design, information technology, merchandising management, and multimedia production and design. Associate degrees are offered in advertising and design, computer graphics, fashion design, information technology, iteractive media, and mrchandising management.

Academic Programs

The programs of the Academy involve both classroom education and supervised activities off campus that are designed to prepare students for entry-level positions in their chosen field. Students must take a minimum of 180 quarter hours of study to earn the baccalaureate degree. Transfer credits are acceptable in all programs. Students must take a minimum of 90 quarter hours to earn the Associate of Applied Science degree and must complete all prescribed courses satisfactorily with a minimum grade point average of 2.0.

The curriculum for each program is reviewed periodically by the faculty members, program directors, and members of the faculty advisory council, who, along with the president and deans, constitute the Curriculum Advisory Committee. Members of the Faculty Advisory Council are experienced professionals in the fields of fashion, interior design, advertising, merchandising, multimedia production and design, computer graphics, interactive media, and information technology. The Faculty Advisory Council provides the Academy with counsel on a variety of subjects and also participates in seminars. These successful practitioners form an essential link between the academic world and the world that students enter upon graduation.

The Academy's programs are arranged into four quarters of eleven weeks each. A normal full-time load is 15 credit hours per quarter. As a result of the career-oriented emphasis of the Academy, course work is highly specialized and prepares students for entry into a career field. From the point at which they begin their studies at the Academy, and continuing through graduation, students are given personal one-on-one academic guidance. Students are regularly advised by the Academy's faculty members regarding their progress in classes.

Academic Facilities

Classrooms are designed to facilitate learning and consist of lecture rooms, drafting labs, design studios, and sewing and pattern-making rooms. Computer labs equipped with Macintosh and IBM-compatible personal computers are used for instruction and practice in computer-aided design (CAD), graphic design, word processing, database management, spreadsheet analysis, and computer-aided pattern drafting.

The library houses a growing collection of approximately 5,500 book volumes and 90 periodical subscriptions to support the major programs of study as well as general education courses. The library's multimedia resources consist of more than 500 videos, DVDs, and CDs with image and sound files. Other components of the collection are electronic resources with access to eBooks, full-text journals, magazines, and newspaper articles. A professional librarian manages the site and assists students in the use of the library's print collection and online databases. The librarian also facilitates student access to local libraries that participate in the INFOPASS program.

The bookstore sells books and supplies used in the courses taught at the Academy. The bookstore attempts to keep a balance of inventory between new and used books whenever possible. The bookstore also coordinates book buy-back periods at the end of each quarter.

Costs

Full-time tuition for the 2003–04 academic year was $13,800 for all programs. Books and supplies ranged from $300 to $2000.

Financial Aid

The Academy helps students find the financial resources they need to achieve their educational goals. The College participates in the Federal Pell Grant, Federal Supplemental Education Opportunity Grant (SEOG), Federal Stafford Student Loan, and the Federal PLUS loan program. In addition to state and federal aid, the Academy has its own scholarship programs.

Faculty

Faculty members of the Academy possess extensive academic and professional credentials. Their experience enables them to teach theoretical principles while emphasizing current practices in the field. Faculty members are sought and retained because they are committed to teaching at the undergraduate level. In and out of the classroom, the faculty is an integral part of the students' career preparation.

Student Government

The Student Council meets quarterly to discuss issues pertaining to student campus life at the college.

Admission Requirements

Pursuant to the mission of the institution, the Academy desires to admit students who possess appropriate credentials and have demonstrated the capacity or potential for successfully completing the educational programs offered by the institution. To that end, the institution evaluates all students and makes admission decisions on an individual basis. To assist the admissions personnel in making informed decisions, an admissions interview is required.

Transfer students meeting admission requirements are accepted. Students must have a transcript from the postsecondary institution previously attended forwarded to the Academy. Credit may be given for a course taken at the previous institution if it is comparable in scope and length to an International Academy course.

Application and Information

Prospective students should apply for admission as soon as possible in order to be officially accepted for a specific program and starting date. Prospective students must have an admissions interview and are given an opportunity to tour the Academy with their families to see its equipment and facilities, during which time, there is also an opportunity to ask questions relating to the Academy's curricula and a student's possible career goals.

At the time of application, the student must complete an enrollment agreement, pay a $50 application fee, complete an attestation of high school graduation or its equivalency or provide proof of high school graduation or its equivalency, and provide proof of immunization as required by Illinois law. Once an applicant has completed and submitted the enrollment agreement, the school reviews the information and informs the applicant of its decision.

For further information, students should contact:

Robyn Palmersheim, Vice President of Admissions
International Academy of Design & Technology
One North State Street, Suite 400
Chicago, Illinois 60602-3300
Telephone: 312-980-9200
        877-222-3369 (toll-free)
Fax: 312-541-3929
E-mail: info@iadtchicago.com
World Wide Web: http://www.iadtchicago.com

IOWA STATE UNIVERSITY OF SCIENCE AND TECHNOLOGY

AMES, IOWA

The University

Iowa State University of Science and Technology (Iowa State), a public, broad-based international university of 27,380 students, was established in 1858 as one of the first U.S. land-grant colleges. It is a member of the prestigious Association of American Universities and is accredited by the North Central Association of Colleges and Schools. All fifty states and 112 countries are represented in the student body, exposing students to ideas from other cultures both in and out of the classroom.

Iowa State has grown in size and reputation to become one of the nation's leading educational institutions and has made significant contributions to the development of the United States and the world. Revolutionary innovations include the world's first electronic digital computer, the digital encoding process that led to the development of facsimile machines, and LoSatSoy, a new cooking oil low in saturated fat. Iowa State's graduates include George Washington Carver, one of the nation's most distinguished educators and plant scientists; Carrie Chapman Catt, a leader in the women's suffrage movement; and John Vincent Atanasoff who, as a faculty member at Iowa State, invented the electronic digital computer.

Nearly 8,000 students live on campus in nineteen residence halls and twelve apartment-style buildings. Each of the nineteen residence halls is divided into houses, which are small-group living arrangements of about 60 residents. Wellness houses, learning communities, honors houses, and alcohol- and smoke-free houses are a few of the options available. The Department of Residence is in the midst of a $105-million renovation and improvement project. In addition, 3,000 undergraduates participate in Iowa State's national award-winning Greek system, which encompasses twenty-seven fraternities, thirteen sororities, and six National Pan-Hellenic chapters conveniently located near the campus.

More than 500 clubs and organizations provide unlimited leadership, social, and cultural opportunities. Annually, 3,000 teams participate in fifty intramural sports, 2,500 people participate in forty sports clubs, and 20,000 students, staff members, and faculty members participate in outdoor recreation activities. Facilities include the Lied Recreation/Athletic Center, which houses twenty courts for basketball and volleyball, a rock climbing wall, a 300-meter track, an artificial turf area, and a weightlifting and fitness center; Beyer Hall; the Physical Education Building; the State Gym; and many outdoor facilities. The Cyclones have eighteen Division I intercollegiate men's and women's sports and belong to the Big 12, one of the premier sports conferences in the country.

Outstanding facilities for the cultural and performing arts include the 2,700-seat Stephens Auditorium, the 452-seat Fisher Theater, and the 15,000-seat Hilton Coliseum. Iowa State attracts the top entertainment acts and world-renowned speakers. Recent performers include Shermie Alexie, Bill Cosby, the Dave Matthews Band, Simon Estes, Mae Jemmison, Jars of Clay, Prince, Wynton Marsalis, Nikki Giovanni, Michael W. Smith, Sarah McLachlan, Aerosmith, Dixie Chicks, Blue Man Group, Tool, Toby Keith, Cabaret, and John Mayer.

Personal support services, available to help students become their best, include the following: assertiveness training; career counseling; communication skills workshops; medical, physical, and learning disabled services; and stress management, study skills, and test-taking workshops.

Iowa State University offers 111 master's programs, eighty-two Ph.D. programs, and one professional degree program—the Doctor of Veterinary Medicine.

Location

Iowa State is located in Ames, just 30 minutes north of Iowa's capital, Des Moines. Minneapolis, Chicago, Kansas City, St. Louis, Omaha, and other metropolitan areas are a short drive from Ames or easily accessible by plane and train.

The campus environment rates high with students and faculty and staff members. The book *The Campus as a Work of Art* rated Iowa State among the twenty-five most beautiful campuses in the nation. The American Society of Landscape Architects recently chose Iowa State as a "medallion site," one of the three best central campuses in the nation. Iowa State students spend most of their time on the 24-acre central campus, part of the 1,984 acres.

Ames was ranked the second-best "micropolitan" area (population 50,000 or fewer) in the nation. Students take advantage of arts groups, recreational facilities, biking and hiking trails, more than eighty restaurants, a great downtown, many shopping areas, and a variety of movie theaters.

Majors and Degrees

Iowa State University offers 101 bachelor's degree programs. The College of Agriculture includes programs in agricultural biochemistry, agricultural business, agricultural education, agricultural extension education, agricultural studies, agricultural systems technology, agronomy, animal ecology, animal science, dairy science, dietetics, entomology, environmental science, food science, forestry, genetics, horticulture, international agriculture, microbiology, nutritional science, pest management, plant health and protection, public service and administration in agriculture, seed science, and zoology. The College of Business offers programs in accounting, finance, management, management information systems, marketing, and transportation and logistics. The College of Design offers programs in architecture, art and design, community and regional planning, graphic design, interior design, and landscape architecture. The College of Education offers programs in early childhood education, elementary education, environmental studies, exercise and sport science, industrial technology, and secondary education. The College of Engineering offers programs in aerospace engineering, agricultural engineering, ceramic engineering, chemical engineering, civil engineering, computer engineering, construction engineering, electrical engineering, engineering applications, engineering science, industrial engineering, mechanical engineering, and metallurgical engineering. The College of Family and Consumer Sciences offers programs in apparel merchandising, design, and production; child and family services; dietetics; early childhood education; family and consumer sciences education; family resource management and consumer sciences; food science; hotel, restaurant, and institution management; housing and the near environment; nutritional science; and studies in family and consumer sciences. The College of Liberal Arts and Sciences is the largest college and offers programs in advertising, African-American studies, American Indian studies, anthropology, astronomy, biochemistry, biology, biology/premedical illustration, biophysics, botany, chemistry, classical studies, computer science, earth science, economics, English, environmental science, environmental studies, French, genetics, geology, German, gerontology, history, interdisciplinary studies, international studies, journalism and mass communication, Latin, liberal studies, linguistics, mathematics, meteorology, music, naval science, performing arts, philosophy, physics, political science, Portuguese, psychology, religious studies, Russian, secondary education, sociology, Spanish, speech communication, statistics, technical communications, technology and social change, women's studies, and zoology.

Academic Programs

Each college provides academic support through advising offices. Additional academic services include academic learning labs, learning communities, learning teams, peer education, supplemental instruction, and tutoring services. The University Honors Program provides academically talented students an opportunity to stretch their minds through individualized programs, special courses and seminars, unique off-campus opportunities, and 24-hour access to the Martin C. Jischke Honors Building, home of the Honors Program. The academic year is divided into two semesters of sixteen weeks each, beginning in late August and ending in early May. A program called Soar in Four guarantees graduation in four years in all majors except architecture and landscape architecture.

Off-Campus Programs

Students can take advantage of internships, cooperative education programs, and research programs, which provide the opportunity for professional work with national and international companies. International exchange programs are available at more than 100 colleges and universities in forty countries. The National Student Exchange program provides students an opportunity to study at one of 177 reciprocating universities around the country.

Academic Facilities

Iowa State's 173 campus buildings include several recent state-of-the-art additions. Among the newest are the Durham Center for Computation and Communication, the Molecular Biology Building, the Martin C. Jischke Honors Building, the Palmer Educational Building, and Howe Hall, the $61-million engineering facility that is the home of the Engineering Teaching and Research Center (ETRC). Construction is complete on Hoover Hall, a new engineering building, and the Gerdin Building, which houses the College of Business. Technology is utilized to provide students the resources to succeed in a competitive global market. Iowa State is home to C4 and C6, two of the world's most advanced virtual reality rooms. C6 is the only six-sided virtual reality environment in the United States and one of three worldwide. Students are provided free e-mail and Internet access and space to create their own Web pages. Students use AccessPlus via the Web for instant access to jobs, grades, schedules, and more. Computing resources include thousands of workstations, 24-hour availability, and mainframe/Internet access from residence hall rooms.

Costs

For the 2004–05 academic year, in-state tuition and fees are $5426 and out-of-state tuition and fees are $15,128 (based upon full-time undergraduate status for two semesters). Room and board are $6121 for two semesters. Books and supplies are estimated at $820 per year.

Financial Aid

Need- and merit-based financial assistance is available to qualified applicants. Approximately 66 percent of students receive some type of financial aid, such as grants, scholarships, loans, and jobs. Students should apply for admission early to receive maximum consideration for merit scholarships. All applicants are encouraged to file the FAFSA by March 1 (for fall

semester enrollment). Links to scholarships and financial aid resources may be found at Iowa State's Web site at http://www.financialaid.iastate.edu.

Faculty

Iowa State has 1,751 faculty members, 77 percent of whom hold doctorates. The student-faculty ratio is 18:1.

Student Government

The Government of the Student Body (GSB) legislates and administers student policy and provides services to meet the needs of students. The functions of GSB are carried out by executives and senators elected by Iowa State students. GSB's primary function is the allocation of student activity fees, through which a number of diverse services and student organizations are funded.

Admission Requirements

Students seeking admission directly from high school must have a minimum of 4 years of English, 3 years of math (including 1 year each of algebra, geometry, and advanced algebra), 3 years of science (including 1 year each of courses from two of the following fields: biology, chemistry, and physics), and 2 years of social studies. In addition, students applying to the College of Liberal Arts and Sciences must have completed an additional year of social studies, for a total of 3 years, plus 2 years of a single foreign language. Grades, class rank, and quality of course work are the most important criteria in the admissions decision.

Transfer applicants are typically admitted if they have a minimum of 24 transferable credit hours and have earned at least a C (2.0) average in all college-level courses attempted. However, some programs may require a transfer grade point average higher than the 2.0 minimum. Higher academic standards may be required of students who are not residents of Iowa, including international students. Applicants who have not completed 24 transferable semester (or 36 quarter) hours prior to enrolling at Iowa State must submit a high school transcript and an ACT or SAT I score and meet all admission requirements for entering freshmen, as well as earn at least a 2.0 average in all college-level courses attempted.

Applicants must submit an application along with a $30 application fee ($50 for international students) and have their secondary school provide an official transcript of their academic record, including credits and grades, rank in class, and certification of graduation. Applicants must also arrange to have their ACT or SAT I scores reported to Iowa State directly from the testing agency. The Test of English as a Foreign Language (TOEFL) is required of international students whose first language is not English. Applicants may be required to submit additional information or data to support their applications.

Application and Information

Students interested in applying for the fall semester should apply during the preceding fall. Students should submit applications for the spring and summer terms six to nine months in advance. Interested students should contact the Office of Admissions at the toll-free number listed below or visit the Web site listed below for an application, a campus visit, financial aid, or other enrollment information.

Office of Admissions
Alumni Hall
Iowa State University of Science and Technology
Ames, Iowa 50011-2010
Telephone: 515-294-3094 (TTY/TDD)
              800-262-3810 (toll-free)
Fax: 515-294-2592
E-mail: admissions@iastate.edu
World Wide Web: http://www.admissions.iastate.edu

KENDALL COLLEGE
EVANSTON, ILLINOIS

The College

Kendall College is a private, career-driven college located in the heart of Chicago that provides its students with a small, personal, and supportive academic environment. The school prepares its students for the "real world" with the skills and attitudes critical for success.

Internships are a key component of each degree program. As a result, Kendall students graduate with a solid liberal college education and hands-on experience in their chosen field. Each area of study is taught with the individual in mind and a low student-faculty ratio.

Outside of class, Kendall is also committed to providing an active social and cultural life for its students. The move to a new facility in Chicago, Illinois, offers students the rich resources of the city of Chicago. The new College residence is located at 320 North Michigan Avenue, just steps from world-class museums, shopping, and entertainment.

Kendall College is accredited by the Commission on Institutions of Higher Education of the North Central Association of Colleges and Schools (NCACS) and the University Senate of the United Methodist Church. The School of Culinary Arts is accredited by the American Culinary Federation (ACF) Accrediting Commission.

Location

Beginning fall 2004, Kendall College offers classes at its new Chicago campus. The 166,000-square-foot building has been redeveloped into a state-of-the-art academic facility. The eight-story tower is part of a 6-acre riverfront campus only minutes from some of the country's best restaurants, hotels, and companies, providing students prime access to internships and work experiences. The facility offers sweeping views of the Chicago skyline, access to newly developed areas on the Chicago River, and all the cultural and social benefits of the third-largest city in the United States.

Majors and Degrees

A Kendall education is designed to make students the most effective and well-rounded professional possible. Kendall College awards Bachelor of Arts (B.A.) degrees in business and technology, culinary arts, early childhood education, hospitality management, and human services. The College also awards the Associate of Applied Science (A.A.S.) degree in baking and pastry arts and culinary arts.

Kendall College offers six major degree programs from which students may choose an area of study: baking and pastry arts, business and technology, culinary arts, early childhood education, hospitality management, and human services.

Kendall also offers concentrations and certificates in each of its major programs. The business and technology program offers concentrations in business administration, marketing, and Web design, and certificates in entrepreneurship and e-marketing. The culinary arts program offers certificates in baking and pastry arts, professional catering, professional personal chef, and professional cookery. Early childhood education offers a concentration in special education approval. The hospitality management program offers one certificate in bed and breakfast operations and five concentrations: convention and meeting planning, culinary management, food and beverage operations, hotel management, and international hospitality management. Students may also pursue concentrations in human services in crime, justice and rehabilitation, gerontology, psychology, or substance abuse treatment studies.

Academic Programs

Kendall College operates on a quarter system. The first quarter term extends from September to early December, the second term extends from January to March, and the third term extends from April to June. Summer sessions are offered from July to September. Students must fulfill a minimum of 92 quarter hours for an associate degree and a minimum of 184 quarter hours for a bachelor degree, and maintain a 2.0 GPA.

Academic Facilities

The Chicago campus provides wireless Internet access, labs with the latest computer equipment, and two distance learning videoconference facilities. Classrooms and study environments are high-tech and flexible, designed to give students a first-class, state-of-the-art setting in which to learn. There are auditoriums and presentation spaces, student lounges, fifteen kitchens, 350 secure parking spaces, and a number of nearby health clubs. As Kendall College settles into the new campus, the College will operate several restaurants to augment the culinary and hospitality programs.

Costs

In 2004–05, full-time tuition and fees in the School of Arts and Sciences are $15,165 for three quarters (12–19 credit hours). Part-time tuition for the arts and sciences program is $460 per credit hour.

Full-time tuition and fees in the School of Culinary Arts are $24,480 for three quarters, including culinary facilities usage. Part-time culinary arts tuition is $475 per credit hour.

Housing is located at 320 North Michigan Avenue. Students may lease double- or triple-occupancy apartments for $9000 per eleven-month lease.

Financial Aid

The College works with each student and develops a needs analysis to determine student eligibility, which then culminates in a financial aid package. It is the goal of Kendall College to seek funding and to package aid to fully meet the needs of all applicants. The financial aid packaging process ensures effective use of available funds, providing fair and equitable treatment of all applicants. Priority is given to applicants who meet the April 1 preferential filing date.

The College administers aid for undergraduates, including need-based, merit-based, and curriculum-specific scholarships; state and federal awards; Federal Supplemental Educational Opportunity Grants (FSEOG); Federal Work-Study Program awards; and opportunities for campus employment.

Faculty

The academic faculty has 34 full-time and 45 part-time members. The student-faculty ratio is approximately 17:1. Faculty members at Kendall College believe students work best when they are actively involved in making choices about their own learning. As Kendall students develop clear ideas of what they wish to study, they are provided with the opportunities to use tutorials to continue their education.

Student Government

Kendall College's Student Government Federation is designed to give students a leadership role and voice in building and improving their campus community. The Student Government Federation is elected annually in the fall term and is composed of a president, vice-president, and a group of senators. This group serves in an advisory capacity to the Board of Trustees, the Faculty Senate and various other faculty committees.

Admission Requirements

Kendall assesses its entrance difficulty level as moderate. Admission to Kendall College is open to men and women of all races and religious affiliations. Each applicant is considered on the basis of probable success at Kendall, as indicated primarily by high school grades, class rank, and ACT or SAT I test scores. A minimum GPA of at least 2.0 and an ACT score of 18 or an SAT I score of at least 850 are required for acceptance. If a student falls below either the minimum GPA or the standardized test requirements, the student must complete an entrance examination and submit two letters of recommendation. An essay accompanying the application is required. Qualities of character are also important at Kendall. Therefore, personal interviews and campus visits are encouraged, though not required, to help determine admission.

Application and Information

Prospective students may obtain applications from the Office of Admissions or via the College Web site listed below. Students may submit the admission application at any time. The Office of Admissions must be sent an official transcript. Some students may be admitted on probation after consulting with the Admissions Committee.

For further information, students should contact:

Office of Admissions
Kendall College
900 North Branch Street
Chicago, Illinois 60622
Telephone: 847-448-2304
            877-588-8860 (toll-free)
Fax: 312-752-2248
E-mail: admissions@kendall.edu
World Wide Web: http://www.kendall.edu

A view of Kendall College's new Riverworks campus in Chicago.

KETTERING UNIVERSITY

FLINT, MICHIGAN

The University

Kettering University (formerly GMI Engineering & Management Institute) offers education for the real world. Nearly 100 percent of Kettering's students receive a job offer or are accepted by graduate schools before receiving their diplomas. Kettering University has a unique partnership that offers students, business, and industry an opportunity found at no other undergraduate college in America. Kettering, a professional cooperative engineering, management, science, and math university, is the only institution that assists incoming freshmen to be selected by companies for cooperative employment, a process initiated for all accepted students. Kettering University successfully integrates the practical aspects of the workplace into the world of higher education through its more than 700 corporate partners, corporations, and agencies located throughout the United States, Canada, and selected countries. Kettering's corporate partners represent most major industrial groups; many are recognized as worldwide leaders in business innovation and manufacturing technology. These corporations share a commitment to "grow their own" engineers and managers by employing exceptionally talented young men and women in one of the nine baccalaureate degree programs. Kettering's corporate partners invest in students' futures by providing a program of progressive work experience that exposes them to processes, products, corporate culture, and the technology necessary to compete in tomorrow's business environment.

Founded in 1919, Kettering University is private and enrolls more than 2,400 undergraduate students. The University is accredited by the North Central Association of Colleges and Schools. Its engineering curricula are accredited by the Accreditation Board for Engineering and Technology, Inc. (ABET). The management program is accredited by the Association of Collegiate Business Schools and Programs (ACBSP).

The combination of academics and professional, paid work experience offered through Kettering University is not only highly effective, it is without equal, even among other cooperative education programs. The advantages of a Kettering education have enabled thousands of graduates to rise to key executive leadership positions in the world's finest corporations.

A varied program of sports, fitness, and recreational activities is offered. A 445-student residence hall and a new apartment complex are located on campus. Recreation facilities include athletic fields, tennis courts, and a recreation center with an Olympic-size, six-lane swimming pool, aerobic fitness rooms, a full line of Nautilus equipment, and basketball, tennis, and racquetball courts. A public golf course is adjacent to the campus.

Professional counseling, support services, and health care are available.

Location

Located in east-central Michigan, 60 miles west of Lake Huron and Canada and 60 miles north of Detroit, Flint is a city of 135,000 residents with a metropolitan area population of 450,000. Flint is particularly proud of its distinctive College and Cultural Center Complex, which is about 1½ miles from campus. Built and endowed entirely by the gifts of private citizens, the center includes the Alfred P. Sloan Museum; the Whiting Auditorium, home of the Flint Symphony and host to leading stage shows and entertainers; the Robert T. Longway Planetarium, Michigan's largest and best-equipped sky show facility; the Flint Institute of Arts; the F. A. Bower Theatre; the Dort Institute of Music; the University of Michigan–Flint Campus; the C. S. Mott Community College; and the Flint Public Library.

Outdoor and indoor recreational opportunities are abundant. Within a few minutes' drive are downhill and cross-country skiing facilities, several fine lakes for the entire range of water sports, a wide selection of good golf courses open to the public, and excellent indoor and outdoor skating rinks.

Majors and Degrees

Kettering University offers a 4½-year, professional cooperative education program with curricula leading to designated Bachelor of Science degrees in Computer Engineering, Electrical Engineering, Industrial Engineering, and Mechanical Engineering degrees; a designated Bachelor of Science in Business Management degree with concentrations in accounting/finance, information systems, manufacturing management, marketing, and materials management; and designated Bachelor of Science degrees in applied mathematics, applied physics, computer science, and environmental chemistry. Minors are available in applied chemistry, applied mathematics, applied optics, computer science, liberal arts, and management.

Academic Programs

Although each program at Kettering University has its own sequence requirements, 160 credit hours are generally required, including thesis credit hours. The program involves nine academic terms and nine co-op terms, two of which are focused on the capstone thesis project, which is done on behalf of the student's co-op employer. Students alternate between eleven-week periods of academic study on the campus in Flint and twelve-week periods of related work experience with their corporate employer. The academic year consists of two 3–month academic terms on campus and two 3–month terms of paid work experience. A typical Kettering University cooperative student may earn up to $65,000 in co-op wages through the complete program.

Academic Facilities

The C.S. Mott Engineering and Science Center—a $42 million facility—opened in summer 2003. This state-of-the-art facility houses a fuel cell lab, an emissions lab, and much more. Kettering University has the traditional laboratory facilities expected of any top engineering school, but also has labs to demonstrate and experiment with a wide range of technologies found in industry—from basic machining to emerging technologies. The instrumentation in some labs is generally found only in graduate school facilities at other colleges. There are manufacturing, laser, radioisotope, heat transfer, electricity and solid-state electronics, metallurgy, computer-aided design (CAD), computer-integrated manufacturing (CIM), acoustics, mechatronics, human factors, digital and analog computer, robotics, holography, and electron microscopy laboratories and the Polymer Optimization Center. The campus is fully networked and allows access to computer resources from dormitory rooms, dedicated labs, and other locations. Course materials are offered online through Blackboard. Each student has unlimited 24-hour access to computer resources and the World Wide Web. The library contains more than 94,000 cataloged volumes and currently subscribes to more than 540 periodicals and various online services. Special facilities include a microfilm area, database search services, record and tape listening and videocassette viewing facilities, and a special collection of SAE, SME, and ASME technical papers.

Costs

Tuition in 2003-04 was $21,184, and room and board were $4984 (nineteen meals per week).

Financial Aid

In addition to all traditional sources of aid, all Kettering students benefit from a special resource that is significant and not need based. One of the many advantages of attending Kettering University is the opportunity for students to earn a salary during their co-op work terms. Co-op income is substantial and can help cover part of the cost of a Kettering education by supplementing the family contribution and the standard forms of need-based and merit-based financial aid. Students who live at home during work experience periods are able to contribute a greater proportion of earnings directly to educational expenses. About 70 percent of students are able to live at home during work terms. The typical range of co-op earnings over the five-year program is $40,000 to $65,000.

Kettering University offers all the traditional forms of financial aid, both need- and merit-based. The new Kettering Merit Scholarship program rewards all qualified applicants. Because of their talents, many students win scholarships from agencies and organizations from their local communities. Michigan residents are often recipients of the Michigan Competitive Scholarship/Tuition Grant. Traditionally, more than 92 percent of the entering class receives some form of financial aid, making a private education at Kettering very affordable.

The primary purpose of financial aid at Kettering University is to supplement a student's unmet financial need after cooperative earnings and parents' contributions. Students who wish to apply for financial aid should complete the Free Application for Federal Student Aid (FAFSA) and request that a copy of the analysis be sent to Kettering University. Aid is given as grants, scholarships, loans, and work-study awards.

Faculty

Kettering University's full-time faculty of 144 members have teaching as their prime responsibility. Most professors in degree disciplines have industrial experience in addition to academic credentials and maintain contact with industry through consulting, sponsored research, and advising on student thesis projects. More than 80 percent of faculty members hold a doctorate. Because only half of the students are on campus at any one time, class sizes are small and opportunities for enrichment and extra help are readily available. Kettering faculty members find the challenge of teaching talented students who share their experiences from co-op especially refreshing and rewarding.

Student Government

Kettering University students enjoy an active college life with a wide range of clubs and organizations and an exciting intramural athletic program. Eleven professional societies are active on campus, and there are fourteen national fraternities and six sororities. More than half of all students are active in fraternities and sororities. Kettering students tend to enjoy competition, whether it be in service activities or on the athletic field. The student government represents the interests and needs of the students and contributes to their educational development in the areas of leadership skills, self-confidence, interpersonal relations, and organizational operations.

Admission Requirements

Admission to Kettering University is competitive and based on scholastic achievement and nonscholastic interests, activities, and achievements. Applicants are required to have earned the following credits (a credit represents two semesters or one year of study): algebra, 2 credits; geometry, 1 credit; trigonometry, ½ credit; laboratory science, 2 credits (physics and chemistry are strongly recommended for all students; at least 1 credit of chemistry or physics is required); and English, 3 credits. A minimum of 16 credits is required; however, the University encourages students to complete at least 20 credits. Applicants must submit results of the SAT I or ACT. (Kettering's ACT code number is 1998; the SAT I code number is 1246.) The staff of the Cooperative Education and Career Services Office initiates the process and assists all enrolled students with the process of securing cooperative employment. The process begins upon confirmation of enrollment and continues until each student is employed.

Most Kettering University students achieve at or near the top 10 percent of their graduating class on traditional criteria such as grades, rank, and test scores. Corporate employers are also very interested in activities, career goals, experiences, leadership, and other personal qualities. Kettering University also welcomes students wishing to transfer from other colleges and universities. The transfer alternative is an excellent way to gain admission for students who do not enroll as freshmen.

Application and Information

Prospective freshmen are encouraged to file their application early in their senior year. Admission decisions for transfer applicants are based on college record for those who have completed at least 30 credits. Applications are accepted all year long; however, early application greatly increases visibility for early employment possibilities in the co-op search process. The application fee is $35. Students can also apply online at the Web site listed below.

Admissions Office
Kettering University
1700 West Third Avenue
Flint, Michigan 48504-4898
Telephone: 810-762-7865
          800-955-4464 (toll-free in the United States
            and Canada)
E-mail: admissions@kettering.edu
World Wide Web: http://www.admissions.kettering.edu

Kettering University graduates expect a good job or entrance into a top graduate school.

LAKE FOREST COLLEGE
LAKE FOREST, ILLINOIS

The College

Lake Forest College is a coeducational undergraduate community of 1,300 students that celebrates the personal growth accompanying the quest for excellence. Founded in 1857, Lake Forest provides a secure residential campus of great beauty and enriches its curriculum with the vibrant resources of Chicago.

A national liberal arts college, Lake Forest prides itself on diversity, with students representing forty-five states and forty-three other countries. International students and members of minority groups comprise more than 25 percent of the Lake Forest student body. With 86 percent of its students living in residence halls, Lake Forest fosters interaction and shared experiences among its diverse population. Lake Forest offers each student the opportunity to develop a variety of life skills.

More than seventy student organizations, groups, and clubs provide the campus with a wide range of extracurricular opportunities. These enriching experiences work in unison with Lake Forest's commitment to high standards of academic excellence and integrity. Ultimately, Lake Forest endeavors to help individuals develop lives of leadership, service, and personal fulfillment.

Location

Thirty miles north of Chicago on Lake Michigan's famed North Shore, Lake Forest College is situated on 107 scenic wooded acres in a residential community. The town of Lake Forest is 25 miles from O'Hare International Airport. Students are within an easy commute to Chicago, a world-class city of nearly 3 million people and a treasure of cultural locations. Chicago has become an extension of the campus. Internships, independent study, research projects, and field trips are readily available through Chicago's vast resources.

Majors and Degrees

Lake Forest College awards the Bachelor of Arts (B.A.) degree in nineteen departments and eight interdisciplinary majors spanning more than 500 courses. Departmental majors are art, biology, business, chemistry, communications, computer science, economics, education (in conjunction with another major), English, French, history, mathematics, music, philosophy, physics, politics, psychology, sociology and anthropology, and Spanish. The interdisciplinary majors are American studies, area studies, Asian studies (including beginning Chinese and Japanese languages), environmental studies, international relations, and Latin American studies. Course work is also available in religion and theater.

Students may create their own majors through the independent scholar program, which enables qualified and motivated students to design and pursue individual degree programs that focus on particular topics or themes rather than on single academic disciplines.

In addition, the College also offers minors. Students can declare a minor in those departmental and nondepartmental programs that have a major, as well as in religion, theater, African-American studies, French civilization, metropolitan studies, and women's gender studies. A minor requires at least four courses.

Lake Forest offers a cooperative degree (3-2) program with the Sever School of Engineering of Washington University (St. Louis). Students may receive a Bachelor of Arts degree from Lake Forest and a Bachelor of Science degree from Washington University.

Academic Programs

Lake Forest College bases its academic calendar on two 15-week semesters, from late August through mid-December and from mid-January through early May. The curriculum establishes an integrated framework for the general education of undergraduate students across four years of study. The curriculum includes general education requirements, which ensure that students receive educational breadth as well as depth while allowing considerable latitude in designing individual programs of study. Also included are requirements for writing and cultural diversity. Students are expected to pass thirty-two courses, fulfill the general education requirements, and complete the requirements of a major.

Off-Campus Programs

In addition to the Internship Program, Lake Forest College provides students with a wide variety of opportunities for off-campus study, both domestic and international. Semester-long options in the United States include the Chicago Semester in the Arts, the Oak Ridge Science Semester, the Urban Studies Program, the Urban Education Program, the Newberry Library Program, and the Washington Semester Program at American University.

There are many options for international study, such as Lake Forest's own international internship programs in Paris and in Santiago (Chile), as well as the Ancient Mediterranean Civilizations Program in Greece and Turkey and the Marine Biology Program in the Bahamas. As a member of the Associated Colleges of the Midwest, Lake Forest also offers programs in such countries as Costa Rica, the Czech Republic, England, India, Italy, Japan, Russia, Tanzania, and Zimbabwe.

Academic Facilities

In fall 2004, Lake Forest College is scheduled to open the doors of a new, twenty-first century library and information technology center. An $18-million expansion and renovation project, the new facility will incorporate the latest concepts, ideas, and technological innovations pertaining to teaching and learning, while providing a comfortable environment for collaboration, including a 24-hour cyber café.

Currently, the Donnelley Library contains more than 300,000 books and government documents and 900 current periodical subscriptions. In addition, the library provides online access to articles from several thousand electronic periodical titles. The library features a strong literacy program where students can gain proficiency with a wide variety of information resources. Lake Forest students and faculty members have online access to the holdings of forty-five academic libraries statewide, and can borrow books online from any of those libraries. The library's Special Collections Unit includes the College Archives and houses rare books and manuscripts.

Information technology services works closely with library staff members to support the information and technology needs of the campus. There are more than 120 public-access computers available for student use in computing labs on campus. The Technology Resource Center, equipped with high-end computing hardware and software, is available for students and faculty members. All residence hall rooms, faculty offices, laboratories, and classrooms, are wired from connections to the College's fiber-optic network. From their residence hall rooms, students have full access to the Internet and all networked campus services. All students receive e-mail accounts and accounts on a College Web server.

Among the fifty-five buildings on campus is the Dixon Science Research Center, designed for student-faculty research. The modern three-story, 7,500-square-foot facility contains thirteen laboratories and two animal holding facilities. State-of-the-art equipment includes a nuclear magnetic resonance spectrometer with a 400-megahertz superconductivity magnet and an electron microscope.

Costs

Comprehensive fees for 2003–04 are $30,170: tuition and fees, $24,406, and room and board, $5764.

Financial Aid

Lake Forest College supports a comprehensive financial aid program. About 85 percent of the students receive need- and merit-based assistance. More than $14 million is awarded annually in Lake Forest College grant and scholarship assistance, with the average aid package totaling $20,650.

The College recognizes distinguished academic performance through the Trustee and Presidential Scholarship Competition. The Deerpath Scholarship Program honors achievement and talent in academics, art, foreign language, leadership, music, science, theater, and writing.

Faculty

At the core of the College stands its distinguished faculty of excellent teachers and accomplished scholars. The College seeks and retains faculty members principally because they enjoy and excel at teaching undergraduates. Faculty members, not graduate assistants, teach the College's courses and provide academic advising. A student-faculty ratio of 12:1 gives students easy access to their teachers, while providing opportunities for informed counsel about individual programs of study.

The faculty's tradition of teaching excellence is matched and supported by its achievement in scholarly research. More than 98 percent hold a Ph.D. or its equivalent. Faculty members have won national teaching awards and have spoken and consulted throughout the United States and abroad. More than 30 percent have published books in their disciplines. Lake Forest faculty members continually receive fellowships and grants from prestigious institutions and foundations in the U.S. and abroad.

Student Government

The first Lake Forest College student body self-governing organization was the Student Council, established in 1917. Today, Student Government is composed of the General Assembly and its subcommittees, the Executive Committee and the four Student Government officers: the president, vice-president, treasurer, and secretary. Student members of other College governing committees also play an active and important role in the Student Government.

Ultimate responsibility for guiding Lake Forest College rests with the Board of Trustees. The Student Government president and vice-president serve as voting members on the full board.

Students at Lake Forest College advise the administration through representation on a variety of committees that deal with the hiring of faculty members, allocation of the budget, department course offerings, and administering a judicial system while also taking a prominent role in enhancing the educational growth and social life of the campus community.

Admission Requirements

Admission to Lake Forest College is competitive and based on a record of achievement in academic studies and extracurricular activities. Selection includes assessment of a student's program of study, academic achievement, aptitude, intellectual curiosity, qualities of character and personality, and activities both within and outside the school setting. Lake Forest College unequivocally selects its students without regard to social background, religious affiliation, race, national origin, gender, handicap, or financial position. This admission policy is manifest in the diverse nature of the student community.

Students are urged to begin the application procedure early in their final year of secondary school. There is no formal closing deadline for receipt of the application. The early notification deadline is December 1. This option is nonbinding but allows the student to receive an admission decision as early as December 20. The early decision (binding) deadline is January 1. Admission decisions are announced no later than the third week of March for all freshman candidates whose applications are complete as of March 1.

Lake Forest recommends a precollege program that includes a minimum of 4 years of English; 3 or more years of mathematics, including trigonometry; in-depth study in one or more foreign languages; and 2 to 4 years of work in both the social and natural sciences. All candidates are required to present the results of either the SAT I or the ACT. The tests may be completed in the candidate's junior or senior year of secondary school. Although an interview is not required, the admission staff welcomes and encourages visits to the campus by prospective students and their families.

Candidates for undergraduate admission may obtain the required application forms by contacting the Admission Office. Lake Forest College also accepts the Common Application in lieu of its own form and gives equal consideration to both. Students may obtain copies of the Common Application from their high schools. Students who wish to defer enrollment should complete the application procedure during the final year of secondary school.

Transfer students are admitted at the beginning of each semester. Transfer applicants should have achieved an overall college average of at least a C or its equivalent and be eligible to return to their previous institutions. When a transfer student is admitted to the College, the maximum credit accepted in transfer is 60 semester hours. All transfer students are required to submit the following credentials: an application for admission, a secondary school transcript, transcripts of all college work completed through the most recent term, and a letter of recommendation from the academic dean or a professor at the current college.

Application and Information

The Admission Office is open from 8:30 a.m. to 5 p.m. on weekdays and 9 a.m. to 1 p.m. on Saturdays throughout the year. For further information, including a campus tour, interview, or an application form, prospective students should contact:

Admission Office
Lake Forest College
555 N. Sheridan Road
Lake Forest, Illinois 60045
Telephone: 847-735-5000
         800-828-4751 (toll-free)
Fax: 847-735-6271
E-mail: admissions@lakeforest.edu
World Wide Web: http://www.lakeforest.edu

LOYOLA UNIVERSITY CHICAGO

CHICAGO, ILLINOIS

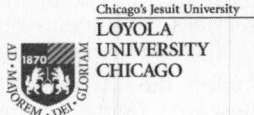

The University

Loyola University Chicago is the most comprehensive Jesuit university in the United States. Founded in 1870 by priests of the Society of Jesus, Loyola continues the Jesuit commitment to education, which is well-grounded in the liberal arts and based on excellence in teaching and research.

Loyola attracts students from all fifty states and seventy-four countries to its nine schools and colleges: the Stritch School of Medicine, the School of Law, the College of Arts and Sciences, the School of Business Administration, the Niehoff School of Nursing, the School of Education, the School of Social Work, the Graduate School, and the School of Professional Studies (for adult and lifelong learning).

Each year, Loyola University Chicago enrolls more than 1,900 freshmen and more than 400 transfer students. These students choose Loyola because of its personal attention, its environment of academic excellence, and its reputation for career preparation. Loyola students take advantage of Chicago as an educational resource, often combining their studies with internships and part-time work experience.

The University seeks to provide an environment that will enhance the academic, social, and spiritual growth of students. More than 125 student organizations, including eleven fraternities and sororities, and extensive recreational sports programs and facilities are provided. NCAA Division I teams include basketball, cross-country, golf, soccer, track, and volleyball for men and basketball, cross-country, golf, soccer, softball, track, and volleyball for women.

Loyola provides thirteen undergraduate residence halls on the Lake Shore Campus. There are both coed and single-sex halls. Freshmen and sophomores are required to live on campus if they do not live at home. There is also convenient and affordable off-campus housing in the immediate vicinity of campus for upperclass students.

Location

The Lake Shore Campus is located 8 miles north of the city's center and sits on the shore of Lake Michigan in the Rogers Park/Edgewater area, a desirable residential neighborhood where many Loyola faculty and staff members reside. Students at the Lake Shore Campus also can take advantage of the city's vast business and cultural resources, with downtown Chicago being less than 20 minutes away via university-run shuttle bus or via convenient public transportation.

Loyola's Water Tower Campus is located on Chicago's "Magnificent Mile," a fashionable area on the near north side. Close to theaters, museums, major corporate and financial institutions, and some of Chicago's most elegant shops and boutiques, the Water Tower Campus is a vibrant educational center.

Majors and Degrees

Loyola's four undergraduate colleges offer the Bachelor of Arts (B.A.), Bachelor of Science (B.S.), Bachelor of Business Administration (B.B.A.), Bachelor of Science in Education (B.S.Ed.), and the Bachelor of Science in Nursing (B.S.N.) degrees. The College of Arts and Sciences offers majors in

anthropology, biology, chemistry (biochemistry), classical civilization, communication (communication and social justice, journalism, and organizational communication/business), computer science, criminal justice, ecology, economics, English (creative writing), environmental studies, environmental sciences (chemistry), fine arts (art history, studio art, and visual communication), French, Greek (ancient), history, international studies, Italian, Latin, mathematics (operations research), mathematics and computer science, music, pharmacy, philosophy, physics, physics and engineering (theoretical physics and applied mathematics), political science, psychology (applied social psychology, human services, natural sciences, and social sciences), social work, sociology, Spanish, statistical science, theology, and women's studies. The School of Business Administration offers majors in accounting, economics, finance, human resource management, information systems management, international business (combined with a second major), marketing, and operations management. The School of Education offers a major in elementary education as well as secondary school certification in eleven majors. The Niehoff School of Nursing offers the Bachelor of Science in Nursing and a baccalaureate completion program for registered nurses, an accelerated B.S.N. program. Five-year dual-degree (bachelor's/ master's) programs are available in applied social psychology, biology/M.B.A., business administration/accountancy, business administration/information systems management, computer science, criminal justice, environmental sciences/M.B.A., mathematics, political science, social work, and sociology.

Interdisciplinary studies include Asian studies, black world studies, Catholic studies, international studies, Latin American studies, medieval studies, neuroscience, peace studies, and psychology of crime and justice.

Preprofessional programs prepare students for future study in bioethics and health policy, cell biology, cell and molecular physiology, divinity, law, medicine, microbiology and immunology, molecular biology, molecular and cellular biochemistry, neurobiology and anatomy, pastoral studies, pharmacology and experimental therapeutics, religious education, and social work. A 3+3 Law Program, in conjunction with the Loyola University School of Law, allows talented undergraduates to enter law school at the conclusion of their junior year of college. An early assurance program to the Loyola Stritch School of Medicine provides students with an articulated admission to medical school.

Academic Programs

Jesuit educators believe that a solid foundation in the liberal arts and sciences is essential for students entering all professions. Loyola's Core Curriculum is designed to give students this foundation. The core requirements vary by college but usually include courses in expressive arts, history, literature, mathematical and natural sciences, philosophy, social sciences, and theology. The core allows students who are undecided about their majors to explore all possibilities before deciding upon a field of study.

Most majors require 128 semester hours for graduation. Exceptionally well-qualified students may apply to the Honors Program. Students may receive credit through the Advanced Placement Program (AP Program) tests, the International

Baccalaureate (I.B.), and certain College-Level Examination Program (CLEP) tests are accepted. Loyola students may participate in the Army and Naval ROTC programs through neighboring universities.

Off-Campus Programs

Loyola offers more than thirty study-abroad programs in nineteen countries. Loyola's Rome Center in Rome, Italy, is the most popular student study-abroad destination. Students may also choose a reciprocal exchange program in Chile, China, England, France, Ireland, Japan, or Mexico, or they may participate in one of several other affiliate programs around the globe.

Academic Facilities

The University's library system, including the Cudahy Library at the Lake Shore Campus and the Lewis Library at the Water Tower Campus, contains more than 1.3 million books and 12,000 periodical subscriptions. Other academic facilities include extensive laboratories for the biology, chemistry, and physics departments; a nursing resource center; and computing facilities on all campuses. The School of Business is located in a $38-million building on the Water Tower Campus.

The Martin D'Arcy Gallery of Medieval and Renaissance Art is located on the Lake Shore Campus along with the Fine Art Department's gallery and studios. The theater department's facilities include the Mullady Theatre, where the most sophisticated computerized lighting system in Chicago was recently installed, and the Studio Theatre, an experimental black-box facility. Loyola's FM radio station provides communication majors with on-campus production experience.

The Medical Center Campus in Maywood, a suburb of Chicago, consists of the Foster G. McGaw Hospital and the Stritch School of Medicine as well as the Mulcahy Outpatient Center, the Russo Surgical Pavilion, and the Cardinal Bernardin Cancer Center.

Costs

For the 2003–04 academic year, tuition for full-time undergraduates was $20,544. Based on double occupancy, room and board costs average $7900. Books and fees total about $1715 per year.

Financial Aid

Loyola attempts to meet the financial need of as many students as possible. Ninety-four percent of Loyola freshman receive some form of aid, including University-funded scholarships and grants, federal and state grants, work-study, and loans. Students are encouraged to file the Free Application for Federal Student Aid (FAFSA) by mid-February in order to receive consideration for all types of aid.

Merit scholarships are awarded to entering freshmen who have outstanding academic records. Presidential, Damen, and Loyola Scholarships are awarded to students who rank at the top of their high school graduating class and score well on the ACT or SAT I. Scholarship amounts for these programs are $5000–$12,500 per year. These awards are renewable for up to three years.

Other scholarships available include competitive awards for students admitted to the Honors Program and students from Jesuit/BVM/Sisters of Christian Charity high schools, National Merit/National Achievement finalists, theater scholarships (awarded by audition), and debate, elementary education, leadership, and public accounting awards.

Transfer students who have completed 30 hours of college credit with an outstanding record of academic achievement may receive a Transfer Academic Scholarship. These awards are renewable for up to three years.

Faculty

More than 95 percent of the University's full-time faculty members hold the Ph.D. or the highest degree in their field. Faculty members generally teach both graduate and undergraduate students, and senior faculty members often teach Core Curriculum courses. At 13:1 the student-faculty ratio is far below the national average, giving undergraduates ready access to faculty members both as teachers and as advisers.

Student Government

Student government at Loyola provides a liaison between students and administration, emphasizes concerns for student rights, and provides a forum for debate, recommendation, and action on issues that pertain to students. Students also take an active role on University policy and advisory committees and as elected representatives in the residence halls.

Admission Requirements

Students seeking admission to Loyola University Chicago are evaluated on the basis of their overall academic record, including ACT or SAT scores. Most Loyola students rank in the upper quarter of their graduating class, but consideration is given to students in the upper half. Candidates should be graduating from an accredited secondary school with a minimum of 15 units, including courses in English, math, social studies, and science. Study of a foreign language is strongly recommended. Students must submit the application for admission along with high school transcripts, test scores, and a secondary school counselor recommendation. Admission counselors are available to meet and talk with students individually either before or after the application is submitted.

Transfer students with 20 semester hours or more of acceptable credit are evaluated on the basis of their college work only. Minimum acceptable grade point averages are 2.0 (C) for the College of Arts and Sciences; 2.0 (C) for the School of Education; and 2.5 (C+) for the Schools of Business Administration and Nursing. Candidates must also have been in good standing at the last college attended.

Application and Information

Applicants are notified of the admission decision three to four weeks after the application, supporting credentials, secondary school counselor recommendation, and $25 application fee are received. The application fee is waived for students who apply online.

Prospective students are encouraged to visit the campus. The Undergraduate Admission Office encourages students to schedule individual appointments and campus tours or to participate in one of the many campus programs offered throughout the year.

To obtain an application and further information and to arrange a visit, students should contact:

Undergraduate Admission Office
Loyola University Chicago
820 North Michigan Avenue
Chicago, Illinois 60611
Telephone: 312-915-6500
          800-262-2373 (toll-free)
E-mail: admission@luc.edu
World Wide Web: http://www.luc.edu/undergrad

MANCHESTER COLLEGE
NORTH MANCHESTER, INDIANA

The College

Manchester College, founded in 1889, is an independent, coeducational, liberal arts college of the Church of the Brethren. Throughout its history, the College has held that values are central in the study of all majors and that the liberal arts provide a foundation of critical skills and sound scholarship.

An emphasis on service produces exceptional graduates who possess both professional ability and personal convictions, prepared for responsible lives that make a difference in the world.

Located at the edge of North Manchester, Indiana, Manchester College is primarily a residential school; 75 percent of the students live on the beautiful 124-acre campus. The academic buildings are constructed around a tree-lined central mall, and manicured flower gardens dot the campus. In addition, the resource-rich 100-acre Koinonia Environmental Retreat Center is located 12 miles from the academic campus.

The undergraduate enrollment is 1,150. Most students are between the ages of 18 and 22. Approximately 85 percent of the full-time students are from Indiana. Students from twenty-three states and twenty-nine countries were also enrolled during 2002–03. Sixteen percent of the students are members of the Church of the Brethren, but many different religious backgrounds are represented, and all are welcomed.

At Manchester, students get to know the members of the College's well-trained, concerned faculty on both a personal and an academic level. Faculty members take the time to assist students in a caring way, both in the classroom and as advisers.

There are five residence halls on campus that provide a variety of living experiences for students to choose from.

Manchester is a member of the National Collegiate Athletic Association Division III and offers nine men's and eight women's sports. The Physical Education and Recreation Center houses physical education classes, a fitness center, intercollegiate and intramural sports, and recreational activities. The College has a very strong intramural program that involves about 80 percent of its students.

In addition to its undergraduate program, Manchester College offers the Master of Accountancy and Master of Arts in contemporary leadership degrees.

Location

Located in the heart of Indiana's beautiful lake country, North Manchester is a thriving community of 6,000 people. It is within a half hour's drive of the Fort Wayne metropolitan area and is only 3½ hours from Chicago. Wide streets with large shade trees, graceful homes, and a beautiful park combine to provide a setting for classic college living.

Majors and Degrees

Manchester College grants Bachelor of Arts and Bachelor of Science degrees. Areas of study include accounting, adapted physical education, art, athletic training, biology, business administration, chemistry, coaching, communication studies, computer science, corporate finance, criminal justice, early childhood education, economics, elementary education, engineering science, English, environmental studies, exercise science, French, gender studies, German, gerontology, health and fitness instruction, history, journalism, mathematics, media studies, medical technology, music, nonprofit management, peace studies, philosophy, physical education, physics, political science, prelaw, premedicine, prenursing, pre–occupational therapy, pre–physical therapy, psychology, religion, secondary education, small-business administration, social work, sociology, Spanish, and theater arts. Individualized interdisciplinary majors can also be arranged to meet a student's particular goals.

Academic Programs

The curriculum reflects a commitment to sound training in a specific area of study, the major, and broad development of skills and understanding through the liberal arts. In addition, students may explore interests different from specific career or professional areas through elective courses. This combination prepares students for careers or graduate school immediately after graduation and equips them for the challenges and changes of the coming century.

Manchester College operates on a 4-1-4 calendar and offers three summer sessions. Qualifying scores on the Advanced Placement Program and College-Level Examination Program tests of the College Board are recognized for college credit or advanced placement.

Off-Campus Programs

Manchester College students may study abroad for a semester or year in thirteen countries: at Philipps-Universität Marburg in Marburg/Lahn (Germany), the Institut International d'Études Françaises of the University of Strasbourg (France), the University of Nancy (France), the University of Barcelona (Spain), St. Mary's College in Cheltenham (England), Hokkai Gakuen University in Sapporo (Japan), the Dalian Institute of Foreign Languages in Dalian (People's Republic of China), the University of La Verne Athens Center (Greece), the Catholic University of Ecuador, the Federal University of Ouro Preto (Brazil), Satya Wacana University (Indonesia), Marmara University (Turkey), Cochin (India), and Universidad Veracruzana (Mexico).

During January session, numerous classes are held off campus. In the past several years, professors have taken classes to India, Africa, England, Mexico, Russia, France, Ghana, Vietnam, Nicaragua, Haiti, Germany, Costa Rica, Cuba, and Hawaii as well as destinations in the continental United States.

Field experiences and internships are offered for credit in accounting, broadcasting, business, criminal justice, early childhood education, elementary education, forensic chemistry, gerontology, health sciences practicum, journalism, peace studies, physical education, political science, psychology, secondary education, and social work.

Academic Facilities

Manchester College has a local area network of 165 IBM-compatible workstations, one for every 6 students. In addition, the Clark Computer Center houses file servers, three computer labs, and an AS400 for student use. PC labs tied to the network are located in each residence hall and the library.

Cordier Auditorium, dedicated in 1978, seats 1,300 people and has modern facilities for staging, lighting, and sound.

The Holl-Kintner Hall of Science has extensive laboratory facilities for biology, botany, physics, and geology as well as four separate chemistry laboratories and a number of research laboratories. Students in astronomy use the 10-inch Newtonian reflector telescope in the Charles S. Morris Observatory.

The Funderburg Library is a newly renovated, three-story building that houses more than 170,000 books, 800 periodicals, and 4,500 audio recordings available for student use. Computer connections allow access to major libraries across the country.

Costs

Tuition for 2003–04 was $17,040 for full-time students. Room and board costs for the residence halls (double occupancy) were $6340. The total charges were $23,380 for the academic year.

Financial Aid

Manchester offers extensive scholarship and grant assistance through institutional resources. Academic awards include Honors, Trustee, Presidential, and Dean's Scholarships. Special scholarships based on academic merit and interest are awarded in art, broadcasting, journalism, music, theater, and the video arts. Service scholarships and modern language scholarships are also awarded. International students can receive scholarships based on academic accomplishments and financial need. Manchester awards significant need-based grants. More than $7 million in College funds were awarded in 2002–03.

Approximately 98 percent of Manchester's students have some type of financial assistance, whether it is a scholarship, a grant, a loan, or campus employment. Questions about financial aid should be referred to the Office of Admissions.

Faculty

Manchester's faculty consists of 72 full-time and 19 part-time members. Ninety-three percent of full-time faculty members hold the highest degrees in their fields, and 94 percent of all courses are taught by full-time faculty members. The primary emphasis of the faculty members is teaching, but many are actively engaged in research as well. Faculty members serve as academic advisers, with a specially trained group of faculty members acting as primary advisers for new students. There is a 14:1 student-faculty ratio.

Student Government

Students at Manchester assume responsibility for the governmental and judicial activities of the College. The Community Council provides a forum for discussion and investigation of community concerns and a channel for evaluating and solving community problems.

Each of the residence halls elects a governing body, which is responsible for providing leadership.

The judicial system of the College includes three courts: the Judicial Board, the Community Court, and an administrative hearing panel. The Student Budget Board is charged with responsibility for receiving requests for funds to support the activity program of the College and for making the necessary appropriations.

The Manchester Activities Council organizes programming of student events. Students are offered a wide variety of leadership and participation opportunities as part of the College's student development program.

Admission Requirements

Manchester College seeks to enroll students whose scholastic record, test scores, and personality give promise of success in college. Graduation from an accredited high school or its equivalent is required.

The College recommends that students take 4 years of English, 3 years of laboratory science, 3 years of mathematics, 2 years of foreign language, and 2 years of social studies in high school. Students may take either the ACT or the SAT I, and personal recommendations from a high school principal or guidance counselor are required.

For transfer students, transcripts of all previous college work are required.

Application and Information

Students may apply for admission prior to each term. Applications are accepted on a rolling basis. There is a nonrefundable $20 application fee.

Interested students and their parents are encouraged to visit Manchester College and meet faculty members, coaches, and current students; sit in on classes; and take a campus tour. Arrangements can be made by writing or calling the Office of Admissions.

For application forms and further information, students may contact:

Office of Admissions
Manchester College
North Manchester, Indiana 46962-0365
Telephone: 800-852-3648 (toll-free)
E-mail: admitinfo@manchester.edu
World Wide Web: http://www.manchester.edu

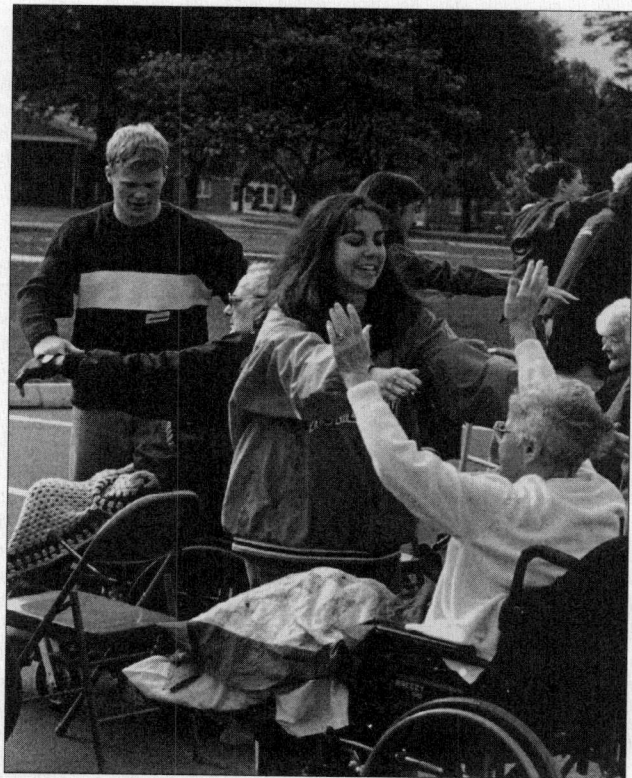

Students from the First Year Colloquium course Bodies in Motion lead residents of Peabody Retirement Community in Tai Chi.

MILWAUKEE SCHOOL OF ENGINEERING
MILWAUKEE, WISCONSIN

The School

Advancing beyond acquisition to the highly sophisticated application of knowledge has been the foundation of the Milwaukee School of Engineering's (MSOE) educational philosophy for more than 100 years. This approach, the university's educational niche, produces graduates who are fully prepared to begin their first jobs and pursue challenging careers. MSOE graduates start their careers as work-ready problem solvers and develop into leaders: creating new products, starting or heading companies, and working to better their communities. MSOE is governed by a Board of Regents of more than 50 members who are elected from leaders in business and industry nationwide who are members of the 200-member MSOE Corporation.

The student body of 2,600 men and women comes from throughout the United States and numerous countries. Since its founding, the university has encouraged the enrollment of students of any race, color, creed, or gender. Approximately half of the full-time students live in three high-rise residence halls.

Representatives from hundreds of firms from throughout the country, including representatives from Fortune 500 companies, visit MSOE during the academic year to interview graduating students for employment and to discuss career opportunities. The university had a 97 percent placement rate over the past five years.

MSOE's Counseling Services Office provides individual assistance for students with educational, personal, or vocational concerns. Free, on-campus tutoring is provided by the Learning Resource Center and Tau Omega Mu, an honorary fraternity founded in 1953 for the purpose of aiding students who need extra help with their studies.

The Student Life and Campus Center provides on-campus recreational activities. This facility houses student activity rooms, student organization offices, a TV viewing area, a marketplace eatery, and a game room. Additional recreation areas can be found in the residence halls and the MSOE Sports Center.

There are more than fifty professional societies, fraternities, and other special interest groups on campus. Many students participate in intramural sports programs. MSOE is a member of the National Collegiate Athletic Association (NCAA) Division III Lake Michigan Conference. The Athletic Department sponsors NCAA student teams in men's baseball, basketball, cross-country, golf, ice hockey, soccer, tennis, indoor and outdoor track and field, volleyball, and wrestling and women's basketball, cross-country, golf, soccer, softball, tennis, indoor and outdoor track and field, and volleyball that compete with teams from other private colleges and universities in the Midwest.

In addition to the undergraduate degree programs listed below, MSOE offers six Master of Science degree programs: engineering, engineering management (accelerated option available), environmental engineering, medical informatics (jointly offered with the Medical College of Wisconsin), perfusion, and structural engineering.

Milwaukee School of Engineering (MSOE) is a member of, and accredited by, the North Central Association of Colleges and Schools. Program-specific accrediting agencies are identified in the MSOE academic catalogs.

Location

The MSOE campus is located in the East Town section of downtown Milwaukee. Nearby are the Bradley Center, the Midwest Express Center, the Marcus Center for the Performing Arts, the theater district, churches of most denominations, major hotels and office buildings, restaurants, and department stores. Famous for its friendly atmosphere, Milwaukee offers students many opportunities for educational, cultural, and professional growth as well as ample employment opportunities. The metropolitan area has more than 15,000 acres of parks and river parkways and miles of bike trails. A few blocks east of the MSOE campus is Lake Michigan, a place of year-round natural beauty. MSOE also offers classes in several other locations in Wisconsin for students who wish to pursue select programs in the evening on a part-time basis.

Majors and Degrees

Four-year programs are offered that lead to Bachelor of Science degrees in business, construction management, engineering (architectural, biomedical, computer, electrical, industrial, mechanical, and software), engineering technology—transfer programs only (electrical and mechanical), international business, management, management information systems, and nursing. A Bachelor of Science or Bachelor of Arts degree is offered in technical communication. A five-year, double-major option is available in a combination of engineering, business, construction management, and technical communication programs. An engineering/environmental engineering dual degree (B.S./M.S. combination) is also available. An RN to B.S.N. program is available through the MSOE School of Nursing. International study opportunities also exist.

Academic Programs

MSOE guarantees graduation in four years for full-time undergraduate students who start on track as freshmen, follow the prescribed curriculum, and meet graduation requirements.

The degree programs at MSOE combine study in degree specialty courses with basic study in sciences, communication, mathematics, and humanities in a high-technology, applications-oriented atmosphere. Students who are admitted with advanced credit to a program leading to a bachelor's degree must complete at least 50 percent of the curriculum in residence at MSOE. MSOE operates on a quarter system. Students average between 16 and 19 credits per quarter, which represent a combination of lecture and laboratory courses. Undergraduate students average 600 hours of laboratory experience.

MSOE offers students the opportunity to participate in the Air Force Reserve Officer Training Corps (AFROTC) program, the Army ROTC program, or the Navy ROTC program, which are offered in conjunction with Marquette University.

Academic Facilities

The Fred Loock Engineering Center adjoins the Allen-Bradley Hall of Science, forming a prime technical education and applied research complex. The Walter Schroeder Library houses more than 60,000 volumes, with collections that represent the specialized curricula of the university. Electronic technology enables the library to connect with libraries, government agencies, and other sources of information throughout the world. Full-time freshmen are required to participate in a Technology Package program that includes a notebook computer and affiliated services. A full range of software is available on these systems and via the local area network linked by a fiber-optic ring around the campus. State-of-the-art electrical, mechanical, industrial, and nursing laboratories complement the respective areas of study. The Rader School of Business has recently moved into a new facility, Rosenberg Hall, with computer technology integrated throughout. The Applied Technology Center™ (ATC) utilizes faculty and student expertise to solve technological problems confronting business and industry. The ATC is heavily involved in the transferring of new technologies into real business practice through the Rapid Prototyping Center (MSOE is the only university in the world to possess the five leading rapid prototyping technologies), Fluid Power Institute™, Photonics and Applied Optics Center, Construction Science and Engineering Center, and the Center for BioMolecular Modeling.

There are more laboratories than classrooms at MSOE, many with industrial sponsorship from such companies as Johnson Controls, Harley-Davidson, Rockwell Automation/Allen-Bradley, Master Lock, Snap-On, General Electric, and Outboard Marine Corporation. The key to the Rapid Prototyping Center's success is a high level of industrial parts design and fabrication activity using stereolithography, laminated-object manufacturing, and fused deposition modeling systems.

Costs

For 2004–05, tuition is $23,034 per year (same as 2003–04) plus $1140 for the Technology Package (notebook computer, software, insurance, maintenance, Internet access, and user services). The cost of room and board in the residence halls is approximately $5610 per year. Books and supplies average $400 per quarter but may be somewhat higher the first quarter.

Financial Aid

Qualified students are assisted by a comprehensive financial aid program, including MSOE and industry-supported scholarships, student loans, and part-time employment; Federal Perkins Loan, Federal Stafford Student Loan, Federal Work-Study, Federal Pell Grant, and Federal Supplemental Educational Opportunity Grant Programs; and state-supported grant programs. Students can also visit MSOE's Web site (listed at the end of this description) for a financial aid estimate.

Faculty

There are more than 200 men and women on the MSOE faculty (full-time and part-time). Many are registered professional engineers, architects, and nurses in Wisconsin and other states. They and their colleagues in nontechnical academic areas are active in related professional societies. The student-faculty ratio is 11:1. MSOE does not utilize teaching assistants.

Student Government

The MSOE Student Government Association (SGA) represents clubs and fraternities as well as residence halls and commuting students. SGA appoints representatives to the Campus Security and Disciplinary Hearing committees and the Alumni Association's Board of Directors.

Admission Requirements

Each applicant to MSOE is reviewed individually on the basis of his or her potential for success as determined by academic preparation. Admission may be gained by submitting an application for admission and the appropriate transcripts. High school students are encouraged to complete math through precalculus (including algebra and geometry), chemistry, biology (nursing), physics, and 4 years of English. All entering freshmen are also required to provide results from the ACT or the SAT.

Transfer opportunities exist into the junior year of the Bachelor of Science in electrical engineering technology, management, mechanical engineering technology, and technical communication programs with the appropriate associate degree or equivalent credits.

Application and Information

Classes start in September, November, March, and late May. Freshman and transfer students may enter at the beginning of any quarter; however, entry in the fall quarter is recommended. An application for admission may be obtained by contacting the address below or by visiting MSOE's Web site listed below. Applicants are encouraged to visit MSOE and have a preadmission counseling interview. Transfer students are required to submit transcripts from all prior institutions attended. An applicant's prior course work is reviewed to determine eligibility for admission. Required course work varies depending on the desired course of study.

Admission Office
Milwaukee School of Engineering
1025 North Broadway
Milwaukee, Wisconsin 53202-3109
Telephone: 414-277-6763
          800-332-6763 (toll-free)
E-mail: explore@msoe.edu
World Wide Web: http://www.msoe.edu

MSOE's undergraduate students average 600 hours of laboratory experience—just one more advantage to an MSOE education.

MISSOURI SOUTHERN STATE UNIVERSITY

JOPLIN, MISSOURI

The University

Missouri Southern State University is a four-year institution that features a liberal arts education with an international perspective. The University focuses on classroom teaching, resulting in a tradition of small classes and close, personal interaction between faculty members and approximately 5,600 students. This approach is maintained through an 18:1 student-teacher ratio. Southern's faculty members come from all over the world, with degrees from prestigious universities and professional experience in the disciplines they teach.

Southern stresses the development of independent learners and their ability to conceptualize, solve problems, manipulate thoughts and patterns, and work cooperatively. These elements, coupled with an international emphasis, enable Southern's graduates to compete successfully in the rapidly changing world. This international emphasis, a distinctive theme of the University's mission, is the focus of the Institute of International Studies, which coordinates all international programs and activities, including a pervasive global dimension in all curricula, study-abroad opportunities for faculty members and students, internships abroad for students, and expanded foreign language offerings.

A wide range of extracurricular activities, designed to support the academic experience and develop leadership abilities, is available for both resident and commuter students. More than 100 organizations, including departmental groups, Greek fraternities and sororities, religious and professional organizations, and honor societies, invite involvement and camaraderie. Also available are music and theater performance activities and many other opportunities. Varsity athletes in sixteen men's and women's sports compete in NCAA Division II. Athletic facilities include a multipurpose 80,000-square-foot athletic center with comfortable chair-back seating for approximately 3,500. The facility features a six-lane, 200-meter indoor track and is home to the Missouri Southern men's and women's basketball teams, who play on the arena's parquet floor. Other facilities include a new sprint turf stadium with an all-weather running track, a swimming pool, racquetball courts, and lighted tennis courts and softball and soccer fields.

The 600 students who live on campus enjoy air-conditioned residence halls. The Student Life Center offers a cafeteria, an aerobics room, a weight/exercise room, laundry facilities, a computer lab, a video game room, and a lounge with a big-screen television and surround sound.

Location

Missouri Southern's 341-acre campus is located in what has been known as the Crossroads of America. Two major cross-country highways intersect in Joplin—U.S. 71 north to south and I-44 east to west. This location allows easy access to major metropolitan cities around the Midwest. However, the University is also in ideal surroundings on the edge of the Ozarks, where recreational opportunities abound. The beautifully landscaped and extremely safe suburban campus rests on the edge of town within walking distance of the region's largest mall. Many movie theaters, restaurants, and athletic and cultural activities provide entertainment throughout the year. Students find employment in businesses throughout Joplin, which is Missouri's fourth-largest metropolitan region, and the surrounding communities. Area businesses also provide internships for students in a variety of disciplines and recruit graduates for permanent positions.

Majors and Degrees

Missouri Southern offers more than 100 degree options for the Bachelor of Science, Bachelor of Arts, Bachelor of Science in Business Administration, Bachelor of Science in Education, and Bachelor of General Studies. Also offered are a few Associate of Arts and Associate of Science degrees. Bachelor's degrees are awarded in accounting, art, athletic training, biology, chemistry, communications, computer-assisted manufacturing technology, computer information science, criminal justice administration, data processing, economics and finance, elementary education, English, environmental health technology, French, general business, German, health promotion and wellness, history, international business, international studies, management, management technology, marketing, mathematics, medical technology, music, nursing, paralegal studies, physical education, physics, political science, psychology, secondary education, social studies, sociology, Spanish, and theater. Associate degrees are awarded in accounting, computer-aided drafting and design, computer analysis, computer-assisted manufacturing technology, computer programming, dental hygiene, environmental health technology, law enforcement, pre-engineering studies, radiologic technology, and respiratory therapy. Certificate programs include basic police recruit studies, computer science and information systems, emergency medical technician studies, and EMT-paramedic studies. Preprofessional programs are offered in dentistry, engineering, law, medicine, optometry, pharmacy, and veterinary medicine.

Academic Programs

Because graduates may change occupations and careers several times during their working lives, all students pursuing a degree complete the core curriculum, a series of courses carefully designed to instill certain lifelong thinking and learning skills. Core courses emphasize critical-thinking, problem-solving, and communications skills; a general understanding of scientific and artistic aspects of this culture; and the ability to function in a global society through knowledge and understanding of other cultures. In both the core and major studies, writing skills and computer literacy are developed, and an international perspective is stressed in every possible course. The baccalaureate degree requires 51 credit hours of the core and a total of 124 hours; the Associate of Arts degree requires 64 hours, with 42 hours from the core; and the Associate of Science degree requires 64 hours, with 26 hours from the core curriculum.

Many broad-based majors offer emphases that allow students a more specialized direction of study. A prestigious Honors Program provides special challenges and opportunities for qualified students who may receive full scholarships for their academic studies.

Off-Campus Programs

Study abroad is an integral part of the University's international approach to education. Three-week summer-study programs on various subjects are available at Oxford and Cambridge Universities in England to qualified students. Many other travel/study opportunities developed by departments last a week to a semester and include language studies, business practices, art, law enforcement, teacher education, and many other disciplines. A significant number of students receive financial assistance for these programs. In addition, students can pay Missouri Southern fees and study abroad for a semester or year at more than 100 colleges and universities throughout the world as part of the International Student Exchange Program (ISEP).

Academic Facilities

Students have access to the most modern facilities. More than $42 million in construction was completed in the last five years. New projects and facilities include a major expansion of the Spiva Library that doubled its size and wired it for the twenty-first century, an 80,000-square-foot athletic center, a new 250-seat black box theater, a major expansion of the Mills Anderson Justice Center, and an extensive refitting of the Ummel Technology Building.

Southern has a safe, modern, and beautifully landscaped campus. The George A. Spiva Library houses more than 238,000 books and 1,200 periodicals. A state and federal government documents collection, a law library, and a 584,000-item microform collection provide additional reference materials for student research. A world of materials and services are available through the library's link with a nationwide computer network of libraries. All functions of the library are automated, so students and professors can access library functions via modem. A vast array of resources is also available in CD-ROM format. State-of-the-art computer labs for student use are located in the library and throughout the campus.

Taylor Auditorium is a 2,000-seat facility equipped with state-of-the-art computerized sound and lighting systems. Theater students train and perform there, as do the University's music groups. Both Matthews Hall Auditorium and Mills Anderson Justice Center Auditorium have 300 seats and are equipped for multimedia presentations, films, and other events. Webster Hall Auditorium, which seats 400, provides performance space for small musical presentations, lectures, and satellite conferences. Webster Hall also has a variety of facilities that give students extraordinarily valuable experiences. Communications students have hands-on opportunities in the production studios of Missouri Southern Television, which broadcasts over the air and on cable. KXMS-FM broadcasts classical music to the region and around the world on the Internet, 24 hours a day.

Costs

Tuition for 2003–04 was $127 per credit hour for Missouri residents and $254 per credit hour for out-of-state students, the lowest in the state of Missouri. Residence halls cost $4000 per semester depending on the meal plan. An added cost-saving feature is the rental of textbooks for $6 per credit hour per semester.

Financial Aid

A wide variety of financial aid options assist students with college costs. More than $21 million is distributed each year to 80 percent of the students, with an average award of more than

$3500. Federal programs include the Federal Pell Grant, Federal Supplemental Educational Opportunity Grant, Federal Work-Study Program, Federal Perkins Loan, and Federal Stafford Loan. Several state programs aid prospective teachers and students with high academic standing. In addition, the University provides a wide range of academic scholarships, performing awards, and student employment opportunities. Special scholarships are available for qualified junior college transfer students, and out-of-state tuition scholarships are offered to students in a designated surrounding area.

Faculty

The whole focus of Missouri Southern's faculty members is teaching and advising undergraduate students. With an 18:1 student-faculty ratio, close personal attention to the individual student's success is integral to the teaching process. Faculty members serve as personal advisers and mentors. Of the 197 full-time faculty members, 123 have doctoral or terminal degrees. Faculty members are actively involved in other campus activities as well as many community endeavors and encourage their students to participate in their communities.

Student Government

The Student Senate is the student governing body of the University. Senate members serve on various Faculty Senate committees as voting members, serve as liaisons with the University administration, and initiate new programs for the academic and cultural benefit of all students. The Campus Activities Board organizes social and cultural activities for the students.

Admission Requirements

Students are admitted to Missouri Southern if they are in the top 25 percent of their high school graduating class or have a minimum composite score of 21 on the ACT or a selection index score of 75. Students are strongly encouraged to complete a 16-unit high school core curriculum consisting of 4 units of English, 3 units each of math and social science, 2 units of science, 1 unit of visual/performing arts, and 3 units of additional core electives (2 years of foreign language is highly recommended). Students whose ACT scores and class rank are below those stated may request a review with the admission selection committee.

Application and Information

The University has a priority deadline of August 1. Students may apply any time during their senior year of high school. There is a $15 nonrefundable application fee. Information on specific academic areas and other University programs is readily available from the Admission Office and online.

Admission Office
Missouri Southern State University
3950 East Newman Road
Joplin, Missouri 64801-1595
Telephone: 417-782-6778
        866-818-MSSU (6778) (toll-free)
Fax: 417-659-4429
E-mail: admissions@mssc.edu
World Wide Web: http://www.mssu.edu

MISSOURI VALLEY COLLEGE

MARSHALL, MISSOURI

The College

Missouri Valley College (MVC) is a private, coeducational, liberal arts college affiliated with the Presbyterian Church (U.S.A.). The College offers a rich tradition of personalized liberal arts education with a focus on career preparation. MVC is situated on 150 acres; its student body in 2004 is made up of 1,425 students from forty-three states and thirty countries. The College is committed to preparing young people to become active and contributing members of society.

Founded in 1889 by a group of Presbyterian and civic leaders in Marshall, Missouri, the College has been accredited by the North Central Association of Colleges and Schools since 1916. Missouri Valley College is approved by the Missouri State Department of Education and the Board of Christian Education of the Presbyterian Church (U.S.A.).

In addition to academic facilities, including the historic Baity Hall, the newly built Technology Center, Ferguson Center, and Collins Science Center, there are four men's dormitories, one women's dormitory, and numerous on-campus houses and apartments available for students. Built in 1991, the Burns Athletic Complex is recognized as one of the premier small-college facilities in the country. The building includes a full recreational area (basketball courts, indoor track, and other facilities) as well as classrooms, locker rooms, a concession area, the Missouri Valley College Athletic Hall of Fame trophy room, and seating to accommodate numerous events.

Missouri Valley College offers many opportunities to be involved on campus and within the community. The College is home to four nationally recognized fraternities and two nationally recognized sororities. The Greek system provides students with the opportunity to develop leadership skills, build career networks, and provide community service. Participants in Greek life also develop close bonds with fellow students through a variety of social activities.

Missouri Valley College competes in the NAIA as a member of the Heart of America Conference. Viking athletic programs include baseball (men), basketball (men and women), cheerleading (men and women), cross-country (men and women), football (men), golf (men and women), rodeo (men and women), soccer (men and women), softball (women), track (men and women), volleyball (men and women), and wrestling (men and women).

Location

Missouri Valley College is located in Marshall, Missouri, a town of about 13,000 residents. Marshall is 1 hour east of the Kansas City metropolitan area and 1 hour west of Columbia, Missouri.

Majors and Degrees

Missouri Valley College is divided into six academic divisions: Arts and Humanities, Business, Education, Human Services, Mathematics and Science, and Social Science.

The Arts and Humanities Division of Missouri Valley College offers Bachelor of Arts degrees in the areas of art, English, mass communication, philosophy and religion, speech communication, and theater. A Bachelor of Fine Arts degree in theater is also available. Courses in English as a second language, French, Latin, music, and Spanish are also offered, and dance, English, music, and theater minors are also available. The division collaborates with the Teacher Education Program to offer certification in English and speech/theater.

The College's Business Division offers Bachelor of Arts and Bachelor of Science degrees in accounting; business administration, with concentrations in agribusiness, finance, management, marketing, and small business development; and economics. The division also offers a two-year Associate of Arts degree in small business

management. Students are encouraged to seek double majors within the division or in a complementary discipline, such as computer information systems. Minors are available in accounting, business administration, and economics.

Offered through the Division of Education and Physical Education, the Missouri Valley College Teacher Education Program is approved by the Missouri State Board of Education and accredited by the North Central Association of Colleges and Schools. MVC offers certification in the following areas: early childhood, elementary grades, middle school, secondary school, and special education cross-categorical. Missouri Valley Teacher Education Program graduates are well represented throughout the nation and have a 95 percent employment rate. MVC also has an athletic training major, and a physical education major is available with K–9, 9–12, and K–12 grade-level certifications.

The Human Services Division offers Bachelor of Arts degrees in human services/agency management and recreation administration. Students may apply for the specialized American Humanics Program, qualifying them to become certified American Humanics graduates. Academic courses stress the knowledge students need to become successful nonprofit youth agency administrators. American Humanics was founded at Missouri Valley College in 1948, and Missouri Valley College is the first institution to bring American Humanics into international light.

In the Mathematics and Science Division, Bachelor of Science degrees are obtainable in biology, computer information systems, and mathematics. MVC also offers a Bachelor of Arts degree in biology. Minors are available in biology, chemistry, and mathematics. The division collaborates with the Teacher Education Program to offer certification to teach science and mathematics.

The Social Science Division offers Bachelor of Arts and Bachelor of Science degrees in the following areas: alcohol and drug studies, criminal justice, history, political science/public administration, psychology, and sociology; a Bachelor of Science degree is offered in social studies education. A prelaw curriculum is an option for those interested in law school. Practicum and internship experiences are available, as are service learning and volunteer opportunities.

MVC also offers an Associate of Arts degree in liberal arts.

Academic Programs

The academic program of Missouri Valley College has been formulated to promote the personal and professional development of every student. The program is intended to ensure the academic growth of the student within a framework of social, physical, and spiritual development.

The academic year consists of two semesters, with summer courses available. While the number of semester hours required for graduation varies with the program chosen, a minimum of 128 hours is required for a degree. A student must complete the required semester hours in a major as well as the basic requirements of the core curriculum. With an emphasis in liberal arts education, the core curriculum provides general education through approximately 40 hours of core classes.

Academic Facilities

The campus of Missouri Valley College has facilities that enhance the quality of the students' academic and social lives. The Technology Center provides students and instructors with classrooms, library space, and a computer lab equipped for the digital age. The new addition to the Technology Center hosts classrooms complete with wireless laptop computers, which have Internet access, and an instructor's station, where a professor can access everything from compact discs and DVDs to the Internet for sharing as part of a presentation. There is also a high-technology version of the old overhead projector that digitizes information and can even convert a three-dimensional object into a computer picture for sharing on the large screen at the front of the room.

Other major construction projects have included renovations of the old chapel on the upper floor of Baity Hall into the Learning Center, with computers and tutors available to students, and an extensive remodeling of Murrell Library.

The main library is located in the Murrell Memorial Library building, and the library annex is located in the Technology Center. This part of the library houses library collections that include art, business and economics, English, humanities, psychology, science and mathematics, and the social sciences. The Eckilson-Mabee Theatre also has been renovated into an extraordinary performance facility. The 274-seat theater is equipped with a Dolby 7.1 surround sound system, a high definition digital projection unit, and an ETC computerized lighting system.

Costs

Tuition and fees at Missouri Valley College for 2003–04 were $13,100 per year, and room and board averaged $5200. A nonrefundable deposit of $500 is required for resident students; a $250 deposit is required for commuter students.

Financial Aid

Financial need may be met through a combination of state, federal, and institutional aid, which is available to all qualified students. Institutional awards and grants are offered in many areas.

To be eligible for financial aid, a student must be admitted to the College. All students receiving federal or state-based program aid must file the Free Application for Federal Student Aid. New students need to file the financial aid application by the date of enrollment. International students are required to fill out a standard Affidavit of Support, in addition to their application for admission, to document their ability to pay their education expenses.

The College participates in the following federally sponsored aid programs: the Federal Pell Grant, Federal Supplemental Educational Opportunity Grant, Federal Work-Study Program, and subsidized and unsubsidized Federal Stafford Student Loan Programs. Missouri Student Grants are available to Missouri students carrying a minimum of 12 hours per semester who can prove financial need. Full-time resident students are able to defray a portion of their college costs by participating in the Missouri Valley College Work & Learn Program on campus. Generally, compensation for this work is credited toward the student's account.

A variety of scholarships are awarded to students who have excelled in fields of study, community activities, or athletic competition. Missouri Valley College's admissions counselors can advise prospective students of the full program of available scholarships.

Faculty

The total number of faculty members the College employs is 113, of whom 71 are full-time. The student-faculty ratio is 18:1, with more than 59 percent of the faculty members holding terminal degrees. The College prides itself on the good rapport and excellent personal relationships students and faculty members share.

Student Government

Students take an active leadership role in a wide variety of campus organizations and activities. Honorary, academic, athletic, and performance organizations and clubs, along with sororities and fraternities, contribute to the quality of student life at MVC. The Student Government Association (SGA), whose mission is to uphold and enhance all areas of student life on campus, also provides student leadership.

Admission Requirements

The College selects freshmen and transfer students who will benefit from the College's full-service program and who demonstrate the potential for academic success. Each application for admission is reviewed individually.

Students seeking admission to Missouri Valley College should earn at least a composite 18 on the ACT or a combined 860 on the SAT, be in the top half of their graduating class, and have at least a 2.0 GPA on a 4.0 scale. Students who do not meet these requirements are considered on a case-by-case basis.

Students should take the following steps to satisfy admission procedures: complete an application form and submit it in person or by mail to the Office of Admissions, along with a $10 nonrefundable application fee; provide the Office of Admissions an official high school transcript indicating graduation from high school (applicants may provide a copy of the General Educational Development (GED) certificate in lieu of transcripts); and provide a copy of the results of either the ACT or SAT. A student's high school counselor may assist in arranging for the test and obtaining the results. Students who have not taken the SAT or ACT by the time of their arrival on campus are contacted by the Office of Admissions and required to take the ACT during their first semester.

Students who wish to transfer from another institution, including those who have completed junior college work, should submit the following materials to ensure that their applications are processed promptly: the Missouri Valley College application for admission; a high school transcript or the recognized equivalent of a high school diploma; official transcripts of all previous collegiate work, including financial aid transcripts; and the ACT or SAT score (not necessary for students with more than 27 transfer hours). Students should provide a copy of the previous college's catalog to ensure proper credit transfer. If official transcripts are not received within a reasonable time, the student's academic and financial aid status may change.

Application and Information

An application and additional information can be obtained by contacting:

Office of Admissions
Missouri Valley College
500 East College Street
Marshall, Missouri 65340

Telephone: 660-831-4000 or 4114
E-mail: admissions@moval.edu
World Wide Web: http://www.moval.edu

Baity Hall, on the campus of Missouri Valley College.

MORNINGSIDE COLLEGE
SIOUX CITY, IOWA

The College

The Morningside College experience cultivates a passion for lifelong learning and a dedication to ethical leadership and civic responsibility. For more than 100 years, the goal of Morningside College has been to provide students with an education of the highest quality. Morningside is rooted in a strong church-related, liberal arts tradition, and its challenge is to prepare students to be flexible in thought, open in attitude, and confident in themselves.

Founded in 1894, Morningside College is a private, four-year, coeducational, liberal arts institution affiliated with the United Methodist Church. The College seeks both students and faculty members representing diverse social, cultural, ethnic, racial, and national backgrounds.

At the graduate level, Morningside confers a Master of Arts in Teaching, with specialization in elementary education, special education, and technology-based learning.

Morningside College's approximately 1,000 students are encouraged to participate in a wide variety of activities, including departmental, professional, and religious organizations; honor societies; and sororities and fraternities. A newspaper, literary magazine, yearbook, and campus radio station are all under student direction. These activities provide students with many opportunities to develop leadership, interpersonal, and social skills. Since nearly all activities on campus are student initiated and student directed, ample opportunities for leadership development exist. Music recitals and concerts, theater productions, and an academic and cultural arts and lecture series are held each semester. Intercollegiate athletics are available for men in baseball, basketball, cross-country, football, golf, soccer, swimming, tennis, and track and field and for women in basketball, cross-country, golf, soccer, softball, swimming, tennis, track, and volleyball. A variety of intramural activities are available.

The Hindman-Hobbs Recreation Center includes a pool, saunas, racquetball courts, a weight room, three basketball courts, and a jogging track as well as classroom facilities and offices.

Location

Morningside College is located on a 41-acre campus in Sioux City, the fourth-largest city in Iowa. The campus is based in a residential section of the community, adjacent to a city park, swimming pool, and tennis courts and within 5 minutes of a major regional shopping mall. The Sioux City metropolitan area offers a blend of urban shopping, commerce, and recreation in a scenic, rural setting. Students find Morningside's Sioux City location to be advantageous in seeking internship opportunities and full- or part-time employment.

Majors and Degrees

The five undergraduate degrees conferred by Morningside College are the Bachelor of Arts, Bachelor of Science, Bachelor of Science in Nursing, Bachelor of Music, and Bachelor of Music Education. Career programs consist of accounting, art, biology, business administration, chemistry, computer science, corporate communications, elementary education, engineering physics, English, graphic arts, history, interdisciplinary studies, mass communications, mathematics, music, nursing, philosophy, photography, political science, psychology, religious studies, Spanish, special education, and theater. Students choosing to teach in secondary school may be certified in most academic majors.

In cooperation with other institutions, Morningside offers preprofessional programs in engineering, law, medical technology, medicine, the ministry, pharmacy, physical therapy, physician assistant studies, and veterinary medicine.

Academic Programs

Morningside operates on a two-semester system; sessions are held from late August to December and from January to early May. Evening classes are offered each semester. A 3-week May interim and two 5-week summer sessions are also available.

Morningside College is committed to the liberal arts as a foundation for every field of concentration at the undergraduate level. Requirements in general education consist of a distribution of studies in the humanities, natural sciences, social sciences, and some interdisciplinary courses.

Special opportunities include a voluntary Honors Program, in which students meet weekly to discuss such focus topics as Ancient Rome and the Eighteenth Century. Friday is Writing Day is a weekly discussion format that allows students and faculty members to read aloud and react to one another's writing.

Every entering full-time student receives a laptop computer that is used in classroom work. Student technology services include high-speed Internet connection, ports in all residence halls and classrooms, Web-accessible personal e-mail accounts, a digital library accessible day and night, specialized computer labs to support academic programs, and wireless network access points in selected areas on campus.

Off-Campus Programs

Morningside students who qualify have the opportunity to take advantage of special programs for off-campus study. Programs are available for a semester or the entire school year. The College has agreements with schools in England, Japan, and Northern Ireland.

Students participate in exchange programs with Kansai Gadai University in Japan, Queen's University, the University of Ulster, and Belfast Institute for Further and Higher Education in Northern Ireland.

In addition, Morningside has opportunities for students to enroll for a semester at American University to study the U.S. government in action. Students may also be nominated for a semester at Drew University to study the United Nations. Students who participate in these programs maintain their enrollment at Morningside College.

Academic Facilities

The Hickman-Johnson-Furrow Library has more than 114,000 volumes, more than 5,000 audio recordings and video materials, and nearly 600 current print periodical subscriptions. Online accessibility includes student/faculty access to more than 10,000 full-text journals. The library's Web-based, integrated online system allows seamless access to numerous subscription databases as well as other online catalogs and Web sites. The library building also houses classrooms, the Mass Communication Department, a media center, and a computer lab.

The Eugene C. Eppley Fine Arts Building is one of the finest music and art facilities in the Midwest. The auditorium seats 1,500 people and is noted for its acoustical qualities and the majestic Sanford Memorial Organ. The MacCollin Classroom Building, adjoining the auditorium, houses offices, art studios, practice rooms, and classrooms for music and art students.

The Helen Levitt Art Gallery adjoins the Eppley Auditorium and is home to the Levitt art collection, which includes work by internationally famous artists.

The Robert M. Lincoln Center houses the College's division of business administration and economics and contains a library, auditorium, microcomputer lab, conference room, and several classrooms.

Costs

Tuition and fees for 2003–04 were $16,350, and room and board were $5260. These figures do not include books and personal expenses.

Financial Aid

In 2002–03, almost $14 million was awarded in financial aid to Morningside students, with an average financial aid package of $16,758. The financial aid resources of federal, state, and College programs are available to Morningside students through a combination of scholarships, grants, loans, and work-study employment. Morningside values students who achieve both in and out of the classroom—people who are thinkers and doers. Morningside Celebration of Excellence Scholarships recognize academic excellence and outstanding service, and awards of up to $10,000 per year are renewable for four years. Morningside also values its ties with alumni and the United Methodist Church, and those awards are also renewable for four years. Students are encouraged to submit the Free Application for Federal Student Aid (FAFSA) as early as possible. The College's code number is 001879. The annual priority deadline for need-based financial aid is March 1.

Faculty

Eighty-four percent of Morningside College's 63 full-time faculty members have earned the terminal degree in their chosen field. The College also employs 48 part-time instructors and has a 14:1 student-faculty ratio.

Student Government

Student government is directly responsible for regulation, supervision, and coordination of student campus activities. The president of the student body is a voting member of the Board of Directors, allowing for student input in decisions facing the Board.

Admission Requirements

Morningside College selects students for admission whose scholastic achievement and personal abilities provide a foundation for success at the college level. While the College seeks students who rank in the upper half of their graduating

class, each application is considered on an individual basis. The student's academic record, class rank, and test scores are considered. Transfer students must have a minimum 2.0 GPA on previous college work to qualify for automatic admission. It is the policy and practice of Morningside College to not discriminate against persons on the basis of age, sex, religion, creed, race, color, national or ethnic origin, sexual orientation, or physical or mental disability.

Application and Information

Rolling admission allows for flexibility; however, prospective students are encouraged to apply as early as possible before the semester in which they wish to enroll. Transfer and international students are welcome. Catalogs, application forms, and financial aid forms are available from the Office of Admissions.

For further information, students should contact:

Office of Admissions
Morningside College
1501 Morningside Avenue
Sioux City, Iowa 51106
Telephone: 712-274-5111
　　　　　800-831-0806 (toll-free)
E-mail: mscadm@morningside.edu
World Wide Web: http://www.morningside.edu

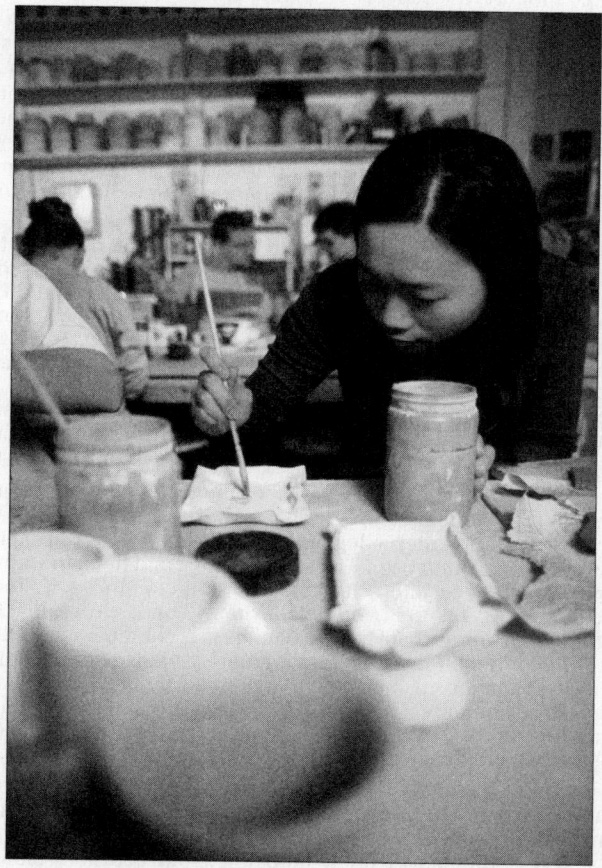

Morningside College provides a welcoming environment for art majors.

MOUNT MERCY COLLEGE
CEDAR RAPIDS, IOWA

The College

Mount Mercy College is distinguished by a unique blend of career preparation and liberal arts, strengthened by a strong emphasis on leadership and service. A Catholic, coeducational four-year college, Mount Mercy is fully accredited by the North Central Association of Colleges and Schools.

Although the College offers a number of professional programs, its career preparation is not limited to those areas. Students majoring in English or history, for example, are just as likely to benefit from internships as students in business or social work. There is a focus on workplace skills such as group process and presentations—competencies that help graduates begin their careers. Mount Mercy believes strongly in a firm liberal arts foundation of analysis, critical thinking, and communication—skills that help graduates adapt to a changing world and find long-term career success.

Through its Emerging Leaders and Campus Ministry programs, the College supports the concept of servant leadership. This tradition of service is a legacy of the Sisters of Mercy, who founded the College in 1928. The College welcomes students of all faiths.

Mount Mercy's high academic quality and its relatively moderate cost make it one of the best values in Midwest higher education. The College offers thirty-five major fields of study, including several interdisciplinary majors. In the College's Partnership program, professors are paired with freshman students to support their transition to college and to enhance the intellectual growth needed to assure academic success.

Student activities include more than thirty clubs and organizations, a student newspaper, a choir, and a pom squad and cheerleaders, along with such annual events as Hillfest and Spring Fling. Each May, commencement exercises are followed by a celebration for graduates and their families on Mount Mercy's hilltop. During the school year, many student activities—including Club Friday, a Friday afternoon gathering of students, faculty members, and staff members—take place in the Lundy Commons, which houses a game room, fitness center, conference rooms, student organization offices, the *Mount Mercy Times* office, lounge areas, and a bookstore.

Mount Mercy College is a member of the National Association of Intercollegiate Athletics (NAIA) and the Midwest Classic Conference. The College offers intercollegiate competition in men's basketball, baseball, cross-country, golf, soccer, and track and field. In women's sports, the College offers basketball, cross-country, golf, soccer, softball, track and field, and volleyball. These programs have combined for more than twenty conference championship Mount Mercy teams and individuals that regularly qualify for regional and national championship events. In addition, Mount Mercy student-athletes are annually recognized as NAIA academic all-Americans. Intramural activities include basketball, cross-country, flag football, golf, softball, and volleyball.

About 400 of Mount Mercy's approximately 1,473 students live in campus housing. The College offers a variety of living arrangements. Mount Mercy's newest residence, which opened in fall 1999, houses 144 students in eight homelike, four-bedroom suites. A network of tunnels connects campus buildings; many students wear shorts all winter.

Location

Mount Mercy is just minutes from downtown Cedar Rapids' museums, malls, movie theaters, and restaurants. Local businesses offer numerous internships and employment opportunities. The 40-acre, tree-lined campus is tucked into a residential neighborhood of well-kept homes, neat lawns, and good neighbors. Mount Mercy's hilltop, with its sweeping view of the city skyline, is said to be the highest point in Linn County. The city bus stops at the College's "front door," providing convenient in-town transportation.

Cedar Rapids is served by six major airlines and is just a 4- or 5-hour drive from Chicago, Minneapolis–St. Paul, Omaha, and St. Louis. Mount Mercy's location in a thriving Midwestern city helps students explore career possibilities and, when they graduate, find promising opportunities. Both economically and culturally, Cedar Rapids offers an outstanding quality of life.

Majors and Degrees

Mount Mercy awards the Bachelor of Arts, Bachelor of Science, Bachelor of Business Administration, Bachelor of Applied Science, Bachelor of Applied Arts, and Bachelor of Science in Nursing degrees.

The Bachelor of Arts degree is awarded to graduates who major in applied philosophy, art, biology, communication, criminal justice, criminal justice/business administration–interdisciplinary, English, English/business administration–interdisciplinary, history, international studies, mathematics, music, music/business administration–interdisciplinary, music education, political science, political science/business administration–interdisciplinary, psychology, psychology/business administration–interdisciplinary, religious studies, secondary education, social work, sociology, sociology/business administration–interdisciplinary, speech/drama, and visual arts/business administration–interdisciplinary.

The Bachelor of Science degree is awarded to graduates who major in biology, business, computer information systems, computer science, elementary education, health services administration, mathematics, medical technology, nursing, and secondary education.

Original endorsements, coupled with the secondary education major, may be completed in art, biology–education, business–marketing/management, English/language arts, history, mathematics–education, music–education, social science American government, social science American history, social science psychology, social science sociology, social science world history, and speech communication theater.

The Bachelor of Business Administration is awarded to graduates who major in accounting, administrative management, business–general (teacher education program), marketing, and secondary education. The Bachelor of Science in Nursing is awarded to graduates in nursing.

The Bachelor of Applied Science and Bachelor of Applied Arts degree programs are designed for students with technical training who wish to broaden their specialized background to include a liberal arts education. The Bachelor of Applied Science degree is awarded to graduates who major in accounting, administrative management, biology, business, computer information systems, computer science, health services administration, marketing, and mathematics. The Bachelor of Applied Arts degree is awarded to graduates who major in art, biology, criminal justice, history, mathematics, music, political science, psychology, religious studies, sociology, and speech drama.

Academic Programs

Mount Mercy College requires 123 semester hours for graduation, with a cumulative grade point average of at least 2.0 (on a 4.0 scale). General education requirements include two courses in English, two in social sciences, and one each in fine arts, history, mathematics, multicultural studies, natural science, philosophy, religious studies, and speech. Students apply for admission to their major program in the spring of the sophomore year. The College gives credit for related experience based on portfolio presentations and for independent study arranged by the student and the instructor. Graduation requirements may vary according to the major field of study.

Special academic opportunities are offered to outstanding students through special honors sections of general education courses. Students graduating in the honors program receive special recognition at commencement.

Mount Mercy's academic year consists of fall and spring semesters, plus a winter term. This four-week term offers required courses as well as exploratory electives, allowing students to make more rapid progress toward their degrees. In addition, two 5-week summer sessions are held.

Off-Campus Programs

Mount Mercy College has an exchange program with the University of Palacky in Olomouc, Czech Republic.

Academic Facilities

The Busse Library provides an inviting study and research environment. Internet access opens other major libraries to students as well. The library houses the computer center; a computer classroom used for instruction in writing, accounting, and computer skills; a media center; individual study carrels; group study rooms; and a variety of other comfortable study areas.

Basile Hall is a new business and biology building that opened in summer 2003, providing thirteen technology-ready classrooms and teaching labs, four seminar rooms, and a computer-teaching laboratory.

All on-campus student rooms and faculty/staff offices are connected to a campus network. The College also has an ICN (Iowa Communications Network) fiber-optics classroom, making it possible for students in more than one location to take the same course, interacting with other students and with the instructor.

Costs

Full-time tuition for the 2003–04 academic year was $16,070, about at the midpoint among Iowa private colleges. Major fees are included in this figure. Room costs were $2164 in residence halls and $2772 in apartments. Two meal plans are offered: the nineteen-meal-per-week plan, which cost $3166, and the fifteen-meal plan, $2944. Estimated annual costs for a resident student, including books, supplies, and personal expenses, were $25,894.

Financial Aid

Nearly all Mount Mercy's new, full-time freshmen receive some form of financial aid, including Mount Mercy scholarships or grants, federal or state grants, loans, on-campus employment, or a combination of these sources. The College awarded twenty-nine Presidential Scholarships of up to $6700 for the 2003–04 school year to high school seniors who had an ACT score of at least 26 and a high school grade point average of at least 3.5. Other awards also are made on the basis of ACT score and GPA. Each year, students who have been admitted to Mount Mercy and identified as Presidential Scholars are invited to campus to compete for the Holland Scholarship, a full-tuition award named for the first president of Mount Mercy. Three Holland Scholarships were awarded for the 2003–04 school year. Students may also apply for the Merit Award, given to entering freshmen and transfer students on the basis of their demonstrated leadership in school and community activities. In addition, scholarships are available to students with records of achievement in art, drama, and music and to those who are planning to major in social work. In 2003–04, the College awarded more than $5 million in institutional scholarships and grants to qualified students.

Students who show financial need may be eligible for the Federal Pell Grant, the Iowa Tuition Grant, Federal Stafford Student Loan, and on-campus employment. Students in work-study positions typically earn from $1000 to $1500 a year.

To apply for Mount Mercy scholarships and grants, students must first be admitted to the College. Early application is advised. The priority deadline for filing the FAFSA (Free Application for Federal Student Aid) is March 1. Students should check other deadlines with their high school counselors or call the Mount Mercy financial aid office.

Faculty

Most of Mount Mercy's 72 full-time and 45 part-time faculty members hold the terminal degree in their fields. Many have been recognized for their achievements: several have been Fulbright Fellows or have received grants from the National Endowment for the Humanities and the National Endowment for the Arts, and many others have been recognized by their professional organizations. With a faculty-student ratio of 14:1, Mount Mercy offers students the opportunity to know their teachers well and to learn from them in an informal, friendly, and supportive environment.

Student Government

The official voice of the student at Mount Mercy is the Student Government Association (SGA). Its officers serve on College committees, and SGA is represented at regular faculty meetings. An SGA petition to the faculty resulted in adding a fall break to the academic calendar. SGA is the body through which all other campus organizations are formed and funded.

Admission Requirements

Mount Mercy admits students whose academic preparation, abilities, interests, and personal qualities give promise of success in college. Applicants are considered on the basis of academic record, class rank, test scores, and recommendations. An Admission Committee reviews the applications of students with minimum qualifications. Students may apply online. To apply, students must submit an application for admission, a transcript of high school credits, scores from ACT or SAT examinations, and a $20 application fee. Transfer students must submit official transcripts from all colleges attended. Mount Mercy College has an agreement with several two-year colleges in Iowa through which degree graduates of these colleges may be admitted to Mount Mercy with junior standing.

Prospective students are encouraged to visit the campus and meet with a faculty member in their area of interest. Special campus visit days are scheduled each year, and individual appointments also may be made. Overnight accommodations in residence halls can be arranged.

Application and Information

Students who wish to be considered for Mount Mercy scholarships and grants should submit their applications for admission as early as possible after their junior year in high school. Admission decisions are made on a rolling basis, and the College notifies students of its decision within ten days of receiving the necessary forms.

Application forms and additional information may be obtained by contacting:

Office of Admission
Mount Mercy College
1330 Elmhurst Drive, NE
Cedar Rapids, Iowa 52402
Telephone: 319-368-6460
            319-363-5270
            800-248-4504 (toll-free)
E-mail: admission@mtmercy.edu
World Wide Web: http://www.mtmercy.edu

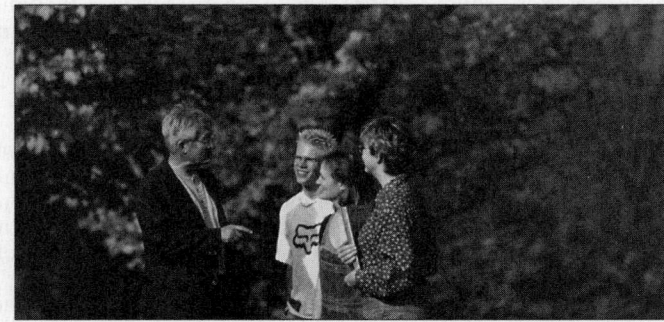

Students talk with a professor on the campus of Mount Mercy.

NORTH CENTRAL COLLEGE
NAPERVILLE, ILLINOIS

The College

Founded in 1861, North Central College has a distinctive heritage as a comprehensive college that educates students in both the liberal arts and sciences and in preprofessional fields.

A private, United Methodist–affiliated institution, the College has long been recognized for academic excellence, with its educational philosophy of incorporating leadership, ethics, and values into academic and cocurricular activities. North Central's 2,500 students include traditional-age undergraduate, part-time, and graduate students. Master's degree programs are offered in business administration, computer science, education, information systems, leadership studies, and liberal studies. New graduate certificates are now available in business foundations, change management, dispute resolution, finance, gender studies, history and nature of science, human resource management, investments and financial planning, leadership studies, management, marketing, multicultural studies, and organizational ethics.

North Central's 56-acre campus has more than twenty major buildings. Facilities include the historic Old Main, built in 1870 and renovated in 1998; the state-of-the-art Cardinal Stadium, which seats 5,500 and is the home to football, soccer and track; and Pfeiffer Hall, a 1,050-seat auditorium. Kaufman Dining Hall serves the entire campus.

Twenty-five states and twenty-five other countries are represented (86 percent of the students are Illinois residents). Twelve percent of the members of the 2003 freshman class were members of minority groups, and 82 percent of freshmen live in one of nine residence halls.

Cocurricular programs parallel many academic majors and include the nationally acclaimed Students in Free Enterprise, Cardinals in Action (a community service organization), campus radio station WONC, Mock Trial, Model United Nations, and forensics. North Central student athletes compete in nineteen NCAA Division III intercollegiate varsity sports within the College Conference of Illinois and Wisconsin. The varsity sports include baseball, basketball, cross-country, football, golf, soccer, swimming, tennis, track and field, and wrestling for men. Women participate in basketball, cross-country, golf, soccer, softball, swimming, tennis, track and field, and volleyball. Students have many options for social activities: programmed events through the College Union Activities Board, residence life activities, an active intramural program, and travel to both downtown Naperville and Chicago. Student services include centers for academic advising, counseling, writing, foreign language, and career development.

Location

North Central is located in a charming historic district in the heart of Naperville, Illinois, a fast growing community of 140,000 residents in the west-suburban area of metropolitan Chicago. The city is a residential community with excellent community services and has become the Midwest center of scientific research and development. It is in the "Silicon Prairie" center of the high-technology Illinois Research and Development Corridor, where some of the nation's largest companies (e.g., BP Amoco, Metropolitan Life, and Ondeo-Nalco Chemical Company) are located. Nearby are Argonne National Laboratory, Fermi National Accelerator Laboratory, and Morton Arboretum. All of

these facilities and industries represent unique resources for North Central students—for internships, jobs, and joint research opportunities.

Chicago is just 29 miles away, and the cultural, artistic, and entertainment venues in this great city make it a rich resource for a North Central education. Students can catch the Burlington Northern Railroad just two blocks from the campus for an easy commute.

Majors and Degrees

North Central College awards the Bachelor of Arts (B.A.) degree in accounting, art, art education, arts and letters, athletic training, biochemistry, biology, broadcast communication, chemistry, classical civilization, computer science, East Asian studies, economics, education (elementary and secondary), English, entrepreneurship and small business management, exercise science, finance, French, German, history, human resource management, humanities, international business, international studies, Japanese, management, management information systems, marketing, mathematics, music, musical theater, music education, organizational communication, philosophy, physical education, physics, political science, print journalism, psychology, religious studies, science, social studies, sociology, sociology and anthropology, Spanish, speech communication, sports management, theater, and urban and suburban studies. The Bachelor of Science (B.S.) degree is awarded in actuarial science, applied mathematics, biochemistry, biology, chemistry, computer science, mathematics, and psychology and in all economics and business areas.

Preprofessional-professional programs are offered in engineering, health sciences, medical physics, medical technology, nursing, and law. A 3-2 engineering program is offered in cooperation with the University of Illinois at Urbana-Champaign, Washington University in St. Louis, Missouri, Iowa State University and the University of Minnesota. Both 2-2 and 3-2 programs in nursing are available in cooperation with Rush University in Chicago. Students may also design other majors that bridge two or more areas of study.

Academic Programs

North Central provides a comprehensive education with the goal of preparing students to live free, ethically responsible, and intellectually rewarding lives. Each student must complete a minimum of 120 credit hours, including all general education requirements and an approved major. CLEP, AP, and IB exams are considered for college credit and/or advanced course placement.

The academic year comprises three 10½-week terms and a monthlong Interim Term between Thanksgiving and the beginning of the new calendar year. Students usually take three courses during each term, while the Interim Term is used for independent study, taking courses, travel, research, work, or simply relaxation. The College actively supports internships as part of career preparation, and the College Scholars Honors Program is open to select students.

Off-Campus Programs

North Central College provides many opportunities for students to study abroad. Students interested in engaging in intensive Spanish study may travel to Costa Rica each fall term for 13 weeks. The 15-week London term allows students to explore European history and understand the changing contemporary

English and continental cultures. Other study-abroad possibilities include exchange programs to Japan, China, Korea, Taiwan, Northern Ireland, and France.

North Central is also one of only twelve colleges and universities in the nation to offer the distinctive Richter Independent Study Fellowship Program, which provides funds of up to $5000 for a single specialized project. Richter Independent Study projects have included travel and research on every continent.

Academic Facilities

WONC (89.1 FM), the College's 1,500-watt radio station, is one of the most powerful student-staffed stations in the Midwest. The station, with three state-of-the-art studios for on-air and audio production work, has won 20 Marconi Awards—more than any other college radio station in the country.

All students and faculty and staff members have access to a voice, video, and data network, including full Internet access from their residence halls, classrooms, computer laboratories, and offices. Ten MB of Web space has been made available to every enrolled student for personal pages, and 55 MB of hard drive space for file storage.

Science equipment available for student research projects includes a fourteen-CPU LINUX parallel processor, computer networking and multimedia labs, a 300-MHz magnetic resonance spectrometer, a gas chromatograph/mass spectrometer, a liquid chromatograph, a pulsed nitrogen laser, a phase-contrast video microscope, PCR thermal cyclers, and environmental chambers. North Central also has state-of-the-art language and market research laboratories.

Costs

For 2004–05, tuition at North Central College is $20,160. Room and board are $6747. Resident students pay a $225 technology fee. The student activity fee is $180, and estimated additional expenses are $425 for books and supplies. Students should also budget personal expenses and transportation costs.

Financial Aid

The Offices of Administration and Financial Aid are committed to assisting students throughout the process of applying for financial aid. Scholarships, loans, grants, and work-study assistance are awarded on the basis of demonstrated financial need and the academic record. Students are required to submit the Free Application for Federal Student Aid (FAFSA). Funds are also available through the Illinois State Monetary Award Program (for Illinois residents only), the Federal Pell Grant Program, Federal Supplemental Educational Opportunity Grant, and the Federal Stafford Student Loan Program. The College awarded more than $12 million from institutional sources for 2003–04. A large portion of those funds was allocated through the academic-based Presidential Scholarship Program. Awards range from $5000 to full tuition, renewable annually. Students may also interview and/or audition for scholarships in science, theatre, forensics, vocal and instrumental music, as well as submit art portfolios.

Faculty

Members of the North Central faculty, 89 percent of whom hold the Ph.D. or another terminal degree, are first—and foremost—teachers. A student-faculty ratio of 14:1 and an average class size of 19 students ensure opportunities for a stimulating exchange of ideas. All faculty members also serve as academic advisers to provide guidance and counseling for students. Students get to know their professors on a personal basis, and the list of independent study projects is extensive. Faculty members teach both undergraduate and graduate courses.

Student Government

All undergraduates are members of the Student Association, which is governed by its elected officers. The Student Association is a vital and influential force in campus activities, and it takes an active role in the development and implementation of policies concerning student life on campus. Representatives of the student body have a voice on faculty, trustee, and administrative committees, while the College Union Activities Board plans social and service events.

Admission Requirements

New students are accepted individually on the basis of their overall academic preparation, character, and potential for success at North Central College. Graduation from an accredited secondary school is a basic requirement for admission. Other criteria used in the selection of prospective students are the high school academic record, personal recommendations of high school counselors, ACT or SAT I scores, and involvement in extracurricular activities. Members of the North Central freshman class of 2003–04 scored an average of 24 on the ACT and ranked in the 75th percentile of their high school graduating class. North Central does not discriminate on the basis of sex, race, ethnic background, age, or physical handicap.

Application and Information

North Central College operates on a rolling admission basis, which allows students to apply at any time during or after their senior year in high school. Students can complete and submit an application for admission on the College's Web site. Applicants receive notification within three weeks after the College receives all documentation. Early application is recommended to ensure availability of campus housing. The application must be accompanied by a $25 fee, an official high school transcript, and official reports of ACT or SAT I scores from the testing agency. For additional information or application forms, students should contact:

Office of Admission
North Central College
30 North Brainard Street
Naperville, Illinois 60540
Telephone: 630-637-5800
         800-411-1861 (toll-free)
Fax: 630-637-5819
E-mail: ncadm@noctrl.edu
World Wide Web: http://www.northcentralcollege.edu

Historic Old Main, built in 1870 and renovated in 1998, houses the Offices of Admission, Financial Aid, and the Registrar.

OHIO WESLEYAN UNIVERSITY
DELAWARE, OHIO

The University

An unusual synthesis of liberal arts learning and preprofessional preparation has set Ohio Wesleyan University (OWU) apart. It is one of the country's five independent four-year colleges to rank among the top twenty in both the number of graduates earning Ph.D.'s and the number who are U.S. business leaders. Founded by the United Methodist Church in 1842, the University is strongly committed to developing the service ethic in students, to fusing theory with its practical applications, and to confronting specific issues of long-range public importance.

Undergraduate enrollment is about 1,850 men and women. Students come to Ohio Wesleyan from forty-four states and forty-five countries, and most reside on the attractive 200-acre campus. OWU ranks fourth in the nation (among schools in its class) in the proportion of students with international origins. Housing options include six large residence halls with special-interest corridors; a number of smaller special-interest units, such as the Tree House and the Peace and Justice House; and eleven fraternity houses. The five sorority houses are nonresidential.

There is a wide range of cocurricular activities. Students initiate discussion groups, service projects, and intramural athletics. Other activities include a fully independent student newspaper, cultural- and ethnic-interest groups such as the Student Union on Black Awareness and the Christian Fellowship, crisis intervention work, the College Republicans and Young Democrats, and prelaw and premed clubs. In the course of a year, students may enjoy more than 100 concerts, plays, dance programs, films, exhibits, and timely speakers. The Theatre and Dance Department stages four major productions and much additional studio work each year, while the Music Department sponsors four large groups and other small ensembles. An impressive campus center is the hub of cocurricular life on campus.

There are twenty-three varsity athletic teams—eleven for men, eleven for women, and a coed sailing team. Many teams often earn NCAA Division III national ranking; recent rankings have included the men's teams in baseball, golf, lacrosse, soccer, and tennis, and the women's cross-country, field hockey, soccer, swimming, and track teams. In 2001 and 2002, the OWU women's soccer team was the NCAA Division III national champion. In recent years, individual All-Americans have been named in these sports and in football, men's cross-country, and men's track. Intramural programs are extensive, and all students have access to racquet sports, swimming, and weight-lifting facilities in the Branch Rickey Physical Education Center. Fitness equipment and health services are housed in the Health and Wellness Center, conveniently located near the residence halls. Off-campus opportunities for backpacking, boating, camping, golf, skiing, and swimming are abundant.

Location

Delaware combines the small-town pace and maple-lined streets of the county seat (population 25,000) with easy access to the state capital, Columbus, the fifteenth-largest city in America. Thirty minutes south of the campus, Columbus provides rich internship opportunities, international research centers, fine dining and shopping, and cultural events that complement campus life. Delaware, founded in 1808, retains a stately, post-Colonial charm in many of its sections. Because the campus is in the town, students find a degree of solitude but not a sense of isolation. About half of the faculty members live a short walk from campus.

Majors and Degrees

Ohio Wesleyan offers the Bachelor of Arts degree in accounting, astronomy, biological sciences (botany, genetics, microbiology, and zoology), chemistry, computer science, economics (including accounting, international business, and management), education

(elementary and secondary licensing in seventeen areas), English literature and writing, environmental science, fine arts, French, geography, geology, German, history, humanities-classics, journalism, mathematics, music (applied or history/literature), neuroscience, philosophy, physical education, physics, politics and government, psychology, religion, sociology/anthropology, Spanish, and theater and dance. Fifteen interdisciplinary majors include black studies, East Asian studies, environmental studies, international studies, urban studies, and gender studies, as well as prelaw and premedicine. Students may also design majors in topical, period, or regional studies.

Two professional degrees are awarded: the Bachelor of Fine Arts in art history, arts education, and studio art, and the Bachelor of Music in music education and performance. Combined-degree (generally 3-2) programs are offered in engineering, medical technology, optometry, and physical therapy.

Academic Programs

Ohio Wesleyan provides opportunities for students to acquire not only depth in a major area but also knowledge about their cultural past through the insight provided by a broad curriculum. At Ohio Wesleyan, education is placed in a context of values, and students are encouraged to develop the intellectual skills of effective communication, independent and logical thought, and creative problem solving. To these ends, students are required to demonstrate competence in English composition and a foreign language (often through placement testing) and to complete distributional study in the natural and social sciences, the humanities, and the arts. With few exceptions, the major requires the completion of eight to fifteen courses; double majors and minors are encouraged. Completion of thirty-four courses is required for graduation.

Advanced placement is available with or without credit. Under the four-year honors program, freshmen may be named Merit Scholars and work individually with faculty mentors on research, directed readings, or original creative work. Upperclass students are also encouraged to participate in independent study. Phi Beta Kappa is one of more than twenty scholastic honorary societies with chapters on campus.

The objectives of an Ohio Wesleyan education are crystallized in the distinctive Sagan National Colloquium, a program focused annually on one issue of compelling public importance, such as "Food: A Harvest of History, Culture, Politics, and Science." Through weekly speakers and semester-long seminars, the colloquium stimulates campuswide dialogue and encourages students to integrate knowledge from many different disciplines and apply what is studied to life. Participants should discover not only what they think about the issue but also why they think as they do and how to make important decisions based on their beliefs.

Off-Campus Programs

Full-semester internships and apprenticeships, as well as programs of advanced research, are actively developed through most departments. Many are approved by the Great Lakes Colleges Association, Inc. (GLCA), a highly regarded academic consortium of twelve independent institutions. Programs include the Philadelphia Center, the GLCA Arts Program in New York, and the Oak Ridge National Laboratory Science Semester. Other cooperative arrangements include the Newberry Library Program, Wesleyan in Washington, and the Drew University United Nations Semester. Research is done locally at the U.S. Department of Agriculture (USDA) Laboratories in Delaware, the nearby Columbus Zoo, and several other sites.

Ohio Wesleyan has been long committed to education for a global society. Consequently, the curriculum has an international perspective, a significant portion of the student body is drawn from other countries, and a wide variety of opportunities are offered overseas. Individual work may be arranged elsewhere, but formal programs are offered in more than twenty countries. These include Ohio Wesleyan's affiliation with the University of Salamanca in Salamanca, Spain, and its program in Strasbourg, France, as well as programs in Africa, China, Colombia, England, India/Nepal, Japan, Russia, and Scotland.

Academic Facilities

The University has recently completed, and exceeded the goal of, a $100-million campaign. This campaign, which has substantially enhanced the endowment, has also provided funding for extensive building renovations, athletic facility enhancements, and technology improvements. The Beeghly Library houses 517,646 volumes, one of the largest collections in the country for a private university of Ohio Wesleyan's size. The library's federal documents depository is among the nation's oldest and largest, providing an additional 200,000 reference publications. Beeghly also offers the Online Computer Library Center's most advanced cataloging system. The collection is enhanced by OhioLINK and CONSORT membership.

The comprehensive academic computing system is accessible to students 24 hours per day, and all residence hall rooms are wired for network and Internet access. University-wide computing systems at Ohio Wesleyan include Linux-based IBM xSeries and RS/6000 servers for e-mail, administrative data processing, Web hosting, and timesharing as well as a Compaq ProLiant server running Windows 2000. Approximately 300 Windows-based microcomputers in more than a dozen public computer laboratories are accessible to the campus community. In the summer of 2003, a new, massively scalable fiber-optic Internet connection (owned by OWU) was installed for the campus.

The first phase of the $34-million new Science Center opened in January 2003. Now completed, it includes a 145,000-square-foot three-level building that houses a wide variety of state-of-the-art instrumentation, including a scanning electron microscope and scanning and transmission electron microscopes, which are co-owned by the USDA Labs. The Woltemade Center for Economics, Business, and Entrepreneurship; the Department of Economics; the Learning Resource Center; and Information Systems are located in the R. W. Corns Building. The University has a state-of-the-art Geographic Information Systems Computer Laboratory. Perkins Observatory houses a 32-inch reflector telescope and two smaller instruments. Two University wilderness preserves cover a total of 100 acres. Other special facilities are the multistage Chappelear Drama Center; Sanborn Hall, home to the Music Department; and Gray Chapel, which houses a Klais concert organ.

Costs

The general fee for 2003–04 was $32,550. This amount covered tuition ($25,080), room ($3530), board ($3580), and fees ($360). Books and personal expenses averaged $1100. Nominal fees are charged for some studio art courses, off-campus study, private music lessons for students who are not majoring in music, and student teaching.

Financial Aid

Nearly all freshmen who demonstrate need have been awarded an aid package. Packages include grant, loan, and employment assistance from Ohio Wesleyan and the standard federal and state programs (such as Federal Pell Grant, Federal Stafford Student Loan, Federal Perkins Loan, and Federal Work-Study). More than two thirds of the student body receive some form of need-based aid, and another quarter receive merit- or non-need-based aid. More than 75 percent of all aid is provided by grants and scholarships. On the average, students on financial aid at Ohio Wesleyan receive more scholarship and grant assistance and rely less on loan support than do students at most other institutions.

Several merit scholarship programs worth as much as $25,080 per year, private loan programs, and flexible payment plans are available without regard to financial need. This year, more than 140 enrolling freshmen received merit awards.

Faculty

The full-time faculty numbers 135, providing a student-faculty ratio of approximately 13:1. All of the full-time faculty members hold the highest degree in their fields. Although committed first to teaching and advising, most faculty members maintain active research programs and publish important articles and books. Some members of the faculty are practicing artists whose contributions include the creation and exhibition of original works of art and theater.

Student Government

Students have a significant voice in the government of campus life. The Wesleyan Council on Student Affairs, more than two thirds of whose members are students, formulates basic policy. Students also sit on judicial boards and nine faculty committees and are represented at all meetings of the Board of Trustees.

Admission Requirements

The admission process is competitive. Each application is carefully studied on an individual basis. Although the applicant's academic record is most important, followed closely by teacher and counselor evaluations and SAT I or ACT scores, many other factors are considered, such as evidence of creativity, community service, and leadership. A sixteen-course preparatory program is required. Four units of English and 3 each of mathematics, social studies, science, and foreign language are recommended, but variations of this program are considered. SAT II Subject Tests are not required but may qualify students for advanced placement. Candidates for the B.Mus. degree must audition (tapes are accepted). Early action, early decision, and transfer admission are offered. Campus interviews are strongly recommended but not required. In 2003, approximately 2,600 applications were received; about 1,900 of the applicants gained admission.

Application and Information

Students are urged to complete the application process as early as possible in the senior year of secondary school, especially if they are applying for financial aid. Once complete credentials (application, transcript, recommendations, and SAT I or ACT scores) are received, decisions are made on a rolling basis after January 1. The student's response is required by May 1. The deadline for early decision application is December 1; the deadline for early action application is December 15. Notification is given within four weeks. After April 1, students are admitted on a space-available, rolling admission basis.

For further information, students should contact:

Office of Admission
Ohio Wesleyan University
Delaware, Ohio 43015

Telephone: 800-922-8953 (toll-free)
Fax: 740-368-3314
E-mail: owuadmit@owu.edu
World Wide Web: http://www.owu.edu

The Hamilton-Williams Campus Center is a magnificent meeting place for the campus community.

OLIVET NAZARENE UNIVERSITY

BOURBONNAIS, ILLINOIS

The University

Olivet Nazarene University (ONU) is a Christian, private, liberal arts university with a strong emphasis on both academic excellence and Christ-centered living. ONU offers one of the finest liberal arts educations in the Midwest, world-class facilities for learning and entertainment, and an atmosphere that promotes fun, relationship building, and spiritual growth.

Olivet's high retention, graduation, and employment/placement rates demonstrate the University's commitment to students' success. The faculty, staff, and administration are dedicated to teaching, encouraging, and mentoring each student as a whole person—academically, socially, and spiritually.

With 4,300 total students (2,200 undergraduates), Olivet offers an ideal student population for a private institution, maintaining diversity without sacrificing personalized attention. Half of the student body comes from the Nazarene denomination, while the remainder come from some thirty other denominations. Most U.S. states are represented, as are twenty-one countries.

The campus offers a championship-caliber athletics department (eighteen intercollegiate men's and women's sports in all) and a large intramural sports program. Music and drama groups involve hundreds of students, and many clubs are organized for a wide variety of interests. Olivet students are also heavily involved in dozens of ministry groups and volunteer efforts, small-group Bible studies, and weekly student-led services.

The University recently completed a number of campus renovations, including construction of the 56,700-square-foot Weber Center, home to the University's Divisions of Education and Social Sciences; a new entrance to the football field; and outdoor athletic facilities. Larsen Fine Arts Center, housing Kresge Auditorium and the Brandenberg Gallery for showcasing students' and outside artists' work, received a complete renovation in 2002. Future plans call for a new chapel and performing arts center.

The University is home to the Chicago Bears' summer training camp and Shine.fm, a 35,000-watt station ranked among the top stations in the nation and staffed by Olivet's broadcasting students.

Location

The University is located just 50 minutes south of Chicago's Loop in the historic village of Bourbonnais. The area includes mall shopping, restaurants, entertainment, and natural recreation centered on the Kankakee River State Park system. Olivet students enjoy many activities nearby and often make the quick trip north to sample the limitless offerings of Chicago and its surroundings.

In addition to recreation, students find numerous opportunities for employment and internships in the area, which is ranked as one of the top locations in the nation for small businesses, and the vast professional resources of Chicago. Students, faculty members, and staff members also find themselves working side by side in local and regional ministry projects. Olivet students are recognized professionally and ministerially as a valuable commodity by area businesses, churches, and parachurch organizations.

Majors and Degrees

Olivet confers Bachelor of Arts (B.A.) and/or Bachelor of Science (B.S.) degrees in the following fields of study (includes all majors, minors, and concentrations): accounting, art, art (education), athletic coaching, athletic training, biblical languages, biblical studies, biochemistry, biology, business administration, chemistry, child development, children's ministry, Christian education, church music, clinical laboratory science, communication studies, computer science, corporate communication, counseling, criminal justice, cross-cultural ministries, dietetics, digital media: graphics, digital media: photography, digital production, drawing/illustration, early childhood education, earth and space science, economics and finance, electrical engineering, elementary education, engineering, English, English (education), environmental science, family and consumer sciences, family and consumer sciences (education), film studies, finance, French, general science, general studies, geobiology, geochemistry, geoengineering, geology, geomathematics, Greek, health education, history, hospitality, housing and environmental design, information systems, international business, journalism, literature, management, marketing, mass communication, mathematics, mathematics (education), mechanical engineering, music, music education, music performance, nursing, painting, personnel psychology, philosophy, physical education/health, physical science, physics, political science, practical ministries, predentistry, prelaw, premedicine, preoptometry, prepharmacy, pre–physical therapy, pre–physician's assistant studies, pre–veterinary medicine, psychology, public policy, radio, religion, religion and philosophy, science (education), secondary education, social science, social science (education), social work, sociology, Spanish, Spanish (education), sports management, systems programming, television/video production, theater, youth ministry, and zoology.

Academic Programs

Olivet seeks to offer an "Education with a Christian Purpose." The University believes this commitment to Christ mandates nothing less than the highest-quality academic programs. Olivet's liberal arts curriculum requires that students complete 53 to 61 hours of general education courses. With the addition of major and minor programs of study, students must complete a minimum of 128 credit hours to obtain a bachelor's degree. Credit may be earned through AP and CLEP tests. Students may also participate in ROTC.

Olivet operates on a two-semester schedule, from August to May. Two summer sessions are also available.

Off-Campus Programs

Olivet students are encouraged to participate in the various off-campus study programs offered each semester. International locations include Beijing, China; San José, Costa Rica; Cairo, Egypt; Oxford, England; western Europe; Irian Jaya, Indonesia; Tokyo, Japan; Moscow, Nizhni Novgorod, and St. Petersburg, Russia; and Sighisoara, Transylvania (Romania). Domestic opportunities include the American Studies Program in Washington, D.C.; the Los Angeles Film Studies Program in Burbank, California; Focus on the Family Institute in Colorado Springs, Colorado; and the AuSable Institute (environmental science) in northern Michigan. Costs are usually comparable to a semester at Olivet, and credit is given for these programs. In addition, financial aid is applicable.

In addition, many Olivet students participate in numerous educational and missions-oriented short-term trips, which are available during the Christmas, spring, and summer breaks.

Academic Facilities

Olivet's 200-acre, $150-million campus offers leading-edge academic facilities. These include high-quality performance halls and athletic arenas; excellent natural science, engineering, and nursing laboratories; "smart" classrooms in most departments; and an observatory. It is one of only a handful of small college campuses in the nation to have a planetarium. Each department uses the top software in its field. More than a dozen campus computer labs are available for student use, and two network ports in each dorm room give students access to e-mail, the Internet, and classroom applications 24 hours a day.

Benner Library and Resource Center provides unlimited access to any material a student needs, either on-site from its more than 225,000 volumes, 1,000 periodicals, and more than 250,000 government documents and CD-ROMs or through the interlibrary loan system.

Costs

Tuition, based on 12 to 18 credit hours, was $14,160 in 2003–04. Room and board, based on double occupancy and the twenty-one-meals-per-week plan, were $5655.

Financial Aid

More than 95 percent of Olivet students receive some form of financial aid each year. Merit- and need-based scholarships range from $500 to full tuition. The Olivet Nazarene University Leadership Scholarship for Freshmen provides a significant award for those students who qualify through an application and essay process.

Olivet's cost is below average for private colleges nationwide, and more than 95 percent of ONU students receive financial aid. The University also participates in all federal and state financial aid programs. The priority deadline for filing the Free Application for Federal Student Aid (FAFSA) is March 1. To apply for aid, students must fill out the FAFSA as well as Olivet's application for financial aid. The student must be an accepted applicant before a financial aid package can be created. Olivet offers a monthly installment plan in addition to the traditional three-payment plan. Olivet believes funding a student's education is a partnership between each family, Olivet, and the state and federal governments. The friendly staff is committed to making an Olivet education affordable to every young person.

Faculty

Olivet's more than 100 full-time faculty members are the key to excellence in and out of the classroom. Teaching is a ministry for these dedicated Christian individuals, and Olivet's student-faculty ratio gives them an opportunity to teach, mentor, and encourage students on a personal level. To that end, the faculty is heavily involved in campus life, whether sponsoring social organizations or participating in talent shows.

Within the traditional liberal arts curriculum, more than 75 percent of Olivet's faculty members have terminal degrees.

Student Government

The Associated Student Council is the student government organization on campus. Its Executive Council consists of a president, vice president of finance, vice president of spiritual life, vice president of social affairs, vice president of women's residential life, vice president of men's residential life, vice president of office management, the *GlimmerGlass* (student newspaper) editor, and the *Aurora* (yearbook) editor. They work alongside the University's administrative team to ensure the health and promotion of campus activities and organizations.

Admission Requirements

Admission to the University is moderately difficult. Students are considered for admission on the basis of their high school GPA, ACT or SAT I scores, and personal recommendations. An ACT score is required for placement in courses. For international students, TOEFL results are an additional factor in the admission decision. Students with low test scores and GPAs may be admitted on a provisional basis. A campus visit and interview are strongly recommended for all prospective students.

Application and Information

Admission is on a rolling basis, although an early decision is required for some scholarships. Students may apply at Olivet's home page on the World Wide Web or in print. The application process includes the written (or electronic) application, high school transcripts, two letters of recommendation, ACT or SAT I scores, and a health form. There is no application fee, but a $30 room deposit places the student on the list for housing.

For more information or to arrange a campus visit, students should contact:

Office of Admissions
Olivet Nazarene University
One University Avenue
Bourbonnais, Illinois 60914

Telephone: 800-648-1463 (toll-free)
E-mail: admissions@olivet.edu
World Wide Web: http://www.olivet.edu

A view of the campus at Olivet Nazarene University.

OTTERBEIN COLLEGE
WESTERVILLE, OHIO

The College

Otterbein College, a private, coeducational institution affiliated with the United Methodist Church, blends the traditional and contemporary and continues to pride itself on offering a broad-based liberal arts education. Its 1,969 full-time and 1,095 part-time students come from all over the United States and several countries, but the majority, including 440 graduate students, are from Ohio. Founded in 1847 with only two buildings on 8 acres of land, Otterbein has since grown to twenty-seven buildings on 140 acres in the heart of historic Westerville, Ohio, a suburb of Columbus.

The College offers a wide range of extracurricular activities. They include theater productions, vocal and instrumental ensembles, religious programming activities, the ca weekly student newspaper, the campus radio station (WOBN), the Otterbein-Westerville television station (WOCC), and intramural and intercollegiate athletics. Otterbein men and women compete in the Ohio Athletic Conference, NCAA Division III. There are eight varsity sports for men and eight for women. The Rike Physical Education–Recreation Center is the home for men's and women's athletics and physical education facilities and includes racquetball and tennis courts, an indoor track, a weight room, and seating for 3,000. The $9.5-million Clements Recreation Center opened in fall 2002. Five local fraternities and six local sororities attract approximately 27 percent of Otterbein's students. Roush Hall, a multipurpose, handicapped-accessible building, houses academic departments, multimedia classrooms, contemporary conference rooms, a gallery, and a computer center.

A Master of Science in Nursing program is offered for students who have completed a four-year baccalaureate program.

A Master of Arts in Teaching (M.A.T.) degree program is available to qualified liberal arts graduates to prepare for teacher certification in elementary education or secondary education—biology (life science), computer science, English, and mathematics. A Master of Arts in Education (M.A.E.) degree program is available to certified teachers. Majors are offered in curriculum and instruction, reading, and teacher leadership and supervision.

Otterbein also offers an M.B.A. program.

Location

Otterbein is located in Westerville, Ohio, 20 minutes from downtown Columbus, one of the fastest-growing cities in the Midwest and Northeast. The College's proximity to Columbus means more than access to entertainment and recreation; as a thriving business center, the city provides many internship opportunities for students that often lead to full-time employment after graduation. The College is easily accessible from Interstates 71 and 270 and is close to the Port Columbus International Airport.

Majors and Degrees

The Bachelor of Arts degree is offered in accounting, broadcasting, business administration, chemistry, computer science, economics, English, equine science, French, health education, history, international studies, journalism, life science, mathematics, music, organizational communication, philosophy, physical education, physics, political science, psychology, public relations, religion, secondary education, sociology, Spanish, speech communication, sports medicine, sports wellness and management, theater, and visual arts. The Bachelor of Science degree is offered in accounting, business administration, chemistry, computer science, equine science, life science, mathematics, physics, psychology, and sports medicine. The Bachelor of Fine Arts is offered in theater with concentrations in acting-directing, design-technical, and musical theater programs. The Bachelor of Music Education prepares students for teaching careers in music. The Bachelor of Science in Education is awarded in early childhood education and middle childhood education. The Bachelor of Science in Nursing degree is also offered. The Bachelor of Music is offered for students interested in performance careers.

Preprofessional programs are offered in dentistry, law, medicine, optometry, and veterinary medicine.

A dual degree in engineering is offered in conjunction with Washington University in St. Louis and Case Western Reserve University in Cleveland.

Minors are offered in accounting, athletic training, black studies, broadcasting, business, chemistry, coaching, computer science, dance, economics, English, French, geology, health sciences, history, mathematics, music, philosophy, physical education, physics, political science, psychology, public relations, religion, sign language, sociology, Spanish, speech communication, visual art, and women's studies. In fall 2002, minors were added in sound production and arts administration.

Academic Programs

Otterbein College offers a program of liberal arts education in the Christian tradition. The College encourages serious dialogue so that students will develop to serve within the community. The fulfillment of this purpose requires students to read well, write well, think clearly, and identify ideas; know how to discuss, listen, and seek data; and have the abilities of synthesis and creativity.

Graduation with a bachelor's degree from the College requires successful completion of 180 quarter hours, of which 50 quarter hours are in core requirements offered under the title of Integrative Studies in Human Nature. The College's quarter calendar lends itself to the wide variety of internships and other off-campus educational opportunities offered by the College. The academic year begins in mid-September and ends in early June.

Through other academic opportunities, students may design an individualized major as well as receive advanced placement by examination and credit through CLEP examinations in some academic areas.

Off-Campus Programs

A variety of off-campus programs are available, including foreign language study in Dijon, France. Semester at Sea, a shipboard-campus program offered in cooperation with the University of Pittsburgh, enables students to take a variety of liberal arts courses while cruising. Study opportunities also exist with the Washington Semester Plan, operated through the American University in Washington, D.C., and with the

Philadelphia Center. The Roehampton Exchange, located in the Wimbledon area of London, England, consists of a federation of four institutions, providing the student with many cultural opportunities.

Academic Facilities

Roush Hall houses state-of-the-art computer labs, classrooms, a multimedia room, a two-story art gallery, and faculty and administrative offices. The Courtright Memorial Library houses 300,000 volumes and 1,015 periodical subscriptions and has an outstanding learning-resource center that includes the studios of the Otterbein-Westerville television station, WOCC. The McFadden-Schear Science Hall has modern laboratories and classrooms and a renovated planetarium and observatory. Cowan Hall houses modern facilities for speech and theater, including WOBN-FM, the campus radio station. The Battelle Fine Arts Center is the home for programs in music, art, and dance and also houses an electronic music laboratory. Historic Towers Hall, a campus landmark since 1870, had an $8.5-million renovation in 1999–2000 and houses classrooms, faculty offices, and updated math and computer science labs.

Costs

For 2003–04, Otterbein's tuition and fees were $20,133. Room and board cost $5952 per year. Books and supplies amount to approximately $600–$700 per year.

Financial Aid

Otterbein offers a wide variety of scholarships and grants, including Presidential Scholar Awards, Otterbein Scholar Awards, Endowed Scholarships, Dean's Scholarships, community service awards, talent awards, Federal Pell Grants, Ohio Instructional Grants, and Ammons-Thomas minority scholarships. In addition, Federal Perkins Loans, Federal Stafford Student Loans, and United Methodist Student Loans are available. To be considered for need-based College financial aid, students must file the Free Application for Federal Student Aid (FAFSA). Otterbein's financial aid policy is to attempt to meet the financial need of each full-time dependent and independent student offered admission who files financial aid forms by April 1.

Approximately 95 percent of Otterbein's students receive some form of financial aid. In addition to its need-based awards, the College offers scholarships to students on the basis of academic ability and proven talent.

Faculty

Otterbein has a faculty of 144 full-time and 105 part-time members (giving a student-faculty ratio of 13:1). Ninety-two percent of the full-time faculty members hold a doctorate or appropriate terminal degree. Faculty members are actively involved in campus governance, committees, and activities. The extensive sabbatical plan at Otterbein helps ensure that the faculty members constantly update and improve their classroom teaching.

Student Government

Otterbein's governance program gives students a voting voice along with faculty and administrators on all campus policymaking and decision-making bodies. Students are elected to the College Senate, to all governance committees, and to the College's Board of Trustees.

Admission Requirements

To be considered for admission to Otterbein College, students must complete and sign an admission application, submit an official copy of their high school transcript, and provide the College with their scores on either the ACT or SAT I. Applicants should have a solid high school academic record with at least 16 college-preparatory units. Otterbein does not discriminate on the basis of sex, race, gender, sexual orientation, age, political affiliation, national origin, or disabling condition in the admission of students, educational policies, financial aid and scholarships, housing, athletics, employment, and other activities. Inquiries regarding compliance with federal nondiscrimination regulations may be directed to the chairperson of the Affirmative Action Committee, the vice president for academic affairs, or the vice president for business affairs.

Students can gain a fuller understanding of student life at Otterbein by spending a day on campus. Prospective students are welcome to visit classes, eat in the Campus Center, and talk informally with Otterbein students and should simply notify the Office of Admission in advance so arrangements can be made.

Application and Information

Students are urged to begin the application process early in their senior year of high school. Applicants are notified of their admission status as soon as their application file is completed. Otterbein College's application is available on the Web at http://www.otterbein.edu.

For further information, students should contact:

Office of Admission
Otterbein College
Westerville, Ohio 43081
Telephone: 614-823-1500
          800-488-8144 or 877-OTTERBEIN (toll-free)
E-mail: uotterb@otterbein.edu

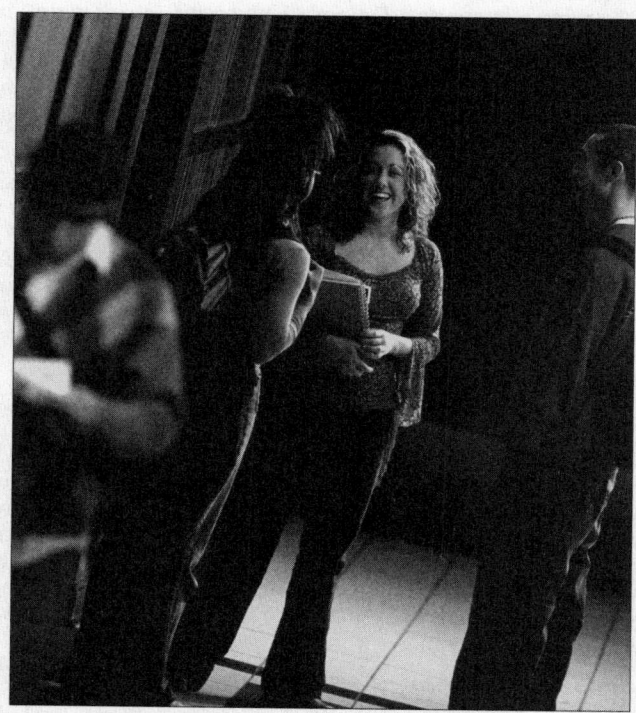

Students on the campus of Otterbein College.

QUINCY UNIVERSITY
QUINCY, ILLINOIS

The University

Quincy University is a private Roman Catholic university of the liberal arts and sciences. It was founded in 1860 by the Franciscan Friars, who have influenced the world by caring about people as people and urging them to fulfill their potential. This spirit is still maintained at Quincy University today. The University prides itself on its personal approach to learning. Small classes, a dedicated faculty, close faculty-student relationships, and a comfortable atmosphere on campus all create an environment conducive to personal growth and development. The University offers courses on both its 52-acre main campus and the 23-acre North Campus, ten blocks away. Shuttle bus service moves students between these campuses regularly.

The 1,200 students come from diverse social and economic backgrounds. Although the majority are from the Midwest, twenty-four states and ten countries are represented in the student body. Quincy University is a residential campus with more than 70 percent of the students living on campus. Campus housing options are varied and include single-sex and coed residence halls, apartments, and houses. Numerous campus organizations offer unlimited opportunities for students to participate in both University and community activities. A National Public Radio station, music performance groups, publications, honor and service societies, a lecture series, and concerts are a few of the many extracurricular opportunities available to students. Eighty percent of the students participate in intramural sports. Quincy University also maintains membership in the NCAA and the Great Lakes Valley Conference. Intercollegiate sports for men are baseball, basketball, football, golf, soccer, tennis, and volleyball. Women's intercollegiate sports are basketball, golf, soccer, softball, tennis, and volleyball.

Career planning and placement counseling is available to students throughout their academic career. Quincy University has an outstanding placement record; more than 96 percent of graduates are placed in jobs or graduate schools within 180 days of graduation. Individual assistance with academic planning, study skills, and tutorial work, as well as personal and vocational counseling, is provided free of charge.

At the graduate level, Quincy University offers programs of study leading to the M.B.A. and M.S.Ed. degrees.

Location

The University is located in a residential section of Quincy, a city of 50,000 people, situated on the bluffs of the Mississippi River. It is within easy traveling time of St. Louis (2 hours), Kansas City (4 hours), and Chicago (4½ hours). Good highways and bus, train, and air service make the area easily accessible from any part of the nation. Quincy has a rich and distinguished tradition in the arts. It is noted for its fine architecture and extensive park system.

Majors and Degrees

Quincy University awards the Bachelor of Arts (B.A.), Bachelor of Fine Arts (B.F.A.), and Bachelor of Science (B.S.) degrees. Programs of study include accounting, art, aviation, aviation management, biology, biological sciences, biological sciences education, business administration, chemistry, clinical laboratory science, computer information systems, communication, computer science, criminal justice, elementary education, English, English education, finance, history, history education, humanities (interdisciplinary), human services, management, marketing, music, music education, nursing, physical education, political science, psychology, social work, special education–learning disabilities, sports management, theology, theology/Franciscan studies, and theology/pastoral ministry. A Bachelor of Science in Nursing (B.S.N.) is available through a cooperative program with Blessing-Riemann College of Nursing.

Minors are available in most programs; concentrations are offered in physics and reading. A certificate program in business and a coaching specialty in physical education are also available.

Preprofessional programs include dentistry, engineering, law, medicine, physical therapy, and veterinary medicine.

Academic Programs

The academic program at Quincy University is based on the belief that liberal arts is the most functional and exciting tradition in education. The curriculum is designed to provide students with the fundamentals of a liberal arts education and at the same time prepare them for a rewarding professional and personal life. The flexible curriculum design allows for double majors or major-minor combinations, student-designed majors, and interdepartmental majors. An honors program, independent studies, special-topics courses, independent research, practicums, and internships are also available to meet the special needs of students.

To be eligible for a baccalaureate degree, a student must complete a minimum of 124 semester hours of university courses with at least a C average. The degree program requires 43 semester hours in general education and "tools" courses, 30–33 hours in a major, and at least 36 hours each in distributed electives and upper-level course work.

Quincy University accepts credit earned through the Advanced Placement Program, the College-Level Examination Program, challenge examinations, and, in some cases, academically related experience.

Off-Campus Programs

Arrangements are made with area schools, health facilities, businesses, and industries for such credit-bearing activities as student teaching, clinical training, internships, and practicums. The University also promotes the Early Exploratory Internship Program to its first- and second-year students, allowing them to gain preprofessional experience with area businesses and agencies. Study abroad is possible through many options, with the academic credit for this study preplanned and integrated into the degree program.

Academic Facilities

The Brenner Library, considered one of the top three private-college libraries in the state of Illinois, houses more than 260,000 volumes and 182,000 microtext items and subscribes to 725 periodicals. Among the outstanding holdings are a rare book collection, the 75,000-volume Bonaventure Collection of early Christian and medieval history and theology, and the 4,000-volume Fraborese Collection on Spanish-American history.

Through the University's membership in the Online Computer Library Center, Quincy University students have access to millions of books in libraries throughout the Midwest and the nation. The library is also equipped with a computerized reference service.

A modern academic complex located at North Campus houses laboratories for chemistry, physics, biology, engineering, and psychology as well as lecture halls and faculty offices. Six computer labs and more than 200 workstations are available for student use. Students also have unlimited access to personal computers, various networks, Internet, and UNIX. Additional special facilities are a radio station; a fully equipped television studio; the Ameritech Center for Communication, a state-of-the-art computer writing lab and classroom; and a newly opened Student Health and Fitness Center.

Costs

The costs for the 2003–04 academic year were $16,850 for tuition (12–18 credit hours), $450 for the student activity/computer fee, $3265 for room (double occupancy), and $2215 for board.

Financial Aid

More than 95 percent of the students at Quincy University receive some form of financial assistance. The University participates in the Federal Pell Grant, Federal Supplemental Educational Opportunity Grant (FSEOG), Federal Perkins Loan, Federal Work-Study (FWS), and Federal Stafford Student Loan programs. Illinois State Grants are available for qualified Illinois residents. Quincy University awards academic scholarships ranging from $500 to full tuition. Need-based grants are also available. Students who wish to apply for aid must complete the Free Application for Federal Student Aid (FAFSA) as well as the brief QU Application for Financial Aid. Notification of financial aid awards is made on a rolling basis. Early application is recommended, and priority is given to students who apply before February 15. Transfer applicants are required to submit a transcript from each college or university attended.

Faculty

The Quincy University faculty is composed of 102 professionals, highly qualified in their respective fields. Although many are engaged in research, teaching is the top priority at Quincy University. The University's favorable student-faculty ratio of 12:1 and its experienced faculty members, many of whom have had actual work experience in their field, bring an added dimension to the classroom. Eighty-six percent of the faculty members have the highest degree possible in their field.

Student Government

Students participate in University governance through representation on most University committees, including the Academic Affairs Committee, Athletic Advisory Committee, Student Life Committee, and University Judicial Board. The Student Senate provides for effective student participation in all aspects of University life.

Admission Requirements

Quincy University encourages applications from students who are serious about enrolling in a coeducational university of the liberal arts and sciences and who have demonstrated through their previous academic work an ability to profit from and contribute to the University. Each applicant for admission is evaluated individually. Primary consideration is given to the student's previous academic record. Quincy University recommends that prospective students take a strong college-preparatory program in high school. The Office of Admissions evaluates the prospective freshman's high school record in the following areas: number of academic courses taken, level of difficulty of courses attempted, type of high school attended, grade point average, standardized test scores, class rank, and extracurricular activities. All freshmen are required to submit SAT I or ACT scores.

Transfer students who have earned fewer than 24 semester hours must submit a high school transcript in addition to their college transcripts and should have maintained an overall grade point average of at least 2.0 (C) during their collegiate years. Transfer students may enter at three times during the year: August, January, or June.

International students must submit a transcript from each secondary and collegiate institution they have attended. All non-English transcripts must be translated into English before submission to the Office of Admissions. All international students must also submit TOEFL scores or demonstrate proficiency in the English language.

Application and Information

All students seeking admission are encouraged to apply early. Applications are evaluated after all required application materials have been received. Notification of admission decisions is made on a rolling basis.

Parents, students, and student groups are always welcome to visit the University. The Office of Admissions welcomes visitors from 8 a.m. to 5 p.m., Monday through Friday. Saturday visitors are welcome by appointment. If possible, campus visits should be scheduled during the academic year, when classes are in session. Accepted students may stay overnight in residence halls during the academic year.

For more information about the University's 143-year tradition of excellence, students should contact:

Director of Admissions
Quincy University
1800 College Avenue
Quincy, Illinois 62301-2699
Telephone: 217-228-5210
        800-688-HAWK (4295) (toll-free)
E-mail: admissions@quincy.edu
World Wide Web: http://www.quincy.edu

Quincy University's new $12-million Student Health and Fitness Center.

RIPON COLLEGE
RIPON, WISCONSIN

The College

One key reason why students choose Ripon College from among the more than 3,500 colleges and universities in the country is that Ripon offers an intensely personal undergraduate education. Since 1851, Ripon has provided a personal liberal arts education that makes a remarkable difference in the lives of students. In recent years, college guides such as *The Princeton Review*, *The Fiske Guide to Colleges*, and Kaplan's *328 Most Interesting Colleges* have noted that Ripon is among those national liberal arts colleges that offer high-quality education at a reasonable cost.

Companies look for college graduates who can adapt to change and who can write, use modern technology with confidence, communicate, and make a contribution to a team. These are the skills that a Ripon education offers students. In 2002, Ripon student Zach Morris became the College's third Rhodes Scholar, and in 2003, two students earned Fulbright Teaching Grants.

Ripon's curricular emphasis focuses on Communicating Plus. This program aims to assist students in the development of superior written and oral communication, critical-thinking, and problem-solving skills.

Ripon is a residential college; 90 percent of its 1,000 students live on campus, and because students remain on the campus after classes have ended, learning occurs around the clock. All students are encouraged to participate in Ripon's numerous extracurricular activities, including the campus radio station and the Student Senate.

Ripon College is fully accredited by the North Central Association of Colleges and Schools.

Location

Ripon College is situated on 250 tree-lined, rolling acres adjacent to downtown Ripon, Wisconsin, a charming turn-of-the-century community of 7,500 people. Ripon is a short drive from Green Bay, Madison, and Milwaukee. A variety of year-round recreational activities are available in Ripon and in Green Lake, a city just 6 miles from the campus.

Majors and Degrees

The Bachelor of Arts is offered in thirty majors: anthropology, art, biology, business administration, chemistry, chemistry-biology, computer science, economics, educational studies, English, environmental studies, exercise science, foreign languages, French, German, global studies, history, Latin American studies, mathematics, music, philosophy, physical science, politics and government, psychobiology, psychology, religion, sociology-anthropology, Spanish, communication, and theater. Self-designed majors and preprofessional programs are also available. Minors are available in most of the departments listed above and in leadership studies and women's studies. In addition, the educational studies department offers certification programs in elementary education, music, physical education, and secondary education.

Under a special program for engineers, a student may study for three years at Ripon and two at an engineering school, receiving a bachelor's degree from each institution. Ripon has formal cooperative engineering programs with Washington University in St. Louis and Rensselaer Polytechnic Institute. A student who desires to go into forestry may study for three years at Ripon and two years at Duke University, receiving both a bachelor's degree and a master's degree. In addition, Ripon College and Rush-Presbyterian-St. Luke's Medical Center in Chicago offer a cooperative program in nursing and allied health sciences in which students spend their first two years at Ripon and then transfer to Rush for their final two years.

Academic Programs

Since its founding, Ripon has been a liberal arts college. Students have the opportunity to study all fields of human knowledge, including the social sciences, the natural sciences, the humanities, and the fine arts. While other colleges have become increasingly specialized, Ripon has remained steadfast in its belief that the liberal arts are the key for a life of both personal and professional success. Ripon operates on a schedule of two 15-week semesters and an optional 3-week "Maymester."

Off-Campus Programs

Ripon's off-campus studies program sends students to such places as Costa Rica, England, France, Germany, Italy, Japan, and Spain to study for a semester. In addition, students can select programs within the U.S., such as the Oak Ridge Laboratory Semester in Tennessee, the Newberry Library Seminar in the Humanities in Chicago, urban studies and urban teaching in Chicago, and study at the Marine Biological Laboratory at Wood's Hole Oceanographic Institution.

Academic Facilities

Ripon's campus combines the best of both historic and modern architecture. The College's three original buildings, constructed between 1851 and 1867, are still used for offices and classes. The Farr Hall of Science, which recently received a $4.4-million renovation and addition, holds a planetarium, a greenhouse, ample laboratory space, and state-of-the-art equipment. On the west side of campus, the C. J. Rodman Center for the Arts and the J. M. Storzer Physical Education Center house a recital hall, a theater, an art gallery, a sculpture garden, a multipurpose gymnasium, a pool, racquetball courts, free-weight and Nautilus rooms, and aerobics rooms. Adjacent to the Storzer Center is the Ceresco Prairie Conservancy, 3½ miles of recreational trails and 130 acres of restored native habitat. Ripon's student center, Harwood Memorial Union, holds a lecture hall, the Pub, a game room, the radio station, and student organization offices.

Costs

The costs for 2004–05 are as follows: tuition, $20,480; room, $2530; board, $2830; activity fee, $240; and additional fees, books, and miscellaneous personal expenses, $1000.

Financial Aid

Ninety percent of Ripon students receive financial assistance that meets 100 percent of their financial need. The average financial aid award equals 78 percent of a student's total costs. Ripon's extensive scholarship program is designed to recognize and reward applicants for their talents and abilities. Currently, seventeen types of scholarships that range from $1000 to full tuition annually are available.

Faculty

Ripon College's student-faculty ratio is 14:1, and the average class size is 20. Ninety-seven percent of the full-time faculty members have earned the highest degree in their fields, and, as a result of their hard work, Ripon has received ten National Science Foundation Grants since 1992 and six Fulbright Fellowships since 1989.

Student Government

The Student Senate, composed of representatives of all resident groups and campus organizations, is the main governing body and administers a budget of more than $100,000 for student organizations and activities. It is an active and influential means of bringing student opinion to bear on College affairs.

Admission Requirements

Important factors considered in the admission process include graduation from an accredited secondary school (or GED equivalent), the secondary school transcript, and results of standardized tests (SAT or ACT).

Application and Information

Prospective students who value a challenging liberal arts and sciences education in a small, caring community are invited to visit the campus, sit in on Ripon classes, and see firsthand how Ripon students and professors interact with one another.

Students who wish to apply to Ripon College should submit a completed application form, a secondary school transcript, results of standardized tests, and the $30 application fee. Ripon College application forms are available from the admission office and at the College's Web site (address below). Ripon participates in the Common Application Plan and accepts photocopies of the Common Application in place of the Ripon College application form. Common Application forms are available in many secondary school guidance offices. Ripon also accepts applications that are made through the Wisconsin Mentor site (http://www.wisconsinmentor.org/admissionapp).

Candidates for fall term consideration are encouraged to apply early. Notification of fall term admission occurs within two weeks of the completion of the student's application. Students applying for spring term consideration should submit applications by December 15. Notification occurs shortly thereafter.

For further information, students should contact:

Dean of Admission
Ripon College
300 Seward Street
P.O. Box 248
Ripon, Wisconsin 54971-0248

Telephone: 800-94-RIPON (toll-free)
E-mail: adminfo@ripon.edu
World Wide Web: http://www.ripon.edu

Ripon College students and their families celebrate commencement on the lawn of Harwood Memorial Union.

ROBERT MORRIS COLLEGE

CHICAGO, O'HARE, DUPAGE, ORLANDO PARK, PEORIA, LAKE COUNTY, AND SPRINGFIELD, ILLINOIS

The College

Robert Morris College (RMC) is a private, not-for-profit, independent college dedicated to providing intensive career education and general education opportunities. Associate degrees, the Bachelor of Business Administration degree, the Bachelor of Applied Science degree in graphic design, and the Bachelor of Applied Science degree in computer studies are awarded. Robert Morris College is accredited by the Higher Learning Commission and is a member of the North Central Association of Colleges and Schools (30 North LaSalle Street, Suite 2400, Chicago, Illinois 60602; telephone: 312-263-0456; Web: http://www.ncahigherlearningcommission.org).

The history of Robert Morris College dates back to the founding of the Moser School, one of the outstanding independent business schools in Chicago, in 1913. Robert Morris College also has origins in Illinois at the site of the former Carthage College. Here, Robert Morris College was chartered and offered associate degrees in both liberal and vocational arts from 1965 to 1974. With the acquisition of the Moser School in 1975, RMC expanded to include business and allied health. The College now provides students with a choice of seven locations: Chicago, O'Hare, DuPage, Orland Park, Peoria, Lake County, and Springfield, Illinois.

RMC offers programs in the School of Business Administration, the School of Health Studies, the School of Computer Studies, the Institute of Culinary Arts, and the Institute of Art and Design. Each of these five divisions uses the most modern computer technology. Acquisition of such technology is imperative to providing real-world, educational experiences that are relevant to the evolving work place.

RMC's unique five-quarter system is designed for continuous learning. It enables students to accelerate their education, completing a bachelor's degree in three years and an associate degree in fifteen months.

The student body of approximately 6,000 is a cross-cultural, ethnic, and racial mix representative of the communities served. Each student works with a team of program directors, instructors, and placement specialists in an effort to achieve educational and career goals. The records of the College's students and graduates are the best indicators of what a prospective student can expect. Seventy percent of RMC students graduate from the programs they begin, compared to significantly lower percentages at other private and public colleges and universities.

The Placement Department, which has offices at each of the College's campuses, continuously cultivates employment opportunities for RMC graduates, with representatives in the business, allied health, art, and computer industries. Last year, 9 out of 10 RMC graduates who requested job placement assistance successfully secured employment in their chosen fields.

Robert Morris College is a member of the National Association of Intercollegiate Athletics (NAIA) and the Chicagoland Collegiate Athletic Conference (CCAC), Division II. The College offers men's and women's basketball, cross-country, golf, and soccer. It also offers men's baseball, men's and women's club hockey, and women's softball, volleyball, and tennis.

Location

Located in the heart of Chicago's bustling cultural and financial districts, the College's main campus is minutes from all that Chicago offers, including the Chicago Board of Trade, Art Institute, Field Museum, Merchandise Mart, lakefront, sports arenas, theaters, and all forms of public transportation. The Chicago campus is readily accessible from all parts of the city and suburbs by bus lines and trains. Parking is available in the immediate vicinity. Robert Morris Center is across the street from the renowned Harold Washington Public Library.

The O'Hare Campus opened to better serve the residents of western Cook and DuPage Counties and to meet the demands of employers in the area. The Springfield campus is located on Montvale Drive, just east of White Oaks Mall. The College is accessible by bus, and ample parking is also available. The recently expanded Orland Park campus now includes a technology center with the latest computer facilities available to industry and education. It is located adjacent to the Orland Square Mall, approximately 30 miles southwest of Chicago. It is accessible via public transportation and I-80 and I-55, which run parallel on the south and north ends of the campus, respectively. Orland Park is becoming a corporate center of the southwest Chicago suburbs, offering students ample opportunity for professional growth through internships and employment.

The DuPage campus opened on the border between Naperville and Aurora and serves students as well as employers along the East-West High Tech Corridor—the heart of rapid technological development and close to a wide range of employers. The Peoria campus in the busy downtown area of the city expands RMC's commitment to serving central Illinois. Beginning fall 2003, classes are available to Lake County area residents at a campus in Waukegan. Students in northern Illinois and southeastern Wisconsin can take advantage of RMC programs in this new setting.

All locations provide students with access to the unlimited variety of business services and enhance the students' understanding of the world of work and the employment process.

Majors and Degrees

The Bachelor of Business Administration degree at Robert Morris College offers concentrations in accounting, health-care management, hospitality management, and management. The Bachelor of Applied Science degree in graphic design offers concentrations in graphic arts and media arts. The Bachelor of Applied Science degree in computer studies offers concentrations in database management, networking, telecommunications management, and Web programming. RMC also awards associate degrees in accounting, business administration, CAD drafting (architectural/mechanical), computer networking, computer programming, culinary arts, fitness specialist, graphic arts, interior design, legal office assistant/paralegal studies, media arts, and medical assisting. More than twenty-six transfer agreements have been established between RMC and community colleges, allowing students who have earned associate degrees elsewhere to complete their bachelor's degrees at RMC by transferring in as a junior. Robert Morris College is the seventh-largest private college/ university in Illinois; tuition is one of the lowest for Illinois private colleges/universities. RMC is the largest granter of baccalaureate degrees in business and awards more associate degrees (all disciplines combined) to members of minority groups than any institution in Illinois. RMC is the sixteenth-largest granter of Bachelor of Business Administration degrees to African Americans and the twenty-eighth to Hispanic Americans in the country.

Academic Programs

The College's academic calendar consists of five quarters, each of which is ten weeks long. The program of study is designed so that students can complete their course work and enter their careers in the shortest time possible: in as little as three years for a bachelor's degree and fifteen months for an associate degree.

By concentrating on the specialized subjects related to the student's chosen career field, the College's curricula provide students with the skills and knowledge necessary to enter the job market. Each major consists of courses prescribed by the College to lead to this objective. An associate degree requires at least 92 quarter hours of credit with a minimum of 56 hours of credit in general education in the areas of communications, humanities, math and science, and social and behavioral science. A minimum of 52 quarter hours of credit are required in career courses, and the remaining hours are electives split between general education and career courses. A bachelor's degree requires a minimum of 188 quarter hours of credit. A minimum of 72 hours of credit are required in general education courses; 100 to 104 hours are required in major course work.

Robert Morris College offers students the opportunity to gain experience in their majors and improve their skills through internships and externships. Placement personnel work closely with students to secure positions related to their fields of study. Internships offer many educational and professional benefits and provide students with the opportunity to earn academic credit for participating in a career-specific work experience.

Off-Campus Programs

Robert Morris College offers students the opportunity to study abroad at the Institute of European Studies in Vienna, Austria; at Regent's College in London, England; and in Florence, Italy.

Academic Facilities

General purpose classrooms; high-tech equipment; specialized laboratories; study, practice, and leisure lounges; fitness centers; and cyber cafés are among the facilities the College provides at each campus. The technology-based library has online capabilities that connect the College's various campuses. Online Internet access offers students advanced research capabilities, sizable collections of reference and resource volumes, and periodical subscriptions. Vertical file information is available in addition to numerous computer and audio resources and a job search center.

Costs

Robert Morris College has one of the lowest tuition rates of any baccalaureate degree–granting private college in the state. Tuition for 2003–04 is $4500 per quarter. Book and supply costs vary by major from $300 to $500 per quarter.

Financial Aid

Robert Morris College participates in the following federal and state financial aid programs: the Federal Pell Grant, Illinois Monetary Award (SSIG/IMA), Federal Supplemental Educational Opportunity Grant (FSEOG), Federal Stafford Student Loan, Federal Perkins Loan, Federal PLUS Loan, and Federal Work-Study (FWS) programs. In addition, the College awards institutional grants on the basis of need, scholarship, residence, academic major, or a combination of these factors. All students must complete a financial planning interview with their admissions counselor, and all are urged to complete the Free Application for Federal Student Aid (FAFSA). Approximately 85 percent of the student body receive some financial assistance. In the 2001–02 academic year, the College awarded more than $12 million in institutional aid.

Faculty

The faculty members at Robert Morris College are selected on the basis of their academic credentials, career experiences in their field, and dedication to giving special attention to every student. All faculty members possess a master's degree in their chosen field, and many possess a Ph.D. in their area of specialization. In addition to teaching courses, faculty members promote the progress of their students through the individualized academic, employment, and personal development counseling they provide.

Student Government

Robert Morris College has no formal student government. Student representatives serve on committees that make recommendations about campus issues. Student organizations and activities are available.

Admission Requirements

All graduates of accredited high schools or the equivalent (GED) are eligible for admission to the College. All candidates are encouraged to have a personal interview with an admissions representative and to have a tour of the campus.

A variety of materials are considered for various applicants. Freshman applicants just graduating from high school must submit their high school record or GED score and test results from the ACT, SAT I, Applied Education Skills Assessment (AESA), Advanced Placement, and SAT II Subject Area tests.

Those enrolling as an adult (age 23 and above) must submit their high school record or GED score; test results from the ACT, SAT I, Applied Education Skills Assessment (AESA), College Level Examination Program (CLEP), and Dantes; and evidence of a successful employment experience.

Transfer students must present a minimum of 12 transferable credit hours from an accredited institution and their academic records from any high schools and colleges previously attended.

International students must forward their official education records, the results from either TOEFL or AESA, and an affidavit of financial support.

Home-schooled students must submit a complete transcript of all classes they have taken, curriculum documentation and its state certification, and results from any standardized examinations they have taken.

Application and Information

Applications can be obtained by contacting the Admissions Office at any of the College's campuses. The completed application and the $20 nonrefundable application fee ($100 nonrefundable application fee for international students) should be sent to the Admissions Office. The College operates on a rolling admissions basis, and students can enroll during any one of the five times offered during the year. For further information, prospective students should visit the Web site below or contact:

Admissions Office
Robert Morris College
401 South State Street
Chicago, Illinois 60605

Admissions Office
Robert Morris College
905 Meridian Lake Drive
Aurora, Illinois 60504

Admissions Office
Robert Morris College
43 Orland Square
Orland Park, Illinois 60462

Admissions Office
Robert Morris College
1000 Tower Lane
Bensenville, Illinois 60108

Admissions Office
Robert Morris College
211 Fulton Street
Peoria, Illinois

Admissions Office
Robert Morris College
3101 Montvale Drive
Springfield, Illinois 62704

Admissions Office
Robert Morris College
Lake County
1507 South Waukegan Road
Lake County, Illinois 60085

Telephone: 800-RMC-5960 (toll-free)
World Wide Web: http://www.robertmorris.edu

ROCKFORD COLLEGE
ROCKFORD, ILLINOIS

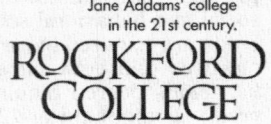

Jane Addams' college
in the 21st century.

The College

Rockford College challenges students to become leaders and make a significant difference in a world that faces incredible challenges. One of Rockford's most distinguished graduates was the prominent social reformer, Jane Addams, who, according to legendary FBI Director J. Edgar Hoover, was "the most dangerous woman in America." In 1931, Rockford's notable alumna was honored for her efforts to promote international peace and justice and became one of the first women to win the Nobel Prize for peace.

At Rockford, students find many of the same things that they can find at other colleges—great professors, wonderful students, and outstanding athletic teams. However, what sets Rockford apart from other schools is the spirit and legacy of Jane Addams. Through Addams' life work, students at Rockford become inspired to think big and to think independently about the important questions they face in this increasingly complex world. Students are inspired to act humanely by learning through service to their community, adapting and responding to both problems and opportunities while holding firm to such principles as integrity and democracy.

The Jane Addams Center for Civic Engagement at Rockford College brings students and faculty and staff members together to make the campus and local communities better places to live. All those working with the Center know that action has the potential to change lives, when what is learned in the classroom is connected to the community.

Interested students are encouraged to visit the campus in person and to check out the College's Web site at the address listed below to see what makes Rockford the special place it is.

Approximately 25 percent of all full-time students participate in the intercollegiate athletic program. The Rockford College Regents are a member of the NCAA Division III and compete in the Northern Illinois and Iowa Conference (NIIC). Women compete in basketball, soccer, softball, tennis, and volleyball. Men compete in baseball, basketball, football, golf, soccer, and tennis.

Location

Rockford is only 75 miles from both Chicago and Milwaukee and is easily accessible by car, bus, and plane. The College is located on a 130-acre wooded campus. The city of Rockford offers students all the advantages of a thriving community: off-campus entertainment includes more than 500 restaurants, concerts and attractions at the MetroCentre, the New American Theater, the Coronado Theater, the Rockford Dance Company, numerous malls and shopping centers, museums, riverside events, and an award-winning park district. Students benefit from volunteer, internship, and employment opportunities in the community. The involvement of students in the community provides unlimited experiences that enhance and complement their Rockford College education.

Majors and Degrees

The Bachelor of Arts degree is awarded in accounting, anthropology/sociology, art (with concentrations in ceramics, drawing, painting, photography, printmaking, and sculpture), art history, biology, business administration (with tracks in management and marketing), chemistry, classics, computer science (management information systems), criminal justice (program in anthropology/sociology), economics (with tracks in finance, international economics, and public policy), education, English, French, German, history, Latin, mathematics, music history and literature, philosophy, physical education (with tracks in business and teaching), political science, psychology, science and mathematics, social sciences, Spanish, theater arts, and urban studies.

The Bachelor of Fine Arts degree is awarded in art (with concentrations in ceramics, drawing, painting, photography, printmaking, and sculpture) and performing arts (musical theater performance).

The Bachelor of Science degree is awarded in accounting, anthropology/sociology, biochemistry, biology, business administration (with tracks in management and marketing), chemistry, computer science (management information systems), economics (with tracks in finance, international economics, and public policy), education, English, history, mathematics, physical education (with tracks in business and teaching), political science, pre–social work (program in anthropology/sociology), psychology, science and mathematics, social sciences, and urban studies.

A four-year NLNAC-accredited Bachelor of Science in Nursing program is offered. A B.S.N. completion program designed specifically for registered nurses is also available.

Preprofessional programs are carefully designed to meet the needs of students who plan to pursue careers in dentistry, engineering (3-2 program), health professions (optometry and physical therapy), law, medicine, pharmacy, and veterinary medicine.

In addition to the majors/programs/degrees listed above, Rockford College also offers minors in the following areas of study: British studies, communication, dance, Greek, human development, military science, peace and conflict studies, physics, and religious studies.

Academic Programs

Education at Rockford College is intended to be both broad-based and preparatory. The liberal arts curriculum allows for a choice of course work with an emphasis on a major. To earn a degree from Rockford College, students must complete at least 124 credit hours. Courses are offered by semester; there are two semesters per year. Summer courses are also available. The Honors Program in Liberal Arts offers extensive study in the humanities, a challenging core curriculum, and rigorous distribution requirements. Entrance to this program is limited and available by application only. The Forum Series offers exposure to great scholars, artists, and ideas. Special features of the College's academic program include Phi Beta Kappa and other scholastic honor societies, the Archaeological Institute of America, faculty seminars, art exhibitions, independent study, academic internships, and an extensive study-abroad program. A freshman seminar program is required for new students.

Off-Campus Programs

Rockford College gives its students an opportunity to study for a semester or a year at Regent's College in London, England, for approximately the same cost as attending the Illinois campus. Regent's College, a residential campus located in Regent's Park, offers a wide variety of courses, including academic internships, in a fully accredited program. The campus is conveniently located close to museums, galleries, theaters, and other attractions. Residence at Regent's College makes travel throughout Britain and on the Continent possible.

Rockford College also participates in programs that allow students to study in Australia, France, Germany, Spain, and other countries.

In the United States, Rockford students may participate in the Washington and United Nations Semesters.

Academic Facilities

Among the major academic buildings on the Rockford College campus is the Howard Colman Library, which houses 170,000 volumes and more than 800 periodical subscriptions. CD-ROM computers provide easy access to library holdings and national indexes; the availability of resources is enhanced by the interlibrary loan system. Private study carrels are provided. The Starr Science Building houses the major science facilities, which include physics laboratories, chemistry teaching and research laboratories with a fully equipped instrumentation lab, biology and psychology teaching and research laboratories, and nursing laboratories. It also houses the student computer lab and language lab. Programs in fine and performing arts are housed in the Clark Arts Center, which has a 570-seat theater with computerized lighting and sound equipment; an experimental theater; an art gallery; a sculpture garden; studios for lithography/ printmaking, drawing, painting, sculpting, and ceramics; a darkroom; and facilities for dance and music. The Seaver Physical Education Building is the campus sports complex. It includes locker rooms, a pool, a basketball court, a free-weight room, a fitness center, a training room, and classrooms. Dayton Hall houses the Learning Resources Center, which offers free tutoring. Scarborough Hall houses classrooms, faculty offices, and the writing center.

Costs

Costs for the 2003–04 academic year were $20,210 for tuition and $4034 for a double room. Several board plans were available, starting at $2547. Books are estimated to cost $900 per year. Miscellaneous expenses, including transportation, vary with individual needs but total approximately $2000 per year.

Financial Aid

Rockford wants to help those students who want to change the world with the cost of their college education. The College believes that a student who is like Jane Addams is an idealist and an activist, one who is willing to make sacrifices—not one who is asking for handouts. Rockford not only shares those values, but supports them with scholarships, grants, and a full array of financial aid programs. Every year, the College awards more than $4 million to students who make a difference.

Approximately 95 percent of students receive financial aid. Students may be considered for financial assistance if they are taking at least 6 credit hours per semester. Merit-based awards, including several full tuition scholarships, are available to full-time students. Need-based awards are determined by the results of the Free Application for Federal Student Aid (FAFSA). These awards include Rockford College grants and institutional loans as well as federal and state funds. Students are encouraged to file for financial aid by June 1. Rockford College students who attend Regent's College are eligible for the above awards.

Faculty

The student-faculty ratio at Rockford College is 12:1. The full-time faculty is composed of more than 80 men and women with outstanding academic backgrounds and varied international experience. Seventy percent hold terminal degrees in their respective fields. Some departments enlist part-time faculty members from the Rockford and Chicago professional communities to augment their programs. An extensive faculty development program helps ensure that the faculty members constantly update and improve their classroom teaching. Faculty members are involved in the lives of their students by serving as academic advisers, club and organization advisers, and mentors. A freshman advising program matches incoming freshmen with full-time faculty members who serve as advisers and mentors.

Student Government

The Rockford College Student Government serves its constituency in all areas of campus life. Students serve on College committees, judge their peers in student court, uphold the campus honor code, monitor campus media, and are consulted regarding changes in College policy. The Entertainment Council is responsible for organizing campus activities, including concerts, lectures, dances, and other social events.

Admission Requirements

Admission to Rockford College is based upon the applicant's potential for success as determined by prior academic preparation and personal achievement and is subject to satisfactory completion of academic work currently in progress. Students may apply upon completion of their junior year of high school. Admission is based on high school GPA, ACT or SAT test results, and class rank.

All applicants must submit an application and a nonrefundable $35 application fee. The fee is waived for students who visit the campus. On-campus interviews and personal statements are highly encouraged. Recommendations may be requested.

International students are welcome to apply; they should contact the Director of International Student Admission for specific application information.

Application and Information

Rockford College uses a rolling admission policy. Students can expect to be notified of decisions within two weeks of receipt of the completed application and all necessary documents.

For further information, students should contact:

Office of Admission
Nelson Hall
Rockford College
5050 East State Street
Rockford, Illinois 61108-2393
Telephone: 815-226-4050
           800-892-2984 (toll-free in the U.S. and
           Canada)
Fax: 815-226-2822
E-mail: admission@rockford.edu
World Wide Web: http://www.rockford.edu

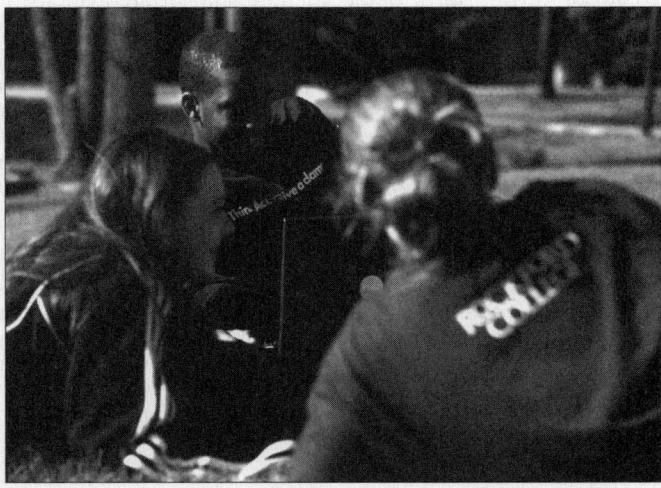

The accessibility of faculty members at Rockford College allows close interaction with students both in and out of the classroom.

SAINT MARY'S COLLEGE
NOTRE DAME, INDIANA

SAINT MARY'S COLLEGE NOTRE DAME, IN

The College

One of the oldest Catholic colleges for women in the United States, Saint Mary's College was founded and continues to be sponsored by the Sisters of the Holy Cross in 1844. The College has long been recognized as a pioneer in exploring with integrity and imagination the roles of women in society. Today, Saint Mary's enjoys a national reputation for academic excellence and vitality of campus life.

With more than 1,600 students from forty-nine states and twelve countries, Saint Mary's brings together women from a wide range of geographical areas, social backgrounds, and educational experiences. International and minority students comprise 8 percent of the student body.

Saint Mary's College's liberal arts emphasis enhances a comprehensive curriculum. Strong programs in the humanities and sciences are complemented by professional programs in business administration, education, nursing, and social work; majors in the fine and performing arts; and courses of preprofessional study that prepare students for law school, medical school, or advanced study in other health professions.

Small classes (median size: 16) and a low student-faculty ratio (12:1) encourage student participation in class discussions, collaboration with faculty members, and preparation for real-world challenges. The College enjoys a unique co-exchange program with the University of Notre Dame.

Approximately 80 percent of Saint Mary's students live on campus in four residence halls, each with its own distinctive character. Upperclass students may live off-campus. Residence halls offer a full calendar of activities, from twice-yearly dances to discussions with professors. The College has a student center, a dining hall, and a clubhouse for extracurricular activities. All residence halls have chapels, and the Church of Loretto is on campus.

As an NCAA Division III school and a member of the Michigan Intercollegiate Athletic Association, Saint Mary's sponsors varsity teams in basketball, cross-country, golf, soccer, softball, swimming and diving, tennis, and volleyball. Club sports, cosponsored with Notre Dame, include equestrian, gymnastics, lacrosse, sailing, skiing, and synchronized swimming. In addition, Saint Mary's offers many intramural sports.

The College's Angela Athletic Facility contains multipurpose courts for tennis, volleyball, and basketball; a training and fitness center; and racquetball courts. The campus has an indoor swimming pool, outdoor tennis courts, athletic fields, and a driving range for golf.

Location

Saint Mary's 275-acre campus, set alongside the Saint Joseph River, has great natural beauty. The College, located just across the street from the University of Notre Dame, just north of the city of South Bend, and just 90 miles from Chicago, is at the hub of much activity. Students from Saint Mary's and Notre Dame form a dynamic intercollegiate community. South Bend provides sites for internships and practicums and opportunities for volunteer service.

Majors and Degrees

Saint Mary's College offers programs leading to the Bachelor of Arts, Bachelor of Science, Bachelor of Fine Arts, Bachelor of Business Administration, and Bachelor of Music degrees.

For a Bachelor of Arts degree, students may choose majors in art, biology, chemistry, communication studies, economics, elementary education, English literature, English writing, French, history, humanistic studies, mathematics, music, philosophy, political science, psychology, religious studies, social work, sociology, Spanish, statistics and actuarial mathematics, and theater.

A Bachelor of Science degree may be obtained in biology, chemistry, computational mathematics, mathematics, medical technology, nursing, and statistics and actuarial mathematics.

The Bachelor of Music degree program, which is a member of the National Association of Schools of Music, offers concentrations in applied music and music education. For talented art students, Saint Mary's offers a Bachelor of Fine Arts degree.

The Bachelor of Business Administration degree program offers a major in business administration (with concentrations in accounting, finance, international business, management, and marketing) and a major in management information systems.

Superior students who are candidates for either a Bachelor of Arts or a Bachelor of Science degree may design a program of study outside of the traditional department structure.

For women interested in engineering fields, a five-year dual-degree program offered in cooperation with the University of Notre Dame leads to a bachelor's degree from Saint Mary's College and a Bachelor of Science in Engineering degree from Notre Dame in one of seven areas.

Saint Mary's education department, accredited by the National Council for Accreditation of Teacher Education, offers certification in elementary and secondary education.

In addition, the College offers more than forty minors in a variety of fields, including American studies, information science, justice studies, Latin American studies, urban studies, and women's studies.

Academic Programs

Graduation from Saint Mary's College requires successful completion of at least 128 semester hours of credit with a minimum quality point average of 2.0. Every student must also complete a comprehensive examination in her major, which may take the form of a thesis, a research or creative project, or a written or oral examination, depending on the discipline. All students must demonstrate writing proficiency by satisfactorily completing a writing-intensive "W" course, usually in the first year, and an advanced portfolio of writings in the major discipline, usually as seniors.

Students spend approximately one third of their time in general education courses in humanities, fine arts, foreign language, natural and social sciences, theology, and philosophy. Remaining course hours are devoted to their major and electives or minors. The College assists those students interested in pursuing independent study or research and internships.

Off-Campus Programs

Through Saint Mary's international study programs, students can study with Irish students at the National University of Ireland Maynooth, just outside Dublin. They can absorb Italian art and culture on Saint Mary's campus in the center of Rome, or experience Southeast Asia and the Far East with the India-based Semester Around the World Program.

Students can spend a month during the summer based in London, earning credit hours while also traveling to other European countries.

Saint Mary's students may also enroll in the Spanish language programs of the Center for Cross-Cultural Study in Seville, Spain, or in the French language and culture study in Dijon, France. A new exchange program with the Australian University of Notre Dame has just begun.

Saint Mary's students may study in Austria, France, Japan, Mexico, and Toledo, Spain, as well as Jerusalem through a cooperative program with the University of Notre Dame.

A student majoring in political science has the opportunity to spend a semester at the American University in Washington, D.C. Saint Mary's also participates in student- and faculty-member exchange programs with the University of Notre Dame and members of the Northern Indiana Consortium for Education.

Academic Facilities

Students have abundant access to computers, the campus network, and the World Wide Web. Residence halls and classrooms are wired for network access. Computer labs for students are located in several campus buildings, and an expanding set of services and support is available. Many faculty members make use of information technology for teaching and research.

The modern Cushwa-Leighton Library houses a fine collection of 210,812 volumes. It includes offices, study areas, an after-hours study lounge, a media center, computer facilities, the College archives, and a rare book room.

In addition to extensive biology, chemistry, and physics lab facilities, laboratories for psychology research and for foreign language study and practice are available to students. Art studios, music practice rooms, the O'Laughlin Auditorium, and Moreau's Little Theatre provide ample space for arts creation, practice, and performance.

The professionally staffed Early Childhood Development Center on campus provides education and psychology majors with an unusual opportunity to work with young children. Other facilities include the Madeleva classroom building, Science Hall, Havican nursing facility, and Moreau Art Galleries.

Costs

The expenses for the 2003–04 academic year were tuition and fees, $21,624; room and board, $7289 (double occupancy); and miscellaneous expenses (books, transportation, and living costs), $2225.

Financial Aid

The College strives to make a Saint Mary's education available for every student by offering eligible students financial aid packages that may include grants, scholarships, work-study, and loans. Competitive scholarships, awarded solely on merit, as well as those determined by a combination of financial need and academic achievement are available. Last year, more than 87 percent of Saint Mary's students received more than $25 million in financial assistance, more than $9.7 million from the College alone.

All applicants for financial assistance must complete the Financial Aid PROFILE and the Free Application for Federal Student Aid (FAFSA) each year that they desire assistance. Applications for assistance must be received at the processing center by March 1 to be given priority consideration. Decisions concerning financial aid are made as soon as possible after a student has been accepted.

Faculty

Saint Mary's has 114 full-time and 75 part-time faculty members. About 96 percent of the faculty members hold earned doctorates or other terminal degrees; of these, most teach first-year students as well as upper-division students. Faculty members work with students in all phases of college life, including academic counseling.

Student Government

Students are active at every level of campus governance and share in community decision making. There are voting representatives on the president's two highest advisory boards, the Student Affairs Council and the Academic Affairs Council. A student is a voting member of the College Board of Trustees. Student government sponsors many extracurricular and cocurricular activities.

Admission Requirements

Applicants for admission to Saint Mary's College should be graduates of an accredited high school and should ordinarily have completed a four-year program of 16 or more academic units. They must include 4 units of English, 3 units of college-preparatory mathematics, 2 units of one foreign language, 2 units of social science, and 2 units of laboratory science. The remaining units should be in college-preparatory courses. An applicant's credentials should include an academic transcript showing current rank and senior-year subjects, a counselor/administrator recommendation, SAT I or ACT scores, and an essay.

Home-schooled students are encouraged to apply for admission and should contact the Admission Office for details.

An interview with an admission officer is recommended. Saint Mary's encourages students to visit the campus. The Admission Office can make arrangements for students who wish to attend classes or stay overnight.

Superior students who have studied for advanced placement may begin sophomore-level courses in their first year. Mature, well-qualified students who wish to enter college after three years of high school may apply for early admission. Saint Mary's College also grants deferred admission upon request to candidates who are accepted in the normal competition.

Application and Information

Saint Mary's has two application and notification programs: early decision and modified rolling admission. Highly qualified students who have selected Saint Mary's as their first choice for admission may apply under the early decision program. The application deadline is November 15, and the notification date is December 15. Students who apply for modified rolling admission and whose application files are complete on or before December 1 are notified of the admission decision in mid-January. Candidates are encouraged to apply by the end of their junior year of high school or in the fall of their senior year. Applications are accepted, however, as long as space is available.

Interested students are encouraged to contact:

Director of Admission
Saint Mary's College
Notre Dame, Indiana 46556-5001
Telephone: 574-284-4587
         800-551-7621 (toll-free)
Fax: 574-284-4841
E-mail: admission@saintmarys.edu
World Wide Web: http://www.saintmarys.edu

SIMPSON COLLEGE
INDIANOLA, IOWA

The College

Simpson College was founded in 1860. The institution was named Simpson College to honor Bishop Matthew Simpson (1811–1884), one of the best-known and most influential religious leaders of his day. The College is coeducational; although it is affiliated with the United Methodist Church, it is nonsectarian in spirit and accepts students without regard to race, color, creed, national origin, religion, sex, age, or disability.

For more than a century, Simpson has played a vital role in the educational, cultural, intellectual, political, and religious life of the nation. The College has thirty-two buildings on 73 acres of beautiful campus and enrolls more than 1,900 students.

Extracurricular activities at Simpson are designed to supplement and reinforce the academic program and contribute toward a total learning experience. Students may participate in student government, publications, music, theater, and social groups. Simpson competes in eighteen intercollegiate sports and has an extensive intramural program for both men and women. Men's and women's athletics at Simpson are governed by the NCAA. Simpson also has chapters of three national fraternities, one local fraternity, and four national sororities.

Location

Simpson is located in the city of Indianola, a residential community of 13,000 people. Indianola is 12 miles south of Des Moines, Iowa's capital city; 12 miles east of Interstate 35; and 15 miles south of Interstates 80 and 235. The Des Moines International Airport is 20 minutes from campus. Five miles south of Indianola is Lake Ahquabi State Park, where swimming and other recreational facilities are available. Every summer, Indianola is the home of the National Hot Air Balloon Classic and of the Des Moines Metropolitan Summer Opera Festival. The location of the residential campus provides the best of both metropolitan and suburban activities.

Majors and Degrees

Simpson College grants Bachelor of Arts and Bachelor of Music degrees in major and career programs, including accounting, art, athletic training, biochemistry, biology, chemistry, computer information systems, computer science, corporate communication, criminal justice, economics, education, English, environmental science, French, German, history, international management, international relations, journalism and mass communication, management, marketing, mathematics, music, music education, music performance, philosophy, physical education, physics, political science, psychology, religion, rhetoric and speech communication, sociology, Spanish, sports administration, and theater arts.

Simpson also offers preprofessional programs in dentistry, engineering, law, medicine, optometry, physical therapy, theology, and veterinary medicine.

Academic Programs

Simpson College operates on a 4-4-1 academic calendar. The first semester starts in late August and ends in mid-December; the second semester starts in mid-January and ends in late April. A three-week session takes place during the month of May. During this period, students have the opportunity to take one class that focuses on a single subject, to study abroad, or to participate in a field experience or internship.

Students must participate in one May Term class or program for each year of full-time study at Simpson College. All students must complete the requirements of the cornerstone studies in liberal arts and competencies in foreign language, math, and writing. To earn the Bachelor of Arts degree, students may take no more than 42 hours in the major department, excluding May Term programs, and 84 hours in the division of the major, including May Term programs. In addition, at least 128 semester hours of course work must be accumulated with a grade point average of C (2.0) or better.

For a Bachelor of Music degree, the same requirements apply, except that 84 hours must be earned in the major, excluding May Terms, and the candidate is limited to 12 additional hours in the division of fine arts. In addition, a minimum of 132 hours of course work must be completed with a cumulative grade point average of C (2.0) or better.

The First Year Program is a broadly inclusive program of orientation, group-building, mentoring, community service, advising, and classroom work structured to help new students adapt to their first year of college. The program begins with summer orientation and extends throughout the full year.

The academic component of the First Year Program is the Liberal Arts Seminar, a joint classroom and advising concept that is unique among first-year programs. The seminars are small in size—no more than 18 first-year students each—and all are taught by students' faculty advisers.

Off-Campus Programs

A variety of programs are offered for off-campus study. Simpson offers semester-long study-abroad programs in London, England; Schorndorf, Germany; and Managua, Nicaragua. During May Term and an optional summer session in June, qualified students may study in Mérida, Mexico, in the Yucatán Peninsula. Students also may study in Paris and other cities in France for a semester or a year or during May Term.

Simpson is an affiliate of the American Institute for Foreign Study, which provides access to carefully planned semester or academic-year study programs in Austria, Britain, China, France, Germany, Italy, and Spain. Additional international travel programs are offered on a regular basis during the May Term as well.

The Washington Semester, offered in conjunction with the American University in Washington, D.C., permits a qualified student to study the political process in the nation's capital. Also available is the United Nations Semester with Drew University in Madison, New Jersey. Students undertake a course of study at Drew and at the United Nations in New York City. With both programs, students maintain enrollment at Simpson. In addition, the Washington Center Internships and Symposia Program consists of semester-long, full-time, supervised work experiences in the nation's capital, supplemented by weekly academic seminars.

Academic Facilities

The George Washington Carver Science Center provides state-of-the-art research facilities, computer labs, and classrooms. The computer labs contain Macintosh and IBM-compatible microcomputers. For academic computing, Simpson has a Compaq DS20E Alpha server computer and a campuswide Ethernet fiber-optic network.

The Henry H. and Thomas H. McNeill Hall houses classrooms for management, accounting, economics, and communication studies. In addition, the hall houses a seminar room and the Pioneer Hi-Bred International Conference Center.

The Amy Robertson Music Center houses the music department and contains the Sven and Mildred Lekberg Recital Hall, ten studios, twenty-two practice rooms, a music computer lab, and the band rehearsal room. A new wing includes a choral rehearsal room, a classroom, and studios.

Dunn Library, a contemporary learning resource center, contains approximately 155,133 volumes, 698 current periodicals, 2,075 DVDs and videotapes, 809 music CDs, and access to more than 6,769 e-books. Additional materials for research can be obtained through a national computer-based interlibrary loan network. The library also provides audiovisual equipment and services to the campus.

The A. H. and Theo Blank Performing Arts Center accommodates Simpson's well-known programs in theater arts and opera and includes the magnificent 500-seat Pote Theatre, with both proscenium and hydraulically controlled thrust stages; a studio theater; the Barborka Gallery; technical facilities and shops; and classrooms.

Wallace Hall reopened in 1996 after a complete internal renovation. Named to the National Register of Historic Places in 1991, Wallace Hall contains facilities for education, psychology, sociology, applied social science, and a biofeedback/psychology laboratory.

Costs

Tuition and fees for 2003–04 were $18,097, a room was $2669, and board was $2892. These figures did not include books, music fees, or personal expenses.

Financial Aid

Simpson College seeks to make it financially possible for qualified students to experience the advantages of a college education. Generous gifts from alumni, trustees, and friends of the College, in addition to state and federal student aid programs, make this opportunity possible. Simpson offers financial aid on both a need and non-need basis. Need is determined by filing the Free Application for Federal Student Aid.

Financial aid granted on a non-need basis includes academic scholarships, which are awarded on the basis of prior academic records, and talent scholarships, which are available in theater, music, and art. The talent scholarships are determined by audition/portfolio.

Faculty

Ninety-two percent of Simpson's 82 full-time faculty members have earned their terminal degrees. At Simpson, faculty members serve as academic advisers as well as teachers and often attend College plays, operas, and athletic events, reinforcing their sincere interest in students. The student-faculty ratio is 14:1.

Student Government

Student involvement in College governance is an integral part of the organization of the College. Students annually elect a president and vice president of the Student Government. The members of each housing unit and the off-campus students elect representatives to the Student Senate. The Student Senate appoints student members to all College committees in which students hold membership. The senate also appoints 4 students-at-large who attend plenary sessions of the Board of Trustees as members on the Student Affairs Committee.

Admission Requirements

Admission to Simpson College is selective and competitive. A strong academic record is essential. Applications are acted upon by an admissions committee, which is elected by the faculty and represents the five academic divisions of the College. These faculty members consider the college-preparatory courses taken, the grades received in those courses, rank in class, and standardized test scores (ACT and/or SAT I), including test subscores. A short time after all required credentials are received, the application is reviewed by the Admissions Committee. Transfer applicants are accepted on the basis of successful completion of academic work at an accredited college or university. In addition, transfer applicants are required to submit official high school transcripts and ACT/SAT I results.

Application and Information

Simpson's rolling admission policy allows flexibility; however, early application is recommended. Transfer and international students are welcome. Students are strongly encouraged to visit the campus.

For additional information or to obtain application materials, students should contact:

Office of Admissions
Simpson College
701 North "C" Street
Indianola, Iowa 50125
Telephone: 515-961-1624
           800-362-2454 (toll-free)
E-mail: admiss@simpson.edu
World Wide Web: http://www.simpson.edu

The George Washington Carver Science Center provides Simpson students with state-of-the-art labs and research facilities.

SOUTHERN ILLINOIS UNIVERSITY CARBONDALE
CARBONDALE, ILLINOIS

The University

Southern Illinois University Carbondale (SIUC), chartered in 1869, is a comprehensive state-supported institution with nationally and internationally recognized instructional, research, and service programs. SIUC is fully accredited by the North Central Association of Colleges and Schools.

SIUC offers more than 150 undergraduate majors, specializations, and minors; four associate degree programs; more than ninety baccalaureate degree programs; more than sixty master's degree programs; thirty-two doctoral programs; and professional degrees in law and medicine. SIUC is a multicampus university and includes the Carbondale campus as well as the SIUC School of Medicine at Springfield and a branch campus in Nakajo, Japan.

During the 2003–04 academic year, SIUC's enrollment reached 21,387, which included 16,366 undergraduate students, 4,343 graduate students, and 678 professional students. The average age of undergraduates is 23. Seven percent of SIUC's enrolled students are international students. Of U.S. students, 13 percent are African American, .3 percent are American Indian/Alaskan, 2 percent are Asian or Pacific Islander, and 1 percent are Hispanic.

Students who are ready to start college but not ready to commit to a specific major can enroll in SIUC's Pre-Major Program. Premajor advisers and career counselors help premajor students plan their education and careers. SIUC faculty members, staff members, and alumni help students arrange internships, cooperative education programs, and work-study programs.

All single incoming freshmen under the age of 21 are required to live on campus their first year at SIUC unless they are living at home with a legal guardian or parent. SIUC has three on-campus residential areas for single students. Each area includes a cafeteria, a post office, laundry facilities, and computer labs. SIUC residence hall dining services provide nineteen meals per week with no limit on quantity at each meal. Optional meal plans are available. Meal hours are long enough to accommodate most schedules, but students with conflicts can arrange for take-out lunches or late plates. Dining services provide a variety of menus and a full-time dietitian to help students who have special dietary needs. Off-campus housing includes many types of privately owned units, including residence halls, apartments, and houses; many are within easy walking distance of the campus.

SIUC intercollegiate sports teams compete at the NCAA Division I level (football is Division I-AA). Conference affiliations include the Missouri Valley and Gateway Conferences. Intercollegiate sports teams include men's and women's basketball, cross-country, diving, golf, swimming, tennis, and track and field; men's baseball and football; and women's softball and volleyball. The campus holds various playfields, several tennis courts, and a campus lake with a beach and a boat dock. SIUC's Student Recreation Center houses an Olympic-size pool; indoor tracks; handball/racquetball and squash courts; a climbing wall; weight rooms; and basketball, volleyball, and tennis courts. It also offers outdoor equipment rental, an aerobic area, walleyball, martial arts, and dance and cardio studios.

The Student Center is one of the largest student centers in the U.S. without a hotel. It contains a bookstore, several restaurants, a craft shop, a bakery, and facilities for bowling and billiards. It is headquarters for 360 active student organizations and the student government office. It holds four ballrooms and an auditorium. On-campus events throughout the year include concerts, plays, festivals, guest speakers, and musicals.

Location

Carbondale is 6 hours south of Chicago, 2 hours southeast of St. Louis, and 3 hours north of Nashville. Four large recreational lakes, the two great rivers (the Mississippi and the Ohio), and the spectacular 270,000-acre Shawnee National Forest are within minutes of the campus. The mid-South climate is ideal for year-round outdoor activities.

Carbondale is a small city of 26,000 people that supports one large enclosed mall, several mini-malls, theaters, and restaurants. Students frequent the shops and restaurants that line Illinois and Grand Avenues.

Majors and Degrees

The University offers associate in applied science degree programs at the College of Applied Sciences and Arts in aviation flight, dental technology, physical therapist assistant studies, and respiratory therapy technology.

The College of Applied Sciences and Arts offers bachelor's degree programs in advanced technical studies, architectural studies, automotive technology, aviation management, aviation technologies, dental hygiene, electronics systems technologies, fire science management, health-care management, information systems technologies, interior design, mortuary science and funeral service, physician assistant studies, and radiologic sciences.

The College of Agriculture offers bachelor's degree programs in agribusiness economics, animal science, food and nutrition, forestry, general agriculture, and plant and soil science.

The College of Business and Administration offers bachelor's degree programs in accounting, business and administration, business economics, finance, management, and marketing.

The College of Education and Human Services offers bachelor's degree programs in communication disorders and sciences, early childhood education, elementary education, fashion design and merchandising, health education, physical education, recreation, rehabilitation services, social studies, social work, special education, and workforce education and development. Teacher preparation is available in art, biological sciences, English, French, German, health education, history, mathematics, music, physical education, secondary education, social studies, Spanish, and special education.

The College of Engineering offers bachelor's degree programs in civil engineering, computer engineering, electrical engineering, engineering technology, industrial technology, mechanical engineering, and mining engineering.

The College of Liberal Arts offers bachelor's degrees in administration of justice, anthropology, art, classics, design, economics, English, foreign language and international trade, French, geography, German, history, linguistics, mathematics, music, paralegal studies, philosophy, political science, psychology, Russian, sociology, Spanish, speech communication, theater, and university studies.

The College of Mass Communication and Media Arts offers bachelor's degrees in cinema and photography, journalism, and radio-television.

The College of Science offers bachelor's degree programs in biological sciences, chemistry, computer science, geology, mathematics, microbiology, physics, physiology, plant biology, zoology, and preprofessional programs in dentistry, medicine, nursing, optometry, osteopathy, pharmacy, physical therapy, physician assistant studies, podiatry, and veterinary medicine.

In addition to many majors offered at SIUC, specializations are offered in all colleges in many areas.

Academic Programs

Each bachelor's degree candidate must earn a minimum of 120 semester hours of credit, including at least 60 at a senior-level institution and the last 30 at SIUC. Each student must maintain at least a C average in all course work at SIUC. Each student must fulfill the University core curriculum and the specific requirements of their degree programs. SIUC awards credit through qualifying extension and correspondence programs, military experience, the High School Advanced Placement Program, the College-Level Examination Program (CLEP), SIUC's proficiency examination program, and work experience.

SIUC offers honors course work and special recognition for students who demonstrate exceptional academic achievement. The Air Force and Army offer ROTC programs at SIUC. SIUC offers three semesters: fall, spring, and summer.

Off-Campus Programs

At Southern Illinois University Carbondale, distance education courses are offered in interactive, print-based and Web-based formats. Print-based (correspondence) and Web-based courses are offered by the Individualized Learning Program (ILP). Web-based courses and Two-Way Interactive Video courses are offered through the Office of Distance Education. Many of the courses offered through the ILP and other distance education courses can be taken to complete the University Studies Degree (B.A.) in the College of Liberal Arts.

Off-campus credit programs are designed to meet the educational needs of adults wishing to pursue a degree but who are unable to travel to the Carbondale campus. Faculty members who teach off-campus courses travel to distant sites to teach SIUC courses.

Contractual services are provided and include specialized educational services to groups, organizations, governmental agencies, and businesses on a cost-recovery basis. These services are provided regionally, nationally, and internationally.

All credit courses offered through these programs carry full SIUC academic credit and are taught by faculty members appointed by the academic departments of the University. Additional information can be found on the Web (http://www.dce.siu.edu/siuconnected).

Academic Facilities

In addition to the 2.4 million volumes, 3.5 million microfilms, and more than 11,000 periodicals currently available in Morris Library, students and faculty members have access to more than 10,000 full-text electronic journals. SIUC students have access to several computer learning centers that are equipped, in all, with more than 1,600 microcomputers. Additional information can be found on the Web (http://www.lib.siu.edu).

Students learn and practice in the Southern Illinois Airport, outdoor laboratories, the student-run *Daily Egyptian* newspaper, WSIU-TV, WSIU-FM, art and natural history museums, a literary magazine, McCleod Theater, Memorial Hospital, a vivarium, the plant biology greenhouses, the University Farms, and the Touch of Nature Environmental Center.

Costs

Tuition and fee charges for the 2003–04 academic year (fall and spring) for students enrolled in 15 or more semester hours were $4920 for Illinois residents and $12,300 for out-of-state residents, including international students. Room and board were $5200. All costs are subject to change. The cost of books and school supplies varies among programs. The average cost is $840 per academic year. Some courses require that students purchase special materials.

Financial Aid

More than $160 million in financial aid was distributed to more than 21,387 SIUC students in fiscal year 2003 through federal, state, and institutionally funded financial aid programs.

To apply for financial aid at SIUC, students should complete a Free Application for Federal Student Aid (FAFSA). Applications that are filed before April 1 receive priority consideration for campus-based aid. The FAFSA can be completed electronically at the U.S. Department of Education's Web site (http://www.fafsa.ed.gov). When completing the FAFSA, students should list Southern Illinois University Carbondale (Federal School Code 001758) as a school of choice.

SIUC has one of the largest student employment programs in the country, with approximately 6,000 students employed each year in a wide variety of job classifications. SIUC offers competitive scholarships based on talent and academic achievement.

Faculty

Faculty members are dedicated to excellence in teaching and to their advancement of knowledge in a wide variety of disciplines and professions. Many faculty members are well-known both nationally and internationally for their varied research contributions. The undergraduate student-faculty ratio is 17:1. There are 894 full-time and 218 part-time instructional faculty members.

Teaching assistants at SIUC are graduate students who assist faculty members in teaching. While some teach introductory undergraduate classes, others provide support to faculty members by assisting in laboratories, monitoring tests, and helping students.

Student Government

The undergraduate student government consists of a president, vice president, executive assistant, and chief of staff. Under the vice president, there are 58 senators: 1 senator per 300 students. Each student has at least 2 representatives: 1–6 for their residential area, and 1–6 for the college in which they are enrolled. Under the 6 commissioners are a list of committees on which a varying number of students sit to represent the student body. The student government writes and passes legislation on University policies, funding, student organizations, and other matters that affect the students and the University.

Admission Requirements

Freshman applicants whose ACT or SAT score is at or above the 50th percentile or whose ACT or SAT score is at or above the 33rd percentile and whose class rank is in the upper half are admitted. Admission standards are subject to change. Freshman applicants must meet course pattern requirements: 4 years of English, 3 years of mathematics, 3 years of laboratory science, 3 years of social science, and 2 years of electives.

Transfer applicants must have an overall grade point average of at least 2.0 on a 4.0 scale, based on work attempted at all institutions and calculated by SIUC grading policies. Transfer applicants must also be eligible to continue at the last institution attended.

Some programs have higher admission requirements or require additional screening for admission. Undergraduates can apply online (http://salukinet.siu.edu/admit/).

Application and Information

Admission is granted on a rolling basis. Application priority deadlines for freshmen are: June 1 for the Summer 2004 Term; April 30 for the Fall 2004 Term; and December 1, 2004 for the Spring 2005 Term. Application priority deadlines for transfer students are: June 1 for the Summer 2004 Term; July 1 for the Fall 2004 Term; and December 1, 2004 for the Fall 2005 Term. The application fee is $30.

Undergraduate Admissions MC 4710
425 Clocktower Drive
Southern Illinois University Carbondale
Carbondale, Illinois 62901
Telephone: 618-536-4405
Fax: 618-453-3250
E-mail: joinsiuc@siu.edu
World Wide Web: http://www.siuc.edu

SIUC's Pulliam Hall.

STEPHENS COLLEGE
COLUMBIA, MISSOURI

The College

Stephens College, founded in 1833 as the nation's second-oldest women's college, is a premier national liberal arts college for women in the Midwest. Stephens is ranked nationally in *U.S. News & World Report* and has repeatedly been selected to the *Princeton Review*'s list of the best colleges in the country. Students from around the globe enrich Stephens with their varied talents, interests, and backgrounds. Stephens students may choose to join one of twelve honorary societies on campus, including Psi Chi, Alpha Epsilon Rho, and Mortar Board, or become involved in student government. Leadership experience is emphasized in all aspects of life at Stephens. Stephens' residence halls provide much of the focus for campus activity. The Searcy House Plan offers a living/learning environment in the humanities to a select group of freshmen each year. Since it began in the 1960s as an experiment funded by the Ford Foundation, the Searcy program has served as a model for similar living/learning communities in colleges and universities across the nation.

In addition to undergraduate degrees, Stephens offers Master's degrees.

Location

Stephens College is located in Columbia, Missouri. Situated halfway between Kansas City and St. Louis, Columbia is the cultural, medical, and business center of mid-Missouri. Often called "College Town, USA," Columbia is also the home of Columbia College and the University of Missouri. Stephens students have easy access to Columbia's shopping, dining, and entertainment offerings.

Majors and Degrees

Stephens College awards the Associate in Arts, Bachelor of Arts, Bachelor of Fine Arts, and Bachelor of Science. Majors include accounting; biology; business administration; creative writing; dance; digital filmmaking; early childhood education; elementary education; English; equestrian business management; equestrian science; fashion communication; fashion design and product development; fashion marketing and management; graphic design/multimedia; health sciences; liberal studies; marketing: public relations and advertising; mass communication (electronic media, journalism, or public relations); psychology; student-initiated majors; and theater arts. The B.F.A. program includes professional-level work in the fine or performing arts plus a strong component in liberal studies.

Academic Programs

The B.A. degree is generally completed in four years. Students pursue depth of study in an academic area, breadth in liberal arts study, and elective course work with guidance from faculty advisers. Academic departments require relevant internships and often provide opportunities for research projects in field settings.

Stephens has introduced many innovative educational concepts into its programs. Stephens emphasizes personalized teaching and development of the individual. Small classes are offered, and most departments offer tutorial projects and readings.

Students in the bachelor's degree programs, either B.A., B.F.A., or B.S., must complete the residence requirement of seven semesters. Students must demonstrate the ability to write proper English or pass two courses in English composition, and must complete at least twelve courses at an advanced level (including five in the major). All degree candidates take eight courses selected from seven areas: natural sciences, social and behavioral sciences, languages and literature, fine arts, history, humanities/religion/philosophy, and mathematics and analytical reasoning. In addition, all degree candidates complete one upper-level liberal arts requirement in each of the following areas: cross-cultural studies, interdisciplinary studies, and moral and ethical issues.

Degree requirements for the Bachelor of Arts include completion of at least eight courses in a department. At least five of these courses must be at or above the 300 level. As many as fifteen courses may be required in the major, but no more than fifteen may count toward a forty-course degree program. Students also may elect to design an interdisciplinary student-initiated Bachelor of Arts major.

The Bachelor of Science degree program requires completion of fifteen to nineteen courses, including a minimum of five courses at or above the 300 level. Bachelor of Science candidates may elect additional courses in the major, but no more than twenty courses may count toward a forty-course degree program. Students also may elect to design an interdisciplinary student-initiated Bachelor of Science major.

Degree requirements for the Bachelor of Fine Arts include completion of twenty to twenty-five courses, including at least five courses at or above the 300 level. B.F.A. candidates may elect additional courses in their major, up to a maximum of twenty-six within a forty-course degree program. The B.F.A. in theater and in dance are completed in three years and two summers.

Through Stephens College School of Graduate and Continuing Education, nontraditional students throughout the country have the opportunity to complete an online program that builds on past learning. Most of Stephens' programs, including courses of study leading to the B.A. degree, are open to Stephens College School of Graduate and Continuing Education students. In addition, the School of Graduate and Continuing Education has programs in business administration; English; health care and a second area; health information administration (the first accredited external degree program in medical record administration in the country); health science and a second area; law, philosophy, and rhetoric; psychology; and student-initiated majors. In addition, Stephens offers graduate degrees in business (through an Internet-based program) and education. Undergraduates in business, fashion marketing/management, and equestrian business management can complete the online M.B.A. through a tuition-paid fellowship, provided they meet certain stipulations.

Stephens also offers numerous partnerships with other institutions wherein students may earn a bachelor's degree from Stephens in three years and a master's degree from another college or university after two additional years. Partnerships currently exist in occupational therapy, physical therapy, physician assistant studies, and accounting.

Off-Campus Programs

Stephens sponsors summer seminars in several countries, including France, Italy, and Japan, as extensions of courses that are regularly offered at the College. Summer-study programs include drama and musical theater at Lake Okoboji, Spirit Lake, Iowa. Stephens also offers study opportunities in Sweden, Ecuador, Korea, and Cambridge, England.

Many other study opportunities are available through global partnerships with other universities.

Academic Facilities

The Hugh Stephens Resources Library contains more than 120,000 volumes. The library is the central building of a quadrangle that includes the Helis Communication Center and the Patricia Barry Television Studio. The E. S. Pillsbury Science Center houses science and mathematics classrooms and laboratories, and the Ellis Learning Laboratories provide modern equipment for individual and group study of foreign languages. Other working laboratories include the student-run Warehouse Theatre, the Johnson Plant Laboratory, and the Audrey Webb Child Study Center, which has an enrollment of approximately 100 children in preschool through third grade.

Costs

For 2004–05, tuition is $18,230, and room costs for single occupancy are $4210. Costs for room and board are subject to change. Additional costs for books, supplies, and personal expenses range between $750 and $1000. The enrollment deposit is $100.

Financial Aid

More than 80 percent of the student body receive some form of assistance through scholarships, grants, loans, or employment. Stephens participates in the Federal Pell Grant, Federal Supplemental Educational Opportunity Grant, Federal Perkins Loan, Federal Stafford Student Loan, and Federal Work-Study programs. Missouri residents are encouraged to apply for aid under the Missouri Student Grant Program. The Free Application for Federal Student Aid (FAFSA) is required for financial aid consideration. Applications for financial aid should be received by March 15. Stephens also offers an early financial aid estimate service.

Faculty

Though most faculty members have come to college teaching via the recognized route of graduate study and scholarship, some have prepared for teaching through work experience, particularly those in applied and performing arts with careers as actors, dancers, musicians, and artists. The faculty is primarily a teaching faculty, and many of the instructors include students in independent scholarly research. Men and women join the Stephens faculty with a commitment to individualized education. They are actively engaged in academic advising and tutorial relationships and frequently spend many more hours working with students outside the classroom than in formal teaching situations. The student-faculty ratio is 10:1.

Student Government

Each student is a member of the Student Government Association (SGA). Working in the SGA provides women with experience in planning and administering cultural, social, and recreational activities and in dealing with academic, residential, and community concerns. The association has executive and legislative powers to govern student activities and to develop and maintain group-living standards. Students also serve as voting members of established faculty committees and in advisory capacities to committees of the Board of Trustees. Stephens has been nationally recognized for the many leadership opportunities it provides for students.

Admission Requirements

Applicants are considered by the Director of Admission and the Admission Committee on an individual basis without regard to race, religion, geographic origin, or handicap. Major factors for admission consideration are the recommendations and academic record, including rank in class, subjects studied, grade point average, proficiency in English, and test scores (SAT I and ACT).

Application and Information

Candidates for admission should submit the application with the $25 application fee and arrange to have transcripts and recommendations mailed to the Office of Admission. Upon receipt of the application, any additional material is mailed to the student. Qualified students are accepted on a rolling admission basis upon receipt of all necessary credentials.

Office of Admission
Campus Box 2121
Stephens College
Columbia, Missouri 65215
Telephone: 573-876-7207
             800-876-7207 (toll-free)
Fax: 573-876-7237
E-mail: apply@stephens.edu
World Wide Web: http://www.stephens.edu

On the Stephens College campus.

TRUMAN STATE UNIVERSITY

KIRKSVILLE, MISSOURI

The University

Truman State University has forged a national reputation for offering an exceptionally high-quality undergraduate education at a competitive price. For the seventh consecutive year, *U.S. News & World Report* has ranked Truman State University as the number one master's-level public institution in the Midwest. In addition, Kaplan's 2004 National Survey of High School Guidance Counselors describes Truman as a "hidden treasure" and one of only fifty-nine universities that offer the best value when weighing the quality of education versus the cost. A commitment to student achievement and learning is at the core of everything the University does. This commitment is evidenced by faculty and staff members who recognize the importance of providing students with the opportunity to interact with their professors both in and out of the classroom. With class sizes averaging only 22 students and 95 percent of freshman courses being taught by full-time faculty members, students find ample opportunity to ask questions of professors as well as interact with their multitalented peers. Truman's academic environment is enhanced by a student body that achieves at remarkable levels. The 2003 freshman class had an ACT midrange of 25 to 30 and an average GPA of 3.75 on a 4.00 scale. In addition, numerous opportunities exist for students to engage in undergraduate research. Each year, approximately 1,000 students work side by side with professors on University research projects, gaining greater confidence, knowledge, and skill in their chosen disciplines. The University offers these students the opportunity to present the results of their research at the annual Undergraduate Research Symposium. In addition, selected students travel to the National Undergraduate Research Symposium to present their research findings. Undergraduate research stipends are also available.

The teaching degree at Truman is the Master of Arts in Education. Students wishing to pursue a teaching career first complete a bachelor's degree in an academic discipline and then apply for admission into professional study at the master's level. Master's programs in special education, elementary education, and secondary education are available.

With more than 200 University organizations available to students, encompassing service, Greek, honorary, professional, religious, social, political, and recreational influences, Truman students have tremendous opportunities to become involved while enrolled at the University. Truman's Student Activities Board provides popular culture entertainment such as current box office films like *Two Weeks Notice, Old School,* and *The Recruit;* special events like MTV's "Campus Invasion;" comedians such as Jimmy Fallon, David Chapelle, and Bill Bellamy; and musical artists like Jimmy Eat World and Lifehouse. In addition, admission to all varsity athletic events, Truman theater productions, and Lyceum Series events is free to Truman students. Recent theater productions have included *Arcadia, A Christmas Carol, Cat on a Hot Tin Roof,* and *Lysistrata.*

Location

Truman State University is located in Kirksville, a town of approximately 17,000, nestled in the northeast corner of Missouri. The town square, located within walking distance of the Truman campus, provides a connection to Kirksville's past. A multiplex movie theater opened on the town square in 2001. Local merchants operate specialized gift, book, and clothing stores, and several restaurants offer a wide selection of American and international cuisine.

The Kirksville Aquatic Center is a great place to have fun and get fit. An indoor/outdoor pool complex, the Aquatic Center, offers a variety of activities, classes, and programs designed to appeal to people of all ages. Inside the complex is a six-lane indoor swimming pool, perfect for swimming, relaxing, or playing a game of water-basketball. The outdoor pool is designed with a zero-depth entry, a 1-meter diving board, and four 25-yard outdoor lap lanes as well as a 20-foot water slide.

The northeast region of Missouri is also home to Thousand Hills State Park. A 3,252-acre state park and 573-acre lake for camping, hiking, biking, fishing, swimming, boating, and water skiing is located within 10 minutes of the Truman campus.

Majors and Degrees

Undergraduate degrees offered by Truman include the Bachelor of Arts (B.A.), Bachelor of Science (B.S.), Bachelor of Music: Performance (B.M.), Bachelor of Fine Arts (B.F.A.), and Bachelor of Science in Nursing (B.S.N.). Truman offers more than forty areas of study in the following disciplines: accounting, agricultural science, art, art history, biology, business administration, chemistry, classics, communication, communication disorders, computer science, economics, English, exercise science, French, German, health science, history, justice systems, mathematics, music, music: performance, nursing, philosophy and religion, physics, political science, psychology, Russian, sociology/anthropology, Spanish, and theater.

Professional paths include but are not limited to dentistry, engineering, law, medicine, optometry, pharmacy, physical therapy, and veterinary medicine.

Academic Programs

Truman is Missouri's premier liberal arts and sciences university and the only highly selective public institution in the state. The Liberal Studies Program is the heart of Truman's curriculum and is intended to serve as a foundation for all major programs of study offered by the University. Truman's mission is to "offer an exemplary undergraduate education, grounded in the liberal arts and sciences, in the context of a public institution of higher learning." Therefore, Truman is providing the kind of education in the liberal arts and sciences that has historically been offered only at private colleges. The program is a blend of two intellectual traditions in higher education, one that emphasizes the traditional thought and learning of the culture as reflected in the classical works produced by it, and the other that emphasizes personal investigation and freedom of discovery. The philosophy behind the Liberal Studies Program is based upon a commitment that Truman has made to provide students with essential skills needed for lifelong learning, breadth across the traditional liberal arts and sciences through exposure to various discipline-based modes of inquiry, and interconnecting perspectives that stress interdisciplinary thinking and integration as well as linkage to other cultures and experiences. All students graduating from Truman must complete 63 or more credit hours in liberal arts and sciences courses.

Truman's Residential College Program brings the University learning community inside the student residence halls. Historically, residential colleges have been places where faculty members and students join together as "friends of learning." At Truman, this living/learning tradition is honored as one means of furthering its specific goals as a public liberal arts university. The Residential College Program seeks to make liberal arts education personally vital and engaging to the whole person.

Truman also offers an especially challenging General Honors Program. This program provides students with the opportunity to select the most rigorous honors courses to satisfy the liberal arts component of their respective programs. Students who successfully complete this program not only benefit from an even richer academic experience at Truman but also receive special recognition at graduation. Departmental honors are also available in several disciplines.

Off-Campus Programs

Each year, more than 300 Truman students participate in enriching and life-changing study-abroad experiences. Truman's own study-abroad programs, combined with programs offered through Truman's membership in the College Consortium for International Studies, International Student Exchange Program, Australearn, and the Council on International Educational Exchange, provide students with study-abroad opportunities in more than thirty-five countries worldwide, including Australia, England, France, Hong Kong, Italy, Russia, Spain, Thailand, and Wales.

In addition, there are several cooperative programs affiliated with biology. Students interested in medical technology may complete classes at one of several medical technology schools in Iowa, Illinois, or Missouri. Truman is also affiliated with the Gulf Coast Research Laboratory at Ocean Springs, Mississippi. Marine biology courses may be taken at the laboratory during the summer with credit awarded at Truman. In-depth study of the Ozark habitats is also available through Truman's affiliation with Reis Biological Station located near Steelville, Missouri.

In cooperation with the Washington Center for Internships and Academic Seminars, Truman offers a wide variety of experiential internships in Washington, D.C. Included are work-experience opportunities in such areas as public administration, the fine and performing arts, foreign affairs/diplomacy, government affairs, criminal justice, international relations, health and human services, environmental policy, business administration, and communications as well as other areas. Placement sites include nonprofit groups, media organizations, Congress, museums, and much more.

Truman requires internships in education, health science, and exercise science and annually offers internship opportunities with the Missouri State Legislature. In recent years, students have completed internships with United States senators, the governor of Missouri, business and industry managers, zoos, broadcast and print media professionals, accountants, advertising agencies, physical therapists, musicians, artists, and the United States Supreme Court.

Academic Facilities

The Truman campus contains forty buildings in an expanse of 140 acres. Featured among these facilities is Pickler Memorial Library. This 449,275-volume facility provides a state-of-the-art library resource for students and faculty members alike. Materials not available in Pickler Memorial Library can be obtained through the Interlibrary Loan Office and MOBIUS.

Improvement to campus facilities have recently included the construction of a $750,000, eight-lane, all-weather track as well as construction of the $8-million Student Recreation Center complete with four athletic courts, an aerobic room, a weight room, an indoor track, and a lounge. In addition, the $7-million renovation to Violette Hall incorporated technologically advanced classrooms, two 100-seat auditoriums, and several student meeting rooms as well as faculty and division offices. The $20-million renovation and 80,000-square-foot addition to Ophelia Parrish Building was completed in summer 2002 and has transformed this facility into the new Fine Arts Center housing art studios, practice facilities, a performing arts center, and a black box theater. The $20-million renovation and expansion of Truman's science facility, Magruder Hall is under way.

Additional facilities include a student media center with a TV studio, a radio station, and print media production facilities, a biofeedback laboratory, an organic chemistry lab, an analytical chemistry lab, an independent learning center for nursing students, an observatory, a greenhouse, a 5,000-seat football stadium, a soccer field, tennis and racquetball courts, a softball diamond, a 3,000-seat arena with three basketball courts and an Olympic-size swimming pool, a multicultural affairs center, a writing center, and a career center.

Costs

Tuition for Missouri residents for the 2003–04 academic year was $4600; out-of-state tuition was $8400. Room and board totals for both Missouri residents and nonresidents were $5072. Additional

fees included a $150 freshman orientation fee, an annual $56 activities fee, a $50 parking fee for those with a vehicle, and the costs of books and personal expenses.

Financial Aid

Truman offers automatic scholarships ranging from $1000 to $2000. Competitive scholarship awards vary from $500 up to full tuition, room, and board, plus a $4000 study-abroad stipend. The application for admission also serves as the application for the automatic and competitive scholarship programs.

Several scholarships are awarded to students for excellence in music, theater, or art. These scholarships are available for instrumental, strings, or vocal music; acting or dramatic production; and studio art or art history. Of special interest to piano students is the Truman Piano Fellowship Competition.

The National Collegiate Athletic Association and the University authorize a limited number of grants to outstanding athletes. The value of this aid may vary with each individual recipient.

Truman accepts the Free Application for Federal Student Aid (FAFSA) and participates in all Federal Title IV financial aid programs. Financial aid estimates are available upon request.

Faculty

Truman State University is committed to teaching the academically talented undergraduate student. The University has 381 full-time faculty members and 23 part-time faculty members. Of these, 98 percent teach undergraduates and 85 percent hold a doctoral degree or the highest terminal degree in their discipline. Most major graduate institutions are represented among the Truman faculty, including Harvard, Princeton, Yale, Berkeley, Oxford, and the Sorbonne. The student-faculty ratio at Truman is 15:1.

Student Government

Student Senate is the official elected governing body of the Student Association representing approximately 6,000 students. Its mission is to represent the views of the Student Association in the formulation of the University policy through legislation and membership on all University committees; to facilitate communication and mutual understanding among the Student Association, faculty and staff members, and administration; to maintain a cohesive vision for the future of the University; and to actively participate in the fulfillment of the University's mission as an exemplary public liberal arts and sciences university.

Admission Requirements

Admission to Truman is competitive. Each applicant is evaluated for admission based upon academic and cocurricular record, ACT or SAT results, and the admission essay. Truman requires the following high school core: 4 units of English, 3 units of mathematics (4 recommended), 3 units of social studies/history, 3 units of natural science, 1 unit of fine arts, and 2 units of the same foreign language.

Application and Information

Students interested in early admission must submit an application by November 15. Notification of acceptance is mailed after December 15. Applications received after November 15 are processed on a rolling basis. The recommended final deadline to apply for the fall semester is March 1. There is no application fee. Students may apply online at the University's Web site. For further information or to schedule a campus visit, students should contact:

Admission Office
Truman State University
205 McClain Hall
100 East Normal
Kirksville, Missouri 63501
Telephone: 660-785-4114
       800-892-7792 (toll-free, Missouri only)
Fax: 660-785-7456
E-mail: admissions@truman.edu
World Wide Web: http://www.truman.edu

THE UNIVERSITY OF FINDLAY
FINDLAY, OHIO

The University

The University of Findlay is a private coeducational institution with 4,711 full- and part-time students. Founded in 1882 by the Churches of God, General Conference, it emphasizes preparation for careers and professions in an educational program that blends liberal arts and career education. Students of many denominations attend Findlay, and religious participation is a matter of personal choice.

Bachelor of Arts degree programs are available in sixty different majors. The Associate of Arts degree is awarded in nearly twenty areas. Master's degrees are offered in athletic training, business administration, education, environmental management, liberal studies, occupational therapy, physical therapy, and teaching English to speakers of other languages (TESOL).

The largest programs at Findlay are in business, education, and health professions. Majors in the sciences and health professions include athletic training, computer science, equestrian studies (English, Western, and equine management), nuclear medicine, occupational therapy, physical therapy, physician assistant studies, premedicine, pre–veterinary medicine, and technology management. Business degrees are founded in a comprehensive core program with eleven different majors, including an individualized major option.

Opportunities for internships and work-related experiences are available in most major fields through the Professional Experiences Program (PEP).

Most of Findlay's students come from Ohio and the surrounding states of Michigan, Indiana, and Pennsylvania. More than thirty other states are also represented. Because of the Intensive English Language Institute located on the campus, many international students are part of the total student body.

Resident students live in eight modern residence halls and several town-house-style apartments. All students eat their meals in an attractive, newly renovated dining hall. Social life at Findlay centers on student organizations, fraternities, and sororities. Findlay has three officially recognized fraternities: Alpha Sigma Phi, Tau Kappa Epsilon, and Theta Chi; there are two sororities: Phi Sigma Sigma and Sigma Kappa. Organizations include department and special interest clubs, the newspaper, musical groups, a radio and TV station, Circle K, and Aristos Eklektos (honors).

Athletic programs are affiliated with NCAA Division II and the Great Lakes Intercollegiate Athletic Conference. Findlay offers thirteen intercollegiate sports for men: baseball, basketball, cross-country, equestrian, football, golf, indoor track and field, outdoor track and field, soccer, swimming and diving, tennis, volleyball, and wrestling. It has eleven varsity sports for women: basketball, cross-country, equestrian, golf, indoor track and field, outdoor track and field, soccer, softball, swimming and diving, tennis, track, and volleyball. Club sport teams include the equestrian and ice hockey teams. Athletic scholarships are available.

Croy Physical Education Center has a 25-meter swimming pool, exercise areas, a gymnasium, offices, and classrooms. The Gardner Fitness Center is a state-of-the-art facility. The 130,000-square-foot Koehler Recreation and Fitness Complex, opened in 1999, contains the Malcolm Athletic Center, with a six-lane, NCAA regulation track and four multipurpose courts; the Clauss Ice Arena; locker rooms; and offices for the athletic department.

Student services include career and placement counseling, the Cosiano Health Center, academic tutoring and personal counseling, and study skills assistance through the Academic Support Center.

Location

Findlay was voted the most livable micropolitan city in Ohio and scored among the top twelve in the United States. It is within easy driving distance of Toledo, Columbus, Detroit, and Fort Wayne. Interstate 75 and the Ohio Turnpike (Interstates 80 and 90) are major highways serving the area. Airports in Toledo, Columbus, and Detroit are convenient. The town of Findlay has 39,000 residents and is home to Marathon Oil Corporation and Cooper Tire and Rubber Company. The Findlay campus consists of more than 200 acres on several sites. A 72-acre campus-owned farm houses pre–veterinary medicine and English equestrian studies. A second 32-acre facility houses the English riding program. Many opportunities exist for students who want business-related and social service agency experience. The University has established strong relationships with the community, which supports athletic and cultural events on the campus. Besides the full program of on-campus activities, off-campus trips to cultural and entertainment events are scheduled. The city of Findlay, which has an excellent business climate, offers part-time job opportunities, volunteer service organizations, and the chance to be involved with the larger civic community. Findlay's campus is attractive, safe, comfortable, and friendly.

Majors and Degrees

The Bachelor of Arts (B.A.) degree is awarded in the following majors: adolescent/young adult/integrated English/language arts, adolescent/young adult/integrated social studies, art, children's book illustration, communication (broadcast journalism emphasis), communication (broadcast telecommunication emphasis), communication (journalism emphasis), communication (organizational communication emphasis), communication (public relations emphasis), criminal justice administration, English, English as an international language, general social studies, graphic communication, health communication, history, interpersonal and public communication, Japanese, law and the liberal arts, middle childhood/language arts and social studies, multi-age/drama/theater, multi-age/Japanese, multi-age/Spanish, multi-age/visual arts, philosophy/applied philosophy, political science, psychology, religious studies, social work, sociology, Spanish, studio art, teaching English to speakers of other languages, technical communication, and theater. Minors are offered in numerous areas.

The Bachelor of Science (B.S.) degree is granted in accounting; adolescent/young adult/earth science; adolescent/young adult/integrated mathematics; adolescent/young adult/life science; athletic training; biology; business administration; business management; computer science; early childhood; economics; environmental, safety, and occupational health management; equestrian studies (English and Western emphases); equine business management; finance; health education; health studies; hospitality management; human resource management; international business; intervention specialist/mild to moderate disabilities; language and international business; marketing; mathematics; medical technology; middle childhood/language arts/math; middle childhood/language arts/science; middle childhood/math/science; middle childhood/math/social studies; middle childhood/science/social studies; multi-age/health education; multi-age/physical education; nuclear medicine technology; occupational therapy; operations and logistics; physical education; physician assistant; physical therapy; premedicine; prenursing; pre–veterinary medicine; recreation therapy; small business/entrepreneurship; strength and conditioning; and technology management.

The Associate of Arts degree is available in accounting, computer science, criminal justice administration (corrections or law enforcement emphases), English as an international language, equestrian studies, financial management, general social studies, human resource management, humanities, management information systems, massage therapy, nuclear medicine technology, office administration, personal training, religious studies, sales/

retail management, small business/entrepreneurship, and technology management. Certificate programs are available in a variety of areas.

Academic Programs

Findlay operates on the semester system. Students must complete at least 124 semester hours with a minimum overall grade point average of 2.0 to earn a bachelor's degree. General education requirements and competency requirements in English, reading, computer literacy, speech, and library use must be fulfilled. The First Year Seminar introduces students to living and learning at Findlay and gives them the opportunity to work with the same teachers and student group in two related courses. The Foundations Program offers students the chance to develop those skills in writing, reading, and thinking needed for their success as college students. Study skills, time management, and academic advising are included. Students are selected for this program at the time of admission. The Honors Program provides additional challenge to those students who qualify on the basis of academic credentials. Study- and travel-abroad programs are offered by various departments. Credit and/or placement can be earned through Advanced Placement (AP) exams.

The Equestrian Program is a well-recognized program of its kind and serves approximately 250 students from throughout the United States and abroad. Majors in equine business management and in English and Western riding are offered. The instruction, both in the classroom and on horseback, makes use of the expertise of recognized national equestrian champions. The pre–veterinary medicine program, using the farm facilities, offers the advantages of hands-on experience with livestock and an internship program in a distinctive curriculum. The pre–veterinary medicine program has a placement rate into veterinary schools that is much higher than the national average.

The Nuclear Medicine Institute provides the training necessary to qualify students for careers in nuclear medicine technology, a growing health-related career field.

The Health Professions Program provides eleven majors, including athletic training, nuclear medicine technology, strength and conditioning, recreation therapy, occupational therapy, physical therapy, and physician assistant studies.

Academic Facilities

The focal point of the Findlay campus is Old Main, which houses classrooms, faculty and administrative offices, the computer center, facilities for various student activities, and the Ritz Auditorium. Shafer Library is a member of a consortium that provides extensive resources to students. The Gardner Fine Arts Pavilion, dedicated in 1994, houses the Mazza Museum of original art from children's books. The University has numerous computer labs. Other academic buildings include the Frost Science Center, with a greenhouse and the Newhard Planetarium, and the Egner Center for the Performing Arts, which houses a 200-seat theater and the student-operated radio and television stations. A 101,000-square-foot athletic complex was completed in January 1999. This facility houses a six-lane indoor track, sand pits for long jump, a state-of-the-art timing system, and a wrestling room. Also under the same roof is an ice arena with a seating capacity of 1,200. Approximately 450 horses are stabled and trained at the equestrian facilities, which offer barns and indoor and outdoor riding arenas.

Costs

Tuition for the 2003–04 academic year totaled $19,052 for most programs, $22,402 for the equestrian programs, and $20,322 for the pre–veterinary medicine program. Room and board cost $7062. The estimated cost for transportation, books, and supplies is $1500.

Financial Aid

Ninety percent of Findlay students receive financial aid. Assistance is based on need as well as scholastic achievement. Factors used in determining aid are the Free Application for Federal Student Aid (FAFSA), grade point average, and ACT or SAT results. Federal and state programs are used with institution grants and scholarships, including sibling grants. The FAFSA must be filed. Notification of aid awards is made on a rolling basis. Work-study jobs are available. Scholarships for high-achieving students and student athletes are offered.

Faculty

The 16:1 student-faculty ratio results in small classes—usually fewer than 30 students. Professors know their students, and every student has a faculty adviser.

Student Government

The Student Government Association (SGA) and the Campus Program Board are involved in planning and implementing student activities. SGA provides leadership experience for students and enhances cooperation among faculty members, the administration, and students. A representative from SGA sits on the Board of Trustees. The Campus Program Board plans activities for recreation and cultural enrichment.

Admission Requirements

Applicants to Findlay should have a college-preparatory high school background, including 4 years of English, 2 to 3 years of mathematics, 2 to 3 years of social studies, and 2 years of sciences. A foreign language is recommended but not required. Results of the ACT or SAT and high school transcripts should be submitted with the application for admission. Transfer students must be eligible to return to the institution last attended and must submit transcripts of all college work. Decisions are made on a rolling basis. Application deadlines are August 1 for fall semester and December 15 for spring semester. A campus visit is strongly recommended. For students not meeting regular minimum admission requirements, Findlay has a Foundations Program, which provides skill building and academic support during the first semester of the freshman year. Findlay is an equal opportunity institution in admission and employment.

Application and Information

For application forms and other information, students may contact:

Office of Undergraduate Admissions
The University of Findlay
1000 North Main Street
Findlay, Ohio 45840
Telephone: 419-434-4732
        800-548-0932 (toll-free)
E-mail: admissions@findlay.edu
World Wide Web: http://www.findlay.edu

Old Main.

UNIVERSITY OF ST. FRANCIS

JOLIET, ILLINOIS

The University

Committed to the success of its students, the University of St. Francis (USF) offers a global perspective to its students, with strong career preparation, a liberal arts base, and the self-confidence to take on the world. About 85 percent of USF graduates find employment or enter graduate school within six months of graduation.

The University of St. Francis offers an intimate, personalized college experience, and students—residents, commuters, adult learners, and graduate students—benefit from an innovative student-centered approach. The University serves some 1,500 students at its Joliet campus. More than 2,800 students throughout the nation are served by programs offered at off-site locations and online.

Some interesting facts about The University of St. Francis include the following: 75 percent of the University's science graduates are women; nearly 25 percent of all students are involved in volunteer programs; 76 percent of students are transfer students; the University has provided Illinois schools with more than 1,000 teachers; the average undergraduate class size is 16; the University offers more than thirty student organizations; and prominent Chicago-based and national companies recruit on the campus each year.

More than sixty areas of undergraduate study are offered in the arts and sciences, business, computer science, education, and nursing. The University also offers undergraduate programs designed for adult learners, such as the Bachelor of Science in professional arts/applied organizational management, the RN-B.S.N. Fast Track program for registered nurses, and the health arts program.

Nine graduate programs are offered: the M.S. in health services administration, M.B.A., M.S. in management, M.S. in training and development, M.S. in nursing, M.S. in physician assistant studies, M.S. in educational leadership, M.S. in teaching and learning, and M.Ed. in education with certification.

USF offers programming nationwide at on-site locations, online, and through faculty-directed distance tutorials. USF is committed to teaching and to providing students with the challenges and support essential to meeting their potential. Small class sizes ensure that students get the individual attention and focus they need. The University's writing and math centers and tutoring programs provide an important support network. Programs for scholars, such as the Biology Fellows Program and various honor societies, provide challenging and relevant educational experiences beyond classroom learning. USF is at the forefront of technology, providing a variety of online research work and experiences to its students.

USF is committed to educating the student as a whole. A variety of student clubs and organizations are available, as are volunteer activities. Student Affairs sponsors many entertainment events as well as the Student Government Association. Schola, the student choir, and *Loquitur*, the University's literary magazine, are popular activities. The University is also host to the annual Undergraduate Conference on English Language and Literature, which draws student presenters from prestigious colleges and universities throughout the nation. Cultural musical events, which bring internationally and nationally acclaimed performers to the University, are sponsored through the Featured Performances series. Exhibits that bring the works of regionally recognized artists to the campus are planned.

During the past twenty years, USF teams have won sixty conference championships, have had sixty-two national tournament appearances, and have won one national championship. USF has six sports programs for men and eight programs for women, as well as ten intramural programs.

Location

USF's main campus is on 16 acres in the midst of a historic residential area known as Joliet's Cathedral area. The University is 35 miles southwest of Chicago (about 45 minutes) and is easily accessible by major roadways and trains. USF is also conveniently located between Argonne National Laboratory and Midewin National Tallgrass Prairie. Both sites provide excellent opportunities for research, internships, and paid cooperative job programs with professionals in many disciplines, including math, natural sciences, education, computer science, and mass communication.

The University's College of Nursing and Allied Health is located 5 minutes from the main campus, adjacent to Provena Saint Joseph Medical Center. The University also holds classes at a variety of health-care facilities throughout the nation and maintains a regional center in Albuquerque, New Mexico, where the M.S. in physician assistant studies and the Master of Science in Nursing with a family nurse practitioner track are offered.

The Regional Education Academy for Leadership (REAL), an initiative of the College of Education, is housed on Jefferson Street in the Twin Oaks office center, approximately 10 minutes from the campus. In partnership with area school districts, REAL offers educational opportunities for area educators at convenient locations throughout the region.

Majors and Degrees

Undergraduate programs of study include accounting, actuarial science, advertising/public relations, American politics, applied organizational management, art, arts–management, arts–marketing, biology, broadcasting/audio-video, commercial/public recreation, computer science, computer science/electronics, elementary education, English, environmental science, finance, general management, health arts, history, human resource management, information technology, management, marketing, mass communications, mathematics, media arts, medical technology, music, nuclear medicine technology, nursing, pastoral ministry, political science, predental, premedical, prepharmacy, pre–physical therapy, pre–veterinary medicine, professional arts/applied organizational management, psychology, public policy, radiation therapy, radiography, recreation administration, secondary education (science, language arts/English, social science, mathematics), social work, special education, studio art, teaching ministry, theology, therapeutic recreation, visual arts, visual arts/graphic design, and Web application development.

Academic Programs

The University of St. Francis offers a comprehensive education designed to introduce the student to various modes and areas of inquiry. The core curriculum includes interdisciplinary courses taken in the freshman through junior years. The relationship of the major to the liberal education courses is addressed in a senior capstone experience in the major. For a baccalaureate degree, a student must earn 128 semester hours. Thirty-two semester hours must be earned at USF. In addition to the overall requirement of at least a 2.0 GPA, a student must achieve a grade of C or better in every course required for the major program. The University also offers Prior Learning Assessment (PLAP), College-Level

Examination Program (CLEP), and advanced placement opportunities. Various honors and internship programs are available.

Academic Facilities

The University's oldest building, Tower Hall, is the focal point of activities, housing interactive learning classrooms, state-of-the-art laboratories, offices, two residence wings, dining facilities, the chapel, the bookstore, and the radio and television stations. St. Albert Hall is home to the Natural Science Learning Center and the University's main computing lab. Marian Hall is a residence hall housing 225 students, a residence wing for science students, lounges, a game room, computing lab, and Information Services offices.

The main campus also includes the three-story library, which offers Internet access and houses the distance learning classroom. Online and off-campus students may fully utilize USF library services through the University's Web site. The recreation center, with seating for 1,500, is a three-level facility that includes basketball, volleyball, and racquetball courts; a Nautilus training and exercise room; a conference room; and a classroom. The Moser Performing Arts Center houses an auditorium, art gallery, studio theater, and music and choir practice rooms. The College of Nursing and Allied Health is housed at a medical center complex about 5 minutes from the Wilcox Street campus.

Costs

In 2003–04, tuition and fees for full-time undergraduates were $16,480 per year; room and board were $6030 per year. Tuition for part-time students was $480 per credit hour; RN-B.S.N. Fast Track, $345 per credit hour; professional arts/applied organizational management, $450 per credit hour; and health arts, $305 per credit hour.

Financial Aid

USF is committed to assisting students in obtaining a high-quality private education. The University spends more than $5 million in institutional aid and scholarships, in addition to nearly $6 million in federal and state assistance, to enable students to attend USF. In order to apply for all forms of federal, state, and USF assistance, students must complete a financial aid application form. USF prefers that students complete the Free Application for Federal Student Aid (FAFSA).

Faculty

The University of St. Francis faculty is committed to teaching. The University has 76 full-time faculty members, more than half of whom have terminal degrees. Forty adjunct faculty members bring a variety of academic and professional experience to the classroom. Faculty advisers are an integral part of the USF experience.

The USF faculty is invested in the success of its students, both academically and personally. Nursing faculty members are strong clinicians. Their intense commitment to health care and to patients ensures that students are challenged academically and offered a personal, caring support system.

Admission Requirements

Although each applicant is considered individually, there are four general requirements for admission to the University of St. Francis as an incoming freshman: satisfactory ACT or SAT I scores; rank in the upper half of their graduating class; at least 16 high school units in academic subjects, or the equivalent of a high school diploma, including 4 units of English, 2 units of mathematics (algebra and geometry), 2 units of social studies, 2 units of science (one with lab), 3 units total with courses from two of three areas (foreign language, computer science, or music/art), and 3 units of electives; and satisfactory scores on the TOEFL from applicants for whom English is a second language.

A $100 registration deposit is required thirty days after acceptance. This deposit is credited to the applicant's bill and is fully refundable until May 1 for students entering in the fall semester or January 1 for students entering in the spring semester.

Students attending other colleges may transfer to the University of St. Francis at any time during their academic careers. A minimum 2.0 GPA and demonstration of college-ready proficiency in math and English are required of transfer students for admission. Students attending community colleges are not required to earn an associate degree to enter. The University has outstanding services for transfer students. Articulation agreements with community colleges ensure a smooth transition to USF.

Application and Information

Freshmen are admitted in the fall and spring. Students should take the ACT or SAT I and visit the campus for an interview by April 1. Entrance exams should be taken in the spring of the junior year or the fall of the senior year in high school. Applications, including a high school transcript and an application fee, should be filed by July 15 for fall entry and December 1 for spring entry. Notification is on a rolling basis. Students transferring from a community college or another senior college or university may seek admission for either the fall or spring semester. Transfer students anticipating enrollment as nursing majors should submit an application for admission and have transcripts forwarded to the Admissions Office from one year to one semester before their projected entry date.

Registered nurses seeking admission to the RN-B.S.N. Fast Track degree completion program must submit the application for admission with the fee, official transcripts from each school attended, a copy of current licensure as an RN, and two letters of reference. Specific prerequisite and major supportive courses are also required.

Health-care professionals (dental hygienists, radiologic technologists, registered nurses, respiratory therapists, and other qualified health-care professionals) seeking admission as a health arts major must submit an application; transcripts of academic credit from all colleges, universities, or diploma programs; proof of current licensure; prior learning documentation of appropriate work experience, as specified; and applicable fees. For information about admissions, prospective students should contact:

University of St. Francis
500 Wilcox Street
Joliet, Illinois 60435
Telephone: 815-740-3400
            800-735-7500 (toll-free)
E-mail: admissions@stfrancis.edu
World Wide Web: http://www.stfrancis.edu

Tower Hall, on the campus of the University of St. Francis.

VANDERCOOK COLLEGE OF MUSIC

CHICAGO, ILLINOIS

The College

VanderCook College of Music traces its roots back to the early 1900s when Hale A. VanderCook opened his downtown studio. By the late 1920s, the studio had developed into what would become one of the first three institutions to offer a degree in instrumental music education. The development of music education in the United States is closely linked to VanderCook's development as an institution.

VanderCook's hands-on curriculum is a practical and fundamental approach to learning. Having only one major, music education, VanderCook students are allowed a greater opportunity to focus on their education. The success of the College is determined by both the advancement of its students and the success of its graduates.

While students are taught all aspects of music, the main focus remains on music education. This is the point at which VanderCook students excel above all others. Their dedication to both education and performance helps make them aware of all areas of music. More than 95 percent of the graduates make their career in the field of music education. VanderCook continues to have a 95 to 100 percent job placement rate.

VanderCook College of Music is accredited by the National Association of Schools of Music, the North Central Association of Colleges and Schools, and the Illinois Board of Higher Education.

VanderCook also offers a Master of Music Education degree and a Master of Music Education degree with teaching certification.

Location

The College is in the South Loop area of Chicago on the campus of the Illinois Institute of Technology, close to the heart of the city's magnificent musical and cultural centers. VanderCook students have the opportunity to hear the world-renowned Chicago Symphony Orchestra, the Lyric Opera, and many other musical performers. Transportation to and from campus is readily accessible with public transportation stops located on campus and a shuttle bus, which runs between campus and the train stations. The city of Chicago is an important extension of the VanderCook campus.

Majors and Degrees

VanderCook College of Music offers one major at the undergraduate level, music education. Upon completing the appropriate course of study, vocal or instrumental, undergraduate students are awarded the Bachelor of Music Education degree.

Academic Programs

VanderCook College of Music trains students in both a musical course of study and in general academic areas. The curriculum is practical, emphasizing the proven fundamentals of music education developed by founder H. A. VanderCook. In addition to studying voice, all students learn to perform and teach seventeen different types of instruments and upon graduation are prepared to teach band, choir, and classroom music.

The academic year, which begins in the fall, is based on a semester system. Students may enter in either fall or spring. (Summer terms are for graduate students only.)

Academic Facilities

The College is housed in a two-story building located on the campus of the Illinois Institute of Technology. The building contains classrooms, an academic library, a music library, a listening laboratory, practice rooms, a recital hall, a conference room, an instrument repair laboratory, and various offices. VanderCook's newly renovated Electronic Music Center contains computer workstations and MIDI hardware that use the latest in computer technology and music software. In addition, VanderCook students have complete access to the student services provided by the Illinois Institute of Technology such as dormitories, the library, the gymnasium, and the recreation center.

Costs

Tuition in 2003–04 was $15,290. Room and board, provided by the Illinois Institute of Technology, totaled $6200, and fees were $370.

Financial Aid

Each student is considered on an individual basis for financial aid. Merit-based scholarships are given for musical talent and are based on competitive auditions. Academic scholarships are also available to qualified students. Scholarships are renewable based on musical growth and participation and also cumulative grade point average. Illinois residents may apply for the Monetary Award Program and Federal Stafford Student Loans are also available.

Faculty

At VanderCook College of Music, all undergraduate classes are taught by either full-time or part-time faculty members who have many years of in-depth, practical experience in the field of music education to share with their students. Faculty members are dedicated to giving individual instruction, made possible by a 6:1 student-teacher ratio.

Admission Requirements

VanderCook College of Music seeks musically proficient students who have demonstrated talent and who desire to become the finest music educators.

Candidates for admission must submit an application and essay along with high school transcripts, ACT or SAT I scores, and three letters of recommendation. Following the application, students should schedule and audition and interview with the Director of Admission.

Transfer students must submit both high school and college transcripts. VanderCook is authorized under federal law to enroll international students. These students must submit TOEFL scores and the I-20 form.

Application and Information

Applications are accepted up to four weeks prior to the beginning of a term, subject to the availability of space.

Information or an application may be obtained by contacting:

Tamara V. Trutwin
Admissions and Student Recruitment
VanderCook College of Music
3140 South Federal Street
Chicago, Illinois 60616-3731
Telephone: 312-225-6288
            800-448-2655 (toll-free)
Fax: 312-225-5211
E-mail: ttrutwin@vandercook.edu
World Wide Web: http://www.vandercook.edu

WARTBURG COLLEGE

WAVERLY, IOWA

The College

Founded in 1852 by German Lutheran immigrants, Wartburg is a college of the Evangelical Lutheran Church in America. Wartburg challenges and nurtures students for lives of leadership and service as a spirited expression of their faith and learning. The College's name honors the Wartburg Castle, a days of the Reformation. The College and the castle have close ties, and the communities of Waverly and Eisenach are sister cities.

Wartburg enrolls 1,775 students from twenty-three states and thirty-two countries. Eighty-five percent of Wartburg's first-year students graduated in the top half of their high school class. The average ACT score for first-year students is 23.7. The campus is 85 percent residential. Living accommodations include traditional residence halls; small manor units; 4-, 6-, and 8-person suites; and town house–style apartments for senior students.

Wartburg students are active in more than 100 campus organizations, including honor societies, interest groups, and department-related clubs. The Wartburg Choir, Castle Singers, and Wind Ensemble make annual concert tours in the United States and travel abroad every third year during the College's one-month May Term. The annual Christmas with Wartburg production attracts more than 6,500 people to performances in Waverly, Cedar Falls, and Des Moines, Iowa. The Wartburg Community Symphony presents a five-concert season. Student publications include a weekly newspaper, a daily information bulletin, a yearbook, and a literary magazine. Students also manage a campus radio station, operate and produce programs for the College's local cable television access channel, and manage the city of Waverly's local channel. The Artist Series brings renowned performing artists to the campus, and a convocation series presents lectures by nationally and internationally recognized speakers. The Art Gallery features touring exhibitions and the work of prominent regional artists. Wartburg is a member of Division III of the National Collegiate Athletic Association. Its nineteen (ten men's, nine women's) athletic teams compete in the Iowa Intercollegiate Athletic Conference and regularly earn conference championships and national rankings. The Physical Education Center provides recreational facilities that include an indoor track, handball and racquetball courts, a weight room, a sauna, a cardiovascular room, and an area that accommodates four basketball courts or five tennis courts. Walston-Hoover Stadium opened in 2001 with seating for 4,000 fans, a lighted FieldTurf football field, and an eight-lane all-weather track. Athletic facilities also include two new soccer fields and a throwing venue for track and field.

Wartburg welcomes students of all faiths and offers many avenues for worship, study, fellowship, service, and outreach. A chapel serves as a center for worship and a home for the College's active campus ministry program. Chapel services are scheduled three times a week, and a midweek Eucharist and Sunday morning service provide a variety of worship formats.

The College is accredited by the Higher Learning Commission of the North Central Association of Colleges and Schools. Individual programs are accredited by the National Council for the Accreditation of Teacher Education, the Council on Social Work Education, the National Association of Schools of Music, and the American Music Therapy Association.

Location

Waverly, a northeast Iowa community of 10,000 residents, is recognized statewide for its progressive businesses and industries. Its quiet neighborhoods, low crime rate, clean air, and friendly atmosphere contribute to a high quality of life. Scenic parks along the Cedar River, shopping areas, restaurants, a hospital, medical clinics, dental offices, and many churches are within walking distance. Students find part-time jobs and internships in Waverly, and local residents attend campus events and support College programs. The Waterloo–Cedar Falls metropolitan area (population 128,000) is 20 minutes from Waverly.

Majors and Degrees

The heart of education at Wartburg College is a four-year liberal arts curriculum. The Bachelor of Arts degree signifies study in the liberal arts with a concentration of courses in a major. The Bachelor of Music degree adds an extended concentration of work in musical performance. The Bachelor of Music Education degree prepares students to teach music or major in music therapy.

Departmental majors are offered in accounting, applied music, art, biochemistry, biology, business administration (finance, international business, management, marketing, and sports management), chemistry, church music, communication arts (electronic media, print media, public relations), communication design, communication studies (speech and theater), computer information systems, computer science, economics, education (Christian day school, early childhood, elementary, and secondary), engineering science, English, fitness management, French, French studies, German, German studies, history, international relations, mathematics, music education (instrumental or vocal), music performance, music therapy, philosophy, physical education, physics, political science, psychology, religion (camping ministry, parish education, urban ministry, and youth and family ministry), social work, sociology, Spanish, Spanish studies, and writing.

Minors are offered in most academic departments and in four interdisciplinary programs: environmental studies, intercultural certification, leadership certification, and women's studies.

Wartburg offers cooperative programs and preprofessional advisement in dentistry, engineering, law, medical technology, medicine, nursing, occupational therapy, optometry, pharmacy, physical therapy, and veterinary medicine.

Wartburg is the only private college in Iowa offering a major in music therapy.

Academic Programs

Academic studies are divided into three relatively equal parts. The Wartburg Plan of Essential Education comprises one third of the classwork and is designed to create liberally educated, ethically minded citizens for the twenty-first century. Essential Education courses emphasize thinking strategies, reasoning skills, fundamental literacies, faith and reflection, health and wellness, and a capstone course that addresses ethical issues in the student's academic major. The second third of work is devoted to a major field of study, consisting of a prescribed group of courses that offer depth of knowledge in a discipline. The final third consists of elective courses, which students may choose from any academic area.

The College's 4-4-1 calendar culminates in the one-month May Term, when students concentrate on one course. May Term classes travel within Iowa, across the country, and abroad.

The Pathways Center coordinates academic advising and support services, providing a one-stop resource for guiding students through college and beyond. Services include academic advising, career services, counseling services, first-year programming, senior-year experience, supplemental instruction, testing services, and the writing/reading/speaking laboratory. A special Exploring Majors program is available to students who have not settled on a major. Wartburg consistently places 95 percent or more of each year's graduating class in jobs or graduate school within seven months of graduation.

Wartburg encourages and fosters academic excellence through close faculty-student relationships and an integrated approach that combines the liberal arts with leadership education, global and multicultural studies, a focus on ethics, and opportunities for service and hands-on learning. The student-faculty ratio is 14:1.

The College recognizes credit through Advanced Placement examinations, the College-Level Examination Program, DANTES, Departmental Challenge Examinations, and work at other institutions. It also awards credit for experiential learning.

Off-Campus Programs

Wartburg West in Denver, Colorado, places students in internships or field experiences related to their majors or in community service organizations. They also take academic courses dealing with religion and urban issues. The Washington Center Program allows students to participate in an academic internship program in Washington, D.C. International exchange programs with Bonn University and Jena University in Germany and International Christian University in Japan enable students to study abroad. French, German, and Spanish majors spend significant time studying abroad. Through the Venture Education Program, cultural immersion experiences are available in Australia, China, England, France, Germany, Ghana, Guyana, Israel/Palestine, Jamaica, Mexico, Spain, and Tanzania. Academic travel and on-site course work are offered each May Term, and students may enroll in internships during any term.

Academic Facilities

Wartburg doubled its science facilities in 2004 with the opening of a new Science Center that houses outstanding science, mathematics, and physics programs. An expansive new Student Center provides facilities for campus dining, student organizations, and student services, as well as a multipurpose performance space for campus programming. The Vogel Library is designed to accommodate all types of learning from individual research to group projects and faculty-student interaction. It houses books, periodicals, and reference materials as well as extensive electronic resources. Librarians teach courses in information literacy as part of the Wartburg Plan of Essential Education. The Classroom Technology Center is the home for the social sciences department and several technology-enhanced classrooms. Students have access to more than 400 Macintosh and PC-compatible microcomputers in open-access and departmental computing clusters throughout the campus. Classrooms and residence halls are connected to the campuswide computer network. The Fine Arts Center provides spacious rehearsal and recital halls, music studios, practice rooms, a music therapy suite, art studios, and an art gallery. Its twenty-one-workstation Presser Music Technology Classroom is equipped with keyboard/ synthesizers and Macintosh computers for music theory, composition, and ear training classes. McElroy Communication Arts Center includes a journalism laboratory with Macintosh computers, a television studio with video capabilities, and a television control room equipped with TV production and digital editing equipment. The College radio station has two on-air production studios, digital audio editing, and computer-controlled programming, and broadcasts over the Internet. Whitehouse Business Center has specially designed rooms for accounting, business, marketing, and economics classes.

Costs

For the 2004–05 academic year, tuition is $18,150, room is $2430, board is $2650, and fees are $400, for a total cost of $23,630.

Financial Aid

Wartburg supports the concept of a socially, culturally, and economically diverse student body, believing that contact with others from various backgrounds better prepares students for contemporary life. The College admits applicants on the basis of academic and personal promise, not the ability to pay. More than 97 percent of students receive financial aid in the form of scholarships, grants, loans, and employment. Merit-based academic and music scholarships are awarded to qualified students. The College allocates more than $11 million annually from its own resources for student aid. The application deadline for financial aid is May 1.

Faculty

The 103 full-time and 59 part-time faculty members form a close living-learning community with students and serve as academic advisers. Eighty-three percent of the full-time faculty members hold an earned doctoral degree or the highest degree in their discipline. Wartburg emphasizes good teaching and also provides faculty research and development opportunities. Many faculty members involve students in their research projects. A sabbatical program permits professors to spend a term or a year on a growth project. Endowments support academic chairs in banking and monetary economics, biology, chaplaincy, choral conducting, communication arts, ethics, global and multicultural studies, and leadership.

Student Government

The Student Senate provides a student voice on campus issues. Its 35 members are selected annually. The Senate selects students to serve on a number of faculty-student committees dealing with all aspects of campus life. Senate members represent student interests to the faculty, administration, and Board of Regents.

Admission Requirements

Applicants are considered according to their potential for academic success, based upon high school rank, breadth and depth of previous study, test scores on the ACT or SAT I, an academic recommendation, and a personal interview with an admission representative. The recommended high school background is 4 years of English, 3 years of mathematics (advanced courses preferred), 3 years of science, 2 years of social science, 2 years of foreign language, and 1 year of computer study. Transfer students and international students should contact the Admissions Office to determine any special admission requirements.

Application and Information

A rolling admission policy is used, and applicants may apply at any time. The Wartburg College application for admission, the $20 application fee, one academic recommendation from a teacher, ACT or SAT I scores, and official copies of high school and college transcripts should be sent to the Admissions Office. The application fee is waived for students who make an official campus visit.

Doug Bowman, Dean of Admissions and Financial Aid
Wartburg College
100 Wartburg Boulevard
P.O. Box 1003
Waverly, Iowa 50677-0903
Telephone: 319-352-8264
        800-772-2085 (toll-free)
Fax: 319-352-8579

The Vogel Library is designed as a learner's library. The library's espresso coffee shop is a popular gathering spot for students and faculty members.

WESTERN MICHIGAN UNIVERSITY

KALAMAZOO, MICHIGAN

The University

Western Michigan University (WMU) has emerged as one of the nation's top public universities and enjoys an international reputation in fields as varied as medieval studies, blind rehabilitation, jazz studies, aviation, paper science, graph theory, and evaluation.

The University is one of only 102 public universities in the nation placed by the Carnegie Foundation for the Advancement of Teaching in its top classification of Doctoral/Research–Universities–Extensive. It also is one of only ninety-seven public universities in the United States to have its own chapter of Phi Beta Kappa, the nation's premier honor society. In addition, *U.S. News & World Report* has ranked WMU as one of America's top 100 public universities for the past five years.

With 29,178 students, WMU is Michigan's fourth-largest university and is among the nation's fifty largest institutions of higher education. Despite its size, complexity, and variety of offerings, WMU is committed to its mission of being a student-centered research university and has worked to maintain a comfortable student-faculty ratio of 16:1. Because of its relatively low tuition and required fees, the University is often listed as one of the country's best buys in higher education.

Founded in 1903, WMU has seven degree-granting colleges: Arts and Sciences, Aviation, the Haworth College of Business, Education, Engineering and Applied Sciences, Fine Arts, and Health and Human Services as well as the Graduate College and Lee Honors College, which is one of the oldest honors programs in the nation. The University offers 254 academic programs, 152 of them at the undergraduate level. Because it has a vibrant graduate component that includes thirty doctoral degree programs, the University attracts faculty members who have been trained at the world's leading universities and who have well-established research and teaching careers.

Over the past decade, WMU has focused on enhancing its out-of-class learning opportunities by expanding its study-abroad programs, internships with organizations around the nation, and regional and national business partnerships. Its on-campus learning environment is bolstered by some of the best instructional, cultural, and recreational facilities in the Midwest. In recent years, more than half a billion dollars in new construction and equipment has transformed the campus, giving students access to acclaimed performance spaces; a state-of-the-art science pavilion; a world-class aviation college; a large, well-equipped student recreation center; and a cutting-edge engineering campus adjacent to a new Business Technology and Research Park.

The University is home to a diverse student body that includes students from all fifty states as well as an international enrollment of more than 1,700 students representing 110 nations. Minority students also are well represented and typically make up about 9 percent of the student body. The University's on-campus enrollment of more than 27,000 includes about 6,200 students who live in twenty-two campus residence halls that offer a variety of living arrangements.

There are more than 375 registered student organizations, including a wide range of Greek, academic honorary, and professional organizations. In addition, the University has nationally recognized arts programs, a lively cultural calendar, and NCAA Division I-A Mid-American and Central Collegiate Hockey Association sports teams. It's nine men's and eleven women's varsity sports, intramural teams, and club sports add vitality to campus life.

Location

Kalamazoo, one of Michigan's larger cities, is at the center of a county whose population exceeds 280,000 residents. The campus is located midway between Detroit and Chicago, about 2½ hours from each city. Commercial transportation includes train, bus, and airline services. The Kalamazoo community offers a wide array of lively entertainment: sports, such as professional baseball, hockey, and soccer; music, from jazz to heavy metal; intimate comedy clubs; and dining, from fast food to international cuisine. West Michigan is also home to numerous thriving businesses, industries, and Fortune 500 companies, including Haworth Inc., the Whirlpool Corp., and the Kellogg Co., and many of these organizations offer internships to WMU students. Kalamazoo is just 45 minutes from Lake Michigan beaches and only 3 to 4 hours from northern Michigan's ski country. Excellent local skiing is only 30 minutes from the campus.

Majors and Degrees

WMU offers bachelor's degree programs in these fields: accountancy; administrative systems; advertising and promotion; aeronautical engineering; Africana studies; American studies; anthropology; art; art education; art history; athletic training; aviation flight science; aviation maintenance technology; aviation science and administration; biochemistry; biology; biomedical sciences; broadcast and cable production; business-oriented chemistry; chemical engineering; chemistry; civil engineering; communication studies; community health education; computer engineering; computer information systems; computer science; computer science–theory and analysis; construction engineering; criminal justice; dance; dietetics; earth science; economics; electrical engineering; elementary education–art, elementary group minors, music, physical education, speech pathology and audiology; engineering graphics and design technology; engineering management technology; English; environmental studies; exercise science; family studies; family studies–child development; finance; food marketing; food service administration; French; general business; geochemistry; geography; geology; geophysics; German; gerontology; global and international studies; graphic design; health education; history; human resource management; hydrogeology; imaging; industrial design; industrial engineering; industrial technology; integrated supply matrix management; interdisciplinary health services; interior design; interpersonal communication; journalism; Latin; management; manufacturing engineering; manufacturing engineering technology; marketing; mathematics; mechanical engineering; media studies; music; music composition; music education; music history; music–jazz studies; music performance; music theater performance; music theory; music therapy; nursing; nursing RN completion; occupational education studies; occupational therapy; organizational communication; paper engineering; paper science; personal financial planning; philosophy; physics; political science; predentistry; prelaw; premedicine; professional studies; psychology; public administration; public history; public relations; recreation; religion; sales and business marketing; school health education; secondary education–art education, biology, chemistry, dietitics, earth science, English, family and consumer sciences, French, geography, German, health education, history, industrial technology, Latin, mathematics, music education, physical education–teacher/coach, physics, political science, secondary education in business, secondary education in marketing, Spanish, technology and design; social work, sociology, Spanish, technology design; special education–emotionally impaired; special education–mentally impaired; speech pathology and audiology; statistics; student-integrated curriculum; student-planned curriculum; student-planned major; technology and design; telecommunications management; textile and apparel studies; theater; theater–design and technical production; theater–performance; theater–theater studies; tourism and travel; travel instruction; and women's studies.

Academic Programs

WMU offers undergraduate students a rich blend of academic majors and minors, as well as its comprehensive general education program and an honors college. These programs ensure that students graduate with the proficiencies and perspectives they need to succeed. The University Curriculum Program is available to students who are undecided about a major and wish to explore WMU's academic offerings. Last fall, more than 2,000 students enrolled in the program, which won a national award for outstanding academic advising. The Lee Honors College provides undergraduates with a unique living/learning environment, offering the intimacy of a small college with the resources of a major university.

Off-Campus Programs

A host of U.S. business-industry partnerships as well as exchange agreements with universities around the world provide numerous training and research opportunities for graduate and undergraduate students alike. The University provides assistance to students seeking internships in their chosen fields of study.

Academic Facilities

The University Libraries, with the fourth-largest holdings in Michigan, and the University Computing Center together provide campuswide access to worldwide information resources, comparable to other top universities in the Midwest. Computer labs are available across the campus, many in residence halls. In addition, WMU is a completely wireless campus.

Costs

WMU is committed to keeping costs as low as possible to ensure that all qualified students have access to the University. WMU's tuition and fees are among the lowest in the state. Costs for 2003–04 were tuition and fees, $5535, and room and board, $6496. Books and supplies and personal and travel expenses vary based on individual factors.

Financial Aid

Last year, more than 24,000 students received financial assistance totaling nearly $175 million. There are three basic types of financial aid: merit-based programs, need-based programs, and student employment.

Merit-based programs include the Medallion Scholarships, which are valued at $32,000 over four years and are the University's most prestigious award for entering freshmen. Other financial aid includes the Army ROTC awards, Michigan National Guard awards, the National Merit Scholarships Award, and numerous sponsored and departmental scholarships for new and currently enrolled students. Merit-based scholarships, ranging in value from $2000 to $6000, also are available to community college transfer students.

Need-based loans, grants, college work-study, and other aid options are provided for students who demonstrate particular financial need. To be considered, students should complete the Free Application for Federal Student Aid (FAFSA).

The student employment option reflects research indicating that students who work part time are more likely to graduate than students who do not work at all. About 40 percent of WMU's students work while in school, and more than 700 jobs are offered through the college work-study program.

WMU provides a tuition payment plan through Academic Management Services (AMS) and Tuition Management Systems (TMS). This allows parents and students to pay college costs in monthly installments. No interest is charged for these services,

which may be renewed annually for $55. Students should contact AMS at 800-556-6684 or TMS at 800-722-4867 for more information.

Faculty

WMU's commitment to academic excellence means that many of its 986 full-time and 203 part-time faculty members conduct research. Tenured professors teach freshman-level courses, and full-time faculty members teach three quarters of all classes. Almost 93 percent of WMU faculty members have earned a doctorate or other terminal degree in their fields.

Student Government

Governance structures include the Western Student Association and its Student Senate and the Residence Hall Association. Each provides students with a wide variety of opportunities for leadership.

Admission Requirements

Admission to the University is based on a combination of factors, including grade point average, ACT scores, number and kinds of college-prep courses, and trend of grades. In addition, students must meet specific course requirements that include 4 years of English; 3 years of mathematics, including intermediate algebra; 3 years of social sciences; and 2 years of biological/physical sciences. Students who do not meet these requirements but are otherwise admissible may still be admitted to WMU and take the necessary courses as University-level work for credit during their first year.

Transfer students with a minimum of 26 transferable hours (39 quarter hours) at the time of application and a GPA of at least 2.0 (C average) are considered for admission. The trend of the most recent grades is also taken into account. Applicants with fewer than 26 transferable hours (39 quarter hours) at the time of application also must submit a high school transcript. In such cases, admission is based on both college and high school records. For more information, students can request a transfer brochure from the Office of Admissions and Orientation.

Application and Information

For an application or additional information, students should contact:

Office of Admissions and Orientation
Western Michigan University
1903 West Michigan Avenue
Kalamazoo, Michigan 49008-5720
Telephone: 269-387-2000
              800-400-4WMU (toll-free)
World Wide Web: http://www.wmich.edu/admi/
              undergradapp/

This imposing clock tower joins Waldo Library, on the right, with the University Computing Center.

WILLIAM WOODS UNIVERSITY

FULTON, MISSOURI

WILLIAM
WOODS
UNIVERSITY

The University

As an independent, selective, coeducational institution, William Woods University (WWU) serves a total enrollment of 1,813 students and offers degrees in more than forty undergraduate and graduate majors in both traditional and nontraditional settings. Chartered in 1870 as an all-female institution serving young women orphaned by the Civil War, the school moved to its Fulton, Missouri, location in 1890, changing its name to Daughter's College of the Christian Church. By the turn of the twentieth century, the school adopted the William Woods College name and began offering undergraduate programs. In 1962, William Woods officially became a four-year liberal arts college, and in 1993, William Woods became a university, awarding graduate degrees. In 1997, the University became a fully coeducational institution.

The diverse student body of William Woods University consists of 912 undergraduate and 901 graduate students from thirty-seven states and seventeen other countries. Eighty-eight percent of the students live in the twelve residence halls on campus.

More than 30,000 students from five nearby colleges and universities offer William Woods students abundant social opportunities in Fulton and the surrounding area. William Woods has more than forty clubs and six national fraternal organizations. Students have the opportunity to participate in a wide range of extracurricular activities. Intercollegiate sports include men's baseball, golf, soccer, and volleyball and women's basketball, golf, soccer, softball, and volleyball.

The Helen Stephens Sports Complex houses a gymnasium, classrooms, a weight room, and a whirlpool and sauna. The University's Weider Fitness Center also contains aerobic fitness equipment for student use.

The on-campus Equine Center includes four stables, two indoor arenas, an outdoor arena, a blacksmith's shop, and a 30-acre cross-country course. The McNutt Student Center, a multipurpose geodesic domed structure, houses the student activities center and the admission office, as well as a 1,251-seat auditorium.

A $1.5 million Center for Human Performance provides a home for the new Department of Human Performance, which includes athletic training, sports management, and physical education. The one-story, 12,000-square-foot facility provides ten times the amount of space previously dedicated to athletic training. It serves the two-fold purpose of providing state-of-the-art care to WWU athletes and, at the same time, enhancing the University's ability to provide clinical experiences for athletic-training students.

The University's Graduate and Adult Studies Division offers programs leading to the Master of Business Administration, Master of Education in administration, Master of Education in curriculum and instruction, and the Education Specialist degree.

Location

The beautiful 170-acre William Woods campus is located in Fulton, Missouri, a historic community of 12,000. William Woods students enjoy the charm and safety that a small town offers, along with the cultural and recreational facilities of nearby cities and educational institutions. Columbia, home of the University of Missouri and its 25,000 students, is 25 miles west. Fulton sits midway between Kansas City and St. Louis and is a scenic hour's drive north of mid-Missouri's premier recreational area, the Lake of the Ozarks.

Majors and Degrees

William Woods University offers programs leading to the Bachelor of Arts, Bachelor of Science, Bachelor of Social Work, and Bachelor of Fine Arts degrees. Majors and minors include accounting, advertising/marketing, art, art education, athletic training, biology, biology education, broadcasting, business administration, chemistry, communications, computer and information systems, criminal justice, early childhood education, economics/finance, elementary education, English, English education, equestrian science, equine administration, film studies, graphic design, history, history education, interdisciplinary studies, international business, interpreting/American Sign Language (ASL), journalism, management, math education, mathematics, middle school education, music, paralegal studies, philosophy, physical education, physical science, political and legal studies, psychology, public relations, secondary education, social work, sociology, Spanish, special education, speech/theater education, sports management, theater, and visual communications. WVU is one of only twenty-five schools in the country to offer a four-year degree in American Sign Language interpreting.

Academic Programs

At William Woods, students are encouraged to develop a comprehensive, global vision of the world. The workplace is expanding globally, and so must a student's education. Academic programs are designed to prepare the graduate for an active role in a profession or graduate study as well as in society. William Woods purposely remains a small university because it wishes to emphasize the recognition of each student as an individual and to provide the advantages of small classes. The University encourages a close relationship between students, professors, and faculty advisers.

A minimum of 122 credit hours is required for the baccalaureate degree; these include both departmental and general education requirements. The University requires all students to complete a core of common studies. These courses include English, communications, mathematics, fine and performing arts, humanities, history, cultural diversity, natural science, and behavioral/social science. In addition, students gain practical experience through internships offered in many programs of study.

The University grants advanced placement and appropriate credit to qualified students on the basis of College Board Advanced Placement examinations, advanced-placement high school courses, CLEP scores, community college courses, International Baccalaureate, or other supporting evidence of superior scholarship and accomplishments. William Woods also offers an honors program, the Mentor-Mentee Program, and accelerated and independent study for advanced students.

Off-Campus Programs

William Woods participates in exchange agreements with four other regional institutions, providing many academic and cocurricular opportunities. Through cooperative agreements and direct affiliations with institutions abroad, opportunities for fully accredited study abroad are available to qualified students. Approved programs currently are available through the following organizations: American Institute for Foreign Study, Council International Education, and Beaver College. Direct affiliation programs are available at the following institutions: Regent's College in London, Espiritu Santo University in Ecuador, Altai State University in Russia, and Nagoya Women's University in Japan.

Academic Facilities

The William Woods University Library contains more than 122,000 printed volumes, more than 4,000 journal titles in printed and full-text electronic form, and thousands of nonprint items, including videos, CD-ROMs, and computer software. A separate law library is located within the library building. WWU is a charter member of MOBIUS, a statewide consortium of academic libraries that provides online patron-initiated borrowing to WWU students and faculty members from all participating libraries in Missouri. WWU has twelve computer labs for instructional and student use. The library, all classroom buildings, and all residence halls have direct connections to the Internet through the campus network. Distance education students also have access to electronic library resources from remote sites.

The Burton Business and Economics Building, a three-level structure of 35,000 square feet, houses the Division of Business and the Departments of Legal Studies and Interpreting/American Sign Language. A model courtroom provides space for mock trials. The campus also has a 40,000-square-foot Center for the Arts, which houses the Division of Visual, Performing and Communication Arts. Built with a glassed-in main foyer and sculpture garden, the facility contains a performance theater, a television studio, an art gallery for exhibitions, foundry and kilns, and computer labs, as well as numerous classrooms dedicated to studio art, jewelry, sculpture, printing, graphic design, photography, ceramics, music, weaving, and other activities.

Costs

Resident student fees for the 2003–04 academic year were as follows: tuition and fees, $14,000, and room and board, $5700. The application fee is $25.

Financial Aid

Approximately 90 percent of the University's students receive some form of financial assistance. William Woods participates in the Federal Pell Grant, Federal Supplemental Educational Opportunity Grant, Gallagher State Grant, Federal Perkins Loan, Federal Stafford Student Loan, and Federal Work-Study programs. Parents of students applying for need-based assistance are required to file the Free Application for Federal Student Aid (FAFSA). In addition to providing awards for achievement in art, athletics, equestrian science, and performing arts, William Woods also offers academic scholarships based on class rank and ACT or SAT I scores. Scholarships are offered to students graduating first in their class as well as to those students who have achieved National Merit Finalist status. William Woods has designed a program intended to make the University more affordable and, at the same time, to encourage and reward campus and community involvement that makes a complete, well-rounded liberal arts background. This $5000 LEAD (Leading, Educating, Achieving, and Developing) award is available to any student, regardless of financial need, who agrees to make a commitment to campus and community involvement. Information, instructions about applying, and necessary forms are available in the Office of Enrollment Services or on the University's Web site, listed below.

Faculty

William Woods has 57 full-time and 12 part-time faculty members; no classes are taught by graduate students. Students enjoy the relaxed and informal atmosphere of small classes conducted by a diverse teaching faculty; the student-faculty ratio is 16:1. Most of the professors are experienced professionals, and more than 84 percent hold Ph.D.'s or other terminal degrees. The faculty's enthusiasm and dedication to students are among the University's greatest assets.

Admission Requirements

The Enrollment Council at William Woods considers each application individually. The council reviews an applicant's high school courses, grades, activities, performance on the SAT I or ACT, rank in class, and personal references. Early admission and early acceptance policies exist at William Woods. Transfer students who have cumulative grade point averages of C (2.0) or above are eligible for acceptance. Enrollment representatives arrange visits for prospective students and their parents. The Office of Enrollment Services arranges campus tours and interviews during the regular school terms and summer months.

William Woods University welcomes qualified students of any race, color, gender, and national or ethnic origin and persons with disabilities, according to the definition in Section 504 of the Rehabilitation Act of 1973.

Application and Information

To apply for admission, students should submit a current application with a $25 application fee, authorize their high school to send an academic transcript to William Woods, and request that SAT I or ACT scores be sent to the University. Students are accepted on a rolling admission basis after all necessary credentials have been received. While there is no deadline for applying, the University encourages students to apply as early as possible. For an application form, financial assistance information, and brochures, students should contact:

Office of Enrollment Services
William Woods University
1 University Avenue
Fulton, Missouri 65251-1098
Telephone: 573-592-4221
       800-995-3159 (toll-free)
E-mail: admissions@williamwoods.edu
World Wide Web: http://www.williamwoods.edu

William Woods is located on a self-contained, 170-acre campus.

YOUNGSTOWN STATE UNIVERSITY

YOUNGSTOWN, OHIO

The University

For almost a century, Youngstown State University (YSU) has prepared its graduates to become leaders in the region, the state, and the nation. Located on a beautiful 140-acre campus near downtown Youngstown, Ohio, YSU offers its students a comprehensive selection of major programs backed by a strong tradition of teaching and scholarship. YSU's diverse student body of 12,698 and a student-faculty ratio of 19:1 provide the personal contact associated with a smaller institution, and its connection to the Ohio state system of higher education enables it to draw on the vast resources of that system. The average undergraduate class size is 27 for lectures and 9 for labs.

Youngstown State seeks to offer its students a vital living and learning environment with a relatively small, cohesive campus and a wealth of curricular and cocurricular activities. Attractive residence halls house close to 1,000 students and include a special residential honors facility. The new University Courtyard Apartments, located adjacent to the campus, offer 400 students spacious, apartment-style living. Campus activities abound, with more than 130 student organizations, including social sororities and fraternities and opportunities for participation in theater, performing groups, student publications, intramural and intercollegiate athletics, and activity planning.

Youngstown State University competes in NCAA athletics. Since 1991, it has captured four Division I-AA national football championships. During the past decade, the women's basketball team won five Mid-Continent Conference titles and played three years in the NCAA tournament. The University fields ten women's and eight men's intercollegiate Division I teams. Fitness and recreational facilities are free to all YSU students in the Beeghly Physical Education Center and the Stambaugh Sports Complex, including track, tennis, swimming, racquetball, basketball, handball, Nautilus, aerobic conditioning, and free weights. A new wellness and recreation center is scheduled to open as part of the student center in 2005.

Of the 12,858 students at YSU, 11,598 are undergraduates. Multicultural students make up 13 percent of the student body and international students hail from fifty-five countries. Students benefit from a wide range of student services: complete tutorial assistance in all subject areas, with special centers for writing, study skills, reading, and mathematics; counseling and health services; career testing, planning, and placement; special programs for multicultural, women, and adult students (those older than 25); and an orientation program that includes mentoring by faculty and staff members and upperclass students.

The University seeks a balance between teaching, service, and scholarly activity that serves both its students and the larger community of scholars. The University is committed to keeping its doors open to all who seek higher education and equally committed to giving students every opportunity to enrich their minds, develop their creativity and problem-solving abilities, and become informed, conscientious citizens of the world.

The University's School of Graduate Studies and Research offers more than thirty master's degree programs, including one in physical therapy, and a doctoral degree in educational leadership.

Location

Youngstown is at the center of a metropolitan area of 600,000, located 60 miles from both Pittsburgh and Cleveland. The campus is within easy driving or walking distance of restaurants, shopping centers, museums, and parks. The University is a major contributor to the city's cultural and recreational vitality, each year presenting hundreds of concerts, exhibits, lectures, performances, and athletic contests. The city offers an outstanding symphony orchestra, three community theaters, a vital arts community, and unlimited recreational options provided by 2,500-acre Mill Creek Park that is located 1 mile from the campus. YSU students can take advantage of close ties to area businesses for internships and work co-op programs, which provide valuable on-the-job experience.

Majors and Degrees

The College of Arts and Sciences offers majors in Africana studies, American studies, anthropology, biology, chemistry, computer information systems, computer science, earth science, economics, English, environmental studies, French, geography, geology, German, history, information technology, Italian, journalism, mathematics, philosophy, physics/astronomy, political science, professional writing and editing, psychology, religious studies, social studies, sociology, and Spanish, as well as predentistry, preforestry, prelaw, premedicine, and pre–veterinary medicine.

The Beeghly College of Education offers majors in adolescent/young adult education (in specialized teaching fields), early and middle childhood education, multiage education (in specialized teaching fields), special education, and vocational education.

The Rayen College of Engineering and Technology offers majors in chemical engineering, civil engineering (structural and transportation option and environmental option), civil and construction engineering technology, drafting and design technology, electrical and computer engineering, electrical engineering technology, electric utility technology, industrial and systems engineering, mechanical engineering, mechanical engineering technology, and power-plant technology.

The College of Fine and Performing Arts offers majors in studio art, art history, music/history and literature, music education, music/performance, music theory, music composition, communications studies, telecommunication studies, and theater.

The Bitonte College of Health and Human Services offers majors in allied health, Army and Air Force ROTC, clinical laboratory science, clinical laboratory technology, community health, criminal justice, dental hygiene, dietetic technology, emergency medical technology, family and consumer sciences education, exercise science, family and consumer studies, food and nutrition, histotechnology, hospitality management, medical assisting technology, merchandising (fashion and interiors), nursing, nursing home administration, physical education, prekindergarten, respiratory care, school health education, social service technology, and social work.

The Williamson College of Business Administration offers majors in accounting, advertising and public relations, business economics, finance, general administration, human resource management, management, management information systems, and marketing management. Associate degrees are offered with concentrations in accounting, finance, labor studies, management, and marketing.

Interdisciplinary minors are offered in gerontology, linguistics, peace and conflict studies, professional ethics, statistics, and women's studies.

Students may also enroll for a combined B.S./M.D. program with the Northeastern Ohio Universities College of Medicine. Each student successfully completing this program is awarded the Bachelor of Science degree from Youngstown State University and the M.D. degree from the College of Medicine.

Academic Programs

Youngstown State University is one of a few comprehensive metropolitan institutions in Ohio that provide associate, baccalaureate, and graduate instruction and continuing education in one location. Currently, the University offers a broad curriculum in the School of Graduate Studies and Research and six colleges: Arts and Sciences, Business Administration, Education, Engineering and Technology, Fine and Performing Arts, and Health and Human Services. The spirit of cooperation among departments and colleges permits students to pursue interdisciplinary majors and minors, to major in one department or college and minor in another, or to pursue double majors. Youngstown State University provides for a broad-based education through a core curriculum of 45 semester hours spread across five areas of concentration and emphasizing the development of writing, speaking, and critical-thinking skills. In addition to fulfilling this general education requirement, each student must complete the major and/or minor requirements and meet the semester hours required for the baccalaureate degree.

Application of associate degree credits to baccalaureate programs is possible within the University. Transfer and dual-admission agreements with two-year institutions and community colleges provide opportunities for transfer into baccalaureate programs at Youngstown State.

An individualized curriculum program is available to students whose needs are not met by existing conventional programs. Students may design curricula to suit their particular needs, allowing alternative paths for earning the undergraduate degrees currently offered.

Off-Campus Programs

YSU offers cooperative/internship education programs in which students participate in both classroom and experiential study via employment in a government, industry, or business setting. Opportunities for international studies for academic credit are available in several majors.

Academic Facilities

Maag Library houses more than a half-million books and more than 200,000 government documents and subscribes to more than 2,500 periodicals and scholarly journals. Online research services provide access to all state university libraries in Ohio and a wide range of other information sources. The library's resources are augmented by the Curriculum Resource Center in the College of Education. A Multimedia Center, housed in Maag Library, offers research materials in a variety of formats.

Comprehensive computing facilities are readily available to students throughout the campus. Scientific laboratories at YSU are fully outfitted with up-to-date instructional and research equipment. Studios and performance halls in the College of Fine and Performing Arts have been recently renovated for acoustic excellence, and the McDonough Museum of Art is an innovative exhibit space for student and faculty work.

Costs

Tuition and fees for an Ohio resident for the 2004 fall semester are $2941 for full-time (12–16 credits) attendance. For students residing in certain counties in New York, West Virginia, and western Pennsylvania, the out-of-state tuition surcharge is reduced, making the total semester cost $4177 for full-time attendance. The charge for University housing, including meals, is $6100 per year. The University estimates books and supplies at $860 per year, and on-campus parking is $68 per semester. Some laboratory and computer classes entail a lab/materials fee, ranging from $35 to $65. All fees and charges are subject to change.

Financial Aid

Financial aid is awarded in four basic forms: scholarships, grants, loans, and on-campus employment. Depending on the student's computed financial need, the award may include a package of any or all of these components in varying amounts. Financial aid applications should be submitted to the University by February 15 for fall-semester assistance and must be resubmitted each year. About 82 percent of Youngstown State's full-time students receive some form of financial aid through a comprehensive program that includes need-based and performance-based aid. Youngstown State prides itself on an exemplary scholarship program that rewards academic performance and promise. The University Scholars program provides full-cost scholarships for 160 high-achieving students, and numerous other scholarships are available under a wide range of criteria.

Faculty

Eighty percent of YSU's 360 full-time faculty members hold the highest degree in their field and most are engaged in active, cutting-edge research that they bring to their instruction. YSU classes are small—76 percent of undergraduate classes have fewer than 30 students—creating many opportunities for class discussion, projects, and interaction between faculty members and students.

Student Government

Student Government exercises the power to conduct student elections, to recommend student representatives to serve on joint faculty-student committees, and to supervise programs funded from its operating budget. Members are elected by the student body to executive positions and to the legislative branch in proportion to the enrollment in each college. Student Government nominates students for two nonvoting gubernatorial appointments to the University Board of Trustees.

Admission Requirements

Ohio residents and residents of Mercer and Lawrence Counties in Pennsylvania must have graduated from a public or chartered high school or passed the General Educational Development (GED) test. Home-schooled applicants should contact the Office of Undergraduate Admissions for information. Nonresidents must have graduated from a public or chartered high school and be ranked in the upper two thirds of their high school class, have a minimum ACT composite score of 17 or a minimum combined SAT score of 820, or have passed the GED test. Transfer applicants must have earned at least a 2.0 accumulated point average and be in good standing at the last institution attended.

Application and Information

Application deadlines vary depending on the semester and the program for which a student is applying. Under the program, students who are admitted by February 15 become eligible for advance advisement and registration for fall classes. Applications must be accompanied by a nonrefundable fee. For more information and an application, students should contact:

Undergraduate Admissions
Youngstown State University
One University Plaza
Youngstown, Ohio 44555
Telephone: 330-941-2000
           330-941-1564 (TTY/TDD)
           877-468-6978 (toll-free)
Fax: 330-941-3674
E-mail: enroll@ysu.edu
World Wide Web: http://www.ysu.edu

YSU's beautiful, safe campus provides a pleasant backdrop for the students' college experience.

Profiles and In-Depth Descriptions of Other Colleges to Consider

Alabama

THE UNIVERSITY OF ALABAMA IN HUNTSVILLE

Huntsville, Alabama

UAH is a coed, public unit of University of Alabama System, founded in 1950, offering degrees at the bachelor's, master's, and doctoral levels and post-master's and postbachelor's certificates. It has a 376-acre campus in Huntsville.

Academic Information The faculty has 447 members (62% full-time), 71% with terminal degrees. The undergraduate student-faculty ratio is 16:1. The library holds 277,878 titles, 1,120 serial subscriptions, and 2,677 audiovisual materials. Special programs include academic remediation, services for learning-disabled students, an honors program, cooperative (work-study) education, advanced placement credit, accelerated degree programs, ESL programs, double majors, independent study, distance learning, summer session for credit, part-time degree programs (daytime, evenings, summer), adult/continuing education programs, internships, and arrangement for off-campus study with Alabama Agricultural and Mechanical University, Oakwood College, Athens State College, John C. Calhoun State Community College. The most frequently chosen baccalaureate fields are business/marketing, engineering/engineering technologies, health professions and related sciences.

Student Body Statistics The student body totals 7,051, of whom 5,481 are undergraduates (798 freshmen). 49 percent are women and 51 percent are men. Students come from 45 states and territories and 55 other countries. 86 percent are from Alabama. 3 percent are international students.

Expenses for 2003–04 *Application fee:* $20. *Area resident tuition:* $926 per term part-time. *State resident tuition:* $4126 full-time, $926 per term part-time. *Nonresident tuition:* $8702 full-time, $1945 per term part-time. Full-time tuition varies according to course load. Part-time tuition varies according to course load. *College room and board:* $5000. *College room only:* $3400. Room and board charges vary according to board plan and housing facility.

Financial Aid Forms of aid include need-based and non-need-based scholarships, athletic grants, and part-time jobs. The average aided 2003–04 undergraduate received an aid package worth an estimated $5560. The application deadline for financial aid is July 31 with a priority deadline of April 1.

Freshman Admission UAH requires a high school transcript, SAT I or ACT scores, and TOEFL scores for international students. The application deadline for regular admission is August 15.

Entrance Difficulty UAH assesses its entrance difficulty level as moderately difficult. For the fall 2003 freshman class, 88 percent of the applicants were accepted.

For Further Information Contact Ms. Ginger Reed, Senior Associate Director of Admissions, The University of Alabama in Huntsville, 301 Sparkman Drive, Huntsville, AL 35899. *Telephone:* 256-824-6426 or 800-UAH-CALL (toll-free). *Fax:* 256-824-6073. *E-mail:* admitme@email.uah.edu. *Web site:* http://www.uah.edu/.

See page 382 for a narrative description.

Florida

FLORIDA GULF COAST UNIVERSITY

Fort Myers, Florida

FGCU is a coed, public, comprehensive unit of State University System of Florida, founded in 1991, offering degrees at the associate, bachelor's, and master's levels. It has a 760-acre campus in Fort Myers.

Academic Information The faculty has 402 members (48% full-time). The undergraduate student-faculty ratio is 16:1. The library holds 282,357 titles, 1,429 serial subscriptions, and 2,421 audiovisual materials. Special programs include academic remediation, services for learning-disabled students, an honors program, cooperative (work-study) education, study abroad, advanced placement credit, accelerated degree programs, double majors, independent study, distance learning, summer session for credit, part-time degree programs (daytime, evenings, weekends, summer), internships, and arrangement for off-campus study. The most frequently chosen baccalaureate fields are business/marketing, education, liberal arts/general studies.

Student Body Statistics The student body totals 5,972, of whom 4,836 are undergraduates (880 freshmen). 63 percent are women and 37 percent are men. Students come from 34 states and territories. 97 percent are from Florida. 0.8 percent are international students.

Expenses for 2003–04 *Application fee:* $30. *State resident tuition:* $2850 full-time, $95 per credit part-time. *Nonresident tuition:* $13,200 full-time, $440 per credit part-time. *Mandatory fees:* $71 full-time, $35.50 per term part-time. Full-time tuition and fees vary according to course load. Part-time tuition and fees vary according to course load. *College room and board:* $8000. *College room only:* $4220. Room and board charges vary according to board plan.

Financial Aid Forms of aid include need-based and non-need-based scholarships, athletic grants, and part-time jobs. The average aided 2002–03 undergraduate received an aid package worth $6313. The application deadline for financial aid is continuous.

Freshman Admission FGCU requires a high school transcript, a minimum 2.0 high school GPA, SAT I or ACT scores, and TOEFL scores for international students. An essay, recommendations, and an interview are required for some. The application deadline for regular admission is March 1.

Transfer Admission The application deadline for admission is rolling.

Entrance Difficulty FGCU assesses its entrance difficulty level as moderately difficult. For the fall 2003 freshman class, 72 percent of the applicants were accepted.

SPECIAL MESSAGE TO STUDENTS

Social Life At Florida Gulf Coast University (FGCU), students may choose from more than 100 clubs, including academic, service, social, and Greek letter; special interest groups; and choral, dance, and theater groups. The Student Government Association (SGA) sponsors popular concerts, including ones hosted by MTV, as well as comedy jams. The SGA also manages campus issues. Residential students enjoy fully furnished apartment style suites with living room, kitchen, bedrooms, and bathrooms. Lakefront campus housing hosts canoeing, kayaking, and waterskiing. Collegiate athletics, intramural sports, and the Wellness Center are integral to campus life.

Academic Highlights Built in 1997, FGCU is one of the most modern, attractive, and technologically advanced campuses in the world. Students are excited about the curriculum emphasis on environmental sustainability and the opportunity to conduct research under the encouraging direction of nationally recruited top professors in their field. In the Survey of Student Engagement, FGCU students rated their active learning experience in the top seventh percentile nationally. Small classes and academic support programs help to ensure academic success. The student-faculty ratio is 18:1. Within the first six months of graduation, 92 percent of FGCU students are employed.

Interviews and Campus Visits Students are invited to visit FGCU in Fort Myers. Campus tours are available daily; reservations are strongly encouraged. Because of its location in southwest Florida and its newness, the campus is extraordinarily accessible to the physically disabled. While interviews and essays are not generally required for admission, a personal statement attached to the application is encouraged and influences admission decisions. The FGCU campus is located on 760 acres of wetlands and uplands that serve as a laboratory for the required environmental colloquium. Lee Transit provides access to downtown Fort Myers, the site of the historic Thomas Edison and Henry Ford Winter Estates museums. FGCU is within easy traveling distance to Gulf beaches, Everglades National Park, Sanibel Island, and Key West. For additional information and to schedule a visit, prospective students should call the Office of Admissions at 239-590-7878 or 888-889-1095 (toll-free), Monday through Friday, 8:00 a.m. to 5:30 p.m. The nearest commercial airport is Southwest Florida International.

For Further Information Write to Margaret S. Sugden Welcome Center, Florida Gulf Coast University, 10501 FGCU Boulevard, Fort Myers, FL 33965-6565. *E-mail:* admissions@fgcu.edu. *Web site:* http://www.fgcu.edu.

UNIVERSITY OF WEST FLORIDA
Pensacola, Florida

UWF is a coed, public, comprehensive unit of State University System of Florida, founded in 1963, offering degrees at the associate, bachelor's, master's, and doctoral levels. It has a 1,600-acre campus in Pensacola.

Academic Information The faculty has 479 members (52% full-time). The undergraduate student-faculty ratio is 22:1. The library holds 414,418 titles, 3,236 serial subscriptions, and 4,303 audiovisual materials. Special programs include services for learning-disabled students, an honors program, cooperative (work-study) education, study abroad, advanced placement credit, ESL programs, independent study, distance learning, summer session for credit, part-time degree programs (daytime, evenings, summer), internships, and arrangement for off-campus study with other members of the State University System of Florida. The most frequently chosen baccalaureate fields are business/marketing, education, protective services/public administration.

Student Body Statistics The student body totals 9,452, of whom 7,911 are undergraduates (940 freshmen). 59 percent are women and 41 percent are men. Students come from 49 states and territories and 85 other countries. 87 percent are from Florida. 1 percent are international students.

Expenses for 2003–04 *Application fee:* $20. *State resident tuition:* $1902 full-time, $63.41 per semester hour part-time. *Nonresident tuition:* $12,930 full-time, $431.01 per semester hour part-time. *Mandatory fees:* $953 full-time, $31.78 per semester hour part-time. Full-time tuition and fees vary according to location. Part-time tuition and fees vary according to location. *College room and board:* $6000. Room and board charges vary according to housing facility.

Financial Aid Forms of aid include need-based and non-need-based scholarships, athletic grants, and part-time jobs. The application deadline for financial aid is continuous.

Freshman Admission UWF requires a high school transcript, a minimum 2.0 high school GPA, SAT I or ACT scores, and TOEFL scores for international students. The application deadline for regular admission is June 30.

Transfer Admission The application deadline for admission is June 30.

Entrance Difficulty UWF assesses its entrance difficulty level as moderately difficult; noncompetitive for applicants with associate degrees from Florida public junior colleges. For the fall 2003 freshman class, 66 percent of the applicants were accepted.

For Further Information Contact Mr. Richard M. Hulett, Director of Admissions, University of West Florida, Admissions, 11000 University Parkway, Pensacola, FL 32514. *Telephone:* 850-474-2230 or 800-263-1074 (toll-free). *Fax:* 850-474-2096. *E-mail:* admissions@uwf.edu. *Web site:* http://uwf.edu/.

See page 386 for a narrative description.

Kentucky

BRESCIA UNIVERSITY
Owensboro, Kentucky

Brescia is a coed, private, Roman Catholic, comprehensive institution, founded in 1950, offering degrees at the associate, bachelor's, and master's levels. It has a 9-acre campus in Owensboro.

Academic Information The faculty has 72 members. The undergraduate student-faculty ratio is 14:1. The library holds 2,466 serial subscriptions and 6,717 audiovisual materials. Special programs include academic remediation, services for learning-disabled students, an honors program, study abroad, advanced placement credit, ESL programs, double majors, independent study, self-designed majors, summer session for credit, part-time degree programs (daytime, weekends, summer), adult/continuing education programs, internships, and arrangement for off-campus study with Kentucky Wesleyan College. The most frequently chosen baccalaureate fields are business/marketing, education, protective services/public administration.

Student Body Statistics The student body totals 790. Students come from 18 states and territories and 19 other countries. 84 percent are from Kentucky. 5.4 percent are international students.

Expenses for 2003–04 *Application fee:* $25. *Comprehensive fee:* $15,620 includes full-time tuition ($10,600), mandatory fees ($220), and college room and board ($4800). *College room only:* $3600. Room and board charges vary according to board plan and housing facility. *Part-time tuition:* varies with course load.

Financial Aid Forms of aid include need-based and non-need-based scholarships, athletic grants, and part-time jobs. The average aided 2002–03 undergraduate received an aid package worth $6494. The priority application deadline for financial aid is March 1.

Freshman Admission Brescia requires an essay, a high school transcript, a minimum 2.5 high school GPA, SAT I or ACT scores, and TOEFL scores for international students. 1 recommendation and an interview are required for some. The application deadline for regular admission is rolling.

Transfer Admission The application deadline for admission is rolling.

Entrance Difficulty Brescia assesses its entrance difficulty level as moderately difficult. For the fall 2003 freshman class, 80 percent of the applicants were accepted.

For Further Information Write to Admissions Office, 811 Frederica Street, Owensboro, KY 42301. *E-mail:* admissions@brescia.edu.

See page 368 for a narrative description.

CUMBERLAND COLLEGE
Williamsburg, Kentucky

Cumberland is a coed, private, Kentucky Baptist, comprehensive institution, founded in 1889, offering degrees at the associate, bachelor's, and master's levels. It has a 50-acre campus in Williamsburg near Knoxville.

Academic Information The faculty has 96 members (93% full-time), 64% with terminal degrees. The undergraduate student-faculty ratio is 16:1. The library holds 191,701 titles, 3,655 serial subscriptions, and 7,043 audiovisual materials. Special programs include academic remediation, an honors program, cooperative (work-study) education, study abroad, advanced placement credit, accelerated degree programs, Freshman Honors College, double majors, independent study, distance learning, self-designed majors, summer session for credit, part-time degree programs (daytime, evenings, summer), adult/continuing education programs, and internships. The most frequently chosen baccalaureate fields are business/marketing, biological/life sciences, education.

Student Body Statistics The student body totals 1,727, of whom 1,604 are undergraduates (414 freshmen). 53 percent are women and 47 percent are men. Students come from 36 states and territories and 21 other

Cumberland College (continued)

countries. 61 percent are from Kentucky. 2 percent are international students. 29 percent of the 2003 graduating class went on to graduate and professional schools.

Expenses for 2004–05 *Application fee:* $30. *Comprehensive fee:* $16,984 includes full-time tuition ($11,498), mandatory fees ($360), and college room and board ($5126). *Part-time tuition:* varies with course load.

Financial Aid Forms of aid include need-based and non-need-based scholarships, athletic grants, and part-time jobs. The average aided 2003–04 undergraduate received an aid package worth an estimated $12,416. The priority application deadline for financial aid is March 1.

Freshman Admission Cumberland requires an essay, a high school transcript, a minimum 2.0 high school GPA, 1 recommendation, and SAT I or ACT scores. An interview and TOEFL scores for international students are recommended. The application deadline for regular admission is rolling.

Entrance Difficulty Cumberland assesses its entrance difficulty level as moderately difficult. For the fall 2003 freshman class, 72 percent of the applicants were accepted.

For Further Information Contact Mrs. Erica Harris, Director of Admissions, Cumberland College, 6178 College Station Drive, Williamsburg, KY 40769. *Telephone:* 606-539-4201 or 800-343-1609 (toll-free). *Fax:* 606-539-4303. *E-mail:* admiss@cumberlandcollege.edu. *Web site:* http://www.cumberlandcollege.edu/.

See page 374 for a narrative description.

TRANSYLVANIA UNIVERSITY
Lexington, Kentucky

Transylvania is a coed, private, four-year college, founded in 1780, affiliated with the Christian Church (Disciples of Christ), offering degrees at the bachelor's level. It has a 35-acre campus in Lexington near Cincinnati and Louisville.

Academic Information The faculty has 91 members (87% full-time), 80% with terminal degrees. The student-faculty ratio is 13:1. The library holds 93,019 titles, 500 serial subscriptions, and 1,860 audiovisual materials. Special programs include study abroad, advanced placement credit, double majors, independent study, self-designed majors, summer session for credit, part-time degree programs (daytime), internships, and arrangement for off-campus study with Washington Center for Internships and Academic Seminars, Kentucky Institute for International Studies. The most frequently chosen baccalaureate fields are business/marketing, psychology, social sciences and history.

Student Body Statistics The student body is made up of 1,134 undergraduates (300 freshmen). 57 percent are women and 43 percent are men. Students come from 32 states and territories and 3 other countries. 80 percent are from Kentucky. 0.3 percent are international students. 32 percent of the 2003 graduating class went on to graduate and professional schools.

Expenses for 2003–04 *Application fee:* $30. *Comprehensive fee:* $23,780 includes full-time tuition ($17,010), mandatory fees ($650), and college room and board ($6120). *College room only:* $3420. Room and board charges vary according to board plan and location. *Part-time tuition:* $1890 per course. *Part-time mandatory fees:* $70 per course.

Financial Aid Forms of aid include need-based and non-need-based scholarships and part-time jobs. The average aided 2003–04 undergraduate received an aid package worth an estimated $15,115. The priority application deadline for financial aid is March 1.

Freshman Admission Transylvania requires an essay, a high school transcript, a minimum 2.75 high school GPA, 2 recommendations, SAT I or ACT scores, and TOEFL scores for international students. An interview is recommended. An interview is required for some. The application deadline for regular admission is February 1 and for early action it is December 1.

Transfer Admission The application deadline for admission is rolling.

Entrance Difficulty Transylvania assesses its entrance difficulty level as very difficult. For the fall 2003 freshman class, 88 percent of the applicants were accepted.

For Further Information Contact Ms. Sarah Coen, Director of Admissions, Transylvania University, 300 North Broadway, Lexington, KY 40508-1797. *Telephone:* 859-233-8242 or 800-872-6798 (toll-free). *Fax:* 859-233-8797. *E-mail:* admissions@transy.edu. *Web site:* http://www.transy.edu/.

See page 380 for a narrative description.

Louisiana

UNIVERSITY OF NEW ORLEANS
New Orleans, Louisiana

UNO is a coed, public unit of Louisiana State University System, founded in 1958, offering degrees at the bachelor's, master's, and doctoral levels and postbachelor's certificates. It has a 345-acre campus in New Orleans.

Academic Information The faculty has 598 members (82% full-time), 65% with terminal degrees. The undergraduate student-faculty ratio is 26:1. The library holds 896,000 titles, 4,950 serial subscriptions, and 125,600 audiovisual materials. Special programs include academic remediation, services for learning-disabled students, an honors program, cooperative (work-study) education, study abroad, advanced placement credit, ESL programs, double majors, independent study, distance learning, self-designed majors, summer session for credit, part-time degree programs, adult/continuing education programs, internships, and arrangement for off-campus study with Southern University at New Orleans, Delgado Community College, Nunez Community College. The most frequently chosen baccalaureate fields are business/marketing, education, liberal arts/general studies.

Student Body Statistics The student body totals 17,360, of whom 13,338 are undergraduates (2,284 freshmen). 56 percent are women and 44 percent are men. Students come from 50 states and territories and 69 other countries. 96 percent are from Louisiana. 2.6 percent are international students.

Expenses for 2004–05 *Application fee:* $20. *State resident tuition:* $3084 full-time, $488 per course part-time. *Nonresident tuition:* $10,128 full-time, $1826 per course part-time. *Mandatory fees:* $150 full-time, $5 per semester hour part-time, $10 per term part-time. Part-time tuition and fees vary according to course load. *College room only:* $4122. Room charges vary according to housing facility.

Financial Aid Forms of aid include need-based and non-need-based scholarships, athletic grants, and part-time jobs. The average aided 2003–04 undergraduate received an aid package worth an estimated $3269. The priority application deadline for financial aid is May 15.

Freshman Admission UNO requires a high school transcript, SAT I or ACT scores, and TOEFL scores for international students. An essay, a minimum 2.0 high school GPA, 3 recommendations, an interview, and 2.0 high school GPA on high school core program are required for some. The application deadline for regular admission is rolling.

Transfer Admission The application deadline for admission is August 28.

Entrance Difficulty UNO assesses its entrance difficulty level as moderately difficult. For the fall 2003 freshman class, 70 percent of the applicants were accepted.

For Further Information Contact Ms. Roslyn S. Sheley, Director of Admissions, University of New Orleans, Lake Front, New Orleans, LA 70148. *Telephone:* 504-280-7013 or 800-256-5866 (toll-free out-of-state). *Fax:* 504-280-5522. *E-mail:* admissions@uno.edu. *Web site:* http://www.uno.edu/.

See page 384 for a narrative description.

New York

CLARKSON UNIVERSITY

Potsdam, New York

Clarkson is a coed, private university, founded in 1896, offering degrees at the bachelor's, master's, and doctoral levels. It has a 640-acre campus in Potsdam.

Academic Information The faculty has 199 members (90% full-time), 84% with terminal degrees. The undergraduate student-faculty ratio is 17:1. The library holds 272,204 titles, 1,656 serial subscriptions, and 2,004 audiovisual materials. Special programs include services for learning-disabled students, an honors program, cooperative (work-study) education, study abroad, advanced placement credit, accelerated degree programs, ESL programs, double majors, independent study, self-designed majors, summer session for credit, part-time degree programs (daytime, summer), internships, and arrangement for off-campus study with Associated Colleges of the St. Lawrence Valley. The most frequently chosen baccalaureate fields are business/marketing, engineering/engineering technologies, interdisciplinary studies.

Student Body Statistics The student body totals 3,105, of whom 2,723 are undergraduates (721 freshmen). 24 percent are women and 76 percent are men. Students come from 39 states and territories and 33 other countries. 77 percent are from New York. 2.6 percent are international students. 29 percent of the 2003 graduating class went on to graduate and professional schools.

Expenses for 2004–05 *Application fee:* $30. *Comprehensive fee:* $33,208 includes full-time tuition ($24,100), mandatory fees ($40), and college room and board ($9068). *College room only:* $4728. Full-time tuition and fees vary according to course load. Room and board charges vary according to housing facility. *Part-time tuition:* $803 per credit. Part-time tuition varies according to course load.

Financial Aid Forms of aid include need-based and non-need-based scholarships, athletic grants, and part-time jobs. The average aided 2003–04 undergraduate received an aid package worth an estimated $16,730. The priority application deadline for financial aid is March 1.

Freshman Admission Clarkson requires a high school transcript, 1 recommendation, SAT I or ACT scores, and TOEFL scores for international students. An interview and SAT II: Subject Test scores are recommended. The application deadline for regular admission is March 15; for early decision plan 1 it is December 1; and for early decision plan 2 it is January 15.

Entrance Difficulty Clarkson assesses its entrance difficulty level as very difficult. For the fall 2003 freshman class, 81 percent of the applicants were accepted.

SPECIAL MESSAGE TO STUDENTS

Social Life Clarkson offers more than 100 clubs and organizations, a 640-acre tree-covered campus, and 600 major cultural or educational events within a 10-mile radius of the campus each year. More than 75 percent of Clarkson students participate in extracurricular activities, and the 6-million-acre Adirondack Park is only minutes away.

Academic Highlights Academics at Clarkson emphasize team project–based learning, hands-on undergraduate research, mastery of technology, and interdisciplinary perspectives. All degree programs develop communication and collaboration skills, with a focus on practical application of knowledge and creative, open-ended problem solving. Every student majoring in business, for example, gains first-hand experience by actually running a business. Undergraduates customize programs through specialized concentrations and minors that broaden career options. Clarkson's relatively small size encourages personal attention and interactions between students and faculty members, flexibility, and interdisciplinary collaboration in learning and research. Strong advising is a hallmark of the academic environment. The

University offers an honors program for high-achieving students, an accelerated three-year bachelor's degree, and co-op education with industry, structured so that participants graduate in four years.

Interviews and Campus Visits Although an interview is not required, Clarkson strongly recommends that students visit the campus and take part in an admission interview. This interview provides an opportunity for an informal exchange of information between the student and an admission staff member. These students are then much better prepared to assess how Clarkson can benefit them. Any student who visits the campus for an interview with an admission counselor receives a fee-waived voucher for a Clarkson application. Clarkson is located in the friendly community of Potsdam, between the beautiful Adirondack Mountains and the St. Lawrence River. The scenic, open campus offers a blend of old and new architecture. New buildings include the Center for Advanced Materials Processing, a new state-of-the-art building for business and liberal arts, and the Cheel Student Center, a combination student union and multipurpose arena facility. There are many prominent sandstone buildings in the community, and the storefronts in Potsdam are an attractive Victorian style. There are also several other colleges in the area. For information about appointments and campus visits, students should call the Office of Undergraduate Admission at 315-268-6479 or 6480 or 800-527-6577 (toll-free), Monday through Friday, 9 a.m. to 4 p.m., or Saturday, 10 a.m. to 2 p.m. The office is located in Holcroft House on campus. The nearest commercial airport is Syracuse-Hancock International.

For Further Information Write to Mr. Brian Grant, Director of Admission, Clarkson University, P.O. Box 5605, Potsdam, NY 13699-5605. *E-mail:* admission@clarkson.edu. *Web site:* http://www.clarkson.edu.

See page 370 for a narrative description.

North Carolina

NORTH CAROLINA AGRICULTURAL AND TECHNICAL STATE UNIVERSITY

Greensboro, North Carolina

North Carolina A&T is a coed, public unit of University of North Carolina System, founded in 1891, offering degrees at the bachelor's, master's, and doctoral levels. It has a 191-acre campus in Greensboro.

Academic Information The faculty has 458 members. The undergraduate student-faculty ratio is 17:1. The library holds 527,252 titles, 5,515 serial subscriptions, and 35,446 audiovisual materials. Special programs include academic remediation, services for learning-disabled students, an honors program, cooperative (work-study) education, study abroad, advanced placement credit, summer session for credit, part-time degree programs (daytime, evenings, summer), adult/continuing education programs, internships, and arrangement for off-campus study with University of North Carolina at Greensboro, Guilford College, Bennett College, High Point University, Greensboro College.

Student Body Statistics The student body totals 8,319, of whom 7,331 are undergraduates (1,771 freshmen). 52 percent are women and 48 percent are men. Students come from 42 states and territories. 80 percent are from North Carolina. 0.8 percent are international students.

Expenses for 2003–04 *Application fee:* $35. *State resident tuition:* $1544 full-time, $64 per credit part-time. *Nonresident tuition:* $10,911 full-time, $455 per credit part-time. *Mandatory fees:* $1178 full-time. *College room and board:* $4968. *College room only:* $2768.

Financial Aid Forms of aid include need-based and non-need-based scholarships, athletic grants, and part-time jobs. The average aided 2003–04 undergraduate received an aid package worth an estimated $5098. The priority application deadline for financial aid is March 15.

Freshman Admission North Carolina A&T requires a high school transcript, a minimum 2.0 high school GPA, and TOEFL scores for international students. SAT I or ACT scores are recommended. The application deadline for regular admission is June 1.

North Carolina Agricultural and Technical State University (continued)

Transfer Admission The application deadline for admission is June 1.
Entrance Difficulty North Carolina A&T assesses its entrance difficulty level as moderately difficult. For the fall 2003 freshman class, 81 percent of the applicants were accepted.

For Further Information Contact Mr. John Smith, Director of Admissions, North Carolina Agricultural and Technical State University, 1601 East Market Street, Webb Hall, Greensboro, NC 27411. *Telephone:* 336-334-7946 or 800-443-8964 (toll-free in-state). *Fax:* 336-334-7478. *E-mail:* uadmit@ncat.edu. *Web site:* http://www.ncat.edu/.

See page 378 for a narrative description.

Pennsylvania

GANNON UNIVERSITY

Erie, Pennsylvania

Gannon is a coed, private, Roman Catholic, comprehensive institution, founded in 1925, offering degrees at the associate, bachelor's, master's, and doctoral levels and post-master's and postbachelor's certificates. It has a 13-acre campus in Erie near Cleveland.

Academic Information The faculty has 285 members (59% full-time), 43% with terminal degrees. The undergraduate student-faculty ratio is 11:1. The library holds 257,670 titles, 9,389 serial subscriptions, and 2,274 audiovisual materials. Special programs include academic remediation, services for learning-disabled students, an honors program, cooperative (work-study) education, study abroad, advanced placement credit, accelerated degree programs, ESL programs, double majors, independent study, distance learning, summer session for credit, part-time degree programs (daytime, evenings, weekends, summer), external degree programs, adult/continuing education programs, internships, and arrangement for off-campus study with Mercyhurst College and Edinboro University. The most frequently chosen baccalaureate fields are business/marketing, education, health professions and related sciences.
Student Body Statistics The student body totals 3,459, of whom 2,435 are undergraduates (613 freshmen). 58 percent are women and 42 percent are men. Students come from 29 states and territories and 20 other countries. 81 percent are from Pennsylvania. 1.4 percent are international students. 22 percent of the 2003 graduating class went on to graduate and professional schools.
Expenses for 2004–05 *Application fee:* $25. *Comprehensive fee:* $24,570 includes full-time tuition ($17,030), mandatory fees ($470), and college room and board ($7070). *College room only:* $3840. Full-time tuition and fees vary according to class time and program. Room and board charges vary according to board plan and housing facility. *Part-time tuition:* $530 per credit. *Part-time mandatory fees:* $15 per credit. Part-time tuition and fees vary according to class time and program.
Financial Aid Forms of aid include need-based and non-need-based scholarships, athletic grants, and part-time jobs. The average aided 2003–04 undergraduate received an aid package worth an estimated $12,740. The priority application deadline for financial aid is March 15.
Freshman Admission Gannon requires a high school transcript, a minimum 2.0 high school GPA, counselor's recommendation, SAT I or ACT scores, and TOEFL scores for international students. An essay is recommended. A minimum 3.0 high school GPA, 3 recommendations, and an interview are required for some. The application deadline for regular admission is rolling.
Transfer Admission The application deadline for admission is rolling.
Entrance Difficulty Gannon assesses its entrance difficulty level as moderately difficult. For the fall 2003 freshman class, 84 percent of the applicants were accepted.

SPECIAL MESSAGE TO STUDENTS

Social Life Gannon's location on the shores of Lake Erie in Pennsylvania's fourth-largest city, Erie, provides something for everyone to enjoy. On campus, students can attend everything from plays, movies, and dances to athletic events. They also take advantage of cultural events and local Erie entertainment. Students may participate in fraternities and sororities, governing groups, academic clubs and organizations, and intercollegiate and intramural sports programs.

Academic Highlights Gannon's friendly academic environment, coupled with a low student-to-faculty ratio of 13:1, fosters achievement. Students can choose from a variety of majors offered in business, humanities, education, science and engineering, and health sciences. Students enrich their education with professional experience offered through summer field courses; studies abroad; local, regional, and national co-ops; and internships. Advanced technologies, like wireless computing, Web-based services, and networked classrooms, enable students to experience cutting-edge technology.

Interviews and Campus Visits The Office of Admissions schedules appointments year-round, Monday through Friday, from 9 a.m. to 3 p.m., and group presentations on select Saturday mornings at 10 a.m. During a campus visit, students can meet with an admissions representative, professors in their intended major, and financial aid representatives. Campus visits also include a campus tour. To schedule a campus visit, prospective students should call 800-GANNON-U (800-426-6668) Ext. 7407.

For Further Information Write to Mr. Christopher Tremblay, Director of Admissions, Gannon University, 109 University Square, Erie, PA 16541. *E-mail:* admissions@gannon.edu. *Web site:* http://www.gannon.edu.

LEHIGH UNIVERSITY

Bethlehem, Pennsylvania

Lehigh is a coed, private university, founded in 1865, offering degrees at the bachelor's, master's, and doctoral levels and post-master's certificates. It has a 1,600-acre campus in Bethlehem near Philadelphia.

Academic Information The faculty has 547 members (79% full-time). The undergraduate student-faculty ratio is 10:1. The library holds 1 million titles, 6,271 serial subscriptions, and 8,415 audiovisual materials. Special programs include services for learning-disabled students, an honors program, cooperative (work-study) education, study abroad, advanced placement credit, accelerated degree programs, ESL programs, double majors, independent study, distance learning, summer session for credit, external degree programs, adult/continuing education programs, internships, and arrangement for off-campus study with members of the Lehigh Valley Association of Independent Colleges, American University. The most frequently chosen baccalaureate fields are business/marketing, engineering/engineering technologies, social sciences and history.
Student Body Statistics The student body totals 6,732, of whom 4,679 are undergraduates (1,125 freshmen). 40 percent are women and 60 percent are men. Students come from 52 states and territories. 32 percent are from Pennsylvania. 2.8 percent are international students. 32 percent of the 2003 graduating class went on to graduate and professional schools.
Expenses for 2004–05 *Application fee:* $60. *Comprehensive fee:* $37,570 includes full-time tuition ($29,140), mandatory fees ($200), and college room and board ($8230). *College room only:* $4700. Room and board charges vary according to board plan and student level. *Part-time tuition:* $1215 per credit.
Financial Aid Forms of aid include need-based and non-need-based scholarships, athletic grants, and part-time jobs. The average aided 2003–04 undergraduate received an aid package worth an estimated $23,533. The application deadline for financial aid is February 1.
Freshman Admission Lehigh requires a high school transcript, 1 recommendation, a graded writing sample, SAT I or ACT scores, and TOEFL scores for international students. An essay, an interview, and SAT II: Subject Test scores are recommended. The application deadline for regular admission is January 1; for early decision plan 1 it is November 15; and for early decision plan 2 it is February 1.

Transfer Admission The application deadline for admission is April 1.

Entrance Difficulty Lehigh assesses its entrance difficulty level as most difficult. For the fall 2003 freshman class, 40 percent of the applicants were accepted.

For Further Information Contact Mr. J. Bruce Gardiner, Interim Dean of Admissions and Financial Aid, Lehigh University, 27 Memorial Drive West, Bethlehem, PA 18015. *Telephone:* 610-758-3100. *Fax:* 610-758-4361. *E-mail:* admissions@lehigh.edu. *Web site:* http://www.lehigh.edu/.

See page 376 for a narrative description.

West Virginia

CONCORD COLLEGE
Athens, West Virginia

Concord is a coed, public, four-year college of State College System of West Virginia, founded in 1872, offering degrees at the associate, bachelor's, and master's levels. It has a 100-acre campus in Athens.

Academic Information The faculty has 189 members (52% full-time), 37% with terminal degrees. The undergraduate student-faculty ratio is 21:1. The library holds 150,151 titles, 227 serial subscriptions, and 4,060 audiovisual materials. Special programs include academic remediation, services for learning-disabled students, an honors program, study abroad, advanced placement credit, accelerated degree programs, ESL programs, double majors, independent study, distance learning, self-designed majors, summer session for credit, part-time degree programs (daytime, evenings, weekends, summer), external degree programs, internships, and arrangement for off-campus study. The most frequently chosen baccalaureate fields are business/marketing, education, social sciences and history.

Student Body Statistics The student body totals 3,026, of whom 2,933 are undergraduates. Students come from 27 states and territories and 14 other countries. 85 percent are from West Virginia.

Expenses for 2003–04 *Application fee:* $0. *State resident tuition:* $3198 full-time, $133 per credit hour part-time. *Nonresident tuition:* $7278 full-time, $303 per credit hour part-time. Full-time tuition varies according to course load. Part-time tuition varies according to course load. *College room and board:* $4938. *College room only:* $2284.

Financial Aid Forms of aid include need-based and non-need-based scholarships, athletic grants, and part-time jobs. The average aided 2003–04 undergraduate received an aid package worth an estimated $6321. The priority application deadline for financial aid is April 15.

Freshman Admission Concord requires a high school transcript, a minimum 2.0 high school GPA, SAT I or ACT scores, and TOEFL scores for international students. An interview and ACT scores are recommended. An essay and an interview are required for some. The application deadline for regular admission is rolling and for nonresidents it is January 15.

Transfer Admission The application deadline for admission is rolling.

Entrance Difficulty Concord assesses its entrance difficulty level as minimally difficult. For the fall 2003 freshman class, 63 percent of the applicants were accepted.

For Further Information Contact Mr. Michael Curry, Vice President of Admissions and Financial Aid, Concord College, 1000 Vermillion Street, Athens, WV 24712. *Telephone:* 304-384-5248 or 888-384-5249 (toll-free). *Fax:* 304-384-9044. *E-mail:* admissions@concord.edu. *Web site:* http://www.concord.edu/.

See page 372 for a narrative description.

BRESCIA UNIVERSITY
OWENSBORO, KENTUCKY

The University

Brescia University prepares its students for successful careers and for service to others. Brescia was founded by the Ursuline Sisters of Mount Saint Joseph in 1950 as a Catholic liberal arts college. It began as the Mount Saint Joseph College for Women at Maple Mount, Kentucky, in 1925. The school is committed to the concept of value-centered education with a strong emphasis on Christian values. The Southern Association of Colleges and Schools accredits Brescia to award associate and baccalaureate degrees, the Master of Science in Management degree, and the Master of Science degree in curriculum and instruction. The University of Louisville offers the Master of Science in Social Work on Brescia's campus. Students pursuing their master's in social work may also complete their field placement work locally where it is convenient for them. All of Brescia's teacher education programs are accredited by the Kentucky Department of Education.

Currently, 790 students are enrolled at the University. Thirty-eight percent are men; 62 percent are women. The average age of full-time students is 23. The cosmopolitan student body comes from as far away as Canada, Cyprus, Japan, Venezuela, and the West Indies, as well as states from Alaska to California. About 74 percent of the students live off campus. Students can choose from a variety of extracurricular activities, including the *Brescia Broadcast* (student newspaper), the Brescia Owensboro Student Catholic Organization, the Locke Society (students with interests in political science and history), the Alpha Chi National Honor Society, the Delta Epsilon Sigma National Catholic Honor Society, the Brescia Student National Education Association, the International Student Organization, and the Ichabod Society (students with interests in all forms of literature). Students may also participate in the Student Government Association, the Brescia Philosophical Society, the Brescia Science Association, the Brescia Writers Group, the Council for Exceptional Children, the Handbell Choir, the Psychology Club, the Spanish Club, the National Speech Language Hearing Association, the Social Work Club, the Math and Computer Club, and the choir. The Brescia Little Theater performs dramatic productions in an intimate setting. The Parents in Action club is open to any student who is currently a parent. Students and faculty members may enjoy lunchtime concerts featuring jazz, blues, and chamber music. Campus facilities include an indoor walking track, a racquetball court, fitness facilities, weight room, and an attractively furnished Study Pavilion.

Location

Brescia University's 9-acre campus is located near downtown Owensboro, Kentucky. The University is just 45 minutes from Evansville, Indiana; 2 hours southwest of Louisville, Kentucky (home of the Kentucky Derby); and 2 hours north of Nashville, Tennessee.

Owensboro is well known as the "Barbecue Capital of the World." Owensboro has a Barbecue Festival in May and a Summer Festival. The Riverpark Center in Owensboro offers a multitude of productions like *Grease, Chicago,* and *Cats.* The Executive Inn Rivermont features nationally known entertainers like Tanya Tucker, Loretta Lynn, and Toby Keith. These events are within walking distance of Brescia's campus.

Majors and Degrees

Brescia University offers an Associate of Arts degree in catechetical leadership ministry, human relations, liberal arts, and pastoral ministry. Brescia also offers the Associate of Science degree in business, engineering studies, and engineering technology. The Bachelor of Arts degree offers a variety of study areas, including art, art education, English, English: emphasis in professional writing, graphic design, history, integrated studies, pastoral ministry, pre–art therapy, psychology, religious studies, social studies, and Spanish. Minors for the Bachelor of Arts degree may be chosen from the following: English, history, pastoral ministry, political science, psychology, religious studies, Spanish, sociology, and women's studies. Majors for the Bachelor of Science degree are accounting, biology, business, business: economics and finance emphasis, business: human resource development or management emphasis, chemistry, communication sciences and disorders, computer and mathematical sciences, early elementary education, general studies, mathematics, medical technology, middle grades education, science with an area of concentration, and special education. Minors for the Bachelor of Science degree are accounting, biology, business, chemistry, computer studies, finance/economics, mathematics, and physics. Brescia also offers the Bachelor of Social Work degree and a dual-degree program in chemistry/chemical engineering through the University of Louisville.

Teacher certification/endorsement is offered in the following areas: art education; early elementary education; middle grades and secondary (8–12) education in English, mathematics, science, social studies, and Spanish; and special education in the areas of learning and behavior disorders and moderate and severe disabilities. Candidates graduate with a license to teach in Kentucky schools. The license is reciprocal in some other states.

Academic Programs

There are two semesters at Brescia—fall and spring. Intersession is offered in May. A summer session is offered in June and in July. In addition, Brescia has a Weekend College program that is divided into four modules. Candidates for the associate degree must earn a minimum of 63 credit hours, with a minimum of 27 hours of general education requirements. Bachelor's degree candidates must earn a minimum of 128 credit hours, of which at least 42 credit hours are in upper-division courses. They must also complete 57 credit hours of general education courses and complete a major program of study, with a 2.5 (C) grade point average or better in all upper-division courses in the major and minor. A cumulative grade point average of at least 2.0 on a 4.0 scale must be achieved. The Center for English as a Second Language (ESL) at Brescia University offers a variety of both full-time and part-time English language courses. The two levels (intermediate and advanced) in the Intensive Summer Session are content-oriented courses that focus on speaking/listening, reading, writing, and the study skills necessary for academic success. Brescia graduates should be committed to the following values: continued personal, intellectual, and spiritual growth; the welfare of others; respect for the physical environment; and respect for the appreciation of the diversity in cultures. Brescia's Ministry Formation Program is the only accredited undergraduate program of its kind in the nation.

Academic Facilities

The Brescia University campus consists of seventeen buildings within a two-block area near downtown Owensboro. Facilities include the library, science building, administration building, campus center, graduate center, and residence halls. The library, campus center, and classroom buildings are accessible to people with disabilities. The library has more than 180,000 volumes and is fully automated, with access to the Kentucky Library Network (300 libraries). Biology and medical technology students view the human body through computer simulations with the powerful ADAM, while mathematics students graph 3-D space curves and solve large systems of equations with Mathematica. Computer science and physics students learn from state-of-the-art IBM hardware and software packages, including the ability to analyze experiments by digital imaging. There are five computer labs available for students on campus. Every student may receive access to the Internet and e-mail. Students in Brescia's modern language classes and the English as a second language program have access to a state-of-the-art digital computer lab.

Costs

Full-time tuition at Brescia is currently $10,600, which is well below the national average. Room and board costs vary; the cost of a double room and a ten-meal plan is $4600. A technology fee of $60 per semester is assessed for each student, and the activity fee is $100 per year. Other fees vary according to the student's course work but are typically $50. New books are estimated to cost about $650. A $100 deposit is required for housing.

Financial Aid

More than 85 percent of Brescia students receive scholarships or financial aid. Students receive aid through the many federal and state programs in which the University participates and through the University's deferred payment plan. Brescia also awards scholarships annually to incoming students on the basis of academic excellence and leadership qualities. Students who wish to be considered for financial aid should complete the Free Application for Federal Student Aid (FAFSA). Preference is given to applications received by March 1. Students may obtain the FAFSA by contacting their high school counselor or the University's Web site listed below.

Faculty

Brescia's faculty consists of 72 full- and part-time members. There are almost equal numbers of men and women, and the faculty includes both lay and religious members. More than 70 percent of the full-time faculty members have earned terminal degrees. A 14:1 student-faculty ratio assures students of individualized attention.

Student Government

Brescia students participate in University governance through the Student Government Association. They are represented on the Board of Trustees committees as well as various other committees.

Admission Requirements

Applications to Brescia are reviewed on an individual basis. Grades and course work receive strong consideration. College-preparatory and liberal arts courses are recommended. Standardized test scores are taken into consideration. Students are asked to submit a high school transcript, showing proof of graduation date, or GED score report and an ACT or SAT score report. Transfer students must submit official transcripts from each college they attended. The Test of English as a Foreign Language (TOEFL) is required for nonnative English speakers.

Application and Information

Applications are considered as they are received. Applications and transcripts should be submitted with a $25 nonrefundable application fee. Admission is on a rolling basis. Applications must be received by March 15 for scholarship consideration. Students may e-mail the admissions staff, individual counselors, and financial aid staff members through Brescia's Web site at the address below.

For further information, students and parents should contact:

Admissions
Brescia University
717 Frederica Street
Owensboro, Kentucky 42301
Telephone: 877-273-7242 (toll-free)
E-mail: admissions@brescia.edu
World Wide Web: http://www.brescia.edu

Brescia Quad in the spring.

CLARKSON UNIVERSITY

POTSDAM, NEW YORK

The University

Clarkson University, founded in 1896, is an independent technological university offering professional programs in business, engineering, liberal arts, and the sciences, including health sciences. Students benefit from a challenging, collaborative culture that develops the technical expertise, management skills, and versatility required in today's knowledge-based economy.

Clarkson has earned a reputation for developing innovative leaders in technology-based fields. It is also known for having a friendly campus where students enjoy personal attention. A rigorous curriculum emphasizes hands-on team projects and real-world, multidisciplinary challenges that develop skills in collaboration, communication, and creative problem solving. About 25 percent of the 2,725 undergraduates are women. Through a comprehensive Graduate School with 385 students, the University offers twenty-two master's degree and nine doctoral programs.

Many extracurricular activities are available to Clarkson students. Its more than 100 organizations include intercollegiate and intramural athletics, student publications (a newspaper and a yearbook), professional and honorary societies, outing club, pep band, jazz band, orchestra, religious clubs, chess club, amateur radio club, automotive association, and photo, drama, ski, cycle, bridge, rifle, international, outing, and table tennis clubs. The University's recreational facilities include a field house, with racquetball courts, a 3,000-square-foot fitness center, and a swimming pool, and a $13-million student center, including a 3,000-seat arena. An outdoor lodge was completed in 2000.

Location

Potsdam, New York (population 9,500), a college community, is located in the St. Lawrence River valley of northern New York. The community is the home of both Clarkson University and the State University of New York College at Potsdam. The village of Potsdam, with a combined student population approaching 7,000, is truly a college town. Students from both institutions attend events on either campus, and many combined social and cultural activities are scheduled during the year. Major international cities, such as Montreal, Quebec, and Ottawa, Ontario, are within a 2-hour drive.

Majors and Degrees

The Bachelor of Science degree is offered in aeronautical engineering, applied mathematics and statistics, biology, biomolecular science, business and technology management, chemical engineering, chemistry, civil engineering, computer engineering, computer science, e-business, electrical engineering, engineering and management, environmental science and policy, financial information and analysis, history, humanities, industrial hygiene–environmental toxicology (environmental and occupational health), information systems and business processes, liberal studies, mathematics, mechanical engineering, physical therapy (prephysical therapy leading to a master's degree), physics, political science, Project Aretè (liberal arts/business), psychology, social sciences, software engineering, and technical communications (telecommunications option). Choices that allow students to begin a general program and choose their major at a later date include business studies, engineering studies, science studies, and university studies. Clarkson offers both an honors program and an accelerated three-year bachelor's degree program. Special advising programs

are offered in prelaw, premedicine, and pre–physical therapy, a program in which the University offers a master's degree. Preprofessional programs are available in dentistry, law, medicine, physical therapy, and veterinary sciences.

Academic Programs

Programs are flexible at Clarkson, enabling undergraduates to customize their studies according to individual interests and goals. Today, many of the most profound advances in knowledge and social progress are occurring at the intersections of previously distinct academic disciplines. Building on a tradition of collaboration, the University has developed an increasing number of interdisciplinary majors, while promoting opportunities for specialization and customization through double majors, minors, concentrations, and electives. Each student must achieve a cumulative GPA of at least 2.0 to qualify for graduation and must earn at least 120 credit hours.

The innovative interdisciplinary programs at Clarkson reflect not only the high quality of faculty members and resources, but also the flexibility and vitality of the highly collaborative academic environment. The curriculum in the interdisciplinary engineering and management program, established in 1954, was the first of its kind to be accredited at any college or university in the nation. Other interdisciplinary degree programs include biomolecular science, environmental science and policy, industrial hygiene–environmental toxicology (environmental and occupational health), Project Aretè (a double major program in business and liberal arts), and software engineering.

Undergraduates in all majors also have opportunities to join multidisciplinary academic teams that compete against intercollegiate peers as they tackle creative problem-solving challenges. Students can choose among fourteen different teams at Clarkson, organized through a program called Student Projects for Engineering Experience and Design (SPEED).

Recent recognition of quality at Clarkson includes the following: winner of the 2002 IBM Linux Scholar Challenge, a worldwide open programming project-based competition; winner of the 2001 Boeing Outstanding Educator Award for its SPEED program; top-twenty ranking in supply chain management in the 2003 and 2004 *U.S. News & World Report*'s "Best Business Programs"; and finalist for the 2002 and 2003 National Undergraduate Entrepreneurship Education Award from the U.S. Association for Small Business Entrepreneurship.

Off-Campus Programs

The Associated Colleges of the St. Lawrence Valley was chartered in 1970 to facilitate cooperative relationships among four distinct institutions: Clarkson University, St. Lawrence University, the State University of New York College at Potsdam, and the State University of New York College of Technology at Canton. Student-oriented objectives include improved coordination of cultural affairs, interlibrary exchange, and cross-registration that allows students to pursue two courses per year at other member colleges at no extra cost.

Academic Facilities

The University's 640-acre wooded campus is the site of forty-six buildings that comprise 1,224,000 square feet of assignable space. Eighty-five percent of these buildings have been built since 1970. Dedicated exclusively to instructional programs are 371,114 square feet, including 52,713 square feet of traditional classrooms and 166,334 square feet assigned as laboratory areas. In the Center for Advanced Materials Processing (a New York State Center for Advanced Technology), there are seventy state-of-the-art research labs. Other labs and research tools include the multidisciplinary engineering and project laboratory for team-based projects, such as the mini-Baja and Formulae SAE racers; a robotics laboratory; a high-voltage lab; electron microscopy; a Class 10 clean room; a polymer fabrication lab; crystal growth labs; and a structural testing lab. School of Arts and Sciences facilities include a virtual reality laboratory, a molecular design laboratory, a human brain electrophysiology laboratory, and other specialized facilities.

Bertrand H. Snell Hall, opened in 2000, houses the School of Business and School of Arts and Sciences administrative offices. Fully networked classrooms and study spaces, collaborative centers for team projects, and videoconferencing capabilities are among its state-of-the-art features. The facility includes three academic centers, available to all students: the Shipley Center for Leadership and Entrepreneurship, the Center for Global Competitiveness, and the Eastman Kodak Center for Excellence in Communication. The Center for Health Sciences at Clarkson is a regional center of excellence for education, treatment, and research in physical rehabilitation and other health sciences.

Costs

For 2004–05, tuition is $24,100; room (2 persons), $4728; and board (all options), $4340. Fees are $400, and books, supplies, travel, and personal expenses vary but may come to approximately $2000.

Financial Aid

More than 90 percent of the student body receive some form of financial aid. This aid includes Clarkson University scholarships; state scholarships and awards; state and federal student loans; industrial, endowed, organizational, and individual scholarships; federal grants; and Federal Work-Study awards. More than half of the freshmen receive renewable scholarships or grants directly from Clarkson.

Faculty

A full-time faculty of 175 serves both the undergraduate and graduate programs, thus enhancing the opportunities for interchange of knowledge among faculty members and students at all levels. The percentage of earned doctorates is high, and some departments are staffed completely by Ph.D.'s. Courses are taught by faculty members, while graduate students assist in laboratory and recitation situations. The faculty-student ratio is 1:16.

Student Government

The Student Senate and the Interfraternity Council combine to form the student government at Clarkson University. The former supervises all extracurricular activities (except athletics) and has responsibility for the allocation of student activity funds and for other appropriate business. The latter prescribes standards and rules for fraternities. Students are involved in the formation of University policies through membership, with faculty and staff representatives, on all important committees.

Admission Requirements

A thorough preparation in mathematics, science, and English is very important in the academic qualifications of a candidate for admission. Candidates for entrance to the Wallace H. Coulter School of Engineering or the School of Arts and Sciences should have successfully completed secondary school courses in physics and chemistry. All candidates for admission are required to take the SAT I or ACT. SAT II Subject Tests are recommended in Writing, Level I or Level II Mathematics, and either Physics or Chemistry (Physics is preferred). The high school record is the most important factor in an admission decision. International students for whom English is a second language must submit a minimum TOEFL score of 550 (paper-based) or 213 (computer-based).

Students achieving scores of 4 or better on the College Board's Advanced Placement examinations are considered for advanced placement and credit in virtually all academic areas. Advanced standing is most common in English, mathematics, and science.

An early decision plan is offered on a "first-choice" basis; this plan does not prohibit the student from making other applications, but it does commit the student to withdraw other applications if accepted at Clarkson. Early admission for students who have completed three years of secondary education is encouraged when the academic record, standardized test scores, and recommendations indicate the student has reached a sufficiently high intellectual and emotional level to perform successfully with other college students.

A personal interview is very helpful to the student in formulating his or her college plans. Interviews on campus should be arranged by letter or telephone at least one week prior to the intended visit. The interview is not required but is strongly recommended, especially for early decision candidates. The admission office is open Monday through Friday, from 9 a.m. to 4 p.m., and Saturday by appointment. The University welcomes visitors to the campus and makes arrangements, as requested, for families to tour and meet with academic and other departments on campus.

Application and Information

Office of Undergraduate Admission
Holcroft House
Clarkson University
P.O. Box 5605
Potsdam, New York 13699-5605
Telephone: 315-268-6479 or 6480
     800-527-6577 (toll-free)
Fax: 315-268-7647
E-mail: admission@clarkson.edu
World Wide Web: http://www.clarkson.edu

Clarkson is a leader in project-based learning, providing students with strong communication skills, leadership ability, and technological skill in their fields.

CONCORD COLLEGE
ATHENS, WEST VIRGINIA

The College

Concord College, a growing state-supported college committed exclusively to undergraduate instruction, was founded 129 years ago. Concord features accredited career-oriented education with a strong liberal arts base and focuses on the needs of the individual student as its fundamental concern. The beautiful 123-acre campus stands on a ridge of the Appalachian Mountains. Four residence halls and adult studio apartments house up to 1,100 students from twenty-eight states, predominantly from the East, South, and Midwest. Concord also has a large international student population, with thirty nations represented. With a total student population of 3,050, Concord serves the needs of active commuter students who join the residential students in following courses of study in the arts and sciences, business administration, teacher education, and such fields as advertising/graphic design and social work. Preparation for advanced and professional study is a Concord hallmark.

Each year, the Alexander Fine Arts Center presents the Artist-Lecture Series, which includes recitals, plays, art exhibitions, and guest speakers. Special events have included the North Carolina Dance Theatre; the West Virginia Symphony; lecturers Dr. Homer Hickam, NASA scientist and author of the book *Rocket Boys* (which was later made into the hit movie *October Sky*), and Dr. Cornel West, a preeminent African-American scholar from Harvard; and professional art exhibits. Theatrical productions range from Shakespeare and Chekhov to Woody Allen.

Students participate in special interest organizations, honor societies, five fraternities, four sororities, the yearbook, and the newspaper and enjoy many student activities, which include comedians, musicians, magicians, and other entertainers. Concord was recently awarded the Great Lakes Regional Award for Outstanding Comprehensive Programming at the NACA conference. In addition, students participate in intramural and intercollegiate sports. Intercollegiate sports for men include baseball, basketball, cross-country, football, golf, soccer, tennis, and track and field. Intercollegiate sports for women include basketball, soccer, softball, tennis, track and field, and volleyball.

Counseling and tutoring are strongly supported through Student Support Services; faculty-supervised developmental labs in English, reading, and mathematics; and twice-a-year individual counseling with faculty advisers. The Student Needs Assistance Program offers extensive academic support that ranges from time management to reducing stress anxiety to testing at the student's best level to perform.

Location

Athens is a small town in southern West Virginia near the Virginia border. Located near Princeton and Bluefield, West Virginia, Athens is 6 miles from I-77 and not far from I-64 and I-81. Athens has easy access to thriving population centers, such as Roanoke, Virginia; Charleston, West Virginia; and Charlotte, North Carolina. Shopping malls and entertainment are also available nearby, and Pipestem State Park Resort offers many recreational opportunities. WinterPlace ski resort is approximately 20 minutes north of the campus and white-water rafting is also nearby.

Majors and Degrees

Concord offers more than eighty-five majors, minors, and programs. The degrees offered at Concord are the Bachelor of Science in Computer Information Systems; the Bachelor of Arts in Communication Arts; the Bachelor of Arts/Bachelor of Science in Interdisciplinary Studies; the Bachelor of Social Work; the Bachelor of Science in Education (with a wide selection of teaching fields); the Bachelor of Science in Medical Technology; the Bachelor of Science in Business Administration; the Bachelor of Science, with majors in athletic training, biology, comprehensive chemistry, GIS and cartography, mathematics, mathematics comprehensive, mathematics/computer science, preprofessional biology, and preprofessional chemistry; and the Bachelor of Arts, with majors in advertising/graphic design, English (with emphases in journalism, literature, and writing), geography, history, history with a concentration in philosophy, political science, preprofessional mentoring programs for law and premed, psychology, sociology, and studio art. Concord offers the Regents Bachelor of Arts degree for adults who cannot interrupt their normal activities to attend college but have gained comparable knowledge outside the classroom. Concord also offers a two-year degree, the Associate of Arts in Office Supervision, and five structured interdisciplinary options, including environmental geosciences, health-care management, leadership and entrepreneurial studies, public administration, and sports management.

Academic Programs

All students must complete a minimum of 128 semester hours with a grade point average of 2.0 (C) or better to receive a degree. A program of general studies, required of all students, includes courses in communication and literature, fine arts, social sciences, natural sciences, mathematics, foreign languages (optional in most majors), and physical education. Credit is awarded for satisfactory scores on the College-Level Examination Program (CLEP), Advanced Placement (AP), and International Baccalaureate tests. An outstanding honors program is also available to qualifying students. Honors courses and independent study projects are available in most departments. Semesters begin in late August and mid-January; there are summer terms as well.

Off-Campus Programs

The Concord College Beckley Center offers a wide range of academic opportunities, from freshman-level courses to the four-year degree in business administration, to students in Raleigh County, West Virginia. Summer internships, which provide valuable professional contacts and experience, are part of the program of study for students majoring in communication arts and advertising/graphic design. Medical technology students must complete a twelve-month internship at an approved hospital. An internship program is available for travel industry management students. Professional fieldwork placements form part of the social work program.

Academic Facilities

An open-stack library and a modern center for academic technologies facilitate research. Students have access to twenty-five computer labs, port-per-pillow fiber optics in the residence halls, the observatory, two spacious theaters, and physical education facilities, including gymnasiums, an indoor swimming pool, a dance studio, well-equipped weight rooms, and squash, handball, and racquetball courts. Laboratories are integral components of programs in the natural sciences, psychology, and geography. The Alexander Fine Arts Center houses facilities for art, music, communications, and dramatic arts studies.

Costs

For the 2003–04 academic year, the tuition and fees for West Virginia residents were $3198, room and board were $4938, books and supplies cost approximately $600, and personal expenses were nearly $1000. For nonresidents, tuition and fees are $7278 per academic year. All other costs were the same. These figures are subject to change.

Financial Aid

Concord College has the most generous scholarship program in the West Virginia State College System. Merit awards, athletic and talent scholarships, transfer scholarships, and scholarships for nontraditional students are readily available for qualifying students. Federal Pell Grants, Federal Supplemental Educational Opportunity Grants, Federal Perkins Loans, West Virginia Higher Education Grants, Federal PLUS loans, and Federal Stafford Student Loans are available through the College. The State Student Assistance Program and the Federal Work-Study Program offer opportunities for student employment. To receive priority, the Free Application for Federal Student Aid (FAFSA) must be on file by April 15.

Concord offers scholarships to international students. The average scholarship covers about 35 percent of the total institutional cost.

Incoming freshmen who are willing to perform community service may apply for the Bonner Scholars Program, which pays up to $3050 per year for four years as long as its criteria are met. Funded by the Corella and Bertram F. Bonner Foundation of Princeton, New Jersey, the award is primarily based on need and prior service.

Approximately 85 percent of freshman students receive scholarship, financial aid, or both. In addition, 65 percent of the entire student body receive some form of financial aid.

Faculty

All members of the faculty teach courses in the program of general studies, and all counsel and advise students. Terminal degrees are held by 61 of the 87 full-time faculty members. In addition, the College employs adjunct instructors who are experts in their fields. The average class size is 25 students.

Student Government

Concord's Student Government Association (SGA) budgets the student activity fee and plans entertainment. The SGA names students to voting membership on administrative councils and committees. Students also fund the SGA Memorial Scholarship. The College Center Board provides on-campus movies, dances, and special programs. The Concord Office of Student Residential Life offers numerous programs and activities in residence halls.

Admission Requirements

Applicants must have an overall grade point average of at least 2.0 (C) at an approved secondary school or a composite score of at least 17 on the ACT examination or 810 on the SAT I examinations, complete an application form, and send a high school transcript. Applicants may gain admission with advanced standing if they obtain qualifying scores on the College Board's AP tests, CLEP tests, or International Baccalaureate (IB) tests. GED test scores may be considered in lieu of the high school diploma.

Applicants must have completed the following secondary units: 4 in English, 3 in social studies (including U.S. history), 3 in mathematics (algebra I and higher), and 3 in laboratory sciences. Foreign language study is strongly recommended.

Transfer students are encouraged to apply for admission and may be eligible for scholarships. In addition, a limited number of talented high school students can be admitted to the summer school to earn college credit. Talented students who have completed the junior year of high school may be eligible for the College's early admission program.

Application and Information

Applications should be submitted by January 15 for early admission consideration and by August 1 for admission for the fall semester, which begins in late August and ends in December.

For further information, students may contact:

Michael Curry
Vice President for Admissions and Financial Aid
Concord College
P.O. Box 1000
Athens, West Virginia 24712
Telephone: 304-384-5248 or 5249
Telephone: 888-384-5249 (toll-free)
E-mail: admissions@concord.edu
World Wide Web: http://www.concord.edu
　　　　　　http://www.concord.edu/Pages/
　　　　　　admissions/

The Administration Building at Concord College.

CUMBERLAND COLLEGE
WILLIAMSBURG, KENTUCKY

The College

For more than 100 years, Cumberland College has been committed to providing a superior education in an exceptional Christian atmosphere at an affordable cost. Emphasis is placed on the growth of the individual student. The College strives to instill in students the desire to be agents of change in the world and to use knowledge for the benefit of others as well as themselves.

Cumberland is a four-year, coed liberal arts college offering a broad curriculum with more than forty programs of undergraduate study from which to choose. A graduate program leading to the Master of Arts in Education is also offered.

The student body consists of 1,700 students representing thirty-eight states and fourteen countries. Most students live on campus in the College's ten residence halls. Each hall is supervised by a director assisted by student staff members.

Extracurricular activities abound, including debate team, theater, musical performance groups, academic societies, Baptist Student Union, Appalachian Ministries, departmental clubs, and intramural sports. Cumberland participates in intercollegiate competition in women's basketball, cross-country, golf, judo, soccer, softball, swimming, tennis, track, volleyball, and wrestling; men's baseball, basketball, cross-country, football, golf, judo, soccer, swimming, tennis, track, and wrestling; and coed cheerleading. The O. Wayne Rollins Convocation/Physical Education Center houses a 2,700-seat athletic arena, a swimming pool, an indoor walking/jogging track, and classrooms. The James H. Taylor II Stadium complex includes a football field, an eight-lane all-weather track, and soccer fields.

Students benefit from such special services as the Career Services Center, Center for Leadership Studies, Student Health Center, Academic Resource Center, and free tutorial assistance.

Cumberland College is accredited by the Commission on Colleges of the Southern Association of Colleges and Schools (1866 Southern Lane, Decatur, Georgia 30033-4097; telephone: 404-679-4501) to award Bachelor of Arts, Bachelor of General Studies, Bachelor of Music, Bachelor of Science, and Master of Arts in Education degrees.

Location

Williamsburg is located in southern Kentucky, 185 miles south of Cincinnati, Ohio, and 70 miles north of Knoxville, Tennessee. The campus is easily accessible from Interstate 75, about 1 mile from Exit 11. Williamsburg is one of Kentucky's older towns and is known for its beautiful homes and the hospitality of its people. The College is situated on three hills above the town and has a panoramic view of the surrounding mountains and Cumberland River Valley, an area known throughout the country for its lovely waterfalls, forests, and lakes. Famed Cumberland Falls State Resort Park is just 20 minutes from campus.

Majors and Degrees

Cumberland College confers the degrees of Bachelor of Arts, Bachelor of Science, Bachelor of General Studies, and Bachelor of Music. Major fields of study are accounting, art, biology, business administration, chemistry, church music, communications and theater arts, computer information systems, education, English, health, history, mathematics, medical technology, movement and leisure studies, music, office administration, philosophy, political science, psychology, religion, social work, and special education.

Minor fields of study can be chosen from major fields or from biblical languages, French, philosophy, physics, and Spanish.

Preprofessional and special curricula are offered in medical technology, military science, predentistry, pre-engineering, prelaw, premedicine, prenursing, preoptometry, prepharmacy, pre–physical therapy, pre–veterinary medicine, and religious vocations.

Academic Programs

Cumberland seeks to provide academic specialization within the broad framework of a liberal arts education. To supplement the in-depth knowledge acquired within each major, 47 semester hours of general studies from the areas of Christian faith and values, cultural and aesthetic values, the English language, humanities, leadership and community service, natural and mathematical sciences, physical education, and social sciences are required. Students must earn 128 semester hours to graduate with a bachelor's degree.

The academic year begins in late August, with the first semester ending in mid-December. The second semester runs from early January to early May. One 5-week undergraduate summer session and two 4-week graduate summer sessions are also offered. Orientation, preregistration, and academic advising by faculty members begin in the summer preceding entrance.

Students may receive credit for successful scores on the Advanced Placement examinations of the College Board, the College-Level Examination Program (CLEP), and special departmental tests. Through the honors program, highly qualified students have the opportunity to undertake advanced independent study.

Academic Facilities

Cumberland's campus contains thirty-two buildings, reflecting antebellum architectural style. The science building features well-equipped biology, chemistry, and physics labs providing graduate-level research opportunities.

The McGaw Music Building contains individual rehearsal and studio areas as well as a recital hall. The Norma Perkins Hagan Memorial Library houses more than 150,500 book titles, 1,630 periodical subscriptions, and 715,878 microform titles. Sophisticated computer equipment provides access to an additional 20 million or more items from many of the nation's outstanding libraries. The instructional media center includes a children's library, a computerized language lab, and a listening library.

Other special academic features include a computer center, an art gallery, a word processing center for English composition, a theater, the Career Services Center, a 600-seat chapel, two large lecture halls, and the Distance Learning Laboratory.

Costs

For 2003–04, the basic academic-year expenses were $11,458 for tuition and fees and $4926 for room and board, for a total of $16,384. There are no additional fees for out-of-state students. The average cost for books and supplies is approximately $300 per semester.

Financial Aid

Cumberland sponsors a large financial aid program that coordinates money from federal, state, private, and College sources. Last year, 95 percent of Cumberland students shared more than $17 million in aid.

To apply for financial aid, it is necessary to complete the Free Application for Federal Student Aid (FAFSA). For further information about financial aid opportunities, students should contact the Director of Financial Aid at 800-532-0828 (toll-free). Applications made by March 15 are given priority for the fall semester.

Numerous scholarships and leadership grants are available.

Faculty

There are 95 full-time and 2 part-time faculty members who are respected scholars and whose primary responsibility is to teach. Courses are not taught by graduate assistants. The student-faculty ratio is 16:1, enabling students to receive ample attention and assistance from professors. Faculty members also serve as advisers to help students in planning their academic programs.

Student Government

The Student Government Association acts as a liaison between the students and the College administration. The organization also plans, implements, and governs various activities and special events each year to enhance the quality of campus social life. Members of the executive and legislative branches are elected by the student body.

Admission Requirements

In compliance with federal law, including provisions of Title IX of the Educational Amendments of 1972 and Section 504 of the Rehabilitation Act of 1973, Cumberland College does not illegally discriminate on the basis of race, sex, color, national or ethnic origin, age, disability, or military service in its administration of education policies, programs, or activities; admissions policies; or employment. Under federal law, the College may discriminate on the basis of religion in order to fulfill its purposes. The College reserves the right to discriminate on the basis of sex in its undergraduate admissions programs. Further, the College reserves the right to deny admission to any applicant whose academic preparation, character, or personal conduct is determined to be inconsistent with the purpose and objectives of the College. Where possible, the College will seek to reasonably accommodate a student's disability. However, the College's obligation to reasonably accommodate a student's disability ends where the accommodation would pose an undue hardship on the College or where the accommodation in question would fundamentally alter the academic program. Inquiries or complaints should be directed to the Vice President for Academic Affairs.

The purpose of the admission process is to identify applicants who are likely to succeed academically at Cumberland College and at the same time contribute positively to the campus community. The process considers such factors as high school records (including courses taken, grade trends, and rank in class), college records (if transferring from another institution), scores on the ACT or on the SAT I, application essay, letters of recommendation, extracurricular activities and honors, and personal contact.

Application and Information

Applicants for admission should contact the admissions office for an application form and return the completed form to the College, along with the appropriate application fee. Applicants should also have official transcripts of all high school and college work sent to the College, along with a copy of the ACT or SAT I scores. Each student is notified regarding official admission within ten working days after the application procedure has been completed.

Students accepted for admission must submit the required enrollment deposit.

Additional information may be obtained by contacting:

Office of Admissions
Cumberland College
Williamsburg, Kentucky 40769
Telephone: 606-539-4241
           800-343-1609 (toll-free)
E-mail: admiss@cumberlandcollege.edu
World Wide Web: http://www.cumberlandcollege.edu

Students on the campus of Cumberland College.

LEHIGH UNIVERSITY
BETHLEHEM, PENNSYLVANIA

The University

Lehigh University is among the nation's most selective, highly ranked private research universities, rich in tradition, with an inspiring history that spans more than 135 years. Lehigh offers a comprehensive education that integrates courses from four colleges and dozens of fields of study to create a dynamic learning environment. At Lehigh, students can choose from nationally recognized programs in the arts and sciences, humanities, business, engineering, and education. Students can customize their college experience to their personal interests by tailoring their majors and academic programs from more than 2,000 courses, with opportunities to take courses outside of their college or major field of study.

Lehigh is the right size—small enough to be personal, yet large enough to be powerful. The school combines learning opportunities found at larger research universities with the personal attention of a smaller, private college. Many students consider Lehigh as everything that college was meant to be. At Lehigh, students have easy access to world-class faculty members who are renowned in their fields but also offer their time and personal attention to help students learn and succeed. With a 9.9:1 student-faculty ratio, a college experience customized to the individual, close mentoring by faculty members, hands-on projects, extensive industry internships, and innovative study, Lehigh students emerge as leaders in careers and life. The University's approximately 4,685 undergraduate students come from nearly every state and more than sixty-five countries. Women comprise 40 percent of the student body, and minorities, 13 percent. More than half ranked in the top 10 percent of their high school class. Seventy percent live on campus in residence halls, in fraternity or sorority houses, in apartments, or in specialty housing. At Lehigh, students gain hands-on, real-world experience and take part in a variety of activities, in and out of the classroom, that build confidence and help students develop as leaders. Lehigh prepares students to succeed in whatever careers they choose.

Twenty-five Division I varsity athletic teams compete primarily in the Patriot League. Lehigh is consistently among the leaders in NCAA graduation rates. Its athletics program was in the top twenty of *U.S. News & World Report's* "America's Best College Sports Programs." There are more than forty club and intramural sports, in which 80 percent of undergraduate students participate. Lehigh supports a vibrant campus life, offering many social and extracurricular activities outside the classroom, with more than 130 different clubs and social organizations to suit virtually any interest—from politics and student government to music, drama, journalism, and religion.

Location

Lehigh's metroburban location in Pennsylvania's Lehigh Valley, the state's third-largest market, provides the best of all worlds. It combines the comfortable, secure setting of a suburban town with convenient access to the excitement of major cultural centers, including Philadelphia (50 miles south) and New York City (75 miles northeast). Lehigh is situated in Bethlehem, Pennsylvania, an ethnically diverse community of 78,000 that offers a variety of cultural events, ethnic restaurants, and sources of entertainment to three quarters of a million people.

Lehigh offers a unique mixture of modern, state-of-the-art facilities and historic, ivy-covered stone buildings. Situated on the side and top of scenic South Mountain in the Saucon Valley, the University's three contiguous campuses, spread over 1,600 acres, rival the most beautiful parks. Amidst tall trees, wooded hills, and colorful landscaping, the Asa Packer Campus is home to more than 100 historic and contemporary structures. The Mountaintop Campus provides additional teaching and research space for the biosciences and the College of Education. The Murray H. Goodman Campus features the 16,000-seat Goodman Stadium for football; the 5,600-seat Stabler Arena for indoor athletics contests, concerts, and special events; Rauch Field House; Ulrich Sports Complex, with both natural grass and artificial turf fields; and extensive outdoor athletic fields for intercollegiate and intramural sports.

Majors and Degrees

The College of Arts and Sciences, the largest college with just under half of the University's faculty members and undergraduates, offers flexible curricula, personal attention to students, and a problem-solving culture. Students explore seventy-seven majors and minors in forty disciplines in eighteen departments spanning the arts, humanities, social sciences, and natural sciences. Departments team on joint ventures in the new Humanities Center, where courses, lectures, and informal gatherings embrace literature, languages, religion studies, philosophy, current events, the history of art, and architecture and music. Another example is the Lehigh Earth Observatory (LEO), in which teams of students work on real-world problems as they study environmental systems and their relationship with society. The modern Zoellner Arts Center is home to Lehigh's outstanding programs of music and theater. Cross-disciplinary programs like Africana studies, classical civilization, computer science and business, design arts, economics, women's studies, and science, technology, and society provide a well-rounded education and a rich variety of career opportunities. The college offers a four-year curriculum in arts and sciences, a five-year curriculum in arts-engineering, double-degree programs, and a combined bachelor's/master's degree program in education.

With its interdisciplinary approach to learning, the College of Business and Economics is powerfully positioned to develop leaders. It provides strong programs at both the graduate and undergraduate levels. Traditional undergraduate business majors, as well as a variety of niche-based, market-driven programs such as supply chain management, computer science and business, and integrated business and engineering, are offered. The Bachelor of Science degree is offered with majors in accounting, business economics, computer science and business, economics, finance, information systems, management, marketing, and supply chain management. The Bachelor of Science degree in business and engineering (BSBE) is offered to those completing the Integrated Business and Engineering (IBE) Honors Program. The business and accounting programs are accredited by AACSB International–The Association to Advance Collegiate Schools of Business.

In the College of Education, undergraduates discover new ways of learning with their world-renowned professors, fellow students, and the children and adults they serve. The College of Education has consistently climbed the ranks among U.S. graduate schools and offers some of the most competitive programs in the country. The college has a strong focus on the use of information technology in education, and faculty members are highly entrepreneurial in creating new learning experiences. The college offers a five-year combined-degree program leading to a B.S. or B.A. in a defined major and elementary or secondary education teaching certification.

The P.C. Rossin College of Engineering and Applied Science is internationally known for the quality of its professors and its research. Students receive a hands-on education and work on cutting-edge research projects with professors and with industry engineers. A co-op program allows students to work eight months for a company and graduate in four years. The college offers the B.S. degree in applied science, arts and engineering (five-year dual-degree program), bioengineering, chemical engineering, civil engineering, computer engineering, computer science, electrical engineering, engineering mechanics, engineering physics, environmental engineering, industrial engineering, information and systems engineering, materials science and engineering, and mechanical engineering. The College of Engineering, with the College of Business and Economics, offers the demanding and popular Integrated Business and Engineering Honors Program and a computer science and business degree. With the College of Arts and Sciences, the engineering college offers an arts/engineering dual degree and a B.S. in bioengineering. The three colleges also offer an award-winning one-year course in integrated product development (IPD), in which student teams make and market products for corporate sponsors.

Academic Programs

Students are expected to maintain regular progress toward the baccalaureate degree by carrying the normal course load of 12 to 18 credit hours each semester. They may, however, accelerate the pace by using Advanced Placement credits, summer-session study, and course overloads, and by gaining credit for courses through examination. Students in good academic standing earn their degrees by meeting the requirements of their specific degree curriculum as well as general University requirements. Students should confer with their advisers on curricular matters.

Off-Campus Programs

Semester and yearlong study-abroad programs are available in Australia, Austria, Belgium, China, Costa Rica, Denmark, Egypt, England, France, Germany, Ghana, Greece, Hungary, Ireland, Israel, Italy, Japan, Kenya, Korea, Mexico, New Zealand, Russia, Scotland, Spain, Sweden, Taiwan, and Wales. Lehigh summer-study programs are available in London and Paris and at other locations in Europe and China. All programs are approved for credit. Internships in other countries are available. Credit for off-campus study may be earned through Urban Semesters in Philadelphia and Washington, D.C., and by cross-registration with a consortium of five other Lehigh Valley colleges.

Academic Facilities

From technology to the arts, Lehigh students learn in outstanding facilities as partners with professors in research and scholarship. The Zoellner Arts Center provides a laboratory for learning, performing, and visual arts for the University and the Lehigh Valley community. Lehigh was one of America's first "wired" campuses, with information network links in every residence, classroom, and office, and with large areas of wireless network access. Library and computing facilities provide access to more than 1.2 million print books and journals as well as a growing array of electronic databases and journals, computer software, and media collections.

Lehigh expects students to meet stringent academic demands, but the University provides support services to ensure each student ample opportunity to succeed. Lehigh's Dean of Students Office directs students toward help with academic or personal problems, legal issues, or general concerns. Lehigh offers a health center, fitness center, counseling service, drug and alcohol counseling service, testing service, and learning center. The University provides career planning and placement throughout students' undergraduate years and offers comprehensive support services for students who are members of minority groups.

Costs

Tuition in 2003–04 was $27,230; average room and board cost $7880.

Financial Aid

Lehigh offers merit scholarships each year based on academics, leadership, or talent in music or theater. Top Lehigh students who graduate and meet certain requirements can take a fifth year of courses, tuition-free, to earn a master's or second bachelor's degree through the President's Scholars program. College selection should be based on educational growth opportunities, not on the price of admission. Financial aid is designed to make college affordable for families unable to meet its costs. Lehigh is committed to providing need-based financial aid.

In 2002–03, Lehigh awarded more than $36 million in University grants and scholarships. Approximately 50 percent of freshmen receive financial aid awards. Financial aid packages are typically made up of a combination of scholarships/need-based grants, loans, and work-study. More than half of all incoming freshmen receive financial aid awards; the average freshman award for the 2002–03 school year was $19,156. Awards based on financial need ranged from $500 to $33,000.

In addition to providing students with extra cash to cover expenses, work-study jobs can also be a great opportunity to enhance a resume. At Lehigh, work-study positions can range from writing press releases in the Office of University Relations to working the front desk at the Student Health Center. Lehigh is a member of College Scholarship Service. To apply for need-based financial aid, the CSS/Profile and FAFSA are required. Financial aid application deadlines come early; the freshmen fall application deadline is January 1.

Faculty

Lehigh's 417 full-time faculty members and 572 total instructional faculty members, 99 percent of whom hold doctoral or other terminal degrees in their fields, are nationally and internationally known leaders in research and scholarship. They are committed first and foremost to undergraduate teaching and advising. It is common for a senior faculty member to teach a freshman course, and close student-faculty advising is the norm. Faculty members often meet with individual students and small groups outside of class, accompany students abroad, and participate in student governance and other activities.

Student Government

The Student Senate is an elected deliberative body that addresses student life and campus issues. Students are ensured access to the highest levels of decision making through two nonvoting representatives to the Board of Trustees.

Admission Requirements

Lehigh encourages men and women of all backgrounds to consider study at the University. All applicants should have completed 4 years of English, 3 or 4 years of mathematics, 2 to 4 years of history and social studies, 2 to 4 years of laboratory science, and 2 years of foreign language. An individual's potential cannot be fully reflected in the accumulation of units in a four-year college-preparatory program, so Lehigh considers a number of criteria in evaluating applicants, especially the strength of the high school record. The University requires either the SAT I or ACT, which must be taken by December of the senior year.

The middle 50 percent of students admitted to Lehigh score between 1210 and 1350 on the SAT I. However, the staff in Lehigh's admissions office works hard to move beyond the numbers and to look at a student's entire profile when making acceptance decisions. Admissions counselors review such factors as Advanced Placement or honors courses, evidence of special talent, and a student's leadership record. To provide prospective students with an opportunity to get to know the University and to determine if Lehigh is a good match, on-campus group or personal interviews are recommended.

Application and Information

Early Decision applications must be filed by November 15; regular applications must be submitted by January 1. For students who determine that Lehigh is their first choice later in the process, the University offers an Early Decision II option with an application deadline of January 1 and a declaration of intent to apply Early Decision II by February 1. Entrance exams should be taken by the January test date. Orientations for prospective students, consisting of general information sessions, campus tours, and personal interviews, are scheduled Monday through Friday. Interviews and tours are also available on some Saturdays. To schedule a visit, contact:

Bruce Gardiner
Interim Dean of Admissions and Financial Aid
Office of Admissions
Lehigh University
27 Memorial Drive West
Bethlehem, Pennsylvania 18015-3094
Telephone: 610-758-3100
Fax: 610-758-4361
E-mail: admissions@lehigh.edu
World Wide Web: http://www.lehigh.edu

NORTH CAROLINA AGRICULTURAL AND TECHNICAL STATE UNIVERSITY

GREENSBORO, NORTH CAROLINA

The University

North Carolina Agricultural and Technical State University was founded in 1891 as one of two land-grant institutions in the state. Originally, it was established to provide postsecondary education and training for black students. Today, the University is a comprehensive institution of higher education with an integrated faculty and student body, and it has been designated a constituent institution of the University of North Carolina, offering degrees at the baccalaureate, master's, and doctoral degree levels. Located on a 191-acre campus, the University has 110 buildings, including single-sex and coeducational residence halls. Of a total undergraduate population of 8,715, 4,165 students are men and 4,550 are women. The total population is approximately 10,030.

North Carolina Agricultural and Technical State University (A&T) provides outstanding academic programs through five undergraduate schools, two colleges, and a graduate school.

The mission of the University is to provide an intellectual setting in which students may find a sense of belonging, responsibility, and achievement that prepares them for roles of leadership and service in the communities where they will live and work. In this sense, the University serves as a laboratory for the development of excellence in teaching, research, and public service. As a result, A&T today stands as an example of well-directed higher education for all students.

Student life at the University is active and purposeful. The broad objective of the program provided by Student Development Services is to aid students in attaining the attitudes, understandings, insights, and skills that enable them to be socially competent. The program places special emphasis on campus relationships and experiences that complement formal instruction. Some of the services available are counseling, housing, health, and placement services. There is a University Student Union, and there are special services for international and minority students, veterans, and handicapped students. The University also provides a well-balanced program of activities to foster the moral, spiritual, cultural, and physical development of its students.

Location

Greensboro, North Carolina, is 300 miles south of Washington, D.C., and 349 miles north of Atlanta. It is readily accessible by air, bus, and automobile. The city offers a variety of cultural and recreational activities and facilities. These include sports events, concerts, bowling, boating, fishing, tennis, golf, and other popular forms of recreation. There are major shopping centers, churches, theaters, and medical facilities near the University. The heavy concentration of factories, service industries, government agencies, and shopping centers provides many job opportunities for students who desire part-time employment.

Majors and Degrees

North Carolina Agricultural and Technical State University grants the following degrees: Bachelor of Arts, Bachelor of Science, Bachelor of Fine Arts, Bachelor of Science in Nursing, and Bachelor of Social Work.

The School of Agriculture and Environmental Sciences offers programs in agricultural and biosystems engineering, agricultural economics, agricultural economics (agricultural business), agricultural education, agricultural education (agricultural extension), agricultural science–earth and environmental science (earth and environmental science, landscape horticulture design, plant science, soil science), agricultural science–natural resources (plant science), animal science, animal science (animal industry), child development, child development–early education and family studies B–K (teaching), family and consumer science (fashion merchandising and design), family and consumer science education, food and nutritional sciences, laboratory animal science, and landscape architecture.

In the College of Arts and Sciences, programs are available in applied mathematics, biology, biology–secondary education, broadcast production, chemistry, chemistry–secondary education, criminal justice, electronic/media journalism, English, English–secondary education, French, French–Romance languages and literatures, French–secondary education, history, history–secondary education, journalism and mass communications, liberal studies, mathematics, mathematics–secondary education, media management, music education, music–general, music–performance, physics, physics–secondary education, political science, print journalism, professional theater, psychology, public relations, sociology, social work, Spanish–Romance languages and literatures, Spanish–secondary education, speech, speech (speech pathology/audiology), visual arts–art education, and visual arts–design.

The School of Business and Economics offers programs in accounting, business education, business education (administrative systems, vocational business education, vocational business education–data processing), economics, finance, management, management (management information systems), marketing, and transportation.

In the School of Education, programs are available in elementary education, health and physical education (fitness/wellness management), health and physical education (teaching), recreation administration, and special education.

In the College of Engineering, programs are offered in architectural engineering, chemical engineering, civil engineering, computer science, electrical engineering, industrial engineering, and mechanical engineering.

The School of Nursing grants the Bachelor of Science in Nursing (B.S.N.) degree.

The School of Technology has programs in construction management, electronics technology, graphic communication systems, manufacturing systems, occupational safety and health, technology education, and vocational industrial education.

Academic Programs

Students must complete a minimum of 124 semester hours to earn a bachelor's degree; the exact number varies with the program. Students are also required to demonstrate competence in English and mathematics.

As complements to the academic programs, the University's Army and Air Force ROTC programs and cooperative education program provide excellent opportunities for students to enrich their educational experiences. The ROTC programs are designed to prepare college graduates for military service careers. The cooperative education program provides an opportunity for qualified students to alternate periods of study on campus and meaningful employment off campus in private industrial or business firms or government agencies.

Academic Facilities

The University library has current holdings that include 507,036 book volumes and bound periodicals, as well as 5,446 current serials. As a select depository in North Carolina for U.S. government documents, the library contains a collection of more than 250,000 official publications. Among the library's other holdings are a collection of audiovisuals and 1,038,474 microforms, archives, and special collections in black studies and teacher-education materials. Special services are provided through formal and informal library instruction, interlibrary loans, and photocopying facilities.

The University's educational support centers are the Learning Assistance Center, the Audiovisual Center, the Closed Circuit Television Facility, a 1,000-watt student-operated educational radio station, the Computer Center, the Reading Center, the Language Laboratory, and the Center for Manpower Research and Training. The H. Clinton Taylor Art Gallery and the African Heritage Center are two exceptional art museums on campus. Throughout the year, these museums have on display a number of special exhibits of sculpture, paintings, graphics, and other media.

Costs

In 2003–04, tuition and fees for North Carolina residents were $2714 per year; for nonresidents of the state, they were $11,635. Board and lodging for the academic year were $4845.

Financial Aid

Through the student financial aid program, the University makes every effort to ensure that no qualified student is denied the opportunity to attend because of a lack of funds. Students who demonstrate financial need and have the potential to achieve academic success at the University may obtain assistance to meet their expenses in accordance with the funds available. Financial aid is awarded without regard to race, religion, color, national origin, or sex. The University provides financial aid for students from four basic sources: grants, scholarships, loans, and employment. To apply for aid, students must submit the Free Application for Federal Student Aid (FAFSA). The priority filing deadline is March 15 for fall semester. North Carolina residents may call 800-443-0835 (toll-free).

Faculty

The University's teaching faculty consists of 600 highly qualified members, of approximately 90 percent hold the doctoral degree or the first professional degree in their discipline. Faculty members are recruited from many areas and backgrounds, thereby bringing together a diverse cadre of academic professionals from many nations.

Student Government

The Student Government Association (SGA), composed of senators elected from the student body, is primarily a policy-recommending group and represents the views and concerns of the students. The president of SGA reports directly to the vice-chancellor for student affairs. In addition, each student organization is represented by a senator, and these senators sit on the Faculty Senate.

Admission Requirements

Applicants for undergraduate admission are considered individually and in accordance with criteria applied flexibly to ensure that applicants with unusual qualifications are not denied admission. However, admission for out-of-state freshman students is competitive due to an 18 percent out-of-state enrollment cap. Students who are applying for admission as freshmen are expected to have completed a college-preparatory program in high school and taken the SAT I or the ACT. General requirements include graduation from an accredited high school with 16 units of credit, with no more than 4 units in vocational subjects and with at least 2 units in physical education; a satisfactory score on the SAT I or ACT; and a respectable GPA and/or class rank. The General Educational Development (GED) test score results or a high school equivalency certificate from the state department of education may be submitted in lieu of the high school transcript for applicants receiving equivalency before January 1988.

North Carolina A&T State University welcomes applications from graduates of accredited community, technical, and junior colleges and from students who wish to transfer from other senior colleges.

Application and Information

The suggested application deadline for students who expect to live on campus is February 1; for commuting students, it is June 1. Applications are processed upon the receipt of the completed application form with the application fee of $35, official transcripts, and SAT I or ACT scores. Out-of-state admission is limited; therefore, applications for admission should be filed by February 1.

To arrange an interview or a visit to the campus, students should contact:

Office of Admissions
B. C. Webb Hall
North Carolina Agricultural and Technical State University
Greensboro, North Carolina 27411
Telephone: 336-334-7946 or 7947
          800-443-8964 (toll-free in North Carolina)
World Wide Web: http://www.ncat.edu

A professor and students in the chemical engineering lab.

TRANSYLVANIA UNIVERSITY
LEXINGTON, KENTUCKY

The University

Transylvania, a small, private liberal arts college of about 1,075 men and women, is consistently ranked among the best of its kind in the nation. The name—from the Latin that means across the woods—refers to the heavily forested Transylvania settlement in which the University was founded in 1780. Transylvania was the first college west of the Allegheny Mountains and the sixteenth in the nation. The University established the first schools of medicine and law in what was then the West and educated the doctors, lawyers, ministers, political leaders, and others who helped shape the young nation. Transylvania also founded the first college literary magazine in the West, *The Transylvanian*, still published by students today. Transylvania's link with early Lexington is symbolized by its administration building, Old Morrison, a registered National Historic Landmark and the central feature on the official seal of the city of Lexington.

After more than 220 years of academic excellence, Transylvania continues as a pioneer in higher education, preparing future leaders in business, government, education, the sciences, and the arts. Students work closely with professors in small classes, many with fewer than 10 students. The student body represents twenty-eight states and eleven countries. A high percentage of graduates attend selective medical, law, and other professional programs.

Transylvania offers more than fifty cocurricular activities, and most students participate in several of these. The Lampas Circle of the national leadership honorary society Omicron Delta Kappa recognizes students for academic excellence and campus leadership. The athletics program includes seven varsity sports for men, eight for women, and more than a dozen intramural sports. Transylvania also has four national sororities and four national fraternities.

Location

Transylvania is located in Lexington, Kentucky, a city of 242,000 and a growing center of commerce, culture, research, and education. Known as the horse capital of the world, Lexington is surrounded by the rolling green pastures of the famous Bluegrass region of central Kentucky. The area is also home to nearly 30,000 college students. Transylvania's parklike campus is just a 5-minute walk from downtown, with easy access to restaurants, shops, and entertainment. The proximity to downtown is also an advantage for students who want convenient part-time jobs and internship opportunities in law offices, accounting firms, hospitals, and other organizations. Transylvania offers its students a shuttle service between the modern Transylvania library and the University of Kentucky libraries every day, and the Lexington Public Library is a few blocks from the campus. Lexington is served by major airlines, and Louisville and Cincinnati are only 80 miles away.

Majors and Degrees

The Bachelor of Arts degree is awarded in the following majors: accounting, art, biology, business administration (specializations in finance; hotel, restaurant, and tourism administration; management; and marketing), chemistry, computer science, drama, economics, education, English, exercise science, French, history, mathematics, music, philosophy, physical education, physics, political science, psychology, religion, sociology, sociology/anthropology, and Spanish. Individually designed majors also may be arranged. Minors are available in most majors and in anthropology; classical studies; communication; European studies; German; hotel, restaurant, and tourism administration; international affairs; multicultural studies; and women's studies. Advising and undergraduate preparation are provided for dentistry, engineering, law, medicine, ministry, pharmacy, physical therapy, and veterinary medicine. A cooperative program in engineering allows students to earn a B.A. in physics or liberal studies from Transylvania in three years and a B.S. in

engineering from the University of Kentucky, Vanderbilt University, or Washington University in two years. A cooperative program in accounting allows students to earn a B.A. in accounting from Transylvania in four years and an M.S. in accounting from the University of Kentucky in one year; graduates qualify to take the CPA exam.

Academic Programs

The academic year is based on a 4-4-1 academic calendar, with two 14-week terms (fall and winter) and a one-month May term. The fall term begins in early September and ends in mid-December. The winter term begins in mid-January and ends in late April. During the May term, students may participate in a variety of programs on or off campus. Students normally take four courses in each of the fall and winter terms and one course in the May term. Thirty-six courses are required to graduate. Freshmen participate in a two-term program called Foundations of the Liberal Arts, which features small-group discussions with a faculty leader; lectures, films, concerts, and other presentations; and a tutorial program in basic communication, critical thinking, and study skills. Special study-skills clinics and workshops are offered on an optional basis. Students must complete requirements designed to ensure broad familiarity with the major areas of learning and human endeavor in the humanities and fine arts, social sciences, natural sciences and mathematics, logic, and languages.

Transylvania grants credit for scores of 4 or 5 on the Advanced Placement examinations of the College Board and at least 5 on the International Baccalaureate program. Detailed information may be obtained from the Office of the Registrar.

Off-Campus Programs

Experiencing diverse cultures through international study is a vital part of a Transylvania education. It is common for Transylvania students to study abroad for a summer, a term, or a year. A program at Regent's College, London, allows students to study there for the same cost and course credit as a semester at Transylvania. Scholarships are available for both semester-long and summer study abroad. Summer study programs, including those in Austria, Brazil, China, Costa Rica, Ecuador, France, Germany, Italy, Japan, Mexico, and Spain, are available through Transylvania's affiliation with the Kentucky Institute for International Studies. Transylvania also cooperates with the English-Speaking Union to offer advanced students scholarships for summer study at Cambridge and Oxford Universities. Students may participate in seminars or internships in Washington, D.C., through the Washington Center. Internships with congressional offices, Kentucky state government, city government, and local firms are easily arranged. Participation in Reserve Officers' Training Corps (Air Force and Army ROTC) is offered in cooperation with the University of Kentucky.

Academic Facilities

Two new Georgian-style buildings combine elegance with high-tech facilities to offer the latest advances in teaching and learning. The Cowgill Center for Business, Economics, and Education includes a multimedia classroom where professors from any discipline can use a large display screen to show the entire class information from one of the twenty-five networked student computers or from a TV, video, CD-ROM, or satellite. A specialized area for education majors includes a laboratory classroom for teacher training. The new Lucille C. Little Theater, used for faculty- and student-directed productions and drama classes, is a technically innovative facility that includes computerized lighting and sound, flexible staging options, and movable seating. The Frances Carrick Thomas/J. Douglas Gay, Jr. Library offers sophisticated computerized databases, which are invaluable for research and can be accessed from any computer connected to

Transylvania's server, including PCs in dorm rooms. The Mitchell Fine Arts Center provides music program facilities, including practice rooms, a recital hall, and an auditorium. It also houses the Career Development Center, which provides free interest testing and helps students research careers, improve job search skills, arrange internships and part-time jobs, and apply to graduate schools. Mitchell also houses a teaching laboratory for the hotel, restaurant, and tourism administration program. A newly acquired building is dedicated to art classes, studios, and a student gallery. Other modern facilities include the L. A. Brown Science Center and the Haupt Humanities Building. The Clive M. Beck Athletic and Recreation Center opened in January 2002. About 80 percent of students live on campus in six residence halls—two for men, one for women, and three for men and women. These include apartment-style living for upperclass students and suite-style rooms. All rooms are air-conditioned and completely furnished and offer private telephone service with voice mail, access to cable television and Transylvania's computer network, ample lounge and study areas, computer labs, and recreational facilities. The dining hall is in the women's residence hall. The William T. Young Campus Center offers a competition-size indoor pool, a gymnasium, a fitness center, and other facilities.

Costs

Transylvania charges an annual tuition that covers fall, winter, and May terms for a normal full-time schedule of courses. Special instruction fees are charged in addition for certain designated courses, such as applied music. For 2002–03, tuition was $16,170, the room and board (double occupancy) cost was $5940, and the general fee was $620.

Financial Aid

Transylvania is committed to providing financial aid to students and their families. Four types of financial assistance are available: scholarships, which are based on academic performance, leadership, and citizenship, and grants, loans, and campus work, which are based on financial need. About 90 percent of Transylvania students receive some form of financial assistance and many receive more than one type of aid. Outstanding entering freshmen may qualify for one of twenty-five William T. Young Scholarships—each worth more than $55,000 over four years—which cover tuition and fees. Submission of Transylvania's Application for Admission and Scholarships by the appropriate deadline is all that is necessary to be considered for all scholarships at Transylvania. Students who are interested in need-based aid must file the Free Application for Federal Student Aid (FAFSA).

Faculty

Transylvania's relatively small size and low student-faculty ratio of 13:1 allow for close, personal attention in teaching and advising. Ninety-seven percent of full-time faculty members hold a doctorate or the highest degree in their field and have come to Transylvania from a variety of graduate and professional schools. Many faculty members are recognized for their scholarship and professional activities, but their central concern is teaching and advising students. Transylvania's commitment to outstanding teaching is reflected in its nationally recognized Bingham Program for Excellence in Teaching. The program seeks to attract and retain gifted teachers through an evaluation process and financial incentives.

Student Government

Students at Transylvania have a high degree of access to the administration and governing board of the University. The Student Government Association serves as a representative government, and students also hold positions on standing committees of the faculty and the Board of Trustees.

Admission Requirements

Each applicant is considered individually on the basis of academic records, SAT I scores and/or ACT scores, activities, interests, essays, and recommendations. Admission is also offered to transfer students, international students (through the SAT I, ACT, or Test of English as a Foreign Language), and nontraditional students. High

school students who graduate at the end of their junior year may also be considered for admission.

Transylvania enrolled 330 new students for the 2001–02 academic year. The middle 50 percent composite ACT score for the freshman class was 24 to 29; the middle 50 percent combined SAT I score was 1100 to 1290. Sixty percent were in the top 10 percent of their high school class.

Application and Information

Submission of a Transylvania Application for Admission and Scholarships or the common application is all that is necessary to be considered for admission and most merit scholarships at Transylvania. Application deadlines vary with particular scholarships and types of financial aid.

The priority admission and scholarships deadline is December 1 for applicants who wish to learn of their acceptance by January 1 and who want to be considered for all Transylvania scholarships. February 1 is the general admission and scholarships deadline for applicants who wish to be considered for all Transylvania scholarships except the William T. Young Scholarship. Applicants who apply after the December 1 priority deadline and by February 1 are considered for admission and scholarships on a rolling basis. Applicants who apply after February 1 are considered on a space-available basis. The deadline for applications for the winter term, which begins in January, is December 5. The same deadlines apply to electronic applications, which may be submitted on the Internet at the Web address listed below.

Students considering Transylvania are urged to visit the campus. High school seniors are encouraged to stay overnight in a dorm with a student admissions assistant. Weekday visits may include a customized campus tour and an opportunity to attend classes; talk with professors, students, and admissions and financial aid counselors; and enjoy meals on campus. Visits should be arranged with the Office of Admissions, preferably one to two weeks in advance. Open houses are held in the fall and winter, and a college planning workshop for high school juniors and sophomores is held in the spring.

For more information and application materials, students should contact:

Office of Admissions
Transylvania University
300 North Broadway
Lexington, Kentucky 40508-1797
Telephone: 859-233-8242
         800-872-6798 (toll-free)
E-mail: admissions@transy.edu
World Wide Web: http://www.transy.edu

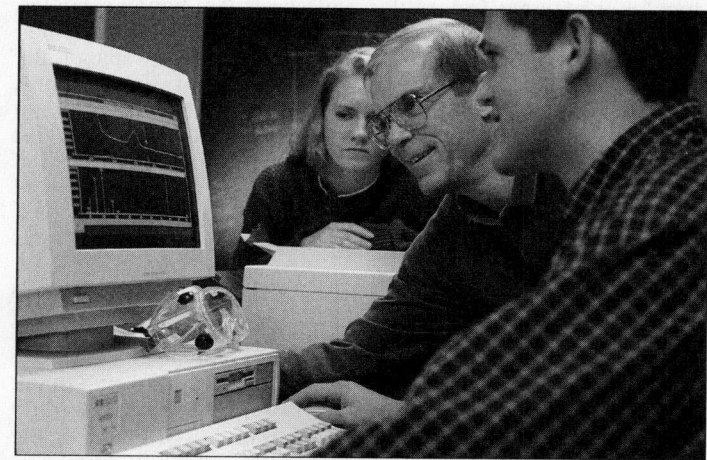

Small class sizes at Transylvania give professors and students the opportunity to work closely together, and many are directly involved in student research projects.

THE UNIVERSITY OF ALABAMA IN HUNTSVILLE

HUNTSVILLE, ALABAMA

The University

The University of Alabama in Huntsville (UAH) is a public, four-year, coeducational institution and is a member of the University of Alabama System. UAH was founded in 1950 as an extension center of the University of Alabama and became an autonomous campus in 1969. UAH has earned national recognition in engineering and the sciences, and its programs in the humanities, fine arts, social sciences, business, and nursing are outstanding. Students interact with some of the most productive researchers in their respective disciplines. Close ties with business, industry, and government give students real-world opportunities and experience. UAH is a partner with more than 100 high-tech industries as well as major federal laboratories such as NASA's Marshall Space Flight Center and the U.S. Army. Its unique location makes possible many co-op opportunities for students to earn much of their college costs and to maximize their employment potential. Students have many opportunities to work with some of the top scientists in the country. UAH is accredited by the Southern Association of Colleges and Schools' Commission on Colleges. In addition, UAH holds professional accreditation from the American Chemical Society; the Computing Sciences Accreditation Board; the Accreditation Board for Engineering and Technology, Inc.; the National League for Nursing Accrediting Commission; the National Association of Schools of Music; and AACSB–The International Association for Management Education.

The fall 2003 enrollment consisted of 5,481 undergraduate and 1,570 graduate students. Seventy-eight percent are from Alabama, 7 percent are from other countries, 52 percent are men, and 48 percent are women. UAH students represent forty-five states and more than eighty-six countries. Of the total undergraduate enrollment, 24 percent are members of ethnic minority groups. The median ACT composite range for entering students was 22-27; the median GPA was 3.4.

UAH has more than 115 active student groups and organizations, including national fraternities and sororities, honor societies, special interest groups, religious organizations, the Student Government Association (SGA), the student-run newspaper, the student-run literary magazine, minority student organizations, international student organizations, the choir, the chorus, a film and lecture series, service organizations, professional interest groups, and intramural athletics. The University is a member of the NCAA Division II and the Gulf South Conference and competes in the following intercollegiate sports: men's baseball, basketball, cross-country, soccer, and tennis and women's basketball, cross-country, soccer, softball, tennis, and volleyball. In addition, UAH competes at the NCAA Division I level in men's ice hockey.

On-campus housing is available for undergraduate and graduate students. The new North Campus Residence Hall opened in fall 2002. The Central Campus Residence Hall is a seven-story residence hall that offers private bedrooms, is located in the center of campus, and is connected to the University Center by an enclosed walkway. Student apartments in Southeast Housing are reserved for upperclassmen and graduate students. Private apartments are available for married students and students with children. Handicapped-accessible apartments are available. Meals are available in the University Center cafeteria.

The Colleges of Administrative Science, Engineering, Liberal Arts, Nursing, and Science and the School of Graduate Studies administer the degree programs of the University. Through the School of Graduate Studies, students may earn the master's degree in accounting, atmospheric science, biological science, chemical engineering, chemistry, civil engineering, computer engineering, computer science, electrical engineering, English, history, industrial and systems engineering, management, management information systems, management of technology, materials science, mathematics, mechanical engineering, nursing, operations research, physics, psychology, public affairs, and software engineering. The Ph.D. degree is awarded in applied mathematics, atmospheric science, biotechnology, civil engineering, computer engineering, computer science, electrical engineering, industrial and systems engineering, materials science, mechanical engineering, optical science and engineering, and physics.

Location

The University of Alabama in Huntsville is located in the Tennessee River Valley of north-central Alabama, 100 miles north of Birmingham and 100 miles south of Nashville, Tennessee. Huntsville is home to more than fifty Fortune 500 companies that specialize in high technology, including aerospace engineering, rocket propulsion, computer technology, weapons systems, telecommunications, software engineering, information systems design, and engineering services. Most of these companies are located in one of the top ten research parks in the world and the second-largest research park in the U.S., Cummings Research Park, which is adjacent to the UAH campus.

Majors and Degrees

The College of Administrative Science awards the Bachelor of Science in Business Administration (B.S.B.A.) degree in the fields of accounting, finance, management, management information systems, and marketing. The College of Engineering awards the Bachelor of Science in Engineering (B.S.E.) degree in the following engineering disciplines: chemical, civil, computer, electrical, industrial and systems, mechanical, and optical. The College of Nursing awards the Bachelor of Science in Nursing (B.S.N.) degree. The Bachelor of Arts (B.A.) degree is awarded by the College of Liberal Arts in the fields of art, communication arts, education, English, foreign languages and international trade, history, music, philosophy, political science, psychology, and sociology. In the College of Science, the Bachelor of Science (B.S.) degree is available in biological science, chemistry, computer science, mathematics, and physics. A Bachelor of Arts degree is available in biological science and mathematics.

Fifth-year certificates are available in accounting, education, and human resource management for individuals who already hold a bachelor's degree in another field. Undergraduate teacher certification programs are offered in the following areas: art education (N–12), elementary education (K–6), and music education (N–12) and in secondary/high school education (4–8 or 7–12), with majors in biology, chemistry, English, French, general science, German, history, language arts, mathematics, physics, Russian, social science, and Spanish.

Academic Programs

The general education course work is designed to broaden intellectual awareness and enhance cultural literacy and analytical thinking. All undergraduates are required to complete course work in English composition, humanities and fine arts, history, social and behavioral sciences, natural and physical sciences, and mathematics. B.A., B.S., B.S.B.A., and B.S.N. degrees require the completion of at least 128 total semester hours; B.S.E. degrees in electrical and industrial and systems engineering require 131; B.S.E. degrees in chemical and civil engineering, 132; B.S.E. degrees in mechanical and optical engineering, 134; and the B.S.E. in computer engineering, 135. A variety of special academic programs and options are available, including academic remediation, accelerated degree completion, cooperative education, cross-registration with other institutions, distance learning, double majors, dual enrollment, English as a second language, an honors program, independent study, internships, and learning disabilities services. Credit is awarded for appropriate scores on CLEP and AP examinations. UAH offers Army ROTC at a participating institution off campus. Special services are available for handicapped students, including note-taking services, readers, tape recorders, tutors, interpreters for the hearing impaired, special transportation, special housing, adaptive equipment, and Braille services. The fall 2004 semester begins August 30 and ends December 16; spring semester 2005 begins January 10 and ends May 3. Two summer sessions are offered and begin May 31 and July 5, 2005.

Academic Facilities

The 376-acre campus is in northwest Huntsville. All academic buildings have been constructed since 1960 and exemplify modern functional design. The UAH library houses more than 300,000 books, serial backfiles, and government documents; more than 1,000 current serials; and more than 550,000 microforms. The UAH Art Gallery hosts art exhibits by local, regional, and national artists as well as by students and faculty members. More than 900 personal computers are available across the campus for student use. Computer labs, one of which is open 24 hours a day, are located in several buildings and are staffed to provide assistance. Access to the University fiber-optic network is available in all buildings, including the Central Campus Residence Hall. Internet access and e-mail are available to all students. UAH has a number of state-of-the-art research labs that are accessible to undergraduates.

Costs

In 2003–04, tuition for undergraduate Alabama residents was $4126 (15 credits each semester) for the academic year. Out-of-state students paid $8702 (15 credits each semester) for the academic year. Undergraduates can expect to spend approximately $720 on books and supplies for the academic year. Undergraduate students pay an estimated $3400 for room, $1600 for board, $1080 for transportation, and $1200 for personal and miscellaneous expenses per year.

Financial Aid

UAH awards nearly $20 million annually in need-based and non-need-based financial aid in the form of scholarships, grants, loans, and campus jobs. The following financial aid programs are available: Federal Stafford Student Loans (subsidized and unsubsidized), Federal PLUS Loans, Consolidation Loans, Federal Pell Grants, Federal Supplemental Educational Opportunity Grants (FSEOG), state scholarships and grants, private scholarships, and institutional scholarships. Non-need-based scholarships are available for athletics, ROTC, academic merit, creative and performing arts, special achievement, leadership skills, and minority status. Students should submit the Free Application for Federal Student Aid (FAFSA) and the UAH financial aid form before April 1 for priority consideration and no later than the final closing date of July 31. Award notifications are made on a rolling basis. The priority date for scholarship application is February 1.

Faculty

Of the 277 full-time instructional faculty members, 87 percent hold the Ph.D. or other terminal degree in their field. The student-faculty ratio is 16:1. Graduate students teach 5 percent of introductory undergraduate courses. The average introductory lecture class size is 29.

Student Government

The primary purpose of the Student Government Association is to help improve the educational environment and promote the welfare of students in all areas of University life. The SGA is responsible for developing and sponsoring programs that enrich the students' cultural, intellectual, and social life. An executive branch, a 15-member legislature, and a 5-member arbitration board are responsible for carrying out the official business of the organization. The SGA sponsors more than 110 clubs and organizations in addition to providing many student services, such as health insurance, special rates for community cultural events, and a student directory.

Admission Requirements

High school graduates may be admitted as regular freshmen based on acceptable high school achievement and standardized test scores (SAT I or ACT), which are considered together. A higher result in one area offsets a lower performance in the other. For example, a minimum high school GPA of 3.0 is required if the ACT composite score is 18 or the combined SAT I score is 850. A high school GPA of 2.0 requires an ACT composite score of 23 or higher or a combined SAT I score of 1050 or higher. Applicants should present a minimum of 20 Carnegie high school units, including 4 units of English, 3 of social studies, 1 of algebra, 1 of geometry, 1 of biology (recommended), 1 of chemistry/physics (required by the Colleges of Engineering and Science and recommended by all other Colleges), 1 of algebra II/trigonometry (one each required by the College of Engineering and recommended by all other Colleges), and sufficient academic electives to meet the required 20 units. First-time freshmen and transfer students are admitted for every academic term. Transfer students with fewer than 18 hours of earned college credit are admitted based on high school transcripts, test scores, and college course work. Transfer students are required to submit transcripts of all university work and have at least a 2.0 average on all work attempted to qualify for regular admission.

Application and Information

Completed applications and a nonrefundable $20 application fee should be sent by August 1 for admission in the fall semester and by December 15 for admission in the spring semester. Admission notifications are sent on a rolling basis.

For an application form and more information, students should contact:

Office of Admissions
The University of Alabama in Huntsville
301 Sparkman Drive
Huntsville, Alabama 35899
Telephone: 256-824-6070
        800-UAH-CALL (toll-free)
Fax: 256-824-6073
E-mail: admitme@uah.edu
World Wide Web: http://www.uah.edu

UNIVERSITY OF NEW ORLEANS

NEW ORLEANS, LOUISIANA

The University

The University of New Orleans (UNO) is part of the rich cultural tapestry of its hometown, which is one of the most extraordinary cities in the world. Established in 1956 to bring publicly supported higher education to the New Orleans area, UNO is fully accredited by the Commission on Colleges of the Southern Association of Colleges and Schools. With an enrollment of 17,360 (13,338 undergraduates and 4,022 graduate students) in fall 2003, UNO offers both undergraduate and graduate degrees through the doctoral level. UNO derives its strength from its urban setting and strives to enhance the economic, social, and cultural amenities of New Orleans through its numerous research projects, outreach programs, and special cooperative agreements. The University of New Orleans attracts students from forty-five states (5.3 percent) and eighty-eight countries, with a majority of the students Louisiana residents (94.7 percent). The diverse student population (35.4 percent of students are members of ethnic minorities) provides an excellent opportunity for personal growth and understanding.

For students who are interested in on-campus housing, UNO offers three unique styles living. Privateer Place overlooks beautiful Lake Pontchartrain and includes a swimming pool and Jacuzzi. Privateer Place contains seventy-two 2-person unfurnished efficiency apartments, 216 furnished two-bedroom apartments, and sixty furnished four-bedroom apartments. Bienville Hall is a coeducational dormitory for single students and has 306 two-person rooms, seventy-eight of which have been recently remodeled. Lafitte Village is married student housing, with 48 one-bedroom apartments and 72 two-bedroom apartments. Waiting lists for Lafitte can be up to a year, so students who are interested in these units should apply early. All complexes have disability-accessible rooms available. Campus dining facilities are conveniently located near all on-campus housing facilities and heavily populated student areas, with various hours of operation. Other student services include six on-campus computer labs that provide free Internet access, a learning resource center that offers additional tutoring services, student counseling services, an on-campus medical office and pharmacy, student legal counseling, and religious centers.

UNO has more than 100 active student organizations on campus, including academic, professional, Greek, social, political, and religious organizations. UNO's newest addition is the University pep band, the UNO Blue Zoo, which performs at all UNO home basketball games and other University-related events. The *Driftwood*, UNO's student newspaper, is published weekly, and the *Ellipsis*, a literary magazine, is published annually.

As a Division I member of the National Collegiate Athletic Association (NCAA), UNO fields men's teams in basketball, baseball, cross-country, golf, tennis, and track and field (indoor and outdoor) and women's teams in basketball, volleyball, cross-country, golf, tennis, and track and field (indoor and outdoor). UNO students can also participate in several recreational and intramural sports. Students have access to a new 85,000-square-foot Wellness Center, which features a 12,000-square-foot cardiovascular, circuit, and free weight training room; an indoor jogging track; racquetball courts; outdoor sundeck; juice bar; and social lounge.

Location

The University's 195-acre main campus is set in one of the most beautiful residential areas on the south shore of Lake Pontchartrain, only minutes from the fun and excitement of downtown New Orleans and the French Quarter. New Orleans is a cosmopolitan city, known for its great Southern hospitality and its unique tourist attractions. Renowned for its Creole and Cajun cuisine, Mardi Gras, and jazz music festivals, New Orleans culture offers a unique environment for students to grow, both socially and academically. Whether exploring the artsy Warehouse District or strolling down stately St. Charles Avenue, New Orleans has something for everyone, and the University of New Orleans is a part of it all.

Many of UNO's hotel, restaurant, and tourism administration majors find internships in the city's best hotels and restaurants. Naval architecture students have access to the nation's largest undergraduate program in naval architecture and marine engineering as well as to the UNO–Avondale Maritime Center. As New Orleans continues to attract computer technology–based businesses to what has been called "the Silicon Bayou," the UNO Research and Technology Park continues to expand, producing more than 8,000 new jobs. Computer science majors are able to network with potential employers in one of the fastest-growing computer technology markets in the country.

Majors and Degrees

Bachelor of Science degrees are offered in accounting; biological sciences; chemistry; civil and environmental engineering; computer science; economics; electrical engineering; environmental science and policy; finance; general business administration; general science; geology; geophysics; hotel, restaurant, and tourism administration; management; marketing; mathematics; mathematics education; mechanical engineering; naval architecture and marine engineering; physics; preprofessional programs; predentistry; premedicine (with biology, chemistry, and psychology tracks); prenursing; pre-occupational therapy studies; pre-pharmacy; pre–physical therapy studies; pre–rehabilitation counseling; pre–respiratory therapy studies; pre–veterinary medicine; psychology; science education; and urban studies and planning.

Bachelor of Arts degrees are offered in anthropology; drama and communications, with drama options including acting, directing, and design and communications options including film, message design, radio, television, and video; economics; elementary education; English; English education; fine arts–history; fine arts–studio (with options that include painting, photography, and sculpture); foreign language education; French; geography; history; human performance and health promotion education; international studies; mathematics education; music (with options including instrumental, jazz studies, theory and composition, and vocal); music education; philosophy; political science; secondary education; social science education; sociology; Spanish; urban and public administration; and women's studies.

A four-year Bachelor of General Studies degree program is available for students who wish to design individual curricula. Credit programs in paralegal studies and medical coding are also offered. Additional interdisciplinary minors are offered in interdisciplinary studies in Africana studies, Asian studies, entrepreneurship, environmental economics, environmental studies, Latin American studies, medical coding, Native American studies, paralegal studies, and print journalism.

Academic Programs

All baccalaureate degree programs require a minimum of 128 semester hours with a minimum grade point average of 2.0 (C) in all work attempted in the college major. Also, all students must successfully complete an approved course demonstrating computer literacy. Other course requirements vary according to program. Programs leading to degrees with honors are offered in most academic majors. Credit for selected courses may be earned either through advanced-standing exams administered by the academic departments or through the College Board's Advanced Placement and College-Level Examination Program tests. College credit may also be gained for certain armed services and other nonacademic training. The academic year is composed of sixteen-week fall and spring semesters and three summer sessions.

Off-Campus Programs

The University of New Orleans Metropolitan College coordinates international study programs in Austria, Costa Rica, the Czech Republic, Ecuador, France, Greece, Honduras, and Italy. UNO's partnership with the University of Innsbruck, Austria, affords students an opportunity to participate in the largest international summer school of any American university in Europe. UNO offers college-credit exchange programs in Brazil and Canada. Students may also attend another school within the continental United States via the National Student Exchange (NSE) for one semester or one year.

UNO offers several off-campus facilities throughout the metropolitan New Orleans area, demonstrating UNO's commitment to community outreach. Off-campus locations offer both credit and noncredit courses, with hours varying from sunrise to evening and weekend classes.

Academic Facilities

The Earl K. Long Library's 1.5-million-volume collection includes approximately 12,000 journals, of which 3,800 are current subscriptions. Microform holdings include microfilm, microcard, and microfiche formats; microtext readers and reader-printers are also available. Other facilities include individual study carrels, a music listening room, computer terminals connected to the Computer Research Center, a Kurzweil reader for the visually impaired, and photocopy services. The Office of Educational Support Services includes a media resources center, which provides important media aids for the instructional staff in classroom presentations, and Television Resources, which coordinates a closed-circuit cable system and TV production studio. WWNO, the first public radio station in Louisiana, is located on the UNO campus.

All enrolled students and faculty and staff members receive a LAN and e-mail account. The University's computer network provides connections to approximately 5,000 locations campuswide. High-speed ResNet service is available to students living in Privateer Place, and a free dial-up Internet modem pool provides access for all off-campus enrolled students and faculty and staff members.

The UNO Lee Circle Centre for the Arts includes the Ogden Museum, which houses the largest collection of Southern art in the world. The center also houses the National D-Day Museum, which includes the world's largest collection of World War II color film. The 70,000-square-foot UNO Studio Center, located 20 minutes from the main campus, houses a professional-quality sound stage, including a 10,000-square-foot studio for University film projects. The UNO Studio Center is also available for professional film projects.

Costs

In 2003–04, combined undergraduate fees for full-time students for the fall and spring semesters were $3084 for Louisiana residents and $10,128 for nonresidents; summer session fees for full-time students were $795 for Louisiana residents and $1345 for nonresidents. Residence hall and board fees totaled $3520 (double occupancy) for the fall and spring semesters. Costs of books and supplies totaled $825 per year. Additional charges include a $20 application fee, a $10 registration fee, field service and laboratory fees (usually $10 to $35) for some courses, a $50 car registration fee, a $30 late application fee, a $30 late registration fee, a $5 per-credit-hour (maximum $75) technology fee, and a $10 per-credit-hour (maximum $120) academic enhancement fee. All fees are subject to change and can be confirmed by calling the Office of Admissions.

Financial Aid

The Office of Student Financial Aid develops financial aid packages to assist students with their educational expenses. This package is usually a combination of grants, loans, student employment, and/or scholarships, which, along with family contribution, help to finance the student's education. To be eligible for most federal financial aid programs, students must enroll for at least 6 credit hours (half-time) in an eligible program (one that leads to a degree or certificate). Approximately 90 percent of all freshmen in fall 2002 who showed financial need and took at least 6 credit hours were offered some form of financial aid. The priority date for the financial aid application is May 1. All applications postmarked on or before January 15 are considered for UNO's numerous academic scholarships. The University of New Orleans also offers scholarships in jazz studies, classical music, fine arts, drama and communications, and creative writing. These scholarships require either an audition or the submission of a portfolio or manuscript along with the scholarship application.

Faculty

UNO has 577 full-time and 267 part-time faculty members, most of whom participate in both graduate and undergraduate instruction and research activity. Graduate students serve as teaching assistants in laboratory courses under the close supervision of the faculty. Approximately 80 percent of the faculty members hold doctorates. Most full-time faculty members devote themselves exclusively to University-related pursuits and are integrally involved in student affairs through counseling, teaching, research, and social activities. The student-faculty ratio is 24:1.

Student Government

Every student enrolled at UNO is a member of the Student Government (SG). SG offers students a way to create effective change, express opinions and concerns, and utilize resources to enhance their educational experiences. Some of the programs SG currently offers and/or sponsors are Student Legal Services, the Academic Travel Fund, 24-hour study hall during finals week, UNO pep band (The Blue Zoo), UNO Soccer Club, Mini Baja, UNO Jazz Night at the UC, musical excursions, UNO Ambassadors Fishing Rodeo, the UNO student literary magazine (*Ellipsis*), recreation and intramural sports, cheerleaders, and Starlettes.

Admission Requirements

Students seeking admission to the University of New Orleans should submit their application as early as possible in their senior year. Admission requirements for fall 2004 include either a composite score of at least 20 on the ACT (950 on the SAT I) or a grade point average (GPA) of at least 2.0 on a 4.0 scale for 17½ specific core courses. Out-of-state students who satisfy the GPA core must also have a minimum composite score of 17 on the ACT or 820 on the SAT I. Transfer students are required to submit official transcripts from each institution previously attended and must have a minimum cumulative 2.0 GPA to be considered for admission. Students with fewer than 24 credit hours must satisfy both freshman and transfer requirements.

Beginning in fall 2005, entering freshmen must meet new admission requirements, including the completion of the Board of Regents core curriculum. Prospective students must also have either a high school cumulative GPA of at least 2.5 (students with less than a 2.0 GPA cannot be admitted) or an ACT composite score of at least 23 (1060 SAT I) or rank in the top 25 percent of their high school graduating class, and students must not have taken more than one developmental/remedial course. Transfer requirements beginning in fall 2005 include the completion of 18 semester hours of nondevelopmental work, a minimum 2.25 cumulative GPA, and completion of all developmental course work before transferring. Students with fewer than 18 semester hours must meet both freshman and transfer requirements.

Application and Information

The University of New Orleans has a rolling admissions policy. The application fee is $20. Priority deadlines for application are as follows: July 1 for the fall semester, November 15 for the spring semester, and May 1 for the summer semester. Deadlines for international students are June 1, October 1, and March 1, respectively.

Office of Admissions
University of New Orleans
Lakefront 103 Administration Building
New Orleans, Louisiana 70148
Telephone: 504-280-6595
        800-256-5-UNO (toll-free)
Fax: 504-280-5522
World Wide Web: http://www.uno.edu/~admi

UNIVERSITY OF WEST FLORIDA

PENSACOLA, FLORIDA

The University

One of the eleven state universities of Florida, the University of West Florida (UWF) enrolls approximately 9,500 students in its Colleges of Arts and Sciences, Business, and Professional Studies. The University of West Florida, which opened in fall 1967, is located on a 1,600-acre nature preserve 10 miles north of downtown Pensacola. The University's facilities, valued at more than $81 million, have been designed to complement the natural beauty of the site.

The University currently enrolls students from forty-seven states and sixty countries. Students and professors enjoy a relationship that is more common at a small, private college. Approximately 940 freshmen began their studies at UWF last year. The middle 50 percent statistics for the class are as follows: high school grade point average ranged from 3.1 to 3.9; SAT I total score ranged from 1020 to 1210; and ACT composite ranged from 21 to 26.

In addition to its undergraduate programs, UWF also offers the master's degree in twenty-nine areas of study and specialist and Ed.D. degrees in education.

UWF operates centers in downtown Pensacola and at Eglin Air Force Base, a branch campus in Fort Walton Beach (in conjunction with a local community college), and a Navy program office at Naval Air Station Pensacola. In addition, UWF owns 152 acres of beachfront property on nearby Santa Rosa Island, adjacent to the Gulf Islands National Seashore. Available for both recreation and research, this property provides special opportunities for students pursuing degrees in marine biology, maritime studies, and coastal zone studies.

The University of West Florida is a member of the NCAA Division II. Men's sports include baseball, basketball, cross-country, golf, soccer, and tennis. Women's sports include basketball, cross-country, golf, soccer, softball, tennis, and volleyball. Students also participate in more than nineteen intramural sports and twenty club sports. The Program Council and the Residence Hall Advisory Council provide activities and events open to the entire campus community. UWF hosts six national sororities and five national fraternities; 110 professional, academic, and religious organizations are open to UWF students.

A natatorium housing an Olympic-size pool adjoins the Field House, center for indoor sports and large-group activities and events. Varsity soccer fields, tennis courts, handball and racquetball courts, jogging trails, picnic areas, and sites for canoeing are available on campus. Varsity baseball and softball fields and a lighted track complete the UWF sports complex. Sailing and waterskiing facilities are nearby, and campus nature trails attract thousands of visitors annually.

Students may choose to live on or off campus. The Office of Housing oversees 1,450 total residence hall spaces that include low-rise residence halls, two- or four-bedroom residence hall apartments that are equipped with modern conveniences, and three new residence halls, one with 300 spaces and the other two with 200 spaces.

There are also various apartment complexes conveniently located just beyond the campus.

Location

Students and visitors alike delight in the beauty of the campus, which is nestled in the rolling hills outside Pensacola, Florida.

Wide verandas, massive moss-draped oaks, and spacious lawns capture the traditional charm and grace of the South, while modern architecture and state-of-the-art facilities blend in naturally among loblolly pines and meandering walkways.

Only minutes from the campus gate are the emerald waters and white beaches of the Gulf of Mexico and the Gulf Islands National Seashore, one of the nation's most beautiful beaches. The Pensacola area attracts vacationers from all around the country to its historic Seville Square, golf tournaments, sailing regattas, restaurants on the bay, and a variety of art and music festivals. WUWF, the University's public radio station, produces a monthly live program, Gulf Coast RadioLive. UWF is 3½ hours from New Orleans, 1 hour from Mobile, 3 hours from Tallahassee, and 5 hours from Atlanta.

Majors and Degrees

The University of West Florida awards the bachelor's degree in forty-four undergraduate programs with many areas of specialization. Undergraduate majors are available in the College of Arts and Sciences in anthropology, art, biology, chemistry, communication arts, computer information systems, computer science, English, environmental studies, fine arts, history, interdisciplinary humanities studies, interdisciplinary information technology, interdisciplinary science, international studies, leisure studies, marine biology, mathematics, medical technology, music, nursing, philosophy, physics, pre-engineering, preprofessional studies, psychology, social sciences (interdisciplinary), studio art, and theater as well as joint computer engineering, electrical engineering, and seven-year predental B.S./D.M.D. programs with the University of Florida.

Undergraduate majors in the College of Business include accounting, economics, finance, management, management information systems, and marketing. The College of Business is accredited by AACSB International–The Association to Advance Collegiate Schools of Business.

The College of Professional Studies, which includes education programs that are accredited by the National Council for Accreditation of Teacher Education (NCATE), offers professional training and majors leading to bachelor's degrees in the following areas: criminal justice; elementary education; engineering technology; health education; health, leisure, and science; legal administration; middle school education; political science; prekindergarten/primary education; prelaw; social work; special education (emotionally handicapped, learning-disabled, mentally handicapped); sports science; and vocational education. There are specialist programs in educational leadership and in curriculum and instruction and a doctoral program in curriculum and instruction.

Academic Programs

A general curriculum is required for entering freshmen and for transfer students without an Associate in Arts degree from a Florida public community college. General studies provide students with a broad foundation in the liberal arts, science, and career and life planning. The academic skills of reading, writing, discourse, critical inquiry, logical thinking, and mathematical reasoning are central elements of the general studies curriculum.

Students of high ability may enter an honors program offering intensive instruction in a more individualized setting. Cooperative education programs are available in nearly every field, allowing

UWF students to get a head start on their careers while paying for their education. Army and Air Force ROTC programs and scholarships are also available.

Off-Campus Programs

The Office of International Education and Programs arranges more than twenty study-abroad and student exchange programs on every continent except Antarctica. Participants may study in Austria, Canada, England, Finland, France, Germany, Japan, Mexico, the Netherlands, and Portugal.

Academic Facilities

The main campus consists of more than 100 buildings. One of the most prominent of these is the five-floor John C. Pace Library, which houses a collection of more than 2.3 million bound volumes and micropieces. Interconnected through computer linkages with state and national libraries for research purposes, the UWF library contains one of the finest special collections about the Gulf Coast area. Some of the items in this collection date back to the fourteenth century, and there are also a manuscript letter signed by Thomas Jefferson, books autographed by Albert Einstein, and materials carried aboard the space shuttle by UWF alumni.

Excellent science and technology laboratories for preprofessional majors, extensive video and film equipment, desktop publishing labs, an AP wire service, and an impressive computer science facility also support students' scholarly endeavors. Microcomputers, minicomputers, a diverse inventory of software, a real-time laboratory, modem linkages to residence halls, and 24-hour-a-day access to the computer center all are available to students in every field of study. Other major facilities include a Center for Fine and Performing Arts, a College of Professional Studies Complex, a Student Services Complex, and a Commons.

Expansion and renovation continue to enhance the main campus. The Commons feature a bookstore, post office, and snack bar. An archaeology building and museum opened in 1999. An expansion and renovation of the student sports and recreation facility is in process.

Costs

For fall 2004, tuition was $95.19 per credit for Florida residents and $462.79 per credit for out-of-state students. Room and board cost total $6000. The cost of books was estimated at $800. Transportation and personal expenses vary according to students' individual needs.

Financial Aid

About 60 percent of UWF students receive some form of financial aid and scholarships. UWF is committed to meeting a student's financial need. Aid is awarded on a first-come, first-served basis.

The Scholarship Program for outstanding freshmen allows students to receive early scholarship commitments as soon as they have decided to enroll in UWF. The John C. Pace Jr. scholarships are awarded to meritorious freshmen and transfers with A.A. degrees from Florida's community colleges. Awards are $1000 per year. Special scholarships for National Achievement Scholars and students with talent in the arts are awarded. Non-Florida tuition grants are awarded to outstanding freshmen and transfer students. These awards reduce the amount of out-of-state fees.

Faculty

Faculty members at the University of West Florida include published authors, scientists engaged in a wide range of research projects, and journalists skilled in advertising and filmmaking. Eighty percent of the faculty members hold doctoral degrees from major institutions throughout the United States.

Student Government

The Student Government Association is authorized to represent the student body in all matters concerning student life. The basic purposes of the student government are to provide students with an opportunity to participate in the decision-making process of the University; to review, evaluate, and allocate all student activity and service fee monies as allowed by state law (annually, some $1 million is allocated by students); to consider and make recommendations on all phases of student life; and to serve as the principal forum for discussion of matters of broad concern to the students.

Admission Requirements

The University of West Florida admits freshman applicants based on high school GPA, completion of college-preparatory courses, and test scores (either the ACT or the SAT I is accepted). Special consideration is given to applicants with special talents. College-preparatory courses should include 4 years of English; 3 each of math, social science, and natural science; 2 of the same foreign language; and 4 academic electives.

Transfer applicants with fewer than 60 hours are required to submit SAT I or ACT test scores and official transcripts from both the college(s) and the high school attended. Students transferring with 60 hours or more must submit their college transcript(s) only.

Application and Information

Students are encouraged to apply early in order to allow time for receipt of transcripts and to receive full consideration for financial aid, scholarships, and housing. Admissions decisions are made on a rolling basis. The University encourages visits to its beautiful campus and offers riding tours Monday through Friday at 10 a.m. and 1 p.m. central standard time. Students can visit the University of West Florida's home page via the Internet at the World Wide Web address listed below. Among the available features are the catalog, Saturday Open House dates, applications for admission, and the course guide for the current term. The Lighthouse Information System allows applicants to view their admission and financial aid status via the Internet.

Additional information and application materials may be obtained by writing or calling:

Office of Admissions
University of West Florida
11000 University Parkway
Pensacola, Florida 32514-5750
Telephone: 850-474-2230
           800-263-1074 (toll-free)
E-mail: admissions@uwf.edu
World Wide Web: http://uwf.edu

The UWF Sailing Club goes out for a day of sun and recreation on Pensacola Bay.

Indexes

Majors and Degrees

Accounting

College	Degree
Academy Coll, MN	A
Adrian Coll, MI	B
AIB Coll of Business, IA	A
Alma Coll, MI	B
Andrews U, MI	B
Aquinas Coll, MI	B
Ashland U, OH	B
Augsburg Coll, MN	B
Augustana Coll, IL	B
Augustana Coll, SD	B
Aurora U, IL	B
Avila U, MO	B
Bacone Coll, OK	A,B
Baker Coll of Allen Park, MI	A
Baker Coll of Auburn Hills, MI	A,B
Baker Coll of Cadillac, MI	A,B
Baker Coll of Clinton Township, MI	A
Baker Coll of Flint, MI	A,B
Baker Coll of Jackson, MI	A,B
Baker Coll of Muskegon, MI	A,B
Baker Coll of Owosso, MI	A,B
Baker Coll of Port Huron, MI	A,B
Baker U, KS	B
Ball State U, IN	B
Bellevue U, NE	B
Bemidji State U, MN	B
Benedictine Coll, KS	B
Benedictine U, IL	B
Bethany Coll, KS	B
Bethel Coll, IN	B
Blackburn Coll, IL	B
Black Hills State U, SD	B
Bluffton Coll, OH	B
Bowling Green State U, OH	B
Bradley U, IL	B
Brescia U, KY	B
Briar Cliff U, IA	B
Bryant and Stratton Coll, WI	A
Buena Vista U, IA	B
Butler U, IN	B
Calumet Coll of Saint Joseph, IN	A,B
Calvin Coll, MI	B
Cameron U, OK	B
Capital U, OH	B
Cardinal Stritch U, WI	B
Carroll Coll, WI	B
Carthage Coll, WI	B
Case Western Reserve U, OH	B
Cedarville U, OH	B
Central Christian Coll of Kansas, KS	A,B
Central Coll, IA	B
Central Methodist Coll, MO	B
Central Michigan U, MI	B
Central Missouri State U, MO	B
Central State U, OH	B
Chicago State U, IL	B
Clarke Coll, IA	B
Clarkson U	B
Cleary U, MI	B
Cleveland State U, OH	B
Coe Coll, IA	B
Coll of Mount St. Joseph, OH	A,B
Coll of Saint Benedict, MN	B
Coll of St. Catherine, MN	B
Coll of Saint Mary, NE	A
The Coll of St. Scholastica, MN	B
Coll of the Ozarks, MO	B
Colorado Tech U Sioux Falls Campus, SD	A,B
Columbia Coll, MO	B
Concordia Coll, MN	B
Concordia U, IL	B
Concordia U, NE	B
Concordia U, St. Paul, MN	B
Concordia U Wisconsin, WI	B
Concord U, WV	B
Cornerstone U, MI	B
Creighton U, NE	B
Culver-Stockton Coll, MO	B
Cumberland Coll, KY	B
Dakota State U, SD	B
Dakota Wesleyan U, SD	B
Dana Coll, NE	B
Davenport U, Dearborn, MI	A,B
Davenport U, Grand Rapids, MI	A,B
Davenport U, Kalamazoo, MI	A,B
Davenport U, Lansing, MI	A,B
Davenport U, Lapeer, MI	A,B
Davenport U, Warren, MI	A,B
Defiance Coll, OH	B
DePaul U, IL	B
Dickinson State U, ND	B
Doane Coll, NE	B
Dominican U, IL	B
Donnelly Coll, KS	A
Dordt Coll, IA	B
Drake U, IA	B
Drury U, MO	B
East Central U, OK	B
Eastern Illinois U, IL	B
Eastern Michigan U, MI	B
Edgewood Coll, WI	B
Elmhurst Coll, IL	B
Emporia State U, KS	B
Eureka Coll, IL	B
Evangel U, MO	A,B
Ferris State U, MI	A,B
Florida Gulf Coast U, FL	B
Fontbonne U, MO	B
Fort Hays State U, KS	B
The Franciscan U, IA	B
Franciscan U of Steubenville, OH	A,B
Franklin Coll, IN	B
Franklin U, OH	A,B
Gallipolis Career Coll, OH	A
Gannon U, PA	B
Globe Coll, MN	A
Goshen Coll, IN	B
Governors State U, IL	B
Grace Bible Coll, MI	B
Grace Coll, IN	B
Graceland U, IA	B
Grace U, NE	B
Grand Valley State U, MI	B
Grand View Coll, IA	B
Greenville Coll, IL	B
Gustavus Adolphus Coll, MN	B
Hamilton Coll, NE	A
Harris-Stowe State Coll, MO	B
Hastings Coll, NE	B
Heidelberg Coll, OH	B
Hickey Coll, MO	A
Hillsdale Coll, MI	B
Hope Coll, MI	B
Huntington Coll, IN	B
Illinois Coll, IL	B
Illinois State U, IL	B
Illinois Wesleyan U, IL	B
Indiana Inst of Technology, IN	A,B
Indiana State U, IN	B
Indiana U Bloomington, IN	B
Indiana U Northwest, IN	B
Indiana U–Purdue U Fort Wayne, IN	B
Iowa State U of Science and Technology, IA	B
Iowa Wesleyan Coll, IA	B
Jamestown Coll, ND	B
John Carroll U, OH	B
Judson Coll, IL	B
Kansas State U, KS	A,B
Kansas Wesleyan U, KS	B
Kaplan Coll, IA	A
Kent State U, OH	B
Kent State U, Salem Campus, OH	A
Kent State U, Tuscarawas Campus, OH	A
Kettering U, MI	B
Kilian Comm Coll, SD	A
Lake Erie Coll, OH	B
Lakeland Coll, WI	B
Lake Superior State U, MI	A,B
Lehigh U, PA	B
Lewis U, IL	B
Lincoln Coll, Lincoln, IL	A
Lincoln U, MO	B
Lindenwood U, MO	B
Loras Coll, IA	B
Lourdes Coll, OH	B
Loyola U Chicago, IL	B
Luther Coll, IA	B
MacCormac Coll, IL	A
MacMurray Coll, IL	B
Madonna U, MI	B
Malone Coll, OH	B
Manchester Coll, IN	A,B
Marian Coll, IN	A,B
Marian Coll of Fond du Lac, WI	B
Marietta Coll, OH	B
Marquette U, WI	B
Martin U, IN	B
Marygrove Coll, MI	A
Maryville U of Saint Louis, MO	B
McKendree Coll, IL	B
McPherson Coll, KS	B
Metropolitan State U, MN	B
Miami U, OH	B
Miami U Hamilton, OH	B
Michigan State U, MI	B
Michigan Technological U, MI	B
MidAmerica Nazarene U, KS	B
Millikin U, IL	B
Minnesota School of Business–Brooklyn Center, MN	A
Minnesota School of Business-Plymouth, MN	A
Minnesota School of Business-Richfield, MN	A
Minnesota State U Mankato, MN	B
Minnesota State U Moorhead, MN	B
Minot State U, ND	B
Missouri Baptist U, MO	B
Missouri Southern State U, MO	A,B
Missouri Valley Coll, MO	B
Missouri Western State Coll, MO	B
Monmouth Coll, IL	B
Morningside Coll, IA	B
Mount Marty Coll, SD	A,B
Mount Mary Coll, WI	B
Mount Mercy Coll, IA	B
Mount Union Coll, OH	B
Mount Vernon Nazarene U, OH	B
Muskingum Coll, OH	B
National American U, SD	A,B
National American U–Sioux Falls Branch, SD	A,B
National-Louis U, IL	B
Nebraska Wesleyan U, NE	B
Newman U, KS	B
North Carolina Ag and Tech State U, NC	B
North Central Coll, IL	B
North Dakota State U, ND	B
Northeastern Illinois U, IL	B
Northeastern State U, OK	B
Northern Illinois U, IL	B
Northern Michigan U, MI	B
Northern State U, SD	B
North Park U, IL	B
Northwestern Coll, IA	B
Northwestern Coll, MN	B
Northwestern Oklahoma State U, OK	B
Northwood U, MI	A,B
Notre Dame Coll, OH	B
Oakland City U, IN	A,B
Oakland U, MI	B
Ohio Dominican U, OH	B
Ohio Northern U, OH	B
The Ohio State U, OH	B
Ohio U, OH	B
Ohio Wesleyan U, OH	B
Oklahoma Baptist U, OK	B
Oklahoma Christian U, OK	B
Oklahoma City U, OK	B
Oklahoma Panhandle State U, OK	B
Oklahoma State U, OK	B
Olivet Coll, MI	B

A—associate degree; B—bachelor's degree

Olivet Nazarene U, IL	B
Oral Roberts U, OK	B
Otterbein Coll, OH	B
Park U, MO	B
Peru State Coll, NE	B
Pittsburg State U, KS	B
Purdue U, IN	B
Purdue U Calumet, IN	B
Purdue U North Central, IN	A
Quincy U, IL	B
Reformed Bible Coll, MI	B
Rochester Coll, MI	B
Rockford Coll, IL	B
Rockhurst U, MO	B
Roosevelt U, IL	B
Saginaw Valley State U, MI	B
St. Ambrose U, IA	B
St. Cloud State U, MN	B
St. Gregory's U, OK	B
Saint John's U, MN	B
Saint Joseph's Coll, IN	B
Saint Louis U, MO	B
Saint Mary-of-the-Woods Coll, IN	B
Saint Mary's U of Minnesota, MN	B
St. Norbert Coll, WI	B
Saint Xavier U, IL	B
Shawnee State U, OH	A
Siena Heights U, MI	A,B
Silver Lake Coll, WI	B
Simpson Coll, IA	B
Southeastern Oklahoma State U, OK	B
Southeast Missouri State U, MO	B
Southern Illinois U Carbondale, IL	B
Southern Illinois U Edwardsville, IL	B
Southern Nazarene U, OK	B
Southwest Baptist U, MO	A,B
Southwestern Oklahoma State U, OK	B
Southwest Missouri State U, MO	B
Spring Arbor U, MI	B
Stephens Coll, MO	B
Tabor Coll, KS	B
Taylor U, IN	B
Tiffin U, OH	A,B
Transylvania U, KY	B
Trinity Christian Coll, IL	B
Trinity International U, IL	B
Tri-State U, IN	A,B
Truman State U, MO	B
Union Coll, NE	A,B
The U of Akron, OH	B
The U of Alabama in Huntsville, AL	B
U of Central Oklahoma, OK	B
U of Cincinnati, OH	A,B
U of Dayton, OH	B
U of Detroit Mercy, MI	B
U of Dubuque, IA	A,B
U of Evansville, IN	B
The U of Findlay, OH	A,B
U of Illinois at Chicago, IL	B
U of Illinois at Springfield, IL	B
U of Illinois at Urbana–Champaign, IL	B
U of Indianapolis, IN	B
The U of Iowa, IA	B
U of Kansas, KS	B

U of Mary, ND	A,B
U of Michigan, MI	B
U of Michigan–Flint, MI	B
U of Minnesota, Crookston, MN	A,B
U of Minnesota, Duluth, MN	B
U of Minnesota, Twin Cities Campus, MN	B
U of Missouri–Columbia, MO	B
U of Missouri–Kansas City, MO	B
U of Missouri–St. Louis, MO	B
U of Nebraska at Omaha, NE	B
U of Nebraska–Lincoln, NE	B
U of New Orleans, LA	B
U of North Dakota, ND	B
U of Northern Iowa, IA	B
U of Northwestern Ohio, OH	A,B
U of Notre Dame, IN	B
U of Oklahoma, OK	B
U of Phoenix–Chicago Campus, IL	B
U of Phoenix–Kansas City Campus, MO	B
U of Phoenix–Metro Detroit Campus, MI	B
U of Phoenix–Oklahoma City Campus, OK	B
U of Phoenix–Tulsa Campus, OK	B
U of Phoenix–West Michigan Campus, MI	B
U of Phoenix–Wisconsin Campus, WI	B
U of Rio Grande, OH	A,B
U of St. Francis, IL	B
U of Saint Francis, IN	B
U of Saint Mary, KS	B
U of St. Thomas, MN	B
U of Sioux Falls, SD	B
The U of South Dakota, SD	B
U of Southern Indiana, IN	B
U of Toledo, OH	A,B
U of Tulsa, OK	B
U of West Florida, FL	B
U of Wisconsin–Eau Claire, WI	B
U of Wisconsin–Green Bay, WI	B
U of Wisconsin–La Crosse, WI	B
U of Wisconsin–Madison, WI	B
U of Wisconsin–Milwaukee, WI	B
U of Wisconsin–Oshkosh, WI	B
U of Wisconsin–Parkside, WI	B
U of Wisconsin–Platteville, WI	B
U of Wisconsin–River Falls, WI	B
U of Wisconsin–Stevens Point, WI	B
U of Wisconsin–Superior, WI	B
U of Wisconsin–Whitewater, WI	B
Upper Iowa U, IA	B
Urbana U, OH	A,B
Ursuline Coll, OH	B
Valparaiso U, IN	B
Viterbo U, WI	B

Walsh Coll of Accountancy and Business Administration, MI	B
Walsh U, OH	A,B
Wartburg Coll, IA	B
Washburn U, KS	B
Washington U in St. Louis, MO	B
Wayne State Coll, NE	B
Wayne State U, MI	B
Webster U, MO	B
Western Illinois U, IL	B
Western Michigan U, MI	B
Westminster Coll, MO	B
Westwood Coll–Chicago Du Page, IL	B
Westwood Coll–Chicago O'Hare Airport, IL	B
Wichita State U, KS	B
Wilberforce U, OH	B
William Jewell Coll, MO	B
William Penn U, IA	B
William Woods U, MO	B
Winona State U, MN	B
Wright State U, OH	B
Xavier U, OH	B
York Coll, NE	B
Youngstown State U, OH	A,B

Accounting and Business/ Management

Central Christian Coll of Kansas, KS	A,B
Illinois State U, IL	B
ITT Tech Inst, Fort Wayne, IN	B
ITT Tech Inst, Indianapolis, IN	B
ITT Tech Inst, Arnold, MO	B
ITT Tech Inst, Earth City, MO	B
Ohio U–Southern Campus, OH	A
Westwood Coll–Chicago Du Page, IL	B
Westwood Coll–Chicago Loop Campus, IL	A,B
Westwood Coll–Chicago O'Hare Airport, IL	B
Westwood Coll–Chicago River Oaks, IL	B

Accounting and Finance

American InterContinental U Online, IL	B
Central Christian Coll of Kansas, KS	A
Drake U, IA	B
Eastern Michigan U, MI	B
Kettering U, MI	B
U of North Dakota, ND	B
Wilberforce U, OH	B

Accounting Related

Central Michigan U, MI	B
Eastern Michigan U, MI	B
Maryville U of Saint Louis, MO	B
Park U, MO	A,B
Saint Mary-of-the-Woods Coll, IN	B
The U of Akron, OH	B

Accounting Technology and Bookkeeping

Baker Coll of Flint, MI	A

Cleary U, MI	A
Davenport U, Dearborn, MI	A
Davenport U, Holland, MI	A
Davenport U, Kalamazoo, MI	A
Davenport U, Lapeer, MI	A
Davenport U, Warren, MI	A
Kent State U, OH	A
Lake Superior State U, MI	A
Ohio U, OH	A
Ohio U–Southern Campus, OH	A
Robert Morris Coll, IL	A
St. Augustine Coll, IL	A
The U of Akron, OH	A
U of Rio Grande, OH	A
Wright State U, OH	A
Youngstown State U, OH	A

Acting

Central Christian Coll of Kansas, KS	A
Coe Coll, IA	B
Coll of the Ozarks, MO	B
Columbia Coll Chicago, IL	B
DePaul U, IL	B
Drake U, IA	B
Ohio U, OH	B
St. Cloud State U, MN	B
The U of Akron, OH	B
U of Northern Iowa, IA	B
Western Michigan U, MI	B
Youngstown State U, OH	B

Actuarial Science

Ball State U, IN	B
Bradley U, IL	B
Butler U, IN	B
Carroll Coll, WI	B
Central Michigan U, MI	B
Drake U, IA	B
Eastern Michigan U, MI	B
Elmhurst Coll, IL	B
Indiana U Northwest, IN	B
Jamestown Coll, ND	B
Maryville U of Saint Louis, MO	B
North Central Coll, IL	B
Northwestern Coll, IA	B
The Ohio State U, OH	B
Ohio U, OH	B
Roosevelt U, IL	B
Tabor Coll, KS	B
U of Central Oklahoma, OK	B
U of Illinois at Urbana–Champaign, IL	B
The U of Iowa, IA	B
U of Michigan–Flint, MI	B
U of Minnesota, Duluth, MN	B
U of Minnesota, Twin Cities Campus, MN	B
U of Nebraska–Lincoln, NE	B
U of Northern Iowa, IA	B
U of St. Thomas, MN	B
U of Wisconsin–Madison, WI	B
U of Wisconsin–Stevens Point, WI	B
Valparaiso U, IN	B
Washburn U, KS	B

Administrative Assistant and Secretarial Science

AIB Coll of Business, IA	A
Bacone Coll, OK	A
Baker Coll of Auburn Hills, MI	A

A—associate degree; B—bachelor's degree

Baker Coll of Cadillac, MI	A		
Baker Coll of Clinton Township, MI	A		
Baker Coll of Flint, MI	A,B		
Baker Coll of Jackson, MI	A		
Baker Coll of Muskegon, MI	A,B		
Baker Coll of Owosso, MI	A,B		
Baker Coll of Port Huron, MI	A,B		
Ball State U, IN	A		
Baptist Bible Coll, MO	A,B		
Black Hills State U, SD	A		
Bryant and Stratton Coll, WI	A		
Central Missouri State U, MO	A		
Dakota State U, SD	A		
Davenport U, Dearborn, MI	A		
Dickinson State U, ND	A		
Dordt Coll, IA	A		
East Central U, OK	B		
Evangel U, MO	A,B		
Faith Baptist Bible Coll and Theological Seminary, IA	A		
Fort Hays State U, KS	A,B		
Gallipolis Career Coll, OH	A		
Globe Coll, MN	A		
God's Bible School and Coll, OH	A		
Grace Coll, IN	A		
Hamilton Coll, NE	A		
Indiana State U, IN	A		
Kent State U, OH	A		
Kent State U, Salem Campus, OH	A		
Kent State U, Tuscarawas Campus, OH	A		
Kilian Comm Coll, SD	A		
Lake Superior State U, MI	A,B		
Lincoln U, MO	A,B		
MacCormac Coll, IL	A		
Mayville State U, ND	A,B		
Minnesota School of Business–Brooklyn Center, MN	A		
Minnesota School of Business-Plymouth, MN	A		
Minnesota School of Business-Richfield, MN	A		
Mount Vernon Nazarene U, OH	A,B		
North Carolina Ag and Tech State U, NC	B		
North Central U, MN	A		
North Dakota State Coll of Science, ND	A		
Northern Michigan U, MI	A		
Northern State U, SD	A,B		
Northwestern Coll, IA	A		
Oakland City U, IN	A		
Ohio U, OH	A		
Ohio U–Chillicothe, OH	A		
Pillsbury Baptist Bible Coll, MN	A,B		
Reformed Bible Coll, MI	A		
Robert Morris Coll, IL	A		
Rochester Comm and Tech Coll, MN	A		
St. Augustine Coll, IL	A		
Southeast Missouri State U, MO	B		
Southwest Baptist U, MO	A		
Tabor Coll, KS	A,B		
Trinity Bible Coll, ND	A,B		
The U of Akron, OH	A		
U of Cincinnati, OH	A		
The U of Findlay, OH	A		

U of Northwestern Ohio, OH	A
U of Rio Grande, OH	A
U of Sioux Falls, SD	A,B
U of Toledo, OH	A
U of Wisconsin–Superior, WI	B
Washburn U, KS	A
Winona State U, MN	A,B
Wright State U, OH	A
Youngstown State U, OH	A,B

Adult and Continuing Education

Dakota Wesleyan U, SD	B
DePaul U, IL	B
Iowa Wesleyan Coll, IA	B
Martin U, IN	B
Pittsburg State U, KS	B
Tabor Coll, KS	B
U of Central Oklahoma, OK	B
U of Toledo, OH	B
Urbana U, OH	B

Adult Development and Aging

Bowling Green State U, OH	B
Eastern Michigan U, MI	B
Madonna U, MI	A,B
Saint Mary-of-the-Woods Coll, IN	A,B
U of Toledo, OH	A

Adult Health Nursing

Wright State U, OH	B

Advertising

American Academy of Art, IL	B
Ball State U, IN	B
Bradley U, IL	B
Central Michigan U, MI	B
Clarke Coll, IA	B
Columbia Coll Chicago, IL	B
Concordia Coll, MN	B
DePaul U, IL	B
Drake U, IA	B
Drury U, MO	B
East Central U, OK	B
Ferris State U, MI	B
Fontbonne U, MO	B
Gannon U, PA	B
Grand Valley State U, MI	B
Hastings Coll, NE	B
The Illinois Inst of Art-Schaumburg, IL	B
Iowa State U of Science and Technology, IA	B
Kent State U, OH	B
Marquette U, WI	B
Metropolitan State U, MN	B
Michigan State U, MI	B
Minneapolis Coll of Art and Design, MN	B
Minnesota State U Moorhead, MN	B
Northwood U, MI	A,B
Ohio U, OH	B
Oklahoma Baptist U, OK	B
Oklahoma Christian U, OK	B
Oklahoma City U, OK	B
Oklahoma State U, OK	B
Pittsburg State U, KS	B
St. Ambrose U, IA	B
St. Cloud State U, MN	B
Simpson Coll, IA	B
Stephens Coll, MO	B
U of Central Oklahoma, OK	B
U of Illinois at Urbana–Champaign, IL	B
U of Kansas, KS	B

U of Missouri–Columbia, MO	B
U of Nebraska–Lincoln, NE	B
U of Oklahoma, OK	B
U of Southern Indiana, IN	B
U of Wisconsin–Madison, WI	B
Washington U in St. Louis, MO	B
Wayne State Coll, NE	B
Webster U, MO	B
William Woods U, MO	B
Winona State U, MN	B
Xavier U, OH	A,B
Youngstown State U, OH	B

Aeronautical/Aerospace Engineering Technology

Central Missouri State U, MO	A,B
Ohio U, OH	A
Purdue U, IN	A
Saint Louis U, MO	B

Aeronautics/Aviation/ Aerospace Science and Technology

Augsburg Coll, MN	B
Eastern Michigan U, MI	B
Indiana State U, IN	A
Kansas State U, KS	B
Kent State U, OH	B
Ohio U, OH	B
Purdue U, IN	A,B
U of Nebraska at Omaha, NE	B
U of North Dakota, ND	B
U of Oklahoma, OK	B

Aerospace, Aeronautical and Astronautical Engineering

Bethel Coll, IN	B
Case Western Reserve U, OH	B
Clarkson U	B
Illinois Inst of Technology, IL	B
Iowa State U of Science and Technology, IA	B
Miami U, OH	B
The Ohio State U, OH	B
Oklahoma State U, OK	B
Purdue U, IN	B
Saint Louis U, MO	B
U of Cincinnati, OH	B
U of Illinois at Urbana–Champaign, IL	B
U of Kansas, KS	B
U of Michigan, MI	B
U of Minnesota, Twin Cities Campus, MN	B
U of Missouri–Rolla, MO	B
U of Notre Dame, IN	B
U of Oklahoma, OK	B
Washington U in St. Louis, MO	B
Western Michigan U, MI	B
Wichita State U, KS	B

African-American/Black Studies

Antioch Coll, OH	B
Coe Coll, IA	B
The Coll of Wooster, OH	B
Denison U, OH	B
DePaul U, IL	B
DePauw U, IN	B
Earlham Coll, IN	B
Eastern Illinois U, IL	B

Eastern Michigan U, MI	B
Grinnell Coll, IA	B
Indiana State U, IN	B
Indiana U Bloomington, IN	B
Indiana U Northwest, IN	B
Kent State U, OH	B
Kenyon Coll, OH	B
Knox Coll, IL	B
Luther Coll, IA	B
Marquette U, WI	B
Martin U, IN	B
Miami U, OH	B
Northwestern U, IL	B
Oberlin Coll, OH	B
The Ohio State U, OH	B
Ohio U, OH	B
Ohio Wesleyan U, OH	B
Purdue U, IN	B
Roosevelt U, IL	B
U of Chicago, IL	B
U of Cincinnati, OH	B
U of Illinois at Chicago, IL	B
The U of Iowa, IA	B
U of Kansas, KS	B
U of Michigan, MI	B
U of Michigan–Flint, MI	B
U of Minnesota, Twin Cities Campus, MN	B
U of Nebraska at Omaha, NE	B
U of Oklahoma, OK	B
U of Toledo, OH	B
U of Wisconsin–Madison, WI	B
U of Wisconsin–Milwaukee, WI	B
Washington U in St. Louis, MO	B
Wayne State U, MI	B
Western Illinois U, IL	B
Wright State U, OH	B
Youngstown State U, OH	B

African Languages

Ohio U, OH	B
U of Wisconsin–Madison, WI	B

African Studies

Antioch Coll, OH	B
Bowling Green State U, OH	B
Carleton Coll, MN	B
Chicago State U, IL	B
DePaul U, IL	B
Indiana U Bloomington, IN	B
Kenyon Coll, OH	B
Northwestern U, IL	B
The Ohio State U, OH	B
Ohio U, OH	B
U of Chicago, IL	B
The U of Iowa, IA	B
U of Kansas, KS	B
U of Michigan, MI	B
U of Minnesota, Twin Cities Campus, MN	B
U of Wisconsin–Madison, WI	B
Washington U in St. Louis, MO	B
Youngstown State U, OH	B

Agribusiness

Andrews U, MI	B
Central Missouri State U, MO	B
Coll of the Ozarks, MO	B
Illinois State U, IL	B
Lindenwood U, MO	B

Majors and Degrees
Agribusiness

North Dakota State U, ND — B
Northwestern Coll, IA — B
South Dakota State U, SD — B
Southeast Missouri State U, MO — B
Southwest Missouri State U, MO — B
U of Illinois at Urbana–Champaign, IL — B

Agricultural and Food Products Processing
Kansas State U, KS — B
The Ohio State U, OH — B

Agricultural/Biological Engineering and Bioengineering
Iowa State U of Science and Technology, IA — B
Kansas State U, KS — B
Michigan State U, MI — B
North Dakota State U, ND — B
The Ohio State U, OH — B
Purdue U, IN — B
South Dakota State U, SD — B
U of Illinois at Urbana–Champaign, IL — B
U of Minnesota, Twin Cities Campus, MN — B
U of Missouri–Rolla, MO — B
U of Nebraska–Lincoln, NE — B
U of Wisconsin–Madison, WI — B
U of Wisconsin–River Falls, WI — B

Agricultural Business and Management
Andrews U, MI — A,B
Capital U, OH — B
Central Christian Coll of Kansas, KS — A
Central Missouri State U, MO — B
Dickinson State U, ND — A,B
Dordt Coll, IA — A,B
Fort Hays State U, KS — B
Grace U, NE — B
Iowa State U of Science and Technology, IA — B
Kansas State U, KS — B
Lincoln U, MO — B
McPherson Coll, KS — B
Michigan State U, MI — B
MidAmerica Nazarene U, KS — A,B
North Carolina Ag and Tech State U, NC — B
North Dakota State U, ND — B
Northwestern Oklahoma State U, OK — B
The Ohio State U, OH — B
Oklahoma Panhandle State U, OK — B
Oklahoma State U, OK — B
Tabor Coll, KS — B
Truman State U, MO — B
U of Minnesota, Crookston, MN — A,B
U of Minnesota, Twin Cities Campus, MN — B
U of Missouri–Columbia, MO — B
U of Nebraska–Lincoln, NE — B
U of Northwestern Ohio, OH — A

U of Wisconsin–Madison, WI — B
U of Wisconsin–Platteville, WI — B
U of Wisconsin–River Falls, WI — B
Upper Iowa U, IA — B
Wayne State Coll, NE — B

Agricultural Business and Management Related
North Dakota State Coll of Science, ND — A

Agricultural Communication/Journalism
Michigan State U, MI — B
Oklahoma State U, OK — B
U of Illinois at Urbana–Champaign, IL — B
U of Missouri–Columbia, MO — B
U of Nebraska–Lincoln, NE — B

Agricultural Economics
Central Missouri State U, MO — B
Kansas State U, KS — B
McPherson Coll, KS — B
Michigan State U, MI — B
North Carolina Ag and Tech State U, NC — B
North Dakota State U, ND — B
The Ohio State U, OH — B
Oklahoma State U, OK — B
Purdue U, IN — B
South Dakota State U, SD — B
Southern Illinois U Carbondale, IL — B
Truman State U, MO — B
U of Illinois at Urbana–Champaign, IL — B
U of Missouri–Columbia, MO — B
U of Nebraska–Lincoln, NE — B
U of Wisconsin–Madison, WI — B

Agricultural/Farm Supplies Retailing and Wholesaling
North Dakota State Coll of Science, ND — A

Agricultural Mechanization
Andrews U, MI — A,B
Central Missouri State U, MO — B
Coll of the Ozarks, MO — B
Iowa State U of Science and Technology, IA — B
Kansas State U, KS — B
North Carolina Ag and Tech State U, NC — B
North Dakota State Coll of Science, ND — A
North Dakota State U, ND — B
Purdue U, IN — B
South Dakota State U, SD — B
U of Illinois at Urbana–Champaign, IL — B
U of Missouri–Columbia, MO — B
U of Nebraska–Lincoln, NE — B

Agricultural Mechanization Related
Coll of the Ozarks, MO — B

Agricultural Power Machinery Operation
U of Minnesota, Crookston, MN — B

Agricultural Production
North Dakota State Coll of Science, ND — A

Agricultural Sciences
Cameron U, OK — B

Agricultural Teacher Education
Andrews U, MI — B
Central Missouri State U, MO — B
Coll of the Ozarks, MO — B
Dordt Coll, IA — B
Iowa State U of Science and Technology, IA — B
North Carolina Ag and Tech State U, NC — B
North Dakota State U, ND — B
The Ohio State U, OH — B
Oklahoma Panhandle State U, OK — B
Oklahoma State U, OK — B
Purdue U, IN — B
South Dakota State U, SD — B
Southwest Missouri State U, MO — B
The U of Akron, OH — B
U of Minnesota, Crookston, MN — B
U of Minnesota, Twin Cities Campus, MN — B
U of Missouri–Columbia, MO — B
U of Nebraska–Lincoln, NE — B
U of Wisconsin–Madison, WI — B
U of Wisconsin–River Falls, WI — B

Agriculture
Andrews U, MI — A,B
Dordt Coll, IA — B
Fort Hays State U, KS — B
Illinois State U, IL — B
Iowa State U of Science and Technology, IA — B
Knox Coll, IL — B
Lincoln U, MO — A,B
North Carolina Ag and Tech State U, NC — B
North Dakota State U, ND — B
Northwestern Oklahoma State U, OK — B
Oklahoma Panhandle State U, OK — A
Oklahoma State U, OK — B
Purdue U, IN — A,B
South Dakota State U, SD — A,B
Southeast Missouri State U, MO — B
Southern Illinois U Carbondale, IL — B
Southwest Missouri State U, MO — B
Truman State U, MO — B
U of Illinois at Urbana–Champaign, IL — B
U of Minnesota, Crookston, MN — A,B
U of Minnesota, Twin Cities Campus, MN — B

U of Missouri–Columbia, MO — B
U of Nebraska–Lincoln, NE — B
U of Wisconsin–Madison, WI — B
U of Wisconsin–River Falls, WI — B
Western Illinois U, IL — B

Agriculture and Agriculture Operations Related
Bethel Coll, IN — B
Michigan State U, MI — B

Agronomy and Crop Science
Andrews U, MI — A,B
Coll of the Ozarks, MO — B
Fort Hays State U, KS — B
Iowa State U of Science and Technology, IA — B
Kansas State U, KS — B
The Ohio State U, OH — B
Oklahoma Panhandle State U, OK — B
Purdue U, IN — B
South Dakota State U, SD — B
Southwest Missouri State U, MO — B
Truman State U, MO — B
U of Illinois at Urbana–Champaign, IL — B
U of Minnesota, Crookston, MN — A,B
U of Minnesota, Twin Cities Campus, MN — B
U of Nebraska–Lincoln, NE — B
U of Wisconsin–Madison, WI — B
U of Wisconsin–Platteville, WI — B
U of Wisconsin–River Falls, WI — B

Agronomy/Crop Science
Coll of the Ozarks, MO — B

Aircraft Powerplant Technology
Kansas State U, KS — A
Northern Michigan U, MI — A

Air Force R.O.T.C./Air Science
The U of Iowa, IA — B

Airframe Mechanics and Aircraft Maintenance Technology
Kansas State U, KS — A
Lewis U, IL — A,B

Airline Flight Attendant
The U of Akron, OH — A

Airline Pilot and Flight Crew
Academy Coll, MN — A
Andrews U, MI — A,B
Baker Coll of Flint, MI — A
Baker Coll of Muskegon, MI — A
Bowling Green State U, OH — B
Central Christian Coll of Kansas, KS — A
Cornerstone U, MI — B
Grace U, NE — B
Indiana State U, IN — B
Kansas State U, KS — A,B
Lewis U, IL — B
Oklahoma State U, OK — B
Quincy U, IL — B

A—associate degree; B—bachelor's degree

St. Cloud State U, MN   B
Saint Louis U, MO   B
Southeastern Oklahoma State
   U, OK   B
Southern Illinois U
   Carbondale, IL   A
U of Dubuque, IA   A,B
Western Michigan U, MI   B
Winona State U, MN   A

Air Traffic Control
St. Cloud State U, MN   B
U of North Dakota, ND   B

**Allied Health and Medical
Assisting Services Related**
Wayne State U, MI   B

**Allied Health Diagnostic,
Intervention, and Treatment
Professions Related**
Cameron U, OK   A
Kent State U, OH   A
The U of Akron, OH   A
U of Toledo, OH   B

**American Government and
Politics**
Drury U, MO   B
Oklahoma Christian U, OK   B
The U of Akron, OH   B

American History
Calvin Coll, MI   B
Central Christian Coll of
   Kansas, KS   A
North Central Coll, IL   B

**American Indian/Native
American Studies**
Bacone Coll, OK   A
Bemidji State U, MN   B
Black Hills State U, SD   B
Creighton U, NE   B
Haskell Indian Nations U,
   KS   B
Lake Superior State U, MI   B
Northeastern State U, OK   B
Northland Coll, WI   B
The U of Iowa, IA   B
U of Minnesota, Duluth, MN   B
U of Minnesota, Twin Cities
   Campus, MN   B
U of North Dakota, ND   B
U of Oklahoma, OK   B
U of Science and Arts of
   Oklahoma, OK   B
The U of South Dakota, SD   B
U of Wisconsin–Eau Claire,
   WI   B
U of Wisconsin–Milwaukee,
   WI   B

American Literature
Haskell Indian Nations U,
   KS   A
Saint Mary's U of Minnesota,
   MN   B
Washington U in St. Louis,
   MO   B

**American Native/Native
American Languages**
Bemidji State U, MN   B

American Sign Language (Asl)
Bethel Coll, IN   A,B
Madonna U, MI   A,B
North Central U, MN   A,B

**American Sign Language
Related**
U of Chicago, IL   B
The U of Iowa, IA   B

American Studies
Albion Coll, MI   B
Ashland U, OH   B
Bowling Green State U, OH   B
Carleton Coll, MN   B
Case Western Reserve U,
   OH   B
Cedarville U, OH   B
Coe Coll, IA   B
Creighton U, NE   B
DePaul U, IL   B
Dominican U, IL   B
Elmhurst Coll, IL   B
Franklin Coll, IN   B
Grinnell Coll, IA   B
Hillsdale Coll, MI   B
Illinois Wesleyan U, IL   B
Kent State U, OH   B
Kenyon Coll, OH   B
Knox Coll, IL   B
Lake Forest Coll, IL   B
Lehigh U, PA   B
Lewis U, IL   B
Miami U, OH   B
Miami U Hamilton, OH   B
Michigan State U, MI   B
Millikin U, IL   B
Minnesota State U
   Moorhead, MN   B
Mount Union Coll, OH   B
Muskingum Coll, OH   B
Northwestern U, IL   B
Oakland U, MI   B
Oklahoma City U, OK   B
Oklahoma State U, OK   B
Roosevelt U, IL   B
St. Cloud State U, MN   B
Saint Louis U, MO   B
St. Olaf Coll, MN   B
Southeast Missouri State U,
   MO   B
Southern Nazarene U, OK   B
U of Chicago, IL   B
U of Dayton, OH   B
The U of Iowa, IA   B
U of Kansas, KS   B
U of Michigan, MI   B
U of Michigan–Dearborn, MI   B
U of Minnesota, Twin Cities
   Campus, MN   B
U of Missouri–Kansas City,
   MO   B
U of Northern Iowa, IA   B
U of Notre Dame, IN   B
U of Rio Grande, OH   B
U of Toledo, OH   B
U of Wisconsin–Madison,
   WI   B
Ursuline Coll, OH   B
Valparaiso U, IN   B
Washington U in St. Louis,
   MO   B
Wayne State U, MI   B
Western Michigan U, MI   B
Wittenberg U, OH   B
Youngstown State U, OH   B

Anatomy
Andrews U, MI   B
Minnesota State U Mankato,
   MN   B

U of Indianapolis, IN   B
Wright State U, OH   B

Ancient/Classical Greek
Carleton Coll, MN   B
Creighton U, NE   B
DePauw U, IN   B
Indiana U Bloomington, IN   B
Kenyon Coll, OH   B
Lawrence U, WI   B
Lehigh U, PA   B
Loyola U Chicago, IL   B
Luther Coll, IA   B
Miami U, OH   B
Ohio U, OH   B
St. Olaf Coll, MN   B
U of Chicago, IL   B
The U of Iowa, IA   B
U of Nebraska–Lincoln, NE   B
U of Notre Dame, IN   B
U of St. Thomas, MN   B
Washington U in St. Louis,
   MO   B

**Ancient Near Eastern and
Biblical Languages**
Bethel Coll, IN   A,B
Concordia U, IL   B
Concordia U, MI   B
Concordia U Wisconsin, WI   B
Cornerstone U, MI   B
Laura and Alvin Siegal Coll
   of Judaic Studies, OH   B
Luther Coll, IA   B
North Central U, MN   A
Oklahoma Baptist U, OK   B
Taylor U, IN   B
U of Chicago, IL   B
York Coll, NE   B

Ancient Studies
Michigan State U, MI   B
St. Olaf Coll, MN   B
Southwest Missouri State U,
   MO   B
The U of Iowa, IA   B
U of Kansas, KS   B

Animal Behavior and Ethology
Carroll Coll, WI   B

Animal Genetics
Ball State U, IN   B
Missouri Southern State U,
   MO   B
The Ohio State U, OH   B
Ohio Wesleyan U, OH   B
U of Minnesota, Twin Cities
   Campus, MN   B
U of Wisconsin–Madison,
   WI   B

**Animal/Livestock Husbandry
and Production**
Dordt Coll, IA   B
Saint Mary-of-the-Woods
   Coll, IN   A,B

Animal Physiology
Minnesota State U Mankato,
   MN   B
Northern Michigan U, MI   B
The U of Akron, OH   B
U of Minnesota, Twin Cities
   Campus, MN   B

Animal Sciences
Andrews U, MI   A
Coll of the Ozarks, MO   B
Dordt Coll, IA   B

Fort Hays State U, KS   B
Iowa State U of Science and
   Technology, IA   B
Kansas State U, KS   B
Michigan State U, MI   B
North Carolina Ag and Tech
   State U, NC   B
North Dakota State U, ND   B
The Ohio State U, OH   B
Oklahoma Panhandle State
   U, OK   B
Oklahoma State U, OK   B
Purdue U, IN   B
South Dakota State U, SD   B
Southern Illinois U
   Carbondale, IL   B
Southwest Missouri State U,
   MO   B
Truman State U, MO   B
U of Illinois at Urbana–
   Champaign, IL   B
U of Minnesota, Crookston,
   MN   A,B
U of Minnesota, Twin Cities
   Campus, MN   B
U of Missouri–Columbia,
   MO   B
U of Nebraska–Lincoln, NE   B
U of Wisconsin–Madison,
   WI   B
U of Wisconsin–Platteville,
   WI   B
U of Wisconsin–River Falls,
   WI   B

**Animation, Interactive
Technology, Video Graphics
and Special Effects**
The Art Insts International
   Minnesota, MN   B
The Illinois Inst of
   Art-Schaumburg, IL   B
ITT Tech Inst, Fort Wayne,
   IN   B
ITT Tech Inst, Indianapolis,
   IN   B
ITT Tech Inst, Newburgh,
   IN   B
ITT Tech Inst, Arnold, MO   B
ITT Tech Inst, Earth City,
   MO   B
ITT Tech Inst, Green Bay,
   WI   B
ITT Tech Inst, Greenfield,
   WI   B
Kent State U, OH   A
Kent State U, Tuscarawas
   Campus, OH   A
School of the Art Inst of
   Chicago, IL   B
U of Dubuque, IA   B

Anthropology
Albion Coll, MI   B
Alma Coll, MI   B
Antioch Coll, OH   B
Augustana Coll, IL   B
Ball State U, IN   B
Beloit Coll, WI   B
Butler U, IN   B
Carleton Coll, MN   B
Case Western Reserve U,
   OH   B
Central Michigan U, MI   B
Chicago State U, IL   B
Cleveland State U, OH   B
Denison U, OH   B

DePaul U, IL	B
DePauw U, IN	B
Drake U, IA	B
Eastern Michigan U, MI	B
Franciscan U of Steubenville, OH	B
Grand Valley State U, MI	B
Grinnell Coll, IA	B
Gustavus Adolphus Coll, MN	B
Hamline U, MN	B
Hanover Coll, IN	B
Heidelberg Coll, OH	B
Illinois State U, IL	B
Indiana State U, IN	B
Indiana U Bloomington, IN	B
Indiana U–Purdue U Fort Wayne, IN	B
Indiana U–Purdue U Indianapolis, IN	B
Iowa State U of Science and Technology, IA	B
Judson Coll, IL	B
Kalamazoo Coll, MI	B
Kansas State U, KS	B
Kent State U, OH	B
Kenyon Coll, OH	B
Knox Coll, IL	B
Lake Forest Coll, IL	B
Lawrence U, WI	B
Lehigh U, PA	B
Loyola U Chicago, IL	B
Luther Coll, IA	B
Macalester Coll, MN	B
Marquette U, WI	B
Miami U, OH	B
Miami U Hamilton, OH	B
Michigan State U, MI	B
Minnesota State U Mankato, MN	B
Minnesota State U Moorhead, MN	B
National-Louis U, IL	B
Northeastern Illinois U, IL	B
Northern Illinois U, IL	B
North Park U, IL	B
Northwestern U, IL	B
Oakland U, MI	B
Oberlin Coll, OH	B
The Ohio State U, OH	B
Ohio U, OH	B
Ohio Wesleyan U, OH	B
Principia Coll, IL	B
Ripon Coll, WI	B
Rockford Coll, IL	B
St. Cloud State U, MN	B
Southeast Missouri State U, MO	B
Southern Illinois U Carbondale, IL	B
Southern Illinois U Edwardsville, IL	B
Southwest Missouri State U, MO	B
Transylvania U, KY	B
U of Chicago, IL	B
U of Cincinnati, OH	B
U of Evansville, IN	B
U of Illinois at Chicago, IL	B
U of Illinois at Springfield, IL	
U of Illinois at Urbana–Champaign, IL	B
U of Indianapolis, IN	B
The U of Iowa, IA	B
U of Kansas, KS	B

U of Michigan, MI	B
U of Michigan–Dearborn, MI	B
U of Michigan–Flint, MI	B
U of Minnesota, Duluth, MN	B
U of Minnesota, Morris, MN	B
U of Minnesota, Twin Cities Campus, MN	B
U of Missouri–Columbia, MO	B
U of Missouri–St. Louis, MO	B
U of Nebraska–Lincoln, NE	B
U of New Orleans, LA	B
U of North Dakota, ND	B
U of Northern Iowa, IA	B
U of Notre Dame, IN	B
U of Oklahoma, OK	B
The U of South Dakota, SD	B
U of Toledo, OH	B
U of Tulsa, OK	B
U of West Florida, FL	B
U of Wisconsin–Madison, WI	B
U of Wisconsin–Milwaukee, WI	B
U of Wisconsin–Oshkosh, WI	B
Washburn U, KS	B
Washington U in St. Louis, MO	B
Wayne State U, MI	B
Webster U, MO	B
Western Michigan U, MI	B
Westminster Coll, MO	B
Wheaton Coll, IL	B
Wichita State U, KS	B
Wright State U, OH	B
Youngstown State U, OH	B

Apparel and Accessories Marketing

Bluffton Coll, OH	B
Youngstown State U, OH	B

Apparel and Textile Marketing Management

Wayne State U, MI	B

Apparel and Textiles

Central Missouri State U, MO	B
Coll of the Ozarks, MO	B
Indiana State U, IN	B
Indiana U Bloomington, IN	B
Iowa State U of Science and Technology, IA	B
Kansas State U, KS	B
Michigan State U, MI	B
North Dakota State U, ND	B
Northern Illinois U, IL	B
The Ohio State U, OH	B
Ohio U, OH	B
Oklahoma State U, OK	B
Purdue U, IN	B
Southern Illinois U Carbondale, IL	B
Southwest Missouri State U, MO	B
The U of Akron, OH	B
U of Missouri–Columbia, MO	B
U of Nebraska–Lincoln, NE	B
U of Northern Iowa, IA	B
U of Wisconsin–Stout, WI	B
Western Michigan U, MI	B
Youngstown State U, OH	B

Appliance Installation and Repair Technology

Dunwoody Coll of Technology, MN	A

Applied Art

American Academy of Art, IL	B
Bemidji State U, MN	B
Carthage Coll, WI	B
Chicago State U, IL	B
Cleveland State U, OH	B
Coll for Creative Studies, MI	B
DePaul U, IL	B
Indiana U Bloomington, IN	B
Lincoln Coll, Lincoln, IL	A
Lindenwood U, MO	B
Marygrove Coll, MI	B
Minnesota State U Mankato, MN	
Minnesota State U Moorhead, MN	B
Mount Vernon Nazarene U, OH	B
Muskingum Coll, OH	B
Northern Michigan U, MI	B
Oakland City U, IN	B
Oklahoma Baptist U, OK	B
Olivet Coll, MI	B
Peru State Coll, NE	B
St. Cloud State U, MN	B
Truman State U, MO	B
The U of Akron, OH	B
U of Dayton, OH	B
U of Michigan, MI	B
U of Sioux Falls, SD	B
U of Toledo, OH	B
U of Wisconsin–Madison, WI	B
Washington U in St. Louis, MO	B
Winona State U, MN	B

Applied Economics

The Coll of St. Scholastica, MN	B
Michigan State U, MI	B
U of Northern Iowa, IA	B

Applied Horticulture

Coll of the Ozarks, MO	B
Iowa State U of Science and Technology, IA	B
Kent State U, OH	A
Kent State U, Salem Campus, OH	A
Oakland City U, IN	A
South Dakota State U, SD	B

Applied Horticulture/Horticultural Business Services Related

Kent State U, Salem Campus, OH	A

Applied Mathematics

Brescia U, KY	B
Case Western Reserve U, OH	B
Central Methodist Coll, MO	A
Clarkson U	B
Coll of Mount St. Joseph, OH	B
Creighton U, NE	B
DePaul U, IL	B
Ferris State U, MI	B
Grand Valley State U, MI	B
Grand View Coll, IA	B

Illinois Inst of Technology, IL	B
Indiana U South Bend, IN	B
Jamestown Coll, ND	B
Kent State U, OH	B
Kettering U, MI	B
Lincoln Coll, Lincoln, IL	A
Maryville U of Saint Louis, MO	B
Metropolitan State U, MN	B
Michigan State U, MI	B
Michigan Technological U, MI	B
North Carolina Ag and Tech State U, NC	B
North Central Coll, IL	B
Northern Illinois U, IL	B
Northern Michigan U, MI	B
Northland Coll, WI	B
Northwestern U, IL	B
Oakland City U, IN	B
Oakland U, MI	B
Ohio U, OH	B
Saint Louis U, MO	B
Shawnee State U, OH	B
The U of Akron, OH	B
U of Central Oklahoma, OK	B
U of Chicago, IL	B
U of Michigan, MI	B
U of Missouri–Rolla, MO	B
U of Missouri–St. Louis, MO	B
U of Northern Iowa, IA	B
U of Sioux Falls, SD	B
U of Tulsa, OK	B
U of Wisconsin–Madison, WI	B
U of Wisconsin–Milwaukee, WI	B
U of Wisconsin–Stout, WI	B
Washington U in St. Louis, MO	B
Wayne State Coll, NE	B
Western Michigan U, MI	B
Winona State U, MN	B
Wright State U, OH	B

Applied Mathematics Related

Carroll Coll, WI	B
Saint Mary's Coll, IN	B
The U of Akron, OH	B
U of Dayton, OH	B
The U of Iowa, IA	B

Aquatic Biology/Limnology

Eastern Michigan U, MI	B

Arabic

The Ohio State U, OH	B
U of Chicago, IL	B
U of Michigan, MI	B
U of Notre Dame, IN	B
Washington U in St. Louis, MO	B

Archeology

The Coll of Wooster, OH	B
Grinnell Coll, IA	B
Lawrence U, WI	B
Minnesota State U Moorhead, MN	B
Oberlin Coll, OH	B
U of Evansville, IN	B
U of Indianapolis, IN	B
U of Michigan, MI	B
U of Missouri–Columbia, MO	B
U of Wisconsin–La Crosse, WI	B

A—associate degree; B—bachelor's degree

Washington U in St. Louis, MO — B
Wheaton Coll, IL — B

Architectural Drafting and CAD/CADD
Baker Coll of Flint, MI — A
Baker Coll of Muskegon, MI — A
Dunwoody Coll of Technology, MN — A
Indiana State U, IN — A
Indiana U–Purdue U Indianapolis, IN — A
U of Toledo, OH — A
Westwood Coll–Chicago Du Page, IL — A
Westwood Coll–Chicago Loop Campus, IL — A
Westwood Coll–Chicago O'Hare Airport, IL — A
Westwood Coll–Chicago River Oaks, IL — A

Architectural Engineering
Andrews U, MI — B
Illinois Inst of Technology, IL — B
Kansas State U, KS — B
Milwaukee School of Engineering, WI — B
North Carolina Ag and Tech State U, NC — B
Oklahoma State U, OK — B
U of Cincinnati, OH — B
U of Kansas, KS — B
U of Missouri–Rolla, MO — B
U of Nebraska at Omaha, NE — B
U of Nebraska–Lincoln, NE — B

Architectural Engineering Technology
Baker Coll of Cadillac, MI — A
Baker Coll of Clinton Township, MI — A
Baker Coll of Owosso, MI — A
Baker Coll of Port Huron, MI — A
Central Christian Coll of Kansas, KS — A
Central Missouri State U, MO — B
Ferris State U, MI — A
Indiana State U, IN — B
Indiana U–Purdue U Fort Wayne, IN — A
Indiana U–Purdue U Indianapolis, IN — B
North Dakota State Coll of Science, ND — A
Northern Michigan U, MI — A
Purdue U, IN — A,B
Purdue U Calumet, IN — A
Purdue U North Central, IN — A
Ranken Tech Coll, MO — A,B
U of Cincinnati, OH — A,B
Washington U in St. Louis, MO — B

Architectural History and Criticism
Miami U Hamilton, OH — B
U of Kansas, KS — B

Architectural Technology
Washington U in St. Louis, MO — B

Architecture
Andrews U, MI — B

Ball State U, IN — B
Central Christian Coll of Kansas, KS — A
Coe Coll, IA — B
Cornell Coll, IA — B
Drury U, MO — B
Eastern Michigan U, MI — B
Illinois Inst of Technology, IL — B
Iowa State U of Science and Technology, IA — B
Judson Coll, IL — B
Kansas State U, KS — B
Kent State U, OH — B
Lawrence Technological U, MI — B
Lehigh U, PA — B
Miami U, OH — B
Miami U Hamilton, OH — B
North Dakota State U, ND — B
The Ohio State U, OH — B
Oklahoma State U, OK — B
Southern Illinois U Carbondale, IL — B
U of Cincinnati, OH — B
U of Detroit Mercy, MI — B
U of Illinois at Chicago, IL — B
U of Kansas, KS — B
U of Michigan, MI — B
U of Minnesota, Twin Cities Campus, MN — B
U of Nebraska–Lincoln, NE — B
U of Notre Dame, IN — B
U of Oklahoma, OK — B
U of Wisconsin–Milwaukee, WI — B
Washington U in St. Louis, MO — B
Western Michigan U, MI — B

Architecture Related
School of the Art Inst of Chicago, IL — B
U of Illinois at Urbana–Champaign, IL — B
U of Oklahoma, OK — B
Washington U in St. Louis, MO — B

Area, Ethnic, Cultural, and Gender Studies Related
Bethel U, MN — B
Coe Coll, IA — B
The Coll of Wooster, OH — B
Columbia Coll Chicago, IL — B
Kent State U, OH — B
U of Chicago, IL — B
Washington U in St. Louis, MO — B

Area Studies
Denison U, OH — B
Eastern Michigan U, MI — B
U of Oklahoma, OK — B

Area Studies Related
Eastern Michigan U, MI — B
Illinois Wesleyan U, IL — B
Kent State U, OH — B
Lewis U, IL — B
Northwestern U, IL — B
Oakland U, MI — B
U of Illinois at Urbana–Champaign, IL — B
U of Oklahoma, OK — B
Washington U in St. Louis, MO — B
Wright State U, OH — B

Army R.O.T.C./Military Science
Drake U, IA — B
Minnesota State U Mankato, MN — B
Purdue U Calumet, IN — B
The U of Iowa, IA — B

Art
Adrian Coll, MI — A,B
Albion Coll, MI — B
Alma Coll, MI — B
Alverno Coll, WI — B
American Academy of Art, IL — B
Andrews U, MI — B
Aquinas Coll, MI — B
Art Academy of Cincinnati, OH — B
Ashland U, OH — A,B
Augsburg Coll, MN — B
Augustana Coll, IL — B
Augustana Coll, SD — B
Bacone Coll, OK — A
Ball State U, IN — B
Bemidji State U, MN — B
Bethany Coll, KS — B
Bethany Lutheran Coll, MN — B
Bethel Coll, IN — B
Bethel U, MN — B
Blackburn Coll, IL — B
Black Hills State U, SD — B
Bluffton Coll, OH — B
Bradley U, IL — B
Brescia U, KY — B
Briar Cliff U, IA — B
Buena Vista U, IA — B
Calvin Coll, MI — B
Cameron U, OK — B
Capital U, OH — B
Cardinal Stritch U, WI — B
Carroll Coll, WI — B
Central Christian Coll of Kansas, KS — A
Central Coll, IA — B
Central Michigan U, MI — B
Central State U, OH — B
Chadron State Coll, NE — B
Clarke Coll, IA — B
Cleveland State U, OH — B
Coe Coll, IA — B
Coll for Creative Studies, MI — B
Coll of Saint Benedict, MN — B
Coll of St. Catherine, MN — B
Coll of Saint Mary, NE — A,B
Coll of the Ozarks, MO — B
Coll of Visual Arts, MN — B
Columbia Coll, MO — B
Columbia Coll Chicago, IL — B
Concordia Coll, MN — B
Concordia U, IL — B
Concordia U, MI — B
Concordia U, NE — B
Concordia U Wisconsin, WI — B
Cornell Coll, IA — B
Creighton U, NE — B
Culver-Stockton Coll, MO — B
Dakota Wesleyan U, SD — B
Dana Coll, NE — B
Defiance Coll, OH — A,B
Denison U, OH — B
DePaul U, IL — B
Dickinson State U, ND — B
Doane Coll, NE — B
Dominican U, IL — B
Dordt Coll, IA — B
Drake U, IA — B
Drury U, MO — B
Earlham Coll, IN — B

East Central U, OK — B
Eastern Illinois U, IL — B
Eastern Michigan U, MI — B
Edgewood Coll, WI — B
Elmhurst Coll, IL — B
Emporia State U, KS — B
Eureka Coll, IL — B
Evangel U, MO — B
Fontbonne U, MO — B
Fort Hays State U, KS — B
Goshen Coll, IN — B
Governors State U, IL — B
Grace Coll, IN — B
Graceland U, IA — B
Grand Valley State U, MI — B
Grand View Coll, IA — B
Greenville Coll, IL — B
Grinnell Coll, IA — B
Gustavus Adolphus Coll, MN — B
Hamline U, MN — B
Hannibal-LaGrange Coll, MO — B
Hanover Coll, IN — B
Hastings Coll, NE — B
Hillsdale Coll, MI — B
Hiram Coll, OH — B
Huntington Coll, IN — B
Illinois Coll, IL — B
Illinois State U, IL — B
Illinois Wesleyan U, IL — B
Indiana State U, IN — B
Indiana U Bloomington, IN — B
Indiana U Northwest, IN — B
Indiana U South Bend, IN — B
Indiana U Southeast, IN — B
Iowa State U of Science and Technology, IA — B
Iowa Wesleyan Coll, IA — B
Jamestown Coll, ND — B
Judson Coll, IL — B
Kalamazoo Coll, MI — B
Kansas State U, KS — B
Kansas Wesleyan U, KS — B
Kent State U, Stark Campus, OH — A
Kenyon Coll, OH — B
Knox Coll, IL — B
Lake Erie Coll, OH — B
Lakeland Coll, WI — B
Lewis U, IL — B
Lincoln U, MO — B
Lindenwood U, MO — B
Lourdes Coll, OH — A,B
Loyola U Chicago, IL — B
Luther Coll, IA — B
MacMurray Coll, IL — B
Madonna U, MI — A,B
Manchester Coll, IN — A,B
Marian Coll, IN — A,B
Marietta Coll, OH — B
Marygrove Coll, MI — B
McKendree Coll, IL — B
McPherson Coll, KS — B
Miami U, OH — B
Miami U Hamilton, OH — B
Michigan State U, MI — B
Milwaukee Inst of Art and Design, WI — B
Minnesota State U Mankato, MN — B
Minnesota State U Moorhead, MN — B
Minot State U, ND — B
Missouri Valley Coll, MO — B
Missouri Western State Coll, MO — B

Monmouth Coll, IL	B	Trinity Christian Coll, IL	B	William Woods U, MO	B	Oberlin Coll, OH	B

Monmouth Coll, IL — B
Morningside Coll, IA — B
Mount Mary Coll, WI — B
Mount Mercy Coll, IA — B
Mount Union Coll, OH — B
Mount Vernon Nazarene U, OH — B
Muskingum Coll, OH — B
National-Louis U, IL — B
Nebraska Wesleyan U, NE — B
Newman U, KS — B
North Central Coll, IL — B
North Dakota State U, ND — B
Northeastern Illinois U, IL — B
Northeastern State U, OK — B
Northern Illinois U, IL — B
Northern Michigan U, MI — B
Northern State U, SD — B
Northland Coll, WI — B
North Park U, IL — B
Northwestern Coll, IA — B
Northwestern U, IL — B
Notre Dame Coll, OH — B
Oakland City U, IN — B
Oberlin Coll, OH — B
Ohio Northern U, OH — B
The Ohio State U, OH — B
Ohio U, OH — B
Oklahoma Baptist U, OK — B
Oklahoma Christian U, OK — B
Oklahoma City U, OK — B
Oklahoma State U, OK — B
Olivet Coll, MI — B
Olivet Nazarene U, IL — B
Ottawa U, KS — B
Otterbein Coll, OH — B
Peru State Coll, NE — B
Pittsburg State U, KS — B
Purdue U, IN — B
Ripon Coll, WI — B
Rockford Coll, IL — B
Roosevelt U, IL — B
Saginaw Valley State U, MI — B
St. Ambrose U, IA — B
St. Cloud State U, MN — B
St. Gregory's U, OK — A
Saint John's U, MN — B
Saint Mary-of-the-Woods Coll, IN — B
Saint Mary's Coll, IN — B
St. Norbert Coll, WI — B
St. Olaf Coll, MN — B
Saint Xavier U, IL — B
School of the Art Inst of Chicago, IL
Shawnee State U, OH — A,B
Siena Heights U, MI — A,B
Silver Lake Coll, WI — B
Simpson Coll, IA — B
South Dakota State U, SD — B
Southeastern Oklahoma State U, OK — B
Southeast Missouri State U, MO — B
Southern Illinois U Carbondale, IL
Southern Illinois U Edwardsville, IL — B
Southwest Baptist U, MO — B
Southwest Missouri State U, MO
Spring Arbor U, MI — B
Sterling Coll, KS — B
Taylor U, IN — B
Transylvania U, KY — B

Trinity Christian Coll, IL — B
Truman State U, MO — B
Union Coll, NE — A
The U of Akron, OH — B
The U of Alabama in Huntsville, AL — B
U of Central Oklahoma, OK — B
U of Chicago, IL — B
U of Cincinnati, OH — B
U of Dayton, OH — B
U of Evansville, IN — B
The U of Findlay, OH — B
U of Illinois at Springfield, IL — B
U of Indianapolis, IN — B
The U of Iowa, IA — B
U of Minnesota, Duluth, MN — B
U of Minnesota, Twin Cities Campus, MN — B
U of Missouri–Columbia, MO — B
U of Missouri–Kansas City, MO — B
U of Nebraska at Omaha, NE — B
U of North Dakota, ND — B
U of Northern Iowa, IA — B
U of Oklahoma, OK — B
U of Rio Grande, OH — A,B
U of Saint Francis, IN — B
U of Saint Mary, KS — B
U of Science and Arts of Oklahoma, OK — B
The U of South Dakota, SD — B
U of Southern Indiana, IN — B
U of Toledo, OH — A,B
U of West Florida, FL — B
U of Wisconsin–Eau Claire, WI — B
U of Wisconsin–Green Bay, WI — A,B
U of Wisconsin–La Crosse, WI — B
U of Wisconsin–Madison, WI — B
U of Wisconsin–Milwaukee, WI — B
U of Wisconsin–Oshkosh, WI — B
U of Wisconsin–Parkside, WI — B
U of Wisconsin–Platteville, WI — B
U of Wisconsin–River Falls, WI — B
U of Wisconsin–Stevens Point, WI — B
U of Wisconsin–Whitewater, WI — B
Upper Iowa U, IA — B
Valley City State U, ND — B
Valparaiso U, IN — B
Viterbo U, WI — B
Wabash Coll, IN — B
Wartburg Coll, IA — B
Washburn U, KS — B
Washington U in St. Louis, MO — B
Wayne State Coll, NE — B
Wayne State U, MI — B
Webster U, MO — B
Western Illinois U, IL — B
Western Michigan U, MI — B
Wheaton Coll, IL — B
Wichita State U, KS — B
William Jewell Coll, MO — B

William Woods U, MO — B
Winona State U, MN — B
Wisconsin Lutheran Coll, WI — B
Wittenberg U, OH — B
Wright State U, OH — B
Xavier U, OH — B
Youngstown State U, OH — B

Art History, Criticism and Conservation

Andrews U, MI — B
Aquinas Coll, MI — B
Art Academy of Cincinnati, OH — B
Augsburg Coll, MN — B
Augustana Coll, IL — B
Baker U, KS — B
Baldwin-Wallace Coll, OH — B
Beloit Coll, WI — B
Blackburn Coll, IL — B
Bowling Green State U, OH — B
Bradley U, IL — B
Calvin Coll, MI — B
Carleton Coll, MN — B
Case Western Reserve U, OH — B
Chicago State U, IL — B
Clarke Coll, IA — B
Coll of Saint Benedict, MN — B
Coll of St. Catherine, MN — B
The Coll of Wooster, OH — B
Concordia Coll, MN — B
Cornell Coll, IA — B
Denison U, OH — B
DePaul U, IL — B
DePauw U, IN — B
Dominican U, IL — B
Drake U, IA — B
Drury U, MO — B
Eastern Michigan U, MI — B
Governors State U, IL — B
Grand Valley State U, MI — B
Gustavus Adolphus Coll, MN — B
Hamline U, MN — B
Hanover Coll, IN — B
Hastings Coll, NE — B
Hiram Coll, OH — B
Hope Coll, MI — B
Indiana U Bloomington, IN — B
Indiana U–Purdue U Indianapolis, IN — B
John Carroll U, OH — B
Kalamazoo Coll, MI — B
Kansas City Art Inst, MO — B
Kent State U, OH — B
Kenyon Coll, OH — B
Knox Coll, IL — B
Lake Forest Coll, IL — B
Lawrence U, WI — B
Lincoln Coll, Lincoln, IL — A
Lindenwood U, MO — B
Lourdes Coll, OH — A,B
Loyola U Chicago, IL — B
Macalester Coll, MN — B
MacMurray Coll, IL — B
Marian Coll, IN — B
Miami U, OH — B
Michigan State U, MI — B
Minnesota State U Mankato, MN — B
Minnesota State U Moorhead, MN — B
Northern Illinois U, IL — B
Northwestern U, IL — B
Oakland U, MI — B

Oberlin Coll, OH — B
The Ohio State U, OH — B
Ohio U, OH — B
Ohio Wesleyan U, OH — B
Oklahoma City U, OK — B
Principia Coll, IL — B
Rockford Coll, IL — B
Roosevelt U, IL — B
St. Cloud State U, MN — B
Saint John's U, MN — B
Saint Louis U, MO — B
St. Olaf Coll, MN — B
School of the Art Inst of Chicago, IL — B
Truman State U, MO — B
The U of Akron, OH — B
U of Chicago, IL — B
U of Cincinnati, OH — B
U of Dayton, OH — B
U of Evansville, IN — B
U of Illinois at Chicago, IL — B
U of Illinois at Urbana–Champaign, IL — B
U of Indianapolis, IN — B
The U of Iowa, IA — B
U of Kansas, KS — B
U of Michigan, MI — B
U of Michigan–Dearborn, MI — B
U of Minnesota, Duluth, MN — B
U of Minnesota, Morris, MN — B
U of Minnesota, Twin Cities Campus, MN — B
U of Missouri–Columbia, MO — B
U of Missouri–Kansas City, MO — B
U of Missouri–St. Louis, MO — B
U of Nebraska at Omaha, NE — B
U of Nebraska–Lincoln, NE — B
U of New Orleans, LA — B
U of Northern Iowa, IA — B
U of Notre Dame, IN — B
U of Oklahoma, OK — B
U of St. Thomas, MN — B
U of Toledo, OH — B
U of Tulsa, OK — B
U of West Florida, FL — B
U of Wisconsin–Madison, WI — B
U of Wisconsin–Milwaukee, WI — B
U of Wisconsin–Superior, WI — B
U of Wisconsin–Whitewater, WI — B
Ursuline Coll, OH — B
Valparaiso U, IN — B
Washburn U, KS — B
Washington U in St. Louis, MO — B
Wayne State U, MI — B
Webster U, MO — B
Western Michigan U, MI — B
Wichita State U, KS — B
Wright State U, OH — B
Youngstown State U, OH — B

Artificial Intelligence and Robotics

Eastern Michigan U, MI — B
U of Cincinnati, OH — A

Arts Management

Adrian Coll, MI — B
Aquinas Coll, MI — B
Benedictine Coll, KS — B

A—associate degree; B—bachelor's degree

Benedictine U, IL — B
Buena Vista U, IA — B
Butler U, IN — B
Columbia Coll Chicago, IL — B
Culver-Stockton Coll, MO — B
Dakota State U, SD — B
DePaul U, IL — B
Drury U, MO — B
Eastern Michigan U, MI — B
Fontbonne U, MO — B
Illinois Wesleyan U, IL — B
Kansas Wesleyan U, KS — B
Luther Coll, IA — B
Millikin U, IL — B
Ohio U, OH — B
Oklahoma City U, OK — B
Quincy U, IL — B
U of Evansville, IN — B
The U of Iowa, IA — B
U of Michigan–Dearborn, MI — B
U of Tulsa, OK — B
U of Wisconsin–Stevens Point, WI — B
Upper Iowa U, IA — B
Viterbo U, WI — B
Wartburg Coll, IA — B
Wright State U, OH — B

Art Teacher Education
Adrian Coll, MI — B
Alma Coll, MI — B
Alverno Coll, WI — B
Andrews U, MI — B
Aquinas Coll, MI — B
Ashland U, OH — B
Augsburg Coll, MN — B
Augustana Coll, IL — B
Augustana Coll, SD — B
Baker U, KS — B
Baldwin-Wallace Coll, OH — B
Ball State U, IN — B
Beloit Coll, WI — B
Bemidji State U, MN — B
Bethany Coll, KS — B
Bethel U, MN — B
Bowling Green State U, OH — B
Brescia U, KY — B
Briar Cliff U, IA — B
Buena Vista U, IA — B
Calumet Coll of Saint Joseph, IN — B
Calvin Coll, MI — B
Cameron U, OK — B
Capital U, OH — B
Cardinal Stritch U, WI — B
Carroll Coll, WI — B
Case Western Reserve U, OH — B
Central Christian Coll of Kansas, KS — A
Central Michigan U, MI — B
Central Missouri State U, MO — B
Central State U, OH — B
Chadron State Coll, NE — B
Chicago State U, IL — B
Clarke Coll, IA — B
Coe Coll, IA — B
Coll of Mount St. Joseph, OH — B
Coll of Saint Benedict, MN — B
Coll of St. Catherine, MN — B
Coll of the Ozarks, MO — B
Concordia Coll, MN — B
Concordia U, IL — B
Concordia U, MI — B
Concordia U, NE — B
Concordia U Wisconsin, WI — B
Concord U, WV — B
Culver-Stockton Coll, MO — B
Cumberland Coll, KY — B
Dakota State U, SD — B
Dakota Wesleyan U, SD — B
Dana Coll, NE — B
Defiance Coll, OH — B
Dickinson State U, ND — B
East Central U, OK — B
Eastern Michigan U, MI — B
Edgewood Coll, WI — B
Elmhurst Coll, IL — B
Evangel U, MO — B
Fontbonne U, MO — B
Fort Hays State U, KS — B
Goshen Coll, IN — B
Grace Coll, IN — B
Graceland U, IA — B
Grand Valley State U, MI — B
Greenville Coll, IL — B
Gustavus Adolphus Coll, MN — B
Hannibal-LaGrange Coll, MO
Hastings Coll, NE — B
Hope Coll, MI — B
Huntington Coll, IN — B
Indiana State U, IN — B
Indiana U Bloomington, IN — B
Indiana U–Purdue U Fort Wayne, IN — B
Indiana U–Purdue U Indianapolis, IN
Iowa Wesleyan Coll, IA — B
Kansas Wesleyan U, KS — B
Kent State U, OH — B
Lawrence U, WI — B
Lewis U, IL — B
Lincoln Coll, Lincoln, IL — A
Lincoln U, MO — B
Lindenwood U, MO — B
Loras Coll, IA — B
Madonna U, MI — B
Malone Coll, OH — B
Manchester Coll, IN — B
Marian Coll, IN — B
Marian Coll of Fond du Lac, WI — B
Maryville U of Saint Louis, MO — B
McKendree Coll, IL — B
McPherson Coll, KS — B
Miami U, OH — B
Miami U Hamilton, OH — B
Michigan State U, MI — B
Millikin U, IL — B
Minnesota State U Mankato, MN — B
Minnesota State U Moorhead, MN — B
Minot State U, ND — B
Missouri Western State Coll, MO — B
Morningside Coll, IA — B
Mount Mary Coll, WI — B
Mount Mercy Coll, IA — B
Mount Vernon Nazarene U, OH — B
Muskingum Coll, OH — B
North Carolina Ag and Tech State U, NC — B
North Central Coll, IL — B
Northeastern State U, OK — B
Northern Illinois U, IL — B
Northern Michigan U, MI — B
Northern State U, SD — B
Northland Coll, WI — B
North Park U, IL — B
Northwestern Coll, IA — B
Northwestern Coll, MN — B
Notre Dame Coll, OH — B
Oakland City U, IN — B
Ohio Dominican U, OH — B
Ohio Northern U, OH — B
The Ohio State U, OH — B
Ohio U, OH — B
Ohio Wesleyan U, OH — B
Oklahoma Baptist U, OK — B
Oklahoma City U, OK — B
Olivet Coll, MI — B
Olivet Nazarene U, IL — B
Oral Roberts U, OK — B
Ottawa U, KS — B
Otterbein Coll, OH — B
Peru State Coll, NE — B
Pittsburg State U, KS — B
Rockford Coll, IL — B
St. Ambrose U, IA — B
St. Cloud State U, MN — B
Saint John's U, MN — B
Saint Joseph's Coll, IN — B
Saint Mary-of-the-Woods Coll, IN — B
Saint Mary's Coll, IN — B
Saint Xavier U, IL — B
School of the Art Inst of Chicago, IL — B
Shawnee State U, OH — B
Siena Heights U, MI — B
Silver Lake Coll, WI — B
Simpson Coll, IA — B
South Dakota State U, SD — B
Southeastern Oklahoma State U, OK — B
Southeast Missouri State U, MO — B
Southern Nazarene U, OK — B
Southwest Baptist U, MO — B
Southwestern Oklahoma State U, OK — B
Southwest Missouri State U, MO — B
Tabor Coll, KS — B
Taylor U, IN — B
Transylvania U, KY — B
Trinity Christian Coll, IL — B
Union Coll, NE — B
The U of Akron, OH — B
U of Central Oklahoma, OK — B
U of Cincinnati, OH — B
U of Dayton, OH — B
U of Evansville, IN — B
The U of Findlay, OH — B
U of Illinois at Chicago, IL — B
U of Illinois at Urbana–Champaign, IL — B
U of Indianapolis, IN — B
The U of Iowa, IA — B
U of Kansas, KS — B
U of Michigan, MI — B
U of Michigan–Dearborn, MI — B
U of Michigan–Flint, MI — B
U of Minnesota, Duluth, MN — B
U of Minnesota, Twin Cities Campus, MN — B
U of Missouri–Columbia, MO — B
U of Nebraska–Lincoln, NE — B
U of North Dakota, ND — B
U of Northern Iowa, IA — B
U of Rio Grande, OH — B
U of Saint Francis, IN — B
U of Sioux Falls, SD — B
The U of South Dakota, SD — B
U of Toledo, OH — B
U of West Florida, FL — B
U of Wisconsin–La Crosse, WI — B
U of Wisconsin–Madison, WI — B
U of Wisconsin–Milwaukee, WI — B
U of Wisconsin–Oshkosh, WI — B
U of Wisconsin–River Falls, WI — B
U of Wisconsin–Stout, WI — B
U of Wisconsin–Superior, WI — B
U of Wisconsin–Whitewater, WI — B
Upper Iowa U, IA — B
Ursuline Coll, OH — B
Valley City State U, ND — B
Valparaiso U, IN — B
Viterbo U, WI — B
Waldorf Coll, IA — B
Wartburg Coll, IA — B
Washburn U, KS — B
Washington U in St. Louis, MO — B
Wayne State U, MI — B
Western Michigan U, MI — B
Wichita State U, KS — B
William Woods U, MO — B
Winona State U, MN — B
Wright State U, OH — B
York Coll, NE — B
Youngstown State U, OH — B

Art Therapy
Alverno Coll, WI — B
Bowling Green State U, OH — B
Brescia U, KY — B
Capital U, OH — B
Edgewood Coll, WI — B
Goshen Coll, IN — B
Marian Coll of Fond du Lac, WI — B
Marygrove Coll, MI — B
Millikin U, IL — B
Mount Mary Coll, WI — B
Ohio U, OH — B
Ohio Wesleyan U, OH — B
U of Indianapolis, IN — B
U of Wisconsin–Superior, WI — B
Webster U, MO — B
Wright State U, OH — B

Asian-American Studies
The Ohio State U, OH — B

Asian Studies
Augustana Coll, IL — B
Beloit Coll, WI — B
Bowling Green State U, OH — B
Carleton Coll, MN — B
Case Western Reserve U, OH — B
Coe Coll, IA — B
Hamline U, MN — B
Illinois Wesleyan U, IL — B
Indiana U Bloomington, IN — B
John Carroll U, OH — B
Kenyon Coll, OH — B
Lake Forest Coll, IL — B
Macalester Coll, MN — B
Mount Union Coll, OH — B
Northwestern U, IL — B
Ohio U, OH — B
St. Olaf Coll, MN — B

U of Chicago, IL — B
U of Cincinnati, OH — B
The U of Iowa, IA — B
U of Michigan, MI — B
U of Northern Iowa, IA — B
U of Toledo, OH — B
U of Wisconsin–Madison, WI — B
Washington U in St. Louis, MO — B
Wayne State U, MI — B
Western Michigan U, MI — B

Asian Studies (East)
Augsburg Coll, MN — B
Denison U, OH — B
DePaul U, IL — B
DePauw U, IN — B
Grinnell Coll, IA — B
Hamline U, MN — B
Indiana U Bloomington, IN — B
John Carroll U, OH — B
Lawrence U, WI — B
Oberlin Coll, OH — B
The Ohio State U, OH — B
Ohio Wesleyan U, OH — B
U of Chicago, IL — B
U of Illinois at Urbana–Champaign, IL — B
U of Minnesota, Twin Cities Campus, MN — B
U of Missouri–Columbia, MO — B
U of St. Thomas, MN — B
Valparaiso U, IN — B
Washington U in St. Louis, MO — B
Wayne State U, MI — B
Wittenberg U, OH — B

Asian Studies (South)
U of Chicago, IL — B
U of Michigan, MI — B
U of Minnesota, Twin Cities Campus, MN — B
U of Missouri–Columbia, MO — B

Asian Studies (Southeast)
Ohio U, OH — B
U of Chicago, IL — B
U of Michigan, MI — B
U of Wisconsin–Madison, WI — B

Astronomy
Benedictine Coll, KS — B
Case Western Reserve U, OH — B
Central Michigan U, MI — B
Drake U, IA — B
Indiana U Bloomington, IN — B
Minnesota State U Mankato, MN — B
Mount Union Coll, OH — B
Northwestern U, IL — B
The Ohio State U, OH — B
Ohio Wesleyan U, OH — B
U of Illinois at Urbana–Champaign, IL — B
The U of Iowa, IA — B
U of Kansas, KS — B
U of Michigan, MI — B
U of Minnesota, Twin Cities Campus, MN — B
U of Oklahoma, OK — B
U of Toledo, OH — B

U of Wisconsin–Madison, WI — B
Valparaiso U, IN — B
Youngstown State U, OH — B

Astrophysics
Augsburg Coll, MN — B
Indiana U Bloomington, IN — B
Lehigh U, PA — B
Michigan State U, MI — B
Ohio U, OH — B
U of Minnesota, Twin Cities Campus, MN — B
U of Oklahoma, OK — B

Athletic Training
Aquinas Coll, MI — B
Ashland U, OH — B
Augsburg Coll, MN — B
Augustana Coll, SD — B
Baldwin-Wallace Coll, OH — B
Ball State U, IN — B
Benedictine Coll, KS — B
Bethany Coll, KS — B
Bethel Coll, KS — B
Bethel U, MN — B *Accred*
Bowling Green State U, OH — B
Buena Vista U, IA — B
Calvin Coll, MI — B
Capital U, OH — B
Carroll Coll, WI — B
Carthage Coll, WI — B
Cedarville U, OH — B
Central Christian Coll of Kansas, KS — A
Central Methodist Coll, MO — B
Central Michigan U, MI — B
Clarke Coll, IA — B
Coe Coll, IA — B
Coll of Mount St. Joseph, OH — B
Concordia U Wisconsin, WI — B
Creighton U, NE — B
Culver-Stockton Coll, MO — B
Dakota Wesleyan U, SD — B
Defiance Coll, OH — B
DePauw U, IN — B
Eastern Michigan U, MI — B
Emporia State U, KS — B
Eureka Coll, IL — B
The Franciscan U, IA — B
Franklin Coll, IN — B
Graceland U, IA — B *Acc*
Grand Valley State U, MI — B
Gustavus Adolphus Coll, MN — B
Hamline U, MN — B
Heidelberg Coll, OH — B
Hope Coll, MI — B
Illinois State U, IL — B
Indiana State U, IN — B
Indiana U Bloomington, IN — B
Kansas State U, KS — B
Kent State U, OH — B
Lake Superior State U, MI — B
Lindenwood U, MO — B
Loras Coll, IA — B
Manchester Coll, IN — B
Marietta Coll, OH — B
Marquette U, WI — B
McKendree Coll, IL — B
Miami U, OH — B
Miami U Hamilton, OH — B
MidAmerica Nazarene U, KS — B
Millikin U, IL — B
Minnesota State U Mankato, MN — B

Missouri Valley Coll, MO — B
Mount Marty Coll, SD — B
Mount Union Coll, OH — B
National American U, SD — B
Nebraska Wesleyan U, NE — B
North Central Coll, IL — B
North Dakota State U, ND — B
Northern Michigan U, MI — B
North Park U, IL — B
Ohio Northern U, OH — B
The Ohio State U, OH — B
Ohio U, OH — B
Oklahoma Baptist U, OK — B
Oklahoma State U, OK — B
Olivet Nazarene U, IL — B
Otterbein Coll, OH — B
Park U, MO — B
Shawnee State U, OH — B
Simpson Coll, IA — B
South Dakota State U, SD — B
Southern Nazarene U, OK — B
Southwest Baptist U, MO — B
Southwestern Coll, KS — B
Southwest Missouri State U, MO — B
Sterling Coll, KS — B
Tabor Coll, KS — B
Taylor U, IN — B
Trinity International U, IL — B
The U of Akron, OH — B
U of Evansville, IN — B
The U of Findlay, OH — B
U of Indianapolis, IN — B
The U of Iowa, IA — B
U of Kansas, KS — B
U of Mary, ND — B
U of Michigan, MI — B
U of Nebraska–Lincoln, NE — B
U of Northern Iowa, IA — B
U of Tulsa, OK — B
U of Wisconsin–Eau Claire, WI — B
U of Wisconsin–La Crosse, WI — B
U of Wisconsin–Stevens Point, WI — B
Upper Iowa U, IA — B
Urbana U, OH — B
Valparaiso U, IN — B
Walsh U, OH — B
William Woods U, MO — B
Winona State U, MN — B *Acc*
Xavier U, OH — B
Youngstown State U, OH — B

Athletic Training/Sports Medicine
U of North Dakota, ND — B

Atmospheric Sciences and Meteorology
Creighton U, NE — B
Iowa State U of Science and Technology, IA — B
Northern Illinois U, IL — B
Northland Coll, WI — B
Ohio U, OH — B
St. Cloud State U, MN — B
Saint Louis U, MO — B
U of Kansas, KS — B
U of Michigan, MI — B
U of Missouri–Columbia, MO — B
U of Nebraska–Lincoln, NE — B
U of North Dakota, ND — B
U of Oklahoma, OK — B

U of Wisconsin–Milwaukee, WI — B
Valparaiso U, IN — B

Atomic/Molecular Physics
Ohio U, OH — B
Saint Mary's U of Minnesota, MN — B
The U of Akron, OH — B

Audio Engineering
Cleveland Inst of Music, OH — B

Audiology and Hearing Sciences
Cleveland State U, OH — B
Indiana U Bloomington, IN — B
Indiana U–Purdue U Fort Wayne, IN — B
Northwestern U, IL — B
Ohio U, OH — A
The U of Akron, OH — B
The U of Iowa, IA — B
U of Oklahoma Health Sciences Center, OK — B

Audiology and Speech-Language Pathology
Andrews U, MI — B
Augustana Coll, SD — B
Ball State U, IN — B
Brescia U, KY — B
Butler U, IN — B
Calvin Coll, MI — B
Central Michigan U, MI — B
Elmhurst Coll, IL — B
Fontbonne U, MO — B
Fort Hays State U, KS — B
Governors State U, IL — B
Illinois State U, IL — B
Indiana State U, IN — B
Indiana U Bloomington, IN — B
Kent State U, OH — B
Marquette U, WI — B
Miami U, OH — B
Miami U Hamilton, OH — B
Michigan State U, MI — B
Minnesota State U Mankato, MN — B
Minnesota State U Moorhead, MN — B
Northeastern State U, OK — B
Northern Michigan U, MI — B
Northern State U, SD — B
Northwestern U, IL — B
The Ohio State U, OH — B
Ohio U, OH — B
Otterbein Coll, OH — B
Purdue U, IN — B
St. Cloud State U, MN — B
Southern Illinois U Edwardsville, IL — B
Southwest Missouri State U, MO — B
The U of Akron, OH — B
U of Central Oklahoma, OK — B
U of Cincinnati, OH — B
U of Illinois at Urbana–Champaign, IL — B
The U of Iowa, IA — B
U of Minnesota, Duluth, MN — B
U of Minnesota, Twin Cities Campus, MN — B
U of North Dakota, ND — B
U of Oklahoma Health Sciences Center, OK — B

A—associate degree; B—bachelor's degree

MN State Univ. - Moorhead
Acc.

U of Toledo, OH — B
U of Tulsa, OK — B
U of Wisconsin–Milwaukee, WI — B
U of Wisconsin–Oshkosh, WI — B
U of Wisconsin–Stevens Point, WI — B
Western Michigan U, MI — B
Wichita State U, KS — B

Audiovisual Communications Technologies Related
Greenville Coll, IL — B

Autobody/Collision and Repair Technology
Dunwoody Coll of Technology, MN — A
North Dakota State Coll of Science, ND — A
Northern Michigan U, MI — A
Ranken Tech Coll, MO — A

Automobile/Automotive Mechanics Technology
Andrews U, MI — A,B
Baker Coll of Flint, MI — A
Central Missouri State U, MO — A
Dunwoody Coll of Technology, MN — A
Ferris State U, MI — A,B
McPherson Coll, KS — A
North Dakota State Coll of Science, ND — A
Northern Michigan U, MI — A
Oakland City U, IN — A
Pittsburg State U, KS — A,B
Ranken Tech Coll, MO — A
U of Northwestern Ohio, OH — A

Automotive Engineering Technology
Central Michigan U, MI — B
Central Missouri State U, MO — B
Indiana State U, IN — B
Minnesota State U Mankato, MN — B
Pittsburg State U, KS — B
Southern Illinois U Carbondale, IL — B
The U of Akron, OH — A

Aviation/Airway Management
Academy Coll, MN — A
Baker Coll of Muskegon, MI — B
Bowling Green State U, OH — B
Indiana State U, IN — B
Lewis U, IL — B
Minnesota State U Mankato, MN — B
The Ohio State U, OH — B
Ohio U, OH — B
Oklahoma State U, OK — B
Park U, MO — A,B
Quincy U, IL — B
St. Cloud State U, MN — B
Saint Louis U, MO — B
Southeastern Oklahoma State U, OK — B
Southern Illinois U Carbondale, IL — B
Southern Nazarene U, OK — B
The U of Akron, OH — A
U of Dubuque, IA — A;B

U of Minnesota, Crookston, MN — A,B
U of North Dakota, ND — B
Western Michigan U, MI — B
Winona State U, MN — B

Avionics Maintenance Technology
Andrews U, MI — A,B
Baker Coll of Flint, MI — A
Coll of the Ozarks, MO — B
Grace U, NE — B
Lewis U, IL — A,B
Moody Bible Inst, IL — B
Northern Michigan U, MI — A
The Ohio State U, OH — B
Oklahoma State U, OK — B
Southern Illinois U Carbondale, IL — B
U of Minnesota, Crookston, MN — A
Western Michigan U, MI — B

Ayurvedic Medicine
Maharishi U of Management, IA — B

Baking and Pastry Arts
Kendall Coll, IL — A

Banking and Financial Support Services
Buena Vista U, IA — B
Central Michigan U, MI — B
Northwood U, MI — A,B
The U of Akron, OH — A
U of Indianapolis, IN — A,B
U of Nebraska at Omaha, NE — B
Youngstown State U, OH — B

Behavioral Sciences
Andrews U, MI — B
Antioch Coll, OH — B
Augsburg Coll, MN — B
Bemidji State U, MN — B
Central Christian Coll of Kansas, KS — A
Concordia U, NE — B
Dakota Wesleyan U, SD — B
Drury U, MO — B
Evangel U, MO — B
Grand Valley State U, MI — B
Indiana U Kokomo, IN — B
Lincoln Coll, Lincoln, IL — A
McPherson Coll, KS — B
Minnesota State U Mankato, MN — B
Mount Marty Coll, SD — B
Mount Mary Coll, WI — B
National-Louis U, IL — B
Northern Michigan U, MI — B
Purdue U Calumet, IN — B
Rochester Coll, MI — B
St. Cloud State U, MN — B
Sterling Coll, KS — B
The U of Akron, OH — B
U of Chicago, IL — B
U of Detroit Mercy, MI — B
U of Kansas, KS — B
U of Mary, ND — B
U of Michigan–Dearborn, MI — B
U of Missouri–Columbia, MO — B
U of Sioux Falls, SD — B
Ursuline Coll, OH — B
Walsh U, OH — B

Bengali
U of Chicago, IL — B

Biblical Studies
Andrews U, MI — B
Barclay Coll, KS — A,B
Bethel Coll, IN — A,B
Bethel U, MN — B
Calvary Bible Coll and Theological Seminary, MO — A,B
Calvin Coll, MI — B
Cedarville U, OH — B
Central Christian Coll of Kansas, KS — A,B
Cornerstone U, MI — B
Crossroads Bible Coll, IN — B
Crossroads Coll, MN — B
Crown Coll, MN — A,B
Evangel U, MO — B
Faith Baptist Bible Coll and Theological Seminary, IA — A,B
Global U of the Assemblies of God, MO — B
God's Bible School and Coll, OH — A
Goshen Coll, IN — B
Grace Bible Coll, MI — B
Grace Coll, IN — A,B
Grace U, NE — A,B
Hannibal-LaGrange Coll, MO — B
Hesston Coll, KS — A
Hillsdale Free Will Baptist Coll, OK — A
Huntington Coll, IN — B
Judson Coll, IL — B
Laura and Alvin Siegal Coll of Judaic Studies, OH — B
Malone Coll, OH — B
Manhattan Christian Coll, KS — A,B
Messenger Coll, MO — B
Moody Bible Inst, IL — B
Mount Vernon Nazarene U, OH — B
North Central U, MN — A,B
North Park U, IL — B
Northwestern Coll, MN — B
Oak Hills Christian Coll, MN — A,B
Oakland City U, IN — B
Oklahoma Baptist U, OK — B
Oklahoma Christian U, OK — B
Olivet Nazarene U, IL — B
Oral Roberts U, OK — B
Pillsbury Baptist Bible Coll, MN — B
Reformed Bible Coll, MI — A,B
Rochester Coll, MI — B
St. Louis Christian Coll, MO — B
Southwest Baptist U, MO — B
Tabor Coll, KS — A,B
Taylor U, IN — B
Taylor U Fort Wayne, IN — B
Trinity Bible Coll, ND — A,B
Trinity International U, IL — B
U of Evansville, IN — B
U of Michigan, MI — B
Vennard Coll, IA — B
Wheaton Coll, IL — B
William Tyndale Coll, MI — A,B
York Coll, NE — B

Bilingual and Multilingual Education
Adrian Coll, MI — B
Calvin Coll, MI — B

Chicago State U, IL — B
Concordia U, St. Paul, MN — B
Goshen Coll, IN — B
Indiana U Bloomington, IN — B
Lehigh U, PA — B
Mount Mary Coll, WI — B
Northeastern Illinois U, IL — B
The U of Akron, OH — B
The U of Findlay, OH — B
U of Michigan–Dearborn, MI — B
U of Wisconsin–Milwaukee, WI — B
Western Illinois U, IL — B

Biochemistry
Alma Coll, MI — B
Andrews U, MI — B
Beloit Coll, WI — B
Benedictine Coll, KS — B
Benedictine U, IL — B
Bradley U, IL — B
Calvin Coll, MI — B
Capital U, OH — B
Carroll Coll, WI — B
Case Western Reserve U, OH — B
Clarkson U — B
Coe Coll, IA — B
Coll of Mount St. Joseph, OH — B
Coll of Saint Benedict, MN — B
Coll of St. Catherine, MN — B
The Coll of St. Scholastica, MN — B
The Coll of Wooster, OH — B
Cornell Coll, IA — B
Denison U, OH — B
DePaul U, IL — B
DePauw U, IN — B
Dominican U, IL — B
Eastern Michigan U, MI — B
Grand Valley State U, MI — B
Grinnell Coll, IA — B
Gustavus Adolphus Coll, MN — B
Hamline U, MN — B
Illinois State U, IL — B
Indiana U Bloomington, IN — B
Iowa State U of Science and Technology, IA — B
Jamestown Coll, ND — B
Kansas State U, KS — B
Kenyon Coll, OH — B
Knox Coll, IL — B
Lakeland Coll, WI — B
Lawrence U, WI — B
Lehigh U, PA — B
Lewis U, IL — B
Loras Coll, IA — B
Loyola U Chicago, IL — B
Madonna U, MI — B
Marietta Coll, OH — B
Marquette U, WI — B
Miami U, OH — B
Miami U Hamilton, OH — B
Michigan State U, MI — B
Michigan Technological U, MI — B
Minnesota State U Mankato, MN — B
Monmouth Coll, IL — B
Nebraska Wesleyan U, NE — B
North Central Coll, IL — B
Northern Michigan U, MI — B
Northwestern U, IL — B
Notre Dame Coll, OH — B
Oakland U, MI — B
Oberlin Coll, OH — B

Ohio Northern U, OH	B
The Ohio State U, OH	B
Oklahoma Christian U, OK	B
Oklahoma City U, OK	B
Oklahoma State U, OK	B
Olivet Coll, MI	B
Olivet Nazarene U, IL	B
Oral Roberts U, OK	B
Otterbein Coll, OH	B
Purdue U, IN	B
Ripon Coll, WI	B
Rockford Coll, IL	B
Saginaw Valley State U, MI	B
Saint John's U, MN	B
Saint Joseph's Coll, IN	A,B
Simpson Coll, IA	B
South Dakota State U, SD	B
Southern Nazarene U, OK	B
Southwestern Coll, KS	B
Spring Arbor U, MI	B
Union Coll, NE	B
U of Chicago, IL	B
U of Cincinnati, OH	B
U of Dayton, OH	B
U of Detroit Mercy, MI	B
U of Evansville, IN	B
U of Illinois at Chicago, IL	B
U of Illinois at Urbana–Champaign, IL	B
The U of Iowa, IA	B
U of Michigan, MI	B
U of Michigan–Dearborn, MI	B
U of Minnesota, Duluth, MN	B
U of Minnesota, Twin Cities Campus, MN	B
U of Missouri–Columbia, MO	B
U of Nebraska–Lincoln, NE	B
U of Northern Iowa, IA	B
U of Notre Dame, IN	B
U of St. Thomas, MN	B
U of Tulsa, OK	B
U of Wisconsin–Madison, WI	B
U of Wisconsin–Milwaukee, WI	B
U of Wisconsin–River Falls, WI	B
Valparaiso U, IN	B
Viterbo U, WI	B
Wartburg Coll, IA	B
Washington U in St. Louis, MO	B
Western Michigan U, MI	B
William Jewell Coll, MO	B
Wisconsin Lutheran Coll, WI	B
Wittenberg U, OH	B
Wright State U, OH	B

Biochemistry/Biophysics and Molecular Biology

Illinois Inst of Technology, IL	B
Michigan State U, MI	B
Monmouth Coll, IL	B
Nebraska Wesleyan U, NE	B
North Dakota State U, ND	B
U of Kansas, KS	B

Biochemistry, Biophysics and Molecular Biology Related

Mount Union Coll, OH	B
Oklahoma State U, OK	B

Bioethics/Medical Ethics

Cleveland State U, OH	B

Bioinformatics

Eastern Michigan U, MI	B

Biological and Biomedical Sciences Related

Capital U, OH	B
Kent State U, OH	B
Lehigh U, PA	B
Monmouth Coll, IL	B
Park U, MO	B
Saint Mary's U of Minnesota, MN	B
U of Illinois at Urbana–Champaign, IL	B
U of Kansas, KS	B
U of North Dakota, ND	B
U of Wisconsin–Parkside, WI	B
Ursuline Coll, OH	B
Washington U in St. Louis, MO	B

Biological and Physical Sciences

Alma Coll, MI	B
Antioch Coll, OH	B
Augsburg Coll, MN	B
Avila U, MO	B
Bemidji State U, MN	B
Brescia U, KY	B
Buena Vista U, IA	B
Calvin Coll, MI	B
Cameron U, OK	B
Cedarville U, OH	B
Central Christian Coll of Kansas, KS	A
Coe Coll, IA	B
Coll of Saint Benedict, MN	B
Concordia U, IL	B
Concordia U, MI	B
Concordia U, St. Paul, MN	B
Crown Coll, MN	A
Donnelly Coll, KS	A
Eastern Michigan U, MI	B
Eureka Coll, IL	B
Fort Hays State U, KS	B
Gannon U, PA	B
Grand Valley State U, MI	B
Grinnell Coll, IA	B
Huntington Coll, IN	B
Indiana U East, IN	A
Indiana U Kokomo, IN	B
Iowa Wesleyan Coll, IA	B
John Carroll U, OH	B
Judson Coll, IL	B
Kent State U, Stark Campus, OH	A
Lehigh U, PA	B
Lincoln Coll, Lincoln, IL	A
Madonna U, MI	A,B
Marian Coll of Fond du Lac, WI	B
Marygrove Coll, MI	B
Maryville U of Saint Louis, MO	B
Michigan State U, MI	B
Minnesota State U Mankato, MN	B
Mount Vernon Nazarene U, OH	B
National-Louis U, IL	B
Northern State U, SD	B
Northland Coll, WI	B
North Park U, IL	B
Northwestern U, IL	B
Oakland City U, IN	B

Ohio U, OH	A
Ohio U–Chillicothe, OH	A
Ohio U–Southern Campus, OH	A
Ohio U–Zanesville, OH	A
Oklahoma Baptist U, OK	B
Oklahoma City U, OK	B
Oklahoma Panhandle State U, OK	B
Olivet Nazarene U, IL	B
Palmer Coll of Chiropractic, IA	B
Peru State Coll, NE	B
Purdue U, IN	B
Purdue U Calumet, IN	B
Rochester Coll, MI	A,B
Rockford Coll, IL	B
Saginaw Valley State U, MI	B
Saint Mary-of-the-Woods Coll, IN	B
St. Norbert Coll, WI	B
Saint Xavier U, IL	B
Shawnee State U, OH	B
Simpson Coll, IA	B
Tabor Coll, KS	B
Tri-State U, IN	A
The U of Akron, OH	B
U of Cincinnati, OH	A
U of Dubuque, IA	B
The U of Findlay, OH	B
U of Michigan–Dearborn, MI	B
U of Northern Iowa, IA	B
U of Saint Francis, IN	B
U of Southern Indiana, IN	B
U of Toledo, OH	B
U of West Florida, FL	B
U of Wisconsin–Platteville, WI	B
U of Wisconsin–Superior, WI	B
U of Wisconsin–Whitewater, WI	B
Upper Iowa U, IA	B
Valparaiso U, IN	A
Walsh U, OH	B
Washburn U, KS	A
Washington U in St. Louis, MO	B
Winona State U, MN	B
Wright State U, OH	B
Xavier U, OH	B
York Coll, NE	B
Youngstown State U, OH	B

Biological Specializations Related

Kent State U, OH	A

Biology/Biological Sciences

Adrian Coll, MI	A,B
Albion Coll, MI	B
Alma Coll, MI	B
Alverno Coll, WI	B
Ancilla Coll, IN	A
Andrews U, MI	B
Antioch Coll, OH	B
Aquinas Coll, MI	B
Ashland U, OH	B
Augsburg Coll, MN	B
Augustana Coll, IL	B
Augustana Coll, SD	B
Aurora U, IL	B
Avila U, MO	B
Baker U, KS	B
Baldwin-Wallace Coll, OH	B
Ball State U, IN	B
Beloit Coll, WI	B

Bemidji State U, MN	B
Benedictine Coll, KS	B
Benedictine U, IL	B
Bethany Coll, KS	B
Bethany Lutheran Coll, MN	B
Bethel Coll, IN	B
Bethel Coll, KS	B
Bethel U, MN	B
Blackburn Coll, IL	B
Black Hills State U, SD	B
Bluffton Coll, OH	B
Bowling Green State U, OH	B
Bradley U, IL	B
Brescia U, KY	B
Briar Cliff U, IA	B
Buena Vista U, IA	B
Butler U, IN	B
Calvin Coll, MI	B
Cameron U, OK	B
Capital U, OH	B
Cardinal Stritch U, WI	B
Carleton Coll, MN	B
Carroll Coll, WI	B
Carthage Coll, WI	B
Case Western Reserve U, OH	B
Cedarville U, OH	B
Central Christian Coll of Kansas, KS	A
Central Coll, IA	B
Central Methodist Coll, MO	B
Central Michigan U, MI	B
Central Missouri State U, MO	B
Central State U, OH	B
Chadron State Coll, NE	B
Chicago State U, IL	B
Clarke Coll, IA	B
Clarkson U	B
Cleveland Chiropractic Coll-Kansas City Campus, MO	A,B
Cleveland State U, OH	B
Coe Coll, IA	B
Coll of Mount St. Joseph, OH	B
Coll of Saint Benedict, MN	B
Coll of St. Catherine, MN	B
Coll of Saint Mary, NE	B
The Coll of St. Scholastica, MN	B
Coll of the Ozarks, MO	B
The Coll of Wooster, OH	B
Columbia Coll, MO	B
Concordia Coll, MN	B
Concordia U, IL	B
Concordia U, MI	B
Concordia U, NE	B
Concordia U, St. Paul, MN	B
Concordia U Wisconsin, WI	B
Concord U, WV	B
Cornell Coll, IA	B
Cornerstone U, MI	B
Creighton U, NE	B
Crown Coll, MN	A,B
Culver-Stockton Coll, MO	B
Cumberland Coll, KY	B
Dakota State U, SD	B
Dakota Wesleyan U, SD	B
Dana Coll, NE	B
Defiance Coll, OH	B
Denison U, OH	B
DePaul U, IL	B
DePauw U, IN	B
Dickinson State U, ND	B

A—associate degree; B—bachelor's degree

Doane Coll, NE	B	Lincoln U, MO	B	Ohio Northern U, OH	B	Truman State U, MO	B
Dominican U, IL	B	Lindenwood U, MO	B	The Ohio State U, OH	B	Union Coll, NE	B
Dordt Coll, IA	B	Logan U-Coll of		The Ohio State U at Lima,		The U of Akron, OH	B
Drake U, IA	B	Chiropractic, MO	B	OH	B	The U of Alabama in	
Drury U, MO	B	Loras Coll, IA	B	Ohio U, OH	B	Huntsville, AL	B
Earlham Coll, IN	B	Lourdes Coll, OH	A,B	Ohio Wesleyan U, OH	B	U of Central Oklahoma, OK	B
East Central U, OK	B	Loyola U Chicago, IL	B	Oklahoma Baptist U, OK	B	U of Chicago, IL	B
Eastern Illinois U, IL	B	Luther Coll, IA	B	Oklahoma Christian U, OK	B	U of Cincinnati, OH	B
Eastern Michigan U, MI	B	Macalester Coll, MN	B	Oklahoma City U, OK	B	U of Dayton, OH	B
Edgewood Coll, WI	B	MacMurray Coll, IL	B	Oklahoma Panhandle State		U of Detroit Mercy, MI	B
Elmhurst Coll, IL	B	Madonna U, MI	B	U, OK		U of Dubuque, IA	A,B
Emporia State U, KS	B	Malone Coll, OH	B	Oklahoma State U, OK	B	U of Evansville, IN	B
Eureka Coll, IL	B	Manchester Coll, IN	B	Olivet Coll, MI	B	The U of Findlay, OH	B
Evangel U, MO	B	Marian Coll, IN	B	Olivet Nazarene U, IL	B	U of Illinois at Chicago, IL	B
Ferris State U, MI	B	Marian Coll of Fond du Lac,		Oral Roberts U, OK	B	U of Illinois at Springfield,	
Fontbonne U, MO	B	WI	B	Ottawa U, KS	B	IL	B
Fort Hays State U, KS	B	Marietta Coll, OH	B	Otterbein Coll, OH	B	U of Illinois at Urbana–	
The Franciscan U, IA	B	Marquette U, WI	B	Park U, MO	B	Champaign, IL	B
Franciscan U of Steubenville,		Martin U, IN	B	Peru State Coll, NE	B	U of Indianapolis, IN	B
OH	B	Marygrove Coll, MI	B	Pittsburg State U, KS	B	The U of Iowa, IA	B
Franklin Coll, IN	B	Maryville U of Saint Louis,		Presentation Coll, SD	A,B	U of Kansas, KS	B
Gannon U, PA	B	MO	B	Principia Coll, IL	B	U of Mary, ND	B
Goshen Coll, IN	B	Mayville State U, ND	B	Purdue U, IN	B	U of Michigan, MI	B
Governors State U, IL	B	McKendree Coll, IL	B	Purdue U Calumet, IN	B	U of Michigan–Dearborn, MI	B
Grace Coll, IN	B	McPherson Coll, KS	B	Purdue U North Central, IN	B	U of Michigan–Flint, MI	B
Graceland U, IA	B	Metropolitan State U, MN	B	Quincy U, IL	B	U of Minnesota, Duluth, MN	B
Grand Valley State U, MI	B	Miami U, OH	B	Ripon Coll, WI	B	U of Minnesota, Morris, MN	B
Grand View Coll, IA	B	Michigan State U, MI	B	Rockford Coll, IL	B	U of Minnesota, Twin Cities	
Greenville Coll, IL	B	Michigan Technological U,		Rockhurst U, MO	B	Campus, MN	B
Grinnell Coll, IA	B	MI	B	Roosevelt U, IL	B	U of Missouri–Columbia,	
Gustavus Adolphus Coll, MN	B	MidAmerica Nazarene U, KS	B	Rose-Hulman Inst of		MO	B
Hamline U, MN	B	Millikin U, IL	B	Technology, IN	B	U of Missouri–Kansas City,	
Hannibal-LaGrange Coll,		Minnesota State U Mankato,		Saginaw Valley State U, MI	B	MO	B
MO	B	MN	B	St. Ambrose U, IA	B	U of Missouri–Rolla, MO	B
Hanover Coll, IN	B	Minnesota State U		St. Cloud State U, MN	B	U of Missouri–St. Louis, MO	B
Hastings Coll, NE	B	Moorhead, MN	B	St. Gregory's U, OK	B	U of Nebraska at Omaha,	
Heidelberg Coll, OH	B	Minot State U, ND	B	Saint John's U, MN	B	NE	B
Hillsdale Coll, MI	B	Missouri Baptist U, MO	B	Saint Joseph's Coll, IN	B	U of Nebraska–Lincoln, NE	B
Hiram Coll, OH	B	Missouri Southern State U,		Saint Louis U, MO	B	U of New Orleans, LA	B
Hope Coll, MI	B	MO	B	Saint Mary-of-the-Woods		U of North Dakota, ND	B
Huntington Coll, IN	B	Missouri Valley Coll, MO	B	Coll, IN	B	U of Northern Iowa, IA	B
Illinois Coll, IL	B	Missouri Western State Coll,		Saint Mary's Coll, IN	B	U of Notre Dame, IN	B
Illinois Inst of Technology, IL	B	MO	B	Saint Mary's U of Minnesota,		U of Rio Grande, OH	A,B
Illinois State U, IL	B	Monmouth Coll, IL	B	MN	B	U of St. Francis, IL	B
Illinois Wesleyan U, IL	B	Morningside Coll, IA	B	St. Norbert Coll, WI	B	U of Saint Francis, IN	B
Indiana State U, IN	B	Mount Marty Coll, SD	B	St. Olaf Coll, MN	B	U of Saint Mary, KS	B
Indiana U Bloomington, IN	B	Mount Mary Coll, WI	B	Saint Xavier U, IL	B	U of St. Thomas, MN	B
Indiana U East, IN	B	Mount Mercy Coll, IA	B	Shawnee State U, OH	A,B	U of Science and Arts of	
Indiana U Kokomo, IN	B	Mount Union Coll, OH	B	Siena Heights U, MI	B	Oklahoma, OK	B
Indiana U Northwest, IN	B	Mount Vernon Nazarene U,		Silver Lake Coll, WI	B	U of Sioux Falls, SD	B
Indiana U–Purdue U Fort		OH	B	Simpson Coll, IA	B	The U of South Dakota, SD	B
Wayne, IN	A,B	Muskingum Coll, OH	B	South Dakota State U, SD	B	U of Southern Indiana, IN	B
Indiana U–Purdue U		National-Louis U, IL	B	Southeastern Oklahoma State		U of Toledo, OH	A,B
Indianapolis, IN	B	Nebraska Wesleyan U, NE	B	U, OK	B	U of Tulsa, OK	B
Indiana U South Bend, IN	A,B	Newman U, KS	B	Southeast Missouri State U,		U of West Florida, FL	B
Indiana U Southeast, IN	B	North Carolina Ag and Tech		MO	B	U of Wisconsin–Green Bay,	
Iowa State U of Science and		State U, NC	B	Southern Illinois U		WI	A,B
Technology, IA	B	North Central Coll, IL	B	Carbondale, IL	B	U of Wisconsin–La Crosse,	
Iowa Wesleyan Coll, IA	B	North Dakota State U, ND	B	Southern Illinois U		WI	B
Jamestown Coll, ND	B	Northeastern Illinois U, IL	B	Edwardsville, IL	B	U of Wisconsin–Madison,	
John Carroll U, OH	B	Northeastern State U, OK	B	Southern Nazarene U, OK	B	WI	B
Judson Coll, IL	B	Northern Illinois U, IL	B	Southwest Baptist U, MO	B	U of Wisconsin–Milwaukee,	
Kalamazoo Coll, MI	B	Northern Michigan U, MI	B	Southwestern Coll, KS	B	WI	B
Kansas State U, KS	B	Northern State U, SD	B	Southwestern Oklahoma		U of Wisconsin–Oshkosh,	
Kansas Wesleyan U, KS	B	Northland Coll, WI	B	State U, OK	B	WI	B
Kent State U, OH	B	North Park U, IL	B	Southwest Missouri State U,		U of Wisconsin–Platteville,	
Kenyon Coll, OH	B	Northwestern Coll, IA	B	MO	B	WI	B
Knox Coll, IL	B	Northwestern Coll, MN	B	Spring Arbor U, MI	B	U of Wisconsin–River Falls,	
Lake Erie Coll, OH	B	Northwestern Oklahoma		Stephens Coll, MO	B	WI	B
Lake Forest Coll, IL	B	State U, OK	B	Sterling Coll, KS	B	U of Wisconsin–Stevens	
Lakeland Coll, WI	B	Northwestern U, IL	B	Tabor Coll, KS	B	Point, WI	B
Lake Superior State U, MI	B	Notre Dame Coll, OH	B	Taylor U, IN	B	U of Wisconsin–Superior, WI	B
Lawrence U, WI	B	Oakland City U, IN	B	Transylvania U, KY	B	U of Wisconsin–Whitewater,	
Lehigh U, PA	B	Oakland U, MI	B	Trinity Christian Coll, IL	B	WI	B
Lewis U, IL	B	Oberlin Coll, OH	B	Trinity International U, IL	B	Upper Iowa U, IA	B
Lincoln Coll, Lincoln, IL	A	Ohio Dominican U, OH	B	Tri-State U, IN	B	Urbana U, OH	B

Ursuline Coll, OH — B
Valley City State U, ND — B
Valparaiso U, IN — B
Viterbo U, WI — B
Wabash Coll, IN — B
Walsh U, OH — B
Wartburg Coll, IA — B
Washburn U, KS — B
Washington U in St. Louis, MO — B
Wayne State Coll, NE — B
Wayne State U, MI — B
Webster U, MO — B
Western Illinois U, IL — B
Westminster Coll, MO — B
Wheaton Coll, IL — B
Wichita State U, KS — B
Wilberforce U, OH — B
William Jewell Coll, MO — B
William Penn U, IA — B
William Woods U, MO — B
Winona State U, MN — B
Wisconsin Lutheran Coll, WI — B
Wittenberg U, OH — B
Wright State U, OH — A,B
Xavier U, OH — B
York Coll, NE — B
Youngstown State U, OH — B

Biology/Biotechnology Laboratory Technician
Cleveland State U, OH — B
Ferris State U, MI — A
Michigan Technological U, MI — B
Minnesota State U Mankato, MN — B
Purdue U Calumet, IN — B
St. Cloud State U, MN — B

Biology Teacher Education
Alma Coll, MI — B
Bethany Coll, KS — B
Bethel U, MN — B
Bowling Green State U, OH — B
Buena Vista U, IA — B
Capital U, OH — B
Carroll Coll, WI — B
Cedarville U, OH — B
Central Christian Coll of Kansas, KS — A
Central Methodist Coll, MO — B
Central Michigan U, MI — B
Central Missouri State U, MO — B
Chadron State Coll, NE — B
Coll of St. Catherine, MN — B
The Coll of St. Scholastica, MN — B
Coll of the Ozarks, MO — B
Concordia Coll, MN — B
Concordia U, IL — B
Concordia U, MI — B
Concordia U, NE — B
Concordia U, St. Paul, MN — B
Cornerstone U, MI — B
Dakota Wesleyan U, SD — B
Dordt Coll, IA — B
East Central U, OK — B
Eastern Michigan U, MI — B
Elmhurst Coll, IL — B
Evangel U, MO — B
Franklin Coll, IN — B
Greenville Coll, IL — B
Gustavus Adolphus Coll, MN — B
Hastings Coll, NE — B

Hope Coll, MI — B
Illinois Wesleyan U, IL — B
Indiana U Bloomington, IN — B
Indiana U Northwest, IN — B
Indiana U–Purdue U Fort Wayne, IN — B
Indiana U South Bend, IN — B
Indiana U Southeast, IN — B
Jamestown Coll, ND — B
Lindenwood U, MO — B
Marian Coll of Fond du Lac, WI — B
Maryville U of Saint Louis, MO — B
Mayville State U, ND — B
McKendree Coll, IL — B
Miami U, OH — B
Minot State U, ND — B
Mount Mary Coll, WI — B
North Dakota State U, ND — B
Northern Michigan U, MI — B
Northwestern Coll, IA — B
Oakland City U, IN — B
Ohio Northern U, OH — B
Ohio U, OH — B
Ohio Wesleyan U, OH — B
Oklahoma Baptist U, OK — B
Pittsburg State U, KS — B
St. Ambrose U, IA — B
St. Gregory's U, OK — B
Saint Xavier U, IL — B
Southwest Missouri State U, MO — B
Taylor U, IN — B
Trinity Christian Coll, IL — B
Union Coll, NE — B
The U of Akron, OH — B
U of Dubuque, IA — B
U of Illinois at Chicago, IL — B
The U of Iowa, IA — B
U of Mary, ND — B
U of Michigan–Flint, MI — B
U of Missouri–Columbia, MO — B
U of Missouri–St. Louis, MO — B
U of Nebraska–Lincoln, NE — B
U of Rio Grande, OH — B
U of Saint Francis, IN — B
U of St. Thomas, MN — B
The U of South Dakota, SD — B
U of Wisconsin–River Falls, WI — B
U of Wisconsin–Superior, WI — B
Valley City State U, ND — B
Valparaiso U, IN — B
Viterbo U, WI — B
Washington U in St. Louis, MO — B
Xavier U, OH — B
York Coll, NE — B
Youngstown State U, OH — B

Biomedical/Medical Engineering
Case Western Reserve U, OH — B
Illinois Inst of Technology, IL — B
Indiana U–Purdue U Indianapolis, IN — B
Kettering U, MI — B
Lehigh U, PA — B
Marquette U, WI — B
Michigan State U, MI — B
Milwaukee School of Engineering, WI — B

Northwestern U, IL — B
Oklahoma State U, OK — B
Oral Roberts U, OK — B
Rose-Hulman Inst of Technology, IN — B
Saint Louis U, MO — B
The U of Akron, OH — B
U of Central Oklahoma, OK — B
U of Illinois at Chicago, IL — B
U of Illinois at Urbana–Champaign, IL — B
The U of Iowa, IA — B
U of Nebraska–Lincoln, NE — B
U of Oklahoma, OK — B
U of Toledo, OH — B
U of Wisconsin–Madison, WI — B
Washington U in St. Louis, MO — B
Wright State U, OH — B

Biomedical Sciences
Antioch Coll, OH — B
Grand Valley State U, MI — B
Marquette U, WI — B
St. Cloud State U, MN — B
St. Gregory's U, OK — B
Stephens Coll, MO — B
U of Michigan, MI — B
U of Wisconsin–Eau Claire, WI — B
U of Wisconsin–Green Bay, WI — B

Biomedical Technology
Andrews U, MI — B
Baker Coll of Flint, MI — A
Indiana U–Purdue U Indianapolis, IN — A
Oral Roberts U, OK — B
Wright State U, OH — B

Biometry/Biometrics
U of Michigan, MI — B

Biophysics
Andrews U, MI — B
Clarkson U — B
Illinois Inst of Technology, IL — B
Iowa State U of Science and Technology, IA — B
Oklahoma City U, OK — B
Saint Mary's U of Minnesota, MN — B
Southwestern Oklahoma State U, OK — B
U of Illinois at Urbana–Champaign, IL — B
U of Michigan, MI — B
U of Southern Indiana, IN — B
Washington U in St. Louis, MO — B

Biopsychology
Hastings Coll, NE — B
Morningside Coll, IA — B
Nebraska Wesleyan U, NE — B
Washington U in St. Louis, MO — B

Biotechnology
Calvin Coll, MI — B
Clarkson U — B
Florida Gulf Coast U, FL — B
Gannon U, PA — B
Kent State U, OH — B
Missouri Southern State U, MO — B

North Dakota State U, ND — B
The Ohio State U, OH — B
Roosevelt U, IL — B
Southeastern Oklahoma State U, OK — B
U of Nebraska at Omaha, NE — B
U of Northern Iowa, IA — B
U of Wisconsin–River Falls, WI — B
Ursuline Coll, OH — B

Botany/Plant Biology
Andrews U, MI — B
Ball State U, IN — B
Iowa State U of Science and Technology, IA — B
Kent State U, OH — B
Lincoln Coll, Lincoln, IL — A
Miami U, OH — B
Michigan State U, MI — B
Minnesota State U Mankato, MN — B
North Dakota State U, ND — B
Northern Michigan U, MI — B
The Ohio State U, OH — B
Ohio U, OH — B
Ohio Wesleyan U, OH — B
Oklahoma State U, OK — B
Purdue U, IN — B
Purdue U Calumet, IN — B
St. Cloud State U, MN — B
Saint Xavier U, IL — B
Southeastern Oklahoma State U, OK — B
Southern Illinois U Carbondale, IL — B
The U of Akron, OH — B
U of Illinois at Urbana–Champaign, IL — B
U of Michigan, MI — B
U of Minnesota, Twin Cities Campus, MN — B
U of Oklahoma, OK — B
U of Wisconsin–Madison, WI — B

Botany/Plant Biology Related
Miami U Hamilton, OH — B

Broadcast Journalism
Adrian Coll, MI — B
Baldwin-Wallace Coll, OH — B
Bemidji State U, MN — B
Bowling Green State U, OH — B
Bradley U, IL — B
Calvary Bible Coll and Theological Seminary, MO — B
Cedarville U, OH — B
Chicago State U, IL — B
Coll of the Ozarks, MO — B
Columbia Coll Chicago, IL — B
Concordia Coll, MN — B
Cornerstone U, MI — A
Drake U, IA — B
Drury U, MO — B
Evangel U, MO — A,B
Fontbonne U, MO — B
Goshen Coll, IN — B
Grace U, NE — B
Grand Valley State U, MI — B
Hastings Coll, NE — B
Huntington Coll, IN — B
Indiana U Bloomington, IN — B
Lewis U, IL — B
Lincoln Coll, Lincoln, IL — A

Lindenwood U, MO — B
Manchester Coll, IN — A
Marquette U, WI — B
Minnesota State U Moorhead, MN — B
Mount Vernon Nazarene U, OH — B
Muskingum Coll, OH — B
North Central Coll, IL — B
North Central U, MN — A,B
Northern Michigan U, MI — B
Ohio U, OH — B
Ohio U–Zanesville, OH — A
Ohio Wesleyan U, OH — B
Oklahoma Baptist U, OK — B
Oklahoma Christian U, OK — B
Oklahoma City U, OK — B
Oklahoma State U, OK — B
Olivet Nazarene U, IL — B
Pittsburg State U, KS — B
Reformed Bible Coll, MI — B
St. Cloud State U, MN — B
St. Gregory's U, OK — B
Southern Nazarene U, OK — B
Stephens Coll, MO — B
The U of Akron, OH — B
U of Central Oklahoma, OK — B
U of Cincinnati, OH — B
U of Dayton, OH — B
U of Detroit Mercy, MI — B
The U of Findlay, OH — B
U of Illinois at Urbana–Champaign, IL — B
U of Kansas, KS — B
U of Missouri–Columbia, MO — B
U of Nebraska at Omaha, NE — B
U of Nebraska–Lincoln, NE — B
U of Northern Iowa, IA — B
U of Oklahoma, OK — B
U of St. Thomas, MN — B
U of Wisconsin–Madison, WI — B
U of Wisconsin–Milwaukee, WI — B
U of Wisconsin–Oshkosh, WI — B
U of Wisconsin–Platteville, WI — B
U of Wisconsin–River Falls, WI — B
U of Wisconsin–Superior, WI — B
Waldorf Coll, IA — B
Wartburg Coll, IA — B
Webster U, MO — B
William Woods U, MO — B
Winona State U, MN — B

Building/Property Maintenance and Management
Park U, MO — A

Business Administration and Management
Academy Coll, MN — A,B
Adrian Coll, MI — A,B
AIB Coll of Business, IA — A
Albion Coll, MI — B
Alma Coll, MI — B
Alverno Coll, WI — B
Ancilla Coll, IN — A
Andrews U, MI — A,B
Antioch Coll, OH — B
Aquinas Coll, MI — B
Argosy U/Chicago, IL — B
Ashland U, OH — B

Augsburg Coll, MN — B
Augustana Coll, IL — B
Augustana Coll, SD — B
Bacone Coll, OK — A,B
Baker Coll of Allen Park, MI — A
Baker Coll of Auburn Hills, MI — A,B
Baker Coll of Cadillac, MI — A,B
Baker Coll of Clinton Township, MI — A,B
Baker Coll of Flint, MI — A,B
Baker Coll of Jackson, MI — A,B
Baker Coll of Muskegon, MI — A,B
Baker Coll of Owosso, MI — A,B
Baker Coll of Port Huron, MI — A,B
Baker U, KS — B
Baldwin-Wallace Coll, OH — B
Ball State U, IN — A,B
Baptist Bible Coll, MO — A,B
Barclay Coll, KS — B
Bellevue U, NE — B
Beloit Coll, WI — B
Bemidji State U, MN — B
Benedictine Coll, KS — B
Benedictine U, IL — A
Bethany Coll, KS — B
Bethany Lutheran Coll, MN — B
Bethel Coll, IN — A,B
Bethel U, MN — B
Blackburn Coll, IL — B
Black Hills State U, SD — B
Bluffton Coll, OH — B
Bradley U, IL — B
Briar Cliff U, IA — B
Butler U, IN — B
Calumet Coll of Saint Joseph, IN — A,B
Calvin Coll, MI — B
Cameron U, OK — A,B
Capital U, OH — B
Cardinal Stritch U, WI — A,B
Carroll Coll, WI — B
Carthage Coll, WI — B
Case Western Reserve U, OH — B
Cedarville U, OH — B
Central Christian Coll of Kansas, KS — A,B
Central Coll, IA — B
Central Methodist Coll, MO — B
Central Michigan U, MI — B
Central Missouri State U, MO — B
Central State U, OH — B
Chadron State Coll, NE — B
Chatfield Coll, OH — A
Chicago State U, IL — B
Clarke Coll, IA — B
Clarkson U — B
Cleary U, MI — B
Cleveland State U, OH — B
Coe Coll, IA — B
Coll of Mount St. Joseph, OH — A,B
Coll of Saint Benedict, MN — B
Coll of St. Catherine, MN — B
Coll of Saint Mary, NE — A,B
The Coll of St. Scholastica, MN — B
Coll of the Ozarks, MO — B
Colorado Tech U Sioux Falls Campus, SD — A,B
Columbia Coll, MO — A,B
Columbia Coll Chicago, IL — B
Concordia Coll, MN — B

Concordia U, IL — B
Concordia U, MI — B
Concordia U, NE — B
Concordia U, St. Paul, MN — B
Concordia U Wisconsin, WI — B
Concord U, WV — A,B
Cornerstone U, MI — B
Crown Coll, MN — A,B
Culver-Stockton Coll, MO — B
Dakota State U, SD — A,B
Dakota Wesleyan U, SD — A,B
Dana Coll, NE — B
Davenport U, Dearborn, MI — A,B
Davenport U, Grand Rapids, MI — A,B
Davenport U, Kalamazoo, MI — A,B
Davenport U, Lansing, MI — A,B
Davenport U, Lapeer, MI — A,B
Davenport U, Warren, MI — A,B
Defiance Coll, OH — A,B
DePaul U, IL — B
Dickinson State U, ND — B
Doane Coll, NE — B
Dominican U, IL — B
Donnelly Coll, KS — A
Dordt Coll, IA — B
Drake U, IA — B
Drury U, MO — B
Earlham Coll, IN — B
East Central U, OK — B
Eastern Illinois U, IL — B
Eastern Michigan U, MI — B
Edgewood Coll, WI — B
Elmhurst Coll, IL — B
Emporia State U, KS — B
Eureka Coll, IL — B
Evangel U, MO — B
Ferris State U, MI — B
Florida Gulf Coast U, FL — B
Fontbonne U, MO — B
Fort Hays State U, KS — B
The Franciscan U, IA — B
Franciscan U of Steubenville, OH — A,B
Franklin U, OH — A,B
Gallipolis Career Coll, OH — A
Gannon U, PA — A,B
Globe Coll, MN — A
Goshen Coll, IN — B
Governors State U, IL — B
Grace Bible Coll, MI — A,B
Grace Coll, IN — B
Graceland U, IA — B
Grace U, NE — B
Grand Valley State U, MI — B
Grand View Coll, IA — B
Greenville Coll, IL — B
Gustavus Adolphus Coll, MN — B
Hamilton Coll, NE — A
Hamline U, MN — B
Hannibal-LaGrange Coll, MO — B
Hanover Coll, IN — B
Harris-Stowe State Coll, MO — B
Haskell Indian Nations U, KS — A,B
Hastings Coll, NE — B
Heidelberg Coll, OH — B
Hesston Coll, KS — A
Hickey Coll, MO — B
Hillsdale Coll, MI — B
Hiram Coll, OH — B
Hope Coll, MI — B
Huntington Coll, IN — B
Illinois Coll, IL — B
Illinois State U, IL — B

Illinois Wesleyan U, IL — B
Indiana Inst of Technology, IN — A,B
Indiana State U, IN — A,B
Indiana U Bloomington, IN — B
Indiana U Northwest, IN — B
Indiana U–Purdue U Fort Wayne, IN — A,B
Iowa State U of Science and Technology, IA — B
Iowa Wesleyan Coll, IA — B
ITT Tech Inst, Fort Wayne, IN — B
ITT Tech Inst, Indianapolis, IN — B
ITT Tech Inst, Arnold, MO — B
ITT Tech Inst, Earth City, MO — B
Jamestown Coll, ND — B
John Carroll U, OH — B
Judson Coll, IL — B
Kansas State U, KS — B
Kansas Wesleyan U, KS — A,B
Kaplan Coll, IA — A,B
Kendall Coll, IL — B
Kent State U, OH — A,B
Kent State U, Salem Campus, OH — A,B
Kent State U, Stark Campus, OH — A
Kent State U, Tuscarawas Campus, OH — A,B
Kettering U, MI — B
Kilian Comm Coll, SD — A
Lake Erie Coll, OH — B
Lakeland Coll, WI — B
Lake Superior State U, MI — A,B
Lawrence Technological U, MI — B
Lehigh U, PA — B
Lewis U, IL — B
Lincoln Coll, Lincoln, IL — A
Lincoln U, MO — B
Lindenwood U, MO — B
Loras Coll, IA — B
Lourdes Coll, OH — A,B
Loyola U Chicago, IL — B
Luther Coll, IA — B
MacCormac Coll, IL — A
MacMurray Coll, IL — A,B
Madonna U, MI — A,B
Maharishi U of Management, IA — B
Malone Coll, OH — B
Manchester Coll, IN — A,B
Manhattan Christian Coll, KS — B
Marian Coll, IN — A,B
Marian Coll of Fond du Lac, WI — B
Marietta Coll, OH — A,B
Marquette U, WI — B
Martin U, IN — B
Marygrove Coll, MI — B
Maryville U of Saint Louis, MO — B
Mayville State U, ND — A,B
McKendree Coll, IL — B
McPherson Coll, KS — B
Messenger Coll, MO — B
Metropolitan State U, MN — B
Miami U, OH — B
Miami U Hamilton, OH — A
Michigan State U, MI — B
Michigan Technological U, MI — B

MidAmerica Nazarene U, KS — A,B
Millikin U, IL — B
Milwaukee School of Engineering, WI — B
Minnesota School of Business–Brooklyn Center, MN — A
Minnesota School of Business–Plymouth, MN — A
Minnesota School of Business–Richfield, MN — A
Minnesota State U Mankato, MN — B
Minnesota State U Moorhead, MN — B
Minot State U, ND — B
Missouri Baptist U, MO — A,B
Missouri Southern State U, MO — A,B
Missouri Valley Coll, MO — A,B
Missouri Western State Coll, MO — A,B
Monmouth Coll, IL — B
Morningside Coll, IA — B
Mount Marty Coll, SD — A,B
Mount Mary Coll, WI — B
Mount Mercy Coll, IA — B
Mount Union Coll, OH — B
Muskingum Coll, OH — B
National American U, SD — A,B
National American U–Sioux Falls Branch, SD — A,B
National-Louis U, IL — B
Nebraska Wesleyan U, NE — B
Newman U, KS — A,B
North Carolina Ag and Tech State U, NC — B
North Central Coll, IL — B
North Central U, MN — A,B
North Dakota State U, ND — B
Northeastern Illinois U, IL — B
Northeastern State U, OK — B
Northern Illinois U, IL — B
Northern Michigan U, MI — A,B
Northern State U, SD — A,B
Northland Coll, WI — B
North Park U, IL — B
Northwestern Coll, IA — B
Northwestern Coll, MN — B
Northwestern Oklahoma State U, OK — B
Northwood U, MI — A,B
Notre Dame Coll, OH — A,B
Oak Hills Christian Coll, MN — B
Oakland City U, IN — A,B
Oakland U, MI — B
Ohio Dominican U, OH — A,B
Ohio Northern U, OH — B
The Ohio State U, OH — B
The Ohio State U at Lima, OH — B
The Ohio State U at Marion, OH — B
The Ohio State U–Mansfield Campus, OH — B
The Ohio State U–Newark Campus, OH — B
Ohio U, OH — A,B
Ohio U–Chillicothe, OH — A,B
Ohio U–Southern Campus, OH — B
Ohio Wesleyan U, OH — B
Oklahoma Baptist U, OK — B
Oklahoma Christian U, OK — B

Oklahoma City U, OK — B
Oklahoma Panhandle State U, OK — A,B
Olivet Coll, MI — B
Olivet Nazarene U, IL — B
Oral Roberts U, OK — B
Ottawa U, KS — B
Otterbein Coll, OH — B
Park U, MO — A,B
Peru State Coll, NE — B
Pillsbury Baptist Bible Coll, MN — B
Pittsburg State U, KS — B
Presentation Coll, SD — A,B
Principia Coll, IL — B
Purdue U, IN — B
Purdue U Calumet, IN — B
Purdue U North Central, IN — A,B
Quincy U, IL — B
Reformed Bible Coll, MI — B
Ripon Coll, WI — B
Robert Morris Coll, IL — A,B
Rochester Coll, MI — B
Rochester Comm and Tech Coll, MN — A
Rockford Coll, IL — B
Rockhurst U, MO — B
Roosevelt U, IL — B
Saginaw Valley State U, MI — B
St. Ambrose U, IA — B
St. Augustine Coll, IL — A
St. Cloud State U, MN — B
St. Gregory's U, OK — A,B
Saint John's U, MN — B
Saint Louis U, MO — B
Saint Mary-of-the-Woods Coll, IN — B
Saint Mary's Coll, IN — B
Saint Mary's U of Minnesota, MN — B
Shawnee State U, OH — A,B
Siena Heights U, MI — A,B
Silver Lake Coll, WI — B
Simpson Coll, IA — B
Southeastern Oklahoma State U, OK — B
Southeast Missouri State U, MO — B
Southern Illinois U Carbondale, IL — B
Southern Illinois U Edwardsville, IL — B
Southern Nazarene U, OK — B
Southwest Baptist U, MO — A,B
Southwestern Coll, KS — B
Southwestern Oklahoma State U, OK — B
Southwest Missouri State U, MO — B
Spring Arbor U, MI — B
Stephens Coll, MO — B
Sterling Coll, KS — B
Tabor Coll, KS — B
Taylor U, IN — A,B
Taylor U Fort Wayne, IN — A,B
Tiffin U, OH — A,B
Transylvania U, KY — B
Trinity Bible Coll, ND — A,B
Trinity Christian Coll, IL — B
Trinity International U, IL — B
Tri-State U, IN — A,B
Truman State U, MO — B
Union Coll, NE — A,B
The U of Akron, OH — A,B

The U of Alabama in Huntsville, AL — B
U of Central Oklahoma, OK — B
U of Cincinnati, OH — A,B
U of Dayton, OH — B
U of Detroit Mercy, MI — B
U of Dubuque, IA — A,B
U of Evansville, IN — B
The U of Findlay, OH — A,B
U of Illinois at Chicago, IL — B
U of Illinois at Springfield, IL — B
U of Indianapolis, IN — A,B
The U of Iowa, IA — B
U of Mary, ND — A,B
U of Michigan, MI — B
U of Michigan–Dearborn, MI — B
U of Michigan–Flint, MI — B
U of Minnesota, Crookston, MN — A,B
U of Minnesota, Duluth, MN — B
U of Minnesota, Morris, MN — B
U of Missouri–Columbia, MO — B
U of Missouri–Kansas City, MO — B
U of Missouri–Rolla, MO — B
U of Missouri–St. Louis, MO — B
U of Nebraska at Omaha, NE — B
U of Nebraska–Lincoln, NE — B
U of New Orleans, LA — B
U of Northern Iowa, IA — B
U of Northwestern Ohio, OH — A,B
U of Oklahoma, OK — B
U of Phoenix–Chicago Campus, IL — B
U of Phoenix–Cleveland Campus, OH — B
U of Phoenix–Kansas City Campus, MO — B
U of Phoenix–Metro Detroit Campus, MI — B
U of Phoenix–Oklahoma City Campus, OK — B
U of Phoenix–St. Louis Campus, MO — B
U of Phoenix–Tulsa Campus, OK — B
U of Phoenix–West Michigan Campus, MI — B
U of Phoenix–Wisconsin Campus, WI — B
U of Rio Grande, OH — A,B
U of St. Francis, IL — B
U of Saint Francis, IN — A,B
U of Saint Mary, KS — B
U of St. Thomas, MN — B
U of Sioux Falls, SD — A,B
The U of South Dakota, SD — B
U of Southern Indiana, IN — B
U of Toledo, OH — A,B
U of Tulsa, OK — B
U of West Florida, FL — B
U of Wisconsin–Eau Claire, WI — B
U of Wisconsin–Green Bay, WI — A,B
U of Wisconsin–La Crosse, WI — B
U of Wisconsin–Madison, WI — B
U of Wisconsin–Milwaukee, WI — B

U of Wisconsin–Oshkosh, WI — B
U of Wisconsin–Parkside, WI — B
U of Wisconsin–Platteville, WI — B
U of Wisconsin–River Falls, WI — B
U of Wisconsin–Stevens Point, WI — B
U of Wisconsin–Stout, WI — B
U of Wisconsin–Superior, WI — B
U of Wisconsin–Whitewater, WI — B
Upper Iowa U, IA — A,B
Urbana U, OH — A,B
Ursuline Coll, OH — B
Valley City State U, ND — B
Vennard Coll, IA — B
Viterbo U, WI — B
Waldorf Coll, IA — B
Walsh Coll of Accountancy and Business Administration, MI — B
Walsh U, OH — A,B
Wartburg Coll, IA — B
Washburn U, KS — B
Washington U in St. Louis, MO — B
Wayne State Coll, NE — B
Wayne State U, MI — B
Webster U, MO — B
Western Illinois U, IL — B
Western Michigan U, MI — B
Westminster Coll, MO — B
Wichita State U, KS — B
Wilberforce U, OH — B
William Jewell Coll, MO — B
William Penn U, IA — B
William Tyndale Coll, MI — B
William Woods U, MO — B
Winona State U, MN — B
Wittenberg U, OH — B
Wright State U, OH — B
Xavier U, OH — B
York Coll, NE — B
Youngstown State U, OH — A,B

Business Administration, Management and Operations Related

Alverno Coll, WI — B
American InterContinental U Online, IL — A,B
Bryant and Stratton Coll, WI — A,B
Capital U, OH — B
Central Michigan U, MI — B
Cleveland State U, OH — B
Cornerstone U, MI — B
Davenport U, Dearborn, MI — B
Davenport U, Grand Rapids, MI — B
Davenport U, Holland, MI — B
Davenport U, Lapeer, MI — B
Davenport U, Warren, MI — B
DePaul U, IL — B
DeVry U, Addison, IL — B
DeVry U, Chicago, IL — B
DeVry U, Tinley Park, IL — B
DeVry U, MO — B
DeVry U, Columbus, OH — B
Malone Coll, OH — B
Mayville State U, ND — B
Miami U Hamilton, OH — B
Missouri Baptist U, MO — B
Oakland City U, IN — B

A—associate degree; B—bachelor's degree

Oakland U, MI	B
St. Augustine Coll, IL	A
Saint Mary-of-the-Woods Coll, IN	B
Trinity Christian Coll, IL	B
U of Notre Dame, IN	B
U of St. Thomas, MN	B
U of Toledo, OH	B
Ursuline Coll, OH	B
Viterbo U, WI	B
Washington U in St. Louis, MO	B

Business Automation/ Technology/Data Entry

Baker Coll of Clinton Township, MI	A
Central Christian Coll of Kansas, KS	A
East Central U, OK	B
Kent State U, OH	A
The U of Akron, OH	A
U of Rio Grande, OH	A
U of Toledo, OH	A
Youngstown State U, OH	A

Business/Commerce

Academy Coll, MN	A
Argosy U/Chicago Northwest, IL	B
Aurora U, IL	B
Avila U, MO	B
Baker Coll of Flint, MI	A
Baker Coll of Jackson, MI	A
Benedictine U, IL	B
Bethel Coll, KS	B
Bowling Green State U, OH	B
Brescia U, KY	A,B
Capella U, MN	B
Capital U, OH	B
Central Christian Coll of Kansas, KS	A,B
Central Michigan U, MI	B
Concordia Coll, MN	B
Concordia U, NE	B
Crown Coll, MN	A
Cumberland Coll, KY	B
Davenport U, Dearborn, MI	B
Davenport U, Gaylord, MI	B
Davenport U, Grand Rapids, MI	B
Davenport U, Holland, MI	B
Davenport U, Kalamazoo, MI	B
Davenport U, Lansing, MI	B
Davenport U, Lapeer, MI	B
Davenport U, Traverse City, MI	B
Davenport U, Warren, MI	B
DePaul U, IL	B
Drake U, IA	B
Eastern Michigan U, MI	B
Franklin Coll, IN	B
Gallipolis Career Coll, OH	A
Gannon U, PA	A
God's Bible School and Coll, OH	A
Grace Coll, IN	B
Harris-Stowe State Coll, MO	B
Hillsdale Free Will Baptist Coll, OK	A,B
Illinois Inst of Technology, IL	B
Indiana U Bloomington, IN	B
Indiana U East, IN	A,B
Indiana U Kokomo, IN	A,B
Indiana U–Purdue U Indianapolis, IN	B
Indiana U South Bend, IN	A,B

Indiana U Southeast, IN	A,B
Kaplan Coll, IA	B
Kent State U, OH	A
Lehigh U, PA	B
Loras Coll, IA	B
Manchester Coll, IN	B
Marygrove Coll, MI	A,B
Maryville U of Saint Louis, MO	B
Miami U, OH	B
Miami U Hamilton, OH	B
Milwaukee School of Engineering, WI	B
Mount Vernon Nazarene U, OH	A,B
North Dakota State Coll of Science, ND	A
Northeastern Illinois U, IL	B
Northern Illinois U, IL	B
Ohio Northern U, OH	B
Ohio U, OH	B
Oklahoma Christian U, OK	B
Oklahoma City U, OK	B
Oklahoma State U, OK	B
Rockhurst U, MO	B
Roosevelt U, IL	B
Saginaw Valley State U, MI	B
St. Ambrose U, IA	B
Saint Joseph's Coll, IN	B
St. Norbert Coll, WI	B
Saint Xavier U, IL	B
Southern Nazarene U, OK	A
Southwest Baptist U, MO	A
Southwest Missouri State U, MO	B
Trinity Christian Coll, IL	B
Union Inst & U, OH	B
The U of Akron, OH	B
U of Central Oklahoma, OK	B
U of Illinois at Urbana–Champaign, IL	B
U of Kansas, KS	B
U of Missouri–Rolla, MO	B
U of Missouri–St. Louis, MO	B
U of Nebraska at Omaha, NE	B
U of North Dakota, ND	B
U of Notre Dame, IN	B
U of Science and Arts of Oklahoma, OK	B
U of Southern Indiana, IN	B
U of Toledo, OH	A,B
U of Wisconsin–Whitewater, WI	B
Washington U in St. Louis, MO	B
Webster U, MO	B
Western Michigan U, MI	B
Wright State U, OH	B
Xavier U, OH	A,B
Youngstown State U, OH	B

Business/Corporate Communications

Aquinas Coll, MI	B
Augustana Coll, SD	B
Calvin Coll, MI	B
Central Christian Coll of Kansas, KS	A
Marietta Coll, OH	B
Morningside Coll, IA	B
Ohio Dominican U, OH	B
Rochester Coll, MI	B
Rockhurst U, MO	B
Simpson Coll, IA	B
Southwestern Coll, KS	B
The U of Findlay, OH	B

U of Mary, ND	B
U of Rio Grande, OH	B
U of St. Thomas, MN	B

Business Family and Consumer Sciences/Human Sciences

The Ohio State U, OH	B

Business, Management, and Marketing Related

Benedictine U, IL	B
Bowling Green State U, OH	B
Central Michigan U, MI	B
Coll of Mount St. Joseph, OH	B
The Coll of St. Scholastica, MN	B
Iowa State U of Science and Technology, IA	B
Nebraska Wesleyan U, NE	B
Ohio U, OH	B
Park U, MO	B
Saint Mary's U of Minnesota, MN	B
The U of Akron, OH	A
U of Phoenix–Kansas City Campus, MO	B
U of Southern Indiana, IN	A
U of Toledo, OH	B

Business/Managerial Economics

Andrews U, MI	B
Augsburg Coll, MN	B
Aurora U, IL	B
Ball State U, IN	B
Beloit Coll, WI	B
Benedictine U, IL	B
Bethany Coll, KS	B
Bowling Green State U, OH	B
Bradley U, IL	B
Buena Vista U, IA	B
Butler U, IN	B
Capital U, OH	B
Cardinal Stritch U, WI	B
Central Christian Coll of Kansas, KS	A
Cleveland State U, OH	B
Coll of the Ozarks, MO	B
The Coll of Wooster, OH	B
DePaul U, IL	B
East Central U, OK	B
Eastern Michigan U, MI	B
Ferris State U, MI	B
Fort Hays State U, KS	B
Gustavus Adolphus Coll, MN	B
Hope Coll, MI	B
Huntington Coll, IN	B
Illinois Coll, IL	B
Indiana U Bloomington, IN	B
Indiana U–Purdue U Fort Wayne, IN	B
Indiana U Southeast, IN	B
Jamestown Coll, ND	B
Kalamazoo Coll, MI	B
Kent State U, OH	B
Lake Forest Coll, IL	B
Lake Superior State U, MI	B
Lehigh U, PA	B
Lewis U, IL	B
Lincoln Coll, Lincoln, IL	A
Loyola U Chicago, IL	B
Marian Coll of Fond du Lac, WI	B
Marquette U, WI	B
Miami U, OH	B

Miami U Hamilton, OH	B
Michigan Technological U, MI	B
Northern State U, SD	B
Northland Coll, WI	B
Northwood U, MI	A,B
The Ohio State U, OH	B
Ohio Wesleyan U, OH	B
Oklahoma City U, OK	B
Oklahoma State U, OK	B
Olivet Nazarene U, IL	B
Otterbein Coll, OH	B
Park U, MO	B
Pittsburg State U, KS	B
Rockford Coll, IL	B
Roosevelt U, IL	B
Saginaw Valley State U, MI	B
Southeast Missouri State U, MO	B
Southern Illinois U Carbondale, IL	B
Southern Illinois U Edwardsville, IL	B
U of Central Oklahoma, OK	B
U of Dayton, OH	B
U of Evansville, IN	B
U of Indianapolis, IN	B
The U of Iowa, IA	B
U of Missouri–Columbia, MO	B
U of Nebraska at Omaha, NE	B
U of Nebraska–Lincoln, NE	B
U of New Orleans, LA	B
U of North Dakota, ND	B
U of Oklahoma, OK	B
The U of South Dakota, SD	B
U of Toledo, OH	B
U of West Florida, FL	B
U of Wisconsin–Platteville, WI	B
U of Wisconsin–Superior, WI	B
U of Wisconsin–Whitewater, WI	B
Urbana U, OH	A,B
Washington U in St. Louis, MO	B
Wayne State Coll, NE	B
Western Illinois U, IL	B
Western Michigan U, MI	B
Wheaton Coll, IL	B
Wilberforce U, OH	B
William Woods U, MO	B
Winona State U, MN	B
Wisconsin Lutheran Coll, WI	B
Wittenberg U, OH	B
Wright State U, OH	B
Xavier U, OH	B
Youngstown State U, OH	B

Business Operations Support and Secretarial Services Related

Ancilla Coll, IN	A
Roosevelt U, IL	B
The U of Akron, OH	A

Business Statistics

Central Missouri State U, MO	B
Cleveland State U, OH	B
Western Michigan U, MI	B
Wright State U, OH	B

Business Systems Analysis/ Design

U of North Dakota, ND	B

Business Systems Networking/ Telecommunications

Globe Coll, MN — A
Minnesota School of Business–Brooklyn Center, MN — A
Minnesota School of Business–Plymouth, MN — A
Minnesota School of Business-Richfield, MN — A

Business Teacher Education

Adrian Coll, MI — B
Baldwin-Wallace Coll, OH — B
Ball State U, IN — B
Bethany Coll, KS — B
Bethel Coll, IN — B
Black Hills State U, SD — B
Bowling Green State U, OH — B
Buena Vista U, IA — B
Calumet Coll of Saint Joseph, IN — B
Central Christian Coll of Kansas, KS — A
Central Michigan U, MI — B
Central Missouri State U, MO — B
Chadron State Coll, NE — B
Chicago State U, IL — B
Coll of the Ozarks, MO — B
Concordia Coll, MN — B
Concordia U, NE — B
Concordia U Wisconsin, WI — B
Concord U, WV — B
Cumberland Coll, KY — B
Dakota State U, SD — B
Dakota Wesleyan U, SD — B
Dana Coll, NE — B
Defiance Coll, OH — B
Dickinson State U, ND — B
Doane Coll, NE — B
Dordt Coll, IA — B
Drake U, IA — B
East Central U, OK — B
Eastern Michigan U, MI — B
Evangel U, MO — B
Ferris State U, MI — B
Fort Hays State U, KS — B
The Franciscan U, IA — B
Goshen Coll, IN — B
Grace U, NE — B
Hannibal-LaGrange Coll, MO — B
Hastings Coll, NE — B
Huntington Coll, IN — B
Illinois State U, IL — B
Indiana State U, IN — B
Kent State U, OH — B
Lakeland Coll, WI — B
Lincoln Coll, Lincoln, IL — A
Lincoln U, MO — B
Lindenwood U, MO — B
Mayville State U, ND — B
McKendree Coll, IL — B
McPherson Coll, KS — B
MidAmerica Nazarene U, KS — B
Minot State U, ND — B
Missouri Baptist U, MO — B
Morningside Coll, IA — B
Mount Mary Coll, WI — B
Mount Vernon Nazarene U, OH — B
Muskingum Coll, OH — B

North Carolina Ag and Tech State U, NC — B
Northeastern State U, OK — B
Northern Michigan U, MI — B
Northern State U, SD — B
Northwestern Coll, IA — B
Northwestern Oklahoma State U, OK — B
Oakland City U, IN — B
Oklahoma Panhandle State U, OK — B
Pillsbury Baptist Bible Coll, MN — B
St. Ambrose U, IA — B
Saint Mary's Coll, IN — B
Siena Heights U, MI — B
Southeastern Oklahoma State U, OK — B
Southeast Missouri State U, MO — B
Southern Nazarene U, OK — B
Southwest Baptist U, MO — B
Southwest Missouri State U, MO — B
Tabor Coll, KS — B
Trinity Christian Coll, IL — B
Union Coll, NE — B
The U of Akron, OH — B
U of Central Oklahoma, OK — B
The U of Findlay, OH — B
U of Illinois at Urbana–Champaign, IL — B
U of Indianapolis, IN — B
U of Minnesota, Twin Cities Campus, MN — B
U of Missouri–Columbia, MO — B
U of Missouri–St. Louis, MO — B
U of Nebraska–Lincoln, NE — B
U of North Dakota, ND — B
U of Northern Iowa, IA — B
U of Rio Grande, OH — B
U of Saint Francis, IN — B
U of Southern Indiana, IN — B
U of Toledo, OH — B
U of Wisconsin–Superior, WI — B
U of Wisconsin–Whitewater, WI — B
Upper Iowa U, IA — B
Valley City State U, ND — B
Viterbo U, WI — B
Wayne State Coll, NE — B
Western Michigan U, MI — B
William Penn U, IA — B
Winona State U, MN — B
Wright State U, OH — B
York Coll, NE — B
Youngstown State U, OH — B

Cad/Cadd Drafting/Design Technology

Eastern Michigan U, MI — B
ITT Tech Inst, Mount Prospect, IL — A
ITT Tech Inst, Fort Wayne, IN — A
ITT Tech Inst, Indianapolis, IN — A
ITT Tech Inst, Newburgh, IN — A
ITT Tech Inst, Arnold, MO — A
ITT Tech Inst, Earth City, MO — A
ITT Tech Inst, NE — A

ITT Tech Inst, Green Bay, WI — A
ITT Tech Inst, Greenfield, WI — A
Kent State U, OH — A
Morrison Inst of Technology, IL — A
Shawnee State U, OH — A
Vatterott Coll, St. Ann, MO — A

Canadian Studies

Franklin Coll, IN — B

Cardiopulmonary Technology

Bacone Coll, OK — A

Cardiovascular Technology

Argosy U/Twin Cities, MN — A
Argosy U/Twin Cities, Eagan, MN — A
Nebraska Methodist Coll, NE — A,B
U of Toledo, OH — A

Caribbean Studies

Northwestern U, IL — B

Carpentry

Northern Michigan U, MI — A
Ranken Tech Coll, MO — A

Cartography

Ball State U, IN — B
East Central U, OK — B
Northern Michigan U, MI — A
Southwest Missouri State U, MO — B
The U of Akron, OH — B
U of Wisconsin–Madison, WI — B
U of Wisconsin–Platteville, WI — B

Cell and Molecular Biology

Eastern Michigan U, MI — B
Grand Valley State U, MI — B
Pittsburg State U, KS — B
Southwest Missouri State U, MO — B
U of Illinois at Urbana–Champaign, IL — B

Cell Biology and Histology

Ball State U, IN — B
Beloit Coll, WI — B
Clarkson U — B
Lindenwood U, MO — B
Northeastern State U, OK — B
Northwestern U, IL — B
Ohio U, OH — B
Oklahoma State U, OK — B
U of Illinois at Urbana–Champaign, IL — B
U of Michigan, MI — B
U of Minnesota, Duluth, MN — B
U of Minnesota, Twin Cities Campus, MN — B
U of Wisconsin–Madison, WI — B
U of Wisconsin–Superior, WI — B
William Jewell Coll, MO — B

Ceramic Arts and Ceramics

Ball State U, IN — B
Bethany Coll, KS — B
Bowling Green State U, OH — B
Chicago State U, IL — B
The Cleveland Inst of Art, OH — B

Coe Coll, IA — B
Coll for Creative Studies, MI — B
Concord U, WV — B
Grand Valley State U, MI — B
Indiana U Bloomington, IN — B
Kansas City Art Inst, MO — B
Lincoln Coll, Lincoln, IL — A
Loyola U Chicago, IL — B
Minnesota State U Mankato, MN — B
Minnesota State U Moorhead, MN — B
Northern Michigan U, MI — B
Ohio Northern U, OH — B
The Ohio State U, OH — B
Ohio U, OH — B
St. Cloud State U, MN — B
School of the Art Inst of Chicago, IL — B
Shawnee State U, OH — B
Trinity Christian Coll, IL — B
The U of Akron, OH — B
U of Evansville, IN — B
The U of Iowa, IA — B
U of Kansas, KS — B
U of Michigan, MI — B
U of Michigan–Flint, MI — B
U of Wisconsin–Milwaukee, WI — B
Washington U in St. Louis, MO — B

Ceramic Sciences and Engineering

The Ohio State U, OH — B
U of Missouri–Rolla, MO — B

Chemical Engineering

Ball State U, IN — A
Bethel Coll, IN — B
Calvin Coll, MI — B
Case Western Reserve U, OH — B
Clarkson U — B
Cleveland State U, OH — B
Ferris State U, MI — A
Illinois Inst of Technology, IL — B
Iowa State U of Science and Technology, IA — B
Kansas State U, KS — B
Lehigh U, PA — B
Michigan State U, MI — B
Michigan Technological U, MI — B
North Carolina Ag and Tech State U, NC — B
Northwestern U, IL — B
The Ohio State U, OH — B
Ohio U, OH — B
Oklahoma State U, OK — B
Purdue U, IN — B
Rose-Hulman Inst of Technology, IN — B
South Dakota School of Mines and Technology, SD — B
Tri-State U, IN — B
The U of Akron, OH — B
The U of Alabama in Huntsville, AL — B
U of Cincinnati, OH — B
U of Dayton, OH — B
U of Illinois at Chicago, IL — B
U of Illinois at Urbana–Champaign, IL — B
The U of Iowa, IA — B
U of Kansas, KS — B

A—associate degree; B—bachelor's degree

U of Michigan, MI — B
U of Minnesota, Duluth, MN — B
U of Minnesota, Twin Cities Campus, MN — B
U of Missouri–Columbia, MO — B
U of Missouri–Rolla, MO — B
U of Nebraska–Lincoln, NE — B
U of North Dakota, ND — B
U of Notre Dame, IN — B
U of Oklahoma, OK — B
U of Toledo, OH — B
U of Tulsa, OK — B
U of Wisconsin–Madison, WI — B
Waldorf Coll, IA — B
Washington U in St. Louis, MO — B
Wayne State U, MI — B
Western Michigan U, MI — B
Winona State U, MN — B
Xavier U, OH — B
Youngstown State U, OH — B

Chemical Physics
Michigan State U, MI — B

Chemical Technology
Indiana U–Purdue U Fort Wayne, IN — A
Lawrence Technological U, MI — A
The U of Akron, OH — A
U of Toledo, OH — A

Chemistry
Adrian Coll, MI — A,B
Albion Coll, MI — B
Alma Coll, MI — B
Alverno Coll, WI — B
Ancilla Coll, IN — A
Andrews U, MI — B
Antioch Coll, OH — B
Aquinas Coll, MI — B
Ashland U, OH — B
Augsburg Coll, MN — B
Augustana Coll, IL — B
Augustana Coll, SD — B
Aurora U, IL — B
Avila U, MO — B
Baker U, KS — B
Baldwin-Wallace Coll, OH — B
Ball State U, IN — B
Beloit Coll, WI — B
Bemidji State U, MN — B
Benedictine Coll, KS — B
Benedictine U, IL — B
Bethany Coll, KS — B
Bethany Lutheran Coll, MN — B
Bethel Coll, IN — A,B
Bethel Coll, KS — B
Bethel U, MN — B
Blackburn Coll, IL — B
Black Hills State U, SD — B
Bluffton Coll, OH — B
Bowling Green State U, OH — B
Bradley U, IL — B
Brescia U, KY — B
Briar Cliff U, IA — B
Buena Vista U, IA — B
Butler U, IN — B
Calvin Coll, MI — B
Cameron U, OK — B
Capital U, OH — B
Cardinal Stritch U, WI — B
Carleton Coll, MN — B
Carroll Coll, WI — B
Carthage Coll, WI — B

Case Western Reserve U, OH — B
Cedarville U, OH — B
Central Christian Coll of Kansas, KS — A
Central Coll, IA — B
Central Methodist Coll, MO — A,B
Central Michigan U, MI — B
Central Missouri State U, MO — B
Central State U, OH — B
Chadron State Coll, NE — B
Chicago State U, IL — B
Clarke Coll, IA — B
Clarkson U — B
Cleveland State U, OH — B
Coe Coll, IA — B
Coll of Mount St. Joseph, OH — B
Coll of Saint Benedict, MN — B
Coll of St. Catherine, MN — B
Coll of Saint Mary, NE — B
The Coll of St. Scholastica, MN — B
Coll of the Ozarks, MO — B
The Coll of Wooster, OH — B
Columbia Coll, MO — B
Concordia Coll, MN — B
Concordia U, IL — B
Concordia U, NE — B
Concord U, WV — B
Cornell Coll, IA — B
Creighton U, NE — B
Culver-Stockton Coll, MO — B
Cumberland Coll, KY — B
Dakota State U, SD — B
Dana Coll, NE — B
Defiance Coll, OH — B
Denison U, OH — B
DePaul U, IL — B
DePauw U, IN — B
Dickinson State U, ND — B
Doane Coll, NE — B
Dominican U, IL — B
Dordt Coll, IA — B
Drake U, IA — B
Drury U, MO — B
Earlham Coll, IN — B
East Central U, OK — B
Eastern Illinois U, IL — B
Eastern Michigan U, MI — B
Edgewood Coll, WI — B
Elmhurst Coll, IL — B
Emporia State U, KS — B
Eureka Coll, IL — B
Evangel U, MO — B
Fort Hays State U, KS — B
Franciscan U of Steubenville, OH — B
Franklin Coll, IN — B
Gannon U, PA — B
Goshen Coll, IN — B
Governors State U, IL — B
Graceland U, IA — B
Grand Valley State U, MI — B
Greenville Coll, IL — B
Grinnell Coll, IA — B
Gustavus Adolphus Coll, MN — B
Hamline U, MN — B
Hannibal-LaGrange Coll, MO — A
Hanover Coll, IN — B
Hastings Coll, NE — B
Heidelberg Coll, OH — B
Hillsdale Coll, MI — B
Hiram Coll, OH — B

Hope Coll, MI — B
Huntington Coll, IN — B
Illinois Coll, IL — B
Illinois Inst of Technology, IL — B
Illinois State U, IL — B
Illinois Wesleyan U, IL — B
Indiana State U, IN — B
Indiana U Bloomington, IN — B
Indiana U Northwest, IN — B
Indiana U–Purdue U Fort Wayne, IN — B
Indiana U–Purdue U Indianapolis, IN — B
Indiana U South Bend, IN — A,B
Indiana U Southeast, IN — B
Iowa State U of Science and Technology, IA — B
Iowa Wesleyan Coll, IA — B
Jamestown Coll, ND — B
John Carroll U, OH — B
Judson Coll, IL — B
Kalamazoo Coll, MI — B
Kansas State U, KS — B
Kansas Wesleyan U, KS — B
Kent State U, OH — B
Kenyon Coll, OH — B
Kettering U, MI — B
Knox Coll, IL — B
Lake Erie Coll, OH — B
Lake Forest Coll, IL — B
Lakeland Coll, WI — B
Lake Superior State U, MI — A
Lawrence Technological U, MI — B
Lawrence U, WI — B
Lehigh U, PA — B
Lewis U, IL — B
Lincoln Coll, Lincoln, IL — A
Lincoln U, MO — B
Lindenwood U, MO — B
Loras Coll, IA — B
Lourdes Coll, OH — A,B
Loyola U Chicago, IL — B
Luther Coll, IA — B
Macalester Coll, MN — B
MacMurray Coll, IL — B
Madonna U, MI — A,B
Malone Coll, OH — B
Manchester Coll, IN — B
Marian Coll, IN — B
Marian Coll of Fond du Lac, WI — B
Marietta Coll, OH — B
Marquette U, WI — B
Martin U, IN — B
Marygrove Coll, MI — B
Maryville U of Saint Louis, MO — B
Mayville State U, ND — B
McKendree Coll, IL — B
McPherson Coll, KS — B
Miami U, OH — B
Miami U Hamilton, OH — B
Michigan State U, MI — B
Michigan Technological U, MI — B
MidAmerica Nazarene U, KS — B
Millikin U, IL — B
Minnesota State U Mankato, MN — B
Minnesota State U Moorhead, MN — B
Minot State U, ND — B
Missouri Baptist U, MO — B
Missouri Southern State U, MO — B

Missouri Western State Coll, MO — B
Monmouth Coll, IL — B
Morningside Coll, IA — B
Mount Marty Coll, SD — B
Mount Mary Coll, WI — B
Mount Union Coll, OH — B
Mount Vernon Nazarene U, OH — B
Muskingum Coll, OH — B
Nebraska Wesleyan U, NE — B
Newman U, KS — B
North Carolina Ag and Tech State U, NC — B
North Central Coll, IL — B
North Dakota State U, ND — B
Northeastern Illinois U, IL — B
Northeastern State U, OK — B
Northern Illinois U, IL — B
Northern Michigan U, MI — B
Northern State U, SD — B
Northland Coll, WI — B
North Park U, IL — B
Northwestern Coll, IA — B
Northwestern Oklahoma State U, OK — B
Northwestern U, IL — B
Notre Dame Coll, OH — B
Oakland City U, IN — B
Oakland U, MI — B
Oberlin Coll, OH — B
Ohio Dominican U, OH — A,B
Ohio Northern U, OH — B
The Ohio State U, OH — B
Ohio U, OH — B
Ohio Wesleyan U, OH — B
Oklahoma Baptist U, OK — B
Oklahoma Christian U, OK — B
Oklahoma City U, OK — B
Oklahoma Panhandle State U, OK — B
Oklahoma State U, OK — B
Olivet Coll, MI — B
Olivet Nazarene U, IL — B
Oral Roberts U, OK — B
Otterbein Coll, OH — B
Park U, MO — B
Peru State Coll, NE — B
Pittsburg State U, KS — B
Principia Coll, IL — B
Purdue U, IN — B
Purdue U Calumet, IN — B
Quincy U, IL — B
Ripon Coll, WI — B
Rockford Coll, IL — B
Rockhurst U, MO — B
Roosevelt U, IL — B
Rose-Hulman Inst of Technology, IN — B
Saginaw Valley State U, MI — B
St. Ambrose U, IA — B
St. Cloud State U, MN — B
St. Gregory's U, OK — B
Saint John's U, MN — B
Saint Joseph's Coll, IN — B
Saint Louis U, MO — B
Saint Mary's Coll, IN — B
Saint Mary's U of Minnesota, MN — B
St. Norbert Coll, WI — B
St. Olaf Coll, MN — B
Saint Xavier U, IL — B
Shawnee State U, OH — B
Siena Heights U, MI — A,B
Simpson Coll, IA — B

South Dakota School of Mines and Technology, SD — B
South Dakota State U, SD — B
Southeastern Oklahoma State U, OK — B
Southeast Missouri State U, MO — B
Southern Illinois U Carbondale, IL — B
Southern Illinois U Edwardsville, IL — B
Southern Nazarene U, OK — B
Southwest Baptist U, MO — B
Southwestern Coll, KS — B
Southwestern Oklahoma State U, OK — B
Southwest Missouri State U, MO — B
Spring Arbor U, MI — B
Tabor Coll, KS — B
Taylor U, IN — B
Transylvania U, KY — B
Trinity Christian Coll, IL — B
Trinity International U, IL — B
Tri-State U, IN — B
Truman State U, MO — B
Union Coll, NE — B
The U of Akron, OH — B
The U of Alabama in Huntsville, AL — B
U of Central Oklahoma, OK — B
U of Chicago, IL — B
U of Cincinnati, OH — B
U of Dayton, OH — B
U of Detroit Mercy, MI — B
U of Evansville, IN — B
U of Illinois at Chicago, IL — B
U of Illinois at Springfield, IL — B
U of Illinois at Urbana–Champaign, IL — B
U of Indianapolis, IN — A,B
The U of Iowa, IA — B
U of Kansas, KS — B
U of Michigan, MI — B
U of Michigan–Dearborn, MI — B
U of Michigan–Flint, MI — B
U of Minnesota, Duluth, MN — B
U of Minnesota, Morris, MN — B
U of Minnesota, Twin Cities Campus, MN — B
U of Missouri–Columbia, MO — B
U of Missouri–Kansas City, MO — B
U of Missouri–Rolla, MO — B
U of Missouri–St. Louis, MO — B
U of Nebraska at Omaha, NE — B
U of Nebraska–Lincoln, NE — B
U of New Orleans, LA — B
U of North Dakota, ND — B
U of Northern Iowa, IA — B
U of Notre Dame, IN — B
U of Oklahoma, OK — B
U of Rio Grande, OH — A,B
U of Saint Francis, IN — B
U of Saint Mary, KS — B
U of St. Thomas, MN — B
U of Science and Arts of Oklahoma, OK — B
U of Sioux Falls, SD — B
The U of South Dakota, SD — B
U of Southern Indiana, IN — B
U of Toledo, OH — B

U of Tulsa, OK — B
U of West Florida, FL — B
U of Wisconsin–Eau Claire, WI — B
U of Wisconsin–Green Bay, WI — A,B
U of Wisconsin–La Crosse, WI — B
U of Wisconsin–Madison, WI — B
U of Wisconsin–Milwaukee, WI — B
U of Wisconsin–Oshkosh, WI — B
U of Wisconsin–Parkside, WI — B
U of Wisconsin–River Falls, WI — B
U of Wisconsin–Stevens Point, WI — B
U of Wisconsin–Superior, WI — B
U of Wisconsin–Whitewater, WI — B
Upper Iowa U, IA — B
Urbana U, OH — B
Valley City State U, ND — B
Valparaiso U, IN — B
Viterbo U, WI — B
Wabash Coll, IN — B
Walsh U, OH — B
Wartburg Coll, IA — B
Washburn U, KS — B
Washington U in St. Louis, MO — B
Wayne State Coll, NE — B
Wayne State U, MI — B
Western Illinois U, IL — B
Western Michigan U, MI — B
Westminster Coll, MO — B
Wheaton Coll, IL — B
Wichita State U, KS — B
Wilberforce U, OH — B
William Jewell Coll, MO — B
Winona State U, MN — B
Wisconsin Lutheran Coll, WI — B
Wittenberg U, OH — B
Wright State U, OH — A,B
Xavier U, OH — B
Youngstown State U, OH — B

Chemistry Related
Coll of Mount St. Joseph, OH — B
Lawrence Technological U, MI — B
Lehigh U, PA — B
Ohio Northern U, OH — B
U of Northern Iowa, IA — B
U of Notre Dame, IN — B
U of Wisconsin–Eau Claire, WI — B
U of Wisconsin–Whitewater, WI — B
Washington U in St. Louis, MO — B
Western Michigan U, MI — B

Chemistry Teacher Education
Alma Coll, MI — B
Bethany Coll, KS — B
Bethel U, MN — B
Buena Vista U, IA — B
Capital U, OH — B
Carroll Coll, WI — B
Central Christian Coll of Kansas, KS — A
Central Methodist Coll, MO — B

Central Michigan U, MI — B
Central Missouri State U, MO — B
Chadron State Coll, NE — B
Coll of St. Catherine, MN — B
The Coll of St. Scholastica, MN — B
Coll of the Ozarks, MO — B
Concordia Coll, MN — B
Concordia U, NE — B
Concordia U, St. Paul, MN — B
Dordt Coll, IA — B
East Central U, OK — B
Eastern Michigan U, MI — B
Elmhurst Coll, IL — B
Evangel U, MO — B
Franklin Coll, IN — B
Greenville Coll, IL — B
Gustavus Adolphus Coll, MN — B
Hastings Coll, NE — B
Hope Coll, MI — B
Illinois Wesleyan U, IL — B
Indiana U Bloomington, IN — B
Indiana U Northwest, IN — B
Indiana U–Purdue U Fort Wayne, IN — B
Indiana U South Bend, IN — B
Kent State U, OH — B
Lindenwood U, MO — B
Marian Coll of Fond du Lac, WI — B
Maryville U of Saint Louis, MO — B
Mayville State U, ND — B
Miami U Hamilton, OH — B
Michigan State U, MI — B
Minot State U, ND — B
Mount Marty Coll, SD — B
North Dakota State U, ND — B
Northern Michigan U, MI — B
Ohio Dominican U, OH — B
Ohio Northern U, OH — B
Ohio Wesleyan U, OH — B
Oklahoma Baptist U, OK — B
Pittsburg State U, KS — B
St. Ambrose U, IA — B
Saint Mary's U of Minnesota, MN — B
Southwest Baptist U, MO — B
Southwest Missouri State U, MO — B
Trinity Christian Coll, IL — B
Union Coll, NE — B
The U of Akron, OH — B
U of Illinois at Chicago, IL — B
The U of Iowa, IA — B
U of Michigan–Flint, MI — B
U of Missouri–Columbia, MO — B
U of Missouri–St. Louis, MO — B
U of Nebraska–Lincoln, NE — B
U of Saint Francis, IN — B
U of St. Thomas, MN — B
U of Wisconsin–River Falls, WI — B
U of Wisconsin–Superior, WI — B
Valley City State U, ND — B
Valparaiso U, IN — B
Viterbo U, WI — B
Washington U in St. Louis, MO — B
Western Michigan U, MI — B
Xavier U, OH — B
Youngstown State U, OH — B

Child Care and Support Services Management
Central Michigan U, MI — B
Central Missouri State U, MO — A
Concordia U, St. Paul, MN — B
Mount Vernon Nazarene U, OH — A
St. Augustine Coll, IL — A
Saint Mary-of-the-Woods Coll, IN — B
Southeast Missouri State U, MO — A
Youngstown State U, OH — A

Child Care/Guidance
Coll of the Ozarks, MO — B

Child Care Provision
Mayville State U, ND — A
Saint Mary-of-the-Woods Coll, IN — A

Child Care Services Management
Cameron U, OK — A

Child Development
Ashland U, OH — B
Bowling Green State U, OH — B
Coll of the Ozarks, MO — B
Concordia Coll, MN — B
Evangel U, MO — A
Ferris State U, MI — A
Franciscan U of Steubenville, OH — A
Goshen Coll, IN — B
Indiana U Bloomington, IN — B
Kansas State U, KS — B
Madonna U, MI — A,B
Miami U, OH — B
Michigan State U, MI — B
Minnesota State U Mankato, MN — B
Missouri Baptist U, MO — B
North Carolina Ag and Tech State U, NC — B
Northern Michigan U, MI — A,B
Ohio U, OH — A,B
Oklahoma Baptist U, OK — B
Oklahoma Christian U, OK — B
Oklahoma State U, OK — B
Olivet Nazarene U, IL — B
Pittsburg State U, KS — B
Purdue U Calumet, IN — A
Reformed Bible Coll, MI — A,B
St. Cloud State U, MN — B
South Dakota State U, SD — B
Stephens Coll, MO — B
The U of Akron, OH — B
U of Central Oklahoma, OK — B
U of Cincinnati, OH — A
U of Illinois at Springfield, IL — B
U of Michigan–Dearborn, MI — B
U of Saint Mary, KS — B
U of Wisconsin–Madison, WI — B
Washburn U, KS — A
Western Michigan U, MI — B
Youngstown State U, OH — A,B

Child Guidance
Coll of the Ozarks, MO — B
Oklahoma Baptist U, OK — B
Reformed Bible Coll, MI — B
Rochester Coll, MI — B

A—associate degree; B—bachelor's degree

Rochester Comm and Tech
Coll, MN — A
Siena Heights U, MI — A,B
U of Central Oklahoma, OK — B

Chinese
Augustana Coll, IL — B
Grinnell Coll, IA — B
Indiana U Bloomington, IN — B
Lawrence U, WI — B
Oakland U, MI — B
The Ohio State U, OH — B
U of Chicago, IL — B
The U of Iowa, IA — B
U of Michigan, MI — B
U of Minnesota, Twin Cities
Campus, MN — B
U of Notre Dame, IN — B
U of Wisconsin–Madison,
WI — B
Washington U in St. Louis,
MO — B

Christian Studies
Bethany Coll, KS — B
Bethel Coll, IN — B
Crown Coll, MN — B
God's Bible School and Coll,
OH — A,B
Hillsdale Coll, MI — B
Lindenwood U, MO — B
Ursuline Coll, OH — B
Vennard Coll, IA — A,B

Cinematography and Film/Video Production
Antioch Coll, OH — B
Coll for Creative Studies, MI — B
Columbia Coll Chicago, IL — B
Grand Valley State U, MI — B
Maharishi U of Management,
IA — B
Minneapolis Coll of Art and
Design, MN — B
Northern Michigan U, MI — B
Ohio U, OH — B
Oklahoma City U, OK — B
School of the Art Inst of
Chicago, IL — B
Southern Illinois U
Carbondale, IL — B
U of Illinois at Chicago, IL — B
The U of Iowa, IA — B
U of Oklahoma, OK — B
Waldorf Coll, IA — B
Webster U, MO — B

City/Urban, Community and Regional Planning
Ball State U, IN — B
DePaul U, IL — B
Eastern Michigan U, MI — B
Indiana U Bloomington, IN — B
Iowa State U of Science and
Technology, IA — B
Miami U, OH — B
Miami U Hamilton, OH — B
Michigan State U, MI — B
Minnesota State U Mankato,
MN — B
Northern Michigan U, MI — B
The Ohio State U, OH — B
St. Cloud State U, MN — B
Saint Louis U, MO — B
Southwest Missouri State U,
MO — B
U of Cincinnati, OH — B

U of Illinois at Urbana–
Champaign, IL — B
U of Missouri–Kansas City,
MO — B
Winona State U, MN — B
Wright State U, OH — B

Civil Engineering
Bethel Coll, IN — B
Bradley U, IL — B
Calvin Coll, MI — B
Case Western Reserve U,
OH — B
Clarkson U — B
Cleveland State U, OH — B
Illinois Inst of Technology, IL — B
Iowa State U of Science and
Technology, IA — B
Kansas State U, KS — B
Lawrence Technological U,
MI — B
Lehigh U, PA — B
Marquette U, WI — B
Michigan State U, MI — B
Michigan Technological U,
MI — B
Minnesota State U Mankato,
MN — B
North Carolina Ag and Tech
State U, NC — B
North Dakota State U, ND — B
Northwestern U, IL — B
Ohio Northern U, OH — B
The Ohio State U, OH — B
Ohio U, OH — B
Oklahoma State U, OK — B
Purdue U, IN — B
Rose-Hulman Inst of
Technology, IN — B
South Dakota School of
Mines and Technology, SD — B
South Dakota State U, SD — B
Southern Illinois U
Carbondale, IL — B
Southern Illinois U
Edwardsville, IL — B
Tri-State U, IN — B
The U of Akron, OH — B
The U of Alabama in
Huntsville, AL — B
U of Cincinnati, OH — B
U of Dayton, OH — B
U of Detroit Mercy, MI — B
U of Evansville, IN — B
U of Illinois at Chicago, IL — B
U of Illinois at Urbana–
Champaign, IL — B
The U of Iowa, IA — B
U of Kansas, KS — B
U of Michigan, MI — B
U of Minnesota, Twin Cities
Campus, MN — B
U of Missouri–Columbia,
MO — B
U of Missouri–Kansas City,
MO — B
U of Missouri–Rolla, MO — B
U of Missouri–St. Louis, MO — B
U of Nebraska at Omaha,
NE — B
U of Nebraska–Lincoln, NE — B
U of New Orleans, LA — B
U of North Dakota, ND — B
U of Notre Dame, IN — B
U of Oklahoma, OK — B
U of Toledo, OH — B

U of Wisconsin–Madison,
WI — B
U of Wisconsin–Milwaukee,
WI — B
U of Wisconsin–Platteville,
WI — B
Valparaiso U, IN — B
Washington U in St. Louis,
MO — B
Wayne State U, MI — B
Western Michigan U, MI — B
Youngstown State U, OH — B

Civil Engineering Related
Bradley U, IL — B
Ohio Northern U, OH — B

Civil Engineering Technology
Ferris State U, MI — A
Fontbonne U, MO — B
Indiana U–Purdue U Fort
Wayne, IN — A
Indiana U–Purdue U
Indianapolis, IN — A
Kansas State U, KS — A
Michigan Technological U,
MI — A
Missouri Western State Coll,
MO — A,B
North Dakota State Coll of
Science, ND — A
Purdue U Calumet, IN — A,B
Purdue U North Central, IN — A
Rochester Comm and Tech
Coll, MN — A
U of Cincinnati, OH — A,B
U of Toledo, OH — A,B
Washington U in St. Louis,
MO — B
Youngstown State U, OH — A,B

Classical, Ancient Mediterranean and Near Eastern Studies and Archaeology
Creighton U, NE — B

Classics and Classical Languages Related
Concordia Coll, MN — B
Lawrence U, WI — B
Saint Louis U, MO — B
U of St. Thomas, MN — B

Classics and Languages, Literatures and Linguistics
Augustana Coll, IL — B
Ave Maria Coll, MI — B
Ball State U, IN — B
Beloit Coll, WI — B
Bowling Green State U, OH — B
Calvin Coll, MI — B
Carleton Coll, MN — B
Carthage Coll, WI — B
Case Western Reserve U,
OH — B
Coe Coll, IA — B
Coll of Saint Benedict, MN — B
The Coll of Wooster, OH — B
Cornell Coll, IA — B
Denison U, OH — B
DePauw U, IN — B
Earlham Coll, IN — B
Franciscan U of Steubenville,
OH — B
Grand Valley State U, MI — B
Grinnell Coll, IA — B
Gustavus Adolphus Coll, MN — B

Hanover Coll, IN — B
Hillsdale Coll, MI — B
Hiram Coll, OH — B
Hope Coll, MI — B
Illinois Wesleyan U, IL — B
Indiana U Bloomington, IN — B
John Carroll U, OH — B
Kalamazoo Coll, MI — B
Kent State U, OH — B
Kenyon Coll, OH — B
Knox Coll, IL — B
Lawrence U, WI — B
Lehigh U, PA — B
Loyola U Chicago, IL — B
Luther Coll, IA — B
Macalester Coll, MN — B
Marquette U, WI — B
Miami U, OH — B
Miami U Hamilton, OH — B
Monmouth Coll, IL — B
North Dakota State U, ND — B
Northwestern U, IL — B
Oakland U, MI — B
Oberlin Coll, OH — B
The Ohio State U, OH — B
Ohio U, OH — B
Ohio Wesleyan U, OH — B
Rockford Coll, IL — B
Saint John's U, MN — B
St. Olaf Coll, MN — B
Southern Illinois U
Carbondale, IL — B
Truman State U, MO — B
The U of Akron, OH — B
U of Chicago, IL — B
U of Cincinnati, OH — B
U of Evansville, IN — B
U of Illinois at Chicago, IL — B
U of Illinois at Urbana–
Champaign, IL — B
The U of Iowa, IA — B
U of Kansas, KS — B
U of Michigan, MI — B
U of Missouri–Columbia,
MO — B
U of Nebraska–Lincoln, NE — B
U of Notre Dame, IN — B
U of Oklahoma, OK — B
U of St. Thomas, MN — B
The U of South Dakota, SD — B
U of Toledo, OH — B
U of Wisconsin–Madison,
WI — B
U of Wisconsin–Milwaukee,
WI — B
Valparaiso U, IN — B
Wabash Coll, IN — B
Washington U in St. Louis,
MO — B
Wayne State U, MI — B
Wright State U, OH — B
Xavier U, OH — B

Clinical Laboratory Science/ Medical Technology
Andrews U, MI — B
Aquinas Coll, MI — B
Augustana Coll, SD — B
Aurora U, IL — B
Ball State U, IN — B
Bemidji State U, MN — B
Benedictine U, IL — B
Blackburn Coll, IL — B
Bowling Green State U, OH — B
Bradley U, IL — B
Brescia U, KY — B
Briar Cliff U, IA — B

Cameron U, OK	B
Carroll Coll, WI	B
Cedarville U, OH	B
Central Michigan U, MI	B
Central Missouri State U, MO	B
Coll of Mount St. Joseph, OH	B
Coll of St. Catherine, MN	B
Coll of St. Catherine–Minneapolis, MN	A
Coll of Saint Mary, NE	B
Coll of the Ozarks, MO	B
Concordia Coll, MN	B
Concord U, WV	B
Culver-Stockton Coll, MO	B
Cumberland Coll, KY	B
Defiance Coll, OH	B
DePaul U, IL	B
Dominican U, IL	B
Dordt Coll, IA	B
Eastern Illinois U, IL	B
Eastern Michigan U, MI	B
Edgewood Coll, WI	B
Elmhurst Coll, IL	B
Eureka Coll, IL	B
Evangel U, MO	B
Ferris State U, MI	B
Fort Hays State U, KS	B
Gannon U, PA	B
Graceland U, IA	B
Grand Valley State U, MI	B
Illinois Coll, IL	B
Illinois State U, IL	B
Indiana State U, IN	B
Indiana U East, IN	A,B
Indiana U Kokomo, IN	B
Indiana U–Purdue U Fort Wayne, IN	B
Indiana U–Purdue U Indianapolis, IN	B
Indiana U Southeast, IN	B
Jamestown Coll, ND	B
Jewish Hospital Coll of Nursing and Allied Health, MO	B
Kansas State U, KS	B
Kent State U, OH	B
Lake Superior State U, MI	B
Lewis U, IL	B
Lincoln U, MO	B
Lindenwood U, MO	B
Loras Coll, IA	B
Madonna U, MI	B
Malone Coll, OH	B
Manchester Coll, IN	B
Marian Coll of Fond du Lac, WI	B
Maryville U of Saint Louis, MO	B
McKendree Coll, IL	B
Miami U, OH	B
Miami U Hamilton, OH	B
Michigan State U, MI	B
Michigan Technological U, MI	B
Minnesota State U Mankato, MN	B
Minnesota State U Moorhead, MN	B
Minot State U, ND	B
Missouri Southern State U, MO	B
Missouri Western State Coll, MO	B

Morningside Coll, IA	B
Mount Marty Coll, SD	B
Mount Mercy Coll, IA	B
Mount Vernon Nazarene U, OH	B
Muskingum Coll, OH	B
National-Louis U, IL	B
North Dakota State U, ND	B
Northeastern State U, OK	B
Northern Illinois U, IL	B
Northern Michigan U, MI	A,B
Northern State U, SD	B
North Park U, IL	B
Northwestern Coll, IA	B
Oakland U, MI	B
Ohio Northern U, OH	B
The Ohio State U, OH	B
Oklahoma Christian U, OK	B
Oklahoma Panhandle State U, OK	B
Oklahoma State U, OK	B
Olivet Nazarene U, IL	B
Peru State Coll, NE	B
Pittsburg State U, KS	B
Purdue U, IN	B
Purdue U Calumet, IN	B
Quincy U, IL	B
Roosevelt U, IL	B
Rush U, IL	B
Saginaw Valley State U, MI	B
St. Cloud State U, MN	B
Saint Joseph's Coll, IN	B
Saint Louis U, MO	B
Saint Mary-of-the-Woods Coll, IN	B
Saint Mary's Coll, IN	B
Saint Mary's U of Minnesota, MN	B
Simpson Coll, IA	B
South Dakota State U, SD	B
Southeastern Oklahoma State U, OK	B
Southeast Missouri State U, MO	B
Southwest Baptist U, MO	B
Southwestern Oklahoma State U, OK	B
Southwest Missouri State U, MO	B
Tabor Coll, KS	B
Taylor U, IN	B
Union Coll, NE	B
The U of Akron, OH	B
U of Central Oklahoma, OK	B
U of Cincinnati, OH	B
U of Evansville, IN	B
The U of Findlay, OH	B
U of Illinois at Chicago, IL	B
U of Indianapolis, IN	B
The U of Iowa, IA	B
U of Kansas, KS	B
U of Mary, ND	B
U of Michigan, MI	B
U of Michigan–Flint, MI	B
U of Minnesota, Twin Cities Campus, MN	B
U of Missouri–St. Louis, MO	B
U of Nebraska Medical Center, NE	B
U of New Orleans, LA	B
U of North Dakota, ND	B
U of Rio Grande, OH	B
U of St. Francis, IL	B
U of Saint Francis, IN	B
U of Sioux Falls, SD	B

U of Toledo, OH	A,B
U of West Florida, FL	B
U of Wisconsin–La Crosse, WI	B
U of Wisconsin–Madison, WI	B
U of Wisconsin–Milwaukee, WI	B
U of Wisconsin–Oshkosh, WI	B
U of Wisconsin–Stevens Point, WI	B
Wartburg Coll, IA	B
Washburn U, KS	B
Wayne State Coll, NE	B
Western Illinois U, IL	B
Wichita State U, KS	B
William Jewell Coll, MO	B
Winona State U, MN	B
Wright State U, OH	B
Xavier U, OH	B
Youngstown State U, OH	B

Clinical/Medical Laboratory Assistant

Northern Michigan U, MI	A
Youngstown State U, OH	A

Clinical/Medical Laboratory Science and Allied Professions Related

Roosevelt U, IL	B
Saint Louis U, MO	B
The U of Akron, OH	A

Clinical/Medical Laboratory Technology

Andrews U, MI	B
Argosy U/Twin Cities, MN	A
Argosy U/Twin Cities, Eagan, MN	A
Baker Coll of Owosso, MI	A
Baldwin-Wallace Coll, OH	B
Dakota State U, SD	A
DePaul U, IL	B
East Central U, OK	B
Ferris State U, MI	A,B
Indiana U Northwest, IN	A
Madonna U, MI	A,B
Marquette U, WI	B
Northern Michigan U, MI	A,B
Northern State U, SD	B
Presentation Coll, SD	A
Purdue U Calumet, IN	B
Rochester Comm and Tech Coll, MN	A
Shawnee State U, OH	A
U of Cincinnati, OH	A
U of Missouri–Kansas City, MO	B
U of Oklahoma, OK	B
U of Rio Grande, OH	A
U of Science and Arts of Oklahoma, OK	B
Winona State U, MN	B
Youngstown State U, OH	A

Clinical/Medical Social Work

U of St. Thomas, MN	B

Clinical Psychology

Blackburn Coll, IL	B
Purdue U Calumet, IN	B
U of Michigan–Flint, MI	B

Clothing/Textiles

Bluffton Coll, OH	B

Bowling Green State U, OH	B
Indiana U Bloomington, IN	A,B
Minnesota State U Mankato, MN	B
North Carolina Ag and Tech State U, NC	B
The Ohio State U, OH	B
Oklahoma State U, OK	B
Olivet Nazarene U, IL	B
The U of Akron, OH	B
U of Central Oklahoma, OK	B
U of Minnesota, Twin Cities Campus, MN	B
U of Wisconsin–Madison, WI	B

Cognitive Psychology and Psycholinguistics

Indiana U Bloomington, IN	B
Lawrence U, WI	B
Northwestern U, IL	B
U of Kansas, KS	B
Washington U in St. Louis, MO	B

Cognitive Science

Lawrence U, WI	B

College Student Counseling and Personnel Services

Eastern Michigan U, MI	B

Commercial and Advertising Art

Academy Coll, MN	A
American Academy of Art, IL	B
Andrews U, MI	A,B
The Art Insts International Minnesota, MN	A,B
Ashland U, OH	B
Baker Coll of Auburn Hills, MI	A
Baker Coll of Clinton Township, MI	A
Baker Coll of Flint, MI	A,B
Baker Coll of Muskegon, MI	A
Baker Coll of Owosso, MI	A,B
Baker Coll of Port Huron, MI	A
Ball State U, IN	B
Bemidji State U, MN	B
Black Hills State U, SD	B
Brescia U, KY	B
Briar Cliff U, IA	B
Buena Vista U, IA	B
Cardinal Stritch U, WI	B
Carroll Coll, WI	B
Carthage Coll, WI	B
Central Michigan U, MI	B
Central Missouri State U, MO	B
Chicago State U, IL	B
The Cleveland Inst of Art, OH	B
Coll for Creative Studies, MI	B
Coll of Visual Arts, MN	B
Columbia Coll Chicago, IL	B
Concordia U, IL	B
Concordia U, NE	B
Concordia U Wisconsin, WI	B
Concord U, WV	B
DePaul U, IL	B
Dominican U, IL	B
Dordt Coll, IA	B
Drake U, IA	B
Edgewood Coll, WI	B

A—associate degree; B—bachelor's degree

Ferris State U, MI	A
Fontbonne U, MO	B
Fort Hays State U, KS	B
Grace Coll, IN	B
Graceland U, IA	B
Grand Valley State U, MI	B
Huntington Coll, IN	B
The Illinois Inst of Art, IL	A,B
Indiana U Bloomington, IN	B
Indiana U–Purdue U Fort Wayne, IN	A,B
International Academy of Design & Technology, IL	A,B
Iowa State U of Science and Technology, IA	B
Judson Coll, IL	B
Kansas City Art Inst, MO	B
Kent State U, OH	B
Lewis U, IL	B
Lincoln Coll, Lincoln, IL	A
Marietta Coll, OH	B
Millikin U, IL	B
Milwaukee Inst of Art and Design, WI	B
Minneapolis Coll of Art and Design, MN	B
Minnesota State U Mankato, MN	B
Minnesota State U Moorhead, MN	B
Missouri Southern State U, MO	B
Morningside Coll, IA	B
Mount Mary Coll, WI	B
Northeastern State U, OK	B
Northern Michigan U, MI	A,B
Northern State U, SD	A
Ohio Northern U, OH	B
The Ohio State U, OH	B
Ohio U, OH	B
Oklahoma Christian U, OK	B
Oklahoma City U, OK	B
Oklahoma State U, OK	B
Olivet Coll, MI	B
Olivet Nazarene U, IL	B
Oral Roberts U, OK	B
Park U, MO	B
Peru State Coll, NE	B
Pittsburg State U, KS	B
Robert Morris Coll, IL	A
Saint Mary's U of Minnesota, MN	B
St. Norbert Coll, WI	B
School of the Art Inst of Chicago, IL	B
Silver Lake Coll, WI	A
Simpson Coll, IA	B
Southwest Baptist U, MO	B
Southwestern Oklahoma State U, OK	B
Taylor U, IN	B
Trinity Christian Coll, IL	B
Truman State U, MO	B
Union Coll, NE	B
The U of Akron, OH	B
U of Central Oklahoma, OK	B
U of Cincinnati, OH	B
U of Dayton, OH	B
U of Evansville, IN	B
U of Illinois at Chicago, IL	B
U of Indianapolis, IN	B
U of Michigan, MI	B
U of Minnesota, Duluth, MN	B
U of Minnesota, Twin Cities Campus, MN	B
U of Saint Francis, IN	A,B
U of Sioux Falls, SD	B
U of Wisconsin–Platteville, WI	B
U of Wisconsin–Stevens Point, WI	B
Upper Iowa U, IA	B
Wartburg Coll, IA	B
Washington U in St. Louis, MO	B
Wayne State Coll, NE	B
Western Michigan U, MI	B
Westwood Coll–Chicago Du Page, IL	A,B
Westwood Coll–Chicago O'Hare Airport, IL	A,B
Wichita State U, KS	B
William Woods U, MO	B
Winona State U, MN	B
Youngstown State U, OH	B

Commercial Photography
Coll for Creative Studies, MI	B
Harrington Coll of Design, IL	A
Minnesota State U Moorhead, MN	B
Ohio U, OH	B
The U of Akron, OH	A

Communication and Journalism Related
Bowling Green State U, OH	B
Bradley U, IL	B
Coll of the Ozarks, MO	B
The Franciscan U, IA	B
Hannibal-LaGrange Coll, MO	B
Illinois Inst of Technology, IL	B
Indiana State U, IN	B
Lehigh U, PA	B
Loyola U Chicago, IL	B
Luther Coll, IA	B
Malone Coll, OH	B
Marquette U, WI	B
Milwaukee School of Engineering, WI	B
Ohio Northern U, OH	B
The Ohio State U, OH	B
Ohio U, OH	B
Oklahoma State U, OK	B
Pittsburg State U, KS	B
Saint Louis U, MO	B
Southeastern Oklahoma State U, OK	B
Sterling Coll, KS	B
Taylor U Fort Wayne, IN	B
The U of Akron, OH	B
U of Illinois at Urbana–Champaign, IL	B
U of Oklahoma, OK	B
U of Wisconsin–Green Bay, WI	B
Valparaiso U, IN	B
Washington U in St. Louis, MO	B
Webster U, MO	B
Wisconsin Lutheran Coll, WI	B

Communication and Media Related
Alma Coll, MI	B
Bellevue U, NE	B
Calumet Coll of Saint Joseph, IN	B
Central Missouri State U, MO	B
Crown Coll, MN	B

Greenville Coll, IL	B
Indiana U–Purdue U Fort Wayne, IN	B
Missouri Western State Coll, MO	B
Northwestern U, IL	B
St. Gregory's U, OK	B
Southwestern Coll, KS	B
Trinity International U, IL	B
Walsh U, OH	B

Communication Disorders
Baldwin-Wallace Coll, OH	B
Bowling Green State U, OH	B
Case Western Reserve U, OH	B
Eastern Illinois U, IL	B
Kansas State U, KS	B
Minnesota State U Mankato, MN	B
Minot State U, ND	B
Northern Illinois U, IL	B
Northwestern U, IL	B
Oklahoma State U, OK	B
St. Cloud State U, MN	B
Southeast Missouri State U, MO	B
Southern Illinois U Carbondale, IL	B
Truman State U, MO	B
The U of Akron, OH	B
U of Kansas, KS	B
The U of South Dakota, SD	B
U of Wisconsin–Eau Claire, WI	B
U of Wisconsin–River Falls, WI	B
Western Illinois U, IL	B

Communication Disorders Sciences and Services Related
Ohio U, OH	B
St. Cloud State U, MN	B
U of Missouri–Columbia, MO	B
U of Oklahoma Health Sciences Center, OK	B

Communication/Speech Communication and Rhetoric
Alverno Coll, WI	B
Antioch Coll, OH	B
Aquinas Coll, MI	B
Augustana Coll, SD	B
Aurora U, IL	B
Avila U, MO	B
Baker Coll of Jackson, MI	A
Baldwin-Wallace Coll, OH	B
Benedictine U, IL	B
Bethany Coll, KS	B
Bethany Lutheran Coll, MN	B
Bethel Coll, IN	B
Bethel U, MN	B
Blackburn Coll, IL	B
Bluffton Coll, OH	B
Bowling Green State U, OH	B
Bradley U, IL	B
Buena Vista U, IA	B
Calumet Coll of Saint Joseph, IN	B
Calvin Coll, MI	B
Cameron U, OK	A,B
Capital U, OH	B
Cardinal Stritch U, WI	B
Carroll Coll, WI	B
Cedarville U, OH	B

Central Christian Coll of Kansas, KS	A
Central Coll, IA	B
Central Methodist Coll, MO	B
Clarkson U	B
Cleveland State U, OH	B
Coll of Mount St. Joseph, OH	A,B
The Coll of St. Scholastica, MN	B
The Coll of Wooster, OH	B
Concordia Coll, MN	B
Concordia U, IL	B
Concordia U, MI	B
Concordia U, NE	B
Creighton U, NE	B
Cumberland Coll, KY	B
Dana Coll, NE	B
DePaul U, IL	B
Doane Coll, NE	B
Elmhurst Coll, IL	B
Emporia State U, KS	B
Fontbonne U, MO	B
Franciscan U of Steubenville, OH	B
Gannon U, PA	B
Governors State U, IL	B
Grace U, NE	B
Hannibal-LaGrange Coll, MO	B
Hastings Coll, NE	B
Hope Coll, MI	B
Huntington Coll, IN	B
Indiana State U, IN	B
Indiana U Bloomington, IN	B
Indiana U East, IN	B
Indiana U Kokomo, IN	B
Indiana U–Purdue U Indianapolis, IN	B
Indiana U Southeast, IN	B
Jamestown Coll, ND	B
Kansas State U, KS	B
Lake Forest Coll, IL	B
Loyola U Chicago, IL	B
Macalester Coll, MN	B
Marian Coll of Fond du Lac, WI	B
Marietta Coll, OH	B
Marquette U, WI	B
Martin U, IN	B
Metropolitan State U, MN	B
Miami U Hamilton, OH	B
Michigan State U, MI	B
Michigan Technological U, MI	B
Millikin U, IL	B
Missouri Baptist U, MO	B
Missouri Southern State U, MO	B
Moody Bible Inst, IL	B
Mount Mary Coll, WI	B
Mount Mercy Coll, IA	B
Mount Union Coll, OH	B
Mount Vernon Nazarene U, OH	B
Nebraska Wesleyan U, NE	B
Northern Illinois U, IL	B
Northern Michigan U, MI	B
Northwestern Coll, MN	B
Northwestern U, IL	B
Notre Dame Coll, OH	B
Oakland U, MI	B
Ohio Dominican U, OH	B
Ohio Northern U, OH	B
The Ohio State U, OH	B
Ohio U, OH	B

Majors and Degrees
Communication/Speech Communication and Rhetoric

Oral Roberts U, OK — B
Park U, MO — B
Presentation Coll, SD — A,B
Purdue U, IN — B
Quincy U, IL — B
Reformed Bible Coll, MI — B
Ripon Coll, WI — B
Rochester Coll, MI — B
Rockhurst U, MO — B
Roosevelt U, IL — B
Saginaw Valley State U, MI — B
Saint Joseph's Coll, IN — B
Saint Louis U, MO — B
Saint Mary's Coll, IN — B
St. Norbert Coll, WI — B
Saint Xavier U, IL — B
Southeastern Oklahoma State U, OK — B
Southeast Missouri State U, MO — B
Southern Nazarene U, OK — A
Southwest Baptist U, MO — B
Southwest Missouri State U, MO — B
Spring Arbor U, MI — B
Tabor Coll, KS — B
Taylor U, IN — B
Tiffin U, OH — B
Trinity Christian Coll, IL — B
Tri-State U, IN — A,B
Truman State U, MO — B
Union Inst & U, OH — B
The U of Akron, OH — B
U of Central Oklahoma, OK — B
U of Indianapolis, IN — B
The U of Iowa, IA — B
U of Michigan–Flint, MI — B
U of Missouri–Columbia, MO — B
U of Missouri–St. Louis, MO — B
U of Nebraska at Omaha, NE — B
U of Nebraska–Lincoln, NE — B
U of New Orleans, LA — B
U of North Dakota, ND — B
U of Northern Iowa, IA — B
U of Oklahoma, OK — B
U of Rio Grande, OH — A,B
U of Saint Francis, IN — B
U of St. Thomas, MN — B
U of Science and Arts of Oklahoma, OK — B
U of Southern Indiana, IN — B
U of Toledo, OH — B
U of Tulsa, OK — B
U of West Florida, FL — B
U of Wisconsin–Eau Claire, WI — B
U of Wisconsin–La Crosse, WI — B
U of Wisconsin–Parkside, WI — B
U of Wisconsin–Stevens Point, WI — B
U of Wisconsin–Whitewater, WI — B
Valparaiso U, IN — B
Washburn U, KS — B
Washington U in St. Louis, MO — B
Wayne State U, MI — B
Western Illinois U, IL — B
Western Michigan U, MI — B
Wheaton Coll, IL — B
Wichita State U, KS — B
William Penn U, IA — B

William Woods U, MO — B
Wisconsin Lutheran Coll, WI — B
Wittenberg U, OH — B
Wright State U, OH — A,B
Youngstown State U, OH — B

Communications Technologies and Support Services Related
Alverno Coll, WI — B
Saint Mary-of-the-Woods Coll, IN — B

Communications Technology
Eastern Michigan U, MI — B
Ferris State U, MI — A
Hastings Coll, NE — B
Kent State U, Tuscarawas Campus, OH — A
Lawrence Technological U, MI — B
Saint Mary-of-the-Woods Coll, IN — B
U of Michigan–Dearborn, MI — B
Vennard Coll, IA — A

Community College Education
Eastern Michigan U, MI — B

Community Health and Preventive Medicine
U of Illinois at Urbana–Champaign, IL — B

Community Health Services Counseling
Bethel U, MN — B
Cleveland State U, OH — B
Cumberland Coll, KY — B
Indiana State U, IN — B
Indiana U–Purdue U Fort Wayne, IN — B
Minnesota State U Moorhead, MN — B
Northeastern Illinois U, IL — B
Ohio U, OH — B
U of Kansas, KS — B
U of Michigan–Flint, MI — B
U of Nebraska at Omaha, NE — B
U of Nebraska–Lincoln, NE — B
U of Northern Iowa, IA — B
U of West Florida, FL — B
Youngstown State U, OH — B

Community Organization and Advocacy
Alverno Coll, WI — B
Bemidji State U, MN — B
Central Michigan U, MI — B
Cleveland State U, OH — B
Concordia U, St. Paul, MN — B
Eastern Michigan U, MI — B
Northern State U, SD — B
North Park U, IL — B
Northwestern U, IL — B
Rockhurst U, MO — B
Roosevelt U, IL — B
Siena Heights U, MI — B
The U of Akron, OH — A,B
The U of Findlay, OH — A
U of Saint Mary, KS — B
U of Toledo, OH — B

Community Psychology
Northwestern U, IL — B
U of Saint Mary, KS — B
Wright State U, OH — B

Comparative Literature
Antioch Coll, OH — B
Beloit Coll, WI — B
Case Western Reserve U, OH — B
The Coll of Wooster, OH — B
DePaul U, IL — B
Hillsdale Coll, MI — B
Indiana U Bloomington, IN — B
Northwestern U, IL — B
Oakland U, MI — B
Oberlin Coll, OH — B
The Ohio State U, OH — B
Roosevelt U, IL — B
St. Cloud State U, MN — B
U of Chicago, IL — B
U of Cincinnati, OH — B
U of Illinois at Urbana–Champaign, IL — B
The U of Iowa, IA — B
U of Michigan, MI — B
U of Michigan–Dearborn, MI — B
U of Minnesota, Twin Cities Campus, MN — B
U of Wisconsin–Madison, WI — B
U of Wisconsin–Milwaukee, WI — B
Washington U in St. Louis, MO — B
William Woods U, MO — B

Computational Mathematics
Indiana U–Purdue U Fort Wayne, IN — B
Marquette U, WI — B
Michigan State U, MI — B
Northern Illinois U, IL — B

Computer and Information Sciences
Academy Coll, MN — A
Alverno Coll, WI — B
Andrews U, MI — B
Aquinas Coll, MI — B
Aurora U, IL — B
Avila U, MO — B
Baker Coll of Allen Park, MI — A
Baker Coll of Muskegon, MI — B
Bellevue U, NE — B
Bethel Coll, IN — B
Bethel U, MN — B
Black Hills State U, SD — A
Bowling Green State U, OH — B
Bradley U, IL — B
Bryant and Stratton Coll, WI — A
Cameron U, OK — B
Carroll Coll, WI — B
Central Christian Coll of Kansas, KS — A
Central Michigan U, MI — B
Central Missouri State U, MO — B
Central State U, OH — B
Clarkson U — B
Cleveland State U, OH — B
Coll of St. Catherine, MN — B
The Coll of St. Scholastica, MN — B
Coll of the Ozarks, MO — B
Columbia Coll, MO — A,B
Concordia U, MI — B
Concordia U, NE — B
Cumberland Coll, KY — B
DePaul U, IL — B
Doane Coll, NE — B

Drury U, MO — B
Dunwoody Coll of Technology, MN — A
Eastern Michigan U, MI — B
Emporia State U, KS — B
Florida Gulf Coast U, FL — B
The Franciscan U, IA — B
Franciscan U of Steubenville, OH — B
Franklin Coll, IN — B
Franklin U, OH — A,B
Gannon U, PA — B
Grace Bible Coll, MI — B
Grace U, NE — B
Grand Valley State U, MI — B
Hannibal-LaGrange Coll, MO — B
Haskell Indian Nations U, KS — A,B
Hastings Coll, NE — B
Herzing Coll, Minneapolis Drafting School Division, MN — A
Indiana State U, IN — B
Indiana U Bloomington, IN — B
Indiana U–Purdue U Indianapolis, IN — B
Iowa State U of Science and Technology, IA — B
Kansas State U, KS — B
Kaplan Coll, IA — A,B
Kent State U, Salem Campus, OH — A
Knox Coll, IL — B
MacCormac Coll, IL — A
Madonna U, MI — A,B
Marygrove Coll, MI — B
Mayville State U, ND — B
Miami U, OH — B
Michigan State U, MI — B
Millikin U, IL — B
Minnesota State U Moorhead, MN — B
Missouri Baptist U, MO — B
Missouri Southern State U, MO — B
Missouri Western State Coll, MO — B
Mount Mercy Coll, IA — B
Mount Vernon Nazarene U, OH — B
Northeastern Illinois U, IL — B
Northern Michigan U, MI — B
Northwestern U, IL — B
Northwood U, MI — B
Oakland U, MI — B
The Ohio State U, OH — B
Oklahoma Baptist U, OK — B
Oklahoma Panhandle State U, OK — A
Oklahoma State U, OK — B
Olivet Coll, MI — B
Park U, MO — B
Pittsburg State U, KS — B
Principia Coll, IL — B
Purdue U, IN — B
Purdue U Calumet, IN — B
Quincy U, IL — B
Ranken Tech Coll, MO — A
Reformed Bible Coll, MI — B
Saginaw Valley State U, MI — B
St. Augustine Coll, IL — A
Saint Joseph's Coll, IN — B
Saint Louis U, MO — B

A—associate degree; B—bachelor's degree

Saint Mary-of-the-Woods
Coll, IN — B
Saint Xavier U, IL — B
Silver Lake Coll, WI — B
South Dakota State U, SD — B
Southeastern Oklahoma State
U, OK — B
Southeast Missouri State U,
MO
Southwestern Oklahoma
State U, OK — B
Sterling Coll, KS — B
Taylor U Fort Wayne, IN — B
Tri-State U, IN — A
The U of Alabama in
Huntsville, AL — B
U of Cincinnati, OH — A,B
U of Detroit Mercy, MI — B
U of Dubuque, IA — B
U of Illinois at Chicago, IL — B
The U of Iowa, IA — B
U of Kansas, KS — B
U of Michigan–Dearborn, MI — B
U of Missouri–Columbia,
MO — B
U of Missouri–St. Louis, MO — B
U of Nebraska–Lincoln, NE — B
U of North Dakota, ND — B
U of Notre Dame, IN — B
U of Oklahoma, OK — B
U of Phoenix–Cleveland
Campus, OH — B
U of Phoenix–Kansas City
Campus, MO — B
U of Phoenix–Tulsa Campus,
OK — B
U of Phoenix–Wisconsin
Campus, WI — B
U of Saint Mary, KS — B
U of St. Thomas, MN — B
U of Science and Arts of
Oklahoma, OK — B
The U of South Dakota, SD — B
U of Southern Indiana, IN — B
U of West Florida, FL — B
U of Wisconsin–Eau Claire,
WI — B
U of Wisconsin–River Falls,
WI — B
U of Wisconsin–Stevens
Point, WI — B
U of Wisconsin–Superior, WI — B
U of Wisconsin–Whitewater,
WI — B
Valley City State U, ND — B
Viterbo U, WI — B
Walsh Coll of Accountancy
and Business
Administration, MI — B
Washington U in St. Louis,
MO — B
Wayne State U, MI — B
Western Illinois U, IL — B
Western Michigan U, MI — B
Wichita State U, KS — B
William Woods U, MO — B
Winona State U, MN — B
Wright State U, OH — B
Youngstown State U, OH — A,B

Computer and Information Sciences and Support Services Related
Academy Coll, MN — A
Cleary U, MI — A

Coll of Mount St. Joseph,
OH — B
Columbia Coll Chicago, IL — B
Greenville Coll, IL — B
International Academy of
Design & Technology, IL — B
Lehigh U, PA — B
Mayville State U, ND — B
Park U, MO — B
Purdue U, IN — B
Ranken Tech Coll, MO — A
Saint Louis U, MO — B
Tiffin U, OH — B
U of Missouri–Rolla, MO — B
U of Notre Dame, IN — B
Valley City State U, ND — B
Washington U in St. Louis,
MO — B

Computer and Information Sciences Related
Bellevue U, NE — B
Central Michigan U, MI — B
DePaul U, IL — B
Donnelly Coll, KS — A
Eastern Illinois U, IL — B
Grace U, NE — B
Indiana State U, IN — B
Madonna U, MI — A
Miami U Hamilton, OH — B
Pittsburg State U, KS — B
U of Northern Iowa, IA — B

Computer and Information Systems Security
Academy Coll, MN — A
Briar Cliff U, IA — B
Dakota State U, SD — B
Davenport U, Dearborn, MI — B
Davenport U, Grand Rapids,
MI — B
Davenport U, Lansing, MI — B
Davenport U, Warren, MI — B
ITT Tech Inst, Mount
Prospect, IL — B
ITT Tech Inst, Fort Wayne,
IN — B
ITT Tech Inst, Indianapolis,
IN — B
ITT Tech Inst, Newburgh,
IN — B
ITT Tech Inst, Arnold, MO — B
ITT Tech Inst, Earth City,
MO — B
ITT Tech Inst, NE — B
ITT Tech Inst, Green Bay,
WI — B
ITT Tech Inst, Greenfield,
WI — B
Westwood Coll–Chicago Du
Page, IL — B
Westwood Coll–Chicago
Loop Campus, IL — B
Westwood Coll–Chicago
O'Hare Airport, IL — B
Westwood Coll–Chicago
River Oaks, IL — B

Computer Engineering
Bethel Coll, IN — B
Capital U, OH — B
Case Western Reserve U,
OH — B
Cedarville U, OH — B
Clarkson U — B
Cleveland State U, OH — B
Dominican U, IL — B

Dordt Coll, IA — B
Eastern Michigan U, MI — B
Grand Valley State U, MI — B
Illinois Inst of Technology, IL — B
Indiana Inst of Technology,
IN — B
Indiana U–Purdue U Fort
Wayne, IN — B
Indiana U–Purdue U
Indianapolis, IN — B
Iowa State U of Science and
Technology, IA — B
Kansas State U, KS — B
Kettering U, MI — B
Lawrence Technological U,
MI — B
Lehigh U, PA — B
Marquette U, WI — B
Miami U Hamilton, OH — B
Michigan State U, MI — B
Michigan Technological U,
MI — B
Milwaukee School of
Engineering, WI — B
Minnesota State U Mankato,
MN — B
Missouri Tech, MO — B
North Dakota State U, ND — B
Northwestern U, IL — B
Ohio Northern U, OH — B
The Ohio State U, OH — B
Ohio U, OH — B
Oklahoma Christian U, OK — B
Oklahoma State U, OK — B
Oral Roberts U, OK — B
Purdue U, IN — B
Purdue U Calumet, IN — B
Rose-Hulman Inst of
Technology, IN — B
St. Cloud State U, MN — B
Saint Mary's U of Minnesota,
MN — B
South Dakota School of
Mines and Technology, SD — B
Southern Illinois U
Carbondale, IL — B
Southern Illinois U
Edwardsville, IL — B
Taylor U, IN — B
Tri-State U, IN — B
The U of Akron, OH — B
The U of Alabama in
Huntsville, AL — B
U of Cincinnati, OH — B
U of Dayton, OH — B
U of Detroit Mercy, MI — B
U of Evansville, IN — B
U of Illinois at Chicago, IL — B
U of Illinois at Urbana–
Champaign, IL — B
U of Kansas, KS — B
U of Michigan, MI — B
U of Minnesota, Duluth, MN — B
U of Missouri–Columbia,
MO — B
U of Missouri–Rolla, MO — B
U of Nebraska at Omaha,
NE — B
U of Nebraska–Lincoln, NE — B
U of Notre Dame, IN — B
U of Oklahoma, OK — B
U of Toledo, OH — B
U of West Florida, FL — B
U of Wisconsin–Madison,
WI — B
Valparaiso U, IN — B

Vatterott Coll, St. Ann, MO — A
Washington U in St. Louis,
MO — B
Western Michigan U, MI — B
Wichita State U, KS — B
Wilberforce U, OH — B
Wright State U, OH — B

Computer Engineering Related
Ohio Northern U, OH — B

Computer Engineering Technologies Related
ITT Tech Inst, Mount
Prospect, IL — A
ITT Tech Inst, Fort Wayne,
IN — A
ITT Tech Inst, Indianapolis,
IN — A
ITT Tech Inst, Newburgh,
IN — A
ITT Tech Inst, Arnold, MO — A
ITT Tech Inst, Earth City,
MO — A
ITT Tech Inst, NE — A
ITT Tech Inst, Green Bay,
WI — A
ITT Tech Inst, Greenfield,
WI — A

Computer Engineering Technology
Andrews U, MI — A,B
Baker Coll of Owosso, MI — A
Central Michigan U, MI — B
DeVry U, Addison, IL — B
DeVry U, Chicago, IL — B
DeVry U, Tinley Park, IL — B
DeVry U, MO — B
DeVry U, Columbus, OH — B
Indiana State U, IN — B
Indiana U–Purdue U Fort
Wayne, IN — B
Kansas State U, KS — A
Kent State U, Tuscarawas
Campus, OH — A
Lake Superior State U, MI — A,B
Madonna U, MI — A
Martin U, IN — B
Minnesota State U Mankato,
MN — B
Missouri Tech, MO — A
National American U, SD — A
Oakland City U, IN — A
Pittsburg State U, KS — B
Purdue U Calumet, IN — A,B
Purdue U North Central, IN — A,B
Ranken Tech Coll, MO — A
Shawnee State U, OH — B
U of Cincinnati, OH — A
U of Dayton, OH — B

Computer Graphics
Academy Coll, MN — A
American Academy of Art, IL — B
The Art Insts International
Minnesota, MN — B
Baker Coll of Cadillac, MI — A
Baker Coll of Flint, MI — B
Capella U, MN — B
Coll for Creative Studies, MI — B
Dakota State U, SD — B
DePaul U, IL — B
Dominican U, IL — B
Globe Coll, MN — A
The Illinois Inst of Art, IL — A,B
International Academy of
Design & Technology, IL — A

Judson Coll, IL	B
Kent State U, OH	A
Minnesota School of Business–Brooklyn Center, MN	A
Minnesota School of Business-Plymouth, MN	A
Minnesota School of Business-Richfield, MN	A
Northern Michigan U, MI	B
Oakland City U, IN	B
Pittsburg State U, KS	B
School of the Art Inst of Chicago, IL	B
South Dakota State U, SD	B
Taylor U, IN	B
U of Dubuque, IA	B

Computer/Information Technology Services Administration Related

Bellevue U, NE	B
Capella U, MN	B
Dordt Coll, IA	B
Eastern Illinois U, IL	B
Hesston Coll, KS	A
Kettering U, MI	B
Lindenwood U, MO	B
The U of Akron, OH	A
Vennard Coll, IA	A
Washington U in St. Louis, MO	B

Computer Management

AIB Coll of Business, IA	A
Coll of Saint Mary, NE	B
Davenport U, Lansing, MI	A
Luther Coll, IA	B
National American U, SD	B
National-Louis U, IL	B
Northwood U, MI	A,B
Oakland City U, IN	A,B
Oklahoma Baptist U, OK	B
Oklahoma State U, OK	B
Rochester Coll, MI	B
Simpson Coll, IA	B
U of Cincinnati, OH	B
Webster U, MO	B

Computer Programming

Academy Coll, MN	A
American InterContinental U Online, IL	B
Ancilla Coll, IN	A
Andrews U, MI	B
Baker Coll of Flint, MI	A,B
Baker Coll of Muskegon, MI	A
Baker Coll of Owosso, MI	A,B
Baker Coll of Port Huron, MI	A
Black Hills State U, SD	A
Creighton U, NE	B
Dakota State U, SD	A
DePaul U, IL	B
Dordt Coll, IA	B
Ferris State U, MI	B
Grace U, NE	B
Grand Valley State U, MI	B
Hamilton Coll, NE	A
Hickey Coll, MO	A
Indiana U East, IN	A
Iowa Wesleyan Coll, IA	B
Kansas State U, KS	A
Kent State U, OH	A,B
Lincoln Coll, Lincoln, IL	A
McPherson Coll, KS	B

Michigan Technological U, MI	B
Minnesota State U Mankato, MN	B
National American U, SD	A,B
National American U–Sioux Falls Branch, SD	A,B
Northern Michigan U, MI	B
Oakland City U, IN	A
Ohio Dominican U, OH	B
Pittsburg State U, KS	B
Purdue U Calumet, IN	A
Purdue U North Central, IN	A
Rockhurst U, MO	B
Southeast Missouri State U, MO	B
Southwestern Coll, KS	B
Taylor U, IN	B
Tiffin U, OH	A
U of Cincinnati, OH	A,B
U of Detroit Mercy, MI	B
U of Indianapolis, IN	A
U of Northwestern Ohio, OH	A
U of Toledo, OH	A,B
Vatterott Coll, St. Ann, MO	A
Westwood Coll–Chicago Du Page, IL	A
Westwood Coll–Chicago Loop Campus, IL	A
Westwood Coll–Chicago O'Hare Airport, IL	A
Westwood Coll–Chicago River Oaks, IL	A
Winona State U, MN	B
Youngstown State U, OH	A,B

Computer Programming Related

Donnelly Coll, KS	A

Computer Programming (Specific Applications)

AIB Coll of Business, IA	A
DePaul U, IL	B
Dunwoody Coll of Technology, MN	A
Hamilton Coll, NE	A
ITT Tech Inst, Mount Prospect, IL	A
ITT Tech Inst, Fort Wayne, IN	A
ITT Tech Inst, Indianapolis, IN	A
ITT Tech Inst, Newburgh, IN	A
ITT Tech Inst, Arnold, MO	A
ITT Tech Inst, Earth City, MO	A
ITT Tech Inst, NE	A
ITT Tech Inst, Green Bay, WI	A
ITT Tech Inst, Greenfield, WI	A
Kent State U, OH	A,B
North Dakota State Coll of Science, ND	A
Oklahoma Baptist U, OK	B
Robert Morris Coll, IL	A
St. Norbert Coll, WI	B
U of Toledo, OH	A
Westwood Coll–Chicago Du Page, IL	B

Westwood Coll–Chicago Loop Campus, IL	B
Westwood Coll–Chicago River Oaks, IL	B

Computer Programming (Vendor/Product Certification)

Davenport U, Dearborn, MI	B
Davenport U, Gaylord, MI	B
Davenport U, Grand Rapids, MI	B
Davenport U, Kalamazoo, MI	B
Davenport U, Warren, MI	B
National American U–Sioux Falls Branch, SD	B

Computer Science

Academy Coll, MN	B
Albion Coll, MI	B
Alma Coll, MI	B
Alverno Coll, WI	B
Andrews U, MI	B
Antioch Coll, OH	B
Aquinas Coll, MI	B
Ashland U, OH	B
Augsburg Coll, MN	B
Augustana Coll, IL	B
Augustana Coll, SD	B
Bacone Coll, OK	A
Baker Coll of Allen Park, MI	A
Baker Coll of Muskegon, MI	B
Baker Coll of Owosso, MI	A,B
Baker U, KS	B
Baldwin-Wallace Coll, OH	B
Ball State U, IN	B
Beloit Coll, WI	B
Bemidji State U, MN	B
Benedictine Coll, KS	B
Benedictine U, IL	B
Bethel Coll, IN	A,B
Bethel Coll, KS	B
Blackburn Coll, IL	B
Black Hills State U, SD	A
Bluffton Coll, OH	B
Briar Cliff U, IA	B
Buena Vista U, IA	B
Butler U, IN	B
Calumet Coll of Saint Joseph, IN	A,B
Calvin Coll, MI	B
Capital U, OH	B
Cardinal Stritch U, WI	B
Carleton Coll, MN	B
Carroll Coll, WI	B
Carthage Coll, WI	B
Case Western Reserve U, OH	B
Cedarville U, OH	B
Central Christian Coll of Kansas, KS	A
Central Coll, IA	B
Central Methodist Coll, MO	A,B
Chicago State U, IL	B
Clarke Coll, IA	B
Clarkson U	B
Cleveland State U, OH	B
Coe Coll, IA	B
Coll of Mount St. Joseph, OH	B
Coll of Saint Benedict, MN	B
Coll of the Ozarks, MO	B
The Coll of Wooster, OH	B
Colorado Tech U Sioux Falls Campus, SD	B
Columbia Coll, MO	B
Concordia Coll, MN	B

Concordia U, IL	B
Concordia U, NE	B
Concordia U Wisconsin, WI	B
Concord U, WV	B
Cornell Coll, IA	B
Creighton U, NE	A,B
Dakota State U, SD	B
Dana Coll, NE	B
Defiance Coll, OH	A,B
Denison U, OH	B
DePaul U, IL	B
DePauw U, IN	B
Dickinson State U, ND	B
Doane Coll, NE	B
Dominican U, IL	B
Donnelly Coll, KS	A
Dordt Coll, IA	B
Drake U, IA	B
Drury U, MO	B
Earlham Coll, IN	B
East Central U, OK	B
Elmhurst Coll, IL	B
Eureka Coll, IL	B
Evangel U, MO	B
Fontbonne U, MO	B
Franciscan U of Steubenville, OH	B
Franklin Coll, IN	B
Gallipolis Career Coll, OH	A
Goshen Coll, IN	B
Governors State U, IL	B
Graceland U, IA	B
Grace U, NE	B
Grand Valley State U, MI	B
Grand View Coll, IA	B
Greenville Coll, IL	B
Grinnell Coll, IA	B
Gustavus Adolphus Coll, MN	B
Hanover Coll, IN	B
Hastings Coll, NE	B
Heidelberg Coll, OH	B
Hillsdale Coll, MI	B
Hiram Coll, OH	B
Hope Coll, MI	B
Huntington Coll, IN	B
Illinois Coll, IL	B
Illinois Inst of Technology, IL	B
Illinois State U, IL	B
Illinois Wesleyan U, IL	B
Indiana Inst of Technology, IN	B
Indiana U–Purdue U Fort Wayne, IN	A,B
Indiana U South Bend, IN	A,B
Indiana U Southeast, IN	A,B
Iowa Wesleyan Coll, IA	B
Jamestown Coll, ND	B
John Carroll U, OH	B
Judson Coll, IL	B
Kalamazoo Coll, MI	B
Kansas Wesleyan U, KS	A,B
Kent State U, OH	B
Kettering U, MI	B
Kilian Comm Coll, SD	A
Lake Forest Coll, IL	B
Lakeland Coll, WI	B
Lake Superior State U, MI	B
Lawrence Technological U, MI	B
Lawrence U, WI	B
Lehigh U, PA	B
Lewis U, IL	B
Lincoln Coll, Lincoln, IL	A
Lincoln U, MO	A
Lindenwood U, MO	B

A—associate degree; B—bachelor's degree

Loras Coll, IA	B
Loyola U Chicago, IL	B
Luther Coll, IA	B
Macalester Coll, MN	B
Madonna U, MI	A,B
Maharishi U of Management, IA	B
Malone Coll, OH	B
Manchester Coll, IN	A,B
Marietta Coll, OH	B
Marquette U, WI	B
Maryville U of Saint Louis, MO	B
McKendree Coll, IL	B
McPherson Coll, KS	B
Metropolitan State U, MN	B
Miami U Hamilton, OH	B
Michigan Technological U, MI	B
MidAmerica Nazarene U, KS	B
Minnesota State U Mankato, MN	B
Minnesota State U Moorhead, MN	B
Minot State U, ND	B
Missouri Southern State U, MO	A,B
Missouri Valley Coll, MO	B
Monmouth Coll, IL	B
Morningside Coll, IA	B
Mount Marty Coll, SD	B
Mount Mary Coll, WI	B
Mount Mercy Coll, IA	B
Mount Union Coll, OH	B
Muskingum Coll, OH	B
Nebraska Wesleyan U, NE	B
North Carolina Ag and Tech State U, NC	B
North Central Coll, IL	B
North Dakota State U, ND	B
Northeastern Illinois U, IL	B
Northeastern State U, OK	B
Northern Illinois U, IL	B
Northern Michigan U, MI	B
Northwestern Coll, IA	B
Northwestern Oklahoma State U, OK	B
Northwestern U, IL	B
Oakland City U, IN	A
Oberlin Coll, OH	B
Ohio Dominican U, OH	B
Ohio Northern U, OH	B
The Ohio State U, OH	B
Ohio U, OH	B
Ohio U–Southern Campus, OH	A
Ohio Wesleyan U, OH	B
Oklahoma Baptist U, OK	B
Oklahoma Christian U, OK	B
Oklahoma City U, OK	B
Oklahoma State U, OK	B
Olivet Coll, MI	B
Olivet Nazarene U, IL	B
Oral Roberts U, OK	B
Otterbein Coll, OH	B
Park U, MO	A,B
Peru State Coll, NE	B
Pittsburg State U, KS	B
Purdue U Calumet, IN	B
Quincy U, IL	B
Ripon Coll, WI	B
Rochester Comm and Tech Coll, MN	A
Rockford Coll, IL	B
Rockhurst U, MO	B
Roosevelt U, IL	B
Rose-Hulman Inst of Technology, IN	B
St. Ambrose U, IA	B
St. Cloud State U, MN	B
Saint John's U, MN	B
Saint Mary's U of Minnesota, MN	B
St. Olaf Coll, MN	B
Saint Xavier U, IL	B
Simpson Coll, IA	B
South Dakota School of Mines and Technology, SD	B
Southern Illinois U Carbondale, IL	B
Southern Illinois U Edwardsville, IL	B
Southern Nazarene U, OK	B
Southwest Baptist U, MO	A,B
Southwestern Coll, KS	B
Southwestern Oklahoma State U, OK	B
Southwest Missouri State U, MO	B
Spring Arbor U, MI	B
Tabor Coll, KS	A,B
Taylor U, IN	B
Transylvania U, KY	B
Trinity Christian Coll, IL	B
Trinity International U, IL	B
Tri-State U, IN	B
Truman State U, MO	B
Union Coll, NE	B
The U of Akron, OH	B
U of Central Oklahoma, OK	B
U of Chicago, IL	B
U of Cincinnati, OH	B
U of Dayton, OH	B
U of Detroit Mercy, MI	B
U of Dubuque, IA	A,B
U of Evansville, IN	B
The U of Findlay, OH	A,B
U of Illinois at Springfield, IL	B
U of Illinois at Urbana–Champaign, IL	B
U of Indianapolis, IN	B
The U of Iowa, IA	B
U of Michigan, MI	B
U of Michigan–Dearborn, MI	B
U of Michigan–Flint, MI	B
U of Minnesota, Duluth, MN	B
U of Minnesota, Morris, MN	B
U of Minnesota, Twin Cities Campus, MN	B
U of Missouri–Columbia, MO	B
U of Missouri–Kansas City, MO	B
U of Missouri–Rolla, MO	B
U of Missouri–St. Louis, MO	B
U of Nebraska at Omaha, NE	B
U of New Orleans, LA	B
U of Northern Iowa, IA	B
U of Rio Grande, OH	A,B
U of St. Francis, IL	B
U of Sioux Falls, SD	B
U of Toledo, OH	B
U of Tulsa, OK	B
U of Wisconsin–Green Bay, WI	B
U of Wisconsin–La Crosse, WI	B
U of Wisconsin–Madison, WI	B
U of Wisconsin–Milwaukee, WI	B
U of Wisconsin–Oshkosh, WI	B
U of Wisconsin–Parkside, WI	B
U of Wisconsin–Platteville, WI	B
U of Wisconsin–River Falls, WI	B
U of Wisconsin–Superior, WI	B
Valparaiso U, IN	B
Walsh U, OH	B
Wartburg Coll, IA	B
Washington U in St. Louis, MO	B
Wayne State Coll, NE	B
Webster U, MO	B
Western Michigan U, MI	B
Westminster Coll, MO	B
Wheaton Coll, IL	B
Wilberforce U, OH	B
William Jewell Coll, MO	B
William Penn U, IA	B
Winona State U, MN	B
Wittenberg U, OH	B
Wright State U, OH	B
Xavier U, OH	B
Youngstown State U, OH	B

Computer Software and Media Applications Related

AIB Coll of Business, IA	A
Ancilla Coll, IN	A
Baldwin-Wallace Coll, OH	B
Dakota Wesleyan U, SD	B
Gallipolis Career Coll, OH	A
Indiana U–Purdue U Fort Wayne, IN	A,B
Kilian Comm Coll, SD	B
Westwood Coll–Chicago Loop Campus, IL	B

Computer Software Engineering

Carroll Coll, WI	B
Clarkson U	B
Globe Coll, MN	A
Michigan Technological U, MI	B
Milwaukee School of Engineering, WI	B
Minnesota School of Business–Brooklyn Center, MN	A
Minnesota School of Business-Plymouth, MN	A
Minnesota School of Business-Richfield, MN	A
Rose-Hulman Inst of Technology, IN	B
South Dakota State U, SD	B
Westwood Coll–Chicago Du Page, IL	A
Westwood Coll–Chicago O'Hare Airport, IL	A

Computer Software Technology

ITT Tech Inst, Fort Wayne, IN	B
ITT Tech Inst, Indianapolis, IN	B
ITT Tech Inst, Newburgh, IN	B
ITT Tech Inst, Arnold, MO	B
ITT Tech Inst, Earth City, MO	B
ITT Tech Inst, Green Bay, WI	B
ITT Tech Inst, Greenfield, WI	B

Computer Systems Analysis

Baker Coll of Flint, MI	A,B
Baldwin-Wallace Coll, OH	B
Davenport U, Dearborn, MI	A,B
Davenport U, Gaylord, MI	A
Davenport U, Grand Rapids, MI	A,B
Davenport U, Holland, MI	A,B
Davenport U, Kalamazoo, MI	A,B
Davenport U, Lansing, MI	A
Davenport U, Warren, MI	A,B
DeVry U, Addison, IL	B
DeVry U, Chicago, IL	B
DeVry U, Tinley Park, IL	B
DeVry U, MO	B
DeVry U, Columbus, OH	B
Kansas State U, KS	A
Kent State U, OH	B
Metropolitan State U, MN	B
Miami U, OH	B
Miami U Hamilton, OH	B
Oklahoma Baptist U, OK	B
Rockhurst U, MO	B
Saginaw Valley State U, MI	B
St. Ambrose U, IA	B
The U of Akron, OH	A
U of Toledo, OH	A

Computer Systems Networking and Telecommunications

Academy Coll, MN	A
AIB Coll of Business, IA	A
Ancilla Coll, IN	A
Aurora U, IL	B
Baker Coll of Allen Park, MI	A
Baker Coll of Flint, MI	A
Baldwin-Wallace Coll, OH	B
Capella U, MN	B
Davenport U, Dearborn, MI	A,B
Davenport U, Gaylord, MI	A
Davenport U, Grand Rapids, MI	A,B
Davenport U, Holland, MI	A,B
Davenport U, Kalamazoo, MI	A,B
Davenport U, Lansing, MI	A,B
Davenport U, Warren, MI	A,B
DePaul U, IL	B
DeVry U, Addison, IL	B
DeVry U, Chicago, IL	B
DeVry U, Tinley Park, IL	B
DeVry U, MO	B
Globe Coll, MN	A
Herzing Coll, Minneapolis Drafting School Division, MN	A
Illinois State U, IL	B
ITT Tech Inst, Fort Wayne, IN	B
ITT Tech Inst, Indianapolis, IN	B
ITT Tech Inst, Newburgh, IN	B
ITT Tech Inst, Arnold, MO	B
ITT Tech Inst, Earth City, MO	B
ITT Tech Inst, NE	B
ITT Tech Inst, Green Bay, WI	B
ITT Tech Inst, Greenfield, WI	B

Minnesota School of
Business–Brooklyn Center,
MN   A

Minnesota School of
Business-Plymouth, MN   A

Minnesota School of
Business-Richfield, MN   A

Northern Michigan U, MI   B

Northwestern Oklahoma
State U, OK   B

Robert Morris Coll, IL   A

Roosevelt U, IL   B

St. Ambrose U, IA   B

The U of Findlay, OH   B

U of St. Francis, IL   B

U of Wisconsin–Stout, WI   B

Westwood Coll–Chicago Du
Page, IL   A,B

Westwood Coll–Chicago
Loop Campus, IL   A,B

Westwood Coll–Chicago
O'Hare Airport, IL   A,B

Westwood Coll–Chicago
River Oaks, IL   A,B

Computer Teacher Education

Alma Coll, MI   B

Baker Coll of Flint, MI   A

Buena Vista U, IA   B

Capital U, OH   B

Central Christian Coll of
Kansas, KS   A

Central Michigan U, MI   B

Concordia U, IL   B

Concordia U, NE   B

Dordt Coll, IA   B

Eastern Michigan U, MI   B

Northern Michigan U, MI   B

Pillsbury Baptist Bible Coll,
MN   B

South Dakota State U, SD   B

Union Coll, NE   B

The U of Akron, OH   B

U of Illinois at Urbana–
Champaign, IL   B

U of Nebraska–Lincoln, NE   B

U of Wisconsin–River Falls,
WI   B

Viterbo U, WI   B

Wright State U, OH   B

Youngstown State U, OH   B

Computer/Technical Support

Gallipolis Career Coll, OH   A

**Computer Technology/
Computer Systems
Technology**

Kent State U, OH   A

Miami U Hamilton, OH   A

Southeast Missouri State U,
MO   A

Southwestern Coll, KS   B

**Computer Typography and
Composition Equipment
Operation**

Baker Coll of Auburn Hills,
MI   A

Baker Coll of Cadillac, MI   A

Baker Coll of Clinton
Township, MI   A

Baker Coll of Flint, MI   A

Baker Coll of Jackson, MI   A

Calumet Coll of Saint Joseph,
IN   A

Lincoln Coll, Lincoln, IL   A

MacCormac Coll, IL   A

Northern Michigan U, MI   A

U of Toledo, OH   A

Conducting

Calvin Coll, MI   B

Central Christian Coll of
Kansas, KS   A

Ohio U, OH   B

Conservation Biology

St. Gregory's U, OK   B

Construction Engineering

Andrews U, MI   B

Bradley U, IL   B

Clarkson U   B

Michigan Technological U,
MI   B

North Dakota State U, ND   B

Purdue U, IN   B

U of Cincinnati, OH   B

Western Michigan U, MI   B

**Construction Engineering
Technology**

Baker Coll of Owosso, MI   A

Bemidji State U, MN   B

Bowling Green State U, OH   B

Central Michigan U, MI   B

Central Missouri State U,
MO   A,B

Eastern Michigan U, MI   B

Ferris State U, MI   A

Indiana U–Purdue U Fort
Wayne, IN   B

Lake Superior State U, MI   A

Lawrence Technological U,
MI   A

Minnesota State U
Moorhead, MN   B

Morrison Inst of Technology,
IL   A

North Dakota State Coll of
Science, ND   A

Northern Michigan U, MI   A,B

Oklahoma State U, OK   B

Pittsburg State U, KS   B

Purdue U Calumet, IN   A,B

Purdue U North Central, IN   A

South Dakota State U, SD   B

Southeast Missouri State U,
MO   B

Southern Illinois U
Carbondale, IL   B

Southern Illinois U
Edwardsville, IL   B

The U of Akron, OH   A

U of Cincinnati, OH   A,B

U of Nebraska at Omaha,
NE   B

U of Nebraska–Lincoln, NE   B

U of Toledo, OH   A,B

U of Wisconsin–Stout, WI   B

Western Michigan U, MI   B

Wright State U, OH   A

**Construction/Heavy
Equipment/Earthmoving
Equipment Operation**

Oklahoma State U, OK   B

Construction Management

Baker Coll of Flint, MI   A

Eastern Michigan U, MI   B

Ferris State U, MI   B

Lawrence Technological U,
MI   B

Michigan State U, MI   B

Milwaukee School of
Engineering, WI   B

Minnesota State U Mankato,
MN   B

North Carolina Ag and Tech
State U, NC   B

North Dakota State U, ND   B

Oklahoma State U, OK   B

Pittsburg State U, KS   B

U of Cincinnati, OH   B

U of Minnesota, Twin Cities
Campus, MN   B

U of Northern Iowa, IA   B

U of Wisconsin–Madison,
WI   B

U of Wisconsin–Platteville,
WI   B

Western Michigan U, MI   B

**Consumer Merchandising/
Retailing Management**

Baker Coll of Owosso, MI   A

Chicago State U, IL   B

East Central U, OK   B

Ferris State U, MI   B

Fontbonne U, MO   B

Governors State U, IL   B

Indiana U Bloomington, IN   B

Lindenwood U, MO   B

MacCormac Coll, IL   A

Madonna U, MI   A,B

Northern Michigan U, MI   B

U of Central Oklahoma, OK   B

U of Toledo, OH   A

Winona State U, MN   B

Youngstown State U, OH   B

**Consumer Services and
Advocacy**

Coll of the Ozarks, MO   B

South Dakota State U, SD   B

U of Wisconsin–Madison,
WI   B

**Cooking and Related Culinary
Arts**

Kendall Coll, IL   A,B

Lexington Coll, IL   A,B

Corrections

Baker Coll of Muskegon, MI   A

Chicago State U, IL   B

Coll of the Ozarks, MO   B

East Central U, OK   B

Lake Superior State U, MI   A,B

Lincoln Coll, Lincoln, IL   A

Marygrove Coll, MI   A

Minnesota State U Mankato,
MN   B

Oklahoma City U, OK   B

Saint Louis U, MO   B

Southeast Missouri State U,
MO   B

Tiffin U, OH   B

The U of Akron, OH   B

U of Indianapolis, IN   A,B

U of Toledo, OH   A

Washburn U, KS   A,B

Winona State U, MN   B

Xavier U, OH   A

Youngstown State U, OH   A,B

**Corrections and Criminal
Justice Related**

American InterContinental U
Online, IL   B

Chadron State Coll, NE   B

Hastings Coll, NE   B

Mount Mary Coll, WI   B

North Dakota State U, ND   B

U of Michigan–Flint, MI   B

U of Phoenix–St. Louis
Campus, MO   B

U of Phoenix–Tulsa Campus,
OK   B

U of Phoenix–West Michigan
Campus, MI   B

Westwood Coll–Chicago Du
Page, IL   B

Westwood Coll–Chicago
O'Hare Airport, IL   B

Westwood Coll–Chicago
River Oaks, IL   B

Cosmetology

Globe Coll, MN   A

Lincoln Coll, Lincoln, IL   A

Minnesota School of
Business–Brooklyn Center,
MN   A

Minnesota School of
Business-Plymouth, MN   A

Minnesota School of
Business-Richfield, MN   A

Counseling Psychology

Central Christian Coll of
Kansas, KS   A

Crossroads Coll, MN   B

Grace Coll, IN   B

Jamestown Coll, ND   B

Kilian Comm Coll, SD   A

Morningside Coll, IA   B

Newman U, KS   B

Northwestern U, IL   B

Rochester Coll, MI   B

Saint Xavier U, IL   B

**Counselor Education/School
Counseling and Guidance**

Central Christian Coll of
Kansas, KS   A

DePaul U, IL   B

East Central U, OK   B

Eastern Michigan U, MI   B

Martin U, IN   B

Oakland U, MI   B

Pittsburg State U, KS   B

Purdue U Calumet, IN   B

St. Cloud State U, MN   B

U of Central Oklahoma, OK   B

U of Wisconsin–Superior, WI   B

Wayne State Coll, NE   B

Wright State U, OH   B

Court Reporting

AIB Coll of Business, IA   A

Kaplan Coll, IA   A

MacCormac Coll, IL   A

Metropolitan Coll, Tulsa, OK   A,B

U of Cincinnati, OH   A

Crafts, Folk Art and Artisanry

Bowling Green State U, OH   B

The Cleveland Inst of Art,
OH   B

Indiana U–Purdue U Fort
Wayne, IN   B

Kent State U, OH   B

A—associate degree; B—bachelor's degree

School	
School of the Art Inst of Chicago, IL	B
The U of Akron, OH	B
U of Illinois at Urbana–Champaign, IL	B

Creative Writing

School	
Antioch Coll, OH	B
Ashland U, OH	B
Augustana Coll, IL	B
Beloit Coll, WI	B
Bethel Coll, IN	A
Bluffton Coll, OH	B
Bowling Green State U, OH	B
Briar Cliff U, IA	B
Capital U, OH	B
Cardinal Stritch U, WI	B
Carroll Coll, WI	B
Central Michigan U, MI	B
Chicago State U, IL	B
Coe Coll, IA	B
Coll of St. Catherine, MN	B
Columbia Coll Chicago, IL	B
Concordia Coll, MN	B
Cornerstone U, MI	B
Denison U, OH	B
DePaul U, IL	B
Drury U, MO	B
Eastern Michigan U, MI	B
Grand Valley State U, MI	B
Haskell Indian Nations U, KS	A
Hastings Coll, NE	B
Indiana U–Purdue U Fort Wayne, IN	B
Kenyon Coll, OH	B
Knox Coll, IL	B
Lincoln Coll, Lincoln, IL	A
Loras Coll, IA	B
Manchester Coll, IN	A
Marquette U, WI	B
Miami U, OH	B
Miami U Hamilton, OH	B
Millikin U, IL	B
Minnesota State U Mankato, MN	B
Northern Michigan U, MI	B
Northland Coll, WI	B
Northwestern Coll, MN	B
Oberlin Coll, OH	B
Ohio Northern U, OH	B
The Ohio State U, OH	B
Ohio U, OH	B
Ohio Wesleyan U, OH	B
Oklahoma Christian U, OK	B
Oklahoma State U, OK	B
Rockhurst U, MO	B
St. Cloud State U, MN	B
Saint Joseph's Coll, IN	B
Saint Mary's Coll, IN	B
Stephens Coll, MO	B
Taylor U, IN	B
U of Chicago, IL	B
U of Evansville, IN	B
The U of Findlay, OH	B
U of Michigan, MI	B
U of Nebraska at Omaha, NE	B
U of St. Thomas, MN	B
U of Wisconsin–Parkside, WI	B
Waldorf Coll, IA	B
Washington U in St. Louis, MO	B
Wayne State Coll, NE	B
Western Michigan U, MI	B

Criminal Justice/Law Enforcement Administration

School	
Adrian Coll, MI	A,B
Ancilla Coll, IN	A
Ashland U, OH	A,B
Aurora U, IL	B
Baldwin-Wallace Coll, OH	B
Ball State U, IN	A,B
Bellevue U, NE	B
Bemidji State U, MN	A,B
Blackburn Coll, IL	B
Bradley U, IL	B
Briar Cliff U, IA	B
Calumet Coll of Saint Joseph, IN	A,B
Carroll Coll, WI	B
Carthage Coll, WI	B
Cedarville U, OH	B
Central Christian Coll of Kansas, KS	A
Central Missouri State U, MO	B
Chicago State U, IL	B
Coll of the Ozarks, MO	B
Columbia Coll, MO	A,B
Concordia U, MI	B
Concordia U Wisconsin, WI	B
Culver-Stockton Coll, MO	B
Dakota Wesleyan U, SD	A,B
Dana Coll, NE	B
Defiance Coll, OH	A,B
Dordt Coll, IA	B
East Central U, OK	B
Edgewood Coll, WI	B
Evangel U, MO	B
Ferris State U, MI	B
Governors State U, IL	B
Grace Coll, IN	B
Graceland U, IA	B
Grand Valley State U, MI	B
Grand View Coll, IA	B
Greenville Coll, IL	B
Gustavus Adolphus Coll, MN	B
Hamline U, MN	B
Hannibal-LaGrange Coll, MO	A,B
Harris-Stowe State Coll, MO	B
Indiana U Northwest, IN	A,B
Indiana U South Bend, IN	A,B
Iowa Wesleyan Coll, IA	B
ITT Tech Inst, Fort Wayne, IN	B
ITT Tech Inst, Indianapolis, IN	B
ITT Tech Inst, Arnold, MO	B
ITT Tech Inst, Earth City, MO	
Kansas Wesleyan U, KS	A,B
Kilian Comm Coll, SD	A
Lake Superior State U, MI	A,B
Lewis U, IL	B
Lincoln Coll, Lincoln, IL	A
Lincoln U, MO	A,B
Lindenwood U, MO	B
Lourdes Coll, OH	A,B
MacMurray Coll, IL	A,B
Marian Coll of Fond du Lac, WI	B
Martin U, IN	B
McKendree Coll, IL	B
Metropolitan State U, MN	B
Michigan State U, MI	B
MidAmerica Nazarene U, KS	B
Missouri Southern State U, MO	B
Missouri Valley Coll, MO	B

School	
Mount Mercy Coll, IA	B
Mount Vernon Nazarene U, OH	B
Muskingum Coll, OH	B
Newman U, KS	B
Northeastern State U, OK	B
Northern Michigan U, MI	A,B
Oakland City U, IN	B
Ohio Dominican U, OH	B
Ohio Northern U, OH	B
Ohio U, OH	B
Ohio U–Chillicothe, OH	B
Ohio U–Southern Campus, OH	A,B
Ohio U–Zanesville, OH	B
Oklahoma City U, OK	B
Olivet Nazarene U, IL	B
Park U, MO	A,B
Peru State Coll, NE	B
Pittsburg State U, KS	B
Purdue U Calumet, IN	B
Rockford Coll, IL	B
St. Cloud State U, MN	B
Saint Louis U, MO	B
Saint Mary's U of Minnesota, MN	B
Siena Heights U, MI	A,B
Simpson Coll, IA	B
Southern Illinois U Carbondale, IL	B
Southwest Baptist U, MO	B
Southwestern Coll, KS	B
Southwestern Oklahoma State U, OK	B
Taylor U Fort Wayne, IN	B
Tiffin U, OH	B
Tri-State U, IN	A,B
Truman State U, MO	B
Union Inst & U, OH	B
The U of Akron, OH	B
U of Central Oklahoma, OK	B
U of Cincinnati, OH	A,B
U of Dayton, OH	B
U of Detroit Mercy, MI	B
U of Dubuque, IA	B
U of Evansville, IN	B
The U of Findlay, OH	A,B
U of Illinois at Springfield, IL	B
U of Indianapolis, IN	A,B
U of Missouri–Kansas City, MO	B
The U of South Dakota, SD	B
U of Wisconsin–Milwaukee, WI	B
U of Wisconsin–Oshkosh, WI	B
U of Wisconsin–Parkside, WI	B
U of Wisconsin–Platteville, WI	B
Urbana U, OH	A,B
Washburn U, KS	A,B
Wayne State Coll, NE	B
Western Illinois U, IL	B
Winona State U, MN	B
Youngstown State U, OH	A,B

Criminal Justice/Police Science

School	
Bemidji State U, MN	B
Cameron U, OK	A
Chicago State U, IL	B
Coll of the Ozarks, MO	B
Defiance Coll, OH	A,B
East Central U, OK	B
Ferris State U, MI	B
Grand Valley State U, MI	B

School	
Kent State U, Tuscarawas Campus, OH	A,B
Lake Superior State U, MI	A,B
Lincoln Coll, Lincoln, IL	A
MacMurray Coll, IL	A,B
Metropolitan State U, MN	B
Minnesota State U Mankato, MN	B
Missouri Southern State U, MO	A
Northeastern State U, OK	B
Northern Michigan U, MI	A,B
Northern State U, SD	B
Northwestern Oklahoma State U, OK	B
Ohio Northern U, OH	B
Ohio U, OH	A
Ohio U–Chillicothe, OH	A
Oklahoma City U, OK	B
Purdue U Calumet, IN	B
Rochester Comm and Tech Coll, MN	A
St. Gregory's U, OK	B
Saint Louis U, MO	B
Saint Mary's U of Minnesota, MN	B
Tiffin U, OH	A,B
Truman State U, MO	B
The U of Akron, OH	A
U of Cincinnati, OH	A,B
U of Mary, ND	B
U of Toledo, OH	A
U of Wisconsin–Milwaukee, WI	B
U of Wisconsin–Superior, WI	A
Washburn U, KS	A,B
Wayne State Coll, NE	B
Winona State U, MN	B
Wright State U, OH	B
Youngstown State U, OH	A,B

Criminal Justice/Safety

School	
Augsburg Coll, MN	B
Aurora U, IL	B
Bethany Coll, KS	B
Bethel Coll, IN	A,B
Bluffton Coll, OH	B
Bowling Green State U, OH	B
Buena Vista U, IA	B
Butler U, IN	B
Capital U, OH	B
Central Christian Coll of Kansas, KS	A
Central Methodist Coll, MO	B
Colorado Tech U Sioux Falls Campus, SD	A,B
Concordia U, St. Paul, MN	B
Florida Gulf Coast U, FL	B
Fort Hays State U, KS	B
The Franciscan U, IA	B
Gannon U, PA	B
Illinois State U, IL	B
Indiana U Bloomington, IN	B
Indiana U East, IN	A
Indiana U Kokomo, IN	A,B
Indiana U–Purdue U Fort Wayne, IN	A,B
Indiana U–Purdue U Indianapolis, IN	A,B
Jamestown Coll, ND	B
Judson Coll, IL	B
Kaplan Coll, IA	A,B
Kent State U, OH	A,B
Lakeland Coll, WI	B
Loras Coll, IA	B
Loyola U Chicago, IL	B
Madonna U, MI	A,B

Manchester Coll, IN	A
Metropolitan State U, MN	B
Michigan State U, MI	B
Minnesota State U Moorhead, MN	B
Minot State U, ND	B
Missouri Baptist U, MO	B
Missouri Western State Coll, MO	A,B
Mount Marty Coll, SD	B
Northeastern Illinois U, IL	B
Northern Michigan U, MI	B
Northwestern Coll, MN	B
Ohio Northern U, OH	B
The Ohio State U, OH	B
Ohio U, OH	B
Olivet Coll, MI	B
Pittsburg State U, KS	B
Quincy U, IL	B
Roosevelt U, IL	B
Saginaw Valley State U, MI	B
St. Ambrose U, IA	B
St. Gregory's U, OK	A
Saint Joseph's Coll, IN	B
Saint Xavier U, IL	B
Southeastern Oklahoma State U, OK	B
Southern Illinois U Edwardsville, IL	B
Southern Nazarene U, OK	B
Southwest Missouri State U, MO	B
Taylor U Fort Wayne, IN	B
Tiffin U, OH	B
The U of Akron, OH	B
U of Central Oklahoma, OK	B
U of Illinois at Chicago, IL	B
U of Nebraska at Omaha, NE	B
U of North Dakota, ND	B
U of Toledo, OH	B
U of West Florida, FL	B
U of Wisconsin–Eau Claire, WI	B
U of Wisconsin–Superior, WI	B
Viterbo U, WI	B
Wayne State U, MI	B
Western Michigan U, MI	B
Wichita State U, KS	B
Xavier U, OH	A,B
Youngstown State U, OH	B

Criminology

Ball State U, IN	A,B
Bethel Coll, KS	B
Cameron U, OK	B
Capital U, OH	B
Central Michigan U, MI	B
Coll of Mount St. Joseph, OH	B
Coll of the Ozarks, MO	B
Dominican U, IL	B
Drury U, MO	B
Eastern Michigan U, MI	B
Indiana State U, IN	A,B
Lincoln Coll, Lincoln, IL	A
Lindenwood U, MO	B
Marquette U, WI	A,B
Maryville U of Saint Louis, MO	B
The Ohio State U, OH	B
Ohio U, OH	B
St. Cloud State U, MN	B
U of Minnesota, Duluth, MN	B
U of Missouri–St. Louis, MO	B

U of Northern Iowa, IA	B
U of Oklahoma, OK	B
U of St. Thomas, MN	B
Upper Iowa U, IA	B
Valparaiso U, IN	B
Western Michigan U, MI	B
William Penn U, IA	B
Wright State U, OH	B

Crop Production

North Dakota State U, ND	B

Culinary Arts

The Art Insts International Minnesota, MN	A,B
Baker Coll of Muskegon, MI	A
Kendall Coll, IL	A,B
Lexington Coll, IL	A,B
Metropolitan State U, MN	B
Northern Michigan U, MI	B
Oakland City U, IN	A
Purdue U Calumet, IN	A
Robert Morris Coll, IL	A
St. Augustine Coll, IL	A
The U of Akron, OH	A

Culinary Arts Related

Lexington Coll, IL	A,B

Cultural Resource Management and Policy Analysis

Eastern Michigan U, MI	B

Cultural Studies

Cornell Coll, IA	B
Kent State U, OH	B
Minnesota State U Mankato, MN	B
The Ohio State U, OH	B
Ohio Wesleyan U, OH	B
Reformed Bible Coll, MI	B
Saint Mary-of-the-Woods Coll, IN	B
St. Olaf Coll, MN	B
U of Wisconsin–Milwaukee, WI	B
Washington U in St. Louis, MO	B

Curriculum and Instruction

Eastern Michigan U, MI	B
Ohio U, OH	B
U of Saint Mary, KS	B
The U of South Dakota, SD	B
Wright State U, OH	B

Customer Service Management

U of Wisconsin–Stout, WI	B

Customer Service Support/Call Center/Teleservice Operation

Davenport U, Dearborn, MI	A
Davenport U, Grand Rapids, MI	A
Davenport U, Holland, MI	A
Davenport U, Kalamazoo, MI	A
Davenport U, Lansing, MI	A
Davenport U, Warren, MI	A
National American U–Sioux Falls Branch, SD	A,B

Cytotechnology

Edgewood Coll, WI	B
Elmhurst Coll, IL	B
The Franciscan U, IA	B
Illinois Coll, IL	B

Indiana U–Purdue U Indianapolis, IN	A,B
Indiana U Southeast, IN	A,B
Jewish Hospital Coll of Nursing and Allied Health, MO	B
Marian Coll of Fond du Lac, WI	
Minnesota State U Moorhead, MN	B
Northern Michigan U, MI	B
Oakland U, MI	B
Roosevelt U, IL	B
Saint Mary's Coll, IN	B
Saint Mary's U of Minnesota, MN	B
The U of Akron, OH	B
U of Kansas, KS	B
U of Missouri–St. Louis, MO	B
U of North Dakota, ND	B
Winona State U, MN	B

Dairy Science

Iowa State U of Science and Technology, IA	B
South Dakota State U, SD	B
U of Wisconsin–Madison, WI	B
U of Wisconsin–River Falls, WI	B

Dance

Alma Coll, MI	B
Antioch Coll, OH	B
Baldwin-Wallace Coll, OH	B
Ball State U, IN	B
Bowling Green State U, OH	B
Butler U, IN	B
Cleveland State U, OH	B
Columbia Coll Chicago, IL	B
Denison U, OH	B
Eastern Michigan U, MI	B
Gustavus Adolphus Coll, MN	B
Hope Coll, MI	B
Indiana U Bloomington, IN	B
Kent State U, OH	B
Kenyon Coll, OH	B
Lake Erie Coll, OH	B
Lincoln Coll, Lincoln, IL	A
Lindenwood U, MO	B
Luther Coll, IA	B
Marygrove Coll, MI	B
Northwestern U, IL	B
Oakland U, MI	B
Oberlin Coll, OH	B
The Ohio State U, OH	B
Ohio U, OH	B
Oklahoma City U, OK	B
St. Gregory's U, OK	B
St. Olaf Coll, MN	B
Southwest Missouri State U, MO	B
Stephens Coll, MO	B
The U of Akron, OH	B
U of Central Oklahoma, OK	B
U of Cincinnati, OH	B
U of Illinois at Urbana–Champaign, IL	B
The U of Iowa, IA	B
U of Kansas, KS	B
U of Michigan, MI	B
U of Minnesota, Twin Cities Campus, MN	B
U of Missouri–Kansas City, MO	B
U of Nebraska–Lincoln, NE	B

U of Oklahoma, OK	B
U of Wisconsin–Milwaukee, WI	B
U of Wisconsin–Stevens Point, WI	B
Washington U in St. Louis, MO	B
Wayne State U, MI	B
Webster U, MO	B
Western Michigan U, MI	B
Wright State U, OH	B

Dance Therapy

Columbia Coll Chicago, IL	B

Data Entry/Microcomputer Applications

Baker Coll of Allen Park, MI	A
Gallipolis Career Coll, OH	A

Data Entry/Microcomputer Applications Related

AIB Coll of Business, IA	A
Baker Coll of Allen Park, MI	A
Donnelly Coll, KS	A

Data Processing and Data Processing Technology

Academy Coll, MN	A
American InterContinental U Online, IL	A
Baker Coll of Auburn Hills, MI	A
Baker Coll of Cadillac, MI	A
Baker Coll of Clinton Township, MI	A
Baker Coll of Flint, MI	A
Baker Coll of Jackson, MI	A
Baker Coll of Muskegon, MI	A
Baker Coll of Owosso, MI	A
Baker Coll of Port Huron, MI	A
Bemidji State U, MN	B
Chicago State U, IL	B
Davenport U, Kalamazoo, MI	A
Donnelly Coll, KS	A
Dordt Coll, IA	A
Indiana U Kokomo, IN	B
Indiana U Northwest, IN	B
Lake Superior State U, MI	A
Lincoln Coll, Lincoln, IL	A
Lincoln U, MO	A
Minnesota State U Mankato, MN	B
Missouri Southern State U, MO	A
Mount Vernon Nazarene U, OH	B
Northern Michigan U, MI	A,B
Northern State U, SD	A
The U of Akron, OH	A
U of Cincinnati, OH	A
U of Southern Indiana, IN	B
U of Toledo, OH	A
Wright State U, OH	A
Youngstown State U, OH	A

Dental Assisting

Herzing Coll, Minneapolis Drafting School Division, MN	A
U of Southern Indiana, IN	A

Dental Hygiene

Argosy U/Twin Cities, MN	A
Argosy U/Twin Cities, Eagan, MN	A

A—associate degree; B—bachelor's degree

Baker Coll of Port Huron, MI — A
Ferris State U, MI — A
Herzing Coll, Minneapolis Drafting School Division, MN — A
Indiana U Northwest, IN — A
Indiana U–Purdue U Fort Wayne, IN — A
Indiana U–Purdue U Indianapolis, IN — A,B
Indiana U South Bend, IN — A
Marquette U, WI — B
Minnesota State U Mankato, MN — A,B
Missouri Southern State U, MO — A
North Dakota State Coll of Science, ND — A
The Ohio State U, OH — B
Rochester Comm and Tech Coll, MN — A
Shawnee State U, OH — A
Southern Illinois U Carbondale, IL — B
U of Detroit Mercy, MI — B
U of Michigan, MI — B
U of Minnesota, Twin Cities Campus, MN — B
U of Missouri–Kansas City, MO — B
U of Nebraska Medical Center, NE — B
U of Oklahoma Health Sciences Center, OK — B
The U of South Dakota, SD — A,B
U of Southern Indiana, IN — A,B
Wichita State U, KS — A,B
Youngstown State U, OH — A

Dental Laboratory Technology
Central Missouri State U, MO — B
Indiana U–Purdue U Fort Wayne, IN — A
Southern Illinois U Carbondale, IL — A

Design and Applied Arts Related
Coll for Creative Studies, MI — B
Lehigh U, PA — B
Ohio U, OH — B
Robert Morris Coll, IL — B
St. Cloud State U, MN — B
School of the Art Inst of Chicago, IL — B
The U of Akron, OH — B
U of Saint Francis, IN — B
U of Wisconsin–Stout, WI — B
Westwood Coll–Chicago Du Page, IL — B
Westwood Coll–Chicago O'Hare Airport, IL — B

Design and Visual Communications
Academy Coll, MN — A
Alma Coll, MI — B
American Academy of Art, IL — B
American InterContinental U Online, IL — B
Bethel Coll, IN — B
Bowling Green State U, OH — B
Coll for Creative Studies, MI — B
Drury U, MO — B

The Illinois Inst of Art-Schaumburg, IL — B
Illinois Inst of Technology, IL — B
International Academy of Design & Technology, IL
Iowa State U of Science and Technology, IA — B
Mount Union Coll, OH — B
Mount Vernon Nazarene U, OH — B
Ohio Northern U, OH — B
The Ohio State U, OH — B
Ohio U, OH — B
Purdue U, IN — B
Saginaw Valley State U, MI — B
St. Ambrose U, IA — B
Saint Mary-of-the-Woods Coll, IN — B
School of the Art Inst of Chicago, IL — B
Southern Illinois U Carbondale, IL — B
Southwest Missouri State U, MO — B
Truman State U, MO — B
U of Kansas, KS — B
U of Michigan, MI — B
U of Notre Dame, IN — B
U of Oklahoma, OK — B
Viterbo U, WI — B
Washington U in St. Louis, MO — B
Westwood Coll–Chicago Du Page, IL — A,B
Westwood Coll–Chicago Loop Campus, IL — B
Westwood Coll–Chicago O'Hare Airport, IL — A,B
Westwood Coll–Chicago River Oaks, IL — B
William Woods U, MO — B

Desktop Publishing and Digital Imaging Design
Davenport U, Dearborn, MI — A
Davenport U, Holland, MI — A
Davenport U, Kalamazoo, MI — A
Davenport U, Lansing, MI — A
Davenport U, Lapeer, MI — A
Davenport U, Warren, MI — A

Developmental and Child Psychology
Central Christian Coll of Kansas, KS — A
Edgewood Coll, WI — B
Lincoln Coll, Lincoln, IL — A
Metropolitan State U, MN — B
Minnesota State U Mankato, MN — B
Northern Michigan U, MI — B
Oklahoma Baptist U, OK — B
Olivet Nazarene U, IL — B
Rochester Comm and Tech Coll, MN — A
Rockford Coll, IL — B
The U of Akron, OH — B
U of Detroit Mercy, MI — B
U of Michigan–Dearborn, MI — B
U of Minnesota, Twin Cities Campus, MN — B
U of Sioux Falls, SD — A
U of Toledo, OH — B
U of Wisconsin–Green Bay, WI — B
U of Wisconsin–Madison, WI — B

Development Economics and International Development
The Ohio State U, OH — B

Diagnostic Medical Sonography and Ultrasound Technology
Argosy U/Twin Cities, MN — A
Argosy U/Twin Cities, Eagan, MN — A
Baker Coll of Auburn Hills, MI — A
Baker Coll of Owosso, MI — A
Baker Coll of Port Huron, MI — A
Coll of St. Catherine, MN — A
Coll of St. Catherine–Minneapolis, MN — A
Nebraska Methodist Coll, NE — A,B
U of Missouri–Columbia, MO — B
U of Nebraska Medical Center, NE — B

Diesel Mechanics Technology
North Dakota State Coll of Science, ND — A
U of Northwestern Ohio, OH — A

Dietetics
Andrews U, MI — B
Ashland U, OH — B
Ball State U, IN — A,B
Bowling Green State U, OH — B
Case Western Reserve U, OH — B
Central Michigan U, MI — B
Central Missouri State U, MO — B
Coll of Saint Benedict, MN — B
Coll of St. Catherine, MN — B
Coll of the Ozarks, MO — B
Concordia Coll, MN — B
Dominican U, IL — B
Eastern Michigan U, MI — B
Fontbonne U, MO — B
Gannon U, PA — B
Indiana U Bloomington, IN — B
Iowa State U of Science and Technology, IA — B
Kansas State U, KS — B
Miami U, OH — B
Miami U Hamilton, OH — B
Michigan State U, MI — B
Minnesota State U Mankato, MN — B
Mount Mary Coll, WI — B
North Carolina Ag and Tech State U, NC — B
North Dakota State U, ND — B
Northern Michigan U, MI — B
The Ohio State U, OH — B
Ohio U, OH — B
Oklahoma State U, OK — B
Olivet Nazarene U, IL — B
Purdue U Calumet, IN — A
Saint John's U, MN — B
South Dakota State U, SD — B
Southwest Missouri State U, MO — B
The U of Akron, OH — B
U of Central Oklahoma, OK — B
U of Dayton, OH — B
U of Illinois at Chicago, IL — B

U of Minnesota, Crookston, MN — A
U of Missouri–Columbia, MO — B
U of North Dakota, ND — B
U of Oklahoma Health Sciences Center, OK — B
U of Wisconsin–Madison, WI — B
U of Wisconsin–Stevens Point, WI — B
U of Wisconsin–Stout, WI — B
Viterbo U, WI — B
Wayne State U, MI — B
Western Michigan U, MI — B
Youngstown State U, OH — A,B

Dietetics and Clinical Nutrition Services Related
Madonna U, MI — B

Dietitian Assistant
Youngstown State U, OH — A

Digital Communication and Media/Multimedia
The Art Insts International Minnesota, MN — A,B
Calvin Coll, MI — B
Clarkson U — B
Grace Bible Coll, MI — B
Huntington Coll, IN — B
The Illinois Inst of Art-Schaumburg, IL — B
Kent State U, OH — B
Lindenwood U, MO — B
Minot State U, ND — B
School of the Art Inst of Chicago, IL — B
U of Northern Iowa, IA — B

Directing and Theatrical Production
Coe Coll, IA — B
Drake U, IA — B
Ohio U, OH — B
Western Michigan U, MI — B

Divinity/Ministry
Baptist Bible Coll, MO — B
Barclay Coll, KS — B
Bethel Coll, IN — B
Cardinal Stritch U, WI — B
Central Christian Coll of Kansas, KS — A,B
Faith Baptist Bible Coll and Theological Seminary, IA — A,B
Global U of the Assemblies of God, MO — B
Grace Coll, IN — B
Grace U, NE — B
Huntington Coll, IN — B
Manhattan Christian Coll, KS — A,B
Messenger Coll, MO — B
MidAmerica Nazarene U, KS — A
North Central U, MN — A,B
North Park U, IL — B
Oakland City U, IN — B
Oklahoma Baptist U, OK — B
Reformed Bible Coll, MI — B
St. Louis Christian Coll, MO — A,B
Tabor Coll, KS — B

Drafting and Design Technology
Baker Coll of Auburn Hills, MI — A
Baker Coll of Cadillac, MI — A

Drafting and Design Technology

Baker Coll of Clinton Township, MI	A
Baker Coll of Flint, MI	A,B
Baker Coll of Muskegon, MI	A,B
Baker Coll of Owosso, MI	A,B
Baker Coll of Port Huron, MI	A
Black Hills State U, SD	A
Central Christian Coll of Kansas, KS	A
Central Missouri State U, MO	A,B
Donnelly Coll, KS	A
East Central U, OK	B
Ferris State U, MI	A
Hamilton Tech Coll, IA	A
Hillsdale Coll, MI	B
Lake Superior State U, MI	A
Lincoln U, MO	A
Missouri Southern State U, MO	A
Morrison Inst of Technology, IL	A
Northern Michigan U, MI	A,B
Northern State U, SD	A,B
Tri-State U, IN	A,B
The U of Akron, OH	A
U of Cincinnati, OH	A
U of Rio Grande, OH	A,B
U of Toledo, OH	A
Wright State U, OH	A
Youngstown State U, OH	A

Drafting/Design Engineering Technologies Related

The U of Akron, OH	A

Drama and Dance Teacher Education

Bowling Green State U, OH	B
Capital U, OH	B
Carroll Coll, WI	B
Central Christian Coll of Kansas, KS	A
Chadron State Coll, NE	B
Coll of St. Catherine, MN	B
Concordia U, NE	B
Dana Coll, NE	B
Dordt Coll, IA	B
Hastings Coll, NE	B
Hope Coll, MI	B
Indiana U–Purdue U Fort Wayne, IN	B
Minnesota State U Moorhead, MN	B
The Ohio State U, OH	B
Ohio Wesleyan U, OH	B
Oklahoma Baptist U, OK	B
The U of Akron, OH	B
The U of Iowa, IA	B
U of St. Thomas, MN	B
The U of South Dakota, SD	B
Valparaiso U, IN	B
Viterbo U, WI	B
Waldorf Coll, IA	B
Washington U in St. Louis, MO	B
William Jewell Coll, MO	B
Youngstown State U, OH	B

Dramatic/Theatre Arts

Adrian Coll, MI	A,B
Albion Coll, MI	B
Alma Coll, MI	B
Antioch Coll, OH	B
Ashland U, OH	B
Augsburg Coll, MN	B
Augustana Coll, IL	B
Augustana Coll, SD	B
Avila U, MO	B
Bacone Coll, OK	A
Baker U, KS	B
Ball State U, IN	B
Beloit Coll, WI	B
Bemidji State U, MN	B
Benedictine Coll, KS	B
Bethany Lutheran Coll, MN	B
Bethel Coll, IN	B
Bethel Coll, KS	B
Bethel U, MN	B
Bowling Green State U, OH	B
Bradley U, IL	B
Briar Cliff U, IA	B
Butler U, IN	B
Calvin Coll, MI	B
Capital U, OH	B
Cardinal Stritch U, WI	B
Carroll Coll, WI	B
Carthage Coll, WI	B
Case Western Reserve U, OH	B
Cedarville U, OH	B
Central Christian Coll of Kansas, KS	A
Central Coll, IA	B
Central Methodist Coll, MO	B
Central Michigan U, MI	B
Central Missouri State U, MO	B
Chadron State Coll, NE	B
Clarke Coll, IA	B
Cleveland State U, OH	B
Coe Coll, IA	B
Coll of Saint Benedict, MN	B
Coll of St. Catherine, MN	B
Coll of the Ozarks, MO	B
The Coll of Wooster, OH	B
Columbia Coll Chicago, IL	B
Concordia Coll, MN	B
Concordia U, IL	B
Concordia U, NE	B
Concordia U, St. Paul, MN	B
Cornell Coll, IA	B
Creighton U, NE	B
Culver-Stockton Coll, MO	B
Cumberland Coll, KY	B
Dakota Wesleyan U, SD	B
Denison U, OH	B
DePaul U, IL	B
DePauw U, IN	B
Dickinson State U, ND	B
Doane Coll, NE	B
Dominican U, IL	B
Dordt Coll, IA	B
Drake U, IA	B
Drury U, MO	B
Earlham Coll, IN	B
Eastern Illinois U, IL	B
Eastern Michigan U, MI	B
Edgewood Coll, WI	B
Elmhurst Coll, IL	B
Emporia State U, KS	B
Eureka Coll, IL	B
Fontbonne U, MO	B
Franklin Coll, IN	B
Gannon U, PA	B
Goshen Coll, IN	B
Graceland U, IA	B
Grand Valley State U, MI	B
Grand View Coll, IA	B
Greenville Coll, IL	B
Grinnell Coll, IA	B
Gustavus Adolphus Coll, MN	B
Hamline U, MN	B
Hannibal-LaGrange Coll, MO	B
Hanover Coll, IN	B
Hastings Coll, NE	B
Heidelberg Coll, OH	B
Hillsdale Coll, MI	B
Hiram Coll, OH	B
Hope Coll, MI	B
Huntington Coll, IN	B
Illinois Coll, IL	B
Illinois State U, IL	B
Illinois Wesleyan U, IL	B
Indiana State U, IN	B
Indiana U Bloomington, IN	A,B
Indiana U Northwest, IN	B
Indiana U–Purdue U Fort Wayne, IN	B
Indiana U South Bend, IN	B
Iowa State U of Science and Technology, IA	B
Jamestown Coll, ND	B
Judson Coll, IL	B
Kalamazoo Coll, MI	B
Kansas State U, KS	B
Kansas Wesleyan U, KS	B
Kent State U, OH	B
Kenyon Coll, OH	B
Knox Coll, IL	B
Lake Erie Coll, OH	B
Lawrence U, WI	B
Lewis U, IL	B
Lincoln Coll, Lincoln, IL	A
Lindenwood U, MO	B
Loyola U Chicago, IL	B
Macalester Coll, MN	B
MacMurray Coll, IL	B
Manchester Coll, IN	B
Marietta Coll, OH	B
Marquette U, WI	B
McPherson Coll, KS	B
Metropolitan State U, MN	B
Miami U, OH	B
Michigan State U, MI	B
Millikin U, IL	B
Minnesota State U Mankato, MN	B
Minnesota State U Moorhead, MN	B
Missouri Southern State U, MO	B
Missouri Valley Coll, MO	B
Monmouth Coll, IL	B
Morningside Coll, IA	B
Mount Mercy Coll, IA	B
Mount Union Coll, OH	B
Mount Vernon Nazarene U, OH	B
Muskingum Coll, OH	B
National-Louis U, IL	B
Nebraska Wesleyan U, NE	B
North Carolina Ag and Tech State U, NC	B
North Central Coll, IL	B
North Central U, MN	A,B
North Dakota State U, ND	B
Northeastern State U, OK	B
Northern Illinois U, IL	B
Northern Michigan U, MI	B
Northern State U, SD	B
North Park U, IL	B
Northwestern Coll, IA	B
Northwestern Coll, MN	B
Northwestern U, IL	B
Oakland U, MI	B
Oberlin Coll, OH	B
Ohio Northern U, OH	B
The Ohio State U, OH	B
Ohio U, OH	B
Ohio Wesleyan U, OH	B
Oklahoma Baptist U, OK	B
Oklahoma Christian U, OK	B
Oklahoma City U, OK	B
Oklahoma State U, OK	B
Oral Roberts U, OK	B
Ottawa U, KS	B
Otterbein Coll, OH	B
Principia Coll, IL	B
Purdue U, IN	B
Ripon Coll, WI	B
Rockford Coll, IL	B
Rockhurst U, MO	B
Roosevelt U, IL	B
Saginaw Valley State U, MI	B
St. Ambrose U, IA	B
St. Cloud State U, MN	B
Saint John's U, MN	B
Saint Louis U, MO	B
Saint Mary-of-the-Woods Coll, IN	B
Saint Mary's Coll, IN	B
Saint Mary's U of Minnesota, MN	B
St. Olaf Coll, MN	B
Shawnee State U, OH	B
Siena Heights U, MI	B
Simpson Coll, IA	B
South Dakota State U, SD	B
Southeastern Oklahoma State U, OK	B
Southeast Missouri State U, MO	B
Southern Illinois U Carbondale, IL	B
Southern Illinois U Edwardsville, IL	B
Southwest Baptist U, MO	B
Southwest Missouri State U, MO	B
Stephens Coll, MO	B
Sterling Coll, KS	B
Taylor U, IN	B
Transylvania U, KY	B
Truman State U, MO	B
The U of Akron, OH	B
U of Central Oklahoma, OK	B
U of Cincinnati, OH	B
U of Dayton, OH	B
U of Detroit Mercy, MI	B
U of Evansville, IN	B
The U of Findlay, OH	B
U of Illinois at Chicago, IL	B
U of Illinois at Urbana–Champaign, IL	B
U of Indianapolis, IN	B
The U of Iowa, IA	B
U of Kansas, KS	B
U of Michigan, MI	B
U of Michigan–Flint, MI	B
U of Minnesota, Duluth, MN	B
U of Minnesota, Morris, MN	B
U of Minnesota, Twin Cities Campus, MN	B
U of Missouri–Columbia, MO	B
U of Missouri–Kansas City, MO	B

A—associate degree; B—bachelor's degree

U of Nebraska at Omaha, NE	B	Bowling Green State U, OH	B	Hannibal-LaGrange Coll, MO	B
U of Nebraska–Lincoln, NE	B	Central Christian Coll of Kansas, KS	A	Harris-Stowe State Coll, MO	B
U of North Dakota, ND	B	Chicago State U, IL	B	Hastings Coll, NE	B
U of Northern Iowa, IA	B	The Cleveland Inst of Art, OH	B	Hillsdale Coll, MI	B
U of Notre Dame, IN	B	Coll for Creative Studies, MI	B	Illinois Coll, IL	B
U of Oklahoma, OK	B	Coll of Visual Arts, MN	B	Indiana State U, IN	B
U of Saint Mary, KS	B	Columbia Coll, MO	B	Indiana U–Purdue U Fort Wayne, IN	A
U of St. Thomas, MN	B	DePaul U, IL	B	Iowa State U of Science and Technology, IA	B
U of Science and Arts of Oklahoma, OK	B	Drake U, IA	B	Kendall Coll, IL	B
U of Sioux Falls, SD	A,B	Governors State U, IL	B	Kent State U, Tuscarawas Campus, OH	A
The U of South Dakota, SD	B	Grace Coll, IN	B	Loras Coll, IA	B
U of Southern Indiana, IN	B	Grand Valley State U, MI	B	Malone Coll, OH	B
U of Toledo, OH	B	Indiana U Bloomington, IN	B	Miami U Hamilton, OH	B
U of Tulsa, OK	B	Indiana U–Purdue U Fort Wayne, IN	B	Mount Union Coll, OH	B
U of West Florida, FL	B	Judson Coll, IL	B	Mount Vernon Nazarene U, OH	B
U of Wisconsin–Eau Claire, WI	B	Lewis U, IL	B	Muskingum Coll, OH	B
U of Wisconsin–Green Bay, WI	A,B	Lincoln Coll, Lincoln, IL	A	Northeastern Illinois U, IL	B
U of Wisconsin–La Crosse, WI	B	Lindenwood U, MO	B	Northern Michigan U, MI	B
U of Wisconsin–Madison, WI	B	Milwaukee Inst of Art and Design, WI	B	Northwestern Coll, MN	B
U of Wisconsin–Milwaukee, WI	B	Minneapolis Coll of Art and Design, MN	B	Notre Dame Coll, OH	B
U of Wisconsin–Oshkosh, WI	B	Minnesota State U Mankato, MN	B	Oakland City U, IN	A
U of Wisconsin–Parkside, WI	B	Northern Michigan U, MI	A,B	Oakland U, MI	B
U of Wisconsin–River Falls, WI	B	The Ohio State U, OH	B	Ohio Dominican U, OH	B
U of Wisconsin–Stevens Point, WI	B	Ohio U, OH	B	Ohio Northern U, OH	B
U of Wisconsin–Superior, WI	B	St. Cloud State U, MN	B	The Ohio State U–Mansfield Campus, OH	B
U of Wisconsin–Whitewater, WI	B	School of the Art Inst of Chicago, IL	B	Ohio U, OH	B
Valparaiso U, IN	B	Shawnee State U, OH	B	Ohio U–Southern Campus, OH	A,B
Viterbo U, WI	B	Trinity Christian Coll, IL	B	Ohio Wesleyan U, OH	B
Wabash Coll, IN	B	The U of Akron, OH	B	Oklahoma Christian U, OK	B
Waldorf Coll, IA	B	U of Evansville, IN	B	Park U, MO	B
Washburn U, KS	B	The U of Iowa, IA	B	Purdue U, IN	B
Washington U in St. Louis, MO	B	U of Michigan, MI	B	Ripon Coll, WI	B
Wayne State Coll, NE	B	U of Missouri–St. Louis, MO	B	St. Ambrose U, IA	B
Wayne State U, MI	B	U of Toledo, OH	B	St. Augustine Coll, IL	A
Webster U, MO	B	Washington U in St. Louis, MO	B	Shawnee State U, OH	B
Western Illinois U, IL	B	Winona State U, MN	B	Southern Illinois U Edwardsville, IL	B
Western Michigan U, MI	B	Wright State U, OH	B	Southern Nazarene U, OK	B
Wichita State U, KS	B			Southwestern Coll, KS	B
William Jewell Coll, MO	B	**Driver and Safety Teacher Education**		Southwest Missouri State U, MO	B
William Woods U, MO	B	U of Northern Iowa, IA	B	Stephens Coll, MO	B
Winona State U, MN	B	William Penn U, IA	B	U of Mary, ND	B
Wisconsin Lutheran Coll, WI	B			U of Michigan–Flint, MI	B
Wittenberg U, OH	B	**Early Childhood Education**		U of Minnesota, Crookston, MN	B
Wright State U, OH	B	Alma Coll, MI	B	U of Missouri–Columbia, MO	B
Youngstown State U, OH	B	Bacone Coll, OK	B	U of Missouri–St. Louis, MO	B
		Baker Coll of Allen Park, MI	A	U of New Orleans, LA	B
Dramatic/Theatre Arts and Stagecraft Related		Baker Coll of Jackson, MI	A	U of North Dakota, ND	B
Baldwin-Wallace Coll, OH	B	Baldwin-Wallace Coll, OH	B	U of Oklahoma, OK	B
Bowling Green State U, OH	B	Bethel Coll, IN	A	U of Science and Arts of Oklahoma, OK	B
DePaul U, IL	B	Bethel U, MN	B	U of West Florida, FL	B
Drake U, IA	B	Capital U, OH	B	U of Wisconsin–Stout, WI	B
Nebraska Wesleyan U, NE	B	Carroll Coll, WI	B	U of Wisconsin–Whitewater, WI	B
Ohio U, OH	B	Cedarville U, OH	B	Ursuline Coll, OH	B
St. Cloud State U, MN	B	Central Methodist Coll, MO	B	Waldorf Coll, IA	B
The U of Akron, OH	B	Cleveland State U, OH	B		
		Coll of Saint Mary, NE	A,B	**East Asian Languages**	
Drawing		Columbia Coll Chicago, IL	B	U of Kansas, KS	B
American Academy of Art, IL	B	Concordia U, NE	B		
Antioch Coll, OH	B	Concordia U, St. Paul, MN	B	**East Asian Languages Related**	
Aquinas Coll, MI	B	Cornerstone U, MI	B	Michigan State U, MI	B
Art Academy of Cincinnati, OH	B	Crown Coll, MN	A,B	Northwestern U, IL	B
Ball State U, IN	B	East Central U, OK	B	Washington U in St. Louis, MO	B
Bethany Coll, KS	B	Eastern Michigan U, MI	B		
		Evangel U, MO	B		
		Florida Gulf Coast U, FL	B		
		Governors State U, IL	B		
		Grace Bible Coll, MI	B		
		Greenville Coll, IL	B		

Ecology

Ball State U, IN	B
Bemidji State U, MN	B
Bradley U, IL	B
Clarkson U	B
Defiance Coll, OH	B
East Central U, OK	B
Iowa State U of Science and Technology, IA	
Kent State U, OH	B
Lawrence U, WI	B
Lehigh U, PA	B
Manchester Coll, IN	B
Michigan Technological U, MI	B
Minnesota State U Mankato, MN	
Missouri Southern State U, MO	B
Northern Michigan U, MI	B
Northland Coll, WI	B
Northwestern U, IL	B
Oberlin Coll, OH	B
St. Cloud State U, MN	B
The U of Akron, OH	B
U of Illinois at Urbana–Champaign, IL	B
U of Michigan, MI	B
U of Michigan–Flint, MI	B
U of Minnesota, Twin Cities Campus, MN	B
U of Northern Iowa, IA	B
U of Rio Grande, OH	B
U of Wisconsin–Milwaukee, WI	B
Winona State U, MN	B

E-Commerce

Eastern Michigan U, MI	
ITT Tech Inst, Mount Prospect, IL	B
ITT Tech Inst, Fort Wayne, IN	B
ITT Tech Inst, Indianapolis, IN	B
ITT Tech Inst, Newburgh, IN	B
ITT Tech Inst, Arnold, MO	B
ITT Tech Inst, Earth City, MO	B
ITT Tech Inst, NE	B
ITT Tech Inst, Green Bay, WI	B
ITT Tech Inst, Greenfield, WI	B
Maryville U of Saint Louis, MO	B
Saint Mary's U of Minnesota, MN	B
U of Southern Indiana, IN	B
Westwood Coll–Chicago Du Page, IL	B
Westwood Coll–Chicago O'Hare Airport, IL	B
Westwood Coll–Chicago River Oaks, IL	B

Econometrics and Quantitative Economics

Miami U Hamilton, OH	B
U of Northern Iowa, IA	B
U of St. Thomas, MN	B
Youngstown State U, OH	B

Economics

Adrian Coll, MI	A,B
Albion Coll, MI	B

Alma Coll, MI	B	Hiram Coll, OH	B	Park U, MO	B	The U of South Dakota, SD	B
Andrews U, MI	B	Hope Coll, MI	B	Pittsburg State U, KS	B	U of Southern Indiana, IN	B
Antioch Coll, OH	B	Huntington Coll, IN	B	Principia Coll, IL	B	U of Toledo, OH	B
Aquinas Coll, MI	B	Illinois Coll, IL	B	Purdue U, IN	B	U of Tulsa, OK	B
Ashland U, OH	B	Illinois State U, IL	B	Purdue U Calumet, IN	B	U of Wisconsin–Eau Claire, WI	B
Augsburg Coll, MN	B	Illinois Wesleyan U, IL	B	Ripon Coll, WI	B	U of Wisconsin–Green Bay, WI	A,B
Augustana Coll, IL	B	Indiana State U, IN	B	Rockford Coll, IL	B	U of Wisconsin–La Crosse, WI	B
Augustana Coll, SD	B	Indiana U Bloomington, IN	B	Rockhurst U, MO	B	U of Wisconsin–Madison, WI	B
Aurora U, IL	B	Indiana U Northwest, IN	B	Roosevelt U, IL	B	U of Wisconsin–Milwaukee, WI	B
Ave Maria Coll, MI	B	Indiana U–Purdue U Fort Wayne, IN	B	Rose-Hulman Inst of Technology, IN	B	U of Wisconsin–Oshkosh, WI	B
Baker U, KS	B	Indiana U–Purdue U Indianapolis, IN	B	Saginaw Valley State U, MI	B	U of Wisconsin–Parkside, WI	B
Baldwin-Wallace Coll, OH	B	Indiana U South Bend, IN	B	St. Ambrose U, IA	B	U of Wisconsin–Platteville, WI	B
Ball State U, IN	B	Indiana U Southeast, IN	B	St. Cloud State U, MN	B	U of Wisconsin–River Falls, WI	B
Beloit Coll, WI	B	Iowa State U of Science and Technology, IA	B	Saint John's U, MN	B	U of Wisconsin–Stevens Point, WI	B
Bemidji State U, MN	B	John Carroll U, OH	B	Saint Joseph's Coll, IN	B	U of Wisconsin–Superior, WI	B
Benedictine Coll, KS	B	Kansas State U, KS	B	Saint Louis U, MO	B	Valparaiso U, IN	B
Benedictine U, IL	B	Kent State U, OH	B	Saint Mary's Coll, IN	B	Wabash Coll, IN	B
Bethel U, MN	B	Kenyon Coll, OH	B	St. Norbert Coll, WI	B	Wartburg Coll, IA	B
Bluffton Coll, OH	B	Knox Coll, IL	B	St. Olaf Coll, MN	B	Washburn U, KS	B
Bowling Green State U, OH	B	Lake Forest Coll, IL	B	Simpson Coll, IA	B	Washington U in St. Louis, MO	B
Bradley U, IL	B	Lake Superior State U, MI	B	South Dakota State U, SD	B	Wayne State U, MI	B
Butler U, IN	B	Lawrence U, WI	B	Southeastern Oklahoma State U, OK	B	Webster U, MO	B
Calvin Coll, MI	B	Lewis U, IL	B	Southeast Missouri State U, MO	B	Western Illinois U, IL	B
Capital U, OH	B	Lincoln Coll, Lincoln, IL	A	Southern Illinois U Carbondale, IL	B	Western Michigan U, MI	B
Carleton Coll, MN	B	Lincoln U, MO	B	Southern Illinois U Edwardsville, IL	B	Westminster Coll, MO	B
Carthage Coll, WI	B	Lindenwood U, MO	B	Southwest Missouri State U, MO	B	Wheaton Coll, IL	B
Case Western Reserve U, OH	B	Loras Coll, IA	B	Taylor U, IN	B	Wichita State U, KS	B
Central Christian Coll of Kansas, KS	A	Loyola U Chicago, IL	B	Transylvania U, KY	B	Wilberforce U, OH	B
Central Coll, IA	B	Luther Coll, IA	B	Truman State U, MO	B	William Jewell Coll, MO	B
Central Methodist Coll, MO	B	Macalester Coll, MN	B	The U of Akron, OH	B	Winona State U, MN	B
Central Michigan U, MI	B	Manchester Coll, IN	B	U of Central Oklahoma, OK	B	Wittenberg U, OH	B
Central Missouri State U, MO	B	Marietta Coll, OH	B	U of Chicago, IL	B	Wright State U, OH	B
Central State U, OH	B	Marquette U, WI	B	U of Cincinnati, OH	B	Xavier U, OH	B
Chicago State U, IL	B	McKendree Coll, IL	B	U of Dayton, OH	B	Youngstown State U, OH	B
Clarke Coll, IA	B	Metropolitan State U, MN	B	U of Detroit Mercy, MI	B		
Cleveland State U, OH	B	Miami U, OH	B	U of Evansville, IN	B	**Economics Related**	
Coe Coll, IA	B	Miami U Hamilton, OH	B	The U of Findlay, OH	B	Eastern Michigan U, MI	B
Coll of Saint Benedict, MN	B	Michigan State U, MI	B	U of Illinois at Chicago, IL	B	Truman State U, MO	B
Coll of St. Catherine, MN	B	Minnesota State U Mankato, MN	B	U of Illinois at Springfield, IL	B	The U of Akron, OH	B
The Coll of Wooster, OH	B	Minnesota State U Moorhead, MN	B	U of Illinois at Urbana–Champaign, IL	B	U of Illinois at Urbana–Champaign, IL	B
Concordia Coll, MN	B	Minot State U, ND	B	The U of Iowa, IA	B	Valparaiso U, IN	B
Concordia U Wisconsin, WI	B	Missouri Valley Coll, MO	B	U of Kansas, KS	B	Wright State U, OH	B
Cornell Coll, IA	B	Missouri Western State Coll, MO	B	U of Michigan, MI	B		
Creighton U, NE	B	Monmouth Coll, IL	B	U of Michigan–Dearborn, MI	B	**Education**	
Denison U, OH	B	Mount Union Coll, OH	B	U of Michigan–Flint, MI	B	Adrian Coll, MI	B
DePaul U, IL	B	Muskingum Coll, OH	B	U of Minnesota, Duluth, MN	B	Albion Coll, MI	B
DePauw U, IN	B	Nebraska Wesleyan U, NE	B	U of Minnesota, Morris, MN	B	Alma Coll, MI	B
Doane Coll, NE	B	North Carolina Ag and Tech State U, NC	B	U of Minnesota, Twin Cities Campus, MN	B	Alverno Coll, WI	B
Dominican U, IL	B	North Central Coll, IL	B	U of Missouri–Columbia, MO	B	Andrews U, MI	B
Drake U, IA	B	North Dakota State U, ND	B	U of Missouri–Kansas City, MO	B	Antioch Coll, OH	B
Drury U, MO	B	Northeastern Illinois U, IL	B	U of Missouri–Rolla, MO	B	Aquinas Coll, MI	B
Earlham Coll, IN	B	Northern Illinois U, IL	B	U of Missouri–St. Louis, MO	B	Ashland U, OH	B
Eastern Illinois U, IL	B	Northern Michigan U, MI	B	U of Nebraska–Lincoln, NE	B	Augsburg Coll, MN	B
Eastern Michigan U, MI	B	Northern State U, SD	B	U of New Orleans, LA	B	Augustana Coll, IL	B
Edgewood Coll, WI	B	Northland Coll, WI	B	U of North Dakota, ND	B	Bacone Coll, OK	A,B
Elmhurst Coll, IL	B	North Park U, IL	B	U of Northern Iowa, IA	B	Baker Coll of Auburn Hills, MI	A
Emporia State U, KS	B	Northwestern Coll, IA	B	U of Notre Dame, IN	B		
Eureka Coll, IL	B	Northwestern U, IL	B	U of Oklahoma, OK	B	Baker Coll of Cadillac, MI	A
Fort Hays State U, KS	B	Oakland U, MI	B	U of Rio Grande, OH	B	Baldwin-Wallace Coll, OH	B
Franciscan U of Steubenville, OH	B	Oberlin Coll, OH	B	U of Saint Francis, IN	B	Ball State U, IN	B
Franklin Coll, IN	B	Ohio Dominican U, OH	B	U of St. Thomas, MN	B	Beloit Coll, WI	B
Goshen Coll, IN	B	The Ohio State U, OH	B	U of Science and Arts of Oklahoma, OK	B	Bemidji State U, MN	B
Graceland U, IA	B	Ohio U, OH	B	U of Sioux Falls, SD	A,B	Benedictine U, IL	B
Grand Valley State U, MI	B	Ohio Wesleyan U, OH	B			Bethany Coll, KS	B
Grinnell Coll, IA	B	Oklahoma State U, OK	B			Bethel Coll, IN	B
Gustavus Adolphus Coll, MN	B	Olivet Coll, MI	B				
Hamline U, MN	B	Olivet Nazarene U, IL	B				
Hanover Coll, IN	B	Otterbein Coll, OH	B				
Hastings Coll, NE	B						
Heidelberg Coll, OH	B						
Hillsdale Coll, MI	B						

A—associate degree; B—bachelor's degree

Bowling Green State U, OH	B	Kendall Coll, IL	B	Saint John's U, MN	B	Wright State U, OH	B

College	Degree
Bowling Green State U, OH	B
Brescia U, KY	B
Briar Cliff U, IA	B
Cameron U, OK	B
Capital U, OH	B
Cardinal Stritch U, WI	B
Carroll Coll, WI	B
Carthage Coll, WI	B
Central Christian Coll of Kansas, KS	A
Central Methodist Coll, MO	B
Central Missouri State U, MO	B
Chicago State U, IL	B
Clarke Coll, IA	B
Cleveland State U, OH	B
Coe Coll, IA	B
Coll of Saint Benedict, MN	B
Coll of St. Catherine, MN	B
Coll of Saint Mary, NE	B
Coll of the Ozarks, MO	B
Columbia Coll, MO	B
Concordia Coll, MN	B
Concordia U, IL	B
Concordia U, NE	B
Concordia U, St. Paul, MN	B
Concordia U Wisconsin, WI	B
Concord U, WV	B
Cornerstone U, MI	B
Dakota State U, SD	B
Dakota Wesleyan U, SD	B
Dana Coll, NE	B
Defiance Coll, OH	B
DePaul U, IL	B
Dickinson State U, ND	B
Donnelly Coll, KS	A
Dordt Coll, IA	B
Drury U, MO	B
Earlham Coll, IN	B
East Central U, OK	B
Edgewood Coll, WI	B
Elmhurst Coll, IL	B
Eureka Coll, IL	B
Evangel U, MO	A,B
Ferris State U, MI	B
Fontbonne U, MO	B
The Franciscan U, IA	B
Goshen Coll, IN	B
Graceland U, IA	B
Grand Valley State U, MI	B
Grinnell Coll, IA	B
Gustavus Adolphus Coll, MN	B
Hamline U, MN	B
Hannibal-LaGrange Coll, MO	B
Hastings Coll, NE	B
Heidelberg Coll, OH	B
Hillsdale Coll, MI	B
Huntington Coll, IN	B
Illinois Coll, IL	B
Illinois Wesleyan U, IL	B
Indiana U Bloomington, IN	B
Indiana U East, IN	B
Indiana U Northwest, IN	B
Indiana U–Purdue U Fort Wayne, IN	B
Indiana U–Purdue U Indianapolis, IN	B
Indiana U South Bend, IN	B
Indiana U Southeast, IN	B
Iowa State U of Science and Technology, IA	B
Iowa Wesleyan Coll, IA	B
John Carroll U, OH	B
Judson Coll, IL	B
Kansas Wesleyan U, KS	B

College	Degree
Kendall Coll, IL	B
Kent State U, OH	A,B
Kent State U, Salem Campus, OH	A,B
Kent State U, Stark Campus, OH	A
Knox Coll, IL	B
Lake Forest Coll, IL	B
Lake Superior State U, MI	B
Lehigh U, PA	B
Lewis U, IL	B
Lincoln Coll, Lincoln, IL	A
Lindenwood U, MO	B
Loras Coll, IA	B
Madonna U, MI	B
Manchester Coll, IN	B
Marian Coll, IN	B
Marian Coll of Fond du Lac, WI	B
Marietta Coll, OH	B
Marquette U, WI	B
Martin U, IN	B
Marygrove Coll, MI	B
Mayville State U, ND	B
McPherson Coll, KS	B
Michigan State U, MI	B
Minnesota State U Mankato, MN	B
Missouri Southern State U, MO	B
Missouri Valley Coll, MO	B
Monmouth Coll, IL	B
Morningside Coll, IA	B
Mount Marty Coll, SD	B
Mount Mary Coll, WI	B
Mount Mercy Coll, IA	B
Mount Vernon Nazarene U, OH	B
Muskingum Coll, OH	B
Newman U, KS	B
North Carolina Ag and Tech State U, NC	B
North Central Coll, IL	B
Northeastern State U, OK	B
Northern Illinois U, IL	B
Northern Michigan U, MI	B
Northern State U, SD	B
Northland Coll, WI	B
North Park U, IL	B
Northwestern U, IL	B
Oakland City U, IN	B
Oakland U, MI	B
Ohio Northern U, OH	B
Ohio U, OH	B
Ohio U–Southern Campus, OH	B
Ohio Wesleyan U, OH	B
Oklahoma Baptist U, OK	B
Oklahoma City U, OK	B
Oklahoma State U, OK	B
Olivet Coll, MI	B
Olivet Nazarene U, IL	B
Oral Roberts U, OK	B
Otterbein Coll, OH	B
Peru State Coll, NE	B
Pillsbury Baptist Bible Coll, MN	B
Pittsburg State U, KS	B
Purdue U, IN	B
Purdue U Calumet, IN	B
Ripon Coll, WI	B
Rockford Coll, IL	B
Rockhurst U, MO	B
Roosevelt U, IL	B
St. Ambrose U, IA	B
St. Cloud State U, MN	B

College	Degree
Saint John's U, MN	B
Saint Louis U, MO	B
Saint Mary-of-the-Woods Coll, IN	B
Saint Mary's Coll, IN	B
Shawnee State U, OH	B
Simpson Coll, IA	B
South Dakota State U, SD	B
Southeastern Oklahoma State U, OK	B
Southern Nazarene U, OK	B
Southwestern Oklahoma State U, OK	B
Tabor Coll, KS	B
Taylor U, IN	B
Trinity Christian Coll, IL	B
Trinity International U, IL	B
Tri-State U, IN	B
Union Coll, NE	B
Union Inst & U, OH	B
The U of Akron, OH	B
U of Cincinnati, OH	B
U of Dayton, OH	B
U of Detroit Mercy, MI	B
The U of Findlay, OH	B
U of Indianapolis, IN	B
U of Michigan, MI	B
U of Michigan–Dearborn, MI	B
U of Michigan–Flint, MI	B
U of Minnesota, Duluth, MN	B
U of Minnesota, Morris, MN	B
U of Minnesota, Twin Cities Campus, MN	B
U of Missouri–Columbia, MO	B
U of Missouri–Kansas City, MO	B
U of Missouri–St. Louis, MO	B
U of Rio Grande, OH	B
U of Saint Francis, IN	B
U of Saint Mary, KS	B
U of Sioux Falls, SD	B
The U of South Dakota, SD	B
U of Southern Indiana, IN	A
U of Toledo, OH	B
U of Tulsa, OK	B
U of Wisconsin–La Crosse, WI	B
U of Wisconsin–Milwaukee, WI	B
U of Wisconsin–Oshkosh, WI	B
U of Wisconsin–Platteville, WI	B
U of Wisconsin–River Falls, WI	B
U of Wisconsin–Stevens Point, WI	B
U of Wisconsin–Superior, WI	B
U of Wisconsin–Whitewater, WI	B
Upper Iowa U, IA	B
Urbana U, OH	B
Valley City State U, ND	B
Waldorf Coll, IA	B
Walsh U, OH	B
Washburn U, KS	B
Washington U in St. Louis, MO	B
Wayne State Coll, NE	B
Webster U, MO	B
William Jewell Coll, MO	B
William Penn U, IA	B
William Woods U, MO	B
Winona State U, MN	B
Wittenberg U, OH	B

College	Degree
Wright State U, OH	B
Xavier U, OH	B
York Coll, NE	B
Youngstown State U, OH	B

Educational Administration and Supervision Related

Kendall Coll, IL	B

Educational, Instructional, and Curriculum Supervision

Wright State U, OH	B

Educational/Instructional Media Design

Ball State U, IN	B
Capital U, OH	B
Eastern Michigan U, MI	B
Ferris State U, MI	A
Indiana State U, IN	B
Lindenwood U, MO	B
St. Cloud State U, MN	B
U of Central Oklahoma, OK	B
U of Toledo, OH	B
U of Wisconsin–Superior, WI	A,B
Western Illinois U, IL	B

Educational Leadership and Administration

Baldwin-Wallace Coll, OH	B
Cleveland State U, OH	B
Eastern Michigan U, MI	B
Eureka Coll, IL	B
Jamestown Coll, ND	B
Kendall Coll, IL	B
Lindenwood U, MO	B
Oakland U, MI	B
Ohio U, OH	B
Oral Roberts U, OK	B
Purdue U Calumet, IN	B
St. Cloud State U, MN	B
U of Central Oklahoma, OK	B
U of Wisconsin–Superior, WI	B
Wright State U, OH	B

Educational Psychology

Eastern Michigan U, MI	B

Education (K-12)

Adrian Coll, MI	B
Augustana Coll, SD	B
Briar Cliff U, IA	B
Coll of Saint Mary, NE	B
The Coll of St. Scholastica, MN	B
Dickinson State U, ND	B
Dominican U, IL	B
Dordt Coll, IA	B
Graceland U, IA	B
Grace U, NE	B
Hamline U, MN	B
Hastings Coll, NE	B
Hillsdale Coll, MI	B
Illinois Coll, IL	B
Jamestown Coll, ND	B
John Carroll U, OH	B
Lake Erie Coll, OH	B
Lewis U, IL	B
Lindenwood U, MO	B
McKendree Coll, IL	B
McPherson Coll, KS	B
Northwestern Coll, IA	B
Ohio Dominican U, OH	B
Ohio Wesleyan U, OH	B
St. Ambrose U, IA	B
Saint Mary-of-the-Woods Coll, IN	B
St. Norbert Coll, WI	B
Southwest Baptist U, MO	B

Majors and Degrees
Education (K-12)

Tabor Coll, KS — B
Trinity International U, IL — B
U of Minnesota, Morris, MN — B
U of St. Thomas, MN — B
U of Wisconsin–Superior, WI — B
Washington U in St. Louis, MO — B

Education (Multiple Levels)
Concordia U Wisconsin, WI — B
Dakota Wesleyan U, SD — B
Lake Superior State U, MI — B
Martin Luther Coll, MN — B
Miami U Hamilton, OH — B
Ohio Northern U, OH — B
Ohio Wesleyan U, OH — B
Oral Roberts U, OK — B
Saint Louis U, MO — B
Shawnee State U, OH — B
The U of Akron, OH — B
U of Nebraska–Lincoln, NE — B
U of Rio Grande, OH — B
Waldorf Coll, IA — B
Wright State U, OH — B
York Coll, NE — B
Youngstown State U, OH — B

Education Related
Bowling Green State U, OH — B
Cleveland State U, OH — B
Concordia U, St. Paul, MN — B
Kendall Coll, IL — B
Kent State U, OH — A
Madonna U, MI — B
Messenger Coll, MO — B
Oakland U, MI — B
Ohio Northern U, OH — B
Park U, MO — B
Pittsburg State U, KS — B
Roosevelt U, IL — B
The U of Akron, OH — A
U of Missouri–Columbia, MO — B
Wright State U, OH — B

Education (Specific Levels and Methods) Related
Bowling Green State U, OH — B
Columbia Coll Chicago, IL — B
Kendall Coll, IL — B
Oakland U, MI — B
St. Cloud State U, MN — B
The U of Akron, OH — B
U of Toledo, OH — B
Washington U in St. Louis, MO — B
Wright State U, OH — B
Xavier U, OH — B

Education (Specific Subject Areas) Related
Avila U, MO — B
Bowling Green State U, OH — B
Bradley U, IL — B
Cameron U, OK — B
Central Michigan U, MI — B
Chadron State Coll, NE — B
Columbia Coll Chicago, IL — B
Eastern Michigan U, MI — B
Hope Coll, MI — B
Madonna U, MI — B
Marquette U, WI — B
Minot State U, ND — B
Ohio U, OH — B
Oklahoma State U, OK — B
Southwest Baptist U, MO — B

Southwest Missouri State U, MO — B
The U of Akron, OH — B
U of Central Oklahoma, OK — B
U of Michigan–Flint, MI — B
U of Nebraska–Lincoln, NE — B
U of Oklahoma, OK — B
U of St. Thomas, MN — B
U of Toledo, OH — B
U of Wisconsin–Eau Claire, WI — B
Wright State U, OH — B

Electrical and Electronic Engineering Technologies Related
Kent State U, OH — A
Lawrence Technological U, MI — A
Miami U Hamilton, OH — A
Pittsburg State U, KS — B
Southern Illinois U Carbondale, IL — B

Electrical and Power Transmission Installation
Dunwoody Coll of Technology, MN — A

Electrical and Power Transmission Installation Related
Vatterott Coll, St. Ann, MO — A

Electrical, Electronic and Communications Engineering Technology
Andrews U, MI — A,B
Baker Coll of Cadillac, MI — A
Baker Coll of Muskegon, MI — A,B
Baker Coll of Owosso, MI — A,B
Bowling Green State U, OH — B
Bradley U, IL — B
Cameron U, OK — A,B
Central Michigan U, MI — B
Central Missouri State U, MO — B
Cleveland State U, OH — B
DeVry U, Addison, IL — A,B
DeVry U, Chicago, IL — A,B
DeVry U, Tinley Park, IL — A,B
DeVry U, MO — A,B
DeVry U, Columbus, OH — A,B
Dunwoody Coll of Technology, MN — A
East Central U, OK — B
Eastern Michigan U, MI — B
Ferris State U, MI — B
Hamilton Tech Coll, IA — A,B
Indiana State U, IN — A,B
Indiana U–Purdue U Fort Wayne, IN — A,B
Indiana U–Purdue U Indianapolis, IN — A,B
ITT Tech Inst, Mount Prospect, IL — B
ITT Tech Inst, Fort Wayne, IN — B
ITT Tech Inst, Indianapolis, IN — B
ITT Tech Inst, Newburgh, IN — B
ITT Tech Inst, Arnold, MO — B
ITT Tech Inst, Earth City, MO — B
ITT Tech Inst, NE — B

ITT Tech Inst, Green Bay, WI — B
ITT Tech Inst, Greenfield, WI — B
Kansas State U, KS — A,B
Kent State U, Tuscarawas Campus, OH — A
Lake Superior State U, MI — A,B
Lawrence Technological U, MI — A
Lincoln U, MO — A
Michigan Technological U, MI — A,B
Milwaukee School of Engineering, WI — B
Minnesota State U Mankato, MN — B
Missouri Tech, MO — A
Missouri Western State Coll, MO — A,B
North Dakota State Coll of Science, ND — A
Northeastern State U, OK — B
Northern Michigan U, MI — A,B
Northern State U, SD — A,B
Ohio U, OH — A
Oklahoma State U, OK — B
Pittsburg State U, KS — A,B
Purdue U, IN — A,B
Purdue U Calumet, IN — A,B
Purdue U North Central, IN — A
Ranken Tech Coll, MO — A
Rochester Comm and Tech Coll, MN — A
Roosevelt U, IL — B
St. Cloud State U, MN — B
South Dakota State U, SD — B
Southeastern Oklahoma State U, OK — B
The U of Akron, OH — A,B
U of Cincinnati, OH — A,B
U of Dayton, OH — B
U of Nebraska–Lincoln, NE — B
U of Toledo, OH — A,B
Vatterott Coll, St. Ann, MO — A
Washburn U, KS — A
Wayne State U, MI — B
Wichita State U, KS — A
Wright State U, OH — A
Youngstown State U, OH — A,B

Electrical, Electronics and Communications Engineering
Bethel Coll, IN — B
Bradley U, IL — B
Calvin Coll, MI — B
Case Western Reserve U, OH — B
Cedarville U, OH — B
Clarkson U — B
Cleveland State U, OH — B
Dominican U, IL — B
Dordt Coll, IA — B
Gannon U, PA — B
Grand Valley State U, MI — B
Illinois Inst of Technology, IL — B
Indiana Inst of Technology, IN — B
Indiana U–Purdue U Fort Wayne, IN — B
Indiana U–Purdue U Indianapolis, IN — B
Iowa State U of Science and Technology, IA — B
Kansas State U, KS — B

Kettering U, MI — B
Lake Superior State U, MI — B
Lawrence Technological U, MI — B
Lehigh U, PA — B
Marquette U, WI — B
Miami U, OH — B
Michigan State U, MI — B
Michigan Technological U, MI — B
Milwaukee School of Engineering, WI — B
Minnesota State U Mankato, MN — B
Missouri Tech, MO — A,B
North Carolina Ag and Tech State U, NC — B
North Dakota State U, ND — B
Northern Illinois U, IL — B
Northwestern U, IL — B
Oakland U, MI — B
Ohio Northern U, OH — B
The Ohio State U, OH — B
Ohio U, OH — B
Oklahoma Christian U, OK — B
Oklahoma State U, OK — B
Oral Roberts U, OK — B
Purdue U, IN — B
Purdue U Calumet, IN — B
Rose-Hulman Inst of Technology, IN — B
Saginaw Valley State U, MI — B
St. Cloud State U, MN — B
Saint Louis U, MO — B
South Dakota School of Mines and Technology, SD — B
South Dakota State U, SD — B
Southern Illinois U Carbondale, IL — B
Southern Illinois U Edwardsville, IL — B
Tri-State U, IN — B
The U of Akron, OH — B
The U of Alabama in Huntsville, AL — B
U of Cincinnati, OH — B
U of Dayton, OH — B
U of Detroit Mercy, MI — B
U of Evansville, IN — B
U of Illinois at Chicago, IL — B
U of Illinois at Urbana–Champaign, IL — B
U of Indianapolis, IN — B
The U of Iowa, IA — B
U of Kansas, KS — B
U of Michigan, MI — B
U of Michigan–Dearborn, MI — B
U of Minnesota, Duluth, MN — B
U of Minnesota, Twin Cities Campus, MN — B
U of Missouri–Columbia, MO — B
U of Missouri–Kansas City, MO — B
U of Missouri–Rolla, MO — B
U of Missouri–St. Louis, MO — B
U of Nebraska at Omaha, NE — B
U of Nebraska–Lincoln, NE — B
U of New Orleans, LA — B
U of Notre Dame, IN — B
U of Oklahoma, OK — B
U of St. Thomas, MN — B
U of Toledo, OH — B
U of Tulsa, OK — B

A—associate degree; B—bachelor's degree

426   www.petersons.com
Peterson's Colleges in the Midwest 2005

U of West Florida, FL — B
U of Wisconsin–Madison, WI — B
U of Wisconsin–Milwaukee, WI — B
U of Wisconsin–Platteville, WI — B
Valparaiso U, IN — B
Washington U in St. Louis, MO — B
Wayne State U, MI — B
Western Michigan U, MI — B
Wichita State U, KS — B
Wilberforce U, OH — B
Wright State U, OH — B
Youngstown State U, OH — B

Electromechanical Technology
Miami U Hamilton, OH — B
Michigan Technological U, MI — A
Northern Michigan U, MI — A
Shawnee State U, OH — A
The U of Akron, OH — A
U of Northern Iowa, IA — B
U of Toledo, OH — A
Wayne State U, MI — B
Wright State U, OH — A

Elementary and Middle School Administration/Principalship
Eastern Michigan U, MI — B
Ohio U, OH — B

Elementary Education
Adrian Coll, MI — B
Albion Coll, MI — B
Alma Coll, MI — B
Alverno Coll, WI — B
Ancilla Coll, IN — A
Andrews U, MI — B
Aquinas Coll, MI — B
Ashland U, OH — B
Augsburg Coll, MN — B
Augustana Coll, IL — B
Augustana Coll, SD — B
Aurora U, IL — B
Avila U, MO — B
Bacone Coll, OK — B
Baker U, KS — B
Baldwin-Wallace Coll, OH — B
Ball State U, IN — B
Baptist Bible Coll, MO — B
Barclay Coll, KS — B
Beloit Coll, WI — B
Bemidji State U, MN — B
Benedictine Coll, KS — B
Benedictine U, IL — B
Bethany Coll, KS — B
Bethany Lutheran Coll, MN — B
Bethel Coll, IN — B
Bethel Coll, KS — B
Bethel Coll, MN — B
Blackburn Coll, IL — B
Black Hills State U, SD — B
Bluffton Coll, OH — B
Bowling Green State U, OH — B
Bradley U, IL — B
Brescia U, KY — B
Briar Cliff U, IA — B
Buena Vista U, IA — B
Butler U, IN — B
Calumet Coll of Saint Joseph, IN — B
Calvary Bible Coll and Theological Seminary, MO — B
Calvin Coll, MI — B

Capital U, OH — B
Cardinal Stritch U, WI — B
Carroll Coll, WI — B
Carthage Coll, WI — B
Central Christian Coll of Kansas, KS — A
Central Coll, IA — B
Central Methodist Coll, MO — B
Central Michigan U, MI — B
Central Missouri State U, MO — B
Chadron State Coll, NE — B
Chicago State U, IL — B
Clarke Coll, IA — B
Cleveland State U, OH — B
Coe Coll, IA — B
Coll of Saint Benedict, MN — B
Coll of St. Catherine, MN — B
Coll of Saint Mary, NE — B
The Coll of St. Scholastica, MN — B
Coll of the Ozarks, MO — B
Concordia Coll, MN — B
Concordia U, IL — B
Concordia U, MI — B
Concordia U, NE — B
Concordia U, St. Paul, MN — B
Concordia U Wisconsin, WI — B
Concord U, WV — B
Cornell Coll, IA — B
Cornerstone U, MI — B
Creighton U, NE — B
Crossroads Bible Coll, IN — B
Crown Coll, MN — B
Culver-Stockton Coll, MO — B
Cumberland Coll, KY — B
Dakota State U, SD — B
Dakota Wesleyan U, SD — B
Dana Coll, NE — B
Defiance Coll, OH — B
DePaul U, IL — B
DePauw U, IN — B
Dickinson State U, ND — B
Doane Coll, NE — B
Dominican U, IL — B
Dordt Coll, IA — B
Drake U, IA — B
Drury U, MO — B
East Central U, OK — B
Eastern Illinois U, IL — B
Eastern Michigan U, MI — B
Edgewood Coll, WI — B
Elmhurst Coll, IL — B
Emporia State U, KS — B
Eureka Coll, IL — B
Evangel U, MO — B
Faith Baptist Bible Coll and Theological Seminary, IA — B
Florida Gulf Coast U, FL — B
Fontbonne U, MO — B
Fort Hays State U, KS — B
The Franciscan U, IA — B
Franciscan U of Steubenville, OH — B
Franklin Coll, IN — B
Gannon U, PA — B
God's Bible School and Coll, OH — A,B
Goshen Coll, IN — B
Governors State U, IL — B
Grace Bible Coll, MI — B
Grace Coll, IN — B
Graceland U, IA — B
Grace U, NE — B
Grand Valley State U, MI — B
Grand View Coll, IA — B

Greenville Coll, IL — B
Grinnell Coll, IA — B
Gustavus Adolphus Coll, MN — B
Hamline U, MN — B
Hannibal-LaGrange Coll, MO — B
Harris-Stowe State Coll, MO — B
Haskell Indian Nations U, KS — B
Hastings Coll, NE — B
Heidelberg Coll, OH — B
Hillsdale Coll, MI — B
Hillsdale Free Will Baptist Coll, OK — A
Hiram Coll, OH — B
Hope Coll, MI — B
Huntington Coll, IN — B
Illinois Coll, IL — B
Illinois State U, IL — B
Illinois Wesleyan U, IL — B
Indiana State U, IN — B
Indiana U Bloomington, IN — B
Indiana U East, IN — B
Indiana U Kokomo, IN — B
Indiana U Northwest, IN — B
Indiana U–Purdue U Fort Wayne, IN — B
Indiana U–Purdue U Indianapolis, IN — B
Indiana U South Bend, IN — B
Indiana U Southeast, IN — B
Iowa State U of Science and Technology, IA — B
Iowa Wesleyan Coll, IA — B
Jamestown Coll, ND — B
John Carroll U, OH — B
Judson Coll, IL — B
Kansas State U, KS — B
Kansas Wesleyan U, KS — B
Kendall Coll, IL — B
Lake Erie Coll, OH — B
Lake Forest Coll, IL — B
Lakeland Coll, WI — B
Lake Superior State U, MI — B
Lewis U, IL — B
Lincoln Coll, Lincoln, IL — A
Lincoln U, MO — B
Lindenwood U, MO — B
Loras Coll, IA — B
Loyola U Chicago, IL — B
Luther Coll, IA — B
MacMurray Coll, IL — B
Madonna U, MI — B
Maharishi U of Management, IA — B
Manchester Coll, IN — B
Marian Coll, IN — B
Marian Coll of Fond du Lac, WI — B
Marietta Coll, OH — B
Marquette U, WI — B
Martin Luther Coll, MN — B
Martin U, IN — B
Maryville U of Saint Louis, MO — B
Mayville State U, ND — B
McKendree Coll, IL — B
McPherson Coll, KS — B
Miami U, OH — B
Michigan State U, MI — B
MidAmerica Nazarene U, KS — B
Millikin U, IL — B
Minnesota State U Mankato, MN — B
Minnesota State U Moorhead, MN — B

Minot State U, ND — B
Missouri Baptist U, MO — B
Missouri Southern State U, MO — B
Missouri Valley Coll, MO — B
Missouri Western State Coll, MO — B
Monmouth Coll, IL — B
Morningside Coll, IA — B
Mount Marty Coll, SD — B
Mount Mary Coll, WI — B
Mount Mercy Coll, IA — B
Mount Vernon Nazarene U, OH — B
Muskingum Coll, OH — B
National-Louis U, IL — B
Nebraska Wesleyan U, NE — B
Newman U, KS — B
North Carolina Ag and Tech State U, NC — B
North Central Coll, IL — B
North Central U, MN — B
North Dakota State U, ND — B
Northeastern Illinois U, IL — B
Northeastern State U, OK — B
Northern Illinois U, IL — B
Northern Michigan U, MI — B
Northern State U, SD — B
Northland Coll, WI — B
North Park U, IL — B
Northwestern Coll, IA — B
Northwestern Coll, MN — B
Northwestern Oklahoma State U, OK — B
Notre Dame Coll, OH — B
Oakland City U, IN — B
Oakland U, MI — B
Ohio Northern U, OH — B
The Ohio State U at Lima, OH — B
The Ohio State U at Marion, OH — B
The Ohio State U–Mansfield Campus, OH — B
The Ohio State U–Newark Campus, OH — B
Ohio U, OH — B
Ohio U–Chillicothe, OH — B
Ohio U–Zanesville, OH — B
Ohio Wesleyan U, OH — B
Oklahoma Baptist U, OK — B
Oklahoma Christian U, OK — B
Oklahoma City U, OK — B
Oklahoma Panhandle State U, OK — B
Oklahoma State U, OK — B
Olivet Coll, MI — B
Olivet Nazarene U, IL — B
Oral Roberts U, OK — B
Ottawa U, KS — B
Otterbein Coll, OH — B
Park U, MO — B
Peru State Coll, NE — B
Pillsbury Baptist Bible Coll, MN — B
Pittsburg State U, KS — B
Principia Coll, IL — B
Purdue U, IN — B
Purdue U Calumet, IN — B
Purdue U North Central, IN — B
Quincy U, IL — B
Reformed Bible Coll, MI — B
Ripon Coll, WI — B
Rockford Coll, IL — B
Rockhurst U, MO — B
Roosevelt U, IL — B

Saginaw Valley State U, MI	B	U of Nebraska at Omaha, NE	B
St. Ambrose U, IA	B	U of Nebraska–Lincoln, NE	B
St. Cloud State U, MN	B	U of New Orleans, LA	B
Saint John's U, MN	B	U of North Dakota, ND	B
Saint Joseph's Coll, IN	B	U of Northern Iowa, IA	B
Saint Mary-of-the-Woods Coll, IN	B	U of Oklahoma, OK	B
Saint Mary's Coll, IN	B	U of Rio Grande, OH	B
Saint Mary's U of Minnesota, MN	B	U of St. Francis, IL	B
St. Norbert Coll, WI	B	U of Saint Francis, IN	B
Saint Xavier U, IL	B	U of Saint Mary, KS	B
Shawnee State U, OH	B	U of St. Thomas, MN	B
Siena Heights U, MI	B	U of Science and Arts of Oklahoma, OK	B
Silver Lake Coll, WI	B	U of Sioux Falls, SD	B
Simpson Coll, IA	B	The U of South Dakota, SD	B
Southeastern Oklahoma State U, OK	B	U of Southern Indiana, IN	B
Southeast Missouri State U, MO	B	U of Toledo, OH	B
		U of Tulsa, OK	B
Southern Illinois U Carbondale, IL	B	U of West Florida, FL	B
Southern Illinois U Edwardsville, IL	B	U of Wisconsin–Eau Claire, WI	B
Southern Nazarene U, OK	B	U of Wisconsin–Green Bay, WI	B
Southwest Baptist U, MO	B	U of Wisconsin–La Crosse, WI	B
Southwestern Coll, KS	B	U of Wisconsin–Madison, WI	B
Southwestern Oklahoma State U, OK	B	U of Wisconsin–Milwaukee, WI	B
Southwest Missouri State U, MO	B	U of Wisconsin–Oshkosh, WI	B
Spring Arbor U, MI	B	U of Wisconsin–Platteville, WI	B
Stephens Coll, MO	B		
Sterling Coll, KS	B	U of Wisconsin–River Falls, WI	B
Tabor Coll, KS	B	U of Wisconsin–Stevens Point, WI	B
Taylor U, IN	B		
Taylor U Fort Wayne, IN	B	U of Wisconsin–Superior, WI	B
Transylvania U, KY	B	U of Wisconsin–Whitewater, WI	B
Trinity Bible Coll, ND	B		
Trinity Christian Coll, IL	B	Upper Iowa U, IA	B
Trinity International U, IL	B	Urbana U, OH	B
Tri-State U, IN	B	Valley City State U, ND	B
Union Coll, NE	B	Valparaiso U, IN	B
The U of Akron, OH	B	Vennard Coll, IA	A,B
The U of Alabama in Huntsville, AL	B	Viterbo U, WI	B
		Waldorf Coll, IA	B
U of Central Oklahoma, OK	B	Walsh U, OH	B
U of Cincinnati, OH	B	Wartburg Coll, IA	B
U of Dayton, OH	B	Washburn U, KS	B
U of Detroit Mercy, MI	B	Washington U in St. Louis, MO	B
U of Dubuque, IA	B		
U of Evansville, IN	B	Wayne State Coll, NE	B
The U of Findlay, OH	B	Wayne State U, MI	B
U of Illinois at Chicago, IL	B	Webster U, MO	B
U of Illinois at Springfield, IL	B	Western Illinois U, IL	B
		Western Michigan U, MI	B
U of Illinois at Urbana–Champaign, IL	B	Westminster Coll, MO	B
U of Indianapolis, IN	B	Wheaton Coll, IL	B
The U of Iowa, IA	B	Wichita State U, KS	B
U of Kansas, KS	B	William Jewell Coll, MO	B
U of Mary, ND	B	William Penn U, IA	B
U of Michigan, MI	B	William Woods U, MO	B
U of Michigan–Dearborn, MI	B	Winona State U, MN	B
U of Michigan–Flint, MI	B	Wisconsin Lutheran Coll, WI	B
U of Minnesota, Duluth, MN	B	Wittenberg U, OH	B
U of Minnesota, Morris, MN	B	Wright State U, OH	B
U of Minnesota, Twin Cities Campus, MN	B	Xavier U, OH	B
		York Coll, NE	B
U of Missouri–Columbia, MO	B	Youngstown State U, OH	B
U of Missouri–Kansas City, MO	B		
U of Missouri–St. Louis, MO	B		

Emergency Care Attendant (Emt Ambulance)

Kent State U, OH	A
Trinity Coll of Nursing and Health Sciences, IL	A

Emergency Medical Technology (Emt Paramedic)

Baker Coll of Cadillac, MI	A
Baker Coll of Clinton Township, MI	A
Baker Coll of Muskegon, MI	A
Ball State U, IN	A
Creighton U, NE	A,B
Hannibal-LaGrange Coll, MO	A
IHM Health Studies Center, MO	A
Indiana U–Purdue U Indianapolis, IN	A
Kent State U, OH	A
Nebraska Methodist Coll, NE	A,B
Shawnee State U, OH	A
Southwest Baptist U, MO	A
U of Minnesota, Twin Cities Campus, MN	A
U of Saint Francis, IN	A
U of Toledo, OH	A
Youngstown State U, OH	A

Energy Management and Systems Technology

Baker Coll of Flint, MI	A
Ferris State U, MI	B
U of Cincinnati, OH	A

Engineering

Baker U, KS	B
Baldwin-Wallace Coll, OH	B
Beloit Coll, WI	B
Bethel Coll, IN	B
Brescia U, KY	A
Briar Cliff U, IA	A
Calvin Coll, MI	B
Carthage Coll, WI	B
Case Western Reserve U, OH	B
Central Christian Coll of Kansas, KS	A
Clarkson U	B
Cleveland State U, OH	B
Coll of the Ozarks, MO	B
Donnelly Coll, KS	A
Dordt Coll, IA	B
Fontbonne U, MO	B
Gannon U, PA	B
Grand Valley State U, MI	B
Hope Coll, MI	B
Indiana U–Purdue U Indianapolis, IN	B
Iowa State U of Science and Technology, IA	B
Kansas Wesleyan U, KS	B
Lake Superior State U, MI	A
Marquette U, WI	B
Michigan State U, MI	B
Michigan Technological U, MI	B
North Dakota State U, ND	B
Northwestern U, IL	B
Oakland U, MI	B
Ohio Northern U, OH	B
Ohio U, OH	B
Oklahoma Christian U, OK	B
Oklahoma State U, OK	B

Olivet Nazarene U, IL	B
Purdue U Calumet, IN	B
St. Cloud State U, MN	B
Union Coll, NE	A
The U of Akron, OH	B
U of Cincinnati, OH	B
U of Detroit Mercy, MI	B
U of Illinois at Urbana–Champaign, IL	B
The U of Iowa, IA	B
U of Michigan, MI	B
U of Michigan–Dearborn, MI	B
U of Oklahoma, OK	B
U of Southern Indiana, IN	B
U of Toledo, OH	B
U of Wisconsin–Madison, WI	B
U of Wisconsin–Milwaukee, WI	B
Wartburg Coll, IA	B
Washington U in St. Louis, MO	B
Western Michigan U, MI	B
Winona State U, MN	B
Wright State U, OH	B
Youngstown State U, OH	A,B

Engineering/Industrial Management

Eastern Michigan U, MI	B
Grand Valley State U, MI	B
Illinois Inst of Technology, IL	B
Kettering U, MI	B
Lake Superior State U, MI	B
Lawrence Technological U, MI	B
Miami U, OH	B
Miami U Hamilton, OH	B
Missouri Tech, MO	B
Saint Louis U, MO	B
South Dakota State U, SD	B
Tri-State U, IN	B
U of Evansville, IN	B
U of Illinois at Chicago, IL	B
U of Missouri–Rolla, MO	B
U of Wisconsin–Stout, WI	B
Western Michigan U, MI	B

Engineering Mechanics

Cleveland State U, OH	B
Dordt Coll, IA	B
Lehigh U, PA	B
Michigan Technological U, MI	B
Oral Roberts U, OK	B
U of Cincinnati, OH	B
U of Illinois at Urbana–Champaign, IL	B
U of Wisconsin–Madison, WI	B

Engineering Physics

Augustana Coll, IL	B
Augustana Coll, SD	B
Aurora U, IL	B
Bemidji State U, MN	B
Bradley U, IL	B
Case Western Reserve U, OH	B
Hope Coll, MI	B
John Carroll U, OH	B
Lehigh U, PA	B
Loras Coll, IA	B
Miami U, OH	B
Miami U Hamilton, OH	B

A—associate degree; B—bachelor's degree

Michigan Technological U, MI	
Morningside Coll, IA	B
North Carolina Ag and Tech State U, NC	B
Northeastern State U, OK	B
The Ohio State U, OH	B
Rose-Hulman Inst of Technology, IN	B
St. Ambrose U, IA	B
Saint Mary's U of Minnesota, MN	B
South Dakota State U, SD	B
Southeast Missouri State U, MO	B
Southwestern Coll, KS	B
Southwestern Oklahoma State U, OK	B
Southwest Missouri State U, MO	B
Taylor U, IN	B
The U of Akron, OH	B
U of Illinois at Chicago, IL	B
U of Illinois at Urbana–Champaign, IL	B
U of Kansas, KS	B
U of Michigan, MI	B
U of Nebraska at Omaha, NE	B
U of Northern Iowa, IA	B
U of Oklahoma, OK	B
U of Toledo, OH	B
U of Tulsa, OK	B
U of Wisconsin–Madison, WI	B
Washington U in St. Louis, MO	B
Wilberforce U, OH	B
Wright State U, OH	B

Engineering Related

Augustana Coll, IL	B
Cleveland State U, OH	B
Dunwoody Coll of Technology, MN	A
Eastern Illinois U, IL	B
Eastern Michigan U, MI	B
Iowa State U of Science and Technology, IA	B
Lehigh U, PA	B
Loras Coll, IA	B
Madonna U, MI	B
Marquette U, WI	B
Northwestern U, IL	B
Ohio Northern U, OH	B
Ohio U, OH	B
Ohio Wesleyan U, OH	B
Park U, MO	B
Principia Coll, IL	B
Purdue U, IN	B
Rose-Hulman Inst of Technology, IN	B
The U of Alabama in Huntsville, AL	B
U of Nebraska–Lincoln, NE	B
Wheaton Coll, IL	B
Wright State U, OH	B

Engineering Science

Benedictine U, IL	B
Bethel U, MN	B
Case Western Reserve U, OH	B
Cleveland State U, OH	B
Franciscan U of Steubenville, OH	B

Iowa State U of Science and Technology, IA	B
Manchester Coll, IN	B
Northwestern U, IL	B
Ohio Wesleyan U, OH	B
U of Cincinnati, OH	A,B
U of Michigan, MI	B
U of Michigan–Flint, MI	B
U of New Orleans, LA	B
Washington U in St. Louis, MO	B
Wright State U, OH	B

Engineering Technologies Related

Cameron U, OK	A,B
Kent State U, OH	A
Ohio U, OH	B
St. Cloud State U, MN	B
The U of Akron, OH	A
U of Southern Indiana, IN	B
Western Michigan U, MI	B

Engineering Technology

Andrews U, MI	A,B
Cleveland State U, OH	B
Dordt Coll, IA	B
Eastern Michigan U, MI	B
Kent State U, Tuscarawas Campus, OH	A
Lake Superior State U, MI	A
Lawrence Technological U, MI	B
Miami U, OH	B
Miami U Hamilton, OH	B
Missouri Tech, MO	A,B
Morrison Inst of Technology, IL	A
Northern Illinois U, IL	B
Oklahoma State U, OK	B
Pittsburg State U, KS	B
Purdue U Calumet, IN	B
St. Cloud State U, MN	B
Southern Illinois U Carbondale, IL	B
Southwestern Oklahoma State U, OK	B
Tri-State U, IN	A
The U of Akron, OH	B
U of West Florida, FL	B
U of Wisconsin–River Falls, WI	B
U of Wisconsin–Stout, WI	B
William Penn U, IA	B
Youngstown State U, OH	B
Youngstown State U, OH	A,B

English

Adrian Coll, MI	A,B
Albion Coll, MI	B
Alma Coll, MI	B
Alverno Coll, WI	B
Andrews U, MI	B
Antioch Coll, OH	B
Aquinas Coll, MI	B
Ashland U, OH	B
Augsburg Coll, MN	B
Augustana Coll, IL	B
Augustana Coll, SD	B
Aurora U, IL	B
Avila U, MO	B
Baker U, KS	B
Baldwin-Wallace Coll, OH	B
Ball State U, IN	B
Beloit Coll, WI	B
Bemidji State U, MN	B
Benedictine Coll, KS	B

Benedictine U, IL	B
Bethany Coll, KS	B
Bethany Lutheran Coll, MN	B
Bethel Coll, IN	B
Bethel Coll, KS	B
Bethel U, MN	B
Blackburn Coll, IL	B
Black Hills State U, SD	B
Bluffton Coll, OH	B
Bowling Green State U, OH	B
Bradley U, IL	B
Brescia U, KY	B
Briar Cliff U, IA	B
Buena Vista U, IA	B
Butler U, IN	B
Calumet Coll of Saint Joseph, IN	A,B
Calvin Coll, MI	B
Cameron U, OK	B
Capital U, OH	B
Cardinal Stritch U, WI	B
Carleton Coll, MN	B
Carroll Coll, WI	B
Carthage Coll, WI	B
Case Western Reserve U, OH	B
Cedarville U, OH	B
Central Christian Coll of Kansas, KS	A
Central Coll, IA	B
Central Methodist Coll, MO	A,B
Central Michigan U, MI	B
Central Missouri State U, MO	B
Central State U, OH	B
Chadron State Coll, NE	B
Chicago State U, IL	B
Clarke Coll, IA	B
Cleveland State U, OH	B
Coe Coll, IA	B
Coll of Mount St. Joseph, OH	B
Coll of Saint Benedict, MN	B
Coll of St. Catherine, MN	B
Coll of Saint Mary, NE	B
The Coll of St. Scholastica, MN	B
Coll of the Ozarks, MO	B
The Coll of Wooster, OH	B
Columbia Coll, MO	B
Concordia Coll, MN	B
Concordia U, IL	B
Concordia U, MI	B
Concordia U, NE	B
Concordia U, St. Paul, MN	B
Concordia U Wisconsin, WI	B
Concord U, WV	B
Cornell Coll, IA	B
Cornerstone U, MI	B
Creighton U, NE	B
Crown Coll, MN	B
Culver-Stockton Coll, MO	B
Cumberland Coll, KY	B
Dakota State U, SD	B
Dakota Wesleyan U, SD	B
Dana Coll, NE	B
Defiance Coll, OH	B
Denison U, OH	B
DePaul U, IL	B
DePauw U, IN	B
Dickinson State U, ND	B
Doane Coll, NE	B
Dominican U, IL	B
Donnelly Coll, KS	A
Dordt Coll, IA	B
Drake U, IA	B

Drury U, MO	B
Earlham Coll, IN	B
East Central U, OK	B
Eastern Illinois U, IL	B
Eastern Michigan U, MI	B
Edgewood Coll, WI	B
Elmhurst Coll, IL	B
Emporia State U, KS	B
Eureka Coll, IL	B
Evangel U, MO	B
Fontbonne U, MO	B
Fort Hays State U, KS	B
The Franciscan U, IA	B
Franciscan U of Steubenville, OH	B
Franklin Coll, IN	B
Goshen Coll, IN	B
Governors State U, IL	B
Grace Coll, IN	B
Graceland U, IA	B
Grand Valley State U, MI	B
Grand View Coll, IA	B
Greenville Coll, IL	B
Grinnell Coll, IA	B
Gustavus Adolphus Coll, MN	B
Hamline U, MN	B
Hannibal-LaGrange Coll, MO	A,B
Hanover Coll, IN	B
Hastings Coll, NE	B
Heidelberg Coll, OH	B
Hillsdale Coll, MI	B
Hillsdale Free Will Baptist Coll, OK	A
Hiram Coll, OH	B
Hope Coll, MI	B
Huntington Coll, IN	B
Illinois Coll, IL	B
Illinois State U, IL	B
Illinois Wesleyan U, IL	B
Indiana State U, IN	B
Indiana U Bloomington, IN	B
Indiana U East, IN	B
Indiana U Kokomo, IN	B
Indiana U Northwest, IN	B
Indiana U–Purdue U Fort Wayne, IN	A,B
Indiana U–Purdue U Indianapolis, IN	B
Indiana U South Bend, IN	B
Indiana U Southeast, IN	B
Iowa State U of Science and Technology, IA	B
Iowa Wesleyan Coll, IA	B
Jamestown Coll, ND	B
John Carroll U, OH	B
Judson Coll, IL	B
Kalamazoo Coll, MI	B
Kansas State U, KS	B
Kansas Wesleyan U, KS	B
Kent State U, OH	B
Kenyon Coll, OH	B
Knox Coll, IL	B
Lake Erie Coll, OH	B
Lake Forest Coll, IL	B
Lakeland Coll, WI	B
Lake Superior State U, MI	B
Lawrence U, WI	B
Lewis U, IL	B
Lincoln Coll, Lincoln, IL	A
Lincoln U, MO	B
Lindenwood U, MO	B
Loras Coll, IA	B
Lourdes Coll, OH	A,B
Loyola U Chicago, IL	B
Luther Coll, IA	B

Macalester Coll, MN	B
MacMurray Coll, IL	B
Madonna U, MI	A,B
Maharishi U of Management, IA	B
Malone Coll, OH	B
Manchester Coll, IN	A,B
Marian Coll, IN	B
Marian Coll of Fond du Lac, WI	B
Marietta Coll, OH	B
Marquette U, WI	B
Martin U, IN	B
Marygrove Coll, MI	B
Maryville U of Saint Louis, MO	B
Mayville State U, ND	B
McKendree Coll, IL	B
McPherson Coll, KS	B
Metropolitan State U, MN	B
Miami U, OH	B
Miami U Hamilton, OH	B
Michigan State U, MI	B
Michigan Technological U, MI	B
MidAmerica Nazarene U, KS	B
Millikin U, IL	B
Minnesota State U Mankato, MN	B
Minnesota State U Moorhead, MN	B
Minot State U, ND	B
Missouri Baptist U, MO	B
Missouri Southern State U, MO	B
Missouri Valley Coll, MO	B
Missouri Western State Coll, MO	B
Monmouth Coll, IL	B
Morningside Coll, IA	B
Mount Marty Coll, SD	B
Mount Mary Coll, WI	B
Mount Mercy Coll, IA	B
Mount Union Coll, OH	B
Mount Vernon Nazarene U, OH	B
Muskingum Coll, OH	B
National-Louis U, IL	B
Nebraska Wesleyan U, NE	B
Newman U, KS	B
North Carolina Ag and Tech State U, NC	B
North Central Coll, IL	B
North Central U, MN	B
North Dakota State U, ND	B
Northeastern Illinois U, IL	B
Northeastern State U, OK	B
Northern Illinois U, IL	B
Northern Michigan U, MI	B
Northern State U, SD	B
Northland Coll, WI	B
North Park U, IL	B
Northwestern Coll, IA	B
Northwestern Coll, MN	B
Northwestern Oklahoma State U, OK	B
Northwestern U, IL	B
Notre Dame Coll, OH	B
Oakland City U, IN	B
Oakland U, MI	B
Oberlin Coll, OH	B
Ohio Dominican U, OH	B
Ohio Northern U, OH	B
The Ohio State U, OH	B

The Ohio State U at Lima, OH	B
The Ohio State U at Marion, OH	B
The Ohio State U–Mansfield Campus, OH	B
The Ohio State U–Newark Campus, OH	B
Ohio U, OH	B
Ohio Wesleyan U, OH	B
Oklahoma Baptist U, OK	B
Oklahoma Christian U, OK	B
Oklahoma City U, OK	B
Oklahoma Panhandle State U, OK	B
Oklahoma State U, OK	B
Olivet Coll, MI	B
Olivet Nazarene U, IL	B
Ottawa U, KS	B
Otterbein Coll, OH	B
Park U, MO	B
Peru State Coll, NE	B
Pittsburg State U, KS	B
Pontifical Coll Josephinum, OH	B
Presentation Coll, SD	A
Principia Coll, IL	B
Purdue U, IN	B
Purdue U Calumet, IN	B
Purdue U North Central, IN	B
Quincy U, IL	B
Ripon Coll, WI	B
Rochester Coll, MI	B
Rockford Coll, IL	B
Rockhurst U, MO	B
Roosevelt U, IL	B
Saginaw Valley State U, MI	B
St. Ambrose U, IA	B
St. Cloud State U, MN	B
St. Gregory's U, OK	B
Saint John's U, MN	B
Saint Joseph's Coll, IN	B
Saint Louis U, MO	B
Saint Mary-of-the-Woods Coll, IN	B
Saint Mary's U of Minnesota, MN	B
St. Norbert Coll, WI	B
St. Olaf Coll, MN	B
Saint Xavier U, IL	B
Shawnee State U, OH	B
Siena Heights U, MI	A,B
Silver Lake Coll, WI	B
Simpson Coll, IA	B
South Dakota State U, SD	B
Southeastern Oklahoma State U, OK	B
Southeast Missouri State U, MO	B
Southern Illinois U Carbondale, IL	B
Southern Illinois U Edwardsville, IL	B
Southern Nazarene U, OK	B
Southwest Baptist U, MO	B
Southwestern Coll, KS	B
Southwestern Oklahoma State U, OK	B
Southwest Missouri State U, MO	B
Spring Arbor U, MI	B
Stephens Coll, MO	B
Sterling Coll, KS	B
Tabor Coll, KS	B
Taylor U, IN	B

Taylor U Fort Wayne, IN	B
Tiffin U, OH	B
Transylvania U, KY	B
Trinity Christian Coll, IL	B
Trinity International U, IL	B
Tri-State U, IN	B
Truman State U, MO	B
Union Coll, NE	B
The U of Akron, OH	B
The U of Alabama in Huntsville, AL	B
U of Central Oklahoma, OK	B
U of Chicago, IL	B
U of Cincinnati, OH	B
U of Dayton, OH	B
U of Detroit Mercy, MI	B
U of Dubuque, IA	A,B
U of Evansville, IN	B
The U of Findlay, OH	B
U of Illinois at Chicago, IL	B
U of Illinois at Springfield, IL	B
U of Illinois at Urbana–Champaign, IL	B
The U of Iowa, IA	B
U of Kansas, KS	B
U of Mary, ND	B
U of Michigan, MI	B
U of Michigan–Dearborn, MI	B
U of Michigan–Flint, MI	B
U of Minnesota, Duluth, MN	B
U of Minnesota, Morris, MN	B
U of Minnesota, Twin Cities Campus, MN	B
U of Missouri–Columbia, MO	B
U of Missouri–Kansas City, MO	B
U of Missouri–Rolla, MO	B
U of Missouri–St. Louis, MO	B
U of Nebraska at Omaha, NE	B
U of Nebraska–Lincoln, NE	B
U of New Orleans, LA	B
U of North Dakota, ND	B
U of Northern Iowa, IA	B
U of Notre Dame, IN	B
U of Oklahoma, OK	B
U of Rio Grande, OH	A,B
U of St. Francis, IL	B
U of Saint Francis, IN	B
U of Saint Mary, KS	B
U of St. Thomas, MN	B
U of Science and Arts of Oklahoma, OK	B
U of Sioux Falls, SD	B
The U of South Dakota, SD	B
U of Southern Indiana, IN	B
U of Toledo, OH	B
U of Tulsa, OK	B
U of West Florida, FL	B
U of Wisconsin–Eau Claire, WI	B
U of Wisconsin–Green Bay, WI	A,B
U of Wisconsin–La Crosse, WI	B
U of Wisconsin–Madison, WI	B
U of Wisconsin–Milwaukee, WI	B
U of Wisconsin–Oshkosh, WI	B
U of Wisconsin–Parkside, WI	B

U of Wisconsin–Platteville, WI	B
U of Wisconsin–River Falls, WI	B
U of Wisconsin–Stevens Point, WI	B
U of Wisconsin–Superior, WI	B
U of Wisconsin–Whitewater, WI	B
Upper Iowa U, IA	B
Urbana U, OH	B
Ursuline Coll, OH	B
Valley City State U, ND	B
Valparaiso U, IN	B
Viterbo U, WI	B
Wabash Coll, IN	B
Waldorf Coll, IA	B
Walsh U, OH	B
Wartburg Coll, IA	B
Washburn U, KS	B
Washington U in St. Louis, MO	B
Wayne State Coll, NE	B
Wayne State U, MI	B
Webster U, MO	B
Western Illinois U, IL	B
Western Michigan U, MI	B
Westminster Coll, MO	B
Wheaton Coll, IL	B
Wichita State U, KS	B
William Jewell Coll, MO	B
William Tyndale Coll, MI	B
William Woods U, MO	B
Winona State U, MN	B
Wisconsin Lutheran Coll, WI	B
Wittenberg U, OH	B
Wright State U, OH	B
Xavier U, OH	A,B
York Coll, NE	B
Youngstown State U, OH	B

English as a Second/Foreign Language (Teaching)

Aquinas Coll, MI	B
Bethel U, MN	B
Calvin Coll, MI	B
Concordia U, NE	B
Concordia U, St. Paul, MN	B
Concordia U Wisconsin, WI	B
Doane Coll, NE	B
Eastern Michigan U, MI	B
Goshen Coll, IN	B
Moody Bible Inst, IL	B
Northwestern Coll, MN	B
Ohio Dominican U, OH	B
Ohio U, OH	B
Oklahoma Christian U, OK	B
Oral Roberts U, OK	B
The U of Findlay, OH	B
The U of Iowa, IA	B
U of Nebraska–Lincoln, NE	B
U of Northern Iowa, IA	B
U of Wisconsin–Oshkosh, WI	B
U of Wisconsin–River Falls, WI	B
William Penn U, IA	B
Wright State U, OH	B

English Composition

Aurora U, IL	B
Bethel U, MN	B
Central Christian Coll of Kansas, KS	A
DePauw U, IN	B
Eastern Michigan U, MI	B

A—associate degree; B—bachelor's degree

College	Degree
Graceland U, IA	B
Jamestown Coll, ND	B
Lakeland Coll, WI	B
Metropolitan State U, MN	B
Miami U Hamilton, OH	B
Mount Union Coll, OH	B
Oakland U, MI	B
Oklahoma Baptist U, OK	B
Rochester Coll, MI	B
U of Illinois at Urbana–Champaign, IL	B
U of Michigan–Flint, MI	B
Wartburg Coll, IA	B
Western Michigan U, MI	B
William Woods U, MO	B

English/French as a Second/Foreign Language (Teaching) Related

College	Degree
Western Michigan U, MI	B

English Language and Literature Related

College	Degree
St. Gregory's U, OK	B
Saint Mary-of-the-Woods Coll, IN	B
Saint Mary's U of Minnesota, MN	B
U of Chicago, IL	B
The U of Iowa, IA	B
U of Oklahoma, OK	B
Viterbo U, WI	B
Washington U in St. Louis, MO	B
Webster U, MO	B

English/Language Arts Teacher Education

College	Degree
Alma Coll, MI	B
Alverno Coll, WI	B
Aquinas Coll, MI	B
Bethany Coll, KS	B
Bethel Coll, IN	B
Bethel U, MN	B
Bowling Green State U, OH	B
Buena Vista U, IA	B
Calumet Coll of Saint Joseph, IN	B
Capital U, OH	B
Carroll Coll, WI	B
Cedarville U, OH	B
Central Christian Coll of Kansas, KS	A
Central Michigan U, MI	B
Central Missouri State U, MO	B
Central State U, OH	B
Chadron State Coll, NE	B
Coll of St. Catherine, MN	B
The Coll of St. Scholastica, MN	B
Coll of the Ozarks, MO	B
Concordia Coll, MN	B
Concordia U, IL	B
Concordia U, MI	B
Concordia U, NE	B
Cornerstone U, MI	B
Crown Coll, MN	B
Culver-Stockton Coll, MO	B
Dakota Wesleyan U, SD	B
Dana Coll, NE	B
East Central U, OK	B
Eastern Michigan U, MI	B
Elmhurst Coll, IL	B
Faith Baptist Bible Coll and Theological Seminary, IA	B
Franklin Coll, IN	B

College	Degree
Grace Coll, IN	B
Greenville Coll, IL	B
Hannibal-LaGrange Coll, MO	B
Hastings Coll, NE	B
Hope Coll, MI	B
Illinois Wesleyan U, IL	B
Indiana U Bloomington, IN	B
Indiana U Northwest, IN	B
Indiana U–Purdue U Fort Wayne, IN	B
Indiana U–Purdue U Indianapolis, IN	B
Indiana U South Bend, IN	B
Indiana U Southeast, IN	B
Jamestown Coll, ND	B
Kent State U, OH	B
Malone Coll, OH	B
Marian Coll of Fond du Lac, WI	B
Marquette U, WI	B
Maryville U of Saint Louis, MO	B
Mayville State U, ND	B
McKendree Coll, IL	B
Miami U, OH	B
Miami U Hamilton, OH	B
MidAmerica Nazarene U, KS	B
Minnesota State U Moorhead, MN	B
Minot State U, ND	B
Missouri Western State Coll, MO	B
Mount Marty Coll, SD	B
Mount Mary Coll, WI	B
Mount Vernon Nazarene U, OH	B
Nebraska Wesleyan U, NE	B
North Dakota State U, ND	B
Northern Michigan U, MI	B
Northwestern Coll, MN	B
Oakland City U, IN	B
Ohio Northern U, OH	B
Oklahoma Baptist U, OK	B
Oklahoma Christian U, OK	B
Oral Roberts U, OK	B
Pillsbury Baptist Bible Coll, MN	B
Pittsburg State U, KS	B
St. Ambrose U, IA	B
St. Gregory's U, OK	B
Saint Mary's U of Minnesota, MN	B
Saint Xavier U, IL	B
Shawnee State U, OH	B
Southeastern Oklahoma State U, OK	B
Southeast Missouri State U, MO	B
Southern Nazarene U, OK	B
Southwest Baptist U, MO	B
Southwestern Oklahoma State U, OK	B
Southwest Missouri State U, MO	B
Trinity Christian Coll, IL	B
Tri-State U, IN	B
Union Coll, NE	B
The U of Akron, OH	B
U of Central Oklahoma, OK	B
U of Dubuque, IA	B
U of Illinois at Chicago, IL	B
U of Illinois at Urbana–Champaign, IL	B
U of Indianapolis, IN	B
U of Mary, ND	B

College	Degree
U of Minnesota, Twin Cities Campus, MN	B
U of Missouri–St. Louis, MO	B
U of Nebraska–Lincoln, NE	B
U of New Orleans, LA	B
U of Oklahoma, OK	B
U of Rio Grande, OH	B
U of St. Francis, IL	B
U of Saint Francis, IN	B
U of St. Thomas, MN	B
The U of South Dakota, SD	B
U of Toledo, OH	B
U of West Florida, FL	B
U of Wisconsin–River Falls, WI	B
U of Wisconsin–Superior, WI	B
Ursuline Coll, OH	B
Valley City State U, ND	B
Valparaiso U, IN	B
Viterbo U, WI	B
Waldorf Coll, IA	B
Washington U in St. Louis, MO	B
Wayne State U, MI	B
Western Michigan U, MI	B
William Penn U, IA	B
William Woods U, MO	B
Wright State U, OH	B
York Coll, NE	B
Youngstown State U, OH	B

English Literature (British and Commonwealth)

College	Degree
Eastern Michigan U, MI	B
Gannon U, PA	B
Indiana U–Purdue U Fort Wayne, IN	B
Oral Roberts U, OK	B
Saint Mary's Coll, IN	B
Washington U in St. Louis, MO	B

Entomology

College	Degree
Iowa State U of Science and Technology, IA	B
Michigan State U, MI	B
The Ohio State U, OH	B
Oklahoma State U, OK	B
Purdue U, IN	B
U of Illinois at Urbana–Champaign, IL	B
U of Wisconsin–Madison, WI	B

Entrepreneurial and Small Business Related

College	Degree
Haskell Indian Nations U, KS	A
Kendall Coll, IL	B

Entrepreneurship

College	Degree
Bacone Coll, OK	B
Baker Coll of Flint, MI	A
Buena Vista U, IA	B
Davenport U, Dearborn, MI	A,B
Davenport U, Gaylord, MI	A,B
Davenport U, Grand Rapids, MI	A,B
Davenport U, Traverse City, MI	B
Davenport U, Warren, MI	A,B
East Central U, OK	B
Iowa State U of Science and Technology, IA	B
Kendall Coll, IL	B
Northern Michigan U, MI	B
Northwood U, MI	A,B
Union Coll, NE	B

College	Degree
The U of Akron, OH	A
U of Illinois at Chicago, IL	B
The U of Iowa, IA	B
U of North Dakota, ND	B
U of Oklahoma, OK	B
U of Phoenix–Kansas City Campus, MO	B
U of Phoenix–Metro Detroit Campus, MI	B
U of St. Thomas, MN	B
U of Southern Indiana, IN	B
U of Toledo, OH	B
Washington U in St. Louis, MO	B

Environmental Biology

College	Degree
Antioch Coll, OH	B
Beloit Coll, WI	B
Bethel Coll, IN	B
Cedarville U, OH	B
Central Methodist Coll, MO	B
Cornerstone U, MI	B
Greenville Coll, IL	B
Grinnell Coll, IA	B
Heidelberg Coll, OH	B
Iowa Wesleyan Coll, IA	B
Marygrove Coll, MI	B
Michigan State U, MI	B
Minnesota State U Mankato, MN	B
Mount Union Coll, OH	B
Northland Coll, WI	B
Ohio U, OH	B
Otterbein Coll, OH	B
Pittsburg State U, KS	B
St. Cloud State U, MN	B
Simpson Coll, IA	B
Tabor Coll, KS	B
Taylor U, IN	B
U of Dayton, OH	B
U of Dubuque, IA	B
Ursuline Coll, OH	B
William Penn U, IA	B
Winona State U, MN	B

Environmental Control Technologies Related

College	Degree
Kent State U, OH	A

Environmental Design/Architecture

College	Degree
Ball State U, IN	B
Bowling Green State U, OH	B
Coll for Creative Studies, MI	B
Kent State U, OH	B
Lawrence Technological U, MI	B
Miami U, OH	B
North Dakota State U, ND	B
Northern Michigan U, MI	A
U of Oklahoma, OK	B

Environmental Education

College	Degree
Northland Coll, WI	B
The Ohio State U, OH	B

Environmental Engineering Technology

College	Degree
Baker Coll of Flint, MI	A
Baker Coll of Owosso, MI	A
Baker Coll of Port Huron, MI	A
Kansas State U, KS	A
Lake Superior State U, MI	B
Ohio U, OH	B
Shawnee State U, OH	B
U of Cincinnati, OH	A
U of Toledo, OH	A

U of Wisconsin–Whitewater, WI	B
Wright State U, OH	B

Environmental/Environmental Health Engineering

Bradley U, IL	B
Clarkson U	B
Gannon U, PA	B
Illinois Inst of Technology, IL	B
Marquette U, WI	B
Michigan Technological U, MI	B
Northwestern U, IL	B
Ohio U, OH	A
Ohio U–Chillicothe, OH	A
South Dakota School of Mines and Technology, SD	B
South Dakota State U, SD	B
U of Michigan, MI	B
U of Missouri–Rolla, MO	B
U of North Dakota, ND	B
U of Notre Dame, IN	B
U of Oklahoma, OK	B
U of Wisconsin–Madison, WI	B
Youngstown State U, OH	B

Environmental Health

Bowling Green State U, OH	B
Clarkson U	B
East Central U, OK	B
Ferris State U, MI	B
Illinois State U, IL	B
Indiana State U, IN	B
Iowa Wesleyan Coll, IA	B
Missouri Southern State U, MO	B
Oakland U, MI	B
Ohio U, OH	B
The U of Akron, OH	A
U of Michigan–Flint, MI	B
U of Wisconsin–Eau Claire, WI	B
Wright State U, OH	B

Environmental Science

Aquinas Coll, MI	B
Bethel U, MN	B
Blackburn Coll, IL	B
Capital U, OH	B
Carroll Coll, WI	B
Central Christian Coll of Kansas, KS	A
Central Methodist Coll, MO	B
Concordia U, St. Paul, MN	B
Drake U, IA	B
East Central U, OK	B
Haskell Indian Nations U, KS	B
Heidelberg Coll, OH	B
Lindenwood U, MO	B
Marietta Coll, OH	B
Maryville U of Saint Louis, MO	B
Miami U Hamilton, OH	B
Michigan State U, MI	B
Monmouth Coll, IL	B
Muskingum Coll, OH	B
Northern Michigan U, MI	B
Northwestern Coll, IA	B
Northwestern U, IL	B
Notre Dame Coll, OH	B
Otterbein Coll, OH	B
Roosevelt U, IL	B
Saint Joseph's Coll, IN	B

Saint Louis U, MO	B
Southeastern Oklahoma State U, OK	B
U of Dubuque, IA	B
U of Illinois at Urbana–Champaign, IL	B
The U of Iowa, IA	B
U of Northern Iowa, IA	B
U of Oklahoma, OK	B
U of St. Francis, IL	B
U of Wisconsin–Green Bay, WI	A,B
Upper Iowa U, IA	B
Valparaiso U, IN	B
Western Michigan U, MI	B
Westminster Coll, MO	B
Wright State U, OH	B

Environmental Studies

Adrian Coll, MI	B
Albion Coll, MI	B
Alverno Coll, WI	B
Antioch Coll, OH	B
Aquinas Coll, MI	B
Ashland U, OH	B
Augustana Coll, IL	B
Aurora U, IL	B
Ball State U, IN	B
Beloit Coll, WI	B
Bemidji State U, MN	B
Benedictine U, IL	B
Black Hills State U, SD	B
Briar Cliff U, IA	B
Calvin Coll, MI	B
Carthage Coll, WI	B
Case Western Reserve U, OH	B
Central Christian Coll of Kansas, KS	A
Central Coll, IA	B
Central Michigan U, MI	B
Clarkson U	B
Cleveland State U, OH	B
Coe Coll, IA	B
Coll of Saint Benedict, MN	B
Columbia Coll, MO	B
Concordia Coll, MN	B
Concordia U, IL	B
Cornell Coll, IA	B
Creighton U, NE	B
Dana Coll, NE	B
Defiance Coll, OH	A,B
Denison U, OH	B
DePaul U, IL	B
DePauw U, IN	B
Dickinson State U, ND	A,B
Doane Coll, NE	B
Dominican U, IL	B
Dordt Coll, IA	B
Drake U, IA	B
Drury U, MO	B
Earlham Coll, IN	B
East Central U, OK	B
Elmhurst Coll, IL	B
Goshen Coll, IN	B
Grinnell Coll, IA	B
Gustavus Adolphus Coll, MN	B
Hamline U, MN	B
Heidelberg Coll, OH	B
Hiram Coll, OH	B
Hope Coll, MI	B
Illinois Coll, IL	B
Illinois Wesleyan U, IL	B
Indiana U Bloomington, IN	B

Iowa State U of Science and Technology, IA	B
John Carroll U, OH	B
Kent State U, OH	A
Kent State U, Salem Campus, OH	A
Kent State U, Tuscarawas Campus, OH	A
Kenyon Coll, OH	B
Knox Coll, IL	B
Lake Erie Coll, OH	B
Lake Forest Coll, IL	B
Lake Superior State U, MI	B
Lawrence U, WI	B
Lehigh U, PA	B
Lewis U, IL	B
Loyola U Chicago, IL	B
Macalester Coll, MN	B
Maharishi U of Management, IA	B
Manchester Coll, IN	B
Marietta Coll, OH	B
Marygrove Coll, MI	B
Maryville U of Saint Louis, MO	B
McPherson Coll, KS	B
Miami U Hamilton, OH	B
Michigan State U, MI	B
Minnesota State U Mankato, MN	B
Muskingum Coll, OH	B
Northeastern Illinois U, IL	B
Northern Michigan U, MI	B
Northern State U, SD	B
Northland Coll, WI	B
Northwestern U, IL	B
Oberlin Coll, OH	B
Ohio Northern U, OH	B
The Ohio State U, OH	B
Ohio U–Chillicothe, OH	A
Ohio Wesleyan U, OH	B
Oklahoma State U, OK	B
Olivet Coll, MI	B
Olivet Nazarene U, IL	B
Pittsburg State U, KS	B
Principia Coll, IL	B
Ripon Coll, WI	B
Roosevelt U, IL	B
Saint John's U, MN	B
St. Olaf Coll, MN	B
Southern Nazarene U, OK	B
Stephens Coll, MO	B
Taylor U, IN	B
Tri-State U, IN	B
U of Chicago, IL	B
U of Cincinnati, OH	A
U of Dayton, OH	B
U of Dubuque, IA	A,B
U of Evansville, IN	B
The U of Findlay, OH	A,B
U of Indianapolis, IN	B
The U of Iowa, IA	B
U of Kansas, KS	B
U of Michigan, MI	B
U of Michigan–Dearborn, MI	B
U of Minnesota, Crookston, MN	B
U of Minnesota, Duluth, MN	B
U of Minnesota, Twin Cities Campus, MN	B
U of Missouri–Columbia, MO	B
U of Nebraska at Omaha, NE	B
U of Nebraska–Lincoln, NE	B

U of New Orleans, LA	B
U of Saint Francis, IN	B
U of Toledo, OH	A,B
U of Tulsa, OK	B
U of West Florida, FL	B
U of Wisconsin–Green Bay, WI	A,B
U of Wisconsin–River Falls, WI	B
Washington U in St. Louis, MO	B
Webster U, MO	B
Western Michigan U, MI	B
Westminster Coll, MO	B
Wheaton Coll, IL	B
Wittenberg U, OH	B
Youngstown State U, OH	B

Equestrian Studies

Lake Erie Coll, OH	B
National American U, SD	B
North Dakota State U, ND	B
Ohio U, OH	A
Otterbein Coll, OH	B
Saint Mary-of-the-Woods Coll, IN	A,B
Stephens Coll, MO	B
Truman State U, MO	B
The U of Findlay, OH	A,B
U of Minnesota, Crookston, MN	A,B
U of Wisconsin–River Falls, WI	B
William Woods U, MO	B

Ethics

U of Michigan–Flint, MI	B

Ethnic, Cultural Minority, and Gender Studies Related

Bowling Green State U, OH	B
Cornell Coll, IA	B
Kenyon Coll, OH	B
Lawrence U, WI	B
Metropolitan State U, MN	B
Miami U Hamilton, OH	B
St. Olaf Coll, MN	B
Washington U in St. Louis, MO	B

European History

Calvin Coll, MI	B

European Studies

Antioch Coll, OH	B
Beloit Coll, WI	B
Central Michigan U, MI	B
Hamline U, MN	B
Hillsdale Coll, MI	B
Ohio U, OH	B
U of Kansas, KS	B
U of Michigan, MI	B
U of Minnesota, Morris, MN	B
U of Minnesota, Twin Cities Campus, MN	B
U of Missouri–Columbia, MO	B
U of Northern Iowa, IA	B
U of Toledo, OH	B
Washington U in St. Louis, MO	B

European Studies (Central and Eastern)

Grinnell Coll, IA	B
Hamline U, MN	B
Indiana U Bloomington, IN	B

A—associate degree; B—bachelor's degree

Kent State U, OH | B
U of Chicago, IL | B
U of Missouri–Columbia, MO | B

European Studies (Western)
Central Coll, IA | B
Grinnell Coll, IA | B
Illinois Wesleyan U, IL | B
The Ohio State U, OH | B
U of Nebraska–Lincoln, NE | B

Evolutionary Biology
Case Western Reserve U, OH | B

Executive Assistant/Executive Secretary
Baker Coll of Allen Park, MI | A
Baker Coll of Flint, MI | A
Cumberland Coll, KY | B
Davenport U, Dearborn, MI | A
Davenport U, Holland, MI | A
Davenport U, Kalamazoo, MI | A
Davenport U, Lansing, MI | A
Davenport U, Lapeer, MI | A
Davenport U, Warren, MI | A
Hickey Coll, MO | A
Robert Morris Coll, IL | A
The U of Akron, OH | A
Youngstown State U, OH | A,B

Exercise Physiology
Baldwin-Wallace Coll, OH | B
Concordia U Wisconsin, WI | B
Miami U Hamilton, OH | B

Experimental Psychology
Blackburn Coll, IL | B
Millikin U, IL | B
Northern Michigan U, MI | B
U of Toledo, OH | B
U of Wisconsin–Madison, WI | B

Facilities Planning and Management
Eastern Michigan U, MI | B
North Dakota State U, ND | B

Family and Community Services
Andrews U, MI | B
Baker Coll of Flint, MI | A
Central Christian Coll of Kansas, KS | A
God's Bible School and Coll, OH | B
Goshen Coll, IN | B
Iowa State U of Science and Technology, IA | B
Michigan State U, MI | B
Oklahoma Christian U, OK | B
Oklahoma State U, OK | B
Olivet Nazarene U, IL | B
U of Minnesota, Twin Cities Campus, MN | B
U of Northern Iowa, IA | B
Youngstown State U, OH | B

Family and Consumer Economics Related
Andrews U, MI | B
Ashland U, OH | B
Baldwin-Wallace Coll, OH | B
Ball State U, IN | B
Chadron State Coll, NE | B
Indiana U Bloomington, IN | B
Iowa State U of Science and Technology, IA | B

Miami U, OH | B
Minnesota State U Mankato, MN | B
Northern Michigan U, MI | B
Oklahoma State U, OK | B
The U of Akron, OH | B
U of Missouri–Columbia, MO | B
U of Nebraska–Lincoln, NE | B
U of Northern Iowa, IA | B
U of Wisconsin–Madison, WI | B
U of Wisconsin–Stevens Point, WI | B
Wayne State Coll, NE | B

Family and Consumer Sciences/Home Economics Teacher Education
Ashland U, OH | B
Ball State U, IN | B
Bluffton Coll, OH | B
Bowling Green State U, OH | B
Central Missouri State U, MO | B
Chadron State Coll, NE | B
Coll of St. Catherine, MN | B
Coll of the Ozarks, MO | B
Concordia U, NE | B
East Central U, OK | B
Ferris State U, MI | B
Fontbonne U, MO | B
Iowa State U of Science and Technology, IA | B
Kent State U, OH | B
Madonna U, MI | B
Miami U, OH | B
Michigan State U, MI | B
Minnesota State U Mankato, MN | B
Mount Vernon Nazarene U, OH | B
North Carolina Ag and Tech State U, NC | B
North Dakota State U, ND | B
Northeastern State U, OK | B
Northern Illinois U, IL | B
Olivet Nazarene U, IL | B
Pittsburg State U, KS | B
South Dakota State U, SD | B
Southeast Missouri State U, MO | B
Southwest Missouri State U, MO | B
The U of Akron, OH | B
U of Central Oklahoma, OK | B
U of Illinois at Springfield, IL | B
U of Minnesota, Twin Cities Campus, MN | B
U of Wisconsin–Madison, WI | B
U of Wisconsin–Stevens Point, WI | B
U of Wisconsin–Stout, WI | B
Wayne State Coll, NE | B
Western Michigan U, MI | B
Youngstown State U, OH | B

Family and Consumer Sciences/Human Sciences
Ashland U, OH | B
Ball State U, IN | B
Bluffton Coll, OH | B
Cameron U, OK | B
Central Missouri State U, MO | B

Coll of St. Catherine, MN | B
Coll of the Ozarks, MO | B
East Central U, OK | B
Eastern Illinois U, IL | B
Eastern Michigan U, MI | B
Fontbonne U, MO | B
Illinois State U, IL | B
Indiana State U, IN | B
Iowa State U of Science and Technology, IA | B
Kent State U, OH | B
Kent State U, Salem Campus, OH | A,B
Madonna U, MI | B
Miami U, OH | B
Michigan State U, MI | B
Minnesota State U Mankato, MN | B
Mount Vernon Nazarene U, OH | A,B
North Carolina Ag and Tech State U, NC | B
Northeastern State U, OK | B
Ohio U, OH | B
Oklahoma State U, OK | B
Olivet Nazarene U, IL | B
Pittsburg State U, KS | B
Purdue U, IN | B
Southeast Missouri State U, MO | B
The U of Akron, OH | B
U of Central Oklahoma, OK | B
U of Nebraska at Omaha, NE | B
U of Wisconsin–Madison, WI | B
Wayne State Coll, NE | B
Western Illinois U, IL | B
Youngstown State U, OH | B

Family and Consumer Sciences/Human Sciences Communication
U of Nebraska at Omaha, NE | B

Family/Community Studies
Coll of the Ozarks, MO | B

Family Resource Management
Bradley U, IL | B
Iowa State U of Science and Technology, IA | B
The Ohio State U, OH | B
Ohio U, OH | B
U of Nebraska at Omaha, NE | B

Family Systems
Central Michigan U, MI | B
Spring Arbor U, MI | B
The U of Akron, OH | B
Western Michigan U, MI | B

Farm and Ranch Management
Iowa State U of Science and Technology, IA | B
Oklahoma Panhandle State U, OK | A
The U of Findlay, OH | B
U of Minnesota, Crookston, MN | B
U of Wisconsin–Madison, WI | B

Fashion/Apparel Design
Coll of St. Catherine, MN | B
Columbia Coll Chicago, IL | B

Columbus Coll of Art & Design, OH | B
Dominican U, IL | B
The Illinois Inst of Art, IL | A,B
Indiana U Bloomington, IN | A,B
International Academy of Design & Technology, IL | A,B
Iowa State U of Science and Technology, IA | B
Kent State U, OH | B
Lindenwood U, MO | B
Michigan State U, MI | B
Minnesota State U Mankato, MN | B
Mount Mary Coll, WI | B
Oklahoma State U, OK | B
School of the Art Inst of Chicago, IL | B
Stephens Coll, MO | B
U of Cincinnati, OH | B
Ursuline Coll, OH | B
Washington U in St. Louis, MO | B

Fashion Merchandising
Ashland U, OH | B
Ball State U, IN | B
Bowling Green State U, OH | B
Central Michigan U, MI | B
Coll of St. Catherine, MN | B
Dominican U, IL | B
East Central U, OK | B
Eastern Michigan U, MI | B
Fontbonne U, MO | B
The Illinois Inst of Art, IL | B
Indiana U Bloomington, IN | B
International Academy of Design & Technology, IL | A,B
Kent State U, OH | B
Lincoln U, MO | B
Lindenwood U, MO | B
Mount Mary Coll, WI | B
Northeastern State U, OK | B
Northwood U, MI | A,B
Oklahoma State U, OK | B
Olivet Nazarene U, IL | B
Pittsburg State U, KS | B
Rochester Comm and Tech Coll, MN | A
South Dakota State U, SD | B
Stephens Coll, MO | B
The U of Akron, OH | A,B
U of Central Oklahoma, OK | B
U of Illinois at Urbana–Champaign, IL | B
U of Wisconsin–Madison, WI | B
Ursuline Coll, OH | B
Wayne State Coll, NE | B
Youngstown State U, OH | B

Fiber, Textile and Weaving Arts
Bowling Green State U, OH | B
The Cleveland Inst of Art, OH | B
Coll for Creative Studies, MI | B
Kansas City Art Inst, MO | B
Northern Michigan U, MI | B
School of the Art Inst of Chicago, IL | B
U of Kansas, KS | B
U of Michigan, MI | B
U of Wisconsin–Milwaukee, WI | B

Film/Cinema Studies

Bowling Green State U, OH	B
Calvin Coll, MI	B
Columbia Coll Chicago, IL	B
Denison U, OH	B
Grand Valley State U, MI	B
Indiana U South Bend, IN	A
Northern Michigan U, MI	B
Northwestern U, IL	B
Oakland U, MI	B
Ohio U, OH	B
Olivet Nazarene U, IL	B
St. Cloud State U, MN	B
School of the Art Inst of Chicago, IL	B
U of Chicago, IL	B
The U of Iowa, IA	B
U of Michigan, MI	B
U of Minnesota, Twin Cities Campus, MN	B
U of Nebraska–Lincoln, NE	B
U of Toledo, OH	B
U of Tulsa, OK	B
U of Wisconsin–Milwaukee, WI	B
Washington U in St. Louis, MO	B
Wayne State U, MI	B
Webster U, MO	B
Wright State U, OH	B

Film/Video and Photographic Arts Related

Coll for Creative Studies, MI	B
Haskell Indian Nations U, KS	A
School of the Art Inst of Chicago, IL	B
The U of Iowa, IA	B

Finance

Academy Coll, MN	A
AIB Coll of Business, IA	A
Ashland U, OH	B
Augsburg Coll, MN	B
Augustana Coll, IL	B
Aurora U, IL	B
Avila U, MO	B
Bacone Coll, OK	B
Ball State U, IN	B
Benedictine U, IL	B
Bowling Green State U, OH	B
Bradley U, IL	B
Brescia U, KY	B
Butler U, IN	B
Capital U, OH	B
Carroll Coll, WI	B
Cedarville U, OH	B
Central Christian Coll of Kansas, KS	A
Central Michigan U, MI	B
Central Missouri State U, MO	B
Central State U, OH	B
Chicago State U, IL	B
Clarkson U	B
Cleary U, MI	B
Cleveland State U, OH	B
Colorado Tech U Sioux Falls Campus, SD	B
Columbia Coll, MO	B
Concordia U, St. Paul, MN	B
Creighton U, NE	B
Culver-Stockton Coll, MO	B
Dakota State U, SD	B
Dakota Wesleyan U, SD	B

Davenport U, Dearborn, MI	A,B
Davenport U, Grand Rapids, MI	A,B
Davenport U, Warren, MI	A,B
Defiance Coll, OH	B
DePaul U, IL	B
Dickinson State U, ND	B
Drake U, IA	B
East Central U, OK	B
Eastern Illinois U, IL	B
Eastern Michigan U, MI	B
Elmhurst Coll, IL	B
Eureka Coll, IL	B
Ferris State U, MI	B
Florida Gulf Coast U, FL	B
Fontbonne U, MO	B
Fort Hays State U, KS	B
Franklin U, OH	B
Gannon U, PA	B
Governors State U, IL	B
Grand Valley State U, MI	B
Hillsdale Coll, MI	B
Illinois Coll, IL	B
Illinois State U, IL	B
Indiana State U, IN	B
Indiana U Bloomington, IN	B
Indiana U–Purdue U Fort Wayne, IN	B
Indiana U South Bend, IN	A
Iowa State U of Science and Technology, IA	B
John Carroll U, OH	B
Kansas State U, KS	B
Kent State U, OH	B
Kettering U, MI	B
Lake Forest Coll, IL	B
Lake Superior State U, MI	B
Lehigh U, PA	B
Lewis U, IL	B
Lindenwood U, MO	B
Loras Coll, IA	B
Loyola U Chicago, IL	B
MacMurray Coll, IL	B
Manchester Coll, IN	B
Marian Coll, IN	A,B
Marian Coll of Fond du Lac, WI	B
Marquette U, WI	B
McKendree Coll, IL	B
McPherson Coll, KS	B
Metropolitan State U, MN	B
Miami U, OH	B
Miami U Hamilton, OH	B
Michigan State U, MI	B
Michigan Technological U, MI	B
Millikin U, IL	B
Minnesota State U Mankato, MN	B
Minnesota State U Moorhead, MN	B
Minot State U, ND	B
Missouri Southern State U, MO	B
Missouri Western State Coll, MO	B
North Central Coll, IL	B
Northeastern Illinois U, IL	B
Northeastern State U, OK	B
Northern Illinois U, IL	B
Northern Michigan U, MI	B
Northern State U, SD	B
North Park U, IL	B
Northwestern Coll, MN	B
Oakland U, MI	B

Ohio Dominican U, OH	B
The Ohio State U, OH	B
Ohio U, OH	B
Oklahoma Baptist U, OK	B
Oklahoma City U, OK	B
Oklahoma State U, OK	B
Olivet Coll, MI	B
Olivet Nazarene U, IL	B
Oral Roberts U, OK	B
Otterbein Coll, OH	B
Pittsburg State U, KS	B
Quincy U, IL	B
Rockford Coll, IL	B
Rockhurst U, MO	B
Roosevelt U, IL	B
Saginaw Valley State U, MI	B
St. Ambrose U, IA	B
St. Cloud State U, MN	B
Saint Louis U, MO	B
Saint Mary's Coll, IN	B
Southeastern Oklahoma State U, OK	B
Southeast Missouri State U, MO	B
Southern Illinois U Carbondale, IL	B
Southern Nazarene U, OK	B
Southwestern Oklahoma State U, OK	B
Southwest Missouri State U, MO	B
Taylor U, IN	B
Tiffin U, OH	B
Trinity Bible Coll, ND	B
Truman State U, MO	B
The U of Akron, OH	B
The U of Alabama in Huntsville, AL	B
U of Central Oklahoma, OK	B
U of Cincinnati, OH	A,B
U of Dayton, OH	B
U of Detroit Mercy, MI	B
U of Evansville, IN	B
U of Illinois at Chicago, IL	B
U of Illinois at Urbana–Champaign, IL	B
The U of Iowa, IA	B
U of Michigan–Dearborn, MI	B
U of Michigan–Flint, MI	B
U of Minnesota, Duluth, MN	B
U of Minnesota, Twin Cities Campus, MN	B
U of Missouri–Columbia, MO	B
U of Missouri–St. Louis, MO	B
U of Nebraska at Omaha, NE	B
U of Nebraska–Lincoln, NE	B
U of New Orleans, LA	B
U of North Dakota, ND	B
U of Northern Iowa, IA	B
U of Notre Dame, IN	B
U of Oklahoma, OK	B
U of St. Francis, IL	B
U of Saint Francis, IN	B
U of St. Thomas, MN	B
The U of South Dakota, SD	B
U of Southern Indiana, IN	B
U of Toledo, OH	B
U of Tulsa, OK	B
U of West Florida, FL	B
U of Wisconsin–Eau Claire, WI	B
U of Wisconsin–La Crosse, WI	B

U of Wisconsin–Madison, WI	B
U of Wisconsin–Milwaukee, WI	B
U of Wisconsin–Oshkosh, WI	B
U of Wisconsin–Parkside, WI	B
U of Wisconsin–River Falls, WI	B
U of Wisconsin–Whitewater, WI	B
Valparaiso U, IN	B
Waldorf Coll, IA	B
Walsh Coll of Accountancy and Business Administration, MI	B
Walsh U, OH	A,B
Wartburg Coll, IA	B
Washburn U, KS	B
Washington U in St. Louis, MO	B
Wayne State Coll, NE	B
Wayne State U, MI	B
Western Illinois U, IL	B
Western Michigan U, MI	B
Wichita State U, KS	B
Wilberforce U, OH	B
Winona State U, MN	B
Wright State U, OH	B
Xavier U, OH	B
Youngstown State U, OH	A,B

Finance and Financial Management Services Related

Grace Bible Coll, MI	B
Park U, MO	B
The U of Akron, OH	B

Financial Planning and Services

Bethany Coll, KS	B
Central Michigan U, MI	B
Jamestown Coll, ND	B
The Ohio State U at Lima, OH	B
Trinity Christian Coll, IL	B

Fine Arts Related

Ancilla Coll, IN	A
Bowling Green State U, OH	B
Coll for Creative Studies, MI	B
Indiana State U, IN	B
Lehigh U, PA	B
Loyola U Chicago, IL	B
Madonna U, MI	B
Mount Vernon Nazarene U, OH	B
School of the Art Inst of Chicago, IL	B
The U of Akron, OH	B
U of Saint Francis, IN	B
U of Science and Arts of Oklahoma, OK	B

Fine/Studio Arts

Alma Coll, MI	B
American Academy of Art, IL	B
Aquinas Coll, MI	B
Art Academy of Cincinnati, OH	B
Ashland U, OH	B
Augsburg Coll, MN	B
Augustana Coll, IL	B
Baker U, KS	B
Baldwin-Wallace Coll, OH	B
Ball State U, IN	B

A—associate degree; B—bachelor's degree

Beloit Coll, WI — B
Bemidji State U, MN — B
Benedictine U, IL — B
Bethel Coll, KS — B
Bowling Green State U, OH — B
Bradley U, IL — B
Calvin Coll, MI — B
Capital U, OH — B
Cardinal Stritch U, WI — B
Carleton Coll, MN — B
Carroll Coll, WI — B
Carthage Coll, WI — B
Central Missouri State U, MO — B
Chicago State U, IL — B
Clarke Coll, IA — B
Coe Coll, IA — B
Coll for Creative Studies, MI — B
Coll of Mount St. Joseph, OH — B
Coll of Saint Benedict, MN — B
Coll of St. Catherine, MN — B
Coll of the Ozarks, MO — B
The Coll of Wooster, OH — B
Columbia Coll Chicago, IL — B
Columbus Coll of Art & Design, OH — B
Concordia Coll, MN — B
Concordia U, NE — B
Concordia U, St. Paul, MN — B
Cumberland Coll, KY — B
Denison U, OH — B
DePaul U, IL — B
DePauw U, IN — B
Dominican U, IL — B
Drake U, IA — B
Drury U, MO — B
Eastern Michigan U, MI — B
Ferris State U, MI — B
Fontbonne U, MO — B
Governors State U, IL — B
Graceland U, IA — B
Grand Valley State U, MI — B
Grand View Coll, IA — B
Hamline U, MN — B
Hiram Coll, OH — B
Hope Coll, MI — B
Illinois State U, IL — B
Indiana U Bloomington, IN — B
Indiana U–Purdue U Fort Wayne, IN — B
Indiana U–Purdue U Indianapolis, IN — B
Indiana U South Bend, IN — B
Indiana U Southeast, IN — B
Iowa Wesleyan Coll, IA — B
Jamestown Coll, ND — B
Judson Coll, IL — B
Kent State U, OH — B
Kenyon Coll, OH — B
Lake Erie Coll, OH — B
Lake Forest Coll, IL — B
Lawrence U, WI — B
Lewis U, IL — B
Lincoln Coll, Lincoln, IL — A
Lindenwood U, MO — B
Loras Coll, IA — B
Macalester Coll, MN — B
MacMurray Coll, IL — B
Maharishi U of Management, IA — B
Malone Coll, OH — B
Manchester Coll, IN — A,B
Marian Coll, IN — B
Marian Coll of Fond du Lac, WI — B

Marietta Coll, OH — B
Martin U, IN — B
Marygrove Coll, MI — B
Maryville U of Saint Louis, MO — B
Miami U, OH — B
Millikin U, IL — B
Minneapolis Coll of Art and Design, MN — B
Minnesota State U Mankato, MN — B
Minnesota State U Moorhead, MN — B
Morningside Coll, IA — B
Northeastern State U, OK — B
Northern Illinois U, IL — B
Northern Michigan U, MI — B
Northland Coll, WI — B
North Park U, IL — B
Northwestern Coll, MN — B
Notre Dame Coll, OH — B
Oakland U, MI — B
Oberlin Coll, OH — B
Ohio Dominican U, OH — B
Ohio Northern U, OH — B
The Ohio State U, OH — B
Ohio U, OH — B
Ohio Wesleyan U, OH — B
Oklahoma Baptist U, OK — B
Oklahoma City U, OK — B
Oklahoma State U, OK — B
Olivet Coll, MI — B
Oral Roberts U, OK — B
Park U, MO — B
Pittsburg State U, KS — B
Principia Coll, IL — B
Rockford Coll, IL — B
Saginaw Valley State U, MI — B
St. Ambrose U, IA — B
St. Cloud State U, MN — B
St. Gregory's U, OK — A,B
Saint John's U, MN — B
Saint Joseph's Coll, IN — B
Saint Louis U, MO — B
Saint Mary-of-the-Woods Coll, IN — B
Saint Mary's U of Minnesota, MN — B
School of the Art Inst of Chicago, IL — B
Shawnee State U, OH — B
Southern Illinois U Carbondale, IL — B
Southern Illinois U Edwardsville, IL — B
Southwest Missouri State U, MO — B
Transylvania U, KY — B
Truman State U, MO — B
Union Coll, NE — B
The U of Akron, OH — B
U of Chicago, IL — B
U of Dayton, OH — B
U of Illinois at Chicago, IL — B
U of Indianapolis, IN — B
The U of Iowa, IA — B
U of Kansas, KS — B
U of Michigan–Flint, MI — B
U of Minnesota, Duluth, MN — B
U of Minnesota, Morris, MN — B
U of Missouri–Kansas City, MO — B
U of Missouri–St. Louis, MO — B
U of Nebraska at Omaha, NE — B
U of Nebraska–Lincoln, NE — B

U of New Orleans, LA — B
U of Northern Iowa, IA — B
U of Notre Dame, IN — B
U of Oklahoma, OK — B
U of Toledo, OH — B
U of Tulsa, OK — B
U of West Florida, FL — B
U of Wisconsin–Milwaukee, WI — B
U of Wisconsin–Oshkosh, WI — B
U of Wisconsin–Stevens Point, WI — B
U of Wisconsin–Superior, WI — B
Ursuline Coll, OH — B
Valparaiso U, IN — B
Viterbo U, WI — B
Washburn U, KS — B
Washington U in St. Louis, MO — B
Webster U, MO — B
Western Illinois U, IL — B
Wilberforce U, OH — B
William Woods U, MO — B
Winona State U, MN — B
Xavier U, OH — B
Youngstown State U, OH — B

Fire Protection and Safety Technology
Oklahoma State U, OK — B
The U of Akron, OH — A
U of Cincinnati, OH — A
U of Nebraska–Lincoln, NE — A
U of Toledo, OH — A

Fire Protection Related
The U of Akron, OH — B

Fire Science
Lake Superior State U, MI — A,B
Madonna U, MI — A,B
U of Cincinnati, OH — A

Fire Services Administration
Southern Illinois U Carbondale, IL — B

Fish/Game Management
Iowa State U of Science and Technology, IA — B
Lake Superior State U, MI — B
Northland Coll, WI — B
Pittsburg State U, KS — B
South Dakota State U, SD — B
Southeastern Oklahoma State U, OK — B
U of Minnesota, Duluth, MN — B
U of Minnesota, Twin Cities Campus, MN — B
U of Missouri–Columbia, MO — B
Winona State U, MN — A

Fishing and Fisheries Sciences and Management
The Ohio State U, OH — B
U of Missouri–Columbia, MO — B

Folklore
Indiana U Bloomington, IN — B
The Ohio State U, OH — B

Food Preparation
Lexington Coll, IL — A,B

Foods and Nutrition Related
Kent State U, OH — B
U of Wisconsin–Stout, WI — B

Food Science
Dominican U, IL — B
Kansas State U, KS — B
Michigan State U, MI — B
North Carolina Ag and Tech State U, NC — B
North Dakota State U, ND — B
The Ohio State U, OH — B
Olivet Nazarene U, IL — B
Purdue U, IN — B
South Dakota State U, SD — B
The U of Akron, OH — B
U of Illinois at Urbana–Champaign, IL — B
U of Missouri–Columbia, MO — B
U of Nebraska–Lincoln, NE — B
U of Wisconsin–Madison, WI — B
U of Wisconsin–River Falls, WI — B

Food Service and Dining Room Management
Lexington Coll, IL — A,B

Food Services Technology
Iowa State U of Science and Technology, IA — B
Madonna U, MI — B
Purdue U Calumet, IN — A

Foodservice Systems Administration
Central Michigan U, MI — B
Dominican U, IL — B
North Dakota State Coll of Science, ND — A
U of Wisconsin–Stout, WI — B
Western Michigan U, MI — B

Foods, Nutrition, and Wellness
Andrews U, MI — B
Ashland U, OH — B
Bluffton Coll, OH — B
Bowling Green State U, OH — B
Coll of Saint Benedict, MN — B
Coll of St. Catherine, MN — B
Coll of the Ozarks, MO — B
Concordia Coll, MN — B
Dominican U, IL — B
Eastern Michigan U, MI — B
Indiana State U, IN — B
Indiana U Bloomington, IN — B
Iowa State U of Science and Technology, IA — B
Kansas State U, KS — B
Kent State U, OH — B
Lincoln Coll, Lincoln, IL — A
Loyola U Chicago, IL — B
Madonna U, MI — A,B
Minnesota State U Mankato, MN — B
Mount Marty Coll, SD — B
North Carolina Ag and Tech State U, NC — B
Northeastern State U, OK — B
Northern Illinois U, IL — B
The Ohio State U, OH — B
Ohio U, OH — B
Oklahoma State U, OK — B
Purdue U, IN — B
Saint John's U, MN — B
Saint Louis U, MO — B
South Dakota State U, SD — B
Southern Illinois U Carbondale, IL — B
The U of Akron, OH — B

U of Central Oklahoma, OK   B
U of Cincinnati, OH   B
U of Dayton, OH   B
U of Michigan, MI   B
U of Minnesota, Twin Cities Campus, MN   B
U of Missouri–Columbia, MO   B
U of Nebraska–Lincoln, NE   B
U of Northern Iowa, IA   B
U of Wisconsin–Madison, WI   B
Wayne State U, MI   B
Youngstown State U, OH   B

Foreign Languages and Literatures
Augustana Coll, SD   B
Cameron U, OK   B
Central Methodist Coll, MO   B
Eastern Illinois U, IL   B
Emporia State U, KS   B
Gannon U, PA   B
Graceland U, IA   B
Greenville Coll, IL   B
Hastings Coll, NE   B
Indiana State U, IN   B
Kansas State U, KS   B
Kenyon Coll, OH   B
Knox Coll, IL   B
Marian Coll of Fond du Lac, WI   B
Millikin U, IL   B
Minnesota State U Moorhead, MN   B
Oakland U, MI   B
Principia Coll, IL   B
Purdue U, IN   B
Roosevelt U, IL   B
Saint Louis U, MO   B
Saint Mary's U of Minnesota, MN   B
Southern Illinois U Edwardsville, IL   B
The U of Alabama in Huntsville, AL   B
U of North Dakota, ND   B
U of Northern Iowa, IA   B
Wayne State U, MI   B
Wright State U, OH   B
Youngstown State U, OH   B

Foreign Languages Related
Marquette U, WI   B
Oakland U, MI   B
Southern Illinois U Carbondale, IL   B
U of Michigan–Flint, MI   B
U of Northern Iowa, IA   B
U of St. Thomas, MN   B

Foreign Language Teacher Education
Bowling Green State U, OH   B
Carroll Coll, WI   B
Central Methodist Coll, MO   B
Dana Coll, NE   B
Gannon U, PA   B
Hastings Coll, NE   B
Kent State U, OH   B
Marquette U, WI   B
Ohio Dominican U, OH   B
Ohio Northern U, OH   B
Ohio Wesleyan U, OH   B
Southeast Missouri State U, MO   B

Southern Nazarene U, OK   B
The U of Akron, OH   B
U of Illinois at Chicago, IL   B
U of Illinois at Urbana–Champaign, IL   B
U of Minnesota, Twin Cities Campus, MN   B
U of Nebraska–Lincoln, NE   B
U of New Orleans, LA   B
U of Northern Iowa, IA   B
U of Oklahoma, OK   B
U of St. Thomas, MN   B
The U of South Dakota, SD   B
U of West Florida, FL   B
Valparaiso U, IN   B
Western Michigan U, MI   B
Wright State U, OH   B
Youngstown State U, OH   B

Forensic Psychology
St. Ambrose U, IA   B
Tiffin U, OH   B

Forensic Science and Technology
Carroll Coll, WI   B
Coll of the Ozarks, MO   B
Columbia Coll, MO   B
Indiana U Bloomington, IN   B
Tri-State U, IN   B
U of Central Oklahoma, OK   B
U of North Dakota, ND   B

Forest/Forest Resources Management
U of Minnesota, Twin Cities Campus, MN   B

Forestry
Coll of Saint Benedict, MN   B
Iowa State U of Science and Technology, IA   B
Michigan State U, MI   B
Michigan Technological U, MI   B
Northland Coll, WI   B
The Ohio State U, OH   B
Oklahoma State U, OK   B
Purdue U, IN   B
Saint John's U, MN   B
Southern Illinois U Carbondale, IL   B
U of Illinois at Urbana–Champaign, IL   B
U of Minnesota, Twin Cities Campus, MN   B
U of Missouri–Columbia, MO   B
U of Wisconsin–Madison, WI   B
U of Wisconsin–Milwaukee, WI   B
U of Wisconsin–Stevens Point, WI   B
Winona State U, MN   A

Forestry Technology
Michigan Technological U, MI   A

French
Adrian Coll, MI   A,B
Albion Coll, MI   B
Alma Coll, MI   B
Andrews U, MI   B
Antioch Coll, OH   B
Aquinas Coll, MI   B

Ashland U, OH   B
Augsburg Coll, MN   B
Augustana Coll, IL   B
Augustana Coll, SD   B
Baker U, KS   B
Baldwin-Wallace Coll, OH   B
Ball State U, IN   B
Beloit Coll, WI   B
Benedictine Coll, KS   B
Bethel U, MN   B
Bowling Green State U, OH   B
Bradley U, IL   B
Butler U, IN   B
Calvin Coll, MI   B
Capital U, OH   B
Cardinal Stritch U, WI   B
Carleton Coll, MN   B
Carthage Coll, WI   B
Case Western Reserve U, OH   B
Central Coll, IA   B
Central Methodist Coll, MO   B
Central Michigan U, MI   B
Central Missouri State U, MO   B
Clarke Coll, IA   B
Cleveland State U, OH   B
Coe Coll, IA   B
Coll of Saint Benedict, MN   B
Coll of St. Catherine, MN   B
Coll of the Ozarks, MO   B
The Coll of Wooster, OH   B
Concordia Coll, MN   B
Cornell Coll, IA   B
Creighton U, NE   B
Denison U, OH   B
DePaul U, IL   B
DePauw U, IN   B
Doane Coll, NE   B
Dominican U, IL   B
Drury U, MO   B
Earlham Coll, IN   B
Eastern Michigan U, MI   B
Edgewood Coll, WI   B
Elmhurst Coll, IL   B
Fort Hays State U, KS   B
Franciscan U of Steubenville, OH   B
Franklin Coll, IN   B
Grace Coll, IN   B
Grand Valley State U, MI   B
Greenville Coll, IL   B
Grinnell Coll, IA   B
Gustavus Adolphus Coll, MN   B
Hamline U, MN   B
Hanover Coll, IN   B
Hillsdale Coll, MI   B
Hiram Coll, OH   B
Hope Coll, MI   B
Illinois Coll, IL   B
Illinois State U, IL   B
Illinois Wesleyan U, IL   B
Indiana State U, IN   B
Indiana U Bloomington, IN   B
Indiana U Northwest, IN   B
Indiana U–Purdue U Fort Wayne, IN   A,B
Indiana U–Purdue U Indianapolis, IN   B
Indiana U South Bend, IN   B
Indiana U Southeast, IN   B
Iowa State U of Science and Technology, IA   B
John Carroll U, OH   B
Kalamazoo Coll, MI   B

Kent State U, OH   B
Kenyon Coll, OH   B
Knox Coll, IL   B
Lake Erie Coll, OH   B
Lake Forest Coll, IL   B
Lawrence U, WI   B
Lehigh U, PA   B
Lincoln U, MO   B
Lindenwood U, MO   B
Loras Coll, IA   B
Loyola U Chicago, IL   B
Luther Coll, IA   B
Macalester Coll, MN   B
Madonna U, MI   B
Manchester Coll, IN   B
Marian Coll, IN   B
Marquette U, WI   B
Miami U, OH   B
Miami U Hamilton, OH   B
Michigan State U, MI   B
Millikin U, IL   B
Minnesota State U Mankato, MN   B
Minot State U, ND   B
Missouri Southern State U, MO   B
Missouri Western State Coll, MO   B
Monmouth Coll, IL   B
Mount Mary Coll, WI   B
Mount Union Coll, OH   B
Muskingum Coll, OH   B
Nebraska Wesleyan U, NE   B
North Carolina Ag and Tech State U, NC   B
North Central Coll, IL   B
North Dakota State U, ND   B
Northeastern Illinois U, IL   B
Northern Illinois U, IL   B
Northern Michigan U, MI   B
Northern State U, SD   B
North Park U, IL   B
Northwestern U, IL   B
Oakland U, MI   B
Oberlin Coll, OH   B
Ohio Northern U, OH   B
The Ohio State U, OH   B
Ohio U, OH   B
Ohio Wesleyan U, OH   B
Oklahoma Baptist U, OK   B
Oklahoma City U, OK   B
Oklahoma State U, OK   B
Oral Roberts U, OK   B
Otterbein Coll, OH   B
Pittsburg State U, KS   B
Principia Coll, IL   B
Purdue U Calumet, IN   B
Ripon Coll, WI   B
Rockford Coll, IL   B
Rockhurst U, MO   B
Roosevelt U, IL   B
Saginaw Valley State U, MI   B
St. Ambrose U, IA   B
St. Cloud State U, MN   B
Saint John's U, MN   B
Saint Louis U, MO   B
Saint Mary-of-the-Woods Coll, IN   B
Saint Mary's Coll, IN   B
Saint Mary's U of Minnesota, MN   B
St. Norbert Coll, WI   B
St. Olaf Coll, MN   B
Simpson Coll, IA   B
South Dakota State U, SD   B

College	Degree
Southeast Missouri State U, MO	B
Southern Illinois U Carbondale, IL	B
Southwest Missouri State U, MO	B
Taylor U, IN	B
Transylvania U, KY	B
Truman State U, MO	B
Union Coll, NE	B
The U of Akron, OH	B
U of Central Oklahoma, OK	B
U of Chicago, IL	B
U of Cincinnati, OH	B
U of Dayton, OH	B
U of Evansville, IN	B
U of Illinois at Chicago, IL	B
U of Illinois at Urbana–Champaign, IL	B
U of Indianapolis, IN	B
The U of Iowa, IA	B
U of Kansas, KS	B
U of Michigan, MI	B
U of Michigan–Dearborn, MI	B
U of Michigan–Flint, MI	B
U of Minnesota, Morris, MN	B
U of Minnesota, Twin Cities Campus, MN	B
U of Missouri–Columbia, MO	B
U of Missouri–Kansas City, MO	B
U of Missouri–St. Louis, MO	B
U of Nebraska at Omaha, NE	B
U of Nebraska–Lincoln, NE	B
U of New Orleans, LA	B
U of North Dakota, ND	B
U of Northern Iowa, IA	B
U of Notre Dame, IN	B
U of Oklahoma, OK	B
U of St. Thomas, MN	B
The U of South Dakota, SD	B
U of Southern Indiana, IN	B
U of Toledo, OH	B
U of Tulsa, OK	B
U of Wisconsin–Eau Claire, WI	B
U of Wisconsin–Green Bay, WI	A,B
U of Wisconsin–La Crosse, WI	B
U of Wisconsin–Madison, WI	B
U of Wisconsin–Milwaukee, WI	B
U of Wisconsin–Oshkosh, WI	B
U of Wisconsin–Parkside, WI	B
U of Wisconsin–Platteville, WI	B
U of Wisconsin–River Falls, WI	B
U of Wisconsin–Stevens Point, WI	B
U of Wisconsin–Whitewater, WI	B
Valparaiso U, IN	B
Wabash Coll, IN	B
Walsh U, OH	B
Wartburg Coll, IA	B
Washburn U, KS	B
Washington U in St. Louis, MO	B
Wayne State Coll, NE	B
Wayne State U, MI	B
Webster U, MO	B
Western Illinois U, IL	B
Western Michigan U, MI	B
Westminster Coll, MO	B
Wheaton Coll, IL	B
Wichita State U, KS	B
William Jewell Coll, MO	B
Winona State U, MN	B
Wittenberg U, OH	B
Wright State U, OH	B
Xavier U, OH	A,B
Youngstown State U, OH	B

French as a Second/Foreign Language (Teaching)

College	Degree
Western Michigan U, MI	B

French Language Teacher Education

College	Degree
Alma Coll, MI	B
Bethel U, MN	B
Carroll Coll, WI	B
Central Michigan U, MI	B
Central Missouri State U, MO	B
Coll of St. Catherine, MN	B
Coll of the Ozarks, MO	B
Concordia Coll, MN	B
Eastern Michigan U, MI	B
Elmhurst Coll, IL	B
Franklin Coll, IN	B
Grace Coll, IN	B
Hope Coll, MI	B
Illinois Wesleyan U, IL	B
Indiana U Bloomington, IN	B
Indiana U Northwest, IN	B
Indiana U–Purdue U Fort Wayne, IN	B
Indiana U–Purdue U Indianapolis, IN	B
Indiana U South Bend, IN	B
Kent State U, OH	B
Lindenwood U, MO	B
Miami U Hamilton, OH	B
Minot State U, ND	B
Missouri Western State Coll, MO	B
North Dakota State U, ND	B
Northern Michigan U, MI	B
Ohio Northern U, OH	B
Ohio U, OH	B
Ohio Wesleyan U, OH	B
Oklahoma Baptist U, OK	B
Oral Roberts U, OK	B
St. Ambrose U, IA	B
Saint Mary's U of Minnesota, MN	B
Southwest Missouri State U, MO	B
The U of Akron, OH	B
U of Illinois at Chicago, IL	B
U of Illinois at Urbana–Champaign, IL	B
U of Indianapolis, IN	B
The U of Iowa, IA	B
U of Michigan–Flint, MI	B
U of Minnesota, Duluth, MN	B
U of Missouri–St. Louis, MO	B
U of Nebraska–Lincoln, NE	B
The U of South Dakota, SD	B
U of Toledo, OH	B
U of Wisconsin–River Falls, WI	B
Valparaiso U, IN	B
Washington U in St. Louis, MO	B
Western Michigan U, MI	B
William Woods U, MO	B
Youngstown State U, OH	B

French Studies

College	Degree
Carleton Coll, MN	B
Case Western Reserve U, OH	B
Coe Coll, IA	B

Funeral Service and Mortuary Science

College	Degree
Cincinnati Coll of Mortuary Science, OH	A,B
Eastern Michigan U, MI	B
Gannon U, PA	B
Lindenwood U, MO	B
Southern Illinois U Carbondale, IL	B
U of Central Oklahoma, OK	B
U of Minnesota, Twin Cities Campus, MN	B
Wayne State U, MI	B
Worsham Coll of Mortuary Science, IL	A

Furniture Design and Manufacturing

College	Degree
Ferris State U, MI	B

General Studies

College	Degree
Alverno Coll, WI	B
Avila U, MO	A,B
Bacone Coll, OK	A
Black Hills State U, SD	A
Calumet Coll of Saint Joseph, IN	A,B
Cameron U, OK	A
Central Christian Coll of Kansas, KS	B
Central Coll, IA	B
Cleveland State U, OH	B
Coll of Saint Mary, NE	A,B
Concordia U, MI	A
Concordia U, St. Paul, MN	A,B
Concordia U Wisconsin, WI	B
Crown Coll, MN	A,B
Cumberland Coll, KY	B
DePaul U, IL	B
Dordt Coll, IA	B
East Central U, OK	B
Emporia State U, KS	B
Florida Gulf Coast U, FL	B
The Franciscan U, IA	B
Franciscan U of Steubenville, OH	A
God's Bible School and Coll, OH	B
Hillsdale Free Will Baptist Coll, OK	A
Indiana State U, IN	A,B
Indiana U Bloomington, IN	A,B
Indiana U East, IN	A,B
Indiana U Kokomo, IN	A,B
Indiana U Northwest, IN	A,B
Indiana U–Purdue U Fort Wayne, IN	A,B
Indiana U–Purdue U Indianapolis, IN	A,B
Indiana U South Bend, IN	A,B
Indiana U Southeast, IN	A,B
Kent State U, OH	B
Kettering Coll of Medical Arts, OH	A
Lawrence Technological U, MI	A
Madonna U, MI	B
Marygrove Coll, MI	B
Mayville State U, ND	B
Mercy Coll of Northwest Ohio, OH	A
Messenger Coll, MO	A
Metropolitan State U, MN	B
Miami U Hamilton, OH	A
Michigan Technological U, MI	B
Minot State U, ND	B
Mount Marty Coll, SD	A,B
Mount Vernon Nazarene U, OH	B
Northwestern U, IL	B
Oakland City U, IN	A,B
Ohio Dominican U, OH	A,B
Ohio Northern U, OH	B
Ohio U, OH	B
Ohio Wesleyan U, OH	B
Oklahoma Panhandle State U, OK	A
Pittsburg State U, KS	B
Rochester Comm and Tech Coll, MN	A
Saginaw Valley State U, MI	B
St. Augustine Coll, IL	A
Shawnee State U, OH	A,B
Shimer Coll, IL	B
Siena Heights U, MI	A,B
Silver Lake Coll, WI	A
South Dakota School of Mines and Technology, SD	A
Southeastern Oklahoma State U, OK	B
Southeast Missouri State U, MO	B
Southern Nazarene U, OK	B
Southwest Baptist U, MO	A
Southwestern Coll, KS	B
U of Dayton, OH	B
U of Mary, ND	B
U of Michigan, MI	B
U of Missouri–Columbia, MO	B
U of Missouri–St. Louis, MO	B
U of Nebraska at Omaha, NE	B
U of New Orleans, LA	B
U of Rio Grande, OH	A
The U of South Dakota, SD	A
U of Toledo, OH	A,B
U of Wisconsin–Green Bay, WI	B
U of Wisconsin–Stevens Point, WI	B
Vennard Coll, IA	A
Western Michigan U, MI	B
York Coll, NE	B

Genetics

College	Degree
Iowa State U of Science and Technology, IA	B
Ohio Wesleyan U, OH	B

Geochemistry

College	Degree
Western Michigan U, MI	

Geography

College	Degree
Aquinas Coll, MI	B
Augustana Coll, IL	B
Ball State U, IN	B
Bemidji State U, MN	B
Bowling Green State U, OH	B
Calvin Coll, MI	B
Carroll Coll, WI	B
Carthage Coll, WI	B
Central Michigan U, MI	B
Central Missouri State U, MO	B
Chicago State U, IL	B

Majors and Degrees

Geography

Concordia U, IL	B
Concordia U, NE	B
Concord U, WV	B
DePaul U, IL	B
Dickinson State U, ND	B
Eastern Illinois U, IL	B
Eastern Michigan U, MI	B
Elmhurst Coll, IL	B
Gustavus Adolphus Coll, MN	B
Illinois State U, IL	B
Indiana State U, IN	B
Indiana U Bloomington, IN	B
Indiana U–Purdue U Indianapolis, IN	B
Indiana U Southeast, IN	B
Kansas State U, KS	B
Kent State U, OH	B
Lincoln Coll, Lincoln, IL	A
Macalester Coll, MN	B
Miami U, OH	B
Miami U Hamilton, OH	B
Michigan State U, MI	B
Minnesota State U Mankato, MN	B
Northeastern Illinois U, IL	B
Northeastern State U, OK	B
Northern Illinois U, IL	B
Northern Michigan U, MI	B
Northwestern U, IL	B
The Ohio State U, OH	B
Ohio U, OH	B
Ohio Wesleyan U, OH	B
Oklahoma State U, OK	B
Pittsburg State U, KS	B
Roosevelt U, IL	B
St. Cloud State U, MN	B
South Dakota State U, SD	B
Southeast Missouri State U, MO	B
Southern Illinois U Carbondale, IL	B
Southern Illinois U Edwardsville, IL	B
Southwest Missouri State U, MO	B
The U of Akron, OH	B
U of Central Oklahoma, OK	B
U of Chicago, IL	B
U of Cincinnati, OH	B
U of Illinois at Urbana–Champaign, IL	B
The U of Iowa, IA	B
U of Kansas, KS	B
U of Michigan, MI	B
U of Michigan–Flint, MI	B
U of Minnesota, Duluth, MN	B
U of Minnesota, Twin Cities Campus, MN	B
U of Missouri–Columbia, MO	B
U of Missouri–Kansas City, MO	B
U of Nebraska at Omaha, NE	B
U of Nebraska–Lincoln, NE	B
U of New Orleans, LA	B
U of North Dakota, ND	B
U of Northern Iowa, IA	B
U of Oklahoma, OK	B
U of St. Thomas, MN	B
U of Toledo, OH	B
U of Wisconsin–Eau Claire, WI	B
U of Wisconsin–La Crosse, WI	B
U of Wisconsin–Madison, WI	B
U of Wisconsin–Milwaukee, WI	B
U of Wisconsin–Oshkosh, WI	B
U of Wisconsin–Parkside, WI	B
U of Wisconsin–Platteville, WI	B
U of Wisconsin–River Falls, WI	B
U of Wisconsin–Stevens Point, WI	B
U of Wisconsin–Whitewater, WI	B
Valparaiso U, IN	B
Wayne State Coll, NE	B
Wayne State U, MI	B
Western Illinois U, IL	B
Western Michigan U, MI	B
Wittenberg U, OH	B
Wright State U, OH	A,B
Youngstown State U, OH	B

Geography Teacher Education

Carroll Coll, WI	B
Concordia U, NE	B
Northern Michigan U, MI	B
Shawnee State U, OH	B
The U of Iowa, IA	B
Valparaiso U, IN	B
Western Michigan U, MI	B

Geological and Earth Sciences/Geosciences Related

Lehigh U, PA	B
Ohio U, OH	B
Southeast Missouri State U, MO	B
The U of Akron, OH	B
U of Northern Iowa, IA	B
U of Oklahoma, OK	B
Western Michigan U, MI	B

Geological Engineering

U of North Dakota, ND	B

Geological/Geophysical Engineering

Michigan Technological U, MI	B
South Dakota School of Mines and Technology, SD	B
The U of Akron, OH	B
U of Minnesota, Twin Cities Campus, MN	B
U of Missouri–Rolla, MO	B

Geology/Earth Science

Adrian Coll, MI	A,B
Albion Coll, MI	B
Antioch Coll, OH	B
Ashland U, OH	B
Augustana Coll, IL	B
Baldwin-Wallace Coll, OH	B
Ball State U, IN	B
Beloit Coll, WI	B
Bemidji State U, MN	B
Bowling Green State U, OH	B
Bradley U, IL	B
Calvin Coll, MI	B
Carleton Coll, MN	B
Case Western Reserve U, OH	B
Central Michigan U, MI	B
Central Missouri State U, MO	B
Cleveland State U, OH	B
The Coll of Wooster, OH	B
Cornell Coll, IA	B
Denison U, OH	B
DePauw U, IN	B
Dickinson State U, ND	B
Earlham Coll, IN	B
Eastern Illinois U, IL	B
Eastern Michigan U, MI	B
Emporia State U, KS	B
Fort Hays State U, KS	B
Grand Valley State U, MI	B
Gustavus Adolphus Coll, MN	B
Hanover Coll, IN	B
Hope Coll, MI	B
Illinois State U, IL	B
Indiana State U, IN	B
Indiana U Bloomington, IN	B
Indiana U East, IN	A
Indiana U Northwest, IN	B
Indiana U–Purdue U Fort Wayne, IN	B
Indiana U–Purdue U Indianapolis, IN	B
Iowa State U of Science and Technology, IA	B
Kansas State U, KS	B
Kent State U, OH	B
Lake Superior State U, MI	B
Lawrence U, WI	B
Lincoln Coll, Lincoln, IL	A
Macalester Coll, MN	B
Marietta Coll, OH	B
Miami U, OH	B
Miami U Hamilton, OH	B
Michigan State U, MI	B
Michigan Technological U, MI	B
Minnesota State U Mankato, MN	B
Minot State U, ND	B
Mount Union Coll, OH	B
Muskingum Coll, OH	B
North Dakota State U, ND	B
Northeastern Illinois U, IL	B
Northern Illinois U, IL	B
Northern Michigan U, MI	B
Northland Coll, WI	B
Northwestern U, IL	B
Oberlin Coll, OH	B
The Ohio State U, OH	B
Ohio U, OH	B
Ohio Wesleyan U, OH	B
Oklahoma State U, OK	B
Olivet Nazarene U, IL	B
Purdue U, IN	B
St. Cloud State U, MN	B
Saint Louis U, MO	B
St. Norbert Coll, WI	B
South Dakota School of Mines and Technology, SD	B
Southern Illinois U Carbondale, IL	B
Southwest Missouri State U, MO	B
The U of Akron, OH	B
U of Cincinnati, OH	B
U of Dayton, OH	B
U of Illinois at Chicago, IL	B
U of Illinois at Urbana–Champaign, IL	B
U of Indianapolis, IN	B
The U of Iowa, IA	B
U of Kansas, KS	B
U of Michigan, MI	B

U of Minnesota, Duluth, MN	B
U of Minnesota, Morris, MN	B
U of Minnesota, Twin Cities Campus, MN	B
U of Missouri–Columbia, MO	B
U of Missouri–Kansas City, MO	B
U of Missouri–Rolla, MO	B
U of Nebraska at Omaha, NE	B
U of Nebraska–Lincoln, NE	B
U of New Orleans, LA	B
U of North Dakota, ND	B
U of Northern Iowa, IA	B
U of Notre Dame, IN	B
U of Oklahoma, OK	B
U of St. Thomas, MN	B
The U of South Dakota, SD	B
U of Southern Indiana, IN	B
U of Toledo, OH	B
U of Tulsa, OK	B
U of Wisconsin–Eau Claire, WI	B
U of Wisconsin–Green Bay, WI	A,B
U of Wisconsin–Madison, WI	B
U of Wisconsin–Milwaukee, WI	B
U of Wisconsin–Oshkosh, WI	B
U of Wisconsin–Parkside, WI	B
U of Wisconsin–Platteville, WI	B
U of Wisconsin–River Falls, WI	B
Valparaiso U, IN	B
Washington U in St. Louis, MO	B
Wayne State U, MI	B
Western Illinois U, IL	B
Western Michigan U, MI	B
Wheaton Coll, IL	B
Wichita State U, KS	B
Winona State U, MN	B
Wittenberg U, OH	B
Wright State U, OH	B
Youngstown State U, OH	B

Geophysics and Seismology

Eastern Michigan U, MI	B
Hope Coll, MI	B
Michigan State U, MI	B
Michigan Technological U, MI	B
Saint Louis U, MO	B
The U of Akron, OH	B
U of Chicago, IL	B
U of Minnesota, Twin Cities Campus, MN	B
U of Missouri–Rolla, MO	B
U of New Orleans, LA	B
U of Oklahoma, OK	B
U of Tulsa, OK	B
U of Wisconsin–Madison, WI	B
Western Michigan U, MI	B
Wright State U, OH	B

German

Adrian Coll, MI	A,B
Albion Coll, MI	B
Alma Coll, MI	B
Antioch Coll, OH	B
Aquinas Coll, MI	B

A—associate degree; B—bachelor's degree

College	Degree
Augsburg Coll, MN	B
Augustana Coll, IL	B
Augustana Coll, SD	B
Baker U, KS	B
Baldwin-Wallace Coll, OH	B
Ball State U, IN	B
Beloit Coll, WI	B
Bemidji State U, MN	B
Bowling Green State U, OH	B
Bradley U, IL	B
Butler U, IN	B
Calvin Coll, MI	B
Carleton Coll, MN	B
Carthage Coll, WI	B
Case Western Reserve U, OH	B
Central Coll, IA	B
Central Michigan U, MI	B
Central Missouri State U, MO	B
Coe Coll, IA	B
Coll of Saint Benedict, MN	B
Coll of the Ozarks, MO	B
The Coll of Wooster, OH	B
Concordia Coll, MN	B
Concordia U Wisconsin, WI	B
Cornell Coll, IA	B
Creighton U, NE	B
Dana Coll, NE	B
Denison U, OH	B
DePaul U, IL	B
DePauw U, IN	B
Doane Coll, NE	B
Dordt Coll, IA	B
Drury U, MO	B
Earlham Coll, IN	B
Eastern Michigan U, MI	B
Elmhurst Coll, IL	B
Fort Hays State U, KS	B
Franciscan U of Steubenville, OH	B
Goshen Coll, IN	B
Grace Coll, IN	B
Graceland U, IA	B
Grand Valley State U, MI	B
Grinnell Coll, IA	B
Gustavus Adolphus Coll, MN	B
Hamline U, MN	B
Hanover Coll, IN	B
Hastings Coll, NE	B
Heidelberg Coll, OH	B
Hillsdale Coll, MI	B
Hiram Coll, OH	B
Hope Coll, MI	B
Illinois Coll, IL	B
Illinois State U, IL	B
Illinois Wesleyan U, IL	B
Indiana State U, IN	B
Indiana U Bloomington, IN	B
Indiana U–Purdue U Fort Wayne, IN	A,B
Indiana U–Purdue U Indianapolis, IN	B
Indiana U South Bend, IN	B
Indiana U Southeast, IN	B
Iowa State U of Science and Technology, IA	B
John Carroll U, OH	B
Kalamazoo Coll, MI	B
Kent State U, OH	B
Kenyon Coll, OH	B
Knox Coll, IL	B
Lake Erie Coll, OH	B
Lakeland Coll, WI	B
Lawrence U, WI	B
Lehigh U, PA	B
Loyola U Chicago, IL	B
Luther Coll, IA	B
Manchester Coll, IN	B
Marquette U, WI	B
Miami U, OH	B
Miami U Hamilton, OH	B
Michigan State U, MI	B
Millikin U, IL	B
Minnesota State U Mankato, MN	B
Minot State U, ND	B
Missouri Southern State U, MO	B
Mount Union Coll, OH	B
Muskingum Coll, OH	B
Nebraska Wesleyan U, NE	B
North Central Coll, IL	B
Northern Illinois U, IL	B
Northern State U, SD	B
Northwestern U, IL	B
Oakland U, MI	B
Oberlin Coll, OH	B
The Ohio State U, OH	B
Ohio U, OH	B
Ohio Wesleyan U, OH	B
Oklahoma Baptist U, OK	B
Oklahoma City U, OK	B
Oklahoma State U, OK	B
Oral Roberts U, OK	B
Principia Coll, IL	B
Purdue U Calumet, IN	B
Ripon Coll, WI	B
Rockford Coll, IL	B
St. Ambrose U, IA	B
St. Cloud State U, MN	B
Saint John's U, MN	B
Saint Louis U, MO	B
St. Norbert Coll, WI	B
St. Olaf Coll, MN	B
Simpson Coll, IA	B
South Dakota State U, SD	B
Southeast Missouri State U, MO	B
Southern Illinois U Carbondale, IL	B
Southwest Missouri State U, MO	B
Truman State U, MO	B
Union Coll, NE	B
The U of Akron, OH	B
U of Central Oklahoma, OK	B
U of Chicago, IL	B
U of Cincinnati, OH	B
U of Dayton, OH	B
U of Evansville, IN	B
U of Illinois at Chicago, IL	B
U of Illinois at Urbana–Champaign, IL	B
U of Indianapolis, IN	B
The U of Iowa, IA	B
U of Michigan, MI	B
U of Michigan–Dearborn, MI	B
U of Minnesota, Morris, MN	B
U of Minnesota, Twin Cities Campus, MN	B
U of Missouri–Columbia, MO	B
U of Missouri–Kansas City, MO	B
U of Missouri–St. Louis, MO	B
U of Nebraska at Omaha, NE	B
U of Nebraska–Lincoln, NE	B
U of North Dakota, ND	B
U of Northern Iowa, IA	B
U of Notre Dame, IN	B
U of Oklahoma, OK	B
U of St. Thomas, MN	B
The U of South Dakota, SD	B
U of Southern Indiana, IN	B
U of Toledo, OH	B
U of Tulsa, OK	B
U of Wisconsin–La Crosse, WI	B
U of Wisconsin–Madison, WI	B
U of Wisconsin–Milwaukee, WI	B
U of Wisconsin–Oshkosh, WI	B
U of Wisconsin–Parkside, WI	B
U of Wisconsin–Platteville, WI	B
U of Wisconsin–River Falls, WI	B
U of Wisconsin–Stevens Point, WI	B
U of Wisconsin–Whitewater, WI	B
Valparaiso U, IN	B
Wabash Coll, IN	B
Wartburg Coll, IA	B
Washburn U, KS	B
Washington U in St. Louis, MO	B
Wayne State Coll, NE	B
Wayne State U, MI	B
Webster U, MO	B
Western Michigan U, MI	B
Wheaton Coll, IL	B
Winona State U, MN	B
Wittenberg U, OH	B
Wright State U, OH	B
Xavier U, OH	A,B

Germanic Languages

Bethel Coll, KS	B
Cleveland State U, OH	B
Eastern Michigan U, MI	B
U of Kansas, KS	B
U of Wisconsin–Eau Claire, WI	B
U of Wisconsin–Green Bay, WI	A,B
Washington U in St. Louis, MO	B

Germanic Languages Related

College	Degree
Calvin Coll, MI	B
Ohio Northern U, OH	B

German Language Teacher Education

College	Degree
Alma Coll, MI	B
Carroll Coll, WI	B
Central Michigan U, MI	B
Central Missouri State U, MO	B
Concordia Coll, MN	B
Concordia U Wisconsin, WI	B
Eastern Michigan U, MI	B
Elmhurst Coll, IL	B
Grace Coll, IN	B
Hope Coll, MI	B
Indiana U Bloomington, IN	B
Indiana U–Purdue U Fort Wayne, IN	B
Indiana U–Purdue U Indianapolis, IN	B
Indiana U South Bend, IN	B
Miami U Hamilton, OH	B
Minot State U, ND	B
Ohio Northern U, OH	B

German Studies

College	Degree
Case Western Reserve U, OH	B
Coe Coll, IA	B
The Coll of Wooster, OH	B

Gerontology

College	Degree
Alma Coll, MI	B
Bowling Green State U, OH	B
Case Western Reserve U, OH	B
Cleveland State U, OH	B
Coll of Mount St. Joseph, OH	A,B
Coll of the Ozarks, MO	B
Dominican U, IL	B
Eastern Michigan U, MI	B
John Carroll U, OH	B
Lindenwood U, MO	B
Madonna U, MI	A,B
Manchester Coll, IN	A
Miami U Hamilton, OH	B
National-Louis U, IL	B
Ohio Dominican U, OH	A
Roosevelt U, IL	B
St. Cloud State U, MN	B
Saint Mary-of-the-Woods Coll, IN	B
Siena Heights U, MI	A
Southeastern Oklahoma State U, OK	B
Southwest Missouri State U, MO	B
The U of Akron, OH	B
U of Evansville, IN	B
U of Nebraska at Omaha, NE	B
U of Northern Iowa, IA	B
U of Toledo, OH	A
Wichita State U, KS	B
Winona State U, MN	A

Graphic and Printing Equipment Operation/ Production

College	Degree
Ball State U, IN	A
Dunwoody Coll of Technology, MN	A
Ferris State U, MI	A,B
Indiana State U, IN	B
Pittsburg State U, KS	B
Western Illinois U, IL	B

Gerontology (continued, right column)

College	Degree
Ohio U, OH	B
Ohio Wesleyan U, OH	B
Oklahoma Baptist U, OK	B
Oral Roberts U, OK	B
St. Ambrose U, IA	B
Southwest Missouri State U, MO	B
The U of Akron, OH	B
U of Illinois at Chicago, IL	B
U of Illinois at Urbana–Champaign, IL	B
The U of Iowa, IA	B
U of Minnesota, Duluth, MN	B
U of Missouri–St. Louis, MO	B
U of Nebraska–Lincoln, NE	B
The U of South Dakota, SD	B
U of Toledo, OH	B
U of Wisconsin–River Falls, WI	B
Valparaiso U, IN	B
Washington U in St. Louis, MO	B
Western Michigan U, MI	B
Youngstown State U, OH	B

Graphic Communications
Carroll Coll, WI	B
Grand View Coll, IA	B
Notre Dame Coll, OH	B
School of the Art Inst of Chicago, IL	B
U of Northern Iowa, IA	B

Graphic Communications Related
The Art Insts International Minnesota, MN	A,B

Graphic Design
Academy Coll, MN	A
Alma Coll, MI	B
Art Academy of Cincinnati, OH	A,B
The Art Insts International Minnesota, MN	A,B
Cedarville U, OH	B
The Cleveland Inst of Art, OH	B
Coll for Creative Studies, MI	B
Coll of Mount St. Joseph, OH	A,B
Columbia Coll, MO	B
Columbus Coll of Art & Design, OH	B
Concordia U Wisconsin, WI	B
Creighton U, NE	B
Dordt Coll, IA	B
Drake U, IA	B
Grand View Coll, IA	B
Hickey Coll, MO	A
Indiana U–Purdue U Fort Wayne, IN	B
Iowa State U of Science and Technology, IA	B
Marietta Coll, OH	B
Maryville U of Saint Louis, MO	B
Miami U Hamilton, OH	B
MidAmerica Nazarene U, KS	B
Missouri Western State Coll, MO	B
Northwestern Coll, MN	B
Ohio Dominican U, OH	B
Ohio Northern U, OH	B
Oklahoma State U, OK	B
Quincy U, IL	B
St. Ambrose U, IA	B
School of the Art Inst of Chicago, IL	B
Shawnee State U, OH	B
Union Coll, NE	A,B
U of Illinois at Chicago, IL	B
U of Illinois at Urbana–Champaign, IL	B
U of Kansas, KS	B
U of Michigan–Flint, MI	B
Ursuline Coll, OH	B
Viterbo U, WI	B
Washington U in St. Louis, MO	B
Westwood Coll–Chicago Du Page, IL	A
Westwood Coll–Chicago Loop Campus, IL	A,B
Westwood Coll–Chicago O'Hare Airport, IL	A
Westwood Coll–Chicago River Oaks, IL	A

Graphic/Printing Equipment
Coll of the Ozarks, MO	B

Greenhouse Management
Kent State U, Salem Campus, OH	A
Rochester Comm and Tech Coll, MN	A

Hazardous Materials Information Systems Technology
Ohio U, OH	A

Hazardous Materials Management and Waste Technology
Ohio U, OH	A

Health and Medical Administrative Services Related
Kent State U, OH	A,B
The U of Akron, OH	A
U of Michigan–Flint, MI	B
Ursuline Coll, OH	B

Health and Physical Education
Baldwin-Wallace Coll, OH	B
Bethel Coll, IN	A,B
Bethel Coll, KS	B
Bethel U, MN	B
Black Hills State U, SD	B
Bluffton Coll, OH	B
Capital U, OH	B
Carroll Coll, WI	B
Cedarville U, OH	B
Central Christian Coll of Kansas, KS	A
Coll of St. Catherine, MN	B
Coll of the Ozarks, MO	B
Concordia Coll, MN	B
Concordia U, NE	B
Concordia U Wisconsin, WI	B
Cumberland Coll, KY	B
Dana Coll, NE	B
Doane Coll, NE	B
Dordt Coll, IA	B
Eastern Michigan U, MI	B
Elmhurst Coll, IL	B
Evangel U, MO	B
Hamline U, MN	B
Haskell Indian Nations U, KS	A
Hastings Coll, NE	B
Iowa State U of Science and Technology, IA	B
Lindenwood U, MO	B
Loras Coll, IA	B
Luther Coll, IA	B
Malone Coll, OH	B
Mayville State U, ND	B
Miami U, OH	B
Minnesota State U Moorhead, MN	B
Mount Vernon Nazarene U, OH	A
Nebraska Wesleyan U, NE	B
Ohio Northern U, OH	B
Ohio U, OH	B
Oklahoma Baptist U, OK	B
Oklahoma State U, OK	B
Olivet Coll, MI	B
Pittsburg State U, KS	B
Robert Morris Coll, IL	A
St. Ambrose U, IA	B
South Dakota State U, SD	B
Southeast Missouri State U, MO	B

Southern Illinois U Edwardsville, IL	B
Southwestern Coll, KS	B
Spring Arbor U, MI	B
Sterling Coll, KS	B
U of Kansas, KS	B
U of Mary, ND	B
U of Missouri–Kansas City, MO	B
U of Nebraska at Omaha, NE	B
U of Northern Iowa, IA	B
U of Oklahoma, OK	B
U of Rio Grande, OH	B
U of St. Thomas, MN	B
U of Science and Arts of Oklahoma, OK	B
U of West Florida, FL	B
U of Wisconsin–Stevens Point, WI	B
Valparaiso U, IN	B
William Penn U, IA	B
Wright State U, OH	B
Youngstown State U, OH	B

Health and Physical Education Related
Avila U, MO	B
Bowling Green State U, OH	B
Briar Cliff U, IA	B
Capital U, OH	B
Coe Coll, IA	B
Concordia U Wisconsin, WI	B
Cornell Coll, IA	B
Gustavus Adolphus Coll, MN	B
Mayville State U, ND	B
Ohio Northern U, OH	B
The U of Akron, OH	B
U of Central Oklahoma, OK	B
U of Minnesota, Twin Cities Campus, MN	B

Health/Health Care Administration
American InterContinental U Online, IL	B
Augustana Coll, SD	B
Baker Coll of Auburn Hills, MI	A,B
Baker Coll of Flint, MI	A,B
Baker Coll of Muskegon, MI	A,B
Baker Coll of Owosso, MI	B
Baker Coll of Port Huron, MI	B
Bellevue U, NE	B
Benedictine U, IL	B
Black Hills State U, SD	B
Bowling Green State U, OH	B
Calumet Coll of Saint Joseph, IN	B
Concordia Coll, MN	B
Concordia U Wisconsin, WI	B
Creighton U, NE	B
Davenport U, Dearborn, MI	B
Davenport U, Lansing, MI	B
Eastern Michigan U, MI	B
Ferris State U, MI	B
The Franciscan U, IA	B
Franklin U, OH	B
Governors State U, IL	B
Harris-Stowe State Coll, MO	B
Hastings Coll, NE	B
Heidelberg Coll, OH	B
Indiana U Northwest, IN	B
Indiana U–Purdue U Indianapolis, IN	B

Indiana U South Bend, IN	B
Lewis U, IL	B
Lindenwood U, MO	B
Madonna U, MI	A,B
Maryville U of Saint Louis, MO	B
Mercy Coll of Health Sciences, IA	B
Mercy Coll of Northwest Ohio, OH	B
Minnesota State U Moorhead, MN	B
National-Louis U, IL	B
Northeastern State U, OK	B
Ohio U, OH	B
Ohio U–Southern Campus, OH	B
Presentation Coll, SD	B
Roosevelt U, IL	B
Saint Louis U, MO	B
Southwestern Oklahoma State U, OK	B
Spring Arbor U, MI	B
U of Cincinnati, OH	B
U of Detroit Mercy, MI	B
U of Evansville, IN	B
U of Illinois at Springfield, IL	B
U of Michigan–Dearborn, MI	B
U of Michigan–Flint, MI	B
U of Minnesota, Crookston, MN	B
U of Northwestern Ohio, OH	B
U of Phoenix–Cleveland Campus, OH	B
U of Phoenix–Kansas City Campus, MO	B
U of Phoenix–Oklahoma City Campus, OK	B
U of Phoenix–Tulsa Campus, OK	B
U of Phoenix–West Michigan Campus, MI	B
U of Wisconsin–Eau Claire, WI	B
U of Wisconsin–Milwaukee, WI	B
Upper Iowa U, IA	B
Ursuline Coll, OH	B
Webster U, MO	B
Western Illinois U, IL	B
Western Michigan U, MI	B
Wichita State U, KS	B
Wilberforce U, OH	B
Winona State U, MN	B
Wright State U, OH	B

Health Information/Medical Records Administration
Baker Coll of Auburn Hills, MI	A,B
Baker Coll of Cadillac, MI	A
Baker Coll of Clinton Township, MI	A
Baker Coll of Flint, MI	A,B
Baker Coll of Jackson, MI	A
Baker Coll of Port Huron, MI	A
Chicago State U, IL	B
Coll of St. Catherine–Minneapolis, MN	A
Coll of Saint Mary, NE	A,B
The Coll of St. Scholastica, MN	B

A—associate degree; B—bachelor's degree

Dakota State U, SD	A,B
Davenport U, Kalamazoo, MI	A
Davenport U, Warren, MI	A
East Central U, OK	B
Ferris State U, MI	A,B
Illinois State U, IL	B
Indiana U Northwest, IN	A,B
Indiana U–Purdue U Indianapolis, IN	B
The Ohio State U, OH	B
Park U, MO	A
Saint Louis U, MO	B
Southwestern Oklahoma State U, OK	B
U of Illinois at Chicago, IL	B
U of Kansas, KS	B
U of Toledo, OH	B
U of Wisconsin–Milwaukee, WI	B
Washburn U, KS	A

Health Information/Medical Records Technology

Baker Coll of Flint, MI	A
Baker Coll of Jackson, MI	A
Coll of St. Catherine, MN	A
Davenport U, Dearborn, MI	A
Davenport U, Holland, MI	A
Davenport U, Lapeer, MI	A
Davenport U, Warren, MI	A
Mercy Coll of Northwest Ohio, OH	A
Missouri Western State Coll, MO	A
North Dakota State Coll of Science, ND	A

Health/Medical Preparatory Programs Related

Ancilla Coll, IN	A
Aurora U, IL	B
Avila U, MO	B
Chadron State Coll, NE	B
Coll of the Ozarks, MO	B
Concordia U, NE	B
Eastern Michigan U, MI	B
Lehigh U, PA	B
Madonna U, MI	B
Maryville U of Saint Louis, MO	B
Roosevelt U, IL	B
St. Cloud State U, MN	B
Union Coll, NE	A
The U of Akron, OH	B
U of Missouri–Columbia, MO	B
Wheaton Coll, IL	B
Wright State U, OH	B

Health Occupations Teacher Education

U of Central Oklahoma, OK	B

Health Professions Related

Baldwin-Wallace Coll, OH	B
Bowling Green State U, OH	B
Bradley U, IL	B
Cleveland State U, OH	B
Oakland U, MI	B
The Ohio State U, OH	B
Ohio U, OH	B
Purdue U, IN	B
U of Northern Iowa, IA	B
U of Saint Francis, IN	B
U of Southern Indiana, IN	B
Washington U in St. Louis, MO	B

Health Science

Alma Coll, MI	B
Ball State U, IN	B
Benedictine U, IL	B
Bradley U, IL	B
The Coll of St. Scholastica, MN	B
Coll of the Ozarks, MO	B
Gannon U, PA	B
Graceland U, IA	B
Grand Valley State U, MI	B
Hiram Coll, OH	B
Kalamazoo Coll, MI	B
Kansas State U, KS	B
Kettering Coll of Medical Arts, OH	B
Manchester Coll, IN	B
Maryville U of Saint Louis, MO	B
Minnesota State U Mankato, MN	B
Newman U, KS	A,B
Northern Illinois U, IL	B
Oakland U, MI	B
Ohio U, OH	B
Oklahoma State U, OK	B
Roosevelt U, IL	B
Truman State U, MO	B
Union Coll, NE	A
Union Inst & U, OH	B
U of Saint Francis, IN	B
U of St. Thomas, MN	B
U of Wisconsin–Milwaukee, WI	B
Waldorf Coll, IA	B
Wayne State U, MI	B
Winona State U, MN	B
Youngstown State U, OH	B

Health Services Administration

Indiana U–Purdue U Fort Wayne, IN	B
Ohio U–Southern Campus, OH	B
Ursuline Coll, OH	B
Washburn U, KS	B

Health Services/Allied Health/Health Sciences

Central Christian Coll of Kansas, KS	A
The Coll of St. Scholastica, MN	B
Florida Gulf Coast U, FL	B
Kent State U, OH	B
The Ohio State U at Lima, OH	B
St. Cloud State U, MN	B
U of Minnesota, Crookston, MN	B
Ursuline Coll, OH	B

Health Teacher Education

Alma Coll, MI	B
Aquinas Coll, MI	B
Ashland U, OH	B
Augsburg Coll, MN	B
Baldwin-Wallace Coll, OH	B
Ball State U, IN	B
Bemidji State U, MN	B
Bethel U, MN	B
Bowling Green State U, OH	B
Briar Cliff U, IA	B
Capital U, OH	B
Carroll Coll, WI	B
Cedarville U, OH	B

Central Christian Coll of Kansas, KS	A
Central Michigan U, MI	B
Central State U, OH	B
Chicago State U, IL	B
Concordia Coll, MN	B
Concordia U, NE	B
Concordia U, St. Paul, MN	B
Concord U, WV	B
Cumberland Coll, KY	B
Defiance Coll, OH	B
Donnelly Coll, KS	A
East Central U, OK	B
Eastern Illinois U, IL	B
Eastern Michigan U, MI	B
Graceland U, IA	B
Gustavus Adolphus Coll, MN	B
Hamline U, MN	B
Heidelberg Coll, OH	B
Illinois State U, IL	B
Indiana State U, IN	B
Indiana U–Purdue U Indianapolis, IN	B
Iowa State U of Science and Technology, IA	B
Kansas Wesleyan U, KS	B
Kent State U, OH	B
Luther Coll, IA	B
Malone Coll, OH	B
Manchester Coll, IN	B
Mayville State U, ND	B
Miami U, OH	B
Miami U Hamilton, OH	B
Minnesota State U Mankato, MN	B
Minnesota State U Moorhead, MN	B
Missouri Baptist U, MO	B
Missouri Valley Coll, MO	B
Mount Vernon Nazarene U, OH	B
Muskingum Coll, OH	B
North Carolina Ag and Tech State U, NC	B
North Dakota State U, ND	B
Northeastern State U, OK	B
Northern Illinois U, IL	B
Northern Michigan U, MI	B
Northern State U, SD	B
Northwestern Oklahoma State U, OK	B
Ohio Northern U, OH	B
Ohio Wesleyan U, OH	B
Otterbein Coll, OH	B
Peru State Coll, NE	B
Pittsburg State U, KS	B
St. Ambrose U, IA	B
St. Cloud State U, MN	B
Southeastern Oklahoma State U, OK	B
Southern Illinois U Carbondale, IL	B
Southern Illinois U Edwardsville, IL	B
Tabor Coll, KS	B
The U of Akron, OH	B
U of Cincinnati, OH	B
U of Dayton, OH	B
U of Minnesota, Duluth, MN	B
U of Nebraska–Lincoln, NE	B
U of Northern Iowa, IA	B
U of Rio Grande, OH	B
U of Saint Francis, IN	B
U of St. Thomas, MN	B
U of Sioux Falls, SD	B
The U of South Dakota, SD	B

U of Toledo, OH	B
U of Wisconsin–La Crosse, WI	B
Urbana U, OH	B
Valley City State U, ND	B
Waldorf Coll, IA	B
Washburn U, KS	B
Western Illinois U, IL	B
Western Michigan U, MI	B
William Penn U, IA	B
Winona State U, MN	B
Wright State U, OH	B
Youngstown State U, OH	B

Heating, Air Conditioning and Refrigeration Technology

Central Missouri State U, MO	A
Dunwoody Coll of Technology, MN	A
North Dakota State Coll of Science, ND	A
Vatterott Coll, St. Ann, MO	A

Heating, Air Conditioning, Ventilation and Refrigeration Maintenance Technology

Dunwoody Coll of Technology, MN	A
Ferris State U, MI	A,B
North Dakota State Coll of Science, ND	A
Northern Michigan U, MI	A
Oakland City U, IN	A
Ranken Tech Coll, MO	A
U of Cincinnati, OH	A
U of Northwestern Ohio, OH	A

Heavy Equipment Maintenance Technology

Ferris State U, MI	A,B
Pittsburg State U, KS	B

Hebrew

Concordia U Wisconsin, WI	B
Laura and Alvin Siegal Coll of Judaic Studies, OH	B
North Central U, MN	A
The Ohio State U, OH	B
U of Michigan, MI	B
U of Minnesota, Twin Cities Campus, MN	B
U of Wisconsin–Madison, WI	B
U of Wisconsin–Milwaukee, WI	B
Washington U in St. Louis, MO	B

Higher Education/Higher Education Administration

Eastern Michigan U, MI	B
Wright State U, OH	B

Hindi

U of Chicago, IL	B

Hispanic-American, Puerto Rican, and Mexican-American/ Chicano Studies

Goshen Coll, IN	B
St. Olaf Coll, MN	B
U of Michigan, MI	B
U of Michigan–Dearborn, MI	B
U of Minnesota, Twin Cities Campus, MN	B

U of Wisconsin–Madison, WI — B
Wayne State U, MI — B

Histologic Technician
Argosy U/Twin Cities, MN — A

Histologic Technology/ Histotechnologist
Argosy U/Twin Cities, Eagan, MN — A
Northern Michigan U, MI — B

Historic Preservation and Conservation
Eastern Michigan U, MI — B
Ursuline Coll, OH — B

History
Adrian Coll, MI — A,B
Albion Coll, MI — B
Alma Coll, MI — B
Alverno Coll, WI — B
Andrews U, MI — B
Antioch Coll, OH — B
Aquinas Coll, MI — B
Ashland U, OH — B
Augsburg Coll, MN — B
Augustana Coll, IL — B
Augustana Coll, SD — B
Aurora U, IL — B
Ave Maria Coll, MI — B
Avila U, MO — B
Bacone Coll, OK — A
Baker U, KS — B
Baldwin-Wallace Coll, OH — B
Ball State U, IN — B
Beloit Coll, WI — B
Bemidji State U, MN — B
Benedictine Coll, KS — B
Benedictine U, IL — B
Bethany Coll, KS — B
Bethany Lutheran Coll, MN — B
Bethel Coll, IN — B
Bethel Coll, KS — B
Bethel U, MN — B
Blackburn Coll, IL — B
Black Hills State U, SD — B
Bluffton Coll, OH — B
Bowling Green State U, OH — B
Bradley U, IL — B
Brescia U, KY — B
Briar Cliff U, IA — B
Buena Vista U, IA — B
Butler U, IN — B
Calvin Coll, MI — B
Cameron U, OK — B
Capital U, OH — B
Cardinal Stritch U, WI — B
Carleton Coll, MN — B
Carroll Coll, WI — B
Carthage Coll, WI — B
Case Western Reserve U, OH — B
Cedarville U, OH — B
Central Christian Coll of Kansas, KS — A
Central Coll, IA — B
Central Methodist Coll, MO — B
Central Michigan U, MI — B
Central Missouri State U, MO — B
Central State U, OH — B
Chadron State Coll, NE — B
Chicago State U, IL — B
Clarke Coll, IA — B

Clarkson U — B
Coe Coll, IA — B
Coll of Mount St. Joseph, OH — B
Coll of Saint Benedict, MN — B
Coll of St. Catherine, MN — B
The Coll of St. Scholastica, MN — B
Coll of the Ozarks, MO — B
The Coll of Wooster, OH — B
Columbia Coll, MO — B
Concordia Coll, MN — B
Concordia U, IL — B
Concordia U, NE — B
Concordia U, St. Paul, MN — B
Concordia U Wisconsin, WI — B
Concord U, WV — B
Cornell Coll, IA — B
Cornerstone U, MI — B
Creighton U, NE — B
Crown Coll, MN — B
Culver-Stockton Coll, MO — B
Cumberland Coll, KY — B
Dakota Wesleyan U, SD — B
Dana Coll, NE — B
Defiance Coll, OH — B
Denison U, OH — B
DePaul U, IL — B
DePauw U, IN — B
Dickinson State U, ND — B
Doane Coll, NE — B
Dominican U, IL — B
Donnelly Coll, KS — A
Dordt Coll, IA — B
Drake U, IA — B
Drury U, MO — B
Earlham Coll, IN — B
East Central U, OK — B
Eastern Illinois U, IL — B
Eastern Michigan U, MI — B
Edgewood Coll, WI — B
Elmhurst Coll, IL — B
Emporia State U, KS — B
Eureka Coll, IL — B
Evangel U, MO — B
Fontbonne U, MO — B
Fort Hays State U, KS — B
Franciscan U of Steubenville, OH — B
Franklin Coll, IN — B
Gannon U, PA — B
Goshen Coll, IN — B
Graceland U, IA — B
Grand Valley State U, MI — B
Grand View Coll, IA — B
Grinnell Coll, IA — B
Gustavus Adolphus Coll, MN — B
Hamline U, MN — B
Hannibal-LaGrange Coll, MO — B
Hanover Coll, IN — B
Hastings Coll, NE — B
Heidelberg Coll, OH — B
Hillsdale Coll, MI — B
Hiram Coll, OH — B
Hope Coll, MI — B
Huntington Coll, IN — B
Illinois Coll, IL — B
Illinois State U, IL — B
Illinois Wesleyan U, IL — B
Indiana State U, IN — B
Indiana U Bloomington, IN — B
Indiana U East, IN — A
Indiana U Northwest, IN — B

Indiana U–Purdue U Fort Wayne, IN — A,B
Indiana U–Purdue U Indianapolis, IN — B
Indiana U South Bend, IN — B
Indiana U Southeast, IN — B
Iowa State U of Science and Technology, IA — B
Iowa Wesleyan Coll, IA — B
Jamestown Coll, ND — B
John Carroll U, OH — B
Judson Coll, IL — B
Kalamazoo Coll, MI — B
Kansas State U, KS — B
Kansas Wesleyan U, KS — B
Kent State U, OH — B
Kenyon Coll, OH — B
Knox Coll, IL — B
Lake Forest Coll, IL — B
Lakeland Coll, WI — B
Lake Superior State U, MI — B
Laura and Alvin Siegal Coll of Judaic Studies, OH — B
Lawrence U, WI — B
Lehigh U, PA — B
Lewis U, IL — B
Lincoln Coll, Lincoln, IL — A
Lincoln U, MO — B
Lindenwood U, MO — B
Loras Coll, IA — B
Lourdes Coll, OH — A,B
Loyola U Chicago, IL — B
Luther Coll, IA — B
Macalester Coll, MN — B
MacMurray Coll, IL — B
Madonna U, MI — B
Malone Coll, OH — B
Manchester Coll, IN — B
Marian Coll, IN — A,B
Marian Coll of Fond du Lac, WI — B
Marietta Coll, OH — B
Marquette U, WI — B
Martin U, IN — B
Marygrove Coll, MI — B
Maryville U of Saint Louis, MO — B
McKendree Coll, IL — B
McPherson Coll, KS — B
Metropolitan State U, MN — B
Miami U, OH — B
Miami U Hamilton, OH — B
Michigan State U, MI — B
MidAmerica Nazarene U, KS — B
Millikin U, IL — B
Minnesota State U Mankato, MN — B
Minnesota State U Moorhead, MN — B
Minot State U, ND — B
Missouri Baptist U, MO — B
Missouri Southern State U, MO — B
Missouri Valley Coll, MO — B
Missouri Western State Coll, MO — B
Monmouth Coll, IL — B
Morningside Coll, IA — B
Mount Marty Coll, SD — B
Mount Mary Coll, WI — B
Mount Mercy Coll, IA — B
Mount Union Coll, OH — B
Mount Vernon Nazarene U, OH — B
Muskingum Coll, OH — B

Nebraska Wesleyan U, NE — B
Newman U, KS — B
North Carolina Ag and Tech State U, NC — B
North Central Coll, IL — B
North Central U, MN — A
North Dakota State U, ND — B
Northeastern Illinois U, IL — B
Northeastern State U, OK — B
Northern Illinois U, IL — B
Northern Michigan U, MI — B
Northern State U, SD — B
Northland Coll, WI — B
North Park U, IL — B
Northwestern Coll, IA — B
Northwestern Coll, MN — B
Northwestern Oklahoma State U, OK — B
Northwestern U, IL — B
Notre Dame Coll, OH — B
Oakland U, MI — B
Oberlin Coll, OH — B
Ohio Dominican U, OH — B
Ohio Northern U, OH — B
The Ohio State U, OH — B
The Ohio State U at Lima, OH —
The Ohio State U at Marion, OH — B
The Ohio State U–Mansfield Campus, OH — B
The Ohio State U–Newark Campus, OH — B
Ohio U, OH — B
Ohio Wesleyan U, OH — B
Oklahoma Baptist U, OK — B
Oklahoma Christian U, OK — B
Oklahoma City U, OK — B
Oklahoma Panhandle State U, OK — B
Oklahoma State U, OK — B
Olivet Coll, MI — B
Olivet Nazarene U, IL — B
Oral Roberts U, OK — B
Ottawa U, KS — B
Otterbein Coll, OH — B
Park U, MO — B
Peru State Coll, NE — B
Pittsburg State U, KS — B
Principia Coll, IL — B
Purdue U, IN — B
Purdue U Calumet, IN — B
Quincy U, IL — B
Ripon Coll, WI — B
Rochester Coll, MI — B
Rockford Coll, IL — B
Rockhurst U, MO — B
Roosevelt U, IL — B
Saginaw Valley State U, MI — B
St. Ambrose U, IA — B
St. Cloud State U, MN — B
St. Gregory's U, OK — B
Saint John's U, MN — B
Saint Joseph's Coll, IN — B
Saint Louis U, MO — B
Saint Mary-of-the-Woods Coll, IN — B
Saint Mary's Coll, IN — B
Saint Mary's U of Minnesota, MN — B
St. Norbert Coll, WI — B
St. Olaf Coll, MN — B
Saint Xavier U, IL — B
Shawnee State U, OH — B
Siena Heights U, MI — B

A—associate degree; B—bachelor's degree

Silver Lake Coll, WI — B
Simpson Coll, IA — B
South Dakota State U, SD — B
Southeastern Oklahoma State U, OK — B
Southeast Missouri State U, MO — B
Southern Illinois U Carbondale, IL — B
Southern Illinois U Edwardsville, IL — B
Southern Nazarene U, OK — B
Southwest Baptist U, MO — B
Southwestern Coll, KS — B
Southwestern Oklahoma State U, OK — B
Southwest Missouri State U, MO — B
Spring Arbor U, MI — B
Sterling Coll, KS — B
Tabor Coll, KS — B
Taylor U, IN — B
Transylvania U, KY — B
Trinity Christian Coll, IL — B
Trinity International U, IL — B
Truman State U, MO — B
Union Coll, NE — B
Union Inst & U, OH — B
The U of Akron, OH — B
The U of Alabama in Huntsville, AL — B
U of Central Oklahoma, OK — B
U of Chicago, IL — B
U of Cincinnati, OH — B
U of Dayton, OH — B
U of Detroit Mercy, MI — B
U of Evansville, IN — B
The U of Findlay, OH — B
U of Illinois at Chicago, IL — B
U of Illinois at Springfield, IL — B
U of Illinois at Urbana–Champaign, IL — B
U of Indianapolis, IN — B
The U of Iowa, IA — B
U of Kansas, KS — B
U of Mary, ND — B
U of Michigan, MI — B
U of Michigan–Dearborn, MI — B
U of Michigan–Flint, MI — B
U of Minnesota, Duluth, MN — B
U of Minnesota, Morris, MN — B
U of Minnesota, Twin Cities Campus, MN — B
U of Missouri–Columbia, MO — B
U of Missouri–Kansas City, MO — B
U of Missouri–Rolla, MO — B
U of Missouri–St. Louis, MO — B
U of Nebraska at Omaha, NE — B
U of Nebraska–Lincoln, NE — B
U of New Orleans, LA — B
U of North Dakota, ND — B
U of Northern Iowa, IA — B
U of Notre Dame, IN — B
U of Oklahoma, OK — B
U of Rio Grande, OH — A,B
U of St. Francis, IL — B
U of Saint Francis, IN — B
U of Saint Mary, KS — B
U of St. Thomas, MN — B
U of Science and Arts of Oklahoma, OK — B
U of Sioux Falls, SD — B

The U of South Dakota, SD — B
U of Southern Indiana, IN — B
U of Toledo, OH — B
U of Tulsa, OK — B
U of West Florida, FL — B
U of Wisconsin–Eau Claire, WI — B
U of Wisconsin–Green Bay, WI — A,B
U of Wisconsin–La Crosse, WI — B
U of Wisconsin–Madison, WI — B
U of Wisconsin–Milwaukee, WI — B
U of Wisconsin–Oshkosh, WI — B
U of Wisconsin–Parkside, WI — B
U of Wisconsin–Platteville, WI — B
U of Wisconsin–River Falls, WI — B
U of Wisconsin–Stevens Point, WI — B
U of Wisconsin–Superior, WI — B
U of Wisconsin–Whitewater, WI — B
Urbana U, OH — B
Ursuline Coll, OH — B
Valley City State U, ND — B
Valparaiso U, IN — B
Wabash Coll, IN — B
Waldorf Coll, IA — B
Walsh U, OH — B
Wartburg Coll, IA — B
Washburn U, KS — B
Washington U in St. Louis, MO — B
Wayne State Coll, NE — B
Wayne State U, MI — B
Webster U, MO — B
Western Illinois U, IL — B
Western Michigan U, MI — B
Westminster Coll, MO — B
Wheaton Coll, IL — B
Wichita State U, KS — B
William Jewell Coll, MO — B
William Penn U, IA — B
William Tyndale Coll, MI — B
William Woods U, MO — B
Winona State U, MN — B
Wisconsin Lutheran Coll, WI — B
Wittenberg U, OH — B
Wright State U, OH — A,B
Xavier U, OH — A,B
York Coll, NE — B
Youngstown State U, OH — B

History and Philosophy of Science and Technology
Case Western Reserve U, OH — B
U of Wisconsin–Madison, WI — B

History of Philosophy
Marquette U, WI — B
Spring Arbor U, MI — B

History Related
Coll of the Ozarks, MO — B
Eastern Michigan U, MI — B
The Franciscan U, IA — B
Marquette U, WI — B
The Ohio State U, OH — B

Ohio U, OH — B
Saint Mary's U of Minnesota, MN — B

History Teacher Education
Alma Coll, MI — B
Buena Vista U, IA — B
Carroll Coll, WI — B
Central Christian Coll of Kansas, KS — A
Central Michigan U, MI — B
Chadron State Coll, NE — B
The Coll of St. Scholastica, MN — B
Coll of the Ozarks, MO — B
Concordia U, IL — B
Concordia U, NE — B
Concordia U Wisconsin, WI — B
Cornerstone U, MI — B
Crown Coll, MN — B
Culver-Stockton Coll, MO — B
Dakota Wesleyan U, SD — B
Dana Coll, NE — B
Dordt Coll, IA — B
East Central U, OK — B
Eastern Michigan U, MI — B
Elmhurst Coll, IL — B
Evangel U, MO — B
Hannibal-LaGrange Coll, MO — B
Hastings Coll, NE — B
Hope Coll, MI — B
Illinois Wesleyan U, IL — B
Jamestown Coll, ND — B
Lindenwood U, MO — B
Marian Coll of Fond du Lac, WI — B
Maryville U of Saint Louis, MO — B
McKendree Coll, IL — B
Minot State U, ND — B
Mount Marty Coll, SD — B
North Dakota State U, ND — B
Northern Michigan U, MI — B
Ohio Northern U, OH — B
Ohio Wesleyan U, OH — B
Oklahoma Baptist U, OK — B
Pittsburg State U, KS — B
St. Ambrose U, IA — B
Saint Xavier U, IL — B
Shawnee State U, OH — B
Southwest Baptist U, MO — B
Southwestern Oklahoma State U, OK — B
Southwest Missouri State U, MO — B
Taylor U, IN — B
Trinity Christian Coll, IL — B
Union Coll, NE — B
The U of Akron, OH — B
U of Central Oklahoma, OK — B
U of Illinois at Chicago, IL — B
The U of Iowa, IA — B
U of Michigan–Flint, MI — B
U of Nebraska–Lincoln, NE — B
U of Rio Grande, OH — B
The U of South Dakota, SD — B
U of Wisconsin–River Falls, WI — B
U of Wisconsin–Superior, WI — B
Valley City State U, ND — B
Valparaiso U, IN — B
Wartburg Coll, IA — B
Washington U in St. Louis, MO — B
Western Michigan U, MI — B

York Coll, NE — B
Youngstown State U, OH — B

Horse Husbandry/Equine Science and Management
Stephens Coll, MO — B

Horticultural Science
Andrews U, MI — A
Bacone Coll, OK — A
Coll of the Ozarks, MO — B
Iowa State U of Science and Technology, IA — B
Kansas State U, KS — B
Kent State U, Salem Campus, OH — A
Michigan State U, MI — B
North Dakota State U, ND — B
The Ohio State U, OH — B
Oklahoma State U, OK — B
Purdue U, IN — B
Southwest Missouri State U, MO — B
Truman State U, MO — B
U of Illinois at Urbana–Champaign, IL — B
U of Minnesota, Crookston, MN — A,B
U of Nebraska–Lincoln, NE — B
U of Wisconsin–Madison, WI — B
U of Wisconsin–River Falls, WI — B

Hospital and Health Care Facilities Administration
Avila U, MO — B
Black Hills State U, SD — B
Central Michigan U, MI — B
Ohio U, OH — B
The U of South Dakota, SD — B
U of Toledo, OH — B
Ursuline Coll, OH — B

Hospitality Administration
Baker Coll of Flint, MI — A
Baker Coll of Owosso, MI — A
Bowling Green State U, OH — B
Central Michigan U, MI — B
Concord U, WV — B
Eastern Michigan U, MI — B
Ferris State U, MI — B
Indiana U–Purdue U Fort Wayne, IN — A,B
Kendall Coll, IL — A,B
Lexington Coll, IL — A,B
Madonna U, MI — B
Metropolitan State U, MN — B
Michigan State U, MI — B
North Dakota State U, ND — B
The Ohio State U, OH — B
The Ohio State U at Lima, OH — B
Roosevelt U, IL — B
Siena Heights U, MI — A,B
Southwest Missouri State U, MO — B
The U of Akron, OH — A
U of Minnesota, Crookston, MN — A
U of New Orleans, LA — B
U of West Florida, FL — B
U of Wisconsin–Stout, WI — B
Washburn U, KS — A
Youngstown State U, OH — A,B

Hospitality Administration Related

Indiana U–Purdue U Indianapolis, IN	B
Kendall Coll, IL	B
Kent State U, OH	B
Lexington Coll, IL	A,B
Purdue U, IN	A

Hospitality and Recreation Marketing

AIB Coll of Business, IA	A
Kendall Coll, IL	B
The U of Akron, OH	A

Hotel and Restaurant Management

Coll of the Ozarks, MO	

Hotel/Motel Administration

Ashland U, OH	B
Baker Coll of Muskegon, MI	A
Baker Coll of Owosso, MI	A
Baker Coll of Port Huron, MI	A
Central Missouri State U, MO	B
Central State U, OH	B
Chicago State U, IL	B
Coll of the Ozarks, MO	B
Concord U, WV	B
Grand Valley State U, MI	B
Indiana U–Purdue U Indianapolis, IN	A
Iowa State U of Science and Technology, IA	B
Kansas State U, KS	B
Kendall Coll, IL	A,B
Lexington Coll, IL	A,B
MacCormac Coll, IL	A
Michigan State U, MI	B
Northwood U, MI	A,B
Oklahoma State U, OK	B
Purdue U, IN	B
Purdue U Calumet, IN	A,B
South Dakota State U, SD	B
The U of Akron, OH	A
U of Central Oklahoma, OK	B
The U of Findlay, OH	B
U of Minnesota, Crookston, MN	A,B
U of Missouri–Columbia, MO	B
Youngstown State U, OH	A,B

Housing and Human Environments

Iowa State U of Science and Technology, IA	B
Ohio U, OH	B
Southwest Missouri State U, MO	B
The U of Akron, OH	B
U of Missouri–Columbia, MO	B
U of Nebraska–Lincoln, NE	B
U of Northern Iowa, IA	B

Human Development and Family Studies

Antioch Coll, OH	B
Ashland U, OH	B
Concordia U, MI	B
Indiana State U, IN	B
Indiana U Bloomington, IN	B
Kansas State U, KS	B
Kent State U, OH	B

Lincoln Coll, Lincoln, IL	A
Miami U, OH	B
National-Louis U, IL	B
North Dakota State U, ND	B
Northern Illinois U, IL	B
Northern Michigan U, MI	B
The Ohio State U, OH	B
Ohio U, OH	B
Oklahoma State U, OK	B
Purdue U, IN	B
St. Olaf Coll, MN	B
South Dakota State U, SD	B
Southern Nazarene U, OK	B
Southwest Missouri State U, MO	B
U of Chicago, IL	B
U of Illinois at Urbana–Champaign, IL	B
U of Missouri–Columbia, MO	B
U of Wisconsin–Stout, WI	B
Youngstown State U, OH	B

Human Development and Family Studies Related

Kent State U, OH	B
U of Toledo, OH	A

Human Ecology

Kansas State U, KS	B

Humanities

Alma Coll, MI	B
Ancilla Coll, IN	A
Antioch Coll, OH	B
Augsburg Coll, MN	B
Aurora U, IL	B
Bacone Coll, OK	A
Bemidji State U, MN	B
Central Christian Coll of Kansas, KS	A
Clarkson U	B
Coll of Saint Benedict, MN	B
Coll of Saint Mary, NE	B
The Coll of St. Scholastica, MN	B
Concordia Coll, MN	B
Concordia U Wisconsin, WI	B
The Franciscan U, IA	B
Franciscan U of Steubenville, OH	B
Gannon U, PA	B
Grace U, NE	B
Grand Valley State U, MI	B
Hope Coll, MI	B
Indiana State U, IN	B
Indiana U Kokomo, IN	B
John Carroll U, OH	B
Kansas State U, KS	B
Kenyon Coll, OH	B
Lawrence Technological U, MI	B
Lehigh U, PA	B
Lincoln Coll, Lincoln, IL	A
Loyola U Chicago, IL	B
Macalester Coll, MN	B
Martin U, IN	B
Michigan State U, MI	B
Michigan Technological U, MI	A
Minnesota State U Mankato, MN	B
Monmouth Coll, IL	B
Muskingum Coll, IL	B
North Central Coll, IL	B
North Dakota State U, ND	B

Northwestern Coll, IA	B
Northwestern U, IL	B
Oakland City U, IN	B
The Ohio State U, OH	B
Ohio U, OH	A
Ohio Wesleyan U, OH	B
Oklahoma Baptist U, OK	B
Oklahoma City U, OK	B
Oklahoma Panhandle State U, OK	B
Pontifical Coll Josephinum, OH	B
Principia Coll, IL	B
Purdue U, IN	B
Purdue U Calumet, IN	B
Quincy U, IL	B
Rockford Coll, IL	B
St. Gregory's U, OK	A,B
Saint John's U, MN	B
Saint Louis U, MO	B
Saint Mary-of-the-Woods Coll, IN	B
Saint Mary's Coll, IN	B
St. Norbert Coll, WI	B
Shawnee State U, OH	A
Shimer Coll, IL	B
Siena Heights U, MI	B
Southeast Missouri State U, MO	B
Tabor Coll, KS	B
Trinity International U, IL	B
Union Inst & U, OH	B
The U of Akron, OH	B
U of Chicago, IL	B
U of Cincinnati, OH	A,B
U of Detroit Mercy, MI	B
The U of Findlay, OH	A
U of Illinois at Urbana–Champaign, IL	B
U of Kansas, KS	B
U of Michigan, MI	B
U of Michigan–Dearborn, MI	B
U of Northern Iowa, IA	B
U of Rio Grande, OH	B
U of Sioux Falls, SD	A
U of Toledo, OH	B
U of West Florida, FL	B
U of Wisconsin–Green Bay, WI	A,B
U of Wisconsin–Parkside, WI	B
Ursuline Coll, OH	B
Valparaiso U, IN	B
Waldorf Coll, IA	B
Washburn U, KS	A
Washington U in St. Louis, MO	B
Wichita State U, KS	A
Wright State U, OH	B

Human Nutrition

Case Western Reserve U, OH	B
Kent State U, OH	B
U of Missouri–Columbia, MO	B

Human Resources Development

Oakland U, MI	B
Trinity International U, IL	B

Human Resources Management

American InterContinental U Online, IL	B
Baker Coll of Owosso, MI	A,B

Ball State U, IN	B
Black Hills State U, SD	B
Bowling Green State U, OH	B
Brescia U, KY	B
Briar Cliff U, IA	B
Capital U, OH	B
Central Christian Coll of Kansas, KS	A
Central Michigan U, MI	B
Central Missouri State U, MO	B
Clarkson U	B
Cleary U, MI	B
Colorado Tech U Sioux Falls Campus, SD	B
Davenport U, Lansing, MI	B
DePaul U, IL	B
East Central U, OK	B
Eastern Michigan U, MI	B
Franklin U, OH	B
Governors State U, IL	B
Grace U, NE	B
Grand Valley State U, MI	B
Hastings Coll, NE	B
Indiana Inst of Technology, IN	B
Indiana State U, IN	B
Judson Coll, IL	B
Lewis U, IL	B
Lindenwood U, MO	B
Loras Coll, IA	B
Loyola U Chicago, IL	B
Madonna U, MI	B
Marietta Coll, OH	B
Marquette U, WI	B
Martin U, IN	B
Metropolitan State U, MN	B
Miami U, OH	B
Michigan State U, MI	B
MidAmerica Nazarene U, KS	B
Millikin U, IL	B
Northeastern Illinois U, IL	B
Northeastern State U, OK	B
Notre Dame Coll, OH	B
Oakland City U, IN	B
The Ohio State U, OH	B
Ohio U, OH	B
Oklahoma Baptist U, OK	B
Oklahoma State U, OK	B
Olivet Nazarene U, IL	B
Purdue U Calumet, IN	B
Rockhurst U, MO	B
Roosevelt U, IL	B
St. Cloud State U, MN	B
Saint Louis U, MO	B
Saint Mary-of-the-Woods Coll, IN	B
Saint Mary's U of Minnesota, MN	B
Silver Lake Coll, WI	B
Southwestern Coll, KS	B
Spring Arbor U, MI	B
Taylor U, IN	B
Trinity Christian Coll, IL	B
Trinity International U, IL	B
The U of Akron, OH	B
U of Central Oklahoma, OK	B
U of Detroit Mercy, MI	B
The U of Findlay, OH	A,B
U of Indianapolis, IN	B
The U of Iowa, IA	B
U of Michigan–Flint, MI	B
U of Minnesota, Duluth, MN	B
U of Nebraska at Omaha, NE	B

A—associate degree; B—bachelor's degree

U of Saint Francis, IN — B
U of St. Thomas, MN — B
U of Toledo, OH — B
U of Wisconsin–Milwaukee, WI — B
U of Wisconsin–Whitewater, WI — B
Urbana U, OH — A,B
Ursuline Coll, OH — B
Valley City State U, ND — B
Washington U in St. Louis, MO — B
Webster U, MO — B
Western Illinois U, IL — B
Western Michigan U, MI — B
Wichita State U, KS — B
Winona State U, MN — B
Wright State U, OH — B
Xavier U, OH — B
York Coll, NE — B

Human Resources Management and Services Related
Capella U, MN — B
Drake U, IA — B
Miami U Hamilton, OH — B
Park U, MO — B
U of Oklahoma, OK — B

Human Services
Adrian Coll, MI — A,B
Albion Coll, MI — B
Baker Coll of Clinton Township, MI — A
Baker Coll of Flint, MI — A
Baker Coll of Muskegon, MI — A
Baldwin-Wallace Coll, OH — B
Bethel Coll, IN — B
Black Hills State U, SD — B
Calumet Coll of Saint Joseph, IN — B
Chatfield Coll, OH — A
Coll of Saint Mary, NE — B
Coll of Saint Mary, NE — A,B
Concordia U, St. Paul, MN — B
Dakota Wesleyan U, SD — B
Doane Coll, NE — B
Florida Gulf Coast U, FL — B
Fontbonne U, MO — B
The Franciscan U, IA — B
Grace Bible Coll, MI — A,B
Graceland U, IA — B
Grand View Coll, IA — B
Hannibal-LaGrange Coll, MO — B
Hastings Coll, NE — B
Indiana Inst of Technology, IN — B
Indiana U East, IN — A
Indiana U–Purdue U Fort Wayne, IN — A,B
Judson Coll, IL — B
Kendall Coll, IL — A,B
Kent State U, OH — A
Kent State U, Salem Campus, OH — A
Lake Superior State U, MI — B
Lindenwood U, MO — B
Metropolitan State U, MN — B
Millikin U, IL — B
Missouri Baptist U, MO — B
Missouri Valley Coll, MO — B
Mount Vernon Nazarene U, OH — A
National-Louis U, IL — B
Ohio U, OH — A

Ohio U–Chillicothe, OH — A
Ohio U–Southern Campus, OH — A
Ottawa U, KS — B
Park U, MO — B
Rochester Comm and Tech Coll, MN — A
Roosevelt U, IL — B
Saint Mary-of-the-Woods Coll, IN — B
Saint Mary's U of Minnesota, MN — B
Siena Heights U, MI — B
Southwest Baptist U, MO — B
Tiffin U, OH — B
U of Cincinnati, OH — A
U of Detroit Mercy, MI — B
U of Minnesota, Morris, MN — B
U of Saint Francis, IN — A
U of Wisconsin–Oshkosh, WI — B
Upper Iowa U, IA — B
Walsh U, OH — A,B
William Penn U, IA — B

Hydrology and Water Resources Science
East Central U, OK — B
Grand Valley State U, MI — B
Heidelberg Coll, OH — B
Lake Superior State U, MI — A
Northern Michigan U, MI — B
Northland Coll, WI — B
U of Wisconsin–Madison, WI — B
U of Wisconsin–Stevens Point, WI — B
Wright State U, OH — B

Illustration
Art Academy of Cincinnati, OH — B
The Cleveland Inst of Art, OH — B
Coll for Creative Studies, MI — B
Columbia Coll, MO — B
Columbus Coll of Art & Design, OH — B
Lawrence Technological U, MI — B
School of the Art Inst of Chicago, IL — B
U of Kansas, KS — B
Washington U in St. Louis, MO — B

Industrial and Organizational Psychology
Clarkson U — B
Madonna U, MI — B
Maryville U of Saint Louis, MO — B
Nebraska Wesleyan U, NE — B
Northern Michigan U, MI — B
Saint Xavier U, IL — B
U of Illinois at Urbana–Champaign, IL — B
Washington U in St. Louis, MO — B
Wright State U, OH — B

Industrial Arts
Andrews U, MI — B
Ball State U, IN — B
Bemidji State U, MN — B
Chicago State U, IL — B
Coll of the Ozarks, MO — B
Fort Hays State U, KS — B

Lincoln U, MO — B
McPherson Coll, KS — B
Minnesota State U Mankato, MN — B
North Carolina Ag and Tech State U, NC — B
Northeastern State U, OK — B
Northern State U, SD — B
Ohio Northern U, OH — B
Oklahoma Panhandle State U, OK — B
Oklahoma State U, OK — B
Pittsburg State U, KS — B
St. Cloud State U, MN — B
Southwestern Oklahoma State U, OK — B
U of Cincinnati, OH — A
U of Wisconsin–Platteville, WI — B
William Penn U, IA — B

Industrial Design
The Cleveland Inst of Art, OH — B
Coll for Creative Studies, MI — B
Columbia Coll Chicago, IL — B
Columbus Coll of Art & Design, OH — B
Ferris State U, MI — A
ITT Tech Inst, Fort Wayne, IN — B
Kansas City Art Inst, MO — B
Milwaukee Inst of Art and Design, WI — B
Northern Michigan U, MI — A,B
Oakland City U, IN — A
The Ohio State U, OH — B
Pittsburg State U, KS — B
U of Cincinnati, OH — B
U of Illinois at Chicago, IL — B
U of Illinois at Urbana–Champaign, IL — B
U of Kansas, KS — B
U of Michigan, MI — B
U of Wisconsin–Platteville, WI — B
Western Michigan U, MI — B

Industrial Electronics Technology
North Dakota State Coll of Science, ND — A

Industrial Engineering
Bethel Coll, IN — B
Bradley U, IL — B
Central Michigan U, MI — B
Central State U, OH — B
Cleveland State U, OH — B
Ferris State U, MI — B
Grand Valley State U, MI — B
Iowa State U of Science and Technology, IA — B
Kansas State U, KS — B
Kent State U, OH — B
Kettering U, MI — B
Lehigh U, PA — B
Marquette U, WI — B
Miami U, OH — B
Michigan Technological U, MI — B
Milwaukee School of Engineering, WI — B
North Carolina Ag and Tech State U, NC — B
North Dakota State U, ND — B
Northern Illinois U, IL — B

Northwestern U, IL — B
The Ohio State U, OH — B
Ohio U, OH — B
Oklahoma State U, OK — B
Purdue U, IN — B
Purdue U Calumet, IN — B
Roosevelt U, IL — B
St. Ambrose U, IA — B
St. Cloud State U, MN — B
South Dakota School of Mines and Technology, SD — B
Southern Illinois U Edwardsville, IL — B
The U of Alabama in Huntsville, AL — B
U of Cincinnati, OH — B
U of Illinois at Chicago, IL — B
U of Illinois at Urbana–Champaign, IL — B
The U of Iowa, IA — B
U of Michigan, MI — B
U of Michigan–Dearborn, MI — B
U of Minnesota, Duluth, MN — B
U of Minnesota, Twin Cities Campus, MN — B
U of Missouri–Columbia, MO — B
U of Missouri–Rolla, MO — B
U of Nebraska–Lincoln, NE — B
U of Oklahoma, OK — B
U of Toledo, OH — A,B
U of Wisconsin–Madison, WI — B
U of Wisconsin–Milwaukee, WI — B
U of Wisconsin–Platteville, WI — B
Wayne State U, MI — B
Western Michigan U, MI — B
Wichita State U, KS — B
Youngstown State U, OH — B

Industrial Production Technologies Related
Central Michigan U, MI — B
Chadron State Coll, NE — B
Indiana State U, IN — B
Kent State U, OH — A
Southwestern Coll, KS — B
The U of Akron, OH — B
U of Nebraska–Lincoln, NE — A,B
U of Wisconsin–Stout, WI — B
Wayne State U, MI — B

Industrial Radiologic Technology
Baker Coll of Owosso, MI — A,B
Ball State U, IN — A
Briar Cliff U, IA — B
Concordia U Wisconsin, WI — B
Ferris State U, MI — A
Fort Hays State U, KS — A
Jamestown Coll, ND — B
Madonna U, MI — B
National-Louis U, IL — B
U of Cincinnati, OH — A
U of Sioux Falls, SD — B
Washburn U, KS — A

Industrial Safety Technology
South Dakota State U, SD — B

Industrial Technology
Baker Coll of Flint, MI — B
Baker Coll of Muskegon, MI — A
Ball State U, IN — A,B
Bemidji State U, MN — B
Black Hills State U, SD — B

Bowling Green State U, OH   B
Bradley U, IL   B
Cameron U, OK   A
Central Missouri State U, MO   A,B
Central State U, OH   B
Cleveland State U, OH   B
Dunwoody Coll of Technology, MN   A
Eastern Illinois U, IL   B
Eastern Michigan U, MI   B
Ferris State U, MI   A,B
Illinois Inst of Technology, IL   B
Illinois State U, IL   B
Indiana State U, IN   B
Indiana U–Purdue U Fort Wayne, IN   A,B
Kansas State U, KS   A
Kent State U, OH   A,B
Kent State U, Salem Campus, OH   A
Kent State U, Tuscarawas Campus, OH   A,B
Lake Superior State U, MI   B
Lawrence Technological U, MI   B
Minnesota State U Mankato, MN   B
Minnesota State U Moorhead, MN   B
North Carolina Ag and Tech State U, NC   B
North Dakota State Coll of Science, ND   A
Northeastern State U, OK   B
Northern Illinois U, IL   B
Northern Michigan U, MI   A,B
Ohio Northern U, OH   B
Ohio U, OH   B
Oklahoma Panhandle State U, OK   A,B
Oklahoma State U, OK   B
Pittsburg State U, KS   B
Purdue U Calumet, IN   A,B
Purdue U North Central, IN   A
Saginaw Valley State U, MI   B
Saint Mary's U of Minnesota, MN   B
South Dakota State U, SD   B
Southeastern Oklahoma State U, OK   B
Southeast Missouri State U, MO   B
Southern Illinois U Carbondale, IL   B
Southwestern Oklahoma State U, OK   B
Tri-State U, IN   A
The U of Akron, OH   A,B
U of Cincinnati, OH   A
U of Dayton, OH   B
U of Nebraska at Omaha, NE   B
U of Nebraska–Lincoln, NE   B
U of North Dakota, ND   B
U of Northern Iowa, IA   B
U of Rio Grande, OH   A,B
U of Toledo, OH   A,B
U of Wisconsin–Platteville, WI   B
Wayne State U, MI   B
Western Illinois U, IL   B
William Penn U, IA   B
Wright State U, OH   A

Information Resources Management
Clarkson U   B
U of Wisconsin–Eau Claire, WI   B

Information Science/Studies
Andrews U, MI   B
Ashland U, OH   B
Baker Coll of Cadillac, MI   A,B
Baker Coll of Clinton Township, MI   A
Baker Coll of Flint, MI   A,B
Baker Coll of Jackson, MI   A,B
Baker Coll of Muskegon, MI   A,B
Baker Coll of Owosso, MI   A,B
Baker Coll of Port Huron, MI   A,B
Baker U, KS   B
Baldwin-Wallace Coll, OH   B
Ball State U, IN   A,B
Bellevue U, NE   B
Bemidji State U, MN   B
Benedictine U, IL   B
Bluffton Coll, OH   B
Bradley U, IL   B
Butler U, IN   B
Calumet Coll of Saint Joseph, IN   A,B
Carroll Coll, WI   B
Cedarville U, OH   B
Central Coll, IA   B
Chadron State Coll, NE   B
Chicago State U, IL   B
Clarke Coll, IA   B
Cleveland State U, OH   B
Colorado Tech U Sioux Falls Campus, SD   A,B
Concordia U, IL   B
Concord U, WV   B
Cornerstone U, MI   B
Culver-Stockton Coll, MO   B
Dakota State U, SD   A,B
DePaul U, IL   B
DeVry U, Addison, IL   B
DeVry U, Chicago, IL   B
DeVry U, Tinley Park, IL   B
DeVry U, MO   B
DeVry U, Columbus, OH   B
Dominican U, IL   B
Drake U, IA   B
Eastern Michigan U, MI   B
Edgewood Coll, WI   B
Emporia State U, KS   B
Ferris State U, MI   B
Fort Hays State U, KS   B
Goshen Coll, IN   B
Grand Valley State U, MI   B
Grand View Coll, IA   B
Harris-Stowe State Coll, MO   B
Heidelberg Coll, OH   B
Illinois Coll, IL   B
Illinois Inst of Technology, IL   B
Indiana Inst of Technology, IN   A,B
Iowa Wesleyan Coll, IA   B
Judson Coll, IL   B
Kansas State U, KS   B
Kansas Wesleyan U, KS   B
Kettering U, MI   B
Lehigh U, PA   B
Lincoln U, MO   B
Loyola U Chicago, IL   B
MacMurray Coll, IL   B
Madonna U, MI   B

Marietta Coll, OH   B
Marquette U, WI   B
McKendree Coll, IL   B
Metropolitan State U, MN   B
Michigan Technological U, MI   B
Minnesota School of Business-Richfield, MN   A
Minnesota State U Mankato, MN   B
Missouri Southern State U, MO   A,B
Missouri Western State Coll, MO   B
Mount Union Coll, OH   B
National American U, SD   A,B
National American U–Sioux Falls Branch, SD   A,B
National-Louis U, IL   B
Nebraska Wesleyan U, NE   B
Newman U, KS   A,B
Northern Michigan U, MI   B
Northland Coll, WI   B
Northwestern Oklahoma State U, OK   B
Northwestern U, IL   B
Notre Dame Coll, OH   B
Oakland City U, IN   A,B
Ohio Dominican U, OH   B
The Ohio State U, OH   B
Oklahoma Baptist U, OK   B
Oklahoma Christian U, OK   B
Oklahoma Panhandle State U, OK   A,B
Oklahoma State U, OK   B
Olivet Nazarene U, IL   B
Ottawa U, KS   B
Pittsburg State U, KS   B
Purdue U Calumet, IN   B
Purdue U North Central, IN   A
Quincy U, IL   B
Rockhurst U, MO   B
St. Ambrose U, IA   B
St. Cloud State U, MN   B
Saint Mary-of-the-Woods Coll, IN   B
Saint Mary's U of Minnesota, MN   B
Siena Heights U, MI   A,B
Silver Lake Coll, WI   B
Simpson Coll, IA   B
South Dakota State U, SD   B
Southeastern Oklahoma State U, OK   B
Southern Illinois U Carbondale, IL   B
Southern Nazarene U, OK   B
Southwest Baptist U, MO   B
Taylor U, IN   B
Tiffin U, OH   B
Trinity Christian Coll, IL   B
Union Coll, NE   A,B
U of Cincinnati, OH   A,B
U of Dayton, OH   B
U of Detroit Mercy, MI   B
U of Indianapolis, IN   A,B
U of Mary, ND   B
U of Michigan–Dearborn, MI   B
U of Michigan–Flint, MI   B
U of Minnesota, Crookston, MN   A,B
U of Missouri–Rolla, MO   B
U of Saint Mary, KS   B
U of Sioux Falls, SD   B
U of Toledo, OH   A,B

U of Tulsa, OK   B
U of Wisconsin–Green Bay, WI   A,B
U of Wisconsin–River Falls, WI   B
U of Wisconsin–Superior, WI   B
Waldorf Coll, IA   B
Wartburg Coll, IA   B
Washburn U, KS   A,B
Washington U in St. Louis, MO   B
Wayne State Coll, NE   B
Wayne State U, MI   B
Webster U, MO   B
Wilberforce U, OH   B
William Jewell Coll, MO   B
Winona State U, MN   B
Wright State U, OH   B
Youngstown State U, OH   A,B

Information Technology
American InterContinental U Online, IL   B
Bellevue U, NE   B
Bluffton Coll, OH   B
Capella U, MN   B
Coll of the Ozarks, MO   B
Globe Coll, MN   A
Illinois Inst of Technology, IL   B
Illinois State U, IL   B
Indiana Inst of Technology, IN   A
International Academy of Design & Technology, IL   A
Kaplan Coll, IA   A,B
Kilian Comm Coll, SD   A
Lawrence Technological U, MI   B
Marian Coll of Fond du Lac, WI   B
Minnesota School of Business–Brooklyn Center, MN   A
Minnesota School of Business–Plymouth, MN   A
National American U–Sioux Falls Branch, SD   A,B
Robert Morris Coll, IL   B
U of Michigan–Flint, MI   B
U of Missouri–Kansas City, MO   B
U of Phoenix–Metro Detroit Campus, MI   B
U of Phoenix–Oklahoma City Campus, OK   B
U of Phoenix–West Michigan Campus, MI   B
U of St. Francis, IL   B
U of Wisconsin–Whitewater, WI   B

Institutional Food Workers
Kendall Coll, IL   A,B
Lexington Coll, IL   A,B

Insurance
Ball State U, IN   B
Bradley U, IL   B
Ferris State U, MI   B
Illinois State U, IL   B
Illinois Wesleyan U, IL   B
Indiana State U, IN   B
Martin U, IN   B
Minnesota State U Mankato, MN   B
The Ohio State U, OH   B

A—associate degree; B—bachelor's degree

Olivet Coll, MI — B
Roosevelt U, IL — B
St. Cloud State U, MN — B
Southwest Missouri State U, MO — B
The U of Akron, OH — B
U of Cincinnati, OH — A,B
U of Minnesota, Twin Cities Campus, MN — B
U of Wisconsin–Madison, WI — B

Intercultural/Multicultural and Diversity Studies
Coll of St. Catherine, MN — B
Evangel U, MO — B
Marquette U, WI — B

Interdisciplinary Studies
Antioch Coll, OH — B
Augsburg Coll, MN — B
Beloit Coll, WI — B
Blackburn Coll, IL — B
Briar Cliff U, IA — B
Calvin Coll, MI — B
Capital U, OH — A
Cardinal Stritch U, WI — A
Carleton Coll, MN — B
Central Coll, IA — B
Central Methodist Coll, MO — A,B
Chadron State Coll, NE — B
Clarkson U — B
Cleveland State U, OH — B
Coe Coll, IA — B
Coll of the Ozarks, MO — B
The Coll of Wooster, OH — B
Columbia Coll Chicago, IL — B
Cornell Coll, IA — B
Cornerstone U, MI — B
Dana Coll, NE — B
DePaul U, IL — B
DePauw U, IN — B
Earlham Coll, IN — B
Eastern Michigan U, MI — B
Elmhurst Coll, IL — B
Franklin U, OH — B
Grand Valley State U, MI — B
Grinnell Coll, IA — B
Gustavus Adolphus Coll, MN — B
Harris-Stowe State Coll, MO — B
Hastings Coll, NE — B
Hillsdale Coll, MI — B
Hillsdale Free Will Baptist Coll, OK — A,B
Hope Coll, MI — B
Illinois Coll, IL — B
Illinois Wesleyan U, IL — B
Iowa State U of Science and Technology, IA — B
John Carroll U, OH — B
Kalamazoo Coll, MI — B
Kansas State U, KS — A
Kent State U, Stark Campus, OH — B
Kenyon Coll, OH — B
Lake Superior State U, MI — B
Luther Coll, IA — B
Macalester Coll, MN — B
Manchester Coll, IN — B
Marquette U, WI — B
Martin Luther Coll, MN — B
Maryville U of Saint Louis, MO — B
McPherson Coll, KS — B
Miami U, OH — B
Millikin U, IL — B

Minneapolis Coll of Art and Design, MN — B
Minnesota State U Moorhead, MN — B
Morningside Coll, IA — B
Mount Union Coll, OH — B
Muskingum Coll, OH — B
Nebraska Wesleyan U, NE — B
North Central U, MN — A,B
Northland Coll, WI — B
Northwestern U, IL — B
Oakland City U, IN — B
Oakland U, MI — B
Oberlin Coll, OH — B
Ohio Dominican U, OH — A,B
Ohio U, OH — B
Ohio U–Southern Campus, OH — A
Oklahoma Baptist U, OK — B
Olivet Nazarene U, IL — B
Purdue U, IN — B
Ripon Coll, WI — B
Rochester Coll, MI — B
St. Cloud State U, MN — B
Saint Mary's Coll, IN — B
St. Norbert Coll, WI — B
Silver Lake Coll, WI — B
South Dakota School of Mines and Technology, SD — B
Southeast Missouri State U, MO — B
Southern Nazarene U, OK — B
Stephens Coll, MO — B
Sterling Coll, KS — B
Tabor Coll, KS — A,B
Taylor U Fort Wayne, IN — B
The U of Akron, OH — A,B
U of Chicago, IL — B
U of Illinois at Springfield, IL — B
The U of Iowa, IA — B
U of Mary, ND — B
U of Michigan, MI — B
U of Michigan–Dearborn, MI — B
U of Minnesota, Crookston, MN — B
U of Minnesota, Duluth, MN — B
U of Missouri–Columbia, MO — B
U of Missouri–Kansas City, MO — B
U of Saint Mary, KS — B
U of St. Thomas, MN — B
U of Sioux Falls, SD — A,B
U of Wisconsin–Green Bay, WI — A,B
U of Wisconsin–Milwaukee, WI — B
U of Wisconsin–Parkside, WI — B
Washington U in St. Louis, MO — B
Wayne State Coll, NE — B
Wayne State U, MI — B
Webster U, MO — B
William Jewell Coll, MO — B
William Woods U, MO — B
Wisconsin Lutheran Coll, WI — B

Interior Architecture
Central Michigan U, MI — B
Central Missouri State U, MO — B
Indiana State U, IN — B
Kansas State U, KS — B
Lawrence Technological U, MI — B

School of the Art Inst of Chicago, IL — B
U of Missouri–Columbia, MO — B
U of Nebraska–Lincoln, NE — B

Interior Design
Adrian Coll, MI — B
The Art Insts International Minnesota, MN — A,B
Baker Coll of Allen Park, MI — A
Baker Coll of Auburn Hills, MI — A
Baker Coll of Clinton Township, MI — A
Baker Coll of Flint, MI — A,B
Baker Coll of Muskegon, MI — A
Baker Coll of Owosso, MI — A
Baker Coll of Port Huron, MI — A
Bethel Coll, IN — B
Central Missouri State U, MO — B
The Cleveland Inst of Art, OH — B
Coll for Creative Studies, MI — B
Coll of Mount St. Joseph, OH — A,B
Columbia Coll Chicago, IL — B
Columbus Coll of Art & Design, OH — B
Concordia U Wisconsin, WI — B
Eastern Michigan U, MI — B
Ferris State U, MI — B
Harrington Coll of Design, IL — A,B
The Illinois Inst of Art, IL — A,B
The Illinois Inst of Art-Schaumburg, IL — B
Indiana U Bloomington, IN — B
Indiana U–Purdue U Fort Wayne, IN — A
Indiana U–Purdue U Indianapolis, IN — B
International Academy of Design & Technology, IL — A,B
Iowa State U of Science and Technology, IA — B
Kansas State U, KS — B
Kent State U, OH — B
Marian Coll, IN — A
Maryville U of Saint Louis, MO — B
Miami U, OH — B
Miami U Hamilton, OH — B
Michigan State U, MI — B
Milwaukee Inst of Art and Design, WI — B
Minnesota State U Mankato, MN — B
Mount Mary Coll, WI — B
North Dakota State U, ND — B
The Ohio State U, OH — B
Oklahoma Christian U, OK — B
Oklahoma State U, OK — B
Park U, MO — B
Pittsburg State U, KS — B
Robert Morris Coll, IL — A
School of the Art Inst of Chicago, IL — B
South Dakota State U, SD — B
Southern Illinois U Carbondale, IL — B
The U of Akron, OH — B
U of Central Oklahoma, OK — B
U of Cincinnati, OH — B
U of Kansas, KS — B

U of Michigan, MI — B
U of Minnesota, Twin Cities Campus, MN — B
U of Northern Iowa, IA — B
U of Oklahoma, OK — B
U of Wisconsin–Madison, WI — B
U of Wisconsin–Stevens Point, WI — B
Ursuline Coll, OH — B
Wayne State Coll, NE — B
Western Michigan U, MI — B
Westwood Coll–Chicago Du Page, IL — B
Westwood Coll–Chicago Loop Campus, IL — B
Westwood Coll–Chicago O'Hare Airport, IL — B
Westwood Coll–Chicago River Oaks, IL — B
William Woods U, MO — B

Intermedia/Multimedia
Academy Coll, MN — A
Art Academy of Cincinnati, OH — B
The Art Insts International Minnesota, MN — A,B
Calumet Coll of Saint Joseph, IN — B
The Cleveland Inst of Art, OH — B
Coll for Creative Studies, MI — B
Columbia Coll Chicago, IL — B
Globe Coll, MN — A
International Academy of Design & Technology, IL — A
Minneapolis Coll of Art and Design, MN — B
Minnesota School of Business–Brooklyn Center, MN — A
Minnesota School of Business-Plymouth, MN — A
Minnesota School of Business-Richfield, MN — A
Robert Morris Coll, IL — A
School of the Art Inst of Chicago, IL — B
U of Michigan, MI — B
Westwood Coll–Chicago Du Page, IL — A,B
Westwood Coll–Chicago Loop Campus, IL — A,B
Westwood Coll–Chicago O'Hare Airport, IL — A,B
Westwood Coll–Chicago River Oaks, IL — A,B

International Agriculture
Iowa State U of Science and Technology, IA — B
MidAmerica Nazarene U, KS — B
U of Missouri–Columbia, MO — B

International Business/Trade/Commerce
Adrian Coll, MI — B
Alma Coll, MI — B
Alverno Coll, WI — B
Aquinas Coll, MI — B
Augsburg Coll, MN — B
Avila U, MO — B
Baker U, KS — B
Benedictine U, IL — B
Bethany Coll, KS — B

Majors and Degrees
International Business/Trade/Commerce

Institution	Degree
Bethel Coll, IN	B
Bowling Green State U, OH	B
Bradley U, IL	B
Buena Vista U, IA	B
Butler U, IN	B
Cardinal Stritch U, WI	B
Cedarville U, OH	B
Central Coll, IA	B
Central Michigan U, MI	B
Clarke Coll, IA	B
Clarkson U	B
Coll of St. Catherine, MN	B
The Coll of St. Scholastica, MN	B
Coll of the Ozarks, MO	B
Columbia Coll, MO	B
Concordia Coll, MN	B
Cornell Coll, IA	B
Creighton U, NE	B
Davenport U, Dearborn, MI	B
Davenport U, Grand Rapids, MI	B
Davenport U, Warren, MI	B
DePaul U, IL	B
Dickinson State U, ND	B
Dominican U, IL	B
Drake U, IA	B
Drury U, MO	B
Eastern Michigan U, MI	B
Elmhurst Coll, IL	B
Ferris State U, MI	B
Gannon U, PA	B
Grace Coll, IN	B
Graceland U, IA	B
Grand Valley State U, MI	B
Gustavus Adolphus Coll, MN	B
Hamline U, MN	B
Hiram Coll, OH	B
Illinois State U, IL	B
Illinois Wesleyan U, IL	B
Iowa State U of Science and Technology, IA	B
Jamestown Coll, ND	B
Judson Coll, IL	B
Lake Erie Coll, OH	B
Lakeland Coll, WI	B
Loras Coll, IA	B
MacCormac Coll, IL	A
Madonna U, MI	B
Marietta Coll, OH	B
Marquette U, WI	B
Marygrove Coll, MI	B
McPherson Coll, KS	B
Metropolitan State U, MN	B
Millikin U, IL	B
Milwaukee School of Engineering, WI	B
Minnesota State U Mankato, MN	B
Minnesota State U Moorhead, MN	B
Minot State U, ND	B
Missouri Southern State U, MO	B
Mount Union Coll, OH	B
Muskingum Coll, OH	B
National-Louis U, IL	B
Nebraska Wesleyan U, NE	B
North Central Coll, IL	B
Northern State U, SD	B
North Park U, IL	B
Northwestern Coll, MN	B
Northwood U, MI	A,B
Ohio Dominican U, OH	B
Ohio Northern U, OH	B
The Ohio State U, OH	B
Ohio U, OH	B
Ohio Wesleyan U, OH	B
Oklahoma Baptist U, OK	B
Oklahoma City U, OK	B
Oklahoma State U, OK	B
Otterbein Coll, OH	B
Roosevelt U, IL	B
St. Ambrose U, IA	B
St. Cloud State U, MN	B
Saint Louis U, MO	B
Saint Mary's Coll, IN	B
Saint Mary's U of Minnesota, MN	B
St. Norbert Coll, WI	B
Saint Xavier U, IL	B
Simpson Coll, IA	B
Taylor U, IN	B
Taylor U Fort Wayne, IN	B
Trinity International U, IL	B
The U of Akron, OH	B
U of Dayton, OH	B
U of Detroit Mercy, MI	B
U of Evansville, IN	B
The U of Findlay, OH	B
U of Indianapolis, IN	B
U of Minnesota, Twin Cities Campus, MN	B
U of Missouri–Columbia, MO	B
U of Missouri–St. Louis, MO	B
U of Nebraska–Lincoln, NE	B
U of Oklahoma, OK	B
U of Rio Grande, OH	B
U of Saint Francis, IN	A
U of St. Thomas, MN	B
U of Toledo, OH	B
U of Tulsa, OK	B
U of Wisconsin–La Crosse, WI	B
Valparaiso U, IN	B
Wartburg Coll, IA	B
Washington U in St. Louis, MO	B
Wayne State Coll, NE	B
Webster U, MO	B
Westminster Coll, MO	B
Wichita State U, KS	B
William Jewell Coll, MO	B
William Woods U, MO	B
Wright State U, OH	B

International Economics

Institution	Degree
Carthage Coll, WI	B
Coll of St. Catherine, MN	B
Eastern Michigan U, MI	B
Hamline U, MN	B
Hiram Coll, OH	B
John Carroll U, OH	B
Lawrence U, WI	B
Ohio U, OH	B
Rockford Coll, IL	B
Taylor U, IN	B
U of Missouri–Columbia, MO	B
U of St. Thomas, MN	B
Valparaiso U, IN	B
Washington U in St. Louis, MO	B
Youngstown State U, OH	B

International Finance

Institution	Degree
The U of Akron, OH	B
Washington U in St. Louis, MO	B

International/Global Studies

Institution	Degree
Alverno Coll, WI	B
Baldwin-Wallace Coll, OH	B
Case Western Reserve U, OH	B
The Coll of St. Scholastica, MN	B
Concordia Coll, MN	B
Grinnell Coll, IA	B
Hanover Coll, IN	B
Hope Coll, MI	B
Illinois Wesleyan U, IL	B
Kenyon Coll, OH	B
Marquette U, WI	B
Miami U Hamilton, OH	B
Michigan State U, MI	B
Nebraska Wesleyan U, NE	B
North Dakota State U, ND	B
U of Chicago, IL	B
The U of Iowa, IA	B
U of Nebraska at Omaha, NE	B
U of New Orleans, LA	B
U of Wisconsin–Whitewater, WI	B

International Marketing

Institution	Degree
Oklahoma Baptist U, OK	B
The U of Akron, OH	B

International Relations and Affairs

Institution	Degree
Adrian Coll, MI	B
Albion Coll, MI	B
Alverno Coll, WI	B
Antioch Coll, OH	B
Aquinas Coll, MI	B
Ashland U, OH	B
Augsburg Coll, MN	B
Augustana Coll, SD	B
Beloit Coll, WI	B
Benedictine U, IL	B
Bethel U, MN	B
Bowling Green State U, OH	B
Bradley U, IL	B
Butler U, IN	B
Calvin Coll, MI	B
Capital U, OH	B
Carleton Coll, MN	B
Carroll Coll, WI	B
Case Western Reserve U, OH	B
Cedarville U, OH	B
Central Michigan U, MI	B
Cleveland State U, OH	B
Coll of St. Catherine, MN	B
The Coll of Wooster, OH	B
Cornell Coll, IA	B
Creighton U, NE	B
Denison U, OH	B
DePaul U, IL	B
Doane Coll, NE	B
Drake U, IA	B
Earlham Coll, IN	B
Edgewood Coll, WI	B
Graceland U, IA	B
Grand Valley State U, MI	B
Hamline U, MN	B
Hastings Coll, NE	B
Heidelberg Coll, OH	B
Hillsdale Coll, MI	B
Illinois Coll, IL	B
Iowa State U of Science and Technology, IA	B
John Carroll U, OH	B
Kent State U, OH	B
Kenyon Coll, OH	B
Knox Coll, IL	B
Lake Forest Coll, IL	B
Lawrence U, WI	B
Lehigh U, PA	B
Lindenwood U, MO	B
Loras Coll, IA	B
Loyola U Chicago, IL	B
Luther Coll, IA	B
Macalester Coll, MN	B
Marian Coll of Fond du Lac, WI	B
Marquette U, WI	B
McKendree Coll, IL	B
Miami U, OH	B
Michigan State U, MI	B
Millikin U, IL	B
Minnesota State U Mankato, MN	B
Missouri Southern State U, MO	B
Mount Mary Coll, WI	B
Mount Mercy Coll, IA	B
Muskingum Coll, OH	B
Northern Michigan U, MI	B
North Park U, IL	B
Northwestern U, IL	B
Ohio Northern U, OH	B
The Ohio State U, OH	B
Ohio U, OH	B
Ohio Wesleyan U, OH	B
Oral Roberts U, OK	B
Otterbein Coll, OH	B
Rockford Coll, IL	B
Rockhurst U, MO	B
Roosevelt U, IL	B
Saginaw Valley State U, MI	B
St. Cloud State U, MN	B
Saint Joseph's Coll, IN	B
Saint Louis U, MO	B
St. Norbert Coll, WI	B
Saint Xavier U, IL	B
Shawnee State U, OH	B
Simpson Coll, IA	B
Southern Nazarene U, OK	B
Stephens Coll, MO	B
Tabor Coll, KS	B
Taylor U, IN	B
Tiffin U, OH	B
Union Coll, NE	B
U of Cincinnati, OH	B
U of Dayton, OH	B
U of Evansville, IN	B
U of Indianapolis, IN	B
U of Kansas, KS	B
U of Michigan, MI	B
U of Michigan–Dearborn, MI	B
U of Minnesota, Duluth, MN	B
U of Minnesota, Twin Cities Campus, MN	B
U of Nebraska–Lincoln, NE	B
U of St. Thomas, MN	B
U of Southern Indiana, IN	B
U of Toledo, OH	B
U of West Florida, FL	B
U of Wisconsin–Madison, WI	B
U of Wisconsin–Milwaukee, WI	B
U of Wisconsin–Oshkosh, WI	B
U of Wisconsin–Parkside, WI	B
U of Wisconsin–Platteville, WI	B

A—associate degree; B—bachelor's degree

U of Wisconsin–Stevens Point, WI
U of Wisconsin–Whitewater, WI B
Valparaiso U, IN B
Wartburg Coll, IA B
Washington U in St. Louis, MO B
Wayne State U, MI B
Webster U, MO B
Westminster Coll, MO B
Wheaton Coll, IL B
William Jewell Coll, MO B
William Woods U, MO B
Winona State U, MN B
Wright State U, OH B
Xavier U, OH B

Islamic Studies
The Ohio State U, OH B
U of Michigan, MI B
Washington U in St. Louis, MO B

Italian
DePaul U, IL B
Dominican U, IL B
Indiana U Bloomington, IN B
Lake Erie Coll, OH B
Loyola U Chicago, IL B
Northwestern U, IL B
Oakland U, MI B
The Ohio State U, OH B
U of Chicago, IL B
U of Illinois at Chicago, IL B
U of Illinois at Urbana–Champaign, IL B
The U of Iowa, IA B
U of Michigan, MI B
U of Minnesota, Twin Cities Campus, MN B
U of Notre Dame, IN B
U of Wisconsin–Madison, WI B
U of Wisconsin–Milwaukee, WI B
Washington U in St. Louis, MO B
Wayne State U, MI B
Youngstown State U, OH B

Japanese
Antioch Coll, OH B
Aquinas Coll, MI B
Augustana Coll, IL B
Ball State U, IN B
DePaul U, IL B
Eastern Michigan U, MI B
Gustavus Adolphus Coll, MN B
Indiana U Bloomington, IN B
Lawrence U, WI B
Lehigh U, PA B
Mount Union Coll, OH B
North Central Coll, IL B
Oakland U, MI B
The Ohio State U, OH B
U of Chicago, IL B
The U of Findlay, OH B
The U of Iowa, IA B
U of Michigan, MI B
U of Minnesota, Twin Cities Campus, MN B
U of Notre Dame, IN B
U of St. Thomas, MN B
U of Wisconsin–Madison, WI B

Washington U in St. Louis, MO B
Winona State U, MN A

Japanese Studies
Case Western Reserve U, OH B
Earlham Coll, IN B
Gustavus Adolphus Coll, MN B

Jazz/Jazz Studies
Augustana Coll, IL B
Capital U, OH B
Central State U, OH B
Chicago State U, IL B
DePaul U, IL B
Drake U, IA B
Hope Coll, MI B
Indiana U Bloomington, IN B
Indiana U South Bend, IN A
Lincoln Coll, Lincoln, IL A
Michigan State U, MI B
North Central Coll, IL B
Northwestern U, IL B
Oberlin Coll, OH B
The Ohio State U, OH B
Roosevelt U, IL B
St. Cloud State U, MN B
U of Cincinnati, OH B
The U of Iowa, IA B
U of Michigan, MI B
U of Minnesota, Duluth, MN B
Webster U, MO B

Jewish/Judaic Studies
DePaul U, IL B
Hamline U, MN B
Indiana U Bloomington, IN B
Laura and Alvin Siegal Coll of Judaic Studies, OH B
Oberlin Coll, OH B
The Ohio State U, OH B
U of Chicago, IL B
U of Cincinnati, OH B
U of Michigan, MI B
U of Minnesota, Twin Cities Campus, MN B
U of Missouri–Kansas City, MO B
Washington U in St. Louis, MO B

Journalism
Andrews U, MI B
Ashland U, OH B
Augustana Coll, SD B
Bacone Coll, OK A
Ball State U, IN A,B
Bemidji State U, MN B
Bethel Coll, IN A
Bowling Green State U, OH B
Bradley U, IL B
Butler U, IN B
Carroll Coll, WI B
Central Christian Coll of Kansas, KS A
Central Michigan U, MI B
Central Missouri State U, MO B
Coll of St. Catherine, MN B
Coll of the Ozarks, MO B
Columbia Coll Chicago, IL B
Concordia Coll, MN B
Creighton U, NE A,B
Dordt Coll, IA B
Drake U, IA B
Drury U, MO B
Eastern Illinois U, IL B

Eastern Michigan U, MI B
Evangel U, MO A,B
Fort Hays State U, KS B
The Franciscan U, IA B
Franklin Coll, IN B
Goshen Coll, IN B
Grace Coll, IN B
Grand Valley State U, MI B
Grand View Coll, IA B
Hastings Coll, NE B
Huntington Coll, IN B
Indiana State U, IN B
Indiana U Bloomington, IN B
Indiana U–Purdue U Indianapolis, IN B
Indiana U Southeast, IN A
Iowa State U of Science and Technology, IA B
Judson Coll, IL B
Kansas State U, KS B
Kent State U, OH B
Lehigh U, PA B
Lewis U, IL B
Lincoln Coll, Lincoln, IL A
Lincoln U, MO B
Lindenwood U, MO B
Loras Coll, IA B
Loyola U Chicago, IL B
Madonna U, MI A,B
Manchester Coll, IN A
Marietta Coll, OH B
Marquette U, WI B
Miami U, OH B
Miami U Hamilton, OH B
Michigan State U, MI B
Minnesota State U Mankato, MN B
Minnesota State U Moorhead, MN B
Mount Vernon Nazarene U, OH B
Muskingum Coll, OH B
North Central U, MN A,B
Northeastern State U, OK B
Northern Illinois U, IL B
Northwestern Coll, MN B
Northwestern U, IL B
Oakland U, MI B
Ohio Northern U, OH B
The Ohio State U, OH B
Ohio U, OH B
Ohio Wesleyan U, OH B
Oklahoma Baptist U, OK B
Oklahoma Christian U, OK B
Oklahoma City U, OK B
Oklahoma State U, OK B
Olivet Coll, MI B
Olivet Nazarene U, IL B
Oral Roberts U, OK B
Otterbein Coll, OH B
Pittsburg State U, KS B
Purdue U Calumet, IN B
Quincy U, IL B
Roosevelt U, IL B
St. Ambrose U, IA B
St. Cloud State U, MN B
St. Gregory's U, OK B
Saint Mary-of-the-Woods Coll, IN B
South Dakota State U, SD B
Southern Illinois U Carbondale, IL B
Southern Nazarene U, OK B
Southwest Missouri State U, MO B
Spring Arbor U, MI B

Tabor Coll, KS B
Truman State U, MO B
Union Coll, NE B
U of Central Oklahoma, OK B
U of Dayton, OH B
U of Detroit Mercy, MI B
The U of Findlay, OH B
U of Illinois at Urbana–Champaign, IL B
The U of Iowa, IA B
U of Kansas, KS B
U of Michigan, MI B
U of Minnesota, Twin Cities Campus, MN B
U of Missouri–Columbia, MO B
U of Nebraska at Omaha, NE B
U of Oklahoma, OK B
U of St. Francis, IL B
U of St. Thomas, MN B
U of Southern Indiana, IN B
U of Toledo, OH B
U of Wisconsin–Eau Claire, WI B
U of Wisconsin–Madison, WI B
U of Wisconsin–Milwaukee, WI B
U of Wisconsin–Oshkosh, WI B
U of Wisconsin–River Falls, WI B
U of Wisconsin–Superior, WI B
U of Wisconsin–Whitewater, WI B
Valparaiso U, IN B
Waldorf Coll, IA B
Wartburg Coll, IA B
Washburn U, KS B
Wayne State Coll, NE B
Wayne State U, MI B
Webster U, MO B
Western Illinois U, IL B
Western Michigan U, MI B
William Penn U, IA B
Winona State U, MN B
Youngstown State U, OH B

Journalism Related
Central State U, OH B
Grace Coll, IN B
Kent State U, OH B
Ohio U, OH B
Roosevelt U, IL B
U of Nebraska–Lincoln, NE B
U of St. Thomas, MN B

Juvenile Corrections
East Central U, OK B
Harris-Stowe State Coll, MO B

Kindergarten/Preschool Education
Alma Coll, MI B
Ashland U, OH B
Augsburg Coll, MN B
Baker Coll of Clinton Township, MI A
Baker Coll of Muskegon, MI A
Baker Coll of Owosso, MI A
Ball State U, IN B
Bethel Coll, IN A
Black Hills State U, SD B
Bluffton Coll, OH B
Bowling Green State U, OH B
Bradley U, IL B

Majors and Degrees
Kindergarten/Preschool Education

College	Degree
Cardinal Stritch U, WI	B
Carroll Coll, WI	B
Central Christian Coll of Kansas, KS	A
Central Methodist Coll, MO	B
Central State U, OH	B
Chatfield Coll, OH	A
Chicago State U, IL	B
Clarke Coll, IA	B
Coll of Mount St. Joseph, OH	A,B
Coll of St. Catherine, MN	B
Columbia Coll Chicago, IL	B
Concordia Coll, MN	B
Concordia U, IL	B
Concordia U, NE	B
Concordia U, St. Paul, MN	B
Concordia U Wisconsin, WI	B
Concord U, WV	B
Crown Coll, MN	A,B
DePaul U, IL	B
Donnelly Coll, KS	A
East Central U, OK	B
Eastern Illinois U, IL	B
Edgewood Coll, WI	B
Elmhurst Coll, IL	B
Evangel U, MO	B
Fontbonne U, MO	B
Fort Hays State U, KS	B
The Franciscan U, IA	B
Goshen Coll, IN	B
Governors State U, IL	B
Hannibal-LaGrange Coll, MO	B
Harris-Stowe State Coll, MO	B
Hesston Coll, KS	A
Hillsdale Coll, MI	B
Illinois State U, IL	B
Indiana U Bloomington, IN	B
Indiana U–Purdue U Indianapolis, IN	
Indiana U South Bend, IN	A
Iowa Wesleyan Coll, IA	B
John Carroll U, OH	B
Judson Coll, IL	B
Kansas Wesleyan U, KS	A
Kendall Coll, IL	A,B
Kent State U, OH	B
Kent State U, Salem Campus, OH	A
Lakeland Coll, WI	B
Lake Superior State U, MI	A
Lincoln Coll, Lincoln, IL	A
Lindenwood U, MO	B
Loras Coll, IA	B
Lourdes Coll, OH	A,B
Loyola U Chicago, IL	B
Manchester Coll, IN	A
Marian Coll, IN	A,B
Marian Coll of Fond du Lac, WI	B
Martin Luther Coll, MN	B
Martin U, IN	B
Marygrove Coll, MI	A,B
Maryville U of Saint Louis, MO	B
McPherson Coll, KS	B
Metropolitan State U, MN	B
Miami U, OH	B
Minnesota State U Mankato, MN	B
Minnesota State U Moorhead, MN	B
Missouri Baptist U, MO	B
Missouri Southern State U, MO	B
Mount Mary Coll, WI	B
Mount Union Coll, OH	B
Mount Vernon Nazarene U, OH	B
Muskingum Coll, OH	B
National-Louis U, IL	B
North Carolina Ag and Tech State U, NC	B
Northeastern Illinois U, IL	B
Northeastern State U, OK	B
Northern Illinois U, IL	B
North Park U, IL	B
Northwestern Coll, MN	B
Northwestern Oklahoma State U, OK	B
Notre Dame Coll, OH	B
Ohio Northern U, OH	B
The Ohio State U–Mansfield Campus, OH	B
Ohio U, OH	B
Ohio U–Southern Campus, OH	A
Ohio Wesleyan U, OH	B
Oklahoma Baptist U, OK	B
Oklahoma Christian U, OK	B
Oklahoma City U, OK	B
Olivet Nazarene U, IL	B
Oral Roberts U, OK	B
Peru State Coll, NE	B
Pittsburg State U, KS	B
Purdue U, IN	B
Purdue U Calumet, IN	A
Roosevelt U, IL	B
St. Cloud State U, MN	B
Saint Mary-of-the-Woods Coll, IN	B
Saint Xavier U, IL	B
Shawnee State U, OH	B
Siena Heights U, MI	A
Silver Lake Coll, WI	B
Simpson Coll, IA	B
South Dakota State U, SD	B
Southeastern Oklahoma State U, OK	B
Southeast Missouri State U, MO	B
Spring Arbor U, MI	B
Stephens Coll, MO	B
Tabor Coll, KS	B
Taylor U, IN	A,B
The U of Akron, OH	B
U of Central Oklahoma, OK	B
U of Cincinnati, OH	B
U of Dayton, OH	B
U of Detroit Mercy, MI	B
U of Illinois at Urbana–Champaign, IL	B
U of Michigan–Dearborn, MI	B
U of Michigan–Flint, MI	B
U of Minnesota, Duluth, MN	B
U of Minnesota, Twin Cities Campus, MN	B
U of Missouri–Columbia, MO	B
U of Missouri–Kansas City, MO	B
U of Northern Iowa, IA	B
U of Rio Grande, OH	A
U of Sioux Falls, SD	A
U of Toledo, OH	B
U of Wisconsin–La Crosse, WI	B
U of Wisconsin–Madison, WI	B
U of Wisconsin–Milwaukee, WI	B
U of Wisconsin–Oshkosh, WI	B
U of Wisconsin–Platteville, WI	B
U of Wisconsin–Stevens Point, WI	B
Waldorf Coll, IA	B
Walsh U, OH	B
Wartburg Coll, IA	B
Washburn U, KS	A,B
Wayne State Coll, NE	B
Webster U, MO	B
William Tyndale Coll, MI	A
Winona State U, MN	B
Wright State U, OH	B
Youngstown State U, OH	B

Kinesiology and Exercise Science

College	Degree
Adrian Coll, MI	B
Alma Coll, MI	B
Augustana Coll, SD	B
Ball State U, IN	B
Bethel Coll, IN	B
Bethel Coll, MN	B
Calvin Coll, MI	B
Capital U, OH	B
Carroll Coll, WI	B
Cedarville U, OH	B
Central Coll, IA	B
Cleveland State U, OH	B
The Coll of St. Scholastica, MN	B
Concordia Coll, MN	B
Concordia U, IL	B
Concordia U, NE	B
Concordia U, St. Paul, MN	B
Cornerstone U, MI	B
Creighton U, NE	B
Dakota State U, SD	B
Defiance Coll, OH	B
DePauw U, IN	B
Dordt Coll, IA	B
Drury U, MO	B
Elmhurst Coll, IL	B
Eureka Coll, IL	B
Florida Gulf Coast U, FL	B
Gannon U, PA	B
Globe Coll, MN	A
Greenville Coll, IL	B
Hamline U, MN	B
Hastings Coll, NE	B
Hope Coll, MI	B
Huntington Coll, IN	B
Iowa Wesleyan Coll, IA	B
Kansas State U, KS	B
Kent State U, OH	B
Lake Superior State U, MI	B
Loras Coll, IA	B
Malone Coll, OH	B
Manchester Coll, IN	A
Marquette U, WI	B
Miami U, OH	B
Michigan State U, MI	B
MidAmerica Nazarene U, KS	B
Minnesota School of Business-Plymouth, MN	A
Minnesota School of Business-Richfield, MN	A
Missouri Southern State U, MO	B
Missouri Western State Coll, MO	B
Mount Union Coll, OH	B
Mount Vernon Nazarene U, OH	B
Nebraska Wesleyan U, NE	B
Northern Michigan U, MI	B
North Park U, IL	B
Northwestern Coll, IA	B
Northwestern Coll, MN	B
Oakland U, MI	B
Ohio Northern U, OH	B
The Ohio State U, OH	B
Ohio U, OH	B
Oklahoma Baptist U, OK	B
Oklahoma City U, OK	B
Olivet Nazarene U, IL	B
Oral Roberts U, OK	B
St. Cloud State U, MN	B
Saint Louis U, MO	B
St. Olaf Coll, MN	B
Southern Nazarene U, OK	B
Transylvania U, KY	B
Truman State U, MO	B
Union Coll, NE	B
U of Dayton, OH	B
U of Evansville, IN	B
U of Illinois at Chicago, IL	B
U of Illinois at Urbana–Champaign, IL	B
The U of Iowa, IA	B
U of Mary, ND	B
U of Michigan, MI	B
U of Minnesota, Duluth, MN	B
U of Nebraska–Lincoln, NE	B
U of Sioux Falls, SD	B
U of Southern Indiana, IN	B
U of Toledo, OH	B
U of Tulsa, OK	B
U of Wisconsin–Eau Claire, WI	B
U of Wisconsin–La Crosse, WI	B
Upper Iowa U, IA	B
Valparaiso U, IN	B
Wayne State Coll, NE	B
Western Michigan U, MI	B
Wheaton Coll, IL	B
Winona State U, MN	B
Youngstown State U, OH	B

Labor and Industrial Relations

College	Degree
Bowling Green State U, OH	B
Cleveland State U, OH	B
Ferris State U, MI	B
Governors State U, IL	B
Grand Valley State U, MI	B
Indiana U Bloomington, IN	A,B
Indiana U Kokomo, IN	A,B
Indiana U Northwest, IN	A,B
Indiana U–Purdue U Indianapolis, IN	A,B
Indiana U South Bend, IN	A,B
Indiana U Southeast, IN	A,B
Rockhurst U, MO	B
Roosevelt U, IL	B
The U of Akron, OH	A
U of Detroit Mercy, MI	B
The U of Iowa, IA	B
U of Wisconsin–Madison, WI	B
U of Wisconsin–Milwaukee, WI	B
Wayne State U, MI	B

A—associate degree; B—bachelor's degree

Winona State U, MN	B
Youngstown State U, OH	A

Labor Studies

Eastern Michigan U, MI	B
Indiana U–Purdue U Fort Wayne, IN	A,B

Landscape Architecture

Ball State U, IN	B
Iowa State U of Science and Technology, IA	B
Kansas State U, KS	B
Michigan State U, MI	B
North Carolina Ag and Tech State U, NC	B
North Dakota State U, ND	B
The Ohio State U, OH	B
Oklahoma State U, OK	B
Purdue U, IN	B
U of Illinois at Urbana–Champaign, IL	B
U of Michigan, MI	B
U of Minnesota, Twin Cities Campus, MN	B
U of Wisconsin–Madison, WI	B

Landscaping and Groundskeeping

Andrews U, MI	B
Oklahoma State U, OK	B
Rochester Comm and Tech Coll, MN	A
South Dakota State U, SD	B
U of Nebraska–Lincoln, NE	B

Land Use Planning and Management

Grand Valley State U, MI	B
Northern Michigan U, MI	B
Northland Coll, WI	B
U of Michigan–Flint, MI	B
U of Wisconsin–Platteville, WI	B
U of Wisconsin–River Falls, WI	B

Laser and Optical Technology

Indiana U Bloomington, IN	A

Latin

Augustana Coll, IL	B
Ball State U, IN	B
Butler U, IN	B
Calvin Coll, MI	B
Carleton Coll, MN	B
The Coll of Wooster, OH	B
Concordia Coll, MN	B
Cornell Coll, IA	B
Creighton U, NE	B
DePauw U, IN	B
Indiana U Bloomington, IN	B
John Carroll U, OH	B
Kent State U, OH	B
Kenyon Coll, OH	B
Lawrence U, WI	B
Lehigh U, PA	B
Loyola U Chicago, IL	B
Luther Coll, IA	B
Macalester Coll, MN	B
Miami U, OH	B
Miami U Hamilton, OH	B
Monmouth Coll, IL	B
Oberlin Coll, OH	B
Ohio U, OH	B
Rockford Coll, IL	B
St. Olaf Coll, MN	B

Southwest Missouri State U, MO	B
U of Chicago, IL	B
The U of Iowa, IA	B
U of Michigan, MI	B
U of Minnesota, Twin Cities Campus, MN	B
U of Missouri–Columbia, MO	B
U of Nebraska–Lincoln, NE	B
U of Notre Dame, IN	B
U of St. Thomas, MN	B
U of Wisconsin–Madison, WI	B
U of Wisconsin–Milwaukee, WI	B
Wabash Coll, IN	B
Washington U in St. Louis, MO	B
Western Michigan U, MI	B
Wichita State U, KS	B

Latin American Studies

Ball State U, IN	B
Beloit Coll, WI	B
Carleton Coll, MN	B
Central Coll, IA	B
Cornell Coll, IA	B
Denison U, OH	B
DePaul U, IL	B
Earlham Coll, IN	B
Grinnell Coll, IA	B
Gustavus Adolphus Coll, MN	B
Hamline U, MN	B
Hanover Coll, IN	B
Illinois Wesleyan U, IL	B
Indiana U Bloomington, IN	B
Kent State U, OH	B
Lake Forest Coll, IL	B
Macalester Coll, MN	B
Oberlin Coll, OH	B
The Ohio State U, OH	B
Ohio U, OH	B
Pontifical Coll Josephinum, OH	B
Ripon Coll, WI	B
St. Cloud State U, MN	B
St. Olaf Coll, MN	B
U of Chicago, IL	B
U of Cincinnati, OH	B
U of Illinois at Chicago, IL	B
U of Illinois at Urbana–Champaign, IL	B
The U of Iowa, IA	B
U of Kansas, KS	B
U of Michigan, MI	B
U of Minnesota, Morris, MN	B
U of Minnesota, Twin Cities Campus, MN	B
U of Missouri–Columbia, MO	B
U of Nebraska at Omaha, NE	B
U of Nebraska–Lincoln, NE	B
U of Northern Iowa, IA	B
U of Toledo, OH	B
U of Wisconsin–Eau Claire, WI	B
U of Wisconsin–Madison, WI	B
U of Wisconsin–Milwaukee, WI	B
Washington U in St. Louis, MO	B

Latin Teacher Education

Bowling Green State U, OH	B

Hope Coll, MI	B
Kent State U, OH	B
Miami U Hamilton, OH	B
Ohio Wesleyan U, OH	B
U of Illinois at Urbana–Champaign, IL	B
The U of Iowa, IA	B
Western Michigan U, MI	B

Law and Legal Studies Related

U of Nebraska–Lincoln, NE	B

Legal Administrative Assistant/Secretary

AIB Coll of Business, IA	A
Baker Coll of Auburn Hills, MI	A
Baker Coll of Clinton Township, MI	A
Baker Coll of Flint, MI	A
Baker Coll of Jackson, MI	A
Baker Coll of Muskegon, MI	A
Baker Coll of Owosso, MI	A
Baker Coll of Port Huron, MI	A
Ball State U, IN	A,B
Bryant and Stratton Coll, WI	A
Davenport U, Dearborn, MI	A
Davenport U, Kalamazoo, MI	A
Dordt Coll, IA	A
Ferris State U, MI	A
Globe Coll, MN	A
Hamilton Coll, NE	A
Hickey Coll, MO	A
MacCormac Coll, IL	A
Minnesota School of Business–Brooklyn Center, MN	A
Minnesota School of Business-Plymouth, MN	A
Minnesota School of Business-Richfield, MN	A
Northern Michigan U, MI	A
Robert Morris Coll, IL	A
Rochester Comm and Tech Coll, MN	A
Shawnee State U, OH	A
Tabor Coll, KS	B
The U of Akron, OH	A
U of Cincinnati, OH	A
U of Detroit Mercy, MI	A,B
U of Northwestern Ohio, OH	A
U of Rio Grande, OH	A
U of Toledo, OH	A
Washburn U, KS	A
Wright State U, OH	A
Youngstown State U, OH	A

Legal Assistant/Paralegal

Avila U, MO	B
Ball State U, IN	A,B
Calumet Coll of Saint Joseph, IN	B
Coll of Mount St. Joseph, OH	A,B
Coll of Saint Mary, NE	A,B
Concordia U Wisconsin, WI	B
Davenport U, Grand Rapids, MI	A,B
Davenport U, Kalamazoo, MI	A,B
Eastern Michigan U, MI	B
Ferris State U, MI	A
Florida Gulf Coast U, FL	B
Gannon U, PA	A,B
Grand Valley State U, MI	B
Hamilton Coll, NE	A

Hamline U, MN	B
Hickey Coll, MO	A
Indiana U South Bend, IN	A
Kaplan Coll, IA	A,B
Kent State U, OH	A,B
Lake Erie Coll, OH	B
Lake Superior State U, MI	A,B
MacCormac Coll, IL	A
Madonna U, MI	A,B
Maryville U of Saint Louis, MO	B
Metropolitan Coll, Tulsa, OK	A
Minnesota School of Business-Richfield, MN	A
Minnesota State U Moorhead, MN	B
Missouri Western State Coll, MO	A
National American U, SD	A,B
National American U–Sioux Falls Branch, SD	A,B
Ohio U–Chillicothe, OH	A
Robert Morris Coll, IL	A
Roosevelt U, IL	B
Saint Mary-of-the-Woods Coll, IN	A,B
Shawnee State U, OH	A
Southern Illinois U Carbondale, IL	B
The U of Akron, OH	A
U of Cincinnati, OH	A
U of Indianapolis, IN	A
U of Northwestern Ohio, OH	A
U of Toledo, OH	A
U of West Florida, FL	A
U of Wisconsin–Superior, WI	B
Ursuline Coll, OH	B
Washburn U, KS	A
Wichita State U, KS	A
William Woods U, MO	A,B
Winona State U, MN	B

Legal Professions and Studies Related

Bethany Coll, KS	B
U of Nebraska–Lincoln, NE	B
U of Tulsa, OK	B

Legal Studies

Central Christian Coll of Kansas, KS	A
Concordia U, IL	B
East Central U, OK	B
Franciscan U of Steubenville, OH	B
Gannon U, PA	B
Grand Valley State U, MI	B
Hamline U, MN	B
Indiana U–Purdue U Fort Wayne, IN	B
Kenyon Coll, OH	B
Lake Superior State U, MI	A,B
MacCormac Coll, IL	A
Northwestern U, IL	B
Oberlin Coll, OH	B
Ohio Dominican U, OH	A
Park U, MO	B
Roosevelt U, IL	B
U of Detroit Mercy, MI	A,B
U of Evansville, IN	B
U of Illinois at Springfield, IL	B
U of Wisconsin–Superior, WI	B
Webster U, MO	B
Winona State U, MN	B

Legal Support Services Related

Central Missouri State U, MO — A

Liberal Arts and Sciences and Humanities Related

Baldwin-Wallace Coll, OH — B
Central Christian Coll of Kansas, KS — B
Malone Coll, OH — B
Ohio U, OH — B
Shimer Coll, IL — B
Southwestern Coll, KS — B
The U of Akron, OH — A,B
U of Nebraska–Lincoln, NE — B
U of North Dakota, ND — B
U of Wisconsin–Whitewater, WI — B
Wright State U, OH — B

Liberal Arts and Sciences/ Liberal Studies

Alma Coll, MI — B
Alverno Coll, WI — A,B
Ancilla Coll, IN — A
Andrews U, MI — A,B
Aquinas Coll, MI — A,B
Ashland U, OH — A,B
Augsburg Coll, MN — B
Augustana Coll, IL — B
Augustana Coll, SD — B
Bacone Coll, OK — A
Ball State U, IN — A,B
Bemidji State U, MN — A,B
Benedictine Coll, KS — B
Bethany Lutheran Coll, MN — A,B
Bethel Coll, IN — A,B
Bethel U, MN — A
Blackburn Coll, IL — B
Bowling Green State U, OH — B
Bradley U, IL — B
Brescia U, KY — A,B
Briar Cliff U, IA — A
Butler U, IN — A
Calumet Coll of Saint Joseph, IN — A,B
Capital U, OH — B
Cardinal Stritch U, WI — A,B
Central Christian Coll of Kansas, KS — B
Chatfield Coll, OH — A
Clarke Coll, IA — A
Clarkson U — B
Cleveland State U, OH — B
Coe Coll, IA — B
Coll of Mount St. Joseph, OH — B
Coll of Saint Benedict, MN — B
Coll of St. Catherine, MN — A
Coll of St. Catherine–Minneapolis, MN — A
The Coll of St. Scholastica, MN — B
Columbia Coll, MO — A,B
Columbia Coll Chicago, IL — B
Conception Seminary Coll, MO — B
Concordia U Wisconsin, WI — B
Cornell Coll, IA — B
Crossroads Coll, MN — A,B
Crown Coll, MN — A,B
Dakota State U, SD — A
Dakota Wesleyan U, SD — A
Defiance Coll, OH — B

Dickinson State U, ND — A,B
Donnelly Coll, KS — A
Eastern Illinois U, IL — B
Edgewood Coll, WI — A,B
Eureka Coll, IL — B
Ferris State U, MI — A
Florida Gulf Coast U, FL — B
Fontbonne U, MO — B
Fort Hays State U, KS — B
The Franciscan U, IA — A,B
Gannon U, PA — A,B
Goshen Coll, IN — B
Governors State U, IL — B
Grace Bible Coll, MI — A
Graceland U, IA — B
Grace U, NE — A,B
Grand Valley State U, MI — B
Grand View Coll, IA — A,B
Greenville Coll, IL — B
Hannibal-LaGrange Coll, MO — B
Haskell Indian Nations U, KS — A
Hastings Coll, NE — B
Hesston Coll, KS — A
Hillsdale Free Will Baptist Coll, OK — A
Holy Cross Coll, IN — A,B
Illinois Coll, IL — B
Illinois State U, IL — B
Indiana State U, IN — A,B
Iowa State U of Science and Technology, IA — B
Iowa Wesleyan Coll, IA — B
Kansas Wesleyan U, KS — B
Kent State U, OH — A,B
Kent State U, Salem Campus, OH — A
Kent State U, Stark Campus, OH — A
Kent State U, Tuscarawas Campus, OH — A,B
Kilian Comm Coll, SD — A
Lake Superior State U, MI — A
Lewis U, IL — B
Lincoln Coll, Lincoln, IL — A
Lindenwood U, MO — B
Loras Coll, IA — A,B
Lourdes Coll, OH — A,B
MacMurray Coll, IL — B
Marian Coll, IN — A
Marian Coll of Fond du Lac, WI — B
Marietta Coll, OH — A,B
Marygrove Coll, MI — A
Maryville U of Saint Louis, MO — B
Metropolitan State U, MN — B
MidAmerica Nazarene U, KS — A
Minnesota State U Mankato, MN — A,B
Minnesota State U Moorhead, MN — A
Missouri Valley Coll, MO — A,B
Monmouth Coll, IL — B
Mount Marty Coll, SD — A,B
Mount Mercy Coll, IA — B
National American U, SD — A
National-Louis U, IL — B
Newman U, KS — A,B
North Central Coll, IL — B
North Central U, MN — A
North Dakota State Coll of Science, ND — A
Northeastern Illinois U, IL — B

Northern Illinois U, IL — B
Northern Michigan U, MI — A,B
Northern State U, SD — A
Northwestern Coll, MN — A
Northwestern U, IL — B
Oak Hills Christian Coll, MN — A
Oakland City U, IN — A
Oakland U, MI — B
Ohio Dominican U, OH — B
The Ohio State U at Lima, OH — A
The Ohio State U at Marion, OH — A
The Ohio State U–Mansfield Campus, OH — A
The Ohio State U–Newark Campus, OH — A
Ohio U, OH — A,B
Ohio U–Chillicothe, OH — A,B
Ohio U–Southern Campus, OH — A
Ohio U–Zanesville, OH — A,B
Oklahoma Christian U, OK — B
Oklahoma City U, OK — B
Oklahoma State U, OK — B
Olivet Coll, MI — B
Olivet Nazarene U, IL — B
Oral Roberts U, OK — B
Park U, MO — A,B
Presentation Coll, SD — A
Purdue U Calumet, IN — B
Purdue U North Central, IN — B
Reformed Bible Coll, MI — A
Rochester Coll, MI — A
Rochester Comm and Tech Coll, MN — A
Roosevelt U, IL — B
Sacred Heart Major Seminary, MI — B
St. Augustine Coll, IL — A
St. Cloud State U, MN — A,B
St. Gregory's U, OK — A,B
St. Louis Christian Coll, MO — A
Saint Mary-of-the-Woods Coll, IN — A,B
St. Olaf Coll, MN — B
Saint Xavier U, IL — B
Shimer Coll, IL — B
Southern Illinois U Carbondale, IL — B
Southern Illinois U Edwardsville, IL — B
Southwestern Coll, KS — B
Spring Arbor U, MI — A
Stephens Coll, MO — A,B
Taylor U Fort Wayne, IN — A
Trinity Bible Coll, ND — A
Trinity International U, IL — B
Tri-State U, IN — A
Union Inst & U, OH — B
The U of Akron, OH — A,B
U of Central Oklahoma, OK — B
U of Chicago, IL — B
U of Cincinnati, OH — A,B
U of Evansville, IN — B
U of Illinois at Springfield, IL — B
U of Illinois at Urbana–Champaign, IL — B
U of Indianapolis, IN — A,B
The U of Iowa, IA — B
U of Kansas, KS — B
U of Michigan, MI — B
U of Michigan–Dearborn, MI — B

U of Michigan–Flint, MI — B
U of Minnesota, Morris, MN — B
U of Missouri–Kansas City, MO — B
U of Nebraska–Lincoln, NE — B
U of Northern Iowa, IA — B
U of Notre Dame, IN — B
U of Oklahoma, OK — B
U of St. Francis, IL — B
U of Saint Francis, IN — A,B
U of Saint Mary, KS — A,B
U of Sioux Falls, SD — B
The U of South Dakota, SD — B
U of Southern Indiana, IN — B
U of Toledo, OH — A,B
U of Tulsa, OK — B
U of Wisconsin–Eau Claire, WI — A
U of Wisconsin–La Crosse, WI — A
U of Wisconsin–Oshkosh, WI — A,B
U of Wisconsin–Platteville, WI — A,B
U of Wisconsin–River Falls, WI — B
U of Wisconsin–Stevens Point, WI — A
U of Wisconsin–Superior, WI — A
U of Wisconsin–Whitewater, WI — A,B
Upper Iowa U, IA — A
Urbana U, OH — A,B
Viterbo U, WI — B
Walsh U, OH — A,B
Washburn U, KS — A,B
Washington U in St. Louis, MO — B
Webster U, MO — B
Western Illinois U, IL — B
Wichita State U, KS — A,B
Wilberforce U, OH — B
William Tyndale Coll, MI — A
Winona State U, MN — A,B
Wittenberg U, OH — B
Wright State U, OH — B
Xavier U, OH — A,B
York Coll, NE — A,B

Library Assistant

Ohio Dominican U, OH — A

Library Science

Chadron State Coll, NE — B
Concord U, WV — B
Northeastern State U, OK — B
St. Cloud State U, MN — B
U of Nebraska at Omaha, NE — B
U of Oklahoma, OK — B

Library Science Related

Bethel U, MN — B

Linguistics

Central Coll, IA — B
Cleveland State U, OH — B
Crown Coll, MN — B
Eastern Michigan U, MI — B
Grinnell Coll, IA — B
Indiana U Bloomington, IN — B
Iowa State U of Science and Technology, IA — B
Judson Coll, IL — B
Lawrence U, WI — B
Macalester Coll, MN — B
Miami U, OH — B

A—associate degree; B—bachelor's degree

College	Degree
Miami U Hamilton, OH	B
Moody Bible Inst, IL	B
Northeastern Illinois U, IL	B
Northwestern U, IL	B
Oakland U, MI	B
The Ohio State U, OH	B
Ohio U, OH	B
St. Cloud State U, MN	B
Southern Illinois U Carbondale, IL	B
U of Chicago, IL	B
U of Cincinnati, OH	B
U of Illinois at Urbana–Champaign, IL	B
The U of Iowa, IA	B
U of Kansas, KS	B
U of Michigan, MI	B
U of Minnesota, Twin Cities Campus, MN	B
U of Missouri–Columbia, MO	
U of Oklahoma, OK	B
U of Toledo, OH	B
U of Wisconsin–Madison, WI	B
U of Wisconsin–Milwaukee, WI	B
Wayne State U, MI	B
Wright State U, OH	B

Linguistics of ASL and Other Sign Languages

College	Degree
Kent State U, OH	B

Literature

College	Degree
Antioch Coll, OH	B
Augustana Coll, IL	B
Ave Maria Coll, MI	B
Beloit Coll, WI	B
Blackburn Coll, IL	B
Capital U, OH	B
Chicago State U, IL	B
Coe Coll, IA	B
Coll of St. Catherine, MN	B
Defiance Coll, OH	B
DePaul U, IL	B
East Central U, OK	B
Eureka Coll, IL	B
Graceland U, IA	B
Grand Valley State U, MI	B
Hastings Coll, NE	B
Indiana U Bloomington, IN	B
John Carroll U, OH	B
Judson Coll, IL	B
Kansas Wesleyan U, KS	B
Kenyon Coll, OH	B
Lake Superior State U, MI	B
Manchester Coll, IN	A
Minnesota State U Mankato, MN	B
Morningside Coll, IA	B
Mount Vernon Nazarene U, OH	B
North Central Coll, IL	B
North Central U, MN	A
North Park U, IL	B
Ohio Wesleyan U, OH	B
Olivet Nazarene U, IL	B
Otterbein Coll, OH	B
Purdue U Calumet, IN	B
Rochester Coll, MI	B
Rockford Coll, IL	B
Roosevelt U, IL	B
Shimer Coll, IL	B
Southern Nazarene U, OK	B
Taylor U, IN	B
The U of Akron, OH	B
U of Cincinnati, OH	B
U of Evansville, IN	B
The U of Iowa, IA	B
U of Michigan, MI	B
U of Missouri–St. Louis, MO	B
U of Toledo, OH	B
U of Wisconsin–Milwaukee, WI	B
Washington U in St. Louis, MO	B
Wayne State Coll, NE	B
Webster U, MO	B
Wilberforce U, OH	B

Logistics and Materials Management

College	Degree
Bowling Green State U, OH	B
Central Michigan U, MI	B
Clarkson U	B
Eastern Michigan U, MI	B
Elmhurst Coll, IL	B
Iowa State U of Science and Technology, IA	B
Michigan State U, MI	B
The Ohio State U, OH	B
Park U, MO	A,B
The U of Akron, OH	A
The U of Findlay, OH	B
U of Toledo, OH	A,B
Wayne State U, MI	B
Wright State U, OH	B

Machine Shop Technology

College	Degree
North Dakota State Coll of Science, ND	A

Machine Tool Technology

College	Degree
Ferris State U, MI	A
Lake Superior State U, MI	A
Missouri Southern State U, MO	A
Ranken Tech Coll, MO	A

Management Information Systems

College	Degree
Academy Coll, MN	A
Augsburg Coll, MN	B
Augustana Coll, SD	B
Aurora U, IL	B
Baker Coll of Flint, MI	B
Ball State U, IN	B
Bellevue U, NE	B
Bethel Coll, KS	B
Bowling Green State U, OH	B
Bradley U, IL	B
Briar Cliff U, IA	B
Buena Vista U, IA	B
Calvin Coll, MI	B
Cameron U, OK	A
Central Michigan U, MI	B
Central Missouri State U, MO	B
Central State U, OH	B
Chicago State U, IL	B
Clarke Coll, IA	B
Clarkson U	B
Cleary U, MI	B
Coll of St. Catherine, MN	B
Coll of Saint Mary, NE	A,B
Colorado Tech U Sioux Falls Campus, SD	A,B
Concordia U, NE	B
Concordia U, St. Paul, MN	B
Cornerstone U, MI	B
Creighton U, NE	B
Davenport U, Dearborn, MI	A,B
Davenport U, Warren, MI	A
DePaul U, IL	B
Dordt Coll, IA	B
East Central U, OK	B
Eastern Illinois U, IL	B
Eastern Michigan U, MI	B
Elmhurst Coll, IL	B
Eureka Coll, IL	B
Ferris State U, MI	B
Florida Gulf Coast U, FL	B
Fontbonne U, MO	B
Franklin U, OH	B
Gannon U, PA	B
Governors State U, IL	B
Grace Coll, IN	B
Graceland U, IA	B
Grand Valley State U, MI	B
Grand View Coll, IA	B
Greenville Coll, IL	B
Herzing Coll, Minneapolis Drafting School Division, MN	B
Illinois Coll, IL	B
Indiana State U, IN	B
Indiana U Bloomington, IN	B
Iowa State U of Science and Technology, IA	B
Jamestown Coll, ND	B
Judson Coll, IL	B
Kaplan Coll, IA	B
Kettering U, MI	B
Lake Superior State U, MI	A
Lehigh U, PA	B
Lewis U, IL	B
Lindenwood U, MO	B
Loras Coll, IA	B
Loyola U Chicago, IL	B
Luther Coll, IA	B
MacMurray Coll, IL	B
Madonna U, MI	B
Marquette U, WI	B
Maryville U of Saint Louis, MO	B
Metropolitan State U, MN	B
Miami U, OH	B
Miami U Hamilton, OH	A
Michigan Technological U, MI	B
Millikin U, IL	B
Milwaukee School of Engineering, WI	B
Minnesota State U Moorhead, MN	B
Minot State U, ND	B
Morningside Coll, IA	B
National American U, SD	B
National American U–Sioux Falls Branch, SD	A,B
Newman U, KS	B
North Central Coll, IL	B
Northern Illinois U, IL	B
Northern Michigan U, MI	A,B
Northern State U, SD	B
Northwestern Coll, MN	B
Northwood U, MI	A,B
Oakland U, MI	B
The Ohio State U, OH	B
Ohio U, OH	B
Oklahoma Baptist U, OK	B
Oklahoma City U, OK	B
Oklahoma State U, OK	B
Oral Roberts U, OK	B
Park U, MO	B
Peru State Coll, NE	B
Robert Morris Coll, IL	A
Rockford Coll, IL	B
St. Augustine Coll, IL	A
St. Gregory's U, OK	B
Saint Joseph's Coll, IN	A,B
Saint Louis U, MO	B
Saint Mary's Coll, IN	B
St. Norbert Coll, WI	B
Shawnee State U, OH	A,B
Southern Illinois U Edwardsville, IL	B
Southern Nazarene U, OK	B
Southwestern Coll, KS	B
Southwest Missouri State U, MO	B
Spring Arbor U, MI	B
Taylor U, IN	A
Tiffin U, OH	B
Trinity Christian Coll, IL	B
Tri-State U, IN	A
The U of Akron, OH	
The U of Alabama in Huntsville, AL	B
U of Cincinnati, OH	B
U of Dayton, OH	B
U of Illinois at Chicago, IL	B
The U of Iowa, IA	
U of Minnesota, Twin Cities Campus, MN	B
U of Missouri–Columbia, MO	
U of Missouri–St. Louis, MO	B
U of Nebraska at Omaha, NE	B
U of New Orleans, LA	B
U of Northern Iowa, IA	B
U of Notre Dame, IN	B
U of Oklahoma, OK	B
U of Phoenix–Chicago Campus, IL	B
U of Phoenix–Cleveland Campus, OH	B
U of Phoenix–Metro Detroit Campus, MI	B
U of Phoenix–Oklahoma City Campus, OK	B
U of Phoenix–St. Louis Campus, MO	B
U of Phoenix–Tulsa Campus, OK	
U of Phoenix–West Michigan Campus, MI	B
U of Sioux Falls, SD	B
U of Toledo, OH	B
U of Tulsa, OK	B
U of West Florida, FL	B
U of Wisconsin–Green Bay, WI	A,B
U of Wisconsin–La Crosse, WI	B
U of Wisconsin–Milwaukee, WI	B
U of Wisconsin–Oshkosh, WI	B
U of Wisconsin–River Falls, WI	B
U of Wisconsin–Whitewater, WI	B
Upper Iowa U, IA	B
Ursuline Coll, OH	B
Viterbo U, WI	B
Wayne State U, MI	B
Webster U, MO	B
Western Illinois U, IL	B
Westminster Coll, MO	B
Wichita State U, KS	B
William Woods U, MO	B
Winona State U, MN	B
Wright State U, OH	A,B

Xavier U, OH — B
Youngstown State U, OH — B

Management Information Systems and Services Related
Bowling Green State U, OH — B
Buena Vista U, IA — B
Carroll Coll, WI — B
Coll of Mount St. Joseph, OH — A,B
Greenville Coll, IL — B
Lewis U, IL — B
Oakland U, MI — B
Purdue U, IN — A,B
Southeastern Oklahoma State U, OK — B
U of Southern Indiana, IN — A

Management Science
Capella U, MN
Central Methodist Coll, MO — B
The Coll of St. Scholastica, MN — B
Columbia Coll, MO — B
Eastern Illinois U, IL — B
Franklin U, OH — B
Grace Bible Coll, MI — B
Lourdes Coll, OH — B
Madonna U, MI — B
Miami U, OH — B
Minnesota State U Mankato, MN — B
Oakland City U, IN — B
Oakland U, MI — B
Ohio Northern U, OH — B
Oklahoma State U, OK — B
Oral Roberts U, OK — B
Rockhurst U, MO — B
Roosevelt U, IL — B
St. Ambrose U, IA — B
St. Gregory's U, OK — B
Saint Louis U, MO — B
Southeastern Oklahoma State U, OK — B
Southern Illinois U Carbondale, IL — B
Southern Nazarene U, OK — B
Southwestern Coll, KS — B
Trinity International U, IL — B
The U of Iowa, IA — B
U of Mary, ND — B
U of Minnesota, Morris, MN — B
U of Missouri–St. Louis, MO — B
U of Nebraska–Lincoln, NE — B
U of Phoenix–Chicago Campus, IL — B
U of Phoenix–Kansas City Campus, MO — B
U of Phoenix–Metro Detroit Campus, MI — B
U of Phoenix–Oklahoma City Campus, OK — B
U of Phoenix–St. Louis Campus, MO — B
U of Phoenix–Tulsa Campus, OK — B
U of Phoenix–West Michigan Campus, MI — B
U of Phoenix–Wisconsin Campus, WI — B
Valparaiso U, IN — B
Wright State U, OH — B

Management Sciences and Quantitative Methods Related
Indiana State U, IN — B

Ohio Northern U, OH — B
The U of Iowa, IA — B
U of Toledo, OH — B
Valparaiso U, IN — B

Manufacturing Engineering
Clarkson U — B
Eastern Michigan U, MI — B
Kent State U, Salem Campus, OH — A
North Dakota State U, ND — B
Northwestern U, IL — B
Southern Illinois U Edwardsville, IL — B
U of Detroit Mercy, MI — B
U of Missouri–Rolla, MO — B
U of Wisconsin–Stout, WI — B

Manufacturing Technology
Eastern Michigan U, MI — B
Illinois Inst of Technology, IL — B
Kent State U, OH — A
Lawrence Technological U, MI — A
Missouri Western State Coll, MO — A
Northern Michigan U, MI — B
Southwestern Coll, KS — B
U of Nebraska at Omaha, NE — B
U of Northern Iowa, IA — B
Western Illinois U, IL — B

Marine Biology and Biological Oceanography
Ball State U, IN — B
Bemidji State U, MN — B
Lincoln Coll, Lincoln, IL — A
Missouri Southern State U, MO — B
Southwestern Coll, KS — B
U of West Florida, FL — B
U of Wisconsin–Superior, WI — B

Marketing/Marketing Management
AIB Coll of Business, IA — A
Alma Coll, MI — B
Alverno Coll, WI — B
American InterContinental U Online, IL — B
Andrews U, MI — B
Ashland U, OH — B
Augsburg Coll, MN — B
Augustana Coll, IL — B
Aurora U, IL — B
Avila U, MO — B
Baker Coll of Allen Park, MI — A
Baker Coll of Auburn Hills, MI — A,B
Baker Coll of Cadillac, MI — A
Baker Coll of Clinton Township, MI — A
Baker Coll of Flint, MI — A,B
Baker Coll of Jackson, MI — A,B
Baker Coll of Muskegon, MI — A,B
Baker Coll of Owosso, MI — A,B
Baker Coll of Port Huron, MI — A,B
Ball State U, IN — A,B
Bellevue U, NE — B
Benedictine U, IL — B
Blackburn Coll, IL — B
Black Hills State U, SD — B
Bradley U, IL — B
Brescia U, KY — B

Buena Vista U, IA — B
Butler U, IN — B
Capital U, OH — B
Carroll Coll, WI — B
Cedarville U, OH — B
Central Christian Coll of Kansas, KS — A
Central Michigan U, MI — B
Central Missouri State U, MO — B
Central State U, OH — B
Chicago State U, IL — B
Clarke Coll, IA — B
Clarkson U — B
Cleary U, MI — B
Cleveland State U, OH — B
Coll of St. Catherine, MN — B
Coll of the Ozarks, MO — B
Colorado Tech U Sioux Falls Campus, SD — B
Columbia Coll, MO — B
Columbia Coll Chicago, IL — B
Concordia U Wisconsin, WI — B
Cornerstone U, MI — B
Creighton U, NE — B
Dakota State U, SD — B
Dakota Wesleyan U, SD — B
Davenport U, Dearborn, MI — A,B
Davenport U, Grand Rapids, MI — A,B
Davenport U, Kalamazoo, MI — A,B
Davenport U, Lansing, MI — A,B
Davenport U, Warren, MI — A,B
Defiance Coll, OH — B
DePaul U, IL — B
Dickinson State U, ND — B
Drake U, IA — B
East Central U, OK — B
Eastern Illinois U, IL — B
Eastern Michigan U, MI — B
Elmhurst Coll, IL — B
Emporia State U, KS — B
Evangel U, MO — B
Ferris State U, MI — B
Florida Gulf Coast U, FL — B
Fontbonne U, MO — B
Fort Hays State U, KS — B
Franklin U, OH — B
Gannon U, PA — B
Governors State U, IL — B
Grace Bible Coll, MI — B
Grand Valley State U, MI — B
Greenville Coll, IL — B
Hannibal-LaGrange Coll, MO — B
Harris-Stowe State Coll, MO — B
Hastings Coll, NE — B
Hillsdale Coll, MI — B
Illinois State U, IL — B
Indiana Inst of Technology, IN — B
Indiana State U, IN — B
Indiana U Bloomington, IN — B
Indiana U–Purdue U Fort Wayne, IN — B
Indiana U South Bend, IN — B
Iowa State U of Science and Technology, IA — B
Jamestown Coll, ND — B
John Carroll U, OH — B
Kansas State U, KS — B
Kendall Coll, IL — B
Kent State U, OH — B
Kettering U, MI — B
Lakeland Coll, WI — B

Lehigh U, PA — B
Lewis U, IL — B
Lincoln Coll, Lincoln, IL — A
Lincoln U, MO — B
Lindenwood U, MO — B
Loras Coll, IA — B
Loyola U Chicago, IL — B
MacCormac Coll, IL — A
MacMurray Coll, IL — B
Madonna U, MI — B
Manchester Coll, IN — B
Marian Coll of Fond du Lac, WI — B
Marietta Coll, OH — B
Marquette U, WI — B
Martin U, IN — B
Marygrove Coll, MI — B
Maryville U of Saint Louis, MO — B
McKendree Coll, IL — B
Metropolitan State U, MN — B
Miami U, OH — B
Miami U Hamilton, OH — A
Michigan State U, MI — B
Michigan Technological U, MI — B
Millikin U, IL — B
Minnesota State U Mankato, MN — B
Minnesota State U Moorhead, MN — B
Minot State U, ND — B
Missouri Baptist U, MO — B
Missouri Southern State U, MO — B
Missouri Valley Coll, MO — B
Missouri Western State Coll, MO — B
Morningside Coll, IA — B
Mount Mary Coll, WI — B
Mount Mercy Coll, IA — B
Mount Vernon Nazarene U, OH — B
Newman U, KS — B
North Central Coll, IL — B
Northeastern Illinois U, IL — B
Northeastern State U, OK — B
Northern Illinois U, IL — B
Northern Michigan U, MI — B
Northern State U, SD — B
North Park U, IL — B
Northwestern Coll, MN — B
Northwood U, MI — B
Notre Dame Coll, OH — B
Oakland U, MI — B
The Ohio State U, OH — B
Ohio U, OH — B
Oklahoma Baptist U, OK — B
Oklahoma Christian U, OK — B
Oklahoma City U, OK — B
Oklahoma State U, OK — B
Olivet Coll, OH — B
Olivet Nazarene U, IL — B
Oral Roberts U, OK — B
Otterbein Coll, OH — B
Park U, MO — B
Peru State Coll, NE — B
Pittsburg State U, KS — B
Purdue U Calumet, IN — B
Purdue U North Central, IN — A
Quincy U, IL — B
Rochester Coll, MI — B
Rockford Coll, IL — B
Rockhurst U, MO — B
Roosevelt U, IL — B

A—associate degree; B—bachelor's degree

St. Ambrose U, IA	B
St. Cloud State U, MN	B
St. Gregory's U, OK	B
Saint Louis U, MO	B
Saint Mary-of-the-Woods Coll, IN	B
Saint Mary's Coll, IN	B
Saint Mary's U of Minnesota, MN	B
Siena Heights U, MI	A,B
Southeastern Oklahoma State U, OK	B
Southeast Missouri State U, MO	B
Southern Illinois U Carbondale, IL	B
Southern Nazarene U, OK	B
Southwestern Oklahoma State U, OK	B
Southwest Missouri State U, MO	B
Stephens Coll, MO	B
Tabor Coll, KS	B
Taylor U, IN	B
Tiffin U, OH	B
Trinity Christian Coll, IL	B
Trinity International U, IL	B
Tri-State U, IN	B
The U of Akron, OH	B
The U of Alabama in Huntsville, AL	B
U of Central Oklahoma, OK	B
U of Cincinnati, OH	A,B
U of Dayton, OH	B
U of Detroit Mercy, MI	B
U of Evansville, IN	B
The U of Findlay, OH	B
U of Illinois at Chicago, IL	B
U of Indianapolis, IN	B
The U of Iowa, IA	B
U of Michigan–Dearborn, MI	B
U of Michigan–Flint, MI	B
U of Minnesota, Duluth, MN	B
U of Minnesota, Twin Cities Campus, MN	B
U of Missouri–Columbia, MO	B
U of Missouri–St. Louis, MO	B
U of Nebraska at Omaha, NE	B
U of Nebraska–Lincoln, NE	B
U of New Orleans, LA	B
U of North Dakota, ND	B
U of Northern Iowa, IA	B
U of Northwestern Ohio, OH	A,B
U of Notre Dame, IN	B
U of Oklahoma, OK	B
U of Phoenix–Chicago Campus, IL	B
U of Phoenix–Cleveland Campus, OH	B
U of Phoenix–Metro Detroit Campus, MI	B
U of Phoenix–St. Louis Campus, MO	B
U of Phoenix–Tulsa Campus, OK	B
U of Phoenix–Wisconsin Campus, WI	B
U of Rio Grande, OH	B
U of St. Francis, IL	B
U of Saint Francis, IN	B
U of St. Thomas, MN	B
U of Sioux Falls, SD	A,B
The U of South Dakota, SD	B

U of Southern Indiana, IN	B
U of Toledo, OH	B
U of Tulsa, OK	B
U of West Florida, FL	B
U of Wisconsin–Eau Claire, WI	B
U of Wisconsin–La Crosse, WI	B
U of Wisconsin–Milwaukee, WI	B
U of Wisconsin–Oshkosh, WI	B
U of Wisconsin–River Falls, WI	B
U of Wisconsin–Superior, WI	B
U of Wisconsin–Whitewater, WI	B
Upper Iowa U, IA	B
Urbana U, OH	A,B
Ursuline Coll, OH	B
Valparaiso U, IN	B
Viterbo U, WI	B
Waldorf Coll, IA	B
Walsh Coll of Accountancy and Business Administration, MI	B
Walsh U, OH	A,B
Wartburg Coll, IA	B
Washburn U, KS	B
Washington U in St. Louis, MO	B
Wayne State U, MI	B
Webster U, MO	B
Western Illinois U, IL	B
Western Michigan U, MI	B
Westwood Coll–Chicago Du Page, IL	B
Westwood Coll–Chicago Loop Campus, IL	B
Westwood Coll–Chicago O'Hare Airport, IL	B
Westwood Coll–Chicago River Oaks, IL	B
Wichita State U, KS	B
Wilberforce U, OH	B
Winona State U, MN	B
Wittenberg U, OH	B
Wright State U, OH	A,B
Xavier U, OH	B
Youngstown State U, OH	A,B

Marketing Related

Bowling Green State U, OH	B
Capella U, MN	B
Central Michigan U, MI	B
Miami U Hamilton, OH	B
The U of Akron, OH	B
U of Illinois at Urbana–Champaign, IL	B
The U of Iowa, IA	B
Washington U in St. Louis, MO	B
Western Michigan U, MI	B

Marketing Research

Ashland U, OH	B
Baker Coll of Jackson, MI	B
Carthage Coll, WI	B
Saginaw Valley State U, MI	B
U of Toledo, OH	B

Marriage and Family Therapy/Counseling

Central Christian Coll of Kansas, KS	A
Grace U, NE	B
Oklahoma Baptist U, OK	B

Massage Therapy

Globe Coll, MN	A
Herzing Coll, Minneapolis Drafting School Division, MN	A
Mercy Coll of Northwest Ohio, OH	A
Minnesota School of Business–Brooklyn Center, MN	A
Minnesota School of Business–Plymouth, MN	A
Minnesota School of Business-Richfield, MN	A
National American U–Sioux Falls Branch, SD	A

Mass Communication/Media

Adrian Coll, MI	A,B
Albion Coll, MI	B
Andrews U, MI	B
Antioch Coll, OH	B
Ashland U, OH	B
Augsburg Coll, MN	B
Augustana Coll, IL	B
Bacone Coll, OK	A
Baker U, KS	B
Baldwin-Wallace Coll, OH	B
Beloit Coll, WI	B
Bemidji State U, MN	B
Benedictine Coll, KS	B
Bethel Coll, KS	B
Bethel U, MN	B
Black Hills State U, SD	A,B
Briar Cliff U, IA	B
Buena Vista U, IA	B
Calvary Bible Coll and Theological Seminary, MO	B
Calvin Coll, MI	B
Central Christian Coll of Kansas, KS	A
Clarke Coll, IA	B
Coll of St. Catherine, MN	B
Coll of the Ozarks, MO	B
The Coll of Wooster, OH	B
Concordia Coll, MN	B
Concordia U, NE	B
Concordia U, St. Paul, MN	B
Concordia U Wisconsin, WI	B
Concord U, WV	B
Cornerstone U, MI	A,B
Culver-Stockton Coll, MO	B
Defiance Coll, OH	B
Denison U, OH	B
DePaul U, IL	B
DePauw U, IN	B
Doane Coll, NE	B
Dominican U, IL	B
Dordt Coll, IA	B
Drake U, IA	B
Drury U, MO	B
East Central U, OK	B
Edgewood Coll, WI	B
Eureka Coll, IL	B
Evangel U, MO	A,B
Ferris State U, MI	B
Fort Hays State U, KS	B
Goshen Coll, IN	B
Governors State U, IL	B
Grace Coll, IN	B
Grace U, NE	B
Grand Valley State U, MI	B
Grand View Coll, IA	B
Greenville Coll, IL	B
Gustavus Adolphus Coll, MN	B
Hamline U, MN	B
Hanover Coll, IN	B

Hastings Coll, NE	B
Heidelberg Coll, OH	B
Hiram Coll, OH	B
Huntington Coll, IN	B
Illinois Coll, IL	B
Illinois State U, IL	B
Indiana U Bloomington, IN	B
Indiana U Northwest, IN	B
Indiana U South Bend, IN	B
Iowa State U of Science and Technology, IA	B
Iowa Wesleyan Coll, IA	B
John Carroll U, OH	B
Judson Coll, IL	B
Kansas Wesleyan U, KS	B
Kent State U, OH	B
Lewis U, IL	B
Lincoln Coll, Lincoln, IL	A
Lindenwood U, MO	B
Loras Coll, IA	B
Madonna U, MI	A,B
Manchester Coll, IN	B
Marian Coll, IN	B
Marquette U, WI	B
Maryville U of Saint Louis, MO	B
McKendree Coll, IL	B
Miami U, OH	B
Miami U Hamilton, OH	B
Michigan State U, MI	B
MidAmerica Nazarene U, KS	B
Minnesota State U Mankato, MN	B
Minnesota State U Moorhead, MN	B
Missouri Southern State U, MO	B
Missouri Valley Coll, MO	B
Morningside Coll, IA	B
Mount Union Coll, OH	B
Mount Vernon Nazarene U, OH	B
Muskingum Coll, OH	B
Newman U, KS	B
North Carolina Ag and Tech State U, NC	B
North Central Coll, IL	B
North Central U, MN	A,B
North Dakota State U, ND	B
Northern Michigan U, MI	B
North Park U, IL	B
Northwestern Coll, IA	B
Northwestern Oklahoma State U, OK	B
Ohio Northern U, OH	B
Oklahoma Baptist U, OK	B
Oklahoma Christian U, OK	B
Oklahoma City U, OK	B
Olivet Coll, MI	B
Olivet Nazarene U, IL	B
Ottawa U, KS	B
Pittsburg State U, KS	B
Principia Coll, IL	B
Purdue U Calumet, IN	B
St. Ambrose U, IA	B
St. Cloud State U, MN	B
Saint Joseph's Coll, IN	B
Saint Mary-of-the-Woods Coll, IN	B
Simpson Coll, IA	B
South Dakota State U, SD	B
Southern Illinois U Edwardsville, IL	B
Southern Nazarene U, OK	B
Southwestern Oklahoma State U, OK	B

Mass Communication/Media

Southwest Missouri State U, MO — B
Stephens Coll, MO — B
Tabor Coll, KS — B
Taylor U, IN — B
Truman State U, MO — B
The U of Akron, OH — B
U of Cincinnati, OH — B
U of Dayton, OH — B
U of Detroit Mercy, MI — B
U of Dubuque, IA — A,B
U of Evansville, IN — B
U of Illinois at Springfield, IL — B
U of Illinois at Urbana–Champaign, IL — B
The U of Iowa, IA — B
U of Mary, ND — B
U of Michigan, MI — B
U of Michigan–Flint, MI — B
U of Minnesota, Twin Cities Campus, MN — B
U of Missouri–Columbia, MO — B
U of Missouri–Kansas City, MO — B
U of Missouri–St. Louis, MO — B
U of Rio Grande, OH — A,B
U of St. Francis, IL — B
U of Saint Francis, IN — B
U of Saint Mary, KS — B
U of Sioux Falls, SD — B
The U of South Dakota, SD — B
U of Toledo, OH — B
U of Wisconsin–Eau Claire, WI — B
U of Wisconsin–Madison, WI — B
U of Wisconsin–Milwaukee, WI — B
U of Wisconsin–Oshkosh, WI — B
U of Wisconsin–Platteville, WI — B
U of Wisconsin–Superior, WI — B
Upper Iowa U, IA — B
Urbana U, OH — B
Valley City State U, ND — B
Valparaiso U, IN — B
Waldorf Coll, IA — B
Wartburg Coll, IA — B
Washburn U, KS — B
Wayne State Coll, NE — B
Wilberforce U, OH — B
William Penn U, IA — B
Winona State U, MN — B
Wright State U, OH — B

Materials Engineering
Case Western Reserve U, OH — B
Clarkson U — B
Illinois Inst of Technology, IL — B
Iowa State U of Science and Technology, IA — B
Lehigh U, PA — B
Michigan Technological U, MI — B
Northwestern U, IL — B
The Ohio State U, OH — B
Purdue U, IN — B
U of Michigan, MI — B
U of Minnesota, Twin Cities Campus, MN — B
U of Missouri–Rolla, MO — B

U of Wisconsin–Milwaukee, WI — B
Winona State U, MN — B
Wright State U, OH — B

Materials Science
Case Western Reserve U, OH — B
Clarkson U — B
Michigan State U, MI — B
Northwestern U, IL — B
The Ohio State U, OH — B
U of Illinois at Urbana–Champaign, IL — B
U of Michigan, MI — B
U of Minnesota, Twin Cities Campus, MN — B

Mathematical Statistics and Probability
Northern Illinois U, IL — B

Mathematics
Adrian Coll, MI — B
Albion Coll, MI — B
Alma Coll, MI — B
Alverno Coll, WI — B
Ancilla Coll, IN — A
Andrews U, MI — B
Antioch Coll, OH — B
Aquinas Coll, MI — B
Ashland U, OH — B
Augsburg Coll, MN — B
Augustana Coll, IL — B
Augustana Coll, SD — B
Aurora U, IL — B
Ave Maria Coll, MI — B
Avila U, MO — B
Bacone Coll, OK — A
Baker U, KS — B
Baldwin-Wallace Coll, OH — B
Ball State U, IN — B
Beloit Coll, WI — B
Bemidji State U, MN — B
Benedictine Coll, KS — B
Benedictine U, IL — B
Bethany Coll, KS — B
Bethel Coll, IN — B
Bethel Coll, KS — B
Bethel U, MN — B
Blackburn Coll, IL — B
Black Hills State U, SD — B
Bluffton Coll, OH — B
Bowling Green State U, OH — B
Bradley U, IL — B
Briar Cliff U, IA — B
Buena Vista U, IA — B
Butler U, IN — B
Calvin Coll, MI — B
Cameron U, OK — B
Capital U, OH — B
Cardinal Stritch U, WI — B
Carleton Coll, MN — B
Carroll Coll, WI — B
Carthage Coll, WI — B
Case Western Reserve U, OH — B
Cedarville U, OH — B
Central Christian Coll of Kansas, KS — A
Central Coll, IA — B
Central Methodist Coll, MO — B
Central Michigan U, MI — B
Central Missouri State U, MO — B
Central State U, OH — B

Chadron State Coll, NE — B
Chicago State U, IL — B
Clarke Coll, IA — B
Clarkson U — B
Cleveland State U, OH — B
Coe Coll, IA — B
Coll of Mount St. Joseph, OH — B
Coll of Saint Benedict, MN — B
Coll of St. Catherine, MN — B
Coll of Saint Mary, NE — B
The Coll of St. Scholastica, MN — B
Coll of the Ozarks, MO — B
The Coll of Wooster, OH — B
Columbia Coll, MO — B
Concordia Coll, MN — B
Concordia U, IL — B
Concordia U, MI — B
Concordia U, NE — B
Concordia U, St. Paul, MN — B
Concordia U Wisconsin, WI — B
Concord U, WV — B
Cornell Coll, IA — B
Cornerstone U, MI — B
Creighton U, NE — A,B
Culver-Stockton Coll, MO — B
Cumberland Coll, KY — B
Dakota State U, SD — B
Dakota Wesleyan U, SD — B
Dana Coll, NE — B
Defiance Coll, OH — B
Denison U, OH — B
DePaul U, IL — B
DePauw U, IN — B
Dickinson State U, ND — B
Doane Coll, NE — B
Dominican U, IL — B
Donnelly Coll, KS — A
Dordt Coll, IA — B
Drake U, IA — B
Drury U, MO — B
Earlham Coll, IN — B
East Central U, OK — B
Eastern Illinois U, IL — B
Eastern Michigan U, MI — B
Edgewood Coll, WI — B
Elmhurst Coll, IL — B
Emporia State U, KS — B
Eureka Coll, IL — B
Evangel U, MO — B
Ferris State U, MI — B
Fontbonne U, MO — B
Fort Hays State U, KS — B
Franciscan U of Steubenville, OH — B
Franklin Coll, IN — B
Gannon U, PA — B
Goshen Coll, IN — B
Grace Coll, IN — B
Graceland U, IA — B
Grand Valley State U, MI — B
Greenville Coll, IL — B
Grinnell Coll, IA — B
Gustavus Adolphus Coll, MN — B
Hamline U, MN — B
Hannibal-LaGrange Coll, MO — B
Hanover Coll, IN — B
Hastings Coll, NE — B
Heidelberg Coll, OH — B
Hillsdale Coll, MI — B
Hillsdale Free Will Baptist Coll, OK — A
Hiram Coll, OH — B

Hope Coll, MI — B
Huntington Coll, IN — B
Illinois Coll, IL — B
Illinois State U, IL — B
Illinois Wesleyan U, IL — B
Indiana State U, IN — B
Indiana U Bloomington, IN — B
Indiana U East, IN — A
Indiana U Kokomo, IN — B
Indiana U Northwest, IN — B
Indiana U–Purdue U Fort Wayne, IN — A,B
Indiana U–Purdue U Indianapolis, IN — B
Indiana U South Bend, IN — B
Indiana U Southeast, IN — B
Iowa State U of Science and Technology, IA — B
Iowa Wesleyan Coll, IA — B
Jamestown Coll, ND — B
John Carroll U, OH — B
Judson Coll, IL — B
Kalamazoo Coll, MI — B
Kansas State U, KS — B
Kansas Wesleyan U, KS — B
Kent State U, OH — B
Kenyon Coll, OH — B
Knox Coll, IL — B
Lake Erie Coll, OH — B
Lake Forest Coll, IL — B
Lakeland Coll, WI — B
Lake Superior State U, MI — B
Lawrence Technological U, MI — B
Lawrence U, WI — B
Lehigh U, PA — B
Lewis U, IL — B
Lincoln Coll, Lincoln, IL — A
Lincoln U, MO — B
Lindenwood U, MO — B
Loras Coll, IA — B
Loyola U Chicago, IL — B
Luther Coll, IA — B
Macalester Coll, MN — B
MacMurray Coll, IL — B
Madonna U, MI — B
Maharishi U of Management, IA — B
Malone Coll, OH — B
Manchester Coll, IN — B
Marian Coll, IN — B
Marian Coll of Fond du Lac, WI — B
Marietta Coll, OH — B
Marquette U, WI — B
Martin U, IN — B
Marygrove Coll, MI — B
Maryville U of Saint Louis, MO — B
Mayville State U, ND — B
McKendree Coll, IL — B
McPherson Coll, KS — B
Miami U, OH — B
Miami U Hamilton, OH — B
Michigan State U, MI — B
Michigan Technological U, MI — B
MidAmerica Nazarene U, KS — B
Millikin U, IL — B
Minnesota State U Mankato, MN — B
Minnesota State U Moorhead, MN — B
Minot State U, ND — B
Missouri Baptist U, MO — B

A—associate degree; B—bachelor's degree

Missouri Southern State U, MO — B
Missouri Valley Coll, MO — B
Missouri Western State Coll, MO — B
Monmouth Coll, IL — B
Morningside Coll, IA — B
Mount Marty Coll, SD — B
Mount Mary Coll, WI — B
Mount Mercy Coll, IA — B
Mount Union Coll, OH — B
Mount Vernon Nazarene U, OH — B
Muskingum Coll, OH — B
National-Louis U, IL — B
Nebraska Wesleyan U, NE — B
Newman U, KS — B
North Carolina Ag and Tech State U, NC — B
North Central Coll, IL — B
North Dakota State U, ND — B
Northeastern Illinois U, IL — B
Northeastern State U, OK — B
Northern Illinois U, IL — B
Northern Michigan U, MI — B
Northern State U, SD — B
Northland Coll, WI — B
North Park U, IL — B
Northwestern Coll, IA — B
Northwestern Coll, MN — B
Northwestern Oklahoma State U, OK — B
Northwestern U, IL — B
Notre Dame Coll, OH — B
Oakland City U, IN — B
Oakland U, MI — B
Oberlin Coll, OH — B
Ohio Dominican U, OH — B
Ohio Northern U, OH — B
The Ohio State U, OH — B
The Ohio State U at Lima, OH — B
Ohio U, OH — B
Ohio Wesleyan U, OH — B
Oklahoma Baptist U, OK — B
Oklahoma Christian U, OK — B
Oklahoma City U, OK — B
Oklahoma Panhandle State U, OK — B
Oklahoma State U, OK — B
Olivet Coll, MI — B
Olivet Nazarene U, IL — B
Oral Roberts U, OK — B
Ottawa U, KS — B
Otterbein Coll, OH — B
Park U, MO — B
Peru State Coll, NE — B
Pittsburg State U, KS — B
Principia Coll, IL — B
Purdue U, IN — B
Purdue U Calumet, IN — B
Ripon Coll, WI — B
Rochester Coll, MI — B
Rockford Coll, IL — B
Rockhurst U, MO — B
Roosevelt U, IL — B
Rose-Hulman Inst of Technology, IN — B
Saginaw Valley State U, MI — B
St. Ambrose U, IA — B
St. Cloud State U, MN — B
St. Gregory's U, OK — B
Saint John's U, MN — B
Saint Joseph's Coll, IN — B
Saint Louis U, MO — B

Saint Mary-of-the-Woods Coll, IN — B
Saint Mary's Coll, IN — B
Saint Mary's U of Minnesota, MN — B
St. Norbert Coll, WI — B
St. Olaf Coll, MN — B
Saint Xavier U, IL — B
Shawnee State U, OH — B
Siena Heights U, MI — B
Silver Lake Coll, WI — B
Simpson Coll, IA — B
South Dakota School of Mines and Technology, SD — B
South Dakota State U, SD — B
Southeastern Oklahoma State U, OK — B
Southeast Missouri State U, MO — B
Southern Illinois U Carbondale, IL — B
Southern Illinois U Edwardsville, IL — B
Southern Nazarene U, OK — B
Southwest Baptist U, MO — B
Southwestern Coll, KS — B
Southwestern Oklahoma State U, OK — B
Southwest Missouri State U, MO — B
Spring Arbor U, MI — B
Sterling Coll, KS — B
Tabor Coll, KS — B
Taylor U, IN — B
Transylvania U, KY — B
Trinity Christian Coll, IL — B
Trinity International U, IL — B
Tri-State U, IN — A,B
Truman State U, MO — B
Union Coll, NE — B
The U of Akron, OH — B
The U of Alabama in Huntsville, AL — B
U of Central Oklahoma, OK — B
U of Chicago, IL — B
U of Cincinnati, OH — B
U of Dayton, OH — B
U of Detroit Mercy, MI — B
U of Evansville, IN — B
The U of Findlay, OH — B
U of Illinois at Chicago, IL — B
U of Illinois at Springfield, IL — B
U of Illinois at Urbana–Champaign, IL — B
U of Indianapolis, IN — B
The U of Iowa, IA — B
U of Kansas, KS — B
U of Mary, ND — B
U of Michigan, MI — B
U of Michigan–Dearborn, MI — B
U of Michigan–Flint, MI — B
U of Minnesota, Duluth, MN — B
U of Minnesota, Morris, MN — B
U of Minnesota, Twin Cities Campus, MN — B
U of Missouri–Columbia, MO — B
U of Missouri–Kansas City, MO — B
U of Missouri–St. Louis, MO — B
U of Nebraska at Omaha, NE — B
U of Nebraska–Lincoln, NE — B
U of New Orleans, LA — B
U of North Dakota, ND — B

U of Northern Iowa, IA — B
U of Notre Dame, IN — B
U of Oklahoma, OK — B
U of Rio Grande, OH — A,B
U of St. Francis, IL — B
U of Saint Mary, KS — B
U of St. Thomas, MN — B
U of Science and Arts of Oklahoma, OK — B
U of Sioux Falls, SD — B
The U of South Dakota, SD — B
U of Southern Indiana, IN — B
U of Toledo, OH — B
U of Tulsa, OK — B
U of West Florida, FL — B
U of Wisconsin–Eau Claire, WI — B
U of Wisconsin–Green Bay, WI — A,B
U of Wisconsin–La Crosse, WI — B
U of Wisconsin–Madison, WI — B
U of Wisconsin–Milwaukee, WI — B
U of Wisconsin–Oshkosh, WI — B
U of Wisconsin–Parkside, WI — B
U of Wisconsin–Platteville, WI — B
U of Wisconsin–River Falls, WI — B
U of Wisconsin–Stevens Point, WI — B
U of Wisconsin–Superior, WI — B
U of Wisconsin–Whitewater, WI — B
Upper Iowa U, IA — B
Ursuline Coll, OH — B
Valley City State U, ND — B
Valparaiso U, IN — B
Viterbo U, WI — B
Wabash Coll, IN — B
Walsh U, OH — B
Wartburg Coll, IA — B
Washburn U, KS — B
Washington U in St. Louis, MO — B
Wayne State Coll, NE — B
Wayne State U, MI — B
Webster U, MO — B
Western Illinois U, IL — B
Western Michigan U, MI — B
Westminster Coll, MO — B
Wheaton Coll, IL — B
Wichita State U, KS — B
Wilberforce U, OH — B
William Jewell Coll, MO — B
William Tyndale Coll, MI — B
William Woods U, MO — B
Winona State U, MN — B
Wisconsin Lutheran Coll, WI — B
Wittenberg U, OH — B
Wright State U, OH — B
Xavier U, OH — B
Youngstown State U, OH — B

Mathematics and Computer Science
Augustana Coll, IL — B
Bethel Coll, IN — B
Brescia U, KY — B
Cardinal Stritch U, WI — B
Central Coll, IA — B
Coll of Saint Benedict, MN — B
Eastern Illinois U, IL — B
Lake Superior State U, MI — B

Lawrence Technological U, MI — B
Lawrence U, WI — B
Loyola U Chicago, IL — B
Saginaw Valley State U, MI — B
St. Gregory's U, OK — B
Saint John's U, MN — B
Saint Joseph's Coll, IN — B
Saint Mary's Coll, IN — B
Saint Mary's U of Minnesota, MN — B
St. Norbert Coll, WI — B
The U of Akron, OH — B
U of Illinois at Chicago, IL — B
U of Illinois at Urbana–Champaign, IL — B
Washington U in St. Louis, MO — B

Mathematics and Statistics Related
Bradley U, IL — B
Coll of Mount St. Joseph, OH — B
Coll of Saint Benedict, MN — B
Miami U Hamilton, OH — B
The Ohio State U, OH — B
Ohio U, OH — B
The U of Akron, OH — B

Mathematics Related
Hillsdale Coll, MI — B
Ohio Northern U, OH — B

Mathematics Teacher Education
Alma Coll, MI — B
Alverno Coll, WI — B
Bethany Coll, KS — B
Bethel Coll, IN — B
Bethel U, MN — B
Black Hills State U, SD — B
Bowling Green State U, OH — B
Buena Vista U, IA — B
Capital U, OH — B
Carroll Coll, WI — B
Cedarville U, OH — B
Central Christian Coll of Kansas, KS — A
Central Michigan U, MI — B
Central Missouri State U, MO — B
Central State U, OH — B
Chadron State Coll, NE — B
Coll of St. Catherine, MN — B
The Coll of St. Scholastica, MN — B
Coll of the Ozarks, MO — B
Concordia Coll, MN — B
Concordia U, IL — B
Concordia U, MI — B
Concordia U, NE — B
Concordia U, St. Paul, MN — B
Cornerstone U, MI — B
Culver-Stockton Coll, MO — B
Dakota Wesleyan U, SD — B
Dana Coll, NE — B
East Central U, OK — B
Eastern Michigan U, MI — B
Elmhurst Coll, IL — B
Franklin Coll, IN — B
Grace Coll, IN — B
Greenville Coll, IL — B
Gustavus Adolphus Coll, MN — B
Hannibal-LaGrange Coll, MO — B
Hastings Coll, NE — B

Hope Coll, MI	B
Illinois Wesleyan U, IL	B
Indiana U Bloomington, IN	B
Indiana U Northwest, IN	B
Indiana U–Purdue U Fort Wayne, IN	B
Indiana U South Bend, IN	B
Indiana U Southeast, IN	B
Jamestown Coll, ND	B
Lindenwood U, MO	B
Madonna U, MI	B
Marian Coll of Fond du Lac, WI	B
Marquette U, WI	B
Maryville U of Saint Louis, MO	B
Mayville State U, ND	B
McKendree Coll, IL	B
Miami U Hamilton, OH	B
MidAmerica Nazarene U, KS	B
Minnesota State U Moorhead, MN	B
Minot State U, ND	B
Mount Marty Coll, SD	B
Mount Mary Coll, WI	B
Mount Vernon Nazarene U, OH	B
North Dakota State U, ND	B
Northern Michigan U, MI	B
Northwestern Coll, MN	B
Northwestern U, IL	B
Oakland City U, IN	B
Oakland U, MI	B
Ohio Dominican U, OH	B
Ohio Northern U, OH	B
Ohio U, OH	B
Ohio Wesleyan U, OH	B
Oklahoma Baptist U, OK	B
Oklahoma Christian U, OK	B
Oral Roberts U, OK	B
Pillsbury Baptist Bible Coll, MN	B
Pittsburg State U, KS	B
St. Ambrose U, IA	B
St. Gregory's U, OK	B
Saint Mary's U of Minnesota, MN	B
Saint Xavier U, IL	B
Shawnee State U, OH	B
Southeastern Oklahoma State U, OK	B
Southeast Missouri State U, MO	B
Southern Nazarene U, OK	B
Southwest Baptist U, MO	B
Southwest Missouri State U, MO	B
Trinity Christian Coll, IL	B
Tri-State U, IN	B
Union Coll, NE	B
The U of Akron, OH	B
U of Central Oklahoma, OK	B
U of Illinois at Chicago, IL	B
U of Indianapolis, IN	B
The U of Iowa, IA	B
U of Mary, ND	B
U of Minnesota, Duluth, MN	B
U of Minnesota, Twin Cities Campus, MN	B
U of Missouri–Columbia, MO	B
U of Missouri–St. Louis, MO	B
U of Nebraska–Lincoln, NE	B
U of New Orleans, LA	B
U of North Dakota, ND	B

U of Northern Iowa, IA	B
U of Oklahoma, OK	B
U of Rio Grande, OH	B
U of St. Francis, IL	B
U of St. Thomas, MN	B
The U of South Dakota, SD	B
U of Toledo, OH	B
U of West Florida, FL	B
U of Wisconsin–River Falls, WI	B
U of Wisconsin–Superior, WI	B
Ursuline Coll, OH	B
Valley City State U, ND	B
Valparaiso U, IN	B
Viterbo U, WI	B
Wartburg Coll, IA	B
Washington U in St. Louis, MO	B
Wayne State U, MI	B
Western Michigan U, MI	B
William Penn U, IA	B
William Woods U, MO	B
Wright State U, OH	B
York Coll, NE	B
Youngstown State U, OH	B

Mechanical Design Technology

Bowling Green State U, OH	B
Ferris State U, MI	A
Lincoln U, MO	A,B
Pittsburg State U, KS	B

Mechanical Drafting

Cameron U, OK	A

Mechanical Drafting and CAD/CADD

Baker Coll of Flint, MI	A
Eastern Michigan U, MI	B
Indiana U–Purdue U Indianapolis, IN	A
Morrison Inst of Technology, IL	A
Purdue U, IN	A,B

Mechanical Engineering

Andrews U, MI	B
Baker Coll of Flint, MI	B
Bethel Coll, IN	B
Bradley U, IL	B
Calvin Coll, MI	B
Case Western Reserve U, OH	B
Cedarville U, OH	B
Clarkson U	B
Cleveland State U, OH	B
Dordt Coll, IA	B
Gannon U, PA	B
Grand Valley State U, MI	B
Illinois Inst of Technology, IL	B
Indiana Inst of Technology, IN	B
Indiana U–Purdue U Fort Wayne, IN	B
Indiana U–Purdue U Indianapolis, IN	B
Iowa State U of Science and Technology, IA	B
Kansas State U, KS	B
Kettering U, MI	B
Lake Superior State U, MI	B
Lawrence Technological U, MI	B
Lehigh U, PA	B
Marquette U, WI	B

Miami U, OH	B
Michigan State U, MI	B
Michigan Technological U, MI	B
Milwaukee School of Engineering, WI	B
Minnesota State U Mankato, MN	B
North Carolina Ag and Tech State U, NC	B
North Dakota State U, ND	B
Northern Illinois U, IL	B
Northern Michigan U, MI	B
Northwestern U, IL	B
Oakland U, MI	B
Ohio Northern U, OH	B
The Ohio State U, OH	B
Ohio U, OH	B
Oklahoma Christian U, OK	B
Oklahoma State U, OK	B
Oral Roberts U, OK	B
Purdue U, IN	B
Purdue U Calumet, IN	B
Rose-Hulman Inst of Technology, IN	B
Saginaw Valley State U, MI	B
St. Cloud State U, MN	B
Saint Louis U, MO	B
South Dakota School of Mines and Technology, SD	B
South Dakota State U, SD	B
Southern Illinois U Carbondale, IL	B
Southern Illinois U Edwardsville, IL	B
Tri-State U, IN	B
The U of Akron, OH	B
The U of Alabama in Huntsville, AL	B
U of Cincinnati, OH	B
U of Dayton, OH	B
U of Detroit Mercy, MI	B
U of Evansville, IN	B
U of Illinois at Chicago, IL	B
U of Illinois at Urbana–Champaign, IL	B
The U of Iowa, IA	B
U of Kansas, KS	B
U of Michigan, MI	B
U of Michigan–Dearborn, MI	B
U of Minnesota, Twin Cities Campus, MN	B
U of Missouri–Columbia, MO	B
U of Missouri–Kansas City, MO	B
U of Missouri–Rolla, MO	B
U of Missouri–St. Louis, MO	B
U of Nebraska–Lincoln, NE	B
U of New Orleans, LA	B
U of North Dakota, ND	B
U of Notre Dame, IN	B
U of Oklahoma, OK	B
U of St. Thomas, MN	B
U of Toledo, OH	B
U of Tulsa, OK	B
U of Wisconsin–Madison, WI	B
U of Wisconsin–Milwaukee, WI	B
U of Wisconsin–Platteville, WI	B
Valparaiso U, IN	B
Washington U in St. Louis, MO	B

Wayne State U, MI	B
Western Michigan U, MI	B
Wichita State U, KS	B
William Penn U, IA	B
Winona State U, MN	B
Wright State U, OH	B
Youngstown State U, OH	B

Mechanical Engineering/ Mechanical Technology

Andrews U, MI	A,B
Baker Coll of Flint, MI	A
Bowling Green State U, OH	B
Central Michigan U, MI	B
Eastern Michigan U, MI	B
Ferris State U, MI	A
Indiana U–Purdue U Fort Wayne, IN	A,B
Indiana U–Purdue U Indianapolis, IN	A,B
Kansas State U, KS	A,B
Kent State U, OH	A
Kent State U, Tuscarawas Campus, OH	A
Lake Superior State U, MI	A,B
Lawrence Technological U, MI	A
Miami U Hamilton, OH	A,B
Michigan Technological U, MI	A,B
Milwaukee School of Engineering, WI	B
Ohio U, OH	B
Oklahoma State U, OK	B
Pittsburg State U, KS	B
Purdue U Calumet, IN	A,B
Purdue U North Central, IN	A,B
Rochester Comm and Tech Coll, MN	A
The U of Akron, OH	A,B
U of Cincinnati, OH	A,B
U of Dayton, OH	B
U of Rio Grande, OH	A,B
U of Toledo, OH	A,B
Wayne State U, MI	B
Western Michigan U, MI	B
Youngstown State U, OH	A,B

Mechanical Engineering Technologies Related

Cleveland State U, OH	B
Indiana State U, IN	B
Purdue U, IN	A,B

Medical Administrative Assistant

Globe Coll, MN	A
Minnesota School of Business–Brooklyn Center, MN	A
Minnesota School of Business-Plymouth, MN	A

Medical Administrative Assistant and Medical Secretary

AIB Coll of Business, IA	A
Baker Coll of Auburn Hills, MI	A,B
Baker Coll of Cadillac, MI	A
Baker Coll of Clinton Township, MI	A
Baker Coll of Flint, MI	A
Baker Coll of Jackson, MI	A
Baker Coll of Muskegon, MI	A
Baker Coll of Owosso, MI	A

A—associate degree; B—bachelor's degree

Baker Coll of Port Huron, MI	A
Bryant and Stratton Coll, WI	A
Davenport U, Dearborn, MI	A
Davenport U, Lansing, MI	A
Davenport U, Lapeer, MI	A
Davenport U, Warren, MI	A
Dickinson State U, ND	A
Gallipolis Career Coll, OH	A
Hamilton Coll, NE	A
Hannibal-LaGrange Coll, MO	A
MacCormac Coll, IL	A
Northern Michigan U, MI	A
Rochester Comm and Tech Coll, MN	A
Tabor Coll, KS	B
The U of Akron, OH	A
U of Cincinnati, OH	A
U of Northwestern Ohio, OH	A
U of Rio Grande, OH	A
Washburn U, KS	A
Wright State U, OH	A
Youngstown State U, OH	A

Medical/Clinical Assistant

Argosy U/Twin Cities, MN	A
Baker Coll of Allen Park, MI	A
Baker Coll of Auburn Hills, MI	A
Baker Coll of Cadillac, MI	A
Baker Coll of Clinton Township, MI	A
Baker Coll of Flint, MI	A
Baker Coll of Jackson, MI	A
Baker Coll of Muskegon, MI	A
Baker Coll of Owosso, MI	A
Baker Coll of Port Huron, MI	A
Bryant and Stratton Coll, WI	A
Colorado Tech U Sioux Falls Campus, SD	A
Davenport U, Lansing, MI	A
Hamilton Coll, NE	A
Herzing Coll, Minneapolis Drafting School Division, MN	A
Kaplan Coll, IA	A
Minnesota School of Business-Richfield, MN	A
National American U–Sioux Falls Branch, SD	A
Ohio U, OH	A
Palmer Coll of Chiropractic, IA	A
Presentation Coll, SD	A
Robert Morris Coll, IL	A
The U of Akron, OH	A
U of Northwestern Ohio, OH	A
U of Toledo, OH	A
Youngstown State U, OH	A

Medical/Health Management and Clinical Assistant

Davenport U, Dearborn, MI	B

Medical Illustration

Alma Coll, MI	B
The Cleveland Inst of Art, OH	B
Iowa State U of Science and Technology, IA	B
Olivet Coll, MI	B

Medical Insurance Coding

Baker Coll of Allen Park, MI	A

Davenport U, Dearborn, MI	A
Davenport U, Holland, MI	A
Davenport U, Kalamazoo, MI	A
Davenport U, Lansing, MI	A
Davenport U, Lapeer, MI	A
Davenport U, Warren, MI	A
Herzing Coll, Minneapolis Drafting School Division, MN	A
Kent State U, Salem Campus, OH	A
Kilian Comm Coll, SD	A

Medical Insurance/Medical Billing

Baker Coll of Allen Park, MI	A
Davenport U, Dearborn, MI	A
Davenport U, Holland, MI	A
Davenport U, Kalamazoo, MI	A
Davenport U, Lansing, MI	A
Davenport U, Warren, MI	A
Kent State U, Salem Campus, OH	A

Medical Laboratory Technology

Argosy U/Twin Cities, Eagan, MN	A
Evangel U, MO	A
Oakland U, MI	B
Rockhurst U, MO	B
Roosevelt U, IL	B
Southeastern Oklahoma State U, OK	B
U of Cincinnati, OH	B
U of Illinois at Springfield, IL	B
U of Oklahoma, OK	B

Medical Microbiology and Bacteriology

Ball State U, IN	B
Bowling Green State U, OH	B
Central Michigan U, MI	B
Indiana U Bloomington, IN	B
Miami U, OH	B
Michigan Technological U, MI	B
Minnesota State U Mankato, MN	B
Missouri Southern State U, MO	B
Northeastern State U, OK	B
Northern Michigan U, MI	B
The Ohio State U, OH	B
Ohio U, OH	B
Ohio Wesleyan U, OH	B
Oklahoma State U, OK	B
Purdue U Calumet, IN	B
St. Cloud State U, MN	B
South Dakota State U, SD	B
The U of Akron, OH	B
U of Cincinnati, OH	B
U of Michigan, MI	B
U of Michigan–Dearborn, MI	B
U of Minnesota, Twin Cities Campus, MN	B
U of Wisconsin–La Crosse, WI	B
U of Wisconsin–Madison, WI	B
U of Wisconsin–Oshkosh, WI	B

Medical Office Assistant

Concordia U Wisconsin, WI	B

Mercy Coll of Health Sciences, IA	A
Vatterott Coll, St. Ann, MO	A

Medical Office Computer Specialist

Baker Coll of Allen Park, MI	A

Medical Office Management

Kilian Comm Coll, SD	A
Minnesota School of Business-Richfield, MN	A
The U of Akron, OH	A
Youngstown State U, OH	A

Medical Radiologic Technology

Argosy U/Twin Cities, Eagan, MN	A
Avila U, MO	B
Bacone Coll, OK	A
Coll of St. Catherine, MN	A
Coll of St. Catherine–Minneapolis, MN	A
Gannon U, PA	A,B
Indiana U Northwest, IN	A,B
Indiana U–Purdue U Indianapolis, IN	A,B
Indiana U South Bend, IN	A
Kent State U, OH	A
Kent State U, Salem Campus, OH	A,B
Marian Coll of Fond du Lac, WI	B
Mercy Coll of Health Sciences, IA	A
Mercy Coll of Northwest Ohio, OH	A
Minot State U, ND	B
Missouri Southern State U, MO	A
Mount Marty Coll, SD	B
The Ohio State U, OH	B
Presentation Coll, SD	A,B
Roosevelt U, IL	B
Shawnee State U, OH	A
Southern Illinois U Carbondale, IL	B
Southwest Missouri State U, MO	B
Trinity Coll of Nursing and Health Sciences, IL	A
The U of Akron, OH	A
U of Michigan–Flint, MI	A,B
U of Missouri–Columbia, MO	B
U of Nebraska Medical Center, NE	B
U of St. Francis, IL	B
U of Saint Francis, IN	A
U of Southern Indiana, IN	A
Wayne State U, MI	B

Medical Staff Services Technology

East Central U, OK	B

Medical Transcription

Baker Coll of Flint, MI	A
Baker Coll of Jackson, MI	A
Davenport U, Holland, MI	A
Davenport U, Lansing, MI	A
Kaplan Coll, IA	A
Kilian Comm Coll, SD	A

Medicinal and Pharmaceutical Chemistry

Butler U, IN	B
Ohio Northern U, OH	B

Medieval and Renaissance Studies

Cornell Coll, IA	B
Eastern Michigan U, MI	B
Hanover Coll, IN	B
Ohio Wesleyan U, OH	B
U of Chicago, IL	B
The U of Iowa, IA	B
U of Michigan, MI	B
U of Michigan–Dearborn, MI	B
U of Nebraska–Lincoln, NE	B
U of Notre Dame, IN	B
U of Toledo, OH	B
Washington U in St. Louis, MO	B

Mental and Social Health Services and Allied Professions Related

U of Toledo, OH	B
Wright State U, OH	B

Mental Health Counseling

Florida Gulf Coast U, FL	B

Mental Health/Rehabilitation

Evangel U, MO	A,B
Governors State U, IL	B
Kansas Wesleyan U, KS	B
Lake Superior State U, MI	A
Newman U, KS	B
Pittsburg State U, KS	A
St. Augustine Coll, IL	A
St. Cloud State U, MN	B
U of Toledo, OH	A
Washburn U, KS	A
Wright State U, OH	B

Merchandising

Michigan State U, MI	B
The U of Akron, OH	A
Youngstown State U, OH	B

Merchandising, Sales, and Marketing Operations Related (General)

Eastern Michigan U, MI	B
The U of Akron, OH	B
Washington U in St. Louis, MO	B

Merchandising, Sales, and Marketing Operations Related (Specialized)

Central Missouri State U, MO	A
The U of Akron, OH	B

Metal and Jewelry Arts

Bowling Green State U, OH	B
The Cleveland Inst of Art, OH	B
Coll for Creative Studies, MI	B
Grand Valley State U, MI	B
Indiana U Bloomington, IN	B
Loyola U Chicago, IL	B
Northern Michigan U, MI	B
School of the Art Inst of Chicago, IL	B
The U of Akron, OH	B
The U of Iowa, IA	B
U of Kansas, KS	B
U of Michigan, MI	B
U of Wisconsin–Milwaukee, WI	B

Metallurgical Engineering

Cleveland State U, OH	B
Illinois Inst of Technology, IL	B

Metallurgical Engineering

Michigan Technological U, MI	B
The Ohio State U, OH	B
South Dakota School of Mines and Technology, SD	B
U of Cincinnati, OH	B
U of Michigan, MI	B
U of Missouri–Rolla, MO	B
U of Wisconsin–Madison, WI	B

Metallurgical Technology

Purdue U Calumet, IN	A
U of Cincinnati, OH	B

Meteorology

Western Illinois U, IL	B

Microbiological Sciences and Immunology Related

Wright State U, OH	B

Microbiology

Iowa State U of Science and Technology, IA	B
Miami U Hamilton, OH	B
Michigan State U, MI	B
North Dakota State U, ND	B
Northern Michigan U, MI	B
Southern Illinois U Carbondale, IL	B
U of Illinois at Urbana–Champaign, IL	B
The U of Iowa, IA	B
U of Kansas, KS	B
U of Missouri–Columbia, MO	B
U of Northern Iowa, IA	B
U of Oklahoma, OK	B

Middle School Education

Alverno Coll, WI	B
Antioch Coll, OH	B
Ashland U, OH	B
Avila U, MO	B
Baldwin-Wallace Coll, OH	B
Bethel Coll, IN	B
Black Hills State U, SD	B
Bluffton Coll, OH	B
Bowling Green State U, OH	B
Brescia U, KY	B
Capital U, OH	B
Carroll Coll, WI	B
Carthage Coll, WI	B
Central Christian Coll of Kansas, KS	A
Central Methodist Coll, MO	B
Central Missouri State U, MO	B
Central State U, OH	B
Chadron State Coll, NE	B
Clarke Coll, IA	B
Cleveland State U, OH	B
Coll of Mount St. Joseph, OH	B
Coll of the Ozarks, MO	B
Concordia U, NE	B
Concordia U, St. Paul, MN	B
Concordia U Wisconsin, WI	B
Cumberland Coll, KY	B
Dakota Wesleyan U, SD	B
Eastern Illinois U, IL	B
Eastern Michigan U, MI	B
Evangel U, MO	B
Fontbonne U, MO	B
The Franciscan U, IA	B
Governors State U, IL	B

Grace U, NE	B
Harris-Stowe State Coll, MO	B
Illinois State U, IL	B
Kent State U, OH	B
Lakeland Coll, WI	B
Lake Superior State U, MI	B
Lincoln Coll, Lincoln, IL	A
Lindenwood U, MO	B
Lourdes Coll, OH	B
Malone Coll, OH	B
Marian Coll of Fond du Lac, WI	B
Marquette U, WI	B
Maryville U of Saint Louis, MO	B
McKendree Coll, IL	B
Miami U, OH	B
MidAmerica Nazarene U, KS	B
Minnesota State U Moorhead, MN	B
Missouri Baptist U, MO	B
Missouri Southern State U, MO	B
Mount Mercy Coll, IA	B
Mount Union Coll, OH	B
Mount Vernon Nazarene U, OH	B
Muskingum Coll, OH	B
Nebraska Wesleyan U, NE	B
Northland Coll, WI	B
Notre Dame Coll, OH	B
Oakland City U, IN	B
Ohio Dominican U, OH	B
Ohio Northern U, OH	B
Ohio U, OH	B
Ohio Wesleyan U, OH	B
Otterbein Coll, OH	B
Peru State Coll, NE	B
St. Cloud State U, MN	B
Shawnee State U, OH	B
Southeast Missouri State U, MO	B
Southern Nazarene U, OK	B
Southwest Baptist U, MO	B
Southwest Missouri State U, MO	B
Taylor U, IN	B
Transylvania U, KY	B
Trinity Christian Coll, IL	B
The U of Akron, OH	B
U of Kansas, KS	B
U of Michigan–Dearborn, MI	B
U of Minnesota, Duluth, MN	B
U of Missouri–Columbia, MO	B
U of Nebraska–Lincoln, NE	B
U of New Orleans, LA	B
U of North Dakota, ND	B
U of Northern Iowa, IA	B
U of St. Thomas, MN	B
U of Sioux Falls, SD	B
The U of South Dakota, SD	B
U of West Florida, FL	B
U of Wisconsin–Platteville, WI	B
Urbana U, OH	B
Ursuline Coll, OH	B
Valparaiso U, IN	B
Waldorf Coll, IA	B
Washington U in St. Louis, MO	B
Webster U, MO	B
Westminster Coll, MO	B
William Woods U, MO	B
Winona State U, MN	B

Wright State U, OH	B
Xavier U, OH	B
York Coll, NE	B
Youngstown State U, OH	B

Military Technologies

Wright State U, OH	B

Mining and Mineral Engineering

South Dakota School of Mines and Technology, SD	B
Southern Illinois U Carbondale, IL	B
U of Missouri–Rolla, MO	B
U of Wisconsin–Madison, WI	B

Missionary Studies and Missiology

Bethel Coll, IN	B
Calvary Bible Coll and Theological Seminary, MO	B
Cedarville U, OH	B
Central Christian Coll of Kansas, KS	A,B
Concordia U, St. Paul, MN	B
Concordia U Wisconsin, WI	B
Crossroads Bible Coll, IN	B
Crossroads Coll, MN	B
Crown Coll, MN	B
Dordt Coll, IA	B
Faith Baptist Bible Coll and Theological Seminary, IA	A,B
Global U of the Assemblies of God, MO	B
God's Bible School and Coll, OH	A,B
Grace U, NE	B
Hillsdale Free Will Baptist Coll, OK	A,B
Manhattan Christian Coll, KS	A,B
Messenger Coll, MO	B
MidAmerica Nazarene U, KS	B
Moody Bible Inst, IL	B
North Central U, MN	A,B
Northwestern Coll, MN	B
Oak Hills Christian Coll, MN	B
Oklahoma Baptist U, OK	B
Oklahoma Christian U, OK	B
Oral Roberts U, OK	B
Pillsbury Baptist Bible Coll, MN	B
Reformed Bible Coll, MI	B
Southern Nazarene U, OK	B
Vennard Coll, IA	B

Modern Greek

Ball State U, IN	B
Butler U, IN	B
Calvin Coll, MI	B
Concordia U Wisconsin, WI	B
Cornell Coll, IA	B
John Carroll U, OH	B
Kenyon Coll, OH	B
Macalester Coll, MN	B
Monmouth Coll, IL	B
North Central U, MN	A
Oberlin Coll, OH	B
The Ohio State U, OH	B
Rockford Coll, IL	B
Saint Louis U, MO	B
The U of Iowa, IA	B
U of Michigan, MI	B

U of Minnesota, Twin Cities Campus, MN	B
U of Missouri–Columbia, MO	B
U of Wisconsin–Madison, WI	B
U of Wisconsin–Milwaukee, WI	B
Wabash Coll, IN	B
Wright State U, OH	B

Modern Languages

Albion Coll, MI	B
Alma Coll, MI	B
Ball State U, IN	B
Beloit Coll, WI	B
Bemidji State U, MN	B
Buena Vista U, IA	B
Carthage Coll, WI	B
Chicago State U, IL	B
Cornell Coll, IA	B
DePaul U, IL	B
Gannon U, PA	B
Greenville Coll, IL	B
Hastings Coll, NE	B
Kenyon Coll, OH	B
Lake Erie Coll, OH	B
Minnesota State U Mankato, MN	B
Monmouth Coll, IL	B
North Central U, MN	A
North Park U, IL	B
Oakland U, MI	B
Olivet Nazarene U, IL	B
Stephens Coll, MO	B
U of Chicago, IL	B
Walsh U, OH	B
Washington U in St. Louis, MO	B
Wayne State Coll, NE	B
Wright State U, OH	B

Molecular Biochemistry

Baker U, KS	B

Molecular Biology

Alverno Coll, WI	B
Ball State U, IN	B
Beloit Coll, WI	B
Benedictine U, IL	B
Bethel U, MN	B
Blackburn Coll, IL	B
Bradley U, IL	B
Clarkson U	B
Coe Coll, IA	B
The Coll of Wooster, OH	B
Kenyon Coll, OH	B
Lehigh U, PA	B
Marquette U, WI	B
Muskingum Coll, OH	B
Northwestern U, IL	B
Ohio Northern U, OH	B
Otterbein Coll, OH	B
Southwest Missouri State U, MO	B
U of Kansas, KS	B
U of Michigan, MI	B
U of Minnesota, Duluth, MN	B
U of Wisconsin–Eau Claire, WI	B
U of Wisconsin–Madison, WI	B
U of Wisconsin–Parkside, WI	B
U of Wisconsin–Superior, WI	B
William Jewell Coll, MO	B

A—associate degree; B—bachelor's degree

Montessori Teacher Education

Oklahoma City U, OK	B

Multi-/Interdisciplinary Studies Related

Baldwin-Wallace Coll, OH	B
Bethel U, MN	B
Bluffton Coll, OH	B
Bowling Green State U, OH	B
Buena Vista U, IA	B
Capital U, OH	B
Cleveland State U, OH	B
Coll of the Ozarks, MO	B
The Coll of Wooster, OH	B
Columbia Coll, MO	B
Columbia Coll Chicago, IL	B
Cornell Coll, IA	B
Cornerstone U, MI	B
DePauw U, IN	B
Eastern Illinois U, IL	B
Eastern Michigan U, MI	B
Emporia State U, KS	B
The Franciscan U, IA	B
Grace Bible Coll, MI	B
Greenville Coll, IL	B
Hastings Coll, NE	B
Hope Coll, MI	B
Illinois Inst of Technology, IL	B
Iowa State U of Science and Technology, IA	B
Kaplan Coll, IA	A
Kent State U, OH	B
Kenyon Coll, OH	B
Knox Coll, IL	B
Lehigh U, PA	B
Marquette U, WI	B
Miami U, OH	B
Miami U Hamilton, OH	B
Missouri Baptist U, MO	B
Missouri Western State Coll, MO	B
North Dakota State U, ND	B
Northwestern U, IL	B
Notre Dame Coll, OH	B
Ohio U, OH	A
Ohio U–Southern Campus, OH	B
Ohio Wesleyan U, OH	B
Otterbein Coll, OH	B
Park U, MO	B
Purdue U, IN	B
Saginaw Valley State U, MI	B
St. Ambrose U, IA	B
St. Cloud State U, MN	B
St. Olaf Coll, MN	B
Southeast Missouri State U, MO	B
Southern Illinois U Carbondale, IL	B
The U of Akron, OH	A
U of Nebraska at Omaha, NE	B
U of North Dakota, ND	B
U of Oklahoma, OK	B
U of Saint Mary, KS	B
U of St. Thomas, MN	B
U of Toledo, OH	A,B
Ursuline Coll, OH	B
Valparaiso U, IN	B
Vennard Coll, IA	B
Viterbo U, WI	B
Washington U in St. Louis, MO	B
Wheaton Coll, IL	B
Wisconsin Lutheran Coll, WI	B
Wright State U, OH	B

Museum Studies

Beloit Coll, WI	B
Oklahoma Baptist U, OK	B
The U of Iowa, IA	B

Music

Adrian Coll, MI	B
Albion Coll, MI	B
Alma Coll, MI	B
Alverno Coll, WI	B
Andrews U, MI	B
Antioch Coll, OH	B
Aquinas Coll, MI	B
Ashland U, OH	B
Augsburg Coll, MN	B
Augustana Coll, IL	B
Augustana Coll, SD	B
Baker U, KS	B
Baldwin-Wallace Coll, OH	B
Ball State U, IN	B
Baptist Bible Coll, MO	B
Beloit Coll, WI	B
Bemidji State U, MN	B
Benedictine Coll, KS	B
Benedictine U, IL	B
Bethany Coll, KS	B
Bethany Lutheran Coll, MN	B
Bethel Coll, IN	A,B
Bethel U, MN	B
Blackburn Coll, IL	B
Black Hills State U, SD	B
Bluffton Coll, OH	B
Bowling Green State U, OH	B
Bradley U, IL	B
Briar Cliff U, IA	B
Butler U, IN	B
Calvary Bible Coll and Theological Seminary, MO	B
Calvin Coll, MI	B
Cameron U, OK	B
Capital U, OH	B
Cardinal Stritch U, WI	B
Carleton Coll, MN	B
Carroll Coll, WI	B
Carthage Coll, WI	B
Case Western Reserve U, OH	B
Cedarville U, OH	B
Central Christian Coll of Kansas, KS	A
Central Coll, IA	B
Central Methodist Coll, MO	B
Central Michigan U, MI	B
Central Missouri State U, MO	B
Central State U, OH	B
Chadron State Coll, NE	B
Chicago State U, IL	B
Clarke Coll, IA	B
Cleveland Inst of Music, OH	B
Cleveland State U, OH	B
Coe Coll, IA	B
Coll of Mount St. Joseph, OH	B
Coll of Saint Benedict, MN	B
Coll of St. Catherine, MN	B
Coll of the Ozarks, MO	B
The Coll of Wooster, OH	B
Columbia Coll Chicago, IL	B
Concordia Coll, MN	B
Concordia U, IL	B
Concordia U, MI	B
Concordia U, NE	B
Concordia U, St. Paul, MN	B
Concordia U Wisconsin, WI	B
Cornell Coll, IA	B
Cornerstone U, MI	B

Creighton U, NE	B
Crown Coll, MN	A,B
Culver-Stockton Coll, MO	B
Cumberland Coll, KY	B
Dakota Wesleyan U, SD	B
Dana Coll, NE	B
Denison U, OH	B
DePaul U, IL	B
DePauw U, IN	B
Dickinson State U, ND	B
Doane Coll, NE	B
Dordt Coll, IA	B
Drake U, IA	B
Drury U, MO	B
Earlham Coll, IN	B
East Central U, OK	B
Eastern Illinois U, IL	B
Eastern Michigan U, MI	B
Edgewood Coll, WI	B
Elmhurst Coll, IL	B
Emporia State U, KS	B
Eureka Coll, IL	B
Evangel U, MO	B
Fort Hays State U, KS	B
The Franciscan U, IA	B
Goshen Coll, IN	B
Grace Bible Coll, MI	A,B
Graceland U, IA	B
Grace U, NE	A,B
Grand Valley State U, MI	B
Grand View Coll, IA	B
Greenville Coll, IL	B
Grinnell Coll, IA	B
Gustavus Adolphus Coll, MN	B
Hamline U, MN	B
Hannibal-LaGrange Coll, MO	B
Hanover Coll, IN	B
Hastings Coll, NE	B
Heidelberg Coll, OH	B
Hillsdale Coll, MI	B
Hillsdale Free Will Baptist Coll, OK	A
Hiram Coll, OH	B
Hope Coll, MI	B
Huntington Coll, IN	B
Illinois Coll, IL	B
Illinois State U, IL	B
Illinois Wesleyan U, IL	B
Indiana State U, IN	B
Indiana U Bloomington, IN	B
Indiana U–Purdue U Fort Wayne, IN	B
Indiana U Southeast, IN	B
Iowa State U of Science and Technology, IA	
Iowa Wesleyan Coll, IA	B
Jamestown Coll, ND	B
Judson Coll, IL	B
Kalamazoo Coll, MI	B
Kansas State U, KS	B
Kent State U, OH	B
Kenyon Coll, OH	B
Knox Coll, IL	B
Lake Erie Coll, OH	B
Lake Forest Coll, IL	B
Lakeland Coll, WI	B
Lawrence U, WI	B
Lehigh U, PA	B
Lewis U, IL	B
Lincoln Coll, Lincoln, IL	A
Lindenwood U, MO	B
Loras Coll, IA	B
Lourdes Coll, OH	A
Loyola U Chicago, IL	B
Luther Coll, IA	B

Macalester Coll, MN	B
MacMurray Coll, IL	B
Madonna U, MI	B
Malone Coll, OH	B
Manchester Coll, IN	B
Marian Coll, IN	A,B
Marian Coll of Fond du Lac, WI	B
Marietta Coll, OH	B
Martin U, IN	B
Marygrove Coll, MI	B
McKendree Coll, IL	B
McPherson Coll, KS	B
Messenger Coll, MO	B
Miami U, OH	B
Miami U Hamilton, OH	B
Michigan State U, MI	B
MidAmerica Nazarene U, KS	B
Millikin U, IL	B
Minnesota State U Mankato, MN	B
Minnesota State U Moorhead, MN	B
Minot State U, ND	B
Missouri Southern State U, MO	B
Missouri Valley Coll, MO	B
Missouri Western State Coll, MO	B
Monmouth Coll, IL	B
Morningside Coll, IA	B
Mount Marty Coll, SD	B
Mount Mary Coll, WI	B
Mount Mercy Coll, IA	B
Mount Union Coll, OH	B
Mount Vernon Nazarene U, OH	A,B
Muskingum Coll, OH	B
Nebraska Wesleyan U, NE	B
North Central Coll, IL	B
North Central U, MN	A,B
North Dakota State U, ND	B
Northeastern Illinois U, IL	B
Northeastern State U, OK	B
Northern Illinois U, IL	B
Northern Michigan U, MI	B
Northern State U, SD	B
Northland Coll, WI	B
North Park U, IL	B
Northwestern Coll, IA	B
Northwestern Coll, MN	B
Northwestern Oklahoma State U, OK	B
Northwestern U, IL	B
Oak Hills Christian Coll, MN	B
Oakland City U, IN	B
Oakland U, MI	B
Oberlin Coll, OH	B
Ohio Northern U, OH	B
The Ohio State U, OH	B
Ohio U, OH	B
Ohio Wesleyan U, OH	B
Oklahoma Baptist U, OK	B
Oklahoma Christian U, OK	B
Oklahoma City U, OK	B
Oklahoma State U, OK	B
Olivet Nazarene U, IL	B
Oral Roberts U, OK	B
Ottawa U, KS	B
Otterbein Coll, OH	B
Peru State Coll, NE	B
Pillsbury Baptist Bible Coll, MN	B
Pittsburg State U, KS	B
Principia Coll, IL	B

Quincy U, IL	B
Ripon Coll, WI	B
Rochester Coll, MI	B
Roosevelt U, IL	B
Saginaw Valley State U, MI	B
St. Ambrose U, IA	B
St. Cloud State U, MN	B
Saint John's U, MN	B
Saint Louis U, MO	B
Saint Mary-of-the-Woods Coll, IN	B
Saint Mary's Coll, IN	B
Saint Mary's U of Minnesota, MN	B
St. Norbert Coll, WI	B
St. Olaf Coll, MN	B
Saint Xavier U, IL	B
Shawnee State U, OH	A
Siena Heights U, MI	B
Silver Lake Coll, WI	B
Simpson Coll, IA	B
South Dakota State U, SD	B
Southeastern Oklahoma State U, OK	B
Southeast Missouri State U, MO	B
Southern Illinois U Carbondale, IL	B
Southern Illinois U Edwardsville, IL	B
Southwest Baptist U, MO	B
Southwestern Coll, KS	B
Southwestern Oklahoma State U, OK	B
Southwest Missouri State U, MO	B
Spring Arbor U, MI	B
Sterling Coll, KS	B
Tabor Coll, KS	B
Taylor U, IN	B
Taylor U Fort Wayne, IN	B
Trinity Bible Coll, ND	A
Trinity Christian Coll, IL	B
Trinity International U, IL	B
Truman State U, MO	B
Union Coll, NE	B
The U of Akron, OH	B
The U of Alabama in Huntsville, AL	B
U of Central Oklahoma, OK	B
U of Chicago, IL	B
U of Cincinnati, OH	B
U of Dayton, OH	B
U of Evansville, IN	B
U of Illinois at Chicago, IL	B
U of Illinois at Urbana–Champaign, IL	B
U of Indianapolis, IN	B
The U of Iowa, IA	B
U of Kansas, KS	B
U of Michigan, MI	B
U of Michigan–Dearborn, MI	B
U of Michigan–Flint, MI	B
U of Minnesota, Duluth, MN	B
U of Minnesota, Morris, MN	B
U of Minnesota, Twin Cities Campus, MN	B
U of Missouri–Columbia, MO	B
U of Missouri–Kansas City, MO	B
U of Missouri–St. Louis, MO	B
U of Nebraska at Omaha, NE	B
U of Nebraska–Lincoln, NE	B

U of New Orleans, LA	B
U of North Dakota, ND	B
U of Northern Iowa, IA	B
U of Notre Dame, IN	B
U of Oklahoma, OK	B
U of Rio Grande, OH	A,B
U of St. Thomas, MN	B
U of Science and Arts of Oklahoma, OK	B
U of Sioux Falls, SD	B
The U of South Dakota, SD	B
U of Toledo, OH	B
U of Tulsa, OK	B
U of Wisconsin–Eau Claire, WI	B
U of Wisconsin–Green Bay, WI	B
U of Wisconsin–La Crosse, WI	B
U of Wisconsin–Madison, WI	B
U of Wisconsin–Milwaukee, WI	B
U of Wisconsin–Oshkosh, WI	B
U of Wisconsin–Parkside, WI	B
U of Wisconsin–Platteville, WI	B
U of Wisconsin–River Falls, WI	B
U of Wisconsin–Stevens Point, WI	B
U of Wisconsin–Superior, WI	B
U of Wisconsin–Whitewater, WI	B
Valley City State U, ND	B
Valparaiso U, IN	B
Viterbo U, WI	B
Wabash Coll, IN	B
Wartburg Coll, IA	B
Washburn U, KS	B
Washington U in St. Louis, MO	B
Wayne State Coll, NE	B
Wayne State U, MI	B
Webster U, MO	B
Western Illinois U, IL	B
Western Michigan U, MI	B
Wheaton Coll, IL	B
Wichita State U, KS	B
William Jewell Coll, MO	B
William Tyndale Coll, MI	B
Winona State U, MN	B
Wisconsin Lutheran Coll, WI	B
Wittenberg U, OH	B
Wright State U, OH	B
Xavier U, OH	B
York Coll, NE	B
Youngstown State U, OH	B

Musical Instrument Fabrication and Repair

Ball State U, IN	B
Indiana U Bloomington, IN	A

Music History, Literature, and Theory

Baldwin-Wallace Coll, OH	B
Butler U, IN	B
Calvin Coll, MI	B
Central Christian Coll of Kansas, KS	A
Central Michigan U, MI	B
The Coll of St. Scholastica, MN	B
The Coll of Wooster, OH	B

Eastern Michigan U, MI	B
Hastings Coll, NE	B
Indiana U Bloomington, IN	B
Lincoln Coll, Lincoln, IL	A
Northwestern U, IL	B
Oberlin Coll, OH	B
The Ohio State U, OH	B
Ohio U, OH	B
Otterbein Coll, OH	B
Rockford Coll, IL	B
Roosevelt U, IL	B
St. Cloud State U, MN	B
Saint Joseph's Coll, IN	B
Trinity International U, IL	B
The U of Akron, OH	B
U of Chicago, IL	B
U of Cincinnati, OH	B
U of Illinois at Urbana–Champaign, IL	B
U of Kansas, KS	B
U of Michigan, MI	B
U of Michigan–Dearborn, MI	B
U of Wisconsin–Milwaukee, WI	B
Washington U in St. Louis, MO	B
Western Michigan U, MI	B
Wheaton Coll, IL	B
Wright State U, OH	B
Youngstown State U, OH	B

Music Management and Merchandising

Butler U, IN	B
Capital U, OH	B
Central Christian Coll of Kansas, KS	A
The Coll of St. Scholastica, MN	B
Coll of the Ozarks, MO	B
Columbia Coll Chicago, IL	B
DePaul U, IL	B
DePauw U, IN	B
Drake U, IA	B
Elmhurst Coll, IL	B
Ferris State U, MI	B
Heidelberg Coll, OH	B
Lewis U, IL	B
Lincoln Coll, Lincoln, IL	A
Madonna U, MI	B
Marian Coll of Fond du Lac, WI	B
Millikin U, IL	B
Minnesota State U Mankato, MN	B
Minnesota State U Moorhead, MN	B
North Park U, IL	B
Ohio Northern U, OH	B
Ohio U, OH	B
Oklahoma City U, OK	B
Oklahoma State U, OK	B
Otterbein Coll, OH	B
Peru State Coll, NE	B
Saint Joseph's Coll, IN	B
Saint Mary's U of Minnesota, MN	B
South Dakota State U, SD	B
Southern Nazarene U, OK	B
Southwestern Oklahoma State U, OK	B
Tabor Coll, KS	B
Taylor U, IN	B
U of Evansville, IN	B
The U of Iowa, IA	B

U of Sioux Falls, SD	B
Valparaiso U, IN	B
Waldorf Coll, IA	B
Wheaton Coll, IL	B
Winona State U, MN	B

Musicology and Ethnomusicology

Bowling Green State U, OH	B
Northwestern U, IL	B
The U of Akron, OH	B

Music Pedagogy

Cedarville U, OH	B
The Coll of St. Scholastica, MN	B
Eastern Michigan U, MI	B
Hastings Coll, NE	B
Lawrence U, WI	B
Michigan State U, MI	B
Oklahoma State U, OK	B
Roosevelt U, IL	B
St. Cloud State U, MN	B
Trinity International U, IL	B
Viterbo U, WI	B

Music Performance

Alma Coll, MI	B
Aquinas Coll, MI	B
Augustana Coll, IL	B
Avila U, MO	B
Baldwin-Wallace Coll, OH	B
Bethel Coll, IN	B
Bethel U, MN	B
Black Hills State U, SD	B
Bowling Green State U, OH	B
Bradley U, IL	B
Buena Vista U, IA	B
Calvin Coll, MI	B
Capital U, OH	B
Cedarville U, OH	B
Central Christian Coll of Kansas, KS	A
Central Methodist Coll, MO	B
Coe Coll, IA	B
The Coll of St. Scholastica, MN	B
The Coll of Wooster, OH	B
Columbia Coll Chicago, IL	B
Concordia Coll, MN	B
Cornerstone U, MI	B
DePaul U, IL	B
DePauw U, IN	B
Dordt Coll, IA	B
Drake U, IA	B
Drury U, MO	B
Eastern Michigan U, MI	B
Grace Bible Coll, MI	B
Hastings Coll, NE	B
Hope Coll, MI	B
Illinois State U, IL	B
Indiana U South Bend, IN	B
Jamestown Coll, ND	B
Kent State U, OH	B
Lawrence U, WI	B
Marygrove Coll, MI	B
Miami U, OH	B
Michigan State U, MI	B
Millikin U, IL	B
Missouri Baptist U, MO	B
Mount Union Coll, OH	B
Nebraska Wesleyan U, NE	B
North Central U, MN	B
Northwestern Coll, MN	B
Northwestern U, IL	B
Oakland City U, IN	B

A—associate degree; B—bachelor's degree

Oakland U, MI — B
Ohio Northern U, OH — B
The Ohio State U, OH — B
Ohio U, OH — B
Ohio Wesleyan U, OH — B
Oral Roberts U, OK — B
Otterbein Coll, OH — B
Pittsburg State U, KS — B
Roosevelt U, IL — B
St. Cloud State U, MN — B
Saint Mary-of-the-Woods Coll, IN — B
Saint Mary's U of Minnesota, MN — B
St. Olaf Coll, MN — B
Saint Xavier U, IL — B
Simpson Coll, IA — B
Southeastern Oklahoma State U, OK — B
Southern Nazarene U, OK — B
Southwest Missouri State U, MO — B
Taylor U, IN — B
Transylvania U, KY — B
Trinity Christian Coll, IL — B
Truman State U, MO — B
Union Coll, NE — B
The U of Akron, OH — B
U of Illinois at Urbana–Champaign, IL — B
U of Indianapolis, IN — B
U of Mary, ND — B
U of Missouri–St. Louis, MO — B
U of Nebraska at Omaha, NE — B
U of North Dakota, ND — B
U of Northern Iowa, IA — B
U of Oklahoma, OK — B
U of West Florida, FL — B
Valparaiso U, IN — B
Viterbo U, WI — B
Waldorf Coll, IA — B
Wartburg Coll, IA — B
Webster U, MO — B
Western Michigan U, MI — B
Wheaton Coll, IL — B
William Jewell Coll, MO — B
William Tyndale Coll, MI — B
Wright State U, OH — B
Youngstown State U, OH — B

Music Related

Alverno Coll, WI — A,B
Bethel Coll, KS — B
Bowling Green State U, OH — B
Calvary Bible Coll and Theological Seminary, MO — B
Capital U, OH — B
Central Michigan U, MI — B
Coll of the Ozarks, MO — B
Globe Coll, MN — A
Greenville Coll, IL — B
Indiana State U, IN — B
Malone Coll, OH — B
Minnesota School of Business–Brooklyn Center, MN — A
Minnesota School of Business–Plymouth, MN — A
Minnesota School of Business-Richfield, MN — A
Northwestern U, IL — B
Ohio Northern U, OH — B
Oklahoma State U, OK — B
Roosevelt U, IL — B
Saint Mary's U of Minnesota, MN — B

St. Olaf Coll, MN — B
School of the Art Inst of Chicago, IL — B
U of Tulsa, OK — B
U of Wisconsin–Green Bay, WI — B
Western Illinois U, IL — B
Wheaton Coll, IL — B

Music Teacher Education

Adrian Coll, MI — B
Alma Coll, MI — B
Alverno Coll, WI — B
Andrews U, MI — B
Aquinas Coll, MI — B
Ashland U, OH — B
Augsburg Coll, MN — B
Augustana Coll, IL — B
Augustana Coll, SD — B
Baker U, KS — B
Baldwin-Wallace Coll, OH — B
Ball State U, IN — B
Baptist Bible Coll, MO — B
Beloit Coll, WI — B
Bemidji State U, MN — B
Benedictine Coll, KS — B
Benedictine U, IL — B
Bethany Coll, KS — B
Bethel Coll, IN — B
Bethel U, MN — B
Bluffton Coll, OH — B
Bowling Green State U, OH — B
Bradley U, IL — B
Buena Vista U, IA — B
Butler U, IN — B
Calvary Bible Coll and Theological Seminary, MO — B
Calvin Coll, MI — B
Capital U, OH — B
Carroll Coll, WI — B
Carthage Coll, WI — B
Case Western Reserve U, OH — B
Cedarville U, OH — B
Central Christian Coll of Kansas, KS — A
Central Coll, IA — B
Central Methodist Coll, MO — B
Central Michigan U, MI — B
Central Missouri State U, MO — B
Central State U, OH — B
Chadron State Coll, NE — B
Chicago State U, IL — B
Clarke Coll, IA — B
Cleveland Inst of Music, OH — B
Coe Coll, IA — B
Coll of Saint Benedict, MN — B
Coll of St. Catherine, MN — B
The Coll of St. Scholastica, MN — B
Coll of the Ozarks, MO — B
The Coll of Wooster, OH — B
Concordia Coll, MN — B
Concordia U, IL — B
Concordia U, MI — B
Concordia U, NE — B
Concordia U, St. Paul, MN — B
Concordia U Wisconsin, WI — B
Concord U, WV — B
Cornell Coll, IA — B
Cornerstone U, MI — B
Crown Coll, MN — B
Culver-Stockton Coll, MO — B
Cumberland Coll, KY — B
Dakota State U, SD — B
Dakota Wesleyan U, SD — B

Dana Coll, NE — B
DePaul U, IL — B
DePauw U, IN — B
Dickinson State U, ND — B
Dordt Coll, IA — B
Drake U, IA — B
East Central U, OK — B
Eastern Michigan U, MI — B
Elmhurst Coll, IL — B
Emporia State U, KS — B
Eureka Coll, IL — B
Evangel U, MO — B
Faith Baptist Bible Coll and Theological Seminary, IA — B
Fort Hays State U, KS — B
The Franciscan U, IA — B
God's Bible School and Coll, OH — B
Goshen Coll, IN — B
Grace Bible Coll, MI — B
Grace Coll, IN — B
Graceland U, IA — B
Grace U, NE — B
Grand Valley State U, MI — B
Greenville Coll, IL — B
Gustavus Adolphus Coll, MN — B
Hamline U, MN — B
Hannibal-LaGrange Coll, MO — B
Hastings Coll, NE — B
Heidelberg Coll, OH — B
Hope Coll, MI — B
Huntington Coll, IN — B
Illinois State U, IL — B
Illinois Wesleyan U, IL — B
Indiana U Bloomington, IN — B
Indiana U–Purdue U Fort Wayne, IN — B
Indiana U South Bend, IN — B
Iowa State U of Science and Technology, IA — B
Iowa Wesleyan Coll, IA — B
Jamestown Coll, ND — B
Judson Coll, IL — B
Kansas State U, KS — B
Kent State U, OH — B
Lakeland Coll, WI — B
Lawrence U, WI — B
Lincoln U, MO — B
Lindenwood U, MO — B
MacMurray Coll, IL — B
Madonna U, MI — B
Malone Coll, OH — B
Manchester Coll, IN — B
Marian Coll, IN — B
Marian Coll of Fond du Lac, WI — B
McKendree Coll, IL — B
McPherson Coll, KS — B
Miami U, OH — B
Miami U Hamilton, OH — B
Michigan State U, MI — B
MidAmerica Nazarene U, KS — B
Millikin U, IL — B
Minnesota State U Mankato, MN — B
Minnesota State U Moorhead, MN — B
Minot State U, ND — B
Missouri Baptist U, MO — B
Missouri Western State Coll, MO — B
Morningside Coll, IA — B
Mount Marty Coll, SD — B
Mount Mary Coll, WI — B
Mount Mercy Coll, IA — B

Mount Union Coll, OH — B
Mount Vernon Nazarene U, OH — B
Muskingum Coll, OH — B
Nebraska Wesleyan U, NE — B
North Carolina Ag and Tech State U, NC — B
North Dakota State U, ND — B
Northeastern State U, OK — B
Northern Illinois U, IL — B
Northern Michigan U, MI — B
Northern State U, SD — B
Northland Coll, WI — B
North Park U, IL — B
Northwestern Coll, IA — B
Northwestern Coll, MN — B
Northwestern Oklahoma State U, OK — B
Northwestern U, IL — B
Oakland City U, IN — B
Oakland U, MI — B
Oberlin Coll, OH — B
Ohio Northern U, OH — B
The Ohio State U, OH — B
Ohio U, OH — B
Ohio Wesleyan U, OH — B
Oklahoma Baptist U, OK — B
Oklahoma Christian U, OK — B
Oklahoma City U, OK — B
Oklahoma State U, OK — B
Olivet Nazarene U, IL — B
Oral Roberts U, OK — B
Ottawa U, KS — B
Otterbein Coll, OH — B
Peru State Coll, NE — B
Pillsbury Baptist Bible Coll, MN — B
Pittsburg State U, KS — B
Quincy U, IL — B
Reformed Bible Coll, MI — B
Ripon Coll, WI — B
Rochester Coll, MI — B
Roosevelt U, IL — B
St. Ambrose U, IA — B
St. Cloud State U, MN — B
Saint John's U, MN — B
Saint Mary-of-the-Woods Coll, IN — B
Saint Mary's Coll, IN — B
Saint Mary's U of Minnesota, MN — B
St. Norbert Coll, WI — B
St. Olaf Coll, MN — B
Saint Xavier U, IL — B
Siena Heights U, MI — B
Silver Lake Coll, WI — B
Simpson Coll, IA — B
South Dakota State U, SD — B
Southeastern Oklahoma State U, OK — B
Southeast Missouri State U, MO — B
Southern Nazarene U, OK — B
Southwest Baptist U, MO — B
Southwestern Coll, KS — B
Southwestern Oklahoma State U, OK — B
Southwest Missouri State U, MO — B
Spring Arbor U, MI — B
Sterling Coll, KS — B
Tabor Coll, KS — B
Taylor U, IN — B
Transylvania U, KY — B
Trinity Christian Coll, IL — B
Trinity International U, IL — B

Union Coll, NE	A,B	Calvin Coll, MI	B	U of Evansville, IN	B	U of Minnesota, Crookston,	
The U of Akron, OH	B	Capital U, OH	B	The U of Iowa, IA	B	MN	A,B
U of Central Oklahoma, OK	B	Cedarville U, OH	B	U of Kansas, KS	B	U of Minnesota, Twin Cities	
U of Cincinnati, OH	B	Central Christian Coll of		U of Minnesota, Twin Cities		Campus, MN	B
U of Dayton, OH	B	Kansas, KS	A	Campus, MN	B	U of Nebraska–Lincoln, NE	B
U of Evansville, IN	B	Central Michigan U, MI	B	U of Missouri–Kansas City,		U of Wisconsin–Madison,	
U of Illinois at Urbana–		Central Missouri State U,		MO	B	WI	B
Champaign, IL	B	MO	B	U of Wisconsin–Eau Claire,		U of Wisconsin–Stevens	
U of Indianapolis, IN	B	Coe Coll, IA	B	WI	B	Point, WI	B
The U of Iowa, IA	B	The Coll of Wooster, OH	B	U of Wisconsin–Milwaukee,			
U of Kansas, KS	B	Concordia Coll, MN	B	WI	B		
U of Mary, ND	B	Cornerstone U, MI	B	U of Wisconsin–Oshkosh,		**Natural Sciences**	
U of Michigan, MI	B	DePaul U, IL	B	WI	B	Antioch Coll, OH	B
U of Michigan–Flint, MI	B	DePauw U, IN	B	Wartburg Coll, IA	B	Augsburg Coll, MN	B
U of Minnesota, Duluth, MN	B	Drury U, MO	B	Western Michigan U, MI	B	Avila U, MO	B
U of Minnesota, Twin Cities		Grace U, NE	B			Bemidji State U, MN	B
Campus, MN	B	Hope Coll, MI	B	**Natural Resource Economics**		Benedictine Coll, KS	B
U of Missouri–Columbia,		Lawrence U, WI	B	Michigan State U, MI	B	Bethel Coll, KS	B
MO	B	Michigan State U, MI	B			Calvin Coll, MI	B
U of Missouri–Kansas City,		Minnesota State U		**Natural Resources and**		Carthage Coll, WI	B
MO	B	Moorhead, MN	B	**Conservation Related**		Case Western Reserve U,	
U of Missouri–St. Louis, MO	B	North Central U, MN	A,B	St. Gregory's U, OK	B	OH	B
U of Nebraska at Omaha,		Northwestern Coll, MN	B	U of Michigan–Flint, MI	B	Central Christian Coll of	
NE	B	Northwestern U, IL	B			Kansas, KS	A
U of Nebraska–Lincoln, NE	B	Oakland U, MI	B	**Natural Resources/**		Coll of Mount St. Joseph,	
U of New Orleans, LA	B	Oberlin Coll, OH	B	**Conservation**		OH	B
U of North Dakota, ND	B	The Ohio State U, OH	B	Carroll Coll, WI	B	Coll of Saint Benedict, MN	B
U of Northern Iowa, IA	B	Ohio U, OH	B	Central Michigan U, MI	B	Coll of Saint Mary, NE	B
U of Rio Grande, OH	B	Oklahoma Baptist U, OK	B	Kent State U, OH	B	The Coll of St. Scholastica,	
U of St. Thomas, MN	B	Oklahoma City U, OK	B	Mount Vernon Nazarene U,		MN	B
U of Sioux Falls, SD	B	Oral Roberts U, OK	B	OH	B	Concordia U, IL	B
The U of South Dakota, SD	B	Roosevelt U, IL	B	Muskingum Coll, OH	B	Concordia U, NE	B
U of Toledo, OH	B	St. Cloud State U, MN	B	Northern Michigan U, MI	B	Concordia U, St. Paul, MN	B
U of Tulsa, OK	B	St. Olaf Coll, MN	B	Northland Coll, WI	B	Defiance Coll, OH	B
U of West Florida, FL	B	Southwest Missouri State U,		Peru State Coll, NE	B	Doane Coll, NE	B
U of Wisconsin–La Crosse,		MO	B	Purdue U, IN	B	Dordt Coll, IA	B
WI	B	Trinity International U, IL	B	Rochester Comm and Tech		Edgewood Coll, WI	B
U of Wisconsin–Madison,		The U of Akron, OH	B	Coll, MN	A	Eureka Coll, IL	B
WI	B	U of Illinois at Urbana–		Southeastern Oklahoma State		Goshen Coll, IN	B
U of Wisconsin–Milwaukee,		Champaign, IL	B	U, OK	B	Grand Valley State U, MI	B
WI	B	The U of Iowa, IA	B	U of Michigan–Flint, MI	B	Haskell Indian Nations U,	
U of Wisconsin–Oshkosh,		U of Kansas, KS	B	U of Minnesota, Crookston,		KS	A
WI	B	U of Michigan, MI	B	MN	A	Iowa Wesleyan Coll, IA	B
U of Wisconsin–River Falls,		U of Nebraska at Omaha,		U of Missouri–Columbia,		Kenyon Coll, OH	B
WI	B	NE	B	MO	B	Lourdes Coll, OH	A
U of Wisconsin–Stevens		U of Northern Iowa, IA	B	U of Nebraska–Lincoln, NE	B	Loyola U Chicago, IL	B
Point, WI	B	U of Oklahoma, OK	B	U of Wisconsin–Milwaukee,		Madonna U, MI	A,B
U of Wisconsin–Superior, WI	B	Valparaiso U, IN	B	WI	B	Minnesota State U Mankato,	
U of Wisconsin–Whitewater,		Wartburg Coll, IA	B	U of Wisconsin–River Falls,		MN	B
WI	B	Washington U in St. Louis,		WI	B	Monmouth Coll, IL	B
Valley City State U, ND	B	MO	B	U of Wisconsin–Stevens		North Central Coll, IL	B
Valparaiso U, IN	B	Webster U, MO	B	Point, WI	B	Northland Coll, WI	B
VanderCook Coll of Music,		Western Michigan U, MI	B	Upper Iowa U, IA	B	North Park U, IL	B
IL	B	Wheaton Coll, IL	B	Washington U in St. Louis,		Oklahoma Baptist U, OK	B
Viterbo U, WI	B	Wilberforce U, OH	B	MO	B	Oklahoma Panhandle State	
Waldorf Coll, IA	B	William Jewell Coll, MO	B	Winona State U, MN	B	U, OK	B
Wartburg Coll, IA	B	Wright State U, OH	B			Olivet Nazarene U, IL	B
Washburn U, KS	B	Youngstown State U, OH	B	**Natural Resources**		Park U, MO	B
Wayne State Coll, NE	B			**Management**		Peru State Coll, NE	B
Webster U, MO	B	**Music Therapy**		The Ohio State U, OH	B	St. Cloud State U, MN	B
Western Michigan U, MI	B	Alverno Coll, WI	B			St. Gregory's U, OK	B
Wheaton Coll, IL	B	Augsburg Coll, MN	B	**Natural Resources**		Saint John's U, MN	B
Wichita State U, KS	B	Baldwin-Wallace Coll, OH	B	**Management and Policy**		Shawnee State U, OH	A,B
William Jewell Coll, MO	B	The Coll of Wooster, OH	B	Bacone Coll, OK	A	Shimer Coll, IL	B
Winona State U, MN	B	Eastern Michigan U, MI	B	Ball State U, IN	B	Siena Heights U, MI	B
Wright State U, OH	B	Indiana U–Purdue U Fort		Bowling Green State U, OH	B	Stephens Coll, MO	B
Xavier U, OH	B	Wayne, IN	B	Fort Hays State U, KS	B	Tabor Coll, KS	B
York Coll, NE	B	Maryville U of Saint Louis,		Grand Valley State U, MI	B	Taylor U, IN	B
Youngstown State U, OH	B	MO	B	Huntington Coll, IN	B	The U of Akron, OH	B
		Michigan State U, MI	B	Iowa State U of Science and		U of Cincinnati, OH	A,B
Music Theory and		Saint Mary-of-the-Woods		Technology, IA	B	The U of Findlay, OH	B
Composition		Coll, IN	B	Lake Superior State U, MI	A	U of Mary, ND	B
Baldwin-Wallace Coll, OH	B	Southwestern Oklahoma		North Dakota State U, ND	B	U of Michigan–Dearborn, MI	B
Bowling Green State U, OH	B	State U, OK	B	Northland Coll, WI	B	U of Nebraska at Omaha,	
Bradley U, IL	B	U of Dayton, OH	B	The Ohio State U, OH	B	NE	B
				U of Michigan, MI	B		

A—associate degree; B—bachelor's degree

U of Science and Arts of
Oklahoma, OK — B
U of Toledo, OH — A,B
U of Wisconsin–River Falls,
WI — B
U of Wisconsin–Stevens
Point, WI — B
Washington U in St. Louis,
MO — B
Wayne State Coll, NE — B
Winona State U, MN — B
York Coll, NE — B

Naval Architecture and Marine Engineering
U of Michigan, MI — B
U of New Orleans, LA — B

Near and Middle Eastern Studies
Indiana U Bloomington, IN — B
Oberlin Coll, OH — B
The Ohio State U, OH — B
U of Chicago, IL — B
U of Michigan, MI — B
U of Minnesota, Twin Cities
Campus, MN — B
U of Toledo, OH — B
Washington U in St. Louis,
MO — B
William Tyndale Coll, MI — B

Neurobiology and Neurophysiology
Andrews U, MI — B

Neuroscience
Baldwin-Wallace Coll, OH — B
Bowling Green State U, OH — B
Carthage Coll, WI — B
Central Michigan U, MI — B
John Carroll U, OH — B
Kenyon Coll, OH — B
Lawrence U, WI — B
Macalester Coll, MN — B
Muskingum Coll, OH — B
Northwestern U, IL — B
Oberlin Coll, OH — B
Ohio Wesleyan U, OH — B
U of Minnesota, Twin Cities
Campus, MN — B
Washington U in St. Louis,
MO — B

Non-Profit Management
Clarkson U — B
Davenport U, Dearborn, MI — A,B
Eastern Michigan U, MI — B
Lakeland Coll, WI — B
Manchester Coll, IN — B
Saint Mary-of-the-Woods
Coll, IN — B
Trinity International U, IL — B

Nuclear Engineering
Kansas State U, KS — B
Purdue U, IN — B
U of Cincinnati, OH — B
U of Illinois at Urbana–
Champaign, IL — B
U of Michigan, MI — B
U of Missouri–Rolla, MO — B
U of Wisconsin–Madison,
WI — B

Nuclear Medical Technology
Ball State U, IN — A
Benedictine U, IL — B
Ferris State U, MI — A,B

Indiana U–Purdue U
Indianapolis, IN — B
Kent State U, OH — A
Kettering Coll of Medical
Arts, OH — A
Loras Coll, IA — B
Oakland U, MI — B
Peru State Coll, NE — B
Roosevelt U, IL — B
St. Cloud State U, MN — B
Saint Louis U, MO — B
Saint Mary's U of Minnesota,
MN — B
U of Cincinnati, OH — B
The U of Findlay, OH — A,B
The U of Iowa, IA — B
U of Missouri–Columbia,
MO — B
U of Nebraska Medical
Center, NE — B
U of Oklahoma Health
Sciences Center, OK — B
U of St. Francis, IL — B
U of Wisconsin–La Crosse,
WI — B

Nurse Anesthetist
Webster U, MO — B

Nursing Administration
Central Methodist Coll, MO — B
Nebraska Wesleyan U, NE — B

Nursing Assistant/Aide and Patient Care Assistant
Central Christian Coll of
Kansas, KS — A

Nursing (Licensed Practical/Vocational Nurse Training)
Central Christian Coll of
Kansas, KS — A
Davenport U, Dearborn, MI — A
Dickinson State U, ND — A
Grace U, NE — A
Kent State U, OH — A
Lincoln Coll, Lincoln, IL — A
North Dakota State Coll of
Science, ND — A
Northern Michigan U, MI — A

Nursing (Registered Nurse Training)
Allen Coll, IA — B
Alverno Coll, WI — B
Andrews U, MI — B
Augsburg Coll, MN — B
Augustana Coll, SD — B
Aurora U, IL — B
Bacone Coll, OK — A,B
Baker Coll of Clinton
Township, MI — A
Baker Coll of Flint, MI — A
Baker Coll of Muskegon, MI — A
Baker Coll of Owosso, MI — A
Baker U, KS — B
Ball State U, IN — A,B
Bellin Coll of Nursing, WI — B
Bemidji State U, MN — B
Bethel Coll, IN — A,B
Bethel Coll, KS — B
Bethel U, MN — B
Blessing-Rieman Coll of
Nursing, IL — B
Bowling Green State U, OH — B
Bradley U, IL — B
Briar Cliff U, IA — B
Calvin Coll, MI — B

Capital U, OH — B
Cardinal Stritch U, WI — A,B
Carroll Coll, WI — B
Case Western Reserve U,
OH — B
Cedarville U, OH — B
Central Christian Coll of
Kansas, KS — A
Central Methodist Coll, MO — B
Central Missouri State U,
MO — B
Chicago State U, IL — B
Cleveland State U, OH — B
Coe Coll, IA — B
Coll of Mount St. Joseph,
OH — B
Coll of Saint Benedict, MN — B
Coll of St. Catherine, MN — B
Coll of St. Catherine–
Minneapolis, MN — A
Coll of Saint Mary, NE — A,B
The Coll of St. Scholastica,
MN — B
Columbia Coll, MO — A
Columbia Coll of Nursing,
WI — B
Concordia Coll, MN — B
Concordia U, IL — B
Concordia U Wisconsin, WI — B
Creighton U, NE — B
Culver-Stockton Coll, MO — B
Dakota Wesleyan U, SD — A
Davenport U, Dearborn, MI — A,B
Davenport U, Warren, MI — B
DePaul U, IL — B
Dickinson State U, ND — B
Donnelly Coll, KS — A
Dordt Coll, IA — B
East Central U, OK — B
Eastern Michigan U, MI — B
Edgewood Coll, WI — B
Elmhurst Coll, IL — B
Emporia State U, KS — B
Eureka Coll, IL — B
Ferris State U, MI — A,B
Florida Gulf Coast U, FL — B
Fort Hays State U, KS — B
Franciscan U of Steubenville,
OH — B
Gannon U, PA — B
Goshen Coll, IN — B
Governors State U, IL — B
Graceland U, IA — B
Grace U, NE — B
Grand Valley State U, MI — B
Grand View Coll, IA — B
Gustavus Adolphus Coll, MN — B
Hannibal-LaGrange Coll,
MO — A,B
Hesston Coll, KS — A
Hillsdale Free Will Baptist
Coll, OK — A
Hope Coll, MI — B
Illinois State U, IL — B
Illinois Wesleyan U, IL — B
Indiana State U, IN — A,B
Indiana U East, IN — A,B
Indiana U Kokomo, IN — A,B
Indiana U Northwest, IN — A,B
Indiana U–Purdue U Fort
Wayne, IN — A,B
Indiana U–Purdue U
Indianapolis, IN — A,B
Indiana U South Bend, IN — A,B
Indiana U Southeast, IN — B
Iowa Wesleyan Coll, IA — B

Jamestown Coll, ND — B
Jewish Hospital Coll of
Nursing and Allied Health,
MO — A,B
Judson Coll, IL — B
Kansas Wesleyan U, KS — A,B
Kent State U, OH — A,B
Kent State U, Salem Campus,
OH — B
Kent State U, Tuscarawas
Campus, OH — A,B
Kettering Coll of Medical
Arts, OH — A
Lake Superior State U, MI — B
Lester L. Cox Coll of
Nursing and Health
Sciences, MO — A,B
Lewis U, IL — B
Lincoln Coll, Lincoln, IL — A
Lincoln U, MO — A,B
Lourdes Coll, OH — B
Loyola U Chicago, IL — B
Luther Coll, IA — B
MacMurray Coll, IL — B
Madonna U, MI — B
Malone Coll, OH — B
Marian Coll, IN — B
Marian Coll of Fond du Lac,
WI — B
Marquette U, WI — B
Maryville U of Saint Louis,
MO — B
McKendree Coll, IL — B
Medcenter One Coll of
Nursing, ND — B
MedCentral Coll of Nursing,
OH — B
Mercy Coll of Health
Sciences, IA — A
Mercy Coll of Northwest
Ohio, OH — A,B
Metropolitan State U, MN — B
Miami U, OH — B
Michigan State U, MI — B
MidAmerica Nazarene U, KS — B
Millikin U, IL — B
Milwaukee School of
Engineering, WI — B
Minnesota State U Mankato,
MN — B
Minnesota State U
Moorhead, MN — B
Minot State U, ND — B
Missouri Southern State U,
MO — B
Missouri Western State Coll,
MO — B
Morningside Coll, IA — B
Mount Marty Coll, SD — B
Mount Mary Coll, WI — B
Mount Mercy Coll, IA — B
Nebraska Methodist Coll,
NE — A,B
Nebraska Wesleyan U, NE — B
Newman U, KS — A,B
North Carolina Ag and Tech
State U, NC — B
North Central U, MN — A
North Dakota State U, ND — B
Northeastern State U, OK — B
Northern Illinois U, IL — B
Northern Michigan U, MI — B
North Park U, IL — B
Northwestern Oklahoma
State U, OK — B
Oakland U, MI — B

Nursing (Registered Nurse Training)

The Ohio State U, OH	B
Ohio U, OH	A,B
Ohio U–Chillicothe, OH	A,B
Ohio U–Southern Campus, OH	A,B
Ohio U–Zanesville, OH	A,B
Oklahoma Baptist U, OK	B
Oklahoma City U, OK	B
Oklahoma Panhandle State U, OK	A,B
Olivet Nazarene U, IL	B
Oral Roberts U, OK	B
Otterbein Coll, OH	B
Park U, MO	A
Pittsburg State U, KS	B
Presentation Coll, SD	A,B
Purdue U, IN	B
Purdue U Calumet, IN	A,B
Purdue U North Central, IN	A,B
Quincy U, IL	B
Research Coll of Nursing, MO	B
Rochester Comm and Tech Coll, MN	A
Rockford Coll, IL	B
Rockhurst U, MO	B
Rush U, IL	B
Saginaw Valley State U, MI	B
St. Ambrose U, IA	B
Saint Anthony Coll of Nursing, IL	B
St. Cloud State U, MN	B
Saint Francis Medical Center Coll of Nursing, IL	B
St. John's Coll, IL	B
Saint John's U, MN	B
Saint Joseph's Coll, IN	B
Saint Louis U, MO	B
St. Luke's Coll, IA	A
Saint Luke's Coll, MO	B
Saint Mary's Coll, IN	B
St. Olaf Coll, MN	B
Saint Xavier U, IL	B
Shawnee State U, OH	A,B
South Dakota State U, SD	B
Southeast Missouri State U, MO	B
Southern Illinois U Edwardsville, IL	B
Southern Nazarene U, OK	B
Southwest Baptist U, MO	A,B
Southwestern Coll, KS	B
Southwestern Oklahoma State U, OK	B
Southwest Missouri State U, MO	B
Trinity Christian Coll, IL	B
Trinity Coll of Nursing and Health Sciences, IL	A,B
Truman State U, MO	B
Union Coll, NE	B
The U of Akron, OH	B
The U of Alabama in Huntsville, AL	B
U of Central Oklahoma, OK	B
U of Cincinnati, OH	A,B
U of Detroit Mercy, MI	B
U of Dubuque, IA	B
U of Evansville, IN	B
U of Illinois at Chicago, IL	B
U of Illinois at Springfield, IL	B
U of Indianapolis, IN	A,B
The U of Iowa, IA	B
U of Kansas, KS	B

U of Mary, ND	B
U of Michigan, MI	B
U of Michigan–Flint, MI	B
U of Minnesota, Twin Cities Campus, MN	B
U of Missouri–Columbia, MO	B
U of Missouri–Kansas City, MO	B
U of Missouri–St. Louis, MO	B
U of Nebraska Medical Center, NE	B
U of North Dakota, ND	B
U of Oklahoma Health Sciences Center, OK	B
U of Phoenix–Oklahoma City Campus, OK	B
U of Phoenix–St. Louis Campus, MO	B
U of Phoenix–Tulsa Campus, OK	B
U of Phoenix–West Michigan Campus, MI	B
U of Rio Grande, OH	A
U of St. Francis, IL	B
U of Saint Francis, IN	A,B
The U of South Dakota, SD	A
U of Southern Indiana, IN	A,B
U of Toledo, OH	A,B
U of Tulsa, OK	B
U of West Florida, FL	B
U of Wisconsin–Eau Claire, WI	B
U of Wisconsin–Madison, WI	B
U of Wisconsin–Milwaukee, WI	B
U of Wisconsin–Oshkosh, WI	B
U of Wisconsin–Parkside, WI	B
Ursuline Coll, OH	B
Valparaiso U, IN	B
Viterbo U, WI	B
Walsh U, OH	A,B
Washburn U, KS	B
Wayne State U, MI	B
Webster U, MO	B
Western Michigan U, MI	B
William Jewell Coll, MO	B
Winona State U, MN	B
Wright State U, OH	B
Youngstown State U, OH	B

Nursing Related

Alverno Coll, WI	B
Avila U, MO	B
Capital U, OH	B
Madonna U, MI	A,B
Minot State U, ND	B
The U of Akron, OH	B
U of Saint Francis, IN	B
U of Toledo, OH	B
Wright State U, OH	B

Nursing Science

Benedictine U, IL	B
Clarke Coll, IA	B
Mercy Coll of Health Sciences, IA	B
Missouri Baptist U, MO	B
The Ohio State U, OH	B
Trinity Coll of Nursing and Health Sciences, IL	A,B
The U of Akron, OH	B
U of Kansas, KS	B

U of Phoenix–Metro Detroit Campus, MI	B
U of Wisconsin–Green Bay, WI	B
Wichita State U, KS	B
Xavier U, OH	B

Nutrition Sciences

Benedictine U, IL	B
Case Western Reserve U, OH	B
Elmhurst Coll, IL	B
Michigan State U, MI	B
U of Missouri–Columbia, MO	B
U of Wisconsin–Green Bay, WI	B

Occupational Health and Industrial Hygiene

Clarkson U	B
Illinois State U, IL	B
Oakland U, MI	B

Occupational Safety and Health Technology

Ball State U, IN	B
Central Missouri State U, MO	B
Ferris State U, MI	A,B
Grand Valley State U, MI	B
Indiana State U, IN	B
Indiana U Bloomington, IN	A
North Carolina Ag and Tech State U, NC	B
Southeastern Oklahoma State U, OK	B
Southwest Baptist U, MO	A,B
U of Central Oklahoma, OK	B
U of Cincinnati, OH	A
U of North Dakota, ND	B
U of Wisconsin–Whitewater, WI	B
Washburn U, KS	A
Wright State U, OH	A

Occupational Therapist Assistant

Baker Coll of Muskegon, MI	A
Coll of St. Catherine, MN	A
Coll of St. Catherine–Minneapolis, MN	A
Grand Valley State U, MI	B
Kent State U, OH	A
North Dakota State Coll of Science, ND	A
U of Saint Francis, IN	A
U of Southern Indiana, IN	A
Wichita State U, KS	A

Occupational Therapy

Augustana Coll, IL	B
Baker Coll of Flint, MI	B
Calvin Coll, MI	B
Carthage Coll, WI	B
Chicago State U, IL	B
Cleveland State U, OH	B
Coll of Saint Benedict, MN	B
Coll of St. Catherine, MN	B
Coll of Saint Mary, NE	B
Concordia Coll, MN	B
Concordia U Wisconsin, WI	B
Eastern Michigan U, MI	B
Elmhurst Coll, IL	B
Florida Gulf Coast U, FL	B
Gannon U, PA	B
Hamline U, MN	B

Illinois Coll, IL	B
Indiana U–Purdue U Indianapolis, IN	B
McKendree Coll, IL	B
Mount Mary Coll, WI	B
Newman U, KS	A
The Ohio State U, OH	B
Saginaw Valley State U, MI	B
Saint John's U, MN	B
Saint Louis U, MO	B
Shawnee State U, OH	A,B
Stephens Coll, MO	B
The U of Findlay, OH	B
U of Kansas, KS	B
U of Minnesota, Twin Cities Campus, MN	B
U of Missouri–Columbia, MO	B
U of Southern Indiana, IN	B
U of Wisconsin–La Crosse, WI	B
U of Wisconsin–Madison, WI	B
U of Wisconsin–Milwaukee, WI	B
Wartburg Coll, IA	B
Wayne State U, MI	B
Western Michigan U, MI	B
Xavier U, OH	B

Oceanography (Chemical and Physical)

Central Michigan U, MI	B
U of Michigan, MI	B

Office Management

Academy Coll, MN	A
Baker Coll of Flint, MI	A,B
Baker Coll of Jackson, MI	A
Central Michigan U, MI	B
Central Missouri State U, MO	B
Davenport U, Dearborn, MI	B
Davenport U, Warren, MI	B
God's Bible School and Coll, OH	A
Indiana State U, IN	B
Lake Superior State U, MI	A
Mayville State U, ND	B
Metropolitan State U, MN	B
Miami U Hamilton, OH	B
Park U, MO	A
Shawnee State U, OH	A
Southeastern Oklahoma State U, OK	B
Southeast Missouri State U, MO	B
Tiffin U, OH	B
U of Nebraska–Lincoln, NE	B
U of Southern Indiana, IN	B
Valley City State U, ND	B
Wright State U, OH	B
Youngstown State U, OH	A,B

Office Occupations and Clerical Services

Ohio U–Southern Campus, OH	A
Wright State U, OH	A
Youngstown State U, OH	A

Operations Management

Aurora U, IL	B
Baker Coll of Flint, MI	A,B
Bowling Green State U, OH	B
Central Michigan U, MI	B

A—associate degree; B—bachelor's degree

Clarkson U — B
Davenport U, Dearborn, MI — B
Davenport U, Grand Rapids, MI — B
DeVry U, Addison, IL — B
DeVry U, Chicago, IL — B
DeVry U, Tinley Park, IL — B
DeVry U, MO — B
DeVry U, Columbus, OH — B
Franklin U, OH — B
Indiana State U, IN — A
Indiana U–Purdue U Fort Wayne, IN — A,B
Indiana U–Purdue U Indianapolis, IN — A,B
Iowa State U of Science and Technology, IA — B
Kent State U, OH — B
Kettering U, MI — B
Loyola U Chicago, IL — B
Metropolitan State U, MN — B
Miami U, OH — B
Michigan State U, MI — B
Michigan Technological U, MI — B
Missouri Baptist U, MO — B
Northern Illinois U, IL — B
Oakland U, MI — B
The Ohio State U, OH — B
Purdue U, IN — A,B
Saginaw Valley State U, MI — B
Tri-State U, IN — B
U of Indianapolis, IN — B
U of Michigan–Flint, MI — B
U of St. Thomas, MN — B
U of Toledo, OH — B
U of Wisconsin–Stout, WI — B
U of Wisconsin–Whitewater, WI — B
Washington U in St. Louis, MO — B
Wright State U, OH — B
Youngstown State U, OH — B

Operations Research
DePaul U, IL — B
Miami U, OH — B
U of Cincinnati, OH — B

Ophthalmic and Optometric Support Services and Allied Professions Related
Concordia Coll, MN — B

Ophthalmic Laboratory Technology
Indiana U Bloomington, IN — A

Ophthalmic/Optometric Services
Gannon U, PA — B
Indiana U Bloomington, IN — B
Northeastern State U, OK — B

Optical Sciences
Saginaw Valley State U, MI — B

Opticianry
Ferris State U, MI — B
The U of Akron, OH — A

Optometric Technician
Indiana U Bloomington, IN — A

Organizational Behavior
Benedictine U, IL — B
Bluffton Coll, OH — B
Calvary Bible Coll and Theological Seminary, MO — B
Carroll Coll, WI — B

The Coll of St. Scholastica, MN — B
Concordia U, St. Paul, MN — B
Cumberland Coll, KY — B
Denison U, OH — B
Greenville Coll, IL — B
Miami U, OH — B
Northwestern U, IL — B
Oakland City U, IN — B
Oakland U, MI — B
St. Ambrose U, IA — B
Saint Louis U, MO — B
U of Michigan–Flint, MI — B
U of Toledo, OH — B
Wayne State U, MI — B

Organizational Communication
Aquinas Coll, MI — B
Buena Vista U, IA — B
Capital U, OH — B
Carroll Coll, WI — B
The Coll of St. Scholastica, MN — B
Creighton U, NE — A
Dana Coll, NE — B
Indiana U–Purdue U Fort Wayne, IN — B
McKendree Coll, IL — B
Ohio Northern U, OH — B
Ohio U–Southern Campus, OH — B
U of Michigan–Flint, MI — B
U of Northern Iowa, IA — B
Valparaiso U, IN — B
Wright State U, OH — B

Ornamental Horticulture
Ferris State U, MI — A
Iowa State U of Science and Technology, IA — B
Kent State U, Salem Campus, OH — A
U of Illinois at Urbana–Champaign, IL — B

Orthotics/Prosthetics
Baker Coll of Flint, MI — A
Eastern Michigan U, MI — B

Painting
American Academy of Art, IL — B
Art Academy of Cincinnati, OH — B
Bethany Coll, KS — B
Bowling Green State U, OH — B
Central Christian Coll of Kansas, KS — A
The Cleveland Inst of Art, OH — B
Coe Coll, IA — B
Coll for Creative Studies, MI — B
Coll of Visual Arts, MN — B
Columbia Coll, MO — B
Drake U, IA — B
Grace Coll, IN — B
Indiana U–Purdue U Fort Wayne, IN — B
Kansas City Art Inst, MO — B
Lewis U, IL — B
Lincoln Coll, Lincoln, IL — A
Milwaukee Inst of Art and Design, WI — B
Minneapolis Coll of Art and Design, MN — B
Minnesota State U Moorhead, MN — B
Ohio Northern U, OH — B
The Ohio State U, OH — B

Ohio U, OH — B
St. Cloud State U, MN — B
School of the Art Inst of Chicago, IL — B
Shawnee State U, OH — B
Trinity Christian Coll, IL — B
The U of Akron, OH — B
U of Illinois at Urbana–Champaign, IL — B
The U of Iowa, IA — B
U of Kansas, KS — B
U of Michigan, MI — B
U of Michigan–Flint, MI — B
U of Missouri–St. Louis, MO — B
Washington U in St. Louis, MO — B
Youngstown State U, OH — B

Paralegal/Legal Assistant
Globe Coll, MN — A
Minnesota School of Business–Brooklyn Center, MN — A
Minnesota School of Business–Plymouth, MN — A

Parks, Recreation and Leisure
Ashland U, OH — B
Bemidji State U, MN — B
Bethany Coll, KS — B
Black Hills State U, SD — B
Bluffton Coll, OH — B
Bowling Green State U, OH — B
Calvin Coll, MI — B
Carthage Coll, WI — B
Central Christian Coll of Kansas, KS — A,B
Central Michigan U, MI — B
Central Missouri State U, MO — B
Central State U, OH — B
Chicago State U, IL — B
Dordt Coll, IA — B
Emporia State U, KS — B
Evangel U, MO — B
Ferris State U, MI — B
Graceland U, IA — B
Greenville Coll, IL — B
Huntington Coll, IN — B
Indiana U Bloomington, IN — B
Lake Superior State U, MI — B
Minnesota State U Mankato, MN — B
Missouri Valley Coll, MO — B
North Carolina Ag and Tech State U, NC — B
North Dakota State U, ND — B
Northern Michigan U, MI — B
Northland Coll, WI — B
Ohio U, OH — B
Oklahoma Baptist U, OK — B
Oklahoma Panhandle State U, OK — A,B
South Dakota State U, SD — B
Southeastern Oklahoma State U, OK — B
Southeast Missouri State U, MO — B
Southern Illinois U Carbondale, IL — B
Southwest Baptist U, MO — B
Southwestern Oklahoma State U, OK — B
Southwest Missouri State U, MO — B
Taylor U, IN — B
U of Dubuque, IA — B

U of Illinois at Urbana–Champaign, IL — B
The U of Iowa, IA — B
U of Michigan, MI — B
U of Minnesota, Duluth, MN — B
U of Missouri–Columbia, MO — B
U of Nebraska at Omaha, NE — B
U of Northern Iowa, IA — B
The U of South Dakota, SD — B
U of Toledo, OH — B
U of Wisconsin–Madison, WI — B
U of Wisconsin–Milwaukee, WI — B
Upper Iowa U, IA — B
Wayne State Coll, NE — B
Wayne State U, MI — B
Western Michigan U, MI — B
William Penn U, IA — B
Winona State U, MN — B

Parks, Recreation and Leisure Facilities Management
Ball State U, IN — B
Central Michigan U, MI — B
Coll of the Ozarks, MO — B
Concord U, WV — B
Eastern Illinois U, IL — B
Eastern Michigan U, MI — B
Grand Valley State U, MI — B
Hannibal-LaGrange Coll, MO — B
Hastings Coll, NE — B
Illinois State U, IL — B
Indiana Inst of Technology, IN — A,B
Indiana State U, IN — B
Indiana U Bloomington, IN — B
Indiana U Southeast, IN — B
Kansas State U, KS — B
Kent State U, OH — B
Lake Superior State U, MI — B
Michigan State U, MI — B
Minnesota State U Mankato, MN — B
Missouri Valley Coll, MO — B
Missouri Western State Coll, MO — B
Mount Marty Coll, SD — B
Northland Coll, WI — B
Oak Hills Christian Coll, MN — B
Ohio U, OH — B
South Dakota State U, SD — B
Tri-State U, IN — B
U of Minnesota, Twin Cities Campus, MN — B
U of North Dakota, ND — B
U of St. Francis, IL — B
U of Wisconsin–La Crosse, WI — B
Western Illinois U, IL — B
Winona State U, MN — B

Parks, Recreation, and Leisure Related
Chadron State Coll, NE — B
Culver-Stockton Coll, MO — B
Franklin Coll, IN — B
Madonna U, MI — B
Malone Coll, OH — B
Roosevelt U, IL — B
U of Toledo, OH — B

Majors and Degrees
Pastoral Counseling and Specialized Ministries Related

Pastoral Counseling and Specialized Ministries Related
Calvary Bible Coll and Theological Seminary, MO — B
Coll of Mount St. Joseph, OH — B
Crossroads Bible Coll, IN — B
Greenville Coll, IL — B
Malone Coll, OH — B
Trinity International U, IL — B
U of Mary, ND — B
Vennard Coll, IA — B

Pastoral Studies/Counseling
Baptist Bible Coll, MO — B
Barclay Coll, KS — B
Bethel Coll, IN — B
Calvary Bible Coll and Theological Seminary, MO — B
Cedarville U, OH — B
Central Christian Coll of Kansas, KS — A,B
Concordia U, IL — B
Concordia U, NE — B
Concordia U Wisconsin, WI — B
Cornerstone U, MI — B
Crown Coll, MN — B
Dordt Coll, IA — B
Faith Baptist Bible Coll and Theological Seminary, IA — B
Global U of the Assemblies of God, MO — B
God's Bible School and Coll, OH — B
Grace Bible Coll, MI — B
Grace Coll, IN — B
Grace U, NE — B
Greenville Coll, IL — B
Hesston Coll, KS — A
Lindenwood U, MO — B
Madonna U, MI — B
Manhattan Christian Coll, KS — B
Messenger Coll, MO — B
Newman U, KS — B
North Central U, MN — A,B
Notre Dame Coll, OH — A,B
Oklahoma Baptist U, OK — B
Olivet Nazarene U, IL — B
Oral Roberts U, OK — B
Pillsbury Baptist Bible Coll, MN — B
Reformed Bible Coll, MI — B
Rochester Coll, MI — B
St. Gregory's U, OK — B
Saint Joseph's Coll, IN — B
Saint Mary-of-the-Woods Coll, IN — B
Southwest Baptist U, MO — B
Southwestern Coll, KS — B
Tabor Coll, KS — B
Taylor U Fort Wayne, IN — B
Trinity Bible Coll, ND — B
Union Coll, NE — B
U of Saint Mary, KS — B
U of Sioux Falls, SD — B
Vennard Coll, IA — B
Walsh U, OH — B
William Tyndale Coll, MI — B

Peace Studies and Conflict Resolution
Antioch Coll, OH — B
Bethel Coll, KS — B
Coll of Saint Benedict, MN — B

DePauw U, IN — B
Earlham Coll, IN — B
Goshen Coll, IN — B
Hamline U, MN — B
Kent State U, OH — B
Manchester Coll, IN — B
Northland Coll, WI — B
Ohio Dominican U, OH — B
The Ohio State U, OH — B
Saint John's U, MN — B
U of Missouri–Columbia, MO — B
U of St. Thomas, MN — B
U of Wisconsin–Milwaukee, WI — B
Wayne State U, MI — B

Perfusion Technology
Rush U, IL — B

Personal and Culinary Services Related
Lexington Coll, IL — A,B

Petroleum Engineering
Marietta Coll, OH — B
U of Kansas, KS — B
U of Missouri–Rolla, MO — B
U of Oklahoma, OK — B
U of Tulsa, OK — B

Pharmacology
U of Cincinnati, OH — B
U of Wisconsin–Madison, WI — B

Pharmacology and Toxicology
Wright State U, OH — B

Pharmacy
Briar Cliff U, IA — B
Butler U, IN — B
Drake U, IA — B
North Dakota State U, ND — B
Ohio Northern U, OH — B
The Ohio State U, OH — B
Purdue U, IN — B
St. Louis Coll of Pharmacy, MO — B
South Dakota State U, SD — B
Southwestern Oklahoma State U, OK — B
U of Cincinnati, OH — B
The U of Iowa, IA — B
U of Kansas, KS — B
U of Michigan, MI — B
U of Missouri–Kansas City, MO — B
U of Toledo, OH — B
U of Wisconsin–Madison, WI — B
Wayne State U, MI — B

Pharmacy Administration/ Pharmaceutics
Drake U, IA — B

Pharmacy, Pharmaceutical Sciences, and Administration Related
Ferris State U, MI — B
Ohio Northern U, OH — B
U of Toledo, OH — B

Pharmacy Technician
Baker Coll of Flint, MI — A
Baker Coll of Jackson, MI — A
Baker Coll of Muskegon, MI — A

North Dakota State Coll of Science, ND — A
U of Northwestern Ohio, OH — A

Philosophy
Albion Coll, MI — B
Alma Coll, MI — B
Alverno Coll, WI — B
Antioch Coll, OH — B
Aquinas Coll, MI — B
Ashland U, OH — B
Augsburg Coll, MN — B
Augustana Coll, IL — B
Augustana Coll, SD — B
Aurora U, IL — B
Ave Maria Coll, MI — B
Baker U, KS — B
Baldwin-Wallace Coll, OH — B
Ball State U, IN — B
Beloit Coll, WI — B
Bemidji State U, MN — B
Benedictine Coll, KS — B
Benedictine U, IL — B
Bethany Coll, KS — B
Bethel Coll, IN — B
Bethel U, MN — B
Bowling Green State U, OH — B
Bradley U, IL — B
Briar Cliff U, IA — B
Butler U, IN — B
Calvin Coll, MI — B
Capital U, OH — B
Carleton Coll, MN — B
Carthage Coll, WI — B
Case Western Reserve U, OH — B
Cedarville U, OH — B
Central Coll, IA — B
Central Methodist Coll, MO — B
Central Michigan U, MI — B
Clarke Coll, IA — B
Cleveland State U, OH — B
Coe Coll, IA — B
Coll of Saint Benedict, MN — B
Coll of St. Catherine, MN — B
Coll of the Ozarks, MO — B
The Coll of Wooster, OH — B
Concordia Coll, MN — B
Concordia U, IL — B
Cornell Coll, IA — B
Cornerstone U, MI — B
Creighton U, NE — B
Dakota Wesleyan U, SD — B
Denison U, OH — B
DePaul U, IL — B
DePauw U, IN — B
Doane Coll, NE — B
Dominican U, IL — B
Donnelly Coll, KS — A
Dordt Coll, IA — B
Drake U, IA — B
Drury U, MO — B
Earlham Coll, IN — B
Eastern Illinois U, IL — B
Eastern Michigan U, MI — B
Elmhurst Coll, IL — B
Eureka Coll, IL — B
Fort Hays State U, KS — B
Franciscan U of Steubenville, OH — B
Franklin Coll, IN — B
Gannon U, PA — B
Grand Valley State U, MI — B
Greenville Coll, IL — B

Grinnell Coll, IA — B
Gustavus Adolphus Coll, MN — B
Hamline U, MN — B
Hanover Coll, IN — B
Hastings Coll, NE — B
Heidelberg Coll, OH — B
Hillsdale Coll, MI — B
Hiram Coll, OH — B
Hope Coll, MI — B
Huntington Coll, IN — B
Illinois Coll, IL — B
Illinois State U, IL — B
Illinois Wesleyan U, IL — B
Indiana State U, IN — B
Indiana U Bloomington, IN — B
Indiana U Northwest, IN — B
Indiana U–Purdue U Fort Wayne, IN — B
Indiana U–Purdue U Indianapolis, IN — B
Indiana U South Bend, IN — B
Indiana U Southeast, IN — B
Iowa State U of Science and Technology, IA — B
Jamestown Coll, ND — B
John Carroll U, OH — B
Judson Coll, IL — B
Kalamazoo Coll, MI — B
Kansas State U, KS — B
Kent State U, OH — B
Kenyon Coll, OH — B
Knox Coll, IL — B
Lake Forest Coll, IL — B
Lawrence U, WI — B
Lehigh U, PA — B
Lewis U, IL — B
Lincoln Coll, Lincoln, IL — A
Lincoln U, MO — B
Loras Coll, IA — B
Loyola U Chicago, IL — B
Luther Coll, IA — B
Macalester Coll, MN — B
MacMurray Coll, IL — B
Madonna U, MI — B
Manchester Coll, IN — B
Marian Coll, IN — B
Marietta Coll, OH — B
Marquette U, WI — B
McKendree Coll, IL — B
McPherson Coll, KS — B
Metropolitan State U, MN — B
Miami U, OH — B
Miami U Hamilton, OH — B
Michigan State U, MI — B
Millikin U, IL — B
Minnesota State U Mankato, MN — B
Minnesota State U Moorhead, MN — B
Missouri Valley Coll, MO — B
Monmouth Coll, IL — B
Morningside Coll, IA — B
Mount Mary Coll, WI — B
Mount Union Coll, OH — B
Mount Vernon Nazarene U, OH — B
Muskingum Coll, OH — B
Nebraska Wesleyan U, NE — B
North Central Coll, IL — B
North Dakota State U, ND — B
Northeastern Illinois U, IL — B
Northern Illinois U, IL — B
Northern Michigan U, MI — B
Northland Coll, WI — B
North Park U, IL — B

A—associate degree; B—bachelor's degree

Northwestern Coll, IA	B
Northwestern U, IL	B
Oakland U, MI	B
Oberlin Coll, OH	B
Ohio Dominican U, OH	B
Ohio Northern U, OH	B
The Ohio State U, OH	B
Ohio U, OH	B
Ohio Wesleyan U, OH	B
Oklahoma Baptist U, OK	B
Oklahoma City U, OK	B
Oklahoma State U, OK	B
Olivet Nazarene U, IL	B
Oral Roberts U, OK	B
Otterbein Coll, OH	B
Pontifical Coll Josephinum, OH	B
Principia Coll, IL	B
Purdue U, IN	B
Purdue U Calumet, IN	B
Quincy U, IL	B
Ripon Coll, WI	B
Rockford Coll, IL	B
Rockhurst U, MO	B
Roosevelt U, IL	B
Sacred Heart Major Seminary, MI	B
St. Ambrose U, IA	B
St. Cloud State U, MN	B
St. Gregory's U, OK	B
Saint John's U, MN	B
Saint Joseph's Coll, IN	B
Saint Louis U, MO	B
Saint Mary's Coll, IN	B
Saint Mary's U of Minnesota, MN	B
St. Norbert Coll, WI	B
St. Olaf Coll, MN	B
Saint Xavier U, IL	B
Siena Heights U, MI	B
Simpson Coll, IA	B
Southeast Missouri State U, MO	B
Southern Illinois U Carbondale, IL	B
Southern Illinois U Edwardsville, IL	B
Southern Nazarene U, OK	B
Southwest Missouri State U, MO	B
Spring Arbor U, MI	B
Stephens Coll, MO	B
Tabor Coll, KS	B
Taylor U, IN	B
Transylvania U, KY	B
Trinity Christian Coll, IL	B
Trinity International U, IL	B
Truman State U, MO	B
The U of Akron, OH	B
The U of Alabama in Huntsville, AL	B
U of Central Oklahoma, OK	B
U of Chicago, IL	B
U of Cincinnati, OH	B
U of Dayton, OH	B
U of Detroit Mercy, MI	B
U of Dubuque, IA	B
U of Evansville, IN	B
The U of Findlay, OH	B
U of Illinois at Chicago, IL	B
U of Illinois at Urbana–Champaign, IL	B
U of Indianapolis, IN	B
The U of Iowa, IA	B
U of Kansas, KS	B
U of Michigan, MI	B

U of Michigan–Dearborn, MI	B
U of Michigan–Flint, MI	B
U of Minnesota, Duluth, MN	B
U of Minnesota, Morris, MN	B
U of Minnesota, Twin Cities Campus, MN	B
U of Missouri–Columbia, MO	B
U of Missouri–Kansas City, MO	B
U of Missouri–Rolla, MO	B
U of Missouri–St. Louis, MO	B
U of Nebraska at Omaha, NE	B
U of Nebraska–Lincoln, NE	B
U of New Orleans, LA	B
U of North Dakota, ND	B
U of Northern Iowa, IA	B
U of Notre Dame, IN	B
U of Oklahoma, OK	B
U of St. Thomas, MN	B
U of Sioux Falls, SD	B
The U of South Dakota, SD	B
U of Southern Indiana, IN	B
U of Toledo, OH	B
U of Tulsa, OK	B
U of West Florida, FL	B
U of Wisconsin–Eau Claire, WI	B
U of Wisconsin–Green Bay, WI	A,B
U of Wisconsin–La Crosse, WI	B
U of Wisconsin–Madison, WI	B
U of Wisconsin–Milwaukee, WI	B
U of Wisconsin–Oshkosh, WI	B
U of Wisconsin–Parkside, WI	B
U of Wisconsin–Platteville, WI	B
U of Wisconsin–Stevens Point, WI	B
Urbana U, OH	B
Ursuline Coll, OH	B
Valparaiso U, IN	B
Wabash Coll, IN	B
Walsh U, OH	B
Wartburg Coll, IA	B
Washburn U, KS	B
Washington U in St. Louis, MO	B
Wayne State U, MI	B
Webster U, MO	B
Western Illinois U, IL	B
Western Michigan U, MI	B
Westminster Coll, MO	B
Wheaton Coll, IL	B
Wichita State U, KS	B
William Jewell Coll, MO	B
Wittenberg U, OH	B
Wright State U, OH	B
Xavier U, OH	B
Youngstown State U, OH	B

Philosophy and Religious Studies Related

Buena Vista U, IA	B
Capital U, OH	B
Coll of the Ozarks, MO	B
Columbia Coll, MO	B
Cumberland Coll, KY	B
Graceland U, IA	B
Greenville Coll, IL	B
Saint Joseph's Coll, IN	B
Southwestern Coll, KS	B

Sterling Coll, KS	B
U of Notre Dame, IN	B
Washington U in St. Louis, MO	B

Philosophy Related

Ohio Northern U, OH	B

Photographic and Film/Video Technology

Kent State U, OH	B
Ohio U, OH	B

Photography

Andrews U, MI	A,B
Art Academy of Cincinnati, OH	B
Ball State U, IN	B
Bethel Coll, IN	B
Bowling Green State U, OH	B
Carroll Coll, WI	B
Central Christian Coll of Kansas, KS	A
Central Missouri State U, MO	B
The Cleveland Inst of Art, OH	B
Coe Coll, IA	B
Coll for Creative Studies, MI	B
Coll of Visual Arts, MN	B
Columbia Coll, MO	B
Columbia Coll Chicago, IL	B
Columbus Coll of Art & Design, OH	B
Dominican U, IL	B
Governors State U, IL	B
Grand Valley State U, MI	B
Indiana U Bloomington, IN	B
Indiana U–Purdue U Fort Wayne, IN	B
Kansas City Art Inst, MO	B
Lincoln Coll, Lincoln, IL	A
Loyola U Chicago, IL	B
Milwaukee Inst of Art and Design, WI	B
Minneapolis Coll of Art and Design, MN	B
Morningside Coll, IA	B
Northern Michigan U, MI	B
Ohio U, OH	B
Pillsbury Baptist Bible Coll, MN	A
Saint Mary-of-the-Woods Coll, IN	B
School of the Art Inst of Chicago, IL	B
Shawnee State U, OH	B
Trinity Christian Coll, IL	B
The U of Akron, OH	B
U of Central Oklahoma, OK	B
U of Dayton, OH	B
U of Illinois at Chicago, IL	B
U of Illinois at Urbana–Champaign, IL	B
The U of Iowa, IA	B
U of Michigan, MI	B
U of Michigan–Flint, MI	B
U of Missouri–St. Louis, MO	B
U of Oklahoma, OK	B
Washington U in St. Louis, MO	B
Webster U, MO	B
Wright State U, OH	B
Youngstown State U, OH	B

Photojournalism

St. Gregory's U, OK	B
U of Missouri–Columbia, MO	B

Physical and Theoretical Chemistry

Lehigh U, PA	B
Michigan State U, MI	B

Physical Education Teaching and Coaching

Adrian Coll, MI	A,B
Albion Coll, MI	B
Alma Coll, MI	B
Aquinas Coll, MI	B
Ashland U, OH	B
Augsburg Coll, MN	B
Augustana Coll, IL	B
Augustana Coll, SD	B
Aurora U, IL	B
Bacone Coll, OK	B
Baker U, KS	B
Baldwin-Wallace Coll, OH	B
Ball State U, IN	B
Bellevue U, NE	B
Bemidji State U, MN	B
Benedictine Coll, KS	B
Bethany Coll, KS	B
Bethel Coll, IN	B
Bethel U, MN	B
Blackburn Coll, IL	B
Bowling Green State U, OH	B
Briar Cliff U, IA	B
Buena Vista U, IA	B
Calvin Coll, MI	B
Capital U, OH	B
Carroll Coll, WI	B
Carthage Coll, WI	B
Cedarville U, OH	B
Central Christian Coll of Kansas, KS	A
Central Methodist Coll, MO	B
Central Michigan U, MI	B
Central Missouri State U, MO	B
Central State U, OH	B
Chadron State Coll, NE	B
Chicago State U, IL	B
Clarke Coll, IA	B
Cleveland State U, OH	B
Coe Coll, IA	B
Coll of Mount St. Joseph, OH	B
Coll of St. Catherine, MN	B
Coll of the Ozarks, MO	B
Concordia Coll, MN	B
Concordia U, IL	B
Concordia U, MI	B
Concordia U, NE	B
Concordia U St. Paul, MN	B
Concordia U Wisconsin, WI	B
Concord U, WV	B
Cornell Coll, IA	B
Cornerstone U, MI	B
Crown Coll, MN	B
Culver-Stockton Coll, MO	B
Cumberland Coll, KY	B
Dakota State U, SD	B
Dakota Wesleyan U, SD	B
Dana Coll, NE	B
Defiance Coll, OH	B
Denison U, OH	B
DePaul U, IL	B
DePauw U, IN	B
Dickinson State U, ND	B
Doane Coll, NE	B

Dordt Coll, IA	B	Northeastern State U, OK	B	U of Missouri–Kansas City, MO		Michigan State U, MI	B

Dordt Coll, IA — B
East Central U, OK — B
Eastern Illinois U, IL — B
Eastern Michigan U, MI — B
Elmhurst Coll, IL — B
Eureka Coll, IL — B
Evangel U, MO — B
Fort Hays State U, KS — B
Franklin Coll, IN — B
Goshen Coll, IN — B
Grace Coll, IN — B
Graceland U, IA — B
Grand Valley State U, MI — B
Greenville Coll, IL — B
Gustavus Adolphus Coll, MN — B
Hamline U, MN — B
Hannibal-LaGrange Coll, MO — B
Hanover Coll, IN — B
Hastings Coll, NE — B
Heidelberg Coll, OH — B
Hillsdale Coll, MI — B
Hillsdale Free Will Baptist Coll, OK — A
Hope Coll, MI — B
Huntington Coll, IN — B
Illinois Coll, IL — B
Illinois State U, IL — B
Indiana State U, IN — B
Indiana U Bloomington, IN — B
Indiana U–Purdue U Indianapolis, IN — B
Iowa Wesleyan Coll, IA — B
Jamestown Coll, ND — B
John Carroll U, OH — B
Judson Coll, IL — B
Kansas Wesleyan U, KS — B
Kent State U, OH — B
Lewis U, IL — B
Lincoln Coll, Lincoln, IL — A
Lincoln U, MO — B
Lindenwood U, MO — B
Loras Coll, IA — B
Luther Coll, IA — B
MacMurray Coll, IL — B
Malone Coll, OH — B
Manchester Coll, IN — B
Marian Coll, IN — B
Mayville State U, ND — B
McKendree Coll, IL — B
McPherson Coll, KS — B
Miami U, OH — B
Miami U Hamilton, OH — B
Michigan State U, MI — B
MidAmerica Nazarene U, KS — B
Millikin U, IL — B
Minnesota State U Mankato, MN — B
Minnesota State U Moorhead, MN — B
Minot State U, ND — B
Missouri Baptist U, MO — B
Missouri Valley Coll, MO — B
Monmouth Coll, IL — B
Mount Marty Coll, SD — B
Mount Union Coll, OH — B
Mount Vernon Nazarene U, OH — B
Muskingum Coll, OH — B
Nebraska Wesleyan U, NE — B
North Carolina Ag and Tech State U, NC — B
North Central Coll, IL — B
North Dakota State U, ND — B
Northeastern Illinois U, IL — B

Northeastern State U, OK — B
Northern Illinois U, IL — B
Northern Michigan U, MI — B
Northern State U, SD — B
North Park U, IL — B
Northwestern Coll, IA — B
Northwestern Coll, MN — B
Northwestern Oklahoma State U, OK — B
Oakland City U, IN — B
Ohio Northern U, OH — B
The Ohio State U, OH — B
Ohio U, OH — B
Ohio Wesleyan U, OH — B
Oklahoma Baptist U, OK — B
Oklahoma Christian U, OK — B
Oklahoma City U, OK — B
Oklahoma Panhandle State U, OK — B
Oklahoma State U, OK — B
Olivet Coll, MI — B
Olivet Nazarene U, IL — B
Oral Roberts U, OK — B
Ottawa U, KS — B
Otterbein Coll, OH — B
Peru State Coll, NE — B
Pillsbury Baptist Bible Coll, MN — B
Pittsburg State U, KS — B
Purdue U, IN — B
Quincy U, IL — B
Ripon Coll, WI — B
Rockford Coll, IL — B
Saginaw Valley State U, MI — B
St. Ambrose U, IA — B
St. Cloud State U, MN — B
Saint Joseph's Coll, IN — B
Simpson Coll, IA — B
South Dakota State U, SD — B
Southeastern Oklahoma State U, OK — B
Southeast Missouri State U, MO — B
Southern Illinois U Carbondale, IL — B
Southern Nazarene U, OK — B
Southwest Baptist U, MO — B
Southwestern Oklahoma State U, OK — B
Southwest Missouri State U, MO — B
Spring Arbor U, MI — B
Sterling Coll, KS — B
Tabor Coll, KS — B
Taylor U, IN — B
Transylvania U, KY — B
Trinity Christian Coll, IL — B
Trinity International U, IL — B
Tri-State U, IN — B
Union Coll, NE — B
The U of Akron, OH — B
U of Central Oklahoma, OK — B
U of Cincinnati, OH — B
U of Dayton, OH — B
U of Dubuque, IA — B
U of Evansville, IN — B
The U of Findlay, OH — B
U of Indianapolis, IN — B
U of Kansas, KS — B
U of Mary, ND — B
U of Michigan, MI — B
U of Minnesota, Duluth, MN — B
U of Minnesota, Twin Cities Campus, MN — B

U of Missouri–Kansas City, MO —
U of Missouri–St. Louis, MO — B
U of Nebraska at Omaha, NE — B
U of Nebraska–Lincoln, NE — B
U of New Orleans, LA — B
U of North Dakota, ND — B
U of Northern Iowa, IA — B
U of Rio Grande, OH — A,B
U of St. Thomas, MN — B
U of Sioux Falls, SD — B
The U of South Dakota, SD — B
U of Southern Indiana, IN — B
U of Toledo, OH — B
U of Wisconsin–La Crosse, WI — B
U of Wisconsin–Madison, WI — B
U of Wisconsin–Oshkosh, WI — B
U of Wisconsin–River Falls, WI — B
U of Wisconsin–Stevens Point, WI — B
U of Wisconsin–Superior, WI — B
U of Wisconsin–Whitewater, WI — B
Upper Iowa U, IA — B
Valley City State U, ND — B
Valparaiso U, IN — B
Waldorf Coll, IA — B
Walsh U, OH — B
Wartburg Coll, IA — B
Washburn U, KS — B
Wayne State Coll, NE — B
Wayne State U, MI — B
Western Illinois U, IL — B
Western Michigan U, MI — B
Westminster Coll, MO — B
Wichita State U, KS — B
William Penn U, IA — B
William Woods U, MO — B
Winona State U, MN — B
Wright State U, OH — B
York Coll, NE — B
Youngstown State U, OH — B

Physical Sciences

Antioch Coll, OH — B
Bacone Coll, OK — A
Bemidji State U, MN — B
Black Hills State U, SD — B
Calvin Coll, MI — B
Central Christian Coll of Kansas, KS — A
Central Michigan U, MI — B
Coe Coll, IA — B
Concordia U, IL — B
Concordia U, NE — B
Defiance Coll, OH — B
Doane Coll, NE — B
Emporia State U, KS — B
Eureka Coll, IL — B
Fort Hays State U, KS — B
Goshen Coll, IN — B
Graceland U, IA — B
Grand Valley State U, MI — B
Grand View Coll, IA — B
Judson Coll, IL — B
Kansas State U, KS — B
Lincoln Coll, Lincoln, IL — A
Loras Coll, IA — B
Mayville State U, ND — B
McPherson Coll, KS — B

Michigan State U, MI — B
Michigan Technological U, MI —
Minnesota State U Mankato, MN — B
Minot State U, ND — B
Oakland U, MI — B
Oklahoma Baptist U, OK — B
Olivet Nazarene U, IL — B
Otterbein Coll, OH — B
Peru State Coll, NE — B
Pittsburg State U, KS — B
Ripon Coll, WI — B
St. Cloud State U, MN — B
Shawnee State U, OH — B
Tri-State U, IN — B
U of Dayton, OH — B
U of Michigan–Dearborn, MI — B
U of Rio Grande, OH — B
U of Toledo, OH — B
U of Wisconsin–River Falls, WI — B
U of Wisconsin–Superior, WI — B
Washington U in St. Louis, MO — B
Wayne State Coll, NE — B
Winona State U, MN — B
Wittenberg U, OH — B

Physical Sciences Related

The Coll of St. Scholastica, MN — B
Eastern Michigan U, MI — B
Ohio U, OH — B

Physical Science Technologies Related

Southwest Missouri State U, MO — B
The U of Akron, OH — A

Physical Therapist Assistant

Baker Coll of Flint, MI — A
Baker Coll of Muskegon, MI — A
Central Christian Coll of Kansas, KS — A
Coll of St. Catherine, MN — A
Coll of St. Catherine–Minneapolis, MN — A
Kent State U, OH — A
Missouri Western State Coll, MO — A
Southern Illinois U Carbondale, IL — A
U of Evansville, IN — A
U of Indianapolis, IN — A
U of Saint Francis, IN — A
Wichita State U, KS — A

Physical Therapy

Andrews U, MI — B
Bowling Green State U, OH — B
Bradley U, IL — B
Briar Cliff U, IA — A
Central Christian Coll of Kansas, KS — A
Clarke Coll, IA — B
Cleveland State U, OH — B
Coll of Mount St. Joseph, OH — B
Coll of Saint Benedict, MN — B
Concordia Coll, MN — B
Concordia U Wisconsin, WI — B
Davenport U, Lansing, MI — A
Donnelly Coll, KS — A
Elmhurst Coll, IL — B
Grand Valley State U, MI — B

A—associate degree; B—bachelor's degree

Gustavus Adolphus Coll, MN   B
Hamline U, MN   B
Indiana U–Purdue U
  Indianapolis, IN   B
Marquette U, WI   B
Mount Vernon Nazarene U,
  OH   B
Northern Illinois U, IL   B
Oakland U, MI   B
The Ohio State U, OH   B
Pittsburg State U, KS   B
St. Cloud State U, MN   B
Saint John's U, MN   B
Saint Louis U, MO   B
Saint Mary's U of Minnesota,
  MN   B
Shawnee State U, OH   A
Simpson Coll, IA   B
U of Cincinnati, OH   A
U of Evansville, IN   A,B
The U of Findlay, OH   B
U of Minnesota, Morris, MN   B
U of Minnesota, Twin Cities
  Campus, MN   B
U of North Dakota, ND   B
U of Toledo, OH   B
U of Wisconsin–Milwaukee,
  WI   B
Washburn U, KS   A
Winona State U, MN   B

Physician Assistant

Augsburg Coll, MN   B
Butler U, IN   B
Central Christian Coll of
  Kansas, KS   A
Elmhurst Coll, IL   B
Gannon U, PA   B
Globe Coll, MN   A
Grand Valley State U, MI   B
Kettering Coll of Medical
  Arts, OH   A,B
Marquette U, WI   B
Minnesota School of
  Business–Brooklyn Center,
  MN   A
Minnesota School of
  Business-Plymouth, MN   A
Peru State Coll, NE   B
Saint Louis U, MO   B
Southern Illinois U
  Carbondale, IL   B
Union Coll, NE   B
The U of Findlay, OH   B
U of Saint Francis, IN   B
U of Wisconsin–La Crosse,
  WI   B
U of Wisconsin–Madison,
  WI   B
Wichita State U, KS   B

Physics

Adrian Coll, MI   A,B
Albion Coll, MI   B
Alma Coll, MI   B
Andrews U, MI   B
Antioch Coll, OH   B
Aquinas Coll, MI   B
Ashland U, OH   B
Augsburg Coll, MN   B
Augustana Coll, IL   B
Augustana Coll, SD   B
Baker U, KS   B
Baldwin-Wallace Coll, OH   B
Ball State U, IN   B
Beloit Coll, WI   B
Bemidji State U, MN   B

Benedictine Coll, KS   B
Benedictine U, IL   B
Bethel Coll, IN   B
Bethel Coll, KS   B
Bethel U, MN   B
Bluffton Coll, OH   B
Bowling Green State U, OH   B
Bradley U, IL   B
Buena Vista U, IA   B
Butler U, IN   B
Calvin Coll, MI   B
Cameron U, OK   B
Carleton Coll, MN   B
Carthage Coll, WI   B
Case Western Reserve U,
  OH   B
Cedarville U, OH   B
Central Coll, IA   B
Central Methodist Coll, MO   B
Central Michigan U, MI   B
Central Missouri State U,
  MO   B
Chadron State Coll, NE   B
Clarkson U   B
Cleveland State U, OH   B
Coe Coll, IA   B
Coll of Saint Benedict, MN   B
Coll of St. Catherine, MN   B
The Coll of Wooster, OH   B
Concordia Coll, MN   B
Cornell Coll, IA   B
Creighton U, NE   B
Cumberland Coll, KY   B
Dakota State U, SD   B
Denison U, OH   B
DePaul U, IL   B
DePauw U, IN   B
Doane Coll, NE   B
Dordt Coll, IA   B
Drake U, IA   B
Drury U, MO   B
Earlham Coll, IN   B
East Central U, OK   B
Eastern Illinois U, IL   B
Eastern Michigan U, MI   B
Elmhurst Coll, IL   B
Emporia State U, KS   B
Fort Hays State U, KS   B
Goshen Coll, IN   B
Grand Valley State U, MI   B
Greenville Coll, IL   B
Grinnell Coll, IA   B
Gustavus Adolphus Coll, MN   B
Hamline U, MN   B
Hanover Coll, IN   B
Hastings Coll, NE   B
Heidelberg Coll, OH   B
Hillsdale Coll, MI   B
Hiram Coll, OH   B
Hope Coll, MI   B
Illinois Coll, IL   B
Illinois Inst of Technology, IL   B
Illinois State U, IL   B
Illinois Wesleyan U, IL   B
Indiana State U, IN   B
Indiana U Bloomington, IN   B
Indiana U–Purdue U Fort
  Wayne, IN   B
Indiana U–Purdue U
  Indianapolis, IN   B
Indiana U South Bend, IN   B
Iowa State U of Science and
  Technology, IA   B
John Carroll U, OH   B
Kalamazoo Coll, MI   B
Kansas State U, KS   B

Kansas Wesleyan U, KS   B
Kent State U, OH   B
Kenyon Coll, OH   B
Kettering U, MI   B
Knox Coll, IL   B
Lake Forest Coll, IL   B
Lawrence Technological U,
  MI   B
Lawrence U, WI   B
Lehigh U, PA   B
Lewis U, IL   B
Lincoln U, MO   B
Loras Coll, IA   B
Loyola U Chicago, IL   B
Luther Coll, IA   B
Macalester Coll, MN   B
MacMurray Coll, IL   B
Manchester Coll, IN   B
Marietta Coll, OH   B
Marquette U, WI   B
Miami U, OH   B
Miami U Hamilton, OH   B
Michigan State U, MI   B
Michigan Technological U,
  MI   B
MidAmerica Nazarene U, KS   B
Millikin U, IL   B
Minnesota State U Mankato,
  MN   B
Minnesota State U
  Moorhead, MN   B
Minot State U, ND   B
Missouri Southern State U,
  MO   B
Monmouth Coll, IL   B
Morningside Coll, IA   B
Mount Union Coll, OH   B
Muskingum Coll, OH   B
Nebraska Wesleyan U, NE   B
North Carolina Ag and Tech
  State U, NC   B
North Central Coll, IL   B
North Dakota State U, ND   B
Northeastern Illinois U, IL   B
Northeastern State U, OK   B
Northern Illinois U, IL   B
Northern Michigan U, MI   B
North Park U, IL   B
Northwestern Oklahoma
  State U, OK   B
Northwestern U, IL   B
Oakland U, MI   B
Oberlin Coll, OH   B
Ohio Northern U, OH   B
The Ohio State U, OH   B
Ohio U, OH   B
Ohio Wesleyan U, OH   B
Oklahoma Baptist U, OK   B
Oklahoma City U, OK   B
Oklahoma State U, OK   B
Oral Roberts U, OK   B
Otterbein Coll, OH   B
Pittsburg State U, KS   B
Principia Coll, IL   B
Purdue U, IN   B
Purdue U Calumet, IN   B
Rockhurst U, MO   B
Rose-Hulman Inst of
  Technology, IN   B
Saginaw Valley State U, MI   B
St. Ambrose U, IA   B
St. Cloud State U, MN   B
Saint John's U, MN   B
Saint Louis U, MO   B
St. Norbert Coll, WI   B
St. Olaf Coll, MN   B

South Dakota School of
  Mines and Technology, SD   B
South Dakota State U, SD   B
Southeastern Oklahoma State
  U, OK   B
Southeast Missouri State U,
  MO   B
Southern Illinois U
  Carbondale, IL   B
Southern Illinois U
  Edwardsville, IL   B
Southern Nazarene U, OK   B
Southwestern Coll, KS   B
Southwestern Oklahoma
  State U, OK   B
Southwest Missouri State U,
  MO   B
Taylor U, IN   B
Transylvania U, KY   B
Truman State U, MO   B
Union Coll, NE   B
The U of Akron, OH   B
The U of Alabama in
  Huntsville, AL   B
U of Central Oklahoma, OK   B
U of Chicago, IL   B
U of Cincinnati, OH   B
U of Dayton, OH   B
U of Evansville, IN   B
U of Illinois at Chicago, IL   B
U of Illinois at Urbana–
  Champaign, IL   B
U of Indianapolis, IN   B
The U of Iowa, IA   B
U of Kansas, KS   B
U of Michigan, MI   B
U of Michigan–Dearborn, MI   B
U of Michigan–Flint, MI   B
U of Minnesota, Duluth, MN   B
U of Minnesota, Morris, MN   B
U of Minnesota, Twin Cities
  Campus, MN   B
U of Missouri–Columbia,
  MO   B
U of Missouri–Kansas City,
  MO   B
U of Missouri–Rolla, MO   B
U of Missouri–St. Louis, MO   B
U of Nebraska at Omaha,
  NE   B
U of Nebraska–Lincoln, NE   B
U of New Orleans, LA   B
U of North Dakota, ND   B
U of Northern Iowa, IA   B
U of Notre Dame, IN   B
U of Oklahoma, OK   B
U of St. Thomas, MN   B
U of Science and Arts of
  Oklahoma, OK   B
The U of South Dakota, SD   B
U of Toledo, OH   B
U of Tulsa, OK   B
U of West Florida, FL   B
U of Wisconsin–Eau Claire,
  WI   B
U of Wisconsin–La Crosse,
  WI   B
U of Wisconsin–Madison,
  WI   B
U of Wisconsin–Milwaukee,
  WI   B
U of Wisconsin–Oshkosh,
  WI   B
U of Wisconsin–Parkside, WI   B
U of Wisconsin–River Falls,
  WI   B

U of Wisconsin–Stevens Point, WI	B
U of Wisconsin–Whitewater, WI	B
Valparaiso U, IN	B
Wabash Coll, IN	B
Wartburg Coll, IA	B
Washburn U, KS	B
Washington U in St. Louis, MO	B
Wayne State U, MI	B
Western Illinois U, IL	B
Western Michigan U, MI	B
Westminster Coll, MO	B
Wheaton Coll, IL	B
Wichita State U, KS	B
William Jewell Coll, MO	B
Winona State U, MN	B
Wittenberg U, OH	B
Wright State U, OH	B
Xavier U, OH	B
Youngstown State U, OH	B

Physics Related

The Coll of Wooster, OH	B
Lawrence Technological U, MI	B
Ohio Northern U, OH	B
Ohio U, OH	B
Oklahoma State U, OK	B
The U of Akron, OH	B
U of Northern Iowa, IA	B
U of Notre Dame, IN	B
Wright State U, OH	B

Physics Teacher Education

Alma Coll, MI	B
Baldwin-Wallace Coll, OH	B
Bethel U, MN	B
Buena Vista U, IA	B
Carroll Coll, WI	B
Cedarville U, OH	B
Central Methodist Coll, MO	B
Central Michigan U, MI	B
Central Missouri State U, MO	B
Chadron State Coll, NE	B
Concordia Coll, MN	B
Concordia U, NE	B
East Central U, OK	B
Eastern Michigan U, MI	B
Elmhurst Coll, IL	B
Greenville Coll, IL	B
Gustavus Adolphus Coll, MN	B
Hastings Coll, NE	B
Hope Coll, MI	B
Illinois Wesleyan U, IL	B
Indiana U Bloomington, IN	B
Indiana U–Purdue U Fort Wayne, IN	B
Indiana U South Bend, IN	B
Mayville State U, ND	B
Miami U Hamilton, OH	B
Minot State U, ND	B
North Dakota State U, ND	B
Northern Michigan U, MI	B
Ohio Dominican U, OH	B
Ohio Northern U, OH	B
Ohio Wesleyan U, OH	B
Pittsburg State U, KS	B
St. Ambrose U, IA	B
Saint Mary's U of Minnesota, MN	B
Shawnee State U, OH	B
Southwest Missouri State U, MO	B

Union Coll, NE	B
The U of Akron, OH	B
U of Illinois at Chicago, IL	B
The U of Iowa, IA	B
U of Michigan–Flint, MI	B
U of Missouri–Columbia, MO	B
U of Missouri–St. Louis, MO	B
U of Nebraska–Lincoln, NE	B
U of Rio Grande, OH	B
U of St. Thomas, MN	B
The U of South Dakota, SD	B
U of Wisconsin–River Falls, WI	B
Valparaiso U, IN	B
Washington U in St. Louis, MO	B
Western Michigan U, MI	B
Xavier U, OH	B
Youngstown State U, OH	B

Physiological Psychology/ Psychobiology

Grand Valley State U, MI	B
Hiram Coll, OH	B
Luther Coll, IA	B
Oberlin Coll, OH	B
Ripon Coll, WI	B
U of Evansville, IN	B
York Coll, NE	B

Physiology

Eastern Michigan U, MI	B
Michigan State U, MI	B
Northern Michigan U, MI	B
Southern Illinois U Carbondale, IL	B
U of Illinois at Urbana–Champaign, IL	B

Piano and Organ

Andrews U, MI	B
Augustana Coll, IL	B
Baldwin-Wallace Coll, OH	B
Ball State U, IN	B
Bethel Coll, IN	A,B
Bowling Green State U, OH	B
Butler U, IN	B
Calvary Bible Coll and Theological Seminary, MO	B
Calvin Coll, MI	B
Capital U, OH	B
Cedarville U, OH	B
Central Christian Coll of Kansas, KS	A
Cleveland Inst of Music, OH	B
Concordia Coll, MN	B
Concordia U, IL	B
Concordia U, NE	B
DePaul U, IL	B
Dordt Coll, IA	B
Drake U, IA	B
East Central U, OK	B
Grace Coll, IN	B
Grace U, NE	B
Grand Valley State U, MI	B
Hannibal-LaGrange Coll, MO	B
Hastings Coll, NE	B
Heidelberg Coll, OH	B
Huntington Coll, IN	B
Illinois Wesleyan U, IL	B
Indiana U Bloomington, IN	B
Indiana U–Purdue U Fort Wayne, IN	B
Lawrence U, WI	B

Lincoln Coll, Lincoln, IL	A
Minnesota State U Mankato, MN	B
Minnesota State U Moorhead, MN	B
Northeastern State U, OK	B
Northern Michigan U, MI	B
Northwestern Coll, MN	B
Northwestern U, IL	B
Oberlin Coll, OH	B
The Ohio State U, OH	B
Ohio U, OH	B
Oklahoma Baptist U, OK	B
Oklahoma City U, OK	B
Olivet Nazarene U, IL	B
Otterbein Coll, OH	B
Pittsburg State U, KS	B
Roosevelt U, IL	B
St. Cloud State U, MN	B
Southern Nazarene U, OK	B
Southwestern Oklahoma State U, OK	B
Spring Arbor U, MI	B
Tabor Coll, KS	B
Taylor U, IN	B
Trinity Christian Coll, IL	B
Truman State U, MO	B
The U of Akron, OH	B
U of Central Oklahoma, OK	B
U of Cincinnati, OH	B
The U of Iowa, IA	B
U of Kansas, KS	B
U of Michigan, MI	B
U of Minnesota, Duluth, MN	B
U of Missouri–Kansas City, MO	B
U of Oklahoma, OK	B
U of Sioux Falls, SD	B
U of Tulsa, OK	B
Valparaiso U, IN	B
Washburn U, KS	B
Webster U, MO	B
William Tyndale Coll, MI	B
Youngstown State U, OH	B

Pipefitting and Sprinkler Fitting

Ranken Tech Coll, MO	A

Plant Molecular Biology

Pittsburg State U, KS	B

Plant Pathology/ Phytopathology

Michigan State U, MI	B
The Ohio State U, OH	B

Plant Physiology

Pittsburg State U, KS	B

Plant Protection and Integrated Pest Management

Iowa State U of Science and Technology, IA	B
North Dakota State U, ND	B
U of Nebraska–Lincoln, NE	B

Plant Sciences

The Ohio State U, OH	B
Oklahoma State U, OK	B
Southern Illinois U Carbondale, IL	B
U of Minnesota, Twin Cities Campus, MN	B
U of Missouri–Columbia, MO	B

Plastics Engineering Technology

Ball State U, IN	B
Ferris State U, MI	A,B
Kent State U, OH	A
Kent State U, Tuscarawas Campus, OH	A
Pittsburg State U, KS	B
Shawnee State U, OH	A,B
Western Michigan U, MI	B

Playwriting and Screenwriting

Columbia Coll Chicago, IL	B
DePaul U, IL	B
Metropolitan State U, MN	B
Ohio U, OH	B
U of Michigan, MI	B

Plumbing Technology

Vatterott Coll, St. Ann, MO	A

Polish

Madonna U, MI	B
U of Illinois at Chicago, IL	B

Political Communication

Nebraska Wesleyan U, NE	B

Political Science and Government

Adrian Coll, MI	A,B
Albion Coll, MI	B
Alma Coll, MI	B
Alverno Coll, WI	B
Andrews U, MI	B
Antioch Coll, OH	B
Aquinas Coll, MI	B
Ashland U, OH	B
Augsburg Coll, MN	B
Augustana Coll, IL	B
Augustana Coll, SD	B
Aurora U, IL	B
Ave Maria Coll, MI	B
Avila U, MO	B
Bacone Coll, OK	A
Baker U, KS	B
Baldwin-Wallace Coll, OH	B
Ball State U, IN	B
Beloit Coll, WI	B
Bemidji State U, MN	B
Benedictine Coll, KS	B
Benedictine U, IL	B
Bethany Coll, KS	B
Bethel U, MN	B
Blackburn Coll, IL	B
Black Hills State U, SD	B
Bowling Green State U, OH	B
Bradley U, IL	B
Briar Cliff U, IA	B
Buena Vista U, IA	B
Butler U, IN	B
Calumet Coll of Saint Joseph, IN	B
Calvin Coll, MI	B
Cameron U, OK	B
Capital U, OH	B
Cardinal Stritch U, WI	B
Carleton Coll, MN	B
Carroll Coll, WI	B
Carthage Coll, WI	B
Case Western Reserve U, OH	B
Cedarville U, OH	B
Central Coll, IA	B
Central Methodist Coll, MO	B
Central Michigan U, MI	B

A—associate degree; B—bachelor's degree

College	Degree
Central Missouri State U, MO	B
Central State U, OH	B
Chicago State U, IL	B
Clarkson U	B
Cleveland State U, OH	B
Coe Coll, IA	B
Coll of Saint Benedict, MN	B
Coll of St. Catherine, MN	B
Coll of the Ozarks, MO	B
The Coll of Wooster, OH	B
Columbia Coll, MO	B
Concordia Coll, MN	B
Concordia U, IL	B
Concord U, WV	B
Cornell Coll, IA	B
Cornerstone U, MI	B
Creighton U, NE	B
Cumberland Coll, KY	B
Denison U, OH	B
DePaul U, IL	B
DePauw U, IN	B
Dickinson State U, ND	B
Doane Coll, NE	B
Dominican U, IL	B
Donnelly Coll, KS	A
Dordt Coll, IA	B
Drake U, IA	B
Drury U, MO	B
Earlham Coll, IN	B
East Central U, OK	B
Eastern Illinois U, IL	B
Eastern Michigan U, MI	B
Edgewood Coll, WI	B
Elmhurst Coll, IL	B
Emporia State U, KS	B
Eureka Coll, IL	B
Evangel U, MO	B
Florida Gulf Coast U, FL	B
Fort Hays State U, KS	B
Franciscan U of Steubenville, OH	B
Franklin Coll, IN	B
Gannon U, PA	B
Goshen Coll, IN	B
Grand Valley State U, MI	B
Grand View Coll, IA	B
Grinnell Coll, IA	B
Gustavus Adolphus Coll, MN	B
Hamline U, MN	B
Hanover Coll, IN	B
Hastings Coll, NE	B
Heidelberg Coll, OH	B
Hillsdale Coll, MI	B
Hiram Coll, OH	B
Hope Coll, MI	B
Illinois Coll, IL	B
Illinois Inst of Technology, IL	B
Illinois State U, IL	B
Illinois Wesleyan U, IL	B
Indiana State U, IN	B
Indiana U Bloomington, IN	B
Indiana U Northwest, IN	B
Indiana U–Purdue U Fort Wayne, IN	A,B
Indiana U–Purdue U Indianapolis, IN	B
Indiana U South Bend, IN	B
Indiana U Southeast, IN	B
Iowa State U of Science and Technology, IA	B
Jamestown Coll, ND	B
John Carroll U, OH	B
Kalamazoo Coll, MI	B
Kansas State U, KS	B
Kent State U, OH	B
Kenyon Coll, OH	B
Knox Coll, IL	B
Lake Forest Coll, IL	B
Lake Superior State U, MI	B
Lawrence U, WI	B
Lehigh U, PA	B
Lewis U, IL	B
Lincoln Coll, Lincoln, IL	A
Lincoln U, MO	B
Lindenwood U, MO	B
Loras Coll, IA	B
Loyola U Chicago, IL	B
Luther Coll, IA	B
Macalester Coll, MN	B
MacMurray Coll, IL	B
Malone Coll, OH	B
Manchester Coll, IN	B
Marian Coll of Fond du Lac, WI	B
Marietta Coll, OH	B
Marquette U, WI	B
Martin U, IN	B
Marygrove Coll, MI	B
McKendree Coll, IL	B
Miami U, OH	B
Miami U Hamilton, OH	B
Michigan State U, MI	B
Millikin U, IL	B
Minnesota State U Mankato, MN	B
Minnesota State U Moorhead, MN	B
Missouri Southern State U, MO	B
Missouri Valley Coll, MO	B
Missouri Western State Coll, MO	B
Monmouth Coll, IL	B
Morningside Coll, IA	B
Mount Mercy Coll, IA	B
Mount Union Coll, OH	B
Muskingum Coll, OH	B
Nebraska Wesleyan U, NE	B
North Carolina Ag and Tech State U, NC	B
North Central Coll, IL	B
North Dakota State U, ND	B
Northeastern Illinois U, IL	B
Northeastern State U, OK	B
Northern Illinois U, IL	B
Northern Michigan U, MI	B
Northern State U, SD	B
North Park U, IL	B
Northwestern Coll, IA	B
Northwestern Oklahoma State U, OK	B
Northwestern U, IL	B
Notre Dame Coll, OH	B
Oakland U, MI	B
Oberlin Coll, OH	B
Ohio Dominican U, OH	B
Ohio Northern U, OH	B
The Ohio State U, OH	B
Ohio U, OH	B
Ohio Wesleyan U, OH	B
Oklahoma Baptist U, OK	B
Oklahoma City U, OK	B
Oklahoma State U, OK	B
Oral Roberts U, OK	B
Ottawa U, KS	B
Otterbein Coll, OH	B
Park U, MO	B
Pittsburg State U, KS	B
Principia Coll, IL	B
Purdue U, IN	B
Purdue U Calumet, IN	B
Quincy U, IL	B
Ripon Coll, WI	B
Rockford Coll, IL	B
Rockhurst U, MO	B
Roosevelt U, IL	B
Saginaw Valley State U, MI	B
St. Ambrose U, IA	B
St. Cloud State U, MN	B
St. Gregory's U, OK	B
Saint John's U, MN	B
Saint Joseph's Coll, IN	B
Saint Louis U, MO	B
Saint Mary's Coll, IN	B
Saint Mary's U of Minnesota, MN	B
St. Norbert Coll, WI	B
St. Olaf Coll, MN	B
Saint Xavier U, IL	B
Simpson Coll, IA	B
South Dakota State U, SD	B
Southeastern Oklahoma State U, OK	B
Southeast Missouri State U, MO	B
Southern Illinois U Carbondale, IL	B
Southern Illinois U Edwardsville, IL	B
Southern Nazarene U, OK	B
Southwest Baptist U, MO	B
Southwestern Oklahoma State U, OK	B
Southwest Missouri State U, MO	B
Stephens Coll, MO	B
Taylor U, IN	B
Transylvania U, KY	B
Truman State U, MO	B
The U of Akron, OH	B
The U of Alabama in Huntsville, AL	B
U of Central Oklahoma, OK	B
U of Chicago, IL	B
U of Cincinnati, OH	B
U of Dayton, OH	B
U of Detroit Mercy, MI	B
U of Evansville, IN	B
The U of Findlay, OH	B
U of Illinois at Chicago, IL	B
U of Illinois at Springfield, IL	B
U of Illinois at Urbana–Champaign, IL	B
U of Indianapolis, IN	B
The U of Iowa, IA	B
U of Kansas, KS	B
U of Michigan, MI	B
U of Michigan–Dearborn, MI	B
U of Michigan–Flint, MI	B
U of Minnesota, Duluth, MN	B
U of Minnesota, Morris, MN	B
U of Minnesota, Twin Cities Campus, MN	B
U of Missouri–Columbia, MO	B
U of Missouri–Kansas City, MO	B
U of Missouri–St. Louis, MO	B
U of Nebraska at Omaha, NE	B
U of Nebraska–Lincoln, NE	B
U of New Orleans, LA	B
U of North Dakota, ND	B
U of Northern Iowa, IA	B
U of Notre Dame, IN	B
U of Oklahoma, OK	B
U of Rio Grande, OH	B
U of St. Francis, IL	B
U of Saint Mary, KS	B
U of St. Thomas, MN	B
U of Science and Arts of Oklahoma, OK	B
U of Sioux Falls, SD	B
The U of South Dakota, SD	B
U of Southern Indiana, IN	B
U of Toledo, OH	A,B
U of Tulsa, OK	B
U of West Florida, FL	B
U of Wisconsin–Eau Claire, WI	B
U of Wisconsin–Green Bay, WI	A,B
U of Wisconsin–La Crosse, WI	B
U of Wisconsin–Madison, WI	B
U of Wisconsin–Milwaukee, WI	B
U of Wisconsin–Oshkosh, WI	B
U of Wisconsin–Parkside, WI	B
U of Wisconsin–Platteville, WI	B
U of Wisconsin–River Falls, WI	B
U of Wisconsin–Stevens Point, WI	B
U of Wisconsin–Superior, WI	B
U of Wisconsin–Whitewater, WI	B
Valparaiso U, IN	B
Wabash Coll, IN	B
Walsh U, OH	B
Wartburg Coll, IA	B
Washburn U, KS	B
Washington U in St. Louis, MO	B
Wayne State Coll, NE	B
Wayne State U, MI	B
Webster U, MO	B
Western Illinois U, IL	B
Western Michigan U, MI	B
Westminster Coll, MO	B
Wheaton Coll, IL	B
Wichita State U, KS	B
Wilberforce U, OH	B
William Jewell Coll, MO	B
William Penn U, IA	B
William Woods U, MO	B
Winona State U, MN	B
Wisconsin Lutheran Coll, WI	B
Wittenberg U, OH	B
Wright State U, OH	B
Xavier U, OH	A,B
Youngstown State U, OH	B

Political Science and Government Related

College	Degree
Buena Vista U, IA	B
Capital U, OH	B
Monmouth Coll, IL	B
The U of Akron, OH	B
U of Northern Iowa, IA	B

Polymer Chemistry

College	Degree
The U of Akron, OH	B
U of Wisconsin–Stevens Point, WI	B
Winona State U, MN	B

Polymer/Plastics Engineering

College	Degree
Ball State U, IN	B

Case Western Reserve U, OH	
Eastern Michigan U, MI	B
Ferris State U, MI	B
Kettering U, MI	B
North Dakota State U, ND	B
The U of Akron, OH	B
Winona State U, MN	B

Portuguese

Indiana U Bloomington, IN	B
The Ohio State U, OH	B
U of Illinois at Urbana–Champaign, IL	
The U of Iowa, IA	B
U of Minnesota, Twin Cities Campus, MN	B
U of Wisconsin–Madison, WI	B

Postal Management

Washburn U, KS	A

Poultry Science

Coll of the Ozarks, MO	B
U of Wisconsin–Madison, WI	B

Pre-Dentistry Studies

Alma Coll, MI	B
Aquinas Coll, MI	B
Ashland U, OH	B
Augsburg Coll, MN	B
Augustana Coll, IL	B
Augustana Coll, SD	B
Baldwin-Wallace Coll, OH	B
Ball State U, IN	B
Beloit Coll, WI	B
Benedictine U, IL	B
Bethel Coll, IN	B
Blackburn Coll, IL	B
Briar Cliff U, IA	B
Calvin Coll, MI	B
Capital U, OH	B
Cardinal Stritch U, WI	B
Carroll Coll, WI	B
Carthage Coll, WI	B
Cedarville U, OH	B
Central Christian Coll of Kansas, KS	A,B
Central Missouri State U, MO	B
Chicago State U, IL	B
Clarkson U	B
Coe Coll, IA	B
Coll of Saint Benedict, MN	B
Coll of St. Catherine, MN	B
Coll of Saint Mary, NE	B
Columbia Coll, MO	B
Concordia Coll, MN	B
Concordia U, IL	B
Concordia U, NE	B
Concordia U Wisconsin, WI	A
Cornerstone U, MI	B
Dakota State U, SD	B
Defiance Coll, OH	B
Dickinson State U, ND	B
Dominican U, IL	B
Dordt Coll, IA	B
Drake U, IA	B
Drury U, MO	B
East Central U, OK	B
Eastern Michigan U, MI	B
Edgewood Coll, WI	B
Elmhurst Coll, IL	B
Eureka Coll, IL	B
Evangel U, MO	B

Gannon U, PA	B
Goshen Coll, IN	B
Graceland U, IA	B
Grand Valley State U, MI	B
Gustavus Adolphus Coll, MN	B
Hamline U, MN	B
Hastings Coll, NE	B
Heidelberg Coll, OH	B
Hillsdale Coll, MI	B
Hiram Coll, OH	B
Huntington Coll, IN	B
Illinois Coll, IL	B
Indiana U Bloomington, IN	B
Indiana U–Purdue U Fort Wayne, IN	B
Indiana U–Purdue U Indianapolis, IN	B
Iowa State U of Science and Technology, IA	B
Iowa Wesleyan Coll, IA	B
John Carroll U, OH	B
Kansas State U, KS	B
Kansas Wesleyan U, KS	B
Kent State U, OH	B
Kenyon Coll, OH	B
Lake Erie Coll, OH	B
Lake Forest Coll, IL	B
Lake Superior State U, MI	B
Lawrence U, WI	B
Lewis U, IL	B
Lindenwood U, MO	B
Loyola U Chicago, IL	B
MacMurray Coll, IL	B
Madonna U, MI	B
Manchester Coll, IN	B
Marian Coll, IN	B
Marian Coll of Fond du Lac, WI	B
Marquette U, WI	B
Mayville State U, ND	B
McKendree Coll, IL	B
McPherson Coll, KS	B
Miami U, OH	B
Michigan Technological U, MI	B
Millikin U, IL	B
Minnesota State U Mankato, MN	B
Minnesota State U Moorhead, MN	B
Missouri Southern State U, MO	B
Missouri Valley Coll, MO	B
Morningside Coll, IA	B
Mount Mary Coll, WI	B
Mount Mercy Coll, IA	B
Mount Vernon Nazarene U, OH	B
Muskingum Coll, OH	B
Newman U, KS	A
North Central Coll, IL	B
Northeastern State U, OK	B
Northern Michigan U, MI	B
Northern State U, SD	B
Northland Coll, WI	B
North Park U, IL	B
Northwestern Oklahoma State U, OK	B
Ohio Northern U, OH	B
Ohio U, OH	B
Ohio Wesleyan U, OH	B
Oklahoma Baptist U, OK	B
Oklahoma City U, OK	B
Oklahoma State U, OK	B
Olivet Coll, MI	B

Olivet Nazarene U, IL	B
Oral Roberts U, OK	B
Otterbein Coll, OH	B
Peru State Coll, NE	B
Pittsburg State U, KS	B
Purdue U Calumet, IN	B
Quincy U, IL	B
Ripon Coll, WI	B
Rockford Coll, IL	B
Roosevelt U, IL	B
St. Cloud State U, MN	B
St. Gregory's U, OK	B
Saint John's U, MN	B
Saint Mary-of-the-Woods Coll, IN	B
St. Norbert Coll, WI	B
Simpson Coll, IA	B
South Dakota State U, SD	B
Southern Nazarene U, OK	B
Southwestern Oklahoma State U, OK	B
Tabor Coll, KS	B
Taylor U, IN	B
Trinity Christian Coll, IL	B
Truman State U, MO	B
The U of Akron, OH	B
U of Dayton, OH	B
U of Detroit Mercy, MI	B
U of Evansville, IN	B
U of Illinois at Chicago, IL	B
U of Indianapolis, IN	B
The U of Iowa, IA	B
U of Minnesota, Duluth, MN	B
U of Minnesota, Morris, MN	B
U of Minnesota, Twin Cities Campus, MN	B
U of Missouri–Rolla, MO	B
U of Missouri–St. Louis, MO	B
U of Nebraska–Lincoln, NE	B
U of Rio Grande, OH	B
U of St. Francis, IL	B
U of Saint Francis, IN	B
U of Sioux Falls, SD	B
U of Toledo, OH	B
U of Wisconsin–Green Bay, WI	
U of Wisconsin–Milwaukee, WI	B
U of Wisconsin–Oshkosh, WI	B
U of Wisconsin–Parkside, WI	B
U of Wisconsin–River Falls, WI	B
Upper Iowa U, IA	B
Urbana U, OH	B
Valley City State U, ND	B
Walsh U, OH	B
Washington U in St. Louis, MO	B
William Jewell Coll, MO	B
William Penn U, IA	B
Winona State U, MN	B
Wittenberg U, OH	B
Wright State U, OH	B
Youngstown State U, OH	B

Pre-Engineering

Brescia U, KY	A
Briar Cliff U, IA	A
Columbia Coll, MO	B
Edgewood Coll, WI	A
Ferris State U, MI	A
Hannibal-LaGrange Coll, MO	A
Marian Coll, IN	A

McPherson Coll, KS	B
Minnesota State U Mankato, MN	A
Missouri Southern State U, MO	A
Newman U, KS	A
Northern State U, SD	A
Purdue U North Central, IN	A
Rochester Comm and Tech Coll, MN	A
St. Gregory's U, OK	A
Shawnee State U, OH	A
Siena Heights U, MI	A
U of Sioux Falls, SD	A
Valley City State U, ND	B
Washburn U, KS	A
Winona State U, MN	A

Pre-Law Studies

Albion Coll, MI	B
Alma Coll, MI	B
Andrews U, MI	B
Antioch Coll, OH	B
Aquinas Coll, MI	B
Ashland U, OH	B
Augsburg Coll, MN	B
Augustana Coll, IL	B
Augustana Coll, SD	B
Baldwin-Wallace Coll, OH	B
Ball State U, IN	B
Beloit Coll, WI	B
Bemidji State U, MN	B
Benedictine U, IL	B
Bethel Coll, IN	B
Blackburn Coll, IL	B
Bowling Green State U, OH	B
Briar Cliff U, IA	B
Calumet Coll of Saint Joseph, IN	A,B
Calvin Coll, MI	B
Cardinal Stritch U, WI	B
Carthage Coll, WI	B
Cedarville U, OH	B
Central Christian Coll of Kansas, KS	B
Chicago State U, IL	B
Clarkson U	B
Coe Coll, IA	B
Coll of Saint Benedict, MN	B
Coll of St. Catherine, MN	B
Coll of Saint Mary, NE	B
Coll of the Ozarks, MO	B
Columbia Coll, MO	B
Concordia Coll, MN	B
Concordia U, IL	B
Concordia U, MI	B
Concordia U, NE	B
Concordia U Wisconsin, WI	B
Cornerstone U, MI	B
Creighton U, NE	B
Crown Coll, MN	B
Dakota State U, SD	B
Defiance Coll, OH	B
DePaul U, IL	B
Dickinson State U, ND	B
Dominican U, IL	B
Dordt Coll, IA	B
Drake U, IA	B
Drury U, MO	B
Earlham Coll, IN	B
East Central U, OK	B
Eastern Michigan U, MI	B
Edgewood Coll, WI	B
Elmhurst Coll, IL	B
Eureka Coll, IL	B

Evangel U, MO	B
Fontbonne U, MO	B
Fort Hays State U, KS	B
The Franciscan U, IA	B
Gannon U, PA	B
Goshen Coll, IN	B
Graceland U, IA	B
Grand Valley State U, MI	B
Grand View Coll, IA	B
Gustavus Adolphus Coll, MN	B
Hamline U, MN	B
Hannibal-LaGrange Coll, MO	B
Hastings Coll, NE	B
Heidelberg Coll, OH	B
Hiram Coll, OH	B
Huntington Coll, IN	B
Illinois Coll, IL	B
Indiana U Bloomington, IN	B
Indiana U–Purdue U Indianapolis, IN	B
Iowa State U of Science and Technology, IA	B
Iowa Wesleyan Coll, IA	B
John Carroll U, OH	B
Judson Coll, IL	B
Kansas Wesleyan U, KS	B
Kenyon Coll, OH	B
Lake Erie Coll, OH	B
Lake Forest Coll, IL	B
Lake Superior State U, MI	B
Lawrence U, WI	B
Lewis U, IL	B
Lindenwood U, MO	B
Loyola U Chicago, IL	B
MacMurray Coll, IL	B
Madonna U, MI	B
Manchester Coll, IN	B
Marian Coll, IN	B
Marian Coll of Fond du Lac, WI	B
Marquette U, WI	B
Mayville State U, ND	B
McKendree Coll, IL	B
Miami U, OH	B
Michigan State U, MI	B
Millikin U, IL	B
Minnesota State U Mankato, MN	B
Minnesota State U Moorhead, MN	B
Missouri Valley Coll, MO	B
Morningside Coll, IA	B
Mount Mary Coll, WI	B
Mount Mercy Coll, IA	B
Mount Vernon Nazarene U, OH	B
Muskingum Coll, OH	B
Newman U, KS	A
North Central Coll, IL	B
Northeastern State U, OK	B
Northern Michigan U, MI	B
Northern State U, SD	B
Northland Coll, WI	B
North Park U, IL	B
Northwestern Oklahoma State U, OK	B
Notre Dame Coll, OH	B
Oakland City U, IN	B
Ohio Northern U, OH	B
Ohio U, OH	B
Ohio Wesleyan U, OH	B
Oklahoma Baptist U, OK	B
Oklahoma Christian U, OK	B
Oklahoma City U, OK	B
Oklahoma State U, OK	B

Olivet Coll, MI	B
Olivet Nazarene U, IL	B
Otterbein Coll, OH	B
Peru State Coll, NE	B
Pittsburg State U, KS	B
Purdue U Calumet, IN	B
Ripon Coll, WI	B
Rockford Coll, IL	B
Roosevelt U, IL	B
St. Cloud State U, MN	B
St. Gregory's U, OK	B
Saint John's U, MN	B
Saint Mary-of-the-Woods Coll, IN	B
St. Norbert Coll, WI	B
Shawnee State U, OH	B
Siena Heights U, MI	B
Simpson Coll, IA	B
South Dakota State U, SD	B
Southern Nazarene U, OK	B
Southwestern Oklahoma State U, OK	B
Stephens Coll, MO	B
Taylor U, IN	B
Taylor U Fort Wayne, IN	B
Tiffin U, OH	B
Tri-State U, IN	B
Truman State U, MO	B
The U of Akron, OH	B
U of Cincinnati, OH	B
U of Dayton, OH	B
U of Detroit Mercy, MI	B
U of Evansville, IN	B
The U of Findlay, OH	B
U of Illinois at Chicago, IL	B
U of Indianapolis, IN	B
The U of Iowa, IA	B
U of Minnesota, Duluth, MN	B
U of Minnesota, Morris, MN	B
U of Minnesota, Twin Cities Campus, MN	B
U of Missouri–Rolla, MO	B
U of Missouri–St. Louis, MO	B
U of Rio Grande, OH	B
U of Saint Francis, IN	B
U of Sioux Falls, SD	B
U of Toledo, OH	B
U of Wisconsin–Milwaukee, WI	B
U of Wisconsin–Oshkosh, WI	B
U of Wisconsin–Parkside, WI	B
U of Wisconsin–River Falls, WI	B
U of Wisconsin–Superior, WI	B
Urbana U, OH	B
Valley City State U, ND	B
Wabash Coll, IN	B
Washburn U, KS	B
Westminster Coll, MO	B
William Jewell Coll, MO	B
William Penn U, IA	B
William Tyndale Coll, MI	B
Winona State U, MN	B
Wittenberg U, OH	B
Wright State U, OH	B
Youngstown State U, OH	B

Pre-Medical Studies

Adrian Coll, MI	B
Albion Coll, MI	B
Alma Coll, MI	B
Andrews U, MI	B
Antioch Coll, OH	B
Aquinas Coll, MI	B
Ashland U, OH	B
Augsburg Coll, MN	B

Augustana Coll, IL	B
Augustana Coll, SD	B
Baldwin-Wallace Coll, OH	B
Ball State U, IN	B
Beloit Coll, WI	B
Bemidji State U, MN	B
Benedictine U, IL	B
Bethel Coll, IN	B
Blackburn Coll, IL	B
Bluffton Coll, OH	B
Briar Cliff U, IA	B
Calvin Coll, MI	B
Capital U, OH	B
Cardinal Stritch U, WI	B
Carroll Coll, WI	B
Carthage Coll, WI	B
Cedarville U, OH	B
Central Christian Coll of Kansas, KS	A,B
Central Missouri State U, MO	B
Chicago State U, IL	B
Clarkson U	B
Coe Coll, IA	B
Coll of Saint Benedict, MN	B
Coll of St. Catherine, MN	B
Coll of Saint Mary, NE	B
Coll of the Ozarks, MO	B
Columbia Coll, MO	B
Concordia Coll, MN	B
Concordia U, IL	B
Concordia U, MI	B
Concordia U, NE	B
Concordia U Wisconsin, WI	A
Concord U, WV	B
Cornerstone U, MI	B
Dakota State U, SD	B
Defiance Coll, OH	B
Dickinson State U, ND	B
Dominican U, IL	B
Dordt Coll, IA	B
Drake U, IA	B
Drury U, MO	B
Earlham Coll, IN	B
East Central U, OK	B
Eastern Michigan U, MI	B
Edgewood Coll, WI	B
Elmhurst Coll, IL	B
Eureka Coll, IL	B
Evangel U, MO	B
Fontbonne U, MO	B
The Franciscan U, IA	B
Gannon U, PA	B
Goshen Coll, IN	B
Graceland U, IA	B
Grand Valley State U, MI	B
Grinnell Coll, IA	B
Gustavus Adolphus Coll, MN	B
Hamline U, MN	B
Hastings Coll, NE	B
Heidelberg Coll, OH	B
Hillsdale Coll, MI	B
Hiram Coll, OH	B
Huntington Coll, IN	B
Illinois Coll, IL	B
Indiana U Bloomington, IN	B
Indiana U–Purdue U Fort Wayne, IN	B
Indiana U–Purdue U Indianapolis, IN	B
Iowa State U of Science and Technology, IA	B
Iowa Wesleyan Coll, IA	B
John Carroll U, OH	B
Judson Coll, IL	B
Kansas State U, KS	B

Kansas Wesleyan U, KS	B
Kenyon Coll, OH	B
Lake Erie Coll, OH	B
Lake Forest Coll, IL	B
Lake Superior State U, MI	B
Lawrence U, WI	B
Lehigh U, PA	B
Lewis U, IL	B
Lindenwood U, MO	B
Lourdes Coll, OH	B
Loyola U Chicago, IL	B
MacMurray Coll, IL	B
Madonna U, MI	B
Manchester Coll, IN	B
Marian Coll, IN	B
Marian Coll of Fond du Lac, WI	B
Marquette U, WI	B
Mayville State U, ND	B
McKendree Coll, IL	B
McPherson Coll, KS	B
Miami U, OH	B
Michigan State U, MI	B
Michigan Technological U, MI	B
Millikin U, IL	B
Minnesota State U Mankato, MN	B
Minnesota State U Moorhead, MN	B
Missouri Southern State U, MO	B
Missouri Valley Coll, MO	B
Morningside Coll, IA	B
Mount Mary Coll, WI	B
Mount Mercy Coll, IA	B
Mount Vernon Nazarene U, OH	B
Muskingum Coll, OH	B
Newman U, KS	A
North Central Coll, IL	B
Northeastern State U, OK	B
Northern Michigan U, MI	B
Northern State U, SD	B
Northland Coll, WI	B
North Park U, IL	B
Northwestern Oklahoma State U, OK	B
Northwestern U, IL	B
Notre Dame Coll, OH	B
Oakland City U, IN	B
Ohio Northern U, OH	B
Ohio U, OH	B
Ohio Wesleyan U, OH	B
Oklahoma Baptist U, OK	B
Oklahoma City U, OK	B
Oklahoma State U, OK	B
Olivet Coll, MI	B
Olivet Nazarene U, IL	B
Oral Roberts U, OK	B
Otterbein Coll, OH	B
Peru State Coll, NE	B
Pittsburg State U, KS	B
Purdue U Calumet, IN	B
Quincy U, IL	B
Ripon Coll, WI	B
Rockford Coll, IL	B
Roosevelt U, IL	B
St. Cloud State U, MN	B
St. Gregory's U, OK	B
Saint John's U, MN	B
Saint Mary-of-the-Woods Coll, IN	B
St. Norbert Coll, WI	B
Shawnee State U, OH	B
Simpson Coll, IA	B

South Dakota State U, SD	B	Central Missouri State U, MO	B	Trinity International U, IL	B	Kansas Wesleyan U, KS	B

South Dakota State U, SD — B
Southern Nazarene U, OK — B
Southwestern Oklahoma State U, OK — B
Stephens Coll, MO — B
Tabor Coll, KS — B
Taylor U, IN — B
Trinity Christian Coll, IL — B
Trinity International U, IL — B
Tri-State U, IN — B
Truman State U, MO — B
The U of Akron, OH — B
U of Cincinnati, OH — B
U of Dayton, OH — B
U of Detroit Mercy, MI — B
U of Evansville, IN — B
The U of Findlay, OH — B
U of Indianapolis, IN — B
The U of Iowa, IA — B
U of Minnesota, Duluth, MN — B
U of Minnesota, Morris, MN — B
U of Minnesota, Twin Cities Campus, MN — B
U of Missouri–Rolla, MO — B
U of Missouri–St. Louis, MO — B
U of Nebraska–Lincoln, NE — B
U of Notre Dame, IN — B
U of Rio Grande, OH — B
U of St. Francis, IL — B
U of Saint Francis, IN — B
U of Sioux Falls, SD — B
U of Toledo, OH — B
U of Wisconsin–Milwaukee, WI — B
U of Wisconsin–Oshkosh, WI — B
U of Wisconsin–Parkside, WI — B
U of Wisconsin–River Falls, WI — B
Upper Iowa U, IA — B
Urbana U, OH — B
Valley City State U, ND — B
Wabash Coll, IN — B
Walsh U, OH — B
Washburn U, KS — B
Washington U in St. Louis, MO — B
Wayne State Coll, NE — B
William Jewell Coll, MO — B
William Penn U, IA — B
Winona State U, MN — B
Wittenberg U, OH — B
Wright State U, OH — B
Youngstown State U, OH — B

Pre-Nursing Studies
Central Christian Coll of Kansas, KS — A
Cleveland State U, OH — B
Concordia U, NE — B
Concordia U Wisconsin, WI — A
Dordt Coll, IA — B
Lindenwood U, MO — B
Missouri Valley Coll, MO — B
Oklahoma City U, OK — B
Oklahoma State U, OK — B
St. Gregory's U, OK — B
Trinity International U, IL — A

Pre-Pharmacy Studies
Ashland U, OH — B
Briar Cliff U, IA — B
Carroll Coll, WI — B
Central Christian Coll of Kansas, KS — A,B

Central Missouri State U, MO — B
Coll of Saint Benedict, MN — B
Coll of the Ozarks, MO — B
Concordia U, NE — B
Dordt Coll, IA — B
East Central U, OK — B
Eastern Michigan U, MI — B
Elmhurst Coll, IL — B
Iowa Wesleyan Coll, IA — B
Madonna U, MI — B
Mayville State U, ND — B
McPherson Coll, KS — B
Missouri Southern State U, MO — B
Missouri Valley Coll, MO — B
Mount Vernon Nazarene U, OH — B
Muskingum Coll, OH — B
Ohio U, OH — B
Oklahoma Baptist U, OK — B
Oklahoma City U, OK — B
Oklahoma State U, OK — B
Roosevelt U, IL — B
St. Cloud State U, MN — B
St. Gregory's U, OK — B
Saint John's U, MN — B
Saint Mary-of-the-Woods Coll, IN — B
Southern Nazarene U, OK — B
Truman State U, MO — B
The U of Akron, OH — B
The U of Iowa, IA — B
U of Minnesota, Duluth, MN — B
U of Minnesota, Morris, MN — B
U of Missouri–St. Louis, MO — B
U of Nebraska–Lincoln, NE — B
U of Saint Francis, IN — B
U of Wisconsin–Parkside, WI — B
U of Wisconsin–River Falls, WI — B
Valley City State U, ND — B
Washington U in St. Louis, MO — B
Wright State U, OH — B
Youngstown State U, OH — B

Pre-Theology/Pre-Ministerial Studies
Alma Coll, MI — B
Ashland U, OH — B
Central Christian Coll of Kansas, KS — B
Coll of Saint Benedict, MN — B
Concordia Coll, MN — B
Concordia U, IL — B
Concordia U, MI — B
Concordia U, NE — B
Cornerstone U, MI — B
Crossroads Bible Coll, IN — B
Grace U, NE — B
Loras Coll, IA — B
Loyola U Chicago, IL — B
Manchester Coll, IN — A
Martin Luther Coll, MN — B
Minnesota State U Mankato, MN — B
Moody Bible Inst, IL — B
Northwestern Coll, MN — B
Ohio Northern U, OH — B
Ohio Wesleyan U, OH — B
Reformed Bible Coll, MI — B
St. Gregory's U, OK — A
Saint John's U, MN — B
Trinity Christian Coll, IL — B

Trinity International U, IL — B
U of Indianapolis, IN — B
U of Rio Grande, OH — B
Viterbo U, WI — B

Pre-Veterinary Studies
Adrian Coll, MI — B
Albion Coll, MI — B
Alma Coll, MI — B
Andrews U, MI — B
Antioch Coll, OH — B
Aquinas Coll, MI — B
Ashland U, OH — B
Augsburg Coll, MN — B
Augustana Coll, IL — B
Augustana Coll, SD — B
Baldwin-Wallace Coll, OH — B
Bemidji State U, MN — B
Benedictine U, IL — B
Bethel Coll, IN — B
Blackburn Coll, IL — B
Briar Cliff U, IA — B
Calvin Coll, MI — B
Capital U, OH — B
Cardinal Stritch U, WI — B
Carroll Coll, WI — B
Carthage Coll, WI — B
Cedarville U, OH — B
Central Christian Coll of Kansas, KS — A,B
Central Missouri State U, MO — B
Chicago State U, IL — B
Clarkson U — B
Coe Coll, IA — B
Coll of Saint Benedict, MN — B
Coll of St. Catherine, MN — B
Coll of Saint Mary, NE — B
Coll of the Ozarks, MO — B
Columbia Coll, MO — B
Concordia Coll, MN — B
Concordia U, NE — B
Concord U, WV — B
Cornerstone U, MI — B
Dakota State U, SD — B
Defiance Coll, OH — B
Dickinson State U, ND — B
Dominican U, IL — B
Dordt Coll, IA — B
Drake U, IA — B
Drury U, MO — B
East Central U, OK — B
Eastern Michigan U, MI — B
Edgewood Coll, WI — B
Elmhurst Coll, IL — B
Eureka Coll, IL — B
Evangel U, MO — B
Gannon U, PA — B
Goshen Coll, IN — B
Grand Valley State U, MI — B
Gustavus Adolphus Coll, MN — B
Hamline U, MN — B
Hastings Coll, NE — B
Heidelberg Coll, OH — B
Hillsdale Coll, MI — B
Hiram Coll, OH — B
Huntington Coll, IN — B
Illinois Coll, IL — B
Indiana U–Purdue U Indianapolis, IN — B
Iowa State U of Science and Technology, IA — B
Iowa Wesleyan Coll, IA — B
John Carroll U, OH — B
Kansas State U, KS — B

Kansas Wesleyan U, KS — B
Kenyon Coll, OH — B
Lake Erie Coll, OH — B
Lake Forest Coll, IL — B
Lake Superior State U, MI — B
Lawrence U, WI — B
Lewis U, IL — B
Lindenwood U, MO — B
Loyola U Chicago, IL — B
MacMurray Coll, IL — B
Madonna U, MI — B
Manchester Coll, IN — B
Marian Coll, IN — B
Marian Coll of Fond du Lac, WI — B
Mayville State U, ND — B
McKendree Coll, IL — B
McPherson Coll, KS — B
Miami U, OH — B
Michigan State U, MI — B
Michigan Technological U, MI — B
Millikin U, IL — B
Minnesota State U Mankato, MN — B
Minnesota State U Moorhead, MN — B
Missouri Southern State U, MO — B
Missouri Valley Coll, MO — B
Morningside Coll, IA — B
Mount Mary Coll, WI — B
Mount Mercy Coll, IA — B
Mount Vernon Nazarene U, OH — B
Muskingum Coll, OH — B
Newman U, KS — A
North Central Coll, IL — B
Northeastern State U, OK — B
Northern Michigan U, MI — B
Northland Coll, WI — B
North Park U, IL — B
Oakland City U, IN — B
Ohio Northern U, OH — B
Ohio U, OH — B
Ohio Wesleyan U, OH — B
Oklahoma Baptist U, OK — B
Oklahoma City U, OK — B
Oklahoma State U, OK — B
Olivet Coll, MI — B
Olivet Nazarene U, IL — B
Otterbein Coll, OH — B
Peru State Coll, NE — B
Pittsburg State U, KS — B
Purdue U Calumet, IN — B
Quincy U, IL — B
Ripon Coll, WI — B
Rockford Coll, IL — B
St. Cloud State U, MN — B
Saint John's U, MN — B
Saint Mary-of-the-Woods Coll, IN — B
St. Norbert Coll, WI — B
Shawnee State U, OH — A
Simpson Coll, IA — B
South Dakota State U, SD — B
Southwestern Oklahoma State U, OK — B
Stephens Coll, MO — B
Taylor U, IN — B
Trinity Christian Coll, IL — B
Tri-State U, IN — B
Truman State U, MO — B
The U of Akron, OH — B
U of Cincinnati, OH — B

A—associate degree; B—bachelor's degree

U of Evansville, IN	B
The U of Findlay, OH	B
U of Illinois at Urbana–Champaign, IL	B
U of Indianapolis, IN	B
The U of Iowa, IA	B
U of Minnesota, Duluth, MN	B
U of Minnesota, Morris, MN	B
U of Minnesota, Twin Cities Campus, MN	B
U of Missouri–St. Louis, MO	B
U of Nebraska–Lincoln, NE	B
U of Rio Grande, OH	B
U of St. Francis, IL	B
U of Saint Francis, IN	B
U of Sioux Falls, SD	B
U of Toledo, OH	B
U of Wisconsin–Oshkosh, WI	B
U of Wisconsin–Parkside, WI	B
U of Wisconsin–River Falls, WI	B
Upper Iowa U, IA	B
Urbana U, OH	B
Valley City State U, ND	B
Wabash Coll, IN	B
Walsh U, OH	B
Washington U in St. Louis, MO	B
Wayne State Coll, NE	B
William Jewell Coll, MO	B
Winona State U, MN	B
Wittenberg U, OH	B
Wright State U, OH	B
Youngstown State U, OH	B

Printing Management

Carroll Coll, WI	B
Central Missouri State U, MO	A,B
U of Wisconsin–Stout, WI	B

Printmaking

Art Academy of Cincinnati, OH	B
Ball State U, IN	B
The Cleveland Inst of Art, OH	B
Coll for Creative Studies, MI	B
Coll of Visual Arts, MN	B
Columbia Coll, MO	B
Drake U, IA	B
Grand Valley State U, MI	B
Indiana U–Purdue U Fort Wayne, IN	B
Kansas City Art Inst, MO	B
Milwaukee Inst of Art and Design, WI	B
Minneapolis Coll of Art and Design, MN	B
Minnesota State U Moorhead, MN	B
Northern Michigan U, MI	B
Ohio Northern U, OH	B
The Ohio State U, OH	B
Ohio U, OH	B
St. Cloud State U, MN	B
School of the Art Inst of Chicago, IL	B
Trinity Christian Coll, IL	B
The U of Akron, OH	B
The U of Iowa, IA	B
U of Kansas, KS	B
U of Michigan, MI	B
U of Michigan–Flint, MI	B
U of Missouri–St. Louis, MO	B

Washington U in St. Louis, MO	B
Youngstown State U, OH	B

Professional Studies

Bemidji State U, MN	B
Briar Cliff U, IA	B
Kent State U, OH	B
Missouri Southern State U, MO	B
Saint Mary-of-the-Woods Coll, IN	B
U of Dubuque, IA	B
U of Oklahoma, OK	B

Psychiatric/Mental Health Services Technology

Franciscan U of Steubenville, OH	B
Lake Superior State U, MI	A
North Dakota State Coll of Science, ND	A
U of Toledo, OH	A

Psychology

Adrian Coll, MI	A,B
Albion Coll, MI	B
Alma Coll, MI	B
Alverno Coll, WI	B
Andrews U, MI	B
Antioch Coll, OH	B
Aquinas Coll, MI	B
Argosy U/Chicago, IL	B
Argosy U/Chicago Northwest, IL	B
Argosy U/Twin Cities, MN	B
Argosy U/Twin Cities, Eagan, MN	B
Ashland U, OH	B
Augsburg Coll, MN	B
Augustana Coll, IL	B
Augustana Coll, SD	B
Aurora U, IL	B
Avila U, MO	B
Baker U, KS	B
Baldwin-Wallace Coll, OH	B
Ball State U, IN	B
Barclay Coll, KS	B
Beloit Coll, WI	B
Bemidji State U, MN	B
Benedictine Coll, KS	B
Benedictine U, IL	B
Bethany Coll, KS	B
Bethany Lutheran Coll, MN	B
Bethel Coll, IN	B
Bethel Coll, KS	B
Bethel U, MN	B
Blackburn Coll, IL	B
Black Hills State U, SD	B
Bluffton Coll, OH	B
Bowling Green State U, OH	B
Bradley U, IL	B
Brescia U, KY	B
Briar Cliff U, IA	B
Buena Vista U, IA	B
Butler U, IN	B
Calumet Coll of Saint Joseph, IN	A,B
Calvin Coll, MI	B
Cameron U, OK	B
Capital U, OH	B
Cardinal Stritch U, WI	B
Carleton Coll, MN	B
Carroll Coll, WI	B
Carthage Coll, WI	B
Case Western Reserve U, OH	B

Cedarville U, OH	B
Central Christian Coll of Kansas, KS	A
Central Coll, IA	B
Central Methodist Coll, MO	A,B
Central Michigan U, MI	B
Central Missouri State U, MO	B
Central State U, OH	B
Chadron State Coll, NE	B
Chicago State U, IL	B
Clarke Coll, IA	B
Clarkson U	B
Cleveland State U, OH	B
Coe Coll, IA	B
Coll of Mount St. Joseph, OH	B
Coll of Saint Benedict, MN	B
Coll of St. Catherine, MN	B
Coll of Saint Mary, NE	B
The Coll of St. Scholastica, MN	B
Coll of the Ozarks, MO	B
The Coll of Wooster, OH	B
Columbia Coll, MO	B
Concordia Coll, MN	B
Concordia U, IL	B
Concordia U, MI	B
Concordia U, NE	B
Concordia U, St. Paul, MN	B
Concordia U Wisconsin, WI	B
Concord U, WV	B
Cornell Coll, IA	B
Cornerstone U, MI	B
Creighton U, NE	B
Crown Coll, MN	A,B
Culver-Stockton Coll, MO	B
Cumberland Coll, KY	B
Dakota Wesleyan U, SD	B
Dana Coll, NE	B
Defiance Coll, OH	B
Denison U, OH	B
DePaul U, IL	B
DePauw U, IN	B
Dickinson State U, ND	B
Doane Coll, NE	B
Dominican U, IL	B
Donnelly Coll, KS	A
Dordt Coll, IA	B
Drake U, IA	B
Drury U, MO	B
Earlham Coll, IN	B
East Central U, OK	B
Eastern Illinois U, IL	B
Eastern Michigan U, MI	B
Edgewood Coll, WI	B
Elmhurst Coll, IL	B
Emporia State U, KS	B
Eureka Coll, IL	B
Evangel U, MO	B
Fontbonne U, MO	B
Fort Hays State U, KS	B
The Franciscan U, IA	B
Franciscan U of Steubenville, OH	B
Franklin Coll, IN	B
Gannon U, PA	B
Goshen Coll, IN	B
Governors State U, IL	B
Grace Coll, IN	B
Graceland U, IA	B
Grace U, NE	B
Grand Valley State U, MI	B
Grand View Coll, IA	B
Greenville Coll, IL	B
Grinnell Coll, IA	B

Gustavus Adolphus Coll, MN	B
Hamline U, MN	B
Hannibal-LaGrange Coll, MO	B
Hanover Coll, IN	B
Hastings Coll, NE	B
Heidelberg Coll, OH	B
Hillsdale Coll, MI	B
Hillsdale Free Will Baptist Coll, OK	A
Hiram Coll, OH	B
Hope Coll, MI	B
Huntington Coll, IN	B
Illinois Coll, IL	B
Illinois Inst of Technology, IL	B
Illinois State U, IL	B
Illinois Wesleyan U, IL	B
Indiana Inst of Technology, IN	B
Indiana State U, IN	B
Indiana U Bloomington, IN	B
Indiana U East, IN	B
Indiana U Kokomo, IN	B
Indiana U Northwest, IN	B
Indiana U–Purdue U Fort Wayne, IN	A,B
Indiana U–Purdue U Indianapolis, IN	B
Indiana U South Bend, IN	B
Indiana U Southeast, IN	B
Iowa State U of Science and Technology, IA	B
Iowa Wesleyan Coll, IA	B
Jamestown Coll, ND	B
John Carroll U, OH	B
Judson Coll, IL	B
Kalamazoo Coll, MI	B
Kansas State U, KS	B
Kansas Wesleyan U, KS	B
Kent State U, OH	B
Kenyon Coll, OH	B
Knox Coll, IL	B
Lake Erie Coll, OH	B
Lake Forest Coll, IL	B
Lakeland Coll, WI	B
Lake Superior State U, MI	B
Lawrence Technological U, MI	B
Lawrence U, WI	B
Lehigh U, PA	B
Lewis U, IL	B
Lincoln Coll, Lincoln, IL	A
Lincoln U, MO	B
Lindenwood U, MO	B
Loras Coll, IA	B
Lourdes Coll, OH	A,B
Loyola U Chicago, IL	B
Luther Coll, IA	B
Macalester Coll, MN	B
MacMurray Coll, IL	B
Madonna U, MI	B
Malone Coll, OH	B
Manchester Coll, IN	B
Marian Coll, IN	A,B
Marian Coll of Fond du Lac, WI	B
Marietta Coll, OH	B
Marquette U, WI	B
Martin U, IN	B
Marygrove Coll, MI	B
Maryville U of Saint Louis, MO	B
McKendree Coll, IL	B
McPherson Coll, KS	B
Metropolitan State U, MN	B
Miami U, OH	B

Miami U Hamilton, OH	B	Purdue U, IN	B	U of Mary, ND	B	Western Illinois U, IL	B

Miami U Hamilton, OH — B
Michigan State U, MI — B
MidAmerica Nazarene U, KS — B
Millikin U, IL — B
Minnesota State U Mankato, MN — B
Minnesota State U Moorhead, MN — B
Minot State U, ND — B
Missouri Baptist U, MO — B
Missouri Southern State U, MO — B
Missouri Valley Coll, MO — B
Missouri Western State Coll, MO — B
Monmouth Coll, IL — B
Morningside Coll, IA — B
Mount Mary Coll, WI — B
Mount Mercy Coll, IA — B
Mount Union Coll, OH — B
Mount Vernon Nazarene U, OH — B
Muskingum Coll, OH — B
National-Louis U, IL — B
Nebraska Wesleyan U, NE — B
Newman U, KS — B
North Carolina Ag and Tech State U, NC — B
North Central Coll, IL — B
North Central U, MN — A,B
North Dakota State U, ND — B
Northeastern Illinois U, IL — B
Northeastern State U, OK — B
Northern Illinois U, IL — B
Northern Michigan U, MI — B
Northern State U, SD — B
Northland Coll, WI — B
North Park U, IL — B
Northwestern Coll, IA — B
Northwestern Coll, MN — B
Northwestern Oklahoma State U, OK — B
Northwestern U, IL — B
Notre Dame Coll, OH — B
Oak Hills Christian Coll, MN — B
Oakland U, MI — B
Oberlin Coll, OH — B
Ohio Dominican U, OH — B
Ohio Northern U, OH — B
The Ohio State U, OH — B
The Ohio State U at Lima, OH — B
The Ohio State U at Marion, OH — B
The Ohio State U–Mansfield Campus, OH — B
The Ohio State U–Newark Campus, OH — B
Ohio U, OH — B
Ohio Wesleyan U, OH — B
Oklahoma Baptist U, OK — B
Oklahoma Christian U, OK — B
Oklahoma City U, OK — B
Oklahoma Panhandle State U, OK — B
Oklahoma State U, OK — B
Olivet Coll, MI — B
Olivet Nazarene U, IL — B
Oral Roberts U, OK — B
Ottawa U, KS — B
Otterbein Coll, OH — B
Park U, MO — B
Peru State Coll, NE — B
Pittsburg State U, KS — B

Purdue U, IN — B
Purdue U Calumet, IN — B
Quincy U, IL — B
Ripon Coll, WI — B
Rochester Coll, MI — B
Rockford Coll, IL — B
Rockhurst U, MO — B
Roosevelt U, IL — B
Saginaw Valley State U, MI — B
St. Ambrose U, IA — B
St. Cloud State U, MN — B
St. Gregory's U, OK — B
Saint John's U, MN — B
Saint Joseph's Coll, IN — B
Saint Louis U, MO — B
Saint Mary-of-the-Woods Coll, IN — B
Saint Mary's Coll, IN — B
Saint Mary's U of Minnesota, MN — B
St. Norbert Coll, WI — B
St. Olaf Coll, MN — B
Saint Xavier U, IL — B
Shawnee State U, OH — B
Siena Heights U, MI — A,B
Silver Lake Coll, WI — B
Simpson Coll, IA — B
South Dakota State U, SD — B
Southeastern Oklahoma State U, OK — B
Southeast Missouri State U, MO — B
Southern Illinois U Carbondale, IL — B
Southern Illinois U Edwardsville, IL — B
Southern Nazarene U, OK — B
Southwest Baptist U, MO — B
Southwestern Coll, KS — B
Southwestern Oklahoma State U, OK — B
Southwest Missouri State U, MO — B
Spring Arbor U, MI — B
Stephens Coll, MO — B
Tabor Coll, KS — B
Taylor U, IN — B
Taylor U Fort Wayne, IN — B
Tiffin U, OH — B
Transylvania U, KY — B
Trinity Christian Coll, IL — B
Trinity International U, IL — B
Tri-State U, IN — B
Truman State U, MO — B
Union Coll, NE — B
Union Inst & U, OH — B
The U of Akron, OH — B
The U of Alabama in Huntsville, AL — B
U of Central Oklahoma, OK — B
U of Chicago, IL — B
U of Cincinnati, OH — B
U of Dayton, OH — B
U of Detroit Mercy, MI — B
U of Dubuque, IA — B
U of Evansville, IN — B
The U of Findlay, OH — B
U of Illinois at Chicago, IL — B
U of Illinois at Springfield, IL — B
U of Illinois at Urbana–Champaign, IL — B
U of Indianapolis, IN — B
The U of Iowa, IA — B
U of Kansas, KS — B

U of Mary, ND — B
U of Michigan, MI — B
U of Michigan–Dearborn, MI — B
U of Michigan–Flint, MI — B
U of Minnesota, Duluth, MN — B
U of Minnesota, Morris, MN — B
U of Minnesota, Twin Cities Campus, MN — B
U of Missouri–Columbia, MO — B
U of Missouri–Kansas City, MO — B
U of Missouri–Rolla, MO — B
U of Missouri–St. Louis, MO — B
U of Nebraska at Omaha, NE — B
U of Nebraska–Lincoln, NE — B
U of New Orleans, LA — B
U of North Dakota, ND — B
U of Northern Iowa, IA — B
U of Notre Dame, IN — B
U of Oklahoma, OK — B
U of Rio Grande, OH — A
U of St. Francis, IL — B
U of Saint Francis, IN — B
U of Saint Mary, KS — B
U of St. Thomas, MN — B
U of Science and Arts of Oklahoma, OK — B
U of Sioux Falls, SD — B
The U of South Dakota, SD — B
U of Southern Indiana, IN — B
U of Toledo, OH — B
U of Tulsa, OK — B
U of West Florida, FL — B
U of Wisconsin–Eau Claire, WI — B
U of Wisconsin–Green Bay, WI — A,B
U of Wisconsin–La Crosse, WI — B
U of Wisconsin–Madison, WI — B
U of Wisconsin–Milwaukee, WI — B
U of Wisconsin–Oshkosh, WI — B
U of Wisconsin–Parkside, WI — B
U of Wisconsin–Platteville, WI — B
U of Wisconsin–River Falls, WI — B
U of Wisconsin–Stevens Point, WI — B
U of Wisconsin–Stout, WI — B
U of Wisconsin–Superior, WI — B
U of Wisconsin–Whitewater, WI — B
Upper Iowa U, IA — B
Urbana U, OH — B
Ursuline Coll, OH — B
Valley City State U, ND — B
Valparaiso U, IN — B
Vennard Coll, IA — B
Viterbo U, WI — B
Wabash Coll, IN — B
Waldorf Coll, IA — B
Walsh U, OH — B
Wartburg Coll, IA — B
Washburn U, KS — B
Washington U in St. Louis, MO — B
Wayne State Coll, NE — B
Wayne State U, MI — B
Webster U, MO — B

Western Illinois U, IL — B
Western Michigan U, MI — B
Westminster Coll, MO — B
Wheaton Coll, IL — B
Wichita State U, KS — B
Wilberforce U, OH — B
William Jewell Coll, MO — B
William Penn U, IA — B
William Tyndale Coll, MI — B
William Woods U, MO — B
Winona State U, MN — B
Wisconsin Lutheran Coll, WI — B
Wittenberg U, OH — B
Wright State U, OH — A,B
Xavier U, OH — A,B
York Coll, NE — B
Youngstown State U, OH — B

Psychology Related
Buena Vista U, IA — B
Loyola U Chicago, IL — B
Madonna U, MI — B
Ohio Northern U, OH — B
U of Michigan–Flint, MI — B
U of St. Thomas, MN — B
U of Toledo, OH — B

Psychology Teacher Education
Alma Coll, MI — B
Carroll Coll, WI — B
Central Christian Coll of Kansas, KS — A
Ohio Wesleyan U, OH — B
Pittsburg State U, KS — B
St. Ambrose U, IA — B
Shawnee State U, OH — B
U of Michigan–Flint, MI — B
U of Missouri–St. Louis, MO — B
Valparaiso U, IN — B
York Coll, NE — B

Psychometrics and Quantitative Psychology
North Dakota State U, ND — B

Public Administration
Augustana Coll, IL — B
Blackburn Coll, IL — B
Bowling Green State U, OH — B
Buena Vista U, IA — B
Calvin Coll, MI — B
Capital U, OH — B
Cedarville U, OH — B
Central Methodist Coll, MO — A,B
Cleveland State U, OH — B
Doane Coll, NE — B
Eastern Michigan U, MI — B
Edgewood Coll, WI — B
Evangel U, MO — B
Ferris State U, MI — B
Governors State U, IL — B
Grand Valley State U, MI — B
Hamline U, MN — B
Harris-Stowe State Coll, MO — B
Heidelberg Coll, OH — B
Indiana U Bloomington, IN — A,B
Indiana U Northwest, IN — A,B
Indiana U–Purdue U Fort Wayne, IN — A,B
Indiana U–Purdue U Indianapolis, IN — A,B
Indiana U South Bend, IN — A,B
Iowa State U of Science and Technology, IA — B
John Carroll U, OH — B
Lewis U, IL — B
Lincoln U, MO — B

A—associate degree; B—bachelor's degree

Lindenwood U, MO — B
Metropolitan State U, MN — B
Miami U, OH — B
Miami U Hamilton, OH — B
Michigan State U, MI — B
Minnesota State U Mankato, MN — B
Missouri Valley Coll, MO — B
Northern Michigan U, MI — B
Northern State U, SD — B
Notre Dame Coll, OH — B
Oakland U, MI — B
Ohio Wesleyan U, OH — B
Park U, MO — B
Roosevelt U, IL — B
Saginaw Valley State U, MI — B
St. Ambrose U, IA — B
St. Cloud State U, MN — B
Siena Heights U, MI — B
Southwest Missouri State U, MO — B
Union Inst & U, OH — B
U of Michigan–Dearborn, MI — B
U of Michigan–Flint, MI — B
U of Missouri–St. Louis, MO — B
U of Northern Iowa, IA — B
U of Oklahoma, OK — B
U of St. Thomas, MN — B
U of Wisconsin–La Crosse, WI — B
U of Wisconsin–Stevens Point, WI — B
U of Wisconsin–Whitewater, WI — B
Upper Iowa U, IA — B
Washburn U, KS — B
Wayne State Coll, NE — B
Wayne State U, MI — B
Winona State U, MN — B
Wright State U, OH — B
Youngstown State U, OH — B

Public Administration and Social Service Professions Related
Coll of Mount St. Joseph, OH — B
Eastern Michigan U, MI — B
Indiana U–Purdue U Fort Wayne, IN — A
Northeastern Illinois U, IL — B
Ohio U, OH — B
Quincy U, IL — B
Roosevelt U, IL — B
The U of Akron, OH — A
U of Phoenix–Kansas City Campus, MO — B
U of Phoenix–Oklahoma City Campus, OK — B
U of Phoenix–St. Louis Campus, MO — B
U of Phoenix–West Michigan Campus, MI — B
U of Saint Francis, IN — A,B

Public Health
Alma Coll, MI — B
Central Michigan U, MI — B
Grand Valley State U, MI — B
Indiana U Bloomington, IN — B
Indiana U–Purdue U Indianapolis, IN — B
Maryville U of Saint Louis, MO —
Minnesota State U Mankato, MN — B
Truman State U, MO — B

U of Cincinnati, OH — B
U of Minnesota, Twin Cities Campus, MN — B
Winona State U, MN — B

Public Health/Community Nursing
Capital U, OH — B
Northern Illinois U, IL — B
Wright State U, OH — B

Public Health Education and Promotion
Malone Coll, OH — B
U of Michigan–Flint, MI — B
U of St. Thomas, MN — B
U of Toledo, OH — B
U of Wisconsin–La Crosse, WI — B

Public Health Related
Malone Coll, OH — B
Maryville U of Saint Louis, MO — B
U of Illinois at Urbana–Champaign, IL — B

Public Policy Analysis
Albion Coll, MI — B
DePaul U, IL — B
Eastern Michigan U, MI — B
Edgewood Coll, WI — B
Grand Valley State U, MI — B
Indiana U Bloomington, IN — A,B
Indiana U–Purdue U Fort Wayne, IN — B
Kenyon Coll, OH — B
Muskingum Coll, OH — B
Northwestern U, IL — B
St. Cloud State U, MN — B
U of Chicago, IL — B
U of Cincinnati, OH — B
U of Toledo, OH — B
U of Wisconsin–Whitewater, WI — B

Public Relations, Advertising, and Applied Communication Related
Buena Vista U, IA — B
Carroll Coll, WI — B
Madonna U, MI — A,B
Marietta Coll, OH — B
Notre Dame Coll, OH — B
Pittsburg State U, KS — B
The U of Akron, OH — B

Public Relations/Image Management
Andrews U, MI — B
Ball State U, IN — B
Bowling Green State U, OH — B
Bradley U, IL — B
Butler U, IN — B
Capital U, OH — B
Cardinal Stritch U, WI — B
Central Michigan U, MI — B
Central Missouri State U, MO — B
Clarke Coll, IA — B
Cleveland State U, OH — B
Coe Coll, IA — B
Coll of the Ozarks, MO — B
Columbia Coll Chicago, IL — B
Concordia Coll, MN — B
Defiance Coll, OH — B
Doane Coll, NE — B
Drake U, IA — B
Drury U, MO — B

East Central U, OK — B
Eastern Michigan U, MI — B
Ferris State U, MI — B
Fort Hays State U, KS — B
Grand Valley State U, MI — B
Greenville Coll, IL — B
Hastings Coll, NE — B
Heidelberg Coll, OH — B
Huntington Coll, IN — B
Illinois State U, IL — B
Indiana U Northwest, IN — B
Kent State U, OH — B
Lewis U, IL — B
Lindenwood U, MO — B
Loras Coll, IA — B
Madonna U, MI — A,B
Marquette U, WI — B
McKendree Coll, IL — B
MidAmerica Nazarene U, KS — B
Minnesota State U Mankato, MN — B
Minnesota State U Moorhead, MN — B
Monmouth Coll, IL — B
Mount Mary Coll, WI — B
Northern Michigan U, MI — B
Northwestern Coll, MN — B
Ohio Dominican U, OH — B
Ohio Northern U, OH — B
Ohio U, OH — B
Ohio U–Zanesville, OH — B
Oklahoma Baptist U, OK — B
Oklahoma Christian U, OK — B
Oklahoma City U, OK — B
Oral Roberts U, OK — B
Otterbein Coll, OH — B
Pittsburg State U, KS — B
Purdue U Calumet, IN — B
Quincy U, IL — B
Rockhurst U, MO — B
Roosevelt U, IL — B
St. Ambrose U, IA — B
St. Cloud State U, MN — B
Saint Mary-of-the-Woods Coll, IN — B
Saint Mary's U of Minnesota, MN — B
Stephens Coll, MO — B
Tabor Coll, KS — B
Taylor U Fort Wayne, IN — B
Trinity Christian Coll, IL — B
Union Coll, NE — B
U of Central Oklahoma, OK — B
U of Dayton, OH — B
U of Detroit Mercy, MI — B
The U of Findlay, OH — B
U of Northern Iowa, IA — B
U of Oklahoma, OK — B
U of Rio Grande, OH — B
U of Sioux Falls, SD — B
U of Southern Indiana, IN — B
U of Wisconsin–Madison, WI — B
U of Wisconsin–River Falls, WI — B
Ursuline Coll, OH — B
Valparaiso U, IN — B
Wartburg Coll, IA — B
Wayne State U, MI — B
Webster U, MO — B
William Penn U, IA — B
William Woods U, MO — B
Winona State U, MN — B
Xavier U, OH — A,B
Youngstown State U, OH — B

Publishing
Benedictine U, IL — B
Graceland U, IA — B
Saint Mary's U of Minnesota, MN — B
U of Missouri–Columbia, MO — B

Purchasing, Procurement/Acquisitions and Contracts Management
Miami U, OH — B
Miami U Hamilton, OH — A
Southwestern Coll, KS — B
Wright State U, OH — B

Quality Control and Safety Technologies Related
Madonna U, MI — A,B

Quality Control Technology
Baker Coll of Cadillac, MI — A
Baker Coll of Flint, MI — A
Baker Coll of Muskegon, MI — A
Bowling Green State U, OH — B
Eastern Michigan U, MI — B
Ferris State U, MI — B
U of Cincinnati, OH — A
Winona State U, MN — B

Radiation Biology
Grand Valley State U, MI — B

Radiation Protection/Health Physics Technology
Argosy U/Twin Cities, MN — A

Radio and Television
Ashland U, OH — A,B
Bemidji State U, MN — B
Bradley U, IL — B
Central Michigan U, MI — B
Central Missouri State U, MO — B
Central State U, OH — B
Chicago State U, IL — B
Columbia Coll Chicago, IL — B
Concordia Coll, MN — B
Drake U, IA — B
East Central U, OK — B
Evangel U, MO — B
Fort Hays State U, KS — B
Gannon U, PA — B
Grand Valley State U, MI — B
Grand View Coll, IA — B
Hastings Coll, NE — B
Indiana State U, IN — B
Indiana U Bloomington, IN — B
Kent State U, OH — B
Lincoln Coll, Lincoln, IL — A
Lindenwood U, MO — B
Marietta Coll, OH — B
Michigan State U, MI — B
Minot State U, ND — B
Muskingum Coll, OH — B
Northwestern Coll, MN — A,B
Northwestern U, IL — B
Ohio Northern U, OH — B
Ohio U, OH — A,B
Ohio U–Zanesville, OH — A
Oklahoma Baptist U, OK — B
Oklahoma Christian U, OK — B
Oklahoma City U, OK — B
Olivet Nazarene U, IL — B
Oral Roberts U, OK — B
Otterbein Coll, OH — B
Pittsburg State U, KS — B
Purdue U Calumet, IN — B
Quincy U, IL — B

Roosevelt U, IL	B
St. Ambrose U, IA	B
St. Cloud State U, MN	B
Southern Illinois U Carbondale, IL	B
Spring Arbor U, MI	B
Stephens Coll, MO	B
U of Central Oklahoma, OK	B
U of Cincinnati, OH	B
U of Dayton, OH	B
U of Detroit Mercy, MI	B
U of Kansas, KS	B
U of Missouri–Columbia, MO	B
U of Northern Iowa, IA	B
U of Sioux Falls, SD	B
U of Southern Indiana, IN	B
U of Wisconsin–Madison, WI	B
U of Wisconsin–Oshkosh, WI	B
U of Wisconsin–River Falls, WI	B
U of Wisconsin–Superior, WI	B
Valparaiso U, IN	B
Washburn U, KS	B
Wayne State U, MI	B
Webster U, MO	B
Western Illinois U, IL	B
Western Michigan U, MI	B
William Woods U, MO	B
Winona State U, MN	B
Xavier U, OH	A,B
Youngstown State U, OH	B

Radio and Television Broadcasting Technology

Eastern Michigan U, MI	B
Lewis U, IL	B
Ohio U, OH	B
Ohio U–Southern Campus, OH	A

Radiologic Technology/Science

Allen Coll, IA	A
Argosy U/Twin Cities, MN	A
Baker Coll of Clinton Township, MI	A
Baker Coll of Muskegon, MI	A
Indiana U Northwest, IN	A,B
Indiana U–Purdue U Fort Wayne, IN	A
Jamestown Coll, ND	B
Kent State U, OH	B
Kettering Coll of Medical Arts, OH	A,B
Nebraska Methodist Coll, NE	A
Newman U, KS	A
North Dakota State U, ND	B
The Ohio State U, OH	B
St. Luke's Coll, IA	A
Southwest Missouri State U, MO	B
The U of Findlay, OH	B
The U of Iowa, IA	B
U of Mary, ND	B
U of Michigan, MI	B
U of Missouri–Columbia, MO	B
U of Nebraska Medical Center, NE	B
U of Oklahoma Health Sciences Center, OK	B

U of St. Francis, IL	B
Washburn U, KS	A

Radio, Television, and Digital Communication Related

Capital U, OH	B
Drake U, IA	B
Madonna U, MI	B

Range Science and Management

Chadron State Coll, NE	B
Fort Hays State U, KS	B
South Dakota State U, SD	B
U of Nebraska–Lincoln, NE	B

Reading Teacher Education

Aquinas Coll, MI	B
Central Missouri State U, MO	B
Chicago State U, IL	B
Dordt Coll, IA	B
Eastern Michigan U, MI	B
Grand Valley State U, MI	B
Northeastern State U, OK	B
Oakland U, MI	B
Ohio U, OH	B
St. Cloud State U, MN	B
U of Central Oklahoma, OK	B
U of Detroit Mercy, MI	B
U of Nebraska–Lincoln, NE	B
U of Northern Iowa, IA	B
U of Wisconsin–Superior, WI	B
Upper Iowa U, IA	B
William Penn U, IA	B
Winona State U, MN	B
Wright State U, OH	B
York Coll, NE	B

Real Estate

Ball State U, IN	B
Ferris State U, MI	A
Indiana U Bloomington, IN	B
Kent State U, OH	A
Miami U Hamilton, OH	A
Minnesota State U Mankato, MN	B
The Ohio State U, OH	B
St. Cloud State U, MN	B
U of Central Oklahoma, OK	B
U of Cincinnati, OH	A,B
U of Missouri–Columbia, MO	B
U of Nebraska at Omaha, NE	B
U of Northern Iowa, IA	B
U of St. Thomas, MN	B
U of Wisconsin–Madison, WI	B
U of Wisconsin–Milwaukee, WI	B

Receptionist

Baker Coll of Allen Park, MI	A

Recording Arts Technology

Columbia Coll Chicago, IL	B

Rehabilitation and Therapeutic Professions Related

Central Michigan U, MI	B
Southern Illinois U Carbondale, IL	B

Rehabilitation Therapy

Baker Coll of Muskegon, MI	B
Wilberforce U, OH	B

Religious Education

Andrews U, MI	B
Aquinas Coll, MI	A,B
Ashland U, OH	B
Baptist Bible Coll, MO	B
Barclay Coll, KS	B
Calvary Bible Coll and Theological Seminary, MO	A,B
Capital U, OH	B
Cardinal Stritch U, WI	B
Cedarville U, OH	B
Coll of Mount St. Joseph, OH	B
Coll of Saint Benedict, MN	B
Concordia U, IL	B
Concordia U, NE	B
Concordia U, St. Paul, MN	B
Cornerstone U, MI	A,B
Crossroads Bible Coll, IN	B
Crossroads Coll, MN	B
Crown Coll, MN	B
Cumberland Coll, KY	B
Defiance Coll, OH	B
Faith Baptist Bible Coll and Theological Seminary, IA	B
Franciscan U of Steubenville, OH	B
Global U of the Assemblies of God, MO	B
Grace Bible Coll, MI	B
Grace U, NE	B
Hannibal-LaGrange Coll, MO	B
Hillsdale Free Will Baptist Coll, OK	A,B
John Carroll U, OH	B
Kansas Wesleyan U, KS	B
Lincoln Coll, Lincoln, IL	A
Malone Coll, OH	B
Manhattan Christian Coll, KS	A,B
Marian Coll, IN	B
Messenger Coll, MO	B
MidAmerica Nazarene U, KS	A,B
Missouri Baptist U, MO	B
Moody Bible Inst, IL	B
Mount Mary Coll, WI	B
Mount Vernon Nazarene U, OH	B
Northwestern Coll, IA	B
Northwestern Coll, MN	B
Oakland City U, IN	B
Oklahoma Baptist U, OK	B
Oklahoma Christian U, OK	B
Oklahoma City U, OK	B
Olivet Nazarene U, IL	B
Pillsbury Baptist Bible Coll, MN	B
Reformed Bible Coll, MI	A,B
Saint John's U, MN	B
St. Louis Christian Coll, MO	B
Saint Mary's U of Minnesota, MN	B
Southern Nazarene U, OK	B
Sterling Coll, KS	B
Taylor U, IN	B
Taylor U Fort Wayne, IN	B
Trinity Christian Coll, IL	B
Union Coll, NE	B
U of Dayton, OH	B
Vennard Coll, IA	B
Viterbo U, WI	B
Wheaton Coll, IL	B
William Tyndale Coll, MI	B
York Coll, NE	B

Religious/Sacred Music

Aquinas Coll, MI	A,B
Augustana Coll, IL	B
Barclay Coll, KS	B
Bethany Lutheran Coll, MN	B
Bethel Coll, IN	B
Bethel U, MN	B
Calvary Bible Coll and Theological Seminary, MO	B
Calvin Coll, MI	B
Cedarville U, OH	B
Coll of the Ozarks, MO	B
Concordia U, IL	B
Concordia U, MI	B
Concordia U, NE	B
Concordia U, St. Paul, MN	B
Crossroads Coll, MN	B
Drake U, IA	B
Evangel U, MO	B
Faith Baptist Bible Coll and Theological Seminary, IA	B
God's Bible School and Coll, OH	B
Grace U, NE	B
Greenville Coll, IL	B
Gustavus Adolphus Coll, MN	B
Hannibal-LaGrange Coll, MO	B
Hillsdale Free Will Baptist Coll, OK	A,B
Malone Coll, OH	B
Manhattan Christian Coll, KS	A,B
Messenger Coll, MO	B
MidAmerica Nazarene U, KS	A,B
Millikin U, IL	B
Missouri Baptist U, MO	B
Moody Bible Inst, IL	B
Mount Vernon Nazarene U, OH	A,B
North Central U, MN	A,B
North Park U, IL	B
Oak Hills Christian Coll, MN	B
Oklahoma Baptist U, OK	B
Oklahoma City U, OK	B
Olivet Nazarene U, IL	B
Oral Roberts U, OK	B
Pillsbury Baptist Bible Coll, MN	B
Saint Joseph's Coll, IN	A,B
St. Louis Christian Coll, MO	B
Southwestern Oklahoma State U, OK	B
Taylor U, IN	B
Trinity International U, IL	B
Valparaiso U, IN	B
Vennard Coll, IA	A
Wartburg Coll, IA	B
William Jewell Coll, MO	B
William Tyndale Coll, MI	B

Religious Studies

Adrian Coll, MI	A,B
Albion Coll, MI	B
Alma Coll, MI	B
Alverno Coll, WI	B
Andrews U, MI	B
Antioch Coll, OH	B
Aquinas Coll, MI	A,B
Ashland U, OH	B
Augsburg Coll, MN	B
Augustana Coll, IL	B
Augustana Coll, SD	B
Avila U, MO	B

A—associate degree; B—bachelor's degree

Baker U, KS	B	Illinois Wesleyan U, IL	B	Simpson Coll, IA	B	Indiana U Northwest, IN	A
Baldwin-Wallace Coll, OH	B	Indiana U Bloomington, IN	B	Southwest Baptist U, MO	B	Indiana U–Purdue U
Ball State U, IN	B	Indiana U–Purdue U		Southwest Missouri State U,		Indianapolis, IN	A,B
Beloit Coll, WI	B	Indianapolis, IN	B	MO	B	Kettering Coll of Medical
Bemidji State U, MN	B	Iowa State U of Science and		Spring Arbor U, MI	B	Arts, OH	A,B
Benedictine Coll, KS	B	Technology, IA	B	Tabor Coll, KS	A,B	Missouri Southern State U,
Bethany Coll, KS	B	Jamestown Coll, ND	B	Taylor U, IN	B	MO	A
Bethel Coll, KS	B	John Carroll U, OH	B	Transylvania U, KY	B	National-Louis U, IL	B
Bluffton Coll, OH	B	Judson Coll, IL	B	Trinity Christian Coll, IL	B	Nebraska Methodist Coll,
Bradley U, IL	B	Kalamazoo Coll, MI	B	Truman State U, MO	B	NE	A,B
Brescia U, KY	A,B	Kansas Wesleyan U, KS	B	Union Coll, NE	B	Newman U, KS	A
Butler U, IN	B	Kenyon Coll, OH	B	U of Chicago, IL	B	North Dakota State U, ND	B
Calumet Coll of Saint Joseph,		Lakeland Coll, WI	B	U of Dayton, OH	B	The Ohio State U, OH	B
IN	A,B	Laura and Alvin Siegal Coll		U of Detroit Mercy, MI	B	Rochester Comm and Tech
Calvin Coll, MI	B	of Judaic Studies, OH	B	U of Dubuque, IA	B	Coll, MN	A
Capital U, OH	B	Lawrence U, WI	B	U of Evansville, IN	B	St. Augustine Coll, IL	A
Cardinal Stritch U, WI	B	Lehigh U, PA	B	The U of Findlay, OH	A,B	St. Luke's Coll, IA	A
Carleton Coll, MN	B	Lewis U, IL	B	U of Illinois at Urbana–		Shawnee State U, OH	A
Carroll Coll, WI	B	Lindenwood U, MO	B	Champaign, IL	B	Southern Illinois U
Carthage Coll, WI	B	Loras Coll, IA	B	U of Indianapolis, IN	B	Carbondale, IL	A
Case Western Reserve U,		Lourdes Coll, OH	A,B	The U of Iowa, IA	B	Southwest Missouri State U,
OH	B	Luther Coll, IA	B	U of Kansas, KS	B	MO	B
Central Christian Coll of		Macalester Coll, MN	B	U of Mary, ND	B	The U of Akron, OH	A
Kansas, KS	A,B	MacMurray Coll, IL	B	U of Michigan, MI	B	U of Kansas, KS	B
Central Coll, IA	B	Madonna U, MI	A,B	U of Minnesota, Twin Cities		U of Mary, ND	B
Central Methodist Coll, MO	B	Manchester Coll, IN	A,B	Campus, MN	B	U of Missouri–Columbia,
Central Michigan U, MI	B	Manhattan Christian Coll,		U of Missouri–Columbia,		MO	B
Clarke Coll, IA	B	KS	B	MO	B	U of Southern Indiana, IN	A
Cleveland State U, OH	B	Marquette U, WI	B	U of Nebraska at Omaha,		U of Toledo, OH	A
Coe Coll, IA	B	Martin U, IN	B	NE	B	Washburn U, KS	B
Coll of Mount St. Joseph,		Marygrove Coll, MI	B	U of North Dakota, ND	B	Youngstown State U, OH	A,B
OH	B	McKendree Coll, IL	B	U of Northern Iowa, IA	B	
The Coll of St. Scholastica,		McPherson Coll, KS	B	U of Oklahoma, OK	B	**Restaurant, Culinary, and**
MN	B	Messenger Coll, MO	B	U of Saint Francis, IN	B	**Catering Management**
Coll of the Ozarks, MO	B	Miami U, OH	B	U of St. Thomas, MN	B	The Art Insts International
The Coll of Wooster, OH	B	Michigan State U, MI	B	U of Sioux Falls, SD	A,B	Minnesota, MN	B
Concordia Coll, MN	B	MidAmerica Nazarene U, KS	A,B	U of Toledo, OH	B	Kendall Coll, IL	B
Concordia U, MI	B	Missouri Baptist U, MO	A,B	U of Tulsa, OK	B	Lexington Coll, IL	A,B
Concordia U Wisconsin, WI	B	Missouri Valley Coll, MO	B	U of West Florida, FL	B	Lindenwood U, MO	B
Cornell Coll, IA	B	Monmouth Coll, IL	B	U of Wisconsin–Eau Claire,		The U of Akron, OH	A
Cornerstone U, MI	B	Morningside Coll, IA	B	WI	B	U of Illinois at Urbana–
Culver-Stockton Coll, MO	B	Mount Marty Coll, SD	A,B	U of Wisconsin–Milwaukee,		Champaign, IL	B
Dakota Wesleyan U, SD	B	Mount Mary Coll, WI	B	WI	B	
Dana Coll, NE	B	Mount Mercy Coll, IA	B	U of Wisconsin–Oshkosh,		**Restaurant/Food Services**
Defiance Coll, OH	B	Mount Union Coll, OH	B	WI	B	**Management**
Denison U, OH	B	Muskingum Coll, OH	B	Urbana U, OH	B	Kendall Coll, IL	B
DePaul U, IL	B	Nebraska Wesleyan U, NE	B	Vennard Coll, IA	A,B	Lexington Coll, IL	A,B
DePauw U, IN	B	North Central Coll, IL	B	Viterbo U, WI	B	Oklahoma State U, OK	B
Doane Coll, NE	B	North Central U, MN	B	Wabash Coll, IN	B	U of Missouri–Columbia,
Dominican U, IL	B	Northland Coll, WI	B	Walsh U, OH	B	MO	B
Dordt Coll, IA	B	North Park U, IL	B	Wartburg Coll, IA	B	Viterbo U, WI	B
Drake U, IA	B	Northwestern Coll, IA	B	Washburn U, KS	B	
Drury U, MO	B	Northwestern U, IL	B	Washington U in St. Louis,		**Retailing**
Earlham Coll, IN	B	Oakland City U, IN	B	MO	B	The U of Akron, OH	B
Edgewood Coll, WI	B	Oakland U, MI	B	Webster U, MO	B	Youngstown State U, OH	B
Eureka Coll, IL	B	Oberlin Coll, OH	B	Western Michigan U, MI	B	
Fontbonne U, MO	B	Ohio Northern U, OH	B	Westminster Coll, MO	B	**Robotics Technology**
The Franciscan U, IA	B	The Ohio State U, OH	B	Wheaton Coll, IL	B	Indiana State U, IN	B
Franklin Coll, IN	B	Ohio Wesleyan U, OH	B	William Jewell Coll, MO	B	Indiana U–Purdue U
Global U of the Assemblies		Oklahoma Baptist U, OK	B	Wittenberg U, OH	B	Indianapolis, IN	A,B
of God, MO	A	Oklahoma Christian U, OK	B	Wright State U, OH	B	ITT Tech Inst, Fort Wayne,
Goshen Coll, IN	B	Oklahoma City U, OK	B	York Coll, NE	B	IN	B
Grace Bible Coll, MI	A	Olivet Nazarene U, IL	B	Youngstown State U, OH	B	ITT Tech Inst, Indianapolis,
Graceland U, IA	B	Oral Roberts U, OK	B			IN	B
Grand View Coll, IA	B	Ottawa U, KS	B	**Religious Studies Related**		ITT Tech Inst, Newburgh,
Greenville Coll, IL	B	Otterbein Coll, OH	B	Ohio Northern U, OH	B	IN	B
Grinnell Coll, IA	B	Presentation Coll, SD	A	Ursuline Coll, OH	B	Lake Superior State U, MI	B
Gustavus Adolphus Coll, MN	B	Principia Coll, IL	B			Purdue U, IN	A,B
Hamline U, MN	B	Ripon Coll, WI	B	**Resort Management**		U of Rio Grande, OH	A,B
Hastings Coll, NE	B	Saint Mary-of-the-Woods		Florida Gulf Coast U, FL	B	
Heidelberg Coll, OH	B	Coll, IN	B	Lakeland Coll, WI	B	**Romance Languages**
Hillsdale Coll, MI	B	Saint Mary's Coll, IN	B			Beloit Coll, WI	B
Hiram Coll, OH	B	St. Norbert Coll, WI	B	**Respiratory Care Therapy**		Carleton Coll, MN	B
Hope Coll, MI	B	St. Olaf Coll, MN	B	Ball State U, IN	A	DePauw U, IN	B
Huntington Coll, IN	B	Saint Xavier U, IL	B	Coll of St. Catherine, MN	B	Eastern Michigan U, MI	B
Illinois Coll, IL	B	Siena Heights U, MI	B	Dakota State U, SD	A,B	Kenyon Coll, OH	B
				Ferris State U, MI	A	Oberlin Coll, OH	B
				Gannon U, PA	A,B	Olivet Nazarene U, IL	B

Ripon Coll, WI	B
U of Chicago, IL	B
U of Cincinnati, OH	B
U of Michigan, MI	B
Washington U in St. Louis, MO	B

Russian

Beloit Coll, WI	B
Bowling Green State U, OH	B
Carleton Coll, MN	B
Cornell Coll, IA	B
Grinnell Coll, IA	B
Gustavus Adolphus Coll, MN	B
Indiana U Bloomington, IN	B
Kent State U, OH	B
Knox Coll, IL	B
Lawrence U, WI	B
Lehigh U, PA	B
Macalester Coll, MN	B
Miami U, OH	B
Miami U Hamilton, OH	B
Michigan State U, MI	B
Northern Illinois U, IL	B
Oakland U, MI	B
Oberlin Coll, OH	B
The Ohio State U, OH	B
Ohio U, OH	B
Oklahoma State U, OK	B
Saint Louis U, MO	B
St. Olaf Coll, MN	B
Truman State U, MO	B
U of Chicago, IL	B
U of Illinois at Chicago, IL	B
U of Illinois at Urbana–Champaign, IL	B
The U of Iowa, IA	B
U of Michigan, MI	B
U of Minnesota, Twin Cities Campus, MN	B
U of Missouri–Columbia, MO	B
U of Nebraska–Lincoln, NE	B
U of Northern Iowa, IA	B
U of Notre Dame, IN	B
U of Oklahoma, OK	B
U of St. Thomas, MN	B
U of Wisconsin–Madison, WI	B
U of Wisconsin–Milwaukee, WI	B
Washington U in St. Louis, MO	B
Wayne State U, MI	B

Russian Studies

Beloit Coll, WI	B
Carleton Coll, MN	B
The Coll of Wooster, OH	B
Concordia Coll, MN	B
DePauw U, IN	B
Grand Valley State U, MI	B
Gustavus Adolphus Coll, MN	B
Hamline U, MN	B
Indiana U Bloomington, IN	B
Iowa State U of Science and Technology, IA	B
Kent State U, OH	B
Knox Coll, IL	B
Lawrence U, WI	B
Lehigh U, PA	B
Macalester Coll, MN	B
Oberlin Coll, OH	B
The Ohio State U, OH	B
St. Olaf Coll, MN	B
U of Chicago, IL	B

U of Illinois at Urbana–Champaign, IL	B
The U of Iowa, IA	B
U of Kansas, KS	B
U of Michigan, MI	B
U of Minnesota, Twin Cities Campus, MN	B
U of Missouri–Columbia, MO	B
U of Northern Iowa, IA	B
U of St. Thomas, MN	B
U of Wisconsin–Milwaukee, WI	B
Washington U in St. Louis, MO	B
Western Michigan U, MI	B
Wittenberg U, OH	B

Safety/Security Technology

Madonna U, MI	A,B
Ohio U, OH	A
Ohio U–Chillicothe, OH	A
U of Central Oklahoma, OK	B
U of Cincinnati, OH	A

Sales and Marketing/Marketing and Distribution Teacher Education

Bowling Green State U, OH	B
Central Christian Coll of Kansas, KS	A
Central Michigan U, MI	B
Eastern Michigan U, MI	B
Kent State U, OH	B
U of Nebraska–Lincoln, NE	B
U of North Dakota, ND	B
U of Wisconsin–Stout, WI	B
Wright State U, OH	B

Sales, Distribution and Marketing

Academy Coll, MN	A
Bacone Coll, OK	B
Baker Coll of Flint, MI	A
Baker Coll of Jackson, MI	A
Black Hills State U, SD	B
Central Michigan U, MI	B
Colorado Tech U Sioux Falls Campus, SD	B
McKendree Coll, IL	B
Metropolitan State U, MN	B
Ohio U, OH	B
Purdue U North Central, IN	A,B
Trinity Christian Coll, IL	B
The U of Findlay, OH	A,B
U of Illinois at Urbana–Champaign, IL	B
U of Wisconsin–Stout, WI	B
U of Wisconsin–Superior, WI	B
Wichita State U, KS	B
Youngstown State U, OH	B

Sanitation Technology

Grand Valley State U, MI	B

Sanskrit and Classical Indian Languages

U of Chicago, IL	B

Scandinavian Languages

Augsburg Coll, MN	B
Augustana Coll, IL	B
Concordia Coll, MN	B
Gustavus Adolphus Coll, MN	B
North Park U, IL	B
St. Olaf Coll, MN	B

U of Minnesota, Twin Cities Campus, MN	B
U of North Dakota, ND	B
U of Wisconsin–Madison, WI	B

Scandinavian Studies

Gustavus Adolphus Coll, MN	B
Luther Coll, IA	B
U of Michigan, MI	B

School Librarian/School Library Media

The Coll of St. Scholastica, MN	B
Ohio Dominican U, OH	B

School Psychology

Fort Hays State U, KS	B

Science Teacher Education

Adrian Coll, MI	B
Alma Coll, MI	B
Alverno Coll, WI	B
Andrews U, MI	B
Antioch Coll, OH	B
Aquinas Coll, MI	B
Ashland U, OH	B
Augustana Coll, IL	B
Baldwin-Wallace Coll, OH	B
Ball State U, IN	B
Beloit Coll, WI	B
Bemidji State U, MN	B
Benedictine U, IL	B
Bethel Coll, IN	B
Bethel U, MN	B
Black Hills State U, SD	B
Bowling Green State U, OH	B
Buena Vista U, IA	B
Calumet Coll of Saint Joseph, IN	B
Calvin Coll, MI	B
Capital U, OH	B
Cardinal Stritch U, WI	B
Carroll Coll, WI	B
Carthage Coll, WI	B
Cedarville U, OH	B
Central Christian Coll of Kansas, KS	A
Central Methodist Coll, MO	B
Central Michigan U, MI	B
Central Missouri State U, MO	B
Central State U, OH	B
Chadron State Coll, NE	B
Chicago State U, IL	B
Coe Coll, IA	B
Coll of Saint Mary, NE	B
The Coll of St. Scholastica, MN	B
Coll of the Ozarks, MO	B
Concordia Coll, MN	B
Concordia U, IL	B
Concordia U, MI	B
Concordia U, NE	B
Concordia U, St. Paul, MN	B
Concordia U Wisconsin, WI	B
Cornerstone U, MI	B
Culver-Stockton Coll, MO	B
Dakota Wesleyan U, SD	B
Dana Coll, NE	B
Defiance Coll, OH	B
Dickinson State U, ND	B
Dordt Coll, IA	B
Drake U, IA	B
East Central U, OK	B
Eastern Michigan U, MI	B

Eureka Coll, IL	B
Evangel U, MO	B
Ferris State U, MI	B
Fort Hays State U, KS	B
The Franciscan U, IA	B
Goshen Coll, IN	B
Governors State U, IL	B
Grace Coll, IN	B
Graceland U, IA	B
Grand Valley State U, MI	B
Hamline U, MN	B
Hannibal-LaGrange Coll, MO	B
Hastings Coll, NE	B
Heidelberg Coll, OH	B
Hope Coll, MI	B
Huntington Coll, IN	B
Illinois Wesleyan U, IL	B
Indiana State U, IN	B
Indiana U Bloomington, IN	B
Indiana U–Purdue U Fort Wayne, IN	B
Indiana U South Bend, IN	B
Indiana U Southeast, IN	B
Judson Coll, IL	B
Kent State U, OH	B
Lakeland Coll, WI	B
Lincoln U, MO	B
Lindenwood U, MO	B
Madonna U, MI	B
Malone Coll, OH	B
Manchester Coll, IN	B
Marian Coll of Fond du Lac, WI	B
Marquette U, WI	B
Miami U, OH	B
Miami U Hamilton, OH	B
Michigan Technological U, MI	B
Minnesota State U Mankato, MN	B
Minnesota State U Moorhead, MN	B
Minot State U, ND	B
Missouri Baptist U, MO	B
Missouri Valley Coll, MO	B
Morningside Coll, IA	B
Mount Mercy Coll, IA	B
Mount Vernon Nazarene U, OH	B
Muskingum Coll, OH	B
Nebraska Wesleyan U, NE	B
North Central Coll, IL	B
North Dakota State U, ND	B
Northern Michigan U, MI	B
Northland Coll, WI	B
Northwestern Oklahoma State U, OK	B
Oakland City U, IN	B
Oakland U, MI	B
Ohio Dominican U, OH	B
Ohio Northern U, OH	B
Ohio U, OH	B
Oklahoma Baptist U, OK	B
Oklahoma Christian U, OK	B
Oklahoma City U, OK	B
Oklahoma Panhandle State U, OK	B
Olivet Nazarene U, IL	B
Oral Roberts U, OK	B
Otterbein Coll, OH	B
Peru State Coll, NE	B
Pillsbury Baptist Bible Coll, MN	B
Pittsburg State U, KS	B

A—associate degree; B—bachelor's degree

Purdue U Calumet, IN — B
Rockford Coll, IL — B
Saginaw Valley State U, MI — B
St. Ambrose U, IA — B
St. Cloud State U, MN — B
Saint Mary's U of Minnesota, MN
Shawnee State U, OH — B
Southeastern Oklahoma State U, OK — B
Southeast Missouri State U, MO — B
Southern Illinois U Edwardsville, IL — B
Southern Nazarene U, OK — B
Southwest Baptist U, MO — B
Southwestern Oklahoma State U, OK — B
Southwest Missouri State U, MO — B
Tabor Coll, KS — B
Taylor U, IN — B
Trinity Christian Coll, IL — B
Tri-State U, IN — B
The U of Akron, OH — B
U of Central Oklahoma, OK — B
U of Cincinnati, OH — A
U of Dayton, OH — B
U of Detroit Mercy, MI — B
U of Evansville, IN — B
The U of Findlay, OH — B
U of Illinois at Chicago, IL — B
U of Indianapolis, IN — B
The U of Iowa, IA — B
U of Michigan–Dearborn, MI — B
U of Minnesota, Duluth, MN — B
U of Minnesota, Twin Cities Campus, MN — B
U of Missouri–Columbia, MO — B
U of Nebraska–Lincoln, NE — B
U of New Orleans, LA — B
U of North Dakota, ND — B
U of Northern Iowa, IA — B
U of Notre Dame, IN — B
U of Oklahoma, OK — B
U of Rio Grande, OH — B
U of St. Francis, IL — B
U of Saint Francis, IN — B
U of St. Thomas, MN — B
U of Sioux Falls, SD — B
The U of South Dakota, SD — B
U of Toledo, OH — B
U of West Florida, FL — B
U of Wisconsin–Eau Claire, WI — B
U of Wisconsin–La Crosse, WI — B
U of Wisconsin–Madison, WI — B
U of Wisconsin–Platteville, WI — B
U of Wisconsin–River Falls, WI — B
U of Wisconsin–Superior, WI — B
U of Wisconsin–Whitewater, WI — B
Upper Iowa U, IA — B
Urbana U, OH — B
Ursuline Coll, OH — B
Valley City State U, ND — B
Valparaiso U, IN — B
Viterbo U, WI — B
Walsh U, OH — B
Washington U in St. Louis, MO — B

Wayne State Coll, NE — B
Wayne State U, MI — B
Western Michigan U, MI — B
Wheaton Coll, IL — B
Wichita State U, KS — B
William Penn U, IA — B
William Woods U, MO — B
Winona State U, MN — B
Wright State U, OH — B
Xavier U, OH — B
York Coll, NE — B
Youngstown State U, OH — B

Science Technologies Related
Lehigh U, PA — B
Madonna U, MI — A,B
U of Wisconsin–Stout, WI — B

Science, Technology and Society
Butler U, IN — B
Cleveland State U, OH — B
Coll of the Ozarks, MO — B
Eastern Michigan U, MI — B
Grinnell Coll, IA — B
Michigan State U, MI — B
Northwestern U, IL — B
Washington U in St. Louis, MO — B

Sculpture
Antioch Coll, OH — B
Aquinas Coll, MI — B
Art Academy of Cincinnati, OH — B
Ball State U, IN — B
Bethany Coll, KS — B
Bowling Green State U, OH — B
The Cleveland Inst of Art, OH — B
Coll for Creative Studies, MI — B
Coll of Visual Arts, MN — B
DePaul U, IL — B
Drake U, IA — B
Grand Valley State U, MI — B
Indiana U Bloomington, IN — B
Indiana U–Purdue U Fort Wayne, IN — B
Kansas City Art Inst, MO — B
Milwaukee Inst of Art and Design, WI — B
Minneapolis Coll of Art and Design, MN — B
Minnesota State U Mankato, MN — B
Minnesota State U Moorhead, MN — B
Northern Michigan U, MI — B
Ohio Northern U, OH — B
The Ohio State U, OH — B
Ohio U, OH — B
St. Cloud State U, MN — B
School of the Art Inst of Chicago, IL — B
Trinity Christian Coll, IL — B
The U of Akron, OH — B
U of Evansville, IN — B
U of Illinois at Urbana–Champaign, IL — B
The U of Iowa, IA — B
U of Kansas, KS — B
U of Michigan, MI — B
U of Michigan–Flint, MI — B
U of Wisconsin–Milwaukee, WI — B

Washington U in St. Louis, MO — B
Western Michigan U, MI — B

Secondary Education
Adrian Coll, MI — B
Albion Coll, MI — B
Alma Coll, MI — B
Andrews U, MI — B
Antioch Coll, OH — B
Aquinas Coll, MI — B
Ashland U, OH — B
Augsburg Coll, MN — B
Augustana Coll, IL — B
Augustana Coll, SD — B
Baldwin-Wallace Coll, OH — B
Ball State U, IN — B
Beloit Coll, WI — B
Bemidji State U, MN — B
Benedictine Coll, KS — B
Benedictine U, IL — B
Bethel Coll, IN — B
Blackburn Coll, IL — B
Black Hills State U, SD — B
Brescia U, KY — B
Briar Cliff U, IA — B
Buena Vista U, IA — B
Butler U, IN — B
Calumet Coll of Saint Joseph, IN — B
Calvary Bible Coll and Theological Seminary, MO — B
Calvin Coll, MI — B
Capital U, OH — B
Cardinal Stritch U, WI — B
Carroll Coll, WI — B
Carthage Coll, WI — B
Cedarville U, OH — B
Central Christian Coll of Kansas, KS — A
Central Coll, IA — B
Central Methodist Coll, MO — B
Central Missouri State U, MO — B
Chadron State Coll, NE — B
Chicago State U, IL — B
Clarke Coll, IA — B
Coe Coll, IA — B
Coll of Saint Benedict, MN — B
Coll of St. Catherine, MN — B
Coll of Saint Mary, NE — B
Coll of the Ozarks, MO — B
Concordia Coll, MN — B
Concordia U, IL — B
Concordia U, MI — B
Concordia U, NE — B
Concordia U, St. Paul, MN — B
Concordia U Wisconsin, WI — B
Concord U, WV — B
Cornell Coll, IA — B
Cornerstone U, MI — B
Dakota State U, SD — B
Dakota Wesleyan U, SD — B
Dana Coll, NE — B
Defiance Coll, OH — B
DePaul U, IL — B
Dickinson State U, ND — B
Doane Coll, NE — B
Dordt Coll, IA — B
Drake U, IA — B
Drury U, MO — B
East Central U, OK — B
Eastern Michigan U, MI — B
Elmhurst Coll, IL — B
Emporia State U, KS — B
Eureka Coll, IL — B
Evangel U, MO — B

Ferris State U, MI — B
Fontbonne U, MO — B
The Franciscan U, IA — B
Gannon U, PA — B
Goshen Coll, IN — B
Grace Bible Coll, MI — B
Graceland U, IA — B
Grace U, NE — B
Grand Valley State U, MI — B
Grinnell Coll, IA — B
Gustavus Adolphus Coll, MN — B
Hamline U, MN — B
Hannibal-LaGrange Coll, MO — B
Harris-Stowe State Coll, MO — B
Hastings Coll, NE — B
Heidelberg Coll, OH — B
Hillsdale Coll, MI — B
Hiram Coll, OH — B
Hope Coll, MI — B
Huntington Coll, IN — B
Illinois Coll, IL — B
Illinois Wesleyan U, IL — B
Indiana U Bloomington, IN — B
Indiana U East, IN — B
Indiana U Northwest, IN — B
Indiana U–Purdue U Fort Wayne, IN — B
Indiana U–Purdue U Indianapolis, IN — B
Indiana U South Bend, IN — B
Indiana U Southeast, IN — B
Iowa State U of Science and Technology, IA — B
Iowa Wesleyan Coll, IA — B
Jamestown Coll, ND — B
John Carroll U, OH — B
Judson Coll, IL — B
Kansas State U, KS — B
Lake Forest Coll, IL — B
Lakeland Coll, WI — B
Lake Superior State U, MI — B
Lawrence U, WI — B
Lewis U, IL — B
Lindenwood U, MO — B
Loras Coll, IA — B
MacMurray Coll, IL — B
Madonna U, MI — B
Maharishi U of Management, IA — B
Manchester Coll, IN — B
Marian Coll, IN — B
Marian Coll of Fond du Lac, WI — B
Marietta Coll, OH — B
Marquette U, WI — B
Martin U, IN — B
Maryville U of Saint Louis, MO — B
McKendree Coll, IL — B
McPherson Coll, KS — B
Miami U, OH — B
Michigan Technological U, MI — B
MidAmerica Nazarene U, KS — B
Minnesota State U Mankato, MN — B
Minnesota State U Moorhead, MN — B
Missouri Southern State U, MO — B
Missouri Valley Coll, MO — B
Monmouth Coll, IL — B
Morningside Coll, IA — B
Mount Marty Coll, SD — B
Mount Mary Coll, WI — B

Majors and Degrees
Secondary Education

Mount Mercy Coll, IA — B
Mount Vernon Nazarene U, OH — B
Muskingum Coll, OH — B
Newman U, KS — B
North Central Coll, IL — B
North Central U, MN — B
Northeastern State U, OK — B
Northern Michigan U, MI — B
Northern State U, SD — B
Northland Coll, WI — B
North Park U, IL — B
Northwestern Coll, IA — B
Northwestern Oklahoma State U, OK — B
Northwestern U, IL — B
Oakland City U, IN — B
Oakland U, MI — B
Ohio Dominican U, OH — B
Ohio Northern U, OH — B
Ohio U, OH — B
Ohio Wesleyan U, OH — B
Oklahoma Baptist U, OK — B
Oklahoma Christian U, OK — B
Oklahoma City U, OK — B
Oklahoma Panhandle State U, OK — B
Oklahoma State U, OK — B
Olivet Coll, MI — B
Olivet Nazarene U, IL — B
Otterbein Coll, OH — B
Peru State Coll, NE — B
Pillsbury Baptist Bible Coll, MN — B
Pittsburg State U, KS — B
Purdue U Calumet, IN — B
Reformed Bible Coll, MI — B
Ripon Coll, WI — B
Rockhurst U, MO — B
Roosevelt U, IL — B
St. Ambrose U, IA — B
St. Cloud State U, MN — B
Saint John's U, MN — B
Saint Joseph's Coll, IN — B
Saint Mary-of-the-Woods Coll, IN — B
Shawnee State U, OH — B
Siena Heights U, MI — B
Simpson Coll, IA — B
South Dakota State U, SD — B
Southeastern Oklahoma State U, OK — B
Southern Nazarene U, OK — B
Southwest Baptist U, MO — B
Southwestern Oklahoma State U, OK — B
Spring Arbor U, MI — B
Tabor Coll, KS — B
Taylor U, IN — B
Trinity Christian Coll, IL — B
Trinity International U, IL — B
Tri-State U, IN — B
Union Coll, NE — B
The U of Akron, OH — B
U of Central Oklahoma, OK — B
U of Cincinnati, OH — B
U of Dayton, OH — B
U of Detroit Mercy, MI — B
U of Dubuque, IA — B
U of Evansville, IN — B
The U of Findlay, OH — B
U of Illinois at Chicago, IL — B
U of Illinois at Springfield, IL — B
U of Indianapolis, IN — B

The U of Iowa, IA — B
U of Kansas, KS — B
U of Michigan, MI — B
U of Michigan–Dearborn, MI — B
U of Minnesota, Morris, MN — B
U of Missouri–Columbia, MO — B
U of Missouri–Kansas City, MO — B
U of Missouri–Rolla, MO — B
U of Missouri–St. Louis, MO — B
U of Nebraska at Omaha, NE — B
U of Rio Grande, OH — B
U of Saint Francis, IN — B
U of Sioux Falls, SD — B
The U of South Dakota, SD — B
U of Toledo, OH — B
U of Wisconsin–La Crosse, WI — B
U of Wisconsin–Madison, WI — B
U of Wisconsin–Milwaukee, WI — B
U of Wisconsin–Oshkosh, WI — B
U of Wisconsin–Platteville, WI — B
U of Wisconsin–River Falls, WI — B
U of Wisconsin–Stevens Point, WI — B
U of Wisconsin–Whitewater, WI — B
Urbana U, OH — B
Valley City State U, ND — B
Valparaiso U, IN — B
Vennard Coll, IA — A,B
Walsh U, OH — B
Wartburg Coll, IA — B
Washington U in St. Louis, MO — B
Webster U, MO — B
Westminster Coll, MO — B
Wichita State U, KS — B
William Jewell Coll, MO — B
William Penn U, IA — B
William Woods U, MO — B
Winona State U, MN — B
Wright State U, OH — B
York Coll, NE — B
Youngstown State U, OH — B

Secondary School Administration/Principalship
Eastern Michigan U, MI — B

Securities Services Administration
Southwestern Coll, KS — B

Security and Loss Prevention
Youngstown State U, OH — A,B

Security and Protective Services Related
Eastern Michigan U, MI — B
Franklin U, OH — B
Lewis U, IL — B
North Dakota State U, ND — B
Ohio U, OH — A
St. Ambrose U, IA — B

Selling Skills and Sales
The U of Akron, OH — A,B
Youngstown State U, OH — B

Sign Language Interpretation and Translation
Bethel Coll, IN — A,B
Coll of St. Catherine, MN — A
Columbia Coll Chicago, IL — B
Goshen Coll, IN — B
Indiana U–Purdue U Indianapolis, IN — B
MacMurray Coll, IL — B
North Central U, MN — A,B
William Woods U, MO — B

Slavic Languages
Indiana U Bloomington, IN — B
Northwestern U, IL — B
U of Chicago, IL — B
U of Illinois at Chicago, IL — B
U of Kansas, KS — B
U of Wisconsin–Madison, WI — B
U of Wisconsin–Milwaukee, WI — B
Wayne State U, MI — B

Slavic Studies
Lawrence U, WI — B
Northwestern U, IL — B

Small Business Administration
Central Christian Coll of Kansas, KS — A,B
Kendall Coll, IL — B
Northern Michigan U, MI — B

Small Engine Mechanics and Repair Technology
North Dakota State Coll of Science, ND — A

Social and Philosophical Foundations of Education
Eastern Michigan U, MI — B
Northwestern U, IL — B
Washington U in St. Louis, MO — B

Social Psychology
Central Christian Coll of Kansas, KS — A
Lawrence U, WI — B
Loyola U Chicago, IL — B
Maryville U of Saint Louis, MO — B
Park U, MO — A,B
U of Wisconsin–Superior, WI — B

Social Sciences
Adrian Coll, MI — A,B
Alma Coll, MI — B
Alverno Coll, WI — B
Ancilla Coll, IN — A
Andrews U, MI — B
Antioch Coll, OH — B
Aquinas Coll, MI — B
Ashland U, OH — B
Augsburg Coll, MN — B
Ball State U, IN — B
Bemidji State U, MN — B
Benedictine Coll, KS — B
Benedictine U, IL — B
Bethany Lutheran Coll, MN — B
Bethel Coll, IN — B
Bethel U, MN — B
Black Hills State U, SD — B
Bluffton Coll, OH — B
Brescia U, KY — B
Buena Vista U, IA — B
Calvin Coll, MI — B

Cardinal Stritch U, WI — B
Carthage Coll, WI — B
Central Christian Coll of Kansas, KS — A
Central Coll, IA — B
Central Michigan U, MI — B
Clarkson U — B
Cleveland State U, OH — B
Coll of Saint Benedict, MN — B
Coll of St. Catherine, MN — B
Coll of Saint Mary, NE — B
The Coll of St. Scholastica, MN — B
Concordia U, MI — B
Concordia U, NE — B
Crown Coll, MN — A
Dana Coll, NE — B
Defiance Coll, OH — B
DePaul U, IL — B
Dickinson State U, ND — B
Doane Coll, NE — B
Dominican U, IL — B
Dordt Coll, IA — B
Eastern Michigan U, MI — B
Edgewood Coll, WI — B
Emporia State U, KS — B
Eureka Coll, IL — B
Evangel U, MO — A,B
Fontbonne U, MO — B
The Franciscan U, IA — B
Governors State U, IL — B
Graceland U, IA — B
Grand Valley State U, MI — B
Gustavus Adolphus Coll, MN — B
Hamline U, MN — B
Judson Coll, IL — B
Kansas State U, KS — B
Kansas Wesleyan U, KS — B
Kent State U, OH — B
Lake Erie Coll, OH — B
Lake Superior State U, MI — B
Lehigh U, PA — B
Lincoln U, MO — B
Marian Coll of Fond du Lac, WI — B
Marygrove Coll, MI — B
Mayville State U, ND — B
McKendree Coll, IL — B
McPherson Coll, KS — B
Metropolitan State U, MN — B
Michigan State U, MI — B
Michigan Technological U, MI — B
Minnesota State U Mankato, MN — B
Minot State U, ND — B
Missouri Baptist U, MO — B
Mount Vernon Nazarene U, OH — B
Muskingum Coll, OH — B
National-Louis U, IL — B
North Carolina Ag and Tech State U, NC — B
North Central Coll, IL — B
North Dakota State U, ND — B
Northern Michigan U, MI — B
Northland Coll, WI — B
North Park U, IL — B
Northwestern Coll, MN — B
Northwestern Oklahoma State U, OK — B
Oakland City U, IN — B
The Ohio State U, OH — B
Ohio U, OH — A,B
Ohio U–Zanesville, OH — A

A—associate degree; B—bachelor's degree

Oklahoma Baptist U, OK	B
Oklahoma Panhandle State U, OK	B
Olivet Coll, MI	B
Olivet Nazarene U, IL	B
Peru State Coll, NE	B
Pittsburg State U, KS	B
Purdue U, IN	B
Rockford Coll, IL	B
Rockhurst U, MO	B
Roosevelt U, IL	B
St. Cloud State U, MN	B
St. Gregory's U, OK	B
Saint John's U, MN	B
Saint Louis U, MO	B
Saint Mary-of-the-Woods Coll, IN	B
Saint Mary's U of Minnesota, MN	B
Saint Xavier U, IL	B
Shawnee State U, OH	A,B
Shimer Coll, IL	B
Siena Heights U, MI	B
Silver Lake Coll, WI	B
Simpson Coll, IA	B
Southern Illinois U Carbondale, IL	B
Southwest Baptist U, MO	B
Spring Arbor U, MI	B
Tabor Coll, KS	B
Taylor U, IN	B
Trinity International U, IL	B
Tri-State U, IN	A,B
Union Coll, NE	B
Union Inst & U, OH	B
The U of Akron, OH	B
U of Chicago, IL	B
U of Cincinnati, OH	A,B
The U of Findlay, OH	A,B
U of Mary, ND	B
U of Michigan, MI	B
U of Michigan–Dearborn, MI	B
U of Michigan–Flint, MI	B
U of Minnesota, Morris, MN	B
U of North Dakota, ND	B
U of Rio Grande, OH	B
U of St. Thomas, MN	B
U of Sioux Falls, SD	A,B
U of Southern Indiana, IN	A,B
U of Toledo, OH	A
U of West Florida, FL	B
U of Wisconsin–Madison, WI	B
U of Wisconsin–Platteville, WI	B
U of Wisconsin–River Falls, WI	B
U of Wisconsin–Stevens Point, WI	B
U of Wisconsin–Superior, WI	B
U of Wisconsin–Whitewater, WI	B
Upper Iowa U, IA	B
Valley City State U, ND	B
Valparaiso U, IN	A
Viterbo U, WI	B
Washington U in St. Louis, MO	B
Wayne State Coll, NE	B
Webster U, MO	B
Western Michigan U, MI	B
William Tyndale Coll, MI	B
Winona State U, MN	B
Wisconsin Lutheran Coll, WI	B
Wittenberg U, OH	B
Youngstown State U, OH	B

Social Sciences Related

Bethel Coll, KS	B
Central Michigan U, MI	B
Cleveland State U, OH	B
Eastern Michigan U, MI	B
Greenville Coll, IL	B
Lehigh U, PA	B
Northwestern U, IL	B
Roosevelt U, IL	B
Saint Mary's U of Minnesota, MN	B
Transylvania U, KY	B
The U of Akron, OH	B
U of West Florida, FL	B
Washington U in St. Louis, MO	B

Social Science Teacher Education

Alma Coll, MI	B
Alverno Coll, WI	B
Buena Vista U, IA	B
Carroll Coll, WI	B
Central Christian Coll of Kansas, KS	A
Central Methodist Coll, MO	B
Central Michigan U, MI	B
Chadron State Coll, NE	B
The Coll of St. Scholastica, MN	B
Concordia U, IL	B
Concordia U, NE	B
Cornerstone U, MI	B
Dana Coll, NE	B
Dordt Coll, IA	B
Eastern Illinois U, IL	B
Eastern Michigan U, MI	B
Emporia State U, KS	B
Grace U, NE	B
Hastings Coll, NE	B
Lindenwood U, MO	B
Marquette U, WI	B
Mayville State U, ND	B
McKendree Coll, IL	B
Michigan State U, MI	B
Millikin U, IL	B
Minot State U, ND	B
Nebraska Wesleyan U, NE	B
North Dakota State U, ND	B
Northern Michigan U, MI	B
Oakland City U, IN	B
Oklahoma Baptist U, OK	B
St. Ambrose U, IA	B
Saint Mary's U of Minnesota, MN	B
Southern Nazarene U, OK	B
Southwest Baptist U, MO	B
Southwestern Oklahoma State U, OK	B
Taylor U, IN	B
Union Coll, NE	B
The U of Akron, OH	B
U of Detroit Mercy, MI	B
U of Illinois at Chicago, IL	B
U of Mary, ND	B
U of Minnesota, Twin Cities Campus, MN	B
U of Nebraska–Lincoln, NE	B
U of Northern Iowa, IA	B
U of Rio Grande, OH	B
The U of South Dakota, SD	B
U of West Florida, FL	B
U of Wisconsin–River Falls, WI	B
U of Wisconsin–Superior, WI	B
Upper Iowa U, IA	B

Valley City State U, ND	B
Valparaiso U, IN	B
Wartburg Coll, IA	B
Washington U in St. Louis, MO	B
Western Michigan U, MI	B
William Penn U, IA	B
York Coll, NE	B
Youngstown State U, OH	B

Social Studies Teacher Education

Alma Coll, MI	B
Alverno Coll, WI	B
Aquinas Coll, MI	B
Augustana Coll, SD	B
Bethany Coll, KS	B
Bethel Coll, IN	B
Bethel U, MN	B
Bowling Green State U, OH	B
Brescia U, KY	B
Calumet Coll of Saint Joseph, IN	B
Capital U, OH	B
Carroll Coll, WI	B
Cedarville U, OH	B
Central Christian Coll of Kansas, KS	A
Central Michigan U, MI	A,B
Central Missouri State U, MO	B
Central State U, OH	B
Coll of St. Catherine, MN	B
Concordia Coll, MN	B
Concordia U, MI	B
Concordia U, St. Paul, MN	B
Cornerstone U, MI	B
Crown Coll, MN	B
Cumberland Coll, KY	B
Dakota Wesleyan U, SD	B
Dordt Coll, IA	B
Eastern Michigan U, MI	B
Franklin Coll, IN	B
Grand Valley State U, MI	B
Greenville Coll, IL	B
Gustavus Adolphus Coll, MN	B
Hastings Coll, NE	B
Hope Coll, MI	B
Illinois State U, IL	B
Indiana State U, IN	B
Indiana U Bloomington, IN	B
Indiana U Northwest, IN	B
Indiana U–Purdue U Fort Wayne, IN	B
Indiana U–Purdue U Indianapolis, IN	B
Indiana U South Bend, IN	B
Indiana U Southeast, IN	B
Kent State U, OH	B
Madonna U, MI	B
Malone Coll, OH	B
Marquette U, WI	B
Miami U, OH	B
Miami U Hamilton, OH	B
MidAmerica Nazarene U, KS	B
Minnesota State U Mankato, MN	B
Minnesota State U Moorhead, MN	B
Mount Vernon Nazarene U, OH	B
Northern Michigan U, MI	B
Northwestern Coll, MN	B
Oakland City U, IN	B
Ohio Dominican U, OH	B
Ohio Northern U, OH	B
Ohio U, OH	B

Ohio Wesleyan U, OH	B
Oklahoma Baptist U, OK	B
Oklahoma Christian U, OK	B
Oral Roberts U, OK	B
Pillsbury Baptist Bible Coll, MN	B
Pittsburg State U, KS	B
St. Gregory's U, OK	B
St. Olaf Coll, MN	B
Shawnee State U, OH	B
Southeastern Oklahoma State U, OK	B
Southeast Missouri State U, MO	B
Southern Nazarene U, OK	B
Southwest Baptist U, MO	B
Tri-State U, IN	B
The U of Akron, OH	B
U of Central Oklahoma, OK	B
U of Detroit Mercy, MI	B
U of Illinois at Urbana–Champaign, IL	B
U of Indianapolis, IN	B
The U of Iowa, IA	B
U of Minnesota, Duluth, MN	B
U of Missouri–Columbia, MO	B
U of Missouri–St. Louis, MO	B
U of New Orleans, LA	B
U of Northern Iowa, IA	B
U of Oklahoma, OK	B
U of St. Francis, IL	B
U of Saint Francis, IN	B
U of St. Thomas, MN	B
U of Toledo, OH	B
U of Wisconsin–Eau Claire, WI	B
U of Wisconsin–La Crosse, WI	B
U of Wisconsin–River Falls, WI	B
U of Wisconsin–Superior, WI	B
Ursuline Coll, OH	B
Viterbo U, WI	B
Waldorf Coll, IA	B
Washington U in St. Louis, MO	B
Wayne State U, MI	B
Wheaton Coll, IL	B
Wright State U, OH	B
York Coll, NE	B
Youngstown State U, OH	B

Social Work

Adrian Coll, MI	B
Andrews U, MI	B
Ashland U, OH	B
Augsburg Coll, MN	B
Augustana Coll, SD	B
Aurora U, IL	B
Avila U, MO	B
Ball State U, IN	B
Bemidji State U, MN	B
Bethany Coll, KS	B
Bethel Coll, KS	B
Bethel U, MN	B
Bluffton Coll, OH	B
Bowling Green State U, OH	B
Bradley U, IL	B
Brescia U, KY	B
Briar Cliff U, IA	B
Buena Vista U, IA	B
Calvin Coll, MI	B
Capital U, OH	B
Carthage Coll, WI	B
Cedarville U, OH	B

Central Christian Coll of Kansas, KS	A	Minot State U, ND	B	U of St. Francis, IL	B	Cameron U, OK	B
Central Michigan U, MI	B	Missouri Western State Coll, MO	B	U of Saint Francis, IN	B	Capital U, OH	B
Central Missouri State U, MO	B	Mount Mary Coll, WI	B	U of St. Thomas, MN	B	Cardinal Stritch U, WI	B
Central State U, OH	B	Mount Mercy Coll, IA	B	U of Sioux Falls, SD	B	Carleton Coll, MN	B
Chadron State Coll, NE	B	Mount Vernon Nazarene U, OH	B	The U of South Dakota, SD	B	Carroll Coll, WI	B
Clarke Coll, IA	B	Nebraska Wesleyan U, NE	B	U of Southern Indiana, IN	B	Carthage Coll, WI	B
Cleveland State U, OH	B	North Carolina Ag and Tech State U, NC	B	U of Toledo, OH	A,B	Case Western Reserve U, OH	B
Coll of Mount St. Joseph, OH	B	Northeastern Illinois U, IL	B	U of West Florida, FL	B	Cedarville U, OH	B
Coll of Saint Benedict, MN	B	Northeastern State U, OK	B	U of Wisconsin–Eau Claire, WI	B	Central Christian Coll of Kansas, KS	A
Coll of St. Catherine, MN	B	Northern Michigan U, MI	B	U of Wisconsin–Green Bay, WI	A,B	Central Coll, IA	B
The Coll of St. Scholastica, MN	B	Northern State U, SD	A	U of Wisconsin–Madison, WI	B	Central Methodist Coll, MO	B
Coll of the Ozarks, MO	B	Northwestern Coll, IA	B	U of Wisconsin–Milwaukee, WI	B	Central Michigan U, MI	B
Columbia Coll, MO	B	Northwestern Oklahoma State U, OK	B	U of Wisconsin–Oshkosh, WI	B	Central Missouri State U, MO	B
Concordia Coll, MN	B	Ohio Dominican U, OH	B	U of Wisconsin–River Falls, WI	B	Central State U, OH	B
Concordia U, IL	B	The Ohio State U, OH	B	U of Wisconsin–Superior, WI	B	Chadron State Coll, NE	B
Concordia U Wisconsin, WI	B	Ohio U, OH	B	U of Wisconsin–Whitewater, WI	B	Chicago State U, IL	B
Concord U, WV	B	Oklahoma Baptist U, OK	B	Ursuline Coll, OH	B	Clarke Coll, IA	B
Cornerstone U, MI	B	Oral Roberts U, OK	B	Valparaiso U, IN	B	Clarkson U	B
Creighton U, NE	B	Pittsburg State U, KS	B	Viterbo U, WI	B	Cleveland State U, OH	B
Cumberland Coll, KY	B	Presentation Coll, SD	B	Wartburg Coll, IA	B	Coe Coll, IA	B
Dana Coll, NE	B	Purdue U Calumet, IN	B	Washburn U, KS	B	Coll of Mount St. Joseph, OH	B
Defiance Coll, OH	B	Quincy U, IL	B	Wayne State U, MI	B	Coll of Saint Benedict, MN	B
Dickinson State U, ND	B	Reformed Bible Coll, MI	B	Western Illinois U, IL	B	Coll of St. Catherine, MN	B
Dordt Coll, IA	B	Rockford Coll, IL	B	Western Michigan U, MI	B	Coll of the Ozarks, MO	B
East Central U, OK	B	Saginaw Valley State U, MI	B	Wichita State U, KS	B	The Coll of Wooster, OH	B
Eastern Michigan U, MI	B	St. Augustine Coll, IL	B	William Woods U, MO	B	Columbia Coll, MO	B
Evangel U, MO	B	St. Cloud State U, MN	B	Winona State U, MN	B	Concordia Coll, MN	B
Ferris State U, MI	B	Saint John's U, MN	B	Wright State U, OH	A,B	Concordia U, IL	B
Fort Hays State U, KS	B	Saint Joseph's Coll, IN	B	Xavier U, OH	B	Concordia U, NE	B
Franciscan U of Steubenville, OH	B	Saint Louis U, MO	B	Youngstown State U, OH	A,B	Concordia U, St. Paul, MN	B
Gannon U, PA	B	Saint Mary's Coll, IN	B			Concord U, WV	B
Goshen Coll, IN	B	St. Olaf Coll, MN	B	**Social Work Related**		Cornell Coll, IA	B
Governors State U, IL	B	Siena Heights U, MI	A,B	Miami U Hamilton, OH	B	Cornerstone U, MI	B
Grace Coll, IN	B	Southeast Missouri State U, MO	B			Creighton U, NE	B
Graceland U, IA	B	Southern Illinois U Carbondale, IL	B	**Sociobiology**		Culver-Stockton Coll, MO	B
Grand Valley State U, MI	B	Southern Illinois U Edwardsville, IL	B	Beloit Coll, WI	B	Dakota Wesleyan U, SD	B
Greenville Coll, IL	B	Southern Nazarene U, OK	B			Dana Coll, NE	B
Haskell Indian Nations U, KS	A	Southwestern Oklahoma State U, OK	B	**Sociology**		Denison U, OH	B
Hope Coll, MI	B	Southwest Missouri State U, MO	B	Adrian Coll, MI	A,B	DePaul U, IL	B
Illinois State U, IL	B	Spring Arbor U, MI	B	Albion Coll, MI	B	DePauw U, IN	B
Indiana State U, IN	B	Taylor U, IN	B	Alma Coll, MI	B	Doane Coll, NE	B
Indiana U Bloomington, IN	B	Taylor U Fort Wayne, IN	B	Andrews U, MI	B	Dominican U, IL	B
Indiana U East, IN	A,B	Trinity Christian Coll, IL	B	Antioch Coll, OH	B	Dordt Coll, IA	B
Indiana U–Purdue U Indianapolis, IN	B	Union Coll, NE	B	Aquinas Coll, MI	B	Drake U, IA	B
Kansas State U, KS	B	Union Inst & U, OH	B	Ashland U, OH	B	Earlham Coll, IN	B
Kilian Comm Coll, SD	A	The U of Akron, OH	B	Augsburg Coll, MN	B	East Central U, OK	B
Lewis U, IL	B	U of Cincinnati, OH	A,B	Augustana Coll, IL	B	Eastern Illinois U, IL	B
Lindenwood U, MO	B	U of Detroit Mercy, MI	B	Augustana Coll, SD	B	Eastern Michigan U, MI	B
Loras Coll, IA	B	The U of Findlay, OH	B	Aurora U, IL	B	Edgewood Coll, WI	B
Lourdes Coll, OH	B	U of Illinois at Chicago, IL	B	Avila U, MO	B	Elmhurst Coll, IL	B
Loyola U Chicago, IL	B	U of Illinois at Springfield, IL	B	Bacone Coll, OK	A	Emporia State U, KS	B
Luther Coll, IA	B	U of Indianapolis, IN	B	Baker U, KS	B	Eureka Coll, IL	B
MacMurray Coll, IL	B	The U of Iowa, IA	B	Baldwin-Wallace Coll, OH	B	Evangel U, MO	B
Madonna U, MI	B	U of Kansas, KS	B	Ball State U, IN	B	Fort Hays State U, KS	B
Malone Coll, OH	B	U of Mary, ND	B	Beloit Coll, WI	B	Franciscan U of Steubenville, OH	B
Manchester Coll, IN	B	U of Michigan–Flint, MI	B	Bemidji State U, MN	B	Franklin Coll, IN	B
Marian Coll of Fond du Lac, WI	B	U of Missouri–Columbia, MO	B	Benedictine Coll, KS	B	Goshen Coll, IN	B
Marquette U, WI	B	U of Missouri–St. Louis, MO	B	Benedictine U, IL	B	Grace Coll, IN	B
Marygrove Coll, MI	B	U of Nebraska at Omaha, NE	B	Bethany Coll, KS	B	Graceland U, IA	B
McKendree Coll, IL	B	U of North Dakota, ND	B	Bethany Lutheran Coll, MN	B	Grand Valley State U, MI	B
Metropolitan State U, MN	B	U of Northern Iowa, IA	B	Bethel Coll, IN	B	Grand View Coll, IA	A
Miami U, OH	B	U of Oklahoma, OK	B	Black Hills State U, SD	B	Greenville Coll, IL	B
Michigan State U, MI	B	U of Rio Grande, OH	A,B	Bluffton Coll, OH	B	Grinnell Coll, IA	B
Minnesota State U Mankato, MN				Bowling Green State U, OH	B	Gustavus Adolphus Coll, MN	B
Minnesota State U Moorhead, MN	B			Bradley U, IL	B	Hamline U, MN	B
				Briar Cliff U, IA	B	Hannibal-LaGrange Coll, MO	B
				Buena Vista U, IA	B	Hanover Coll, IN	B
				Butler U, IN	B	Hastings Coll, NE	B
				Calvin Coll, MI	B	Hillsdale Coll, MI	B

A—associate degree; B—bachelor's degree

Hiram Coll, OH	B
Hope Coll, MI	B
Huntington Coll, IN	B
Illinois Coll, IL	B
Illinois State U, IL	B
Illinois Wesleyan U, IL	B
Indiana State U, IN	B
Indiana U Bloomington, IN	B
Indiana U East, IN	B
Indiana U Kokomo, IN	B
Indiana U Northwest, IN	B
Indiana U–Purdue U Fort Wayne, IN	B
Indiana U–Purdue U Indianapolis, IN	B
Indiana U South Bend, IN	B
Indiana U Southeast, IN	B
Iowa State U of Science and Technology, IA	B
John Carroll U, OH	B
Judson Coll, IL	B
Kalamazoo Coll, MI	B
Kansas State U, KS	B
Kansas Wesleyan U, KS	B
Kent State U, OH	B
Kenyon Coll, OH	B
Knox Coll, IL	B
Lake Erie Coll, OH	B
Lake Forest Coll, IL	B
Lakeland Coll, WI	B
Lake Superior State U, MI	B
Lehigh U, PA	B
Lewis U, IL	B
Lincoln Coll, Lincoln, IL	A
Lincoln U, MO	B
Lindenwood U, MO	B
Loras Coll, IA	B
Lourdes Coll, OH	A,B
Loyola U Chicago, IL	B
Luther Coll, IA	B
Macalester Coll, MN	B
Madonna U, MI	B
Manchester Coll, IN	B
Marian Coll, IN	B
Marian Coll of Fond du Lac, WI	B
Marquette U, WI	B
Martin U, IN	B
Maryville U of Saint Louis, MO	B
McKendree Coll, IL	B
McPherson Coll, KS	B
Miami U, OH	B
Miami U Hamilton, OH	B
Michigan State U, MI	B
MidAmerica Nazarene U, KS	B
Millikin U, IL	B
Minnesota State U Mankato, MN	B
Minnesota State U Moorhead, MN	B
Minot State U, ND	B
Missouri Southern State U, MO	B
Missouri Valley Coll, MO	B
Monmouth Coll, IL	B
Mount Mercy Coll, IA	B
Mount Union Coll, OH	B
Mount Vernon Nazarene U, OH	B
Muskingum Coll, OH	B
Nebraska Wesleyan U, NE	B
Newman U, KS	B
North Carolina Ag and Tech State U, NC	B
North Central Coll, IL	B
North Dakota State U, ND	B
Northeastern Illinois U, IL	B
Northeastern State U, OK	B
Northern Illinois U, IL	B
Northern Michigan U, MI	B
Northern State U, SD	B
Northland Coll, WI	B
North Park U, IL	B
Northwestern Coll, IA	B
Northwestern Oklahoma State U, OK	B
Northwestern U, IL	B
Oakland U, MI	B
Oberlin Coll, OH	B
Ohio Dominican U, OH	B
Ohio Northern U, OH	B
The Ohio State U, OH	B
Ohio U, OH	B
Ohio Wesleyan U, OH	B
Oklahoma Baptist U, OK	B
Oklahoma City U, OK	B
Oklahoma State U, OK	B
Olivet Coll, MI	B
Ottawa U, KS	B
Otterbein Coll, OH	B
Park U, MO	B
Peru State Coll, NE	B
Pittsburg State U, KS	B
Principia Coll, IL	B
Purdue U, IN	B
Purdue U Calumet, IN	B
Ripon Coll, WI	B
Rockford Coll, IL	B
Rockhurst U, MO	B
Roosevelt U, IL	B
Saginaw Valley State U, MI	B
St. Ambrose U, IA	B
St. Cloud State U, MN	B
St. Gregory's U, OK	B
Saint John's U, MN	B
Saint Joseph's Coll, IN	B
Saint Louis U, MO	B
Saint Mary's Coll, IN	B
Saint Mary's U of Minnesota, MN	B
St. Norbert Coll, WI	B
St. Olaf Coll, MN	B
Saint Xavier U, IL	B
Shawnee State U, OH	B
Simpson Coll, IA	B
South Dakota State U, SD	B
Southeastern Oklahoma State U, OK	B
Southeast Missouri State U, MO	B
Southern Illinois U Carbondale, IL	B
Southern Illinois U Edwardsville, IL	B
Southern Nazarene U, OK	B
Southwest Baptist U, MO	B
Southwest Missouri State U, MO	B
Spring Arbor U, MI	B
Tabor Coll, KS	B
Taylor U, IN	B
Transylvania U, KY	B
Trinity Christian Coll, IL	B
Truman State U, MO	B
The U of Akron, OH	B
The U of Alabama in Huntsville, AL	B
U of Central Oklahoma, OK	B
U of Chicago, IL	B
U of Cincinnati, OH	B
U of Dayton, OH	B
U of Detroit Mercy, MI	B
U of Dubuque, IA	A,B
U of Evansville, IN	B
The U of Findlay, OH	B
U of Illinois at Chicago, IL	B
U of Illinois at Springfield, IL	B
U of Illinois at Urbana–Champaign, IL	B
The U of Iowa, IA	B
U of Kansas, KS	B
U of Michigan, MI	B
U of Michigan–Dearborn, MI	B
U of Michigan–Flint, MI	B
U of Minnesota, Duluth, MN	B
U of Minnesota, Morris, MN	B
U of Minnesota, Twin Cities Campus, MN	B
U of Missouri–Columbia, MO	B
U of Missouri–Kansas City, MO	B
U of Missouri–St. Louis, MO	B
U of Nebraska at Omaha, NE	B
U of Nebraska–Lincoln, NE	B
U of New Orleans, LA	B
U of North Dakota, ND	B
U of Northern Iowa, IA	B
U of Notre Dame, IN	B
U of Oklahoma, OK	B
U of Rio Grande, OH	A,B
U of Saint Mary, KS	B
U of St. Thomas, MN	B
U of Science and Arts of Oklahoma, OK	B
U of Sioux Falls, SD	B
The U of South Dakota, SD	B
U of Southern Indiana, IN	B
U of Toledo, OH	B
U of Tulsa, OK	B
U of West Florida, FL	B
U of Wisconsin–Eau Claire, WI	B
U of Wisconsin–La Crosse, WI	B
U of Wisconsin–Madison, WI	B
U of Wisconsin–Milwaukee, WI	B
U of Wisconsin–Oshkosh, WI	B
U of Wisconsin–Parkside, WI	B
U of Wisconsin–River Falls, WI	B
U of Wisconsin–Stevens Point, WI	B
U of Wisconsin–Superior, WI	B
U of Wisconsin–Whitewater, WI	B
Upper Iowa U, IA	B
Urbana U, OH	B
Ursuline Coll, OH	B
Valparaiso U, IN	B
Viterbo U, WI	B
Walsh U, OH	B
Wartburg Coll, IA	B
Washburn U, KS	B
Wayne State Coll, NE	B
Wayne State U, MI	B
Webster U, MO	B
Western Illinois U, IL	B
Western Michigan U, MI	B
Westminster Coll, MO	B
Wheaton Coll, IL	B
Wichita State U, KS	B
Wilberforce U, OH	B
William Penn U, IA	B
Winona State U, MN	B
Wittenberg U, OH	B
Wright State U, OH	A,B
Xavier U, OH	A,B
Youngstown State U, OH	B

Soil Conservation

Ball State U, IN	B
The Ohio State U, OH	B
U of Minnesota, Crookston, MN	A
U of Wisconsin–Stevens Point, WI	B

Soil Science and Agronomy

Michigan State U, MI	B
North Dakota State U, ND	B
U of Minnesota, Twin Cities Campus, MN	B
U of Nebraska–Lincoln, NE	B
U of Wisconsin–River Falls, WI	B

South Asian Languages

Northwestern U, IL	B
Oakland U, MI	B
U of Chicago, IL	B

Spanish

Adrian Coll, MI	A,B
Albion Coll, MI	B
Alma Coll, MI	B
Andrews U, MI	B
Antioch Coll, OH	B
Aquinas Coll, MI	B
Ashland U, OH	B
Augsburg Coll, MN	B
Augustana Coll, IL	B
Augustana Coll, SD	B
Baker U, KS	B
Baldwin-Wallace Coll, OH	B
Ball State U, IN	B
Beloit Coll, WI	B
Bemidji State U, MN	B
Benedictine Coll, KS	B
Benedictine U, IL	B
Bethel Coll, KS	B
Bethel U, MN	B
Blackburn Coll, IL	B
Black Hills State U, SD	B
Bluffton Coll, OH	B
Bowling Green State U, OH	B
Bradley U, IL	B
Brescia U, KY	B
Briar Cliff U, IA	B
Buena Vista U, IA	B
Butler U, IN	B
Calvin Coll, MI	B
Capital U, OH	B
Cardinal Stritch U, WI	B
Carleton Coll, MN	B
Carroll Coll, WI	B
Carthage Coll, WI	B
Case Western Reserve U, OH	B
Cedarville U, OH	B
Central Christian Coll of Kansas, KS	A
Central Coll, IA	B
Central Methodist Coll, MO	B
Central Michigan U, MI	B
Central Missouri State U, MO	B
Chadron State Coll, NE	B
Chicago State U, IL	B

College	Degree
Clarke Coll, IA	B
Cleveland State U, OH	B
Coe Coll, IA	B
Coll of Saint Benedict, MN	B
Coll of St. Catherine, MN	B
Coll of the Ozarks, MO	B
The Coll of Wooster, OH	B
Concordia Coll, MN	B
Concordia U, MI	B
Concordia U, NE	B
Concordia U Wisconsin, WI	B
Cornell Coll, IA	B
Cornerstone U, MI	B
Creighton U, NE	B
Dakota Wesleyan U, SD	B
Dana Coll, NE	B
Denison U, OH	B
DePaul U, IL	B
DePauw U, IN	B
Dickinson State U, ND	B
Doane Coll, NE	B
Dominican U, IL	B
Dordt Coll, IA	B
Drury U, MO	B
Earlham Coll, IN	B
Eastern Michigan U, MI	B
Edgewood Coll, WI	B
Elmhurst Coll, IL	B
Evangel U, MO	B
Fort Hays State U, KS	B
Franciscan U of Steubenville, OH	B
Franklin Coll, IN	B
Goshen Coll, IN	B
Grace Coll, IN	B
Graceland U, IA	B
Grand Valley State U, MI	B
Greenville Coll, IL	B
Grinnell Coll, IA	B
Gustavus Adolphus Coll, MN	B
Hamline U, MN	B
Hanover Coll, IN	B
Hastings Coll, NE	B
Heidelberg Coll, OH	B
Hillsdale Coll, MI	B
Hiram Coll, OH	B
Hope Coll, MI	B
Illinois Coll, IL	B
Illinois State U, IL	B
Illinois Wesleyan U, IL	B
Indiana State U, IN	B
Indiana U Bloomington, IN	B
Indiana U Northwest, IN	B
Indiana U–Purdue U Fort Wayne, IN	A,B
Indiana U–Purdue U Indianapolis, IN	B
Indiana U South Bend, IN	B
Indiana U Southeast, IN	B
Iowa State U of Science and Technology, IA	B
John Carroll U, OH	B
Kalamazoo Coll, MI	B
Kansas Wesleyan U, KS	B
Kent State U, OH	B
Kenyon Coll, OH	B
Knox Coll, IL	B
Lake Erie Coll, OH	B
Lake Forest Coll, IL	B
Lakeland Coll, WI	B
Lawrence U, WI	B
Lehigh U, PA	B
Lincoln Coll, Lincoln, IL	A
Lindenwood U, MO	B
Loras Coll, IA	B
Loyola U Chicago, IL	B
Luther Coll, IA	B
Macalester Coll, MN	B
MacMurray Coll, IL	B
Madonna U, MI	B
Malone Coll, OH	B
Manchester Coll, IN	B
Marian Coll, IN	B
Marian Coll of Fond du Lac, WI	B
Marietta Coll, OH	B
Marquette U, WI	B
McPherson Coll, KS	B
Miami U, OH	B
Miami U Hamilton, OH	B
Michigan State U, MI	B
MidAmerica Nazarene U, KS	B
Millikin U, IL	B
Minnesota State U Mankato, MN	B
Minnesota State U Moorhead, MN	B
Minot State U, ND	B
Missouri Southern State U, MO	B
Missouri Western State Coll, MO	B
Monmouth Coll, IL	B
Morningside Coll, IA	B
Mount Mary Coll, WI	B
Mount Union Coll, OH	B
Mount Vernon Nazarene U, OH	B
Muskingum Coll, OH	B
Nebraska Wesleyan U, NE	B
North Central Coll, IL	B
North Dakota State U, ND	B
Northeastern Illinois U, IL	B
Northeastern State U, OK	B
Northern Illinois U, IL	B
Northern Michigan U, MI	B
Northern State U, SD	B
North Park U, IL	B
Northwestern Coll, IA	B
Northwestern Coll, MN	B
Northwestern Oklahoma State U, OK	B
Northwestern U, IL	B
Oakland U, MI	B
Oberlin Coll, OH	B
Ohio Northern U, OH	B
The Ohio State U, OH	B
Ohio U, OH	B
Ohio Wesleyan U, OH	B
Oklahoma Baptist U, OK	B
Oklahoma Christian U, OK	B
Oklahoma City U, OK	B
Oklahoma State U, OK	B
Olivet Nazarene U, IL	B
Oral Roberts U, OK	B
Otterbein Coll, OH	B
Park U, MO	B
Pittsburg State U, KS	B
Principia Coll, IL	B
Purdue U Calumet, IN	B
Ripon Coll, WI	B
Rockford Coll, IL	B
Rockhurst U, MO	B
Roosevelt U, IL	B
Saginaw Valley State U, MI	B
St. Ambrose U, IA	B
St. Cloud State U, MN	B
Saint John's U, MN	B
Saint Louis U, MO	B
Saint Mary-of-the-Woods Coll, IN	B
Saint Mary's Coll, IN	B
Saint Mary's U of Minnesota, MN	B
St. Norbert Coll, WI	B
St. Olaf Coll, MN	B
Saint Xavier U, IL	B
Siena Heights U, MI	B
Simpson Coll, IA	B
South Dakota State U, SD	B
Southeast Missouri State U, MO	B
Southern Illinois U Carbondale, IL	B
Southern Nazarene U, OK	B
Southwest Baptist U, MO	B
Southwest Missouri State U, MO	B
Spring Arbor U, MI	B
Taylor U, IN	B
Transylvania U, KY	B
Trinity Christian Coll, IL	B
Truman State U, MO	B
Union Coll, NE	B
The U of Akron, OH	B
U of Central Oklahoma, OK	B
U of Chicago, IL	B
U of Cincinnati, OH	B
U of Dayton, OH	B
U of Evansville, IN	B
The U of Findlay, OH	B
U of Illinois at Chicago, IL	B
U of Illinois at Urbana–Champaign, IL	B
U of Indianapolis, IN	B
The U of Iowa, IA	B
U of Kansas, KS	B
U of Michigan, MI	B
U of Michigan–Dearborn, MI	B
U of Michigan–Flint, MI	B
U of Minnesota, Duluth, MN	B
U of Minnesota, Morris, MN	B
U of Minnesota, Twin Cities Campus, MN	B
U of Missouri–Columbia, MO	B
U of Missouri–Kansas City, MO	B
U of Missouri–St. Louis, MO	B
U of Nebraska at Omaha, NE	B
U of Nebraska–Lincoln, NE	B
U of New Orleans, LA	B
U of North Dakota, ND	B
U of Northern Iowa, IA	B
U of Notre Dame, IN	B
U of Oklahoma, OK	B
U of St. Thomas, MN	B
The U of South Dakota, SD	B
U of Southern Indiana, IN	B
U of Toledo, OH	B
U of Tulsa, OK	B
U of Wisconsin–Eau Claire, WI	B
U of Wisconsin–Green Bay, WI	A,B
U of Wisconsin–La Crosse, WI	B
U of Wisconsin–Madison, WI	B
U of Wisconsin–Milwaukee, WI	B
U of Wisconsin–Oshkosh, WI	B
U of Wisconsin–Parkside, WI	B
U of Wisconsin–Platteville, WI	B
U of Wisconsin–River Falls, WI	B
U of Wisconsin–Stevens Point, WI	B
U of Wisconsin–Whitewater, WI	B
Valley City State U, ND	B
Valparaiso U, IN	B
Viterbo U, WI	B
Wabash Coll, IN	B
Walsh U, OH	B
Wartburg Coll, IA	B
Washburn U, KS	B
Washington U in St. Louis, MO	B
Wayne State Coll, NE	B
Wayne State U, MI	B
Webster U, MO	B
Western Illinois U, IL	B
Western Michigan U, MI	B
Westminster Coll, MO	B
Wheaton Coll, IL	B
Wichita State U, KS	B
William Jewell Coll, MO	B
William Woods U, MO	B
Winona State U, MN	B
Wisconsin Lutheran Coll, WI	B
Wittenberg U, OH	B
Wright State U, OH	B
Xavier U, OH	A,B
Youngstown State U, OH	B

Spanish and Iberian Studies

College	Degree
Coe Coll, IA	B

Spanish Language Teacher Education

College	Degree
Alma Coll, MI	B
Bethel U, MN	B
Buena Vista U, IA	B
Carroll Coll, WI	B
Cedarville U, OH	B
Central Christian Coll of Kansas, KS	A
Central Michigan U, MI	B
Central Missouri State U, MO	B
Chadron State Coll, NE	B
Coll of St. Catherine, MN	B
Concordia Coll, MN	B
Concordia U, NE	B
Concordia U Wisconsin, WI	B
Dordt Coll, IA	B
Eastern Michigan U, MI	B
Elmhurst Coll, IL	B
Evangel U, MO	B
Franklin Coll, IN	B
Grace Coll, IN	B
Greenville Coll, IL	B
Hope Coll, MI	B
Illinois Wesleyan U, IL	B
Indiana U Bloomington, IN	B
Indiana U Northwest, IN	B
Indiana U–Purdue U Fort Wayne, IN	B
Indiana U–Purdue U Indianapolis, IN	B
Indiana U South Bend, IN	B
Kent State U, OH	B
Lindenwood U, MO	B
Malone Coll, OH	B
Marian Coll of Fond du Lac, WI	B

A—associate degree; B—bachelor's degree

Miami U Hamilton, OH B
MidAmerica Nazarene U, KS B
Minnesota State U
    Moorhead, MN B
Minot State U, ND B
Missouri Western State Coll,
    MO B
North Dakota State U, ND B
Northern Michigan U, MI B
Notre Dame Coll, OH B
Ohio Northern U, OH B
Ohio U, OH B
Ohio Wesleyan U, OH B
Oklahoma Baptist U, OK B
Oral Roberts U, OK B
St. Ambrose U, IA B
Saint Mary's U of Minnesota,
    MN B
Saint Xavier U, IL B
Southeastern Oklahoma State
    U, OK B
Southern Nazarene U, OK B
Southwest Baptist U, MO B
Southwest Missouri State U,
    MO B
Taylor U, IN B
The U of Akron, OH B
U of Illinois at Chicago, IL B
U of Illinois at Urbana–
    Champaign, IL B
U of Indianapolis, IN B
The U of Iowa, IA B
U of Michigan–Flint, MI B
U of Minnesota, Duluth, MN B
U of Missouri–St. Louis, MO B
U of Nebraska–Lincoln, NE B
The U of South Dakota, SD B
U of Toledo, OH B
U of Wisconsin–River Falls,
    WI B
Valley City State U, ND B
Valparaiso U, IN B
Viterbo U, WI B
Washington U in St. Louis,
    MO B
Western Michigan U, MI B
Youngstown State U, OH B

Special Education
Ashland U, OH B
Augustana Coll, SD B
Avila U, MO B
Ball State U, IN B
Benedictine Coll, KS B
Benedictine U, IL B
Black Hills State U, SD B
Bowling Green State U, OH B
Brescia U, KY B
Buena Vista U, IA B
Calvin Coll, MI B
Capital U, OH B
Cardinal Stritch U, WI B
Carthage Coll, WI B
Cedarville U, OH B
Central Missouri State U,
    MO B
Central State U, OH B
Chadron State Coll, NE B
Chicago State U, IL B
Clarke Coll, IA B
Cleveland State U, OH B
Coll of Mount St. Joseph,
    OH B
Coll of Saint Mary, NE B
Concordia U, NE B
Concord U, WV B
Culver-Stockton Coll, MO B

Cumberland Coll, KY B
Dakota State U, SD B
Dakota Wesleyan U, SD B
Dana Coll, NE B
Defiance Coll, OH B
Doane Coll, NE B
East Central U, OK B
Eastern Illinois U, IL B
Eastern Michigan U, MI B
Elmhurst Coll, IL B
Evangel U, MO B
Florida Gulf Coast U, FL B
Fontbonne U, MO B
Gannon U, PA B
Grace Coll, IN B
Grand Valley State U, MI B
Greenville Coll, IL B
Hastings Coll, NE B
Heidelberg Coll, OH B
Huntington Coll, IN B
Illinois State U, IL B
Indiana State U, IN B
Indiana U Bloomington, IN B
Indiana U South Bend, IN B
Indiana U Southeast, IN B
John Carroll U, OH B
Kansas Wesleyan U, KS B
Kent State U, OH B
Lewis U, IL B
Lincoln U, MO B
Lindenwood U, MO B
Loyola U Chicago, IL B
MacMurray Coll, IL B
Madonna U, MI B
Manchester Coll, IN B
Marian Coll, IN B
McPherson Coll, KS B
Miami U, OH B
Miami U Hamilton, OH B
Michigan State U, MI B
Minnesota State U
    Moorhead, MN B
Missouri Southern State U,
    MO B
Missouri Valley Coll, MO B
Morningside Coll, IA B
Mount Marty Coll, SD B
Mount Vernon Nazarene U,
    OH B
Muskingum Coll, OH B
Nebraska Wesleyan U, NE B
North Carolina Ag and Tech
    State U, NC B
Northeastern Illinois U, IL B
Northeastern State U, OK B
Northern Illinois U, IL B
Northern Michigan U, MI B
Northern State U, SD B
Northwestern Oklahoma
    State U, OK B
Oakland U, MI B
Ohio Dominican U, OH B
The Ohio State U, OH B
Ohio U, OH B
Oklahoma Baptist U, OK B
Oral Roberts U, OK B
Peru State Coll, NE B
Purdue U Calumet, IN B
Quincy U, IL B
Roosevelt U, IL B
Saginaw Valley State U, MI B
St. Augustine Coll, IL A
St. Cloud State U, MN B
Saint Mary-of-the-Woods
    Coll, IN B
Shawnee State U, OH B

Southeast Missouri State U,
    MO B
Southern Illinois U
    Carbondale, IL B
Southern Illinois U
    Edwardsville, IL B
Southwestern Oklahoma
    State U, OK B
Southwest Missouri State U,
    MO B
Tabor Coll, KS B
Trinity Christian Coll, IL B
U of Central Oklahoma, OK B
U of Cincinnati, OH B
U of Dayton, OH B
U of Detroit Mercy, MI B
U of Evansville, IN B
The U of Findlay, OH B
U of Illinois at Urbana–
    Champaign, IL B
U of Minnesota, Duluth, MN B
U of Missouri–St. Louis, MO B
U of Northern Iowa, IA B
U of Oklahoma, OK B
U of St. Francis, IL B
U of Saint Francis, IN B
The U of South Dakota, SD B
U of Toledo, OH B
U of West Florida, FL B
U of Wisconsin–Eau Claire,
    WI B
U of Wisconsin–Madison,
    WI B
U of Wisconsin–Milwaukee,
    WI B
U of Wisconsin–Oshkosh,
    WI B
U of Wisconsin–Superior, WI B
U of Wisconsin–Whitewater,
    WI B
Ursuline Coll, OH B
Walsh U, OH B
Wayne State Coll, NE B
Wayne State U, MI B
Webster U, MO B
Western Illinois U, IL B
William Penn U, IA B
William Woods U, MO B
Winona State U, MN B
Xavier U, OH B
York Coll, NE B
Youngstown State U, OH B

Special Education (Administration)
East Central U, OK B
Wright State U, OH B

Special Education (Early Childhood)
U of Northern Iowa, IA B

Special Education (Emotionally Disturbed)
Augsburg Coll, MN B
Bradley U, IL B
Central Michigan U, MI B
Eastern Michigan U, MI B
Hope Coll, MI B
Loras Coll, IA B
Marygrove Coll, MI B
Minnesota State U
    Moorhead, MN B
Oklahoma Baptist U, OK B
Trinity Christian Coll, IL B
U of Detroit Mercy, MI B

U of Toledo, OH B
Wright State U, OH B

Special Education (Gifted and Talented)
Wright State U, OH B

Special Education (Hearing Impaired)
Augustana Coll, SD B
Bowling Green State U, OH B
Eastern Michigan U, MI B
MacMurray Coll, IL B
Michigan State U, MI B
Minot State U, ND B
Ohio U–Chillicothe, OH A
U of Nebraska–Lincoln, NE B
U of Science and Arts of
    Oklahoma, OK
U of Toledo, OH B

Special Education (Mentally Retarded)
Bowling Green State U, OH B
Bradley U, IL B
Central Michigan U, MI B
Eastern Michigan U, MI B
Loras Coll, IA B
Minnesota State U
    Moorhead, MN B
Minot State U, ND B
Northern Michigan U, MI B
Oakland City U, IN B
Oklahoma Baptist U, OK B
Silver Lake Coll, WI B
Trinity Christian Coll, IL B
The U of Akron, OH B
U of Mary, ND B
U of Northern Iowa, IA B
U of Rio Grande, OH B
U of West Florida, FL B
Western Michigan U, MI B
Wright State U, OH B

Special Education (Multiply Disabled)
Bowling Green State U, OH B
Ohio U, OH B
The U of Akron, OH B
U of Detroit Mercy, MI B
U of Northern Iowa, IA B
U of Toledo, OH B
Wright State U, OH B

Special Education (Orthopedic and Other Physical Health Impairments)
Eastern Michigan U, MI B
Wright State U, OH B

Special Education Related
Minot State U, ND A,B
Southeastern Oklahoma State
    U, OK B
The U of Akron, OH B
U of Missouri–Columbia,
    MO B
U of Nebraska–Lincoln, NE B
U of Southern Indiana, IN B
U of Toledo, OH B
Wright State U, OH B

Special Education (Specific Learning Disabilities)
Aquinas Coll, MI B
Baldwin-Wallace Coll, OH B
Bowling Green State U, OH B
Bradley U, IL B
Eastern Michigan U, MI B

Hope Coll, MI — B
Malone Coll, OH — B
Michigan State U, MI — B
Minnesota State U Moorhead, MN — B
Northwestern U, IL — B
Notre Dame Coll, OH — B
Oklahoma Baptist U, OK — B
Silver Lake Coll, WI — B
Trinity Christian Coll, IL — B
The U of Akron, OH — B
U of Detroit Mercy, MI — B
U of Rio Grande, OH — B
U of Toledo, OH — B
Wright State U, OH — B
Youngstown State U, OH — B

Special Education (Speech or Language Impaired)
Eastern Michigan U, MI — B
Minot State U, ND — B
The U of Akron, OH — B
U of Nebraska at Omaha, NE — A
U of Toledo, OH — B
Wayne State U, MI — B

Special Education (Vision Impaired)
Eastern Michigan U, MI — B
U of Toledo, OH — B
Western Michigan U, MI — B

Special Products Marketing
Ball State U, IN — A,B
Concord U, WV — B
Dominican U, IL — B
Ferris State U, MI — A
Iowa State U of Science and Technology, IA — B
Lindenwood U, MO — B
Madonna U, MI — B
Northern Michigan U, MI — A,B
Purdue U Calumet, IN — A
U of Minnesota, Crookston, MN — A
Wayne State Coll, NE — B

Speech and Rhetoric
Ashland U, OH — B
Augsburg Coll, MN — B
Augustana Coll, IL — B
Baker U, KS — B
Ball State U, IN — B
Bemidji State U, MN — B
Blackburn Coll, IL — B
Black Hills State U, SD — B
Bowling Green State U, OH — B
Bradley U, IL — B
Butler U, IN — B
Calvin Coll, MI — B
Capital U, OH — B
Carthage Coll, WI — B
Cedarville U, OH — B
Central Michigan U, MI — B
Central Missouri State U, MO — B
Chadron State Coll, NE — B
Coe Coll, IA — B
Coll of Saint Benedict, MN — B
Coll of St. Catherine, MN — B
Coll of the Ozarks, MO — B
Concordia Coll, MN — B
Concordia U, NE — B
Cornell Coll, IA — B
Cornerstone U, MI — B

Creighton U, NE — B
Cumberland Coll, KY — B
Defiance Coll, OH — B
Denison U, OH — B
Dickinson State U, ND — B
Doane Coll, NE — B
Drake U, IA — B
East Central U, OK — B
Eastern Illinois U, IL — B
Eastern Michigan U, MI — B
Evangel U, MO — B
Ferris State U, MI — A
Governors State U, IL — B
Graceland U, IA — B
Greenville Coll, IL — B
Gustavus Adolphus Coll, MN — B
Hannibal-LaGrange Coll, MO — B
Hastings Coll, NE — B
Hillsdale Coll, MI — B
Illinois Coll, IL — B
Illinois State U, IL — B
Indiana U Bloomington, IN — B
Indiana U South Bend, IN — B
Iowa State U of Science and Technology, IA — B
Judson Coll, IL — B
Kansas Wesleyan U, KS — B
Kent State U, OH — B
Lewis U, IL — B
Madonna U, MI — A,B
Manchester Coll, IN — B
Marietta Coll, OH — B
Marquette U, WI — B
McKendree Coll, IL — B
Miami U, OH — B
Minnesota State U Mankato, MN — B
Minnesota State U Moorhead, MN — B
Minot State U, ND — B
Missouri Valley Coll, MO — B
Monmouth Coll, IL — B
Mount Mercy Coll, IA — B
Nebraska Wesleyan U, NE — B
North Carolina Ag and Tech State U, NC — B
North Central Coll, IL — B
North Dakota State U, ND — B
Northeastern Illinois U, IL — B
Northern Michigan U, MI — B
Northern State U, SD — B
North Park U, IL — B
Northwestern Coll, IA — B
Northwestern Oklahoma State U, OK — B
Northwestern U, IL — B
Ohio U, OH — B
Oklahoma Baptist U, OK — B
Oklahoma Christian U, OK — B
Oklahoma City U, OK — B
Oklahoma State U, OK — B
Olivet Nazarene U, IL — B
St. Cloud State U, MN — B
Saint John's U, MN — B
Simpson Coll, IA — B
South Dakota State U, SD — B
Southeast Missouri State U, MO — B
Southern Illinois U Carbondale, IL — B
Southern Illinois U Edwardsville, IL — B
Southern Nazarene U, OK — B
Truman State U, MO — B

The U of Akron, OH — B
The U of Alabama in Huntsville, AL — B
U of Dubuque, IA — B
U of Illinois at Chicago, IL — B
U of Illinois at Urbana–Champaign, IL — B
The U of Iowa, IA — B
U of Kansas, KS — B
U of Michigan, MI — B
U of Michigan–Dearborn, MI — B
U of Minnesota, Morris, MN — B
U of Nebraska at Omaha, NE — B
U of Northern Iowa, IA — B
U of Sioux Falls, SD — B
U of Wisconsin–La Crosse, WI — B
U of Wisconsin–Platteville, WI — B
U of Wisconsin–River Falls, WI — B
U of Wisconsin–Superior, WI — B
U of Wisconsin–Whitewater, WI — B
Wabash Coll, IN — B
Washburn U, KS — B
Wayne State Coll, NE — B
William Jewell Coll, MO — B
Winona State U, MN — B
Youngstown State U, OH — B

Speech-Language Pathology
Augustana Coll, IL — B
Baker Coll of Muskegon, MI — A
Central Missouri State U, MO — B
Eastern Michigan U, MI — B
Indiana State U, IN — A
Miami U, OH — B
Miami U Hamilton, OH — B
Northern Michigan U, MI — B
Northwestern U, IL — B
Rockhurst U, MO — B
St. Cloud State U, MN — B
Saint Xavier U, IL — B
The U of Akron, OH — B
U of Nebraska–Lincoln, NE — B
U of Northern Iowa, IA — B
U of Oklahoma Health Sciences Center, OK — B
U of Science and Arts of Oklahoma, OK — B
U of Toledo, OH — B
U of Wisconsin–Whitewater, WI — B
Wayne State U, MI — B

Speech Teacher Education
Buena Vista U, IA — B
Capital U, OH — B
Central Christian Coll of Kansas, KS — A
Central Michigan U, MI — B
Central Missouri State U, MO — B
Chadron State Coll, NE — B
Coll of St. Catherine, MN — B
Concordia U, IL — B
Concordia U, MI — B
Concordia U, NE — B
Dana Coll, NE — B
Dordt Coll, IA — B
East Central U, OK — B
Evangel U, MO — B
Hastings Coll, NE — B

Indiana U Bloomington, IN — B
Indiana U–Purdue U Fort Wayne, IN — B
Indiana U–Purdue U Indianapolis, IN — B
Minnesota State U Moorhead, MN — B
North Dakota State U, ND — B
Northwestern Oklahoma State U, OK — B
Oklahoma Baptist U, OK — B
Pillsbury Baptist Bible Coll, MN — B
St. Ambrose U, IA — B
Southeast Missouri State U, MO — B
Southern Nazarene U, OK — B
Southwest Baptist U, MO — B
Taylor U, IN — B
The U of Akron, OH — B
U of Indianapolis, IN — B
The U of Iowa, IA — B
U of Michigan–Flint, MI — B
U of Northern Iowa, IA — B
U of Rio Grande, OH — B
The U of South Dakota, SD — B
William Jewell Coll, MO — B
York Coll, NE — B
Youngstown State U, OH — B

Speech/Theater Education
Augustana Coll, SD — B
Bemidji State U, MN — B
Briar Cliff U, IA — B
Culver-Stockton Coll, MO — B
Dickinson State U, ND — B
Graceland U, IA — B
Hamline U, MN — B
Hastings Coll, NE — B
Lewis U, IL — B
McKendree Coll, IL — B
McPherson Coll, KS — B
Missouri Western State Coll, MO — B
Northwestern Coll, IA — B
Oklahoma City U, OK — B
St. Ambrose U, IA — B
Southwest Baptist U, MO — B
U of Minnesota, Morris, MN — B
U of St. Thomas, MN — B
Wartburg Coll, IA — B
William Woods U, MO — B
York Coll, NE — B

Speech Therapy
Augustana Coll, IL — B
Fontbonne U, MO — B
Indiana U Bloomington, IN — B
Northeastern State U, OK — B
Northwestern U, IL — B
Ohio U, OH — B
St. Cloud State U, MN — B
U of Oklahoma Health Sciences Center, OK — B
U of Toledo, OH — B
U of Wisconsin–Madison, WI — B
U of Wisconsin–River Falls, WI — B

Sport and Fitness Administration
Augustana Coll, SD — B
Baldwin-Wallace Coll, OH — B
Ball State U, IN — B
Bemidji State U, MN — B

A—associate degree; B—bachelor's degree

Bethel Coll, IN — B
Black Hills State U, SD — B
Bluffton Coll, OH — B
Bowling Green State U, OH — B
Buena Vista U, IA — B
Cedarville U, OH — B
Central Christian Coll of Kansas, KS — A
Central Methodist Coll, MO — B
Central Michigan U, MI — B
Cleveland State U, OH — B
Concordia U, NE — B
Concordia U Wisconsin, WI — B
Cornerstone U, MI — B
Crown Coll, MN — B
Defiance Coll, OH — B
Eastern Michigan U, MI — B
Elmhurst Coll, IL — B
Graceland U, IA — B
Greenville Coll, IL — B
Hastings Coll, NE — B
Indiana U Bloomington, IN — B
Iowa Wesleyan Coll, IA — B
Judson Coll, IL — B
Lake Superior State U, MI — A
Lindenwood U, MO — B
Loras Coll, IA — B
Luther Coll, IA — B
MacMurray Coll, IL — B
Malone Coll, OH — B
Marian Coll of Fond du Lac, WI — B
Miami U, OH — B
MidAmerica Nazarene U, KS — B
Millikin U, IL — B
Minnesota State U Mankato, MN — B
Minnesota State U Moorhead, MN — B
Minot State U, ND — B
Missouri Baptist U, MO — B
Missouri Valley Coll, MO — B
Mount Union Coll, OH — B
Mount Vernon Nazarene U, OH — B
National American U, SD — B
Nebraska Wesleyan U, NE — B
North Dakota State U, ND — B
Northern Michigan U, MI — B
Northwood U, MI — A,B
Notre Dame Coll, OH — B
Ohio Northern U, OH — B
Ohio U, OH — B
Olivet Coll, MI — B
Olivet Nazarene U, IL — B
Otterbein Coll, OH — B
Principia Coll, IL — B
Quincy U, IL — B
Rochester Coll, MI — B
St. Ambrose U, IA — B
Shawnee State U, OH — B
Simpson Coll, IA — B
Southeast Missouri State U, MO — B
Southern Nazarene U, OK — B
Southwest Baptist U, MO — B
Southwestern Coll, KS — B
Spring Arbor U, MI — B
Taylor U, IN — B
Tri-State U, IN — B
Union Coll, NE — B
U of Dayton, OH — B
The U of Iowa, IA — B
U of Michigan, MI — B
U of Minnesota, Crookston, MN — B

U of Saint Mary, KS — B
U of Tulsa, OK — B
U of Wisconsin–La Crosse, WI — B
U of Wisconsin–Parkside, WI — B
Valparaiso U, IN — B
Wartburg Coll, IA — B
Wayne State Coll, NE — B
William Penn U, IA — B
Winona State U, MN — B
Xavier U, OH — B
Youngstown State U, OH — B

Statistics
Bowling Green State U, OH — B
Case Western Reserve U, OH — B
Central Michigan U, MI — B
Clarkson U, IN — B
DePaul U, IL — B
Eastern Michigan U, MI — B
Grand Valley State U, MI — B
Indiana U–Purdue U Fort Wayne, IN — B
Iowa State U of Science and Technology, IA — B
Kansas State U, KS — B
Kenyon Coll, OH — B
Kettering U, MI — B
Lehigh U, PA — B
Lincoln Coll, Lincoln, IL — A
Loyola U Chicago, IL — B
Luther Coll, IA — B
Marquette U, WI — B
Miami U, OH — B
Miami U Hamilton, OH — B
Michigan State U, MI — B
Michigan Technological U, MI — B
North Dakota State U, ND — B
Northwestern U, IL — B
Oakland U, MI — B
Ohio Northern U, OH — B
Ohio Wesleyan U, OH — B
Oklahoma State U, OK — B
Purdue U, IN — B
Roosevelt U, IL — B
St. Cloud State U, MN — B
The U of Akron, OH — B
U of Chicago, IL — B
U of Illinois at Chicago, IL — B
U of Illinois at Urbana–Champaign, IL — B
The U of Iowa, IA — B
U of Michigan, MI — B
U of Minnesota, Morris, MN — B
U of Missouri–Columbia, MO — B
U of Missouri–Kansas City, MO — B
U of Wisconsin–Madison, WI — B
U of Wisconsin–Milwaukee, WI — B
Washington U in St. Louis, MO — B
Western Michigan U, MI — B
Winona State U, MN — B
Wright State U, OH — B

Statistics Related
Ohio Northern U, OH — B

Structural Engineering
Clarkson U — B
U of Toledo, OH — B
Western Michigan U, MI — B

Substance Abuse/Addiction Counseling
Bacone Coll, OK — A
Calumet Coll of Saint Joseph, IN — A,B
Coll of St. Catherine, MN — B
Graceland U, IA — B
Indiana U–Purdue U Fort Wayne, IN — B
Kansas Wesleyan U, KS — B
Martin U, IN — B
Metropolitan State U, MN — B
Minot State U, ND — B
National-Louis U, IL — B
Newman U, KS — A,B
St. Augustine Coll, IL — A
St. Cloud State U, MN — B
The U of Akron, OH — A
U of Detroit Mercy, MI — B
U of Mary, ND — B
The U of South Dakota, SD — B
U of Toledo, OH — A

Surgical Technology
Baker Coll of Clinton Township, MI — A
Baker Coll of Flint, MI — A
Baker Coll of Jackson, MI — A
Baker Coll of Muskegon, MI — A
Mercy Coll of Health Sciences, IA — A
Presentation Coll, SD — A
Rochester Comm and Tech Coll, MN — A
Trinity Coll of Nursing and Health Sciences, IL — A
The U of Akron, OH — A
U of Saint Francis, IN — A

Survey Technology
Ferris State U, MI — A,B
Kansas State U, KS — A
Michigan Technological U, MI — B
Morrison Inst of Technology, IL — A
The Ohio State U, OH — B
Purdue U, IN — B
The U of Akron, OH — A,B
U of Wisconsin–Madison, WI — B

Swedish
Augustana Coll, IL — B

System Administration
Academy Coll, MN — A
AIB Coll of Business, IA — A
Bethel Coll, KS — B
Dordt Coll, IA — B
U of Minnesota, Crookston, MN — B

System, Networking, and Lan/Wan Management
Academy Coll, MN — A
American InterContinental U Online, IL — B
Baker Coll of Auburn Hills, MI — A
Carroll Coll, WI — B
ITT Tech Inst, Mount Prospect, IL — A
ITT Tech Inst, Indianapolis, IN — A
ITT Tech Inst, Newburgh, IN — A
ITT Tech Inst, Arnold, MO — A

ITT Tech Inst, Earth City, MO — A
ITT Tech Inst, NE — A
ITT Tech Inst, Green Bay, WI — A
ITT Tech Inst, Greenfield, WI — A
Southern Nazarene U, OK — B
U of Minnesota, Crookston, MN — B
Westwood Coll–Chicago Du Page, IL — B
Westwood Coll–Chicago O'Hare Airport, IL — B
Westwood Coll–Chicago River Oaks, IL — B

Systems Engineering
Case Western Reserve U, OH — B
Missouri Tech, MO — A,B
Oakland U, MI — B
The Ohio State U, OH — B
Ohio U, OH — B
U of Detroit Mercy, MI — B
U of Missouri–Rolla, MO — B
Washington U in St. Louis, MO — B
Wright State U, OH — B

Systems Science and Theory
Indiana U Bloomington, IN — B
Miami U, OH — B
Washington U in St. Louis, MO — B
Wright State U, OH — B

Tamil
U of Chicago, IL — B

Taxation
Capital U, OH — B
Globe Coll, MN — A
Minnesota School of Business–Brooklyn Center, MN — A
Minnesota School of Business-Plymouth, MN — A
Minnesota School of Business-Richfield, MN — A

Teacher Assistant/Aide
Alverno Coll, WI — A
Dordt Coll, IA — A
The U of Akron, OH — A

Technical and Business Writing
Bowling Green State U, OH — B
Cedarville U, OH — B
Chicago State U, IL — B
Clarkson U — B
Ferris State U, MI — A,B
Grand Valley State U, MI — B
Illinois Inst of Technology, IL — B
Iowa State U of Science and Technology, IA — B
Madonna U, MI — B
Metropolitan State U, MN — B
Miami U, OH — B
Miami U Hamilton, OH — B
Michigan State U, MI — B
Michigan Technological U, MI — B
Mount Mary Coll, WI — B
Northern Michigan U, MI — B
Northwestern Coll, MN — B
Ohio Northern U, OH — B
Oklahoma State U, OK — B

Pittsburg State U, KS   B
Southwest Missouri State U, MO   B
U of Michigan–Flint, MI   B
U of Wisconsin–Stout, WI   B
Webster U, MO   B
Youngstown State U, OH   B

Technical Teacher Education
Bowling Green State U, OH   B
Eastern Illinois U, IL   B
North Dakota State Coll of Science, ND   A
The Ohio State U, OH   B
The U of Akron, OH   B
U of Missouri–Columbia, MO   B
U of Wisconsin–Stout, WI   B
Valley City State U, ND   B
Wayne State U, MI   B
Wright State U, OH   B

Technology/Industrial Arts Teacher Education
Central Michigan U, MI   B
Central Missouri State U, MO   B
Chadron State Coll, NE   B
Coll of the Ozarks, MO   B
Concordia U, NE   B
Eastern Michigan U, MI   B
Illinois State U, IL   B
Kent State U, OH   B
Lindenwood U, MO   B
Missouri Southern State U, MO   B
Northern Michigan U, MI   B
The Ohio State U, OH   B
Oklahoma Panhandle State U, OK   B
Pittsburg State U, KS   B
Purdue U, IN   B
St. Cloud State U, MN   B
Southeast Missouri State U, MO   B
Southwestern Oklahoma State U, OK   B
U of Nebraska–Lincoln, NE   B
U of Northern Iowa, IA   B
U of Wisconsin–Stout, WI   B
Valley City State U, ND   B
Viterbo U, WI   B
Western Michigan U, MI   B

Telecommunications
Ball State U, IN   B
Bowling Green State U, OH   B
Butler U, IN   B
Coll of Saint Mary, NE   A
Grand Valley State U, MI   B
Indiana U Bloomington, IN   B
Michigan State U, MI   B
Ohio U, OH   B
Oklahoma Baptist U, OK   B
Roosevelt U, IL   B
U of Wisconsin–Platteville, WI   B
Western Michigan U, MI   B
Winona State U, MN   B
Youngstown State U, OH   B

Theatre Design and Technology
Coe Coll, IA   B
Columbia Coll Chicago, IL   B
DePaul U, IL

Indiana U Bloomington, IN   A
Ohio U, OH   B
Oklahoma City U, OK   B
The U of Akron, OH   B
U of Kansas, KS   B
U of Michigan, MI   B
U of Northern Iowa, IA   B
U of Rio Grande, OH   A
Webster U, MO   B
Western Michigan U, MI   B
William Woods U, MO   B
Wright State U, OH   B
Youngstown State U, OH   B

Theatre Literature, History and Criticism
Buena Vista U, IA   B
DePaul U, IL   B
Northwestern U, IL   B
Ohio U, OH   B
U of Northern Iowa, IA   B
Washington U in St. Louis, MO   B

Theatre/Theatre Arts Management
East Central U, OK   B
Eastern Michigan U, MI   B
Haskell Indian Nations U, KS   A
Luther Coll, IA   B
Miami U Hamilton, OH   B
Ohio Northern U, OH   B
Ohio U, OH   B
St. Cloud State U, MN   B
The U of Iowa, IA   B
Western Michigan U, MI   B

Theological and Ministerial Studies Related
Bacone Coll, OK   A
Brescia U, KY   A,B
God's Bible School and Coll, OH   B
Messenger Coll, MO   B
Northwestern Coll, MN   B
Pillsbury Baptist Bible Coll, MN   A
Quincy U, IL   B
Southwest Baptist U, MO   B
U of Saint Francis, IN   A,B

Theology
Andrews U, MI   B
Augsburg Coll, MN   B
Ave Maria Coll, MI   B
Briar Cliff U, IA   A,B
Calumet Coll of Saint Joseph, IN   B
Calvin Coll, MI   B
Cedarville U, OH   B
Central Christian Coll of Kansas, KS   A,B
Coll of Saint Benedict, MN   B
Coll of St. Catherine, MN   B
Concordia U, IL   B
Concordia U, NE   B
Concordia U, St. Paul, MN   B
Concordia U Wisconsin, WI   B
Creighton U, NE   A,B
Crossroads Coll, MN   B
Crown Coll, MN   B
Dakota Wesleyan U, SD   B
Dordt Coll, IA   B
Elmhurst Coll, IL   B

Franciscan U of Steubenville, OH   A,B
Gannon U, PA   B
Global U of the Assemblies of God, MO   B
Grace Bible Coll, MI   B
Hanover Coll, IN   B
Hillsdale Free Will Baptist Coll, MI   B
Huntington Coll, IN   B
Laura and Alvin Siegal Coll of Judaic Studies, OH   B
Loyola U Chicago, IL   B
Manhattan Christian Coll, KS   B
Marian Coll, IN   A,B
Martin Luther Coll, MN   B
Mount Vernon Nazarene U, OH   B
Newman U, KS   B
North Park U, IL   B
Notre Dame Coll, OH   B
Oakland City U, IN   B
Ohio Dominican U, OH   A,B
Oklahoma Baptist U, OK   B
Olivet Nazarene U, IL   B
Oral Roberts U, OK   B
Quincy U, IL   B
Reformed Bible Coll, MI   B
Rockhurst U, MO   B
Sacred Heart Major Seminary, MI   A
St. Ambrose U, IA   B
St. Gregory's U, OK   B
Saint John's U, MN   B
St. Louis Christian Coll, MO   B
Saint Louis U, MO   B
Saint Mary-of-the-Woods Coll, IN   B
Saint Mary's U of Minnesota, MN   B
Silver Lake Coll, WI   B
Southern Nazarene U, OK   B
Taylor U, IN   B
Trinity Christian Coll, IL   B
Union Coll, NE   B
U of Dubuque, IA   B
U of Mary, ND   B
U of Notre Dame, IN   B
U of St. Francis, IL   B
U of Saint Mary, KS   B
Valparaiso U, IN   B
Vennard Coll, IA   B
Walsh U, OH   B
William Tyndale Coll, MI   A,B
Wisconsin Lutheran Coll, WI   B
Xavier U, OH   A,B

Theology and Religious Vocations Related
Coll of Mount St. Joseph, OH   B
Crossroads Coll, MN   B
Missouri Baptist U, MO   B

Therapeutic Recreation
Ashland U, OH   B
Central Michigan U, MI   B
Coll of Mount St. Joseph, OH   B
Eastern Michigan U, MI   B
Grand Valley State U, MI   B
Indiana Inst of Technology, IN   A,B
Indiana U Bloomington, IN   B

Indiana U–Purdue U Fort Wayne, IN   B
Lake Superior State U, MI   B
Minnesota State U Mankato, MN   B
Northland Coll, WI   B
Ohio U, OH   B
Pittsburg State U, KS   B
St. Cloud State U, MN   B
Southwestern Oklahoma State U, OK   B
The U of Findlay, OH   B
The U of Iowa, IA   B
U of Wisconsin–La Crosse, WI   B
U of Wisconsin–Milwaukee, WI   B
Winona State U, MN   B

Tibetan
U of Chicago, IL   B

Tool and Die Technology
Dunwoody Coll of Technology, MN   A

Tourism and Travel Services Management
AIB Coll of Business, IA   A
Baker Coll of Flint, MI   A
Baker Coll of Muskegon, MI   A
Ball State U, IN   B
Black Hills State U, SD   A,B
Concord U, WV   B
Grand Valley State U, MI   B
Kaplan Coll, IA   A
Lincoln Coll, Lincoln, IL   A
MacCormac Coll, IL   A
Northeastern State U, OK   B
Ohio U, OH   A
Robert Morris Coll, IL   A
St. Cloud State U, MN   A
The U of Akron, OH   A
U of Northwestern Ohio, OH   A
Western Michigan U, MI   B
Youngstown State U, OH   B

Tourism and Travel Services Marketing
AIB Coll of Business, IA   A
Central Missouri State U, MO   B
Ohio U–Southern Campus, OH   A
U of Missouri–Columbia, MO   B
Western Michigan U, MI   B

Tourism Promotion
AIB Coll of Business, IA   A
Bowling Green State U, OH   B

Tourism/Travel Marketing
Eastern Michigan U, MI   B
Ohio U, OH   A

Toxicology
Ashland U, OH   B
Clarkson U   B
Eastern Michigan U, MI   B
Minnesota State U Mankato, MN   B
U of Wisconsin–Madison, WI   B

A—associate degree; B—bachelor's degree

Trade and Industrial Teacher Education

Ball State U, IN	B
Bemidji State U, MN	B
Concordia U, NE	B
Dakota State U, SD	B
Indiana State U, IN	A,B
Iowa State U of Science and Technology, IA	B
Kent State U, OH	B
Madonna U, MI	B
North Carolina Ag and Tech State U, NC	B
Northeastern State U, OK	B
Oklahoma State U, OK	B
Pittsburg State U, KS	B
Purdue U, IN	A
Southern Illinois U Carbondale, IL	B
U of Central Oklahoma, OK	B
U of Nebraska–Lincoln, NE	B
U of Toledo, OH	B
U of West Florida, FL	B
Upper Iowa U, IA	B
Western Illinois U, IL	B
Wright State U, OH	B

Transportation Technology

Baker Coll of Flint, MI	A
North Carolina Ag and Tech State U, NC	B
U of Cincinnati, OH	A,B
U of Toledo, OH	A

Turf and Turfgrass Management

Kent State U, Salem Campus, OH	A
North Dakota State U, ND	B
The Ohio State U, OH	B
Rochester Comm and Tech Coll, MN	A
U of Minnesota, Crookston, MN	B

Turkish

U of Chicago, IL	B

Urban Education and Leadership

Harris-Stowe State Coll, MO	B
U of Missouri–Kansas City, MO	B

Urban Studies/Affairs

Aquinas Coll, MI	B
Augsburg Coll, MN	B
Calvary Bible Coll and Theological Seminary, MO	B
Cleveland State U, OH	B
The Coll of Wooster, OH	B
Crossroads Bible Coll, IN	B
DePaul U, IL	B
Elmhurst Coll, IL	B
Hamline U, MN	B
Harris-Stowe State Coll, MO	B
Indiana U Bloomington, IN	B
Lehigh U, PA	B
Macalester Coll, MN	B
Minnesota State U Mankato, MN	B
Mount Mercy Coll, IA	B
Northeastern Illinois U, IL	B
North Park U, IL	B
Northwestern U, IL	B
Ohio Wesleyan U, OH	B
Rockford Coll, IL	B
Roosevelt U, IL	B

St. Cloud State U, MN	B
Saint Louis U, MO	B
Southern Nazarene U, OK	B
Taylor U Fort Wayne, IN	B
U of Cincinnati, OH	B
U of Minnesota, Duluth, MN	B
U of Minnesota, Twin Cities Campus, MN	B
U of Missouri–Kansas City, MO	B
U of New Orleans, LA	B
U of Toledo, OH	B
U of Wisconsin–Green Bay, WI	A,B
U of Wisconsin–Madison, WI	B
U of Wisconsin–Milwaukee, WI	B
U of Wisconsin–Oshkosh, WI	B
Washington U in St. Louis, MO	B
Wayne State U, MI	B
Wittenberg U, OH	B
Wright State U, OH	B

Urdu

U of Chicago, IL	B

Vehicle and Vehicle Parts and Accessories Marketing

Northwood U, MI	A,B

Vehicle/Equipment Operation

Baker Coll of Flint, MI	A

Vehicle Maintenance and Repair Technologies Related

North Dakota State Coll of Science, ND	A

Veterinary/Animal Health Technology

Argosy U/Twin Cities, MN	A
Baker Coll of Cadillac, MI	A
Baker Coll of Jackson, MI	A
Baker Coll of Muskegon, MI	A
Michigan State U, MI	B
Minnesota School of Business-Richfield, MN	A
North Dakota State U, ND	B
Purdue U, IN	A,B
U of Nebraska–Lincoln, NE	B

Veterinary Sciences

Northland Coll, WI	B

Veterinary Technology

Argosy U/Twin Cities, Eagan, MN	A
Globe Coll, MN	A
Michigan State U, MI	B
Minnesota School of Business–Brooklyn Center, MN	A
Minnesota School of Business-Plymouth, MN	A
National American U, SD	A

Violin, Viola, Guitar and Other Stringed Instruments

Augustana Coll, IL	B
Ball State U, IN	B
Butler U, IN	B
Capital U, OH	B
Cleveland Inst of Music, OH	B
DePaul U, IL	B
Grand Valley State U, MI	B
Hastings Coll, NE	B
Heidelberg Coll, OH	B

Illinois Wesleyan U, IL	B
Lawrence U, WI	B
Northern Michigan U, MI	B
Northwestern U, IL	B
Oberlin Coll, OH	B
Oklahoma City U, OK	B
Olivet Nazarene U, IL	B
Otterbein Coll, OH	B
Pittsburg State U, KS	B
Roosevelt U, IL	B
St. Cloud State U, MN	B
The U of Akron, OH	B
U of Central Oklahoma, OK	B
U of Cincinnati, OH	B
The U of Iowa, IA	B
U of Kansas, KS	B
U of Michigan, MI	B
U of Missouri–Kansas City, MO	B
U of Oklahoma, OK	B
U of Wisconsin–Milwaukee, WI	B
Washburn U, KS	B
Youngstown State U, OH	B

Visual and Performing Arts

American Academy of Art, IL	B
Antioch Coll, OH	B
Bethel Coll, KS	B
The Franciscan U, IA	B
Indiana U East, IN	A
Iowa State U of Science and Technology, IA	B
Lehigh U, PA	B
Loras Coll, IA	B
Northwestern U, IL	B
Oakland U, MI	B
Ohio Northern U, OH	B
Ohio U, OH	B
Quincy U, IL	B
St. Gregory's U, OK	B
St. Olaf Coll, MN	B
School of the Art Inst of Chicago, IL	B
South Dakota State U, SD	B
Southeast Missouri State U, MO	B
Southwest Missouri State U, MO	B
U of Michigan, MI	B
U of Michigan–Flint, MI	B
U of Rio Grande, OH	B
U of St. Francis, IL	B
U of Saint Mary, KS	B
Viterbo U, WI	B
Wichita State U, KS	B

Visual and Performing Arts Related

Baldwin-Wallace Coll, OH	B
Cameron U, OK	B
Coll of Visual Arts, MN	B
Illinois State U, IL	B
Illinois Wesleyan U, IL	B
Ohio Northern U, OH	B
St. Cloud State U, MN	B
School of the Art Inst of Chicago, IL	B
The U of Akron, OH	B
U of Oklahoma, OK	B

Vocational Rehabilitation Counseling

Emporia State U, KS	B
U of Wisconsin–Stout, WI	B
Wright State U, OH	B

Voice and Opera

Andrews U, MI	B
Augustana Coll, IL	B
Ball State U, IN	B
Bethel Coll, IN	B
Black Hills State U, SD	B
Bowling Green State U, OH	B
Butler U, IN	B
Calvary Bible Coll and Theological Seminary, MO	B
Calvin Coll, MI	B
Capital U, OH	B
Cedarville U, OH	B
Central Christian Coll of Kansas, KS	A
Clarke Coll, IA	B
Cleveland Inst of Music, OH	B
Concordia Coll, MN	B
Concordia U, IL	B
Concordia U, NE	B
DePaul U, IL	B
Dordt Coll, IA	B
Drake U, IA	B
East Central U, OK	B
Eastern Michigan U, MI	B
Eureka Coll, IL	B
Grace U, NE	B
Grand Valley State U, MI	B
Hannibal-LaGrange Coll, MO	B
Hastings Coll, NE	B
Heidelberg Coll, OH	B
Huntington Coll, IN	B
Illinois Wesleyan U, IL	B
Indiana U Bloomington, IN	B
Indiana U–Purdue U Fort Wayne, IN	B
Judson Coll, IL	B
Lawrence U, WI	B
Lincoln Coll, Lincoln, IL	A
Lindenwood U, MO	B
MidAmerica Nazarene U, KS	B
Millikin U, IL	B
Minnesota State U Mankato, MN	B
Minnesota State U Moorhead, MN	B
Mount Mercy Coll, IA	B
Northeastern State U, OK	B
Northern Michigan U, MI	B
Northern State U, SD	B
North Park U, IL	B
Northwestern Coll, MN	B
Northwestern U, IL	B
Oberlin Coll, OH	B
The Ohio State U, OH	B
Ohio U, OH	B
Oklahoma Baptist U, OK	B
Oklahoma Christian U, OK	B
Oklahoma City U, OK	B
Olivet Nazarene U, IL	B
Otterbein Coll, OH	B
Peru State Coll, NE	B
Pittsburg State U, KS	B
Rochester Coll, MI	B
Roosevelt U, IL	B
St. Cloud State U, MN	B
Southern Nazarene U, OK	B
Southwestern Oklahoma State U, OK	B
Tabor Coll, KS	B
Taylor U, IN	B
Trinity Christian Coll, IL	B
Truman State U, MO	B
The U of Akron, OH	B
U of Central Oklahoma, OK	B

U of Cincinnati, OH — B
U of Illinois at Urbana–Champaign, IL — B
The U of Iowa, IA — B
U of Kansas, KS — B
U of Michigan, MI — B
U of Missouri–Kansas City, MO — B
U of Nebraska at Omaha, NE — B
U of Oklahoma, OK — B
U of Sioux Falls, SD — B
U of Tulsa, OK — B
U of Wisconsin–Milwaukee, WI — B
Valparaiso U, IN — B
Washburn U, KS — B
Washington U in St. Louis, MO — B
Webster U, MO — B
Wilberforce U, OH — B
William Tyndale Coll, MI — B
Winona State U, MN — B
Youngstown State U, OH — B

Water Quality and Wastewater Treatment Management and Recycling Technology
Lake Superior State U, MI — A
Wright State U, OH — A

Water Resources Engineering
Central State U, OH — B

Water, Wetlands, and Marine Resources Management
U of Minnesota, Crookston, MN — B

Web/Multimedia Management and Webmaster
Academy Coll, MN — A
Baker U, KS — B
Dana Coll, NE — B
Davenport U, Dearborn, MI — A,B
Davenport U, Grand Rapids, MI — A,B
Davenport U, Holland, MI — A,B
Davenport U, Kalamazoo, MI — A,B
Davenport U, Warren, MI — A,B
Grace U, NE — B
Greenville Coll, IL — B
ITT Tech Inst, Mount Prospect, IL — A
ITT Tech Inst, Fort Wayne, IN — A
ITT Tech Inst, Indianapolis, IN — A
ITT Tech Inst, Newburgh, IN — A
ITT Tech Inst, Arnold, MO — A
ITT Tech Inst, Earth City, MO — A
ITT Tech Inst, NE — A
ITT Tech Inst, Green Bay, WI — A
ITT Tech Inst, Greenfield, WI — A
U of Dubuque, IA — B
U of St. Francis, IL — B
Westwood Coll–Chicago Du Page, IL — B
Westwood Coll–Chicago Loop Campus, IL — B

Westwood Coll–Chicago O'Hare Airport, IL — B
Westwood Coll–Chicago River Oaks, IL — B

Web Page, Digital/Multimedia and Information Resources Design
Academy Coll, MN — A
The Art Insts International Minnesota, MN — A,B
Baker Coll of Allen Park, MI — A
Bellevue U, NE — B
Capella U, MN — B
The Cleveland Inst of Art, OH — B
Columbia Coll Chicago, IL — B
Dakota State U, SD — B
Dana Coll, NE — B
DePaul U, IL — B
Franklin U, OH — B
Globe Coll, MN — A
The Illinois Inst of Art-Schaumburg, IL — B
ITT Tech Inst, Mount Prospect, IL — A
ITT Tech Inst, Fort Wayne, IN — A
ITT Tech Inst, Indianapolis, IN — A
ITT Tech Inst, Newburgh, IN — A
ITT Tech Inst, Arnold, MO — A
ITT Tech Inst, Earth City, MO — A
ITT Tech Inst, NE — A
ITT Tech Inst, Green Bay, WI — A
ITT Tech Inst, Greenfield, WI — A
Minnesota School of Business–Brooklyn Center, MN — A
Minnesota School of Business-Plymouth, MN — A
Minnesota School of Business-Richfield, MN — A
National American U–Sioux Falls Branch, SD — B
Nebraska Wesleyan U, NE — B
Robert Morris Coll, IL — A
School of the Art Inst of Chicago, IL — B
Silver Lake Coll, WI — B
U of Dubuque, IA — B
U of Wisconsin–Stevens Point, WI — B
Westwood Coll–Chicago Loop Campus, IL — B

Welding Technology
Dunwoody Coll of Technology, MN — A
Ferris State U, MI — A,B
North Dakota State Coll of Science, ND — A
Oakland City U, IN — A
U of Toledo, OH — A
Vatterott Coll, St. Ann, MO — A

Western Civilization
Central Christian Coll of Kansas, KS — A
Grand Valley State U, MI — B
Lincoln Coll, Lincoln, IL — A

Wildlife and Wildlands Science and Management
Coll of the Ozarks, MO — B
Fort Hays State U, KS — B
Grand Valley State U, MI — B
Lake Superior State U, MI — B
Northland Coll, WI — B
The Ohio State U, OH — B
Oklahoma State U, OK — B
Peru State Coll, NE — B
Pittsburg State U, KS — B
Purdue U, IN — B
Purdue U Calumet, IN — B
South Dakota State U, SD — B
Southeastern Oklahoma State U, OK — B
Southwest Missouri State U, MO — B
U of Minnesota, Crookston, MN — A,B
U of Missouri–Columbia, MO — B
U of Wisconsin–Madison, WI — B
U of Wisconsin–Stevens Point, WI — B
Winona State U, MN — A,B

Wildlife Biology
Baker U, KS — B
Ball State U, IN — B
Central Christian Coll of Kansas, KS — A
Grand Valley State U, MI — B
Kansas State U, KS — B
Northeastern State U, OK — B
Northern Michigan U, MI — B
Northland Coll, WI — B
Ohio U, OH — B
St. Cloud State U, MN — B
U of Michigan, MI — B
U of Michigan–Flint, MI — B
Winona State U, MN — B

Wind/Percussion Instruments
Augustana Coll, IL — B
Ball State U, IN — B
Bowling Green State U, OH — B
Butler U, IN — B
Capital U, OH — B
Chicago State U, IL — B
Cleveland Inst of Music, OH — B
Concordia U, IL — B
DePaul U, IL — B
Grand Valley State U, MI — B
Illinois Wesleyan U, IL — B
Indiana U Bloomington, IN — B
Lawrence U, WI — B
Minnesota State U Mankato, MN — B
Minnesota State U Moorhead, MN — B
Northern Michigan U, MI — B
Northwestern U, IL — B
Oberlin Coll, OH — B
Oklahoma Baptist U, OK — B
Oklahoma Christian U, OK — B
Oklahoma City U, OK — B
Olivet Nazarene U, IL — B
Otterbein Coll, OH — B
Peru State Coll, NE — B
Pittsburg State U, KS — B
Roosevelt U, IL — B
Southwestern Oklahoma State U, OK — B
The U of Akron, OH — B

U of Central Oklahoma, OK — B
U of Cincinnati, OH — B
The U of Iowa, IA — B
U of Kansas, KS — B
U of Michigan, MI — B
U of Missouri–Kansas City, MO — B
U of Oklahoma, OK — B
U of Sioux Falls, SD — B
U of Wisconsin–Milwaukee, WI — B

Women's Studies
Albion Coll, MI — B
Antioch Coll, OH — B
Augsburg Coll, MN — B
Augustana Coll, IL — B
Beloit Coll, WI — B
Bowling Green State U, OH — B
Carleton Coll, MN — B
Case Western Reserve U, OH — B
Central Michigan U, MI — B
Coll of St. Catherine, MN — B
The Coll of Wooster, OH — B
Cornell Coll, IA — B
Denison U, OH — B
DePaul U, IL — B
DePauw U, IN — B
Earlham Coll, IN — B
Eastern Michigan U, MI — B
Grand Valley State U, MI — B
Grinnell Coll, IA — B
Hamline U, MN — B
Illinois Wesleyan U, IL — B
Indiana U Bloomington, IN — B
Indiana U–Purdue U Fort Wayne, IN — A,B
Indiana U South Bend, IN — B
Iowa State U of Science and Technology, IA — B
Kansas State U, KS — B
Kenyon Coll, OH — B
Knox Coll, IL — B
Macalester Coll, MN — B
Marquette U, WI — B
Metropolitan State U, MN — B
Minnesota State U Mankato, MN — B
Nebraska Wesleyan U, NE — B
Northeastern Illinois U, IL — B
Northwestern U, IL — B
Oakland U, MI — B
Oberlin Coll, OH — B
The Ohio State U, OH — B
Ohio Wesleyan U, OH — B
Purdue U Calumet, IN — B
Roosevelt U, IL — B
Saint Louis U, MO — B
St. Olaf Coll, MN — B
The U of Iowa, IA — B
U of Kansas, KS — B
U of Michigan, MI — B
U of Michigan–Dearborn, MI — B
U of Minnesota, Duluth, MN — B
U of Minnesota, Morris, MN — B
U of Minnesota, Twin Cities Campus, MN — B
U of Nebraska at Omaha, NE — B
U of Nebraska–Lincoln, NE — B
U of New Orleans, LA — B
U of Oklahoma, OK — B
U of St. Thomas, MN — B
U of Toledo, OH — B

A—associate degree; B—bachelor's degree

U of Wisconsin–Madison, WI	B
U of Wisconsin–Milwaukee, WI	B
U of Wisconsin–Whitewater, WI	B
Washington U in St. Louis, MO	B
Wayne State U, MI	B
Western Illinois U, IL	B
Western Michigan U, MI	B
Wichita State U, KS	B
Wright State U, OH	B

Wood Science and Wood Products/Pulp and Paper Technology

Miami U, OH	B
Pittsburg State U, KS	B
U of Minnesota, Twin Cities Campus, MN	B
U of Wisconsin–Stevens Point, WI	B

Word Processing

Baker Coll of Allen Park, MI	A

Work and Family Studies

Miami U Hamilton, OH	B
Ursuline Coll, OH	B

Youth Ministry

Andrews U, MI	B
Benedictine Coll, KS	B
Bethel Coll, IN	B
Bethel Coll, KS	B
Bethel U, MN	B
Bluffton Coll, OH	B
Calvary Bible Coll and Theological Seminary, MO	B
Cedarville U, OH	B
Central Christian Coll of Kansas, KS	A,B
Concordia U Wisconsin, WI	B
Crossroads Bible Coll, IN	B
Crossroads Coll, MN	B
Dordt Coll, IA	B
Grace Bible Coll, MI	B
Grace U, NE	B
Greenville Coll, IL	B
Lindenwood U, MO	B
Malone Coll, OH	B
Messenger Coll, MO	B

North Central U, MN	B
Northwestern Coll, MN	B
Pillsbury Baptist Bible Coll, MN	B
Saint Mary's U of Minnesota, MN	B
Southwest Baptist U, MO	B
Taylor U Fort Wayne, IN	B
Trinity International U, IL	B
Vennard Coll, IA	B

Youth Services

Indiana U–Purdue U Fort Wayne, IN	B

Zoology/Animal Biology

Andrews U, MI	B
Ball State U, IN	B
Central Christian Coll of Kansas, KS	A
Iowa State U of Science and Technology, IA	B
Kent State U, OH	B
Lincoln Coll, Lincoln, IL	A
Miami U, OH	B
Miami U Hamilton, OH	B

Michigan State U, MI	B
North Dakota State U, ND	B
Northeastern State U, OK	B
Northern Michigan U, MI	B
Northland Coll, WI	B
The Ohio State U, OH	B
Ohio U, OH	B
Ohio Wesleyan U, OH	B
Oklahoma State U, OK	B
Olivet Nazarene U, IL	B
Southeastern Oklahoma State U, OK	B
Southern Illinois U Carbondale, IL	B
The U of Akron, OH	B
U of Michigan, MI	B
U of Oklahoma, OK	B
U of Wisconsin–Madison, WI	B
U of Wisconsin–Milwaukee, WI	B
Winona State U, MN	B

Zoology/Animal Biology Related

Oklahoma State U, OK	B

Athletic Programs and Scholarships

Archery

Case Western Reserve U, OH	M, W
Miami U, OH	M, W
North Dakota State U, ND	M, W
Purdue U, IN	M, W

Badminton

Carleton Coll, MN	M, W
Dickinson State U, ND	M, W
Purdue U, IN	M, W
The Coll of Wooster, OH	M, W
Washington U in St. Louis, MO	M, W

Baseball

Adrian Coll, MI	M
Albion Coll, MI	M
Alma Coll, MI	M
Ancilla Coll, IN	M(s)
Aquinas Coll, MI	M(s)
Ashland U, OH	M(s)
Augsburg Coll, MN	M
Augustana Coll, SD	M(s)
Augustana Coll, IL	M
Aurora U, IL	M
Avila U, MO	M(s)
Bacone Coll, OK	M(s)
Baker U, KS	M(s)
Baldwin-Wallace Coll, OH	M
Ball State U, IN	M(s)
Barclay Coll, KS	M
Bellevue U, NE	M(s)
Beloit Coll, WI	M
Bemidji State U, MN	M(s)
Benedictine Coll, KS	M(s)
Benedictine U, IL	M
Bethany Coll, KS	M(s)
Bethany Lutheran Coll, MN	M
Bethel Coll, IN	M(s)
Bethel U, MN	M
Blackburn Coll, IL	M
Blessing-Rieman Coll of Nursing, IL	M(s), W(s)
Bluffton Coll, OH	M
Bowling Green State U, OH	M(s)
Bradley U, IL	M(s)
Brescia U, KY	M(s)
Briar Cliff U, IA	M(s)
Buena Vista U, IA	M
Butler U, IN	M(s)
Calumet Coll of Saint Joseph, IN	M
Calvin Coll, MI	M
Cameron U, OK	M(s)
Capital U, OH	M
Cardinal Stritch U, WI	M
Carleton Coll, MN	M
Carroll Coll, WI	M
Carthage Coll, WI	M
Case Western Reserve U, OH	M
Cedarville U, OH	M(s)
Central Christian Coll of Kansas, KS	M(s)
Central Coll, IA	M

Central Methodist Coll, MO	M(s)
Central Michigan U, MI	M(s)
Central Missouri State U, MO	M(s)
Chicago State U, IL	M
Clarke Coll, IA	M
Clarkson U	
Cleveland State U, OH	M(s)
Coe Coll, IA	M
Coll of Mount St. Joseph, OH	M
Coll of the Ozarks, MO	M(s)
Concord U, WV	M(s)
Concordia Coll, MN	M
Concordia U, MI	M(s)
Concordia U, NE	M(s)
Concordia U, IL	M
Concordia U Wisconsin, WI	M
Concordia U, St. Paul, MN	M(s)
Cornell Coll, IA	M
Creighton U, NE	M(s)
Crossroads Coll, MN	M
Crown Coll, MN	M
Culver-Stockton Coll, MO	M(s)
Cumberland Coll, KY	M(s)
Dakota State U, SD	M
Dakota Wesleyan U, SD	M(s)
Dana Coll, NE	M(s)
DePauw U, IN	M
Defiance Coll, OH	M
Denison U, OH	M
Dickinson State U, ND	M(s)
Doane Coll, NE	M(s)
Dominican U, IL	M
Dordt Coll, IA	M(s)
Earlham Coll, IN	M
East Central U, OK	M(s)
Eastern Illinois U, IL	M(s)
Eastern Michigan U, MI	M(s)
Edgewood Coll, WI	M
Elmhurst Coll, IL	M
Emporia State U, KS	M(s)
Eureka Coll, IL	M
Evangel U, MO	M(s)
Florida Gulf Coast U, FL	M(s)
Fontbonne U, MO	M
Fort Hays State U, KS	M(s)
Franklin Coll, IN	M
Gannon U, PA	M(s)
Goshen Coll, IN	M(s)
Grace Coll, IN	M(s)
Graceland U, IA	M(s)
Grand Valley State U, MI	M(s)
Grand View Coll, IA	M(s)
Greenville Coll, IL	M
Grinnell Coll, IA	M
Gustavus Adolphus Coll, MN	M
Hamline U, MN	M
Hannibal-LaGrange Coll, MO	M(s)
Hanover Coll, IN	M
Harris-Stowe State Coll, MO	M(s)
Hastings Coll, NE	M(s)
Heidelberg Coll, OH	M

Hesston Coll, KS	M(s)
Hillsdale Coll, MI	M(s)
Hillsdale Free Will Baptist Coll, OK	M
Hiram Coll, OH	M
Hope Coll, MI	M
Huntington Coll, IN	M(s)
Illinois Coll, IL	M
Illinois Inst of Technology, IL	M(s)
Illinois State U, IL	M(s)
Illinois Wesleyan U, IL	M
Indiana Inst of Technology, IN	M(s)
Indiana State U, IN	M(s)
Indiana U Bloomington, IN	M(s)
Indiana U Northwest, IN	M
Indiana U Southeast, IN	M
Indiana U–Purdue U Fort Wayne, IN	M(s)
Iowa Wesleyan Coll, IA	M(s)
Jamestown Coll, ND	M(s)
John Carroll U, OH	M
Judson Coll, IL	M(s)
Kalamazoo Coll, MI	M
Kansas State U, KS	M(s)
Kansas Wesleyan U, KS	M(s)
Kent State U, OH	M(s)
Kenyon Coll, OH	M
Knox Coll, IL	M
Lake Erie Coll, OH	M
Lake Forest Coll, IL	M
Lakeland Coll, WI	M
Lawrence U, WI	M
Lehigh U, PA	M(s)
Lewis U, IL	M(s)
Lincoln Coll, Lincoln, IL	M(s)
Lincoln U, MO	M(s)
Lindenwood U, MO	M(s)
Loras Coll, IA	M
Luther Coll, IA	M
MacMurray Coll, IL	M
Macalester Coll, MN	M
Madonna U, MI	M(s)
Malone Coll, OH	M(s)
Manchester Coll, IN	M
Marian Coll, IN	M(s)
Marian Coll of Fond du Lac, WI	M
Marietta Coll, OH	M
Marquette U, WI	M
Martin Luther Coll, MN	M
Maryville U of Saint Louis, MO	M
Mayville State U, ND	M(s)
McKendree Coll, IL	M(s)
Miami U, OH	M(s)
Miami U Hamilton, OH	M
Michigan State U, MI	M
MidAmerica Nazarene U, KS	M(s)
Millikin U, IL	M
Milwaukee School of Engineering, WI	M
Minnesota State U Mankato, MN	M(s)

M—for men; W—for women; (s)—scholarship offered

Minot State U, ND	M(s)	Simpson Coll, IA	M	U of St. Francis, IL	M(s)
Missouri Baptist U, MO	M(s)	South Dakota State U, SD	M(s)	U of St. Thomas, MN	M
Missouri Southern State U, MO	M(s)	Southeast Missouri State U, MO	M(s)	U of Toledo, OH	M(s)
Missouri Valley Coll, MO	M(s)	Southeastern Oklahoma State U, OK	M(s)	U of West Florida, FL	M(s)
Missouri Western State Coll, MO	M(s)	Southern Illinois U Carbondale, IL	M(s)	U of Wisconsin–La Crosse, WI	M
Monmouth Coll, IL	M	Southern Illinois U Edwardsville, IL	M(s)	U of Wisconsin–Milwaukee, WI	M
Morningside Coll, IA	M(s)			U of Wisconsin–Oshkosh, WI	M
Mount Marty Coll, SD	M(s)	Southern Nazarene U, OK	M(s)	U of Wisconsin–Parkside, WI	M(s)
Mount Mercy Coll, IA	M	Southwest Baptist U, MO	M(s)	U of Wisconsin–Platteville, WI	M
Mount Union Coll, OH	M	Southwest Missouri State U, MO	M(s)	U of Wisconsin–Stevens Point, WI	M
Mount Vernon Nazarene U, OH	M(s)	Southwestern Oklahoma State U, OK	M(s)	U of Wisconsin–Stout, WI	M
Muskingum Coll, OH	M	Spring Arbor U, MI	M(s)	U of Wisconsin–Superior, WI	M
Nebraska Wesleyan U, NE	M	St. Ambrose U, IA	M(s)	U of Wisconsin–Whitewater, WI	M
Newman U, KS	M(s)	St. Cloud State U, MN	M(s)	Upper Iowa U, IA	M
North Carolina Ag and Tech State U, NC	M(s)	St. Gregory's U, OK	M(s)	Urbana U, OH	M(s)
North Central Coll, IL	M	St. Louis Christian Coll, MO	M	Valley City State U, ND	M(s)
North Dakota State U, ND	M(s)	St. Norbert Coll, WI	M	Valparaiso U, IN	M(s)
North Park U, IL	M	St. Olaf Coll, MN	M	Viterbo U, WI	M(s)
Northeastern State U, OK	M(s)	Sterling Coll, KS	M(s)	Wabash Coll, IN	M
Northern Illinois U, IL	M(s)	Tabor Coll, KS	M(s)	Waldorf Coll, IA	M(s)
Northern State U, SD	M	Taylor U, IN	M(s)	Walsh U, OH	M(s)
Northland Coll, WI	M	The Coll of St. Scholastica, MN	M	Wartburg Coll, IA	M
Northwestern Coll, MN	M	The Coll of Wooster, OH	M	Washburn U, KS	M(s)
Northwestern Coll, IA	M(s)	The Franciscan U, IA	M(s)	Washington U in St. Louis, MO	M
Northwestern Oklahoma State U, OK	M(s)	The Ohio State U, OH	M(s)	Wayne State Coll, NE	M(s)
Northwestern U, IL	M(s)	The U of Akron, OH	M(s)	Wayne State U, MI	M
Northwood U, MI	M(s)	The U of Alabama in Huntsville, AL	M(s)	Webster U, MO	M
Oakland City U, IN	M(s)	The U of Findlay, OH	M(s)	Western Illinois U, IL	M(s)
Oakland U, MI	M(s)	The U of Iowa, IA	M(s)	Western Michigan U, MI	M(s)
Oberlin Coll, OH	M	The U of South Dakota, SD	M(s)	Westminster Coll, MO	M
Ohio Dominican U, OH	M(s)	Tiffin U, OH	M(s)	Wheaton Coll, IL	M
Ohio Northern U, OH	M	Transylvania U, KY	M	Wichita State U, KS	M(s)
Ohio U, OH	M(s)	Tri-State U, IN	M	William Jewell Coll, MO	M(s)
Ohio U–Chillicothe, OH	M	Trinity Bible Coll, ND	M	William Penn U, IA	M(s)
Ohio U–Zanesville, OH	M	Trinity Christian Coll, IL	M(s)	William Woods U, MO	M(s)
Ohio Wesleyan U, OH	M	Trinity International U, IL	M(s)	Winona State U, MN	M(s)
Oklahoma Baptist U, OK	M(s)	Truman State U, MO	M(s)	Wisconsin Lutheran Coll, WI	M
Oklahoma City U, OK	M(s)	U of Central Oklahoma, OK	M(s)	Wittenberg U, OH	M
Oklahoma Panhandle State U, OK	M(s)	U of Chicago, IL	M	Wright State U, OH	M(s)
Oklahoma State U, OK	M(s)	U of Dayton, OH	M(s)	Xavier U, OH	M(s)
Olivet Coll, MI	M	U of Detroit Mercy, MI	M(s)	York Coll, NE	M(s)
Olivet Nazarene U, IL	M(s)	U of Dubuque, IA	M	Youngstown State U, OH	M(s)
Oral Roberts U, OK	M(s)	U of Evansville, IN	M(s)		
Ottawa U, KS	M(s)	U of Illinois at Chicago, IL	M(s)	**Basketball**	
Otterbein Coll, OH	M	U of Illinois at Urbana–Champaign, IL	M(s)	Adrian Coll, MI	M, W
Park U, MO	M(s)	U of Indianapolis, IN	M(s)	Albion Coll, MI	M, W
Peru State Coll, NE	M(s)	U of Kansas, KS	M(s)	Alma Coll, MI	M, W
Pillsbury Baptist Bible Coll, MN	M	U of Mary, ND	M(s)	Alverno Coll, WI	W
Pittsburg State U, KS	M(s)	U of Michigan, MI	M(s)	Ancilla Coll, IN	M(s), W(s)
Presentation Coll, SD	M	U of Minnesota, Crookston, MN	M(s)	Aquinas Coll, MI	M(s), W(s)
Principia Coll, IL	M	U of Minnesota, Duluth, MN	M(s)	Ashland U, OH	M(s), W(s)
Purdue U, IN	M(s)	U of Minnesota, Morris, MN	M	Augsburg Coll, MN	M, W
Quincy U, IL	M(s)	U of Minnesota, Twin Cities Campus, MN	M(s)	Augustana Coll, SD	M(s), W(s)
Research Coll of Nursing, MO	M(s)	U of Missouri–Columbia, MO	M(s)	Augustana Coll, IL	M, W
Ripon Coll, WI	M	U of Missouri–Rolla, MO	M(s)	Aurora U, IL	M, W
Robert Morris Coll, IL	M(s)	U of Missouri–St. Louis, MO	M(s)	Avila U, MO	M(s), W(s)
Rochester Coll, MI	M(s)	U of Nebraska at Omaha, NE	M(s)	Bacone Coll, OK	M(s), W(s)
Rochester Comm and Tech Coll, MN	M	U of Nebraska–Lincoln, NE	M(s)	Baker U, KS	M(s), W(s)
Rockford Coll, IL	M	U of New Orleans, LA	M(s)	Baldwin-Wallace Coll, OH	M, W
Rockhurst U, MO	M(s)	U of North Dakota, ND	M(s)	Ball State U, IN	M(s), W(s)
Rose-Hulman Inst of Technology, IN	M	U of Northern Iowa, IA	M(s)	Baptist Bible Coll, MO	M, W
Saginaw Valley State U, MI	M(s)	U of Notre Dame, IN	M(s)	Barclay Coll, KS	M, W
Saint John's U, MN	M	U of Oklahoma, OK	M(s)	Bellevue U, NE	M(s)
Saint Joseph's Coll, IN	M(s)	U of Rio Grande, OH	M(s)	Beloit Coll, WI	M, W
Saint Louis U, MO	M(s)	U of Saint Francis, IN	M(s)	Bemidji State U, MN	M(s), W(s)
Saint Mary's U of Minnesota, MN	M	U of Saint Mary, KS	M(s)	Benedictine Coll, KS	M(s), W(s)
		U of Science and Arts of Oklahoma, OK	M(s)	Benedictine U, IL	M, W
Saint Xavier U, IL	M(s)	U of Sioux Falls, SD	M(s)	Bethany Coll, KS	M(s), W(s)
Shawnee State U, OH	M	U of Southern Indiana, IN	M(s)	Bethany Lutheran Coll, MN	M, W
Siena Heights U, MI	M(s)			Bethel Coll, IN	M(s), W(s)
				Bethel Coll, KS	M(s), W(s)
				Bethel U, MN	M, W
				Black Hills State U, SD	M(s), W(s)
				Blackburn Coll, IL	M, W
				Blessing-Rieman Coll of Nursing, IL	M(s), W(s)

Bluffton Coll, OH	M, W	Faith Baptist Bible Coll and		Malone Coll, OH	M(s), W(s)
Bowling Green State U, OH	M(s), W(s)	Theological Seminary, IA	M, W	Manchester Coll, IN	M, W
Bradley U, IL	M(s), W(s)	Ferris State U, MI	M(s), W(s)	Manhattan Christian Coll, KS	M, W
Brescia U, KY	M(s), W(s)	Florida Gulf Coast U, FL	M(s), W(s)	Marian Coll, IN	M(s), W(s)
Briar Cliff U, IA	M(s), W(s)	Fontbonne U, MO	M, W	Marian Coll of Fond du Lac, WI	M, W
Buena Vista U, IA	M, W	Fort Hays State U, KS	M(s), W(s)	Marietta Coll, OH	M, W
Butler U, IN	M(s), W(s)	Franklin Coll, IN	M, W	Marquette U, WI	M(s), W(s)
Calumet Coll of Saint Joseph, IN	M, W	Gannon U, PA	M(s), W(s)	Martin Luther Coll, MN	M, W
Calvary Bible Coll and		Goshen Coll, IN	M(s), W(s)	Marygrove Coll, MI	M, W
Theological Seminary, MO	M, W	Grace Bible Coll, MI	M, W	Maryville U of Saint Louis, MO	M, W
Calvin Coll, MI	M, W	Grace Coll, IN	M(s), W(s)	Mayville State U, ND	M(s), W(s)
Cameron U, OK	M(s), W(s)	Grace U, NE	M, W	McKendree Coll, IL	M(s), W(s)
Capital U, OH	M, W	Graceland U, IA	M(s), W(s)	McPherson Coll, KS	M, W
Cardinal Stritch U, WI	M, W	Grand Valley State U, MI	M(s), W(s)	Messenger Coll, MO	M, W
Carleton Coll, MN	M, W	Grand View Coll, IA	M(s), W(s)	Miami U, OH	M(s), W(s)
Carroll Coll, WI	M, W	Greenville Coll, IL	M, W	Miami U Hamilton, OH	M, W
Carthage Coll, WI	M, W	Grinnell Coll, IA	M, W	Michigan State U, MI	M(s), W(s)
Case Western Reserve U, OH	M, W	Gustavus Adolphus Coll, MN	M, W	Michigan Technological U, MI	M(s), W(s)
Cedarville U, OH	M(s), W(s)	Hamline U, MN	M, W	MidAmerica Nazarene U, KS	M(s), W(s)
Central Christian Coll of Kansas,		Hannibal-LaGrange Coll, MO	M(s), W(s)	Millikin U, IL	M, W
KS	M(s), W(s)	Hanover Coll, IN	M, W	Milwaukee School of	
Central Coll, IA	M, W	Harris-Stowe State Coll, MO	M(s), W(s)	Engineering, WI	M, W
Central Methodist Coll, MO	M(s), W(s)	Haskell Indian Nations U, KS	M, W	Minnesota State U Mankato,	
Central Michigan U, MI	M(s), W(s)	Hastings Coll, NE	M(s), W(s)	MN	M(s), W(s)
Central Missouri State U, MO	M(s), W(s)	Heidelberg Coll, OH	M, W	Minnesota State U Moorhead,	
Central State U, OH	M(s), W(s)	Hesston Coll, KS	M(s), W(s)	MN	M(s), W(s)
Chadron State Coll, NE	M(s), W(s)	Hillsdale Coll, MI	M(s), W(s)	Minot State U, ND	M(s), W(s)
Chicago State U, IL	M(s), W(s)	Hillsdale Free Will Baptist Coll,		Missouri Baptist U, MO	M(s), W(s)
Clarke Coll, IA	M, W	OK	M, W	Missouri Southern State U, MO	M(s), W(s)
Clarkson U	M, W	Hiram Coll, OH	M, W	Missouri Valley Coll, MO	M(s), W(s)
Cleveland State U, OH	M(s), W(s)	Hope Coll, MI	M, W	Missouri Western State Coll,	
Coe Coll, IA	M, W	Huntington Coll, IN	M(s), W(s)	MO	M(s), W(s)
Coll of Mount St. Joseph, OH	M, W	Illinois Inst of Technology, IL	M(s), W(s)	Monmouth Coll, IL	M, W
Coll of Saint Benedict, MN	W	Illinois State U, IL	M(s), W(s)	Moody Bible Inst, IL	M, W
Coll of Saint Mary, NE	W(s)	Illinois Wesleyan U, IL	M, W	Morningside Coll, IA	M(s), W(s)
Coll of St. Catherine, MN	W	Indiana Inst of Technology, IN	M(s), W(s)	Mount Marty Coll, SD	M(s), W(s)
Coll of the Ozarks, MO	M(s), W(s)	Indiana State U, IN	M(s), W(s)	Mount Mary Coll, WI	W
Columbia Coll, MO	M(s), W(s)	Indiana U Bloomington, IN	M(s), W(s)	Mount Mercy Coll, IA	M, W
Concord U, WV	M(s), W(s)	Indiana U Northwest, IN	M	Mount Union Coll, OH	M, W
Concordia Coll, MN	M, W	Indiana U South Bend, IN	M(s), W(s)	Mount Vernon Nazarene U, OH	M(s), W(s)
Concordia U, MI	M(s), W(s)	Indiana U Southeast, IN	M(s), W(s)	Muskingum Coll, OH	M, W
Concordia U, NE	M(s), W(s)	Indiana U–Purdue U Fort		Nebraska Wesleyan U, NE	M, W
Concordia U, IL	M, W	Wayne, IN	M(s), W(s)	Newman U, KS	M(s), W(s)
Concordia U Wisconsin, WI	M, W	Indiana U–Purdue U		North Carolina Ag and Tech	
Concordia U, St. Paul, MN	M(s), W(s)	Indianapolis, IN	M(s), W(s)	State U, NC	M(s), W(s)
Cornell Coll, IA	M, W	Iowa State U of Science and		North Central Coll, IL	M, W
Cornerstone U, MI	M(s), W(s)	Technology, IA	M(s), W(s)	North Central U, MN	M, W
Creighton U, NE	M(s), W(s)	Iowa Wesleyan Coll, IA	M(s), W(s)	North Dakota State Coll of	
Crossroads Coll, MN	M, W	Jamestown Coll, ND	M(s), W(s)	Science, ND	M(s), W(s)
Crown Coll, MN	M, W	John Carroll U, OH	M, W	North Dakota State U, ND	M(s), W(s)
Culver-Stockton Coll, MO	M(s), W(s)	Judson Coll, IL	M, W	North Park U, IL	M, W
Cumberland Coll, KY	M(s), W(s)	Kalamazoo Coll, MI	M, W	Northeastern State U, OK	M(s), W(s)
Dakota State U, SD	M(s), W(s)	Kansas State U, KS	M(s), W(s)	Northern Illinois U, IL	M(s), W(s)
Dakota Wesleyan U, SD	M(s), W(s)	Kansas Wesleyan U, KS	M(s), W(s)	Northern Michigan U, MI	M(s), W(s)
Dana Coll, NE	M(s), W(s)	Kent State U, OH	M(s), W(s)	Northern State U, SD	M(s), W(s)
Davenport U, Grand Rapids, MI	W	Kent State U, Tuscarawas		Northland Coll, WI	M, W
DePaul U, IL	M(s), W(s)	Campus, OH	M, W	Northwestern Coll, MN	M, W
DePauw U, IN	M, W	Kenyon Coll, OH	M, W	Northwestern Coll, IA	M(s), W(s)
Defiance Coll, OH	M, W	Knox Coll, IL	M, W	Northwestern Oklahoma State	
Denison U, OH	M, W	Lake Erie Coll, OH	M, W	U, OK	M(s), W(s)
Dickinson State U, ND	M(s), W(s)	Lake Forest Coll, IL	M, W	Northwestern U, IL	M(s), W(s)
Doane Coll, NE	M(s), W(s)	Lake Superior State U, MI	M(s), W(s)	Northwood U, MI	M(s), W(s)
Dominican U, IL	M, W	Lakeland Coll, WI	M, W	Notre Dame Coll, OH	M(s), W(s)
Dordt Coll, IA	M(s), W(s)	Lawrence U, WI	M, W	Oak Hills Christian Coll, MN	M, W
Drake U, IA	M(s), W(s)	Lehigh U, PA	M(s), W	Oakland City U, IN	M(s), W(s)
Drury U, MO	M(s)	Lewis U, IL	M(s), W(s)	Oakland U, MI	M(s), W(s)
Earlham Coll, IN	M, W	Lincoln Coll, Lincoln, IL	M(s), W(s)	Oberlin Coll, OH	M, W
East Central U, OK	M(s), W(s)	Lincoln U, MO	M(s), W(s)	Ohio Dominican U, OH	M(s), W(s)
Eastern Illinois U, IL	M(s), W(s)	Lindenwood U, MO	M(s), W(s)	Ohio Northern U, OH	M, W
Eastern Michigan U, MI	M(s), W(s)	Loras Coll, IA	M, W	Ohio U, OH	M(s), W(s)
Edgewood Coll, WI	M, W	Loyola U Chicago, IL	M(s), W(s)	Ohio U–Chillicothe, OH	M, W
Elmhurst Coll, IL	M, W	Luther Coll, IA	M, W	Ohio U–Southern Campus, OH	M, W
Emporia State U, KS	M(s), W(s)	MacMurray Coll, IL	M, W	Ohio U–Zanesville, OH	M, W
Eureka Coll, IL	M, W	Macalester Coll, MN	M, W	Ohio Wesleyan U, OH	M, W
Evangel U, MO	M(s), W(s)	Madonna U, MI	M(s), W(s)	Oklahoma Baptist U, OK	M(s), W(s)

M—for men; W—for women; (s)—scholarship offered

Oklahoma Christian U, OK	M(s), W(s)
Oklahoma City U, OK	M(s), W(s)
Oklahoma Panhandle State U, OK	M(s), W(s)
Oklahoma State U, OK	M(s), W(s)
Olivet Coll, MI	M, W
Olivet Nazarene U, IL	M(s), W(s)
Oral Roberts U, OK	M(s), W(s)
Ottawa U, KS	M(s), W(s)
Otterbein Coll, OH	M, W
Park U, MO	M(s), W(s)
Peru State Coll, NE	M(s), W(s)
Pillsbury Baptist Bible Coll, MN	M, W
Pittsburg State U, KS	M(s), W(s)
Presentation Coll, SD	M, W
Principia Coll, IL	M, W
Purdue U, IN	M(s), W(s)
Purdue U Calumet, IN	M(s), W(s)
Quincy U, IL	M(s), W(s)
Research Coll of Nursing, MO	M(s), W(s)
Ripon Coll, WI	M, W
Robert Morris Coll, IL	M(s), W(s)
Rochester Coll, MI	M(s), W(s)
Rochester Comm and Tech Coll, MN	M, W
Rockford Coll, IL	M, W
Rockhurst U, MO	M(s), W(s)
Rose-Hulman Inst of Technology, IN	M, W
Saginaw Valley State U, MI	M(s), W(s)
Saint John's U, MN	M
Saint Joseph's Coll, IN	M(s), W(s)
Saint Louis U, MO	M(s), W(s)
Saint Mary's Coll, IN	W
Saint Mary's U of Minnesota, MN	M, W
Saint Mary-of-the-Woods Coll, IN	W(s)
Saint Xavier U, IL	M(s)
Shawnee State U, OH	M, W
Siena Heights U, MI	M(s), W(s)
Silver Lake Coll, WI	W
Simpson Coll, IA	M, W
South Dakota School of Mines and Technology, SD	M(s), W(s)
South Dakota State U, SD	M(s), W(s)
Southeast Missouri State U, MO	M(s), W(s)
Southeastern Oklahoma State U, OK	M(s), W(s)
Southern Illinois U Carbondale, IL	M(s), W(s)
Southern Illinois U Edwardsville, IL	M(s), W(s)
Southern Nazarene U, OK	M(s), W(s)
Southwest Baptist U, MO	M(s), W(s)
Southwest Missouri State U, MO	M(s), W(s)
Southwestern Coll, KS	M(s), W(s)
Southwestern Oklahoma State U, OK	M(s), W(s)
Spring Arbor U, MI	M(s), W(s)
St. Ambrose U, IA	M(s), W(s)
St. Cloud State U, MN	M(s), W(s)
St. Gregory's U, OK	M(s), W(s)
St. Louis Christian Coll, MO	M
St. Louis Coll of Pharmacy, MO	M, W
St. Norbert Coll, WI	M, W
St. Olaf Coll, MN	M, W
Stephens Coll, MO	W
Sterling Coll, KS	M(s), W(s)
Tabor Coll, KS	M(s), W(s)
Taylor U, IN	M(s), W(s)
Taylor U Fort Wayne, IN	M, W
The Coll of St. Scholastica, MN	M, W
The Coll of Wooster, OH	M, W
The Franciscan U, IA	M(s), W(s)
The Ohio State U, OH	M(s), W(s)

The Ohio State U at Lima, OH	M, W
The U of Akron, OH	M(s), W(s)
The U of Alabama in Huntsville, AL	M(s), W(s)
The U of Findlay, OH	M(s), W(s)
The U of Iowa, IA	M(s), W(s)
The U of South Dakota, SD	M(s), W(s)
Tiffin U, OH	M(s), W(s)
Transylvania U, KY	M, W
Tri-State U, IN	M, W
Trinity Bible Coll, ND	M, W
Trinity Christian Coll, IL	M(s), W(s)
Trinity International U, IL	M(s), W(s)
Truman State U, MO	M(s), W(s)
Union Coll, NE	M, W
U of Central Oklahoma, OK	M(s), W(s)
U of Chicago, IL	M, W
U of Cincinnati, OH	M(s), W(s)
U of Dayton, OH	M(s), W(s)
U of Detroit Mercy, MI	M(s), W(s)
U of Dubuque, IA	M, W
U of Evansville, IN	M(s), W(s)
U of Illinois at Chicago, IL	M(s), W(s)
U of Illinois at Springfield, IL	M(s), W(s)
U of Illinois at Urbana–Champaign, IL	M(s), W(s)
U of Indianapolis, IN	M(s), W(s)
U of Kansas, KS	M(s), W(s)
U of Mary, ND	M(s), W(s)
U of Michigan, MI	M(s), W(s)
U of Michigan–Dearborn, MI	M(s), W(s)
U of Minnesota, Crookston, MN	M(s), W(s)
U of Minnesota, Duluth, MN	M(s), W(s)
U of Minnesota, Morris, MN	M, W
U of Minnesota, Twin Cities Campus, MN	M(s), W(s)
U of Missouri–Columbia, MO	M(s), W(s)
U of Missouri–Kansas City, MO	M(s), W(s)
U of Missouri–Rolla, MO	M(s), W(s)
U of Missouri–St. Louis, MO	M(s), W(s)
U of Nebraska at Omaha, NE	M(s), W(s)
U of Nebraska–Lincoln, NE	M(s), W(s)
U of New Orleans, LA	M(s), W(s)
U of North Dakota, ND	M(s), W(s)
U of Northern Iowa, IA	M(s), W(s)
U of Notre Dame, IN	M(s), W(s)
U of Oklahoma, OK	M(s), W(s)
U of Rio Grande, OH	M(s), W(s)
U of Saint Francis, IN	M(s), W(s)
U of Saint Mary, KS	M(s), W(s)
U of Science and Arts of Oklahoma, OK	M(s), W(s)
U of Sioux Falls, SD	M(s), W(s)
U of Southern Indiana, IN	M(s), W(s)
U of St. Francis, IL	M(s), W(s)
U of St. Thomas, MN	M, W
U of Toledo, OH	M(s), W(s)
U of Tulsa, OK	M(s), W(s)
U of West Florida, FL	M(s), W(s)
U of Wisconsin–Eau Claire, WI	M, W
U of Wisconsin–Green Bay, WI	M(s), W(s)
U of Wisconsin–La Crosse, WI	M, W
U of Wisconsin–Madison, WI	M(s), W(s)
U of Wisconsin–Milwaukee, WI	M(s), W(s)
U of Wisconsin–Oshkosh, WI	M, W
U of Wisconsin–Parkside, WI	M(s), W(s)
U of Wisconsin–Platteville, WI	M, W
U of Wisconsin–River Falls, WI	M, W
U of Wisconsin–Stevens Point, WI	M, W
U of Wisconsin–Stout, WI	M, W
U of Wisconsin–Superior, WI	M, W
U of Wisconsin–Whitewater, WI	M, W
Upper Iowa U, IA	M, W
Urbana U, OH	M(s), W(s)
Ursuline Coll, OH	W(s)

Valley City State U, ND	M(s), W(s)
Valparaiso U, IN	M(s), W(s)
Vennard Coll, IA	M, W
Viterbo U, WI	M(s), W(s)
Wabash Coll, IN	M
Waldorf Coll, IA	M(s), W(s)
Walsh U, OH	M(s), W(s)
Wartburg Coll, IA	M, W
Washburn U, KS	M(s), W(s)
Washington U in St. Louis, MO	M, W
Wayne State Coll, NE	M(s), W(s)
Wayne State U, MI	M(s), W(s)
Webster U, MO	M, W
Western Illinois U, IL	M(s), W(s)
Western Michigan U, MI	M(s), W(s)
Westminster Coll, MO	M, W
Wheaton Coll, IL	M, W
Wichita State U, KS	M(s), W(s)
Wilberforce U, OH	M, W
William Jewell Coll, MO	M(s), W(s)
William Penn U, IA	M(s), W(s)
William Woods U, MO	W(s)
Winona State U, MN	M(s), W(s)
Wisconsin Lutheran Coll, WI	M, W
Wittenberg U, OH	M, W
Wright State U, OH	M(s), W(s)
Xavier U, OH	M(s), W(s)
York Coll, NE	M(s), W(s)
Youngstown State U, OH	M(s), W(s)

Bowling

Central Missouri State U, MO	M, W
Clarkson U	M, W
Indiana State U, IN	M, W
Lehigh U, PA	M, W
Lindenwood U, MO	M(s), W(s)
McKendree Coll, IL	M(s), W(s)
Newman U, KS	M(s), W(s)
North Dakota State U, ND	M, W
Saginaw Valley State U, MI	M(s)
Southwest Missouri State U, MO	M, W
St. Cloud State U, MN	M, W
The U of Alabama in Huntsville, AL	M, W
U of Minnesota, Duluth, MN	M, W
U of Nebraska–Lincoln, NE	M, W
U of Wisconsin–Whitewater, WI	M, W(s)
Wichita State U, KS	M, W
Winona State U, MN	M, W

Crew

Beloit Coll, WI	M, W
Bowling Green State U, OH	M
Butler U, IN	M, W
Carleton Coll, MN	M, W
Case Western Reserve U, OH	M, W
Coll of Saint Benedict, MN	W
Creighton U, NE	W(s)
DePauw U, IN	M, W
Denison U, OH	M
Drake U, IA	W
Eastern Michigan U, MI	W(s)
Grand Valley State U, MI	M, W
Indiana U Bloomington, IN	W(s)
John Carroll U, OH	M, W
Kansas State U, KS	W(s)
Lawrence U, WI	M, W
Lehigh U, PA	M
Macalester Coll, MN	M, W
Marietta Coll, OH	M, W
Marquette U, WI	M, W
Michigan State U, MI	W(s)
Northern Michigan U, MI	M, W
Oklahoma City U, OK	M, W
Purdue U, IN	M, W
Saint John's U, MN	M
Saint Louis U, MO	M, W

Saint Mary's Coll, IN	W
St. Cloud State U, MN	M, W
The U of Iowa, IA	M, W(s)
U of Cincinnati, OH	M, W
U of Dayton, OH	W
U of Kansas, KS	M, W(s)
U of Michigan, MI	W
U of Nebraska–Lincoln, NE	W(s)
U of Notre Dame, IN	W(s)
U of St. Thomas, MN	M, W
U of Tulsa, OK	W(s)
U of Wisconsin–Madison, WI	M(s), W(s)
Wabash Coll, IN	M
Washburn U, KS	M, W
Washington U in St. Louis, MO	M, W
Wheaton Coll, IL	M, W
Wichita State U, KS	M, W
Wittenberg U, OH	M, W
Xavier U, OH	M, W

Cross-Country Running

Adrian Coll, MI	M, W
Albion Coll, MI	M, W
Alma Coll, MI	M, W
Alverno Coll, WI	W
Aquinas Coll, MI	M(s), W(s)
Ashland U, OH	M(s), W(s)
Augsburg Coll, MN	M, W
Augustana Coll, SD	M(s), W(s)
Augustana Coll, IL	M, W
Bacone Coll, OK	M(s), W(s)
Baker U, KS	M(s), W(s)
Baldwin-Wallace Coll, OH	M, W
Ball State U, IN	M(s), W(s)
Beloit Coll, WI	M, W
Bemidji State U, MN	W
Benedictine Coll, KS	M(s), W(s)
Benedictine U, IL	M, W
Bethany Coll, KS	M(s), W(s)
Bethany Lutheran Coll, MN	M, W
Bethel Coll, IN	M(s), W(s)
Bethel Coll, KS	M(s), W(s)
Bethel U, MN	M, W
Black Hills State U, SD	M(s), W(s)
Blackburn Coll, IL	M, W
Bluffton Coll, OH	M, W
Bowling Green State U, OH	M(s), W(s)
Bradley U, IL	M(s), W(s)
Briar Cliff U, IA	M(s), W(s)
Buena Vista U, IA	M, W
Butler U, IN	M(s), W(s)
Calvin Coll, MI	M, W
Capital U, OH	M, W
Cardinal Stritch U, WI	M, W
Carleton Coll, MN	M, W
Carroll Coll, WI	M, W
Carthage Coll, WI	M, W
Case Western Reserve U, OH	M, W
Cedarville U, OH	M(s), W(s)
Central Christian Coll of Kansas, KS	M(s), W(s)
Central Coll, IA	M, W
Central Methodist Coll, MO	M(s), W(s)
Central Michigan U, MI	M(s), W(s)
Central Missouri State U, MO	M(s), W(s)
Central State U, OH	M(s), W(s)
Chicago State U, IL	M(s), W(s)
Clarke Coll, IA	M, W
Clarkson U	M, W
Cleveland State U, OH	W(s)
Coe Coll, IA	M, W
Coll of Mount St. Joseph, OH	M, W
Coll of Saint Benedict, MN	W
Coll of Saint Mary, NE	W(s)
Coll of St. Catherine, MN	W

Concord U, WV	M(s), W(s)
Concordia Coll, MN	M, W
Concordia U, NE	M(s), W(s)
Concordia U, IL	M, W
Concordia U Wisconsin, WI	M, W
Concordia U, St. Paul, MN	M(s), W(s)
Cornell Coll, IA	M, W
Cornerstone U, MI	M(s), W(s)
Creighton U, NE	M(s), W(s)
Crown Coll, MN	M, W
Cumberland Coll, KY	M(s), W(s)
Dakota State U, SD	M(s), W(s)
Dakota Wesleyan U, SD	M(s), W(s)
Dana Coll, NE	M(s), W(s)
DePaul U, IL	M(s), W(s)
DePauw U, IN	M, W
Defiance Coll, OH	M, W
Denison U, OH	M, W
Dickinson State U, ND	M(s), W(s)
Doane Coll, NE	M(s), W(s)
Dominican U, IL	M, W
Dordt Coll, IA	M(s), W(s)
Drake U, IA	M(s), W(s)
Drury U, MO	M(s), W(s)
Earlham Coll, IN	M, W
East Central U, OK	M(s), W(s)
Eastern Illinois U, IL	M(s), W(s)
Eastern Michigan U, MI	M(s), W(s)
Edgewood Coll, WI	M, W
Elmhurst Coll, IL	M, W
Emporia State U, KS	M(s), W(s)
Evangel U, MO	M(s), W(s)
Ferris State U, MI	M(s), W(s)
Florida Gulf Coast U, FL	M, W
Fontbonne U, MO	M, W
Fort Hays State U, KS	M(s), W(s)
Franklin Coll, IN	M, W
Gannon U, PA	M(s), W(s)
Goshen Coll, IN	M(s), W(s)
Grace Coll, IN	M(s), W(s)
Graceland U, IA	M(s), W(s)
Grand Valley State U, MI	M(s), W(s)
Grand View Coll, IA	M(s), W(s)
Greenville Coll, IL	M, W
Grinnell Coll, IA	M, W
Gustavus Adolphus Coll, MN	M, W
Hamline U, MN	M, W
Hannibal-LaGrange Coll, MO	M(s), W(s)
Hanover Coll, IN	M, W
Haskell Indian Nations U, KS	M, W
Hastings Coll, NE	M(s), W(s)
Heidelberg Coll, OH	M, W
Hillsdale Coll, MI	M(s), W(s)
Hiram Coll, OH	M, W
Hope Coll, MI	M, W
Huntington Coll, IN	M(s), W(s)
Illinois Coll, IL	M, W
Illinois Inst of Technology, IL	M(s), W(s)
Illinois State U, IL	M(s), W(s)
Illinois Wesleyan U, IL	M, W
Indiana State U, IN	M(s), W(s)
Indiana U Bloomington, IN	M(s), W(s)
Indiana U–Purdue U Fort Wayne, IN	M(s), W(s)
Indiana U–Purdue U Indianapolis, IN	M(s), W(s)
Iowa State U of Science and Technology, IA	M(s), W(s)
Jamestown Coll, ND	M(s), W(s)
John Carroll U, OH	M, W
Judson Coll, IL	M(s), W(s)
Kalamazoo Coll, MI	M, W
Kansas State U, KS	M(s), W(s)
Kansas Wesleyan U, KS	M(s), W(s)
Kent State U, OH	M(s), W(s)

Kenyon Coll, OH	M, W
Knox Coll, IL	M, W
Lake Erie Coll, OH	M, W
Lake Forest Coll, IL	M, W
Lake Superior State U, MI	M(s), W(s)
Lakeland Coll, WI	M, W
Lawrence U, WI	M, W
Lehigh U, PA	M(s), W(s)
Lewis U, IL	M(s), W(s)
Lincoln U, MO	M(s), W(s)
Lindenwood U, MO	M(s), W(s)
Loras Coll, IA	M, W
Loyola U Chicago, IL	M(s), W(s)
Luther Coll, IA	M, W
MacMurray Coll, IL	M, W
Macalester Coll, MN	M, W
Malone Coll, OH	M(s), W(s)
Manchester Coll, IN	M, W
Marian Coll, IN	M(s), W(s)
Marietta Coll, OH	M, W
Marquette U, WI	M(s), W(s)
Martin Luther Coll, MN	M, W
Maryville U of Saint Louis, MO	M, W
McKendree Coll, IL	M(s), W(s)
McPherson Coll, KS	M, W
Miami U, OH	M(s), W(s)
Michigan State U, MI	M(s), W(s)
Michigan Technological U, MI	M, W
MidAmerica Nazarene U, KS	M(s), W(s)
Millikin U, IL	M, W
Milwaukee School of Engineering, WI	M, W
Minnesota State U Mankato, MN	M(s), W(s)
Minnesota State U Moorhead, MN	M, W
Minot State U, ND	M(s), W(s)
Missouri Baptist U, MO	M(s), W(s)
Missouri Southern State U, MO	M(s), W(s)
Missouri Valley Coll, MO	M(s), W(s)
Monmouth Coll, IL	M, W
Morningside Coll, IA	M(s), W(s)
Mount Marty Coll, SD	M(s), W(s)
Mount Mercy Coll, IA	M, W
Mount Union Coll, OH	M, W
Muskingum Coll, OH	M, W
Nebraska Wesleyan U, NE	M, W
Newman U, KS	M(s), W(s)
North Carolina Ag and Tech State U, NC	M(s), W(s)
North Central Coll, IL	M, W
North Central U, MN	M, W
North Dakota State U, ND	M(s), W(s)
North Park U, IL	M, W
Northern Illinois U, IL	W
Northern Michigan U, MI	W(s)
Northern State U, SD	M(s), W(s)
Northland Coll, WI	M, W
Northwestern Coll, MN	M, W
Northwestern Coll, IA	M(s), W(s)
Northwestern Oklahoma State U, OK	M(s), W(s)
Northwestern U, IL	W(s)
Northwood U, MI	M(s), W(s)
Notre Dame Coll, OH	M(s), W(s)
Oakland City U, IN	M(s), W(s)
Oakland U, MI	M(s), W(s)
Oberlin Coll, OH	M, W
Ohio Northern U, OH	M, W
Ohio U, OH	M(s), W(s)
Ohio Wesleyan U, OH	M, W
Oklahoma Baptist U, OK	M(s), W(s)
Oklahoma Christian U, OK	M(s), W(s)
Oklahoma Panhandle State U, OK	W(s)

M—for men; W—for women; (s)—scholarship offered

Oklahoma State U, OK	M(s), W(s)
Olivet Coll, MI	M, W
Olivet Nazarene U, IL	M(s), W(s)
Oral Roberts U, OK	M(s), W(s)
Ottawa U, KS	M(s), W(s)
Otterbein Coll, OH	M, W
Park U, MO	M(s), W(s)
Pittsburg State U, KS	M(s), W(s)
Presentation Coll, SD	M, W
Principia Coll, IL	M, W
Purdue U, IN	M(s), W(s)
Ripon Coll, WI	M, W
Robert Morris Coll, IL	M(s), W(s)
Rose-Hulman Inst of Technology, IN	M, W
Saginaw Valley State U, MI	M(s), W(s)
Saint John's U, MN	M
Saint Joseph's Coll, IN	M(s), W(s)
Saint Louis U, MO	M(s), W(s)
Saint Mary's Coll, IN	W
Saint Mary's U of Minnesota, MN	M, W
Saint Xavier U, IL	W(s)
Shawnee State U, OH	M, W
Siena Heights U, MI	M(s), W(s)
Simpson Coll, IA	M, W
South Dakota School of Mines and Technology, SD	M(s), W(s)
South Dakota State U, SD	M(s), W(s)
Southeast Missouri State U, MO	M(s), W(s)
Southeastern Oklahoma State U, OK	W(s)
Southern Illinois U Carbondale, IL	M(s), W(s)
Southern Illinois U Edwardsville, IL	M(s), W(s)
Southern Nazarene U, OK	M(s), W(s)
Southwest Baptist U, MO	M(s), W(s)
Southwest Missouri State U, MO	M(s), W(s)
Southwestern Coll, KS	M(s), W(s)
Southwestern Oklahoma State U, OK	W(s)
Spring Arbor U, MI	M(s), W(s)
St. Ambrose U, IA	M(s), W(s)
St. Cloud State U, MN	M(s), W
St. Gregory's U, OK	M(s), W(s)
St. Louis Coll of Pharmacy, MO	M, W
St. Norbert Coll, WI	M, W
St. Olaf Coll, MN	M, W
Sterling Coll, KS	M(s), W(s)
Tabor Coll, KS	M(s), W(s)
Taylor U, IN	M(s), W(s)
The Coll of St. Scholastica, MN	M, W
The Coll of Wooster, OH	M, W
The Franciscan U, IA	M(s), W(s)
The Ohio State U, OH	M(s), W(s)
The U of Akron, OH	M(s), W(s)
The U of Alabama in Huntsville, AL	M(s), W(s)
The U of Findlay, OH	M(s), W(s)
The U of Iowa, IA	M(s), W(s)
The U of South Dakota, SD	M(s), W(s)
Tiffin U, OH	M(s), W(s)
Transylvania U, KY	M, W
Tri-State U, IN	M, W
Trinity Christian Coll, IL	M(s), W(s)
Truman State U, MO	M(s), W(s)
U of Central Oklahoma, OK	M(s), W(s)
U of Chicago, IL	M, W
U of Cincinnati, OH	M(s), W(s)
U of Dayton, OH	M(s), W(s)
U of Detroit Mercy, MI	M(s), W(s)
U of Dubuque, IA	M, W
U of Evansville, IN	M(s), W(s)
U of Illinois at Chicago, IL	M(s), W(s)

U of Illinois at Urbana–Champaign, IL	M(s), W(s)
U of Indianapolis, IN	M(s), W(s)
U of Kansas, KS	M(s), W(s)
U of Mary, ND	M(s), W(s)
U of Michigan, MI	M(s), W(s)
U of Minnesota, Duluth, MN	M(s), W(s)
U of Minnesota, Morris, MN	W
U of Minnesota, Twin Cities Campus, MN	M(s), W(s)
U of Missouri–Columbia, MO	M(s), W(s)
U of Missouri–Kansas City, MO	M(s), W(s)
U of Missouri–Rolla, MO	M(s), W(s)
U of Nebraska at Omaha, NE	W(s)
U of Nebraska–Lincoln, NE	M(s), W(s)
U of New Orleans, LA	M(s), W(s)
U of North Dakota, ND	M, W
U of Northern Iowa, IA	M(s), W(s)
U of Notre Dame, IN	M(s), W(s)
U of Oklahoma, OK	M(s), W(s)
U of Rio Grande, OH	M(s), W(s)
U of Saint Francis, IN	M(s), W(s)
U of Sioux Falls, SD	M(s), W(s)
U of Southern Indiana, IN	M(s), W(s)
U of St. Francis, IL	W(s)
U of St. Thomas, MN	M, W
U of Toledo, OH	M(s), W(s)
U of Tulsa, OK	M(s), W(s)
U of West Florida, FL	M(s), W(s)
U of Wisconsin–Eau Claire, WI	M, W
U of Wisconsin–Green Bay, WI	M(s), W(s)
U of Wisconsin–La Crosse, WI	M, W
U of Wisconsin–Madison, WI	M(s), W(s)
U of Wisconsin–Milwaukee, WI	M(s), W(s)
U of Wisconsin–Oshkosh, WI	M, W
U of Wisconsin–Parkside, WI	M(s), W(s)
U of Wisconsin–Platteville, WI	M, W
U of Wisconsin–River Falls, WI	M, W
U of Wisconsin–Stevens Point, WI	M, W
U of Wisconsin–Stout, WI	M, W
U of Wisconsin–Superior, WI	M, W
U of Wisconsin–Whitewater, WI	M, W
Valparaiso U, IN	M(s), W(s)
Wabash Coll, IN	M
Walsh U, OH	M(s), W(s)
Wartburg Coll, IA	M, W
Washington U in St. Louis, MO	M, W
Wayne State Coll, NE	M(s), W(s)
Wayne State U, MI	M(s), W(s)
Webster U, MO	W
Western Illinois U, IL	M(s), W(s)
Western Michigan U, MI	M(s), W(s)
Wheaton Coll, IL	M, W
Wichita State U, KS	M(s), W(s)
Wilberforce U, OH	M, W
William Jewell Coll, MO	M(s), W(s)
William Penn U, IA	M(s), W(s)
William Woods U, MO	M(s), W(s)
Winona State U, MN	M, W(s)
Wisconsin Lutheran Coll, WI	M, W
Wittenberg U, OH	M, W
Wright State U, OH	M(s), W(s)
Xavier U, OH	M(s), W(s)
York Coll, NE	M(s), W(s)
Youngstown State U, OH	M(s), W(s)

Equestrian Sports

Ball State U, IN	M, W
Carleton Coll, MN	M, W
Chadron State Coll, NE	M, W
Denison U, OH	M, W
Earlham Coll, IN	M, W
Hillsdale Coll, MI	W
Hiram Coll, OH	M, W
Kenyon Coll, OH	M, W
Lehigh U, PA	M, W

Miami U, OH	M, W
Michigan State U, MI	M, W
National American U, SD	M(s), W(s)
Northern Michigan U, MI	M, W
Oberlin Coll, OH	M, W
Ohio U, OH	M, W
Ohio Wesleyan U, OH	M, W
Oklahoma Panhandle State U, OK	M(s), W(s)
Oklahoma State U, OK	W(s)
Otterbein Coll, OH	M, W
Purdue U, IN	M, W
Saint Mary's Coll, IN	W
Saint Mary-of-the-Woods Coll, IN	W(s)
Southwest Missouri State U, MO	M, W
Southwestern Oklahoma State U, OK	M(s), W(s)
Taylor U, IN	M, W
Truman State U, MO	M, W
U of Wisconsin–River Falls, WI	M, W
Washington U in St. Louis, MO	M, W
William Woods U, MO	M, W
Wittenberg U, OH	W

Fencing

Beloit Coll, WI	M, W
Bradley U, IL	M, W
Carleton Coll, MN	M, W
Case Western Reserve U, OH	M, W
Cleveland State U, OH	M(s), W(s)
Kenyon Coll, OH	M, W
Lake Forest Coll, IL	M, W
Lawrence U, WI	M, W
Macalester Coll, MN	M, W
Marquette U, WI	M, W
Miami U, OH	M, W
Michigan Technological U, MI	M, W
Northwestern U, IL	W(s)
Oberlin Coll, OH	M, W
Purdue U, IN	M, W
Saint Louis U, MO	M, W
St. Cloud State U, MN	M, W
The Ohio State U, OH	M(s), W(s)
U of Detroit Mercy, MI	M(s), W(s)
U of Kansas, KS	M, W
U of Nebraska–Lincoln, NE	M, W
U of Notre Dame, IN	M(s), W(s)
Washington U in St. Louis, MO	M, W
Wayne State U, MI	M(s), W(s)
Winona State U, MN	M, W
Xavier U, OH	M, W

Field Hockey

Ball State U, IN	W(s)
Carleton Coll, MN	W
Central Michigan U, MI	W(s)
DePauw U, IN	W
Denison U, OH	W
Earlham Coll, IN	W
Hanover Coll, IN	W
Indiana U Bloomington, IN	W
Kent State U, OH	W(s)
Kenyon Coll, OH	W
Lehigh U, PA	W(s)
Lindenwood U, MO	W(s)
Miami U, OH	W(s)
Michigan State U, MI	W(s)
Northwestern U, IL	W(s)
Oberlin Coll, OH	W
Ohio U, OH	W(s)
Ohio Wesleyan U, OH	W
Saint Louis U, MO	W(s)
Saint Mary's Coll, IN	W
Southwest Missouri State U, MO	W(s)
The Coll of Wooster, OH	W
The Ohio State U, OH	W(s)

Field Hockey

The U of Iowa, IA	W(s)
Transylvania U, KY	W
U of Michigan, MI	W(s)
Washington U in St. Louis, MO	W
Wheaton Coll, IL	W
Wittenberg U, OH	W

Football

Adrian Coll, MI	M
Albion Coll, MI	M
Alma Coll, MI	M
Ashland U, OH	M(s)
Augsburg Coll, MN	M
Augustana Coll, SD	M(s)
Augustana Coll, IL	M
Aurora U, IL	M
Avila U, MO	M(s)
Bacone Coll, OK	M(s)
Baker U, KS	M(s)
Baldwin-Wallace Coll, OH	M
Ball State U, IN	M(s)
Beloit Coll, WI	M
Bemidji State U, MN	M(s)
Benedictine Coll, KS	M(s)
Benedictine U, IL	M
Bethany Coll, KS	M(s)
Bethel Coll, KS	M(s)
Bethel U, MN	M
Black Hills State U, SD	M(s)
Blackburn Coll, IL	M
Blessing-Rieman Coll of Nursing, IL	M(s)
Bluffton Coll, OH	M
Bowling Green State U, OH	M(s)
Briar Cliff U, IA	M(s)
Buena Vista U, IA	M
Butler U, IN	M
Capital U, OH	M
Carleton Coll, MN	M
Carroll Coll, WI	M
Carthage Coll, WI	M
Case Western Reserve U, OH	M
Central Coll, IA	M
Central Methodist Coll, MO	M(s)
Central Michigan U, MI	M(s)
Central Missouri State U, MO	M(s)
Chadron State Coll, NE	M(s)
Coe Coll, IA	M
Coll of Mount St. Joseph, OH	M
Concord U, WV	M(s)
Concordia Coll, MN	M
Concordia U, NE	M(s)
Concordia U, IL	M
Concordia U Wisconsin, WI	M
Concordia U, St. Paul, MN	M(s)
Cornell Coll, IA	M
Crown Coll, MN	M
Culver-Stockton Coll, MO	M(s)
Cumberland Coll, KY	M(s)
Dakota State U, SD	M(s)
Dakota Wesleyan U, SD	M(s)
Dana Coll, NE	M(s)
DePauw U, IN	M
Defiance Coll, OH	M
Denison U, OH	M
Dickinson State U, ND	M(s)
Doane Coll, NE	M(s)
Drake U, IA	M
Earlham Coll, IN	M
East Central U, OK	M(s)
Eastern Illinois U, IL	M(s)
Eastern Michigan U, MI	M(s)
Elmhurst Coll, IL	M
Emporia State U, KS	M(s)
Eureka Coll, IL	M
Evangel U, MO	M(s)
Ferris State U, MI	M(s)
Fort Hays State U, KS	M(s)
Franklin Coll, IN	M
Gannon U, PA	M
Graceland U, IA	M(s)
Grand Valley State U, MI	M(s)
Greenville Coll, IL	M
Grinnell Coll, IA	M
Gustavus Adolphus Coll, MN	M
Hamline U, MN	M
Hanover Coll, IN	M
Haskell Indian Nations U, KS	M
Hastings Coll, NE	M(s)
Heidelberg Coll, OH	M
Hillsdale Coll, MI	M(s)
Hiram Coll, OH	M
Hope Coll, MI	M
Illinois Coll, IL	M
Illinois State U, IL	M(s)
Illinois Wesleyan U, IL	M
Indiana State U, IN	M(s)
Indiana U Bloomington, IN	M(s)
Iowa State U of Science and Technology, IA	M(s)
Iowa Wesleyan Coll, IA	M(s)
Jamestown Coll, ND	M(s)
John Carroll U, OH	M
Kalamazoo Coll, MI	M
Kansas State U, KS	M(s)
Kansas Wesleyan U, KS	M(s)
Kent State U, OH	M(s)
Kenyon Coll, OH	M
Knox Coll, IL	M
Lake Forest Coll, IL	M
Lakeland Coll, WI	M
Lawrence U, WI	M
Lehigh U, PA	M(s), W
Lincoln U, MO	M(s)
Lindenwood U, MO	M(s)
Loras Coll, IA	M
Luther Coll, IA	M
MacMurray Coll, IL	M
Macalester Coll, MN	M
Malone Coll, OH	M(s)
Manchester Coll, IN	M
Marietta Coll, OH	M
Marquette U, WI	M
Martin Luther Coll, MN	M
Mayville State U, ND	M(s)
McKendree Coll, IL	M(s)
McPherson Coll, KS	M
Miami U, OH	M(s)
Michigan State U, MI	M(s)
Michigan Technological U, MI	M(s)
MidAmerica Nazarene U, KS	M(s)
Millikin U, IL	M
Minnesota State U Mankato, MN	M(s)
Minnesota State U Moorhead, MN	M(s)
Minot State U, ND	M(s)
Missouri Southern State U, MO	M(s)
Missouri Valley Coll, MO	M(s)
Missouri Western State Coll, MO	M(s)
Monmouth Coll, IL	M
Morningside Coll, IA	M(s)
Mount Union Coll, OH	M
Muskingum Coll, OH	M
Nebraska Wesleyan U, NE	M
North Carolina Ag and Tech State U, NC	M(s)
North Central Coll, IL	M
North Dakota State Coll of Science, ND	M(s)
North Dakota State U, ND	M(s)
North Park U, IL	M
Northeastern State U, OK	M(s)
Northern Illinois U, IL	M(s)
Northern Michigan U, MI	M(s)
Northern State U, SD	M(s)
Northwestern Coll, MN	M
Northwestern Coll, IA	M(s)
Northwestern Oklahoma State U, OK	M(s)
Northwestern U, IL	M(s)
Northwood U, MI	M(s)
Oberlin Coll, OH	M
Ohio Dominican U, OH	M(s)
Ohio Northern U, OH	M
Ohio U, OH	M(s)
Ohio Wesleyan U, OH	M
Oklahoma Panhandle State U, OK	M(s)
Oklahoma State U, OK	M(s)
Olivet Coll, MI	M
Olivet Nazarene U, IL	M(s)
Ottawa U, KS	M(s)
Otterbein Coll, OH	M
Peru State Coll, NE	M(s)
Pittsburg State U, KS	M(s)
Principia Coll, IL	M
Purdue U, IN	M(s)
Ripon Coll, WI	M
Rochester Comm and Tech Coll, MN	M
Rockford Coll, IL	M
Rose-Hulman Inst of Technology, IN	M
Saginaw Valley State U, MI	M(s)
Saint John's U, MN	M
Saint Joseph's Coll, IN	M(s)
Saint Xavier U, IL	M(s)
Simpson Coll, IA	M
South Dakota School of Mines and Technology, SD	M(s)
South Dakota State U, SD	M(s)
Southeast Missouri State U, MO	M(s)
Southeastern Oklahoma State U, OK	M(s)
Southern Illinois U Carbondale, IL	M(s)
Southern Nazarene U, OK	M(s)
Southwest Baptist U, MO	M(s)
Southwest Missouri State U, MO	M(s)
Southwestern Coll, KS	M(s)
Southwestern Oklahoma State U, OK	M(s)
St. Ambrose U, IA	M(s)
St. Cloud State U, MN	M(s)
St. Norbert Coll, WI	M
St. Olaf Coll, MN	M
Sterling Coll, KS	M(s)
Tabor Coll, KS	M(s)
Taylor U, IN	M(s)
The Coll of Wooster, OH	M
The Ohio State U, OH	M(s)
The U of Akron, OH	M(s)
The U of Findlay, OH	M(s)
The U of Iowa, IA	M(s)
The U of South Dakota, SD	M(s)
Tiffin U, OH	M(s)
Tri-State U, IN	M
Trinity Bible Coll, ND	M
Trinity International U, IL	M(s)
Truman State U, MO	M(s)
U of Central Oklahoma, OK	M(s)
U of Chicago, IL	M

M—for men; W—for women; (s)—scholarship offered

U of Cincinnati, OH	M(s)
U of Dayton, OH	M
U of Dubuque, IA	M
U of Illinois at Urbana–Champaign, IL	M(s)
U of Indianapolis, IN	M(s)
U of Kansas, KS	M(s)
U of Mary, ND	M(s)
U of Michigan, MI	M(s)
U of Minnesota, Crookston, MN	M(s)
U of Minnesota, Duluth, MN	M(s)
U of Minnesota, Morris, MN	M
U of Minnesota, Twin Cities Campus, MN	M(s)
U of Missouri–Columbia, MO	M(s)
U of Missouri–Rolla, MO	M(s)
U of Nebraska at Omaha, NE	M(s)
U of Nebraska–Lincoln, NE	M(s)
U of North Dakota, ND	M(s)
U of Northern Iowa, IA	M(s)
U of Notre Dame, IN	M(s)
U of Oklahoma, OK	M(s)
U of Saint Francis, IN	M(s)
U of Saint Mary, KS	M(s)
U of Sioux Falls, SD	M(s)
U of St. Francis, IL	M(s)
U of St. Thomas, MN	M
U of Toledo, OH	M(s)
U of Tulsa, OK	M(s)
U of Wisconsin–Eau Claire, WI	M
U of Wisconsin–La Crosse, WI	M
U of Wisconsin–Madison, WI	M(s)
U of Wisconsin–Oshkosh, WI	M
U of Wisconsin–Platteville, WI	M
U of Wisconsin–River Falls, WI	M
U of Wisconsin–Stevens Point, WI	M
U of Wisconsin–Stout, WI	M
U of Wisconsin–Whitewater, WI	M
Upper Iowa U, IA	M
Urbana U, OH	M(s)
Valley City State U, ND	M(s)
Valparaiso U, IN	M
Wabash Coll, IN	M
Waldorf Coll, IA	M(s)
Walsh U, OH	M(s)
Wartburg Coll, IA	M
Washburn U, KS	M(s)
Washington U in St. Louis, MO	M
Wayne State Coll, NE	M(s)
Wayne State U, MI	M(s)
Western Illinois U, IL	M(s)
Western Michigan U, MI	M(s)
Westminster Coll, MO	M
Wheaton Coll, IL	M
William Jewell Coll, MO	M(s)
William Penn U, IA	M(s)
Winona State U, MN	M(s)
Wisconsin Lutheran Coll, WI	M
Wittenberg U, OH	M
Youngstown State U, OH	M(s)

Golf

Adrian Coll, MI	M, W
Albion Coll, MI	M, W
Alma Coll, MI	M, W
Ancilla Coll, IN	M(s)
Aquinas Coll, MI	M(s), W(s)
Ashland U, OH	M(s), W(s)
Augsburg Coll, MN	M, W
Augustana Coll, SD	M, W
Augustana Coll, IL	M, W
Aurora U, IL	M
Avila U, MO	W(s)
Bacone Coll, OK	M(s), W(s)
Baker U, KS	M(s), W(s)
Baldwin-Wallace Coll, OH	M, W

Ball State U, IN	M(s)
Beloit Coll, WI	M, W
Bemidji State U, MN	M, W
Benedictine Coll, KS	M(s), W(s)
Benedictine U, IL	M
Bethany Coll, KS	M(s)
Bethany Lutheran Coll, MN	M, W
Bethel Coll, IN	M(s), W(s)
Bethel Coll, KS	M(s), W(s)
Bethel U, MN	M
Blackburn Coll, IL	M, W
Bluffton Coll, OH	M
Bowling Green State U, OH	M(s), W(s)
Bradley U, IL	M(s), W(s)
Brescia U, KY	M(s), W(s)
Briar Cliff U, IA	M(s), W(s)
Buena Vista U, IA	M, W
Butler U, IN	M(s), W(s)
Calvin Coll, MI	M, W
Cameron U, OK	M(s)
Capital U, OH	M, W
Carleton Coll, MN	M, W
Carroll Coll, WI	M, W
Carthage Coll, WI	M, W
Cedarville U, OH	M(s)
Central Christian Coll of Kansas, KS	M(s), W(s)
Central Coll, IA	M, W
Central Methodist Coll, MO	M(s), W(s)
Central Missouri State U, MO	M(s)
Central State U, OH	M(s), W(s)
Chadron State Coll, NE	W(s)
Chicago State U, IL	M, W
Clarke Coll, IA	M, W
Clarkson U	M
Cleveland State U, OH	M(s)
Coe Coll, IA	M, W
Coll of Mount St. Joseph, OH	M, W
Coll of Saint Benedict, MN	W
Coll of Saint Mary, NE	W(s)
Concord U, WV	M(s)
Concordia Coll, MN	M, W
Concordia U, NE	M(s), W(s)
Concordia U, IL	M
Concordia U Wisconsin, WI	M, W
Concordia U, St. Paul, MN	W(s)
Cornell Coll, IA	M, W
Cornerstone U, MI	M(s)
Creighton U, NE	M(s), W(s)
Crossroads Coll, MN	M, W
Crown Coll, MN	M, W
Culver-Stockton Coll, MO	M(s), W(s)
Cumberland Coll, KY	M(s), W(s)
Dakota State U, SD	M, W
Dakota Wesleyan U, SD	M(s), W(s)
Dana Coll, NE	W(s)
Davenport U, Grand Rapids, MI	M
DePaul U, IL	M(s), W
DePauw U, IN	M, W
Defiance Coll, OH	M, W
Denison U, OH	M
Dickinson State U, ND	M(s), W(s)
Doane Coll, NE	M(s), W(s)
Dordt Coll, IA	M(s)
Drake U, IA	M(s)
Drury U, MO	M(s), W(s)
East Central U, OK	M(s), W
Eastern Illinois U, IL	M(s), W(s)
Eastern Michigan U, MI	M(s), W(s)
Edgewood Coll, WI	M, W
Elmhurst Coll, IL	M, W
Eureka Coll, IL	M, W
Evangel U, MO	M(s), W(s)
Ferris State U, MI	M(s), W(s)
Florida Gulf Coast U, FL	M(s), W(s)
Fontbonne U, MO	M, W

Fort Hays State U, KS	M(s)
Franklin Coll, IN	M, W
Gannon U, PA	M(s), W(s)
Goshen Coll, IN	M(s)
Grace Coll, IN	M(s)
Graceland U, IA	M(s), W(s)
Grand Valley State U, MI	M(s), W(s)
Grand View Coll, IA	M(s), W(s)
Grinnell Coll, IA	M, W
Gustavus Adolphus Coll, MN	M, W
Hannibal-LaGrange Coll, MO	M(s)
Hanover Coll, IN	M, W
Haskell Indian Nations U, KS	M
Hastings Coll, NE	M(s), W(s)
Heidelberg Coll, OH	M, W
Hillsdale Coll, MI	M(s)
Hiram Coll, OH	M, W
Hope Coll, MI	M, W
Huntington Coll, IN	M(s)
Illinois Coll, IL	M, W
Illinois State U, IL	M(s), W(s)
Illinois Wesleyan U, IL	M, W
Indiana U Bloomington, IN	M(s), W(s)
Indiana U Northwest, IN	M, W
Indiana U–Purdue U Indianapolis, IN	M(s), W
Iowa State U of Science and Technology, IA	M(s), W(s)
Jamestown Coll, ND	M(s), W(s)
John Carroll U, OH	M, W
Kalamazoo Coll, MI	M, W
Kansas State U, KS	M(s), W(s)
Kansas Wesleyan U, KS	M(s), W(s)
Kent State U, OH	M(s), W(s)
Kent State U, Tuscarawas Campus, OH	M, W
Kenyon Coll, OH	M
Knox Coll, IL	M, W
Lake Erie Coll, OH	M
Lake Superior State U, MI	M
Lakeland Coll, WI	M, W
Lawrence U, WI	M
Lehigh U, PA	M(s), W(s)
Lewis U, IL	M(s), W(s)
Lincoln Coll, Lincoln, IL	M(s), W(s)
Lincoln U, MO	M(s)
Lindenwood U, MO	M(s), W(s)
Loras Coll, IA	M, W
Loyola U Chicago, IL	M(s), W(s)
Luther Coll, IA	M, W
MacMurray Coll, IL	M, W
Macalester Coll, MN	M, W
Madonna U, MI	M(s), W(s)
Maharishi U of Management, IA	M, W
Malone Coll, OH	M(s), W(s)
Manchester Coll, IN	M, W
Marian Coll, IN	M(s), W(s)
Marian Coll of Fond du Lac, WI	M, W
Marquette U, WI	M(s)
Martin Luther Coll, MN	M
Maryville U of Saint Louis, MO	M
McKendree Coll, IL	M(s), W(s)
Miami U, OH	M(s)
Miami U Hamilton, OH	M
Michigan State U, MI	M(s), W(s)
Millikin U, IL	M, W
Milwaukee School of Engineering, WI	M, W
Minnesota State U Mankato, MN	M(s), W(s)
Minnesota State U Moorhead, MN	M, W
Minot State U, ND	M, W
Missouri Baptist U, MO	M(s)
Missouri Southern State U, MO	M(s)
Missouri Valley Coll, MO	M(s), W(s)

Missouri Western State Coll, MO	M(s), W
Monmouth Coll, IL	M, W
Morningside Coll, IA	M(s), W(s)
Mount Marty Coll, SD	M(s), W(s)
Mount Mercy Coll, IA	M, W
Mount Union Coll, OH	M, W
Mount Vernon Nazarene U, OH	M(s)
Muskingum Coll, OH	M, W
Nebraska Wesleyan U, NE	M, W
Newman U, KS	M(s), W(s)
North Central Coll, IL	M, W
North Dakota State U, ND	M, W(s)
North Park U, IL	M
Northeastern State U, OK	M(s), W(s)
Northern Illinois U, IL	M(s), W(s)
Northern Michigan U, MI	M(s)
Northern State U, SD	M, W(s)
Northwestern Coll, MN	M, W
Northwestern Coll, IA	M(s), W(s)
Northwestern U, IL	M(s), W(s)
Northwood U, MI	M(s), W(s)
Oakland City U, IN	M, W
Oakland U, MI	M(s), W(s)
Oberlin Coll, OH	M, W
Ohio Dominican U, OH	M(s), W(s)
Ohio Northern U, OH	M, W
Ohio U, OH	M(s), W(s)
Ohio U–Chillicothe, OH	M, W
Ohio U–Zanesville, OH	M, W
Ohio Wesleyan U, OH	M
Oklahoma Baptist U, OK	M(s), W(s)
Oklahoma Christian U, OK	M(s)
Oklahoma City U, OK	M(s), W(s)
Oklahoma Panhandle State U, OK	M(s)
Oklahoma State U, OK	M(s), W(s)
Olivet Coll, MI	M, W
Olivet Nazarene U, IL	M(s)
Oral Roberts U, OK	M(s), W(s)
Ottawa U, KS	M(s)
Otterbein Coll, OH	M, W
Park U, MO	W
Pillsbury Baptist Bible Coll, MN	M, W
Pittsburg State U, KS	M(s)
Presentation Coll, SD	M, W
Principia Coll, IL	M
Purdue U, IN	M(s), W(s)
Quincy U, IL	M(s), W(s)
Research Coll of Nursing, MO	M(s), W(s)
Ripon Coll, WI	M, W
Robert Morris Coll, IL	M(s), W(s)
Rochester Comm and Tech Coll, MN	M, W
Rockford Coll, IL	M
Rockhurst U, MO	M(s), W(s)
Rose-Hulman Inst of Technology, IN	M, W
Saginaw Valley State U, MI	M(s)
Saint John's U, MN	M
Saint Joseph's Coll, IN	M(s), W(s)
Saint Louis U, MO	M(s)
Saint Mary's U of Minnesota, MN	M, W
Saint Xavier U, IL	M(s)
Shawnee State U, OH	M
Siena Heights U, MI	M(s)
Simpson Coll, IA	M, W
South Dakota School of Mines and Technology, SD	M, W
South Dakota State U, SD	M, W
Southeast Missouri State U, MO	M(s)
Southern Illinois U Carbondale, IL	M(s), W(s)

Southern Illinois U Edwardsville, IL	W(s)
Southern Nazarene U, OK	M(s), W(s)
Southwest Baptist U, MO	M(s)
Southwest Missouri State U, MO	M(s), W(s)
Southwestern Coll, KS	M(s), W(s)
Southwestern Oklahoma State U, OK	M(s), W(s)
Spring Arbor U, MI	M(s)
St. Ambrose U, IA	M(s), W(s)
St. Cloud State U, MN	M, W(s)
St. Gregory's U, OK	M(s), W(s)
St. Norbert Coll, WI	M, W
St. Olaf Coll, MN	M, W
Tabor Coll, KS	M(s), W(s)
Taylor U, IN	M(s)
The Coll of Wooster, OH	M
The Franciscan U, IA	M(s)
The Ohio State U, OH	M(s), W(s)
The Ohio State U at Lima, OH	M
The U of Akron, OH	M(s)
The U of Findlay, OH	M(s), W(s)
The U of Iowa, IA	M(s), W(s)
Tiffin U, OH	M(s), W(s)
Transylvania U, KY	M, W
Tri-State U, IN	M, W
Truman State U, MO	M(s), W(s)
U of Central Oklahoma, OK	M(s)
U of Cincinnati, OH	M(s)
U of Dayton, OH	M(s), W(s)
U of Detroit Mercy, MI	M(s), W(s)
U of Dubuque, IA	M, W
U of Evansville, IN	M(s)
U of Illinois at Urbana–Champaign, IL	M(s), W(s)
U of Indianapolis, IN	M(s), W(s)
U of Kansas, KS	M(s), W(s)
U of Mary, ND	M(s), W(s)
U of Michigan, MI	M(s), W(s)
U of Minnesota, Crookston, MN	M(s), W
U of Minnesota, Morris, MN	M, W
U of Minnesota, Twin Cities Campus, MN	M(s), W(s)
U of Missouri–Columbia, MO	M(s), W(s)
U of Missouri–Kansas City, MO	M(s), W(s)
U of Missouri–St. Louis, MO	M(s), W(s)
U of Nebraska at Omaha, NE	W
U of Nebraska–Lincoln, NE	M(s), W(s)
U of New Orleans, LA	M(s), W(s)
U of North Dakota, ND	M, W
U of Northern Iowa, IA	M(s), W(s)
U of Notre Dame, IN	M(s), W(s)
U of Oklahoma, OK	M(s), W(s)
U of Saint Francis, IN	M(s)
U of Sioux Falls, SD	M(s), W(s)
U of Southern Indiana, IN	M(s), W(s)
U of St. Francis, IL	M(s), W(s)
U of St. Thomas, MN	M, W
U of Toledo, OH	M(s), W(s)
U of Tulsa, OK	M(s), W(s)
U of West Florida, FL	M(s)
U of Wisconsin–Eau Claire, WI	M, W
U of Wisconsin–Madison, WI	M(s), W(s)
U of Wisconsin–Oshkosh, WI	W
U of Wisconsin–Parkside, WI	M(s)
U of Wisconsin–Platteville, WI	M
U of Wisconsin–Stevens Point, WI	W
U of Wisconsin–Superior, WI	W
U of Wisconsin–Whitewater, WI	W
Upper Iowa U, IA	M, W
Urbana U, OH	M(s)
Ursuline Coll, OH	W(s)
Wabash Coll, IN	M
Waldorf Coll, IA	M(s), W(s)

Walsh U, OH	M(s), W(s)
Wartburg Coll, IA	M, W
Washburn U, KS	M(s)
Wayne State Coll, NE	M(s), W(s)
Wayne State U, MI	M(s)
Webster U, MO	M
Western Illinois U, IL	M(s), W
Western Michigan U, MI	W(s)
Westminster Coll, MO	M, W
Wheaton Coll, IL	M, W
Wichita State U, KS	M(s), W(s)
Wilberforce U, OH	M, W
William Jewell Coll, MO	M(s), W(s)
William Penn U, IA	M(s)
William Woods U, MO	M(s), W(s)
Winona State U, MN	M(s), W(s)
Wisconsin Lutheran Coll, WI	M, W
Wittenberg U, OH	M, W
Wright State U, OH	M(s)
Xavier U, OH	M(s), W(s)
York Coll, NE	M(s), W(s)
Youngstown State U, OH	M(s), W

Gymnastics

Ball State U, IN	W(s)
Bowling Green State U, OH	W(s)
Carleton Coll, MN	W
Central Michigan U, MI	W(s)
Eastern Michigan U, MI	W(s)
Gustavus Adolphus Coll, MN	W
Hamline U, MN	W
Illinois State U, IL	W(s)
Iowa State U of Science and Technology, IA	W(s)
Kent State U, OH	W(s)
Miami U, OH	M, W
Michigan State U, MI	M(s), W(s)
Northern Illinois U, IL	W(s)
Purdue U, IN	M, W
Saint Mary's Coll, IN	W
Southeast Missouri State U, MO	W(s)
The Ohio State U, OH	M(s), W(s)
The U of Iowa, IA	M(s), W(s)
U of Illinois at Chicago, IL	M(s), W(s)
U of Illinois at Urbana–Champaign, IL	M(s), W(s)
U of Michigan, MI	M(s), W(s)
U of Minnesota, Twin Cities Campus, MN	M(s), W(s)
U of Missouri–Columbia, MO	W(s)
U of Nebraska–Lincoln, NE	M(s), W(s)
U of Oklahoma, OK	M(s), W(s)
U of Wisconsin–Eau Claire, WI	W
U of Wisconsin–La Crosse, WI	W
U of Wisconsin–Oshkosh, WI	W
U of Wisconsin–Stout, WI	W
U of Wisconsin–Whitewater, WI	W
Washington U in St. Louis, MO	M, W
Western Michigan U, MI	W(s)
Winona State U, MN	W(s)

Ice Hockey

Augsburg Coll, MN	M, W
Ball State U, IN	M
Beloit Coll, WI	M, W
Bemidji State U, MN	M(s), W(s)
Bethel U, MN	M, W
Bowling Green State U, OH	M(s)
Bradley U, IL	M
Butler U, IN	M
Calvin Coll, MI	M
Carleton Coll, MN	M, W
Carthage Coll, WI	M
Case Western Reserve U, OH	M, W
Clarkson U	M(s), W(s)
Coll of Saint Benedict, MN	W

M—for men; W—for women; (s)—scholarship offered

Coll of St. Catherine, MN	W
Concordia Coll, MN	M, W
Davenport U, Grand Rapids, MI	M
Denison U, OH	M
Dordt Coll, IA	M(s)
Ferris State U, MI	M(s)
Grand Valley State U, MI	M
Gustavus Adolphus Coll, MN	M, W
Hamline U, MN	M
Hillsdale Coll, MI	M
Hope Coll, MI	M
John Carroll U, OH	M
Kenyon Coll, OH	M, W
Kettering U, MI	M
Lake Forest Coll, IL	M, W
Lake Superior State U, MI	M(s)
Lawrence U, WI	M, W
Lehigh U, PA	M
Lindenwood U, MO	M(s), W(s)
Loras Coll, IA	M
Macalester Coll, MN	M, W
Marian Coll of Fond du Lac, WI	M
McKendree Coll, IL	M
Miami U, OH	M(s)
Michigan State U, MI	M(s), W
Michigan Technological U, MI	M(s), W
Milwaukee School of Engineering, WI	M
Minnesota State U Mankato, MN	M(s), W(s)
Minot State U, ND	M
North Dakota State U, ND	M
Northern Michigan U, MI	M(s), W
Northland Coll, WI	M
Northwestern Coll, MN	M
Northwood U, MI	M
Oakland U, MI	M, W
Oberlin Coll, OH	M, W
Ohio U, OH	M
Ohio Wesleyan U, OH	M
Purdue U, IN	M
Ripon Coll, WI	M, W
Robert Morris Coll, IL	M(s), W(s)
Saint John's U, MN	M
Saint Louis U, MO	M, W
Saint Mary's U of Minnesota, MN	M, W
Southwest Missouri State U, MO	M
St. Cloud State U, MN	M(s), W(s)
St. Norbert Coll, WI	M
St. Olaf Coll, MN	M, W
The Coll of St. Scholastica, MN	M
The Ohio State U, OH	M(s), W(s)
The U of Alabama in Huntsville, AL	M(s)
The U of Findlay, OH	M(s), W(s)
The U of Iowa, IA	M
U of Michigan, MI	M(s)
U of Minnesota, Crookston, MN	M(s)
U of Minnesota, Duluth, MN	M(s), W
U of Minnesota, Twin Cities Campus, MN	M(s), W(s)
U of Missouri–St. Louis, MO	M
U of Nebraska at Omaha, NE	M(s)
U of North Dakota, ND	M(s), W(s)
U of Notre Dame, IN	M(s)
U of Southern Indiana, IN	M
U of St. Thomas, MN	M, W
U of Wisconsin–Eau Claire, WI	M, W
U of Wisconsin–Madison, WI	M(s), W(s)
U of Wisconsin–Platteville, WI	M
U of Wisconsin–River Falls, WI	M, W
U of Wisconsin–Stevens Point, WI	M, W
U of Wisconsin–Stout, WI	M, W
U of Wisconsin–Superior, WI	M, W
U of Wisconsin–Whitewater, WI	M, W
Washington U in St. Louis, MO	M
Wayne State U, MI	M, W
Western Michigan U, MI	M(s)
Wheaton Coll, IL	M
Wichita State U, KS	M, W
Winona State U, MN	M
Wittenberg U, OH	M

Lacrosse

Augustana Coll, IL	M
Beloit Coll, WI	M, W
Butler U, IN	M(s)
Calvin Coll, MI	M, W
Carleton Coll, MN	M, W
Clarkson U	M, W
Coll of Saint Benedict, MN	W
Denison U, OH	M, W
Dordt Coll, IA	M
Earlham Coll, IN	M
Gannon U, PA	W(s)
Gustavus Adolphus Coll, MN	M
Hillsdale Coll, MI	M
Hope Coll, MI	M
Illinois Wesleyan U, IL	M
John Carroll U, OH	M, W
Kenyon Coll, OH	M, W
Kettering U, MI	M
Lake Forest Coll, IL	M, W
Lawrence U, WI	M, W
Lehigh U, PA	M(s), W(s)
Lindenwood U, MO	M(s), W(s)
Marietta Coll, OH	M
Marquette U, WI	M
Miami U, OH	M
Michigan State U, MI	M
Northern Michigan U, MI	M
Northwestern U, IL	W(s)
Oberlin Coll, OH	M, W
Ohio U, OH	M, W
Ohio Wesleyan U, OH	M, W
Purdue U, IN	M, W
Saint John's U, MN	M
Saint Louis U, MO	M, W
Southwest Missouri State U, MO	M
Taylor U, IN	M, W
The Coll of Wooster, OH	M, W
The Ohio State U, OH	M(s), W(s)
The U of Iowa, IA	M, W
Truman State U, MO	M, W
U of Minnesota, Duluth, MN	M, W
U of Notre Dame, IN	M(s), W(s)
U of St. Thomas, MN	M, W
U of Wisconsin–Madison, WI	W(s)
U of Wisconsin–Whitewater, WI	M
Wabash Coll, IN	M
Washington U in St. Louis, MO	M, W
Wheaton Coll, IL	M, W
Wittenberg U, OH	M, W
Xavier U, OH	M, W

Racquetball

Miami U, OH	M, W
Michigan Technological U, MI	M, W
Purdue U, IN	M, W
Southwest Missouri State U, MO	M, W
Wichita State U, KS	M, W

Riflery

Denison U, OH	M, W
Hillsdale Coll, MI	M, W
Lindenwood U, MO	M(s), W(s)
Michigan Technological U, MI	M, W
North Dakota State U, ND	M, W
Purdue U, IN	M, W
Rose-Hulman Inst of Technology, IN	M, W
Saint John's U, MN	M
Southwest Missouri State U, MO	M, W
The Ohio State U, OH	M, W
The U of Akron, OH	M, W
U of Missouri–Kansas City, MO	M(s), W(s)
U of Nebraska–Lincoln, NE	W(s)
U of Wisconsin–Oshkosh, WI	M, W
Xavier U, OH	M(s), W(s)

Rugby

Ball State U, IN	M, W
Butler U, IN	M
Carleton Coll, MN	M, W
Central Missouri State U, MO	M, W
Clarkson U	M, W
Coll of Saint Benedict, MN	W
DePauw U, IN	M
Denison U, OH	M, W
Earlham Coll, IN	M
Eastern Illinois U, IL	W(s)
Grand Valley State U, MI	M, W
Gustavus Adolphus Coll, MN	M, W
Hiram Coll, OH	M, W
John Carroll U, OH	M, W
Kenyon Coll, OH	M, W
Lake Forest Coll, IL	M
Lawrence U, WI	W
Lehigh U, PA	M
Loras Coll, IA	M
Macalester Coll, MN	M, W
Marquette U, WI	M, W
Miami U, OH	M
Michigan State U, MI	M, W
North Dakota State U, ND	M, W
Northern Michigan U, MI	M, W
Oberlin Coll, OH	M, W
Ohio U, OH	M, W
Ohio Wesleyan U, OH	M, W
Purdue U, IN	M, W
Ripon Coll, WI	M
Saint John's U, MN	M
Saint Louis U, MO	M
Simpson Coll, IA	M, W
St. Cloud State U, MN	M, W
Tabor Coll, KS	M
The Coll of Wooster, OH	M, W
The U of Iowa, IA	M, W
Truman State U, MO	M, W
U of Cincinnati, OH	M
U of Kansas, KS	M, W
U of Minnesota, Duluth, MN	M, W
U of Southern Indiana, IN	M
U of Wisconsin–Madison, WI	M
U of Wisconsin–Platteville, WI	M
U of Wisconsin–River Falls, WI	M, W
U of Wisconsin–Whitewater, WI	M, W
Wabash Coll, IN	M
Washington U in St. Louis, MO	M, W
Wichita State U, KS	M
Winona State U, MN	M, W
Wittenberg U, OH	M, W
Xavier U, OH	M, W

Sailing

Ball State U, IN	M, W
Carleton Coll, MN	M, W
Denison U, OH	M, W
Grand Valley State U, MI	M, W
Hiram Coll, OH	M, W
John Carroll U, OH	M, W
Miami U, OH	M, W
Michigan State U, MI	M, W
Ohio Wesleyan U, OH	M, W
Purdue U, IN	M, W
Saint Mary's Coll, IN	W
The U of Iowa, IA	M, W
U of Wisconsin–Madison, WI	M, W

Wabash Coll, IN	M	Calumet Coll of Saint Joseph, IN	M, W	Harris-Stowe State Coll, MO	M(s), W(s)
Washington U in St. Louis, MO	M, W	Calvary Bible Coll and		Hastings Coll, NE	M(s), W(s)
		Theological Seminary, MO	M	Heidelberg Coll, OH	M, W
Skiing (Cross-Country)		Calvin Coll, MI	M, W	Hesston Coll, KS	M(s)
Carleton Coll, MN	M, W	Capital U, OH	M, W	Hillsdale Coll, MI	M, W
Clarkson U	M, W	Cardinal Stritch U, WI	M, W	Hiram Coll, OH	M, W
Coll of Saint Benedict, MN	W	Carleton Coll, MN	M, W	Hope Coll, MI	M, W
Concordia Coll, MN	M, W	Carroll Coll, WI	M, W	Huntington Coll, IN	M(s), W(s)
Gustavus Adolphus Coll, MN	M, W	Carthage Coll, WI	M, W	Illinois Coll, IL	M, W
Macalester Coll, MN	M, W	Case Western Reserve U, OH	M, W	Illinois Inst of Technology, IL	M(s), W(s)
Michigan State U, MI	M, W	Cedarville U, OH	M(s), W(s)	Illinois State U, IL	W(s)
Michigan Technological U, MI	M, W	Central Christian Coll of Kansas,		Illinois Wesleyan U, IL	M, W
Northern Michigan U, MI	M(s), W(s)	KS	M(s), W(s)	Indiana Inst of Technology, IN	M(s), W(s)
Saint John's U, MN	M	Central Coll, IA	M, W	Indiana State U, IN	M, W
St. Cloud State U, MN	M, W(s)	Central Methodist Coll, MO	M(s), W(s)	Indiana U Bloomington, IN	M(s), W(s)
St. Olaf Coll, MN	M, W	Central Michigan U, MI	W(s)	Indiana U–Purdue U Fort	
U of Wisconsin–Green Bay, WI	M(s), W(s)	Central Missouri State U, MO	M, W(s)	Wayne, IN	M(s), W(s)
		Clarke Coll, IA	M, W	Indiana U–Purdue U	
Skiing (Downhill)		Clarkson U	M, W	Indianapolis, IN	M(s), W(s)
Carleton Coll, MN	M, W	Cleveland State U, OH	M(s)	Iowa State U of Science and	
Clarkson U	M, W	Coe Coll, IA	M, W	Technology, IA	W(s)
Denison U, OH	M, W	Coll of Mount St. Joseph, OH	W	Iowa Wesleyan Coll, IA	M(s), W(s)
Grand Valley State U, MI	M, W	Coll of Saint Benedict, MN	W	Jamestown Coll, ND	W(s)
John Carroll U, OH	M, W	Coll of Saint Mary, NE	W(s)	John Carroll U, OH	M, W
Lehigh U, PA	M, W	Coll of St. Catherine, MN	W	Judson Coll, IL	M(s), W(s)
Loras Coll, IA	M	Columbia Coll, MO	M(s)	Kalamazoo Coll, MI	M, W
Marquette U, WI	M, W	Concord U, WV	W(s)	Kansas Wesleyan U, KS	M(s), W(s)
Michigan State U, MI	M	Concordia Coll, MN	M, W	Kent State U, OH	W(s)
Michigan Technological U, MI	M, W	Concordia U, MI	M(s), W(s)	Kenyon Coll, OH	M, W
Northern Michigan U, MI	M, W(s)	Concordia U, NE	M(s), W(s)	Kettering U, MI	M
Purdue U, IN	M, W	Concordia U, IL	M, W	Knox Coll, IL	M, W
Saint Mary's Coll, IN	W	Concordia U Wisconsin, WI	M, W	Lake Erie Coll, OH	M, W
St. Cloud State U, MN	M, W	Concordia U, St. Paul, MN	M, W(s)	Lake Forest Coll, IL	M, W
St. Olaf Coll, MN	M, W	Cornell Coll, IA	M, W	Lakeland Coll, WI	M, W
U of Minnesota, Duluth, MN	M, W	Cornerstone U, MI	M(s), W(s)	Lawrence U, WI	M, W
U of St. Thomas, MN	M, W	Creighton U, NE	M(s), W(s)	Lehigh U, PA	M(s), W(s)
Winona State U, MN	M, W	Crown Coll, MN	M, W	Lewis U, IL	M(s), W(s)
		Culver-Stockton Coll, MO	M(s), W(s)	Lincoln Coll, Lincoln, IL	M(s), W(s)
Soccer		Cumberland Coll, KY	M(s), W(s)	Lincoln U, MO	M(s)
Adrian Coll, MI	M, W	Dana Coll, NE	M(s), W(s)	Lindenwood U, MO	M(s), W(s)
Albion Coll, MI	M, W	DePaul U, IL	M(s), W(s)	Loras Coll, IA	M, W
Alma Coll, MI	M, W	DePauw U, IN	M, W	Loyola U Chicago, IL	M(s), W(s)
Alverno Coll, WI	W	Defiance Coll, OH	M, W	Luther Coll, IA	M, W
Aquinas Coll, MI	M(s), W(s)	Denison U, OH	M, W	MacMurray Coll, IL	M, W
Ashland U, OH	M(s), W(s)	Doane Coll, NE	M(s), W(s)	Macalester Coll, MN	M, W
Augsburg Coll, MN	M, W	Dominican U, IL	M, W	Madonna U, MI	M(s), W(s)
Augustana Coll, SD	W(s)	Dordt Coll, IA	M(s), W(s)	Maharishi U of Management, IA	M, W
Augustana Coll, IL	M, W	Drake U, IA	M(s), W(s)	Malone Coll, OH	M(s), W(s)
Aurora U, IL	M, W	Drury U, MO	M(s), W(s)	Manchester Coll, IN	M, W
Avila U, MO	M(s), W(s)	Earlham Coll, IN	M, W	Manhattan Christian Coll, KS	M, W
Bacone Coll, OK	M(s), W(s)	East Central U, OK	W(s)	Marian Coll, IN	M(s), W(s)
Baker U, KS	M(s), W(s)	Eastern Illinois U, IL	M(s), W(s)	Marian Coll of Fond du Lac, WI	M, W
Baldwin-Wallace Coll, OH	M, W	Eastern Michigan U, MI	W(s)	Marietta Coll, OH	M, W
Ball State U, IN	M, W	Edgewood Coll, WI	M, W	Marquette U, WI	M(s), W(s)
Baptist Bible Coll, MO	M	Elmhurst Coll, IL	W	Martin Luther Coll, MN	M, W
Barclay Coll, KS	M	Emporia State U, KS	W(s)	Maryville U of Saint Louis, MO	M, W
Bellevue U, NE	M(s), W	Faith Baptist Bible Coll and		Mayville State U, ND	M(s), W(s)
Beloit Coll, WI	M, W	Theological Seminary, IA	M, W	McKendree Coll, IL	M(s), W(s)
Bemidji State U, MN	W(s)	Ferris State U, MI	W(s)	Miami U, OH	M, W(s)
Benedictine Coll, KS	M(s), W(s)	Fontbonne U, MO	M, W	Michigan State U, MI	M(s), W
Benedictine U, IL	M, W	Franklin Coll, IN	M, W	Michigan Technological U, MI	M, W
Bethany Coll, KS	M(s), W(s)	Gannon U, PA	M(s), W(s)	MidAmerica Nazarene U, KS	M(s), W(s)
Bethany Lutheran Coll, MN	M, W	Goshen Coll, IN	M(s), W(s)	Millikin U, IL	M, W
Bethel Coll, IN	M(s), W(s)	Grace Bible Coll, MI	M	Milwaukee School of	
Bethel Coll, KS	M(s), W(s)	Grace Coll, IN	M(s), W(s)	Engineering, WI	M, W
Bethel U, MN	M, W	Grace U, NE	M	Minnesota State U Mankato,	
Blackburn Coll, IL	M, W	Graceland U, IA	M(s), W(s)	MN	W(s)
Blessing-Rieman Coll of		Grand Valley State U, MI	M, W(s)	Minnesota State U Moorhead,	
Nursing, IL	M(s), W(s)	Grand View Coll, IA	M(s), W(s)	MN	W(s)
Bluffton Coll, OH	M, W	Greenville Coll, IL	M, W	Missouri Baptist U, MO	M(s), W(s)
Bowling Green State U, OH	M(s)	Grinnell Coll, IA	M, W	Missouri Southern State U, MO	M(s), W(s)
Bradley U, IL	M(s), W	Gustavus Adolphus Coll, MN	M, W	Missouri Valley Coll, MO	M(s), W(s)
Brescia U, KY	M(s), W(s)	Hamline U, MN	M, W	Monmouth Coll, IL	M, W
Briar Cliff U, IA	M(s), W(s)	Hannibal-LaGrange Coll, MO	M(s), W(s)	Moody Bible Inst, IL	M
Buena Vista U, IA	M, W	Hanover Coll, IN	M, W	Morningside Coll, IA	M(s), W(s)
Butler U, IN	M(s), W(s)				

M—for men; W—for women; (s)—scholarship offered

Mount Marty Coll, SD	M(s)
Mount Mary Coll, WI	W
Mount Mercy Coll, IA	M, W
Mount Union Coll, OH	M, W
Mount Vernon Nazarene U, OH	M(s), W(s)
Muskingum Coll, OH	M, W
Nebraska Wesleyan U, NE	M, W
Newman U, KS	M(s), W(s)
North Central Coll, IL	M, W
North Central U, MN	M, W
North Dakota State U, ND	M, W(s)
North Park U, IL	M, W
Northeastern State U, OK	M(s), W(s)
Northern Illinois U, IL	M(s), W(s)
Northern Michigan U, MI	W(s)
Northern State U, SD	W(s)
Northland Coll, WI	M, W
Northwestern Coll, MN	M, W
Northwestern Coll, IA	M(s), W(s)
Northwestern Oklahoma State U, OK	W(s)
Northwestern U, IL	M(s), W(s)
Northwood U, MI	M(s), W(s)
Notre Dame Coll, OH	M(s), W(s)
Oakland City U, IN	M, W
Oakland U, MI	M(s), W(s)
Oberlin Coll, OH	M, W
Ohio Dominican U, OH	M(s), W(s)
Ohio Northern U, OH	M, W
Ohio U, OH	M, W(s)
Ohio Wesleyan U, OH	M, W
Oklahoma Christian U, OK	M(s), W(s)
Oklahoma City U, OK	M(s), W(s)
Oklahoma State U, OK	W
Olivet Coll, MI	M, W
Olivet Nazarene U, IL	M(s), W(s)
Oral Roberts U, OK	M(s), W(s)
Ottawa U, KS	M(s), W(s)
Otterbein Coll, OH	M, W
Park U, MO	M(s), W(s)
Pillsbury Baptist Bible Coll, MN	M
Presentation Coll, SD	M, W
Principia Coll, IL	M, W
Purdue U, IN	M, W(s)
Quincy U, IL	M(s), W(s)
Research Coll of Nursing, MO	M(s), W(s)
Ripon Coll, WI	M, W
Robert Morris Coll, IL	M(s), W(s)
Rochester Coll, MI	M(s), W(s)
Rochester Comm and Tech Coll, MN	W
Rockford Coll, IL	M, W
Rockhurst U, MO	M(s), W(s)
Rose-Hulman Inst of Technology, IN	M, W
Saginaw Valley State U, MI	M(s), W(s)
Saint John's U, MN	M
Saint Joseph's Coll, IN	M(s), W(s)
Saint Louis U, MO	M(s), W(s)
Saint Mary's Coll, IN	W
Saint Mary's U of Minnesota, MN	M, W
Saint Mary-of-the-Woods Coll, IN	W(s)
Saint Xavier U, IL	M(s), W(s)
Shawnee State U, OH	M, W
Siena Heights U, MI	M(s), W(s)
Simpson Coll, IA	M, W
South Dakota State U, SD	W(s)
Southern Illinois U Edwardsville, IL	M(s), W(s)
Southern Nazarene U, OK	M(s), W(s)
Southwest Baptist U, MO	M(s), W(s)
Southwest Missouri State U, MO	M(s), W(s)
Southwestern Coll, KS	M(s), W(s)

Southwestern Oklahoma State U, OK	W(s)
Spring Arbor U, MI	M(s), W(s)
St. Ambrose U, IA	M(s), W(s)
St. Cloud State U, MN	M, W(s)
St. Gregory's U, OK	M(s), W(s)
St. Norbert Coll, WI	M, W
St. Olaf Coll, MN	M, W
Stephens Coll, MO	W
Sterling Coll, KS	M(s), W(s)
Tabor Coll, KS	M(s), W(s)
Taylor U, IN	M(s), W(s)
Taylor U Fort Wayne, IN	M
The Coll of St. Scholastica, MN	M, W
The Coll of Wooster, OH	M, W
The Franciscan U, IA	M(s), W(s)
The Ohio State U, OH	M(s), W(s)
The U of Akron, OH	M(s), W
The U of Alabama in Huntsville, AL	M(s), W(s)
The U of Findlay, OH	M(s), W(s)
The U of Iowa, IA	M, W(s)
Tiffin U, OH	M(s), W(s)
Transylvania U, KY	M, W
Tri-State U, IN	M, W
Trinity Christian Coll, IL	M(s), W(s)
Trinity International U, IL	M(s), W(s)
Truman State U, MO	M(s), W(s)
U of Central Oklahoma, OK	W
U of Chicago, IL	M, W
U of Cincinnati, OH	M(s), W(s)
U of Dayton, OH	M(s), W(s)
U of Detroit Mercy, MI	M(s), W(s)
U of Dubuque, IA	M, W
U of Evansville, IN	M(s), W
U of Illinois at Chicago, IL	M(s)
U of Illinois at Springfield, IL	M(s)
U of Illinois at Urbana–Champaign, IL	W(s)
U of Indianapolis, IN	M(s), W(s)
U of Kansas, KS	W(s)
U of Mary, ND	M(s), W(s)
U of Michigan, MI	M, W(s)
U of Minnesota, Crookston, MN	W(s)
U of Minnesota, Duluth, MN	M, W(s)
U of Minnesota, Morris, MN	W
U of Minnesota, Twin Cities Campus, MN	W(s)
U of Missouri–Columbia, MO	W(s)
U of Missouri–Kansas City, MO	M(s)
U of Missouri–Rolla, MO	M(s), W(s)
U of Missouri–St. Louis, MO	M(s), W(s)
U of Nebraska at Omaha, NE	W
U of Nebraska–Lincoln, NE	W(s)
U of Northern Iowa, IA	W(s)
U of Notre Dame, IN	M(s), W(s)
U of Oklahoma, OK	W(s)
U of Rio Grande, OH	M(s)
U of Saint Francis, IN	M(s), W(s)
U of Saint Mary, KS	M(s), W(s)
U of Science and Arts of Oklahoma, OK	M(s), W(s)
U of Sioux Falls, SD	M(s), W(s)
U of Southern Indiana, IN	M(s), W(s)
U of St. Francis, IL	M(s), W(s)
U of St. Thomas, MN	M, W
U of Toledo, OH	W(s)
U of Tulsa, OK	M(s), W(s)
U of West Florida, FL	M(s), W(s)
U of Wisconsin–Eau Claire, WI	W
U of Wisconsin–Green Bay, WI	M(s), W(s)
U of Wisconsin–La Crosse, WI	W
U of Wisconsin–Madison, WI	M(s), W(s)
U of Wisconsin–Milwaukee, WI	M(s), W(s)
U of Wisconsin–Oshkosh, WI	M, W
U of Wisconsin–Parkside, WI	M(s), W(s)

U of Wisconsin–Platteville, WI	M, W
U of Wisconsin–River Falls, WI	M, W
U of Wisconsin–Stevens Point, WI	W
U of Wisconsin–Stout, WI	M, W
U of Wisconsin–Superior, WI	M, W
U of Wisconsin–Whitewater, WI	M, W
Upper Iowa U, IA	M, W
Urbana U, OH	M(s), W(s)
Ursuline Coll, OH	W(s)
Valparaiso U, IN	M(s), W(s)
Vennard Coll, IA	M
Viterbo U, WI	M(s), W(s)
Wabash Coll, IN	M
Waldorf Coll, IA	M(s), W(s)
Walsh U, OH	M(s), W(s)
Wartburg Coll, IA	M, W
Washburn U, KS	W
Washington U in St. Louis, MO	M, W
Wayne State Coll, NE	M, W(s)
Webster U, MO	M, W
Western Illinois U, IL	M(s), W(s)
Western Michigan U, MI	M(s), W(s)
Westminster Coll, MO	M, W
Wheaton Coll, IL	M, W
Wichita State U, KS	M, W
William Jewell Coll, MO	M(s), W(s)
William Penn U, IA	M(s), W(s)
William Woods U, MO	M(s), W(s)
Winona State U, MN	M, W(s)
Wisconsin Lutheran Coll, WI	M, W
Wittenberg U, OH	M, W
Wright State U, OH	M(s), W(s)
Xavier U, OH	M(s), W(s)
York Coll, NE	M(s), W(s)
Youngstown State U, OH	W

Softball

Adrian Coll, MI	W
Albion Coll, MI	W
Alma Coll, MI	W
Alverno Coll, WI	W
Ancilla Coll, IN	W(s)
Aquinas Coll, MI	W(s)
Ashland U, OH	M, W(s)
Augsburg Coll, MN	W
Augustana Coll, SD	W(s)
Augustana Coll, IL	W
Aurora U, IL	W
Avila U, MO	W(s)
Bacone Coll, OK	W(s)
Baker U, KS	W(s)
Baldwin-Wallace Coll, OH	W
Ball State U, IN	W(s)
Bellevue U, NE	W(s)
Beloit Coll, WI	W
Bemidji State U, MN	W(s)
Benedictine Coll, KS	W(s)
Benedictine U, IL	W
Bethany Coll, KS	W(s)
Bethany Lutheran Coll, MN	W
Bethel Coll, IN	W
Bethel U, MN	W
Blackburn Coll, IL	W
Bluffton Coll, OH	W
Bowling Green State U, OH	W(s)
Bradley U, IL	W(s)
Brescia U, KY	W(s)
Briar Cliff U, IA	W(s)
Buena Vista U, IA	W
Butler U, IN	W(s)
Calumet Coll of Saint Joseph, IN	W
Calvin Coll, MI	W
Cameron U, OK	W(s)
Capital U, OH	W
Cardinal Stritch U, WI	W
Carleton Coll, MN	W

Carroll Coll, WI	W	Hillsdale Free Will Baptist Coll,		Mount Union Coll, OH	W
Carthage Coll, WI	W	OK	W	Mount Vernon Nazarene U, OH	W(s)
Case Western Reserve U, OH	W	Hiram Coll, OH	W	Muskingum Coll, OH	W
Cedarville U, OH	W(s)	Hope Coll, MI	W	Nebraska Wesleyan U, NE	W
Central Christian Coll of Kansas,		Huntington Coll, IN	W(s)	Newman U, KS	W(s)
KS	W(s)	Illinois Coll, IL	W	North Carolina Ag and Tech	
Central Coll, IA	W	Illinois State U, IL	W(s)	State U, NC	W
Central Methodist Coll, MO	W(s)	Illinois Wesleyan U, IL	W	North Central Coll, IL	W
Central Michigan U, MI	W(s)	Indiana Inst of Technology, IN	W(s)	North Dakota State U, ND	W(s)
Central Missouri State U, MO	W(s)	Indiana State U, IN	W(s)	North Park U, IL	W
Clarke Coll, IA	W	Indiana U Bloomington, IN	W(s)	Northeastern State U, OK	W(s)
Cleveland State U, OH	W(s)	Indiana U Northwest, IN	W	Northern Illinois U, IL	W(s)
Coe Coll, IA	W	Indiana U–Purdue U Fort		Northern Michigan U, MI	W
Coll of Mount St. Joseph, OH	W	Wayne, IN	W(s)	Northern State U, SD	W(s)
Coll of Saint Benedict, MN	W	Indiana U–Purdue U		Northland Coll, WI	W
Coll of Saint Mary, NE	W(s)	Indianapolis, IN	W(s)	Northwestern Coll, MN	W
Coll of St. Catherine, MN	W	Iowa State U of Science and		Northwestern Coll, IA	W(s)
Columbia Coll, MO	W(s)	Technology, IA	W(s)	Northwestern Oklahoma State	
Concord U, WV	W	Iowa Wesleyan Coll, IA	W(s)	U, OK	W(s)
Concordia Coll, MN	W	Jamestown Coll, ND	W(s)	Northwestern U, IL	W(s)
Concordia U, MI	W(s)	John Carroll U, OH	W	Northwood U, MI	W(s)
Concordia U, NE	W(s)	Judson Coll, IL	W(s)	Notre Dame Coll, OH	W(s)
Concordia U, IL	W	Kalamazoo Coll, MI	W	Oakland City U, IN	W(s)
Concordia U Wisconsin, WI	W	Kansas Wesleyan U, KS	W(s)	Oakland U, MI	W(s)
Concordia U, St. Paul, MN	W(s)	Kent State U, OH	W(s)	Oberlin Coll, OH	W
Cornell Coll, IA	W	Kenyon Coll, OH	W	Ohio Dominican U, OH	W(s)
Cornerstone U, MI	W(s)	Knox Coll, IL	W	Ohio Northern U, OH	W
Creighton U, NE	W(s)	Lake Erie Coll, OH	W	Ohio U, OH	W(s)
Crossroads Coll, MN	W	Lake Forest Coll, IL	W	Ohio U–Zanesville, OH	W
Crown Coll, MN	W	Lake Superior State U, MI	W	Ohio Wesleyan U, OH	W
Culver-Stockton Coll, MO	W(s)	Lakeland Coll, WI	W	Oklahoma Baptist U, OK	W(s)
Cumberland Coll, KY	W(s)	Lawrence U, WI	W	Oklahoma Christian U, OK	W(s)
Dakota State U, SD	W	Lehigh U, PA	W(s)	Oklahoma City U, OK	W(s)
Dakota Wesleyan U, SD	W(s)	Lewis U, IL	W(s)	Oklahoma Panhandle State U,	
Dana Coll, NE	W(s)	Lincoln Coll, Lincoln, IL	W(s)	OK	W(s)
DePaul U, IL	W(s)	Lincoln U, MO	W(s)	Oklahoma State U, OK	W(s)
DePauw U, IN	W	Lindenwood U, MO	W(s)	Olivet Coll, MI	W
Defiance Coll, OH	W	Loras Coll, IA	W	Olivet Nazarene U, IL	W(s)
Denison U, OH	W	Loyola U Chicago, IL	W(s)	Ottawa U, KS	W(s)
Dickinson State U, ND	W(s)	Luther Coll, IA	W	Otterbein Coll, OH	W
Doane Coll, NE	W(s)	MacMurray Coll, IL	W	Park U, MO	W(s)
Dominican U, IL	W	Macalester Coll, MN	W	Peru State Coll, NE	W(s)
Dordt Coll, IA	W(s)	Madonna U, MI	W(s)	Pillsbury Baptist Bible Coll, MN	W
Drake U, IA	W(s)	Malone Coll, OH	W(s)	Pittsburg State U, KS	W(s)
East Central U, OK	W(s)	Manchester Coll, IN	W	Presentation Coll, SD	W
Eastern Illinois U, IL	W(s)	Marian Coll, IN	W(s)	Purdue U, IN	W(s)
Eastern Michigan U, MI	W(s)	Marian Coll of Fond du Lac, WI	W	Purdue U North Central, IN	W
Edgewood Coll, WI	W	Marietta Coll, OH	W	Quincy U, IL	W
Elmhurst Coll, IL	W	Marquette U, WI	W	Ripon Coll, WI	W
Emporia State U, KS	W(s)	Martin Luther Coll, MN	W	Robert Morris Coll, IL	W(s)
Eureka Coll, IL	W	Maryville U of Saint Louis, MO	W	Rochester Coll, MI	W(s)
Evangel U, MO	W(s)	Mayville State U, ND	W(s)	Rochester Comm and Tech Coll,	
Ferris State U, MI	W(s)	McKendree Coll, IL	W(s)	MN	W
Florida Gulf Coast U, FL	W(s)	McPherson Coll, KS	W	Rockford Coll, IL	W
Fontbonne U, MO	W	Miami U, OH	W(s)	Rose-Hulman Inst of	
Fort Hays State U, KS	W	Michigan State U, MI	W	Technology, IN	W
Franklin Coll, IN	W	MidAmerica Nazarene U, KS	W(s)	Saginaw Valley State U, MI	W(s)
Gannon U, PA	W(s)	Millikin U, IL	W	Saint Joseph's Coll, IN	W(s)
Goshen Coll, IN	W(s)	Milwaukee School of		Saint Louis U, MO	W(s)
Grace Coll, IN	W(s)	Engineering, WI	W	Saint Mary's Coll, IN	W
Graceland U, IA	W(s)	Minnesota State U Mankato,		Saint Mary's U of Minnesota,	
Grand Valley State U, MI	W(s)	MN	W(s)	MN	W
Grand View Coll, IA	W(s)	Minnesota State U Moorhead,		Saint Mary-of-the-Woods Coll,	
Greenville Coll, IL	W	MN	W(s)	IN	W(s)
Grinnell Coll, IA	W	Minot State U, ND	W(s)	Saint Xavier U, IL	W(s)
Gustavus Adolphus Coll, MN	W	Missouri Baptist U, MO	W(s)	Shawnee State U, OH	W
Hamline U, MN	W	Missouri Southern State U, MO	W(s)	Siena Heights U, MI	W(s)
Hannibal-LaGrange Coll, MO	W(s)	Missouri Valley Coll, MO	W(s)	Simpson Coll, IA	W
Hanover Coll, IN	W	Missouri Western State Coll,		South Dakota State U, SD	W(s)
Haskell Indian Nations U, KS	W	MO	W(s)	Southeast Missouri State U, MO	W(s)
Hastings Coll, NE	W(s)	Monmouth Coll, IL	W	Southeastern Oklahoma State U,	
Heidelberg Coll, OH	W	Morningside Coll, IA	W(s)	OK	W(s)
Hesston Coll, KS	W(s)	Mount Marty Coll, SD	W(s)	Southern Illinois U Carbondale,	
Hillsdale Coll, MI	W(s)	Mount Mary Coll, WI	W	IL	W(s)
		Mount Mercy Coll, IA	W		

M—for men; W—for women; (s)—scholarship offered

Southern Illinois U Edwardsville, IL	W(s)
Southern Nazarene U, OK	W(s)
Southwest Baptist U, MO	W(s)
Southwest Missouri State U, MO	W(s)
Southwestern Coll, KS	W(s)
Southwestern Oklahoma State U, OK	W(s)
Spring Arbor U, MI	W(s)
St. Ambrose U, IA	W(s)
St. Cloud State U, MN	W(s)
St. Gregory's U, OK	W(s)
St. Norbert Coll, WI	W
St. Olaf Coll, MN	W
Sterling Coll, KS	W(s)
Tabor Coll, KS	W(s)
Taylor U, IN	W(s)
Taylor U Fort Wayne, IN	W
The Coll of St. Scholastica, MN	W
The Coll of Wooster, OH	W
The Franciscan U, IA	W(s)
The Ohio State U, OH	W(s)
The U of Akron, OH	W(s)
The U of Alabama in Huntsville, AL	W
The U of Findlay, OH	W(s)
The U of Iowa, IA	W(s)
The U of South Dakota, SD	W(s)
Tiffin U, OH	W(s)
Transylvania U, KY	W
Tri-State U, IN	W
Trinity Christian Coll, IL	W(s)
Trinity International U, IL	W(s)
Truman State U, MO	W(s)
U of Central Oklahoma, OK	W(s)
U of Chicago, IL	W
U of Dayton, OH	W
U of Detroit Mercy, MI	W(s)
U of Dubuque, IA	W
U of Evansville, IN	W
U of Illinois at Chicago, IL	W(s)
U of Illinois at Springfield, IL	W(s)
U of Indianapolis, IN	W(s)
U of Kansas, KS	W(s)
U of Mary, ND	W(s)
U of Michigan, MI	W(s)
U of Minnesota, Crookston, MN	W(s)
U of Minnesota, Duluth, MN	W(s)
U of Minnesota, Morris, MN	W
U of Minnesota, Twin Cities Campus, MN	W(s)
U of Missouri–Columbia, MO	W(s)
U of Missouri–Kansas City, MO	W(s)
U of Missouri–Rolla, MO	W(s)
U of Missouri–St. Louis, MO	W(s)
U of Nebraska at Omaha, NE	W(s)
U of Nebraska–Lincoln, NE	W(s)
U of North Dakota, ND	W(s)
U of Northern Iowa, IA	W(s)
U of Notre Dame, IN	W(s)
U of Oklahoma, OK	W(s)
U of Rio Grande, OH	W(s)
U of Saint Francis, IN	W(s)
U of Saint Mary, KS	W(s)
U of Science and Arts of Oklahoma, OK	W(s)
U of Sioux Falls, SD	W(s)
U of Southern Indiana, IN	W(s)
U of St. Francis, IL	W(s)
U of St. Thomas, MN	W
U of Toledo, OH	W(s)
U of Tulsa, OK	W(s)
U of West Florida, FL	W(s)
U of Wisconsin–Eau Claire, WI	W
U of Wisconsin–Green Bay, WI	W(s)
U of Wisconsin–La Crosse, WI	W

U of Wisconsin–Madison, WI	W(s)
U of Wisconsin–Oshkosh, WI	W
U of Wisconsin–Parkside, WI	W(s)
U of Wisconsin–Platteville, WI	W
U of Wisconsin–River Falls, WI	W
U of Wisconsin–Stevens Point, WI	W
U of Wisconsin–Stout, WI	W
U of Wisconsin–Superior, WI	W
U of Wisconsin–Whitewater, WI	W
Upper Iowa U, IA	W
Urbana U, OH	W(s)
Ursuline Coll, OH	W(s)
Valley City State U, ND	W(s)
Valparaiso U, IN	W(s)
Viterbo U, WI	W(s)
Waldorf Coll, IA	W(s)
Walsh U, OH	W(s)
Wartburg Coll, IA	W
Washburn U, KS	W(s)
Washington U in St. Louis, MO	W
Wayne State Coll, NE	W(s)
Wayne State U, MI	W(s)
Webster U, MO	W
Western Illinois U, IL	W(s)
Western Michigan U, MI	W(s)
Westminster Coll, MO	W
Wheaton Coll, IL	W
Wichita State U, KS	W(s)
William Jewell Coll, MO	W(s)
William Penn U, IA	W(s)
William Woods U, MO	W(s)
Winona State U, MN	W(s)
Wisconsin Lutheran Coll, WI	W
Wittenberg U, OH	W
Wright State U, OH	W(s)
York Coll, NE	W(s)
Youngstown State U, OH	W(s)

Squash

Denison U, OH	M, W
Kenyon Coll, OH	M, W
Lehigh U, PA	M
Michigan Technological U, MI	M, W
Purdue U, IN	M, W

Swimming

Albion Coll, MI	M, W
Alma Coll, MI	M, W
Ashland U, OH	M(s), W(s)
Augustana Coll, IL	M, W
Baldwin-Wallace Coll, OH	M, W
Ball State U, IN	M(s), W(s)
Beloit Coll, WI	M, W
Benedictine U, IL	M, W
Bowling Green State U, OH	M(s), W(s)
Buena Vista U, IA	M, W
Butler U, IN	M, W
Calvin Coll, MI	M, W
Carleton Coll, MN	M, W
Carroll Coll, WI	M, W
Carthage Coll, WI	M, W
Case Western Reserve U, OH	M, W
Clarkson U	M, W
Cleveland State U, OH	M(s), W(s)
Coe Coll, IA	M, W
Coll of Saint Benedict, MN	W
Coll of St. Catherine, MN	W
Concordia Coll, MN	W
Cumberland Coll, KY	M(s), W(s)
DePauw U, IN	M, W
Denison U, OH	M, W
Drury U, MO	M(s), W(s)
Eastern Illinois U, IL	M(s), W(s)
Eastern Michigan U, MI	M(s), W(s)
Eureka Coll, IL	M, W
Gannon U, PA	M(s), W(s)

Grand Valley State U, MI	M(s), W(s)
Grinnell Coll, IA	M, W
Gustavus Adolphus Coll, MN	M, W
Hamline U, MN	M, W
Hillsdale Coll, MI	W(s)
Hiram Coll, OH	M, W
Hope Coll, MI	M, W
Illinois Inst of Technology, IL	M(s), W(s)
Illinois State U, IL	W(s)
Illinois Wesleyan U, IL	M, W
Indiana State U, IN	M, W
Indiana U Bloomington, IN	M(s), W(s)
Indiana U–Purdue U Indianapolis, IN	M(s), W(s)
Iowa State U of Science and Technology, IA	M(s), W(s)
John Carroll U, OH	M, W
Kalamazoo Coll, MI	M, W
Kenyon Coll, OH	M, W
Knox Coll, IL	M, W
Lake Forest Coll, IL	M, W
Lawrence U, WI	M, W
Lehigh U, PA	M(s), W(s)
Lewis U, IL	M(s), W(s)
Lincoln Coll, Lincoln, IL	M(s), W(s)
Lindenwood U, MO	M(s), W(s)
Loras Coll, IA	M, W
Luther Coll, IA	M, W
MacMurray Coll, IL	M, W
Macalester Coll, MN	M, W
Marquette U, WI	M, W
Miami U, OH	M(s), W(s)
Michigan State U, MI	M(s), W(s)
Michigan Technological U, MI	M, W
Millikin U, IL	M, W
Minnesota State U Mankato, MN	M(s), W(s)
Monmouth Coll, IL	M, W
Morningside Coll, IA	M(s), W(s)
Mount Union Coll, OH	M, W
North Carolina Ag and Tech State U, NC	W(s)
North Central Coll, IL	M, W
Northern Illinois U, IL	M(s), W(s)
Northern Michigan U, MI	W(s)
Northwestern U, IL	M(s), W(s)
Oakland U, MI	M(s), W(s)
Oberlin Coll, OH	M, W
Ohio Northern U, OH	M, W
Ohio U, OH	M(s), W(s)
Ohio Wesleyan U, OH	M, W
Olivet Coll, MI	M, W
Principia Coll, IL	M, W
Purdue U, IN	M(s), W(s)
Ripon Coll, WI	M, W
Rose-Hulman Inst of Technology, IN	M, W
Saint John's U, MN	M
Saint Louis U, MO	M(s), W(s)
Saint Mary's Coll, IN	W
Saint Mary's U of Minnesota, MN	M, W
Simpson Coll, IA	M, W
South Dakota State U, SD	M(s), W(s)
Southern Illinois U Carbondale, IL	M(s), W(s)
Southwest Missouri State U, MO	M(s), W(s)
St. Cloud State U, MN	M(s), W(s)
St. Norbert Coll, WI	W
St. Olaf Coll, MN	M, W
Stephens Coll, MO	W
The Coll of Wooster, OH	M, W
The Ohio State U, OH	M(s), W(s)
The U of Findlay, OH	M(s), W(s)
The U of Iowa, IA	M(s), W(s)
The U of South Dakota, SD	M(s), W

Swimming

Transylvania U, KY	M, W	Bethel U, MN	M, W	Huntington Coll, IN	M(s), W(s)
Truman State U, MO	M(s), W(s)	Blackburn Coll, IL	W	Illinois Coll, IL	M, W
U of Chicago, IL	M, W	Bluffton Coll, OH	M, W	Illinois State U, IL	M(s), W(s)
U of Cincinnati, OH	M(s), W(s)	Bowling Green State U, OH	M(s), W(s)	Illinois Wesleyan U, IL	M, W
U of Evansville, IN	M(s), W(s)	Bradley U, IL	M(s), W(s)	Indiana State U, IN	M(s), W(s)
U of Illinois at Chicago, IL	M(s), W(s)	Brescia U, KY	W(s)	Indiana U Bloomington, IN	M(s), W(s)
U of Illinois at Urbana–Champaign, IL	W(s)	Buena Vista U, IA	M, W	Indiana U Southeast, IN	M, W
U of Indianapolis, IN	M(s), W(s)	Butler U, IN	M(s), W(s)	Indiana U–Purdue U Fort Wayne, IN	M(s), W(s)
U of Kansas, KS	W(s)	Calvin Coll, MI	M, W	Indiana U–Purdue U Indianapolis, IN	M(s), W(s)
U of Michigan, MI	M(s), W(s)	Cameron U, OK	M(s), W(s)	Iowa State U of Science and Technology, IA	W(s)
U of Minnesota, Morris, MN	W	Capital U, OH	M, W	John Carroll U, OH	M, W
U of Minnesota, Twin Cities Campus, MN	M(s), W(s)	Carleton Coll, MN	M, W	Judson Coll, IL	M(s), W(s)
U of Missouri–Columbia, MO	M(s), W(s)	Carroll Coll, WI	M, W	Kalamazoo Coll, MI	M, W
U of Missouri–Rolla, MO	M(s)	Carthage Coll, WI	M, W	Kansas State U, KS	W(s)
U of Nebraska at Omaha, NE	W	Case Western Reserve U, OH	M, W	Kansas Wesleyan U, KS	M(s), W(s)
U of Nebraska–Lincoln, NE	W(s)	Cedarville U, OH	M(s), W(s)	Kenyon Coll, OH	M, W
U of North Dakota, ND	M, W(s)	Central Christian Coll of Kansas, KS	M(s), W(s)	Knox Coll, IL	M, W
U of Northern Iowa, IA	W(s)	Central Coll, IA	M, W	Lake Forest Coll, IL	M, W
U of Notre Dame, IN	M(s), W(s)	Central State U, OH	M(s), W(s)	Lake Superior State U, MI	M(s), W(s)
U of St. Thomas, MN	M, W	Chicago State U, IL	M, W	Lakeland Coll, WI	M, W
U of Toledo, OH	M(s), W(s)	Clarke Coll, IA	M, W	Lawrence U, WI	M, W
U of Wisconsin–Eau Claire, WI	M, W	Clarkson U	M, W	Lehigh U, PA	M(s), W(s)
U of Wisconsin–Green Bay, WI	M(s), W(s)	Cleveland State U, OH	W(s)	Lewis U, IL	M(s), W(s)
U of Wisconsin–La Crosse, WI	M, W	Coe Coll, IA	M, W	Lincoln Coll, Lincoln, IL	M, W
U of Wisconsin–Madison, WI	M(s), W(s)	Coll of Mount St. Joseph, OH	M, W	Lincoln U, MO	W(s)
U of Wisconsin–Milwaukee, WI	M(s), W(s)	Coll of Saint Benedict, MN	W	Lindenwood U, MO	M(s), W(s)
U of Wisconsin–Oshkosh, WI	M, W	Coll of St. Catherine, MN	W	Loras Coll, IA	M, W
U of Wisconsin–River Falls, WI	M, W	Concord U, WV	M(s), W(s)	Luther Coll, IA	M, W
U of Wisconsin–Stevens Point, WI	M, W	Concordia Coll, MN	M, W	MacMurray Coll, IL	M, W
U of Wisconsin–Whitewater, WI	M, W	Concordia U, NE	M(s), W(s)	Macalester Coll, MN	M, W
Valparaiso U, IN	M(s), W(s)	Concordia U, IL	M, W	Malone Coll, OH	M(s), W(s)
Wabash Coll, IN	M	Concordia U Wisconsin, WI	M, W	Manchester Coll, IN	M, W
Washington U in St. Louis, MO	M, W	Cornell Coll, IA	M, W	Manhattan Christian Coll, KS	M, W
Wayne State U, MI	M(s), W(s)	Creighton U, NE	M(s), W(s)	Marian Coll, IN	M(s), W(s)
Webster U, MO	M, W	Crossroads Coll, MN	M, W	Marian Coll of Fond du Lac, WI	M, W
Western Illinois U, IL	M(s), W(s)	Cumberland Coll, KY	M(s), W(s)	Marietta Coll, OH	M, W
Wheaton Coll, IL	M, W	DePaul U, IL	M(s), W(s)	Marquette U, WI	M(s), W(s)
Wichita State U, KS	M, W	DePauw U, IN	M, W	Martin Luther Coll, MN	M, W
Wittenberg U, OH	M, W	Defiance Coll, OH	M, W	Maryville U of Saint Louis, MO	M, W
Wright State U, OH	M(s), W(s)	Denison U, OH	M, W	McKendree Coll, IL	M(s), W(s)
Xavier U, OH	M(s), W(s)	Doane Coll, NE	M, W	Miami U, OH	M, W
Youngstown State U, OH	W	Dominican U, IL	M, W	Miami U Hamilton, OH	M, W
		Dordt Coll, IA	M(s), W(s)	Michigan State U, MI	M(s), W(s)
Table Tennis		Drake U, IA	M(s), W(s)	Michigan Technological U, MI	M, W(s)
Bradley U, IL	M, W	Drury U, MO	M(s), W(s)	Millikin U, IL	M, W
Hiram Coll, OH	M, W	Earlham Coll, IN	M, W	Milwaukee School of Engineering, WI	M, W
Michigan Technological U, MI	M, W	East Central U, OK	M(s), W(s)	Minnesota State U Mankato, MN	M(s), W(s)
Purdue U, IN	M, W	Eastern Illinois U, IL	M(s), W(s)	Minnesota State U Moorhead, MN	W
The U of Iowa, IA	M, W	Eastern Michigan U, MI	W(s)	Missouri Southern State U, MO	W(s)
Washington U in St. Louis, MO	M, W	Edgewood Coll, WI	M, W	Missouri Valley Coll, MO	M(s), W(s)
		Elmhurst Coll, IL	M, W	Missouri Western State Coll, MO	W(s)
Tennis		Emporia State U, KS	M(s), W(s)	Monmouth Coll, IL	M, W
Adrian Coll, MI	M, W	Eureka Coll, IL	M, W	Morningside Coll, IA	M(s), W(s)
Albion Coll, MI	M, W	Evangel U, MO	M(s), W(s)	Mount Mary Coll, WI	W
Alma Coll, MI	M, W	Ferris State U, MI	M(s), W(s)	Mount Union Coll, OH	M, W
Ancilla Coll, IN	M(s), W(s)	Florida Gulf Coast U, FL	M(s), W(s)	Muskingum Coll, OH	M, W
Aquinas Coll, MI	M(s), W(s)	Fontbonne U, MO	M, W	Nebraska Wesleyan U, NE	M, W
Ashland U, OH	M, W	Fort Hays State U, KS	W(s)	Newman U, KS	M(s), W(s)
Augustana Coll, SD	M, W	Franklin Coll, IN	M, W	North Carolina Ag and Tech State U, NC	M(s), W(s)
Augustana Coll, IL	M, W	Goshen Coll, IN	M(s), W(s)	North Central Coll, IL	M, W
Aurora U, IL	M, W	Grace Coll, IN	M(s), W(s)	North Park U, IL	W
Baker U, KS	M(s), W(s)	Graceland U, IA	M(s), W(s)	Northeastern State U, OK	W(s)
Baldwin-Wallace Coll, OH	M, W	Grand Valley State U, MI	M(s), W(s)	Northern Illinois U, IL	M(s), W(s)
Ball State U, IN	M(s), W(s)	Greenville Coll, IL	M, W	Northern State U, SD	M, W(s)
Barclay Coll, KS	M, W	Grinnell Coll, IA	M, W	Northwestern Coll, MN	M, W
Beloit Coll, WI	M, W	Gustavus Adolphus Coll, MN	M, W	Northwestern Coll, IA	M(s), W(s)
Bemidji State U, MN	W(s)	Hamline U, MN	M, W	Northwestern U, IL	M(s), W(s)
Benedictine Coll, KS	M(s), W(s)	Hanover Coll, IN	M, W		
Benedictine U, IL	W	Hastings Coll, NE	M(s), W(s)		
Bethany Coll, KS	M(s), W(s)	Heidelberg Coll, OH	M, W		
Bethany Lutheran Coll, MN	M, W	Hesston Coll, KS	M, W		
Bethel Coll, IN	M(s), W(s)	Hillsdale Coll, MI	W(s)		
Bethel Coll, KS	M(s), W(s)	Hiram Coll, OH	M, W		
		Hope Coll, MI	M, W		

M—for men; W—for women; (s)—scholarship offered

Northwood U, MI	M(s), W(s)
Notre Dame Coll, OH	M(s)
Oakland U, MI	W(s)
Oberlin Coll, OH	M, W
Ohio Dominican U, OH	M(s), W(s)
Ohio Northern U, OH	M, W
Ohio U–Zanesville, OH	M, W
Ohio Wesleyan U, OH	M, W
Oklahoma Baptist U, OK	M(s), W(s)
Oklahoma Christian U, OK	M(s), W(s)
Oklahoma State U, OK	M(s), W(s)
Olivet Coll, MI	M, W
Olivet Nazarene U, IL	M(s), W(s)
Oral Roberts U, OK	M(s), W(s)
Otterbein Coll, OH	M, W
Principia Coll, IL	M, W
Purdue U, IN	M(s), W(s)
Quincy U, IL	M(s), W(s)
Research Coll of Nursing, MO	M(s), W(s)
Ripon Coll, WI	M, W
Robert Morris Coll, IL	W(s)
Rockford Coll, IL	M, W
Rockhurst U, MO	M(s), W(s)
Rose-Hulman Inst of Technology, IN	M, W
Saginaw Valley State U, MI	W(s)
Saint John's U, MN	M
Saint Joseph's Coll, IN	M(s), W(s)
Saint Louis U, MO	M(s), W(s)
Saint Mary's Coll, IN	W
Saint Mary's U of Minnesota, MN	M, W
Shawnee State U, OH	W
Simpson Coll, IA	M, W
South Dakota School of Mines and Technology, SD	M
South Dakota State U, SD	M, W
Southeast Missouri State U, MO	W(s)
Southeastern Oklahoma State U, OK	M(s), W(s)
Southern Illinois U Carbondale, IL	M(s), W(s)
Southern Illinois U Edwardsville, IL	M(s), W(s)
Southern Nazarene U, OK	M(s), W(s)
Southwest Baptist U, MO	M(s), W(s)
Southwest Missouri State U, MO	M(s), W(s)
Southwestern Coll, KS	M(s), W(s)
Spring Arbor U, MI	M(s), W(s)
St. Ambrose U, IA	M(s), W(s)
St. Cloud State U, MN	M(s), W(s)
St. Norbert Coll, WI	M, W
St. Olaf Coll, MN	M, W
Stephens Coll, MO	W
Tabor Coll, KS	M(s), W(s)
Taylor U, IN	M(s), W(s)
The Coll of St. Scholastica, MN	M, W
The Coll of Wooster, OH	M, W
The Ohio State U, OH	M(s), W(s)
The U of Akron, OH	M(s), W(s)
The U of Alabama in Huntsville, AL	M(s), W(s)
The U of Findlay, OH	M(s), W(s)
The U of Iowa, IA	M(s), W(s)
The U of South Dakota, SD	M(s), W(s)
Tiffin U, OH	M(s), W(s)
Transylvania U, KY	M, W
Tri-State U, IN	M, W
Truman State U, MO	M(s), W(s)
U of Central Oklahoma, OK	M(s), W(s)
U of Chicago, IL	M, W
U of Cincinnati, OH	M(s), W(s)
U of Dayton, OH	M(s), W(s)
U of Detroit Mercy, MI	W(s)
U of Dubuque, IA	M, W
U of Evansville, IN	M(s), W(s)

U of Illinois at Chicago, IL	M(s), W(s)
U of Illinois at Springfield, IL	M(s), W(s)
U of Illinois at Urbana–Champaign, IL	M(s), W(s)
U of Indianapolis, IN	M(s), W(s)
U of Kansas, KS	W(s)
U of Mary, ND	M(s), W(s)
U of Michigan, MI	M(s), W(s)
U of Minnesota, Crookston, MN	W(s)
U of Minnesota, Duluth, MN	M(s), W(s)
U of Minnesota, Morris, MN	M, W
U of Minnesota, Twin Cities Campus, MN	M(s), W(s)
U of Missouri–Columbia, MO	W(s)
U of Missouri–Kansas City, MO	M(s), W(s)
U of Missouri–St. Louis, MO	M(s), W(s)
U of Nebraska at Omaha, NE	W
U of Nebraska–Lincoln, NE	M(s), W(s)
U of New Orleans, LA	M(s), W(s)
U of North Dakota, ND	W
U of Northern Iowa, IA	M, W
U of Notre Dame, IN	M(s), W(s)
U of Oklahoma, OK	M(s), W(s)
U of Saint Francis, IN	W(s)
U of Sioux Falls, SD	M(s), W(s)
U of Southern Indiana, IN	M(s), W(s)
U of St. Francis, IL	M(s), W(s)
U of St. Thomas, MN	M, W
U of Toledo, OH	M(s), W(s)
U of Tulsa, OK	M(s), W(s)
U of West Florida, FL	M(s), W(s)
U of Wisconsin–Eau Claire, WI	M, W
U of Wisconsin–Green Bay, WI	M(s), W(s)
U of Wisconsin–La Crosse, WI	M, W
U of Wisconsin–Madison, WI	M(s), W(s)
U of Wisconsin–Milwaukee, WI	M(s), W(s)
U of Wisconsin–Oshkosh, WI	M, W
U of Wisconsin–River Falls, WI	W
U of Wisconsin–Stevens Point, WI	W
U of Wisconsin–Stout, WI	W
U of Wisconsin–Whitewater, WI	M, W
Upper Iowa U, IA	M, W
Ursuline Coll, OH	W(s)
Valparaiso U, IN	M(s), W(s)
Wabash Coll, IN	M
Walsh U, OH	M(s), W(s)
Wartburg Coll, IA	M, W
Washburn U, KS	M(s), W(s)
Washington U in St. Louis, MO	M, W
Wayne State U, MI	M(s), W(s)
Webster U, MO	M, W
Western Illinois U, IL	M(s), W(s)
Western Michigan U, MI	M(s), W(s)
Westminster Coll, MO	M, W
Wheaton Coll, IL	M, W
Wichita State U, KS	M(s), W(s)
William Jewell Coll, MO	M(s), W(s)
Winona State U, MN	M(s), W(s)
Wisconsin Lutheran Coll, WI	W
Wittenberg U, OH	M, W
Wright State U, OH	M(s), W(s)
Xavier U, OH	M(s), W(s)
Youngstown State U, OH	M(s), W(s)

Track and Field

Adrian Coll, MI	M, W
Albion Coll, MI	M, W
Alma Coll, MI	M, W
Aquinas Coll, MI	M(s), W(s)
Ashland U, OH	M(s), W(s)
Augsburg Coll, MN	M, W
Augustana Coll, SD	M(s), W(s)
Augustana Coll, IL	M, W
Bacone Coll, OK	M(s), W(s)
Baker U, KS	M(s), W(s)
Baldwin-Wallace Coll, OH	M, W

Ball State U, IN	M(s), W(s)
Beloit Coll, WI	M, W
Bemidji State U, MN	M(s), W(s)
Benedictine Coll, KS	M(s), W(s)
Benedictine U, IL	M, W
Bethany Coll, KS	M(s), W(s)
Bethel Coll, IN	M(s), W(s)
Bethel Coll, KS	M(s), W(s)
Bethel U, MN	M, W
Black Hills State U, SD	M(s), W(s)
Bluffton Coll, OH	M, W
Bowling Green State U, OH	M(s), W(s)
Bradley U, IL	W(s)
Briar Cliff U, IA	M(s), W(s)
Buena Vista U, IA	M, W
Butler U, IN	M, W
Calvin Coll, MI	M, W
Capital U, OH	M, W
Carleton Coll, MN	M, W
Carroll Coll, WI	M, W
Carthage Coll, WI	M, W
Case Western Reserve U, OH	M, W
Cedarville U, OH	M(s), W(s)
Central Coll, IA	M, W
Central Methodist Coll, MO	M(s), W(s)
Central Michigan U, MI	M(s), W(s)
Central Missouri State U, MO	M(s), W(s)
Central State U, OH	M(s), W(s)
Chadron State Coll, NE	M(s), W(s)
Chicago State U, IL	M(s), W(s)
Cleveland State U, OH	W(s)
Coe Coll, IA	M, W
Coll of Mount St. Joseph, OH	M, W
Coll of Saint Benedict, MN	W
Coll of St. Catherine, MN	W
Concord U, WV	M(s), W(s)
Concordia Coll, MN	M, W
Concordia U, NE	M(s), W(s)
Concordia U, IL	M, W
Concordia U Wisconsin, WI	M, W
Concordia U, St. Paul, MN	M(s), W(s)
Cornell Coll, IA	M, W
Cornerstone U, MI	M(s), W(s)
Cumberland Coll, KY	M(s), W(s)
Dakota State U, SD	M(s), W(s)
Dakota Wesleyan U, SD	M(s), W(s)
Dana Coll, NE	M(s), W(s)
DePaul U, IL	M(s), W(s)
DePauw U, IN	M, W
Defiance Coll, OH	M, W
Denison U, OH	M, W
Dickinson State U, ND	M(s), W(s)
Doane Coll, NE	M(s), W(s)
Dordt Coll, IA	M(s), W(s)
Drake U, IA	M(s), W(s)
Earlham Coll, IN	M, W
East Central U, OK	M, W
Eastern Illinois U, IL	M(s), W(s)
Eastern Michigan U, MI	M(s), W(s)
Elmhurst Coll, IL	M, W
Emporia State U, KS	M(s), W(s)
Eureka Coll, IL	M, W
Evangel U, MO	M(s), W(s)
Ferris State U, MI	M(s), W(s)
Fort Hays State U, KS	M(s), W(s)
Franklin Coll, IN	M, W
Goshen Coll, IN	M(s), W(s)
Grace Coll, IN	M(s), W(s)
Graceland U, IA	M(s), W(s)
Grand Valley State U, MI	M(s), W(s)
Greenville Coll, IL	M, W
Grinnell Coll, IA	M, W
Gustavus Adolphus Coll, MN	M, W
Hamline U, MN	M, W
Hanover Coll, IN	M, W
Harris-Stowe State Coll, MO	W(s)

Haskell Indian Nations U, KS	M, W
Hastings Coll, NE	M(s), W(s)
Heidelberg Coll, OH	M, W
Hillsdale Coll, MI	M(s), W(s)
Hiram Coll, OH	M, W
Hope Coll, MI	M, W
Huntington Coll, IN	M(s), W(s)
Illinois Coll, IL	M, W
Illinois State U, IL	M(s), W(s)
Illinois Wesleyan U, IL	M, W
Indiana State U, IN	M(s), W(s)
Indiana U Bloomington, IN	M(s), W(s)
Indiana U–Purdue U Fort Wayne, IN	W(s)
Iowa State U of Science and Technology, IA	M(s), W(s)
Iowa Wesleyan Coll, IA	M(s), W(s)
Jamestown Coll, ND	M(s), W(s)
John Carroll U, OH	M, W
Kansas State U, KS	M(s), W(s)
Kansas Wesleyan U, KS	M(s), W(s)
Kent State U, OH	M(s), W(s)
Kenyon Coll, OH	M, W
Knox Coll, IL	M, W
Lake Superior State U, MI	M(s), W(s)
Lawrence U, WI	M, W
Lehigh U, PA	M(s), W(s)
Lewis U, IL	M(s), W(s)
Lincoln U, MO	M(s), W(s)
Lindenwood U, MO	M(s), W(s)
Loras Coll, IA	M, W
Loyola U Chicago, IL	M(s), W(s)
Luther Coll, IA	M, W
Macalester Coll, MN	M, W
Malone Coll, OH	M(s), W(s)
Manchester Coll, IN	M, W
Marian Coll, IN	M(s), W(s)
Marietta Coll, OH	M, W
Marquette U, WI	M(s), W(s)
Martin Luther Coll, MN	M, W
McKendree Coll, IL	M(s), W(s)
McPherson Coll, KS	M, W
Miami U, OH	M(s), W(s)
Michigan State U, MI	M(s), W(s)
Michigan Technological U, MI	M, W
MidAmerica Nazarene U, KS	M(s), W(s)
Millikin U, IL	M, W
Milwaukee School of Engineering, WI	M, W
Minnesota State U Mankato, MN	M(s), W(s)
Minnesota State U Moorhead, MN	M(s), W(s)
Minot State U, ND	M(s), W(s)
Missouri Southern State U, MO	M(s), W(s)
Missouri Valley Coll, MO	M(s), W(s)
Monmouth Coll, IL	M, W
Morningside Coll, IA	M(s), W(s)
Mount Marty Coll, SD	M(s), W(s)
Mount Mercy Coll, IA	M, W
Mount Union Coll, OH	M, W
Muskingum Coll, OH	M, W
Nebraska Wesleyan U, NE	M, W
North Carolina Ag and Tech State U, NC	M(s), W(s)
North Central Coll, IL	M, W
North Central U, MN	M, W
North Dakota State U, ND	M(s), W(s)
North Park U, IL	M, W
Northern Michigan U, MI	W(s)
Northern State U, SD	M(s), W(s)
Northwestern Coll, MN	M, W
Northwestern Coll, IA	M(s), W(s)
Northwood U, MI	M(s), W(s)
Notre Dame Coll, OH	M(s), W(s)

Oberlin Coll, OH	M, W
Ohio Northern U, OH	M, W
Ohio U, OH	M(s), W(s)
Ohio Wesleyan U, OH	M, W
Oklahoma Baptist U, OK	M(s), W(s)
Oklahoma Christian U, OK	M(s), W(s)
Oklahoma State U, OK	M(s), W(s)
Olivet Coll, MI	M, W
Olivet Nazarene U, IL	M(s), W(s)
Oral Roberts U, OK	M(s), W(s)
Ottawa U, KS	M(s), W(s)
Otterbein Coll, OH	M, W
Park U, MO	M(s), W(s)
Pittsburg State U, KS	M(s), W(s)
Principia Coll, IL	M, W
Purdue U, IN	M(s), W(s)
Ripon Coll, WI	M, W
Rose-Hulman Inst of Technology, IN	M, W
Saginaw Valley State U, MI	M(s), W(s)
Saint John's U, MN	M
Saint Joseph's Coll, IN	M(s), W(s)
Saint Mary's U of Minnesota, MN	M, W
Siena Heights U, MI	M(s), W(s)
Simpson Coll, IA	M, W
South Dakota School of Mines and Technology, SD	M(s), W(s)
South Dakota State U, SD	M(s), W(s)
Southeast Missouri State U, MO	M(s), W(s)
Southern Illinois U Carbondale, IL	M(s), W(s)
Southern Illinois U Edwardsville, IL	M(s), W(s)
Southern Nazarene U, OK	M(s), W(s)
Southwest Baptist U, MO	M, W
Southwest Missouri State U, MO	M(s), W(s)
Southwestern Coll, KS	M(s), W(s)
Spring Arbor U, MI	M(s), W(s)
St. Ambrose U, IA	M(s), W(s)
St. Cloud State U, MN	M(s), W(s)
St. Gregory's U, OK	M(s), W(s)
St. Norbert Coll, WI	M, W
St. Olaf Coll, MN	M, W
Sterling Coll, KS	M(s), W(s)
Tabor Coll, KS	M(s), W(s)
Taylor U, IN	M(s), W(s)
The Coll of Wooster, OH	M, W
The Franciscan U, IA	M(s), W(s)
The Ohio State U, OH	M(s), W(s)
The U of Akron, OH	M(s), W(s)
The U of Alabama in Huntsville, AL	M, W
The U of Findlay, OH	M(s), W(s)
The U of Iowa, IA	M(s), W(s)
The U of South Dakota, SD	M(s), W(s)
Tiffin U, OH	M(s), W(s)
Tri-State U, IN	M, W
Trinity Christian Coll, IL	M(s), W(s)
Trinity International U, IL	M, W
Truman State U, MO	M(s), W(s)
U of Chicago, IL	M, W
U of Cincinnati, OH	M(s), W
U of Dayton, OH	W(s)
U of Detroit Mercy, MI	M(s), W(s)
U of Dubuque, IA	M, W
U of Illinois at Chicago, IL	M(s), W(s)
U of Illinois at Urbana–Champaign, IL	M(s), W(s)
U of Indianapolis, IN	M(s), W(s)
U of Kansas, KS	M(s), W(s)
U of Mary, ND	M(s), W(s)
U of Michigan, MI	M(s), W(s)
U of Minnesota, Duluth, MN	M(s), W(s)
U of Minnesota, Morris, MN	M, W

U of Minnesota, Twin Cities Campus, MN	M(s), W(s)
U of Missouri–Columbia, MO	M(s), W(s)
U of Missouri–Kansas City, MO	M(s), W(s)
U of Missouri–Rolla, MO	M(s), W(s)
U of Nebraska–Lincoln, NE	M(s), W(s)
U of New Orleans, LA	M(s), W(s)
U of North Dakota, ND	M(s), W(s)
U of Northern Iowa, IA	M(s), W(s)
U of Notre Dame, IN	M(s), W(s)
U of Oklahoma, OK	M(s), W(s)
U of Rio Grande, OH	M(s), W(s)
U of Saint Francis, IN	M(s), W(s)
U of Sioux Falls, SD	M(s), W(s)
U of St. Francis, IL	W(s)
U of St. Thomas, MN	M, W
U of Toledo, OH	M(s), W(s)
U of Tulsa, OK	M(s), W(s)
U of Wisconsin–Eau Claire, WI	M, W
U of Wisconsin–La Crosse, WI	M, W
U of Wisconsin–Madison, WI	M(s), W(s)
U of Wisconsin–Milwaukee, WI	M(s), W(s)
U of Wisconsin–Oshkosh, WI	M, W
U of Wisconsin–Parkside, WI	M(s), W(s)
U of Wisconsin–Platteville, WI	M, W
U of Wisconsin–River Falls, WI	M, W
U of Wisconsin–Stevens Point, WI	M, W
U of Wisconsin–Stout, WI	M, W
U of Wisconsin–Superior, WI	M, W
U of Wisconsin–Whitewater, WI	M, W
Upper Iowa U, IA	M, W
Wabash Coll, IN	M
Walsh U, OH	M(s), W(s)
Wartburg Coll, IA	M, W
Washington U in St. Louis, MO	M, W
Wayne State Coll, NE	M(s), W(s)
Western Illinois U, IL	M(s), W(s)
Western Michigan U, MI	M(s), W(s)
Wheaton Coll, IL	M, W
Wichita State U, KS	M(s), W(s)
William Jewell Coll, MO	M(s), W(s)
William Penn U, IA	M(s), W(s)
William Woods U, MO	M, W
Winona State U, MN	W(s)
Wisconsin Lutheran Coll, WI	M, W
Wittenberg U, OH	M, W
Wright State U, OH	W(s)
York Coll, NE	M(s), W(s)
Youngstown State U, OH	M(s), W(s)

Volleyball

Adrian Coll, MI	W
Albion Coll, MI	M, W
Alma Coll, MI	W
Alverno Coll, WI	W
Aquinas Coll, MI	W(s)
Ashland U, OH	W(s)
Augsburg Coll, MN	W
Augustana Coll, SD	W(s)
Augustana Coll, IL	M, W
Aurora U, IL	W
Avila U, MO	W(s)
Bacone Coll, OK	M(s), W(s)
Baker U, KS	W(s)
Baldwin-Wallace Coll, OH	W
Ball State U, IN	M(s), W(s)
Baptist Bible Coll, MO	W
Barclay Coll, KS	W
Bellevue U, NE	W(s)
Beloit Coll, WI	W
Bemidji State U, MN	W(s)
Benedictine Coll, KS	W(s)
Benedictine U, IL	W
Bethany Coll, KS	W(s)

M—for men; W—for women; (s)—scholarship offered

Bethany Lutheran Coll, MN	W	Edgewood Coll, WI	W	Manchester Coll, IN	W
Bethel Coll, IN	W(s)	Elmhurst Coll, IL	W	Manhattan Christian Coll, KS	W
Bethel Coll, KS	W(s)	Emporia State U, KS	W(s)	Marian Coll, IN	W(s)
Bethel U, MN	M, W	Eureka Coll, IL	W	Marian Coll of Fond du Lac, WI	W
Black Hills State U, SD	W(s)	Evangel U, MO	W(s)	Marietta Coll, OH	W
Blackburn Coll, IL	W	Faith Baptist Bible Coll and		Marquette U, WI	M, W(s)
Blessing-Rieman Coll of		Theological Seminary, IA	W	Martin Luther Coll, MN	W
Nursing, IL	M(s), W(s)	Ferris State U, MI	W(s)	Maryville U of Saint Louis, MO	W
Bluffton Coll, OH	W	Florida Gulf Coast U, FL	W(s)	Mayville State U, ND	W(s)
Bowling Green State U, OH	M, W(s)	Fontbonne U, MO	W	McKendree Coll, IL	W(s)
Bradley U, IL	W(s)	Fort Hays State U, KS	W(s)	McPherson Coll, KS	W
Brescia U, KY	W(s)	Franklin Coll, IN	W	Messenger Coll, MO	W
Briar Cliff U, IA	W(s)	Gannon U, PA	W(s)	Miami U, OH	M, W(s)
Buena Vista U, IA	W	Goshen Coll, IN	W(s)	Miami U Hamilton, OH	W
Butler U, IN	W(s)	Grace Bible Coll, MI	W	Michigan State U, MI	M, W(s)
Calumet Coll of Saint Joseph, IN	M, W	Grace Coll, IN	W(s)	Michigan Technological U, MI	W(s)
Calvary Bible Coll and		Grace U, NE	W	MidAmerica Nazarene U, KS	W(s)
Theological Seminary, MO	W	Graceland U, IA	M(s), W(s)	Millikin U, IL	W
Calvin Coll, MI	W	Grand Valley State U, MI	M, W(s)	Milwaukee School of	
Cameron U, OK	W(s)	Grand View Coll, IA	W(s)	Engineering, WI	M, W
Capital U, OH	W	Greenville Coll, IL	W	Minnesota State U Mankato,	
Cardinal Stritch U, WI	M, W	Grinnell Coll, IA	W	MN	W(s)
Carleton Coll, MN	M, W	Gustavus Adolphus Coll, MN	M, W	Minnesota State U Moorhead,	
Carroll Coll, WI	W	Hamline U, MN	W	MN	W(s)
Carthage Coll, WI	W	Hannibal-LaGrange Coll, MO	W(s)	Minot State U, ND	W(s)
Case Western Reserve U, OH	M, W	Hanover Coll, IN	W	Missouri Baptist U, MO	M(s), W(s)
Cedarville U, OH	W(s)	Harris-Stowe State Coll, MO	W(s)	Missouri Southern State U, MO	W(s)
Central Christian Coll of Kansas,		Haskell Indian Nations U, KS	W	Missouri Valley Coll, MO	M(s), W(s)
KS	W(s)	Hastings Coll, NE	W(s)	Missouri Western State Coll,	
Central Coll, IA	W	Heidelberg Coll, OH	M, W	MO	W(s)
Central Methodist Coll, MO	W(s)	Hesston Coll, KS	W(s)	Monmouth Coll, IL	W
Central Michigan U, MI	W(s)	Hillsdale Coll, MI	W(s)	Moody Bible Inst, IL	M, W
Central Missouri State U, MO	W(s)	Hiram Coll, OH	W	Morningside Coll, IA	W(s)
Central State U, OH	W(s)	Hope Coll, MI	M, W	Mount Marty Coll, SD	W(s)
Chadron State Coll, NE	W(s)	Huntington Coll, IN	W(s)	Mount Mary Coll, WI	W
Chicago State U, IL	W(s)	Illinois Coll, IL	W	Mount Mercy Coll, IA	W
Clarke Coll, IA	M, W	Illinois Inst of Technology, IL	W(s)	Mount Union Coll, OH	W
Clarkson U	M, W	Illinois State U, IL	W(s)	Mount Vernon Nazarene U, OH	W(s)
Cleveland State U, OH	W(s)	Illinois Wesleyan U, IL	M, W	Muskingum Coll, OH	W
Coe Coll, IA	W	Indiana State U, IN	M, W(s)	National American U, SD	W(s)
Coll of Mount St. Joseph, OH	W	Indiana U Bloomington, IN	W(s)	Nebraska Wesleyan U, NE	W
Coll of Saint Benedict, MN	W	Indiana U Northwest, IN	W	Newman U, KS	M(s), W(s)
Coll of Saint Mary, NE	W(s)	Indiana U Southeast, IN	W(s)	North Carolina Ag and Tech	
Coll of St. Catherine, MN	W	Indiana U–Purdue U Fort		State U, NC	W(s)
Coll of the Ozarks, MO	W(s)	Wayne, IN	M(s), W(s)	North Central Coll, IL	W
Columbia Coll, MO	W(s)	Indiana U–Purdue U		North Central U, MN	W
Concord U, WV	W(s)	Indianapolis, IN	W(s)	North Dakota State Coll of	
Concordia Coll, MN	M, W	Iowa State U of Science and		Science, ND	W(s)
Concordia U, MI	W(s)	Technology, IA	W(s)	North Dakota State U, ND	M, W(s)
Concordia U, NE	W(s)	Iowa Wesleyan Coll, IA	W(s)	North Park U, IL	M, W
Concordia U, IL	W	Jamestown Coll, ND	W(s)	Northern Illinois U, IL	W(s)
Concordia U Wisconsin, WI	W	John Carroll U, OH	M, W	Northern Michigan U, MI	W(s)
Concordia U, St. Paul, MN	W(s)	Judson Coll, IL	W(s)	Northern State U, SD	W(s)
Cornell Coll, IA	M, W	Kalamazoo Coll, MI	W	Northland Coll, WI	W
Cornerstone U, MI	W(s)	Kansas State U, KS	W(s)	Northwestern Coll, MN	W
Creighton U, NE	W(s)	Kansas Wesleyan U, KS	W(s)	Northwestern Coll, IA	W(s)
Crossroads Coll, MN	M, W	Kent State U, OH	W(s)	Northwestern U, IL	W(s)
Crown Coll, MN	W	Kenyon Coll, OH	W	Northwood U, MI	W(s)
Culver-Stockton Coll, MO	W(s)	Kettering U, MI	M	Notre Dame Coll, OH	W(s)
Cumberland Coll, KY	W(s)	Knox Coll, IL	W	Oak Hills Christian Coll, MN	M, W
Dakota State U, SD	W(s)	Lake Erie Coll, OH	W	Oakland City U, IN	W(s)
Dakota Wesleyan U, SD	W(s)	Lake Forest Coll, IL	M, W	Oakland U, MI	W(s)
Dana Coll, NE	W(s)	Lake Superior State U, MI	W(s)	Oberlin Coll, OH	M, W
DePaul U, IL	W(s)	Lakeland Coll, WI	M, W	Ohio Dominican U, OH	W(s)
DePauw U, IN	W	Lawrence U, WI	M, W	Ohio Northern U, OH	W
Defiance Coll, OH	W	Lehigh U, PA	M, W(s)	Ohio U, OH	M, W(s)
Denison U, OH	W	Lewis U, IL	M(s), W(s)	Ohio U–Chillicothe, OH	W
Dickinson State U, ND	W(s)	Lincoln Coll, Lincoln, IL	W(s)	Ohio U–Zanesville, OH	W
Doane Coll, NE	W(s)	Lindenwood U, MO	M(s), W(s)	Ohio Wesleyan U, OH	M, W
Dominican U, IL	W	Loras Coll, IA	M, W	Olivet Coll, MI	W
Dordt Coll, IA	W(s)	Loyola U Chicago, IL	M(s), W(s)	Olivet Nazarene U, IL	W(s)
Drake U, IA	W(s)	Luther Coll, IA	W	Oral Roberts U, OK	W(s)
Drury U, MO	W(s)	MacMurray Coll, IL	W	Ottawa U, KS	W(s)
Earlham Coll, IN	M, W	Macalester Coll, MN	M, W	Otterbein Coll, OH	W
Eastern Illinois U, IL	W(s)	Madonna U, MI	W(s)	Park U, MO	M(s), W(s)
Eastern Michigan U, MI	W(s)	Malone Coll, OH	W(s)	Peru State Coll, NE	W(s)

College	
Pillsbury Baptist Bible Coll, MN	W
Pittsburg State U, KS	W(s)
Presentation Coll, SD	W
Principia Coll, IL	W
Purdue U, IN	M, W(s)
Quincy U, IL	M(s), W(s)
Research Coll of Nursing, MO	W(s)
Ripon Coll, WI	W
Robert Morris Coll, IL	W(s)
Rochester Coll, MI	
Rochester Comm and Tech Coll, MN	W
Rockford Coll, IL	M, W
Rockhurst U, MO	W(s)
Rose-Hulman Inst of Technology, IN	W
Saginaw Valley State U, MI	W(s)
Saint John's U, MN	M
Saint Joseph's Coll, IN	W(s)
Saint Louis U, MO	M, W(s)
Saint Mary's Coll, IN	W
Saint Mary's U of Minnesota, MN	W
Saint Xavier U, IL	W(s)
Shawnee State U, OH	W
Siena Heights U, MI	W(s)
Simpson Coll, IA	W
South Dakota School of Mines and Technology, SD	W(s)
South Dakota State U, SD	W(s)
Southeast Missouri State U, MO	W(s)
Southeastern Oklahoma State U, OK	W(s)
Southern Illinois U Carbondale, IL	W(s)
Southern Illinois U Edwardsville, IL	W(s)
Southern Nazarene U, OK	W(s)
Southwest Baptist U, MO	W(s)
Southwest Missouri State U, MO	M, W(s)
Southwestern Coll, KS	W(s)
Spring Arbor U, MI	W(s)
St. Ambrose U, IA	M(s), W(s)
St. Cloud State U, MN	M, W(s)
St. Louis Christian Coll, MO	W
St. Louis Coll of Pharmacy, MO	W
St. Norbert Coll, WI	W
St. Olaf Coll, MN	W
Stephens Coll, MO	W
Sterling Coll, KS	W(s)
Tabor Coll, KS	W(s)
Taylor U, IN	M, W(s)
Taylor U Fort Wayne, IN	W
The Coll of St. Scholastica, MN	W
The Coll of Wooster, OH	M, W
The Franciscan U, IA	W(s)
The Ohio State U, OH	M(s), W(s)
The U of Akron, OH	W(s)
The U of Alabama in Huntsville, AL	W(s)
The U of Findlay, OH	M(s), W(s)
The U of Iowa, IA	M, W(s)
The U of South Dakota, SD	W(s)
Tiffin U, OH	W(s)
Transylvania U, KY	W
Tri-State U, IN	W
Trinity Bible Coll, ND	W
Trinity Christian Coll, IL	M(s), W(s)
Trinity International U, IL	W(s)
Truman State U, MO	M, W(s)
Union Coll, NE	W
U of Central Oklahoma, OK	W(s)
U of Chicago, IL	W
U of Cincinnati, OH	W(s)
U of Dayton, OH	W(s)
U of Dubuque, IA	W
U of Evansville, IN	W(s)
U of Illinois at Chicago, IL	W(s)
U of Illinois at Springfield, IL	W(s)
U of Illinois at Urbana–Champaign, IL	W(s)
U of Indianapolis, IN	W(s)
U of Kansas, KS	W(s)
U of Mary, ND	W(s)
U of Michigan, MI	W(s)
U of Michigan–Dearborn, MI	W(s)
U of Minnesota, Crookston, MN	W(s)
U of Minnesota, Duluth, MN	M, W(s)
U of Minnesota, Morris, MN	W
U of Minnesota, Twin Cities Campus, MN	W(s)
U of Missouri–Columbia, MO	W(s)
U of Missouri–Kansas City, MO	W(s)
U of Missouri–St. Louis, MO	W(s)
U of Nebraska at Omaha, NE	W(s)
U of Nebraska–Lincoln, NE	W(s)
U of New Orleans, LA	W(s)
U of North Dakota, ND	W(s)
U of Northern Iowa, IA	W(s)
U of Notre Dame, IN	W(s)
U of Oklahoma, OK	W(s)
U of Rio Grande, OH	W(s)
U of Saint Francis, IN	W(s)
U of Saint Mary, KS	W(s)
U of Sioux Falls, SD	W(s)
U of Southern Indiana, IN	W(s)
U of St. Francis, IL	W(s)
U of St. Thomas, MN	W
U of Toledo, OH	W(s)
U of Tulsa, OK	W(s)
U of West Florida, FL	W
U of Wisconsin–Eau Claire, WI	W
U of Wisconsin–Green Bay, WI	W(s)
U of Wisconsin–La Crosse, WI	W
U of Wisconsin–Madison, WI	W(s)
U of Wisconsin–Milwaukee, WI	M, W(s)
U of Wisconsin–Oshkosh, WI	W
U of Wisconsin–Parkside, WI	W(s)
U of Wisconsin–Platteville, WI	M, W
U of Wisconsin–River Falls, WI	M, W
U of Wisconsin–Stevens Point, WI	W
U of Wisconsin–Stout, WI	M, W
U of Wisconsin–Superior, WI	W
U of Wisconsin–Whitewater, WI	M, W
Upper Iowa U, IA	M, W
Urbana U, OH	W(s)
Ursuline Coll, OH	W(s)
Valley City State U, ND	W(s)
Valparaiso U, IN	W(s)
Vennard Coll, IA	W
Viterbo U, WI	W(s)
Waldorf Coll, IA	W(s)
Walsh U, OH	W(s)
Wartburg Coll, IA	W
Washburn U, KS	W(s)
Washington U in St. Louis, MO	M, W
Wayne State Coll, NE	W(s)
Wayne State U, MI	W(s)
Webster U, MO	W
Western Illinois U, IL	W(s)
Western Michigan U, MI	W(s)
Westminster Coll, MO	W
Wheaton Coll, IL	M, W
Wichita State U, KS	M, W(s)
William Jewell Coll, MO	W(s)
William Penn U, IA	W
William Woods U, MO	M(s), W(s)
Winona State U, MN	M, W(s)
Wisconsin Lutheran Coll, WI	M, W
Wittenberg U, OH	M, W
Wright State U, OH	W(s)
Xavier U, OH	M, W(s)
Youngstown State U, OH	W(s)

Water Polo

College	
Ball State U, IN	M
Bowling Green State U, OH	M, W
Carleton Coll, MN	M, W
Grand Valley State U, MI	M, W
Hope Coll, MI	M, W
Illinois Wesleyan U, IL	M
Indiana U Bloomington, IN	W(s)
Lake Forest Coll, IL	M
Lindenwood U, MO	M(s), W(s)
Macalester Coll, MN	M, W
Michigan State U, MI	M, W
Michigan Technological U, MI	M, W
Oberlin Coll, OH	M, W
Ohio U, OH	M, W
Purdue U, IN	M, W
Saint John's U, MN	M
Saint Mary's Coll, IN	W
The U of Findlay, OH	M, W
U of Michigan, MI	W
Wabash Coll, IN	M
Washington U in St. Louis, MO	M, W
Wheaton Coll, IL	W

Weight Lifting

College	
Bowling Green State U, OH	M, W
Ohio U, OH	M
Purdue U, IN	M, W
U of Minnesota, Duluth, MN	M, W
U of Wisconsin–River Falls, WI	M, W
U of Wisconsin–Whitewater, WI	M

Wrestling

College	
Ashland U, OH	M(s)
Augsburg Coll, MN	M
Augustana Coll, SD	M(s)
Augustana Coll, IL	M
Bacone Coll, OK	M(s)
Baldwin-Wallace Coll, OH	M
Ball State U, IN	M
Bethel Coll, IN	M(s)
Briar Cliff U, IA	M(s)
Buena Vista U, IA	M
Carleton Coll, MN	M
Case Western Reserve U, OH	M
Central Coll, IA	M
Central Michigan U, MI	M(s)
Central Missouri State U, MO	M(s)
Chadron State Coll, NE	M(s)
Cleveland State U, OH	M(s)
Coe Coll, IA	M
Coll of Mount St. Joseph, OH	M
Concordia Coll, MN	M
Concordia U Wisconsin, WI	M
Cornell Coll, IA	M
Cumberland Coll, KY	M(s), W(s)
Dakota Wesleyan U, SD	M(s)
Dana Coll, NE	M(s)
Dickinson State U, ND	M(s)
Eastern Illinois U, IL	M(s)
Eastern Michigan U, MI	M(s)
Elmhurst Coll, IL	M
Fort Hays State U, KS	M(s)
Gannon U, PA	M(s)
Grand Valley State U, MI	M
Heidelberg Coll, OH	M
Illinois Coll, IL	M
Indiana U Bloomington, IN	M(s)
Iowa State U of Science and Technology, IA	M(s)
Jamestown Coll, ND	M(s)

M—for men; W—for women; (s)—scholarship offered

John Carroll U, OH	M	Northwestern Coll, IA	M(s)
Kent State U, OH	M(s)	Northwestern U, IL	M(s)
Knox Coll, IL	M	Ohio Northern U, OH	M
Lakeland Coll, WI	M	Ohio U, OH	M(s)
Lawrence U, WI	M	Oklahoma State U, OK	M(s)
Lehigh U, PA	M(s)	Olivet Coll, MI	M
Lincoln Coll, Lincoln, IL	M(s)	Purdue U, IN	M(s)
Lindenwood U, MO	M(s)	Ripon Coll, WI	M, W
Loras Coll, IA	M	Rochester Comm and Tech Coll, MN	M
Luther Coll, IA	M	Rose-Hulman Inst of Technology, IN	M
MacMurray Coll, IL	M	Saint John's U, MN	M
Manchester Coll, IN	M	Simpson Coll, IA	M
McKendree Coll, IL	M(s)	South Dakota State U, SD	M(s)
Miami U, OH	M	Southern Illinois U Edwardsville, IL	M(s)
Michigan State U, MI	M(s)	Southwest Missouri State U, MO	M
Millikin U, IL	M	St. Cloud State U, MN	M(s)
Milwaukee School of Engineering, WI	M	St. Olaf Coll, MN	M
Minnesota State U Mankato, MN	M(s)	The Ohio State U, OH	M(s)
Minnesota State U Moorhead, MN	M(s)	The U of Findlay, OH	M(s)
Missouri Baptist U, MO	M(s)	The U of Iowa, IA	M(s)
Missouri Valley Coll, MO	M(s), W(s)	Trinity Bible Coll, ND	M
Mount Union Coll, OH	M	Truman State U, MO	M(s)
Muskingum Coll, OH	M	U of Central Oklahoma, OK	M(s)
North Central Coll, IL	M	U of Chicago, IL	M
North Dakota State U, ND	M(s)	U of Dubuque, IA	M
Northern Illinois U, IL	M(s)	U of Illinois at Urbana–Champaign, IL	M(s)
Northern State U, SD	M(s)		

U of Indianapolis, IN	M(s)
U of Mary, ND	M(s)
U of Michigan, MI	M(s)
U of Minnesota, Twin Cities Campus, MN	M(s)
U of Missouri–Columbia, MO	M(s)
U of Nebraska at Omaha, NE	M(s)
U of Nebraska–Lincoln, NE	M(s)
U of Northern Iowa, IA	M(s)
U of Oklahoma, OK	M(s)
U of Wisconsin–Eau Claire, WI	M
U of Wisconsin–La Crosse, WI	M
U of Wisconsin–Madison, WI	M(s)
U of Wisconsin–Oshkosh, WI	M
U of Wisconsin–Parkside, WI	M(s)
U of Wisconsin–Platteville, WI	M
U of Wisconsin–Stevens Point, WI	M
U of Wisconsin–Whitewater, WI	M, W
Upper Iowa U, IA	M
Wabash Coll, IN	M
Waldorf Coll, IA	M(s)
Wartburg Coll, IA	M
Washburn U, KS	M
Wheaton Coll, IL	M
Wichita State U, KS	M
William Penn U, IA	M(s)
Winona State U, MN	M
Xavier U, OH	M

ROTC Programs

Allen Coll, IA	A(c)	
Alma Coll, MI	A(c)	
Alverno Coll, WI	A(c), AF(c)	
Augsburg Coll, MN	A(c), N(c), AF(c)	
Aurora U, IL	A(c)	
Avila U, MO	A(c)	
Baker U, KS	A(c), AF(c)	
Baldwin-Wallace Coll, OH	A(c), AF(c)	
Ball State U, IN	A	
Baptist Bible Coll, MO	A(c)	
Bellevue U, NE	A(c), AF(c)	
Bellin Coll of Nursing, WI	A(c)	
Benedictine Coll, KS	A	
Benedictine U, IL	A(c)	
Bethany Lutheran Coll, MN	A(c)	
Bethel Coll, IN	A(c), AF(c)	
Bethel U, MN	A(c), AF(c)	
Black Hills State U, SD	A	
Bowling Green State U, OH	A, AF	
Bradley U, IL	A	
Butler U, IN	A(c), AF(c)	
Calvin Coll, MI	A(c)	
Cameron U, OK	A	
Capital U, OH	A, AF(c)	
Carroll Coll, WI	AF(c)	
Carthage Coll, WI	A(c), AF(c)	
Case Western Reserve U, OH	A(c), AF(c)	
Cedarville U, OH	A(c), AF(c)	
Central Methodist Coll, MO	A(c), AF(c)	
Central Michigan U, MI	A	
Central Missouri State U, MO	A, AF(c)	
Central State U, OH	A	
Chicago State U, IL	A, N(c), AF(c)	
Clarkson U	A, AF	
Cleveland Inst of Music, OH	A(c), AF(c)	
Cleveland State U, OH	A(c), AF(c)	
Coe Coll, IA	A(c), AF(c)	
Coll of Mount St. Joseph, OH	A(c), AF(c)	
Coll of Saint Benedict, MN	A(c)	
Coll of St. Catherine, MN	AF(c)	
Coll of Saint Mary, NE	A(c), AF(c)	
The Coll of St. Scholastica, MN	AF(c)	
Coll of the Ozarks, MO	A	
Colorado Tech U Sioux Falls Campus, SD	A(c)	
Columbia Coll, MO	A(c), N(c), AF(c)	
Concordia Coll, MN	A(c), AF(c)	
Concordia U, MI	A(c), AF(c)	
Concordia U, NE	A(c), AF(c)	
Concordia U, St. Paul, MN	A(c), AF(c)	
Cornerstone U, MI	A(c)	
Creighton U, NE	A, AF(c)	
Cumberland Coll, KY	A	
Dakota State U, SD	AF(c)	
Dana Coll, NE	A(c), AF(c)	
Davenport U, Lansing, MI	A(c)	
Denison U, OH	A(c)	
DePaul U, IL	A	
DePauw U, IN	A(c), AF(c)	
DeVry U, Columbus, OH	A(c)	
Doane Coll, NE	A(c), AF(c)	
Drake U, IA	A, AF(c)	
Drury U, MO	A(c)	
Eastern Illinois U, IL	A	
Eastern Michigan U, MI	A, N(c), AF(c)	
Elmhurst Coll, IL	A(c), AF(c)	
Evangel U, MO	A	
Ferris State U, MI	A(c)	
Fontbonne U, MO	A(c)	
Franklin Coll, IN	A(c)	
Franklin U, OH	A(c), AF(c)	
Gannon U, PA	A	
Governors State U, IL	A(c), AF(c)	
Grace U, NE	A(c), AF(c)	
Grand View Coll, IA	A(c), AF(c)	
Gustavus Adolphus Coll, MN	A(c)	
Hamline U, MN	AF(c)	
Harris-Stowe State Coll, MO	AF(c)	
Haskell Indian Nations U, KS	AF(c)	
Heidelberg Coll, OH	A(c), AF(c)	
Holy Cross Coll, IN	A(c), AF(c)	
Illinois Inst of Technology, IL	A, N, AF	
Illinois State U, IL	A	
Illinois Wesleyan U, IL	A(c)	
Indiana State U, IN	A, AF	
Indiana U Bloomington, IN	A, AF	
Indiana U Kokomo, IN	A(c)	
Indiana U Northwest, IN	A	
Indiana U–Purdue U Indianapolis, IN	A, N(c), AF(c)	
Indiana U South Bend, IN	A(c), N(c), AF(c)	
Indiana U Southeast, IN	A(c), AF(c)	
Iowa State U of Science and Technology, IA	A, N, AF	
John Carroll U, OH	A	
Kalamazoo Coll, MI	A(c)	
Kansas State U, KS	A, AF	
Kent State U, OH	A, AF	
Kent State U, Salem Campus, OH	A(c), AF(c)	
Kent State U, Stark Campus, OH	A(c), AF(c)	
Kent State U, Tuscarawas Campus, OH	A(c), AF(c)	
Lawrence Technological U, MI	A(c), AF(c)	
Lehigh U, PA	A	
Lewis U, IL	A(c), AF(c)	
Lincoln U, MO	A	
Lindenwood U, MO	A, AF(c)	
Lourdes Coll, OH	A(c)	
Loyola U Chicago, IL	A(c), N(c)	
Macalester Coll, MN	N(c), AF(c)	
Malone Coll, OH	A(c), AF(c)	
Manhattan Christian Coll, KS	A(c), AF(c)	
Marian Coll, IN	A(c)	
Marian Coll of Fond du Lac, WI	A	
Marquette U, WI	A, N, AF	
Maryville U of Saint Louis, MO	A(c)	
Mayville State U, ND	AF(c)	
McKendree Coll, IL	A(c), AF(c)	
Miami U, OH	A(c), N, AF	
Miami U Hamilton, OH	N(c), AF(c)	
Michigan State U, MI	A, AF	
Michigan Technological U, MI	A, AF	
MidAmerica Nazarene U, KS	A(c), AF(c)	
Milwaukee School of Engineering, WI	A(c), N(c), AF(c)	
Minnesota State U Mankato, MN	A	
Minnesota State U Moorhead, MN	A(c), AF(c)	
Missouri Baptist U, MO	A(c)	
Missouri Valley Coll, MO	A(c)	
Missouri Western State Coll, MO	A	
Monmouth Coll, IL	A(c)	
Mount Marty Coll, SD	A(c)	
Mount Mary Coll, WI	A(c)	
Mount Union Coll, OH	A(c), AF(c)	
National American U, SD	A(c)	
Nebraska Methodist Coll, NE	A(c)	
Nebraska Wesleyan U, NE	A(c), AF(c)	
North Carolina Ag and Tech State U, NC	A, AF	
North Central Coll, IL	A(c), AF(c)	
North Central U, MN	A(c), AF(c)	
North Dakota State U, ND	A, AF	
Northeastern Illinois U, IL	A(c), AF(c)	
Northeastern State U, OK	A	
Northern Illinois U, IL	A, AF(c)	
Northern Michigan U, MI	A	
Northwestern Coll, MN	A(c), AF(c)	
Northwestern U, IL	A(c), N, AF(c)	
Oakland U, MI	AF(c)	
Ohio Dominican U, OH	A(c)	
Ohio Northern U, OH	A(c), AF(c)	
The Ohio State U, OH	A, AF	
The Ohio State U at Lima, OH	A(c), N(c), AF(c)	
The Ohio State U at Marion, OH	A(c), N(c), AF(c)	
The Ohio State U–Mansfield Campus, OH	A(c), N(c), AF(c)	
The Ohio State U–Newark Campus, OH	A(c), N(c), AF(c)	
Ohio U, OH	A, AF	
Ohio U–Chillicothe, OH	A(c), AF(c)	
Ohio Wesleyan U, OH	A(c)	
Oklahoma Baptist U, OK	AF(c)	
Oklahoma Christian U, OK	A(c), AF(c)	
Oklahoma City U, OK	A(c), AF(c)	
Oklahoma State U, OK	A, AF	
Olivet Nazarene U, IL	A	
Oral Roberts U, OK	AF(c)	
Otterbein Coll, OH	A(c), AF(c)	
Park U, MO	A	
Pittsburg State U, KS	A	
Purdue U, IN	A, N, AF	
Purdue U Calumet, IN	A(c)	
Research Coll of Nursing, MO	A(c)	
Ripon Coll, WI	A	
Rockford Coll, IL	A(c)	
Rockhurst U, MO	A(c)	
Rose-Hulman Inst of Technology, IN	A, AF	
St. Cloud State U, MN	A	
St. Gregory's U, OK	A(c), N(c), AF(c)	
Saint John's U, MN	A	
St. Louis Coll of Pharmacy, MO	A(c), AF(c)	
Saint Louis U, MO	A(c), AF	
Saint Mary-of-the-Woods Coll, IN	A(c), AF(c)	
Saint Mary's Coll, IN	A(c), N(c), AF(c)	
St. Norbert Coll, WI	A(c)	
Saint Xavier U, IL	AF(c)	

A—Army; N—Navy; AF—Air Force; (c)—available through a cooperating host institution

South Dakota School of Mines and Technology, SD	A
South Dakota State U, SD	A, AF
Southeast Missouri State U, MO	AF
Southern Illinois U Carbondale, IL	A, AF
Southern Illinois U Edwardsville, IL	A, AF
Southern Nazarene U, OK	A(c), AF(c)
Southwest Baptist U, MO	A(c)
Southwest Missouri State U, MO	A
Stephens Coll, MO	A(c), AF(c)
Tiffin U, OH	A(c), AF(c)
Transylvania U, KY	A(c), AF(c)
Truman State U, MO	A
The U of Akron, OH	A, AF
The U of Alabama in Huntsville, AL	A(c)
U of Central Oklahoma, OK	A
U of Chicago, IL	A(c), AF(c)
U of Cincinnati, OH	A, AF
U of Dayton, OH	A, AF(c)
U of Detroit Mercy, MI	A(c)
U of Dubuque, IA	A
The U of Findlay, OH	A(c), AF(c)
U of Illinois at Chicago, IL	A, N(c), AF(c)
U of Illinois at Urbana–Champaign, IL	A, AF
U of Indianapolis, IN	A(c)
The U of Iowa, IA	A, AF
U of Kansas, KS	A, N, AF
U of Michigan, MI	A, AF
U of Michigan–Dearborn, MI	A(c), N(c), AF(c)
U of Minnesota, Crookston, MN	AF(c)
U of Minnesota, Duluth, MN	AF
U of Minnesota, Twin Cities Campus, MN	A, N, AF
U of Missouri–Columbia, MO	A, N, AF
U of Missouri–Kansas City, MO	A
U of Missouri–Rolla, MO	A, AF
U of Missouri–St. Louis, MO	A(c), AF(c)
U of Nebraska at Omaha, NE	A(c), AF
U of Nebraska–Lincoln, NE	A, N, AF
U of Nebraska Medical Center, NE	A(c), AF(c)
U of New Orleans, LA	A(c), N(c), AF(c)
U of North Dakota, ND	A, AF
U of Northern Iowa, IA	A
U of Notre Dame, IN	A, N, AF
U of Oklahoma, OK	A, AF
U of Oklahoma Health Sciences Center, OK	A(c), AF(c)
U of Rio Grande, OH	A(c)
U of Saint Mary, KS	A(c)
U of St. Thomas, MN	A(c), N(c), AF
The U of South Dakota, SD	A
U of Southern Indiana, IN	A
U of Toledo, OH	A, AF(c)
U of Tulsa, OK	AF(c)
U of West Florida, FL	A, AF
U of Wisconsin–Green Bay, WI	A
U of Wisconsin–La Crosse, WI	A
U of Wisconsin–Madison, WI	A
U of Wisconsin–Oshkosh, WI	A
U of Wisconsin–Parkside, WI	A(c)
U of Wisconsin–Stevens Point, WI	A
U of Wisconsin–Superior, WI	AF(c)
U of Wisconsin–Whitewater, WI	A, AF
Valparaiso U, IN	AF
Viterbo U, WI	A(c)
Wabash Coll, IN	A(c)
Washburn U, KS	A, AF(c)
Washington U in St. Louis, MO	A, AF(c)
Wayne State Coll, NE	A(c)
Wayne State U, MI	AF(c)
Webster U, MO	A(c), AF(c)
Western Illinois U, IL	A
Western Michigan U, MI	A
Westminster Coll, MO	A(c), AF(c)
Wheaton Coll, IL	A, AF(c)
Wilberforce U, OH	A(c), AF(c)
William Woods U, MO	A(c), N(c), AF(c)
Winona State U, MN	A(c)
Wisconsin Lutheran Coll, WI	A(c), N(c), AF(c)
Wittenberg U, OH	A(c), AF(c)
Wright State U, OH	A, AF
Xavier U, OH	A, AF(c)
York Coll, NE	A(c), N(c), AF(c)
Youngstown State U, OH	A, AF(c)

Alphabetical Listing of Colleges and Universities

In this index, the page locations of the profiles are printed in regular type, **Special Messages** in *italics*, and **In-Depth Descriptions** in **bold type**.

Alphabetical Listing of Colleges and Universities

Alphabetical Listing of Colleges and Universities